❦ THE LITERATURE OF LESBIANISM ❦

EDITED BY TERRY CASTLE

The Literature of Lesbianism

A HISTORICAL ANTHOLOGY FROM ARIOSTO TO STONEWALL

COLUMBIA UNIVERSITY PRESS NEW YORK

Columbia University Press

Publishers Since 1893

New York   Chichester, West Sussex

Copyright © 2003 Terry Castle

All rights reserved

Library of Congress Cataloging-in-Publication Data

The literature of lesbianism : a historical anthology from Ariosto to Stonewall / edited by
    Terry Castle.
        p. cm.
    Includes bibliographical references.
    ISBN 0-231-12510-0 (alk. paper)
        1. Lesbians—Literary collections. 2. Lesbians' writings. 3. Lesbianism. I. Castle, Terry.

PN6071.L47L58 2003
808.8′0353—dc21

2002041491

In memory of Jeannette Foster (1895–1981), a great scholar

CONTENTS

The Nineteenth Century   349

ACKNOWLEDGMENTS

This anthology has been embarrassingly long in the making, and I owe deep and heart-felt thanks to the many people who have helped me—both practically and spiritually—during its protracted, sometimes elephantine birthing. First and foremost I would like to thank Jennifer Crewe at Columbia University Press for her unflagging enthusiasm and support for the project. As I have come to know well over the past two decades, Jennifer is an editor of uncommon vision, curiosity, energy, and decency and I am permanently in her debt. I am likewise deeply grateful to the outstanding editorial and production staff at Columbia—in particular Ann Miller, Susan Heath, Susan Pensak, and Chang Jae Lee. It has been a great pleasure to work with all of them.

My other intellectual and personal debts are numerous. Any anthologist must build, humblingly, on the learning and scholarship of others, and I am honored to pay tribute to some of the scholars of the past thirty or forty years whose work has had a shaping influence on my own. Towering indeed must be my debt to the lesbian literary historian Jeannette Howard Foster (1895–1981), an independent scholar of immense, unsung erudition who spent most of her professional life as a librarian at the Kinsey Institute. I am sorry never to have met Miss Foster in person: one suspects she was both an elegant and courageous woman. I first encountered her classic bibliography *Sex Variant Women in Literature*—issued privately at her own expense in 1956, at a time when no reputable publisher would touch the subject of female homosexuality—when I was an undergraduate toiling away on the Friday night graveyard shift at the circulation desk of my college library in the early 1970s. Along with the Kama Sutra, the collected works of Havelock Ellis and Henry Miller, and a dubious over-sized tome entitled *Erotic Paintings of the World*, Foster's richly learned study, a true labor of love, was hidden away in a special, noncirculating, "Triple X-rated" stack behind the front desk. Many were the otherwise moribund evenings I spent perusing it: my first—and still most treasured—introduction to the literature of lesbianism. I have dedicated this volume to Foster's memory: she has influenced it in myriad ways, tangible and intangible.

The work of other scholars has been equally cherishable. Anyone working in contemporary gay and lesbian literary studies owes an enormous, ever-compounding debt to the trailblazing investigators of the 1970s and 1980s. The present volume has been shaped indeed—deeply and ineluctably—by the exemplary scholarship of Shari Benstock, the late John Boswell, the late Alan Bray, the late Germaine Brée, Judith Brown, Vern Bullough, George Chauncey Jr., Stephen Coote, Louis Crompton, Joan DeJean, K. J. Dover, Lillian Faderman, Sandra Gilbert and Susan Gubar, Jonathan Goldberg, Barbara Grier, David M. Halperin, Simon Karlinsky, Jonathan Ned Katz, Karla Jay, Jane Marcus, the late Elaine Marks, Esther Newton, George S. Rousseau, Jane Rule, the late Vito Russo, Eve Kosofsky Sedgwick, Catharine Stimpson, Claude J. Summers, Janet Todd, Randolph Trumbach, Martha Vicinus, Jeffrey Weeks, Edmund White, and the late Jack Winkler. I am tremendously grateful for their pioneering accomplishments.

For valuable assistance of a practical nature—translations, bibliographic leads, copies of rare or unpublished material, technical help, and many other instances of intellectual and personal generosity—I would like to thank Linda Anderson, Robin Becker, Gillian Beer, John Bender, Corinne Blackmer, Eavan Boland, Alyce Boster, Joe Bristow, Erin Carlston, the late Diane Cleaver, Norma Cole, Peter Davidson, Millicent Dillon, Laura Doan, Emma Donoghue, Andrew Elfenbein, Jane Emery, Lillian Faderman, Sophie Fuller, Marjorie Garber, Carolyn Heilbrun, renée hoogland, Richard Howard, Annamarie Jagose, Nicholas Jenkins, Barbara Johnson, Graham Johnson, Rob Kaufman, Margo Leahy, Seth Lerer, Dagmar Logie, Linda Long, Liz Maguire, Diane Middlebrook, Nancy K. Miller, Erin Mouré, Randy Nakayama, Marjorie Perloff, Horace Porter, Lou Roberts, Patricia J. Smith, Susan Sontag, Simon Stern, Jane Stevenson, Catharine Stimpson and Elizabeth Wood, Jennifer Summit, John Tinker, James Grantham Turner, Ruth Vanita, Beth Vesel, Elizabeth S. Wahl, and Leon Wieseltier. (Whatever residual errors in information, taste, or intellectual perspective remain, I should note, are strictly and eternally my own.) For permission to reprint several key works in this anthology I would like to pay particular thanks to the late Paul Bowles, Diana S. Burgin, Barbara Grier, Nigel Nicolson, and Susanna Pinney.

To many colleagues, past and present, at Stanford University I owe my gratitude—especially Keith Baker, George Dekker, John Etchemendy, John Hennessy, and Condoleeza Rice. Each of the aforementioned provided generous institutional and administrative support over the past few years and I deeply appreciate their kindness and commitment. Many thanks also to members of the Department of English at the University of California, Berkeley—especially Carolyn Dinshaw, Catherine Gallagher, Jeff Knapp, and James Turner—for kindly inviting me to teach a graduate seminar on the literature of lesbianism in 1992. The Berkeley course was a crucial early opportunity to explore the historical genealogy of lesbian writing in an especially stimulating intellectual environment and I am grateful to have had the chance to do so.

For the many kindnesses of friends and family—much less easily quantified—any expressions of gratitude must be pitifully inadequate. Nonetheless I would like to thank (always) Paul Alkon, Tamara Bernstein, my sister Tracy Castle, Bridget Castle, John and Joan Castle, Neil and Jane Goodhead, Linda Kerr, Kristin Midelfort, Stephen Orgel and Randy Nakayama, my mother Mavis K. Parker, Rob Polhemus and Carol Shloss, Brenda Pratt, Beverley Talbott, Mary Ann Tilotta, and Blakey Vermeule. The last-named has, too—as she must now know—my wild and unstinting devotion.

A NOTE ON THE TEXTS

I have drawn in this anthology—gratefully indeed—from a large number of published and unpublished sources. For each selection here, the source text used is noted in the first entry under "Further Reading." After the source text, I have cited other works by the same author, followed by selected books and articles (listed by year of publication) dealing with his or her work. Unless otherwise noted, I have not altered or modernized source texts except to correct obvious misprints and solecisms. Formal acknowledgment for all copyrighted sources, including names of editors and translators, appears at the end of the volume.

INTRODUCTION

. . . the strongest emotion known, that of a woman for a woman.
—Honoré de Balzac, *Cousine Bette*

In approaching a subject as weighted with controversy as female homosexuality, one should try to set out one's own intellectual point of view as clearly as possible. *The Literature of Lesbianism* is both a portentous and a somewhat cheeky-sounding title for a Columbia University Press anthology; it has not been chosen lightly. I am fully aware of its provocations. Some of these are intrinsic to the subject matter and thus unavoidable. Regarding any moral queasiness my title may evoke in the traditionally minded, I have little to say: those who find lesbianism distasteful or indelicate or question the value of a tome on the subject—even from such an esteemed press as Columbia—are advised to stop reading now. You will find little here to like. The guiding presumption of this volume is that love between women is a topic of serious and abiding human significance—bound up in as yet unfathomed ways with our deepest beliefs about nature and culture, sexuality and desire, femininity and masculinity, women and men. When it comes to tracing out the literary and cultural manifestations of the lesbian "idea" since the Renaissance, moral judgments are an irrelevance.

Of greater concern is a potential semantic ambiguity in my title. I would like to stress at the outset that this volume is *not* a collection of "writings by lesbians." Over the past thirty years such identity-driven collections have been de rigueur, of course, often for ideological reasons. Even as they serve to enlighten the general public, anthologies of literary works by one's chosen "people" can play, obviously, a powerfully inspirational and self-affirming psychological function for members of minority groups. Literature seems to answer the need for a tribal history and to confirm one's importance in the world. Certainly since the late 1960s and early 1970s, when lesbian and gay civil rights groups began to proliferate in Europe and North America on a new and historic scale, it has been important—even psychically necessary—for many women who love women to legitimate their sexual unorthodoxy by seeking out works of literature written by individuals whom they imagine to be like themselves.[1]

I do not wish to disparage what has been a moving and illuminating search for literary forebears. On the contrary: over the past three decades the "lesbian writers" approach—the gathering and grouping of works by female authors presumed (in some sense) to have loved members of their own sex—has vastly enriched our understanding of literary history since the Renaissance. Forgotten women writers have been rescued from oblivion, with sometimes startling intellectual consequences. We have been made aware, for instance, of an entire school of seventeenth and eighteenth-century women poets inspired by the theme of "romantic" female friendship: the elaborate love-panegyrics of Katherine Philips (1632–1664), Anne Killigrew (1660–1685), Anne Finch (1661–1720), and Anna Seward (1742–1809)—all floridly addressed to other women—pose a complex challenge to traditional notions about feminine "love poetry" and its supposedly heterosexual norms. We have rediscovered the lives and writings of a wild cohort of tomboys, transvestists, "roaring girls" and female sexual renegades—from the cross-dressing Charlotte Charke (1713–1760), whose 1755 memoir of her career en travesti reads like an aberrant Defoe novel, to the astounding Anne Lister (1791–1840), whose voluminous coded diaries, deciphered in the 1980s, are a mind-boggling revelation of real-life lesbian intrigue in the same provincial-genteel world of Regency England described in the fiction of Jane Austen.

We have learned about nineteenth- and twentieth-century imitators of Sappho: Letitia Elizabeth Landon (1802–1838), Elizabeth Oakes Smith (1806–1893), Caroline Norton (1808–1877), Catharine Amy Dawson (1865–1934), "Michael Field" (fl. late nineteenth century), Renée Vivien (1877–1909), Natalie Clifford Barney (1876–1972), "Marie Madeleine" (1881–1944), Rose O'Neill (1874–1944), Sophia Parnok (1885–1933). And about "lesbian coming of age novelists" from the teens and 1920s and 1930s: Clemence Dane (1887–1965), Radclyffe Hall (1880–1943), Christa Winsloe (1888–1944), "Henry Handel Richardson" (1870–1946), Rose Allatini (1890–1980?), Dorothy Baker (1907–1968), Dorothy Strachey (1865–1960). Nor have the rediscoveries been restricted to some conventionally imagined literary mainstream. In particular, thanks to the recovery of lost or suppressed manuscripts, diaries, and letters (and enlightened publishing ventures such as the Schomburg Library of Nineteenth-Century Black Women Writers), a number of African-American lesbian and bisexual writers—including Angelina Weld Grimké (1880–1958), Alice Dunbar Nelson (1875–1935), Nella Larsen (1891–1964), and Lorraine Hansberry (1930–1965)—have also begun lately to come more clearly into view.

The quest after a lost lesbian "tradition" has in turn encouraged critics and scholars to look at certain well-known female authors anew. While no doubt controversial, recent "lesbian-friendly" accounts of the lives and works of Jane Austen, Emily Dickinson, Willa Cather, Katherine Mansfield, H.D., Virginia Woolf, Colette, Djuna Barnes, Elizabeth Bowen, Iris Murdoch, and Elizabeth Bishop—to name only some of the more sensational cases—have been eye-opening.[2] Hidden chains of female-female influence have come glintingly to the fore. To read Woolf's gender-bending *Orlando* (1928) in the light of Lady Mary Wortley Montagu's Turkish *Embassy Letters* (1716–18), or Dorothy Strachey's schoolgirl romance *Olivia* (1948) in relation to Charlotte Brontë's *Villette* (1853), is to sense at once the homoerotic undercurrents linking women writers across the centuries.

For an anthologist, however, the "writings by lesbians" approach has one spectacular defect—already on view in the slippery paragraphs above. Who counts as a "lesbian writer" and who doesn't? *Webster's Ninth* defines *lesbian*, briskly enough, as a woman "characterized by a tendency to direct sexual desire toward another of the same sex." Yet this seemingly no-nonsense formula in fact begs a raft of questions. What precisely does it mean, for a start, to "direct sexual desire toward another of the same sex"? To write another woman a romantic poem? To fantasize about making love to her? To share the same bed with her? To live with her for fifty years? To bring her to orgasm? Even were this fundamental question to be settled—and it never will be—there would still be the issue of historical information. What about authors of whose intimate lives we know little or nothing? Where to put the great Sappho herself, for example, who lives on in literary history largely as a threadbare assemblage of textual fragments, scholarly guesswork, and titillating rumors? Can the requisite "tendency" be deduced solely from an author's writing? From the fact that she *writes* about lesbianism? But what then about men who write about lesbianism? Or female authors who take up lesbian themes but declare themselves asexual or bisexual or heterosexual or in some other fashion *not*-lesbian? How much weight should we give to a writer's self-description?

A few examples will show how exasperating, editorially speaking, such issues can be. Consider the aforementioned seventeenth-century English love poet Katherine Philips. In the early 1650s Philips—known to her contemporaries as the "Matchless Orinda"—wrote a series of startlingly passionate "Platonick" verses to a female friend she called "Lucasia." "Lucasia" has been identified: her real name was Anne Owen. But beyond the fact that Philips (herself a married woman) was deeply distressed by Owen's subsequent engagement to an Irishman, we know virtually nothing about their relationship. It is difficult to discount the ardor of Philips's verses or the hints they give of an intense (if ambiguous) emotional bond between the two women. "No Bridegroom's nor Crown-conqueror's mirth / To mine compar'ed can be"—the poet boasts in "To My Excellent Friend Lucasia, on Our Friendship"—"They have but pieces of this Earth, / I've all the World in thee." Yet in the absence of any thoroughgoing information about Philips's private life, to label her a "lesbian" in the modern dictionary sense seems at once presumptuous and anachronistic.

Even with better-known writers we may find ourselves reluctant to pronounce upon the intimate feelings of those long dead. What to do, for example, with the spinster-genius Emily Dickinson (1830–1886)? This much-revered American poet almost certainly loved members of her own sex—most anguishingly, her sister-in-law Sue Gilbert. Yet like so many gifted women of the nineteenth century, Dickinson was also a lifelong celibate. (She was famous for dressing only in white and sequestering herself for years in her parents' house in Amherst, Massachusetts.) One would hate to exclude Dickinson's verses from the historical archive of lesbian writing. Extraordinary poetic fragments such as "Her sweet Weight on my Heart a Night" or "Going—to—Her!" seem, once again, from a present-day vantage point, exorbitantly sapphic. But can we blithely categorize as "lesbian" a woman who seems never to have acted on a single erotic desire in her life? Even as her poems bear cryptic witness to urgings of the flesh—that fierce "Intemperance" by which "to be undone / Is dearer than Redemption"—Dickinson took her chastity with her, nunlike, to the grave. It seems churlish to violate—if only symbolically—such self-legislated, self-gathering purity.

Then there is the writer who acts on her desires but refuses to be labeled. The twentieth-century novelist Djuna Barnes (1892–1982), author of the lesbian classic *Nightwood* (1936), was in many ways Dickinson's antithesis: a woman for whom sexual daring, even recklessness, was a given. It is well known that *Nightwood*—a hallucinatory reverie on the torment suffered by an American woman in France at the hands of a promiscuous female lover—was inspired by Barnes's own turbulent eight-year liaison with Thelma Wood, a painter with whom she lived in Paris in the 1920s. (Wood's name is embedded, like ancient cellulose, in the novel's darkly sylvan title.) Yet until her death in 1982, Barnes detested being called a lesbian writer. "I am not a lesbian," she was wont to declare in old age; "I just loved Thelma." And she was scathing—however comically—about younger women who found consolation in *Nightwood*'s strangely glamorous emotional universe. As one of the novelist's friends wrote after her death, Barnes recognized

> that what she had written in *Nightwood*, intentional or not, was regarded by many as a novel with a strong lesbian theme and was influential in ways she had not intended. This concerned her. It was acceptable for the strong literary qualities of the book to influence someone, but it was another matter if the book gave meaning or solace to young women, unknown to her, who were casting about in search of justification for their sexuality. "I don't want the responsibility of changing anyone's life," she would often say, "I don't want to make a lot of little lesbians!" She would tell me, "Girls used to kneel outside my door and beg to be let in and when they'd finally depart, they usually left flowers on the doorstep. One was so insistent, she just wouldn't leave, I had to telephone the police to take her away." This seemed somewhat drastic action to me, but it was perfectly acceptable to Barnes.[3]

Who is to say such vehemence is unjustified? That Barnes was *wrong* about herself? However self-deceiving such disavowals may appear (and many lesbian and gay readers have found Barnes's comments painfully hypocritical), the moral force behind them—Barnes's right to her own self-righteousness—remains difficult to gainsay.

With other writers, finally, even when there is no outright denial, the lesbian "tag" can still seem an impertinence—a kind of imposition from without. Witness the celebrated British novelist Virginia Woolf (1882–1941). Woolf was hardly what one would call rampantly heterosexual: having been molested by her two half-brothers as a child, she evinced little desire as an adult for sexual relations with men. Her thirty-year marriage to the writer and publisher Leonard Woolf, though sustaining, was largely passionless. She fell repeatedly in love with women and is known to have had at least one consummated lesbian relationship—with the androgynous poet and novelist Vita Sackville-West. This liaison later inspired what many consider Woolf's most "sapphic" piece of writing—the 1928 fantasy novel, *Orlando*, which she dedicated to Sackville-West.

With all of this in view, might we not fairly describe Woolf, pace *Webster*'s, as *lesbian* in orientation? Alas, and without prejudice, Woolf herself would not have thought so. In letters and diaries she inevitably distinguished herself from "Sapphists" like Sackville-West, whose single-minded pursuit of women (carried out with the blessing of her husband, Harold Nicolson) Woolf saw as relentless and all-consuming. "These Sapphists *love* women," Woolf wrote in 1922 after meeting Vita; "friendship is never untinged with amorosity."[4] Her own feelings, she decided, were of a different order: more subtle and hesitant, harder to pin down or define.

Woolf's distinction rings true: the more we read about her and the somewhat feral Sackville-West, the less like, psychologically speaking, the two women appear. But it also disconcerts. Must we then conclude that Sackville-West was a lesbian and Woolf not? Or that Sackville-West was somehow *more* of a lesbian than Woolf? If so, by how much? And what then of *Orlando*? Woolf's tongue-in-cheek fiction about a sex-changing hero (flagrantly modeled on Vita) is far more critical of heterosexual orthodoxies than any of Sackville-West's own ponderously conventional novels. Might not the fact of Woolf's having produced this palpably "lesbian" masterpiece—like Barnes with *Nightwood*—bring her firmly into the "Sapphist" camp even if she never really *did* much?

I belabor, of course, what will seem to some absurd, ill-shaped, or obnoxious questions. Yet it seems necessary to point up, if only by these crude rhetorical means, the difficulties that assail the anthologist who attempts to define lesbian writing through some circular appeal to the erotic lives of its producers. At the very least the "literature by lesbians" mode ineluctably entangles one in gossipy biographical conundrums unlikely to be resolved in our own day or any other. More damagingly, even as we labor (with greater or lesser unease) to pigeonhole individual women, we are confronted with the aggravating ambiguities of the term *lesbian* itself: its psychic and behavioral imprecision, its obscure historical reach, its annoying failure to refer unequivocally, precisely at those moments when one wants most that it should.[5]

I

My own approach is different: less ideologically fraught, perhaps, and I hope less compromising. Instead of presuming at the outset what lesbianism *is*—then trying to find writers who somehow fit the bill—I start with the assumption that it is precisely the category itself that is in need of historical examination. How (and when) did it first become possible in modern Western culture to *think* about erotic desire between women? From whence derive our sometimes wildly contradictory notions of what lesbianism *is* and how it can be recognized? And how to comprehend, more broadly, the curious and enduring intellectual fascination that fantasies of love between women have exerted over the Western popular imagination since the Renaissance?

Literature can enlighten us on such points, but not because it reflects any "truth" about individual women's lives. Granted, certain works in this volume may offer a fleeting imaginative purchase on what it was like to love another woman in Europe or America at different times over the past four hundred years. But the texts included here do not in themselves constitute anything like a documentary history of lesbian life. I make no claim to present the real "voices" of lesbians. On the contrary, I have sought to shift attention *away* from lesbianism-as-lived-experience (however narrowly or loosely defined) toward lesbianism-as-theme: as *locus communis*, as site of collective imaginative inquiry, as topic of cultural conversation. Far more useful than chasing down the elusive facts of dead women's lives, it seems to me, is to begin exploring the "idea" of lesbianism itself—its conceptual origins, how it has been transmitted, transformed, and collectively embellished, how it has served over the centuries *as something to talk about*. I am less interested in what lesbianism is, in other words, than in what people have said about it—its role as rhetorical and cultural topos.

This shift in approach has several dramatic consequences—the most startling of which for some readers will be that I include numerous works in this anthology written by men. The lesbian "idea" has never been the exclusive intellectual property of the female sex. Indeed, as will already be obvious to anyone who has perused the table of contents, my rough thesis is that in the modern West the collective mental discovery—that *women might love and desire one another as men loved and desired them*—is first visibly registered in the writings of men: those humanist poets and scholars of sixteenth- and seventeenth-century Europe who confronted (to their mixed pleasure and unease) a burgeoning imagery of female-female eros in the recently recovered texts of Sappho, Ovid, Martial, Juvenal, and other Greek and Roman authors of antiquity. To the extent that anyone "owned" the lesbian idea in the Renaissance, if one may speak in such peculiar terms, it was primarily a male possession. (The pervasiveness of female illiteracy in earlier centuries and the general exclusion of women before 1800 from the ferociously male-dominated world of intellectual exchange help to explain, obviously, why we have so few early writings by *women* about female same-sex love.) This pattern of symbolic ownership would only be disrupted around the beginning of the twentieth century, with the fervently sapphophilic writing of Renée Vivien, Natalie Barney, Gertrude Stein, H.D., Radclyffe Hall, Amy Lowell, Virginia Woolf, and many others.

Yes—of course—women have often written about passion between women. And often enough too, despite all the problems of definition, one can indeed sense in such writing an unambiguous authorial investment—that the woman who produced it was inspired by some lived "lesbian" experience of her own. Strange would be that reader who finished Radclyffe Hall's classic lesbian potboiler, *The Well of Loneliness* (1928), without ever wondering if its author had not at some point fallen in love with another woman. But by choosing as my title *The Literature of Lesbianism* I mean to suggest something far more capacious than the relatively small corpus of works that would result were one to cast about for "authentic" lesbian-authored texts. One of the most provocative discoveries I have made while compiling this anthology has been just how commonplace—if not indispensable—the lesbian theme has been in modern Western writing. From Ariosto, Shakespeare, Ben Jonson, John Donne, Andrew Marvell, and Aphra Behn to Coleridge, Balzac, Proust, Strindberg, Henry James, Thomas Hardy, Woolf, Ernest Hemingway, D. H. Lawrence, Katherine Mansfield, and Elizabeth Bowen (and I choose these names more or less at random), virtually every author of note since the Renaissance has written something, somewhere, touching on the subject of love between women. A final advantage of the "literature of lesbianism" rubric, then: how easily it converts into the "lesbianism of literature"—a phenomenon that this work should also do something to illustrate.

2

As for my somewhat odd-looking subtitle, *From Ariosto to Stonewall*, I can elucidate it best by developing further—if at first a bit abstractly—what I mean by the lesbian "idea." The term is not chosen at random. On the contrary, I use it precisely to bring to mind that celebrated branch of scholarly investigation known as the *history of ideas*—the study of how collective beliefs, mental attitudes, and philosophical presuppositions arise and evolve over time. If lesbianism, as I am suggesting, is in at least one important sense an *idea*, then it follows that we may trace the ways in which this idea took shape historically, became part of the shared *mentalité* of modern life. It has its own biography, so to speak, embedded in literary and cultural history—and like any other idea shaping modern Western consciousness, we may see where it begins and where it lives and what it portends—if not yet where it ends.

   This is not to say that the official "history of ideas" has ever, until very recently, taken note of it. A basic paradox confronting anyone seeking historical enlightenment on the subject of female homosexuality must be this: that while same-sex eros has been a recurrent topic of fantasy and exploration in imaginative literature at least since classical antiquity (one need only look to the ancient Greeks and Romans for confirmation), scholarly recognition of this fact has been almost entirely wanting until our own time. Indeed, the paradox is even stranger: even as the number of literary and artistic works devoted to the lesbian theme has increased (spectacularly, over the last three hundred years), the topic of female same-sex love has been repeatedly ruled out of bounds, as a subject radically unsuitable for polite intellectual inquiry. We have the numerous entrenched religious and cultural proscriptions against female homosexuality to thank, undoubtedly, for this state of affairs. Academic critics and historians—their pretensions to boldness and dispatch notwithstanding—are perhaps those members of society *least* likely to test accepted wisdom or challenge received notions of intellectual and social decorum. (Nietzsche, after all, had to leave his academic post in order to think freely and "like the gods.") As always, the poets and painters and mythographers venture first where pedants dare not. The upshot is clear, if regrettable: precisely as the lesbian "idea" has intensified its hold on our collective psychic life—and the literature and art of the past three or four centuries bear abundant witness, in my view, to this monumentally seductive phenomenon—female same-sex love has remained, among professors, pundits, naysayers, and other arbiters of official taste, a taboo subject, one too fraught with anxiety to allow for general acknowledgment, let alone any extended study or examination.

A few examples from exactly that period in which the history of ideas was established as a modern academic discipline—the 1930s to 1960s—may serve to epitomize the pattern of avoidance. In the introduction to his pioneering, now classic book, *The Great Chain of Being: A Study in the History of Ideas* (1936), the literary historian Arthur O. Lovejoy famously defined the goal of the evolving intellectual discipline known as the history of ideas as the demonstration of how certain "unit-ideas" take hold of a social group, "attain a wide diffusion" and "become a part of the stock of many minds."[6] In the learned treatise that followed he traced how the archaic notion of metaphysical *hierarchy*—originating with Plato and the Greeks and emblazoned in the popular Renaissance image of the Great Chain of Being—carried down through the centuries and continued to exert a powerful conceptual influence over Western civilization well into the nineteenth century. Precisely through the exploration of such "primary and persistent or recurrent dynamic units of the history of thought," Lovejoy argued, one might arrive at a deeper understanding of both literary and cultural history and the conceptual links binding them together.[7]

In the decades following the Second World War other scholars took up Lovejoy's project in different ways. In *European Literature and the Latin Middle Ages* (1948), a magisterial study of ancient rhetoric and its influence on Western culture, the Swiss philologist Ernst Robert Curtius demonstrated how a traditional body of conventional "topics" (the so-called topoi or "commonplaces") derived from classical rhetoric had shaped European philosophical and literary discourse since the early Middle Ages. Curtius's "topics" (Nature is a Book, The World is a Stage, Time Flies, *Carpe Diem*, Appearances are Deceiving, All That is Beautiful Must Die, and so on) are similar indeed to Lovejoy's "ideas": each stands in for a complex of cultural meaning so widely disseminated and deeply internalized as to become part of the shared conceptual framework of modern civilized life. Like Lovejoy, Curtius saw the study of these "intelligible units" of culture as profoundly enriching: even as one explored the "advances in historical knowledge" metaphorically embedded in literature and philosophy over the centuries, one replicated in oneself that "widening and clarification of consciousness" undergone by humanity as a whole since ancient times.[8]

The massive *Dictionary of the History of Ideas: Studies of Selected Pivotal Ideas,* a five-volume compendium published in 1968, represents an even more ambitious, if not breathtaking, elaboration on the Lovejovian intellectual scheme. Here, arranged in alphabetical order and marshaled under various subheadings, are what its mid-century editors considered, without blush, the foundational concepts of Western civilization. These included various ancient philosophical notions (Appearance and Reality, Atomism, Catharsis, Causation, Death, Determinism, Free Will, Happiness, Harmony, Justice, Tragedy, *Ut Pictura Poesis*, Utopia, etc.), as well as a grab-bag of modern additions (Academic Freedom, Alienation, Art for Art's Sake, Biologism, Constitutionalism, Deism, Existentialism, The Faust Theme, Historical and Dialectical Materialism, International Peace, Liberalism, Machiavellianism, Nationalism, Oriental Ideas in American Thought, Primitivism, Relativity, Romanticism, Utilitarianism, Victorian Sensibility and Sentiment, and so on). For each "idea" or idea cluster, the editors provided a short account of its history, how it was promulgated across different social groups or classes, and where it fits "in the whole organic and cultural setting of thought."[9]

The editors of the *Dictionary* attempted to disarm potential criticism by acknowledging in their introduction that their roll call of important ideas was hardly exhaustive:

> We cannot emphasize too strongly the point expressed in the subtitle of our work, that we are presenting a varied array of *selected* pivotal topics in intellectual history and of methods of writing about such topics. Although the number of topics discussed is large, we do not pretend that these volumes represent the entire range of intellectual history. To attempt a complete history of ideas would be to attempt (of course, in vain) to exhaust the history of the human mind; hence, the limited number of topics dealt with, and even these contain lacunae which we hope will encourage further studies.[10]

And yet it is worth pointing out how drastically selective the whole history-of-ideas approach has been when it comes to matters dealing with sexuality in general and homosexuality in particular. Lovejoy made no mention of what would now be called "sexual knowledge" in his otherwise monumental adumbration of European intellectual history; Curtius, apart from a brief excursus on sodomy in classical antiquity and the complaints lodged against it by the medieval poet and theologian Alain de Lille (1128–1202), virtually ignored that vast corpus of erotic satire, fable, and speculation now seen as one of the most important legacies of the classical humanist tradition.[11] While the *Dictionary of the History of Ideas* devotes full-scale entries to such relatively marginal or specialized notions as Spontaneous Generation, Literary Attitudes Toward Mountains, Positivism in Latin America, the Wisdom of the Fool, and Causation in Islamic Thought, it has no entry for Sex, Sexuality, Gender, Heterosexuality, Homosexuality, or indeed Lesbianism. Social Attitudes Toward Women, the only entry in the volume under which the latter subject might possibly be broached, makes no mention of sexuality, homo- or hetero-, or the central role of sexual themes in both the philosophical and popular imagination.

Missing until recently from intellectual history has been any concerted investigation into how ideas having to do with the erotic life—as opposed to, say, metaphysics or politics or epistemology—have taken shape in culture and been disseminated over time. Which is not to say we haven't had a complex, awe-inspiring, and permanently scandalous investigation of this cognitive process in relation to *individual* psychic life: Freud's writings are nothing less than a sweeping attempt to describe how in infancy and early childhood we internalize various complex "ideas" about sexual generation, our own bodies and desires, and the bodies and desires of other people. But the social and cultural context in which such conceptual work is supposed to take place has seldom been acknowledged or described.[12]

It is true, of course, that matters have changed dramatically over the past thirty years or so—thanks in large part to the extraordinarily influential books of the French philosopher and social theorist Michel Foucault. However belatedly, the work of acknowledgment and description has begun. Foucault's *The History of Sexuality*, the first volume of which (*La Volunté de savoir*) was translated into English in 1978, was not only the first major work of European intellectual history to explore questions of sexual knowledge in relation to culture at large, it also helped to license a host of groundbreaking studies, in particular, of male homosexuality—among which K. J. Dover's *Greek Homosexuality* (1978), John Boswell's *Christianity, Social Tolerance, and Homosexuality: Gay People in Western Europe from the Beginning of the Christian Era to the Fourteenth Century* (1980), Alan Bray's *Homosexuality in Renaissance England* (1982), Eve Kosofsky Sedgwick's *Between Men: English Literature and Male Homosocial Desire* (1985), and David Halperin's *One Hundred Years of Homosexuality and Other Essays on Greek Love* (1990) are perhaps the best known.[13]

When it comes to the history of the lesbian "idea," however, the breakthroughs have been more scattered. Yes, there have been a handful of pioneering works: Jeannette Foster's *Sex Variant Women in Literature* (1955) and Lillian Faderman's *Surpassing the Love of Men: Romantic Friendship and Love Between Women from the Renaissance to the Present* (1981), and its sequel, *Odd Girls and Twilight Lovers: A History of Lesbian Life in Twentieth-Century America* (1991), remain indispensable for anyone making a broad first foray into the subject.[14] And over the past few years a number of more specialized scholarly books have appeared, the relevance of which to the subject at hand is immediately apparent: Joan DeJean's *Fictions of Sappho, 1546–1937* (1989), Emma Donoghue's *Passions Between Women: British Lesbian Culture 1668–1801* (1993), Page duBois's *Sappho Is Burning* (1995), Bernadette J. Brooten's *Love Between Women: Early Christian Responses to Female Homoeroticism* (1996), Ruth Vanita's *Sappho and the Virgin Mary: Same-Sex Love and the English Literary Imagination* (1996), Jane McIntosh Snyder's *Lesbian Desire in the Lyrics of Sappho* (1997), Patricia Juliana Smith's *Lesbian Panic: Homoeroticism in Modern British Women's Fiction* (1997), Yopie Prins's *Victorian Sappho* (1999), Laura Doan's *Fashioning Sapphism: The Origins of a Modern English Lesbian Culture* (2000), Margaret Reynolds's *The Sappho Companion* (2000), and Harriette Andreadis's *Sappho in Early Modern England: Female Same-Sex Literary Erotics, 1550–1714* (2001). Yet it still might be argued that we lack any comprehensive history of the lesbian topos in modern Western culture, just as we have lacked any truly syncretic collections of relevant primary texts.

It has been my primary goal in this anthology to repair some of this neglect. The diverse, unbowdlerized, even Lovejovian assortment of works following herewith is meant—in the simplest and most direct way—to illuminate the history of a *thought*: *the collective apprehension that women might intimately conjoin for their own sexual pleasure or the sexual pleasure of others*. As "thoughts" go, this one both is and isn't obvious. Nowadays, as self-congratulatory moderns, we tend to take the lesbian idea for granted—just as we may also assume that lesbianism itself has always been around in some form or another. (As indeed it may have been; but that is neither here nor there.) Like male homosexuality, sexual love between women has become eminently "thinkable" in contemporary Western society. Indeed, as a quick troll through the newspapers or a sampling of television talk shows will reveal, we think—and talk—about the subject with compulsive, sometimes tedious, regularity. So familiar in fact has the notion of erotic desire between women become—so much a part, in Lovejoy's terms, "of the stock of many minds"—that it is difficult for us to imagine a time when it was *not* thinkable, or what one might call only *partially* thinkable.

Thinkability, however, is variable over time. The routinization of the lesbian idea in the late twentieth century, I contend, should be seen as just that: as the end result of a long and gradual historical transformation of consciousness that began in Western society in the late Renaissance. Imaginative literature was crucially involved in this historic expansion of awareness. For many centuries, roughly from the collapse of the Roman empire to the later Middle Ages, it was *not* obvious that women might desire other women; had it been otherwise, there would be numerous texts (poems, plays, stories) floating about to tell us so. But few such texts exist. Apart from the fleeting references that survive in the theological arcana of late antiquity (and here the magnificent archival work of Bernadette Brooten has been of compelling interest), even the most meticulous researchers have failed to turn up much popular writing on female same-sex love between the sixth and the sixteenth centuries.[15] This is in marked contrast to what one finds after 1500. In the past five centuries, female same-sex love has become more and more visible as a Western cultural preoccupation, even as lesbian-themed writing—celebratory and scurrilous, polite and prurient—has proliferated in both public and private spheres.

What accounted for this dramatic shift in attention? No single explanation, of course, can possibly account for such an arresting yet ultimately enigmatic cultural transformation. The subtle, broad-based changes in Western European social life associated with modernization—the slow liberation of women from reproductive and economic servitude, the gradual attenuation of Judeo-Christian religious strictures against unorthodox sexual behavior, the rise of revolutionary new notions of feminine moral, psychological, and erotic autonomy (as are found for example in the writings of the eighteenth-century French *philosophes*), and undoubtedly, the rebellious behavior of certain notorious public women (from the "roaring girls" of Renaissance London to the cross-dressing Queen Christina of Sweden and bisexual Marie Antoinette in the seventeenth and eighteenth centuries)—all contributed to the routinization of the lesbian topos. As women came increasingly to be regarded as free agents—with lives and aspirations apart from men—new erotic destinies, previously unknown, were imagined for them. In popular fancy autonomous women became capable of *anything*. The attribution of erotic agency to women was crucial, of course, to the elaboration of cultural fantasies about female same-sex love: the slow-to-dawn collective presumption that women might experience sexual desire—of any sort—was a necessary prerequisite, obviously, to the idea that women might feel sexual desire for each other.

At the same time, however, the significance of various literary developments cannot be ignored. I begin this anthology in 1531, with an excerpt from Ariosto's *Orlando Furioso*, because it was then, roughly speaking—during Ariosto's lifetime and in the decades following—that lesbianism became openly, if ambivalently, "thinkable" for the first time since late antiquity. The fateful appearance in the sixteenth century of new translations of key classical texts—Sappho's fragments, Ovid's *Metamorphoses* and *Heroides*, Martial's *Epigrams*, and Juvenal's *Satires* above all—was a central catalyst, I am convinced, in the cognitive revolution that brought female homosexuality back into view in early modern Europe. Indeed, by foregrounding female same-sex love in startling, provocative, and often wildly scabrous forms, the resuscitated texts of Greek and Roman antiquity did nothing less than make the lesbian topos widely available again to Western consciousness. Confronted with the example of the "libertine" ancients, Renaissance writers and their successors in turn felt free—even philosophically impelled—to continue the mental exploration of this most unruly yet fascinating of human passions.

The recovery of the poet Sappho and her works can be taken as emblematic of this process of revival and recognition. As the reader of this anthology will quickly discover, Sappho of Lesbos (c. 610–580 B.C.) remains a talismanic presence in the history of lesbian writing—the phantasmagoric icon of all it has ever been and all that it might become. Yet as the British classical scholar David M. Robinson was the first to elucidate in the 1920s, Sappho's fame (or infamy) has fluctuated dramatically over the centuries. In ancient times through roughly the end of the Roman period she was universally revered as the greatest poet next to Homer. (Ditto the most scandalous: an Anacreontic fragment written a generation after her death was the first work to lampoon her supposed lesbian affairs.) Plato, writing in the third century B.C., hailed her as the "Tenth Muse"; Antipater of Thessaloniki, in the first century B.C., described her as one of the "earthly Muses" and "the ornament of the fair-tressed Lesbians."[16] In ancient Rome, both Horace and Catullus composed Latin imitations of her poems. By the early part of the first century, the legend of her suicidal passion for the handsome boatman Phaon—she was supposed to have leapt to her death from the White Rocks of Leukas on the Greek mainland out of disappointed love for him—was sufficiently well known for Ovid to dramatize it in "Sappho to Phaon," epistle 15 of his *Heroides*; and Lucian alluded to her in his second-century *Dialogi meritricii*. In the third century, some six hundred years after her death, her renown was such that there was an attempt at a collected edition of her songs: a group of Greek scholars at Alexandria gathered together all of her surviving lyrics, organized them according to metrical scheme into nine books, and transcribed them onto papyrus scrolls.

Sappho's fame went into drastic eclipse, however, following the collapse of the Roman Empire. The vast majority of her poems were lost (what survives today represents only a fraction of what she is believed to have written); and references to her life and writings fell off sharply in the later Christian era. Tzetzes, a twelfth-century Byzantine scholar, speaks of Sappho's poems as having been "destroyed" by time; and with the exception of a few brief entries in the *Etymologicum magnum* (c. 1000 A.D.) and the lexicon known as the Suda, she is absent from medieval dictionaries and encyclopedias. Neither Dante nor Chaucer nor the early Provençal poets mention her. Whether or not one believes the curious tale of the "burning of Sappho"—the claim that her surviving manuscripts were put to the torch, either by the Christian patriarch Gregory of Nazianzos in 380 A.D., or by Pope Gregory VII in Constantinople and Rome in 1073, or by Crusaders in the twelfth century—it can be made to stand as a suggestive metaphor for her near-total disappearance from medieval writing.[17] At best Sappho was a person of whom one did well not to speak ("a love-crazed female fornicator who even sings about her own licentiousness," according to the early Christian writer Tatian);[18] more often than not, she was simply forgotten.

All this had changed—intoxicatingly—by the mid-sixteenth century. Sappho had begun to come teasingly back into view in early Renaissance Italy: Petrarch paid brief homage to her in his *Triumph of Love* (c. 1353) and *Tenth Eclogue* (1357); and Boccaccio included her in his *Of Famous Women* (1363–73). In France, the poet and scholar Christine de Pisan eulogized her in *The Book of the City of Ladies* (1404–5). Octavien de Saint-Gelais's popular 1505 translation of Ovid's *Heroides*, with its fanciful retelling of the Sappho/Phaon legend, in turn helped to revive interest in her life and loves. But the first real philological breakthrough took place in 1546, when the French humanist publisher Robert Estienne issued the first printed text of a Sappho poem—the so-called "Hymn to Aphrodite"—in an edition of Greek rhetorical treatises by Dionysios of Halicarnassus. Four years later his son Henri Estienne began translating all the extant Sapphic fragments into Latin, several of which he published, together with the poems of Anacreon, in 1550 and 1556. (The first French translation of a Sappho poem was by Rémi Belleau, also in 1556.) Henri Estienne's subsequent masterwork—*Poetae Graeci Principes* (1566) containing the Greek texts of almost forty Sapphic fragments with Latin translations facing—continues to be regarded as one of the lasting accomplishments of Renaissance classical scholarship.[19]

The labors of the Estiennes bore abundant fruit. Over the next two centuries, even as additional fragments of her verse continued to turn up, new translations and adaptations of Sappho multiplied. Among poets her influence was immediate and profound. In France, avant-gardists such as Pierre Ronsard and Louise Labé produced Sappho imitations inspired by the Estienne and Belleau translations; in England, Sir Philip Sidney adapted one of her poems—the celebrated love lyric known as Fragment 31—in the *Old Arcadia* (1584). Other writers dramatized her legendary amours. John Lyly and John Donne both produced works on Sappho herself in the later sixteenth century: Lyly's play *Sapho and Phao* appeared in 1584; and Donne's heroic epistle "Sapho to Philaenis" around 1598. Meanwhile her textual recovery went on apace. The first great phase of Sappho's reassimilation culminated with two magisterial late-seventeenth-century compilations of her work: Tanneguy Le Fèvre's annotated Greek edition of 1660, and his daughter Anne Le Fèvre Dacier's Greek-French edition of 1681, *Les Poésies d'Anacréon et de Sapho*. In England, where translations of various Sappho poems had appeared in 1652, 1680, and 1695, Dacier's edition in turn inspired the first modern English collections, Ambrose Philips's *The Works of Anacreon and Sappho* (1713) and John Addison's *Sapphus Odae fragmenta* (1735).

The rediscovery of Sappho and her work meant ineluctably a confrontation with the "idea" of lesbianism. Not only did various biographical sources mention putative love affairs with women (even if only, like Ovid, to impugn or discount them) the poems themselves seemed to bear witness to such as well. Above all, the great Fragment 31, originally preserved in the Greek Christian critic Longinus's third-century treatise *On the Sublime* and Sappho's most famous lyric over the centuries, stood out as a sensational—if cryptic—paean to a female beloved. Usually known as "Peer of the Gods" or "To the Beloved" in English, the poem features a female speaker who gazes longingly at a young woman sitting next to a man at a banquet feast. The speaker expresses her envy of the man and the amorous distress the sight of the girl arouses in her. What follows is a modern rendering by the American translator Jim Powell:

> In my eyes he matches the gods, that man who
> sits there facing you—any man whatever—
> listening from closeby, to the sweetness of your
>   voice as you talk, the
>
> sweetness of your laughter: yes, that—I swear it—
> sets the heart to shaking inside my breast, since
> once I look at you for a moment, I can't
>   speak any longer,
>
> but my tongue breaks down, and then all at once a
> subtle fire races inside my skin, my
> eyes can't see a thing and a whirring whistle
>   thrums at my hearing,
>
> cold sweat covers me and a trembling takes
> ahold of me all over: I'm greener than the

grass is and appear to myself to be little
    short of dying.

But all must be endured, since even a poor [. . .][20]

So authentically "felt" seemed the poetic emotion here, so sensually charged the language of the Greek original, it was hardly surprising that commentators such as Tanneguy Le Fèvre were inclined (despite the Phaon story) to regard Sappho as incontrovertibly homosexual in her tastes. "I mean, Monsieur," wrote Le Fèvre in his 1664 *Abrégé des vies des poètes grecs*, a pedagogical work addressed to the twelve-year-old Comte de Limoges, "that Sappho was of a very amorous complexion, and that not being satisfied with that which other women find in the company of men who are not disagreeable to them, she wanted to have mistresses."[21]

This is not to say, of course, that "confrontation" with the lesbian idea affected every reader in the same way or indeed resolved into Le Fèvre's worldly complacency. In Sappho's case, many translators over the years—starting with Le Fèvre's own daughter Anne Le Fèvre Dacier—energetically denied or discounted the evidences for the poet's lesbianism. As Joan DeJean points out in *Fictions of Sappho 1546–1937*, French and later German commentators were particularly resistant to the homoerotic interpretation of Sappho's verses. In her own annotations on the poet's life, published twenty years after her father's, Madame Dacier dismissed rumors of Sappho's affairs with women as "calumnies" put forth by envious rivals determined to "blacken" her reputation. In a similarly repressive move she retitled Fragment 31 "À son amie" (To her Friend) instead of the more accurate "À une aimée" (To a Beloved), thereby weakening considerably the poem's possible erotic charge. The poem itself is described merely as "an ode that [Sappho] wrote for one of her friends"—as if it were merely, in DeJean's words, "a platonic celebration of the joys of friendship."[22]

Such acts of editorial obfuscation became fairly common in the later eighteenth and nineteenth century. In nineteenth-century England and Germany, for example, scholarly commentators attempted to explain away Sappho's love verses to women by insisting that she had been the headmistress of a kind of all-female academy on Lesbos and that her passionate effusions were simply a reflection of the pedagogical affection she felt for her students. Other would-be rehabilitators depicted her as the charismatic yet chaste leader of a religious cult devoted to Aphrodite. And still others attempted to obscure the stories of sapphic "vice" by way of (sometimes protracted) rhetorical flights. Even David Robinson, sophisticated critic though he was, was capable (as late as 1924) of some truly fantastical mumbo jumbo in defense of Sappho's sexual reputation:

The moral purity of Sappho shines in its own light. She expresses herself, no doubt, in very passionate language, but passionate purity is a finer article than the purity of prudery, and Sappho's passionate expressions are always under the control of her art. A woman of bad character and certainly a woman of such a variety of bad character as scandal . . . has attributed to Sappho might express herself passionately and might run on indefinitely with erotic imagery. But Sappho is never erotic. There is no language to be found in her songs which a pure woman might not use, and it would be practically impossible for a bad woman to subject her expressions to the marvellous niceties of rhythm, accent, and meaning which Sappho everywhere exhibits. Immorality and loss of self-control never subject themselves to perfect literary and artistic taste. It is against the nature of things that a woman who has given herself up to unnatural and inordinate practices which defy the moral instinct and throw the soul into disorder, practices which harden and petrify the soul, should be able to write in perfect obedience to the laws of vocal harmony, imagination, and arrangement of the details of thought. The nature of things does not admit of such an inconsistency.[23]

Sappho's love of certain flowers, he concluded, was a final "luminous testimony" of her virtue: "a bad woman as well as a pure woman might love roses, but a bad woman does not love the small and hidden wild flowers of the field, the dainty anthrysc and the clover, as Sappho did." No flowers of evil there.[24]

The fatal flaw in such maneuvering, of course, was that by disclaiming sapphic "vice" one ended up calling attention—perversely—to the very phenomenon one sought to disavow. Even as commentators such as Dacier and Robinson denied particulars (*Sappho was not a lesbian*), they ended up confirming the more fundamental point: that *lesbianism itself existed*. The battle might be won, in other words, but the war was lost: for the more forcefully one argued that Sappho (or any other woman) was not a lover of women the more distinct (and ultimately assimilable) one made the notion of same-sex love itself. This is a paradox to which we will return: the way in which would-be banishers of the lesbian idea have often ended up facilitating its entry into cultural consciousness by making it more "talkable."

The same paradoxical process, the reader will see, has often been at work in literary explorations of the lesbian idea. Take, for example, the girls-disguised-as-boys sex-comedies of the English Renaissance. In John Lyly's *Gallathea* (1592) two girls who have been disguised as boys since infancy meet and fall in love with one another, each believing the other is *really* a boy. When the true sex of each girl is revealed—to the shock and embarrassment of all—the Goddess of Love changes one of them into a real boy so that they can marry and live happily after all. Yes, a kind of normalization is achieved: Lyly's heroines are "not lesbians." But for a while—the duration of the play in fact—we have been forced to imagine that they might be. Whether we wish to or not, Lyly makes us contemplate, quite literally, the possibility of two young women "in love." In an analogous way, one suspects, the very prolixities of the "Sappho was not a lesbian" school made lesbianism itself—the "unnatural and inordinate practice" under attack—all the more "thinkable" for intelligent readers.

Sappho's fragments were not the only classical texts, however, to prompt such epiphanies. Martial's Epigram 67, with its obscene assault on the girl-loving Philaenis;

Juvenal's Sixth Satire, in which drunken Roman matrons "ride" one another like horses in the moonlight; and Ovid's ever popular *Metamorphoses*, with its cohort of gods and mortals who don disguises and by accident or design attract members of their own sex—each contributed over the decades to the gradual routinization of the lesbian topos.[25] Classical works continued to underwrite explorations of the lesbian theme well into the twentieth century. Sappho alone inspired a seemingly endless flow of homoerotically inflected works: Madeleine de Scudéry's *Les Femmes illustres, ou Les Harangues héroiques* (1642) and *Artamène, ou Le Grand Cyrus* (1653); Alexander Pope's *Sappho to Phaon* (1712); the anonymous *Sappho-an* (c. 1735) and "Dialogue between Sappho and Ninon de l'Enclos in the Shades" (1773); Madame de Staël's *Corinne* (1807); Samuel Taylor Coleridge's "Alcaeus to Sappho" (1800); the "Femme damnées" poems in Charles Baudelaire's *Les Fleurs du mal* (1857); A. C. Swinburne's "Anactoria" (1866) and *Lesbia Brandon* (1867); Paul Verlaine's *Scènes de l'amour sapphique* (1867); Thomas Hardy's *Desperate Remedies* (1871); "Michael Field's" *Long Ago* (1889); Pierre Louÿs's *Chansons de Bilitis* (1894); Walter Pater's "Myth of Demeter and Persephone" (1894); the poems of Renée Vivien, Natalie Barney, Marina Tsvetaeva, Amy Lowell, and Hilda Doolittle; Hope Mirrlees's *Madeleine: One of Love's Jansenists* (1919); Compton Mackenzie's *Extraordinary Women* (1928); Colette's *The Pure and The Impure* (1932); Marguerite Yourcenar's *Sappho, ou suicide* (1937); and on and on.[26]

What happens to the lesbian idea in the twentieth century? I end this anthology with works written or published around the time of Stonewall—the celebrated 1969 fracas in which a number of homosexual men and women in New York's Greenwich Village fought back police who had stormed a local gay bar, the Stonewall Inn, in an attempt to close it down. The decision to end here, with the event now usually regarded as the *beginning* of the contemporary gay and lesbian liberation movement, may strike some as a paradoxical or capricious one—like the corollary decision to exclude from this collection any living writers. But besides its obvious symbolic meanings, Stonewall offers a convenient emblem, in my view, for the historic resolution of that large cultural transformation I have sought to outline here: the absorption into collective awareness of the lesbian idea. Put most bluntly, the years around Stonewall—the late 1960s and early 1970s—saw the first normalization of homosexual behavior in Western society since the Greeks. If hardly relieved of its power to scandalize (and there will always be those who find in the idea of same-sex love an incitement to hatred and mayhem), homosexuality, male and female, was nonetheless publicly recognized in a host of official ways. Consensual homosexual relations between men were decriminalized in Britain in 1967; in the United States, sodomy statutes were overturned in a host of states by the mid-1970s. The American Psychiatric Association removed homosexuality from its list of mental illnesses in 1974; the U.S. Civil Service Commission removed its ban on hiring homosexual employees the following year. The 1970s saw the first openly homosexual person elected to public office in the United States (Massachusetts state assemblywoman Elaine Noble) and the establishment of antidiscrimination laws in Boston, San Francisco, Houston, Detroit, Washington, D.C., and other large American cities.[27] Such acts taken together represented a radical reorganization of cultural proto-cols: the establishment of diplomatic relations, one might say, between the great coun-try of heterosexuality and the breakaway state of homosexuality.

Such changes, however, can be seen as the end result of rather more protracted developments over the centuries—above all, the integration into human thought of the realization that same-sex love not only exists, across time and across societies, but shows no signs of going away. In the case of lesbianism, recognition has come only after centuries of official denial—a denial so profound at times that the law itself has held back acknowledgment until our own day. (Statutes prohibiting male homosexual acts have existed since the Middle Ages; lesbianism, however, has seldom if ever been explicitly outlawed—the fear being that any act of proscription would simply call more attention to it.)[28] Lesbian writing—of all sorts—has proliferated since Stonewall, and a host of existing books and anthologies track its courses.[29] But in an important sense, such writing has been merely a kind of postscript or underscoring: of the coming to consciousness of the lesbian idea itself. Few would balk these days at the thought that Sappho might have had homosexual love affairs; indeed, Greek homosexuality has become a topic of learned discussion among classical scholars. Nor indeed have hun-dreds of revelations about the same-sex liaisons of various prominent female figures of the past century—Jane Addams, Alice James, Willa Cather, Virginia Woolf, H.D., Amy Lowell, Edna St. Vincent Millay, Stein, Bishop, Marina Tsvetaeva, Berenice Abbott, Ma Rainey, Edith Hamilton, Jane Harrison, Babe Didrickson, Romaine Brooks, Katherine Mansfield, Colette, Josephine Baker, Vita Sackville-West, Elizabeth Bowen, Bessie Smith, Djuna Barnes, Alla Nazimova, Margaret Anderson, Eleanor Roosevelt, Anna Freud, Greta Garbo, Marlene Dietrich, Daphne Du Maurier, Eva Le Gallienne, Coco Chanel, Mary Renault, Lorraine Hansberry, Jane Bowles, Carson McCullers, Simone de Beauvoir, Marguerite Yourcenar, Patricia Highsmith, Rachel Carson, Margaret Mead, Janet Flanner, Anne Sexton, Iris Murdoch, Brigid Brophy, Barbara Jordan, Billie Jean King, Martina Navratilova—provoked the mass outrage or denial that they might once have. On the contrary, to judge by the success of recent biographies responsible for "outing" their subjects, such revelations seem to bring gen-eral pleasure to the reading public.[30]

I end with Stonewall, therefore, as a way of marking symbolically the twentieth-century routinization of the lesbian idea: its entry into serious public discourse, its col-lective acceptance as a legitimate topic for discussion, its integration into "the life of many minds"—the beginning of its transformation, in effect, into the *mundane*. For mundane it now becomes, after a thousand years of mixed feelings and eloquence great and grim.

3

A happy ending, then, for the truth lovers. But let us pursue this business of cognitive routinization in a little more detail—by way of some of the specific items included here. I have arranged the texts in this anthology chronologically, usually according to first appearance or date of publication, though in a few unusual cases (Lady Mary Wortley Montagu, Angelina Weld Grimké, Marina Tsvetaeva, Vita Sackville-West) by date of composition.[31] Items are likewise grouped by century, for navigational purposes. When it comes to examining the divers ways in which the lesbian "idea" has manifested itself over time, however, large period distinctions are not necessarily immediately helpful. To be sure, one can generalize about sheer output: as female same-sex love has become ever more "talkable," so the quantity of lesbian-themed texts produced has increased over time. (Even without the inclusion of works by living writers, this volume contains more items from the twentieth century than any other.) Yet it would be simplistic to make broad claims about "seventeenth-century" or "eighteenth-century" treatments of the lesbian topos, as opposed to, say, "nineteenth-century" or "twentieth-century" treatments. From the Renaissance on Western writers have engaged with the lesbian theme in a myriad of complex and often contradictory ways. This complexity of response—decade to decade—must inevitably be registered by anyone hoping to understand its literary or cultural history.

More useful indeed are affective distinctions. And here one may begin to categorize works by type and trace a movement from what one might call inaugural—possibly primitive—to more sophisticated responses. The classic "first response" to the notion of love between women (one perhaps linked to the evolutionary shock of the first primate who witnessed homoerotic play among his kin in the antediluvian forests) is one of astonishment, resolving into the concept *monster*. *Monster* in the old-fashioned or root sense, that is: meaning simply a sight provoking awe or wonder. (Etymologically, *monster* derives from the Latin *monstrare*, to show.) As one might expect, this sort of response is most often to be found in sixteenth- and seventeenth-century works, when authors and readers alike were struggling to absorb, among other things, the cognitive *surprise* of Greco-Roman homosexuality. The core discovery encapsulated here is that it is possible to *run against the course of nature*. Thus in a number of Renaissance writings, for example, the writer claims to have heard "a strange story"—about a woman in such-and-such a town who has changed sex, about a gallant soldier discovered to be female, about a woman who married a woman, about a peasant girl with a five-inch clitoris or a thick beard like a man's. He (seldom a she) may present his tale as one in a collection of odd yarns—about birds with two heads, a lamb with the face of a boy, a griffin seen in Lombardy or the Lowlands—or it may stand alone as single uncanny event. The sixteenth-century physician Ambroise Paré's *On Monsters and Marvels* (1573) is a perfect example of this kind of believe-it-or-not writing: in a catalogue of "things that appear outside the course of Nature," he sets stories about women who have married women alongside tales about demons, tritons, fur-covered boys, and marvelous beasts whose blood can cure wounds. Lesbianism here is the result of a physiological freak: women with such desires, Paré tells us, are said to be either "hermaphrodites" or women who have "degenerated into men"—i.e., females whose genitals have somehow fallen from the womb, to hang outside their bodies like men's. Like unicorns and mermen and women who give birth to stones, they are bizarre aberrations—part of a brave "New World" of mysterious, dumbfounding, and unprecedented things. Though his interest may masquerade as clinical curiosity, the writer's overriding attitude is one of seduced credulity: his goal is to seduce the reader likewise.[32]

This neophyte or "shock" response survives in a number of subsequent writings included here—in Montaigne's travel journal (in which is related the famous case of the woman-turned-man Marie Germain); in the anonymous eighteenth-century antimasturbation treatise known as the *Onania* (c. 1725), whose author dwells with puerile excitement on tales of women with hypertrophied clitorises; even in Henry Fielding's potboiling pamphlet *The Female Husband* (1746) about a male impersonator who marries several women in order to sate her "monstrous" lusts. The wish to associate female homosexuality with physiological oddities such as distended genitalia or supposedly masculine features—an explanatory fantasia that would survive into the writings of the late-nineteenth-century sexologists Richard von Krafft-Ebing and Havelock Ellis—seems inevitably a part of a "naive" or reflexive response to the lesbian idea. Such anatomical myths persist here and there even in contemporary postindustrial societies—wherever, in fact, there are unlettered or unsophisticated people. The survival of terms such as *morphodite* or *mophrodite* or *she-male* in rural or backwoods America—bewildered neighbors applied such words to the lesbian male impersonator Brandon Teena, murdered in Humboldt, Nebraska, in 1993—bespeaks the ongoing appeal, for those lacking any notion of psychology, of the idea that women who desire women must have something freakish about their bodies in order for them to love the way they do.[33]

Such primal naïveté seldom lasts for long, however, without turning into something else: namely, an opinion. In the same way that a soccer goalie, confronted by the prospect of a penalty kick, must commit his body either to the right or to the left—even before the kicker has kicked the ball—the individual newly confronted by the lesbian "monster" must incline, it would seem, in one direction or the other: toward sympathetic interest (the monster is lovable) or hostile self-distancing (the monster is detestable). One either adores or despises, rhapsodizes or condemns. Writers can be categorized according to which affective impulse predominates in their work. Drawing on classical prototypes, we might label the first attitude the "Sapphic" or "sublime" response—in that it has been the professed admirers of Sappho, typically, who have expatiated most empathetically on the vicissitudes of female same-sex love. The second might be labeled the "Roman" or "satiric" attitude—after those classical writers, notably Martial and Juvenal, who first evolved the brilliantly toxic genre of the antilesbian diatribe.

There are a number of things to say about these two attitudes. First and foremost, though cultural stereotypes might prompt one to think otherwise, writers do not fall neatly into "Sapphic" or "Roman" categories according to biological sex. Granted, one can always find authors who epitomize positive or negative attitudes in an almost cartoonishly male or female fashion. There are male writers, for example, with an aversion to female homosexuality so fixed and phobic one might think them chromosomally damaged. It is hard to imagine a more bluntly phallocentric satire, for example, than the

French Renaissance poet François de Maynard's "Tribades, or Lesbia," a brief yet noxious lampoon from 1646 on the digital depravities of one Phyllis:

> If your finger could shoot its wad
> With all it knows to do to date
> Sweet Phyllis, there's no debate
> That readily it could masquerade
> For something much too crude to name.
>
> To have, as is your pride,
> A hand so white and clean
> How in the hell do you keep it preened
> When the tub in which you slide
> It has such strange soap, I mean?

A sad and lonely boy? On the contrary. Jumping three centuries, Maynard finds a soul mate in the British novelist Wyndham Lewis, whose virulent-surreal portrait of a "Lesbian-Ape" in *The Apes of God* (1930) seems motivated by a similarly entrenched sex-bound disgust:

> Before him stood a severe masculine figure. In general effect it was a bavarian youth-movement elderly enthusiast. She was beyond question somewhat past mark-of-mouth. But this was a woman, as in fact she had appeared in the typed description. Of that he felt tolerably certain, because of the indefinable something that could only be described as "masculine." An heroic something or other in the bold blue eye, that held an eyeglass, that reminded him of the Old Guard or the Death-or-Glory Boys, in the house of Mr. Brian Macdonnell, secured for him certainty of the sex at least without further worry. It was She. This was Miss Ansell.
>
> She was wiry and alert with hennaed hair bristling, en brosse. In khaki-shorts, her hands were in their pockets, and her bare sunburnt legs were all muscle and no nonsense at all. There was something that reminded Dan of Dick Whittingdon, for she was bald, he remarked with a deep blush, on the top of her head. Only there, the resemblance ended it seemed, for whereas Dick was anxious, that was easy to see, to disguise his naked scalp, *this* strong-minded person had a peculiar air of being proud of it all the time (to be bald, like the ability to grow a moustache, was a masculine monopoly). A march had been stolen, with her masculine calvity. But a strawberry-pink pull-over was oddly surmounted by a stiff Radcliffe-Hall [*sic*] collar, of antique masculine cut—suggestive of the masculine hey-day, when men were men starched-up and stiff as pokers, in their tandems and tilburys. The bare brown feet were strapped into spartan sandals. A cigarette-holder half a foot long protruded

from a firm-set jaw. It pointed at Dan, sparkling angrily as the breath was compressed within its bore.

One could hardly ask for a more lurid excursion ride through the dank swamps of male paranoia. In the "haggard old bachelor-girl in sports-shorts"—who nonetheless shoots a wad—misogynist head-bangers across the centuries (and Hemingway is sometimes another) come face-to-face with their own worst fears.

In turn, through the looking-glass, are those female writers, such as the late-eighteenth-century poet Anna Seward, whose sickly celebrations of "vestal" devotion between women are kitsch in a vulgar nice-lady way that seems incorrigibly feminine. Witness the following sample stanzas from Seward's 1796 paean to Eleanor Butler and Sarah Ponsonby—two noble Irishwomen who, spurning their wealthy families, eloped to Wales together in 1778 and subsequently became famous as the "Ladies of Llangollen":

> Now with a Vestal lustre glows the VALE,
> Thine, sacred FRIENDSHIP, permanent as pure;
> In vain the stern Authorities assail,
> In vain Persuasion spreads her silken lure,
> High-born, and high-endow'd, the peerless Twain,
> Pant for coy Nature's charms 'mid silent dale, and plain.
>
> Thro' ELEANORA, and her ZARA's mind,
> Early tho' genius, taste, and fancy flow'd,
> Tho' all the graceful Arts their powers combin'd,
> And her last polish brilliant Life bestow'd,
> The lavish Promiser, in Youth's soft morn,
> Pride, Pomp, and Love, her friends, the sweet Enthusiasts scorn.
>
> Then rose the Fairy Palace of the Vale,
> Then bloom'd around it the Arcadian bowers;
> Screen'd from the storms of Winter, cold and pale,
> Screen'd from the fervors of the sultry hours,
> Circling the lawny crescent, soon they rose,
> To letter'd ease devote, and Friendship's blest repose.

Only a respectable woman, one might argue, could make the phrase "pant for coy Nature's charms" sound so appallingly prurient.

Less kitsch—perhaps—the voluptuous reveries of the modern French writer Violette Leduc. Nevertheless, in the florid descriptions of lesbian lovemaking in her autobiographical novel, *La Bâtarde* (1964), it is equally difficult to imagine the writing hand (or the touching hand) as anything but female:

The hand stripped the velvet off my arm, halted near the vein in the crook of the elbow, fornicated there among the traceries, moved downward to the wrist, right to the tips of the nails, sheathed my arm once more in a long suède glove, fell from my shoulder like an insect, and hooked itself into the armpit. I was stretching my neck, listening for what answers my arm was giving the wanderer. The hand, still seeking to persuade me, was bringing my arm, my armpit, into their real existence. The hand was wandering through whispering snow-capped bushes, over the last frosts on the meadows, over the first buds as they swelled to fullness. The springtime that had been crying its impatience with the voice of tiny birds under my skin was now curving and swelling into flower. Isabelle, stretched out upon the darkness, was fastening my feet with ribbons, unwinding the swaddling bands of my alarm. With hands laid flat upon the mattress, I was immersed in the selfsame magic task as she. She was kissing what she had caressed and then, light as a feather duster, the hand began to flick, to brush the wrong way all that it had smoothed before. The sea monster in my entrails quivered. Isabelle was drinking at my breast, the right, the left, and I drank with her, sucking the milk of darkness when her lips had gone. The fingers were returning now, encircling and testing the warm weight of my breast. The fingers were pretending to be waifs in a storm; they were taking shelter inside me. A host of slaves, all with the face of Isabelle, fanned my brow, my hands.

Alike—if in nothing else—in their sexual chauvinism, Seward and Leduc figure love between women as an ecstatic ultrafeminine pastoral: a burgeoning "Vale of Friendship" in the one, a slow, besotting touch in the other. The pretty little flowers are blooming everywhere. In other words: no men need apply.

But it's been the ones who have crossed over—who don't conform to stereotype—who have made four hundred years of Western writing about lesbianism so unpredictable and strange. Not all "Sapphists" are women; not all "Romans" are men. The sharp and the soft commingle. Any number of women, for example, have been as eager as men to lay on the darts. Sharp indeed is the treatment of "Harriot Freke," a dueling, chortling, feminist cross-dresser who appears in Maria Edgeworth's 1801 novel, *Belinda*. Edgeworth lampoons her relentlessly: as half mad and blustering and mannish—a freak of a woman who can't keep her hands off girls. Freke succeeds with one, a feckless young lady named Miss Moreton, but fails with the novel's heroine, the virtuous and book-loving Belinda:

"What have you here?" continued Mrs. Freke, . . . exclaiming as she reviewed each of the books on the table in their turns, in the summary language of presumptuous ignorance. "Smith's *Theory of Moral Sentiments*—milk and water! Moore's *Travels*—hasty pudding! La Bruyère—nettle porridge! This is what you were at when I came in, was it not?" said she, taking up a book in which she saw Belinda's mark, "Essay on the Inconsistency of Human Wishes." "Poor thing! who bored you with this task?"

"Mr. Percival recommended it to me, as one of the best essays in the English language." "The devil! They seem to have put you in a course of the bitters—a course in the woods might do your business better. Do you ever hunt? Let me take you out with me some morning. You'd be quite an angel on horseback; or let me drive you out some day in my unicorn." Belinda declined this invitation, and Mrs. Freke strode away to the window to conceal her mortification, threw up the sash, and called out to her groom, "Walk those horses about, blockhead!"

No disappointment unmans her for long, however. "Fun and Freke for ever, huzza!" is her motto—delivered with belching horse-laugh—and she is soon on her way to new and deplorable conquests.

Other women writers treat the subject with less buffoonery, perhaps, but are just as deeply disturbed by it. A stock character in early-twentieth-century British and American women's fiction, for example, is the seductive older woman (often a teacher of some sort) who preys emotionally on a younger one. In Clemence Dane's *Regiment of Women* (1917), the vain yet charismatic girls' school teacher, Clare Hartill (whose personality combines "the temper of a Calvinist with the tastes of a Renascence bishop"), is one version of the type: the havoc she wreaks in the life of a younger colleague is at once fascinating and repellent. Other examples include Victoria Vanderleyden, the predatory seductress known as "V.V." in Naomi-Royde Smith's *The Tortoise-Shell Cat* (1925), the arrogant, brittle, and ice-cold Geraldine Manners in Rosamond Lehmann's *Dusty Answer* (1927), and the glamorous but destructive Mademoiselle Julie in Dorothy Strachey's *Olivia* (1949).

What is striking in these novels—and there are many more of them besides the ones excerpted here—is the noticeable hostility, overt or covert, informing the portrait of the older woman. It is a hostility, one suspects, born of familiarity: the storyteller seems to write out of her own bitterness and disillusionment. (Such novels are almost always autobiographical in tone and told from the viewpoint of the younger woman.) An unwelcome insight, perhaps, but one ineluctably confirmed in a number of works in this anthology: that certain female writers, even some of those who have lived it, find erotic love between women *unbearable*—so much so, in fact, that they have to write about it again and again. One of the most articulate writers ever to be inspired by the subject was undoubtedly the Russian poet Marina Tsvetaeva (1892–1941), whose tormented affair with her fellow poet Sophia Parnok has only recently made its way into biographies. Yet from the excoriating "Girlfriend" poems of 1915, addressed to Parnok, to the obsessive anguish of "Letter to the Amazon," a brooding reverie on homosexuality and motherhood written in the 1930s, Tsvetaeva's writings about same-sex love are painfully demoralizing. Earnest lesbian readers who think the world owes them its "validation" should be warned off at once; for all they will encounter here—besides beauty and genius—are someone else's worst heartache and the blistering onrush of the old, sad doubts.[34]

By contrast, certain male writers approach the lesbian topos with an oddly vivifying tenderness. Shakespeare, not surprisingly, is magnificently paranoia-free: when girls in his comedies fall "accidentally" in love with other girls-masquerading-as-boys, their confusion is never treated farcically or maliciously or voyeuristically. On the contrary, such erotic beguilement seems to evoke in him a mysterious empathy and delight. The comic mixup is inevitably resolved—Olivia in *Twelfth Night*, enamored by mistake of the cross-dressing Viola, will end up marrying Viola's twin brother—but not before the play itself has been immeasurably enriched by its detour through the precincts of female-female desire. The desire itself is humanized in turn; made part of a rich Shakespearean tapestry of sublunary loves. To carp about the expediency of the ending (how convenient! a twin brother!) or to yearn for some continuation of Olivia's passion for Viola beyond the duration of the play, is to miss the main point: that Shakespeare has created a dream machine capable of endlessly replicating—in and of itself—a deliriously sapphic effect. Each time the play is staged, Olivia will fall in love with Viola. The magic is in the soft pressure such a comedy exerts on everyday consciousness—in the imaginative space it makes for homoerotic emotion. We are indeed in the land of "as you like it" or "what you will"—where the man of one's dreams is to be found, first and foremost, in another girl and then in a fellow who looks just like her.

Shakespeare is hardly alone in his equanimity, however. Donne, Waller, Casanova, Théophile Gautier, Baudelaire, Pierre Louÿs, Swinburne, Hardy, James, Catulle Mendès, Proust, Ronald Firbank, Edouard Bourdet, Compton Mackenzie, H. E. Bates—all embrace in varying degree the empathetic "Sapphic" mode. Different writers all, but each finds something intoxicating in the subject of female homoeroticism and conveys his *bouleversement* to the reader. Not without criticism, one hastens to add, or without a certain dialectical tension: Baudelaire's images of lesbian amorosity in *Les Fleurs du mal* (1857) gleam with melodramatic portent. Hardy's treatment of the seductive Miss Aldclyffe in *Desperate Remedies* (1871) fairly percolates with ambivalence; as does James's view of the girl-adoring spinster, Olive Chancellor, in *The Bostonians* (1886). But in each case there is something emancipating in the encounter between male writer and sapphic Muse—a sort of mad permission-granting that can sometimes resolve (as in Gautier or Firbank) into profound emotional gratification. She lets him be himself, while also providing that psychic arousal from which a complex human art is born.

Which makes this a good moment, perhaps, to say something about pornography. Some readers, and especially female readers, may take offense at certain items in this collection that verge (or worse) on the obscene: various anonymous "dildo poems" from the seventeenth and eighteenth centuries, the "warm" selections from Chorier, Cleland, Diderot, and Sade, the lascivious extract from the anonymous nineteenth-century sexual autobiography *My Secret Life*. My own attitude is somewhat less judg-mental. No history of the lesbian topos, in my view, can afford to ignore the subject's pornographic redactions; they are simply too numerous and historically important to discount. One of the things that I hope this anthology might do is break down in some degree the artificial boundary set up between so-called polite and pornographic treat-ments of the lesbian theme. Practically speaking, the two sorts of writing are often dif-ficult to distinguish: witness the ambiguous excerpts here from Delarivier Manley's 1709 "secret history," *The New Atalantis* (1709), or the anonymous, supposedly thera-peutic moral tract, *Satan's Harvest Home* (1749). Nor does the distinction help very much in thinking about readers or reception history. Despite what is often asserted, it is not true, for example, that in past centuries only women read polite works and only men read pornographic ones. Common sense alone would suggest that given the wide-spread diffusion of certain sexually explicit texts in early modern Europe—of Aretino's *Dialogues* (1534–36), *The School of Venus* (1655), Nicolas Chorier's *Satyra Sotadica* (1660–78), *The Whores Rhetorick* (1683), *Aristotle's Master-piece* (1684), *Ona-nia, or The Heinous Sin of Self-Pollution* (1710), and John Cleland's *Memoirs of a Woman of Pleasure* (1748–49)—literate women in earlier periods had rather more access to "forbidden" books than has ever been officially recognized.[35] When it came to lesbian texts, female readers undoubtedly counted among the cognoscenti. Mrs. Thrale, the ultrarespectable friend of Samuel Johnson, seems to have gleaned her fairly extensive knowledge of Marie Antoinette's rumored lesbian affairs by way of the numerous obscene pamphlets that proliferated on the subject in France and England in the 1780s and early 1790s; Anne Lister, an upper-class Yorkshire sapphist of the 1820s, pursued several of her conquests by engaging them first in conversation about the naughtier effusions of Martial and Juvenal, which she had parsed in the original Latin.[36]

Similarly, with the long view in mind, an honest critic should be prepared to acknowledge that pornographic texts—whether Martial or Chorier or Cleland—have contributed in significant ways to the overall cultural assimilation of the lesbian idea. It does no good to fuss and fume about it: women who love other women owe something of their present-day political and social visibility to the fact that countless men over the centuries have found the idea of erotic love between women exhilarating. Lesbian images have proliferated far and wide in modern Western culture at least in part because such images have always been—for reasons yet to be satisfactorily explained—deeply titillating to men. (In a recent catalogue raisonné of the erotic sketches of the sculptor Auguste Rodin, nearly 30 out of 107 images depict female-female couples. By contrast, there are two images of male-female couples. The rest are female nudes.)[37] However sordid or gross some of the results—and many underground images of female same-sex love are cankerous indeed—male pornographers must be credited with giving female homosexuality over the centuries a starkly palpable representational life. By their graphic insistence that such intimacy was possible—*in the flesh*—they helped make the lesbian topos part of the mental landscape of modern civilization.

Granted, the complaint will be made that the pornographic vision of lesbianism is still intolerably sexist: not only because women's pleasure is viewed instrumentally, either as secondary to men's or completely irrelevant, but because lesbianism is typically represented as a kind of inferior option—a mere "warm-up" or prelude to heterosexual action. Cleland's *Memoirs of a Woman of Pleasure* might be considered typical in this respect. In the episode excerpted in this volume, the young Fanny Hill, Cleland's jolly but virginal heroine, having decided to live in a brothel and become a prostitute, is voluptuously "broken in" by a fellow whore named Phoebe. Fanny is initially excited by lesbian lovemaking, but after spying on a tryst between another girl and one of the regulars, tires of such "foolery from woman to woman" and moves on (with comic precipitancy) to a series of majestically endowed male lovers. Poor Phoebe is left in the lurch; her charming bedmate never returns. Sapphic love has its place as an appetizer, in other words, but cannot compete with the more nutritious "solid food" of male-female intercourse.

An annoying teleology, no doubt—but the pornographic universe is hardly the all-encompassing degradation to lesbian dignity that it is sometimes imagined to be. Obscene books like Cleland's undoubtedly did much, still, to massage the lesbian idea into being. Once again, as with Shakespearean comedy, it is crucial not to give too much ideological force to mere "framing" details or the mechanical conventions of dénouement. It is true that if a female character appears *en travesti* in a literary work before 1900 we know she will ultimately be unmasked—just as it is true that in order for such a play or story to move to a decorous conclusion, homoerotic desires must be converted into heterosexual ones. The central thing, however, is that *the possibility of divergence is broached*. In the Phoebe/Fanny episode, Cleland, like Shakespeare in *Twelfth Night*, gives us something new—and startling—to think about. If only fleetingly, the routine copulation of male and female is challenged by *something else*. And as in life, the shock of the new cannot be erased by fiat, even when the storyteller tries to convince us, after the fact, that it wasn't so startling after all.

I stress the positive, here and elsewhere, because it is my sense that over the course of literary history, the "Sapphic" sensibility ultimately wins out over the "Roman"—even as civil society itself moves toward a gradual social, political, and psychic accommodation with its homosexual elements. To proceed in sequence through the items in this anthology is to witness a slow but unmistakable shift toward the pole of sympathetic interest and emotional identification: the monster is gradually humanized. The trend is already visible by 1700: in certain writings from the early eighteenth century, the semi-automatic vilification of *tribade* or *amazon*—so central a mode in the libertine writing of the Renaissance—begins to give way to something gentler, more encompassing and exploratory. And here without question the impact of women's writing must be measured. The contributions of "Sapphic" men notwithstanding, female authors—ever more visible in the literary marketplace from the mid-seventeenth century on—played a crucial role not only in the modern dissemination of the lesbian "idea" but in its eventual rehabilitation. Despite the occasional traducer from within the ranks (and the pained inquiries of a Tsvetaeva must not be forgotten), women writers were largely responsible for the twentieth-century legitimation of the topos—its subjective infusion, after the rhapsodic sapphic model, with a new moral, psychological, and metaphysical pathos.

This "beautification" process can be tracked across a broad arc of writings in this volume—most noticeably, perhaps, in women's lyric poetry. For the woman poet, the assumption of the Sapphic mantle has meant just this: the sympathetic revelation of one's love—ardent, mesmeric, entangling—for another woman. Not every female-to-female lyric poem, of course, has been overtly erotic; so great was the taboo on the expression of such feeling in earlier centuries that many of the poems in this volume celebrate female-female love-bonds only in the most spiritualized and philosophical terms. It remains a topic of debate how much the highly stylized poetry of seventeenth- and eighteenth-century "romantic friendship"—represented here by the verses of Anne de Rohan, Katherine Philips, Anne Killigrew, Elizabeth Singer Rowe, Anne Finch, Pauline de Simiane, Anna Seward, and Mary Matilda Betham, among others—can or should be read as "lesbian" in impulse or inspiration. My own feeling (intuitive rather than forensic) is that with certain writers it is impossible not to. Perusing her exalted yet infatuated verses on the Ladies of Llangollen, it is hard to conclude that Anna Seward, for example, was anything but a raving dyke—of the most ladylike sort, of course. But with other writers one is less sure. Even so, in that they helped to habituate Western civilization to the idea of passionate emotion between women, even the most chaste exponents of romantic friendship can be said to have prepared the way for later and more daring writers: for "Michael Field," Renée Vivien, Natalie Barney, "Marie Madeleine," Amy Lowell, and Gertrude Stein at the turn of the century and after; for Adrienne Rich, Audre Lorde, May Swenson, Judy Grahn, Olga Broumas, Marilyn Hacker, Eileen Myles, and Brenda Shaughnessy in our own day.[38]

In the poems anthologized here from the later nineteenth and early twentieth century the signs of moral and aesthetic transvaluation are everywhere. A new erotic freedom shapes the writing of lesbian sensuality: first (as always), in the writings of men, in the flamboyantly "Sapphic" verses of Baudelaire, Verlaine, and Swinburne and exotic fantasy-concoctions such as Pierre Louÿs's *Chansons de Bilitis* and Catulle Mendès's prose poem *Lila et Colette*. But women too embrace the new dispensation—the liberating feeling that one might just as well go ahead and *talk* about it. Beginning in the 1880s, with the publication of several books by the Jewish poet Amy Levy, some of whose love lyrics may have been inspired by Olive Schreiner, and of *Long Ago* (1889), an exquisite volume of Sappho imitations by the two women who wrote together as "Michael Field" (Katherine Bradley and Edith Cooper), autobiographically inflected lesbian love poetry grew more and more common. By 1900, with the openly "Mytilenean" experiments of Vivien and Barney, it was almost, indeed, something of a literary cliché. Lesbian poetry at the turn of the century often came loaded up with lurid fin-de-siècle trappings: witness the camp Swinburnean effusions of the German poet "Marie Madeleine":

All night I saw your vision bright;
Within me snarled the Brute and stirred;
My longing cried to you unheard
Throughout the night—throughout the night.

To you, unwilling amorist!
To you—whose nimble strength I broke!
O how your sleeping passions woke,
And how you knelt to me, and kissed!

I longed for you, remembering
Your body's dear abandonment,
Your sultry boudoir's aching scent,
The wounding rapture and the sting.

"I know it all," you smile and say.
But then you know not how, possest,
I longed to leave upon your breast
The fang-marks of the beast of prey.

("Beneath the Surface")

Yet the campiness itself suggests a new psychic freedom. It had become in a funny way almost "respectable" for a woman to flirt with the lesbian topos—to be as bohemian and louche (and as silly) as any man. Civilization was encroaching; the shock value of the theme was diminishing; even a woman might risk a succès de scandale. By the time Sir Compton Mackenzie came to satirize poets of the "Marie Madeleine" school in his 1928 comic novel, *Extraordinary Women*, by way of the cigar-smoking Aurora ("Rory") Fremantle—a burly English denizen of the island of Capri who writes arty homosexual love lyrics under the pen name of "Demonassa" and moons over lady boxers—the persecution jig was mostly up. Not even the famous censorship trial in the same year of Radclyffe Hall's *The Well of Loneliness* could put a stop for long to an ever increasing (and mostly equably received) flow of sapphically oriented verses.

In fiction, however, the changes were no less profound. From Diderot and Gautier to Balzac and Zola and even James, the "lesbian novel" had been a largely masculine and potboiling enterprise. Beginning in the first decades of the twentieth century, however, women both usurped and deepened the genre. The impetus, again, was often autobiographical, with Woolf's intimate reveries in *Mrs. Dalloway* (1925) setting the pattern for sophisticated sapphic self-exploration. The defensive, overwrought mode adopted by Radclyffe Hall in *The Well* was not, aesthetically speaking, a huge success, nor in the end a particularly fruitful model for other women writers. The most intelligent and interesting female writers of the first half of the twentieth century simply went about their business—even when that business included, by the by, an affirmation of lesbian loves. From her first foray into print in 1900, Colette, for example, wrote elegantly and knowledgeably about the seductiveness of women; her early *Claudine* novels made no bones about the ways women wooed or, in so wooing, comforted one another. But the subtle aplomb of her later works was even more subversive. In the extraordinary *Ces Plaisirs* (known in English as *The Pure and the Impure*), her disarming personal reflection from 1932 on those pleasures "which are lightly called physical," Colette astonishes by precisely what she takes for granted: the sheer "everydayness" of lesbian relations in modern life. Love between women intrigues her, no question, and prompts the requisite stylistic flights—witness the delicately inosculatory excerpt here on the poet-libertine Renée Vivien. But it has ceased, absolutely, to surprise. It is part of the human domain—as "natural" indeed as any other expression of physical desire.

One is struck by a similar absence of fuss in other women's writing—the refusal to overdramatize. In the novels and short stories of Katherine Mansfield, Elizabeth Bowen, Sylvia Townsend Warner—and later the ineffable Jane Bowles—women (or girls) fall in love with one another with little authorial comment: the "pash" has its own internal logic and duration. And whatever the fate of a such a feeling, it will be profoundly woven into the psychic fabric of the heroine's life. Even in such a structurally unstable and ambivalent work as Rosamond Lehmann's *Dusty Answer* (1927), in which the susceptible young heroine has to be converted to heterosexuality in the novel's second half, it is nonetheless striking how "normal" a part of life her homoerotic yearnings are made to seem. Against an idyllic Cambridge backdrop, it would appear, it is perfectly understandable that two female undergraduates might wish to bathe together naked in a secret pond, then curl up together for the rest of the day in sensual and warming amity.

Yet perhaps the most telling evidence of the feminine rehabilitation of the lesbian "idea" is to be found, finally, in autobiography itself—in those works in which the urge to testify has become too strong to be hidden behind allegory or coy fictionalizing. It is significant, surely, that some of the most provocative modern works in this anthology are autobiographical in nature and stark in their sexual honesty. Vita Sackville-West's 1920 memoir about her reckless love affair with Violet Trefusis, a work that went undiscovered and unpublished for over fifty years, is one of the least adorned of such accounts—bald to the point of guilelessness—but also unforgettable in its brusque admission of erotic unorthodoxy. We know little of "Diana Frederics," the putative author of *Diana: A Strange Autobiography* (1939), but her tale of sensual awakening likewise impresses by its directness and by how she moves from a paralyzing conviction of her "abnormality" to an odd negative pride in her difference. (I do not incline to the view, obviously, of the work as a male-authored hoax.)

The thought had never occurred to me before, but now I wondered why I'd never seen either a drab or a stupid-looking lesbian, and I imagined several reasons. First of all, a stupid girl probably would never ascertain her abnormality if she were potentially homosexual—a fact not at all strange on second thought. Further, the girl who did come to understand her inversion was likely to have character in her face, if no degree of beauty. The very fact of her abnormality assured her of that; her expression would be crossed by a subtle something, according to the degree of her disillusionment. No woman could adjust herself to lesbianism without developing exceptional qualities of courage.

And in Valentine Ackland's *For Sylvia*, the private account of her erotic and emotional history that Ackland wrote for her lover, the novelist Sylvia Townsend Warner, in 1949, we find a similar matter-of-factness, infusing even passages of the tenderest feeling:

> After about a week, during which I had felt shy and tried to behave as if I were not, while we were talking through the partition between our narrow bed-rooms, I said sadly, "I sometimes think I am utterly unloved." And Sylvia thought she heard such heart-break melancholy in my voice, and with that passionate immediacy of succour which matches, through all her character, and makes her have the most purely beautiful heart I have ever known   perhaps that has ever existed—she sprang up and came through the connecting door and fell on her knees by my bed and took me in her arms. I do not know what happened then, except that in a moment or so she was in my bed and I was holding and kissing her and we were already deeply in love—and never since then have we ceased to love each other, with each year of our joined lives we have loved more, and more truly.

It is true that Sackville-West, "Diana Frederics," and Ackland never openly acknowledged their sexual noncomformity. It was still not safe—in the uncharted years before Stonewall—to make the truth known publicly without the cloak of partial secrecy or pseudonymity. (Both Sackville-West's and Ackland's memoirs were published posthumously—Sackville-West's in 1973, and Ackland's in 1985.) And not surprisingly, even with such protections in place, moments of self-doubt and self-chastisement creep in. Both Sackville-West and Ackland berate themselves for hypocrisy and bad faith; "Diana," a reader of Krafft-Ebing's sexology, is inclined to give way at times to fairly dire asides on the "Third Sex," among whose motley, B movie ranks she invariably counts herself. But in the urge to commemorate—to say to a reader *I loved thus*—each writer nonetheless skirts the central inhibition and affirms, in the most personal and searching way, the human valence of lesbian feeling.

And slowly but surely it became possible for women to write autobiographically without built-in baffles or disguises. In Margaret Anderson's *My Thirty Years' War* (1930) some vestigial coquetry lingers, but Anderson is on the whole frank about the quasi-marital nature of her relationships with Jane Heap and Georgette Leblanc. Mabel Dodge Luhan's *Intimate Memories* (1933) lives unabashedly up to its title; even today, it is hard to think of another work in which budding sensual feeling between girls has been described more clearly or sympathetically. And though I made sport of it earlier, Violette Leduc's *La Bâtarde* remains a stunning and gorgeous and revolutionary work—the most forthright of lesbian memoirs, and a courageous testament to the tormented yet ardent nature of its author.

I conclude this anthology with a piece of autobiographical writing—Janet Flanner's moving 1975 memorial to Alice B. Toklas, the life companion of the celebrated American writer Gertrude Stein. (Stein had died in 1946; Toklas lived on, mostly in the Paris apartment on the Rue de Fleurus that she and Stein had shared for forty years, until her own death in 1967.) Along with their other accomplishments, Gertrude Stein and Alice B. Toklas deserve to be considered two of the great public "normalizers" of the lesbian idea in this century. Even as they became increasingly famous—they began hosting their renowned salon together in 1910—they did nothing to deny or conceal their spousal relationship; indeed, in the presence of Picasso, Joyce, Hemingway, F. Scott Fitzgerald, and countless others, Toklas was happy to play the devoted "wife" to Stein's robust, quasi-masculine "genius." Stein in turn celebrated their bond in her writing—obliquely perhaps in the more experimental works, but with untroubled insouciance in the best-selling 1932 memoir, *The Autobiography of Alice B. Toklas*. Perhaps the most striking thing about them was Stein's comfortable public cultivation—with Toklas's deadpan collaboration—of her sensationally unfeminine appearance. It was a signal moment in my own adolescence to be wrenched out of inattention in a tenth-grade English class when the rickety old "educational" film we were watching about writers in Paris between the wars cut briefly to some extraordinary silent footage of Stein in her apartment: huge, close-cropped, unsexable, surrounded by friends and admirers, subtly engaged with the flickering camera, the Stone Butch at the Wedding Feast. There had been no more scintillating evidence, in my youthful experience, that one might look like a freak and nonetheless be loved and rewarded for exactly who one was.

In their refusal to hide themselves away or ingratiate beyond the granting of a formidable intellectual hospitality, Stein and Toklas got people used to them and to the style of human intimacy they so vividly embodied. For half a century they acted as if nothing strange had happened and everyone who met them agreed that nothing had. Phobias were checked at the door. The same spirit of complaisance—of everybody who was anybody united in charmed civility—is present in Flanner's valedictory reminiscence of Toklas. Flanner, the Paris correspondent for the *New Yorker* since 1925 and herself a lover of women, knew Stein and Toklas well and was a loyal friend to Toklas through the latter's long bereavement and infirm final years. Her own *souvenir*, with its fifty-year backward glance, touches most by its tactful yet invincible affirmation of the "concentrated amity" in which two women may live. Flanner avoids all pretense or gratuitous excitement: the facts of the two interwoven lives are given plainly, with the purity of a Bunyan or Aubrey. Indeed, she writes as though the noble future were already upon us—the one where prurience is unknown and the long-enduring physical happiness of two persons of the same sex a matter for rejoicing. Flanner was morally outraged, of course, that anyone would try to wrest away from Toklas in her dying years her last mementos of Stein—the great modern picture collection that Stein had willed to her—but she never says so in so many words. Hers is writing indeed in which the lesbian "idea" is so deeply assimilated, so thoroughly and everywhere implicit, as not to need expounding. Such worldly equanimity will no doubt strike some as utopian or wishful (just what one might expect from a woman who lived most of her adult life in rooms in the Paris Ritz) but I cannot help but find in Flanner's essay an inspiring tribute to "private love"—in all its forms—and to life itself pursued without hysteria or spleen.

4

My emphasis on the large-scale process of cognitive routinization is not meant, of course, to obviate more traditional ways of looking at the works collected here, nor do I intend to make the lesbian "idea" itself seem more monolithic or formulaic than it really is. On the contrary, it is my hope that the sometimes comically diverse assortment of writings here (by a sheer accident of chronology the diaries of the dear little Ladies of Llangollen follow immediately upon the sulphurous exhalations of the Marquis de Sade) will open itself to further, more localized researches. On the way to my conclusion, therefore, let me point briefly to some areas of general literary and historical interest that the collection as a whole may illuminate.

First, the philological. How has love between women been *named* in Western culture? Various works here suggest that dictionaries have not always been accurate on this point. The editors of the *Oxford English Dictionary* (*OED*), the authoritative reference work on historical English usage, trace the use of *lesbianism* as a term for sexual love between women only back to 1870. *Lesbian*, it is asserted, was not used adjectivally to refer to sexual relations between women before 1890; it did not appear as a noun until 1925. Before then, we are advised, the word meant simply "of or pertaining to the island of Lesbos, in the northern part of the Grecian archipelago." The related term *sapphism*, signifying "unnatural relations between women"—after Sappho, "who was accused of this vice"—is traced back only to 1890; and *Sapphist*, the word used by Virginia Woolf to describe Vita Sackville-West, to 1901.

At the very least, various works in this volume help to roll back these conservative datings. The use of *Lesbian* or *lesbian* in connection with female homosexual practices can be traced back at least to the seventeenth century—as the title of François de Maynard's *Tribades, or Lesbia* (1646) may suggest. "'Tis said how that Sappho the Lesbian was a very high mistress in this art [of cuckolding other women's husbands]," writes Pierre de Bourdeilles, the Seigneur de Brantôme, in his *Lives of Gallant Ladies* (1665–66); "and that in after times the Lesbian dames have copied her therein, and continued the practice to the present day. So Lucian saith: such is the character of the Lesbian women, which will not suffer men at all." Likewise, *sapphic* and *sapphist* have had a longer history than the *OED* records: the translator of a 1762 edition of Plato referred to two women as "Sapphic Lovers"; and the diarist Hester Thrale Piozzi, writing disparagingly in her journal in 1789 about the rumored homosexuality of the French queen Marie Antoinette, described her as "the Head of a Set of Monsters call'd by each other *Sapphists*, who boast her example; and deserve to be thrown with the He Demons that haunt each other likewise, into Mount Vesuvius."[39] An anonymous lampoon here from 1735, the never-before-reprinted *Sappho-An* ("An Heroic Poem of Three Cantos, in the Ovidian Style, describing the Pleasures which the FAIR SEX Enjoy with Each Other"), suggests that a crude metonymic association between the name of the Greek poet and female same-sex love was established in English popular writing as far back indeed as the third decade of the eighteenth century.

Other works allow us to track the dissemination of more ancient terms, inherited from the Greek and Latin. Several of the early writers anthologized here, notably the libertine Nicolas Chorier, in the *Dialogues on the Arcana of Love and Venus by Luisa Sigea Toletana* (1660–78), offer their own mock-pedantic excurses on lesbian nomenclature:

> At first this custom [licentiousness between women] was common especially among the Lesbians: Sappho enhanced this name and thus dignifies it. How often have Andromeda, Athis, Anactorie, Mnais, and Girim, her pet loves, rubbed loins with hers! The Greeks call famous women of this kind Tribades; the Latins named them Frictrices and Subigitatrices. But Philaenis is regarded as having invented the practice, because she abandoned herself utterly to this pleasure. And since she was a woman of high renown she was able by her practice to advise the women and little girls around her of the use of a voluptuousness unknown before her time. They are called Tribades by the Greeks τριβάδης = to rub), and by the Latins, Frictrices (*fricare* = to rub), from the rubbing together of bodies: Subigitatrices (*subigitare* = to bounce up and down) from the more violent movement.

And true enough, *Tribade, tribadism*, and *tribadry* appear in a host of classically inflected works in this volume—in "T.W.'s" "To Mr. J.D." (c. 1633), in Ben Jonson's "Epigram on the Court Pucelle" (1640), in the Seigneur de Brantôme's *Lives of Gallant Ladies* (1665–66), in the *Supplement to the Onania* (c. 1725). *Frictrice*—or *fricatrice*, as it is more commonly spelled in English and French texts—turns up in Brantôme and the *Onania* and lurks punningly in the name of Fricamona, the lesbian love-addict in Diderot's *Les Bijoux indiscrets* (1748).

Slang terms crop up in a number of works. *Tommy*, an eighteenth-century synonym for a masculine-looking lover of women, appears in the 1773 poem *The Adulteress*: it would seem to preserve some of this meaning in Willa Cather's 1896 comic short story "Tommy, the Unsentimental," about a virile young woman who looks like a "lanky boy" and assists girls in need in a small Western prairie town in the late nineteenth century. Other slang words are more graphic. In an eponymous chapter on the subject in the moralizing pamphlet *Satan's Harvest Home* (1749), lesbian lovemaking is vividly maligned as *the game of flatts*. According to Emma Donoghue, the phrase derives from the seventeenth- and eighteenth-century word for playing cards—*flats*—and is meant to suggest the rubbing together of two female pudenda. "Walter," the pseudonymous author of the Victorian pornographic memoir *My Secret Life* (1882–94), uses a related verb, *flat fucking*, to refer, obscenely, to the venereal conjunction of two women.

Perhaps most intriguing are the terms *odd* and *queer*, which appear throughout the centuries in homoerotic contexts and seem to have been part of an argot of sexual non-conformity from early on. Sapphically shaded uses of *odd* turn up in the 1699 poem "Venus's Reply"; in the transvestite actress Charlotte Charke's autobiography in 1755; in Anne Lister's secret lesbian diaries of the 1820s (Lister describes her sexual desire for other women as her "oddity" or "odd freak"); in James's *The Bostonians* (1886); and Radclyffe Hall's *The Well of Loneliness*. As for *queer*—sometimes said to have taken on its homosexual connotations only in the twentieth century—Lister uses it throughout her diary to refer to the female genitalia, typically conjoining it with the deliciously Anglo-Saxon verb *to grubble*:

> My knees & thighs shook, my breathing & everything told her what was the matter. She said she did me no good. I said it was a little headache & I should go to sleep. I then leaned on her bosom &, pretending to sleep, kept puttering about & rubbing the surface of her queer. Then made several gentle efforts to put my hand up her petticoats which, however, she prevented. But she so crossed her legs & leaned against me that I put my hand over & grubbled her on the outside of her petticoats till she was evidently a little excited.

Here and elsewhere, we seem to uncover a sexual vernacular in the making—both frank in its anatomical correlatives and subversive in its co-optation of "normal" or conventional speech.

Words and their meanings are not the only subjects to be illuminated in the various works collected here, however: the sympathetic reader will learn as much about the topography of lesbian desire as its philology. Where, speaking quite literally, does love between women take place? Episodes such as the one above between Anne Lister and her lover Mrs. Barlow—their liaison began in a women-only pension in Paris in which both were lodging in 1825—remind us that certain real-world spaces and locales have been especially conducive to the elaboration of both lesbian lives and lesbian plots. And not surprisingly, numerous works here can be grouped, as it were, topographically— according to historically informed conventions of setting and placement.

Overall, the literary representation of female homosexuality has conventionally depended on what might be called the "islanding" or physical and social isolation of women: their segregation or seclusion in some location or institution relatively apart from the world of men, whether convent, harem, school, rural retreat, or lodging place. The demands of verisimilitude make such settings appropriate, of course, for the development of homoerotically charged plot lines; literary homosexuality, whether male or female, blossoms most energetically in the absence of opposite-sex competition. Yet one also suspects some unconscious symbolic homage to Sappho and her girlfriends: the island of Lesbos—that *gynecium*, or all-female sacred space—remains the mythological reference point around which much contemporary lesbian narrative continues to revolve. It is perhaps significant, after all, that in the legends, Sappho's final debacle—the love-suicide over Phaon—is said in Ovid and elsewhere to have taken place in Leucadia on the Greek mainland. Just as the mythical giant Antaeus's physical strength depended on his keeping part of his body in contact with the ground beneath him, so Sappho's power as homoerotic icon would seem to depend, symbolically, on her remaining on her native Lesbian soil.

In seventeenth- and eighteenth-century texts the "island" is typically a nunnery or convent, reflecting, of course, the sociological realities of the early modern era. (Before 1800 there were few other environments in which women might live in groups in the absence of men.) Male writers—notably those of an anti-Catholic persuasion—tended to treat such places satirically, as hothouses of corruption, sybaritism, and "unnatural" vice. Thus the decadent nuns in Andrew Marvell's *Upon Appleton House* (1650), avid to entice the beautiful young Isabella Thwaites to join their order, glorify the decidedly irreligious pleasures awaiting her in convent life:

> "Nor is our order yet so nice,
> Delight to banish as a vice.
> Here pleasure piety doth meet,
> One perfecting the other sweet;
> So through the mortal fruit we boil
> The sugar's uncorrupting oil;
> And that which perished while we pull,
> Is thus preservèd clear and full.
>
> "For such indeed are all our arts;
> Still handling Nature's finest parts.
> Flowers dress the altars; for the clothes,
> The sea-born amber we compose;
> Balms for the grieved we draw; and pastes
> We mold, as baits for curious tastes.
> What need is here of man? unless
> These as sweet sins we should confess.
>
> "Each night among us to your side
> Appoint a fresh and virgin bride,
> Whom if Our Lord at midnight find,
> Yet neither should be left behind;

Where you may lie as chaste in bed,
As pearls together billetted;
All night embracing arm in arm,
Like crystal pure in cotton warm. [. . .]"

The extraordinary image of "crystal pure in cotton warm" concludes as fine a pickup speech as any in contemporary lesbian pulp fiction.

Eighteenth-century convent literature manages to be both homophobic and pornographic at once. In Diderot's flagrantly lubricious novel, *The Nun* (1760), the heroine is forced into a nunnery by her cruel parents and then seduced by the fantastical "Madame ***," her depraved Mother Superior. In the anonymous *Anecdotes of a Convent* from 1771, the heroine is an English orphan living in a French convent who becomes infatuated with another girl. The fact that the other "girl" turns out to be a man in disguise—a young nobleman who has been raised there since infancy and doesn't even realize that he *is* a man—hardly diminishes the reigning atmosphere of sickly perversity. Yet even as we acknowledge the lurid fascination of such tales, it should be remembered that women themselves often experienced actual convent life very differently—as a dignified and emancipating alternative to marriage and family life. Creative women in particular tended to flourish in the intense emotional ambience of the female ecclesiastical community. Some of the most ardent lesbian love poems in this volume—and one can call them nothing else—were written by the sequestered Mexican nun Sor Juana Inés de la Cruz (1648–1695) and dedicated to her great convent patroness and friend, the Condesa de Paredes.

Beginning in the nineteenth century the girls' school or women's college largely usurps the convent as prime fictional locus for the exploration of lesbian themes, even as educational establishments for women became more and more common in Britain and America and on the Continent. In nineteenth- and twentieth-century narrative especially, from Charlotte Brontë's *Villette* to Leduc's *La Bâtarde*, the girls' school remains the preeminent "institutional" site for homoerotic plot-making, especially in works by women. Colette, Clemence Dane, Rosamond Lehmann, Mabel Dodge Luhan, "Henry Handel Richardson," and Dorothy Strachey are among the many female writers represented here who have exploited the girls' school setting; any number of others—Dorothy Sayers, Angela Brazil, Olive Moore, Christa Winsloe, Lillian Hellman, Antonia White, Dorothy Baker, Josephine Tey, May Sarton, Rosemary Manning, Brigid Brophy, Nancy Spain, Muriel Spark, Fleur Jaeggy, Christine Crow, Catharine Stimpson, Florence King—might also have been included. The stories that unfold in classic girls' school fiction vary in tone and feeling. Some are euphoric tales of triumphant adolescent bonding. (Though unrepresented here for reasons of space, Angela Brazil's vast and delirious series of early-twentieth-century schoolgirl romances must be considered one of the great homoerotic ventures in all of women's popular fiction.)[40] Others are dysphoric stories of exploitation and betrayal, in which a charismatic teacher casts a spell over a student, or an older or more sophisticated girl entangles one younger or more naive. In the latter, as noted earlier, the autobiographical element is typically strong, with the seductive teacher or older girl—Clare Hartill in Dane's *Regiment of Women*, Mademoiselle Julie in Strachey's *Olivia*—represented more critically than any other character. Yet whatever the emotional register—and many schoolgirl fictions end painfully indeed, with the death or defection of the love object—the schoolgirl fiction remains one of the indispensable imaginative vehicles by which the lesbian topos has infiltrated modern literary and cultural life.[41]

There are other "islanding" spaces one might mention: in Naomi Royde-Smith's *The Tortoise-Shell Cat* (1925) the heroine meets her unpleasant seductress "V.V." in a seedy Chelsea women's boarding house; the Thistle Hotel, the setting of Katherine Mansfield's 1907 short story "Leves Amores," is a similarly removed and down-at-the-heels establishment. In H. E. Bates's "Breeze Anstey" (1937), as in D. H. Lawrence's *The Fox*, the lesbian heroine and her companion live out in the countryside, where they run a small farm together. (In Bates's tale, as in Lawrence's, the tranquillity of this rural redoubt—"with an acre of land, on the edge of a forest"—is shattered when a man arrives and proceeds to alienate one woman from the other.) In Ronald Firbank's *The Flower Beneath the Foot* (1923) the setting for the coupling of "Vi," the imperious Countess of Tolga, and her faithful friend and acolyte, Mademoiselle Olga Blumenghast, is out at sea, on a "steady wide-bottomed boat" called the *Calypso*. In some cases the metaphoric "island" of lesbianism is a literal island too—as in Compton Mackenzie's 1928 roman à clef, *Extraordinary Women*, in which the gay-friendly isle of "Sirène" (modeled on post–World War I Capri) becomes a comic modern surrogate for Sappho's fabled Lesbos.

Yet perhaps the most "sapphic" locale of all is not, paradoxically, an island at all—unless in a loose symbolic sense, in the view of those who wash up there and become intoxicated by its liberating spaces. Where else in fiction do women meet and love? As Stein might have said, in Paris Paris France of course.

The reader will have noted that I have included a number of French works in this anthology; a special word must be said about them. For whatever reasons—whether due to that strain of worldliness and moral realism present in French society since the Middle Ages, the relatively high status of women, or the freethinking intellectual traditions associated with the Enlightenment and French Revolution—French writing of the past three or four centuries has been distinguished by an unparalleled sexual frankness and sophistication. So often indeed has female homosexuality been thematized in French literature one might be forgiven for imagining love between women almost a kind of French invention, like champagne or foie gras. As early as 1800—or so Anne Lister's diaries would suggest—Paris was established as a mecca for homosexually inclined Englishwomen; by the mid-nineteenth century, almost all of the influential imaginative writing on the subject was emanating from the French capital. One can hardly speak of any lesbian-themed writing after 1850 *un*touched by the French influence. It is impossible to appreciate what Swinburne does with the topic in *Poems and Ballads* (1866), or James in *The Bostonians*, or Hall in *The Well of Loneliness*, without knowing the works of Balzac, Gautier, Baudelaire, Zola, Maupassant, Rachilde, Louÿs, or (later) Proust and Colette.

By the first decades of the twentieth century the real and symbolic connections between France and *l'amour sapphique* had become ever more visible. Many prominent Anglo-American lesbian and bisexual writers were already living as temporary or permanent exiles in France: Natalie Barney, Renée Vivien, Gertrude Stein, Mabel Dodge Luhan, Djuna Barnes, Violet Trefusis, Margaret Anderson, Janet Flanner, and "Diana Frederics" were all Paris residents at one time or another.[42] France retained its famously relaxed publishing laws: lesbian books censored in England, for example, were easily obtainable across the Channel. (By the time it was banned in Great Britain under the Obscene Publications Act in November 1928, *The Well of Loneliness* was already selling one hundred copies a day in Paris.)[43] Yet the franco-sapphic connection was registered most evocatively in imaginative literature. Given the cosmopolitan nature of French society, it is hardly surprising that in countless twentieth-century Anglo-American novels and short stories France should figure as the geographic locus par excellence both for lesbian self-discovery and psychological healing and emancipation.

Radclyffe Hall's fiction illustrates the symbolic pattern in a paradigmatic if crude fashion. In the 1926 short story, "Miss Ogilvie Finds Herself," reprinted here, the eponymous heroine first recognizes her unorthodox sexual nature while serving in France in an all-female ambulance unit in the First World War. (The ambulance unit or nursing station, incidentally, might be considered another of those "islanding" environments so common in lesbian-themed fiction.) In *The Well*, published two years later, the heroine, Stephen Gordon, meets her first female lover under the same circumstances. "Miss Ogilvie," it is true, ends absurdly—with the demobbed Miss Ogilvie, at home again in England, undergoing a kind of past-life regression to a previous existence as a Stone Age caveman in Devon. Hall obviously did not know what to do with Ogilvie once she had her back in her native land again. She plunges her into a fantasy world, then kills her off. (The hapless lady veteran is found dead in a cave.) By contrast, in the later work, it has become clear what the newly fledged lover of women must do in order to survive: *get back to France as soon as possible*. Stephen Gordon's lesbian life only begins in earnest when she has made France her permanent home.

The Well is conventionally said to end unhappily: in its melodramatic final pages Stephen gives her lover Mary up to a man under the masochistic delusion that she cannot satisfy her. Yet by leaving Stephen still ensconced at novel's end in Paris—where she owns a flat, like the real-life Natalie Barney, on the chic Rue Jacob—Hall not so subtly dilutes the gall and wormwood. Even as Stephen torments herself over her imagined failings, her ongoing residence in the modern-day capital of lesbian desire suggests that all is not lost and that some repaired future may indeed be imagined for her. France is the place where one goes on living—where indeed it is possible to thrive. Post-Lesbos, it is as close to a lesbian homeland as the Western literary imagination has invented.

Topography leads by turns to topology and the characteristic motifs of lesbian-themed writing. I can only gesture briefly at these: the literature of female same-sex love awaits its Vladimir Propp or Stith Thompson—that scholar capable of uncovering and systematizing all the myriad "secondary" tropes, topoi, and subtopics associated with the central lesbian idea. Some of these, it is true, have been indexed in passing by critics over the past few years. A great deal has been written lately, for example, about the "maternal" or "sororal" dynamics of lesbian writing and the tendency of modern authors in particular to represent female same-sex love in psychological terms, as a displaced version of mother-daughter or sisterly bonds. The convent or girls' school story easily lends itself, obviously, to such symbolic ramification; a work such as Diderot's *The Nun*, in which the villainess is a seductive "Mother Superior" and the heroine her bewildered "child," positively invites us to explore it as pre-oedipal fantasy or dysphoric mother-daughter romance. But many works here open themselves to interpretation of this sort. A powerful mother-daughter dynamic inflects the archetypal love story of Ruth and Naomi in the Old Testament Book of Ruth—as it does, less blatantly, the sapphic fictions of Hardy, Woolf, Bowen, Mansfield, and Barnes. Sororal fantasies animate much of the conventional literature of female romantic friendship, not to mention the far richer poetic divagations of Emily Dickinson, Elizabeth Barrett Browning, and Christina Rossetti. In his celebrated 1920 case history, "The Psychogenesis of a Case of Homosexuality in a Woman," Freud would link, of course, the rebellious unfoldings of the sapphic heart with atavistic psychic needs. Yet for better or worse, virtually every element in Freud's theory—including the central role of the maternal "romance" in the genesis of lesbian desire—has always been present, if less systematically, in the sapphically inflected stories and poems of the Western tradition.

Another popular subtopic of late has been the relationship between lesbianism and the supernatural—a linkage to which the numerous lesbian vampires, bogeys, and ghosts in contemporary films and horror stories continue to testify. (The female vampire or lamia, initiating girls with a swift, sharp, yet deeply erotic bite on the neck, has long been an iconic surrogate for the lesbian seductress.) I have included here the founding work in the so-called lesbian-gothic genre—Samuel Taylor Coleridge's kinky and magisterial *Christabel* (1816). I must confess, however, having relieved myself on the subject elsewhere, to a certain ennui with the now (to my mind) somewhat clichéd figure of the lesbian spook. While this volume contains its quotient of sapphic "weird tales"—including Christina Rossetti's creepy fable-in-verse, *Goblin Market* (1862), and Elizabeth Stuart Phelps's morbid "Since I Died" (1873)—I could not bring myself to reprint Sheridan Le Fanu's overrated *Carmilla* (1872), a somewhat tedious vampire yarn about a Transylvanian lady with a hankering for pulchritudinous young females.

Other motifs, less shopworn, hold out more interest. Beginning with Lady Mary Wortley Montagu's celebrated *Embassy Letters* (1716–18), a number of works presented here illuminate the role that fantasies of racial and cultural difference have played in the evolution of the lesbian idea. The legacy has been a complex one. Age-old Western European associations between the dark-skinned races, for example, and sexual "vice" have undoubtedly helped to perpetrate malignant cultural stereotypes over the centuries. (The anonymous 1749 author of the invective-laden *Satan's Harvest Home* denounces tribadism as a Turkish import; other eighteenth-century xenophobes traced it to North Africa or the Tropics.) At the same time some writers have found in the foreign or exotic a way of exploring lesbian themes with relative, even liberating, impunity. The feverishly homoerotic "Kashmiri" verses of Adela Florence Nicolson (1865–1904), for example, seem palpably inspired by some overheated personal vision of "Eastern loves": her four books of poems, all published under the pen name "Laurence Hope," mix throbbing lesbian decadence à la Swinburne or Baudelaire with wild Orientalist fantasia. Constance Fenimore Woolson's extraordinary 1876 short story, "Felipa," in which two women visiting Florida with a male companion are irrevocably changed by an encounter with a volatile Minorcan fishing girl ("offspring of the ocean and the heats"), is a sober and haunting meditation on cross-cultural desire; so too the excerpt here from Jane Bowles's 1943 novel, *Two Serious Ladies*, in which an alienated American woman in Panama, Mrs. Copperfield, falls passively in love with the brown-skinned Pacifica. Nor, one should quickly add, have the intersections between race and female homosexuality been explored strictly from a white or European perspective: still other works here—the secret love poems of Angelina Weld Grimké, the excerpt from Nella Larsen's brilliant and mysterious *Passing* (1929), the fearless and forthright blues lyrics of Ma Rainey and Bessie Jackson—open up, from the inside as it were, the fascinating yet little-charted thematics of female same-sex love in African-American culture before the Civil Rights Movement and Stonewall.

A clutch of texts here shed light on the characteristic motifs—what one might call the erotics—of lesbian desire itself. By *erotics* I don't mean so much how lesbian lovemaking per se is described; outside the realm of pornography, few authors before the mid-twentieth century are particularly explicit on the subject. (Pornographic writers can themselves be fanciful: Sade, for instance, inevitably shows his tribades ejaculating lustily like men.) I refer, more broadly, to the lesbian idea's sensual correlatives—the physical tropes and representative actions by which writers have conventionally signaled the presence of female homoerotic feeling. A good example is the nude bathing or swimming scene—an episode so common as to amuse by the regularity with which it occurs. The modern association between bathing and female homoeroticism dates at least back to the early eighteenth century. Lady Mary Wortley Montagu's famous 1717 letter describing the voluptuous all-female *bagnio* at Constantinople established the connection; in Anthony Hamilton's popular *Memoirs of the Life of Count Grammont*, published a year later, Miss Hobart, a would-be sapphic seductress at the court of Charles II, begins an assault on a young woman by suggesting that they "retire to the bathing closet" so as to "enjoy a little conversation, secure from any impertinent visit."

In his celebrated Sapphic hoax of 1894, *The Songs of Bilitis*, Pierre Louÿs immerses the reader in a veritable Ladies' Bathing Pond of watery metaphor:

> Child, keep watch upon the door, and do not let any passers-by
>   come in, for I and six young girls with lovely arms are going
>   secretly to bathe in the basin's tepid pool.
> We only want to laugh and swim a while. Let lovers stay outside.
>   We'll drench our legs in the water, and, seated on the marble
>   edge, play dice.
> We'll play ball too. But let no lovers enter; our hair is too wet, our
>   throats have gooseflesh and the ends of our fingers are wrinkled.
> Besides, whoever found us naked would regret it! Bilitis is not
>   Athene, but she only shows herself at her own hours and she
>   punishes eyes that are too ardent.
>
> *("The Bath")*

The reader will find similar wet dreams in Lawrence's *The Rainbow* (1915), Lehmann's *Dusty Answer*, H. E. Bates's "Breeze Anstey," and Bowles's *Two Serious Ladies*. "The Bathe," a 1934 short story by the gifted (female) Australian writer "Henry Handel Richardson," exploits the traditional aquatic topos in a magnificently comic and parodic form.[44]

The main point of such scenes—witness *The Rainbow*, in which Lawrence's adolescent heroine, Ursula Brangwen, joins her adored school-mistress, Miss Inger, for a nocturnal river swim during a thunderstorm—is to hint at sexual desire (and sometimes even its consummation) without describing it in so many words:

"I think I shall go and bathe," said Miss Inger, out of the cloud-black darkness.

"At night?" said Ursula.

"It is best at night. Will you come?"

"I should like to."

"It is quite safe—the grounds are private. We had better undress in the bungalow, for fear of the rain, then run down."

Shyly, stiffly, Ursula went into the bungalow and began to remove her clothes. The lamp was turned low, she stood in the shadow. By another chair Winifred Inger was undressing.

Soon the naked, shadowy figure of the elder girl came to the younger.

"Are you ready?" she said.

"One moment."

Ursula could hardly speak. The other naked woman stood by, stood near, silent. Ursula was ready.

They ventured out into the darkness, feeling the soft air of night upon their skins.

"I can't see the path," said Ursula.

"It is here," said the voice, and the wavering, pallid figure was beside her, a hand grasping her arm. And the elder held the younger close against her, close, as they went down, and by the side of the water, she put her arms round her, and kissed her. And she lifted her in her arms, close, saying softly:

"I shall carry you into the water."

Ursula lay still in her mistress's arms, her forehead against the beloved, maddening breast.

"I shall put you in," said Winifred.

But Ursula twined her body about her mistress.

After a while the rain came down on their flushed, hot limbs, startling, delicious. A sudden, ice-cold shower burst in a great weight upon them. They stood up to it with pleasure. Ursula received the stream of it upon her breasts and her belly and her limbs. It made her cold, and a deep, bottomless silence welled up in her, as if bottomless darkness were returning upon her.

So the heat vanished away, she was chilled as if from a waking up. She ran indoors, a chill, non-existent thing, wanting to get away. She wanted the light, the presence of other people, the external connection with the many. Above all she wanted to lose herself among natural surroundings.

The prose of the foregoing is ambiguous enough to make it unclear, indeed, whether Ursula and Winifred actually end up in the water at all: the odd hiatus between "But Ursula twined her body about her mistress" and the paragraph beginning "After a while" may signify some silent coupling at river's edge. (Ursula's chthonic Lawrentian chills likewise suggest the rigors of intimate connection: the ponderous description of the "bottomless darkness" returning "upon her" sounds like Lawrence-speak for postcoital *tristesse*.) Yet whether outright lovemaking occurs or not, the proximity of water seems ineluctably to nurture lesbian feeling. Like the ancient springs of Lesbos, fictional ponds, seas, baths, fountains, and streams "give birth" to same-sex passion. "I wanted to see you in the swimming pool," wrote Amy Lowell in a 1914 love poem to Ada Dwyer Russell:

> White and shining in the silver-flecked water.
> While the moon rode over the garden,
> High in the arch of night,
> And the scent of the lilacs was heavy with stillness.
>
> Night, and the water, and you in your whiteness,
>   bathing!
>   (*"In the Garden"*)

Given the insistence of the bathing motif it is hardly surprising that the leading alternative publisher of lesbian romantic fiction in the United States today—the lesbian equivalent of the Harlequin Press or Mills and Boone—should go by the name of the Naiad Press.

Yet the reader will discover other recurrent sexual images here too. The combing, caressing, or washing of another woman's hair is another standard metaphoric indicator of homoerotic feeling: in works as disparate as Gautier's *Mademoiselle de Maupin*, Hardy's *Desperate Remedies*, Renée Vivien's "Words to My Friend," and Djuna Barnes's "Cassation," tender contact with the beloved's hair seems either to anticipate or to commemorate, synecdochally, the contact of loving bodies. "While I was leaning over the back of her chair as she did her embroidery," writes Gautier's heroine of her courtesan-lover Rosette, "I used to curl my round my fingers the little stray fair curls on her round plump neck, or I smoothed her hair, held taut by a comb, with the back of my hand, and I gave it back its lustre—or else it was some other pretty gesture which you know I often make to my women friends." "Oh delicately winding tendrils / On your moist temple!" writes the Russian poet Sophia Parnok in "You Sleep, My Companion-Lover" (c. 1915): "Oh violets!"

In a rather more sinister vein, various writers here associate lesbian sexuality with the eating of candy, crystallized fruit, or other cloyingly sweet foods. The motif is commonly invoked in order to disparage—to hint that while same-sex love may please, it also fails to nourish. In Andrew Marvell's *Upon Appleton House*, as we have seen, the nuns try to lure Isabella Thwaites into their convent by proffering boiled fruits; in Hamilton's *Life of Count Grammont* (1713), the mannish Miss Hobart attempts to seduce the dim-witted Miss Temple, her fellow lady-in-waiting, by plying her with delicious "sweetmeats." Similar images can be found in Diderot's *The Nun*, Gautier's *Mademoiselle de Maupin*, Zola's *Nana*, James's *The Bostonians*, and Strachey's *Olivia*. In the last-named work, during a trip to Paris to see the Comédie Française, Mademoiselle Julie feeds the infatuated narrator, her pet student, on "cakes and chocolates" from a "fashionable pastry-cook's."

Yet in certain contexts suspiciously "sweet" things, and oral satisfaction generally, function more complexly. In Christina Rossetti's surreal *Goblin Market* the pretty heroine Laura falls under an evil spell when she eats the strange "orchard fruits" ("Sweet to tongue and sound to eye") forced upon her by a band of goblin men:

> Sweeter than honey from the rock,
> Stronger than man-rejoicing wine,
> Clearer than water flowed that juice;
> She never tasted such before,
> How should it cloy with length of use?
> She sucked and sucked and sucked the more
> Fruits which that unknown orchard bore;
> She sucked until her lips were sore;
> Then flung the empty rinds away
> But gathered up one kernel-stone,
> And knew not was it night or day
> As she turned home alone.

Forlorn, enfeebled, and near death, Laura is released from her spell only after her sister, Lizzie, seeks out the goblin men and lets them tempt her with the same fruits, which she refuses to eat. When Lizzie returns, covered in the sticky juices that the goblins, in their eagerness, have "syrupped" all about her face and neck, she invites Laura to save herself through a frenzied (almost sexual) ritual of consumption:

> She cried "Laura," up the garden,
> "Did you miss me?
> Come and kiss me.
> Never mind the bruises,
> Hug me, kiss me, suck my juices
>
> Squeezed from goblin fruits for you,
> Goblin pulp and goblin dew.
> Eat me, drink me, love me;
> Laura, make much of me:
> For your sake I have braved the glen
> And had to do with goblin merchant men."

In the bizarre coupling that follows—saccharine in the most ravishing sense ("she kissed and kissed her with a hungry mouth")—we seem to contemplate an act of love for which goblin "juice" is mere pretext.

And then, finally, there are those odd, miscellaneous, yet sensually fraught images that repeat themselves, uncannily, from text to text. A favorite motif across the centuries is the kiss or caress on the shoulder:

> She pulled my sleeve and kissed my arm all the way up from fingertips to shoulder.
>
> (*Denis Diderot*, The Nun)

> I was moved, and I caressed Rosette once or twice with more than usual affection; my hand had moved down from her hair to her velvet neck, and from there to her round smooth shoulder which I gently stroked, following its trembling lines. The child was quivering at my touch like a clavichord at a musician's fingers; her flesh was shuddering, and it suddenly moved, and loving tremors ran all down her body.
>
> (*Théophile Gautier*, Mademoiselle de Maupin)

> When Clare arrived, radiant in a shining red gown, Irene had not finished dressing. But her smile scarcely hesitated as she greeted her, saying: "I always

seem to keep C.P. time, don't I? We hardly expected you to be able to come. Felise will be pleased. How nice you look."

Clare kissed a bare shoulder, seeming not to notice a slight shrinking.

(*Nella Larsen*, Passing)

It is this unresolved and undemanding sensuality [between women] that finds happiness in an exchange of glances, an arm laid on a shoulder, and is thrilled by the odor of sun-warmed wheat caught in a head of hair.

(*Colette*, The Pure and the Impure)

She put her hands on Cecile's bare arms and as she twisted her round, bent down and kissed her shoulder. A long deliberate kiss on the naked creamy shoulder. An unknown pang of astonishing violence stabbed me. I hated Cecile. I hated Mlle. Julie. As she raised her eyes from the kiss, she saw me watching her. Had she noticed me before? I don't know. Now, I thought, she was mocking me.

(*Dorothy Strachey*, Olivia)

The hand rested on my neck: a frosty sun whitened my hair. The hand followed my veins, downward. The hand stopped. My pulse beat against the mound of Venus of Isabelle's hand. The hand moved up again: it was drawing circles, overflowing in the void, it was spreading its sweet ripples even wider around my left shoulder, while my right shoulder lay abandoned to the breathing of the other girls. I was discovering the velvet smoothness of my bones, the glow hidden in my flesh, the infinity of forms I possessed. The hand was trailing a mist of dreams across my skin. The heavens beg when someone strokes your shoulder: the heavens were begging now.

(*Violette Leduc*, La Bâtarde)

Such reiteration, one feels, can hardly be accidental: we seem to enter here upon a private yet communal erotic phenomenology. While any judgment as to the import of such a detail must remain speculative, one is struck by the fact that the kiss on the shoulder, as opposed, say, to the kiss on the cheek or even the mouth, is a flagrantly erotic gesture—impossible to confuse with the everyday niceties of female homosocial intimacy. A kiss on the mouth *can* be a sexual overture, of course, but often is nothing more than a gesture of friendship or comfortable kinship. (Executed quickly, in public, it can seem utterly drained of erotic content.) To kiss on the shoulder, however, is unmistakably to start things up, to go adventuring, to become a seductive agent. Even as it makes "the heavens beg," the motif has been yet another means by which authors have gotten the lesbian idea *across*—have put the idea, so to speak, in our heads. In pondering the significance of such motifs—and there are many, many others to which one might point—we replay in little that primal recognition on which the writing of lesbianism depends: that one woman may desire another—and nowhere more satisfyingly, perhaps, than when less rather than more is said, and gestures take on the frisson of avowal.

5

And thus to a final, positively Sapphic pathos. Unlike the pleasure betokened by the moonlight swim, the sweet thing on the tongue, the kiss on the shoulder, no *anthology*—crude and ill-featured object that it is—will ever satisfy so fully. However large or ambitious it becomes, and this volume is engorged indeed, there will always be something missing: some crucial text—astonishingly omitted!—on which the captious reader or reviewer can bear down with outraged delight. Why did she leave out X? Why isn't Y here? What happened to Z? This is as it should be. The anthologist's motto might well be *nemini placebo*—I will please no one. No one but a masochist should take on such a bittersweet lot: you have to revel in feeling chagrined.

There are undoubtedly numerous works of literature I might have included here but did not—works that might have helped indeed to underscore my larger theme, the "routinization" of the lesbian idea. Some of my omissions have had to do with copyright restrictions. According to the terms of Radclyffe Hall's will, for example, it is not possible to excerpt from *The Well of Loneliness*. Other omissions result from the fact that the word *lesbianism* in the title of a book can still provoke panic in individuals committed to the impoverishment of understanding: Edna St. Vincent Millay's estate continues to prohibit the reprinting of her poems in any remotely sapphic context. Others reflect, I am sure, various personal quirks and failings. There are hundreds of romantic friendship poems written by women in the eighteenth and nineteenth centuries; but I can't help feeling that if you've read eight or ten of them you've read them all. After a while I simply fail to swoon at yet another Ephelia to Ardelia, Parthenia to Flavia, Logorrhea to Aphasia. I'd rather be reading Balzac—or Emily Dickinson.

Still, such omissions notwithstanding, it is my hope that what is included here will suffice, if nothing else, to call attention to the important place that the lesbian topos has occupied in Western literature since the Renaissance. The story I have sought to tell is one of abundance rather than scarcity. Since the mid-sixteenth century there has been a *lot* of writing about love between women. In asserting this I know I run counter to lingering conceptions of female homosexuality as an "invisible" or largely inaccessible cultural phenomenon. The myth of lesbian invisibility is deeply entrenched in official critical discourse. Perhaps because Sappho and her grievously fragmented corpus offer so poignant an image of *damaged goods*—of the etiolation and mystification of some "lost" lesbian tradition, vanished like a literary Atlantis—we have been inclined to underestimate the sheer power and fecundity of lesbianism as a modern artistic theme. Certainly the reflexive tendency among conventional literary critics has been to view the subject of love between women as frail, marginal, strange, and hard to get a grip on before the twentieth century—a site of conceptual absence rather than of presence. Thus even the most sympathetic accounts of lesbian literary history still tend to treat the pre-1900 lesbian "canon" (insofar as far as it is recognized at all) as sparse, obscure, incomplete, disfigured, or defaced—both by authorial reticence and the malign forces of social and political repression.

One does not wish to underplay the deadening force of taboo and fear and pro-scription; one does not wish to overplay it either. Sappho's oeuvre is undoubtedly frag-mentary, but enough of it remains for her to be recognized not only as lesbian writing's "onlie begetter" but as possibly the greatest lyric poet the world has ever seen. Similarly, even if we take into account the "assault" on literary sapphism in the early Christian era and the relative scarcity of medieval materials, enough relevant texts have survived from 1550 on to construct a fairly lavish genealogy for the lesbian topos itself. What begins to surprise after a while is precisely how *much* has been written on the theme in modern times, rather than how little, and how complexly various fantasies of love between women have functioned, and continue to function, in the Western imagination.

I hope the selections in this anthology may prove as enlightening as they were to their first readers—if not in exactly the same way. To work chronologically through the texts accumulated here is in one sense to reenact the cognitive process that I have argued has been taking place in Western consciousness since the Renaissance: the col-lective psychic assimilation of the lesbian idea. To read on from Montaigne's *Travel Journal* (1581), say, to Graham Greene's "Chagrin in Three Parts" (1967) is to move from a world of bizarre she-males with monstrous clitorises to one in which you find yourself eavesdropping on the *raffinée* lady (with girlfriend) sipping cocktails at the table next to you in a restaurant. The volume is in some ways about becoming sagacious and blasé and letting all the old shock and scandal drop away.

It would be less than honest to suggest, however, that this is all that this volume is about, or indeed that I have no emotional investment of my own in the material col-lected here. Of the three great forms of human desire—man for woman, man for man, and woman for woman—it is incontrovertibly the case that the third has yet to be treated with the intellectual respect, existential weight, and moral and aesthetic gravi-tas of the other two. It has been my hope that this collection might help, if in a limited and bookish fashion, to alter that situation in some degree. Not, obviously, by merely rehearsing some sentimentalized vision of female same-sex relations, or by ignoring the numerous authors, male and female, who have treated the topic in a less than ideal-izing manner. True, I tend to see even the most scurrilous appropriations of the lesbian theme in a somewhat forgiving historical light—as part of that slow, often paradoxical, yet ultimately liberating process by which the idea of love between women has become collectively "thinkable." But I also believe that whatever one's personal stake in the matter, being serious about the history of the lesbian topos involves confronting the worst that has been said, along with the best. It is precisely in the richness of the Western response to female homosexuality that we begin to register the historic power of the topos—its moral and imaginative scope, its crucial influence on modernity, its occasional sublimity.

With what eyes? reads one of Sappho's most haunting fragments. With what eyes, indeed, to peruse the assortment of pleas, plaints, paeans, and perfidies collected here? With "Sapphic" eyes, one hopes—no matter what one's official sex or public relation to the enigmas of sexual orientation. By which I mean with eyes open and human enough to take it all in: the Earth and her beautiful garlands, love aborted and love found. With no man present, Eros, as Sappho knew, can be bittersweet. (He can also— as in Firbank or Stein or Greene—be wildly amusing.) But he is nonetheless a god, to whom paying tribute is advised. Sappho paid up first, and showed the rest of us the way.

NOTES

1. For various historical perspectives on the twentieth-century gay and lesbian liberation movement, see John Lauritsen and David Thorstad, *The Early Homosexual Rights Movement, 1864–1935* (New York: Times Change, 1974); James D. Steakley, *The Homosexual Emancipation Movement in Germany* (New York: Arno, 1975); Jeffrey Weeks, *Coming Out: Homosexual Politics in Britain, from the Nineteenth Century to the Present* (London and New York: Quartet, 1977); Lillian Faderman, *Surpassing the Love of Men: Romantic Friendship and Love Between Women from the Renaissance to the Present* (New York: William Morrow, 1981) and *Odd Girls and Twilight Lovers: A History of Lesbian Life in Twentieth-Century America* (New York: Columbia University Press, 1991); Toby Marotta, *The Politics of Homosexuality* (Boston: Houghton Mifflin, 1981); John D'Emilio, *Sexual Politics, Sexual Communities: The Making of a Homosexual Minority in the United States, 1940–1970* (Chicago: University of Chicago Press, 1983); John D'Emilio and Estelle B. Freedman, *Intimate Matters: A History of Sexuality in America* (New York: Harper and Row, 1988); Martin Duberman, Martha Vicinus and George Chauncey, Jr., eds., *Hidden from History: Reclaiming the Gay and Lesbian Past* (New York: Penguin, 1990); Martha Vicinus, "They Wonder to Which Sex I Belong": The Historical Roots of the Modern Lesbian Identity," *Feminist Studies* 18 (fall 1992): 467–97, rpt. in Henry Abelove, Michèle Aina Barale, and David M. Halperin, eds., *The Lesbian and Gay Studies Reader* (New York and London: Routledge, 1993), pp. 432–52.

2. A (very) small sampling: Richard B. Sewall, *The Life of Emily Dickinson* (Cambridge: Harvard University Press, 1974); Paula Bennett, *Emily Dickinson: Woman Poet* (Iowa City: University of Iowa Press, 1991); Judith Farr, *The Passion of Emily Dickinson* (Cambridge: Harvard University Press, 1992); Sharon O'Brien, *Willa Cather: The Emerging Voice* (New York: Random House, 1987); Hermione Lee, *Willa Cather: A Life Saved Up* (London: Virago, 1989) and *Virginia Woolf* (New York: Knopf, 1996); Claire Tomalin, *Katherine Mansfield: A Secret Life* (New York: Viking Penguin, 1987); Barbara Guest, *HERself Defined: The Poet H.D. and Her World* (Glasgow: William Collins, 1984); Susan Stanford Friedman, *Penelope's Web: Gen-*

der, Modernity, H.D.'s Fiction (Cambridge: Cambridge University Press, 1990); Jane Marcus, *Virginia Woolf and the Languages of Patriarchy* (Bloomington and Indianapolis: Indiana University Press, 1987); Susanne Raitt, *Vita and Virginia: The Work and Friendship of V. Sackville-West and Virginia Woolf* (Oxford: Clarendon, 1993); Philip Herring, *Djuna: The Life and Work of Djuna Barnes* (New York: Viking, 1995); Carolyn J. Allen, *Following Djuna: Women Lovers and the Erotics of Loss* (Bloomington: Indiana University Press, 1996); Victoria Glendinning, *Elizabeth Bowen* (New York: Knopf, 1978); renée c. hoogland, *Elizabeth Bowen: A Reputation in Writing* (New York and London: New York University Press, 1994); Brett C. Millier, *Elizabeth Bishop: Life and the Memory of It* (Berkeley and Los Angeles: University of California Press, 1993); Ruth Vanita, *Sappho and the Virgin Mary: Same-Sex Love and the English Literary Imagination* (New York: Columbia University Press, 1996); Patricia Juliana Smith, *Lesbian Panic: Homoeroticism in Modern British Women's Fiction* (New York: Columbia University Press, 1997); Erin G. Carlston, *Thinking Fascism: Sapphic Modernism and Fascist Modernity* (Stanford: Stanford University Press, 1998). On recent controversies over Jane Austen's sexuality, see Terry Castle, "Sister-Sister," *London Review of Books*, 2 August 1995; rpt. in Jane Hindle, ed., *London Review of Books: An Anthology* (London and New York: Verso, 1996), pp. 138–48; Claudia L. Johnson, "The Divine Miss Jane: Jane Austen, Janeites, and the Discipline of Novel Studies," in Deidre Lynch, ed., *Janeites: Austen's Disciples and Devotees* (Princeton and Oxford: Princeton University Press, 2000), pp. 25–44; and Peter Monaghan, "With Sex and Sensibility, Scholars Redefine Jane Austen," *Chronicle of Higher Education*, 17 August 2001, p. A10.

3. Hank O'Neal, *"Life Is Painful, Nasty and Short . . . In My Case It Has Only Been Painful and Nasty": Djuna Barnes, 1978–1981, An Informal Memoir* (New York: Paragon House, 1990), p. 172.

4. Anne Olivier Bell and Andrew McNeillie, eds., *The Diary of Virginia Woolf* (London: Hogarth, 1975–1980), 3:51.

5. Though I pass by it glancingly here, the reader should be alert to the fact that much has been written lately on precisely this subject. For a varied and sometimes tendentious discussion of the historical genealogy of the term *lesbian*, see Emma Donoghue, *Passions between Women: British Lesbian Culture 1668–1801* (London: Scarlet, 1993); Faderman, *Odd Girls and Twilight Lovers*; Marjorie Garber, *Vice Versa: Bisexuality and the Eroticism of Everyday Life* (New York and London: Routledge, 1993); Jonathan Ned Katz, *The Invention of Heterosexuality* (New York: Dutton, 1995); and Vicinus, "They Wonder to Which Sex I Belong." Other writers have challenged the term on philosophical grounds: Judith Butler offers a brilliant, sometimes unnerving exposé of the epistemological problems involved in its usage in "Imitation and Gender Insubordination," in Diana Fuss, ed., *Inside/Out: Lesbian Theories, Gay Theories* (New York and London: Routledge, 1991), pp. 13–31, and *Bodies That Matter: On the Discursive Limits of "Sex"* (New York and London: Routledge, 1993).

6. Arthur O. Lovejoy, *The Great Chain of Being: A Study in the History of Ideas* (Cambridge: Harvard University Press, 1936), p. 19.

7. Lovejoy, *Great Chain of Being*, p. 7.

8. Ernst Robert Curtius, *European Literature and the Latin Middle Ages*, trans. Willard R. Trask (New York and Evanston: Harper and Row, 1953), p. 3.

9. Philip P. Wiener, et al., eds., *Dictionary of the History of Ideas: Studies of Selected Pivotal Ideas* (New York: Charles Scribner's Sons, 1973), 1:vii.

10. Ibid.

11. See Paula Findlen, "Humanism, Politics, and Pornography in Renaissance Italy," in Lynn Hunt, ed., *The Invention of Pornography: Obscenity and the Origins of Modernity, 1500–1800* (New York: Zone, 1993), pp. 49–108.

12. Before the 1970s the only academic discipline in which one might explore sexual themes in a broader cultural context was anthropology: *Coming of Age in Samoa*, Margaret Mead's pioneering study of sexual attitudes among young adults in Samoa, in the Western Pacific, first appeared, for example, in 1928. (Mead's work was deeply controversial of course—in part because she spoke frankly about the easy acceptance, in Polynesian village life, of homosexual relations between boys and young men.) Yet precisely because anthropology focused on the putatively foreign and exotic—societies supposedly more savage, primitive, backward, or undeveloped than the European—its heuristic power was somewhat limited. Its intellectual provocations were tolerated, one suspects, mainly because the "us-them" distinction was so integral a part of the enterprise. As Mead herself would discover, it might be (marginally) allowable to describe homosexual behavior on a remote Pacific island, but that did not mean one might acknowledge its existence in the modern United States or indeed anywhere else in the "civilized" world.

13. Foucault's *History of Sexuality* is available in English in three volumes, all translated by Robert Hurley: *The History of Sexuality: An Introduction* (New York: Pantheon, 1978); *The Use of Pleasure* (New York: Pantheon, 1986); and *The Care of the Self* (New York, Pantheon, 1986). Numerous scholars have written about Foucault's influence on gay and lesbian literary studies. Two who take his measure most eloquently are Page duBois, whose *Sappho Is Burning* (Berkeley and Los Angeles: University of California Press, 1995) registers the impact of Foucault's ideas on Sappho studies, and David Halperin, whose *Saint Foucault: Towards a Gay Hagiography* (New York and London: Oxford University Press, 1995) offers a powerful overall assessment of his influence on the historiography and politics of gay and lesbian sexuality.

14. Foster (1895–1981), a librarian at the famed Kinsey Institute for Sex Research at Indiana University, published her exhaustive bibliography of lesbian-themed writing at her own expense in 1956. It was subsequently reprinted by the Diana Press in 1975 and Naiad Press in 1985, but is now once again out of print. My debt to Foster will be immediately obvious to anyone who knows her pioneering work. Long before anyone was ready to listen, Foster not only defined the Anglo-European lesbian literary canon but wrote about it with a wit, erudition, and civilized insight yet to be matched by her successors. Along with Faderman, whose outstanding books on the history of modern lesbianism have likewise become classics, Foster is an important "ghost" haunting this volume—a model of style, daring, and intellectual grace whose scholarly accomplishment deserves grateful commemoration.

15. See Bernadette J. Brooten, *Love Between Women: Early Christian Responses to Female Homoeroticism* (Chicago and London: University of Chicago Press, 1996). It is true, as Brooten so illuminatingly shows, that female homoeroticism was much in the minds of the early Church fathers—far more so than one might ever have supposed—and that a rich body of theological

and legal commentary on love between women has existed since late Roman times. When I speak of a dearth of literary material relating to love between women before 1500, I refer to those texts conventionally understood to be "literature"—works designed to engage the reader primarily on an imaginative and human level rather than a forensic or pietistic or theological one. It remains difficult to find writings by ordinary women before 1500 that one would feel comfortable identifying as "lesbian" in anything like the modern sense. Certain medieval devotional works, it is true—Hildegard of Bingen's twelfth-century liturgical songs, her church pageant the *Ordo Virtutum*, or some of the prayers and visions produced by Catholic nuns in celebration of the Virgin Mary and the female saints—might be said, at a stretch, to contain oddly "homoerotic" elements. I omit such works here, however, because they remain cryptic and little-understood texts and, in my view, require exhaustive historical and theological contextualization before one can begin to speculate on possible psychosexual dimensions. I have likewise excluded legal and bureaucratic documents such as the trial records reproduced by the historian Judith Brown in *Immodest Acts: A Lesbian Nun in Renaissance Italy* (New York: Oxford University Press, 1985), her remarkable study of an Italian nun excommunicated for engaging in sexual acts with another nun in 1618–19. Illuminating though they are, ecclesiastical records such as those relating to Brown's Sister Benedetta Carlini had neither the popular diffusion nor the explicitly hedonistic cast of more widely known "literary" and vernacular texts such as Ariosto's *Orlando Furioso* or Sidney's *Arcadia*. Among literary and cultural historians the topic of love between women in medieval Europe remains largely unexplored. For some groundbreaking forays, however, see John Boswell, *Christianity, Social Tolerance, and Homosexuality: Gay People in Western Europe from the Beginning of the Christian Era to the Fourteenth Century* (Chicago: University of Chicago Press, 1980); Louis Crompton, "The Myth of Lesbian Impunity: Capital Laws from 1270 to 1791," in Salvatore J. Licata and Robert P. Peterson, eds., *Historical Perspectives on Homosexuality* (New York: Haworth, 1981), pp. 11–25; E. Ann Matter, "My Sister, My Spouse: Woman-Identified Women in Medieval Christianity," *Journal of Feminist Studies in Religion* 2 (1986): 81–93; rpt. in Judith Plaskow and Carol Christ, eds., *Weaving the Visions: New Patterns in Feminist Spirituality* (San Francisco: Harper and Row, 1986); Carolyn Dinshaw, *Chaucer's Sexual Poetics* (Madison: University of Wisconsin Press, 1989); Angelica Rieger, "Was Bieris de Romans Lesbian?: Women's Relations with Each Other in the World of the Troubadours," in William D. Paden, ed., *The Voice of the Trobairitz: Perspectives on the Women Troubadours* (Philadelphia: University of Pennsylvania Press, 1989), pp. 73–89; Jacqueline Murray, "Twice Marginal and Twice Invisible: Lesbians in the Middle Ages," in Vern L. Bullough and James A. Brundage, eds., *Handbook of Medieval Sexuality* (New York: Garland, 1996), pp. 191–222; and Kathleen M. Blumreich, "Lesbian Desire in the Old French *Romans de Silence*," *Arthuriana* 7 (1997): 47–62.

16. Cited in Jane McIntosh Snyder, *Sappho* (New York and Philadelphia: Chelsea House, 1995), p. 35. In compiling the information here on Sappho's posthumous reputation I draw gratefully on a number of works: David M. Robinson, *Sappho and Her Influence* (Boston: Marshall Jones Co., 1924); Édith Mora, *Sappho: Histoire d'un poète et traduction intégrale de l'oeuvre* (Paris: Flammarion, 1966); Beram Saklatvala, *Sappho of Lesbos: Her Works Restored* (London: Charles

Skilton, 1968); Joan DeJean, *Fictions of Sappho, 1546–1937* (Chicago: University of Chicago Press, 1989); Peter Jay and Caroline Lewis, eds., *Sappho Through English Poetry* (London: Anvil, 1996); Brooten's *Love Between Women*; duBois's *Sappho is Burning*; Ellen Greene, ed., *Re-Reading Sappho: Reception and Transmission* (Berkeley: University of California Press, 1997); Yopie Prins, *Victorian Sappho* (Princeton: Princeton University Press, 1999); Margaret Reynolds, *The Sappho Companion* (New York: Palgrave, 2001); and in particular, Snyder's recent study, *Lesbian Desire in the Lyrics of Sappho* (New York: Columbia University Press, 1997).

17. On the legends of Sapphic conflagration, see Henry Tristam, "The Burning of Sappho," *Dublin Review*, 197 (1935): 137–49. As its title suggests, the metaphor of poems put to the torch operates powerfully in Page duBois's brilliant postmodern reflection on Sappho's poetic legacy in *Sappho Is Burning*.

18. Snyder, *Sappho*, p. 35.

19. For a reliable if bare-bones chronology of Sappho editions and translations through 1962, see Mora, *Sappho*, pp. 445–53. For a more thorough commentary—on early French versions of Sappho especially—see DeJean, *Fictions of Sappho*, chapters 1 and 2. While I do not always agree with DeJean—she overestimates, I think, the effectiveness of seventeenth and eighteenth-century editorial attempts to "heterosexualize" Sappho—my debt to her erudite, meticulous, and wonderfully interesting study is profound.

20. Jim Powell, *Sappho, a Garland: The Poems and Fragments of Sappho* (New York: Farrar, Straus and Giroux, 1993), pp. 23–24.

21. DeJean, *Fictions of Sappho*, p. 55.

22. Ibid., p. 57.

23. Robinson, *Sappho and Her Influence*, p. 44.

24. The fiction of the "chaste Sappho" had powerful advocates well into the twentieth century. See, for example, Théodore Reinach's "Pour mieux connaître Sappho" (1911), J.-M.-F. Bascoul's *La Chaste Sappho de Lesbos et le mouvement féministe à Athènes au quatrième siècle avant J.C.* (1911), and Mario Meunier's *Sappho et Anacréon* (1932). As Reinach put it, "in order to find a stain on this poetry, one must begin by putting it there." DeJean, *Fictions of Sappho*, pp. 251–53.

25. On the role of recovered classical texts in reviving the lesbian topos in English literature, see Ros Ballaster, " 'The Vices of Old Rome Revived': Representations of Female Same-Sex Desire in Seventeenth- and Eighteenth-Century England," in Suzanne Raitt, ed., *Volcanos and Pearl Divers: Essays in Lesbian Feminist Studies* (Binghamton, N.Y.: Haworth, 1995), pp. 13–36. For a consideration of the influence of the Greek and Roman classics on Western erotic writing and art, more generally, see Edgar Wind, *Pagan Mysteries in the Renaissance* (London: Faber and Faber, 1968); James M. Saslow, *Ganymede in the Renaissance: Homosexuality in Art and Society* (New Haven: Yale University Press, 1986); Peter Wagner, *Eros Revived: Erotica of the Enlightenment in England and America* (London: Paladin Grafton, 1990); Leonard Barkan, *Transuming Passion: Ganymede and the Erotics of Humanism* (Stanford: Stanford University Press, 1991); and the various essays collected in Lynn Hunt, ed., *The Invention of Pornography: Obscenity and the Origins of Modernity, 1500–1800* (New York: Zone, 1993), especially Paula Findlen's "Humanism, Politics, and Pornography in Renaissance Italy," pp. 49–108.

26. DeJean concludes her survey of Sappho's influence on French writing with Yourcenar. For the history of Sappho's influence on English literature see Robinson, *Sappho and Her Influence*, Vanita, *Sappho and the Virgin Mary*, and Prins, *Victorian Sappho*.

27. See D'Emilio and Freedman, *Intimate Matters*, pp. 323–25.

28. It would be inaccurate to say that female homosexual acts went entirely unpunished in earlier centuries: for instances to the contrary see Crompton, "The Myth of Lesbian Impunity"; Brown, *Immodest Acts*, pp. 6–20; Brigitte Eriksson, "A Lesbian Execution in Germany, 1721: The Trial Records," *Journal of Homosexuality* 6 (1980/81): 27–40; and Theo van der Meer, "Tribades on Trial: Female Same-Sex Offenders in Late Eighteenth-Century Amsterdam," *Journal of the History of Sexuality* 1 (1991): 424–44. Still, lawmakers over the past five centuries have generally been reluctant to legislate against lesbian acts—often out of fear that publicizing such "unnatural practices" through interdiction would cause them to spread. When it was suggested in 1921 that the British House of Lords rewrite the 1885 Criminal Law Amendment Act prohibiting "gross indecency" between men so as to make it apply to women too, the revision was refused in part on the grounds that "to adopt a Clause of this kind"—as one member put it—"would harm by introducing into the minds of innocent people the most revolting thoughts." Similar anxieties may have prevented Nazi officials in the 1930s from including lesbianism in Paragraph 75—the infamous statute banning male homosexuality in Germany during the Third Reich. See Jeffrey Weeks, *Coming Out: Homosexual Politics in Britain, from the Nineteenth Century to the Present* (London: Quartet, 1977), pp. 106–107; Susan M. Edwards, *Female Sexuality and the Law* (Oxford: Martin Robinson, 1981), pp. 43–45; Sheila Jeffreys, *The Spinster and Her Enemies: Feminism and Sexuality, 1880–1930* (London: Pandora, 1985), pp. 113–15; Richard Plant, *The Pink Triangle: The Nazi War Against Homosexuals* (New York: Henry Holt, 1986), pp. 114–16; and Doan, *Fashioning Sapphism*, pp. 32–37 and 51–63.

29. A number of excellent anthologies focus on lesbian writing of the past two or three decades. Indeed, my decision to end my own volume with writings from around the time of Stonewall was informed in part by my sense that British and American lesbian writing after 1969 is already well represented in existing compilations. See, for example, Felice Picano, ed., *A True Likeness: Lesbian and Gay Writing Today* (New York: Seahorse, 1980); Barbara Smith, ed., *Home Girls: A Black Feminist Anthology* (New York: Kitchen Table, Women of Color, 1983); Margaret Cruikshank, ed., *New Lesbian Writing* (San Francisco: Grey Fox, 1984); Carl Morse and Joan Larkin, eds., *Gay and Lesbian Poetry in Our Time: An Anthology* (New York: St. Martin's, 1988); Don Shewey, ed., *Out Front: Contemporary Gay and Lesbian Plays* (New York: Grove, 1988); Anna Livia and Lilian Mohin, eds., *The Pied Piper: Lesbian Feminist Fiction* (London: Onlywomen, 1989); *Lesbian Love Stories* (Freedom, Cal.: Crossing, 1989); Joan Nestle and Naomi Holoch, eds., *Women on Women: An Anthology of American Lesbian Short Fiction* (New York: Penguin, 1990), *Women on Women 2: An Anthology of American Lesbian Short Fiction* (New York: Penguin, 1993), and *Women on Women 3: A New Anthology of American Lesbian Short Fiction* (New York: Penguin, 1996); Makeda Silvera, ed., *Piece of My Heart: A Lesbian of Colour Anthology* (Toronto: Sister Vision, 1991); Berta Freistadt and Pat O'Brien, eds., *Language of Water, Language of Fire: A Celebration of Lesbian and Gay Poetry* (London: Oscar's, 1992); Robert Dessaix, ed., *Australian Gay and Lesbian Writing: An Anthology* (Melbourne and Oxford: Oxford

University Press, 1993); Margaret Reynolds, ed., *Penguin Book of Lesbian Short Stories* (New York: Viking, 1994); Juanita Ramos, ed., *Compañeras: Latina Lesbians* (New York: Routledge, 1994); Randy Turoff, ed., *Lesbian Words: State of the Art* (New York: Masquerade, 1995); Catherine E. McKinley and L. Joyce DeLaney, eds., *Afrekete: An Anthology of Black Lesbian Writing* (New York: Anchor, 1995); E. J. Levy, ed., *Tasting Life Twice: Literary Lesbian Fiction by New American Writers* (New York: Avon, 1995); Emma Wilson, ed., *Sexuality and Masquerade: The Dedalus Book of Sexual Ambiguity* (Sawtry, Cambridgeshire: Dedalus, 1996). Nearly half of the works reprinted in Lillian Faderman's *Chloe Plus Olivia: An Anthology of Lesbian Literature from the Seventeenth Century to the Present* (New York: Viking, 1994) are by contemporary writers.

30. See Daniel Vaillancourt, "The Dying Game," *The Advocate*, 13 October 1998, pp. 61–63.

31. On a few occasions I have moved a writer slightly out of chronological sequence in order to create a pairing or cluster of related texts; thus excerpts from two Harlem Renaissance novels, Nella Larsen's *Passing* (1929) and Blair Niles's *Strange Brother* (1931), appear next to one another, though Niles's work should technically follow the selections from Margaret Anderson's *My Thirty Years' War* and Wyndham Lewis's *The Apes of God* (both 1930).

32. For a useful overview of the medieval and Renaissance literature of monsters and marvels, see Stephen Greenblatt, *Marvelous Possessions: The Wonder of the New World* (Chicago: University of Chicago Press, 1991) and Lorraine Daston and Katharine Park, *Wonders and the Order of Nature, 1150–1750* (New York: Zone, 1998).

33. Interviewing rural Midwestern friends and relatives of the celebrated male-impersonating jazz musician Billy Tipton in the early 1990s, Tipton's biographer, Diane Wood Middlebrook, encountered several who referred to Tipton—whose real sex was only discovered after her death—as a "he-she" or "hermorphadite" (*sic*). See *Suits Me: The Double Life of Billy Tipton* (Boston: Houghton Mifflin, 1998), pp. 84–89 and 135–40.

34. Diana Lewis Burgin's discussion of Tsvetaeva's and Parnok's relationship in *Sophia Parnok: The Life and Work of Russia's Sappho* (New York and London: New York University Press, 1994) is a model of sympathetic scholarship; one can only hope that Tsvetaeva's critics and biographers—most of whom have been loath up to this point to engage very directly with Tsvetaeva's lesbian writings—will in turn begin to pursue this central aspect of her oeuvre.

35. On the wide dissemination of such texts in seventeenth- and eighteenth-century Britain—and in particular *Aristotles Master-Piece* and the *Onania*—see Roy Porter and Lesley Hall, *The Facts of Life: The Creation of Sexual Knowledge in Britain, 1650–1950* (New Haven and London: Yale University Press, 1995), pp. 33–64 and 96–100; and James Grantham Turner, *Libertines and Radicals in Early Modern London: Sexuality, Politics, and Literary Culture, 1630–1685* (Cambridge: Cambridge University Press, 2002).

36. On the pornographic pamphlet campaign against Marie Antoinette see Lynn Hunt, "The Many Bodies of Marie Antoinette," in Lynn Hunt, ed., *Eroticism and the Body Politic* (Baltimore: Johns Hopkins University Press, 1991), pp. 108–30. I have written elsewhere about Lister's familiarity with the Roman satirists; see Terry Castle, *The Apparitional Lesbian: Female Homosexuality and Modern Culture* (New York: Columbia University Press, 1993), pp. 102–103.

37. Anne-Marie Bonnet, ed., *Auguste Rodin: Erotic Watercolors* (New York: Stewart, Tabori and Chang, 1995). On the extraordinary popularity of lesbian imagery in late-nineteenth-century art and literature, see Faderman, *Surpassing the Love of Men,* and Bram Dijkstra, *Idols of Perversity: Fantasies of Feminine Evil in Fin-de-Siècle Culture* (New York and Oxford: Oxford University Press, 1986).

38. For a representative sampling of poems by these and other contemporary lesbian poets see Faderman, *Chloe Plus Olivia.*

39. Hester Thrale Piozzi, *Thraliana: The Diary of Mrs. Hester Lynch Thrale, 1776–1809,* ed. Katharine C. Balderstone (Oxford: Clarendon, 1951), 2:742. For other early appearances of *lesbian* and *sapphist* see Donoghue, *Passions Between Women,* pp. 2–4, 7, 149–50, 254, and 259.

40. Representative Brazil titles (she wrote over fifty books for children and young girls) include *The Fortunes of Philippa* (1906), *The Nicest Girl in the School* (1910), *A Fourth Form Friendship* (1912), *The Jolliest Term on Record* (1915), *Monitress Merle* (1922), and *Captain Peggy* (1924). While a helpful introduction to the girls' school genre, Mary Cadogan's *You're a Brick, Angela: A New Look at Girls' Fiction from 1829 to 1975* (London: Victor Gollancz, 1976) resolutely avoids any discussion of the almost comically homoerotic aspects of Brazil's novels.

41. Jeannette Foster lists numerous examples in *Sex Variant Women in Literature.* For further discussion, see Castle, *The Apparitional Lesbian,* pp. 85–86; and Corinne E. Blackmer, "*The Finishing Touch* and the Tradition of Girls' School Fictions," *Review of Contemporary Fiction* 15 (1995): 32–39.

42. Numerous volumes of literary and social history confirm the enlivening role of Paris in early-twentieth-century lesbian life; see in particular Shari Benstock, *The Women of the Left Bank: Paris, 1900–1940* (Austin: University of Texas Press, 1986); Andrea Weiss, *Paris Was a Woman: Portraits from the Left Bank* (London: Pandora, 1995); Christine Bard, *Les Garçonnes: Modes et fantasmes des Années folles* (Paris: Flammarion, 1998); and Erin G. Carlston, *Thinking Fascism: Sapphic Modernism and Fascist Modernity* (Stanford: Stanford University Press, 1998).

43. The association between France and scandalous writing was already well established by 1900. Writing in the British medical journal *The Lancet* in 1901, a contributor observed, à propos of the moral superiority of English fiction over its Continental rivals, that "as yet in this country the novelist . . . has not arrived at the treatment in romances of excessive morphiomania, or Sapphism, or vaginismus, all of which diseases will be found in the French novels." See *The Lancet,* 1 June 1901, p. 1548.

44. The importance of the motif in recent lesbian-themed writing has not gone unnoticed; Bonnie Zimmerman discusses some of its manifestations in *The Safe Sea of Women: Lesbian Fiction, 1969–1989* (Boston: Beacon, 1990).

❧ *The Sixteenth and Seventeenth Century* ❧

LUDOVICO ARIOSTO (1474–1533)

From *Orlando furioso* (1532)

The Italian Renaissance poet Ludovico Ariosto was born in Reggio and spent much of his life in Ferrara in the service of Cardinal Ippolito and Duke Alfonso I of Este. His great romantic epic in verse, *Orlando furioso*, a celebration of the house of Este and its legendary ancestor Ruggiero, appeared in 1532 and remains one of the founding works of the modern Western literary tradition. The poem's cultivated vision of human nature, sumptuous use of language, and richly entertaining flow of incident make it a work of permanent artistic importance.

Orlando furioso also offers one of the classic early treatments of what one might call "accidental" or "disguised" female homosexuality. The epic as a whole revolves around the adventures of Orlando, one of Charlemagne's knights, during the holy war against the Saracens. An important subplot has to do, however, with the love of Ruggiero, a knight fighting on the Moorish side, for the heroic female warrior Bradamante. In the excerpt below, from canto 25 of the poem, Ruggiero rescues a "strange knight" (Bradamante's twin brother, Ricciardetto) from a conflagration. When the knight shows his face, Ruggiero is momentarily puzzled, mistaking him for his beloved Bradamante. Ricciardetto quickly explains that ever since Bradamante had her hair cut short after receiving a head wound in battle, he and she have been confused with one another. He then relates a dizzying instance of such confusion involving the beautiful princess Fiordispina. The comical tale he tells—of Fiordispina's deluded passion for Bradamante and how he himself has taken advantage of it—mingles salaciousness and art in equal measure.

Ariosto was not the first modern European writer to exploit the motif of the woman-falling-in-love-with-woman-in-male-disguise. The anonymous thirteenth-century French romance *Huon de Bordeaux* may have been one of Ariosto's sources: in that work, the disguised female knight, Ide, serves valiantly in the forces of the Holy Roman Emperor, and then—to her embarrassment—is given the hand of the Emperor's daughter in marriage as a reward. Her identity is ultimately exposed, but not before the Emperor's daughter, who hasn't a clue about her groom's real sex, suffers bitterly over the feeble "clyppynge and kyssynge" with which Ide tries to satisfy her after their wedding. Ariosto's rendering of a similar situation—deliciously complicated by the figure of the libidinous twin brother, Ricciardetto—is considerably more elaborate, as if the poet were determined to extract from the episode the maximum (pseudo-)sapphic frisson. Lesbianism, one could say, here enters the world of Western literary discourse as sophisticated authorial joke. The imagery of same-sex love flashes vividly before the reader's eyes, even as it is subsumed—cunningly—within the containing framework of heterosexual romance.

FURTHER READING: Ludovico Ariosto, *Orlando furioso*, trans. Barbara Reynolds (Harmondsworth, Middlesex: Penguin, 1977); Charles Peter Brand, *Ludovico Ariosto: A Preface to the Orlando Furioso* (Edinburgh: Edinburgh University Press, 1974); Peter De Sa Wiggins, *Figures in Ariosto's Tapestry: Character and Design in the Orlando Furioso* (Baltimore, Md.: Johns Hopkins University Press, 1986); Albert Russell Ascoli, *Ariosto's Bitter Harmony: Crisis and Evasion in the Italian Renaissance* (Princeton: Princeton University Press, 1987); Barbara Pavlock, *Eros, Imitation, and the Epic Tradition* (Ithaca, N.Y.: Cornell University Press, 1990); Daniel Javitch, *Proclaiming a Classic: The Canonization of Orlando Furioso* (Princeton: Princeton University Press, 1991); Valeria Finucci, *The Lady Vanishes: Subjectivity and Representation in Castiglione and Ariosto* (Stanford: Stanford University Press, 1992); Judith Bryce, "Gender and Myth in the *Orlando furioso*," *Italian Studies* 47 (1992): 41–50.

Ruggiero said, "I see my lady's face,
Her features beautiful beyond compare,
I see her lovely aspect and her grace,
The sweetness of her voice I do not hear.
These words of gratitude I cannot place.
Such thanks to me, her lover, strange appear.
If this is Bradamant, how can it be
That she forgets my name so soon, and me?"

In order to be sure, he shrewdly said:
"Have I not seen you somewhere else ere now?
I've turned the matter over in my head,
And still I can't remember when or how.
Tell me if you remember it instead.
Your name might be of help, if you'll allow.
Reveal it, then, that I may know whom I
Have rescued from the death you were to die."

"It may be you have seen me once before,"
The youth replied, "when, where, I do not know,

Since many different regions I explore;
Seeking adventure, through the world I go.
You may have seen my sister when she wore
Full armour and a sword; we two are so
Alike (for we were born on the same day)
That who is which, our parents cannot say.

"You're not the first; it causes us great mirth
That many folk commit the same mistake.
My father, brothers, she who at one birth
Produced us, the same error often make.
Short hair I have, my sister once no dearth
Of tresses had which for adornment's sake
She twisted round her head in a long braid;
And this between us some distinction made.

"But she was wounded in the head one day
(How this occurred would take too long to tell),
And when a holy hermit passed that way,
He cropped her hair so that the wound might heal.
Now which of us is which no one can say,
If we our names and sex do not reveal:
I Ricciardetto, Bradamante she,
Born of the Montalbano family.

"Such joy at first, such torment in the end
My likeness to my sister brought me to,
I could relate, if you an ear would lend,
A strange event that would astonish you."
No history or tale could more commend
Itself, no anecdote, Ruggiero knew,
More please him than a narrative wherein
His love appeared; he begged him to begin.

And thus he did: "My sister, not long since,
Was riding through these woods, unhelmeted,
And, overtaken by some Saracens,
By one of them was wounded in the head.
A passing hermit, using his good sense,
Observing how extensively she bled,
Cut off her golden hair; then on she rode,
Close-cropped as any man, about the wood.

"Thus wandering, she reached a shady fount.
Her wound had weakened her, so she drew rein,
And when she had descended from her mount
She pulled her helmet off and on the green
Young grass soon fell asleep. I'll now recount
The most delightful tale that's ever been:
Out hunting with her friends that very day,
Fair Fiordispina chanced to pass that way.

"She saw my sister as she rested there,
In armour fully clad, save for her face;
A sword was at her side, where women wear
A distaff; as she views the manly grace
Of one she takes to be a cavalier,
Her heart is vanquished, and to join the chase
She first invites her, then contrives ere long
To separate her from the merry throng.

"Alone with her, where no one could surprise
Them in that leafy, solitary nook,
Her anguished soul reflected in her eyes,
The damsel then began to show with look
And words and gestures and with ardent sighs
Her passion for my sister, whom she took
To be a man; she pales, then, blushing red,
She steals a kiss, so greatly she's misled.

"My sister understood the maid believed
She was a man, and it was evident
Such burning love could never be relieved
By her. 'Better' (so ran her argument)
'This damsel should at once be undeceived
Than she should think me so indifferent.
Better a woman I should prove, and kind,
Than seem a man for love so disinclined.'

"And this was right, for base it were and weak,
And worthy of a statue, not a man,
When such a lovely maid her love should speak,
So sweet and melting in her languid pain,
To sit inertly by, as mild and meek
As a young owl by day; so she began

To tell the maid she was a woman, not
A manly cavalier as she had thought;

"That, like Camilla and Hippolyta,
She went in search of glory in the life
Of arms; that in Arzilla, in Africa,
She had been born and bred for martial strife,
And trained from childhood in the arts of war.
No spark of love is quenched; it is as if
The remedy has been applied too late.
The damsel's wound is deep and desperate.

"That face on this account is no less fair;
That glance, that grace of manner are the same.
The damsel's heart does not return from where
It sunned itself in the belovèd beam
Of those entrancing eyes; seeing her wear
That manly armour which has earned such fame,
Her longing may be yet fulfilled, she thinks,
Then sighs and into deepest sorrow sinks.

"Whoever heard her mourn and weep that day
His own lament would have combined with hers.
'What cruel torments,' she began to say,
'Have ever been, than which mine are not worse?
Of any other love I could allay
The pain by hope of solace in due course;
The rose I'd gather which sharp thorns defend.
Only my present longing has no end.

"'Love, if to torture me was your intent,
If you so envied me my happy state,
Could you, as is your wont, not be content
With many another lover's wretched fate?
In all the world of nature, you invent
A female lover for a female mate!
Women their hearts to women do not lose,
Nor doe to doe, nor ewe to other ewes.

"'On land, on sea, in heaven, I alone
Must bear a blow of such severity;
You mean by my example shall be shown

The last extreme of your authority.
The wife of Ninus, who desired her son,
Your victim was; Myrrha with infamy
Desired her father, Pasiphae the bull,
Yet mine the maddest folly is of all.

"'The mother, hoping to seduce the boy,
Succeeded in her scheme, so I have heard,
And Pasiphae achieved a lustful joy
Inside a wooden cow among the herd.
If Daedalus should all his skills employ
And fly to my assistance like a bird,
This knot would be too intricate for him.
The master-hand of Nature is supreme.'

"So bitterly she grieves in her despair,
No solace can she find in her laments.
She beats her face, she twists and breaks her hair,
And on herself, herself revenge attempts.
My sister, looking on, cannot forbear
To weep at what such sorrow represents.
She seeks to turn her from her vain desire,
To no avail; she cannot quench the fire.

"Not comfort Fiordispina needs, but aid,
And, unconsoled, she grows the more distressed.
The daylight now would soon begin to fade,
As redder flamed the sun towards the West;
The time had come for them to leave the glade.
Since both considered this was for the best,
The damsel to her home near by invited
My sister, lest they both become benighted.

"She could not find it in her to refuse
And so together they approached this town,
Where I by burning was about to lose
My life, had you not mowed the rabble down.
All courtesy the gracious damsel shows
To Bradamante; and a woman's gown
She gives her, so that everybody can
Observe she is a woman, not a man.

"For, understanding that she would obtain
No solace from my sister's virile air,
She judged it would be ill-advised to gain
A name for dalliance with a cavalier.
She also hoped that it would dull the pain
Which armour had inflicted on her fair
Young, unsuspecting, palpitating breast,
To see her thus in women's garments dressed.

"They lay together in the selfsame bed,
But not the same repose; for while one sleeps,
The other groans and, still uncomforted,
With longing is on fire, the more she weeps;
And if she slumbers, by her dreams she's led
To Fancy's realm, where promises Love keeps,
Where Fate's decrees fond lovers do not vex,
And where her Bradamante has changed sex.

"As when a sick man with a raging thirst,
If he should fall asleep, will toss and turn
And, with his lips as fevered as at first,
Will dream of drinking deep at beck or burn,
So in her dreams, when grief has done its worst,
Her longings gain the boon for which they yearn;
But on awaking, with her hand she gropes,
And finds once more that vain are all her hopes.

"What vows, what prayers she uttered every night
To her Mahomet and to every god,
That, working wondrous miracles, they might
To manhood change her love from womanhood!
But all in vain; the heavens mocked her plight.
The long hours passed and Phoebus from the flood
Now slowly lifted up his golden head
And on the waking world his radiance shed.

"The day arrived when more reluctant yet
Fair Fiordispina from her couch arose,
For Bradamante said, with feigned regret,
She must depart (from this impasse she knows
There is no other exit than retreat).

The damsel offers her before she goes
A Spanish horse, with trappings all of gold,
A surcoat also, broidered gay and bold.

"The damsel bore her company a while,
Then, weeping, to her castle went her way.
My sister galloped on, mile after mile,
And Montalbano reached that very day.
Our mother once again began to smile;
Her brothers gathered round to hear her say
What had befallen her, for we had feared
The worst, no tidings of her having heard.

"We gazed astonished at her close-cropped hair,
Which formerly was wound about her head.
Her strangely-broidered surcoat made us stare.
She told us everything, just as I said:
How she was wounded in the forest, where
A hermit passed who, seeing how she bled,
Cut off her tresses that the wound might heal;
And now no more discomfort did she feel.

"And how, while she was sleeping by a fount,
A beautiful young maid came riding by,
Who took her for a knight and bade her mount
And join the huntsmen's merry hue and cry;
And how the maid then drew her from the hunt.
No detail did she spare us or deny.
The story stirred us to our very souls,
To think how nothing the poor maid consoles.

"Of Fiordispina I was well aware,
In Saragossa I'd seen her and in France.
Her lovely eyes, her rounded cheek, her hair
Were to my taste and often drew my glance;
And yet not long I let it linger there,
For hopeless love is folly; now that Chance
Provided access to an open door,
The flame leapt up as ardent as before.

"So from new strands of hope Love weaves his net.
(No other threads at present can he use.)

He catches me and shows how I may get
My heart's desire, how by a simple ruse
I may succeed; if I'm content to let
My likeness to my sister so bemuse
Beholders that they think I am my twin,
The damsel also may be taken in.

"Shall I or shall I not? I ponder well.
To follow pleasure where it leads seems good.
But no one of my secret plan I tell:
To seek advice on this I am too shrewd.
My sister's arms I found when evening fell
(Those she had worn when riding through the wood);
I put them on and rode her horse away,
Not waiting for the light of the new day.

"That very night I leave (Love being my guide)
To find fair Fiordispina once again.
I reach the end at last of my long ride
Just as the sun is rising from the main.
The eager servants one with th'other vied
To carry the glad tidings to their queen;
Hoping to curry favour and earn grace,
They hurried off to her at a great pace.

"They all mistook me, as just now you did,
For Bradamante, being deceived the more
By her apparel and the Spanish steed
On which she galloped off the day before.
And soon towards me Fiordispina sped;
Such joy and happiness her visage wore,
So festive was her welcome and so fond,
No one in all the world was more jocund.

"Throwing her lovely arms about my neck,
She clasps me sweetly and imprints a kiss
Upon my mouth (I swear it was no peck!).
Imagine if Love's arrow now can miss!
Straight to my heart, its flight receives no check.
Then to her room (no harm she sees in this)
She hurries me and there, from helm to spurs,
Disarms me and no help allows but hers.

"Then ordering a robe, ornate and fair,
She spreads its folds and in it dresses me
As if I were a woman; on my hair
She puts a net of golden filigree.
The modest glance, the bashful look I wear,
My every gesture femininity
Proclaim; and though my voice too manly is,
I use it so that no one notices.

"A hall we entered next, where many folk
Awaited us, ladies and chevaliers.
They paid us honour and respect, and spoke
As when great ladies or a queen appears;
And up my sleeve, as at a secret joke,
I laughed at some who (this is for your ears),
Not knowing what I hid beneath my gown,
With languid glances looked me up and down.

"The night was far advanced, the hour grew late;
The servants long ago had cleared the board,
At which the guests and household always ate
The choicest viands, fit for any lord.
The lovely Fiordispina did not wait
For me, who longed for her, to speak the word,
But, as she rose from table, graciously
To sleep with her that night invited me.

"When all the waiting-women moved away,
And pages who escorted us to bed
Had left the sconces flaming bright as day,
'My lady, do not be surprised,' I said,
While we in night-attire together lay,
'Though on my homeward path you saw me sped
(And when I would come back God only knew),
To see me now so soon returned to you.

"'I'll tell you first just why I had to leave.
Next, why I have returned will be explained.
If, lady, I'd had reason to believe
Your ardour would have cooled had I remained,
No greater joy or sweetness than to live
And die in serving you could I have gained;

But as my presence caused you grief and woe,
I judged it best at last that I should go.

"'But Fortune made me wander all about
Among the tangled branches of a glade;
And suddenly I heard a piercing shout
As if a frightened damsel called for aid.
I did not hesitate for long in doubt:
Beside a crystal lake, a bare-limbed maid
Who dangled from a rod-and-line I saw.
A cruel troll prepared to eat her raw.

"'I rushed towards the monster, sword in hand
(Nor could I help the damsel otherwise).
That evil fisherman will never land
Another catch; the maid, to my surprise,
Leapt back into the water from the strand.
"You'll be rewarded handsomely" she cries,
"And anything you care to ask, I'll grant;
I am a nymph; this crystal lake I haunt.

"'"I am possessed of wondrous potency:
The elements and Nature I can bend.
Ask what you will and leave the rest to me,
If you would know how far my powers extend.
The fire to ice, air to solidity,
Will change, the moon above to earth descend
To hear my song; with simple words alone
The globe I can dislodge and stop the sun."

"'No treasure did I ask, no gold require,
No wish had I to dominate mankind,
Nor to a superhuman strength aspire,
Nor fame in military conquests find.
Only the means I ask that your desire
May be fulfilled; and so whatever kind
Of spell or influence she needs to use,
I do not specify, but let her choose.

"'No sooner had I uttered my request,
Than once again she dived beneath the lake,
And put her magic talents to the test:

The only answer she would deign to make
Was to splash water at me, as in jest!
At once I see, I feel—there's no mistake—
I know, though credit it I scarcely can,
I'm changing from a woman to a man.

"'If it were not that here and now straightway,
You can confirm it, you would doubt it too.
As female once and now as male today,
My pleasure it will be to pleasure you.
Command me, for I long but to obey,
And gladly will I serve the whole night through.'
And, taking then her hand in mine, I made
Her test and prove the truth of what I said.

"Like one who, lacking hope, for long has pined
For some loved object, lost (or found too late),
Who, sighing, cannot put it from his mind,
And moans and groans and rails against his fate,
Who if he unexpectedly should find
What he desires, having been desperate
So long and by ill fortune so ill-used,
At first incredulous, would stand confused,

"So Fiordispina, when she feels and sees
What she has been desiring for so long,
Her touch, her eyes, can scarcely trust; she is
Afraid that after all she must be wrong
Or sleeping; to dispel these fantasies,
Good proof I gave her, adequate and strong.
'Dear God,' she said, 'if this is dreaming, make
Me always dream and let me never wake.'

"No roll of drums is heard, no trumpetings
These love-opponents forth to battle send,
But dove-like kisses and sweet murmurings
Give signal to go forward or ascend.
Our weapons are not arrows, nor yet slings.
No scaling-ladders here assistance lend.
I leap upon the fort and am not slow
To plant my standard and subdue my foe.

"If on the previous night that bed had been
A vestibule of sighing and laments,
Tonight, although unaltered is the scene,
Sweet games and smiles and joy are the events.
The sinuous acanthus ne'er was seen
To twine on columns and on pediments,
As we, who clasp each other face to face,
With arms and legs our breasts and thighs embrace.

"At first the secret stayed between us two.
For several months our pleasure was secure.
But someone then observed our rendezvous
And after that it was not long before
The king, her father, heard of it; and you,
Who rescued me, require to hear no more.
You saw the flames; you understand the rest.
God sees the pain which leaves my heart distressed."

This was the story Ricciardetto told
As on they rode together through the night,
Breasting a rising terrain, sheer and bold,
Surrounded by ravines to left and right.
A narrow, rocky pathway, like an old
And rusty key, turned slowly to the height
To reach a citadel, called Agrismonte,
Guarded by Aldigier of Chiaramonte.

PONTUS DE TYARD (1521–1605)

"Elegy for a Lady Fallen for Another Lady" (1573)

Born into a noble Burgundian family in 1521, the French poet Pontus de Tyard is remembered today as a member of the Pléiade—the celebrated group of sixteenth-century writers, led by Pierre de Ronsard and Joachim Du Bellay, who sought to revitalize French poetry by returning to classical models. He was raised as a churchman and served as chaplain to Henri III and Bishop of Chalon-sur-Saône. His first book of verse, *Erreurs amoureuses*, appeared in 1549; his *Vers lyriques* in 1555; and a volume of collected works, *Oeuvres poétiques*, in 1573. His final work was *Douze fables de fleuves ou fontaines*, containing twelve of his sonnets (1585).

The comically melodramatic "Élégie pour une dame enamourée d'une autre dame" (Elegy for a Lady Fallen for Another Lady)—from *Oeuvres poétiques*—purports to be the lament of a female speaker who has fallen in love, to her own disgust and amazement, with another woman. In typical Renaissance fashion, the god of Love is blamed for this catastrophe, which according to the speaker is without historical or mythological precedent. Paradoxically enough, Pontus de Tyard invokes the history of male homoeroticism (the stories of Damon and Pythias, Aeneas and Achates, Hercules and Nestor, and the like) precisely in order to disparage female-female eros. No comparable stories, he suggests, legitimate the speaker's unruly passion. Thus "love" between women remains chimerical, it seems, even as its overheated victim declaims.

FURTHER READING: Pontus de Tyard, *Oeuvres poétiques* (Paris, 1573); Louis Perceau, ed., *Le Cabinet secret du Parnasse: Recueil de poésies libres, rares ou peu connues, pour servir de Supplément aux Oeuvres dites complètes des poètes français*, 4 vols. (Paris: Au Cabinet du Livre, 1935); Eva Kushner, "The Role of Platonic Symbols in the Poetry of Pontus de Tyard," *Yale French Studies* 47 (1972): 124–43; Hugo Sonneville, *Pontus de Tyard: Bibliographie chronologique (1549–1978)*, *Zeitschrift für Franzözische Sprache und Literatur* 90 (1980): 321–46; Jean-Claude Carron, *Discours de l'errance amoureuse: Une lecture de Canzoniere de Pontus de Tyard* (Paris: J. Vrin, 1986); Elizabeth S. Wahl, *Invisible Relations: Representations of Female Intimacy in the Age of Enlightenment* (Stanford: Stanford University Press, 1998).

I have ever fixed Love and honour's bright part
As the only two ardors that burn in my heart,
Could such a magnificent flame ignite
That no brighter Soul could ever alight,
But I knew not how to envision in Thought
How the two fires at once could be wrought
For, as much as beauty is the stuff of Love,
And in Honour entire lies beauty entire,
I could not see how this very beauty
Could be part of both Love and integrity.
Thus I spake: My beauty in honour within myself doth lie,
But not that beauty which bound to love am I,
For the sole beauty to myself of value
Would be nought but mine own honour true,
Yet the Lover outside the self must not rest
But seek the beauty afforded Love through conquest:
Thus only honour's heat will exist in me;
Must I thus flee the ardor of the other Deity?

Alas! Love's beauty, would I choose you over men?
Aha! no; I know too well this century we are in:
Man loves beauty, and honour doth mock, not cherish;
When beauty pleases him, honour doth perish.
So, as one of one honour alone dearly curious,
And free, I disdained all flame amorous,
When Love by my freedom took offense,
And handed me a decoy immune to my defense.

It enriches the Mind; the mouth it refines,
It sweetens your speech; in your eye it reclines;
In your hair it weaves a knot that fain does amaze,
That binds me to you; it fans a blaze,
(Alas! who will believe?) with such new heat,
That my heart—a woman's—alas! for another woman beats.

Never more softly Love did cruise
Into another heart, with honor unbruised
Retaining there its untarnished beauty
The Lover enjoying this belovèd beauty
In the same subject, o Felicity above,
If lightly had it pleased you not lightly to love!

But cruelest Love, having wounded me bereft,
Dislodged all within me and emptiness left,
Emptied of Love, no affection it fashioned,
While filling my heart with miserable passion
And by fair spite, I must cry out my plea,
You're an ingrate, and your freedom mocks me.
Where is your pledged troth, the oaths you did lend,
Where from your speeches are the words that pretend
Like a python that feints and attracts,
That knew how to chain me by ear to those pacts?

Alas! How I've spilled my guts in vain!
How I fled every other Love the same!
How in vain you (scornful one) I chose,
As my one delight, as my life's rose!
How in vain did I think the time ahead
Would by miracle through the centuries us wed
And that, unique example in French history,
Our Love would serve as eternal memory
Proof that Love of woman by woman may arise
And from all manly Lovers seize the prize.

A Damon for Pythias, an Aeneas for Achates,
A Hercules for Nestor, Cherephon for Socrates,
Hoppius for Diamantus, have shown us yet
That Love of man for man is wholly met.
Of Love of man for woman does proof so abound
There is no need for me to cast around
But of woman for woman there is not yet
In the empire of Love, a trove so richly set,
And it cannot be found, as your flight bespeaks!
Since to my faith yours in return was weak,
For never beneath the sun was greater purity,
Nor hotter heat in fire, nor sweeter lick in honey,
No greater bounty found in all of nature,
Than in my heart, where Love had come for nurture!
But harder than the Rock Gibraltar is your heart's rule;
More even than a barbarous Scythian is it cruel.
And Ursa Major has seen less ice eternal
Than you have in your veins; nor does Nocturnal
Morpheus' shifting visage alter its line
As much as thought transforms in your inconstant mind.

Alas! How spite does from me mine own self remove!
Open up to Love, ingrate, open up to Love!
Suffer that the sweet barb that pierced our heart
Might once more enter yours, too much unhurt;
Seek out in your speech the affection it once drove;
And retie the sweet knot in which was wove
The common bond that you to me once led,
And let our hands rejoin in vows we pled,
The vow that in my spirit is secure,
That even in death will endure.
But if a new Love enfold you in its fire,
I implore Counter-Love, Anteros, a God so dire
That before the pain within my heart immure
I be transformed, achieving one thing more
Than what I was before, to wit, that my voice alone
Despondent, endure when through this wood I roam
Where in a little time my weeping pain
Would flow in a river or shower from a fountain,
While I tell both Stag and Buck behorned,
Alone in tufted woods, ingrate, of your scorn,
That you might of a subject all unworthy be consumed,
To pine forlornly, languish, and in your love be doomed!

AMBROISE PARÉ (1510?–1590)

"Memorable Stories About Women Who Have Degenerated Into Men" (1573)

The sixteenth-century French writer and surgeon Ambroise Paré was born in Bourg-Hersant in Maine and began his official medical career in Paris at the Hôtel-Dieu in 1533. By 1554 he had become a member of the Royal College of Surgeons and a leading practitioner, well known especially for his progressive methods for treating gunshot wounds and amputations. Besides *Des Monstres et prodigues* (On Monsters and Marvels), his influential 1573 tract on reproduction and so-called monstrous or unusual births, he wrote treatises on surgical techniques, the transmission of plague, embalming, and medical jurisprudence. His *Collected Works* appeared in three editions, in 1575, 1578, and 1582. He married twice and had numerous children.

The strange anecdotes reported in *On Monsters and Marvels* about women who have "turned into" men reflect common Renaissance medico-anatomical beliefs. According to the ancient Greek physician Galen, whose teachings on anatomy were widely disseminated in the sixteenth and seventeenth centuries, men and women shared identically structured genitalia, only the female genitals were inverted and held inside the body instead of hanging out. Sometimes, following strenuous exertion, a woman's genitals might "escape," resulting in her transformation into a man. Paré provides several examples of such accidental transformation, including the famous case of the hermaphrodite Marie (Germain) Garnier, who changed into a man after too-vigorous exercise and subsequently married a woman. Both Michel de Montaigne in his *Journal de voyage* (1580–81) and Jacques Duval in his *Traité des hermaphrodits* (1612) would later take up the same case.

Paré's work is important in the early literature of lesbianism because it summarizes so neatly one of the primary "medical" explanations for female homosexuality in earlier centuries: that it was the result of some congenital abnormality (hermaphroditism or clitoral hypertrophy) or the accidental descent of the female "testes." Later ages, of course, would explain the phenomenon of women loving women psychologically; but for Paré and his contemporaries female same-sex love was inevitably linked with the real or imagined peculiarities of gross anatomy.

FURTHER READING: Ambroise Paré, *Des Monstres et prodigues*, ed. Jean Ceard (Geneva: Droz, 1971); —, *On Monsters and Marvels*, trans. Janis L. Palliser (Chicago: University of Chicago Press, 1982); Marie-Jo Bonnet, *Un Choix sans équivoque: Recherches historiques sur les relations amoureuses entre les femmes vvie-xx siècle* (Paris: Denoël, 1981); Lorraine Daston and Katharine Park, "Hermaphrodites in Renaissance France," *Critical Matrix* 1 (1985): 1–19; —, *Wonders and the Order of Nature, 1150–1750* (New York: Zone, 1998); Stephen Greenblatt, "Fiction and Friction," in *Shakespearean Negotiations: The Circulation of Social Energy in Renaissance England* (Berkeley and Los Angeles: University of California Press, 1988); Thomas Laqueur, *Making Sex: Body and Gender from the Greeks to Freud* (Cambridge: Harvard University Press, 1990); Ann Rosalind Jones and Peter Stallybrass, "Fetishizing Gender: Constructing the Hermaphrodite in Renaissance Europe," in Julia Epstein and Kristina Straub, eds., *Body Guards: The Cultural Politics of Gender Ambiguity* (New York: Routledge, 1991); Patricia Parker, "Gender Ideology, Gender Change: The Case of Marie Germain," *Critical Inquiry* 19 (Winter 1993): 337–364.

Amatus Lusitanus tells that there was, in a burg named Esgueira, a girl called Marie Pacheca, who, arriving at the time of life when girls begin their monthlies, instead of the above-mentioned monthlies, a male member came out of her, which was formerly hidden within, and hence she changed from female to male; for which reason she was clothed in men's clothes and her name was changed from Marie to Manuel. This male person traded for a long time in India, where, having acquired great fame and great wealth, upon returning [to Portugal] got married; nevertheless, this author [Lusitanus] doesn't know whether he had children; it is true (says he) that he remained without a beard.

Antoine Loqueneux, tax [or rent] receiver for the King in Saint Quentin, not long ago assured me he had seen a man in the Inn of the Swan in Reims, sixty years of age, who, so it seems, people had taken to be a girl until he was fourteen; but while disporting himself and frolicking, having gone to bed with a chambermaid, his male genital parts came to be developed; the father and the mother, recognizing him to be such, had him by authority of the Church change his name from Jeanne to Jean, and male attire was given to him.

Also being in the retinue of the King at Vitry-le-François in Champagne, I saw a certain person (a shepherd) named Germain Garnier—some called him Germain Marie, because when he had been a girl he had been called Marie—a young man of average size, stocky, and very well put together, wearing a red, rather thick beard, who, until he was fifteen years of age, had been held to be a girl, given the fact that no mark of masculinity was visible in him, and furthermore that along with the girls he even dressed like a woman. Now having attained the aforestated age, as he was in the fields and was rather robustly chasing his swine, which were going into a wheat field, [and] finding a ditch, he wanted to cross over it, and having leaped, at that very moment the genitalia and the male rod came to be developed in him, having ruptured the ligaments by which previously they had been held enclosed and locked in (which did not happen to him without pain), and, weeping, he returned from the spot to his mother's house, saying that his guts had fallen out of his belly; and his mother was very astonished at this spectacle. And having brought together Physicians and Surgeons in order to get an opinion on this, they found that she was a man, and no longer a girl; and presently, after having reported to the Bishop—who was the now defunct Cardinal of Lenoncort—and by his authority, an assembly having been called, the shepherd received a man's name: and instead of Marie (for so was he previously named), he was called Germain, and men's clothing was given to him; and I believe that he and his mother are still living.

Pliny (Book 7, Chapter 4) says similarly that a girl became a boy and was for this reason confined on a deserted and uninhabited island, by the decision and order of the Aruspices (or soothsayers). It seems to me that these prophets had not any cause to do this, for the reasons given above; still they estimated that such a monstrous thing was a bad augury and presage for them, which was the reason for driving monsters away and exiling them.

The reason why women can degenerate into men is because women have as much hidden within the body as men have exposed outside; leaving aside, only, that women don't have so much heat, nor the ability to push out what by the coldness of their temperament is held as if bound to the interior. Wherefore if with time, the humidity of childhood which prevented the warmth from doing its full duty being exhaled for the most part, the warmth is rendered more robust, vehement, and active, then it is not an unbelievable thing if the latter, chiefly aided by some violent movement, should be able to push out what was hidden within. Now since such a metamorphosis takes place in Nature for the alleged reasons and examples, we therefore never find in any true story that any man ever became a woman, because Nature tends always toward what is most perfect and not, on the contrary, to perform in such a way that what is perfect should become imperfect.

MICHEL DE MONTAIGNE (1533–1592)

From *The Journal of Montaigne's Travels in Italy by Way of Switzerland and Germany* (1581)

The great Renaissance essayist Michel de Montaigne was born into a wealthy merchant family in Périgord in 1533 and educated at Bordeaux, where he studied law and served as a judge between 1555 and 1570. The closest emotional attachment of his life—his friendship with the humanist scholar Etienne de La Boétie—began during these years. After La Boétie's death in 1563, Montaigne married but never ceased to mourn the loss of his friend. Some scholars speculate that La Boétie was his homosexual lover, but no real evidence exists to support the theory. Montaigne's first major literary endeavor was a translation of Raymond Sebond's *Theologia Naturalis*, published in 1569. In 1570 he resigned his judgeship and retired to his country birthplace, the Château de Montaigne, where he began writing his famous *Essais*—the master work of reflection, anecdote, and canny self-exploration that would make him celebrated across Europe. His rustication, however, was never total: in later years he served twice as mayor of Bordeaux, traveled in Germany and Italy, and carried out several diplomatic missions for Henri de Navarre, the future King Henri IV. He published the first of two books of his *Essais* in 1580; a revised edition appeared in 1582. Upon his death in 1592 he left his manuscripts to his adopted daughter, Marie de Gournay, who published his complete essays in three volumes in 1595.

Given Montaigne's lifelong interest in strange tales and scientific curiosities—not to mention his own possibly ambivalent sexual nature—it is not surprising that his writings sometimes touch on the theme of sexual irregularity. In the journal he kept of his trip to Germany and Italy (1580–81) he preserved two stories of freakish lust. The first has to do with a male impersonator executed for her immoral impositions on other women; the other is the famous tale of Marie (Germain) Garnier—the countrywoman from the Marne who supposedly "became" a man after too strenuous physical exertion. (According to the Galenic model of sexual differentiation to which Montaigne and many of his contemporaries subscribed, women were simply "men" with genitals inverted and held inside the body. A too sudden movement could dislodge this internal genital apparatus, resulting in the extrusion of a penis and scrotum.) The story of Marie/Germain had already appeared, as Montaigne himself notes, in Ambroise Paré's *Des Monstres et prodigues* (1573). Montaigne's version was not known until 1774—

when his journal was first discovered and published—but it helped to give the story wide currency in the nineteenth and early twentieth century.

FURTHER READING: Michel de Montaigne, *The Journal of Montaigne's Travels in Italy by Way of Switzerland and Germany in 1580 and 1581*, 3 vols., trans. W. G. Waters (London: John Murray, 1903); —, *The Complete Essays of Montaigne*, trans. Donald Frame (Stanford: Stanford University Press, 1957); Lorraine Daston and Katharine Park, "Hermaphrodites in Renaissance France," *Critical Matrix* 1 (1985): 1–19; —, *Wonders and the Order of Nature, 1150–1750* (New York: Zone, 1998); Stephen Greenblatt, "Fiction and Friction," in *Shakespearean Negotiations: The Circulations of Social Energy in Elizabethan England* (Berkeley and Los Angeles: University of California Press, 1988); Thomas Laqueur, *Making Sex: Body and Gender from the Greeks to Freud* (Cambridge: Harvard University Press, 1990); Ann Rosalind Jones and Peter Stallybrass, "Fetishizing Gender: Constructing the Hermaphrodite in Renaissance Europe," in Julia Epstein and Kristina Straub, eds., *Body Guards: The Cultural Politics of Gender Ambiguity* (New York: Routledge, 1991); Patricia Parker, "Gender Ideology, Gender Change: The Case of Marie Germain," *Critical Inquiry* 19 (winter 1993), 337–64.

On the morrow we set out after dinner and slept at Vitry le François, seven leagues farther on.

This is a small town on the banks of the Marne, built some thirty-five or forty years ago in place of the former town, which had been burnt. It still keeps its original form, pleasant and well proportioned, and in the midst thereof is a large square, one of the finest in France. During our sojourn there, three marvellous stories were told to us. One was that Madame the Dowager de Guise de Bourbon, who was living at the age of eighty-seven years, could still go afoot for the distance of a quarter of a league. Another was, that a short time ago, execution had been done at Montirandet, a place close by, upon one condemned for a certain offense. Several years before, seven or eight girls belonging to Chaumont-en-Bassigni had secretly determined to put on male attire, and to live the life of men. Amongst these one, called Mary, came from Vitry aforenamed. She got her living by weaving, passing as a well-favoured young man, and on friendly terms with every one. She engaged herself to marry a woman of Vitry, who is still alive, but on account of some strife which arose between them, the match went no further. Afterwards, having gone to Montirandet, and still following the weaver's calling, she fell in love again with a certain woman, with whom she married and lived, as the story goes, contentedly four or five months. But, having been recognized by some one living at Chaumont, and the matter having been brought to the notice of the courts, she was condemned to be hanged; whereupon she declared she would liefer suffer thus than live a woman's life. She was hanged on the charge of using unlawful appliances to remedy the defects of her sex.

The third story is of a man still living named Germain, of humble condition, and engaged in no employment. Up to the age of twenty-two years he had been regarded by all the townsfolk as a girl, albeit the chin was more hairy than that of other girls, for which reason she was called *Marie la barbue*. It came to pass one day when she put forth all her strength in taking a leap, that the distinctive signs of manhood showed themselves, whereupon the Cardinal of Lenoncourt, at that time bishop of Châlons, gave him the name of Germain. This personage is still unmarried, and has a large thick beard. We could not see him because he was away at the village where he lived. A popular song, sung by the girls of the place, warns all girls against taking long strides lest they should become men like Marie Germain. Report says that Ambrose Paré has taken note of this tale in his book on surgery. It is certainly true, and testimony thereof was given to M. de Montaigne by the chief officials of the town. We left this place after breakfast on Sunday morning and travelled to Bar, a distance of nine leagues.

ANONYMOUS

"Poem XLIX" from *The Maitland Quarto Manuscript* (1586)

The following lesbian love poem—its female speaker begs to change her sex so that she may marry her beloved—appears in a collection of early Scottish poems known as *The Maitland Quarto Manuscript* (1586). It has been attributed to Marie Maitland, daughter of the man under whose auspices the collection was put together, Sir Richard Maitland, Keeper of the Great Seal of Scotland and courtier to the Scottish kings James V and James VI. Marie, one of four daughters and three sons, appears to have been both well-educated and renowned for her poetry; another poem in the Maitland collection ("To Your Self") compares her to Sappho and Olimpia Morata, a fifteenth-century Latin poet and learned lady. Maitland later married Alexander Lauder of Hatton; and her son, George Lauder, also became a poet of some distinction.

The fact that unlike other poems in the Maitland Manuscript, "Poem XLIX" is written in italic script—the hand in which literate women of the period learned to write—suggests at the very least that its author was female. Whoever she was, she was well-versed in the elaborate, often homoerotic conventions of Renaissance friendship poetry. The idealizing comparison of herself and her friend with various celebrated (male) couples of antiquity—Perithous and Theseus, Achilles and Patroclus, Achates and Aeneas, Titus and Joseph, David and Jonathan—points to the influence of Continental models. What separates this poem from others of its type, however, is indeed the female-female situation, signaled first in the highly *un*conventional reference to the Biblical Ruth and Naomi. (In *Ruth* 1:16, Ruth, the Moabite daughter-in-law of Naomi, refuses to leave her mother-in-law after the death of her husband, Naomi's son. Her famous declaration—"whither thou goest, I will go, and where thou lodgest, I will lodge: thy people shall be my people, and thy god my God"—has often yielded itself to lesbian literary appropriation.) Certainly, the stark fervor with which the poet makes her plea for a sex change in stanza 6 ("Would mighty Jove grant me the hap / With you to have your Brutus' part / And, metamorphosing our shape, / My sex into his will convert") comes as both a moral and generic shock to the reader; so too the confident apotheosis the poet predicts for herself and her beloved "madame."

The text below is a modernized version of the Middle Scots original; the original scansion has not been preserved.

FURTHER READING: W. A. Craigie, ed., *The Maitland Quarto Manuscript: Containing Poems by Sir Richard Maitland, Arbuthnot, and Others,* The Scottish Text Society, n.s., volume 9 (London: William Blackwood, 1920); Agnes Mure Mackenzie, *An Historical Survey of Scottish Literature to 1714* (London: Alexander Machelrose, 1933); Laurens J. Mills, *One Soul in Bodies Twain: Friendship in Tudor Literature and Stuart Drama* (Bloomington, Indiana: Principia Press, 1937); Valerie Traub, "The (In)significance of 'Lesbian' Desire in Early Modern England," in Susan Zimmerman, ed., *Erotic Politics: Desire on the Renaissance Stage* (New York: Routledge, 1992), pp. 15–69; Jane Farnsworth, "Female Desire in 'Poem XLIX,'" *Studies in English Literature,* 36 (1996), 57–72; Sara Mendelson and Patricia Crawford, *Women in Early Modern Europe, 1550–1720* (Oxford: Clarendon, 1998); Peter Davidson and Jane Stevenson, eds., *Early Modern Women Poets* (Oxford: Oxford University Press, 2001).

As Phoebus in his sphere's height
Outdoes the cape crepuscular,
And Phoebe all the stars' light,
Your splendour, so madame I ween,
Does only pass all feminine
In sapience superlative,
Indued with virtues so divine,
Like learned Pallas come again.

And, as by hidden virtue unknown,
The adamant draws the iron to it,
Your courteous nature so has drawn
My heart, yours to continue still:
So great joy does my spirit fulfill
Contemplating your perfection.
You wield me wholly at your will
And ravish my affection.

Your peerless Virtue does provoke,
And loving kindness so does move,
My Mind to friendship reciproc,
That truth shall try so far above

The ancient heroes' love
As shall be thought prodigious:
And plain experience shall prove
More holy and religious.

In amity, Perithous
To Theseus was not so true,
Nor to Achilles Patroclus,
Nor Pylades to true Orest,
Nor yet Achates' love so leased
To good Aeneas, nor such friendship
David to Jonathan professed,
Nor Titus true to kind Josippus.

Nor yet Penelope, I wis,
So loved Ulysses in her days,
Nor Ruth the kind Moabitess
Naomi, as the scripture says:
Nor Portia, whose worthy praise
In Roman histories we read,
Who did devour the fiery coals
To follow Brutus to the death.

Would mighty Jove give me the chance
With you to have your Brutus' part
And, metamorphosing our shape,
My sex into his will convert:
No Brutus then could cause us smart
As we do now, unhappy women;
Then should we both, with joyful heart,
Honour and bless the band of Hymen.

Yea certainly we should efface
Pollux and Castor's memory;
And if that they deservèd place
Among the stars for loyalty,
Then our more perfect amity
More worthy recompense should merit:
In heaven eternal deity
Among the gods to inherit.

As we are, though to our woe,
Nature and Fortune do conjure;

And Hymen also be our foe,
Yet love of virtue does procure
Friendship and amity so sure,
With so great fervency and force,
So constantly which shall endure,
That none but death shall us divorce.

And though adversity us vex,
Yet by our friendship shall be seen
There is more constancy in our sex
Than ever among men has been—
No trouble, torment, grief, or pain
Nor earthly thing shall us dissever;
Such constancy shall us maintain
In perfect amity forever.

SIR PHILIP SIDNEY (1554–1586)

From *The Countess of Pembroke's Arcadia* (1590)

The Renaissance courtier-poet Sir Philip Sidney, the son of Queen Elizabeth I's lord governor of Ireland, was born at Penshurst Palace in Kent in 1554 and educated at Oxford and on the Continent. In his early twenties he traveled widely in France, Germany, Poland, Italy, Austria, and Ireland on various royal diplomatic missions. A contretemps with the queen in 1579 led to his disgrace, however, and he was forced to withdraw to the country home of his sister, the Countess of Pembroke, where he devoted himself to literary labors. The celebrated sonnet cycle *Astrophel and Stella* (1581–83), *An Apology for Poetry* (1584), and the first version of the prose romance known as *The Arcadia* (1580–84) all date from this period. In 1583 Sidney was reconciled with Queen Elizabeth and knighted; he married Frances Walsingham the same year. He met his death heroically, while serving as a cavalry officer in the battle of Zutphen in the Netherlands in 1586. After his death *The Arcadia* was published by his friend Fulke Greville in a so-called new or revised version (1590), incorporating, among other things, numerous emendations by Sidney's sister.

The *Arcadia* is an important work in the literary history of lesbianism for both philological and thematic reasons. The central narrative has to do with Pyrocles, son of the king of Macedon, who is in love with Philoclea, the beautiful daughter of Basilius and Gynecia, the king and queen of Arcadia. On the advice of an oracle, the Arcadian royal family have taken up residence in a secluded forest and Pyrocles must disguise himself as a young woman (Cleophila in the *Old Arcadia*, Zelmane in the *New*) in order to be near his beloved. His impersonation, however, has several unintended effects. The entire family falls in love with him: first Basilius, who thinks he is a woman; then Gynecia, who suspects (rightly) that he may be a man; and then Philoclea herself, who— believing him to be female—is painfully confounded by her "impossible" yearnings.

Stylistically speaking, the *Arcadia* is the first major work of English literature to show the influence of the ancient Greek writer Sappho, whose poetry, preserved in fragmentary form in various classical sources, was gradually rediscovered and disseminated across Western Europe over the course of the sixteenth century. It is possible that Sidney knew the pioneering Greek and Latin edition of Sappho's poems published by Henri Estienne in 1566. In the verses "If Mine Eyes Can Speak To Do Hearty Errand," declaimed by "Cleophila" (Pyrocles) to Philoclea in the section entitled *The First Eclogues* in the *Old Arcadia*, Sidney experimented with the metrical form first used by Sappho, the so-called sapphic stanza: three lines of eleven syllables each ($-\cup/--/-\cup\cup/-\cup/-\cup$) followed by a fourth containing five syllables ($-\cup\cup/-\cup$):

> If mine eyes can speak to do hearty errand,
> Or mine eyes' language she do hap to judge of,
> So that eyes' message be of her receivèd,
> Hope we do live yet.

Still even more strikingly, in another of Cleophila's love plaints—"My Muse What Ails This Ardour" from *The Second Eclogues*—Sidney directly imitated Sappho's famous Fragment 31 ("Peer of the Gods"):

> My muse what ails this ardour?
> My eyes be dim, my limbs shake,
> My voice is hoarse, my throat scorched,
> My tongue to this my roof cleaves,
> My fancy amazed, my thoughts dulled,
> My heart doth ache, my life faints,
> My soul begins to take leave.

It is fitting, of course, that both of these poems are directed—or at least *seem* to be directed, from the perspective of *Arcadia*'s beguiled characters—from one woman to another.

Indeed, the sexual-disguise plot of the *Arcadia* yields a number of quasi-homo-erotic episodes. In the scene below from book 2 of the *New Arcadia*, the Arcadian queen Gynecia, her daughter Philoclea, and Pyrocles (here disguised as the beautiful female warrior "Zelmane") are involved in a somewhat comical coach accident. Gynecia, slightly injured, asks Zelmane—whom she guesses to be a man and with whom she is wildly in love—to stay with her that night in the hunting lodge to which they have retired. Jealous of Zelmane's interest in Philoclea, she orders Philoclea off to sleep elsewhere, with her sister Pamela. Philoclea, who has also fallen in love with Zelmane but has no inkling of her beloved's real sex, reluctantly complies, indulging as she goes in painful private meditations on her passion for the mysterious "Amazon." In her con-fused lamentations—she has been led to believe that being in love with a woman is monstrous and is thus mortified both by her own and her *mother's* desire for Zelmane—Sidney offers an early epitome of what is sometimes called "lesbian panic": the grip-ping fear that one's erotic longings are at once utterly reprehensible and the deepest part of one's being.

FURTHER READING: Sir Philip Sidney, *The Countess of Pembroke's Arcadia* (*The Old Arcadia*), ed. Katherine Duncan-Jones (Oxford: Oxford University Press, 1985); —, *The Countess of Pembroke's Arcadia*, ed. Victor Skretkowicz (Oxford and New York: Oxford University Press, 1987); David M. Robinson, *Sappho and Her Influence* (Boston: Marshall Jones, 1924); Walter R. Davis, *Sidney's Arcadia: A Map of Arcadia: Sidney's Romance in its Tradition* (New Haven: Yale University Press, 1965); Nancy Lindheim, *The Structures of Sidney's Arcadia* (Toronto and London: University of Toronto Press, 1982); Clare Kinney, "The Masks of Love: Desire and Metamorphosis in Sidney's *New Arcadia*," *Criticism* 33 (1991): 461–90; Margaret M. Sullivan, "Amazons and Aristocrats: The Function of Pyrocles' Amazon Role in Sidney's Revised *Arcadia*," in Jean R. Brink, Maryanne C. Horowitz, and Allison P. Coudert, eds., *Playing with Gender: A Renaissance Pursuit* (Urbana: University of Illinois Press, 1991); Katherine J. Roberts, *Fair Ladies: Sir Philip Sidney's Female Characters* (New York: Peter Lang, 1993); Peter Jay and Caroline Lewis, eds., *Sappho Through English Poetry* (London: Anvil, 1996); Ellen Greene, ed., *Re-Reading Sappho: Reception and Transmission* (Berkeley: University of California Press, 1997).

Divers of which flights Basilius showing to Zelmane, thus was the richesse of the time spent, and the day deceased before it was thought of, till night, like a degenerating successor, made his departure the better remembered. And therefore, so constrained, they willed Dametas to drive homeward; who half sleeping, half musing about the mending of a vine-press, guided the horses so ill, that the wheel coming over a great stub of a tree, it overturned the coach, which though it fell violently upon the side where Zelmane and Gynecia sat, yet for Zelmane's part, she would have been glad of the fall which made her bear the sweet burthen of Philoclea, but that she feared she might receive some hurt. But indeed, neither she did, nor any of the rest, by reason they kept their arms and legs within the coach, saving Gynecia, who with the only bruise of the fall had her shoulder put out of joint—which, though by one of the falconers' cunning it was set well again, yet with much pain was she brought to the lodge; and pain fetching his ordinary companion, a fever, with him, drave her to entertain them both in her bed.

But neither was the fever of such impatient heat as the inward plague-sore of her affection, nor the pain half so noisome as the jealousy she conceived of her daughter Philoclea, lest this time of her sickness might give apt occasion to Zelmane, whom she misdoubted. Therefore she called Philoclea to her, and though it were late in the night, commanded her in her ear to go to the other lodge and send Miso to her, with whom she would speak, and she lie with her sister Pamela; the meanwhile Gynecia kept Zelmane with her, because she would be sure she should be out of the lodge before she licensed Zelmane. Philoclea, not skilled in anything better than obedience, went quietly down; and the moon then full, not thinking scorn to be a torch-bearer to such beauty, guided her steps—whose motions bare a mind which bare in itself far more stirring motions.

And alas, sweet Philoclea, how hath my pen till now forgot thy passions, since to thy memory principally all this long matter is intended? Pardon the slackness to come to those woes, which having caused in others, thou didst feel in thyself. The sweet-minded Philoclea was in their degree of well doing to whom the not knowing of evil serveth for a ground of virtue, and hold their inward powers in better form with an unspotted simplicity than many, who rather cunningly seek to know what goodness is than willingly take into themselves the following of it. But as that sweet and simple breath of heavenly goodness is the easier to be altered because it hath not passed through the worldly wickedness, nor feelingly found the evil that evil carries with it, so now the Lady Philoclea, whose eyes and senses had received nothing but according as the natural course of each thing required (which tender youth had obediently lived under her parents' behests without framing out of her own will the forechoosing of anything), when now she came to appoint (wherein her judgement was to be practised in knowing faultiness by his first tokens), she was like a young fawn, who coming in the wind of the hunters, doth not know whether it be a thing or no to be eschewed— whereof at this time she began to get a costly experience.

For after that Zelmane had a while lived in the lodge with her, and that her only being a noble stranger had bred a kind of heedful attention, her coming to that lonely place (where she had nobody but her parents) a willingness of conversation, her wit and behaviour a liking and silent admiration, at length, the excellency of her natural gifts joined with the extreme shows she made of most devout honouring Philoclea (carrying thus in one person the only two bands of goodwill, loveliness and lovingness) brought forth in her heart a yielding to a most friendly affection; which when it had gotten so full possession of the keys of her mind that it would receive no message from her senses without that affection were the interpreter, then straight grew an exceeding delight still to be with her, with an unmeasurable liking of all that Zelmane did—matters being so turned in her that, where at first, liking her manners did breed goodwill, now goodwill became the chief cause of liking her manners, so that within a while Zelmane was not prized for her demeanour, but the demeanour was prized because it was Zelmane's.

Then followed that most natural effect of conforming oneself to that which she did like, and not only wishing to be herself such another in all things, but to ground an imitation upon so much an esteemed authority; so that the next degree was to mark all Zelmane's doings, speeches, and fashions, and to take them into herself as a pattern of worthy proceeding, which when once it was enacted, not only by the commonalty of passions, but agreed unto by her most noble thoughts, and that by reason itself (not yet experienced in the issues of such matters) had granted his royal assent, then friendship, a diligent officer, took care to see the statute thoroughly observed. Then grew on that not only she did imitate the soberness of her countenance, the gracefulness of her speech, but even their particular gestures; so that, as Zelmane did often eye her, she would often eye Zelmane, and as Zelmane's eyes would deliver a submissive but vehement desire in their look, she, though as yet she had not the desire in her, yet should her eyes answer in like-piercing kindness of a look. Zelmane, as much as Gynecia's jealousy would suffer, desired to be near Philoclea; Philoclea, as much as Gynecia's jealousy would suffer, desired to be near Zelmane. If Zelmane took her hand and softly strained it, she also, thinking the knots of friendship ought to be mutual, would with a sweet fastness show she was loath to part from it. And if Zelmane sighed, she would sigh also. When Zelmane was sad, she deemed it wisdom, and therefore she would be sad too. Zelmane's languishing countenance, with crossed arms, and sometimes cast-up eyes, she thought to have an excellent grace, and therefore she also willingly put on the same countenance; till at the last, poor soul, ere she were aware, she accepted not only the band, but the service; not only the sign, but the passion signified. For whether it were that her wit in continuance did find that Zelmane's friendship was full of impatient desire, having more than ordinary limits, and therefore she was content to second Zelmane, though herself knew not the limits, or that in truth true love, well considered, have an infective power, at last she fell in acquaintance with love's harbinger, wishing.

First she would wish that they two might live all their lives together like two of Diana's nymphs—but that wish she thought not sufficient, because she knew there would be more nymphs besides them who also would have their part in Zelmane. Then would she wish that she were her sister, that such a natural band might make her more special to her—but against that, she considered that though being her sister, if she happened to be married, she should be robbed of her. Then, grown bolder, she would wish either herself or Zelmane a man, that there might succeed a blessed marriage betwixt them—but when that wish had once displayed his ensign in her mind, then followed whole squadrons of longings that so it might be, with a main battle of mislikings and repinings against their creation that so it was not. Then dreams by night began to bring more unto her than she durst wish by day, whereout waking, did make her know herself the better by the image of those fancies. But as some diseases, when they are easy to be cured they are hard to be known, but when they grow easy to be known they are almost impossible to be cured, so the sweet Philoclea, while she might prevent it she did not feel it, now she felt it when it was past preventing—like a river, no rampires being built against it till already it have overflowed, for now indeed love pulled off his mask, and showed his face unto her, and told her plainly that she was his prisoner.

Then needed she no more paint her face with passions, for passions shone thorough her face. Then her rosy colour was often increased with extraordinary blushing, and so, another time, perfect whiteness ascended to a degree of paleness—now hot, then cold, desiring she knew not what, nor how, if she knew what. Then her mind, though too late, by the smart was brought to think of the disease, and her own proof taught her to know her mother's mind, which, as no error gives so strong assault as that which comes armed in the authority of a parent, so greatly fortified her desires, to see that her mother had the like desires. And the more jealous her mother was, the more she thought the jewel precious which was with so many looks guarded. But that prevailing so far as to keep the two lovers from private conference, then began she to feel the sweetness of a lover's solitariness, when freely with words and gestures, as if Zelmane were present, she might give passage to her thoughts, and so as it were utter out some smoke of those flames, wherewith else she was not only burned but smothered.

As this night, that going from the one lodge to the other (by her mother's commandment) with doleful gestures and uncertain paces, she did willingly accept the time's offer to be a while alone, so that going a little aside into the wood where many times before she had delighted to walk, her eyes were saluted with a tuft of trees so close set together as, with the shade the moon gave thorough it, it might breed a fearful kind of devotion to look upon it. But true thoughts of love banish all vain fancy of superstition. Full well she did both remember and like the place, for there had she often with their shade beguiled Phoebus of looking upon her; there had she enjoyed herself often, while she was mistress of herself, and had no other thoughts but such as might arise out of quiet senses. But the principal cause that invited her remembrance was a goodly white marble stone that should seem had been dedicated in ancient time to the sylvan gods; which she finding there a few days before Zelmane's coming, had written these words upon it as a testimony of her mind against the suspicion her captivity made her think she lived in. The writing was this:

> You living powers enclosed in stately shrine
> Of growing trees, you rural gods that wield
> Your sceptres here, if to your ears divine
> A voice may come which troubled soul doth yield,
>   This vow receive, this vow O gods maintain:
>   My virgin life no spotted thought shall stain.
>
> Thou purest stone, whose pureness doth present
> My purest mind; whose temper hard doth show
> My tempered heart; by thee my promise sent
> Unto myself let after-livers know.
>   No fancy mine, nor others' wrong suspect
>   Make me, O virtuous shame, thy laws neglect.
>
> O chastity, the chief of heav'nly lights,
> Which makst us most immortal shape to wear,
> Hold thou my heart, establish thou my sprites;
> To only thee my constant course I bear.
>   Till spotless soul unto thy bosom fly,
>   Such life to lead, such death I vow to die.

But now that her memory served as an accuser of her change, and that her own handwriting was there to bear testimony against her fall, she went in among those few trees, so closed in the tops together as they might seem a little chapel; and there might she by the help of the moonlight perceive the goodly stone which served as an altar in that woody devotion. But neither the light was enough to read the words, and the ink was already foreworn and in many places blotted; which, as she perceived, "Alas," said she, "fair marble, which never receivedst spot but by my writing, well do these blots become a blotted writer; but pardon her which did not dissemble then, although she have changed since. Enjoy, enjoy the glory of thy nature which can so constantly bear the marks of my inconstancy!"

And herewith hiding her eyes with her soft hand, there came into her head certain verses which, if she had had present commodity, she would have adjoined as a retractation to the other. They were to this effect:

> My words, in hope to blaze my steadfast mind,
> This marble chose, as of like temper known:
> But lo, my words defaced, my fancies blind,
> Blots to the stone, shame to myself I find;
>   And witness am, how ill agree in one,
>   A woman's hand with constant marble stone.
>
> My words full weak, the marble full of might;
> My words in store, the marble all alone;
> My words black ink, the marble kindly white;
> My words unseen, the marble still in sight,
>   May witness bear, how ill agree in one,
>   A woman's hand with constant marble stone.

But seeing she could not see means to join as then this recantation to the former vow, laying all her fair length under one of the trees, for a while she did nothing but turn up and down, as if she had hoped to turn away the fancy that mastered her, and hid her face, as if she could have hidden herself from her own fancies. At length, with a whispering note to herself, "O me, unfortunate wretch," said she, "what poisonous heats be these which thus torment me? How hath the sight of this strange guest invaded my soul? Alas, what entrance found this desire, or what strength had it thus to conquer me?"

Then, a cloud passing between her sight and the moon, "O Diana," said she, "I would either the cloud that now hides the light of my virtue would as easily pass away as you will quickly overcome this let; or else that you were for ever thus darkened, to serve for an excuse of my outrageous folly."

Then looking to the stars, which had perfitly as then beautified the clear sky, "My parents," said she, "have told me that in these fair heavenly bodies there are great hidden deities which have their working in the ebbing and flowing of our estates. If it be so, then, O you stars, judge rightly of me, and if I have with wicked intent made myself a prey to fancy, or if by any idle lusts I framed my heart fit for such an impression, then let this plague daily increase in me till my name be made odious to womankind. But if extreme and unresistable violence have oppressed me, who will ever do any of you sacrifice, O you stars, if you do not succor me? No, no, you will not help me. No, no, you cannot help me! Sin must be the mother, and shame the daughter of my affection. And yet are these but childish objections, simple Philoclea. It is the impossibility that doth torment me; for unlawful desires are punished after the effect of enjoying, but unpossible desires are punished in the desire itself. Oh, then, oh ten times unhappy that I am, since where in all other hope kindleth love, in me despair should be the bellows of my affection! and of all despairs, the most miserable, which is drawn from impossibility. The most covetous man longs not to get riches out of a ground which never can bear anything. Why? Because it is impossible. The most ambitious wight vexeth not his wits to climb into heaven. Why? Because it is impossible. Alas, then, O love, why doost thou in thy beautiful sampler set such a work for my desire to take out, which is as much impossible? And yet, alas, why do I thus condemn my fortune before I hear what she can say for herself? What do I, silly wench, know what love hath prepared for me? Do I not see my mother as well, at least as furiously as myself, love Zelmane? And should I be wiser than my mother? Either she sees a possibility in that which I think impossible, or else impossible loves need not misbecome me. And do I not see Zelmane, who doth not think a thought which is not first weighed by wisdom and virtue—doth not she vouchsafe to love me with like ardour? I see it. Her eyes depose it to be true. What then? And if she can love poor me, shall I think scorn to love such a woman as Zelmane? Away, then, all vain examinations of why and how. Thou lovest me, excellent Zelmane, and I love thee!" And with that, embracing the very ground whereon she lay, she said to herself (for even to herself she was ashamed to speak it out in words), "O my Zelmane! Govern and direct me, for I am wholly given over unto thee."

JOHN LYLY (1554?–1606)

From *Gallathea* (1592)

John Lyly, the son of an ecclesiastical official, is thought to have been born in Kent. He was educated at Oxford and Cambridge, and by 1578 was living in London, where he worked as "servant" (possibly secretary) to the Earl of Oxford. He published *Euphues: The Anatomy of Wit*, the first half of his famous prose romance *Euphues*, in 1578. The second half, *Euphues and his England*, appeared in 1580. In 1584 two of his plays, *Campaspe* and *Sapho and Phao*, were given court performances by the boys of Saint Paul's and the Children of the Chapel. Between 1589 and his death in 1606, he wrote five more plays—*Endimion* (1591), *Gallathea* and *Midas* (1592), *Mother Bombie* (1594), and *The Woman in the Moone* (1597)—and served as M.P. for Hindon and Aylesbury. He is remembered today as the prime exemplar of the so-called euphuistic English prose style—a style characterized by repetition, inversion, and the heavy use of oxymoron and antithesis.

Lyly's *Gallathea*—first performed at Greenwich before Queen Elizabeth in 1588 and printed in 1592—is perhaps the most "Sapphic" in implication of any English Renaissance drama. The story is an odd mixture of classical and native English elements. Neptune, angered at the desecration of his temples near the Humber estuary in the north of England, demands that a virgin be sacrificed every five years to assuage his wrath. Two inhabitants of the region, Tityrus and Melebeus, are prompted—unbeknownst to one another—to disguise their daughters as boys so that neither will be sacrificed. The two girls, Phyllida and Gallathea, meet while in disguise and fall in love, each believing the other to be a boy. After numerous complications—including a comic debate between Diana, Venus, and Cupid, all of whom become embroiled in the messy situation—Neptune is persuaded to forego the quintennial sacrifice and Phyllida and Gallathea are revealed as young women. Each continues to swear her passionate love for the other, however, and by way of removing the obvious impediment to their marriage, Venus agrees to turn one of them into a man.

Of crucial importance in the play's resolution—excerpted below—is Venus's reference to "Iphis and Ianthes." In Ovid's *Metamorphoses* (9.666–797), Iphis is a young girl who has been raised as a boy to protect her from her father, who has threatened to kill any child of his unlucky enough to be born female. When Iphis and Ianthe fall in love, the goddess Isis intervenes and changes Iphis into a man so that the two can marry. Lyly, like other Renaissance writers before and after, uses the Ovidian precedent to license his own transgressive erotic scenario. Even as one woman is "made man" through a final Ovidian metamorphosis, love between women is legitimated, it would seem, as a topic for polite literary exploration. For Elizabethan audiences the homo-erotic frisson of Lyly's comedy would of course have been intensified by the universally accepted phenomenon of boy actors taking female parts: when both Phyllida and Gallathea are played by boys—as was undoubtedly the case in 1588—their wooing scenes take on male as well as female homosexual potentialities.

FURTHER READING: John Lyly, *Gallathea and Midas*, ed. Anne Begor Lancashire (Lincoln: University of Nebraska Press, 1969); Leah Scragg, "Shakespeare, Lyly, and Ovid: The Influence of *Gallathea* on *A Midsummer Night's Dream*," *Shakespeare Survey* 30 (1977): 125–34; Robert J. Meyer, " 'Pleasure Reconciled to Virtue': The Mystery of Love in Lyly's *Gallathea*," *Studies in English Literature* 21 (1981): 193–208; Phyllis Rackin, "Androgyny, Mimesis, and the Marriage of the Boy Heroine on the English Renaissance Stage," *PMLA* 102 (1987): 29–41; Jean Howard, "Cross-Dressing, the Theatre, and Gender Struggle in Early Modern England," *Shakespeare Quarterly* 39 (1988): 114–40; Bruce Smith, *Homosexual Desire in Shakespeare's England: A Cultural Poetics* (Chicago and London: University of Chicago Press, 1991); Stephen Orgel, *Impersonations: The Performance of Gender in Renaissance England* (Cambridge: Cambridge University Press, 1996); John Franceschina, *Homosexualities in the English Theatre: From Lyly to Wilde* (Westport, Ct.: Greenwood, 1997).

Enter Tityrus, Melebeus *at one door*, Gallathea *and* Phyllida *at another*
NEPTUNE: But soft, what be these?
TITYRUS: Those that have offended thee to save their daughters.
NEPTUNE: Why, had you a fair daughter?
TITYRUS: Ay, and Melebeus a fair daughter.
NEPTUNE: Where be they?
MELEBEUS: In yonder woods, and methinks I see them coming.
NEPTUNE: Well, your deserts have not gotten pardon, but these goddesses' jars.
MELEBEUS: This is my daughter, my sweet Phyllida.
TITYRUS: And this is my fair Gallathea.
GALLATHEA: Unfortunate Gallathea, if this be Phyllida!
PHYLLIDA: Accursed Phyllida, if that be Gallathea!
GALLATHEA: And wast thou all this while enamored of Phyllida, that sweet Phyllida?
PHYLLIDA: And couldst thou dote upon the face of a maiden, thyself being one, on the face of fair Gallathea?
NEPTUNE: Do you both, being maidens, love one another?

GALLATHEA: I had thought the habit agreeable with the sex, and so burned in the fire of mine own fancies.

PHYLLIDA: I had thought that in the attire of a boy there could not have lodged the body of a virgin, and so was inflamed with a sweet desire which now I find a sour deceit.

DIANA: Now, things falling out as they do, you must leave these fond, fond affections. Nature will have it so, necessity must.

GALLATHEA: I will never love any but Phyllida. Her love is engraven in my heart with her eyes.

PHYLLIDA: Nor I any but Gallathea, whose faith is imprinted in my thoughts by her words.

NEPTUNE: An idle choice, strange and foolish, for one virgin to dote on another, and to imagine a constant faith where there can be no cause of affection. How like you this, Venus?

VENUS: I like well and allow it. They shall both be possessed of their wishes, for never shall it be said that Nature or Fortune shall overthrow love and faith. Is your love unspotted, begun with truth, continued with constancy, and not to be altered till death?

GALLATHEA: Die, Gallathea, if thy love be not so.

PHYLLIDA: Accursed be thou, Phyllida, if thy love be not so.

DIANA: Suppose all this, Venus; what then?

VENUS: Then shall it be seen that I can turn one of them to be a man, and that I will.

DIANA: Is it possible?

VENUS: What is to love or the mistress of love unpossible? Was it not Venus that did the like to Iphis and Ianthes? How say ye, are ye agreed, one to be a boy presently?

PHYLLIDA: I am content, so I may embrace Gallathea.

GALLATHEA: I wish it, so I may enjoy Phyllida.

MELEBEUS: Soft, daughter, you must know whether I will have you a son.

TITYRUS: Take me with you, Gallathea. I will keep you as I begat you, a daughter.

MELEBEUS: Tityrus, let yours be a boy, and if you will, mine shall not.

TITYRUS: Nay, mine shall not, for by that means my young son shall lose his inheritance.

MELEBEUS: Why, then get him to be made a maiden, and then there is nothing lost.

TITYRUS: If there be such changing, I would Venus could make my wife a man.

MELEBEUS: Why?

TITYRUS: Because she loves always to play with men.

VENUS: Well, you are both fond, therefore agree to this changing or suffer your daughters to endure hard chance.

MELEBEUS: How say you, Tityrus, shall we refer it to Venus?

TITYRUS: I am content, because she is a goddess.

VENUS: Neptune, you will not dislike it?

NEPTUNE: Not I.

VENUS: Nor you, Diana?

DIANA: Not I.

VENUS: Cupid shall not.

CUPID: I will not.

VENUS: Then let us depart. Neither of them shall know whose lot it shall be till they come to the church door. One shall be; doth it suffice?

PHYLLIDA: And satisfy us both, doth it not, Gallathea?

GALLATHEA: Yes, Phyllida.

[*Enter* Rafe, Robin, *and* Dick]

RAFE: Come, Robin. I am glad I have met with thee, for now we will make our father laugh at these tales.

DIANA: What are these that so malapertly thrust themselves into our companies?

ROBIN: Forsooth, madam, we are fortune-tellers.

VENUS: Fortunetellers! Tell me my fortune.

RAFE: We do not mean fortunetellers, we mean fortune-tellers. We can tell what fortune we have had these twelve months in the woods.

DIANA: Let them alone, they be but peevish.

VENUS: Yet they will be as good as minstrels at the marriage, to make us all merry.

DICK: Ay, ladies, we bear a very good consort.

VENUS: Can you sing?

RAFE: Basely.

VENUS: And you?

DICK: Meanly.

VENUS: And what can you do?

ROBIN: If they double it, I will treble it.

VENUS: Then shall ye go with us, and sing Hymen before the marriage. Are you content?

RAFE: Content? Never better content, for there we shall be sure to fill our bellies with capons' rumps or some such dainty dishes.

VENUS: Then follow us.

[*Exeunt all but* Gallathea]

THE EPILOGUE

GALLATHEA: Go all, 'tis I only that conclude all. You ladies may see that Venus can make constancy fickleness, courage cowardice, modesty lightness, working things impossible in your sex and tempering hardest hearts like softest wool. Yield, ladies, yield to love, ladies, which lurketh under your eyelids whilst you sleep and playeth with your heartstrings whilst you wake, whose sweetness never breedeth satiety, labor weariness, nor grief bitterness. Cupid was begotten in a mist, nursed in clouds, and sucking only upon conceits. Confess him a conqueror, whom ye ought to regard, sith it is unpossible to resist, for this is infallible, that love conquereth all things but itself, and ladies all hearts but their own.

[*Exit*]

WILLIAM SHAKESPEARE (1564–1616)

From *As You Like It* (1600) and *Twelfth Night* (1602)

William Shakespeare, England's greatest playwright, was born in Stratford-on-Avon in 1564. His father, John Shakespeare, is described in contemporary documents as a "husbandman" or "yeoman" and may have been a glover and wool-dealer; his mother, Mary, was the daughter of a well-to-do farmer. He attended the Stratford Grammar School, and married Anne Hathaway, by whom he had three children, in 1582. His whereabouts between 1585 and 1592 are unknown, though at some point he left Stratford and moved to London where he established himself as an actor and playwright in the company known as the Lord Chamberlain's Men. His earliest plays, *The Comedy of Errors* and *Titus Andronicus*, are thought to have been written in 1589. During the 1590s he produced a raft of brilliant works: the history plays *Henry VI, Part I* (1590–92), *Henry VI, Part II* (1590–91), *Henry VI, Part III* (1590–92), *Richard III* (1592–93), *King John* (1594), *Richard II* (1595–97), *Henry IV, Part I* (1596–97), *Henry IV, Part II* (1596–97), and *Henry V* (1599); the comedies *The Taming of the Shrew* (1593), *Two Gentlemen of Verona* (1592–93), *Love's Labours Lost* (1594), *A Midsummer Night's Dream* (1594–95), *The Merchant of Venice* (1596), *The Merry Wives of Windsor* (1597) and *Much Ado About Nothing* (1598–99); and the tragedies *Romeo and Juliet* (1595) and *Julius Caesar* (1599). In the same decade he also wrote his celebrated *Sonnets* (published in 1609) and the poems *Venus and Adonis* and *The Rape of Lucrece* (1593).

In 1599 the Lord Chamberlain's Men—their name was changed to the King's Men after the accession of James I in 1603—moved to the newly constructed Globe Theatre on the south bank of the Thames. Most of Shakespeare's later plays were performed there. He composed many of his greatest works around 1600 and after: the comedies *As You Like It* (1600), *Twelfth Night* (1602), *Troilus and Cressida* (1601–2), *All's Well That Ends Well* (1602–3), and *Measure for Measure* (1604); and the tragedies *Hamlet* (1601–2), *Othello* (1604), *King Lear* (1605), *Macbeth* (1606), and *Antony and Cleopatra* (1607). These were followed by the lesser-known tragedies *Timon of Athens* (1605–9) and *Coriolanus* (1608), then by the comic romances of his last years, *Pericles* (1608), *Cymbeline* (1609–10), *The Winter's Tale* (1611), and *The Tempest* (1611). The Globe burned to the ground in 1613. By that time, however, Shakespeare had already retired to Stratford, where he lived until his death in 1616. The earliest collected edition of his works was the First Folio (1623), edited by two of his fellow actors. Further folio editions appeared in 1632, 1663, 1664, and 1685.

Like Lyly's *Gallathea*, Shakespeare's *As You Like It* and *Twelfth Night* might be considered "honorary" sapphic comedies. Both plays feature charismatic cross-dressing heroines who inspire ardor in unwitting females. In *As You Like It*, the heroine, Rosalind, disguises herself as a boy in order to pass safely through the forest of Arden in search of her lover, Orlando. She is accompanied by her faithful friend, Celia, who says, reminiscingly, of their childhood:

> . . . we still have slept together,
> Rose at an instant, learn'd, play'd, sat together,
> And wheresoe'er we went, like Juno's swans,
> Still we went coupled and inseparable.

While in disguise as "Ganymede"—the name of a beautiful youth in Greek mythology beloved of Zeus—Rosalind accidentally excites the passion of Phoebe, a country lass being courted by the shepherd Silvius. Only when Rosalind's sex is revealed and her marriage to Orlando assured will Phoebe accept Silvius—as second-best.

In *Twelfth Night*, the heroine, Viola, is separated from her twin brother, Sebastian, when they are shipwrecked off the coast of Illyria. Disguised as the page "Cesario," Viola joins the service of the Duke Orsino, who is in love with a lady named Olivia. When Viola/Cesario is sent to woo Olivia on Orsino's behalf, Olivia immediately falls in love with her. The mix-up here is only resolved when Olivia encounters Sebastian, and thinking *him* "Cesario," marries him on the spot. The Duke Orsino, disappointed in his suit for the hand of Olivia, is persuaded to turn his amorous attentions to Viola, still in male attire but now revealed as a woman after all.

Given the extraordinarily attractive *illusion* of female same-sex love on which the plot of each play depends, it is not surprising that *As You Like It* and *Twelfth Night* have played a talismanic role in lesbian literary tradition. In Théophile Gautier's scandalous 1835 novel, *Mademoiselle de Maupin*, for example, a country-house production of *As You Like It* functions as sapphic aphrodisiac: the cross-dressing heroine, Madeleine de Maupin, seduces her hostess, Rosette, after playing Rosalind to Rosette's Phoebe. In Virginia Woolf's lesbian fantasy novel, *Orlando* (1928), the androgynous Orlando— born a man in the Elizabethan age and transformed into a woman in the eighteenth century—is a hallucinatory amalgam of *both* Shakespeare's Orlando and Rosalind. And in Brigid Brophy's *The King of a Rainy Country* (1956), the young heroine kisses her first love, the seductive Cynthia, while assisting backstage at a school performance of the same Shakespearean play.

Twelfth Night has had a similar importance, particularly in the area of character names. After *Sappho* and *Diana*, *Olivia* is perhaps the most "lesbian-sounding" name one can give a female character in English literature: it virtually tags the bearer as a lover of women. Thus Woolf, in *A Room of One's Own* (1928), celebrates the subversive desire of "Chloe and Olivia"; Radclyffe Hall, in *The Well of Loneliness* (1928), gives her homosexual heroine, Stephen Gordon, "Olivia" as a middle name. Most memorably, perhaps, Olivia is the name of the love-stricken protagonist in the eponymous *Olivia* (1949), Dorothy Strachey's autobiographical novel about an adolescent girl infatuated with her schoolmistress. (Strachey also published the work under the pseudonym "Olivia.") In the 1970s the first lesbian-owned record company in the United States took the name Olivia Records. And still more recently—so long the Shakespearean reach—*Olivia* has been adopted as the name of a cruise ship line specializing in luxury tours for lesbian couples.

FURTHER READING: William Shakespeare, *The Complete Works*, ed. Stanley Wells and Gary Taylor (Oxford: Clarendon, 1986); Jean Howard, "Cross-Dressing, the Theatre, and Gender Struggle in Early Modern England," *Shakespeare Quarterly* 39 (1988), 418–40; Bruce R. Smith, *Homosexual Desire in Shakespeare's England: A Cultural Poetics* (Chicago: University of Chicago Press, 1991); Valerie Traub, *Desire and Anxiety: Circulations of Sexuality in Shakespearean Drama* (London and New York: Routledge, 1992) and "The (In)significance of Lesbian Desire in Early Modern England," in Susan Zimmerman, ed., *Erotic Politics: Desire on the Renaissance Stage* (London and New York: Routledge, 1992); Lisa Jardine, "Twins and Travesties: Gender, Dependency, and Sexual Availability in *Twelfth Night*," in Zimmerman, ed., *Erotic Politics*, pp. 27–38; Kate Chedzgoy, *Shakespeare's Queer Children: Sexual Politics and Contemporary Culture* (Manchester: Manchester University Press, 1995); Jonathan Crewe, "In the Field of Dreams: Transvestism in *Twelfth Night* and *The Crying Game*," *Representations* 50 (1995): 101–21; Stephen Orgel, *Impersonations: The Performance of Gender in Renaissance England* (Cambridge: Cambridge University Press, 1996).

As You Like It (3.v.)

[Another part of the forest
Enter silvius and phebe]
SILVIUS: Sweet Phebe, do not scorn me, do not, Phebe.
    Say that you love me not, but say not so
    In bitterness. The common executioner,
    Whose heart the accustomed sight of death makes hard,
    Falls not the ax upon the humbled neck
    But first begs pardon. Will you sterner be
    Than he that dies and lives by bloody drops?
[*Enter* rosalind, celia, *and* corin, *behind*]
PHEBE: I would not be thy executioner.

I fly thee, for I would not injure thee.
Thou tell'st me there is murder in mine eye.
'Tis pretty, sure, and very probable,
That eyes, that are the frail'st and softest things,
Who shut their coward gates on atomies,
Should be called tyrants, butchers, murderers!
Now I do frown on thee with all my heart,
And if mine eyes can wound, now let them kill thee.
Now counterfeit to swoon, why, now fall down.
Or if thou canst not, oh, for shame, for shame,
Lie not, to say mine eyes are murderers!
Now show the wound mine eye hath made in thee.
Scratch thee but with a pin and there remains
Some scar of it. Lean but upon a rush,
The cicatrice and capable impressure
Thy palm some moment keeps. But now mine eyes,
Which I have darted at thee, hurt thee not,
Nor, I am sure, there is no force in eyes
That can do hurt.

SILVIUS: O dear Phebe,
If ever—as that ever may be near—
You meet in some fresh cheek the power of fancy,
Then shall you know the wounds invisible
That love's keen arrows make.

PHEBE: But till that time
Come not thou near me. And when that time comes,
Afflict me with thy mocks, pity me not,
As till that time I shall not pity thee.

ROSALIND: And why, I pray you? Who might be your mother
That you insult, exult, and all at once
Over the wretched? What though you have no beauty—
As, by my faith, I see no more in you
Than without candle may go dark to bed—
Must you be therefore proud and pitiless?
Why, what means this? Why do you look on me?
I see no more in you than in the ordinary
Of nature's salework. 'Od's my little life,
I think she means to tangle my eyes too!
No, faith, proud mistress, hope not after it.
'Tis not your inky brows, your black silk hair,
Your bugle eyeballs, nor your cheek of cream,
That can entame my spirits to your worship.

You foolish shepherd, wherefore do you follow her
Like foggy south, puffing with wind and rain?
You are a thousand times a properer man
Than she a woman. 'Tis such fools as you
That makes the world full of ill-favored children.
'Tis not her glass, but you, that flatters her,
And out of you she sees herself more proper
Than any of her lineaments can show her.
But, mistress, know yourself. Down on your knees
And thank Heaven, fasting, for a good man's love.
For I must tell you friendly in your ear,
Sell when you can. You are not for all markets.
Cry the man mercy, love him, take his offer.
Foul is most foul, being foul to be a scoffer.
So take her to thee, shepherd. Fare you well.

PHEBE: Sweet youth, I pray you, chide a year together.
I had rather hear you chide than this man woo.

ROSALIND: He's fallen in love with your foulness and she'll fall in love with my anger.
If it be so, as fast as she answers thee with frowning looks, I'll sauce her with bitter
words. Why look you so upon me?

PHEBE: For no ill will I bear you.

ROSALIND: I pray you do not fall in love with me,
For I am falser than vows made in wine.
Besides, I like you not. If you will know my house,
'Tis at the tuft of olives here hard by.
Will you go, Sister? Shepherd, ply her hard.
Come, Sister. Shepherdess, look on him better,
And be not proud. Though all the world could see,
None could be so abused in sight as he.
Come, to our flock.

[*Exeunt* rosalind, celia *and* corin]

PHEBE: Dead shepherd, now I find thy saw of might—
"Who ever loved that loved not at first sight?"

SILVIUS: Sweet Phebe—

PHEBE: Ha, what say'st thou, Silvius?

SILVIUS: Sweet Phebe, pity me.

PHEBE: Why, I am sorry for thee, gentle Silvius.

SILVIUS: Wherever sorrow is, relief would be.
If you do sorrow at my grief in love,
By giving love your sorrow and my grief
Were both extermined.

PHEBE: Thou hast my love. Is not that neighbourly?

SILVIUS: I would have you.

PHEBE: Why, that were covetousness.
　　Silvius, the time was that I hated thee,
　　And yet it is not that I bear thee love.
　　But since that thou canst talk of love so well,
　　Thy company, which erst was irksome to me,
　　I will endure, and I'll employ thee too.
　　But do not look for further recompense
　　Than thine own gladness that thou art employed.

SILVIUS: So holy and so perfect is my love,
　　And I in such a poverty of grace,
　　That I shall think it a most plenteous crop
　　To glean the broken ears after the man
　　That the main harvest reaps. Loose now and then
　　A scattered smile, and that I'll live upon.

PHEBE: Know'st thou the youth that spoke to me erewhile?

SILVIUS: Not very well, but I have met him oft,
　　And he hath bought the cottage and the bounds
　　That the old carlot once was master of.

PHEBE: Think not I love him, though I ask for him.
　　'Tis but a peevish boy, yet he talks well.
　　But what care I for words? Yet words do well
　　When he that speaks them pleases those that hear.
　　It is a pretty youth—not very pretty—
　　But, sure, he's proud, and yet his pride becomes him.
　　He'll make a proper man. The best thing in him
　　Is his complexion, and faster than his tongue
　　Did make offense his eye did heal it up.
　　He is not very tall, yet for his years he's tall.
　　His leg is but so so, and yet 'tis well.
　　There was a pretty redness in his lip,
　　A little riper and more lusty red
　　Than that mixed in his cheek, 'twas just the difference
　　Betwixt the constant red and mingled damask.
　　There be some women, Silvius, had they marked him
　　In parcels as I did, would have gone near
　　To fall in love with him. But for my part,
　　I love him not nor hate him not, and yet
　　I have more cause to hate him than to love him.
　　For what had he to do to chide at me?
　　He said mine eyes were black and my hair black,
　　And, now I am remembered, scorned at me.

I marvel why I answered not again.
But that's all one, omittance is no quittance.
I'll write to him a very taunting letter,
And thou shalt bear it. Wilt thou, Silvius?

SILVIUS: Phebe, with all my heart.

PHEBE: I'll write it straight,
The matter's in my head and in my heart.
I will be bitter with him and passing short.
Go with me, Silvius.
[*Exeunt*]

From *Twelfth Night* (3.i.)

OLIVIA: Let the garden door be shut, and leave me to my hearing.
[*Exeunt* sir toby, sir andrew, *and* maria]
Give me your hand, sir.

VIOLA: My duty, madam, and most humble service.

OLIVIA: What is your name?

VIOLA: Cesario is your servant's name, fair Princess.

OLIVIA: My servant, sir! 'Twas never merry world
Since lowly feigning was called compliment.
You're servant to the Count Orsino, youth.

VIOLA: And he is yours, and his must needs be yours.
Your servant's servant is your servant, madam.

OLIVIA: For him, I think not on him. For his thoughts,
Would they were blanks rather than filled with me!

VIOLA: Madam, I come to whet your gentle thoughts
On his behalf.

OLIVIA: Oh, by your leave, I pray you,
I bade you never speak again of him.
But would you undertake another suit,
I had rather hear you to solicit that
Than music from the spheres.

VIOLA: Dear lady—

OLIVIA: Give me leave, beseech you. I did send,
After the last enchantment you did here,
A ring in chase of you. So did I abuse
Myself, my servant, and, I fear me, you.
Under your hard construction must I sit,
To force that on you, in a shameful cunning,

Which you knew none of yours. What might you think?
Have you not set mine honor at the stake
And baited it with all the unmuzzled thoughts
That tyrannous heart can think? To one of your receiving
Enough is shown. A cypress, not a bosom,
Hides my heart. So let me hear you speak.

VIOLA: I pity you.

OLIVIA: That's a degree to love.

VIOLA: No, not a grize, for 'tis a vulgar proof
That very oft we pity enemies.

OLIVIA: Why, then, methinks 'tis time to smile again.
O world, how apt the poor are to be proud!
If one should be a prey, how much the better
To fall before the lion than the wolf!
[*Clock strikes*]
The clock upbraids me with the waste of time.
Be not afraid, good youth, I will not have you.
And yet, when wit and youth is come to harvest,
Your wife is like to reap a proper man.
There lies your way, due west.

VIOLA: Then westward ho!
Grace and good disposition attend your ladyship!
You'll nothing, madam, to my lord by me?

OLIVIA: Stay.
I prithee tell me what thou think'st of me.

VIOLA: That you do think you are not what you are.

OLIVIA: If I think so, I think the same of you.

VIOLA: Then think you right. I am not what I am.

OLIVIA: I would you were as I would have you be!

VIOLA: Would it be better, madam, than I am?
I wish it might, for now I am your fool.

OLIVIA: Oh, what a deal of scorn looks beautiful
In the contempt and anger of his lip!
A murderous guilt shows not itself more soon
Than love that would seem hid. Love's night is noon.
Cesario, by the roses of the spring,
By maidhood, honor, truth, and everything,
I love thee so, that, mauger all thy pride,
Nor wit nor reason can my passion hide.
Do not extort thy reasons from this clause,
For that I woo, thou therefore hast no cause,

But rather reason thus with reason fetter,
Love sought is good, but given unsought is better.

VIOLA: By innocence I swear, and by my youth,
I have one heart, one bosom, and one truth,
And that no woman has; nor never none
Shall mistress be of it, save I alone.
And so adieu, good madam. Nevermore
Will I my master's tears to you deplore.

OLIVIA: Yet come again, for thou perhaps mayst move
That heart which now abhors to like his love.

[*Exeunt*]

THE KING JAMES BIBLE (1611)

The Book of Ruth

While the Bible has often provided ammunition for antihomosexual bigots—the Old Testament story about the destruction of Sodom and Gomorrah (Gen. 18–19) and the Levitican passage proscribing "unlawful lusts" between men (Lev. 18:22) come immediately to mind—some of its most memorable episodes open themselves to less prejudicial interpretation. The story of David and Jonathan, recounted in the first and second books of Samuel, has long been taken by homophile readers as an endorsement of love between men: David's lament upon the death of Jonathan ("The beauty of Israel is slain upon the high places; how are the mighty fallen! . . . I am very distressed for thee, my brother Jonathan; very pleasant hast thou been unto me: thy love was wonderful, surpassing the love of women" [2 Sam. 1:19–26]) has resonated in gay male literary history from the Renaissance to the present.

The Old Testament story of Ruth and Naomi has played a similar role in the lesbian literary tradition. In *Sex Variant Women in Literature* (1956), Jeannette Foster described this "Hebrew prose masterpiece" as the first of a "line of delicate portrayals, by authors seemingly blind to their full significance, of an attachment which, however innocent, is nevertheless still basically variant." And as Raymond-Jean Frontain points out in a recent essay on the Bible and homosexuality, the story of Ruth's devotion to Naomi—a love hardly diminished by Ruth's strategic marriage to her kinsman, the wealthy farmer Boaz—has authorized a number of twentieth-century lesbian narratives:

> In Helen Anderson's *Pity for Women* (1937) . . . protagonists Ann and Judith recite Ruth's words ["whither thou goest, I will go: and where thou lodgest, I will lodge: thy people shall be my people, and thy God my God" (Ruth 1:16)] while attempting to ceremonialize their union. The thematic center of Isabel Miller's *Patience and Sarah* (1969), perhaps the first self-consciously lesbian-feminist American novel to have commercial success, is the painting that Patience, an artist, makes for their home. She "painted Boaz and Ruth and Naomi, Boaz distant, very small, his back turned, leaving. I call it 'Where Thou Lodgest, I Will Lodge.'" Patience is at first concerned that, despite the

camouflage offered by a biblical subject, visitors might be upset by the passion of the two women's embrace depicted in the scene. Her conclusion to proceed with the painting anyway both reenacts the courage of the biblical women to persevere together and dramatizes the inspiration that that courage has been to lesbian lovers and artists.

The text below is from the so-called King James or Authorized Version of the Bible, the translation of the Hebrew Bible commissioned by James I in 1611. The ornate seventeenth-century prose style—the magnificent rhythms of which have become permanently lodged in English poetic tradition—endows the biblical narrative with a rhetorical grandeur and nobility unmatched in any subsequent translation.

FURTHER READING: *The New King James Bible* (Nashville, Tenn.: T. Nelson, 1982); Edward F. Campbell Jr., *Ruth: A New Translation with Introduction, Notes, and Commentary*, vol. 7 of *The Anchor Bible* (Garden City, N.Y.: Doubleday, 1975); Jeannette Foster, *Sex Variant Women in Literature* (1956; rpt. Tallahassee, Fla.: Naiad, 1985); Derrick Sherwin Bailey, *Homosexuality and the Western Christian Tradition* (Hamden, Conn.: Archon, 1975); John Boswell, *Christianity, Social Tolerance, and Homosexuality: Gay People in Western Europe from the Beginning of the Christian Era to the Fourteenth Century* (Chicago: University of Chicago Press, 1980); David L. Jeffrey, ed., *A Dictionary of Biblical Tradition in English Literature* (Grand Rapids, Mich.: Eerdmans, 1992); Raymond-Jean Frontain, "The Bible," in Claude J. Summers, ed., *The Gay and Lesbian Literary Heritage: A Reader's Companion to the Writers and Their Works from Antiquity to the Present* (New York: Henry Holt, 1995), pp. 92–100; Bernadette J. Brooten, *Love Between Women: Early Christian Responses to Female Homoeroticism* (Chicago: University of Chicago Press, 1996); Mishael Caspi, *Women on the Biblical Road: Ruth, Naomi, and the Female Journey* (Lanham, Md.: University Press of America, 1996); Ruth Vanita, *Sappho and the Virgin Mary: Same-Sex Love and the English Literary Imagination* (New York: Columbia University Press, 1996).

CHAPTER I

1   NOW it came to pass in the days when the judges ruled, that there was a famine in the land. And a certain man of Beth-lehem-judah went to sojourn in the country of Moab, he, and his wife, and his two sons.

2   And the name of the man *was* Elimelech, and the name of his wife Naomi, and the name of his two sons Mahlon and Chilion, Ephrathites of Beth-lehem-judah. And they came into the country of Moab, and continued there.

3   And Elimelech Naomi's husband died; and she was left, and her two sons.

4   And they took them wives of the women of Moab; the name of the one *was* Orpah, and the name of the other Ruth: and they dwelled there about ten years.

5   And Mahlon and Chilion died also both of them; and the woman was left of her two sons and her husband.

6   Then she arose with her daughters in law, that she might return from the country of Moab: for she had heard in the country of Moab how that the Lord had visited his people in giving them bread.

7   Wherefore she went forth out of the place where she was, and her two daughters in law with her; and they went on the way to return unto the land of Judah.

8   And Naomi said unto her two daughters in law, Go, return each to her mother's house: the Lord deal kindly with you, as ye have dealt with the dead, and with me.

9   The Lord grant you that ye may find rest, each *of you* in the house of her husband. Then she kissed them; and they lifted up their voice, and wept.

10 And they said unto her, Surely we will return with thee unto thy people.

11 And Naomi said, Turn again, my daughters: why will ye go with me? *are* there yet *any more* sons in my womb, that they may be your husbands?

12 Turn again, my daughters, go *your way;* for I am too old to have an husband. If I should say, I have hope, *if* I should have an husband also to night, and should also bear sons;

13 Would ye tarry for them till they were grown? would ye stay for them from having husbands? nay, my daughters; for it grieveth me much for your sakes that the hand of the Lord is gone out against me.

14 And they lifted up their voice, and wept again: and Orpah kissed her mother in law; but Ruth clave unto her.

15 And she said, Behold, thy sister in law is gone back unto her people, and unto her gods: return thou after thy sister in law.

16 And Ruth said, Intreat me not to leave thee, *or* to return from following after thee: for whither thou goest, I will go; and where thou lodgest, I will lodge: thy people *shall be* my people, and thy God my God:

17 Where thou diest, will I die, and there will I be buried: the Lord do so to me, and more also, *if ought* but death part thee and me.

18 When she saw that she was stedfastly minded to go with her, then she left speaking unto her.

19 So they two went until they came to Beth-lehem. And it came to pass, when they were come to Beth-lehem, that all the city was moved about them, and they said. *Is* this Naomi?

20 And she said unto them, call me not Naomi, call me Mara: for the Almighty hath dealt very bitterly with me.

21 I went out full, and the Lord hath brought me home again empty: why *then* call ye me Naomi, seeing the Lord hath testified against me, and the Almighty hath afflicted me?

22　So Naomi returned, and Ruth the Moabitess, her daughter in law, with her, which returned out of the country of Moab: and they came to Beth-lehem in the beginning of barley harvest.

CHAPTER 2

1　AND Naomi had a kinsman of her husband's, a mighty man of wealth, of the family of Elimelech; and his name *was* Boaz.

2　And Ruth the Moabitess said unto Naomi. Let me now go to the field, and glean ears of corn after *him* in whose sight I shall find grace. And she said unto her, Go, my daughter.

3　And she went, and came, and gleaned in the field after the reapers: and her hap was to light on a part of the field *belonging* unto Boaz, who *was* of the kindred of Elimelech.

4　And, behold, Boaz came from Beth-lehem, and said unto the reapers, The Lord be with you. And they answered him, The Lord bless thee.

5　Then said Boaz unto his servant that was set over the reapers, Whose damsel *is* this?

6　And the servant that was set over the reapers answered and said, It *is* the Moabitish damsel that came back with Naomi out of the country of Moab:

7　And she said, I pray you, let me glean and gather after the reapers among the sheaves: so she came, and hath continued even from the morning until now, that she tarried a little in the house.

8　Then said Boaz unto Ruth, Hearest thou not, my daughter? Go not to glean in another field, neither go from hence, but abide here fast by my maidens:

9　*Let* thine eyes *be* on the field that they do reap, and go thou after them: have I not charged the young men that they shall not touch thee? and when thou art athirst, go unto the vessels, and drink of *that* which the young men have drawn.

10　Then she fell on her face, and bowed herself to the ground, and said unto him, Why have I found grace in thine eyes, that thou shouldest take knowledge of me, seeing I *am* a stranger?

11　And Boaz answered and said unto her, It hath fully been shewed me, all that thou hast done unto thy mother in law since the death of thine husband: and *how* thou hast left thy father and thy mother, and land of thy nativity, and art come unto a people which thou knewest not heretofore.

12　The Lord recompense thy work, and a full reward be given thee of the Lord God of Israel, under whose wings thou art come to trust.

13　Then she said, Let me find favour in thy sight, my lord; for that thou hast comforted me, and for that thou hast spoken friendly unto thine handmaid, though I be not like unto one of thine handmaidens.

14　And Boaz said unto her, At mealtime come thou hither, and eat of the bread, and dip thy morsel in the vinegar. And she sat beside the reapers: and he reached her parched *corn,* and she did eat, and was sufficed, and left.

15   And when she was risen up to glean, Boaz commanded his young men, saying. Let her glean even among the sheaves, and reproach her not:

16   And let fall also *some* of the handfuls of purpose for her, and leave *them,* that she may glean *them,* and rebuke her not:

17   So she gleaned in the field until even, and beat out that she had gleaned: and it was about an ephah of barley.

18   And she took *it* up, and went into the city: and her mother in law saw what she had gleaned: and she brought forth, and gave to her that she had reserved after she was sufficed.

19   And her mother in law said unto her, Where hast thou gleaned to day? and where wroughtest thou? blessed be he that did take knowledge of thee. And she shewed her mother in law with whom she had wrought, and said, The man's name with whom I wrought to day *is* Boaz.

20   And Naomi said unto her daughter in law, Blessed *be* he of the Lord, who hath not left off his kindness to the living and to the dead. And Naomi said unto her, The man *is* near of kin unto us, one of our next kinsmen.

21   And Ruth the Moabitess said, He said unto me also, Thou shalt keep fast by my young men, until they have ended all my harvest.

22   And Naomi said unto Ruth her daughter in law, *It is* good, my daughter, that thou go out with his maidens, that they meet thee not in any other field.

23   So she kept fast by the maidens of Boaz to glean unto the end of barley harvest and of wheat harvest; and dwelt with her mother in law.

CHAPTER 3

1   THEN Naomi her mother in law said unto her, My daughter, shall I not seek rest for thee, that it may be well with thee?

2   And now *is* not Boaz of our kindred, with whose maidens thou wast? Behold, he winnoweth barley to night in the threshingfloor.

3   Wash thyself therefore, and anoint thee, and put thy raiment upon thee, and get thee down to the floor: *but* make not thyself known unto the man, until he shall have done eating and drinking.

4   And it shall be, when he lieth down, that thou shall mark the place where he shall lie, and thou shalt go in, and uncover his feet, and lay thee down; and he will tell thee what thou shalt do.

5   And she said unto her, All that thou sayest unto me I will do.

6   And she went down unto the floor, and did according to all that her mother in law bade her.

7   And when Boaz had eaten and drunk, and his heart was merry, he went to lie down at the end of the heap of corn: and she came softly, and uncovered his feet, and laid her down.

8   And it came to pass at midnight, that the man was afraid, and turned himself: and, behold, a woman lay at his feet.

9   And he said, Who *art* thou? And she answered, I *am* Ruth thine handmaid: spread therefore thy skirt over thine handmaid; for thou *art* a near kinsman.

10 And he said, Blessed *be* thou of the Lord, my daughter: *for* thou hast shewed more kindness in the latter end than at the beginning, inasmuch as thou followedst not young men, whether poor or rich.

11 And now, my daughter, fear not; I will do to thee all that thou requirest: for all the city of my people doth know that thou *art* a virtuous woman.

12 And now it is true that I *am thy* near kinsman: howbeit there is a kinsman nearer than I.

13 Tarry this night, and it shall be in the morning, *that* if he will perform unto thee the part of a kinsman, well; let him do the kinsman's part: but if he will not do the part of a kinsman to thee, then will I do the part of a kinsman to thee, *as* the Lord liveth: lie down until the morning.

14 And she lay at his feet until the morning: and she rose up before one could know another. And he said, Let it not be known that a woman came into the floor.

15 Also he said, Bring the veil that *thou hast* upon thee, and hold it. And when she held it, he measured six *measures* of barley, and laid *it* on her: and she went into the city.

16 And when she came to her mother in law, she said, Who *art* thou, my daughter? And she told her all that the man had done to her.

17 And she said, These six *measures* of barley gave he me; for he said to me, Go not empty unto thy mother in law.

18 Then said she, Sit still, my daughter, until thou know how the matter will fall: for the man will not be in rest, until he have finished the thing this day.

CHAPTER 4

1   THEN went Boaz up to the gate, and sat him down there: and, behold, the kinsman of whom Boaz spake came by; unto whom he said, Ho, such a one! turn aside, sit down here. And he turned aside, and sat down.

2   And he took ten men of the elders of the city, and said, Sit ye down here. And they sat down.

3   And he said unto the kinsman, Naomi, that is come again out of the country of Moab, selleth a parcel of land, which *was* our brother Elimelech's:

4   And I thought to advertise thee, saying, Buy *it* before the inhabitants, and before the elders of my people. If thou wilt redeem *it,* redeem *it:* but if thou wilt not

redeem *it, then* tell me, that I may know: for *there is* none to redeem *it* beside thee; and I *am* after thee. And he said, I will redeem *it*.

5   Then said Boaz, What day thou buyest the field of the hand of Naomi, thou must buy *it* also of Ruth the Moabitess, the wife of the dead, to raise up the name of the dead upon his inheritance.

6   And the kinsman said, I cannot redeem *it* for myself, lest I mar mine own inheritance: redeem thou my right to thyself; for I cannot redeem *it*.

7   Now this *was the manner* in former time in Israel concerning redeeming and concerning changing, for to confirm all things; a man plucked off his shoe, and gave *it* to his neighbour: and this *was* a testimony in Israel.

8   Therefore the kinsman said unto Boaz, Buy *it* for thee. So he drew off his shoe.

9   And Boaz said unto the elders, and *unto* all the people, Ye *are* witnesses this day, that I have bought all that *was* Elimelech's, and all that *was* Chilion's and Mahlon's, of the land of Naomi.

10   Moreover Ruth the Moabitess, the wife of Mahlon, have I purchased to be my wife, to raise up the name of the dead upon his inheritance, that the name of the dead be not cut off from among his brethren, and from the gate of his place: ye *are* witnesses this day.

11   And all the people that *were* in the gate, and the elders, said, *We are* witnesses. The Lord make the woman that is come into thine house like Rachel and like Leah, which two did build the house of Israel: and do thou worthily in Ephratah, and be famous in Beth-lehem:

12   And let thy house be like the house of Pharez, whom Tamar bare unto Judah, of the seed which the Lord shall give thee of this young woman.

13   So Boaz took Ruth, and she was his wife: and when he went in unto her, the Lord gave her conception, and she bare a son.

14   And the women said unto Naomi, Blessed *be* the Lord, which hath not left thee this day without a kinsman, that his name may be famous in Israel.

15   And he shall be unto thee a restorer of *thy* life, and a nourisher of thine old age: for thy daughter in law, which loveth thee, which is better to thee than seven sons, hath born him.

16   And Naomi took the child, and laid it in her bosom, and became nurse unto it.

17   And the women her neighbours gave it a name, saying, There is a son born to Naomi; and they called his name Obed: he *is* the father of Jesse, the father of David.

18   Now these *are* the generations of Pharez: Pharez begat Hezron.

19   And Hezron begat Ram, and Ram begat Amminadab,

20   And Amminadab begat Nahshon, and Nahshon begat Salmon,

21   And Salmon begat Boaz, and Boaz begat Obed,

22   And Obed begat Jesse, and Jesse begat David.

ANNE DE ROHAN (1584–1646)

"On a Lady Named Beloved" (1617)

Anne de Rohan was the daughter of Viscount René de Rohan, Prince of Léon, and Catherine de Parthenay, the noted French Huguenot poet, dramatist, satirist, and translator. Like her mother, Anne de Rohan was a cultivated woman, well versed in classical and modern literature, and a staunch defender of the Protestant faith during the bloody religious strife preceding and following the Edict of Nantes. At the siege of La Rochelle in 1627 both she and her mother were made prisoners of war: her mother died in captivity. Rohan's works include elegies to her mother and sister and to Henriette de Savoie. Her best-known work is *Stances sur la mort du Roy* (1610), written after Henry IV's assassination the same year.

The 1617 poem "On a Lady Named Beloved" ("Sur une dame nommée Aimée") appeared in the first collection devoted to Anne de Rohan's work, *Poésies d'Anne de Rohan-Soubise*, in 1862. Though short, it is significant: it is perhaps the first French poem written by a woman to make direct allusion to the newly rediscovered verses of Sappho. Of the various Sappho fragments introduced to French readers in the sixteenth century via the editions of Robert Estienne (1546), Henri Estienne (1554, 1556), and Rémi Belleau (1556), the best known and most translated was Fragment 31, conventionally known in English as "Peer of the Gods." Its popular French title was—and remains to this day—"À l'aimée" (To the Beloved). In addressing her own lover as "*Aimée*" Anne de Rohan at once associates herself with the scandalous poet of Lesbos and makes it clear that the person she addresses is female. (Unlike the gender-neutral English "beloved," the French word *aimée* can only refer grammatically to a female object of desire.) Unfortunately, of the circumstances inspiring the poem we know nothing, nor indeed how widely it was circulated.

FURTHER READING: Anne de Rohan, *Poésies d'Anne de Rohan-Soubise et lettres d'Éléonore de Rohan-Montbazon* (Paris, 1862); Joan DeJean, *Fictions of Sappho 1546–1937* (Chicago: University of Chicago Press, 1989); Jane McIntosh Snyder, *Lesbian Desire in the Lyrics of Sappho* (New York: Columbia University Press, 1997);

Elizabeth S. Wahl, *Invisible Relations: Representations of Female Intimacy in the Age of Enlightenment* (Stanford: Stanford University Press, 1998).

Beauty, it would be a great wrong,
If, for your worthy graces,
I had been dealt the lover's fate;
For anyone but you, my dear Beloved,

All the Olympic torches,
Illuminated in their course,
Are not lovelier ornaments
Than the eyes of my beautiful Beloved.

Cupid, delighted with those eyes,
His right hand armed with an arrow
Shot into my troubled heart
The ardent desire to love my Beloved.

I know not whether they be heavens or gods
Whose power from me is hidden
And compels me, both near and far,
To die so as to love my Beloved.

To see them, they seem like the heavens,
Of azure color are they,
But by their effects they're like gods,
Forcing me yet to love that Beloved.

For me, then, they're both heavens and gods,
Because of their hidden power
And luminous appearance,
For I hold nothing dearer than my Beloved.

ANONYMOUS

From *Hic Mulier; or, The Man-Woman* (1620)

Hic Mulier; or, The Man-Woman: Being a Medicine to Cure the Coltish Disease of the Staggers in the Masculine-Feminines of Our Times is an anonymous seventeenth-century English pamphlet attacking the "coltish disease" of women dressing in men's clothes. It is not clear whether the pamphlet was written in response to actual cases of female transvestism or merely reflects the fear that such a fashion *might* take hold. Ever since Elizabeth I had worn armor during her famous speech to the troops at Tilbury Dock before the invasion of the Spanish Armada in 1588, daring upper-class English-women had occasionally sported items of masculine costume such as doublets or poniards. Yet apart from a few notable miscreants such as the cross-dressing "roaring girl" and cutpurse Mary Frith, outright transvestism seems to have been rare. No matter: contemporary moralists viewed even the slightest hint of "Man-Womanishness" as a frightening threat to social and political stability. In the same year that the *Hic Mulier* appeared, 1620, no less an authority than James I instructed the Anglican clergy "to inveigh vehemently in their sermons against women wearing broad-brimmed hats, painted doublets, short hair, and even some of them poniards." If "pulpit admonitions" failed, he warned, "another course [would have to] be taken."

Broadly speaking, pamphlets such as the *Hic Mulier* were part of an ongoing Puritan backlash against "immodesty" that would culminate in the Cromwellian ascendancy of the 1640s. But the work also reinforced emerging cultural taboos on same-sex attachment. (The pamphlet was immediately followed by *Haec Vir: or, The Womanish-Man*, a companion work attacking male effeminacy.) Though the author of the *Hic Mulier* never says so in so many words, he implies that the female adoption of male garb prompts unnatural acts. She who dons the breeches goes against "kind" and soon gives over her "hands" to "ruffianly and uncivil actions."

FURTHER READING: *Hic Mulier: or, the Man-Woman: Being a Medicine to Cure the Coltish Disease of the Staggers in the Masculine-Feminines of Our Times* (The Rota: Exeter University Press, 1973); Barbara J. Baines, ed., *Three Pamphlets on the Jacobean Antifeminist Controversy* (Delmar, N.Y.: Scholars' Facsimiles, 1978); Sandra Clark, "*Hic*

Mulier, Haec Vir, and the Controversy over Masculine Women," *Studies in Philology* 82 (1985): 157–83; Linda Woodbridge, *Women and the English Renaissance* (Urbana: University of Illinois Press, 1986); Valerie R. Lucas, "*Hic Mulier*: The Female Transvestite in Early Modern England," *Renaissance and Reformation/Renaissance et Réforme* 12 (1988): 65–84; Rudolf M. Dekker and Lotte C. Van de Pol, *The Tradition of Female Transvestism in Early Modern Europe* (New York: St. Martin's, 1989); Marjorie Garber, *Vested Interests: Cross-Dressing and Cultural Anxiety* (New York and London: Routledge, 1992); Susan Frye, "The Myth of Elizabeth I at Tilbury," *Sixteenth-Century Journal* 23 (1992): 95–114; —, *Elizabeth I: The Competition for Representation* (Oxford: Oxford University Press, 1993); Stephen Orgel, *Impersonations: The Performance of Gender in Shakespeare's England* (Cambridge: Cambridge University Press, 1996); Ann Rosalind Jones and Peter Stallybrass, *Renaissance Clothing and the Materials of Memory* (Cambridge and New York: Cambridge University Press, 2000).

Come then, you masculine-women, for you are my subject, you that have made Admiration an ass, and fooled him with a deformity never before dreamed of, that have made yourselves stranger things than ever Noah's ark unladed, or Nile engendered; whom to name, he that named all things might study an age to give you a right attribute; whose like are not found in any antiquarian's study, in any sea-man's travel, nor in any painter's cunning; you that are stranger than strangeness itself; whom wisemen wonder at, boys shout at, and goblins themselves start at; you that are the gilt dirt which embroiders playhouses, the painted statues which adorn caroches, and the perfumed carrion that bad men feed on in brothels: 'Tis of you I intreat, and of your monstrous deformity: you that have made your bodies like antic boscage, or *Crotesco* work, not half man, half woman; half fish, half flesh; half beast, half monster; but all odious, all devil, that have cast off the ornaments of your sexes to put on the garments of shame; that have laid by the bashfulness of your natures to gather the impudence of harlots; that have buried silence to revive slander; that are all things but that which you should be, and nothing less than friends to virtue and goodness; that have made the foundation of your highest detested work from the lowest despised creatures that record can give testimony of: the one cut from the commonwealth at the gallows; the other is well known. From the first you got the false armory of yellow starch (for to wear yellow on white, or white upon yellow, is by the rules of heraldry baseness, bastardy, and indignity); the folly of imitation, the deceitfulness of flattery, and the grossest baseness of all baseness, to do whatsoever a greater power will command you. From the other, you have taken the monstrousness of your deformity in apparel, exchanging the modest attire of the comely hood, *caul*, coif, handsome dress or kerchief, to the cloudy ruffianly broadbrimmed hat and wanton feather, the modest upper parts of a concealing straight gown to the loose lascivious open embracement of a French doublet, being all unbuttoned to entice, all of one shape to hide deformity, and extreme short waisted to give a most easy way to every luxurious action; the glory of a fair large hair to the shame of most ruffi-anly short locks; the side, thick-gathered, and close guarding *safeguards*, to the short, weak, thin, loose, and every hand-entertaining short *bases*; for needles, swords; for prayer books, *bawdy jigs*; for modest gestures, giant-like behaviours; and for women's modesty, all mimic and apish incivility. These are your founders, from these you took your copies, and (without amendment) with these you will come to perdition.

The modest comeliness in which they were? Why, did ever these mermaids, or rather mer-monsters, that were the carman's block, the Dutchman's feather *upse-van-musse*, the poor man's pate pouled by a treene dish, the French doublet trussed with points, to Mary Anbry's light nether skirts, the fool's Baudrick, and the devil's poniard. Did they ever know comeliness, or modesty? Fie, no, they never walked in those paths, for these at the best are sure but rags of gentry torn from better pieces for their foul stains, or else the adulterate branches of rich stocks that, taking too much sap from the root, are cut away and employed in base uses; or, if not so, they are the stinking vapours drawn from dunghills which, nourished in the higher regions of the air, become meteors and false fires blazing and flashing therein, and amazing men's minds with their strange propor-tions until, the substance of their pride being spent, they drop down again to the place from whence they came, and there rot and consume unpitied, and unremembered.

And questionless it is true that such were the first beginners of these last deformi-ties, for from any purer blood would have issued a purer birth; there would have been some spark of virtue, some excuse for imitation; but this deformity has no agreement with goodness, nor no difference against the weakest reason: it is all base, all barbarous. Base, in respect it offends man in the example, and God in the most unnatural use; bar-barous, in that it is exorbitant from nature, and an antithesis to kind, going astray (with ill-favored affectation) both in attire, in speech, in manners, and (it is to be feared) in the whole courses and stories of their actions. What can be more barbarous than, with the gloss of mumming art, to disguise the beauty of their creations? To mould their bodies to every deformed fashion, their tongues to vile and horrible profanations, and their hands to ruffianly and uncivil actions; to have their gestures as piebald and as mot-ley various as their disguises, their souls fuller of infirmities than a horse or prostitute, and their minds languishing in those infirmities. If this be not barbarous, make the rude Scithian, the untamed Moore, the naked Indian, or the wild Irish, lords and rulers of well-governed cities.

GEORGE SANDYS (1578–1644)

From *Ovid's Metamorphosis Englished* (1626)

The Renaissance poet George Sandys, one of the first English translators of Ovid's *Metamorphoses*, was educated at St. Mary Hall, Oxford, and later traveled in Italy, Turkey, Egypt, and Palestine. He spent five years in North America in the 1620s as treasurer to the Virginia Company. In addition to his Ovid, he is remembered today for a *Paraphrase upon the Psalmes* (1636) and a verse translation of Grotius's *Christ's Passion, A Tragedy* (1640).

Rediscovered by the West in the Middle Ages and much translated over the next few centuries, Ovid's *Metamorphoses*, a compendium of Greek and Roman myths about shape-shifting gods and goddesses, played an extraordinarily influential role in the imaginative rediscovery of homosexuality in early modern Europe. The poem is full of episodes involving real or feigned same-sex desires. In the well-known story of Zeus and Ganymede (10.147–69), for example, the god Zeus, infatuated with the lovely mortal boy Ganymede, assumes the shape of an eagle in order to snatch Ganymede up to Olympus to serve as his cupbearer. In the episode of Artemis and Callisto (2.399–538), Zeus disguises himself as the goddess Artemis in order to woo Artemis's beloved maiden attendant, Callisto. And in the story of Iphis and Ianthe (9.668–799), presented in Sandys's translation below, Iphis, who has been raised secretly as a boy to protect her from the wrath of her father, falls passionately in love with the beautiful Ianthe. Even as Iphis bemoans the "pious fraud" that renders her love for Ianthe "foolish" ("No cow a cow, no mare a mare pursues") the goddess Isis intervenes, changing Iphis into a real boy so that the two can marry and consummate their love.

Like Sappho's poetic fragments, Plato's *Symposium*, Juvenal's *Sixth Satire*, and various other rediscovered relics of classical antiquity, Ovid's tales of irregular love, revived by Sandys and others, prompted a revitalization of the homosexual theme for the first time in centuries. Granted, homosexual desire is inevitably presented as something to be transmuted or exorcized—primordially through a comic deus ex machina. But in the process of "appearing in order to disappear" it also gains an inaugural space for itself in the collective imagination. The rich history of homoerotic literary fantasy since the Renaissance bespeaks the fructive power of the Ovidian cognitive model.

FURTHER READING: George Sandys, *Ovid's Metamorphosis Englished* (London, 1626); Lee T. Pearcy, *The Mediated Man: English Translations of Ovid 1560–1700* (Hamden, Conn.: Archon, 1984); Deborah Rubin, *Ovid's Metamorphosis Englished: George Sandys as Translator and Mythographer* (New York: Garland, 1985).

The fame of this so wonderful a fate
Had fill'd *Crete's* hundred Cities; if of late
The change of *Iphis*, generally known,
Had not produc'd a wonder of their own.
For *Phaestus*, near to *Gnossus*, fostered
One, *Lygdus*, of unnoted parents bred:
However, free. Nor did his wealth exceed
His parentage: yet both in word and deed
Sincerely just, and of a blameless life.
Who thus bespake his now down-lying wife:
"Two things I wish: that you your belly lay
With little pain; and that it prove a boy.
A daughter is too chargeable, and we
Too poor to match her. If a girl it be,
I charge, what I abhor (o Piety
Forgive me!) that, as soon as born, it die."
This having utter'd; the Commanded wept
And the Commander; tears no measure kept.
Yet *Telethusa* still with fruitless prayer,
Desires he would not in the Gods despair.
But he too constant. Now her time was come,
And the ripe burden vext her heavy womb:
When *Inachis*, with all her sacred band;
In dead of night, o'er stood, or seem'd to stand
Besides her bed. Her brows a crown adorns,
With ears of shining corn, and *Cynthian* horns.
Barking *Anubis*, and *Bubastis* bright,
Black *Apis* spotted variously with white,
He whose mouth-sealing finger silence taught,
Timbrels, *Osiris* never enough sought,
And foreign serpents, whose dire touch constrain
A deadly slumber, consummate her train.
Then (as awake, and seeing) the Divine
Thus said: "O *Telethusa*, One of mine;

Reject these cares, thy husband disobey:
And when *Lucina* shall thy belly lay,
Foster what ere it be. A Deity
Auxiliary to Distress am I;
Ready to help, and easily implor'd:
Nor shall it grieve thee that thou hast ador'd
Ungrateful *Isis*." This admonished,
She leaves the room. When, rising in her bed,
Her hands to Heaven glad *Telethusa* threw:
And humbly prays her vision may prove true.
Increasing throes at length a girl disclos'd,
Both by the father and the world suppos'd
To be a boy; so closely hid: and known
But to the Mother, and the nurse alone.
He pays his vows, and of his Father's name
It *Iphis* calls; which much rejoic'd the dame,
To both sex common; nor deceives thereby:
Who still with pious fraud conceals her lie.
A boy in show; whose looks should you assign
To boy or girl, love would in either shine.
At thirteen years her Father her affi'd
To yellow-tressed *Ianthe*: she the pride
Of *Phaestian* virgins for unequal'd fair:
Telestes' daughter, and his only heir,
Like young, like beautiful, together bred,
Inform'd alike, alike accomplish'd:
Like darts at once their simple bosoms strike;
Alike their wounds; their hopes, o far unlike!
The day they expect. *Ianthe* thought time ran
Too slow; and takes her *Iphis* for a man.
Poor *Iphis* loves, despairs; despair ejects
Far fiercer flames: a maid, a maid affects.
    "What will become of me" (she weeping said)
"Whom new, unknown, prodigious loves invade!
If pitiful, the Gods should have destroy'd:
Or else have given what might have been enjoy'd.
No Cow a Cow, no Mare a Mare pursues:
But Harts their gentle Hinds, and Rams their Ewes:
So Birds together pair. Of all that move,
No Female suffers for a Female love.
O would I had no being! Yet, that all
Abhorr'd by Nature should in *Crete* befall;

Sol's lust-incensed daughter lov'd a Bull:
They male and female. Mine, o far more full
Of uncouth fury! for she pleas'd her blood;
And stood his error in a Cow of wood:
She, to deceive, had an adulterer.
Should all the world their daring wits confer:
Should *Daedalus* his waxen wings renew,
And hither fly; what could his cunning do!
Can art convert a virgin to a boy?
Or fit *Ianthe* for a maiden's joy?
No, fix thy mind; compose thy vast desires:
O quench these ill-advis'd and foolish fires!
Or know thy self, or Self-deceit accuse:
What may be, seek; and love as virgins use.
Hope wings Desire; hope *Cupid*'s flight sustains;
Thy Sex thee hope denies. No watch restrains
Our dear embrace, nor husband's jealousies,
Nor rigorous Sires; nor she her self denies:
Yet not to be enjoy'd. Nor canst thou be
Happy in her; though men and Gods agree!
Now also all to my desires accord:
What they can give, the easy Gods afford;
What me, my father, hers, her self, would please,
Displeaseth Nature; stronger than all these.
She, she forbids. That day begins to shine;
Long wish'd! wherein *Ianthe* must be mine:
And yet not mine. Of mortals most accurst!
I starve at feasts, and in the river thirst.
Juno, o *Hymen*, wherefore are you come?
We both are Brides: but where is the Bridegroom?"
    Here ended. Nor less burns the other Maid;
Who, *Hymen*, for thy swift appearance pray'd.
Yet *Telethusa* fears what thou affects;
Protracting time: oft want of health objects;
Ill-boding dreams, and auguries oft feigns:
But now no colour for excuse remains.
Their nuptial rites, put off with such delay;
Were to be solemniz'd the following day.
When she unbinds, hers, and her daughter's hair;
And holding by the Altar form'd this prayer:
"*Isis*; who *Paraetonium*, *Pharoah*'s isle,
Smooth *Mareotis*, and seven-channel'd *Nile*,

Cheer'st with thy presence: thy poor suppliants hear:
O help in these extremes, and cure our fear!
Thee Goddess, thee of old; these ensigns, I
Have seen, and know: thy lamps, attendancy,
And sounding Timbrels: and have thee obey'd.
To me, impunity; life, to this maid,
Thy saving counsel gave: to both renew
Thy timely pity." Tears her words pursue.
The Goddess shakes her Altar; when the gate
Shook on the hinges: horns that imitate
The waxing Moon's, through all the Temple flung
A sacred splendor: noiseful Timbrels rung.
The Mother, glad of this successful sign,
Though not secure, returns from *Isis'* shrine.
Whom *Iphis* follows with a larger pace
Than usual; nor had so white a face.
Her strength augments; her look more bold appears;
Her short'ning curls scarce hang beneath her ears;
More courage hath, than, when a wench, she had:
For thou, of late a Wench, art now a Lad.
Gifts to the temple bear, and *Io* sing!
Sing Joy! Their gifts they to the Temple bring;
And add a title; in one verse display'd:
What *Iphis* vow'd a Wench, A Boy he pay'd.
The Morning Night dismasks with welcome flame:
When *Juno*, *Venus*, and free *Hymen* came
To grace their marriage; who, with gifts divine,
Iphis the Boy, to his *Ianthe* join.

JOHN DONNE (1572–1631)

"Sapho to Philaenis" (1633)

John Donne, greatest of the so-called metaphysical English poets, was the son of
Roman Catholic parents and educated at Oxford and Cambridge. He renounced his
Catholicism in the 1590s and sailed with Essex on two expeditions to Cadiz and the
Azores in 1596 and 1597. Upon returning, he moved in high circles; his first poems,
the *Satires* and *Elegies*, on religious and political themes, were circulated at court in the
1590s. Between 1598 and 1600 Donne served as secretary to Sir Thomas Egerton,
Keeper of the Great Seal, but fell into disgrace in 1601 after secretly marrying Anne
More, the sixteen-year-old niece of Egerton's wife. Many of his most celebrated love
poems—"The Ecstasy," "A Valediction: Forbidding Mourning," "The Sun Rising,"
and "The Flea"—appear to have been written around this time. These were followed
by the two *Anniversaries* (*The Anatomy of the World* [1611] and *The Progress of the Soul*
[1612]), and later, by a series of sacred sonnets. In 1615, having regained royal patronage, Donne took holy orders, becoming reader in divinity at Lincoln's Inn (1619) and
dean of St. Paul's (1621). His major religious prose work, the *Devotions*, was published
in 1624. In the last part of his life Donne wrote a set of extraordinary sermons, now
considered masterpieces of English baroque prose style. His poems, uncollected in his
lifetime, were published in 1633.

It is not known when Donne composed "Sapho to Philaenis." Loosely modeled on
Ovid's *Heroides*—a series of imaginary letters between great lovers of antiquity—the
poem has been described as "the first female homosexual love poem in English." The
speaker is the ancient Greek poet Sappho; her addressee, Philaenis, a beautiful maiden
she longs to seduce. Although Donne borrows the name Philaenis, meaning "female
friend," from one of the most scabrous antilesbian satires of antiquity—epigram 67 of
book 7 of Martial's *Epigrams*—his handling of the amorous situation is curiously sympathetic. Not only does he try to imagine Sappho's passion from the inside ("Likeness
begets such strange self-flattery, / That touching myself, all seems done to thee"), he
pointedly modifies Ovid's heterosexualized version of her myth. In Ovid, Sappho
renounces her female lovers when she falls in love with the handsome boatman Phaon.
After Phaon spurns her, she commits suicide by jumping off a cliff. By contrast, in
Donne, Sappho's love for Philaenis *supplants* that for "Phao"—

> Such was my Phao awhile, but shall be never,
> As thou, wast, art, and, oh, maist be ever.

—and any suicidal urges are forgotten. Critics remain divided over how deep this revisionary "sapphophilia" goes—and indeed what Donne, in assuming the Sapphic persona, meant to convey about his own poetic art—but in rewriting Sappho's tragic fate he nonetheless intervened powerfully and distinctively in the evolving literary history of the lesbian topos.

FURTHER READING: John Donne, *The Poems of John Donne*, ed. Herbert J. C. Grierson, 2 vols. (Oxford: Clarendon, 1912); —, *The Complete English Poems of John Donne*, ed. A. J. Smith (New York: St. Martin's, 1974); David M. Robinson, *Sappho and Her Influence* (Boston: Marshall Jones, 1924); Barbara Correll, "Symbolic Economies and Zero-Sum Erotica: Donne's 'Sapho to Philaenis,'" *ELH: Journal of English Literary History* 62 (1982): 487–507; James Holstun, "'Will You Rent Our Ancient Love Asunder?': Lesbian Elegy in Donne, Marvell, and Milton," *ELH: Journal of English Literary History* 54 (1987): 835–67; Joan DeJean, *Fictions of Sappho: 1546–1937* (Chicago and London: University of Chicago Press, 1989); Elizabeth Harvey, *Ventriloquized Voices: Feminist Theory and English Renaissance Texts* (New York and London: Routledge, 1992); Janel Mueller, "Lesbian Erotics: The Utopian Trope of Donne's 'Sapho to Philaenis,'" in Claude J. Summers, ed., *Homosexuality in Renaissance and Enlightenment England* (New York: Harrington Park, 1992); Stella P. Revard, "The Sapphic Voice in Donne's 'Sapho to Philaenis,'" in Claude J. Summers and Ted-Larry Pebworth, eds., *Renaissance Discourses of Desire* (Columbia: University of Missouri Press, 1993); Paula Blank, "Comparing Sapho to Philaenis: John Donne's 'Homopoetics,'" *PMLA* 110 (1995): 358–68; Peter Jay and Caroline Lewis, eds., *Sappho Through English Poetry* (London: Anvil, 1996); Ellen Greene, ed., *Re-Reading Sappho: Reception and Transmission* (Berkeley: University of California Press, 1997); Joan McIntosh Snyder, *Lesbian Desire in the Lyrics of Sappho* (New York: Columbia University Press, 1997); Elizabeth S. Wahl, *Invisible Relations: Representations of Female Intimacy in the Age of Enlightenment* (Stanford: Stanford University Press, 1998); Margaret Reynolds, *The Sappho Companion* (New York: Palgrave, 2000); Harriette Andreadis, *Sappho in Early Modern England: Female Same-Sex Literary Erotics* (Chicago: University of Chicago Press, 2001).

> Where is that holy fire, which *Verse* is said
> To have? is that inchanting force decai'd?
> *Verse* that drawes *Natures* workes, from *Natures* law,
> Thee, her best worke, to her worke cannot draw.

Have my teares quench'd my old *Poetique* fire;
  Why quench'd they not as well, that of *desire?*
Thoughts, my mindes creatures, often are with thee,
  But I, their maker, want their libertie.
Onely thine image, in my heart, doth sit,
  But that is waxe, and fires environ it.
My fires have driven, thine have drawne it hence;
  And I am rob'd of *Picture*, *Heart*, and *Sense.*
Dwells with me still mine irksome *Memory,*
  Which, both to keepe, and lose, grieves equally.
That tells me'how faire thou art: Thou are so faire,
  As *gods*, when *gods* to thee I doe compare,
Are grac'd thereby; And to make blinde men see,
  What things *gods* are, I say they'are like to thee.
For, if we justly call each silly *man*
  A *litle world*, What shall we call thee than?
Thou are not soft, and cleare, and strait, and faire,
  As *Down*, as *Stars*, *Cedars*, and *Lillies* are,
But thy right hand, and cheek, and eye, only
  Are like thy other hand, and cheek, and eye.
Such was my *Phao* awhile, but shall be never,
  As thou, wast, art, and, oh, maist be ever.
Here lovers sweare in their *Idolatrie,*
  That I am such; but *Griefe* discolors me.
And yet I grieve the lesse, least *Griefe* remove
  My beauty, and make me'unworthy of thy love.
Plaies some soft boy with thee, oh there wants yet
  A mutuall feeling which should sweeten it.
His chinne, a thorny hairy unevennesse
  Doth threaten, and some daily change possesse.
Thy body is a naturall *Paradise,*
  In whose selfe, unmanur'd, all pleasure lies,
Nor needs *perfection*; why shouldst thou than
  Admit the tillage of a harsh rough man?
Men leave behinde them that which their sin showes,
  And are, as theeves trac'd, which rob when it snowes.
But of our dallyance no more signes there are,
  Then *fishes* leave in streames, or *Birds* in aire.
And betweene us all sweetnesse may be had;
  All, all that *Nature* yields, or *Art* can adde.
My two lips, eyes, thighs, differ from thy two,
  But so, as thine from one another doe;

And, oh, no more; the likenesse being such,
  Why should they not alike in all parts touch?
Hand to strange hand, lippe to lippe none denies;
  Why should they brest to brest, or thighs to thighs?
Likenesse begets such strange selfe flatterie,
  That touching my selfe, all seemes done to thee.
My selfe I embrace, and mine owne hands I kisse,
  And amorously thanke my selfe for this.
Me, in my glasse, I call thee; But alas,
  When I would kisse, teares dimme mine *eyes*, and *glasse*.
O cure this loving madnesse, and restore
  Me to mee; thee, my *half*, my *all*, my *more*.
So may thy cheekes red outweare scarlet dye,
  And their white, whitenesse of the *Galaxy*,
So may thy mighty, amazing beauty move
  Envy in all *women*, and in all *men*, *love*,
And so be *change*, and *sicknesse*, farre from thee,
  As thou by comming neere, keep'st them from me.

"T. W."

"To Mr. J.D." (c. 1633)

"To Mr. J.D. [John Donne]," by the unidentified "T.W.," was first printed in the 1633 edition of Donne's poems. Donne wrote several verse letters to "Mr. T.W."; the present poem would appear to be one of T.W.'s replies. The poem is an elaborate paean to Donne's poetic gifts, which T.W. represents, modestly, as far superior to his own. The only "heat" to be found in his own verses, T.W. confesses, is that which results from Donne's "liberal beams" falling upon them. As the poem proceeds, the imagery of male poetic interchange becomes bizarrely sapphic. Donne is figured as a lesbian lover who gets a "Song" upon T.W. by coupling with T.W.'s "Muse" in an act of "chaste and mystic tribadery." The reference to Bassa ("Bassa's adultery no fruit did leave") heightens the element of kink: in Martial's *Epigrams* (1.40) Bassa is a lustful Roman matron who cuckolds her husband with young girls:

> Oh, horrible! You dare two cunts unite!
> > To play the man, unnatural dreams you nourish!
> Only the Sphinx could read this riddle right:
> > With males renounced, adultery can flourish.

FURTHER READING: John Donne, *The Satires, Epigrams and Verse Letters*, ed. W. Milgate (Oxford: Clarendon, 1967); Bruce R. Smith, *Homosexual Desire in Renaissance England: A Cultural Poetics* (Chicago and London: University of Chicago Press, 1991); Jonathan Goldberg, *Sodometries: Renaissance Texts, Modern Sexualities* (Stanford: Stanford University Press, 1992); George Klawitter, "Verse Letters to T.W. from John Donne, 'By You My Love Is Sent,'" in Claude J. Summers, ed., *Homosexuality in Renaissance and Enlightenment England: Literary Representations in Historical Context* (New York: Harrington Park, 1992), pp. 85–102; Alan Bray, "Homosexuality and the Signs of Male Friendship in Elizabethan England," in Jonathan Goldberg, ed. *Queering the Renaissance* (Durham and London: Duke University Press, 1994), pp. 40–61; —, *Homosexuality in Renaissance England*, 2d ed. (New York: Columbia University Press,

1995); Harriette Andreadis, *Sappho in Early Modern England: Female Same-Sex Erotics, 1550–1714* (Chicago: University of Chicago Press, 2001).

> Thou sendest me prose and rhymes, I send for those
> Lines, which being neither, seem nor verse or prose.
> They're lame and harsh, and have no heat at all
> But what thy liberal beams on them let fall.
> The nimble fire which in thy brain doth dwell
> Is it that fire of heaven or that of hell?
> It doth beget and comfort like heaven's eye
> And like hell's fire it burns eternally.
> And those whom in thy fury and judgment
> Thy verse shall scourge, like hell it will torment.
> Have mercy on me and my sinful Muse,
> Which rubbed and tickled with thine, could not choose
> But spend some of her pith and yield to be
> One in that chaste and mystic tribadry.
> Bassa's adultery no fruit did leave,
> Nor theirs which their swollen thighs did nimbly weave,
> And with new arms and mouths embrace and kiss
> Though they had issue was not like to this.
> Thy Muse, O strange and holy Lechery,
> Being a Maid still, got this Song on me.

BEN JONSON (1572–1637)

"Epigram on the Court Pucelle" (1640)

The poet and playwright Ben Jonson, stepson to a bricklayer, was born in London and educated at Westminster School. In the early 1590s he worked in his stepfather's business and also saw action as a soldier in Flanders. In 1597 he joined Henslowe's theater company as an actor-playwright. His first play, *Every Man in His Humour*, was produced in 1598 with his colleague William Shakespeare in the cast. Then followed a series of successful comedies—*Every Man Out of His Humour* (1599), *Cynthia's Revels* (1600), *The Poetaster* (1601), *Volpone* (1606), *Epicoene, or the Silent Woman* (1609), *The Alchemist* (1610), *Bartholomew Fair* (1614), and *The Devil is an Ass* (1616). His tragedy *Sejanus*, adapted from classical models, was first staged at the Globe Theater in 1603. Between 1605 and 1630 Jonson produced a series of lavish court masques in collaboration with the architect Inigo Jones. He was granted a royal pension in 1616. His last masques—produced without Jones, with whom he quarreled—were performed in 1633–34. He died in 1637, much fêted by his fellow poets, and was buried in Westminster Abbey.

The short satire "An Epigram on the Court Pucelle" first appeared in the collection of poems known as *The Underwood*, published posthumously in the 1640 folio of Jonson's works. The poem is thought to be an attack on Cecilia Bulstrode (1584–1609), a young learned lady at the court of James I. Of particular interest in the poem is Jonson's use of the term *tribade*. Derived from the Greek verb for "to rub," the word appears prominently in classical Roman satire, where it denotes a woman who engages in sexual acts with another woman. Jonson's would appear to be one of its first usages in English. (He is also, interestingly, one of the first English writers to use its Latin equivalent—*fricatrice*—in *Volpone* 4.2.53–57.) By presenting Bulstrode as lascivious tribade "forcing" (or raping) her unwilling muse, Jonson makes a misogynistic linkage that will become common—if not automatic—in later seventeenth- and eighteenth-century lampoons on learned women. Just as Bulstrode subverts male intellectual authority, so is she presumed to subvert—monstrously—male sexual prerogatives as well.

FURTHER READING: Ben Jonson, *The Complete Poems*, ed. George Parfitt (New Haven: Yale University Press, 1982); Annabel Patterson, "Lyric and Society in Jonson's *Underwood*," in Chavia Hosek and Patricia Parker, eds., *Lyric Poetry: Beyond New Criticism* (Ithaca, N.Y.: Cornell University Press, 1985), pp. 148–63; Jongsook Lee, "Who is Cecilia, What Was She?: Cecilia Bulstrode and Jonson's Epideictics," *Journal of English and Germanic Philology* 85 (1986): 20–34; David Riggs, *Ben Jonson* (Cambridge: Harvard University Press, 1989); Valerie Traub, "The (In)significance of Lesbian Desire in Early Modern England," in Susan Zimmerman, ed., *Erotic Politics: Desire on the Renaissance Stage* (London and New York: Routledge, 1992); Elizabeth S. Wahl, *Invisible Relations: Representations of Female Intimacy in the Age of Enlightenment* (Stanford: Stanford University Press, 1998).

Does the court pucelle then so censure me,
  And thinks I dare not her? Let the world see.
What though her chamber be the very pit
  Where fight the prime cocks of the game, for wit?
And that as any are struck, her breath creates
  New in their stead, out of the candidates?
What though with tribade lust she force a muse,
  And in an epicoene fury can write news
Equal with that which for the best news goes,
  As airy light, and as like wit as those?
What though she talk, and can at once with them
  Make state, religion, bawdry, all a theme?
And as lip-thirsty, in each word's expense,
  Doth labour with the phrase more than the sense?
What though she ride two mile on holidays
  To church, as others do to feasts and plays,
To show their 'tires, to view and to be viewed?
  What though she be with velvet gowns endued,
And spangled petticoats brought forth to eye,
  As new rewards of her old secrecy?
What though she hath won on trust, as many do,
  And that her truster fears her: must I too?
I never stood for any place: my wit
  Thinks itself nought, though she should value it.
I am no statesman, and much less divine;
  For bawdry, 'tis her language, and not mine.
Farthest I am from the idolatry
  To stuffs and laces: those my man can buy.

And trust her I would least, that hath foreswore
  In contract twice; what can she perjure more?
Indeed, her dressing some man might delight,
  Her face there's none can like by candle-light.
Not he that should the body have, for case
  To his poor instrument, now out of grace.
Shall I advise thee, pucelle? Steal away
  From court, while yet thy fame hath some small day;
The wits will leave you, if they once perceive
  You cling to lords, and lords, if them you leave
For sermoneers: of which now one, now other
  They say you weekly invite with fits of the mother,
And practise for a miracle; take heed
  This age would lend no faith to Darrel's deed:
Or if it would, the court is the worst place,
  Both for the mothers and the babes of grace;
For there the wicked in the chair of scorn
  Will call it a bastard, when a prophet's born.

EDMUND WALLER (1606–1687)

"On the Friendship Betwixt Two Ladies" (1645)

The English poet Edmund Waller, born into an aristocratic Buckinghamshire family, was educated at Eton and Cambridge and elected to Parliament in his teens. An ardent Royalist during the Civil War, he was banished to the Continent for several years after leading a quixotic plot to reclaim London for Charles I. Pardoned by Oliver Cromwell in 1651, he returned to England and was later reelected to Parliament, where he served for the rest of his life. He was twice married but cherished an unreciprocated passion for Lady Dorothea Sidney, who appears as "Saccharissa" in many of his love lyrics. Waller's major works include *Poems* (1645), *A Panegyric to My Lord Protector* (1655), *Instructions to a Painter* (1666), and *Of Divine Love* (1685). Dryden, Pope, and Johnson all admired his poetry greatly and credited him with perfecting the English heroic couplet. Many of his shorter poems have been set to music—most memorably, the exquisite "Go, Lovely Rose."

"On the Friendship Betwixt Two Ladies," a witty complaint-poem addressed to a pair of female sweethearts, was published in the *Poems* of 1645. Though Waller at one point chides his subjects for acting like "debtors" who do not "mean to pay"—they are enticing to men yet only have eyes for each other—the poem is notable for its (relative) lack of satiric venom. Indeed, in the final affirmation of the couple's passion, Waller seems to anticipate some of the eulogistic female-friendship poems of the later seventeenth and eighteenth centuries.

FURTHER READING: Edmund Waller, *Poems, &c. Written upon Several Occasions, and to Several Persons* (London, 1645); Warren L. Chernaik, *The Poetry of Limitation: A Study of Edmund Waller* (New Haven: Yale University Press, 1968); Jack Glenn Gilbert, *Edmund Waller* (Boston: Twayne, 1979); A. B. Chambers, *Andrew Marvell and Edmund Waller* (University Park: Pennsylvania State University Press, 1991).

Tell me, lovely, loving pair!
Why so kind, and so severe?
Why so careless of our care,
Only to yourselves so dear?

By this cunning change of hearts,
You the power of love control;
While the boy's deluded darts
Can arrive at neither soul.

For in vain to either breast
Still beguiled love does come,
Where he finds a foreign guest,
Neither of your hearts at home.

Debtors thus with like design,
When they never mean to pay,
That they may the law decline,
To some friend make all away.

Not the silver doves that fly,
Yoked in Cytherea's car;
Not the wings that lift so high,
And convey her son so far;

Are so lovely, sweet, and fair,
Or do more ennoble love;
Are so choicely matched a pair,
Or with more consent do move.

FRANÇOIS DE MAYNARD (1582–1646)

"Tribades, or Lesbia" (1646)

The French poet and politician François de Maynard, sometimes known as Le Président Maynard, was born in Toulouse in 1582 and served in his early years as secretary to Marguerite de Valois. Between 1611 and 1627 he administered the fort of Aurillac in the Auvergne, a labor for which he received the title of "Président." In 1634 he became one of the founding members of the Académie Française; in 1635 he traveled to Rome as secretary to the Comte de Noailles. Disgraced by Richelieu in 1636, he was forced into retirement and did not receive another court appointment until Richelieu's death, when the minister Séguier named him Privy Councillor. His collected poems appeared in 1646; Maynard himself died the same year. Some "priapic" verses attributed to him surfaced in the nineteenth century and were published in 1864.

In "Tribades, or Lesbia," a satiric attack on an unnamed woman who uses her finger as a penis, Maynard aims at calumny and achieves it. The flippantly obscene idiom is borrowed from the Roman poets Martial, Juvenal, and Catullus. At the same time, however, the poem shows traces of a distinctly modern male neurosis: an anxious phallocentrism akin to that sometimes found—three hundred years hence—in the lesbian-themed writings of Hemingway, Lawrence, and Wyndham Lewis.

FURTHER READING: François de Maynard, *Oeuvres* (Paris, 1646); —, *Priapées*, ed. Jules Gay (Geneva, 1864); *Les Lettres de François de Maynard, Président au Présidial d'Aurillac, Membre de l'Académie Française*, ed. Paul Durand-Lapie (Paris: Imprimerie nationale, 1901); —, *Des Oeuvres poétiques* (Paris: Sansot, 1909); Louis Perceau, ed., *Le Cabinet secret du Parnasse: Recueil de poésies libres, rares ou peu connues, pour servir de Supplément aux Oeuvres dites complètes des poètes français*, 4 vols. (Paris: Au Cabinet du Livres, 1935); Yves Giraud, "Aspects de l'epigramme chez Maynard," *Maynard et son temps* (Toulouse: Assoc. des Pubs. de l'Université de Toulouse—Le Mirail, 1976); Petra Strien, "Aspects de la satire chez Maynard," *Cahiers Maynard* 10 (1980): 43–51.

Your gorgeous eyes are sorely wrecked
& migraine's not the wind that's bitten
But rather Clymena's fierce delect
And your fingers, better fitting
In an open fly than a glove or mitten.

If your finger could shoot its wad
With all it knows to do to date
Sweet Phyllis, there's no debate
That readily it could masquerade
For something much too crude to name.

To have, as is your pride,
A hand so white and clean
How in hell do you keep it preened
When the tub in which you slide
It has such strange soap, I mean?

ANDREW MARVELL (1621–1678)

From *Upon Appleton House* (1650)

Like his coevals Milton and Waller, the English metaphysical poet Andrew Marvell was as much politician as writer. Born near Hull and educated at Cambridge and abroad, he was a vehement supporter of Oliver Cromwell during the English Civil War. His first important poem was the laudatory *Horatian Ode upon Cromwell's Return from Ireland* (1650). In 1650 Marvell became the tutor of the daughter of Lord Fairfax, at Nun Appleton in Yorkshire, where he began composing verses on pastoral and personal themes. Some of his most famous works—"The Garden," "The Hill and Grove at Billborow," "To His Coy Mistress," "Damon the Mower," and his lavish paean to his patron Fairfax's estate, "Upon Appleton House"—date from this period. From 1653 to 1657 he tutored Cromwell's nephew William Dutton; and in 1657 assisted Milton in the Latin secretaryship to the council. "The Bermudas," "The Anniversaries," and "On the Death of Oliver Cromwell" were written in these years. In 1659 Marvell was elected to Parliament, where he gained a reputation as a fearless critic of Charles II. Marvell's contemporaries saw him as primarily as a satirist and opposition pamphleteer; only in the twentieth century have his outstanding—if idiosyncratic—gifts as a lyric poet come fully into view.

The celebrated country-house poem "Upon Appleton House" contains an important sapphic episode. As part of his poetical history of the Fairfax family seat, Marvell relates the story of Isabella Thwaites, a wealthy orphan who married Sir William Fairfax, an ancestor of Marvell's patron, in 1518. Thwaites had been raised by Cistercian nuns at a convent near Nun Appleton, and upon her engagement to Sir William, the convent prioress attempted to obstruct the marriage by shutting Thwaites up inside the convent walls. The young Fairfax rescued his fiancée, however, and after the dissolution of the monasteries during the Reformation the nunnery was absorbed into the Fairfax family holdings. Marvell makes of this episode a kind of potted patriarchal (and Protestant) foundation myth, in which the "subtle nuns" are cast as corrupt would-be seductresses and Sir William as Thwaites's noble heterosexual liberator. No reader of Marvell's day would have missed the sexual insinuation in the nuns' coy pleas (ll. 185–92) or the meaning of the line in which "vice" is described as infecting the convent's "very wall" (l. 216). While the poet stages the encounter between Thwaites and the nuns as social comedy—the fey humor is typically Marvellian—the poem as whole nonetheless deserves to be considered part of that influential corpus of "homoeroticized" anticlerical writing extending from Chaucer (with his sodomitical Pardoner) to Diderot and the Marquis de Sade.

FURTHER READING: Andrew Marvell, *The Poems and Letters of Andrew Marvell*, ed. H. M. Margoliouth, 2 vols. (Oxford: Clarendon, 1963); Lee Erickson, "Marvell's *Upon Appleton House* and the Fairfax Family," *English Literary Renaissance* 9 (1979): 158–68; Patsy Griffin, "'Twas No Religious House till Now': Marvell's *Upon Appleton House*," *Studies in English Literature* 28 (1988): 61–76; James Holstun, " 'Will You Rent Our Ancient Love Asunder?': Lesbian Elegy in Donne, Marvell, and Milton," *ELH: Journal of English Literary History* 54 (1987): 835–67; and Emma Donoghue, *Passions Between Women: British Lesbian Culture 1668–1801* (London: Scarlet, 1993).

> While with slow eyes we these survey,
> And on each pleasant footstep stay,
> We opportunely may relate
> The progress of this house's fate.
> A nunnery first gave it birth
> (For virgin buildings oft brought forth);
> And all that neighbor-ruin shows
> The quarries whence this dwelling rose.
>
> Near to this gloomy cloister's gates
> There dwelt the blooming virgin Thwaites;
> Fair beyond measure, and an heir
> Which might deformity make fair.
> And oft she spent the summer suns
> Discoursing with the subtle nuns;
> Whence in these words one to her weaved
> (As 'twere by chance) thoughts long conceived.
>
> "Within this holy leisure we
> Live innocently as you see.
> These walls restrain the world without,
> But hedge our liberty about:
> These bars inclose that wider den

Of those wild creatures, callèd men;
The cloister outward shuts its gates,
And, from us, locks on them the grates.

"Here we, in shining armor white,
Like virgin Amazons do fight:
And our chaste lamps we hourly trim,
Lest the great Bridegroom find them dim.
Our orient breaths perfumèd are
With incense of incessant prayer:
And holy-water of our tears
Most strangely our complexion clears:

"Not tears of grief; but such as those
With which calm pleasure overflows;
Or pity, when we look on you
That live without this happy vow.
How should we grieve that must be seen
Each one a Spouse, and each a Queen;
And can in Heaven hence behold
Our brighter robes and crowns of gold?

"When we have prayèd all our beads,
Someone the holy legend reads;
While all the rest with needles paint
The face and graces of the saint.
But what the linen can't receive
They in their lives do interweave;
This work the saints best represents;
That serves for altar's ornaments.

"But much it to our work would add
If here your hand, your face we had.
By it we would Our Lady touch;
Yet thus She you resembles much.
Some of your features, as we sewed,
Through every shrine should be bestowed:
And in one beauty we would take
Enough a thousand saints to make.

"And (for I dare not quench the fire
That me does for your good inspire)

'Twere sacrilege a man t' admit
To holy things, for Heaven fit.
I see the angels in a crown
On you the lilies show'ring down;
And round about you glory breaks,
That something more than human speaks.

"All beauty, when at such a height,
Is so already consecrate.
Fairfax I know; and long ere this
Have marked the youth, and what he is.
But can he such a rival seem
For whom you Heav'n should disesteem?
Ah, no! and 'twould more honor prove
He your *devoto* were, than love.

"Here live belovèd, and obeyed,
Each one your sister, each your maid.
And, if our rule seem strictly penned,
The rule itself to you shall bend.
Our Abbess too, now far in age,
Doth your succession near presage.
How soft the yoke on us would lie,
Might such fair hands as yours it tie!

"Your voice, the sweetest of the choir,
Shall draw Heav'n nearer, raise us higher:
And your example, if our head,
Will soon us to perfection lead.
Those virtues to us all so dear,
Will straight grow sanctity when here:
And that, once sprung, increase so fast
Till miracles it work at last.

"Nor is our order yet so nice,
Delight to banish as a vice.
Here pleasure piety doth meet,
One perfecting the other sweet;
So through the mortal fruit we boil
The sugar's uncorrupting oil;
And that which perished while we pull,
Is thus preservèd clear and full.

"For such indeed are all our arts;
Still handling Nature's finest parts.
Flowers dress the altars; for the clothes,
The sea-born amber we compose;
Balms for the grieved we draw; and pastes
We mold, as baits for curious tastes.
What need is here of man? unless
These as sweet sins we should confess.

"Each night among us to your side
Appoint a fresh and virgin bride,
Whom if Our Lord at midnight find,
Yet neither should be left behind;
Where you may lie as chaste in bed,
As pearls together billeted;
All night embracing arm in arm,
Like crystal pure in cotton warm.

"But what is this to all the store
Of joys you see, and may make more!
Try but a while, if you be wise;
The trial neither costs, nor ties."
Now, Fairfax, seek her promised faith!
Religion that dispensèd hath;
Which she henceforward does begin:
The nun's smooth tongue has sucked her in.

Oft, though he knew it was in vain,
Yet would he valiantly complain:
"Is this that sanctity so great,
An art by which you finelier cheat?
Hypocrite witches, hence *avant*,
Who though in prison yet enchant!
Death only can such thieves make fast,
As rob though in the dungeon cast.

"Were there but, when this house was made,
One stone that a just hand had laid,
It must have fall'n upon her head
Who first thee from thy faith misled.
And yet, how well soever meant,
With them 'twould soon grow fraudulent:

For like themselves they alter all,
And vice infects the very wall.

"But sure those buildings last not long,
Founded by folly, kept by wrong.
I know what fruit their gardens yield,
When they it think by night concealed.
Fly from their vices. 'Tis thy state,
Not thee, that they would consecrate.
Fly from their ruin. How I fear
Though guiltless lest thou perish there!"

What should he do? He would respect
Religion, but not right neglect;
For first religion taught him right,
And dazzled not but cleared his sight.
Sometimes resolved his sword he draws,
But reverenceth then the laws:
For Justice still that Courage led
First from a judge, then soldier bred.

Small honor would be in the storm.
The Court him grants the lawful form;
Which licensed either peace or force,
To hinder the unjust divorce.
Yet still the nuns his right debarred,
Standing upon their holy guard.
Ill-counseled women, do you know
Whom you resist, or what you do?

Is not this he whose offspring fierce
Shall fight through all the universe;
And with successive valor try
France, Poland, either Germany;
Till one, as long since prophesied,
His horse through conquered Britain ride?
Yet, against fate, his spouse they kept,
And the great race would intercept.

Some to the breach against their foes
Their wooden saints in vain oppose.
Another bolder stands at push

With their old holy-water brush.
While the disjointed Abbess threads
The jingling chain-shot of her beads.
But their loud'st cannon were their lungs;
And sharpest weapons were their tongues.

But, waving these aside like flies,
Young Fairfax through the wall does rise.
Then th' unfrequented vault appeared,
And superstitions vainly feared.
The relics false were set to view;
Only the jewels there were true—
But truly bright and holy Thwaites
That weeping at the altar waits.

But the glad youth away her bears
And to the nuns bequeaths her tears:
Who guiltily their prize bemoan,
Like gypsies that a child hath stol'n.
Thenceforth (as when th' enchantment ends
The castle vanishes or rends)
The wasting cloister with the rest
Was in one instant dispossessed.

DENIS SANGUIN DE SAINT-PAVIN (1595–1670)

"Two Beauties, Tender Lovers" (c. 1650)

The French libertine poet Saint-Pavin, holder of numerous court and ecclesiastical preferments during the reigns of Louis XIII and Louis XIV, was born to noble parents and educated by Jesuits. In his youth he served as clerk to the diocese of Paris; he was later chaplain to Louis XIV. A more secular cleric could scarcely be imagined. A professed atheist and frequenter of salons, he fathered an illegitimate child, pursued the famous courtesan Ninon de l'Enclos, wrote lascivious verses, and supported a number of mistresses over the years. Later in life he also won the nickname "Roi de Sodome" (King of Sodom) on account of alleged homosexual excesses. Some writers believe he underwent a religious conversion toward the end of his life, though little biographical evidence supports this view.

Saint-Pavin's more respectable poems were published after his death in collections in 1692 and 1759. The licentious verse did not see the light of day, however, until Paulin Paris edited the *Recueil complet des poésies de Saint-Pavin, comprenant toutes les pièces jusqu'à présent connues et un plus grand nombre de pièces inédites* in 1861. "Two Beauties, Tender Lovers" ("Deux belles s'ayment tendrement")—a waspish attack on a pair of sapphic lovers—was first published in the Paris volume.

FURTHER READING: Denis Sanguin de Saint-Pavin, *Recueil complet des poésies de Saint-Pavin, comprenant toutes les pièces jusqu'à présent connues et un plus grand nombre de pièces inédites*, ed. Paulin Paris (Paris, 1861); Louis Perceau, ed., *Le Cabinet secret du Parnasse: Recueil de poésies libres, rares ou peu connues, pour servir de Supplément aux Oeuvres dites complètes des poètes français*, vol. 4 (Paris: Au Cabinet du Livres, 1935); Elizabeth S. Wahl, *Invisible Relations: Representations of Female Intimacy in the Age of Enlightenment* (Stanford: Stanford University Press, 1998).

Two beauties, tender lovers,
One attends the other equally,
Equally wounded by the same
Affliction, suffering equally.

Uncomplaining in their torment
Both ceaselessly do sigh:
Now the one lover is mistress,
Now the mistress is lover.

Whatever they do for pleasure,
Their hearts are not content,
Wasting thus their daily treasure,

These Innocents, in self-abuse,
Seek pointlessly in their loving
Pleasures which to us they do refuse.

NICOLAS CHORIER (1612–1692)

From *Dialogues on the Arcana of Love and Venus by Luisa Sigea Toletana* (*Satyra Sotadica Arcanis Amoris et Veneris*) (1660–1678)

The seventeenth-century man of letters and pornographer extraordinaire Nicolas Chorier was born in Vienne near Lyon in 1612. He trained as a lawyer in his native town, married in 1642, and was later called to the bar in Grenoble in 1659. His wealth and respectable position did not keep him from committing various impudences, however: in 1661 he stole a collection of charters from the ecclesiastical archives in Grenoble then sold them back (at a high price) to the cardinal of Grenoble. In 1678 and 1680 he received the titles of Comte Palatin de l'Eglise Romaine and Comte Palatin de Padoue.

Chorier's works include a conduct book, *Philosophie de l'honnête homme pour la conduite de ses sentiments et de ses actions* (1648), several learned histories of the Dauphiné region (1654, 1658, 1671), and a set of memoirs discovered in 1847. He is best remembered today, however, as the author of one of the most obscene Latin works of the later Renaissance, the infamous *Aloisiae Sigeae Toletanae satyra sotadica de arcanis Amoris et Veneris*, usually known in English as "Tullia and Octavia." The title, literally translated, means "The Sotadic Satire on Secret Loves and Lusts of Luisa Sigée of Toledo." Sotades was a Greek satirist known for his coarseness; Luisa Sigée, the purported author of the work, the learned daughter of a Frenchman who resided in Toledo in the sixteenth century. Chorier always denied his authorship: the *Satira* was printed secretly at Grenoble or Lyon in 1659 or 1660. From its first publication it was wildly popular. It was translated into French and English several times in the 1680s and over the next ninety years went through fifteen Latin editions as well.

The book consists of a series of dialogues on sex between Tullia, a recently married Roman matron, and her virginal fifteen-year-old cousin, Octavia. Over the course of the work, prompted by Octavia's comically ignorant questions, Tullia discourses learnedly on a host of subjects—masturbation, the mechanics of defloration, the nature of the clitoris, flogging and fellatio, dildos and sodomy. Their second colloquy—which takes place in Tullia's bed—is devoted to the topic of lesbianism. While initiating Octavia (quite literally) into the venereal enjoyments possible between woman and woman, Tullia embarks on an elaborate disquisition on the history of tribadistic practices, complete with scholarly etymologies and learned references to Ovid,

Lucretius, Horace, and Petronius. Female homosexuality turns out to be both practical (it won't make you pregnant) and chic: "the Italian, Spanish, and French women love one another; and if shame did not restrain them, they would all rush headlong against each other in rut." Later in the *Satira* Tullia returns to the lesbian theme: in dialogue 7 ("Little Histories") she offers a rousing defence of Sappho and her naked girls—"the most spiritual of all the Greeks."

FURTHER READING: Nicolas Chorier, *Satire sotadique de Luisa Sigea de Tolède*, trans. A. Berry (Paris: Or du Temps, 1969); —, *Dialogues on the Arcana of Love and Venus*, trans. D. A. McKenzie (Lawrence, Kan.: Coronado, 1974); David Foxon, *Libertine Literature in England 1660–1745* (New Hyde Park, N.Y.: University, 1965); Roger Thompson, *Unfit for Modest Ears: A Study of Pornographic, Obscene and Bawdy Works Written or Published in England in the Second Half of the Seventeenth Century* (London: Macmillan, 1979); Emma Donoghue, *Passions Between Women: British Lesbian Culture 1668–1801* (London: Scarlet, 1993); James Grantham Turner, " 'Alouisa Sigea' in France and England: Female Authorship and the Reception of Chorier's Erotica," in *Oeuvres et Critiques* 20 (1995): 281–94; —, *Libertines and Radicals in Early Modern London: Sexuality, Politics, and Literary Culture, 1630–1685* (Cambridge: Cambridge University Press, 2001); Lise Leibacher-Ouvrard, "Transtextualité et construction de la sexualité: La *Satyra Sotadica* de Chorier," *L'Esprit créateur* 35 (1995): 51–66; Elizabeth S. Wahl, *Invisible Relations: Representations of Female Intimacy in the Age of Enlightenment* (Stanford: Stanford University Press, 1998).

Dialogue 2, "The Lesbians"

OCTAVIA: Now we are in your bed, that same bed where you have wanted me to spend the night when your husband Callias was away—wanted me not merely at your side, but in your arms.

TULLIA: I have at times spent sleepless nights for love of you; I have been wasting away; my love for you has entered all my veins—I have been consumed with fire.

OCTAVIA: You loved me once and now love me no more?

TULLIA: Oh, but I do love you, dear cousin, and am dying wretchedly for want of that love.

OCTAVIA: You are really dying when you know that I would lay down my life for you? What sickness of mind is this? For I cannot doubt that you are in bodily good health.

TULLIA: I love you the way you love Caviceus.

OCTAVIA: Speak clearly; what riddles are you spinning?

TULLIA: Put aside all modesty—comely, handsome though it be.

OCTAVIA: When you wanted me to get into your bed stark naked (which I have done) just as you told me I should have to do the moment I am handed over for Caviceus' pleasure—did I not readily drop all shame?

TULLIA: Once even the queen of the Lydians said: "I have both taken off my tunic and laid aside all shame."

OCTAVIA: You have persuaded me to overcome my timidity and with your help I have mastered myself.

TULLIA: Give me a loving kiss, oh dearest of maidens!

OCTAVIA: Why not? As many as you wish and however you wish.

TULLIA: Oh! The divine shape of your lips! Oh, eyes brighter than light! Oh, your Venus-like beauty!

OCTAVIA: And you are throwing aside the covers? I don't know what I should fear, what I should ask you, if you were not my Tullia. Here I am stark naked; what next?

TULLIA: Oh, ye Gods! I only wish you would let me play the role of Caviceus!

OCTAVIA: What's that? Both my tits, will Caviceus fondle them like that? Will he heap kisses upon kisses without end? Will he, like you, bite my lips, my throat, my breasts?

TULLIA: These, my heart of hearts, will be but the preludes to the combat and the courses at the flowering banquet of Venus.

OCTAVIA: But stop now! You are running your hand over my whole body; you are thrusting your hand lower. Why are you handling my thighs? Ah, ah, ah, but please, Tullia, why are you fingering that spot? And you cannot let it out of your piercing gaze.

TULLIA: I view this field of Venus with curious longing. To be sure it is not broad or spacious, but full of the sweetest delights where inexhaustible Venus will exhaust the forces of your Mars.

OCTAVIA: You are insane, Tullia! Oh, if you were Caviceus, I should really be in danger. For, straddling me as you are, why do you want to examine my whole body before and behind? There is nothing about me that outshines your beauty; take a look at yourself if you want to see something you may love and should praise.

TULLIA: If I denied that I were gifted with some beauty, I should be silly and not modest. Then, too, I am in the prime of life for I have just celebrated my eighteenth birthday. Callias as yet has fathered only one child by me. If my body can give you any pleasure, enjoy it. I would not be against it.

OCTAVIA: Nor I, either. Enjoy what pleasure in me as you may. I am all for it. But I know you can find no delight in a virgin like me. Nor can I find pleasure in you either even if you really were the marvelous garden of all delicacies and attractions.

TULLIA: But indeed you have a garden where Caviceus will in rapture graze and feed on the most delicious fruits.

OCTAVIA: But I do not have a garden like yours which abounds in the same fruits. Now, what is this thing you call a garden? Where is it placed? What are those fruits?

TULLIA: Now I perceive your wantonness: of course you rub your garden on mine, you are well acquainted with your own, as I with mine.

OCTAVIA: Do you perhaps mean by this word "garden" that spot that you are clutching in your right hand and teasing with your fingers and tickling with your fingernails—in order to arouse desire in me?

TULLIA: That's right, cousin. Since you have no experience, you are ignorant of its use; but I'll see that you know what's what!

OCTAVIA: If I should learn it out of wedlock, I should not be chaste. And I should not be worthy of your love since I should be different from you. But tell me what that "use" would be. First of all, stretch out on the bed. Seated up as you are, you are only causing inconvenience to both of us.

TULLIA: I'll do as you wish. Now prick up your ears. For Caviceus will erect the more easily and frequently, the more carefully you listen to what I have to say: may Venus grant it! Take up the omen, Octavia!

OCTAVIA: I do take it up. But you are roaring with laughter? I really don't see the harm in these words.

TULLIA: But you will feel the delights that I wish on your garden with this omen.

OCTAVIA: I am deaf to what you mean.

TULLIA: May Venus grant that you hear and understand. This garden of yours which I hope will always, in spring and in winter, abound in the flowers and fruits of Venus, is the spot, cousin, under the hillock of your belly, now covered only by down, which will soon turn to moss; it is called the *pubis*. This down, when it first begins to bloom, is the sign that the girl's maidenhead is ready for man and ripe for Venus. The Latins call it: a skiff (*cymbam*), a ship (*navim*), a sea shell (*concham*), a forest pasture (*saltum*) a Clitorian fountain (*clitoriam*), a gate (*portam*), a door (*ostium*), the port (*portum*), the inter-thigh (*interfemineum*), the town of Lanuvium (*Lanuvium*), the virginal (*virginale*), the sheath (*vagina*), a cunt (*facandrum*), a ploughshare (*vomer*), a plowed field (*agrum*), a furrow (*sulcum*), a ghost (*larvam*), a ring (*anulum*). The Greeks called it: a cunt (αλδοῖον), a delta (δέλτα), a pig (χοῖρος), and a hearth (ἐσχάρα). Julia, the daughter of Augustus, used to say that she bore Agrippa children resembling her husband as closely as possible because she never carried travellers in her ship unless it was already full. ἐσχάρα is a hearth and chimney; χοῖρος, a boar, δέλτα a letter thus called by the Greeks, but the form of the letter is very different from the form of our garden. I hope, my cousin, that tonight you will leave my arms wiser than if you had been sleeping on Parnassus, so that you can make love in Greek, too: you have learned it all from Juvenal.

OCTAVIA: I should rather be learned like you, cousin, than satiated with sensuality. When I think how young and learned you are, I should wish you were Caviceus. How happily I would spread out for you all the dowry of my person!

TULLIA: Sweet maid, take me in your arms for I am mad with love for you. Allow my eyes and fondlings a free rein wherever it is possible. Caviceus will lose nothing, nor you either. Oh, how vain my efforts; whatever I attack I am miserable. Oh, how I am dying for love of you!

OCTAVIA: Embrace your love and give free rein to the passion of your soul. What you wish is my desire, too.

TULLIA: Then open this garden of yours to me so that I can be its mistress; for otherwise it would be useless to me since I don't have a key to open its gate, nor a hammer to bash it in, nor a foot that could kick it in.

OCTAVIA: Of course I'll give it to you since I am all yours. Do I have any right that is not yours? But you are throwing yourself upon me: what does it mean?

TULLIA: Please don't pull back; open your thighs.

OCTAVIA: And now I have. And you have me now all to yourself! You press your mouth against mine, your bosom against mine, and your womb against mine; oh, I wish I could wrap myself around you as you are entwined around me.

TULLIA: Lift your legs up higher, place your thighs on mine. I'll teach you a new Venus, as you are a new hand. How sweetly you give in! I wish I could command as well as you obey.

OCTAVIA: Ah! Ah! Tullia, my darling, my mistress, how you are bouncing me up and down, how you are shaking me! I wish these candles were snuffed. I am ashamed to have this light see how I am submitting.

TULLIA: Just see what you should do. Every time I bounce down, you should bounce up; imitate me and put some life in your buttocks, raise them as high as you can. Are you afraid you'll give up your soul?

OCTAVIA: Really, you are wearing me out with these thompings. You are smothering me; could I endure such savage attacks from just anybody but you?

TULLIA: Grab on, squeeze closer, Octavia; receive . . . lo, lo, it is spitting, my heart burns, ah, ah, ah!

OCTAVIA: Your garden is setting mine on fire, pull back.

TULLIA: Cheer up, my goddess. I have been a husband to you, my spouse! my wife!

OCTAVIA: Would God you were my husband! What a loving wife you would have. What a fond husband would be mine. But really you have watered my garden with rain; I feel all wet from it. What filth did you pour over me, Tullia?

TULLIA: I have indeed done the job. And love has, in blind fury, poured the venereal foam from the dark hold of my ship into your virginal skiff. But has ever sharper voluptuousness titillated your senses to your inmost being?

OCTAVIA: As Venus may love me, if you want the truth, I'd like to say that I have experienced hardly any voluptuousness from what you have just subjected me to. I was a bit more moved on feeling you so over transported, and a few sparks of your flames slightly ignited that spot which you were hurting with your frequent bouncing. But these rather warned against the flame than lighted it. But tell me truly, Tullia: does this same malady also captivate other women's souls and cause them to long for and assail little girls?

TULLIA: Unless they are stupid and have hearts of stone, they yearn for and assail them. For what is more charming than a rosy and cultured young lady like you? Thus Iphis, before she was changed into a boy, burned for Ianthe:

> Despair is Iphis' lot, bemoaning the maid
> She cannot have and this fires up her flames
> And sorely then the maid for maid does burn.
> And scarcely holding back her tears she says:
> "A strange and unknown love has mastered me,
> A Venus strange to all. If the Gods wish
> To spare me, let their doom destroy me now!
> They have not willed my death so let them mete
> Me out a flame compatible with Nature.
> No father's harshness nor her will is bent
> On balking my request, and still I may
> Not have her to enjoy; whatever happens,
> I can know no happiness, though Gods and men
> Should go to work on my behalf. Today
> Again my vows ascended to the heavens
> And kindly gods have given what they could . . .
> What I desire, my father, Ianthe's father
> And good Ianthe too desire, but Nature,
> Unwilling, is more powerful than all.
> It's Nature alone that is noxious to me.
> The longed for time comes on, the wedding day
> Is now at hand, and Ianthe will soon be mine.
> It shall not be: for we shall thirst amid
> The waves.—Nuptial Juno and then, Hymen,
> Why do you come to these solemnities?
> Pray, who shall lead as bridegroom then, since both
> Of us are brides?"

I'll have to admit, Octavia, that we are nearly all of us a great bunch of bitches. Do you hear the Petronian Quartilla? "May Juno strike me down if I ever remember that I was a maiden; when I was only a child I was corrupted by my playmates, and then as the years passed, I had affairs with grown-up lads, until I have finally arrived at my present age."

OCTAVIA: Until today, and you know that very well, Tullia, I have led a life chaste in body and soul. You call me a simpleton and a fool. But I already feel tinged with lust and the desire of Venus. I am really grateful to fiery Venus that my wedding day is not far off: for I really think that, when men sleep with us, it is in their embraces alone that we can attain a true and solid voluptuousness.

TULLIA: Do you judge rightly and will you feel so tomorrow night! May the Lampsacine entertainment make you happy! But a swollen belly, child-bearing and delivery usually follow the overly free sports of men with us and lashings with the swollen prick. Outside of marriage, this passion which invites and urges little girls to complete coition is fraught with dangers and misfortunes. On the contrary, everything gets on freely and joyfully under Hymen. The newly married girls cover their heads with the same veil with which they also cover the crimes of their lust; under this veil, they conceal themselves the more easily from the sharp eyes of the law and the public. And so, Octavia, maidens and those leading a single life must find some other path to that voluptuousness toward which you see all species of animated beings, as Lucretius says, borne by an impetuosity which nothing, except the force of Venus, can soothe. It is, then, not at all strange that a maiden should be loved by a maiden; for even the greatest of Heroes once found stimulants of their lust in their own sex.

OCTAVIA: But you who have enjoyed a man are no longer a virgin; you are free to enjoy all manner of pleasure. How is it that you are in love with me, that you are seeking pleasure in that way by which Venus outwits Venus?

TULLIA: My friend Pomponia at first (for I will keep no secrets from you) began thus, some years ago, to urge herself freely and licentiously upon me, as we had been very intimate with each other since early childhood: no woman was ever more lascivious or artful at the same time. My soul was aghast at such a thing from the beginning; but little by little I became accustomed to what I used to call a torture. Pomponia would set me the example. She not only accommodated her bodily enjoyment to my petulance but also gave me orders and showed herself a very mild courtesan towards me and a procuress toward herself. When, at last, I had long practiced this enjoyment, I could hardly get on without it. But, darling Octavia, since you have shafted innumerable arrows through my heart, I have been so transported with your love, I am still so inflamed with it, that, except for you, I look with contempt on everything else, even my own Callias. And I feel that every pleasure rests within your embraces. Do not for this reason consider me worse than others, for this caprice is rooted in almost every corner of the earth. The Italian, Spanish, and French women love one another; and if shame did not restrain them, they would all rush headlong against each other in rut. At first this custom was common especially among the Lesbians: Sappho enhanced this name and thus dignifies it. How often have Andromeda, Athis, Anactorie, Mnais, and Girim, her pet loves, rubbed loins with hers! The Greeks call famous women of this kind Tribades; the Latins named them Frictrices and Subigitratices. But Philainis is regarded as having invented the practice, because she abandoned herself utterly to this pleasure. And since she was a woman of high renown she was able by her practice to advise the women and little girls around her of the use of a voluptuousness unknown before her time. They are called Tribades by the Greeks (τριβειν = to rub), and by the Latins, Frictrices (*fricare* = to rub), from the rubbing together of bodies:

Subigitatrices (*subigitare* = to bounce up and down) from the more violent movement. Finally, dear Octavia, it is the role of a woman who is not foolish and whose heart throbs in her breast, to act and be acted upon.

OCTAVIA: Heavens! You are saying strange things, but they are equally funny and absurd. You are, then, today both *tribax* and *frictrix* and *subigitatrix*. But what do you call me?

TULLIA: My tender, honeyed, golden Cypris. At least I have not meddled with anything that might lessen your purity, nothing by which I might have broken in this little door of yours, to pluck the flower of your maidenhead.

OCTAVIA: How could you have done that?

TULLIA: The women of Miletus used to make themselves pricks out of leather eight inches long and broad in proportion. The author, Aristophanes, tells us that the women of his day used to use them. Even nowadays this tool plays a considerable role in the feminine boudoir of Italian and especially Spanish as well as Asiatic women and is regarded as their most precious bit of paraphernalia. They hold it in the highest esteem.

OCTAVIA: I don't understand it or its use.

TULLIA: You will later on. But let us talk about something else now.

From Dialogue 7, "Historiettes"

TULLIA: Love is a Proteus who loves metamorphosis. The angry Solons of this world shout that is obscene to speak of such things and to depict them; they forbid it. But they do not prohibit any arguments over different means of combat and fighting battles. They don't concern themselves over something that might cause the destruction of the human race: they get angry about those things that concern its propagation. Oh! the stupid beasts! They prefer to see the human race destroy itself by every means, than to see it perpetuate itself. Thieves also love sorrow and death, and detest understanding and life. What madness! What insanity! The inhabitants of Lesbos, the most spiritual of all the Greeks, were far more wise. Sappho, the tenth Muse, was in fact a Lesbian. On their coins they had engraved amorous poses, and even those postures no longer in use. They minted these pieces openly. It was an occasion for a public consecration. I myself have seen in Rome in the house of Donna Orsini, two medals, one in bronze, the other in silver, minted, so they say, on the island of Lesbos. On one, Sappho, naked in the arms of another naked young girl, engages in amorous combat in the manner of the Tribades; on another a naked man, leaning on his right knee, supports a naked young girl and pierces her with his javelin; she willingly assists him by spreading her thighs.

ANONYMOUS

From *The Life and Death of Mrs. Mary Frith, Commonly Called Moll Cutpurse* (1662)

Mary Frith (1584?–1659), a.k.a. Moll Cutpurse, a notorious cross-dresser and pick-pocket in early seventeenth-century London, is the subject of the anonymously authored *Life and Death of Mrs. Mary Frith* (1662). A blazing "tomrig or rumpscuttle" in childhood, she continued to wear male dress as an adult, scandalizing contemporaries with her resolutely unfeminine appearance. Sometime around 1610 she turned to a high-profile life of crime, supporting herself as thief, fence, and bawd in the area around Cheapside and St. Paul's. A pamphlet about her, now presumed lost, *The Madde Pranckes of Merry Moll of the Banckside, with her Walks in Mans apparel, and to what Purpose*, was listed in the Stationers' Register in 1610. She was the inspiration behind Middleton and Dekker's comedy *The Roaring Girle or Moll Cut-purse* (1610) and is men-tioned in Thomas Freeman's *Rubbe and a Great Cast* (1614), Nathaniel Field's *Amends for Ladies* (1618), and John Taylor the Water Poet's *A Prodigal Country Gallant* in *The Water Cormorant* (1622). Daniel Defoe may have based the character of Moll Flanders, the trickster-heroine of his 1722 novel of the same name, in part upon her.

Of Frith's amorous inclinations we know nothing, though her masculine tastes and apparent antipathy to marriage suggest a possibly unorthodox sexual makeup. (Have-lock Ellis included her in his *Studies in the Psychology of Sex* as an example of "the homosexual diathesis.") Certainly the po-faced repetitiousness with which the author of the *Life and Death* harps upon her failure to attract *male* lovers, as in the excerpt below, invites the reader to speculate about female ones. Some of Frith's later success as a procuress may have been due to her power to interest susceptible women in her pri-vate concerns: like the eighteenth-century transvestite Charlotte Charke, she seems to have been born butch, with all the uncanny charisma that such a birthright entails.

FURTHER READING: Randall Nakayama, ed., *The Life and Death of Mrs. Mary Frith, Commonly Called Moll Cutpurse* (1662; rpt. New York and London: Garland, 1993); Jeannette Foster, *Sex Variant Women in Literature* (1956; rpt. Tallahassee, Fla.: Naiad, 1985); Rudolf M. Dekker and Lotte C. Van de Pol, *The Tradition of Female Transvestism in Early Modern Europe* (New York: St. Martin's, 1989); Marjorie Garber, *Vested Interests: Cross-Dressing and Cultural Anxiety* (New York: Routledge, 1992).

Under these benevolent and kind stars she grew up to some maturity of years, seasoned all along with such rudiments as these, to be put in use as soon as occasion should present; she was now a lusty and sturdy wench, and fit to put out to service, having not a competency of her own left her by friends to maintain her of herself; but this went against the grain and the hair, as we use to say: she was too great a libertine and lived too much in common to be enclosed in the limits of a private domestic life.

A quarterstaff was fitter to her hand than a distaff, stave and tail instead of spinning and reeling; she would go to the alehouse when she had made shift for some little stock, and spend her penny, and come into anyone's company, and club another till she had any left, and then she was fit for any enterprise.

She could not endure the bakehouse, nor that magpie chat of the wenches; she was not for mincing obscenity, but would talk freely whatever came uppermost; a spice she had even then of profane dissolute language, which in her old days amounted to downright swearing, which was in her not so malicious as customary.

Washing, wringing and starching were as welcome as fasting days unto her; or in short, any household work; but above all she had a natural abhorrence to the tending of children, to whom she ever had an averseness in her mind equal to the sterility and barrenness in her womb, never being made a mother to our best information.

At this age we spoke of before, she was not much taxed with any looseness or debauchery in that kind; whether the virility and manliness of her face and aspect took off any man's desires that way (which may be very rational and probable), or that besides her uncompliable and rougher temper of body and mind also, which in the female sex is usually persuasive and winning, not daring or peremptory (though her disposition can hardly find a suitable term for an indifferent expression of the manage of her life), she herself also from the more importunate and prevailing sway of her inclinations, which were masculine and robust, could not intend those venereal impurities and pleasures: as stronger meats are more palatable and nutritive to strong bodies than *quelque choses* and things of variety, which may perchance move an appetite, provoke a longing, but are easily refrained from by any considerate good fellow that knows what is the lastingest friend to *good drink and good company:* her motto.

She could not but know, moreover (for I suppose her of a very competent discretion and sagacity of mind as well as maturity and suitable growth at those years), that such prostitutions were the most unsatisfactory, that like an accidental scuffle or broil might end in danger, but never in love, to which she was no way so happily formed, nor was so much a woman as vainly to expect it.

Several romances there are of many knights who carried their ladies away in disguise from their parents and native countries, most commonly in the habits of a page or some such manservant: certainly it must be a stupified and far advanced affection which can admire, or fancy, or but admit the view of so unnatural a shape, the reverse of sexes in the most famed beauties, and to whose excellencies and luster the world were devoted. How unsightly and dreadful is the hinder region of the air in the sable breeches of a dropping cloud? What an uncomely mantle is that heap of waters which covers the ground, and deluges and invades the dry land? That which so much offends us in the boisterousness of the elements cannot but be disgustful to mankind in the immodesty of either sex's attire and dress.

Hercules, Nero and Sardanapalus, how are they laughed at and exploded for their effeminacy and degenerated dissoluteness in this extravagant debauchery? The first is portrayed with a distaff in his hand, the other recorded to be married as a wife and all the conjugal and matrimonial rites performed at the solemnity of the marriage, the other lacks the luxury of a pen as loose as his female riots to describe them. These were all monsters or monster killers, and have no parallels either in old or modern histories till such time as our Moll Cutpurse approached this example; but her heroic impudence has quite undone every romance—for never was any woman so like her in her clothes.

Generally we are so much acquainted with ourselves, and so often do dislike the effect of too much familiarity, that though we cannot alter the inside, yet we diversify the outside with all the borrowed pomp of art in our habits; no doubt Moll's converse with herself (whose disinviting eyes and look sank inwards to her breast when they could have no regard abroad) informed her of her defects, and that she was not made for the pleasure or delight of man; and therefore since she could not be honored with him she would be honored by him in that garb and manner of raiment he wore—some wenches have been got with child with the only shaking of the breeches; whereof having no great hopes, she resolved to usurp and invade the doublet, and vie and brave manhood, which she could not tempt nor allure.

I have the rather insisted on this because it was the chief remark of her life, as beginning and ending it; for from the first entrance into a competency of age she would wear it, and to her dying day she would not leave it off till the infirmity and weakness of nature had brought her abed to her last travail, changed it for a waistcoat and her petticoats for a winding sheet.

These were no amiable or obliging vests, they wanted of a mutual correspondence and agreement with themselves, so unlikely were they to beget it abroad and from others: they served properly as a fit covering, not any disguise of her (according to the primitive invention of apparel), wherein every man might see the true dimensions and proportions of body, only hers showed the mind too.

So that by this odd dress it came that no man can say or affirm that ever she had a sweetheart, or any such fond thing to dally with her. A good mastiff was the only thing she then affected and joyed in, in whose fawnings and familiarity she took as much delight as the proudest she ever gloried in the courtship, admiration, attraction and flatteries of her adored beauty. She was not wooed nor solicited by any man, and therefore she was honest, though still in a reserved obedience and future service, either personally or by proxy to Venus.

KATHERINE PHILIPS (1632–1664)

"To My Excellent Lucasia, on Our Friendship," "Parting with Lucasia: A Song," "Orinda to Lucasia," "Friendship's Mysteries: To my Dearest Lucasia," "Injuria Amici" (1664)

Katherine Philips, the seventeenth-century English poet known to admiring contemporaries as the "Matchless Orinda," was born in London. Her father, John Fowler, was a prosperous merchant; her mother's name was Katherine Oxenbridge. Philips was sent to Mrs. Salmon's boarding school in Hackney when she was eight, where she met Mary Aubrey ("Rosania"), the subject and dedicatee of some of her earliest surviving poems. At sixteen, following her father's death and mother's remarriage, she married a stepkinsman, James Philips, a man nearly forty years her senior. They moved to his estate in Wales, where she gave birth to a son and a daughter. Though fond of her elderly husband—"Antenor" in her poems—Philips drew her primary emotional sustenance from various young women of the neighborhood with whom she took to socializing. She dubbed her coterie her "Society of Friendship" and celebrated its members in perfervid yet "Platonick" love verse. Each woman had a poetical nickname: Philips herself was "Orinda"; her closest friend, the adored Anne Owen, was known as "Lucasia." Philips addressed a sheaf of passionate poems to Owen in the 1650s and was deeply resentful when Owen married an Irishman in 1662.

Philips first came to public attention in 1661 when the poet Henry Vaughan praised her in his *Olor Iscanus*. She subsequently translated Corneille's *La Mort de Pompée*; the work was performed, to great acclaim, in Dublin in 1663. Philips seems not to have intended her more personal poems for publication; she was incensed—or claimed to be—by the appearance of an unauthorized volume entitled *Poems. By the Incomparable, Mrs. K.P.* in 1664. Her dismay notwithstanding, the collection made her a celebrity. She was frequently compared to Dryden, and several of her lyrics were set to music by the Cavalier composer Henry Lawes. After her sudden death—of smallpox when she was only thirty-three—her friend Sir Charles Cotterell, Master of Ceremonies at Charles II's court, published an authorized edition of her works in 1667. This was followed by further editions in 1669, 1678, and 1710. Her verses also appeared in *Poems by Eminent Ladies* (1755). Her fame continued unabated into the nineteenth century: in 1817 Keats praised her poem "To Mrs. M.A. Upon Parting" in a letter to J.H. Reynolds.

Philips's ardent paeans to "Lucasia," "Rosania," "M.A.," and other young women register the growing importance of female romantic friendship in post-Restoration

English society. Intense emotional bonds—feverish, fantastical, oddly eroticized, yet also usually deeply sublimated—became increasingly common between educated middle-class women in the seventeenth and eighteenth century, even, paradoxically, as the cultural taboos against homosexuality intensified. The extravagant diction in Philips's poems is characteristic: women caught up in such hectic attachments were wont to speak of the exalting "flames" of their love for one another, of the merging of their "souls," of the moral and spiritual perfection of the bond shared with the "beloved Friend." Such relationships were tolerated, one suspects, precisely because they were figured as non-carnal. As one literary historian has written, "the flame is always pure, the relationship strictly Platonic, a meeting of souls, never the flesh." Subsequent exponents of the "romantic friendship" school included Anne Killigrew (1660–1685), Anne Finch (1661–1720), Elizabeth Singer Rowe (1674–1737), Anna Seward (1742–1809), and Sarah Scott (1723–1795), author of the utopian feminist novel *Millenium Hall* (1762).

The poems themselves read strangely to modern eyes, so intimate and overheated is their rhetoric. It would be cynical indeed to question the chastity of the tie between "Orinda" and her "Lucasia," yet Philips's poems carry an undeniably homoerotic charge. And herein the rub. In that the literature of romantic friendship helped to habituate Western civilization to the notion of passion between women, it was not entirely distinct in its cultural effects from contemporary pornography. For all their superficial dissimilarities, works such as Philips's "Orinda to Lucasia" and rampant scurrilities such as Nicolas Chorier's *Satyra Sotadica* (1660) or Samuel Butler's "Dildoides" (c. 1672) were part of the same cognitive revolution: that coming-into-view—culturally, linguistically, juridically, epistemologically and psychically—of women's desire for one another.

FURTHER READING: Katherine Philips, *Poems By the Most Deservedly Admired Mrs. Katherine Philips the Matchless Orinda* (London, 1667); Patrick Thomas, ed., *The Collected Works of Katherine Philips, the Matchless Orinda*, 3 vols. (Stump Cross, Essex: Stump Cross, 1990); John Aubrey, *Brief Lives*, ed. Andrew Clark, 2 vols. (Oxford: Clarendon Press, 1898); Myra Reynolds, *The Learned Lady in England 1650–1760* (Boston and New York: Houghton Mifflin, 1920); Philip W. Souers, *The Matchless Orinda* (Cambridge: Harvard University Press, 1931); R. K. Alspach, "The Matchless Orinda," *Modern Language Notes* 52 (1937): 116–17; Lillian Faderman, *Surpassing the Love of Men: Romantic Friendship and Love Between Women from the Renaissance to the Present* (New York: William Morrow, 1981); Elaine Hobby, *Virtue of Necessity: English Women's Writing 1649–1688* (London: Virago 1988); —, "Katherine Philips: Seventeenth-Century Lesbian Poet," in Elaine Hobby and Chris White, eds., *What Lesbians Do in Books* (London: Women's, 1991), pp. 183–204; Harriet Andreadis, "The Sapphic-Platonics of Katherine Philips, 1632–1664," *Signs: Journal of Women in Culture and Society* 15 (1989): 34–60; —, *Sappho in Early Modern England: Female Same-Sex Literary Erotics, 1550–1714* (Chicago: University of Chicago Press, 2001); Dorothy Mermin, "Women Becoming Poets: Katherine Philips, Aphra Behn, Anne Finch," *ELH: Journal of English Literary History* 57 (1990): 335–356; Arlene M. Stiebel, "Not Since Sappho: The Erotic in Poems of Katherine Philips and Aphra Behn," in Claude J. Summers, ed., *Homosexuality in Renaissance and Enlightenment England* (Binghamton, N.Y.: Haworth, 1992); Emma Donoghue, *Passions Between Women: British Lesbian Culture 1668–1801* (London: Scarlet, 1993); Betty Rizzo, *Companions Without Vows: Relationships Among Eighteenth-Century British Women* (Athens: University of Georgia Press, 1994); Lisa L. Moore, *Dangerous Intimacies: Toward a Sapphic History of the British Novel* (Durham, N.C.: Duke University Press, 1997).

To My Excellent Lucasia, on Our Friendship

I did not live until this time
   Crown'd my felicity,
When I could say without a crime
   I am not thine, but Thee.

This Carcass breath'd, and walkt, and slept,
   So that the World believ'd
There was a Soul the Motions kept;
   But they were all deceiv'd.

For as a Watch by art is wound
   To motion, such was mine:
But never had *Orinda* found
   A Soul till she found thine;

Which now inspires, *cures* and supplies,
   And guides my darkened Breast:
For thou art all that I can prize,
   My Joy, my Life, my Rest.

No Bridegroom's nor Crown-conqueror's mirth
   To mine compar'd can be:
They have but pieces of this Earth,
   I've all the World in thee.

Then let our Flames still light and shine,
   And no false fear controul,
As innocent as our Design,
   Immortal as our Soul.

Parting with Lucasia: A Song

Well, we will do that rigid thing
    Which makes Spectators think we part;
Though absence hath for none a sting
    But those who keep each other's heart.

And when our Sense is dispossest,
    Our labouring Souls will heave and pant,
And gasp for one another's breast
    Since their Conveyances they want.

Nay, we have felt the tedious smart
    Of absent Friendship, and do know
That when we die we can but part;
    And who knows what we shall do now?

Yet I must go: we will submit,
    And so our own disposers be;
For while we nobly suffer it,
    We triumph o'er Necessity.

By this we shall be truly great,
    If having other things o'ercome,
To make our victory compleat
    We can be Conquerors at home.

Nay then to meet we may conclude,
    And all Obstructions overthrow,
Since we our Passion have subdu'd,
    Which is the strongest thing I know.

Orinda to Lucasia

Observe the weary birds e're night be done,
How they would fain call up the tardy Sun,
    With Feathers hung with dew,
    And trembling voices too,
They court their glorious Planet to appear,
That they may find recruits of spirits there.

The drooping flowers hang their heads,
And languish down into their beds:
While Brooks more bold and fierce than they,
Wanting those beams, from whence
All things drink influence,
Openly murmur and demand the day.
Thou my *Lucasia* art far more to me,
Than he to all the under-world can be;
From thee I've heat and light,
Thy absence makes my night.
But ah! my Friend, it now grows very long,
The sadness weighty, and the darkness strong:
My tears (its dew) dwell on my cheeks,
And still my heart thy dawning seeks,
And to thee mournfully it cries,
That if too long I wait,
Ev'n thou may'st come too late,
And not restore my life, but close my eyes.

Friendship's Mysteries: To My Dearest Lucasia

Come, my *Lucasia,* since we see
That Miracles Men's faith do move,
By wonder and by prodigy
To the dull angry world let's prove
There's a Religion in our Love.

For though we were design'd t'agree,
That Fate no liberty destroyes,
But our Election is as free
As Angels, who with greedy choice
Are yet determin'd to their joyes.

Our hearts are doubled by the loss,
Here Mixture is Addition grown;
We both diffuse, we both ingross:
And we whose minds are so much one,
Never, yet ever are alone.

We court our own Captivity
    Than Thrones more great and innocent:
'Twere banishment to be set free,
    Since we wear fetters whose intent
    Not Bondage is, but Ornament.

Divided joyes are tedious found,
    And griefs united easier grow:
We are ourselves but by rebound,
    And all our Titles shuffled so,
    Both Princes, and both Subjects too.

Our Hearts are mutual Victims laid,
    While they (such power in Friendship lies)
Are Altars, Priests, and off'rings made:
    And each Heart which thus kindly dies,
    Grows deathless by the Sacrifice.

Injuria amici

Lovely apostate! what was my offence?
Or am I punished for obedience?
Must thy strange rigours find as strange a time?
The act and season are an equal crime.
Of what thy most ingenious scorns could do,
Must I be subject and spectator too?
Or were the sufferings and sins too few
To be sustained by me, performed by you?
Unless (with Nero) your uncurbed desire
Be to survey the Rome you set on fire.
While wounded for and by your power, I
At once your martyr and your prospect die.
This is my doom, and such a riddling fate
As all impossibles doth complicate:
For obligation here is injury,
Constancy crime, friendship a heresy;
And you appear so much on ruin bent,
Your own destruction gives you now content:
For our twin-spirits did so long agree,

You must undo your self to ruin me.
And like some frantic goddess, you're inclined
To raze the temple where you were enshrined;
And (what's the miracle of cruelty!)
Kill that which gave you immortality.
While glorious friendship, whence your honour springs,
Lies gasping in the crowd of common things;
And I'm so odious, that for being king
Doubled and studied murders are designed.
Thy sin's all paradox! for shouldst thou be
Thy self again, 'twould be severe to me;
For thy repentance, coming now so late,
Would only change, and not relieve the fate.
So dangerous is the consequence of ill,
Thy least of crimes is too cruel still;
For of thy smiles I should yet more complain,
If I should live to be betrayed again.
Live then (fair tyrant) in security,
From both my kindness and revenge be free;
While I, who to the swains had sung your fame,
And taught each echo to repeat your name,
Will now my private sorrows entertain,
To rocks and rivers (not to you) complain.
And though before our union cherished me,
'Tis now my pleasure that we disagree;
For from my passion your last rigours grew,
And you kill me, because I worshipped you.
But my worst vows shall be your happiness,
And ne'er to be disturbed by my distress.
And though it would my sacred flames pollute,
To make my heart a scorned prostitute;
Yet I'll adore the author of my death,
And kiss the hand that robs me of my breath.

PIERRE DE BOURDEILLES, SEIGNEUR DE BRANTÔME (C. 1540–1614)

From *Lives of Gallant Ladies* (1665–1666)

Pierre de Bourdeilles, commonly known as the Seigneur de Brantôme, was born into a noble French family in Périgord. Designed by his parents for the priesthood, he turned to soldiering at an early age and traveled widely in Italy, Spain, Portugal, England, and Scotland, where he was part of the retinue of Mary, Queen of Scots. He fought in the Wars of Religion in the 1580s on the Catholic side but is known to have been at least somewhat sympathetic to the Protestant reformers. In 1589 an injury led him to retire and devote himself to his voluminous memoirs, subsequently published in 1665–66. According to an early-twentieth-century biographer, the latter work "gave an admirable picture of the general court-life of the time, with its unblushing and undisguised profligacy. There is not an *homme illustre* or a *dame galante* in all his gallery of portraits who is not stained with vice; and yet the whole is narrated with the most complete unconsciousness that there is anything objectionable in their conduct."

The work known as *Lives of Gallant Ladies* (*Vies des dames galantes*) is the second of the four parts into which Brantôme's memoirs were divided after his death. (The other three parts are [1] *Vies des dames illustres de France de son temps*; [3] *Vies des hommes illustres et grands capitans françois*; and [4] *Vies des hommes illustres et grands capitaines étrangers*.) Similar in flavor to works by Boccaccio and Rabelais, *Gallant Ladies* mixes anecdotes about notorious women with libertine reflections on marriage, cuckoldry, and sexual mores around the world. In chapter 16, devoted entirely to lesbianism, Brantôme takes up the question of whether married women who have sex with one another—"sleeping together in one bed, and doing what is called *donna con donna*"—are technically speaking committing adultery. His answer on the specific point is equivocal, but his overall attitude clear. Female same-sex love is popular, he admits: one finds instances of it in every part of the world. Yet it is also insipid—a "frivolous and empty" pleasure that most women will forego in an instant for male caresses. "How many of these Lesbian dames have I seen," he somewhat laboriously jests, "who, for all their customs and habits, yet fail not at the last to go after men!" Perhaps the only really amusing passage in this otherwise fairly dire piece of misogynistic writing is the curious zoological assertion that weasels are "touched with this sort of love, and delight female with female to unite and dwell together."

FURTHER READING: Pierre de Bourdeilles de Brantôme, *Receuil des dames, poésies et tombeaux* (Paris: Gallimard, 1991); ———, *Lives of Fair and Gallant Ladies* (New York: Panurge, n.d.); R. D. Cottrell, *Brantôme: The Writer as Portraitist of his Age* (Geneva: Droz, 1970); Herbert de Ley, " 'Dans les règles du plaisir . . .': Transformations of Sexual Knowledge in Seventeenth-Century France," in Wolfgang Leiner, ed., *Onze nouvelles études sur l'image de la femme dans la littérature française du dix-septième siècle* (Tübingen: G. Narr Verlag, 1984); Elizabeth S. Wahl, *Invisible Relations: Representations of Female Intimacy in the Age of Enlightenment* (Stanford: Stanford University Press, 1998).

Now will I further ask this one question only, and never another, one which mayhap hath never yet been enquired into of any, or possibly even thought of,—to wit, whether two ladies that be in love one with the other, as hath been seen aforetime, and is often seen nowadays, sleeping together in one bed, and doing what is called *donna con donna*, imitating in fact that learned poetess Sappho, of Lesbos, whether these can commit adultery, and between them make their husbands cuckold.

Of a surety do they commit this crime, if we are to believe Martial in Epigram CXIX of his First Book. Therein doth he introduce and speak of a woman by name Bassa, a tribad, reproaching the same greatly in that men were never seen to visit her, in such wise that folk deemed her a second Lucretia for chasteness. But presently she came to be discovered, for that she was observed to be constantly welcoming at her house beautiful women and girls; and 'twas found that she herself did serve these and counterfeit a man. And the poet, to describe this, doth use the words, *geminos committere cunnos*. And further on, protesting against the thing, he doth signify the riddle and give it out to be guessed and imagined, in this Latin line:

Hic, ubi vir non est, ut sit adulterium.

I knew once a courtesan of Rome, old and wily if ever there was one, that was named Isabella de Luna, a Spanish woman, which did take in this sort of friendship another courtesan named Pandora. This latter was eventually married to a butler in the Cardinal d'Armaignac's household, but without abandoning her first calling. Now this same Isabella did keep her, and extravagant and ill-ordered as she was in speech, I have oft times heard her say how that she did cause her to give her husbands more horns than all the wild fellows she had ever had. I know not in what sense she did intend this, unless she did follow the meaning of the epigram of Martial just referred to.

'Tis said how that Sappho the Lesbian was a very high mistress in this art, and that in after times the Lesbian dames have copied her therein, and continued the practice to the present day. So Lucian saith: such is the character of the Lesbian women, which will not suffer men at all. Now such women as love this practice will not suffer men, but devote themselves to other women and are called *tribads*, a Greek word. These tribads are called in Latin *fricatrices*, and in French the same, that is women who do the way of *donne con donne*.

Juvenal again speaks of these women, when he saith:

. . . frictum Grissantis adorat

talking of such a tribad, who adored and loved the embraces of one Grissas.

The excellent and diverting Lucian hath a chapter on this subject, and saith therein how that women do come mutually together. Moreover this name of tribad, which doth elsewhere occur but rarely as applied to these women, is freely employed by him throughout, and he saith that the female sex must needs be like the notorious Philaenis, who was used to parody the actions of manly love. At the same time he doth add, 'tis better far for a woman to be given up to a lustful affection for playing the male, than it is for a man to be womanish; so utterly lacking in all courage and nobility of character doth such an one show himself. Thus the woman, according to this, which doth counterfeit the man, may well be reputed to be more valorous and courageous than another, as in truth I have known some such to be, as well in body as in spirit.

Well, by what I have heard say, there be in many regions and lands plenty of such dames and Lesbian devotees,—in France, in Italy, in Spain, Turkey, Greece and other places. And wherever the women are kept secluded, and have not their entire liberty, this practice doth greatly prevail.

The Turkish women go to the baths more for this than for any other reason, and are greatly devoted thereto. Even the courtesans, which have men at their wish and at all times, still do employ this habit, seeking out the one the other, as I have heard of sundry doing in Italy and in Spain. In my native France women of the sort are common enough; yet it is said to be no long time since they first began to meddle therewith, in fact that the fashion was imported from Italy by a certain lady of quality, whom I will not name.

Several others have I known which have given account of the same manner of loves, amongst whom I have heard tell of a noble lady of the great world, who was superlatively given this way, and who did love many ladies, courting the same and serving them as men are wont. So would she take them and keep them at bed and board, and give them whatever they would. Her husband was right glad and well content thereat, as were many other husbands I have known, all of whom were right glad their wives did follow after this sort of affection rather than that of men, deeming them to be thus less wild. But indeed I think they were much deceived; for by what I have heard said, this is but an apprenticeship, to come later to the greater one with men.

How many of these Lesbian dames have I seen who, for all their customs and habits, yet fail not at the last to go after men! Even Sappho herself, the mistress of them all, did she not end by loving her fond favorite Phaon, for whose sake she died? For after all, as I have heard many fair ladies declare, there is nothing like men. All these other things do but serve them but in the lack of men. And if they but find a chance and opportunity free from scandal, they will straight quit their comrades and go throw their arms round some good man's neck.

I have known in my time two very fair and honorable damsels of a noble house, cousins of one another, which having been used to lie together in one bed for the space of three years, did grow so well accustomed to this, that at the last getting the idea the said pleasure was but a meagre and imperfect one compared with that to be had with men, they did determine to try the latter, and soon became downright harlots. And this was the answer a very honorable damsel I knew did once make to her lover, when he asked her if she did never follow this way with her lady friend,—"No, no!" she replied, "I like men too well."

I have heard of an honorable gentleman who, desiring one day at Court to seek in marriage a certain very honorable damsel, did consult one of her kinswomen thereon. She told him frankly he would but be wasting his time for, as she did herself tell me, such and such a lady, naming her, ('twas one I had already heard talk of) will never suffer her to marry. Instantly I did recognize the hang of it, for I was well aware how she did keep this damsel at bed and board, and did guard her carefully. The gentleman did thank the said cousin for her good advice and warning, not without a merry gibe or two at herself the while, saying she did herein put in a word or two for herself as well as for the other, for that she did take her little pleasures now and again under the rose. But this she did stoutly deny to me.

This doth remind me of certain women which do thus and actually love these friends so dearly they would not share them for all the wealth in the world, neither with Prince nor great noble, with comrade or friend. They are as jealous of them as a beggarman of his drinking barrel; yet even he will offer this to any that would drink. But this lady was fain to keep the damsel all to herself, without giving one scrap to others.

'Tis said how that weasels are touched with this sort of love, and delight female with female to unite and dwell together. And so in hieroglyphic signs, women loving one another with this kind of affection were represented of yore by weasels. I have heard tell of a lady which was used always to keep some of these animals, for that she did take pleasure in watching her little pets together.

Still excuse may be made for maids and widows for loving these frivolous and empty pleasures, preferring to devote themselves to these than to go with men and come to dishonor, or else to lose their pains altogether, as some have done and do every day. Moreover they deem they do not so much offend God, and are not such great harlots, as if they had to do with the men, maintaining there is a great difference betwixt throwing water in a vessel and merely watering about it and round the rim. However I refer me to them; I am neither their judge nor their husband. These last may find it ill, but generally I have never seen any but were right glad their wives should be companionable with their lady friends. And in very deed this is a very different thing from that with men, and, let Martial say what he please, this alone will make no man cuckold. 'Tis no gospel text, this word of a foolish poet. In this at any rate he saith true, that 'tis much better for a woman to be masculine and a very Amazon and lewd after this fashion, than for a man to be feminine, like Sardanapalus or Heliogabalus, and many another their fellows in sin. For the more manlike she is, the braver is she. But concerning all this, I must refer me to the decision of wiser heads.

Monsieur du Gua and I were reading one day in a little Italian book, called the *Book of Beauty*, writ in the form of a dialogue by the Signor Angelo Firenzuola, a Florentine, and fell upon a passage wherein he saith that women were originally made by Jupiter and created of such nature that some are set to love men, but others the beauty of one another. But of these last, some purely and holily, and as an example of this the author doth cite the very illustrious Marguerite of Austria, which did love the fair Laodamia Fortenguerre, but others again wantonly and lasciviously, like Sappho the Lesbian, and in our own time at Rome the famous courtesan Cecilia of Venice. Now this sort do of their nature hate to marry, and fly the conversation of men all ever they can.

Hereupon did Monsieur du Gua criticise the author, saying 'twas a falsehood that the said fair lady, Marguerite of Austria, did love the other fair dame of a pure and holy love. For seeing she had taken up her rather than others which might well be equally fair and virtuous as she, 'twas to be supposed it was to use her for her pleasures, neither more nor less than other women that do the like. Only to cover up her naughtiness, she did say and publish abroad how that her love for her was a pure and holy love, as we see many of her fellows do, which do dissemble their lewdness with suchlike words.

This was what Monsieur du Gua did remark thereanent; and if any man doth wish to discuss the matter farther, well! he is at liberty to do so.

This same fair Marguerite was the fairest Princess was ever in all Christendom in her day. Now beauty and beauty will ever feel mutual love of one sort or another, but wanton love more often than the other. She was married three times, having at her first wedlock espoused King Charles VIII of France, secondly John, son of the King of Aragon, and thirdly the Duke of Savoy, surnamed the Handsome. And men spake of them as the handsomest pair and fairest couple of the time in all the world. However the Princess did have little profit of this union, for that he died very young, and at the height of his beauty, for the which she had very deep sorrow and regret, and for that cause would never marry again.

She it was had that fair church built which lyeth near Bourg en Bresse, one of the most beautiful and noble edifices in Christendom. She was aunt to the Emperor Charles, and did greatly help her nephew; for she was ever eager to allay all differences, as she and the Queen Regent did at the treaty of Cambrai, whereunto both of them did assemble and met together there. And I have heard tell from old folk, men and women, how it was a beauteous sight there to see these two great Princesses together.

Cornelius Agrippa hath writ a brief treatise on the virtue of women, and all in panegyric of this same Marguerite. The book is a right good one, as it could not but be on so fair a subject, and considering its author, who was a very notable personage.

I have heard a tale of a certain great lady, a Princess, which among all her maids of honor did love one above all and more than the rest. At first were folk greatly surprised at this, for there were plenty of others did surpass her in all respects. But eventually 'twas discovered she was a hermaphrodite.

I have heard a certain great lady also named as being hermaphrodite. She hath a virile member, but very tiny; yet hath she more of the woman's complexion, and I know, by having seen her, she is very fair. I have heard sundry famous doctors declare they have seen plenty suchlike women.

Well, this is all I shall say on the subject of this chapter, one I could have made a thousand times longer than I have done, having matter so ample and lengthy, that if all the cuckold husbands and their wives that do make them so, were to hold hands, and form a ring, I verily believe this would be great enough to surround and encircle a good half of the globe.

Yet would I not inveigh over much against honorable and modest wives, which have borne themselves virtuously and faithfully in the fealty sacredly sworn to their husbands; and I do hope anon to write a separate chapter to their praise, and give the lie to Master Jean de Meung. Now this poet in his *Roman de la Rose* did write these words: *Toutes vous autres femmes . . .*

> Estes ou fustes,
> D'effet ou de volonté, putes.

By these verses he did incur such ill will on the part of the Court ladies of that day, that by a plot sanctioned of the Queen and with her privity, these did undertake one day to whip the poet, and did strip him stark naked. But as all stood ready to strike, he did beseech them that at any rate the greatest whore of all should begin first. Then each for very shame durst not strike first; and in this wise he did escape the whip. Myself have seen the story represented in an old tapestry among the ancient furnishings of the Louvre.

APHRA BEHN (1640–1689)

"To the Fair Clorinda, Who Made Love to Me, Imagin'd More than Woman," "Verses Designed by Mrs. A. Behn to be Sent to a Fair Lady, that Desired She Would Absent Herself to Cure her Love" (1684)

The extravagantly gifted novelist, poet, and playwright Aphra Behn, the first woman to earn her living by her pen, remains one of the most colorful if outré figures in English literary history. The facts of her life are disputed. She was probably born in Kent and was possibly the daughter of Bartholemew and Elizabeth Johnson. In her early twenties she traveled to Surinam with her father and lived on Sir Robert Harley's plantation; she may have witnessed the bloody slave uprising later commemorated in her prose romance *Oroonoko* (1688). Returning to England in 1664, she married a Mr. Behn, a Dutch merchant thought to have subsequently died of the plague. In 1666 Charles II dispatched her as a spy to Antwerp, from whence she successfully relayed information about Dutch invasion plans. Several of her later tales, notably *The History of the Nun* and *The Fair Jilt* (both 1688), have Flemish settings.

In financial distress after her return to London, Behn took to supporting herself as a playwright. Over the next two decades she had eighteen plays (possibly more) produced on the London stage. The best known are *The Forced Marriage* (1670), *The Dutch Lover* (1673), *The Rover* (1677), *Sir Patient Fancy* (1678), *The Feigned Courtezan* (1679), *The Lucky Chance* (1686), and *The Emperor of the Moon* (1686). Her patrons and supporters included Sir Thomas Gower, the Duke of Buckingham, James II, the actress Nell Gwynn, and the poets Dryden and Rochester. In the 1670s she became openly and painfully involved with the bisexual lawyer John Hoyle, who along with Rochester may be a model for the promiscuous hero of *The Rover*. (Hoyle is believed to be the author of the epitaph on Behn's stone in Westminster Abbey: "Here lies a proof that wit can never be / Defence enough against mortality.") Not surprisingly, given her free living, fiercely royalist sympathies, and the audacity of her writing—she daringly defended women's right to professional and sexual independence—Behn became a notorious figure and the subject of numerous personal attacks.

Toward the end of her life Behn turned increasingly to poetry and prose. Her poems include several panegyrics on the Stuart family—*A Pindaric on the Death of our Late Sovereign, A Poem . . . to . . . Catherine Queen Dowager, A Pindaric Poem on the Happy Coronation* (all 1685), and *A Congratulatory Poem to . . . Queen Mary* (1688)—as well as satires, love poems, and songs. The verse collection *Poems Upon Several Occa-*

sions appeared in 1684. Between 1684 and 1687 Behn composed a wildly popular three-part epistolary novel, *Love Letters Between a Nobleman and His Sister*, based on a contemporary scandal, the elopement of Forde Grey, Lord Grey of Werke, with his sister-in-law, Lady Henriette Berkeley. Despite crippling arthritis, Behn remained prolific until her death in 1689. In her last year she produced *The Fair Jilt*, *The History of the Nun*, and *Oroonoko*, as well as translations of Fontenelle's *The History of the Oracles* and *A Discovery of New Worlds*, and the French romantic tale *Agnes de Castro*. After her death a number of her unpublished works were issued, along with an anonymous biographical account, *Memoirs of the Life of Mrs Behn*, some of which, it is believed, may have been composed by Behn herself.

"Astraea"—as Behn was known—took a lively interest in female charms, and over the course of her career wrote a number of witty love poems addressed to women. She shows neither embarrassment nor coyness in these verses; indeed, they have a kind of worldliness and esprit that would become all too rare in women's writing in the coming century. Behn herself seems to have inhabited a theatrical and bohemian milieu on the fringes of the Stuart court in which love between women was simply one of a number of sophisticated erotic options: she dedicated *The History of the Nun*, for example, to Hortense Mancini, the notoriously bisexual mistress of Charles II.

FURTHER READING: Aphra Behn, *The Works of Aphra Behn*, ed. Montague Summers, 6 vols. (London: William Heinemann, 1915); —, *The Works of Aphra Behn*, ed. Janet Todd, 7 vols. (London: William Pickering, 1992–); —, *Oroonoko and Other Writings*, ed. Paul Salzman (Oxford and New York: Oxford University Press, 1994); Virginia Woolf, *A Room of One's Own* (London: Hogarth, 1929); Sara Heller Mendelson, *The Mental World of Stuart Women* (Brighton: Harvester, 1967); Maureen Duffy, *The Passionate Shepherdess: Aphra Behn, 1640–1689* (London: Jonathan Cape, 1977); Angeline Goreau, *Reconstructing Aphra: A Social Biography of Aphra Behn* (New York: Dial, 1980); Mary Ann O'Donnell, *Aphra Behn: An Annotated Bibliography of Primary and Secondary Sources* (New York, Garland, 1986); Mary Ann O'Donnell, Bernard Dhuicq, and Guyonne Leduc, eds., *Aphra Behn: Identity, Alterity, Ambiguity* (Paris: Harmattan, 2000); Janet Todd, *The Sign of Angellica: Women, Writing and Fiction 1660–1800* (London: Virago, 1989); —, *The Secret Life of Aphra Behn* (London: André Deutsch, 1996); —, *The Critical Fortunes of Aphra Behn* (Columbia, S.C.: Camden House, 1998); —, ed., *Aphra Behn Studies* (Cambridge: Cambridge University Press, 1996); Dorothy Mermin, "Women Becoming Poets: Katherine Philips, Aphra Behn, Anne Finch," *ELH: Journal of English Literary History* 57 (1990): 335–55; Ros Ballaster, *Seductive Forms: Women's Amatory Fiction, 1684–1740* (Oxford: Clarendon, 1992); Catherine Gallagher, *Nobody's Story: The Vanishing Acts of Women Writers in the Marketplace 1670–1820* (Berkeley and Los Angeles: University of California Press, 1994); Jane Spencer, *Aphra Behn's Afterlife* (Oxford and New York: Oxford University Press, 2000).

To the Fair Clorinda, Who Made Love to Me, Imagin'd More
Than Woman.

Fair lovely Maid, or if that Title be
Too weak, too Feminine for Nobler thee,
Permit a Name that more Approaches Truth:
And let me call thee, Lovely Charming Youth.
This last will justifie my soft complaint,
While that may serve to lessen my constraint;
And without Blushes I the Youth persue,
When so much beauteous Woman is in view.
Against thy Charms we struggle but in vain
With thy deluding Form thou giv'st us pain,
While the bright Nymph betrays us to the Swain.
In pity to our Sex sure thou wert sent,
That we might Love, and yet be Innocent:
For sure no Crime with thee we can commit;
Or if we shou'd—thy Form excuses it.
For who, that gathers fairest Flowers believes
A Snake lies hid beneath the Fragrant Leaves.

    Thou beauteous Wonder of a different kind,
Soft *Cloris* with the dear *Alexis* join'd;
When e'r the Manly part of thee, wou'd plead
Thou tempts us with the Image of the Maid,
While we the noblest Passions do extend
The Love to *Hermes*, *Aphrodite* the Friend.

Verses Design'd by Mrs. A. Behn to be Sent to a Fair Lady,
that Desir'd She Would Absent Herself to Cure her Love.

In vain to Woods and Deserts I retire,
To shun the lovely Charmer I admire,
Where the soft Breezes do but fann my Fire!
In vain in Grotto's dark unseen I lie,
Love pierces where the Sun could never spy.
No place, no Art his *Godhead* can exclude,
The *Dear* Distemper reigns in Solitude:
Distance, alas, contributes to my Grief;
No more, of what fond Lovers call, Relief

Than to the wounded Hind does sudden Flight
From the chast Goddesses pursuing Sight:
When in the Heart the fatal Shaft remains,
And darts the Venom through our bleeding Veins.
If I resolve no longer to submit
My self a wretched Conquest to your Wit,
More swift than fleeting Shades, ten thousand Charms
From your bright Eyes that Rebel Thought disarms:
The more I strugl'd, to my Grief I found
My self in *Cupid's* Chains more surely bound:
Like Birds in Nets, the more I strive, I find
My self the faster in the Snare confin'd.

SOR JUANA INÉS DE LA CRUZ (1648–1695)

"Accompanying a Ring Bearing the Portrait of la Señora Condesa de Paredes. She Explains," "Inés, Dear, with your love I am *Enraptured*" (c. 1685)

Sor Juana Inés de la Cruz—known to contemporaries as the "Tenth Muse" or "Phoenix of Mexico," and perhaps the greatest of all Spanish-speaking woman poets—was born in the viceroyalty of the New Spain, near present-day Mexico City, probably in 1648. Her birth name was Juana de Asbaje y Ramirez de Santinalla. She was illegitimate but nonetheless well educated and ambitious: she became a lady-in-waiting at the court of the Marquesa de Mancera around 1664. In 1669, after a varied experience of court life, she joined the Convent of the Unshod Carmelites but left a short time later in order to join the less restrictive Convent of Santa Paula of the order of San Jeronimo. Over the next two decades, despite repeated harassment from her ecclesiastical superiors, she composed poetry and music, amassed a library of four thousand books (one of the largest in Spanish Mexico), composed music, carried out scientific research, and entertained literary and intellectual visitors at the convent. She became famous around the Spanish-speaking globe for her plays, songs, and devotional writings. In 1690, however, she went too far. In response to provocation from an antagonistic bishop, she produced two controversial prose works, the autobiographical *Cartá Atenagórica* (*Athenagoric Letter*) and *La Respuesta de la poetisa a la muy ilustre Sor Filotea de la Cruz* (*Response to the Most Illustrious Poetess Sor Filotea de la Cruz*). In both treatises she argued passionately for female intellectual emancipation. For this temerity, she was again rebuked by church officials and forced to give up her library and musical instruments. She died not long after, in 1695, during a devastating outbreak of plague in her convent.

Among Sor Juana's fascinating, often startling writings are a number of love poems. At least three of them, including "Accompanying a Ring Bearing the Portrait of la Señora Condesa de Paredes. She Explains," were inspired by her noble patroness of the 1680s, María Luisa Manrique de Lara y Gonzaga, Condesa de Paredes, and Marquesa de la Laguna. The relationship between Sor Juana and the Condesa de Paredes, undoubtedly fervent, has inspired much recent speculation: the Argentinian film director Maria Luisa Bemberg explored its homoerotic dimensions in a moving 1990 film about Sor Juana, *I, the Worst of All*.

The gongoristic poem "Inés, Dear, With Your Love I Am *Enraptured*" is one of "Five Burlesque Sonnets" Sor Juana composed to predetermined rhymes. Father Alfonso Méndez Plancarte, Sor Juana's first modern editor, found it "gross" and "unworthy" of her. One can't help but feel that the baroque freedom of the sentiments may have had something to do with his discomfort.

FURTHER READING: Sor Juana Inés de la Cruz, *Obras completas de Sor Juana Inés de la Cruz*, Alfonso Méndez Plancarte and Alberto G. Salceda, eds., 4 vols. (Mexico: Fondo de Cultura Económica, 1951–57); ——, *Poems, Protest, and a Dream: Selected Writings*, trans. Margaret Sayers Peden, intro. by Ilan Stavans (Harmondsworth, Middlesex: Penguin, 1997); Georgina Sabat de Rivers, *El 'Sueño' de Sor Juana Inés de la Cruz: Tradiciones literarias y originalidad* (London: Tamesis, 1976); Marie-Cécile Bénassy-Berling, *Humanisme et religion chez Sor Juana Inés de la Cruz: La Femme et la culture au XVIIième siècle* (Paris: Sorbonne, Éditions Hispaniques, 1982); Octavio Paz, *Sor Juana: or, The Traps of Faith*, trans. Margaret Sayers Peden (Cambridge: Harvard University Press, 1988); Jean Franco, *Plotting Women: Gender and Representation in Mexico* (New York: Columbia University Press, 1989); George Henry Tavard, *Juana Inés de la Cruz and the Theology of Beauty* (Notre Dame, Ind.: University of Notre Dame Press, 1991); Stephanie Merrim, *Early Modern Women's Writing and Sor Juana Inés de la Cruz* (Nashville, Tenn.: Vanderbilt University Press, 1999); ——, ed., *Feminist Perspectives on Sor Juana Inés de la Cruz* (Detroit: Wayne State University Press, 1991).

Accompanying a Ring Bearing the Portrait of la Señora Condesa de Paredes. She Explains.

This portrait traced by arrogance
was nonetheless by love inspired,
whereon a clumsy hand conspired
to give emotion utterance:
no bursting breast can countenance
for long the presence of perfection,
but needs must spill out its affection;
then let your index finger show
the miniature, that all may know
the ring indexes my subjection.

Inés, Dear, with your love I am *Enraptured*. One of Five
Burlesque Sonnets in Which the Poetess Was Circumscribed
by Rhymes Which Had Been Determined; Composed in a
Moment of Relaxation.

Inés, dear, with your love I am *enraptured*,
and as object of your love, I am *enthralled*,
when gazing on your beauty I am *captured*,
but when I find you jealous, want to *bawl*.

I die of jealousy if others you *entangle*,
I tremble at your grace, your step *sublime*,
because I know, Inés, that you could *mangle*,
the humors of my systematic *chyme*.

When I hold your dainty hand, I am *aquiver*,
in your anger, feel that I must soon *expire*,
if you venture from your home I am *adither*,

so I say, Inés, to one thing I *aspire*,
that your love and my good wine will draw you *hither*,
and to tumble you to bed I can *conspire*.

ANNE KILLIGREW (1660–1685)

"On a Picture Painted by Herself, Representing Two Nymphs of Diana's, One in a Posture to Hunt, the Other Bathing," "On the Soft and Gentle Motions of Eudora" (1686)

Anne Killigrew, dead of smallpox at twenty-five, long owed her place in literary history to the fact that she was the subject of the famous Dryden ode, "To the Pious Memory of the Accomplished Young Lady, Mrs. Anne Killigrew, Excellent in the Two Sister Arts of Poesy and Painting." In recent years, however, her own poetry has attracted interest. She was the daughter of Sir Henry Killigrew, chaplain of the Duke of York, later James II; her father's influence led to her appointment as maid of honor to Mary of Modena, James's wife. At Mary's court she became friends with Anne Finch, Countess of Winchilsea, and won praise for both her piety and verses. She was also an accomplished artist and among her surviving works are portraits of James and Mary, several classical scenes, and two episodes from the life of John the Baptist. Following her early death, her poems were edited by her father and published in 1686. An engraving of a painted self-portrait was used as the frontispiece.

Like her contemporaries Katherine Philips and Anne Finch, Killigrew found the theme of female friendship deeply beguiling. The exotic love verses "On the Soft and Gentle Motions of Eudora"—with their elaborate metaphysical play on sound and silence—were found among Killigrew's papers after her death and are usually attributed to her. (A few modern editors question the attribution on the basis of a note in an early edition of her works: "These Three following ODES being found among Mrs Killigrews Papers, I was willing to Print though none of hers.") The poem about Diana's nymphs seems to have been meant to accompany one of Killigrew's paintings; though the painting is now lost, the poem nonetheless offers a powerful image of same-sex bonding and feminine self-sufficiency. The lunar goddess Diana has often been associated with female homosexuality. Virginal, athletic, and coolly indifferent to men, she epitomizes a kind of primal female noncompliance—a refusal, at the level of myth, of the forces of compulsory heterosexuality.

FURTHER READING: Anne Killigrew, *Poems by Mrs Anne Killigrew* (London, 1686; rpt. Gainesville, Fla.: Scholars' Facsimiles, 1967); Ann Messenger, *His and Hers: Essays in Restoration and Eighteenth-Century Literature* (Lexington: University Press of Kentucky, 1986); Elaine Hobby, *Virtue of Necessity: English Women's Writing 1649–1688* (London: Virago, 1988); Germaine Greer, *Slip-Shod Sybils: Recognition, Rejection, and the Woman Poet* (London: Viking, 1995); Harriette Andreadis, *Sappho in Early Modern England: Female Same-Sex Literary Erotics, 1550–1714* (Chicago: University of Chicago Press, 2001).

On a Picture Painted by Herself, Representing Two Nymphs of Diana's, One in a Posture to Hunt, the Other Bathing

We are Diana's virgin-train,
Descended of no mortal strain;
Our bows and arrows are our goods,
Our palaces, the lofty woods,
The hills and dales, at early morn,
Resound and echo with our horn;
We chase the hind and fallow-deer,
The wolf and boar both dread our spear;
In swiftness we outstrip the wind,
An eye and thought we leave behind;
We fawns and shaggy satyrs awe;
To sylvan powers we give the law:
Whatever does provoke our hate,
Our javelins strike, as sure as fate;
We bathe in springs, to cleanse the soil,
Contracted by our eager toil;
In which we shine like glittering beams,
Or crystal in the crystal streams;
Though Venus we transcend in form,
No wanton flames our bosoms warm!
If you ask where such wights do dwell,
In what blest clime, that so excel?
The poets only that can tell.

On the Soft and Gentle Motions of Eudora

Divine Thalia strike the harmonious lute,
But with a stroke so gentle as may suit
The silent gliding of the hours,

Or yet the calmer growth of flowers;
The ascending of the falling dew,
Which none can see, though all find true.
For thus alone,
Can be shown,
How downy, now smooth,
Eudora doth move,
How silken her actions appear,
The air of her face,
Of a gentler grace
Than those that do stroke the ear.
Her address so sweet,
So modestly meet,
That 'tis not the loud though tunable string,
Can show forth so soft, so noiseless a thing!
O this to express from thy hand must fall,
Then music's self, something more musical.

JOHN DRYDEN (1631–1700)

From *The Satires of Decimus Junius Juvenalis* (1693)

John Dryden, English poet, critic, playwright, and one of the most distinguished men of letters of the seventeenth century, was born into a dissenting family in Northamptonshire and educated at Trinity College, Cambridge. His first important works were poetical: the *Heroic Stanzas* (1659) on the death of Oliver Cromwell and *Astraea Redux* (1660) on the return of Charles II. His first play, *The Wild Gallant*, was staged in 1663; he married Lady Elizabeth Howard the same year. In 1667 after the publication of *Annus Mirabilis*, a celebration of the British naval victory over the Dutch, Dryden was named poet laureate. In the 1670s he produced a number of plays—both light comedies such as *Marriage à la Mode* (1673) and *The Mock-Astrologer* (1678), and heroic verse dramas, of which *The Conquest of Granada* (1672), *Aurengzebe* (1676), and the Shakespearean pastiche *All for Love* (1678) remain the best known.

In the 1680s Dryden turned to political and literary satire with *Absalom and Achitophel* (1681), a lampoon on the unsuccessful Monmouth Rebellion, and *MacFlecknoe* (1682), an attack on fellow playwright Thomas Shadwell. He also underwent a period of protracted religious uncertainty: the 1682 poem *Religio Laici* is a somewhat ambivalent defence of Anglicanism; *The Hind and the Panther*, from the following year, reflects his conversion to Catholicism. (Upon refusing to take the oath of conformity after the Glorious Revolution of 1688 he was stripped of his laureateship by William III.) He produced some of his greatest poems in the 1690s, including the second of two odes for St. Cecilia's Day, *Alexander's Feast*, in 1697. In his last years Dryden devoted himself mainly to translations and adaptations—producing elegantly Englished versions of Persius and Juvenal, Virgil's *Aeneid*, and parts of Homer and Lucretius, as well as a compilation of tales from Chaucer, Ovid and Boccaccio called *Fables, Ancient and Modern* (1699).

Juvenal's Sixth Satire, "On Women," was notorious in the seventeenth and eighteenth centuries for its grossly scandalous passages—notably the no-holds-barred attack (ll. 299–333) on certain tribadistic Roman "dames" who urinate on statues and "ride" one another like horses during drunken moonlit orgies. Dryden's version of the offending passage in his 1693 translation is forthright in a way that Victorian translators would later abjure:

With Musick rais'd, they spread abroad their Hair;
And toss their Heads like an enamour'd Mare:
Lausella lays her Garland by, and proves
The mimick Leachery of Manly Loves.

The redaction here is by no means literal: a more exact translation of Juvenal's *inque vices equitant, ac luna teste moventur* (line 311) might be Peter Green's "Then, while the Moon looks down on their motions, they take turns to ride each other." Yet Dryden keeps intact the poem's moral shock, along with its powerful informational content. For notwithstanding the grotesquerie of its imagery, Juvenal's diatribe was an instructive text for homosexual women before 1900. Not only did the work confirm the existence of same-sex passion, it served as a kind of code-text through which one's own sexual unorthodoxy might be signaled. Thus the early nineteenth-century diarist Anne Lister, who, after hinting at her secret lesbianism to another woman in Yorkshire in the 1820s, wrote in her journal, "Miss Pickford has read the Sixth Satyr of Juvenal. She understands these matters well enough." Whether Lister knew her Juvenal through Dryden is not clear; given the renown of his translation, it is possible she did.

FURTHER READING: James Kinsley, ed., *The Poems of John Dryden*, 4 vols. (Oxford: Clarendon, 1958); Juvenal, *The Sixteen Satires*, trans. Peter Green (Harmondsworth, Middlesex: Penguin, 1974); Felicity Nussbaum, *The Brink of All We Hate: English Satires on Women 1660–1745* (Lexington: University Press of Kentucky, 1984); James A. Winn, " 'Complying with the Times': Dryden's Satires of Juvenal and Persius (1693)," *Eighteenth-Century Life* 21 (1988): 76–87; Rachel Miller, " 'Physics for the Great': Dryden's Satiric Translations of Juvenal, Persius, and Boccaccio," *Philological Quarterly* 68 (1989): 53–75; Ros Ballaster, " 'The Vices of Old Rome Revived': Representations of Female Same-Sex Desire in Seventeenth and Eighteenth Century England," in Suzanne Raitt, ed., *Volcanos and Pearl Divers: Essays in Lesbian Feminist Studies* (Binghamton, N.Y.: Haworth, 1995), pp. 13–36; Tanya Caldwell, "Dryden's Sixth Satire of Juvenal and the Sexual Politics of Monarchy," *Philological Quarterly* 75 (1996): 23–41.

What care our Drunken Dames to whom they spread?
Wine, no distinction makes of Tail or Head.
Who lewdly Dancing at a Midnight-Ball,
For hot Eringoes, and Fat Oysters call:
Full Brimmers to their Fuddled Noses thrust;
Brimmers the last Provocatives of Lust.
When Vapours to their swimming Brains advance,

And double Tapers on the Tables Dance.
  Now think what Bawdy Dialogues they have,
What *Tullia* talks to her confiding Slave;
At Modesty's old Statue: when by Night,
They make a stand, and from their Litters light;
The Good Man early to the Levee goes,
And treads the Nasty Paddle of his Spouse.
  The Secrets of the Goddess nam'd the Good,
Are even by Boys and Barbers understood:
Where the Rank Matrons, Dancing to the Pipe,
Gig with their Bums, and are for Action ripe;
With Musick rais'd, they spread abroad their Hair;
And toss their Heads like an enamour'd Mare:
Lausella lays her Garland by, and proves
The mimick Leachery of Manly Loves.
Rank'd with the Lady, the cheap Sinner lies;
For here not Blood, but Virtue gives the prize.
Nothing is feign'd, in this Venereal Strife;
'Tis downright Lust, and Acted to the Life.
So full, so fierce, so vigorous, and so strong;
That, looking on, wou'd make old *Nestor* Young.
Impatient of delay, a general sound,
An universal Groan of Lust goes round;
For then, and only then, the Sex sincere is found.
Now is the time of Action; now begin,
They cry, and let the lusty Lovers in.
The Whoresons are asleep; Then bring the Slaves,
And Watermen, a Race of strong-back'd Knaves.

ELIZABETH SINGER ROWE (1674–1737)

"Love and Friendship: A Pastoral" (1696)

The poet Elizabeth Singer Rowe, born in Somerset, was the daughter of a dissenting minister, and much of her verse—especially that written after the death of her husband, Thomas Rowe, in 1715—is overtly religious, even mystical in nature. But a number of Rowe's early poems, written under the nom de plume "Philomela" and published in her 1696 *Poems on Several Occasions* when she was only twenty-two, celebrate female romantic friendship. Several are dedicated to Frances Thynne, later the Countess of Hertford, and a poet in her own right. Perfervid effusions such as "Love and Friendship: A Pastoral" exhibit all the classic tensions of late seventeenth- and early eighteenth-century female homophilic verse. Cast as a pastoral dialogue between two shepherdesses, Amaryllis and Sylvia, the poem seemingly contrasts male-female "love" with female-female "friendship," yet its pedantically maintained symmetrical structure actually works to suggest an equivalence between heterosexual and homosexual affection.

FURTHER READING: Elizabeth Singer Rowe, *Miscellaneous Works*, 2 vols. (London, 1739); Madeleine Forell Marshall, *The Poetry of Elizabeth Singer Rowe* (Lewiston: Edwin Mellen, n.d.); H. S. Hughes, "Elizabeth Rowe and the Countess of Hertford," *Publications of the Modern Language Association* 59 (1944): 726–46; H. F. Strecher, *Elizabeth Singer Rowe: The Poetess of Frome* (Berne: Herbert Lang, 1973).

AMARYLLIS:
    While from the skies the ruddy sun descends;
    And rising night the ev'ning shade extends:
    While pearly dews o'erspread the fruitful field;
    And closing flowers reviving odours yield;
    Let us, beneath these spreading trees, recite
    What from our hearts our muses may indite.

Nor need we, in this close retirement, fear,
Least any swain our am'rous secrets hear.

SYLVIA:

To ev'ry shepherd I would mine proclaim;
Since fair *Aminta* is my softest theme:
A stranger to the loose delights of love,
My thoughts the nobler warmth of friendship prove;
And while its pure and sacred fire I sing,
Chaste goddess of the groves, thy succour bring.

AMARYLLIS:

Propitious god of love, my breast inspire
With all thy charms, with all thy pleasing fire:
Propitious god of love, thy succour bring;
Whilst I thy darling, thy *Alexis* sing,
Alexis, as the op'ning blossoms fair,
Lovely as light, and soft as yielding air.
For him each virgin sighs, and on the plains
The happy youth above each rival reigns;
With such an air, and such a graceful mien,
No shepherd dances on the flow'ry green:
Nor to the echoing groves, and whisp'ring springs,
In sweeter strains the tuneful *Conon* sings;
When loud applauses fill the crouded groves,
And *Phoebus* the superior song approves.

SYLVIA:

Beauteous *Aminta* is as early light,
Breaking the melancholy shades of night.
When she is near, all anxious trouble flies:
And our reviving hearts confess her eyes.
Young love, and blooming joy, and gay desires,
In ev'ry breast the beauteous nymph inspires:
But on the plain when she no more appears,
The plain a dark and gloomy prospect wears.
In vain the streams roll on; the eastern breeze
Dances in vain among the trembling trees.
In vain the birds begin their ev'ning song,
And to the silent night their notes prolong:
Nor groves, nor chrystal streams, nor verdant field
Can wonted pleasure in her absence yield.

AMARYLLIS:

Alexis absent, all the pensive day,
In some obscure retreat I lonely stray:

All day to the repeating caves complain,
In mournful accents, and a dying strain.
Dear, lovely youth! I cry to all around:
Dear, lovely youth! the flatt'ring vales resound.

SYLVIA:

On flow'ry banks, by ev'ry murm'ring stream,
Aminta is my muse's softest theme:
'Tis she that does my artful notes refine,
And with her name my noblest verse shall shine.

AMARYLLIS:

I'll twine fresh garlands for *Alexis*' brows,
And consecrate to him my softest vows:
The charming youth shall my *Apollo* prove;
Adorn my songs, and tune my voice to love.

ANONYMOUS

"Venus's Reply" (1699)

The following doggerel poem is a reply to "The Women's Complaint to Venus" (1699), a satiric piece lamenting the prevalence of sodomy in England. Both poems can be found in *A Collection of the Most Choice and Private Poems, Lampoons, &c., from the Withdrawal of the Late King James 1688 to the year 1701, Collected by a Person of Quality*, in the Brotherton Collection at Leeds. (One scholar has suggested that the collection may be the work of Sarah Cowper, a well-connected Hertfordshire lady.) While next to worthless artistically, "Venus's Reply" is of considerable historical and etymological interest. The "game of Flatts" was a common slang phrase for lesbian sex in the eighteenth century: this may represent its first appearance in print. Similarly, the poem contains what may be the earliest usage in English literature of the adjective "odd" (stanza 6) in connection with lesbianism. Like *queer* and *dyke*, the word *odd* has often had covert sapphic connotations. In her 1755 autobiography, the notorious actress and male impersonator Charlotte Charke described herself as an "odd mortal"; her off-stage adventures in masculine dress, she told her eighteenth-century readers, made for a history of consummate "oddity." In the 1820s, the lesbian diarist Anne Lister, referred to her secretly harbored passion for women as her "odd freak": after encountering a similarly inclined lady in 1823 she reported feeling distinctly "oddish." By the later nineteenth century odd had become, in many quarters, a not-so-subtle codeword for lesbian tendencies. In Henry James's *The Bostonians* (1886), Olive Chancellor, the wealthy spinster whose tragic infatuation with a charismatic younger woman drives the narrative, is several times described as "very odd" indeed. The character of Rhoda Nunn, the ascetic feminist in George Gissing's *The Odd Women* (1893), is shaded with similar ambiguities: Gissing's depiction of her putative passion for the cynical bachelor Everard Barfoot remains spectacularly unconvincing. Even in Radclyffe Hall's pioneering lesbian novel of 1928, *The Well of Loneliness*, odds and oddities abound: when Stephen Gordon, Hall's androgynous heroine, refuses a male suitor, her mother's friends whisper "that she had always been odd, and now for some reason she seemed odder than ever."

FURTHER READING: *A Collection of the Most Choice and Private Poems, Lampoons, &c., from the Withdrawal of the Late King James 1688 to the Year 1701, Collected by a Person of Quality* (1701); Terry Castle, *The Apparitional Lesbian: Female Homosexuality and Modern Culture* (New York: Columbia University Press, 1993); Emma Donoghue, *Passions Between Women: British Lesbian Culture 1668–1801* (London: Scarlet, 1993).

Why Nymphs these pitiful stories,
    But you are too to blame,
    And have got a new game
Call'd Flatts with a swinging Clitoris.

Besides I have heard of wax tapers
    With which you get up
    And each other Tup
To cure the Green Sickness and Vapours.

I am told by a delicate Seignior
    Some Matrons do ease
    Their Lust, and so please
They've not been laid with these ten years.

Your Frogmore frolicks discover
    Some Reasons of Art
    So play the man's part
You are for no Masculine Lover.

At all which I am so offended
    My Son at Men's hearts
    Will throw no more darts
Till your Lust and your lives are amended.

Forsake but these odd ways of sinning,
    And I'll undertake
    The arrantest Rake
Shall swinge you as at the beginning.

❧ *The Eighteenth Century* ❧

[MARY] DELARIVIER MANLEY (1663–1724)

"The Ladies of the New Cabal" from *The New Atalantis* (1709)

Delarivier Manley, English novelist, playwright, political journalist, and ardent Tory propagandist during the early years of the eighteenth century, is best known today for her lubricious political allegory, *Secret Memoirs and Manners of Several Persons of Quality, of Both Sexes. From the New Atalantis, an Island in the Mediterranean* (1709). Modeled on the Baronne d'Aulnoy's *Mémoires de la cour d'Espagne* (1679–81) and other seventeenth-century French scandal-memoirs, the book purports to describe life on the imaginary island of Atalantis but is in fact an intricately wrought satire on political and erotic intrigues at the court of Queen Anne. As in her earlier *Secret History of Queen Zarah and the Zarazians* (1705) and the autobiographical *Adventures of Rivella* (1714), Manley attacks prominent Whig leaders of the day, including the Duke of Marlborough and his charismatic wife, Sarah Churchill, one-time favorite of the sapphically inclined Queen Anne.

Eighteenth-century political satirists frequently used sexual innuendo, including rumors of homosexuality, as a way of undermining opponents. Queen Anne's enemies made much both of her volatile intimacy with Sarah Churchill and her later infatuation with a relatively obscure lady-in-waiting, Abigail Hill:

> Wheneas Q— A— of great renown
> Great Britain's scepter swayed,
> Besides the Church, she dearly loved
> A dirty Chamber-maid.

In the "Ladies of the New Cabal" section of the *New Atalantis*—when "Lady Intelligence," in converse with her friend "Astrea," describes the various amorous intrigues taking place among the members of an all-female aristocratic secret society—Manley adopts similar smear tactics. By hinting at the Cabalists' "criminal" fondness for one another, she satirizes a number of women associated with Anne's court, notably the Whig sympathizer and playwright Catherine Trotter (Daphne), who dedicated several works to the Queen. At the same time, the bizarre little gynocosm depicted by Manley has its attractive, even utopian aspects. As several commentators have noted, the "New

Cabal" resembles the homoerotic "Society of Friendship" imagined by the poet Katherine Philips in the 1660s and bears a striking similarity to a number of later, often utopian literary and artistic visions of eroticized all-female communities.

FURTHER READING: Mary Delarivier Manley, *Secret Memoirs and Manners of Several Persons of Quality of Both Sexes, From the New Atalantis, an Island in the Mediterranean, Written Originally in Italian* (1709; rpt. Harmondsworth, Middlesex: Penguin, 1991); Patricia Koster, ed., *The Novels of Mary Delarivier Manley*, 2 vols. (Gainesville, Fla.: Scholars' Facsimiles, 1971); Fidelis Morgan, *A Woman of No Character: An Autobiography of Mrs. Manley* (London: Faber and Faber, 1986); Jane Spencer, *The Rise of the Woman Novelist from Aphra Behn to Jane Austen* (Oxford: Basil Blackwell, 1986); Rosalind Ballaster, *Seductive Forms: Women's Amatory Fiction 1684–1740* (Oxford: Clarendon, 1992); Lisa L. Moore, *Dangerous Intimacies: Toward a Sapphic History of the British Novel* (Durham, N.C.: Duke University Press, 1997); Paula McDowell, *The Women of Grub Street: Press, Politics, and Gender in the London Literary Marketplace* (Oxford and New York: Clarendon, 1998).

ASTREA: Does your Ladyship's intelligence extend to the knowledge of those ladies (we know 'em to be such by their voices) who fill those three coaches that run along the gravel-road on the right hand of us? They laugh loud and incessantly. 'Tis certain they have neither the spleen nor vapours! or, for the present seem to have forgot 'em. Can any persons be more at their ease? Sure these seem to unknow that there is a certain portion of misery and disappointments allotted to all men, which one time or other will assuredly overtake 'em. The very consideration is sufficient, in my opinion, to put a damp upon the serenest, much more a tumultuous joy.

INTELLIGENCE: That is afflicting themselves unprofitably. Nothing ought to hinder a man from enjoying the present, no reflection of the future carry away his relish of the instant, if it be innocently employed. To one of right understanding it will certainly happen thus; provided he be free of bodily pains, which, notwithstanding the vain celebrated apathy of the stoics, none was ever found to be insensible of and, whoever has pretended to the contrary, must be as ridiculous as affected.

But to satisfy your Excellency, these ladies are of the new Cabal, a sect (however innocent in it self) that does not fail from meeting its share of censure from the world. Alas! what can they do? How unfortunate are women? If they seek their diversion out of themselves and include the other sex, they must be criminal? If in themselves (as those of the new Cabal), still they are criminal? Though censurers must carry their imaginations a much greater length than I am able to do mine, to explain this hypothesis with success. They pretend to find in these the vices of old Rome revived and quote you certain detestable authors who (to amuse posterity) have introduced you lasting monuments of vice, which could only subsist in imagination and can, in reality, have no other foundation that what are to be found in the dreams of poets and the ill nature of those censurers, who will have no diversions innocent, but what themselves advance!

Oh how laudable! how extraordinary! how wonderful! is the uncommon happiness of the Cabal? They have wisely excluded that rapacious sex who, making a prey of the honour of ladies, find their greatest satisfaction (some few excepted) in boasting of their good fortune, the very chocolate-house being witnesses of their self-love where, promiscuously among the known and unknown, they expose the letters of the fair, explain the mysterious and refine upon the happy part, in their redundancy of vanity consulting nothing but what may feed the insatiable hydra!

The Cabal run no such dangers, they have all the happiness in themselves! Two beautiful ladies joined in an excess of amity (no word is tender enough to express their new delight) innocently embrace! For how can they be guilty? They vow eternal tenderness, they exclude the men, and condition that they will always do so. What irregularity can there be in this? 'Tis true, some things may be strained a little too far, and that causes reflections to be cast upon the rest. One of the fair could not defend herself from receiving an importunate visit from a person of the troublesome sex. The lady who was her favourite came unexpectedly at the same time upon another. Armida heard her chair set down in the hall and presently knew her voice, enquiring with precipitation who was above? Having observed a common coach at the gate without a livery, the lover became surprised to the last degree to see Armida's. She trembled! she turned pale! she conjured him to pass into her closet and consent to be concealed till the lady was gone! His curiosity made him as obliging as she could desire; he was no sooner withdrawn, but his fair rival entered the chamber enraged, her voice shrill, her tone inquisitive and menacing, the extremes of jealousy in her eyes and air. "Where is this inconstant—where is this ungrateful girl—? What happy wretch is it upon whom you bestow my rites? To whom do you deliver the possession of my kisses and embraces? Upon whom bestow that heart so invaluable and for which I have paid the equivalent?—Come let us see this monster to whom my happiness is sacrificed—Are you not sufficiently warned by the ruin of so many? Are you also eager to be exposed, to be undone, to be food for vanity, to fill the detestable creatures with vain glory! What recompense?—ah, what satisfaction!—Can there be in any heart of theirs, more than in mine—Have they more tenderness—more endearments—their truth cannot come in comparison! Besides, they find their account in treachery and boasting, their pride is gratified, whilst our interest is in mutual secrecy, in natural justice and in mutual constancy."

Such excursions as these have given occasion to the enemies of the Cabal to refine, as much as they please, upon the mysteries of it. There are, who will not allow of innocency in any intimacies, detestable censurers who, after the manner of the Athenians, will not believe so great a man as Socrates (him whom the oracle delivered to be the wisest of all men) could see every hour the beauty of an Alcibiades without taxing his sensibility. How did they recriminate for his affection, for his cares, his tenderness to the lovely youth? How have they delivered him down to posterity as blameable for too guilty a passion for his beautiful pupil?—Since then it is not in the fate of even so wise a man to avoid the censure of the busy and the bold, care ought to be taken by others (less fortified against occasion of detraction, in declining such unaccountable intimacies) to prevent the ill-natured world's refining upon their mysterious innocence.

The persons who passed us in those three coaches were returning from one of their private, I was going to say silent, meetings, but far be it from me to detract from any of the attributes of the sex. The Lady L---- and her daughters make four of the cabal. They have taken a little lodging about twelve furlongs from Angela in a place obscure and pleasant with a magazine of good wine and necessary conveniences as to chambers of repose, a tolerable garden and the country in prospect. They wear away the indulgent happy hours according to their own taste. Their coaches and people (of whom they always take as few with them as possible) are left to wait at the convenient distance of a field in length, an easy walk to their bower of bliss. The day and hour of their *rendezvous* is appointed beforehand; they meet, they caress, they swear inviolable secrecy and amity. The glass corroborates their endearments. They momently exclude the men: fortify themselves in the precepts of virtue and chastity against all their detestable undermining arts: arraign without pity or compassion those who have been so unfortunate as to fall into their snare: propagate their principles of exposing them without mercy: give rules to such of the Cabal who are not married how to behave themselves to such who they think fit they should marry, no such weighty affair being to be accomplished without the mutual consent of the society, at the same time lamenting the custom of the world, that has made it convenient (nay, almost indispensable) for all ladies once to marry. To those that have husbands, they have other instructions, in which this is sure to be one: to reserve their heart, their tender amity for their fair friend, an article in this well-bred, wilfully undistinguishing age which the husband seems to be rarely solicitous of.

Those who are in their opinion so happy as to be released from the imposing matrimonial fetters are thought the ornament of the Cabal and by all most happy. They claim an ascendant, a right of governing, of admitting or extending; in both they are extremely nice, with particular reserve to the constitution of the novice, they strictly examine her genius, whether it have fitted her for the mysteries of the Cabal, as if she may be rendered insensible on the side of Nature. Nature, who has the trick of making them dote on the opposite improving sex, for if her foible be found directed to what Nature inspires, she is unanimously excluded, and particular injunctions bestowed upon all members of this distinguishing society from admitting her to their bosom, or initiating her in the mysteries of their endearments.

Secrecy is also a material article. This they inviolably promise, nor is it the least part of the instruction given to a new bride, lest she let her husband into a mystery (however innocent) that may expose and ridicule the community as it happened in the case of the beautiful virgin Euphelia. No sooner did she appear as attendant to the Queen, but all the eyes of all the circle were directed to her. The men adored, the ladies would have discovered something to destroy that adoration if it had been possible, except the Marchioness de Lerma who, bold and masculine, loudly taxed these invidious spectators of ill nature and malice. She took the fair maid into especial consideration, sheltered her under her distinguished protections and, in short, introduced her into the Cabal of which, they say, the Marchioness was one of the first founders in Atalantis, having something so robust in her air and mien that the other sex would have certainly claimed her for one of theirs, if she had not thought fit to declare her self by her habit (alone) to be of the other, insomuch that I have often heard it lamented by the curious, who have taxed themselves of negligence, and were intimate with her lord, when living, that they did not desire him to explain upon that query.

Euphelia flourished under the shine of so great a favourite. The Marquis de los Minos fell in love with her. There was nothing to obstruct his happiness but the Marchioness de Lerma's jealousy. Enraged to lose her beautiful pupil, she traversed her advancement all that lay in her power, but the honour of such a marriage being conspicuous on the young virgin's side, she was forced to give up the secrets of the Cabal and sacrifice the marchioness's honour to preserve the opinion of her own.

Some few such discoveries have happened to cast a taint upon the innocency of the Cabal. How malicious is the world? Who would not avoid their censure if it were possible? We must do justice to the endeavours of the witty Marchioness of Sandomire when she used to mask her diversions in the habit of the other sex and, with her female favourite, Ianthe, wander through the gallant quarter of Atalantis in search of adventures. But what adventures? Good heaven! none that could in reality wound her chastity! Her virtue sacred to her lord and the marriage bed was preserved inviolable! For what could reflect back upon it with any prejudice in the little liberties she took with her own sex whom she used to cajole with the affected seeming gallantry of the other, engage and carry them to the public gardens, and houses of entertainment with music and all diversions? These creatures of hire failed not to find their account in obliging the Marchioness's and Ianthe's peculiar taste, by all the liberties that belonged to women of their loose character and indigence. Though I should look upon it as an excess of mortification were I the marchioness to see the corruption of the sex and to what extremes vice may step by step lead those who were born and probably educated in the road of innocence. It may be surely counted an inhumane curiosity and shows a height of courage, more blameable than otherwise, not to be dejected at the brutality, the degeneracy, of those of our own specie.

The Viceroy of Peru's lady has a more extensive taste, her circle admitting the eminent of both sexes. None can doubt of her condescension to the men and, because she will leave nothing undiscovered or unattempted in the map of tenderness, she has encouraged the warbling Lindamira (low as is her rank) to explain to her the *terra incognita* of the Cabal. Not one of 'em but think themselves honoured by a person of her distinction and agreeable merit. To complete their happiness they seem to wish (but I doubt it is in vain) that it were possible to exclude the other sex and engross her wholly to their own. But, alas! what hopes? Her heart, her eyes, her air, call for other approbations, the admiration of the men! In her alone that diffusive vanity is pardonable, is taking. She undoubtedly knows herself born to a greater capacity of giving happiness than ought to fall to the share of one mortal and, therefore, in her just and equal distribution of beauty, she seems to leave none of her numerous favourites solid reason of complaint, that they are not in their turn considered as they deserve.

One of the ladies of the Cabal, that is in the leading coach, is a writer. The Chevalier Pierro, without having much wit of his own, married her for hers. A strange paradox! for what is music to the deaf, beauty to the blind, or the best Italian strains, to a person without ear or judgement? Yet this was the Chevalier's case and he made an admirable husband, believing (as he ought) that his wife was never in the wrong, nor himself in the right, but when she said so. Her wit was the leading card, which he was sure to follow and, like a lover (rather than a husband) never renounced. Add to this his youth, good shape and an air of the world, which might make him in most companies be esteemed a genteel man, though with the addition, even of gratitude, Zara could not find her happiness in him but, because she would do nothing against her duty, and was a slave professed to outward honour and virtue, she obliged the Marquis ------ (who did her the courtesy of some of his superficial gallantries) to dress in the habit of her own sex. Thus was the marine lover introduced into her very innermost apartment, the cabinet sacred to the Muses and her self, where her obsequious husband durst never approach uncalled, nor was, but upon eminent days of grace, admitted.

The Marquis, who had a thousand adventures in his head, could not rest long upon any one. Besides, he had a left-hand wife that took up the real tenderness of his heart. What he bestowed upon others was but by way of comparison to endear her the more to him, and as a foil to set off the lustre of her charms. He soon grew weary of Zara's affair, not finding it possible to come up to the height of her lovesick, romantic expectations. She, who had all the Muses in her head, wanted to be caressed in a poetical manner; her lover, by her good will, should not be less than Apollo in his attributes of flame and fancy. Thus would she have been adored, but that was not to be expected from the Marquis, whose heart was engaged. Nor could any but a poet answer the extravagancies of a poetess's expectation. Seignior Mompellier was newly become the fashion (his very just and admirable poem having with applause introduced him); this was a lover indeed worth ten thousand of the vulgar. Nor was cruelty one of his defects; the fair sex never had reason to complain of him that way. Zara, to the utmost extent of her poetical capacity, gave him to know in printed heroics that she did justice to his extreme merit, not doubting, after this advance, but he would be grateful to her. But whether her not being a beauty, or the Seignior's having wit enough for himself and a mistress too, caused him to slight that talent and to neglect his good fortune, 'tis certain she now speaks of him in terms that no ways answer her beginning admiration.

Thus discouraged by the men, she fell into the taste of the Cabal. Daphne was her favourite: Daphne, who when she first set out to travel the road of gallantry, had all the reason in the world to expect a lucky journey, for her first guide (if you will believe her self) was no less a person than Count Fortunatus. She had a relation of hers that sued for a post in the Count's brigade; some small acquaintance with his lady introduced her so far as his antichamber, where she made one of the petitioners. I have heard several divided in opinion as to her person, whether she should be esteemed pretty or indifferent. Her cheeks are by much too sanguine: neither with that advantage does the white assume gloss enough to pass for a good complexion: her eyes light and round but brisk, and sometimes form themselves into a becoming look. Her teeth indeed are admirable. As to her stature, 'tis low; her shape would be well turned, if something of a certain stiffness, which suffers no part of the person to move without the whole, were not unbecoming to all. But she has an air of youth and innocence which has been of excellent use to her in those occasions she has since had to impose upon the world as to matters of conduct, her aspect being so fortunate, that one must wait to be convinced by proof, before one could believe of her what the generality of the world are already so well acquainted with. The Count immediately, by that very air, distinguished and liked her. He approached with a resolution of granting, even before she asked. Thus it was no hard matter for her to succeed. But because the place was too public for what he designed, he softly bid her be in a coach at six a clock, before the temple of Minerva, and he would not fail to attend her there, where they might have more liberty than at present to enquire into the merits of her relation's cause and pretensions.

This was not stumbling in the dark to one of Daphne's conversation with the world; she knew it amounted to a rendezvous, which she ought not to agree to without resolving to pay the price the Count would undoubtedly set upon what she intended to request and he to grant, but, having the pretence of business to veil her modesty, as thin as was that veil and as easily seen through, she assumed it and went to the meeting.

It appears strange to me that, considering the Count's power and riches, she did not make her fortune by his fondness. But I think there yet wants an example of elevated generosity in him to any of his mistresses, though the world can't dispute but that he has had many, his way to pay the favour being to desire the lady to study if there is any thing in his power by which he may oblige any relation or friend of hers and that he will not fail to grant it. Thus every way a husband of his money, his reputation and grandeur procure him the good fortune he desires, though, were the ladies with whom he has a mind to converse, of my taste they would think his own very handsome person a reward sufficient for all the charms they can bestow.

After the first run of the Count's favour, Daphne was forced to descend; all were not Fortunatus's that she saw her self obliged to endure. Then it was that she wrote for the stage, sometimes with ill fortune, sometimes with indifferent and but once with success, for which she was obliged to the long and experience and good judgement of that excellent tragedian Roscius, who was grown old in the arms (if I may call it) and approbation of his audience. Roscius, a sincere friend and man of honour, not to be corrupted even by the way of living and manners of those he hourly conversed with: Roscius, born for every thing that he thinks fit to undertake, has wit and morality, fire and judgement, sound sense and good nature: Roscius, who would have still been eminent in any station of life he had been called to, only unhappy to the world, in that it is not possible for him to bid time stand still and to permit him to endure for ever, the ornament of the stage, the delight of his friends and the regret of all who shall one day have the misfortune to lose him.

See what it is to be so great a man as is the Count Fortunatus, whose favour is esteemed such a piece of good fortune that the very ladies can't possess it without boasting. They who disdain to have their virtue so much as suspected for any other do not forbear to proclaim the sacrifice they have made to him. How else had the world been acquainted with his affair with Daphne and others? The Count himself (reserved and in good correspondence with his wife) would never make these matters his discourse. The Count, who does not seem by his aspect to bear about him a desire to those inferior diversions, born for something more great and noble than the embraces of a puny girl, speaks only of war and state, of the camp and cabinet and, when he descends to talk of his darling inclination, it is only the love of riches that bespeaks his praise and to which all other things must, in his opinion, submit.

I could enumerate, were it not too tedious, many of Daphne's adventures, by which she was become the diversion of as many of the town as found her to their taste and would purchase. Yet she still assumed an air of *Virtue pretended* and was ever eloquent (according to her stiff manner) upon the foible of others. She also fitted her self with an excellent mask called religion, having as often changed and as often professed her self a votary to that shrine, where was to be found the most apparent interest, or which priest had the greatest art of persuading. One of Ceres at length fell to her share, young, scarce initiated in her mysteries and not at all in the profits. But a husband was Daphne's business, the only means to prevent her from falling (when her youth and charms were upon the wing) into extreme contempt.

Zara, who had introduced her to the Cabal, but with infinite anxiety suffered that any lover should dare to engage where she had fixed her heart. But because narrow circumstances do not always suffer people to do what they would, Daphne was still forced to have lovers, though if you believe her professions to her fair friend, they had no part in her inclinations. In short, they seemed to live only for each other. Zara, whose poetical genius did not much lead her to the better economy of her family, soon found the inconveniences of it. The poor Chevalier, her husband, stemmed the tide as long as it was possible; at length obliged by his indifferent circumstances to put himself into the army and campaigns abroad, he left his lady at full liberty to pursue, with an uninterrupted *goust*, her taste of amity and the Cabal.

But Daphne's marriage crossed her delights. How does she exclaim against that breach of friendship in the fair? How regret the authority of a husband, who has boldly dared to carry his wife into the country? Where she now sets up for regularity and intends to be an ornament to that religion, which she had once before abandoned and newly again professed. She will write no more for the stage; 'tis profane, indiscreet, unpardonable. Controversy engrosses all her hours: the Muses must give place. If she have any fancy or judgement we may justly expect to see something excellent from a hand so well fitted (if experience can fit) to paint the defects and beauties of those many opinions she has so often and so zealously embraced.

There are others of the Cabal that lavish vast sums upon their *inamorettas*, with the empressment, diligence and warmth of a beginning lover. I could name a widow or two, who have almost undone themselves by their profuseness, so sacred and invincible is their principle of amity that misfortunes cannot shake. In this little commonwealth is no property; whatever a lady possesses is, *sans ceremone*, at the service and for the use of her fair friend, without the vain nice scruple of being obliged. 'Tis her right; the other disputes it not, no, not so much as in thought. They have no reserve; mutual love bestows all things in common, 'twould be against the dignity of the passion and unworthy such exalted, abstracted notions as theirs. How far laudable your Divinities will conclude of these tender amities, (with all possible submission) I refer to your better judgements and undisputed prerogative of setting the stamp of approbation, or dislike, upon all things.

ASTREA: It is something so new and uncommon, so laudable and blameable, that we don't know how to determine, especially wanting light even to guess at what you call the mysteries of the Cabal. If only tender friendship, inviolable and sincere, be the regard, what can be more meritorious or a truer emblem of their happiness above? 'Tis by imitation, the nearest approach they can make, a feint, a distant landshape of immortal joys. But if they carry it a length beyond what nature designed and fortify themselves by these new-formed amities against the hymenial union, or give their husbands but a second place in their affections and cares, 'tis wrong and to be blamed. Thus far as to the merit of the thing it self, but when we look with true regard to the world, if it permit a shadow of suspicion, a bare imagination, that the mysteries they pretend have any thing in 'em contrary to kind, and that strict modesty and virtue do not adorn and support their conversation, 'tis to be avoided and condemned, lest they give occasion for obscene laughter, new invented satire, fanciful jealousies and impure distrusts in that nice, unforgiving sex, who arbitrarily decide that woman was only created (with all her beauty, softness, passions and complete tenderness) to adorn the husband's reign, perfect his happiness, and propagate the kind.

JOSEPH ADDISON (1672–1719)

Spectator No. 223 (1711)

The essayist, poet, playwright, and politician Joseph Addison, the son of an Anglican dean, was educated at Charterhouse and Oxford, where he won prizes for Latin poetry. After a year as a fellow of Magdalen College, Oxford, he went on a tour of the continent from 1699 to 1703. Upon returning to London, he attracted public notice with his poem *The Campaign*, a bracing celebration of the British victory at Blenheim. Staunchly Whig in political sympathies, he was appointed under secretary of state in 1706 and elected to Parliament in 1708. After two years as chief secretary to the lord lieutenant of Ireland, he lost his post following the Tory victory in 1711 and turned to journalism. In collaboration with a former schoolmate, Richard Steele—editor of the London literary journal *The Tatler*—he began *The Spectator*, a popular newspaper devoted to politics, culture, and literature. Written in a lively, genteel, and accessible style, the paper appealed greatly to middle-class readers, especially women, and was an immediate success. It ran three times weekly from March 1711 to December 1712—then again (for eighty issues) in 1714—and inspired a host of imitations at home and abroad. Addison wrote most of the essays himself—on everything from free trade, Whig politics, and the Stamp Act to marriage, coquettes, cosmetics, fans, Locke's philosophy, witchcraft, the Italian opera, and Milton's *Paradise Lost*. Along with his partner, Steele, he must be considered the first great master of the English informal, or conversational, essay.

In 1713 Addison composed the tragic drama *Cato*, one of the most admired plays of the eighteenth century. In the same year he joined with other leading Whig writers to form the Kit-Kat Club; its members were later commemorated in a famous series of portraits by Sir Godfrey Kneller. Following the Whig return to power in 1715, Addison served as chief secretary for Ireland and then became a lord commissioner of trade in 1716. He married the Countess of Warwick the same year and fathered a daughter, Charlotte. In 1717 he was appointed secretary of state but, in increasingly poor health, was forced to resign his post in 1718. A bitter falling-out with Steele exacerbated his decline. He approached death with equanimity—his last words to his stepson, "See in what peace a Christian can die," became famous across Europe—and he was buried with great pomp in Westminster Abbey. A number of writings were published posthumously, including the first collected edition of his works in 1721.

Although not a scholar or philologist like his contemporary Anne Le Fèvre Dacier, Sappho's French translator, Addison was one of the most important popularizers of Sappho's poetry in the eighteenth century. He first wrote about the Greek poet in *Spectator* 223, an essay devoted—if somewhat sketchily—to her life and works. Conscious of his female and non-classically trained readers, he appended Ambrose Philips's translation of the so-called "Hymn to Aphrodite" (Fragment 1) so that "if the ladies have a mind to know the manner of writing practised by the so much celebrated Sappho, they may here see it in its genuine and natural beauty, without any foreign or affected ornaments." In a subsequent essay, *Spectator* 229, he reprinted Philips's translation of the equally celebrated Fragment 31 ("Blest as th'immortal gods is he"), the poem attributed to Sappho in Longinus's *On the Sublime*. Sappho is also mentioned in the comical *Spectator* 233, devoted to famous men and women of antiquity who killed themselves by leaping from the "promontory of Leucate into the Ionian Sea, in order to cure themselves of the passion of love."

In *Spectator* 223, reproduced below, Addison makes no mention of Sappho's purported lesbianism, perhaps out of deference to the sensibilities of his female readers. He focuses instead on her fabled passion for Phaon. Something in the arch manner in which he treats this love affair, however—Phaon is said to have "occasioned great calamities to this poetical lady"—suggests a more sophisticated apprehension. Addison himself read Greek and undoubtedly knew that several of Sappho's amorous poems were in fact addressed to women and girls.

FURTHER READING: Joseph Addison, *The Works of Joseph Addison*, ed. Richard Hurd, 6 vols. (London: George Bell, 1854–56); —, *The Spectator*, ed. Donald F. Bond, 5 vols. (Oxford: Clarendon, 1965); David M. Robinson, *Sappho and Her Influence* (Boston: Marshall Jones, 1924); Lee Andrew Elioseff, *The Cultural Milieu of Addison's Literary Criticism* (Austin: University of Texas Press, 1963); Édith Mora, *Sappho: Histoire d'un poète et traduction intégrale de l'oeuvre* (Paris: Flammarion, 1966); Peter Smithers, *The Life of Joseph Addison*, 2d ed. (Oxford: Clarendon, 1968); Robert M. Otten, *Joseph Addison* (Boston: Twayne, 1982); Joan DeJean, *Fictions of Sappho, 1546–1937* (Chicago: University of Chicago Press, 1989); Peter Jay and Caroline Lewis, eds., *Sappho Through English Poetry* (London: Anvil, 1996); Margaret Reynolds, *The Sappho Companion* (New York: Palgrave, 2001).

> *O suavis animal! qualem bonam*
> *Antehac fuisse, tales cùm sint reliquiæ!*
> Phæd.

When I reflect upon the various fate of those multitudes of ancient writers who flourished in Greece and Italy, I consider time as an immense ocean, in which many noble authors are entirely swallowed up, many very much shattered and damaged, some quite disjointed and broken into pieces, while some have wholly escaped the common wreck; but the number of the last is very small.

> Apparent rari nantes in gurgite vasto.

Among the mutilated poets of antiquity, there is none whose fragments are so beautiful as those of Sappho. They give us a taste of her way of writing, which is perfectly conformable with that extraordinary character we find of her, in the remarks of those great critics who were conversant with her works when they were entire. One may see by what is left of them, that she followed nature in all her thoughts, without descending to those little points, conceits, and turns of wit, with which many of our modern lyrics are so miserably infected. Her soul seems to have been made up of love and poetry: she felt the passion in all its warmth, and described it in all its symptoms. She is called by ancient authors the Tenth Muse; and by Plutarch is compared to Cacus, the son of Vulcan, who breathed out nothing but flame. I do not know by the character that is given of her works, whether it is not for the benefit of mankind that they are lost. They were filled with such bewitching tenderness and rapture, that it might have been dangerous to have given them a reading.

An inconstant lover, called Phaon, occasioned great calamities to this poetical lady. She fell desperately in love with him, and took a voyage into Sicily, in pursuit of him, he having withdrawn himself thither on purpose to avoid her. It was in that island, and on this occasion, she is supposed to have made the Hymn to Venus, with a translation of which I shall present my reader. Her hymn was ineffectual for the procuring that happiness which she prayed for in it. Phaon was still obdurate, and Sappho so transported with the violence of her passion, that she was resolved to get rid of it at any price.

There was a promontory in Acarnania called Leucate, on the top of which was a little temple dedicated to Apollo. In this temple it was usual for despairing lovers to make their vows in secret, and afterwards to fling themselves from the top of the precipice into the sea, where they were sometimes taken up alive. This place was therefore called The Lover's Leap; and whether or no the fright they had been in, or the resolution that could push them to so dreadful a remedy, or the bruises which they often received in their fall, banished all the tender sentiments of love, and gave their spirits another turn; those who had taken this leap were observed never to relapse into that passion. Sappho tried the cure, but perished in the experiment.

After having given this short account of Sappho so far as it regards the following Ode, I shall subjoin the translation of it as it was sent me by a friend, whose admirable pastorals and winter-piece have been already so well received. The reader will find in it that pathetic simplicity which is so peculiar to him, and so suitable to the Ode he has here translated. This Ode in the Greek (besides those beauties observed by Madame Dacier) has several harmonious turns in the words, which are not lost in the English. I must further add, that the translation has preserved every image and sentiment of Sappho, notwithstanding it has all the ease and spirit of an original. In a word, if the ladies have a mind to know the manner of writing practised by the so much celebrated Sappho, they may here see it in its genuine and natural beauty, without any foreign or affected ornaments.

An Hymn To Venus

I
O Venus, beauty of the skies,
To whom a thousand temples rise,
Gaily false in gentle smiles,
Full of love-perplexing wiles:
O goddess! from my heart remove
The wasting cares and pains of love.

II
If ever thou hast kindly heard
A song in soft distress preferred,
Propitious to my tuneful vow,
O gentle goddess, hear me now.
Descend, thou bright, immortal guest,
In all thy radiant charms confest.

III
Thou once didst leave Almighty Jove,
And all the golden roofs above:
The car thy wanton sparrows drew,
Hovering in air they lightly flew;
As to my bower they winged their way;
I saw their quivering pinions play.

IV
The birds dismist (while you remain)
Bore back their empty car again:
Then you, with looks divinely mild,
In every heavenly feature smiled,
And asked what new complaints I made,
And why I called you to my aid!

V

What phrensy in my bosom raged,
And by what cure to be assuaged?
What gentle youth I would allure,
Whom in my artful toils secure?
Who does thy tender heart subdue,
Tell me, my Sappho, tell me who?

VI

Though now he shuns thy longing arms,
He soon shall court thy slighted charms;
Though now thy offerings he despise,
He soon to thee shall sacrifice;
Though now he freeze, he soon shall burn.
And be thy victim in his turn.

VII

Celestial visitant, once more
Thy needful presence I implore!
In pity come and ease my grief,
Bring my distempered soul relief,
Favour thy suppliant's hidden fires,
And give me all my heart desires.

Madame Dacier observes there is something very pretty in that circumstance of this Ode, wherein Venus is described as sending away her chariot upon her arrival at Sappho's lodgings, to denote that it was not a short, transient visit which she intended to make her. This Ode was preserved by an eminent Greek critic, who inserted it entire in his works, as a pattern of perfection in the structure of it.

Longinus has quoted another Ode of this great poetess, which is likewise admirable in its kind, and has been translated by the same hand with the foregoing one. I shall oblige my reader with it in another paper. In the mean while, I cannot but wonder that these two finished pieces have never been attempted before by any of our countrymen. But the truth of it is, the compositions of the ancients, which have not in them any of those unnatural witticisms that are the delight of ordinary readers, are extremely difficult to render into another tongue, so as the beauties of the original may not appear weak and faded in translation.

AMBROSE PHILIPS (1675–1749)

Sappho Fragment 31 ("Blest as th'immortal Gods is he") (1711)

The poet and translator Ambrose Philips, maligned in his day as "Namby Pamby Philips" for the sentimentality of his verses, is now remembered—if at all—as one of the more hapless dunces in Alexander Pope's 1743 satirical poem *The Dunciad*. Yet he is a surprisingly important figure in the history of Sappho translations. A fellow of St. John's College, Cambridge, Philips first won public notice for his *Pastorals* (1710) and English translation of Racine's *Andromaque* (retitled *The Distrest Mother*) produced in 1712. In 1711 Joseph Addison published Philips's translations of Sappho's Fragment 1 ("Hymn to Venus") and Fragment 31 ("Blest as th'immortal Gods is he") in *The Spectator*, numbers 223 and 229. Philips's annotated edition of *The Works of Anacreon and Sappho* appeared in 1713, containing not only translations of all Sappho's extant verses but a biographical note on "the Lesbian dame." Unlike Sappho's famous French translator, Anne Le Fèvre Dacier, whose widely influential translation of Sappho's odes had appeared in 1681, Philips made no attempt to deny or disguise Sappho's unconventional love life. Tradition held, he noted, "that her Amorous Humour was not satisfied with the Addresses of Men; but that she was willing to have her Mistresses too, as well as her *Gallants*." Nor did his translation of Fragment 31 in any way "heterosexualize" the poetic situation: we seem to hear a woman's voice, lamenting (as in the Greek original) the defection of a female beloved, who has left her for that man at whose side she sits at the banquet feast.

FURTHER READING: Ambrose Philips, *Pastorals* (London, 1710); —, et al., *The Works of Anacreon, and Sappho. Done from the Greek, by Several Hands. With Their lives Prefix'ed. To Which Is Added, The Prize of Wisdom. A Dialogue Between Anacreon and Aristotle. By M. Fontenelle. Also Bion's Idyllium, upon the Death of Adonis. By the Earl of Winchilsea* (London, 1713); —, *Pastorals, Epistles, Odes, and Other Original Poems, with Translations from Pindar, Anacreon, and Sappho* (London, 1765); David M. Robinson, *Sappho and Her Influence* (Boston: Marshall Jones, 1924); Joan DeJean, *Fictions of Sappho, 1546–1937* (Chicago: University of Chicago Press, 1989); Emma Donoghue, *Pas-*

sions Between Women: British Lesbian Culture 1668–1801 (London: Scarlet, 1993); Margaret Reynolds, *The Sappho Companion* (New York: Palgrave, 2001).

Blest as th'immortal Gods is he,
The Youth who fondly sits by thee,
And hears and sees thee all the while,
Softly speak, and sweetly smile.

'Twas this depriv'd my Soul of Rest,
And rais'd such Tumults in my Breast;
For while I gaz'd, in Transport tost,
My Breath was gone, my Voice was lost:

My Bosom glow'd; the subtle Flame
Ran quick thro' all my vital Frame;
O'er my dim Eyes a Darkness hung;
My Ears with hollow Murmurs rung.

In dewy Damps my Limbs were chill'd
My Blood with gentle Horrors thrill'd;
My feeble Pulse forgot to play;
I fainted, sunk, and dy'd away.

ALEXANDER POPE (1688–1744)

"Sappho to Phaon" (1712)

Alexander Pope, the greatest English poet of the eighteenth century, was the son of a London linen draper and raised as a Roman Catholic. At twelve he suffered a debilitating illness (possibly tuberculosis of the spine), which left him deformed and painfully disabled all his life; he never grew higher than four foot six inches. Physical affliction seems to have been a spur to ambition, however: he began publishing serious poetry in his teens. His *Pastorals*, written when he was sixteen, appeared in 1709; his first great poem, the *Essay on Criticism*, in 1711. The latter was an extraordinary popular success and quickly won him a central place in London literary society. In 1712 he published the first version of *The Rape of the Lock*, the finest mock-heroic poem in the English language: a second expanded version of this comic masterpiece appeared in 1714. A life-long friendship with the satirist Jonathan Swift began in 1713—the same year he joined with Swift, John Gay, John Arbuthnot, and other literary men of the day to form the "Scriblerus Club." The group subsequently produced a series of wickedly funny public satires under the name "Martin Scriblerus." Pope's early successes culminated with a magnificent verse translation of Homer's *Iliad* (1715–20)—a work that sold so well in subscription that he was able to buy a suburban estate at Twickenham on the river Thames, where he lived comfortably for the rest of his life.

Pope had a volatile temperament, and both his public and private lives were turbulent. Though never to marry and acutely self-conscious about his physical handicaps, he nonetheless had several intense intellectual and emotional relationships with women, the most rebarbative of which involved the poet Lady Mary Wortley Montagu, with whom he had a bitter falling out in the 1720s. A more stable and long-lasting attachment was that with Martha Blount, the faithful spinster-friend to whom he dedicated the oft-quoted "Of the Characters of Women," the second of his *Moral Essays* of the 1730s. His relations with men were typically tricky, rivalrous, and splenetic. He was notoriously untrustworthy in business dealings and became famous for his devastating satirical attacks on publishers or critics who aroused his enmity. As his enemies multiplied over the years, he became the target of many scurrilous lampoons, to which he inevitably replied in kind.

Yet despite these ups and downs, he was indisputably the dominant literary figure of his age. In 1725 he published a translation of the *Odyssey* and an edition of Shakespeare; the brilliant short satire *Peri Bathous, Or the Art of Sinking in Poetry* appeared in 1727. 1728 saw the publication of the first version of the *Dunciad*, his massive mock-epic verse assault on the bad writers of the day, whom he identified by name. (He would revise the poem for the rest of his life, adding new "Dunces" as they appeared on the literary scene.) During the 1730s he also began a series of more reflective and philosophical works: the four *Moral Essays* (1731–35), the celebrated *Essay on Man* (1733–34), and numerous imitations of Horace's satires and epistles (1733–38). *The Epistle to Arbuthnot*—his last great short poem and in its way a moving summation of his writing life—appeared in 1735; and the final, supremely scatological versions of *The Dunciad* in 1742 and 1743, just before his death in 1744.

Pope's 1712 translation of "Sappho to Phaon" from Ovid's *Heroides* is easy to overlook among the mighty masterpieces of Pope's early career. (It was one of three Ovidian works he translated; the other two were "Vertumnus and Pomona" and "The Fable of Dryope.") Its poetical merits are no doubt considerable, but it wins its place in lesbian literary history—not surprisingly—on account of its subject matter. Like Ovid's original, the poem purports to reveal the final love pangs of the great poet Sappho of Lesbos, its speaker. Lesbian readers may well be dismayed by Ovid's (and Pope's) male-centered rendering of the Sappho myth: she is seen at the end of her life, passionately lamenting her betrayal by Phaon, a feckless Greek youth who has loved her and abandoned her. Confronted with the painful remnants of her desire—

> I view the grotto, once the scene of love,
> The rocks around, the hanging roofs above,
> That charmed me more, with native moss o'ergrown,
> Than Phrygian marble, or the Parian stone;
> I find the shades that veiled our joys before;
> But, Phaon gone, those shades delight no more.

—one might be forgiven indeed for dismissing the poem as simply one in a long and dire tradition of male "heterosexualizations" of Sappho.

But the poem might also be viewed less prejudicially. True, we are invited to believe that Pope's Sappho, like Ovid's, has given herself over to a man. Yet, unlike other English translators of the poem, Pope acknowledges his heroine's homosexual attachments as well. His is not simply a heterosexist whitewash: he is frank, for example, about those "Lesbian dames"—"dear objects of my guilty love"—who have previously inspired Sappho's verses. To the degree that the Ovid-Pope Sappho is presented as *bisexual* in libidinal makeup—in renouncing her girlfriends she also calls our attention to them—her status as sexual outlaw is indelibly preserved.

At a more basic level the poem might be said to confirm as powerfully as any other the magnetizing psychic power that the lesbian figure—emblematically embodied in

Sappho—has exerted on male Western writers since antiquity. For the male poet, Sappho has always been the object of a complex set of identifications, anxieties, projections, and fantasies. Neither mother nor lover, she is yet the one who seems to hold the key, as it were, to poetry itself. To speak in her voice—however fantastically or deceitfully—is somehow to return to the point of origin, to grasp the talisman of the poetic, to shout one's presence to the void. Sappho has to be netted, to be sure, and male poets struggle to contain her within the elaborate webs of rhetorical impersonation and dissimulation. Yet even in a poem such as Pope's, designed to contain her, the sheer force by which she asserts herself, makes herself unforgettable, suggests that her immortality—inseparable from her lesbianism—is already assured.

FURTHER READING: Alexander Pope, *The Works of Alexander Pope*, ed. John Wilson Croker (London: John Murray, 1871–1886); —, *The Twickenham Edition of the Works of Alexander Pope*, ed. John Butt et al., 10 vols. (New Haven: Yale University Press, 1939–61); David M. Robinson, *Sappho and Her Influence* (Boston: Marshall Jones, 1924); Edith Sitwell, *Alexander Pope* (London: Faber and Faber, 1930); George W. Sherburn, *The Early Career of Alexander Pope* (Oxford: Clarendon, 1934); Reuben Brower, *Alexander Pope* (Oxford: Clarendon, 1959); Édith Mora, *Sappho: Histoire d'un poète et traduction intégrale de l'oeuvre* (Paris: Flammarion, 1966); G. F. C. Plowden, *Pope on Classic Ground* (Athens: Ohio University Press, 1983); Maynard Mack, *Alexander Pope: A Life* (New York: Norton, 1985); Rachel Trickett, "The *Heroides* and the English Augustans," in Charles Martindale, ed., *Ovid Renewed: Ovidian Influence on Literature and Art from the Middle Ages to the Twentieth Century* (Cambridge: Cambridge University Press, 1988), pp. 191–204; Emma Donoghue, *Passions Between Women: British Lesbian Culture, 1668–1801* (London: Scarlet, 1993); Margaret Reynolds, *The Sappho Companion* (New York: Palgrave, 2001).

> Say, lovely youth, that dost my heart command,
> Can Phaon's eyes forget his Sappho's hand?
> Must then her name the wretched writer prove,
> To thy remembrance lost, as to thy love?
> Ask not the cause that I new numbers choose,
> The lute neglected, and the lyric muse;
> Love taught my tears in sadder notes to flow,
> And tuned my heart to elegies of woe.
> I burn, I burn, as when through ripened corn
> By driving winds the spreading flames are borne!
> Phaon to Ætna's scorching fields retires,
> While I consume with more than Ætna's fires!

No more my soul a charm in music finds;
Music has charms alone for peaceful minds.
Soft scenes of solitude no more can please,
Love enters there, and I'm my own disease.
No more the Lesbian dames my passion move,
Once the dear objects of my guilty love;
All other loves are lost in only thine,
Ah youth ungrateful to a flame like mine!
Whom would not all those blooming charms surprise,
Those heav'nly looks, and dear deluding eyes?
The harp and bow would you like Phœbus bear,
A brighter Phœbus Phaon might appear;
Would you with ivy wreathe your flowing hair,
Not Bacchus' self with Phaon could compare:
Yet Phœbus loved, and Bacchus felt the flame,
One Daphne warmed, and one the Cretan dame;
Nymphs that in verse no more could rival me,
Than ev'n those gods contend in charms with thee.
The muses teach me all their softest lays,
And the wide world resounds with Sappho's praise.
Though great Alcæus more sublimely sings,
And strikes with bolder rage the sounding strings,
No less renown attends the moving lyre,
Which Venus tunes, and all her loves inspire;
To me what nature has in charms denied,
Is well by wit's more lasting flames supplied.
Though short my stature, yet my name extends
To heav'n itself, and earth's remotest ends.
Brown as I am, an Ethiopian dame
Inspired young Perseus with a gen'rous flame;
Turtles and doves of diff'ring hues unite,
And glossy jet is paired with shining white.
If to no charms thou wilt thy heart resign,
But such as merit, such as equal thine,
By none, alas! by none thou can'st be moved,
Phaon alone by Phaon must be loved!
Yet once thy Sappho could thy cares employ,
Once in her arms you centered all your joy:
No time the dear remembrance can remove,
For oh! how vast a memory has love?
My music, then, you could for ever hear,
And all my words were music to your ear.

You stopped with kisses my enchanting tongue,
And found my kisses sweeter than my song.
In all I pleased, but most in what was best;
And the last joy was dearer than the rest.
Then with each word, each glance, each motion fired,
You still enjoyed, and yet you still desired,
Till all dissolving in the trance we lay,
And in tumultuous raptures died away.
The fair Sicilians now thy soul inflame;
Why was I born, ye gods, a Lesbian dame?
But ah! beware, Sicilian nymphs! nor boast
That wand'ring heart which I so lately lost;
Nor be with all those tempting words abused,
Those tempting words were all to Sappho used.
And you that rule Sicilia's happy plains,
Have pity, Venus, on your poet's pains!
Shall fortune still in one sad tenor run,
And still increase the woes so soon begun?
Inured to sorrow from my tender years,
My parent's ashes drank my early tears;
My brother next, neglecting wealth and fame,
Ignobly burned in a destructive flame:
An infant daughter late my griefs increased,
And all a mother's cares distract my breast.
Alas! what more could fate itself impose,
But thee, the last and greatest of my woes?
No more my robes in waving purple flow,
Nor on my hand the sparkling diamonds glow;
No more my locks in ringlets curled diffuse
The costly sweetness of Arabian dews,
Nor braids of gold the varied tresses bind,
That fly disordered with the wanton wind:
For whom should Sappho use such arts as these?
He's gone, whom only she desired to please!
Cupid's light darts my tender bosom move,
Still is there cause for Sappho still to love:
So from my birth the sisters fixed my doom,
And gave to Venus all my life to come;
Or, while my muse in melting notes complains,
My yielding heart keeps measure to my strains.
By charms like thine which all my soul have won,
Who might not—ah! who would not be undone?

For those Aurora Cephalus might scorn,
And with fresh blushes paint the conscious morn.
For those might Cynthia lengthen Phaon's sleep,
And bid Endymion nightly tend his sheep.
Venus for those had rapt thee to the skies,
But Mars on thee might look with Venus' eyes.
O scarce a youth, yet scarce a tender boy!
O useful time for lovers to employ!
Pride of thy age, and glory of thy race,
Come to these arms, and melt in this embrace!
The vows you never will return, receive;
And take at least the love you will not give.
See, while I write, my words are lost in tears!
The less my sense, the more my love appears.
Sure 'twas not much to bid one kind adieu,
(At least to feign was never hard to you,)
Farewell, my Lesbian love, you might have said;
Or coldly thus, "Farewell, O Lesbian maid!"
No tear did you, no parting kiss receive,
Nor knew I then how much I was to grieve.
No lover's gift your Sappho could confer,
And wrongs and woes were all you left with her.
No charge I gave you, and no charge could give,
But this, "Be mindful of our loves, and live."
Now by the Nine, those pow'rs adored by me,
And Love, the god that ever waits on thee,
When first I heard (from whom I hardly knew)
That you were fled, and all my joys with you,
Like some sad statue, speechless, pale I stood,
Grief chilled my breast, and stopped my freezing blood;
No sigh to rise, no tear had pow'r to flow,
Fixed in a stupid lethargy of woe:
But when its way th' impetuous passion found,
I rend my tresses, and my breast I wound;
I rave, then weep; I curse, and then complain;
Now swell to rage, now melt in tears again.
Not fiercer pangs distract the mournful dame,
Whose first-born infant feeds the fun'ral flame.
My scornful brother with a smile appears,
Insults my woes, and triumphs in my tears;
His hated image ever haunts my eyes;
"And why this grief? thy daughter lives," he cries.

Stung with my love, and furious with despair,
All torn my garments, and my bosom bare,
My woes, thy crimes, I to the world proclaim;
Such inconsistent things are love and shame!
'Tis thou art all my care and my delight,
My daily longing, and my dream by night:
Oh night more pleasing than the brightest day,
When fancy gives what absence takes away,
And, dressed in all its visionary charms,
Restores my fair deserter to my arms!
Then round your neck in wanton wreaths I twine,
Then you, methinks, as fondly circle mine:
A thousand tender words I hear and speak;
A thousand melting kisses give, and take:
Then fiercer joys, I blush to mention these,
Yet, while I blush, confess how much they please.
But when, with day, the sweet delusions fly,
And all things wake to life and joy, but I,
As if once more forsaken, I complain,
And close my eyes to dream of you again:
Then frantic rise, and like some fury rove
Through lonely plains, and through the silent grove,
As if the silent grove, and lonely plains,
That knew my pleasures, could relieve my pains.
I view the grotto, once the scene of love,
The rocks around, the hanging roofs above,
That charmed me more, with native moss o'ergrown,
Than Phrygian marble, or the Parian stone;
I find the shades that veiled our joys before;
But, Phaon gone, those shades delight no more.
Here the pressed herbs with bending tops betray
Where oft entwined in am'rous folds we lay;
I kiss that earth which once was pressed by you,
And all with tears the with'ring herbs bedew.
For thee the fading trees appear to mourn,
And birds defer their songs till thy return:
Night shades the groves, and all in silence lie,
All but the mournful Philomel and I:
With mournful Philomel I join my strain,
Of Tereus she, of Phaon I complain.
A spring there is, whose silver waters show,
Clear as a glass, the shining sands below:

A flow'ry lotos spreads its arms above,
Shades all the banks, and seems itself a grove;
Eternal greens the mossy margin grace,
Watched by the sylvan genius of the place:
Here as I lay, and swelled with tears the flood,
Before my sight a wat'ry virgin stood:
She stood and cried, "O you that love in vain!
Fly hence, and seek the fair Leucadian main;
There stands a rock, from whose impending steep
Apollo's fane surveys the rolling deep;
There injured lovers, leaping from above,
Their flames extinguish, and forget to love.
Deucalion once with hopeless fury burned,
In vain he loved, relentless Pyrrha scorned:
But when from hence he plunged into the main,
Deucalion scorned, and Pyrrha loved in vain.
Haste, Sappho, haste, from high Leucadia throw
Thy wretched weight, nor dread the deeps below!"
She spoke, and vanished with the voice—I rise,
And silent tears fall trickling from my eyes.
I go, ye nymphs! those rocks and seas to prove;
How much I fear, but ah, how much I love!
I go, ye nymphs, where furious love inspires;
Let female fears submit to female fires.
To rocks and seas I fly from Phaon's hate,
And hope from seas and rocks a milder fate.
Ye gentle gales, beneath my body blow,
And softly lay me on the waves below!
And thou, kind Love, my sinking limbs sustain,
Spread thy soft wings, and waft me o'er the main,
Nor let a lover's death the guiltless flood profane!
On Phœbus' shrine my harp I'll then bestow,
And this inscription shall be placed below,
"Here she who sung, to him that did inspire,
Sappho to Phœbus consecrates her lyre;
What suits with Sappho, Phœbus, suits with thee;
The gift, the giver, and the god agree."
But why, alas, relentless youth, ah! why
To distant seas must tender Sappho fly?
Thy charms than those may far more pow'rful be,
And Phœbus' self is less a god to me.
Ah! canst thou doom me to the rocks and sea,

Oh! far more faithless and more hard than they?
Ah! canst thou rather see this tender breast
Dashed on these rocks, than to thy bosom pressed?
This breast which once, in vain! you liked so well;
Where the loves played, and where the muses dwell.
Alas! the muses now no more inspire,
Untuned my lute, and silent is my lyre.
My languid numbers have forgot to flow,
And fancy sinks beneath a weight of woe.
Ye Lesbian virgins, and ye Lesbian dames,
Themes of my verse, and objects of my flames,
No more your groves with my glad songs shall ring,
No more these hands shall touch the trembling string:
My Phaon's fled, and I those arts resign:
(Wretch that I am, to call that Phaon mine!)
Return, fair youth, return, and bring along
Joy to my soul, and vigour to my song:
Absent from thee, the poet's flame expires;
But ah! how fiercely burn the lover's fires!
Gods! can no prayers, no sighs, no numbers move
One savage heart, or teach it how to love?
The winds my prayers, my sighs, my numbers bear,
The flying winds have lost them all in air!
Oh when, alas! shall more auspicious gales
To these fond eyes restore thy welcome sails!
If you return—ah why these long delays?
Poor Sappho dies, while careless Phaon stays.
O launch the bark, nor fear the wat'ry plain;
Venus for thee shall smooth her native main.
O launch thy bark, secure of prosp'rous gales;
Cupid for thee shall spread the swelling sails.
If you will fly—(yet ah! what cause can be,
Too cruel youth, that you should fly from me?)
If not from Phaon I must hope for ease,
Ah let me seek it from the raging seas:
To raging seas unpitied I'll remove,
And either cease to live or cease to love!

ANNE FINCH, COUNTESS OF WINCHILSEA (1661–1720)

"Friendship between Ephelia and Ardelia" (1713)

The poet Anne Finch, born into a noble family in Berkshire, was orphaned as a child and raised by an uncle. At the age of twenty she became Maid of Honour to Mary of Modena, the wife of the Duke of York, later James II. At Mary's court—where fellow ladies-in-waiting included the poet Anne Killigrew—she met and married Heneage Finch, subsequently the Earl of Winchilsea. After James's abdication and banishment in 1688, Finch and her husband retired to the Kentish countryside, where Finch devoted herself to writing. She contributed four poems to Charles Gildon's *New Collection of Poems on Several Occasions* (1701) and won approbation for her verses from both Swift and Pope. She later published poems in Pope's *Poems on Several Occasions* (1717). Finch composed in different poetic styles and genres but is best-known for pensive works such as *The Spleen* (1701) and *A Nocturnal Reverie* (1713). As various critics have pointed out in recent years, feminist sentiments surface often and eloquently in her work.

Although happily married, Finch—like Katherine Philips before her—wrote a number of poems celebrating passionate female friendship. "Friendship between Ephelia and Ardelia," which appeared in her *Miscellany Poems on Several Occasions, Written by a Lady* (1713), is a characteristic effort. The poem is notable for its use of resemblance and repetition, witnessed in the rhyming names, Ardelia and Ephelia, and in the tautological return of Ardelia's phrase "'Tis to love, as I love you." The poem's spare, hallucinatory repetitions work to connect love between women with sameness and mirroring: in loving another woman, the poet suggests, one really loves oneself. Finch's poems were greatly admired later in the century by the poet William Wordsworth, who would subsequently eulogize the Ladies of Llangollen—the eighteenth century's female romantic couple par excellence.

FURTHER READING: Anne Finch, *Miscellany Poems on Several Occasions* (London, 1713); Myra Reynolds, ed., *Poems of Anne Finch* (Chicago, 1903); George Ballard, *Memoirs of Several Ladies of Great Britain Who Have Been Celebrated for their Writings, or Skill in the Learned Languages, Arts, and Sciences* (1752; rpt. Detroit, Mich.: Wayne

State University Press, 1985); Dorothy Mermin, "Women Becoming Poets: Katherine Philips, Aphra Behn, and Anne Finch," *ELH: Journal of English Literary History* 57 (1990): 335–55; Barbara McGovern, *Anne Finch and her Poetry: A Critical Biography* (Athens: University of Georgia Press, 1992); Charles H. Hinnant, "Feminism and Femininity: A Reconsideration of Anne Finch's 'Ardelia's Answer to Ephelia,'" *The Eighteenth-Century: Theory and Interpretation* 33 (Summer 1992): 119–32; ——, *The Poetry of Anne Finch: An Essay in Interpretation* (Newark: University of Delaware Press, 1994); Peter Jay and Caroline Lewis, eds., *Sappho Through English Poetry* (London: Anvil, 1997); Harriette Andreadis, *Sappho in Early Modern England: Female Same-Sex Literary Erotics, 1550–1714* (Chicago: University of Chicago Press, 2001).

EPHELIA: What Friendship is, Ardelia, show.
ARDELIA: 'Tis to love as I love you.
EPHELIA: This account, so short (though kind),
     Suits not my enquiring mind.
     Therefore farther now repeat:
     What is Friendship when complete?
ARDELIA: 'Tis to share all joy and grief;
     'Tis to lend all due relief
     From the tongue, the heart, the hand;
     'Tis to mortgage house and land;
     For a friend be sold a slave;
     'Tis to die upon a grave,
     If a friend therein do lie.
EPHELIA: This indeed, though carried high;
     This, though more than e'er was done
     Underneath the rolling sun,
     This has all been said before.
     Can Ardelia say no more?
ARDELIA: Words indeed no more can show:
     But 'tis to love, as I love you.

ANTHONY HAMILTON (1646?–1720)

From *Memoirs of the Life of Count Grammont* (1713)

Anthony Hamilton, third son of Sir George Hamilton and brother-in-law to the celebrated Comte de Grammont (1621–1707), published his *Mémoires de la vie du Comte de Grammont*—an entertaining (if unreliable) account of life at the court of Charles II—anonymously in Cologne in 1713. The work was subsequently edited (in French) by Horace Walpole and translated into English in 1714 by Abel Boyer; Boyer's translation was in turn revised and reissued by Sir Walter Scott in 1811. The work is in two parts. The first part deals with the rakish Grammont's life at the French court—he was banished in 1662 after trying to seduce one of Louis XIV's mistresses—and was perhaps dictated by Grammont himself. The second part, dealing with Grammont's two-year residence at the English court, where he cut a glamorous and dissipated figure, seems to have been authored solely by Hamilton.

The *Memoirs* is adorable in its way; Voltaire thought it brilliant and Edward Gibbon wrote that "it is a favourite work with all persons who have any pretensions to taste." It owes its place in the canon of lesbian writing, however, to one of its least savory episodes: that of Mary Hobart, maid of honor to the Duchess of York, and her ill-fated sexual pursuit of Miss Anne Temple, another lady-in-waiting. Hamilton's portrait of Hobart is undoubtedly unflattering: she is a meddler and trickster, who preys on young women without regard to reputation or morals, and her eventual humiliation—by her arch-rival, the Earl of Rochester—must be taken as one of the more misogynistic episodes in Restoration literature. Yet in Hamilton's defense, it might be pointed out, neither Rochester nor Miss Temple is presented very favorably either. In Hamilton's terminally jaded world, cunning, hypocrisy, and the ability to *blaguer*—as when Hobart lectures her "dear Temple" on why she should avoid men at all costs, and Rochester in particular—seem to be the only human capacities worthy of respect.

Of the real Mary Hobart little is known. One modern writer describes her as having been "masculine" and "not very young" at the time of the Temple escapade; but no other source than Hamilton is educed for this. She was the daughter of a Yorkshire baronet; the contretemps with Rochester is likely to have taken place in 1665 or 1666 when Rochester first came to court. Pepys describes meeting Miss Temple at a royal ball on 15 November 1666; she later married Sir Charles Lyttelton and had thirteen children.

In her *Life of Anthony Hamilton*, Ruth Clark suggests that the German writer Friedrich Gottlob Wetzel may have drawn on the details of the Hobart-Temple-Rochester intrigue in his *Rache für Rache* (1778).

FURTHER READING: Anthony Hamilton, *Memoirs of Count Grammont*, 2 vols. (London, 1811); Ruth Clark, *Anthony Hamilton (Author of Memoirs of Count Grammont): His Life and Works and His Family* (London: John Lane, 1921); Vivian de Sola Pinto, *Rochester: Portrait of a Restoration Poet* (1935; rpt. Freeport, N.Y.: Books for Libraries Press, 1971); Emma Donoghue, *Passions Between Women: British Lesbian Culture, 1668–1801* (London: Scarlet, 1993); Jeremy Lamb, *So Idle a Rogue: The Life and Death of Lord Rochester* (London: Allison and Busby, 1993); Harold Love, "Hamilton's Memoirs of the Life of Count Grammont and the Reading of Rochester," *Restoration: Studies in English Literary Culture 1660–1700* 19 (1995): 95–102.

[*Description of Miss Hobart and her Unusual Tastes.*]

Miss Hobart's character was at that time as uncommon in England, as her person was singular, in a country where, to be young, and not to be in some degree handsome, is a reproach: she had a good shape, rather a bold air; and a great deal of wit, which was well cultivated, without having much discretion. She was likewise possessed of a great deal of vivacity, with an irregular fancy: there was a great deal of fire in her eyes, which, however, produced no effect upon the beholders; and she had a tender heart, whose sensibility some pretended was alone in favour of the fair sex.

Miss Bagot was the first that gained her tenderness and affection, which she returned at first with equal warmth and sincerity; but perceiving that all her friendship was insufficient to repay that of Miss Hobart, she yielded the conquest to the governess's niece, who thought herself as much honoured by it, as her aunt thought herself obliged by the care she took of the young girl.

It was not long before the report, whether true or false, of this singularity, spread through the whole court, where people, being yet so uncivilized as never to have heard of that kind of refinement in love of ancient Greece, imagined that the illustrious Hobart, who seemed so particularly attached to the fair sex, was in reality something more than she appeared to be.

Satirical ballads soon began to compliment her upon these new attributes; and upon the insinuations that were therein made, her companions began to fear her. The governess, alarmed at these reports, consulted Lord Rochester upon the danger to which her niece was exposed. She could not have applied to a fitter person: he immediately advised her to take her niece out of the hands of Miss Hobart; and contrived matters so well, that she fell into his own. The duchess [of York], who had too much generosity not to treat as visionary what was imputed to Miss Hobart, and too much justice to condemn her upon the faith of lampoons, removed her from the society of the maids of honour, to be an attendant upon her own person. [. . .]

> [*Miss Hobart's Pursuit of Miss Temple. her plan of seduction thwarted by her rival, lord rochester, with the help of Miss Temple's niece, Miss Sarah, and Rochester's friend Killigrew.*]

Though Miss Temple's person was particularly engaging, it was nevertheless eclipsed by that of Miss Jennings; but she was still more excelled by the other's superior mental accomplishments. Two persons, very capable to impart understanding, had the gift been communicable, undertook at the same time to rob her of the little she really possessed: these were Lord Rochester and Miss Hobart: the first began to mislead her, by reading to her all his compositions, as if she alone had been a proper judge of them. He never thought proper to flatter her upon her personal accomplishments; but told her, that if heaven had made him susceptible of the impressions of beauty, it would not have been possible for him to have escaped her chains; but not being, thank God, affected with any thing but wit, he had the happiness of enjoying the most agreeable conversation in the world, without running any risk. After so sincere a confession, he either presented to her a copy of verses, or a new song, in which, whoever dared to come in competition in any respect with Miss Temple, was laid prostrate before her charms, most humbly to solicit pardon: Such flattering insinuations so completely turned her head, that it was a pity to see her.

The duchess took notice of it, and well knowing the extent of both their geniuses, she saw the precipice into which the poor girl was running head-long without perceiving it; but as it is no less dangerous to forbid a connection that is not yet thought of, than it is difficult to put an end to one that is already well established, Miss Hobart was charged to take care, with all possible discretion, that these frequent and long conversations might not be attended with any dangerous consequences: with pleasure she accepted the commission, and greatly flattered herself with success.

She had already made all necessary advances, to gain possession of her confidence and friendship; and Miss Temple, less suspicious of her than of Lord Rochester, made all imaginable returns. She was greedy of praise, and loved all manner of sweet-meats, as much as a child of nine or ten years old: her taste was gratified in both these respects. Miss Hobart having the superintendance of the duchess's baths, her apartment joined them, in which there was a closet stored with all sorts of sweet-meats and liqueurs: the closet suited Miss Temple's taste, as exactly as it gratified Miss Hobart's inclination, to have something that could allure her.

Summer, being now returned, brought back with it the pleasures and diversions that are its inseparable attendants. One day, when the ladies had been taking the air on horseback, Miss Temple, on her return from riding, alighted at Miss Hobart's, in order to recover her fatigue at the expence of the sweet-meats, which she knew were there at her service; but before she began, she desired Miss Hobart's permission to undress herself, and change her linen in her apartment; which request was immediately complied with: "I was just going to propose it to you," said Miss Hobart, "not but that you are as charming as an angel in your riding-habit; but there is nothing so comfortable as a loose dress, and being at one's ease: you cannot imagine, my dear Temple," continued she, embracing her, "how much you oblige me by this free unceremonious conduct; but above all, I am enchanted with your particular attention to cleanliness: how greatly you differ in this, as in many other things, from that silly creature Jennings! Have you remarked how all our court fops admire her for her brilliant complexion, which perhaps, after all, is not wholly her own; and for blunders, which are truly original, and which they are such fools as to mistake for wit: I have not conversed with her long enough to perceive in what her wit consists; but of this I am certain, that if it is not better than her feet, it is no great matter. What stories have I heard of her sluttishness! No cat ever dreaded water so much as she does: Fie upon her! Never to wash for her own comfort, and only to attend to those parts which must necessarily be seen, such as the neck and hands."

Miss Temple swallowed all this with even greater pleasure than the sweet-meats; and the officious Hobart, not to lose time, was helping her off with her clothes, while the chamber-maid was coming. She made some objections to this at first, being unwilling to occasion that trouble to a person, who, like Miss Hobart, had been advanced to a place of dignity; but she was over-ruled by her, and assured, that it was with the greatest pleasure she shewed her that small mark of civility. The collation being finished, and Miss Temple undressed: "Let us retire," said Miss Hobart, "to the bathing closet, where we may enjoy a little conversation, secure from any impertinent visit." Miss Temple consented, and both of them sitting down on a couch: "You are too young, my dear Temple," said she, "to know the baseness of men in general, and too short a time acquainted with the court, to know the character of its inhabitants. I will give you a short sketch of the principal persons, to the best of my knowledge, without injury to any one; for I abominate the trade of scandal.

"In the first place, then, you ought to set it down as an undoubted fact, that all courtiers are deficient, either in honesty, good sense, judgment, wit, or sincerity; that is to say, if any of them by chance possess some one of these qualities, you may depend upon it he is defective in the rest: sumptuous in their equipages, deep play, a great opinion of their own merit, and contempt of that of others, are their chief characteristics.

"Interest or pleasure are the motives of all their actions: those who are led by the first, would sell God Almighty, as Judas sold his Master, and that for less money. I could relate you a thousand noble instances of this, if I had time. As for the sectaries of pleasure, or those who pretend to be such, for they are not all so bad as they endeavour to make themselves appear, these gentlemen pay no manner of regard, either to promises, oaths, law, or religion; that is to say, they are literally no respecters of persons; they care neither for God nor man, if they can but gain their ends. They look upon maids of hon-our only as amusements, placed expressly at court for their entertainment; and the more merit any one has, the more she is exposed to their impertinence, if she gives any ear to them; and to their malicious calumnies, when she ceases to attend to them. As for hus-bands, this is not the place to find them; for unless money or caprice make up the match, there is but little hopes of being married: virtue and beauty in this respect here are equally useless. Lady Falmouth is the only instance of a maid of honour well married without a portion; and if you were to ask her poor weak husband for what reason he married her, I am persuaded that he can assign none, unless it be her great red ears, and broad feet. As for the pale Lady Yarborough, who appeared so proud of her match, she is wife, to be sure, of a great country bumpkin, who, the very week after their marriage, bid her take her farewell of the town for ever, in consequence of five or six thousand pounds a-year he enjoys on the borders of Cornwall. Alas! poor Miss Blague! I saw her go away about this time twelvemonth, in a coach with four such lean horses, that I can-not believe she is yet half way to her miserable little castle. What can be the matter! all the girls seem afflicted with the rage of wedlock, and however small their portion of charms may be, they think it only necessary to shew themselves at court, in order to pick and chuse their men: but was this in reality the case, the being a wife is the most wretched condition imaginable for a person of nice sentiments. Believe me, my dear Temple, the pleasures of matrimony are so inconsiderable, in comparison with its inconveniences, that I cannot imagine how any reasonable creature can resolve upon it; rather fly, therefore, from this irksome engagement than court it. Jealousy, formerly a stranger to these happy isles, is now coming into fashion, with many recent examples of which you are acquainted. However brilliant the phantom may appear, suffer not yourself to be caught by its splendour, and never be so weak as to transform your slave into your tyrant: as long as you preserve your own liberty, you will be mistress of that of others. [. . .]

"Lord Rochester is, without contradiction, the most witty man in all England; but then he is likewise the most unprincipled, and devoid even of the least tincture of hon-our: he is dangerous to our sex alone; and that to such a degree, that there is not a woman who gives ear to him three times, but she irretrievably loses her reputation. No woman can escape him, for he has her in his writings, though his other attacks be inef-fectual; and in the age we live in, the one is as bad as the other, in the eye of the public. In the mean time nothing is more dangerous than the artful insinuating manner with which he gains possession of the mind: he applauds your taste, submits to your senti-ments, and at the very instant that he himself does not believe a single word of what he is saying, he makes you believe it all. I dare lay a wager, that from the conversation you have had with him, you thought him one of the most honourable and sincerest men liv-ing: for my part, I cannot imagine what he means by the assiduity he pays you: not but your accomplishments are sufficient to excite the adoration and praise of the whole world; but had he even been so fortunate as to have gained your affections, he would not know what to do with the loveliest creature at court: for it is a long time since his debauches have brought him to order, with the assistance of the favours of all the common street-walkers. See, then, my dear Temple, what horrid malice possesses him, to the ruin and confusion of innocence! A wretch! to have no other design in his addresses and assiduities to Miss Temple, but to give a greater air of probability to the calumnies with which he has loaded her. You look upon me with astonishment, and seem to doubt the truth of what I advance; but I do not desire you to believe me without evidence: Here," said she, drawing a paper out of her pocket, "see what a copy of verses he has made in your praise, while he lulls your credulity to rest, by flattering speeches, and feigned respect."

After saying this, the perfidious Hobart shewed her half a dozen couplets full of strained invective and scandal, which Rochester had made against the former maids of honour. This severe and cutting lampoon was principally levelled against Miss Price, whose person he took to pieces in the most frightful and hideous manner imaginable. Miss Hobart had substituted the name of Temple instead of Price, which she made to agree, both with the measure and tune of the song. This effectually answered Hobart's intentions: the credulous Temple no sooner heard her sing the lampoon, but she firmly believed it to be made upon herself; and in the first transports of her rage, having nothing so much at heart as to give the lie to the fictions of the poet: "Ah! as for this, my dear Hobart," said she, "I can bear it no longer: I do not pretend to be so handsome as some others; but as for the defects that villain charges me with, I dare say, my dear Hobart, there is no woman more free from them: we are alone, and I am almost inclined to convince you by ocular demonstration." Miss Hobart was too complaisant to oppose this motion; but, although she soothed her mind by extolling all her beauties, in opposition to Lord Rochester's song, Miss Temple was almost driven to distraction by rage and astonishment, that the first man she ever attended to, should, in his conversation with her, not even make use of a single word of truth, but that he should likewise have the unparalleled cruelty, falsely to accuse her of defects; and not being able to find words capable of expressing her anger and resentment, she began to weep like a child.

Miss Hobart used all her endeavours to comfort her, and chid her for being so much hurt with the invectives of a person, whose scandalous impostures were too well known to make any impression: she however advised her never to speak to him any more, for that was the only method to disappoint his designs; that contempt and silence were, on such occasions, much preferable to any explanation, and that if he could once obtain a hearing, he would be justified, but she would be ruined. [. . .]

Lord Rochester had a faithful spy near these nymphs: this was Miss Sarah, who, by his advice, and with her aunt's consent, was reconciled with Miss Hobart, the more effectually to betray her: he was informed by this spy, that Miss Hobart's maid, being suspected of having listened to them in the closet, had been turned away; that she had taken another, whom, in all probability, she would not keep long, because, in the first place, she was ugly, and, in the second, she eat the sweetmeats that were prepared for Miss Temple. Although this intelligence was not very material, Sarah was nevertheless praised for her punctuality and attention; and a few days afterwards, she brought him news of real importance.

Rochester was by her informed, that Miss Hobart and her new favourite designed, about nine o'clock in the evening, to walk in the Mall, in the Park; that they were to change clothes with each other, to put on scarfs, and wear black masks: she added, that Miss Hobart had strongly opposed this project, but that she was obliged to give way at last, Miss Temple having resolved to indulge her fancy.

Upon the strength of this intelligence, Rochester concerted his measures: he went to Killigrew, complained to him of the trick which Miss Hobart had played him, and desired his assistance in order to be revenged: this was readily granted, and having acquainted him with the measures he intended to pursue, and given him the part he was to act in this adventure, they went to the Mall.

Presently after appeared our two nymphs in masquerade: their shapes were not very different, and their faces, which were very unlike each other, were concealed with their masks. The company was but thin in the Park; and as soon as Miss Temple perceived them at a distance, she quickened her pace in order to join them, with the design, under her disguise, severely to reprimand the perfidious Rochester; when Miss Hobart stopping her: "Where are you running to?" said she; "have you a mind to engage in conversation with these two devils, to be exposed to all the insolence and impertinence for which they are so notorious?" These remonstrances were entirely useless: Miss Temple was resolved to try the experiment: and all that could be obtained from her, was, not to answer any of the questions Rochester might ask her.

They were accosted just as they had done speaking: Rochester fixed upon Hobart, pretending to take her for the other; at which she was overjoyed; but Miss Temple was extremely sorry she fell to Killigrew's share, with whom she had nothing to do: he perceived her uneasiness, and, pretending to know her by her clothes: "Ah! Miss Hobart," said he, "be so kind as look this way if you please: I know not by what chance you both came hither, but I am sure it is very apropos for you, since I have something to say to you, as your friend and humble servant."

This beginning raising her curiosity, Miss Temple appeared more inclined to attend him; and Killigrew perceiving that the other couple had insensibly proceeded some distance from them: "In the name of God," said he: "what do you mean by railing so against Lord Rochester, whom you know to be one of the most honourable men at court, and whom you nevertheless described as the greatest villain, to the person whom of all others he esteems and respects the most? What do you think would become of you, if he knew that you made Miss Temple believe she is the person alluded to in a certain song, which you know as well as myself was made upon the clumsy Miss Price, above a year before the fair Temple was heard of? Be not surprised that I know so much of the matter; but pay a little attention, I pray you, to what I am now going to tell you out of pure friendship: your passion and inclinations for Miss Temple are known to every one but herself; for whatever methods you used to impose upon her innocence, the world does her the justice to believe that she would treat you as Lady Falmouth did, if the poor girl knew the wicked designs you had upon her: I caution you, therefore, against making any farther advances, to a person, too modest to listen to them: I advise you likewise to take back your maid again, in order to silence her scandalous tongue; for she says every where, that she is with child, that you are the occasion of her being in that condition, and accuses you of behaving towards her with the blackest ingratitude, upon trifling suspicions only: you know very well, these are no stories of my own invention; but that you may not entertain any manner of doubt, that I had all this from her own mouth, she has told me your conversation in the bathing-room, the characters you there drew of the principal men at court, your artful malice in applying so improperly a scandalous song to one of the loveliest women in all England; and in what manner the innocent girl fell into the snare you had laid for her, in order to do justice to her charms. But that which might be of the most fatal consequences to you in that long conversation, is the revealing certain secrets, which, in all probability, the duchess did not entrust you with, to be imparted to the maids of honour: reflect upon this, and neglect not to make some reparation to Sir ------ Lyttleton, for the ridicule with which you were pleased to load him. I know not whether he had his information from your femme-de-chambre, but I am very certain that he has sworn he will be revenged, and he is a man that keeps his word; for after all, that you may not be deceived by his look, like that of a Stoic, and his gravity, like that of a judge, I must acquaint you, that he is the most passionate man living. Indeed, these invectives are of the blackest and most horrible nature: he says it is most infamous, that a wretch like yourself should find no other employment than to blacken the characters of gentlemen, to gratify your jealousy; that if you do not desist from such conduct for the future, he will immediately complain of you; and that if her royal highness will not do him justice, he is determined to do himself justice, and to run you through the body with his own sword, though you were even in the arms of Miss Temple; and that it is most scandalous that all the maids of honour should get into your hands before they can look around them.

"These things, madam, I thought it my duty to acquaint you with: you are better able to judge than myself, whether what I have now advanced be true, and I leave it to your own discretion to make what use you think proper of my advice; but were I in your situation, I would endeavour to reconcile Lord Rochester and Miss Temple. Once more I recommend to you to take care that your endeavours to mislead her innocency, in order to blast his honour, may not come to his knowledge; and do not estrange from her a man who tenderly loves her, and whose probity is so great, that he would not even suffer his eyes to wander towards her, if his intention was not to make her his wife."

Miss Temple observed her promise most faithfully during this discourse: she did not even utter a single syllable, being seized with such astonishment and confusion, that she quite lost the use of her tongue.

Miss Hobart and Lord Rochester came up to her, while she was still in amazement at the wonderful discoveries she had made; things in themselves, in her opinion, almost incredible, but to the truth of which she could not refuse her assent, upon examining the evidences and circumstances on which they were founded. Never was confusion equal to that with which her whole frame was seized by the foregoing recital.

Rochester and Killigrew took leave of them before she recovered from her surprise; but as soon as she had regained the free use of her senses, she hastened back to St. James's, without answering a single question that the other put to her; and having locked herself up in her chamber, the first thing she did, was immediately to strip off Miss Hobart's clothes, lest she should be contaminated by them; for after what she had been told concerning her, she looked upon her as a monster, dreadful to the innocence of the fair sex, of whatever sex she might be: she blushed at the familiarities she had been drawn into with a creature, whose maid was with child, though she never had been in any other service but her's: she therefore returned her all her clothes, ordered her servant to bring back all her own, and resolved never more to have any connection with her. Miss Hobart, on the other hand, who supposed Killigrew had mistaken Miss Temple for herself, could not comprehend what could induce her to give herself such surprising airs, since that conversation; but being desirous to come to an explanation, she ordered Miss Temple's maid to remain in her apartments, and went to call upon Miss Temple herself, instead of sending back her clothes; and being desirous to give her some proof of friendship before they entered upon expostulations, she slipt softly into her chamber, when she was in the very act of changing her linen, and embraced her. Miss Temple finding herself in her arms before she had taken notice of her, every thing that Killigrew had mentioned, appeared to her imagination: she fancied that she saw in her looks the eagerness of a satyr, or, if possible, of some monster still more odious; and disengaging herself with the highest indignation from her arms, she began to shriek and cry in the most terrible manner, calling both heaven and earth to her assistance.

The first whom her cries raised were the governess and her niece. It was near twelve o'clock at night: Miss Temple in her shift, almost frightened to death, was pushing back with horror Miss Hobart, who approached her with no other intent than to know the occasion of those transports. As soon as the governess saw this scene, she began to lecture Miss Hobart with all the eloquence of a real duenna: she demanded of her, whether she thought it was for her that her royal highness kept the maids of honour? whether she was not ashamed to come at such an unseasonable time of night into their very apartments to commit such violences? and swore that she would, the very next day, complain to the duchess. All this confirmed Miss Temple in her mistaken notions; and Hobart was obliged to go away at last, without being able to convince or bring to reason creatures, whom she believed to be either distracted or mad. The next day Miss Sarah did not fail to relate this adventure to her lover, telling him how Miss Temple's cries had alarmed the maids of honour's apartment, and how herself and her aunt, running to her assistance, had almost surprised Miss Hobart in the very act.

Two days after, the whole adventure, with the addition of several embellishments, was made public: the governess swore to the truth of it, and related in every company what a narrow escape Miss Temple had experienced, and that Miss Sarah, her niece, had preserved her honour, because, by Lord Rochester's excellent advice, she had forbidden her all manner of connection with so dangerous a person. Miss Temple was afterwards informed, that the song that had so greatly provoked her, alluded to Miss Price only: this was confirmed to her by every person, with additional execrations against Miss Hobart, for such a scandalous imposition. Such great coldness after so much familiarity, made many believe, that this adventure was not altogether a fiction.

PAULINE DE SIMIANE (1676–1737)

"Madrigal," "Letter to Madame la Marquise de S——, On Sending Her Tobacco" (1715)

Like her English contemporaries Anne Finch and Elizabeth Singer Rowe, Pauline de Grignan, the Marquise de Simiane—godchild of the Cardinal de Retz and grand-daughter of Madame de Sévigné—wrote poems addressed to women in which professions of friendship are often tinged with erotic feeling. In "Madrigal," from her anonymously published *Porte-feuille de Mme ***, contenant diverses odes, idylles et sonnets* (1715), Simiane's mock complaint to a female friend is given a distinctly homoerotic cast by way of a witty allusion to Diana and Endymion. The poem is followed by a "Letter to Madame la Marquise de S ——, On Sending Her Tobacco," a verse epistle addressed to Simiane by "Mme de C----"—an unidentified member of her circle.

FURTHER READING: Pauline de Simiane, *Porte-feuille de Madame ***, contenant diverses odes, idylles et sonnets, des imitations de Jean Second, L'histoire de coeur de Loulou; et autres opuscules, tant en prose qu'en vers* (Paris, 1715); Domna C. Stanton, ed., *The Defiant Muse: French Feminist Poems from the Middle Ages to the Present* (New York: Feminist, 1986).

Madrigal

You kiss me like a sister,
Kisses filled with sweetness;
Yet you must allow me to condemn them,
For I'm only mortal, my Diane;
Why treat me like Apollo great?
I'd be so happy with Endymion's fate.

Letter to Madame la Marquise de S——, on Sending Her Tobacco

I've not forgotten you chose me
  To gratify one of the senses
  That's generally said to be
  Immaterial to life's pleasures.
Thus, despite the rumors spread abroad,
  If you truly had the longing
  To satisfy them one and all,
I think that in this fancy
  Your heart, without a pause,
  Would not have chosen for the task
  A pitiful friend like me;
But you have needs of modest size;
In you, only the sense of smell is unfulfilled.
And yet do you imagine that my eyes
Away from you suffer any less?
Still, I cannot bear to see you penitent,
And will relieve your pain. As reward
  For my tobacco and my care,
All I ask, my lovable Corinne,
Is that your hand sometimes choose
  To trace for me with tenderness
  All of your pleasures, all your fine times.

LADY MARY WORTLEY MONTAGU (1689–1762)

From the *Embassy Letters* (1716–18)

The brilliant, mercurial eighteenth-century woman of letters, Lady Mary Wortley Montagu, was the daughter of the Earl (later Duke) of Kingston and his wife Lady Mary Fielding. As a child she read widely in her father's library and taught herself Latin; she began writing poetry in her teens. At the age of twenty-three she eloped with Edward Wortley Montagu, a wealthy M.P., by whom she subsequently had two children. Her first published work was an essay printed anonymously in Addison and Steele's *Spectator* (no. 573) in 1713. After Wortley was named ambassador to the Ottoman Empire, Lady Mary accompanied him on a two-year journey to Constantinople, during which time she wrote a celebrated series of letters describing Turkish society and customs. Upon her return in 1718, she became, among other things, a pioneering advocate for smallpox inoculation, a practice she had first encountered in Turkey.

Despite the many practical and psychological obstacles facing women writers in the period—and her own aristocratic diffidence about publication—Lady Mary became a formidable figure in London literary life in the 1720s and 1730s. She wrote a play (never performed) called *Simplicity, A Comedy*, published several anonymous essays in the political journal *The Nonsense of Common-Sense*, and formed an intense friendship with the poet Alexander Pope. After she rebuffed Pope's amorous advances in 1729, the friendship ended disastrously and the two thereafter waged a bitter slanging match in a series of savage and widely circulated lampoons. In 1736 Lady Mary fell violently in love with the bisexual Italian writer and adventurer, Francesco Algarotti. In the hope that Algarotti would come to live with her, she left her husband—from whom she had long been estranged—and moved to Venice, where she resided for the next three years. Algarotti never returned her passion, but by then she had resigned herself to Mediterranean exile. She lived subsequently in Brescia, Avignon, and Padua, where she was much fêted by visiting English aristocrats on the Grand Tour. She was not forgotten in England either: her *Six Town Eclogues. With Some Poems* appeared in 1747. A year before her death, she arranged for the posthumous publication of her letters, including those written during her sojourn in Turkey. She returned to England that same year and after a brief reentry into court life died in 1762.

Although a few of the *Embassy Letters* circulated privately in during Lady Mary's lifetime—those written to Pope, for example—they were not published as a group until 1763. They were an immediate success and frequently reprinted over the next two centuries. Much admired by other writers, including such epicene stylists as Samuel Johnson, Byron, and Virginia Woolf, they offer a vibrant portrait of Turkish life and manners, as seen by a sensitive if highly privileged observer. The famous 1717 letter below from Lady Mary to her daughter, describing the Turkish women's bath house at Sophia, has had an influential place in the history of lesbian iconography. Openly admiring of the beauty of Turkish women—she writes appreciatively elsewhere of the charms of the Ottoman sultana Fatima—Lady Mary describes the *bagnio* as a kind of informal, Adam-less Eden: a she-paradise or *gynecium*, where women repose in a state of exquisite sensual ease, delighting narcissistically in their own and one another's bodies. The homerotic elements in her description were not lost on later writers and artists. Jean Auguste Dominique Ingres's famous painting *Le Bain turc* (1862), showing a bevy of voluptuously entangled Turkish women at the bath, naked except for their necklaces and bracelets, was inspired outright by the bagnio letter and has subsequently become a stereotypic if risible image of female-female eros. Virginia Woolf undoubtedly had Lady Mary and the Turkish bath in mind while writing her homosexual romance, *Orlando* (1928). In the crucial middle section of that novel the androgynous hero, Orlando—modeled on Woolf's lover and friend, Vita Sackville-West—travels as an ambassador to Constantinople in the early eighteenth century, where she undergoes a sex change from male to female. This strange metamorphosis, which turns Orlando from heterosexual man to lesbian woman, seems prompted in part by several visits Orlando pays to the city's harems and seraglios. During these secret excursions into female space Orlando wears a flowing "Turkish" costume similar to that in which Lady Mary had herself painted by Jonathan Richardson in 1725.

FURTHER READING: Lady Mary Wortley Montagu, *The Complete Letters of Mary Wortley Montagu*, ed. Robert Halsband, 3 vols. (Oxford: Clarendon, 1965–67); —, *Essays and Poems and Simplicity. A Comedy*, ed. Robert Halsband and Isobel Grundy (Oxford: Clarendon, 1977); —, *Lady Mary Wortley Montagu/Turkish Embassy Letters*, ed. Malcom Jack (Athens: University of Georgia Press, 1993); Robert Halsband, *The Life of Lady Mary Wortley Montagu* (Oxford: Clarendon, 1956); Patricia Meyer Spacks, "Female Rhetorics," in Shari Benstock, ed., *The Private Self: Theory and Practice of Women's Autobiographical Writings* (Chapel Hill: University of North Carolina Press, 1988), pp. 177–91; Joseph Lew, "Lady Mary's Portable Seraglio," *Eighteenth-Century Studies* 24 (Summer 1991): 432–50; Marcia Pointon, "Killing Pictures," in John Barrell, ed., *Painting and Politics: New Essays on British Art 1700–1850* (Oxford and New York: Oxford University Press, 1992), pp. 39–72; Ruth Bernard Yeazell, "Public Baths and Private Harems: Lady Mary Wortley Montagu and the Origins of Ingres' *Bain Turc*," *Yale Journal of Criticism* 7 (1994): 111–38; —, *Harems of the Mind: Passages of Western*

Art and Literature (New Haven: Yale University Press, 2000); Srinivas Aravamudan, "Lady Mary Wortley Montagu in the Hammam: Masquerade, Womanliness, and Levantinization," *ELH: Journal of English Literary History* 62 (1995): 69–104; Isobel Grundy, *Lady Mary Wortley Montagu* (Oxford and New York: Oxford University Press, 1999).

Adrianople, 1 April 1717

I am now got into a new world where everything I see appears to me a change of scene, and I write to your Ladyship with some content of mind, hoping at least that you will find the charm of novelty in my letters and no longer reproach me that I tell you nothing extraordinary. I won't trouble you with a relation of our tedious journey, but I must not omit what I saw remarkable at Sophia, one of the most beautiful towns in the Turkish Empire and famous for its hot baths that are resorted to both for diversion and health. I stopped here one day on purpose to see them. Designing to go incognito, I hired a Turkish coach. These *voitures* are not at all like ours, but much more convenient for the country, the heat being so great that glasses would be very troublesome. They are made a good deal in the manner of the Dutch coaches, having wooden lattices painted and gilded, the inside being painted with baskets and nosegays of flowers, intermixed commonly with little poetical mottoes. They are covered all over with scarlet cloth, lined with silk and very often richly embroidered and fringed. This covering entirely hides the persons in them, but may be thrown back at pleasure and the ladies peep through the lattices. They hold four people very conveniently, seated on cushions, but not raised.

In one of these covered wagons I went to the bagnio about ten o'clock. It was already full of women. It is built of stone in the shape of a dome with no windows but in the roof, which gives light enough. There was five of these domes joined together, the outmost being less than the rest and serving only as a hall where the porteress stood at the door. Ladies of quality generally give this woman the value of a crown or ten shillings, and I did not forget that ceremony. The next room is a very large one, paved with marble, and all round it raised two sofas of marble, one above another. There were four fountains of cold water in this room, falling first into marble basins and then running on the floor in little channels made for that purpose, which carried the streams into the next room, something less than this, with the same sort of marble sofas, but so hot with steams of sulphur proceeding from the baths joining to it, 'twas impossible to stay there with one's clothes on. The two other domes were the hot baths, one of which had cocks of cold water turning into it to temper it to what degree of warmth the bathers have a mind to.

I was in my travelling habit, which is a riding dress, and certainly appeared very extraordinary to them, yet there was not one of 'em that showed the least surprise or impertinent curiosity, but received me with all the obliging civility possible. I know no

European court where the ladies would have behaved themselves in so polite a manner to a stranger. I believe in the whole there were two hundred women and yet none of those disdainful smiles or satiric whispers that never fail in our assemblies when anybody appears that is not dressed exactly in fashion. They repeated over and over to me, "Uzelle, pek uzelle," which is nothing but, "Charming, very charming." The first sofas were covered with cushions and rich carpets, on which sat the ladies, and on the second their slaves behind 'em, but without any distinction of rank by their dress, all being in the state of nature, that is, in plain English, stark naked, without any beauty or defect concealed, yet there was not the least wanton smile or immodest gesture amongst 'em. They walked and moved with the same majestic grace which Milton describes of our General Mother. There were many amongst them as exactly proportioned as ever any goddess was drawn by the pencil of Guido or Titian, and most of their skins shiningly white, only adorned by their beautiful hair divided into many tresses hanging on their shoulders, braided either with pearl or riband, perfectly representing the figures of the Graces.

I was here convinced of the truth of a reflection that I had often made, that if 'twas the fashion to go naked the face would be hardly observed. I perceived that the ladies with the finest skins and most delicate shapes had the greatest share of my admiration, though their faces were sometimes less beautiful than those of their companions. To tell you the truth, I had wickedness enough to wish secretly that Mr Jervas could have been there invisible. I fancy it would have very much improved his art to see so many fine women naked in different postures, some in conversation, some working, others drinking coffee or sherbet, and many negligently lying on their cushions while their slaves (generally pretty girls of seventeen or eighteen) were employed in braiding their hair in several pretty manners. In short, 'tis the women's coffee-house, where all the news of the town is told, scandal invented, etc. They generally take this diversion once a week, and stay there at least four or five hours without getting cold by immediate coming out of the hot bath into the cool room, which was very surprising to me. The lady that seemed the most considerable amongst them entreated me to sit by her and would fain have undressed me for the bath. I excused myself with some difficulty, they being all so earnest in persuading me. I was at last forced to open my skirt and show them my stays, which satisfied 'em very well, for I saw they believed I was so locked up in that machine that it was not in my own power to open it, which contrivance they attributed to my husband. I was charmed with their civility and beauty and should have been very glad to pass more time with them, but Mr Wortley resolving to pursue his journey the next morning early I was in haste to see the ruins of Justinian's church, which did not afford me so agreeable a prospect as I had left, being little more than a heap of stones.

Adieu, madam. I am sure I have now entertained you with an account of such a sight as you never saw in your life and what no book of travels could inform you of. 'Tis no less than death for a man to be found in one of these places.

ANONYMOUS

"Cloe to Artimesa" (1720)

The anonymous poem "Cloe to Artimesa," a provocative brief in favor of female (erotic?) bonding, first appeared in A. Hammond's *A New Miscellany* in 1720. In the confident assertion that love relations between women are more civilized than those between women and men ("in ourselves we find / Pleasures for their gross senses too refined") the speaker articulates a fantasy about female homoeroticism that would be put forward again by Natalie Clifford Barney, Renée Vivien, and other sapphic chauvinists in the late nineteenth and early twentieth century. Given the anti-male sentiments expressed, the choice of the name "Artimesa" may also be significant—recalling as it does both the virgin goddess Artemis, famed for her hunting skills and indifference to men, and the bloodthirsty Artemisia, ruler of Halicarnassus and ally of Xerxes, who led troops into battle during the assault on Athens in the Persian Wars. When spurned by a lover, Dardanus, she was reputed to have put out his eyes.

FURTHER READING: A. Hammond, *A New Miscellany* (London, 1720); Roger Lonsdale, ed., *Eighteenth-Century Women Poets: An Oxford Anthology* (Oxford and New York: Oxford University Press, 1989); Emma Donoghue, *Passions Between Women: British Lesbian Culture 1668–1801* (London: Scarlet, 1993).

> While vulgar souls their vulgar love pursue,
> And in the common way themselves undo;
> Impairing health and fame, and risking life,
> To be a mistress or, what's worse, a wife:
> We, whom a nicer taste has raised above
> The dangerous follies of such slavish love,
> Despise the sex, and in our selves we find
> Pleasures for their gross senses too refined.
> Let brutish men, made by our weakness vain,

Boast of the easy conquest they obtain;
Let the poor loving wretch do all she can,
And *all* won't please th' ungrateful tyrant, Man;
We'll scorn the monster and his mistress too,
And show the world what women ought to do.

ANONYMOUS

Monsieur Thing's Origin: or, Seignior D----o's Adventures in Britain (1722)

The following rather illiterate obscene poem, published anonymously in 1722, is one of several mock-heroic "dildo poems" written in the 1720s and 1730s in imitation of Samuel Butler's "Dildoides" (1672) and the Earl of Rochester's *The Dildo* (1678). Other contemporary works on the topic included *The Bauble* (1721), *The History of Signor Del Dildo* (1732), and the grossly pornographic *A Voyage to Lethe. By Captain Samuel Cock, Sometime Commander of the Good Ship Charming Polly. Dedicated to the Right Worshipful Adam Cock, Esq., of Black Mary's Hole, Coney Skin Merchant* (1741). Detailing the surreal adventures of little "Seignior D----o" (who is represented as hailing from France), the poem at once parodies the conventions of picaresque fiction and testifies to a growing pornographic fascination with female homosexuality. While "Seignior D----o" is not exclusively a plaything for sapphists—old maids and wives with impotent husbands also find him useful—he achieves his comic apotheosis at the hands of two sex-crazed girls ("vile and lustful elves") who take turns "acting the man" with his help. Like other pornographic squibs of the early eighteenth century, the poem is a fairly dire example of claggy bad faith: it ends, somewhat incoherently, with a generalized warning about the danger of homosexual practices.

FURTHER READING: *Monsieur Thing's Origin: or, Seignior D----o's Adventures in Britain* (London, 1722); Felicity Nussbaum, *The Brink of All We Hate: English Satires on Women, 1650–1750* (Lexington: University Press of Kentucky, 1984); Peter Wagner, "The Discourse on Sex—or Sex as Discourse: Eighteenth-Century Medical and Paramedical Erotica," in G. S. Rousseau and Roy Porter, eds., *Sexual Underworlds of the Enlightenment* (Manchester: Manchester University Press, 1987), pp. 46–68; ——, *Eros Revived: Erotica of the Enlightenment in England and America* (London: Paladin Grafton, 1990); Lynn Hunt, ed., *The Invention of Pornography: Obscenity and the Origins of Modernity, 1500–1800* (New York: Zone, 1993).

Astrea's kind, who taught me how to choose
This comic thesis, for my present muse.
Whoe'er they be, that do desire to trace
His pedigree, it's of the Gallic race:
Some say it was the Duchess Mazarine
Was first contriver of this fine machine;
From Italy it was that first it came,
And from that country it had first its name:
But if my information is but true,
A place it came from nearer to our view.
To France he owes his birth or first extraction,
By doctors there he had his first creation,
And is originally of that nation.
Experienced Asculapians did design
Him for the use of infants feminine,
Until they were fit to be put to nurses
Of males, most proper for to steer their course.
He first was made, to put a help to nature,
But art of nature now has got the better:
His first progeny, and designed descent
Was to relieve the poor and innocent;
But now converted to worse intent.

Satire be kind, and be not too severe,
But lightly speak of Seignior's character:
Then once take wing, and soar o'er Albion's isle,
To see how virtue there seems in exile,
And view how D----o females there beguile.
Behold kind Virtue weeping from on high,
Tears dropping from her, as from gloomy sky,
With eyes dejected, on the Isles of Britain
Bare-faced could not behold, but with a mask on:
Leering she gazes from her airy mansions,
Blushes to see strange introduced inventions.

When Seignior first at London did arrive,
Was put to shifts to know how to contrive,
Or find a place where's family should live.

At length all day after they had been trudging,
Tired with fatigue, in seeking of a lodging,
Were showed a toy-shop, nigh to Covent Garden.

Where for some time they lived in private room,
But soon became unto the public known,
Because his qualities were really such,
Could with small help do little or do much:
For his capacity, made denizen,
'Twas thus Monsieur became an Englishman,
Before 'twas long, the number did increase,
So the last brood were to choose a new place,
That he should not be taken for a clown,
A station chose, in middle of the town,
In toy-shop large, and nigh unto a church,
In Fleet Street did this lovely creature perch.

Although he is not like to owl or bat,
He's downy, smooth, and soft as any rat:
And though he is no bird of paradise,
Can do the lady's business in a trice:
He's often by 'em so caressed and fondled,
No child by them was e'er so dearly dandled,
Or e'er poor thing made use or better handled.

The engine does come up so near to nature,
Can spout so pleasing, betwixt wind and water,
Warm milk, or any liquid softer,
Slow as they please, or, if they please, much faster.

In little time Monsieur came to be known,
Then soon was visited by ev'ry one:
It was the darling of their great desire
To see our foreigner, in his attire;
As it's polite, to visit out of hand
A stranger new come from a foreign land.

No sooner Monsieur grew to be of fame,
But as soon was received by city dame:
The serpent sooner did not beguile Eve,
Than the kind sex blind Seignior did receive.

They brought him quick to truckle to their bow,
To feel what hidden treasures they'd below:
Then afterwards they taught him to ascend
Towards a port, where pleasures did portend:

When they had brought him so near happiness,
They forced him in the summit of their bliss;
And after they had tasted, made a drudge
Worse than a waterman, who wears a badge,
Or ticket-porter in the street that plies,
Burdened with loads, is in no worse disguise,
Than to their lust he is a sacrifice.

   By this time his good qualities were known,
And much became beloved by most of 'em:
A merchant's wife prevailed on him to sit,
His picture coveted, to please her wit.
So Monsieur chose to be picted on glass:
How you would laugh, to see how like a ta----e,
And ladies smile, as they did by it pass.
This greatly did explain their kind good humour,
From respect they paid unto his honour;
For not a soul of them, as they passed by,
But at the picture they would cast an eye.

   Soon after this, he lodged in merchant's house,
And did make friends between him and his spouse:
He undertook the merchant's wife to please,
Then the old doted fool lived at his ease;
All that she wanted, was to please her creature,
It was so brimming full of her good nature.
Our Seignior's duty was no sooner done,
Than the lascivious heart of her he'd won.
She boldly worked him up unto an oil,
So did she make the creature slave and toil;
She wrought him till he was just out of breath
And harassed Seignior almost unto death;
Until he was forced to choose a new place,
To alter somewhat of his slavish case.

   Then he removed, to lodge with an old maid;
No sooner came, her virtue was betrayed:
So soon as he had popped but up his head,
Her modesty was vanished, and quite fled.
As soon as Monsieur had kissed wrinkled Nancy,
He so did tickle, and please Trulla's fancy,
That pleased her thoughts at the first very touch,

Her inclinations he'd gained very much:
Tired with Old Hag, he went away by stealth,
He took his flight, and left her by herself.

Clear as Monsieur was, and free to range,
His tour he took towards the Great Exchange;
Ingratiated himself into the favour
Of milliners by complaisant behaviour:
He pitched his tent between two partners,
Indeed he took them not for to be whores;
But like two cows a-playing in a field,
While the other seemed to yield:
This was itself complete encouragement,
To show what they'd be at and their intent
Fully explained what it was that they meant.

One of these girls tied Monsieur to her middle,
To try if she the secret could unriddle:
She acted man, being in a merry mood,
Striving to please her partner as she could;
And thus they took it in their turns to please
Their lustful inclinations to appease,
Until Monsieur was almost suffocated
With that, of all things, that at last he hated.
So did he leave these vile and lustful elves,
To run the frisk together by themselves.

Monsieur by chance came into a christening room,
Where he had like to have received his doom:
The midwife bellowing, open mouthed she cried,
"If you're encouraged, villain, we're destroyed:"
The bedstaff took, and in her furious whim,
With all her force designed to sling at him.
The parson present, in this angry rage
He interposed, her passion to assuage,
As likewise he did that of furious nurse's
Whose mouth was open'd, nothing but for curses.
But all agreed to turn immediately
Poor Seignior out, as common enemy.
From hence Monsieur took moving to the court,
To see what pastime there was, or what sport:
So came he to the hand of lady's maid,

With whom some little time our Monsieur stayed,
She like cade lamb was pleased, with Monsieur played.
No sooner had she tasted of his favour,
But she embraced the sweetness of his savour;
To him alone she showed her good behaviour.

By this time Monsieur having thus infused
His friendship in the maid, she introduced
Him to her kind mistress's first acquaintance,
As a fine thing of noted worth and sense:
So that the lady was to make a trial
Of Monsieur's skill, which was without denial
The best, most pleasing thing as e'er she felt,
Ever since she near to the court had dwelt.
If e'er you see a proud ambitious cit,
And she pretend to triumph as a wit;
You may be sure that Seignior is her friend,
On him alone she only does depend.

Or e'er you meet a proud and scornful maid,
And she but feign that virtue is her trade;
Then be assured, the jilt is such a one,
Who shares of Seignior's smile, and not his frown,
And does make use of him to please her own:
Yet it's in women's nature to be civil,
If they're not instigated by the devil,
Or in the way, Monsieur he is the rival.

No doubt but this uncouth contrived new fashion
Was to destroy the end of the creation;
Like that foul sin which is as bad in men,
For which God did the Eastern World condemn.

ANONYMOUS

From *A Supplement to the Onania, or the Heinous Sin of
Self-Pollution* (c. 1725)

The *Onania*, a lurid early-eighteenth-century diatribe against masturbation first published anonymously around 1708, has sometimes been attributed to the clergyman Balthasar Bekker. It was extremely popular in its day, running through nineteen editions and spawning several sequels, including the equally squalid *Supplement to the Onania*, added in the seventh edition and expanded in subsequent editions. Collected in the various editions of the *Supplement* are, among other things, "Divers Remarkable LETTERS to the AUTHOR, from Such of Both SEXES, Who Had Injur'd Themselves by SELF-POLLUTION, Lamenting Their Impotencies, and Diseases Thereby." In one edition of *Onania* published after 1725 the author included several letters relating to lesbianism, beginning with that of a young woman who claims, regretfully, to have engaged in acts of "self-pollution" with a debauched chambermaid. As a result of such "filthiness," she opines, she has developed a grotesquely enlarged clitoris that stands out "as long or longer than my Thumb." Letters describing similar oddities follow, to which the author appends his own pseudoscientific commentary and dire warnings. While undoubtedly intended to titillate, the *Supplement*'s tales of distended genitalia and rampaging female lusts point up how prevalent physiological explanations for homosexuality were in the early modern period—and how crudely they might be formulated. The "enlarged clitoris" theory of lesbianism would not be challenged until the later nineteenth century, and even then it occasionally resurfaces in the writings of Havelock Ellis and other turn-of-the-century sexologists.

FURTHER READING: Anonymous, *Onania, or the Heinous Sin of Self-Pollution and A Supplement to the Onania*, (London, n.d.; rpt. London and New York: Garland, 1986); Peter Wagner, "The Veil of Science and Mortality: Some Pornographic Aspects of the 'Onania,'" *British Journal for Eighteenth-Century Studies* 4 (1983): 179–84; —, *Eros Revived: Erotica of the Enlightenment in England and America* (London: Secker and Warburg, 1988); Thomas Laqueur, *Making Sex: Body and Gender from the Greeks to Freud* (Cambridge: Harvard University Press, 1990); Emma Donoghue, *Passions Between Women: British Lesbian Culture, 1668–1801* (London: Scarlet, 1993); Roy Porter and Lesley Hall, *The Facts of Life: The Creation of Sexual Knowledge in Britain, 1650–1950* (New Haven and London: Yale University Press, 1995).

To the Commendable Author of the *Onania*

Oct. 16, 1725.

Sir

This Letter comes from a young Female Creature, but an old Transgressor in the Practice of that filthy Pleasure which you have so justly exploded and condemned, in your ingenious Book of *Onania*, which I happily met with about 10 days ago: But in all the Cases therein enumerated, there is not one that is parallel to mine, which as my welfare requires it, I must be obliged to relate, and is what I question, Sir, whether you have ever once met with: Nor could I tell it, though at the same time I bless the Opportunity, but that I am sure you no more know the Writer of it, nor ever will, than I know the Author of *Onania*, or desire it. I began, Sir, the folly at 11 Years of Age, was taught it by my Mother's Chamber Maid, who lay with me from that Time all along till now, which is full seven Years, and so intimate were we in the Sin, that we took all Opportunities of committing it, and invented all the ways we were capable of to heighten the Titillation, and gratify our sinful Lusts the more. We, in short, pleasured one another, as well as each our selves, but whether by the hard usage of my Parts by her, or my self, or both, or whether from any thing in Nature more in my make, than is customary to the Sex, I don't know, but for above half a Year past I have had a Swelling that thrusts out from my Body, as big, and almost as hard, and as long or longer than my Thumb, which inclines me to excessive lustful Desires, and from it there issues a moisture or slipp'riness to that degree that I am almost continually wet, and sometimes have such a forcing, as if something of a large Substance was coming from me, which greatly frightens both me and my Maid. She went to a Midwife about it, but did not, she says, tell her of our Practice; the Midwife said it was a bearing down of the Womb, by weakness, and told her what I should do, which I did, but to no purpose. Ever since I have been so, I have not had the Course of Nature, have a great pain in my Back, and my Belly is swell'd, am not near as strong as I was, my Countenance much paler, and Appetite less. It has almost distracted me, and unfits me for my Learning, and am afraid I am so hurt, as that it cannot be remedied. O! that I should be so wicked, I, who have had a much nobler Education (and should know better) than is common to most of my Sex; that am vers'd in the Classicks, and design'd by my Friends, who are very rich, for something above the common station of my Sex; I say, that I should so filthily debase my self, wrong my Body, and, which is worse, my Soul, is surprizing even to my self. Had I read more the Bible, and less in *Martial, Juvenal, Ovid* &c. it had been better for me, but those Books, *Rochester,* and Plays, at first debauch'd my silly Fancy. But I hope, as now, both my self and Maid have, on consulting your curious discourse of *Self-Pollution,* abandon'd the Practice, and resolv'd, through God's Grace, to commit it no more, we shall find Pardon, and my infirm Body, from your Hands, good Sir, Relief. She ails nothing, is a strong Wench of twenty seven, my self of tender make, and naturally inclin'd to be weakly, and but just turned of eighteen. I have with this, sent you a Guinea Fee, and desire your Cordial Advice, what I had best to do, and your Opinion of my Case, seal'd up safe, directed for Mrs. *E. N.* and I will send for it tomorrow Morning, at the Bookseller's where this is left; and, Sir, I must needs desire you to send me this Letter back, that I may have the Satisfaction of committing it to the Flames my self. According, to your Answer, you shall hear further from,

> *Sir*
> *Your ever obliged, and*
> *Most obedient humble Servant,*
> *E. N.*

Not, Sir, but you may copy my Letter first, and if you think worth while, to print it also in your next Edition, as a caution to others; but would not that my Hand be seen by any besides your self the circumstances of the Relation, so as not to be known 'tis me, I having taken care of and guarded against.

This young Lady's Case, through the height of her Lust, and force and frequency of abusing herself, and probably the unnatural propendance of the Part, is no more, according to the Account she gives, than a relaxation of the *Clitoris,* a thing common to many of the Sex, both in the single and married, who are Vigorous and Lustful, and have given up themselves to the Practice of *Self-Pollution* for any time. In some Women it extends it self, and is enlarged when inflated to the exact likeness and size of a human *Penis* erect, except that it has no perforation, (though it really looks, by the natural Impression at the end, as if there was a Passage) nor is altogether so long, but yet it erects and falls as that does, in proportion to the venereal Desire or Inclination of the Woman.

I have had in my time one or two under this Circumstance, by the same Practice, for Cure, who upon their living afterwards Chaste, and using some astringent Foments, and a few Internals, to regulate the inordinate and enraged Venereal Desires, have been brought to rights and the Parts restored to their pristine, natural State and Condition. [. . .]

As there are many Women, who from excessive Lust and abuse of the Parts have this propension of the *Clitoris,* so there are others, who are born with it, both to their Trouble and Shame.

Dr. Drake, in his Book of Anatomy, tells us, that the extraordinary Size, and laxness of the *Clitoris*, hanging out of the Body in some Infants, has made the Women mistake Children for those sort of Monsters they call Hermophrodites. Of this sort, says he, I had one brought to me upon another Occasion, whose *Clitoris* hung out of the Body so far, at about three Years old, that it resembled very much a *Penis*, but it wanted the Perforation, and instead of that, just behind it, the Urine issued out at a Hole, which was nothing else but the corner of the *Rima*, the *Clitoris* filling all the rest of the Orifice; so that the Parents mistook it for a Boy, christened it as such, and esteem'd it so, when it was brought to me; but the Neighbours who had notice of this appearance, call'd it an Hermophrodite. *Regner de Graef* also says, he saw a Girl new born, whose *Clitoris* had such a resemblance to a Man's *Penis*, that the Midwife, and the rest of the Women there present, took it for a Boy, and baptiz'd it as such.

It is certain, that in some Women, especially those who are very salacious, the *Clitoris* is so vastly extended, that by hanging out of the Passage, it is mistaken for a *Penis*, such have been called *Fricatrices*: By *Caelius Aurelianus, Tribades*: By *Plautus, Subigatrices*, and accounted Hermophrodites, because, as said before, they have been able to perform the Actions of Men with other Women. *Amatus* relates of two *Turkish* Women of *Thessalonica*; and *De Castro* says, he has also seen some Women at *Lisbon*, punish'd for the like most filthy Wickedness. In *Creophagi*, in *Arabia*, they circumcise the Women that are so, by cutting away a certain *Apophosis* of musculous Skin, that descends from the superior Part of the *Matrix*, which suffers Erection, in Coition. *Lusitanus* tells us, Obs. 82, that a most renowned and very honest Virgin, having naturally a propended *Clitoris*, which so provoked her to Venery, by only its unavoidable rubbing against her Linnen, as she moved, that it gave great trouble and affliction to her Soul, insomuch, that with the Consent of her Parents, this Physician was applied to, to cut it off, which he says, with the help of two skillful Surgeons, was done, and she cured and well ever after.

I have read, that in *France*, there are a People, who have a great propension of the *Clitoris*, naturally, and are equally able to make use of those of both Sexes, and that the Laws there, leave to their Choice, which Sex to make use of, after which, the use of the other is absolutely forbidden them. And we read that in *Florida* and *Virginia*, there is a Nation, which have the Generative Parts of both Sexes: To confirm the same, those that will take the pains to consult the Works of *Jacobus de Moyne*, may see a Description of them, in certain Figures; but it seems they are a People that are hated by the very *Indians*, and by them made servile, to carry Burdens, and do Offices instead of Beasts, they being very strong and able Bodied. *Platerus* says, he saw a *Clitoris* in a Woman, as big and as long as the Neck of a Goose. *Riolanus* and *Schenkius*, two noted Physicians, both say, they have observed it as long in a Woman as a Man's Finger. *Plempius* writes of one *Helena*, a Woman, that lay with several Women, and vitiated several Virgins with that Part. *Diemerbroek* says, he himself saw, in a certain Woman at *Montfort*, a *Clitoris*, as long and thick as the ordinary *Penis* of a Man, which came to be of that magnitude, after she had lain-in, three or four times.

The following History, says an Author, made a mighty Noise both at *Paris* and *Tholouse*. A certain young Woman at *Tholouse*, had a relaxation of the *Vagina*, resembling a Man's *Penis*, and some pretended that she abused it that way, it being six Inches in length, and four in Circumference in the middle, where it was very hard. It gradually encreas'd from her Childhood: She was searched by the Physicians there, who gave their Opinion, it was a real *Penis*; upon which the Magistrates of the Town, ordered her to go in Man's Habit. In this Equipage she came to *Paris*, where she got Money by showing herself, till upon other assurances that she was a Woman, and a promise of being cured, she was brought into the *Hotel Dieu*, where the descent was soon reduc'd, and she forc'd to resume her Female Dress, to her great regret.

Very rarely, or hardly ever do we hear of what *Bauhinus*, a Physician, has observ'd concerning a *Clitoris*, that it became bony, in a *Venetian* Courtezan, which by reason of its extream hardness, did so hurt her Lovers, in *Coition*, that many times, by reason of Inflammations thereby, they were forced to fly to the Surgeons for help.

An Hermophrodite, is by all look'd upon as a Creature of vile Deformity, bringing a Shame upon both Sexes; and in old Times, wherever found, were drowned, or made away with, such Monsters not being thought by them fit to live.

In *Jul. Obseq. lib. prod.* there is an Account, that at *Luna*, at the time that *L. Metellus*, and *Q. Fabius*, were Consuls, there was born an Hermophrodite, which by the Command of the Southsayers, was cast into the Sea, and the like others were served in other Countries, as soon as discover'd, as at *Umbria*, *Ferretinnum*, *Fore Vessonem*, *Rome*, *Saturnia*, &c.

Caliphanes reports, that beyond the *Nasamones*, and about *Matchlies*, there are ordinarily found Hermophrodites, which so much resemble both Sexes, that they have carnal Knowledge one of another by turns; and this, by an Expression in the young Lady's Letter aforegoing, and which introduced all this Discourse about the *Clitoris*, seems to be part of the Practice between her, and her Bedfellow the Chambermaid.

ANONYMOUS

"The Female Cabin Boy" (c. 1730)

The folk ballad "The Female Cabin Boy" is one of many traditional Anglo-American songs and ballads in which a woman dresses as a man or boy in order to pass as a soldier or sailor. Typically, the woman in question is in search of a lost husband or lover and disguises herself in order to find him. In "The Female Cabin Boy" this respectable motive is lacking, however, and the "pretty female" in male attire exerts a comically devastating force on everyone around her. In eight short verses the author manages to create a microcosm of sexual confusion in which desires of every kind—including sapphic—seem to flourish simultaneously.

FURTHER READING: G. Malcolm Laws, *American Balladry from British Broadsides: A Guide for Students and Collectors of Traditional Song*, Publications of the American Folklore Society, Bibliographical and Special Series, vol. 8 (Philadelphia: American Folklore Society, 1957); Diane Dugaw, *Warrior Women and Popular Balladry 1650–1850* (Cambridge: Cambridge University Press, 1989); Julie Wheelwright, *Amazons and Military Maids: Women Who Dressed as Men in Pursuit of Life, Liberty and Happiness* (London: Pandora, 1989).

It's of a pretty female as you shall understand,
She had a mind of roving into a foreign land
Attired in sailor's clothing she boldly did appear,
And engaged with the captain to serve him for one year.

She engaged with the captain as cabin boy to be,
The wind it was in favor so they soon put out to sea
The captain's lady being on board who seem'd it to enjoy,
So glad the captain had engaged the pretty cabin boy.

So nimble was that pretty maid & done her duty well
But mark what followed often the thing itself will tell
The captain with that pretty maid did oft times kiss and toy,
For he soon found out the secret of the female cabin boy.

Her cheeks appeared like roses and with her side locks curled
The sailors often smiled and said he looks just like a girl,
By eating captain's biscuit her colour did destroy,
And the waist did swell of pretty Nell the pretty cabin boy.

As thro' the Bay of Biscay their gallant ship did plow,
One night among the sailors there was a pretty row,
They bundled from their hammocks it did their rest destroy,
And they swore about the groaning of the handsome cabin boy.

O doctor, O doctor the cabin boy did cry,
The sailors swore by all was good the cabin boy would die,
The doctor ran with all his might and smiling at the fun,
For to think a sailor lad should have a daughter or son.

The sailors when they heard the joke they all began to stare,
The child belong'd to none of them they solemnly did swear,
The lady to the captain said, my dear I wish you joy,
For it's either you or I betray'd the handsome cabin boy.

So they all took a bumper and drank success to trade,
And likewise to the cabin boy, tho' neither man nor maid,
And if the waves should rise again the sailors to destroy,
Why then we must ship some sailors like the handsome cabin boy.

JOHN ADDISON (N.D.)

Translation of Sappho Fragments No. 31 "(Happy as a God Is He")
and No. 130 ("Dire Love, Sweet-Bitter Bird of Prey!") (1735)

The eighteenth-century translator John Addison is known only by the two works he published in the 1730s: *The Works of Anacreon, Translated into English Verse; with Notes Explanatory and Poetical. To Which Are Added the Odes, Fragments, and Epigrams of Sappho* (1735) and *The Works of Petronius Arbiter . . . Translated from the Original Latin* (1736). The former work—containing a short biographical note on Sappho and some of the best and most accurate eighteenth-century translations of her poems into English—is sometimes misattributed to Joseph Addison.

Unlike his namesake, who in 1711 offered a somewhat bowdlerized version of Sappho's life story in an essay on her in *The Spectator*, John Addison was frank about what was known of his subject's amorous predilections:

> she married one *Cercolas*, a Gentleman of great Wealth and Power in the Isle of *Andros*, by whom she had a Daughter nam'd *Cleis*; but he leaving her a Widow very Young, she would never accept of any second Match; not enduring to confine that Passion to one Person, which as the Ancients tell us, was too violent in her to be restrain'd even to one Sex.

Of the homoerotically fraught Fragment 130 ("Dire Love, Sweet-Bitter Bird of Prey!") he acknowledged quite plainly that "this Ode was written by *Sappho* upon two favourite Maids, of whom she was jealous."

Though cast, like Ambrose Philips's, in the somewhat generalized poetic idiom of the day, Addison's translations are generally faithful, with Fragment 130 especially catching something of Sappho's fragile yet unmistakable address.

FURTHER READING: John Addison, *The Works of Anacreon, Translated into English Verse; with Notes Explanatory and Poetical. To Which Are Added the Odes, Fragments, and Epigrams of Sappho* (London, 1735); ----, *The Works of Petronius Arbiter . . . Translated from the Original Latin* (London, 1736); David M. Robinson, *Sappho and Her Influence* (Boston: Marshall Jones, 1924); Édith Mora, *Sappho: Histoire d'un poète et traduc-*

tion intégrale de l'oeuvre (Paris: Flammarion, 1966); Joan DeJean, *Fictions of Sappho 1546–1937* (Chicago: University of Chicago Press, 1989); Peter Jay and Caroline Lewis, eds., *Sappho Through English Poetry* (London: Anvil, 1996); Margaret Reynolds, *The Sappho Companion* (New York: Palgrave, 2001).

Fragment no. 31

Happy as a God is he,
That fond Youth, who plac'd by thee,
Hears and sees thee sweetly gay,
Talk and smile his Soul away.

That it was alarm'd my Breast,
And depriv'ed my Heart of Rest.
For in speechless Raptures tost,
While I gaz'd, my Voice was lost.

The soft Fire with flowing Rein,
Glided swift thro' ev'ry Vein;
Darkness o'er my Eyelids hung;
In my Ears faint Murmurs rung.

Chilling Damps my Limbs bedew'd;
Gentle Tremors thrill'd my Blood;
Life from my pale Cheeks retir'd;
Breathless, I almost expir'd.

Fragment no. 130

Dire Love, sweet-bitter Bird of Prey!
  Whom nothing can controul,
Ah me! dissolves my Life away,
  And melts my inmost Soul.

The charming *Atthis*, who so late
  To *Sappho* vow'd her Care;
Now makes *Andromeda* her Fate,
  And leaves me to despair.

ANONYMOUS

From *The Sappho-an* (c. 1735)

The Sappho-an, subtitled "An Heroic Poem, of Three Cantos. In the Ovidian Style, describing the pleasures which the fair sex enjoy with each other. According to the modern and most polite taste. Found amongst the papers of a lady of quality, a great promoter of Jaconitism," might be considered a kind of lesbian origin myth. Borrowing the burlesque mock-heroic couplet form made popular in the first decades of the eighteenth century by Alexander Pope, the anonymous poet describes an imaginary colloquy between the goddesses of Olympus and the poet Sappho on how best to satisfy overweening female lusts. (It is taken for granted that men are insufficient to the task.) After various means are suggested and rejected—dogs, eunuchs, carrots, and so on—Sappho ends the debate by introducing the company to the dildo, that "wondrous machine" of "burnish'd iv'ry" invented by a "curious artist" expressly for women's pleasure. She then proceeds to demonstrate its uses on Io, priestess of Juno, who responds with predictable enthusiasm.

A significant element in the poem, reflected in the title, is the unblushing characterization of Sappho as the originator of female homosexual practices. At least one modern literary historian has argued that seventeenth- and eighteenth-century writers usually represented Sappho as heterosexual, following Ovid's account of her in the *Heroides* as the spurned lover of Phaon. Only after the self-conscious "lesbianizing" of Sappho by nineteenth-century writers such as Baudelaire and Verlaine, it has been suggested, did homosexuality become a central feature of the Sapphic biographical myth. Yet underground works such as *The Sappho-an*, or the anonymous "Dialogue Between Sappho and Ninon de L'Enclos" (1773), would seem to contradict such assertions. Contemporary satiric references, such as Pope's sneering description of Lady Mary Wortley Montagu as a "dirty-smocked Sappho" in his *Epistle to a Lady* (1735), should perhaps in consequence be read as carrying a specifically antihomosexual valence.

The meaning of "Jaconitism" in the subtitle of the poem is obscure, as are a number of topical references in the poem. The poet may intend some allusion to Jacobitism—political pamphleteers had sometimes attributed lesbianism to the Stuart monarch Queen Anne.

In the excerpts below from Cantos 2 and 3, Hermes, the messenger god, seeks to warn Zeus and his fellow Olympians that their wives and consorts, in the borrowed guise of "British beauties," are holding a suspicious conclave with Sappho. The gods, however, are too wrapped up in "toying with boys" to pay any attention. Hermes retreats in disgust while the goddesses, led by Juno, eagerly foregather for Sappho's lecture-demonstration. The poem concludes with a sad coda in which the poet confesses—to her dying shame—that she too has employed a "stupid tool" on occasion and now recommends heterosexual copulation instead.

FURTHER READING: *The Sappho-an. An Heroic Poem, of Three Cantos. In the Ovidian Style, describing the pleasures which the fair sex enjoy with each other. According to the modern and most polite taste. Found among the papers of a lady of quality, a great promoter of Jaconitism* (London, n.d.); David M. Robinson, *Sappho and Her Influence* (Boston: Marshall Jones, 1924); Édith Mora, *Sappho: Histoire d'un poète et traduction intégrale de l'oeuvre* (Paris: Flammarion, 1966); Felicity Nussbaum, *The Brink of All We Hate: English Satires on Women, 1650–1750* (Lexington: University Press of Kentucky, 1984); Peter Wagner, "The Discourse on Sex—or Sex as Discourse: Eighteenth-Century Medical and Paramedical Erotica," in G. S. Rousseau and Roy Porter, eds., *Sexual Underworlds of the Enlightenment* (Manchester: University of Manchester Press, 1987), pp. 46–68; ——, *Eros Revived: Erotica of the Enlightenment in England and America* (London: Paladin Grafton, 1990); Joan DeJean, *Fictions of Sappho 1546–1937* (Chicago: University of Chicago Press, 1989); Peter Jay and Caroline Lewis, eds., *Sappho Through English Poetry* (London: Anvil, 1996); Jane McIntosh Snyder, *Sappho* (New York and Philadelphia: Chelsea House, 1995); ——, *Lesbian Desire in the Lyrics of Sappho* (New York: Columbia University Press, 1997); Margaret Reynolds, *The Sappho Companion* (New York: Palgrave, 2001).

FROM CANTO 2

Soon as the feathered messenger of Jove
Had done what all the goddesses approve;
Wisely reflecting on the ills to come,
And dreading to mankind some fatal doom,
He wisely ruminates within his breast
What scheme to form, how to detect 'em best,
"For sure," quote Hermes, "well I know the sex,
And such a congress must e'en Jove perplex;
Two women seldom meet but ills ensue,
From twelve we must expect some plague that's new."

Away he flies to where the gods in bow'rs
Quaff and repose themselves on beds of flow'rs:
With each his catamite—O! frothy joy,
Which in the action doth itself destroy.

When Hermes thus: "Immortals rouse, attend,
Or let your empire o'er the females end,
No more at your command stretched out they'll lie,
Heave the fond sigh, and roll the wanton eye;
What is the main design I'm yet to know,
But pleasure is the plan on which they go;
O think betimes, that whilst ye're toying here
With boys, o'erthrowing love in its career,
O! my prophetic soul! they may invent
Some secret way to give themselves content."

His message plays unheeded round their ears,
Dissolved in luxury, they laugh at fears;
And vainly fancy they shall still retain
The privilege, both ports at will to gain.

Hermes disgusted, in a rage withdrew,
And to the conclave door in silence flew;
Amazed he stood, firm as his statue fixed,
To see with goddesses plain mortals mixed;
But 'twas deceit, a cunning disguise,
To screen their persons from discerning eyes,
Celestial dazzling brightness laid aside,
They came in loose array and human pride,
From British beauties that enchant the soul,
The grace, the stature, shape, and form they stole.

Juno herself, with features stern and strong,
High nose, thin lips, and chin acute and long,
Whilst spread about some bristly hairs appear,
Such as when yonkers their first off'rings shear;
Her dress was female, but her manly step
Seem'd as she'd wrestle, throw the bar, or leap;
From C----rt----r these she borrow'd, lusty maid,
Who makes the H----ck----y husbands all afraid,
For neither science comes to her amiss,
The spouse she'll bully, and the wife she'll kiss.

Fair Cytherea next advancing slow
To the assembly makes a graceful bow;
Her braided locks with ribbands interwove,
To wanton in the breezes vainly strove;
A thin transparent mantle lightly pressed
With purple hue her gently rising breast;
Her azure zone so carelessly was tied,
As if it courted what it once denied;
And wishing to be loose, would fain reveal
The font of love, which shades embrowned conceal;
But to delude the eye with fond surprise,
The waving robe just shows her iv'ry thighs;
Thus in a dishabille, best choice of dress,
All in the goddess lady M---- confess;
Alike prepared when pleasure beams the eye,
Rapture to give, or in high joy to die;
Ripe with her wrongs and injured husband's brow
Marked for revenge her votive tablets show.

From sylvan scenes of hawthorn glens and trees,
The huntress nymph appears bare to the knees,
Her manlike sinews, hardened by the chase,
Strain, stretch, and crack at thoughts of the embrace;
Yet man she scorns, and whilst she inward burns,
Nature's strong current on itself returns.
Diana thus bold Philony appears,
Whose loud toned pack the Hampshire forests fears.
From them retreating to the inmost shade,
Where no bold eyes their privacy invade;
She with her nymphs their lovely limbs unbind
To be all o'er kissed by the bawdy wind.
Or, laving in the stream, to water give
Th' embraces man most gladly would receive;
In vain they beat the wave, the wave supplies
Fresh warmth, from whence more wanton they arise;
Then stretched on verdant banks in pairs they lie,
And to posteriors friendly birch apply;
The gentle titillation swells the veins
'Till oozing ichor leaves some faintish stains:
Imperfect bliss! mere miniature of joy!
Formed to raise longings and high lust destroy.

From noisy cities where the busy throng,
Impetuous roll their loaded cars along,
See Vesta turret-crowned, experienced dame,
Who knew in private to conceal her shame;
Prim and demure as any quaking saint,
Who wears no lace nor patch, and rails at paint.
With plain stuff-gown, pinched coif and slender waist
She seems like B----m----d's daughter blushing chaste.

To her succeeds the goddess of the fields,
Bright Ceres who her golden harvest yields;
She like a country dame in russet clad
With jocund air that speaks the heart full glad,
In lusty strides the private conclave seeks
And quite abrupt to the assembly breaks.

Her daughter Proserpine behind her creeps,
With skin all tinged by the infernal deeps,
In a Creolian form; her large black eyes
Indicate nothing can her lust suffice;
The flame that in her vitals burns has drained
The balm of nature, and her visage stained;
Her lips, quite parched, demand the juicy kiss,
And every thirsty charm gaps wide for bliss;
As the faint earth cracks out, scorched up and dry,
Begging the moisture of the giving sky:
In this disguise appeared old Pluto's bride,
That if by mortal eyes the goddess had been spied;
None could the true minute resemblance catch,
But take her for the lady of the watch.

Mark yon fell dame who, tott'ring in her gait,
Steps solemn on fond to preserve her state,
Cybele hight, the mother of the gods
Who long has reveled in their dark abodes,
A matron's image shrouds her shriveled skin,
With furrowed brows and features lank and thin;
Yet still her palsied hand would grasp the chief
That floods her veins and renovates her life;
But long debarred from that to art she flies,
And the kind bosom of a virgin tries;

Whose rising sap with genial juices crowned,
Make her faint spirits from their dotage bound;
Her arid limbs entwined, close suction ply,
And drain the melting porous nymph quite dry;
Who yields her vigour to relieve the crone,
And whilst she gives her vigour taints her own;
So tea and spices though they're closely pent
Receive the neighb'ring filth's obnoxious scent.

Behind her Hebe comes in bloom of youth
Formed for congenial love, soft joys and truth;
Blushing and radiant as the rosy morn,
When heav'nly smiles doth nature's face adorn,
Arrayed in ev'ry grace to charm mankind,
To clasp the youth in am'rous folds inclined.
But, ah! too soon those beauties all will fade:
And lust perfidious sully the bright maid
No jocund bridegroom leaps into her arms,
But the old dotard rifles all her charms,
'Till like a dying flow'r she pines and droops,
And in mid-age with impotence she stoops,
From her sunk cheeks declines the lively dye,
And faintly rolls the heavy languid eye.

With lustful shell-fish crowned, from the green deep
The sea-born Naiads climb the azure steep,
From various quarters a strange group appears,
Some warm in youth, some trembling with their years,
All rush like nature to the common flame;
All prone to venery, defying shame.

To close the scene, quite ripe for am'rous sport
The Lesbian, though no goddess, fills the court:
Man's solid bliss she to the full had tried,
Nor to the other sex her aid denied;
Awful she rushes in and claims a part
To add new vigour to the blunted dart;
Amazed the conclave sat, her threat'ning front
Carried dismay and insolence upon't:
For Phaon still she sighed, a tender boy,
Who spurned her hostile love and warrior joy;

For nature in exuberance of lust
Her parts had formed adapt to either gust:
The wide receiver, most capacious space!
With ease the largest chieftain could embrace,
And when the trembling damsel lay supine
To seeming virile force she could incline,
Nature benevolent thrust forth elate
The part that forms to bliss, or goads to hate.
Hence ev'ry hero, on her bosom fell
And how she tickled girls they best can tell.
"Forgive this rude intrusion," now she cries,
"Ripe to redress our sex's wrongs I rise:
A nobler way remains in nature's womb
To fix our joys eternally to come.
Attend whilst I relate the diff'rent ways,
That each to ease her stinging pains essays:
For not a Hippomania can more fierce,
Than woman's wants the very vitals pierce.

     "How some with animals their lusts retain,
Whose supple tongues the saline juices drain:
Hence mark the shock whose ears the carpet sweep
On couch or velvet cushion wont to sleep;
Whose gloating eyes the females all survey,
Prompt on their beds or in their laps to play;
As most the nimble feet he strains his throat,
And wantons underneath the petticoat.
Or if the hand he licks 'tis proof most strong,
Each morn a nobler office claims his tongue.
Other like fair Bodena when the down,
Of love adorns the nether copple crown,
To view the image that affords delight;
Steals from her father's lodge concealed by night,
And gives the son of Mars a pilfered crown,
To have the chief, erect, in triumph shown;
Or mounting on the leads beneath surveys,
Where silver Thames in soft meanders strays,
And there with eager eyes she courses o'er,
The bathing youths that wanton near the shore;
Fondly she sees the bold Priapus lave,
Untamed by rigour of the rolling wave;

The lofty ensign fans her glowing fires,
And lustful pug must quench her lewd desires.

   "Or need I tell when May's sweet breath invites,
To early pleasures, rural calm delights,
How the bright nymph more blooming than the day
Mounts her fleet steed in virid loose array,
The happy pummels wantonly arise
And by the motion triturate her t----s,
The gentle friction mimic joys produce,
And softly oozes the superfluous juice.

   "'Twould tire the muse to mention all the toys,
With which they imitate substantial joys,
In Britain's isle a queen most highly famed
And for distinction's sake the virgin named,
Contrived an easy chair where in full pride
She'd mount aloft and quite triumphant ride:
Secret she kept it long, but prying eyes
Of priesthood soon the mimic cheat decries,
From Italy the pois'nous drug they choose
And o'er the arms its baneful drops infuse,
The chandler's art oft feeds a double flame,
First lights to bed and then her lust doth tame.
Warmed by the prurient hot corroding place,
The frequent motion working on apace;
Soon as the coming joy with her is felt
The giving candle condescends to melt.
From these mean arts afford them some relief
Oh mitigate their pain and hush their grief;
A train of girls your nod all suppliant wait,
Expecting you to fix their future fate;
And humble beg some method you'd invent
To wound their foes and give themselves content.
My poor endeavours shall support the claim,
Love is my life, and love is all my aim;
Man's rough, ungrateful sex henceforth I scorn,
May all like me, their cold embraces spurn;
Woman to woman's breast can best supply
The stream of love, when once the pulse beats high.
Come then ye virgins of the tender make,
Of unfelt joys and circling bliss partake."

Thus Sappho spoke, and at the grateful close,
A pleasing murmur through th' assembly rose,
Mild as when o'er the rill, or through the trees,
In whispers gently swells the vernal breeze,
They smiled assent, and from her starry throne,
Great Juno thus her sentiments made known:
"Celestial sisters! arbiters of fate!
Know from my soul sincerely *man* I hate;
No more the scrubbing of a rustic kiss
Shall rough my face, rude antidote to bliss.
Freedom to all is given; your schemes propose;
At liberty your secret thoughts disclose;
Say, who the noblest science can improve,
With arts unknown to dull, mechanic love;
Let homely wives plod on in one slow track,
And take what nature gives upon their back;
Unpracticed in the skill to vary joy,
By one continual tenderness they cloy;
Be't yours to bound, to leap, your limbs to spread,
And wanton lewdly on the genial bed;
Satiate with man all nature's stock explore,
And pluck assistance from her endless store.
Begin; who first our infant hopes can rear,
Shall in a full assembly transport share."

When Ceres thus: "'Tis mine to till the ground,
Where vegetables of all sorts abound;
Nor think alone by food they man sustain,
The food of man shall ease the females' pain:
For this the carrot rears its verdant head,
Hiding its sandy root in Tellus' bed;
Thence too, close clinging to its native earth,
The friendly parsnip is dug up to birth;
These when some tender hand has washed them clean,
Ye all are well acquainted what they mean;
What need we more? If man will poorly swerve
From nature's rules, for us let carrots serve."

With indignation fired and red'ning eye,
The goddess queen this practice doth defy:
"Born of the earth," she cries, "from dirt you seek
Feeble employment, and a tool most weak.

Let country dames void of politer taste,
On roots, or any thing thus break their fast;
We study to improve the active sport,
And find diversion for the belles at c----t;
Man we despise—but in our better plan
Let us in miniature out-ape the man.

"See from the bath the supple eunuch rise,
The loss of substance better found supplies;
Deprived of balmy juice in virile pride,
He fears not the most tempting to bestride;
All night he labours at the luscious joy,
Nor can the coming morn his bliss destroy;
Better with him luxuriant give the flow,
Than water plants inanimate to grow.
If that you seek, young Ganimede attends,
Whence comes no danger, for no show'r descends;
One road he keeps, one constant track pursues,
To him no pleasure, you, no pain accrues."

Modest in decent pride young Hebe rose,
And thus; "A virgin may her thoughts disclose;
Oft with the tempting boy I've loosely played,
And o'er his limbs my wanton hands have strayed,
Whilst he in free indulgence hath confessed,
Jove in another mode hath love expressed.
Beware then, ladies, how ye here engage,
Nor trust the Ganimedes of this vile age;
Who trust the men their secrets to explore,
Will yours disclose when once the conflict's o'er."

The maiden's caution gladly all approve,
And join to form some other shape of love;
Italian mimicry they all despise,
Some new invention must bear off the prize.

FROM CANTO 3

Still on, Pierian nymph, the theme pursue,
Undraw the veil and bring it all to view,
Fly round the toilette and the couch display;

Illicit love the darling theft betray:
For longer nice the sportive girl disguise,
When she in secret the gay engine tries.

　　When Hebe ceased, alert, with manly air,
Sappho arose from off her iv'ry chair,
Beneath her robe the sacred prize she held,
Whose large protub'rance was but ill concealed.

　　"Cease, cease," she cries, "your needless search suspend,
Well versed in love, let me the conflict end;
A curious artist that through nature pried,
Has ev'ry wish our hearts could form supplied;
He gives us man without the plague of males,
Which will untired remain when nature fails;
The conscious blush must rise whene'er I think
What arts we use when drooping standards sink;
In vain the lily hand with genial fire
Strives with fresh heat the mortals to inspire;
When round their limbs robust we gently twine,
And fondly hope to make the centers join;
Repugnant to our joys, the ruler, dead,
Hangs like a fading flow'r its livid head;
Nor can our heaving breasts new strength excite,
The darting tongue no longer can invite;
When we to rushing joy go boldly on,
Supine and indolent they tumble down;
Balked in our bliss, we to reproaches fly,
And noise and tumult for kind sighs supply;
No more we clasp him in our tender arms,
No more his colder breast our bosom warms;
Who then such frail felicity would trust,
Or value those imperfect efforts most;
When solid joys are always at command,
And court the pressure of your eager hand?
For this the burnish'd iv'ry rears its head,
Waiting for coral of a lovely red;
Or if too rude the polished engine seems,
The velvet cov'ring keeps it from extremes;
Its shape complete, nor can ye aught despise,
For to your choice they shall adapt the size."

She said, and with a more majestic mien
Produc'd at once the wonderful machine.
Not more the Greeks rejoic'd when Ilium's fate,
Which on its stol'n Palladium did await,
The sly Ulysses cautiously drew out
And charmed the wond'ring chiefs and vulgar rout.

With rapture all beheld it and applause
In Io's loud, the silent image draws.
Immediate trial is the next demand,
The trial claims a gently trembling hand;
Kind Sappho soon administers her aid,
And drives the dart into the yielding maid.
Fond of the scheme they strive t'improve its use,
And each will the most pleasing method choose.

Fond to expose her leg the huntress-queen
Close to her buskin fixes the machine;
With limbs expanded moves the nimble heel,
And feeds the part which most she should conceal.[. . .]

Soon as the Lesbian had, with triumph crowned,
And nimble fingers, served th' assembly round,
Each gave her sentiments, and firmly strove
The young advent'rer in each shape t'improve.

Love's goddess from her taper waist alone,
Bestows the beauty-giving azure zone;
Whilst round the female hips that gift is felt,
At distance falls the new-invented belt,
Proud of its better place, the hero struts,
And on the rolling air of manhood puts;
Now strikes the iv'ry belly with its head,
And now bent down upon the thigh is spread;
But when to action called, fierce in the front
He points his mark prepared to face the brunt.

Still there remains another nice essay,
Moisture alone can flaming fire allay;
And what the turgid veins with rapture fill,
Is love descending in soft trickling rills;

When every pore its genial balm collects,
And through one pipe the flowing stream ejects.
To gain this point their skill is at a stand,
The engine drops and shrinks the tender hand,
Till fair Minerva, patroness of arts,
The best improvement to the fair imparts,
A spring she adds, whose property is such,
That at the middle finger's single touch,
Through a small tube is instantly conveyed,
Warm nature to the essence-yielding maid,
Which drawn from dugs distended kindly gives
Lacteal juice to widows, girls or wives.

Thus finished and complete, it long had served
Celestial nymphs, and chastity preserved.
In time our earthly ladies found its use,
Unwilling the least moment's prime to lose.
In China first the supple thing took birth,
And after tea, afforded them new mirth;
Confucius there philosophy first taught,
And thence this cargo was to Europe brought;
Fathers of all may well their annals boast,
The seasons and inventions we have lost;
Lust to supply, and luxury to aid,
These are thy great advantages, O! trade!

Soon Spaniards and Italians make it known,
And privately adopt it as their own.
The French, that ever am'rous, dancing crew,
With vigour to its cold embraces flew,
And claimed their darling of its succour vain,
'Till Britain felt a Stuart's happy reign;
Returning Charles this blessing brought and more,
To fill the magazine of lech'ry's store.
These all the ladies of his court enjoyed,
Though for disguise a hogshead were destroyed;
Of this facetious Butler loudly sings,
Best poet to the bawdiest of k----gs.

Oh! could I trace the dear succession down,
How it the country raided, and spread the town,

As outside nervous should my verses prove,
Yet softer than the milk-distilling love.

    Like sects, opposed, the stronger root it took,
And soon the chief of women men forsook;
They change their habits, alter ev'ry air,
And see in Joseph's puny miss appear;
The bold virago mankind seems to ape,
And for that purpose varies ev'ry shape;
The yielding girl to gentler postures turns,
And gives to woman what to man she scorns.

    The diff'rent symptoms take: the female rake,
The cock of hat and furzy wig bespeak;
She rides her trotting nag aside 'tis true;
But ye pale-looking nymphs how rides she you?
Full flushed, and of the Amazonian kind,
She dreads no storms, nor fears the rougher wind,
All morn most briskly she pursues the chase,
Then on your couch imprints the lewd embrace.

    With languid eyes, and feeble, trembling pulse,
That baffles all the skill of Sl----ne or H----se,
For ever lazy, and for ever dull,
Craving eternally, yet never full;
Stretched on a couch, or lolling in a chair,
The indigent receiver doth appear.
The sport awhile may sick'ning life sustain,
But soon 'tis o'er, and endless is the pain.

    Would ye, young girls, who glow with health and love,
The blissful minutes of your lives improve,
Ne'er throw the balm of luscious love away,
And voluntary dwindle to decay;
Nor bathe a stupid tool, when the same joys,
May bring ye pretty girls and chatt'ring boys;
Rather avow your love, confess your flame,
And nature boldly own, devoid of shame.
Let the mean herd, the shaggy, pallid crew,
Their forced, their made-up bliss at home pursue;
Woman was made for man, so nature meant,

And ev'ry fibre answers the intent;
Who sins against it the creation wrongs,
Must rank with beasts, nor to mankind belongs.

By sad experience taught, I dying speak,
If my former wicked vows should break,
Forgive me, saints of H----ckney, with regret
I think of the false transports I have met;
O! let the fair who thus have lost their bloom,
May yet have years of pregnancy to come,
Some nobler method seek; see where the sacred fain
Stands wide their private births to entertain;
Better to fix the growing substance there,
Than let their children all expand in air:
Though prudes will censure and old maidens talk,
Ne'er screen your bliss, nor flowing transports balk,
Spite of all shame, style one *Young Cupid's Grove*,
And this dull practice, the *Dark Grave of Love*.

SAMUEL RICHARDSON (1689–1761)

From *Pamela* (1740–41) and *Sir Charles Grandison* (1753–54)

The novelist Samuel Richardson, author of *Clarissa*, the eighteenth century's supreme fictional masterpiece, was born in London and apprenticed in youth to a printer. An astute businessman, he subsequently set up his own printing business in Fleet Street and became official printer to the House of Commons. In 1740, after publishing a "little volume of letters, in a common style, on such subjects as might be of use to country readers who are unable to indite for themselves," he was inspired to write an epistolary fiction. The result was *Pamela: or, Virtue Rewarded*, which immediately became a bestseller and spawned numerous imitations and parodies. *Clarissa* followed in 1747–48 and established him— along with Henry Fielding—as the preeminent British novelist of the day. His third and final novel, *Sir Charles Grandison* (1753–54), though inferior to *Clarissa*, was also widely praised. He married twice and had eleven children, none of whom survived infancy. He was also noted for his "flower-garden of ladies," a circle of intimate (platonic) female friends from whom he sought advice about his literary compositions. The bluestocking writers Hester Mulso Chapone and Mary Delany were a part of this dainty yet enthusiastic coterie.

Richardson was clearly fascinated by intense, erotically tinged relationships between women. He sometimes portrayed such relationships satirically—though not inevitably. In *Clarissa* his delineation of the passionate intimacy between the doomed heroine, Clarissa, and her friend Anna Howe became the model for a host of later idealizing depictions of female romantic friendship. Grieving over Clarissa's coffin after Clarissa has been raped and destroyed by the seducer Lovelace, Anna affirms that she and her friend will "meet and rejoice together where no villainous *Lovelaces*, no hardhearted *relations*, will ever shock our innocence, or ruffle our felicity." Richardson's fictional description of female romantic friendship proved extraordinarily influential: similarly fervent bonds link female characters in Rousseau's *La Nouvelle Héloïse* (1761), Sarah Scott's *A Description of Millenium Hall* (1762), Mary Wollstonecraft's *Mary: A Fiction* (1788), and Eliza Fenwick's *Secresy* (1795).

Even as he extolled female platonic friendship, however, Richardson anathematized openly sexualized relations between women. Aggressively "man-like" females, in particular, seem to have both fascinated and repelled him. In the first excerpt below, from *Pamela*, the heroine—a virtuous servant girl—describes in a letter written to her parents being unpleasantly fondled by a repulsive "she-male" named Mrs. Jewkes. Jewkes, it turns out, is in league with Pamela's "naughty" master, Mr. B., who hopes to seduce his beautiful housemaid. Jewkes is ultimately harmless—the hints of sexual inversion in her character remain undeveloped—but Pamela's description of her is lurid enough. With her "hoarse, man-like voice" and sinister-comical manner, Mrs. Jewkes foreshadows a favorite stock character in later eighteenth-century libertine writing: the sexually ambiguous older woman who preys indecently on young girls. Less benign versions of the type appear in novels by Richardson's French admirers— Diderot, Laclos, and the Marquis de Sade.

A younger "she-male" character appears in *Sir Charles Grandison*. In one of the novel's opening scenes, the heroine, Harriet Byron, is making her debut in fashionable London society. (She describes the process in a series of humorous letters to a friend.) Conspicuous among her new acquaintances is the odd Miss Barnevelt—a kind of brazen, boisterous throwback to the Renaissance "roaring girl." When a handsome young baronet, Sir Hargrave Pollexfen, subsequently joins the party, Miss Barnevelt at once begins to compete with him—"unnaturally"—for Harriet's bemused attentions. The tone remains light—*Grandison* much influenced Jane Austen—but the Barnevelt portrait is nonetheless disturbing: too close to grotesquerie to be entirely comfortable.

FURTHER READING: Samuel Richardson, *Pamela: or, Virtue Rewarded* (Harmondsworth, Middlesex: Penguin, 1980); —, *Clarissa: or The History of a Young Lady* (Harmondsworth, Middlesex: Penguin, 1985); *The History of Sir Charles Grandison* (Oxford and New York: Oxford University Press, 1986); T. C. Duncan Eaves and Ben D. Kimpel, *Samuel Richardson: A Biography* (London: Oxford University Press, 1971); Tassie Gwilliam, *Samuel Richardson's Fictions of Gender* (Stanford: Stanford University Press, 1993); George E. Haggerty, *Unnatural Affections: Women and Fiction in the Later Eighteenth Century* (Bloomington: Indiana University Press, 1998).

From *Pamela* (1740–41)

And this I found, when I desired, as soon as I came in, to speak with the mistress of the house. She came to me; and I said, I am a poor unhappy young body, that want your advice and assistance; and you seem to be a good sort of a gentlewoman, that would assist an oppressed innocent person. Yes, madam, said she, I hope you guess right; and I have the happiness to know something of the matter before you speak. Pray call my sister Jewkes.—Jewkes! Jewkes! thought I; I have heard of that name; I don't like it.

Then the wicked creature appeared, whom I had never seen but once before, and I was terrified out of my wits. No stratagem, thought I, not *one!* for a poor innocent girl; but everything to turn out against me; that is hard indeed!

So I began to pull in my horns, as they say, for I saw I was now worse off than at the farmer's.

The naughty woman came up to me with an air of confidence, and kissed me: See, sister, said she, here's a charming creature! Would she not tempt the best lord in the land to run away with her? Oh frightful thought I; here's an avowal of the matter at once: I am now gone, that's certain. And so was quite silent and confounded; and seeing no help for it (for she would not part with me out of her sight), I was forced to set out with her in the chariot; for she came thither on horseback with a man-servant, who rode by us the rest of the way, leading her horse: and now I gave over all thoughts of redemption, and was in a desponding condition indeed.

Well, thought I, here are strange pains taken to ruin a poor innocent, helpless, and even *worthless* young body. This plot is laid too deep, and has been too long hatching, to be baffled, I fear. But then I put my trust in God, who I knew was able to do everything for me, when all other possible means should fail: and in Him I was resolved to confide.

You may see—(Yet, oh! that kills me; for I know not whether *ever* you can see what I now write or no—Else you will see)—what sort of woman that Mrs. Jewkes is, compared to good Mrs. Jervis, by this:—

Every now and then she would be staring in my face, in the chariot, and squeezing my hand, and saying, Why, you are very pretty, my silent dear! And once she offered to kiss me. But I said, I don't like this sort of carriage, Mrs. Jewkes; it is not like two persons of one sex. She fell a laughing very confidently, and said, That's prettily said, I vow! Then thou hadst rather be kissed by the other sex? 'I fackins, I commend thee for that!

I was sadly teased with her impertinence and bold way; but no wonder; she was an innkeeper's housekeeper, before she came to my master; and those sort of creatures don't want confidence, you know: and indeed she made nothing to talk boldly on twenty occasions; and said two or three times, when she saw the tears every now and then, as we rid, trickle down my cheeks, I was sorely hurt, truly, to have the handsomest and finest young gentleman in five countries in love with me!

So I find I am got into the hands of a wicked procuress; and if I was not safe with good Mrs. Jervis, and where everybody loved me, what a dreadful prospect have I now before me, in the hands of a woman that seems to delight in filthiness!

Oh, dear sirs! what shall I do! What shall I do!—Surely, I shall never be equal to all these things! [. . .]

Now I will give you a picture of this wretch: She is a broad, squat, pursy, *fat thing*, quite ugly, if anything human can be so called; about forty years old. She has a huge hand, and an arm as thick as my waist, I believe. Her nose is fat and crooked, and her brows grow down over her eyes; a dead spiteful, grey, goggling eye, to be sure she has. And her face is flat and broad; and as to colour, looks like as if it had been pickled a month in saltpetre: I daresay she drinks:—She has a hoarse, man-like voice, and is as thick as she is long; and yet looks so deadly strong, that I am afraid she would dash me at her foot in an instant, if I was to vex her.—So that with a heart more ugly than her face, she frightens me sadly; and I am undone to be sure, if God does not protect me; for she is very wicked—indeed she is.

From *Sir Charles Grandison* (1753–54)

FRIDAY NIGHT

Some amusement, my Lucy, the day has afforded: Indeed more than I could have wished. A large pacquet, however, for Selby-House.

Lady Betty received us most politely. She had company with her, to whom she introduced us, and presented me in a very advantageous character.

Shall I tell you how their first appearance struck me, and what I have since heard and observed of them?

The first I shall mention was Miss Cantillon; very pretty; but visibly proud, affected, and conceited.

The second Miss Clements; plain; but of a fine understanding, improved by reading; and who having no personal advantages to be vain of, has, by the cultivation of her mind, obtained a preference in every one's opinion over the fair Cantillon.

The third was Miss Barnevelt, a lady of masculine features, and whose mind bely'd not those features; for she has the character of being loud, bold, free, even fierce when opposed; and affects at all times such airs of contempt of her own sex, that one almost wonders at her condescending to wear petticoats.

The gentlemen's names were Walden and Singleton; the first, an Oxford scholar of family and fortune; but quaint and opinionated, despising every one who has not had the benefit of an University education.

Mr. Singleton is an harmless man; who is, it seems, the object of more ridicule, even down to his very name, among all his acquaintance, than I think he by any means ought, considering the apparent inoffensiveness of the man, who did not give *himself* his intellects; and his constant good humour, which might intitle him to better quarter; the rather too as he has one point of knowledge, which those who think themselves his superiors in understanding, do not always attain, the knowledge of himself; for he is humble, modest, ready to confess an inferiority to every one: And as laughing at a jest is by some taken for high applause, he is ever the first to bestow that commendation on what others say; tho' it must be owned, he now-and-then mistakes for a jest what is none: Which, however, may be generally more the fault of the speakers than of Mr.

Singleton; since he takes his cue from their smiles, especially when those are seconded by the laugh of one of whom he has a good opinion.

Mr. Singleton is in possession of a good estate, which makes amends for many defects: He has a turn, it is said, to the well-managing of it; and nobody understands his own interest better than he; by which knowledge, he has opportunities to lay obligations upon many of those, who behind his back think themselves intitled by their supposed superior sense to deride him: And he is ready enough to oblige in this way: But it is always on such securities, that he has never given cause for spendthrifts to laugh at him on that account.

It is thought that the friends of the fair Cantillon would not be averse to an alliance with this gentleman: While I, were I *his* Sister, should rather wish, that he had so much wisdom in his weakness, as to devote himself to the worthier Pulcheria Clements (Lady Betty's wish as well as mine) whose fortune, tho' not despicable, and whose humbler views, would make her think herself repaid the obligation she would lay him under by her accceptance of him.

No-body, it seems, thinks of an *husband* for Miss Barnevelt. She is sneeringly spoken of rather as a *young fellow*, than as a woman; and who will one day look out for a *wife* for herself. One reason indeed, she every-where gives, for being satisfied with being a woman; which is, *that she cannot be married to a WOMAN.*

An odd creature, my dear. But see what women get by going out of character. Like the Bats in the fable, they are look'd upon as mortals of a doubtful species, hardly owned by either, and laugh'd at by both.

This was the company, and all the company besides us, that Lady Betty expected. But mutual civilities had hardly passed, when Lady Betty, having been called out, return'd, introducing, as a gentleman, who would be acceptable to every one, Sir Hargrave Pollexfen. He is, whisper'd she to me, as he saluted the rest of the company, in a very gallant manner, a young Baronet of a very large estate, the greatest part of which has lately come to him by the death of a Grandmother, and two Uncles, all very rich.

When he was presented to me, by name, and I to him, this was his speech: And are at last my eyes bless'd with the sight of a young Lady so celebrated for her graces of person and mind? Much did I hear, when I was at the last Northampton races, of Miss Byron: But little did I expect to find report fall so short of what I see.

Miss Cantillon bridled, play'd with her fan, and look'd as if she thought herself slighted; a little scorn intermingled with the airs she gave herself.

Miss Clements smiled, and look'd pleased, as if she enjoyed, good-naturedly, a compliment made to one of the sex which she adorns by the goodness of her heart.

Miss Barnevelt said, she had from the moment I first enter'd beheld me with the eye of a Lover. And freely taking my hand, squeezed it.—Charming creature! said she, as if addressing a country innocent, and perhaps expecting me to be cover'd with blushes and confusion.

HENRY FIELDING (1707–1754)

The Female Husband (1746)

The great eighteenth-century English novelist Henry Fielding, born in Somerset and educated at Eton, began his literary career as a playwright in London in the 1720s. He achieved considerable public renown for his comic plays and farces, the best-known of which today are perhaps *The Tragedy of Tragedies: or Tom Thumb* (1730), *Pasquin* (1736), and *The Historical Register* (1737), a satiric attack on the Prime Minister, Robert Walpole. After Walpole placed censorship restrictions on the English stage, Fielding was forced to abandon playwriting and turned to the practice of law. In 1741, the success of Samuel Richardson's sentimental novel *Pamela* (1740–41) prompted Fielding to write a parody—*Shamela*—the first of a series of brilliant comic fictions. Over the next decade, while continuing to serve as a lawyer and magistrate, he produced the novels *Joseph Andrews* (1742), *Jonathan Wild* (1743), *Tom Jones* (1749), and *Amelia* (1751). In 1752 he began a critical paper, *The Covent-Garden Journal*, but had to abandon it when his health suddenly deteriorated. Suffering from tuberculosis—and perhaps syphilis— he sailed to Portugal in the hopes of recovering his strength but died in Lisbon in 1754. His *Journal of a Voyage to Lisbon* was issued posthumously.

Fielding published the potboiling pamphlet known as *The Female Husband* anonymously in 1746. It is based on the case of Mary Hamilton, a real-life cross-dresser whose trial in Bath for vagrancy earlier that same year was overseen by one of Fielding's lawyer cousins. Hamilton was born in Somerset and lived afterward in Scotland. At fourteen she left home disguised as a man and traveled the country as a quack doctor. In May 1746 she returned to Somerset and took up lodgings at Wells under the name of "Dr. Charles Hamilton." There she married Mary Price, the niece of her landlady, but after three months of marriage—which apparently included sexual relations—Mary Price realized the fraud and had Hamilton arrested. The law being at a loss to find a precedent for her "uncommon notorious cheat," Hamilton was convicted on a clause in the vagrancy act. She was sentenced to public whippings in four Somerset towns and six months in Bridewell. After her sentencing, she disappears from the historical record.

Fielding, who never met Hamilton, filled out the basic facts of her story with his own mock-heroic inventions and satiric embellishments. (Hamilton's birthplace is changed, for example, from Somerset to the "Isle of Man.") The resulting piece—a kind of lesbian "rogue's biography"—is both amusing and somewhat confusing. The heavy-handed moralizing at the beginning and end, intended no doubt to make the work more acceptable to the censorious, sits oddly with the otherwise facetious treatment of Hamilton's lesbianism *en travesti*. Fielding's ambivalence may have had a personal source: the fictional Hamilton, who comes off as rather more charming than dangerous, may be based on one of Fielding's friends, the mercurial transvestite comic actress Charlotte Charke, with whom he worked at the Haymarket Theatre in London in the 1730s.

FURTHER READING: Henry Fielding, *The Female Husband and Other Writings*, ed. Claude E. Jones (Liverpool: Liverpool University Press, 1960); Sheridan Baker, "Henry Fielding's *The Female Husband*: Fact and Fiction," *PMLA* 74 (1959):213–24; Terry Castle, "Matters Not Fit to Be Mentioned": Fielding's *The Female Husband*," *ELH: Journal of English Literary History* 49 (1982):602–22, rpt. in *The Female Thermometer: Eighteenth-Century Culture and the Invention of the Uncanny* (New York and Oxford: Oxford University Press, 1995); Rudolf M. Dekker and Lotte C. Van de Pol, *The Tradition of Female Transvestism in Early Modern Europe* (New York: St. Martin's, 1989); Emma Donoghue, *Passions Between Women: British Lesbian Culture, 1668–1801* (London: Scarlet, 1993), Jill Campbell, *Natural Masques: Gender and Identity in Fielding's Plays and Novels* (Stanford: Stanford University Press, 1995).

That propense inclination which is for very wise purposes implanted in the one sex for the other, is not only necessary for the continuance of the human species; but is, at the same time, when govern'd and directed by virtue and religion, productive not only of corporeal delight, but of the most rational felicity.

But if once our carnal appetites are let loose, without those prudent and secure guides, there is no excess and disorder which they are not liable to commit, even while they pursue their natural satisfaction; and, which may seem still more strange, there is nothing monstrous and unnatural, which they are not capable of inventing, nothing so brutal and shocking which they have not actually committed.

Of these unnatural lusts, all ages and countries have afforded us too many instances; but none I think more surprising than what will be found in the history of Mrs. *Mary*, otherwise Mr. *George Hamilton*.

This heroine in iniquity was born in the Isle of *Man*, on the 16th Day of *August*, 1721. Her father was formerly a serjeant of grenadiers in the Foot-Guards, who having the good fortune to marry a widow of some estate in that island, purchased his discharge from the army, and retired thither with his wife.

He had not been long arrived there before he died, and left his wife with child of this *Mary*; but her mother, tho' she had not two months to reckon, could not stay till she was delivered, before she took a third husband.

As her mother, tho' she had three husbands, never had any other child, she always express'd an extraordinary affection for this daughter, to whom she gave as good an education as the island afforded; and tho' she used her with much tenderness, yet was the girl brought up in the strictest principles of virtue and religion; nor did she in her younger years discover the least proneness to any kind of vice, much less give cause of suspicion that she would one day disgrace her sex by the most abominable and unnatural pollutions. And indeed she hath often declared from her conscience, that no irregular passion ever had any place in her mind, till she was first seduced by one *Anne Johnson*, a neighbour of hers, with whom she had been acquainted from her childhood; but not with such intimacy as afterwards grew between them.

This *Anne Johnson* going on some business to *Bristol*, which detained her there near half a year, became acquainted with some of the people called *Methodists*, and was by them persuaded to embrace their sect.

At her return to the Isle of *Man*, she soon made an easy convert of *Molly Hamilton*, the warmth of whose disposition rendered her susceptible enough of Enthusiasm, and ready to receive all those impressions which her friend the *Methodist* endeavoured to make on her mind.

These two young women became now inseparable companions, and at length bedfellows: For *Molly Hamilton* was prevail'd on to leave her mother's house, and to reside entirely with Mrs. *Johnson*, whose fortune was not thought inconsiderable in that cheap country.

Young Mrs. *Hamilton* began to conceive a very great affection for her friend, which perhaps was not returned with equal faith by the other. However, Mrs. *Hamilton* declares her love, or rather friendship, was totally innocent, till the temptations of *Johnson* first led her astray. This latter was, it seems, no novice in impurity, which, as she confess'd, she had learnt and often practiced at *Bristol* with her methodistical sisters.

As *Molly Hamilton* was extremely warm in her inclinations, and as those inclinations were so violently attached to Mrs. *Johnson*, it would not have been difficult for a less artful woman, in the most private hours, to turn the ardour of enthusiastic devotion into a different kind of flame.

Their conversation, therefore, soon became in the highest manner criminal, and transactions not fit to be mention'd passed between them.

They had not long carried on this wicked crime before Mrs. *Johnson* was again called by her affairs to visit *Bristol*, and her friend was prevail'd on to accompany her thither.

Here when they arrived, they took up their lodgings together, and lived in the same detestable manner as before; till an end was put to their vile amours, by the means of one *Rogers*, a young fellow, who by his extraordinary devotion (for he was a very zealous

Methodist) or by some other charms, (for he was very jolly and handsome) gained the heart of Mrs. *Johnson*, and married her.

This amour, which was not of any long continuance before it was brought to a conclusion, was kept an entire secret from Mrs. *Hamilton*; but she was no sooner informed of it, than she became almost frantic, she tore her hair, beat her breasts, and behaved in as outrageous a manner as the fondest husband could who had unexpectedly discovered the infidelity of a beloved wife.

In the midst of these agonies she received a letter from Mrs. *Johnson*, in the following words, or as near them as she can possibly remember.

Dear Molly,

I know you will condemn what I have now done; but I condemn myself much more for what I have done formerly: For I take the whole shame and guilt of what hath passed between us on myself. I was indeed the first seducer of your innocence, for which I ask GOD's pardon and yours. All the amends I can make you, is earnestly to beseech you, in the name of the Lord, to forsake all such evil courses, and to follow my example now, as you before did my temptation, and enter as soon as you can into that holy state into which I was yesterday called. In which, tho' I am yet but a novice, believe me, there are delights infinitely surpassing the faint endearments we have experienc'd together. I shall always pray for you, and continue your friend.

This letter rather increased than abated her rage, and she resolved to go immediately and upbraid her false friend; but while she was taking this resolution, she was informed that Mr. *Rogers* and his bride were departed from *Bristol* by a messenger, who brought her a second short note, and a bill for some money from Mrs. *Rogers*.

As soon as the first violence of her passion subsided, she began to consult what course to take, when the strangest thought imaginable suggested itself to her fancy. This was to dress herself in men's cloaths, to embarque for *Ireland*, and commence Methodist teacher.

Nothing remarkable happened to her during the rest of her stay at *Bristol*, which adverse winds occasioned to be a whole week, after she had provided herself with her dress; but at last having procured a passage, and the wind becoming favourable, she set sail for *Dublin*.

As she was a very pretty woman, she now appeared a most beautiful youth. A circumstance which had its consequences aboard the ship, and had like to have discovered her, in the very beginning of her adventures.

There happened to be in the same vessel with this adventurer, a Methodist, who was bound to the same place, on the same design with herself.

These two being alone in the cabin together, and both at their devotions, the man in the extasy of his enthusiasm, thrust one of his hands into the other's bosom. Upon which, in her surprize, she gave so effeminate a squawl, that it reached the Captain's ears, as he was smoaking his pipe upon deck. Hey day, says he, what have we a woman in the ship! and immediately descended into the cabbin, where he found the two Methodists on their knees.

Pox on't, says the Captain, I thought you had had a woman with you here; I could have sworn I had heard one cry out as if she had been ravishing, and yet the Devil must have been in you, if you could convey her in here without my knowledge.

I defy the Devil and all his works, answered the He Methodist. He has no power but over the wicked; and if he be in the ship, thy oaths must have brought him hither: for I have heard thee pronounce more than twenty since I came on board; and we should have been at the bottom before this, had not my prayers prevented it.

Don't abuse my vessel, cried the Captain, she is as safe a vessel, and as good a sailer as ever floated, and if you had been afraid of going to the bottom, you might have stay'd on shore and been damn'd.

The Methodist made no answer, but fell a groaning, and that so loud, that the Captain giving him a hearty curse or two, quitted the cabbin, and resumed his pipe.

He was no sooner gone, than the Methodist gave farther tokens of brotherly love to his companion, which soon became so importunate and troublesome to her, that after having gently rejected his hands several times, she at last recollected the sex she had assumed, and gave him so violent a blow in the nostrils, that the blood issued from them with great impetuosity.

Whether fighting be opposite to the tenets of this sect (for I have not the honour to be deeply read in their doctrines) or from what other motive it proceeded, I will not determine; but the Methodist made no other return to this rough treatment, than by many groans, and prayed heartily to be delivered soon from the conversation of the wicked; which prayers were at length so successful, that, together with a very brisk gale, they brought the vessel into *Dublin* harbour.

Here our adventurer took a lodging in a back-street near *St. Stephen's Green*, at which place she intended to preach the next day; but had got a cold in the voyage, which occasioned such a hoarseness that made it impossible to put that design in practice.

There lodged in the same house with her, a brisk widow of near 40 Years of age, who had buried two husbands, and seemed by her behaviour to be far from having determined against a third expedition to the land of matrimony.

To this widow our adventurer began presently to make addresses, and as he at present wanted tongue to express the ardency of his flame, he was obliged to make use of actions of endearment, such as squeezing, kissing, toying, etc.

These were received in such a manner by the fair widow, that her lover thought he had sufficient encouragement to proceed to a formal declaration of his passion. And this she chose to do by letter, as her voice still continued too hoarse for uttering the soft accents of love.

A letter therefore was penned accordingly in the usual stile, which, to prevent any miscarriages, Mrs. *Hamilton* thought proper to deliver with her own hands; and immediately retired to give the adored lady an opportunity of digesting the contents alone, little doubting of an answer agreeable to her wishes, or at least such a one as the coyness of the sex generally dictates in the beginning of an amour, and which lovers, by long experience, know pretty well how to interpret.

But what was the gallant's surprize, when in return to an amorous epistle, she read the following sarcasms, which it was impossible for the most sanguine temper to misunderstand, or construe favourably.

Sir,

I was greatly astonished at what you put into my hands. Indeed I thought, when I took it, it might have been an Opera song, and which for certain reasons I should think, when your cold is gone, you might sing as well as *Farinelli*, from the great resemblance there is between your persons. I know not what you mean by encouragement to your hopes; if I could have conceived my innocent freedoms could have been so misrepresented, I should have been more upon my guard: but you have taught me how to watch my actions for the future, and to preserve myself even from any suspicion of forfeiting the regard I owe to the memory of the best of men, by any future choice. The remembrance of that dear person makes me incapable of proceeding farther.

And so firm was this resolution, that she would never afterwards admit of the least familiarity with the despairing Mrs. *Hamilton*; but perhaps that destiny which is remarked to interpose in all matrimonial things, had taken the widow into her protection: for in a few days afterwards, she was married to one *Jack Strong*, a cadet in an *Irish* regiment.

Our adventurer being thus disappointed in her love, and what is worse, her money drawing towards an end, began to have some thoughts of returning home, when fortune seemed inclined to maker her amends for the tricks she had hitherto played her, and accordingly now threw another Mistress in her way, whose fortune was much superior to the former widow, and who received Mrs. *Hamilton*'s addresses with all the complaisance she could wish.

This Lady, whose name was *Rushford*, was the widow of a rich cheesemonger, who left her all he had, and only one great grand-child to take care of, whom, at her death, he recommended to be her Heir; but wholly at her own power and discretion.

She was now in the sixty eighth year of her age, and had not, it seems, entirely abandoned all thoughts of the pleasures of this world: for she was no sooner acquainted with Mrs. *Hamilton*, but, taking her for a beautiful lad of about eighteen, she cast the eyes of affection on her, and having pretty well outlived the bashfulness of her youth, made little scruple of giving hints of her passion of her own accord.

It has been observed that women know more of one another than the wisest men (if ever such have been employed in the study) have with all their art been capable of discovering. It is therefore no wonder that these hints were quickly perceived and understood by the female gallant, who animadverting on the conveniency which the old gentlewoman's fortune would produce in her present situation, very gladly embraced the opportunity, and advancing with great warmth of love to the attack, in which she was received almost with open arms, by the tottering citadel, which presently offered to throw open the gates, and surrender at discretion.

In her amour with the former widow, Mrs. *Hamilton* had never had any other design than of gaining the lady's affection, and then discovering herself to her, hoping to have had the same success which Mrs. *Johnson* had found with her: but with this old lady, whose fortune only she was desirous to possess, such views would have afforded very little gratification. After some reflection, therefore, a device entered into her head, as strange and surprizing, as it was wicked and vile; and this was actually to marry the old woman, and to deceive her, by means which decency forbids me even to mention.

The wedding was accordingly celebrated in the most public manner, and with all kind of gaiety, the old woman greatly triumphing in her shame, and instead of hiding her own head for fear of infamy, was actually proud of the beauty of her new husband, for whose sake she intended to disinherit her poor great-grandson, tho' she had derived her riches from her husband's family, who had always intended this boy as his heir. Nay, what may seem very remarkable, she insisted on the parson's not omitting the prayer in the matrimonial service for fruitfulness; drest herself as airy as a girl of eighteen, concealed twenty years of her age, and laughed and promoted all the jokes which are usual at weddings; but she was not so well pleased with a repartee of her great-grandson, a pretty and a smart lad, who, when somebody jested on the bridegroom because he had no beard, answered smartly: There should never be a beard on both-sides: For indeed the old lady's chin was pretty well stocked with bristles.

Nor was this bride contented with displaying her shame by a public wedding dinner, she would have the whole ceremony compleated, and the stocking was accordingly thrown with the usual sport and merriment.

During the three first days of the marriage, the bride expressed herself so well satisfied with her choice, that being in company with another old lady, she exulted so much in her happiness, that her friend began to envy her, and could not forbear inveighing against effeminacy in men; upon which a discourse arose between the two ladies, not proper to be repeated, if I knew every particular; but ended at the last, in the unmarried lady's declaring to the bride, that she thought her husband looked more like a woman than a man. To which the other replied in triumph, he was the best man in *Ireland*.

This and the rest which past, was faithfully recounted to Mrs. *Hamilton* by her wife, at their next meeting, and occasioned our young bridegroom to blush, which the old lady perceiving and regarding as an effect of youth, fell upon her in a rage of love like a tygress, and almost murdered her with kisses.

One of our English Poets remarks in the case of a more able husband than Mrs. *Hamilton* was, when his wife grew amorous in an unseasonable time.

> *The doctor understood the call,*
> *But had not always wherewithal.*

So it happened to our poor bridegroom, who having not at that time *the wherewithal* about her, was obliged to remain meerly passive, under all this torrent of kindness of his wife, but this did not discourage her, who was an experienced woman, and thought she had a cure for this coldness in her husband, the efficacy of which, she might perhaps have essayed formerly. Saying therefore with a tender smile to her husband, I believe you are a woman, her hands began to move in such direction, that the discovery would absolutely have been made, had not the arrival of dinner, at that very instant, prevented it.

However, as there is but one way of laying the spirit of curiosity, when once raised in a woman, *viz.* by satisfying it, so that discovery, though delayed, could not now be long prevented. And accordingly the very next night, the husband and wife had not been long in bed together, before a storm arose, as if drums, guns, wind and thunder were all roaring together. Villain, rogue, whore, beast, cheat, all resounded at the same instant, and were followed by curses, imprecations and threats, which soon waked the poor great-grandson in the garret; who immediately ran down stairs into his great-grandmother's room. He found her in the midst of it in her shift, with a handful of shirt in one hand, and handful of hair in the other, stamping and crying, I am undone, cheated, abused, ruined, robbed by a vile jade, impostor, whore. . . . What is the matter, dear Madam, answered the youth; O child, replied she, undone! I am married to one who is no man. My husband? a woman, a woman, a woman. Ay, said the grandson, where is she? . . . Run away, gone, said the great-grandmother, and indeed so she was: For no sooner was the fatal discovery made than the poor female bridegroom, whipt on her breeches, in the pockets of which, she had stowed all the money she could, and slipping on her shoes, with her coat, waist-coat and stockings in her hands, had made the best of her way into the street, leaving almost one half of her shirt behind, which the enraged wife had tore from her back.

As Mrs. *Hamilton* well knew that an adventure of that kind would soon fill all *Dublin*, and that it was impossible for her to remain there undiscovered, she hastened away to the Key, where by good fortune, she met with a ship just bound to *Dartmouth*, on board of which she immediately went, and sailed out of the harbour, before her pursuers could find out or overtake her.

She was a full fortnight in her passage, during which time, no adventure occurred worthy remembrance. At length she landed at *Dartmouth*, where she soon provided herself with linnen, and thence went to Totness, where she assumed the title of a doctor of physic, and took lodgings in the house of one Mrs. *Baytree*.

Here she soon became acquainted with a young girl, the daughter of one Mr. *Ivythorn*, who had the green sickness; a distemper which the doctor gave out he could cure by an infallible *nostrum*.

The doctor had not been long intrusted with the care of this young patient before he began to make love to her: for though her complexion was somewhat faded with her distemper, she was otherwise extremely pretty.

This Girl became an easy conquest to the doctor, and the day of their marriage was appointed, without the knowledge, or even suspicion of her father, or of an old aunt who was very fond of her, and would neither of them have easily given their consent to the match, had the doctor been as good a Man as the niece thought him.

At the day appointed, the doctor and his mistress found means to escape very early in the morning from *Totness*, and went to a town called *Ashburton* in *Devonshire*, where they were married by a regular Licence which the doctor had previously obtained.

Here they staid two days at a public house, during which time the Doctor so well acted his part, that his bride had not the least suspicion of the legality of her marriage, or that she had not got a husband for life. The third day they returned to *Totness*, where they both threw themselves at Mr. *Ivythorn*'s feet, who was highly rejoic'd at finding his daughter restor'd to him, and that she was not debauched, as he had suspected of her. And being a very worthy good-natur'd man, and regarding the true interest and happiness of his daughter more than the satisfying his own pride, ambition or obstinacy, he was prevailed on to forgive her, and to receive her and her husband into his house, as his children, notwithstanding the opposition of the old aunt, who declared she would never forgive the wanton slut, and immediately quitted the house, as soon as the young couple were admitted into it.

The Doctor and his wife lived together above a fortnight, without the least doubt conceived either by the wife, or by any other person of the Doctor's being what he appeared; till one evening the Doctor having drank a little too much punch, slept somewhat longer than usual, and when he waked, he found his wife in tears, who asked her husband, amidst many sobs, how he could be so barbarous to have taken such advantage of her ignorance and innocence, and to ruin her in such a manner? The Doctor being surprized and scarce awake, asked her what he had done. Done, says she, have you not married me a poor young girl, when you know, you have not . . . you have not . . . what you ought to have. I always thought indeed your shape was something odd, and have often wondered that you had not the least bit of beard; but I thought you had been a man for all that, or I am sure I would not have been so wicked to marry you for the world. The Doctor endeavoured to pacify her, by every kind of promise, and telling her she would have all the pleasures of marriage without the inconveniences. No, no, said she, you shall not persuade me to that, nor will I be guilty of so much wickedness on any account. I will tell my Papa of you as soon as I am up; for you are no husband of mine, nor will I ever have any thing more to say to you. Which resolution the Doctor finding himself unable to alter, she put on her cloaths with all the haste she could, and taking a horse, which she had bought a few days before, hastened instantly out of the town, and made the best of her way, thro' bye-roads and across country, into *Somersetshire*, missing *Exeter*, and every other great town which lay in the road.

And well it was for her, that she used both this haste and precaution: For Mr. *Ivythorn* having heard his daughter's story, immediately obtained a warrant from a justice of peace, with which he presently dispatch'd the proper officers; and not only so, but set forward himself to *Exeter*, in order to try if he could learn any news of his son-in-law, or apprehend her there; till after much search being unable to hear any tidings of her, he was obliged to set down contented with his misfortune, as was his poor daughter to submit to all the ill-natured sneers of her own sex, who were often witty at her expence, and at the expence of their own decency.

The Doctor having escaped, arrived safe at *Wells* in *Somersetshire*, where thinking herself at a safe distance from her pursuers, she again sat herself down in quest of new adventures.

She had not been long in this city, before she became acquainted with one *Mary Price*, a girl of about eighteen years of age, and of extraordinary beauty. With this girl, hath this wicked woman since her confinement declared, she was really much in love, as it was possible for a man ever to be with one of her own sex.

The first opportunity our Doctor obtain'd of conversing closely with this new mistress, was at a dancing among the inferior sort of people, in contriving which the Doctor had herself the principal share. At that meeting the two lovers had an occasion of dancing all night together; and the Doctor lost no opportunity of shewing his fondness, as well by his tongue as by his hands, whispering many soft things in her ears, and squeezing as many soft things into her hands, which, together with a good number of kisses, &c. so pleased and warmed this poor girl, who never before had felt any of those tender sensations which we call love, that she retired from the dancing in a flutter of spirits, which her youth and ignorance could not well account for; but which did not suffer her to close her eyes, either that morning or the next night.

The Day after that the Doctor sent her the following letter.

My Dearest Molly,
Excuse the fondness of that expression; for I assure you, my angel, all I write to you proceeds only from my heart, which you have so entirely conquered, and made your own, that nothing else has any share in it; and, my angel, could you know what I feel when I am writing to you, nay even at every thought of my Molly, I know I should gain your pity if not your love; if I am so happy to have already succeeded in raising the former, do let me have once more an opportunity of seeing you, and that soon, that I may breathe forth my soul at those dear feet, where I would willingly die, if I am not suffer'd to lie there and live. My sweetest creature, give me leave to subscribe myself

Your fond, doating,
Undone SLAVE.

This letter added much to the disquietude which before began to torment poor Molly's breast. She read it over twenty times, and, at last, having carefully survey'd every part of the room, that no body was present, she kissed it eagerly. However, as she was perfectly modest, and afraid of appearing too forward, she resolved not to answer this first letter; and if she met the Doctor, to behave with great coldness towards him.

Her mother being ill, prevented her going out that day; and the next morning she received a second letter from the Doctor, in terms more warm and endearing than before, and which made so absolute a conquest over the unexperienc'd and tender heart of this poor girl, that she suffered herself to be prevailed on, by the intreaties of her lover, to write an answer, which nevertheless she determin'd should be so distant and cool, that the woman of the strictest virtue and modesty in *England* might have no reason to be asham'd of having writ it; of which letter the reader hath here an exact copy:

Sur,

I Haf recevd boath your too litters, and sur I ham much surprise hat the loafe you priten to have for so pur a garl as mee. I kan nut beleef you wul desgrace yourself by marring sutch a yf as mee, and Sur I wool nut be thee hore of the gratest man in the kuntry. For thof mi vartu his all I haf, yit hit is a potion I ham rissolv to kare to mi housband, soe noe moor at present, from your umble savant to cummand.

The Doctor received this letter with all the ecstasies any lover could be inspired with, and, as Mr. *Congreve* says in his *Old Batchelor*, Thought there was more eloquence in the false spellings, with which it abounded, than in all *Aristotle*. She now resolved to be no longer contented with this distant kind of conversation, but to meet her mistress face to face. Accordingly that very afternoon she went to her mother's house, and enquired for her poor *Molly*, who no sooner heard her lover's voice than she fell a trembling in the most violent manner. Her sister who opened the door informed the Doctor she was at home, and let the impostor in; but *Molly* being then in dishabille, would not see him till she had put on clean linnen, and was arrayed from head to foot in as neat, tho' not so fine a manner, as the highest court lady in the kingdom could attire herself in, to receive her embroider'd lover.

Very tender and delicate was the interview of this pair, and if any corner of *Molly*'s heart remain'd untaken, it was now totally subdued. She would willingly have postponed the match somewhat longer, from her strict regard to decency; but the earnestness and ardour of her lover would not suffer her, and she was at last obliged to consent to be married within two days.

Her sister, who was older than herself, and had over-heard all that had past, no sooner perceiv'd the Doctor gone, than she came to her, and wishing her joy with a sneer, said much good may it do her with such a husband; for that, for her own part, she would almost as willingly be married to one of her own sex, and made some remarks not so proper to be here inserted. This was resented by the other with much warmth. She said she had chosen for herself only, and that if she was pleased, it did not become people to trouble their heads with what was none of their business. She was indeed so extremely enamoured, that I question whether she would have exchanged the Doctor for the greatest and richest match in the world.

And had not her affections been fixed in this strong manner, it is possible that an accident which happened the very next night might have altered her mind; for being at another dancing with her lover, a quarrel arose between the Doctor and a man there present, upon which the other seizing the former violently by the collar, tore open her wastecoat, and rent her shirt, so that all her breast was discovered, which, tho' beyond expression beautiful in a woman, were of so different a kind from the bosom of a man, that the married women there set up a great titter; and tho' it did not bring the Doctor's sex into an absolute suspicion, yet caused some whispers, which might have spoiled the match with a less innocent and less enamoured virgin.

It had however no such effect on poor *Molly*. As her fond heart was free from any deceit, so was it entirely free from suspicion; and accordingly, at the fixed time she met the Doctor, and their nuptials were celebrated in the usual form.

The mother was extremely pleased at this preferment (as she thought it) of her daughter. The joy of it did indeed contribute to restore her perfectly to health, and nothing but mirth and happiness appeared in the faces of the whole family.

The new married couple not only continued, but greatly increased the fondness which they had conceived for each other, and poor *Molly*, from some stories she told among her acquaintances, the other young married women of the town, was received as a great fibber, and was at last universally laughed at as such among them all.

Three months past in this manner, when the Doctor was sent for to *Glastonbury* to a patient (for the fame of our adventurer's knowledge in physic began now to spread) when a person of *Totness* being accidentally present, happened to see and know her, and having heard upon enquiry, that the Doctor was married at *Wells*, as we have above mentioned, related the whole story of Mr. *Ivythorn*'s daughter, and the whole adventure at *Totness*.

News of this kind seldom wants wings; it reached *Wells*, and the ears of the Doctor's mother before her return from *Glastonbury*. Upon this the old woman immediately sent for her daughter, and very strictly examined her, telling her the great sin she would be guilty of, if she concealed a fact of this kind, and the great disgrace she would bring on her own family, and even on her whole sex, by living quietly and contentedly with a husband who was in any degree less a man than the rest of his neighbours.

Molly assured her mother of the falsehood of this report; and as it is usual for persons who are too eager in any cause, to prove too much, she asserted some things which staggered her mother's belief, and made her cry out, O child, there is no such thing in human nature.

Such was the progress this story had made in *Wells*, that before the Doctor arrived there, it was in every body's mouth; and as the Doctor rode through the streets, the mob, especially the women, all paid their compliments of congratulation. Some laughed at her, others threw dirt at her, and others made use of terms of reproach not fit to be commemorated. When she came to her own house, she found her wife in tears, and having asked her the cause, was informed of the dialogue which had past between her and her mother. Upon which the Doctor, tho' he knew not yet by what means the discovery had been made, yet too well knowing the truth, began to think of using the same method, which she had heard before put in practice, of delivering herself from any impertinence; for as to danger, she was not sufficiently versed in the laws to apprehend any.

In the mean time the mother, at the solicitation of some of her relations, who, notwithstanding the stout denial of the wife, had given credit to the story, had applied herself to a magistrate, before whom the *Totness* man appeared, and gave evidence as is before mentioned. Upon this a warrant was granted to apprehend the Doctor, with which the constable arrived at her house, just as she was meditating her escape.

The husband was no sooner seized, but the wife threw herself into the greatest agonies of rage and grief, vowing that he was injured, and that the information was false and malicious, and that she was resolved to attend her husband wherever they conveyed him.

And now they all proceeded before the Justice, where a strict examination being made into the affair, the whole happened to be true, to the great shock and astonishment of every body; but more especially of the poor wife, who fell into fits, out of which she was with great difficulty recovered.

The whole truth having been disclosed before the Justice, and something of too vile, wicked and scandalous a nature, which was found in the Doctor's trunk, having been produced in evidence against her, she was committed to *Bridewell*, and Mr. *Gold*, an eminent and learned counsellor at law, who lives in those parts, was consulted with upon the occasion, who gave his advice that she should be prosecuted at the next sessions, on a clause in the vagrant act, *for having by false and deceitful practices endeavoured to impose on some of his Majesty's subjects.*

As the Doctor was conveyed to *Bridewell*, she was attended by many insults from the mob; but what was more unjustifiable, was the cruel treatment which the poor innocent wife received from her own sex, upon the extraordinary accounts which she had formerly given of her husband.

Accordingly at the ensuing sessions of the peace for the county of *Somerset*, the Doctor was indicted for the abovementioned diabolical fact, and after a fair trial convicted, to the entire satisfaction of the whole court.

At the trial the said *Mary Price* the wife, was produced as a witness, and being asked by the council, whether she had ever any suspicion of the Doctor's sex during the whole time of the courtship, she answered positively in the negative. She was then asked how long they had been married, to which she answered three months; and whether they had cohabited the whole time together? to which her reply was in the affirmative. Then the council asked her, whether during the time of this cohabitation, she imagined the Doctor had behaved to her as a husband ought to his wife? Her modesty confounded her a little at this question; but she at last answered she did imagine so. Lastly, she was asked when it was that she first harboured any suspicion of her being imposed upon? To which she answered, she had not the least suspicion till her husband was carried before a magistrate, and there discovered, as hath been said above.

The prisoner having been convicted of this base and scandalous crime, was by the court sentenced to be publickly and severely whipt four several times, in four market towns within the county of *Somerset*, to wit, once in each market town, and to be imprisoned, &c.

These whippings she has accordingly undergone, and very severely have they been inflicted, insomuch, that those persons who have more regard to beauty than to justice, could not refrain from exerting some pity toward her, when they saw so lovely a skin scarified with rods, in such a manner that her back was almost flead; yet so little effect had the smart or shame of this punishment on the person who underwent it, that the very evening she had suffered the first whipping, she offered the gaoler money, to procure her a young girl to satisfy her most monstrous and unnatural desires.

But it is to be hoped that this example will be sufficient to deter all others from the commission of any such foul and unnatural crimes: for which, if they should escape the shame and ruin which they so well deserve in this world, they will be most certain of meeting with their full punishment in the next: for unnatural affections are equally vicious and equally detestable in both sexes, nay, if modesty be the peculiar characteristick of the fair sex, it is in them most shocking and odious to prostitute and debase it.

In order to caution therefore that lovely sex, which, while they preserve their natural innocence and purity, will still look most lovely in the eyes of men, the above pages have been written, which, that they might be worthy of their perusal, such strict regard hath been had to the utmost decency, that notwithstanding the subject of this narrative be of a nature so difficult to be handled inoffensively, not a single word occurs through the whole, which might shock the most delicate ear, or give offence to the purest chastity.

JOHN CLELAND (1709–1789)

From *Memoirs of a Woman of Pleasure* (1748–49)

John Cleland, the son of a Scottish army officer and an Englishwoman of Dutch-Jewish ancestry, was born in 1710 and educated at the Westminster School. At seventeen he joined the army and went to India, where he worked his way up from foot soldier to a position in the East India Company. After twelve years in India he returned to England, feuded with his mother over money, and was imprisoned for debt in 1748. Popular legend holds that Cleland composed his most famous work, the eminently lascivious *Memoirs of a Woman of Pleasure*—also known as *Fanny Hill*—during his year-long incarceration in the Fleet Prison. (It may, in fact, have been written earlier, around 1731.) Published in two volumes in 1748 and 1749, the book was an immediate success and much pirated in England and abroad. Cleland failed to benefit from its success, however, and for the rest of his life struggled to earn a living as a hack writer in London. He produced at least eighteen works over the next twenty years—novels, plays, critical essays, linguistic studies, and numerous translations, including *An Historical and Physical Dissertation on the Case of Catherine Vizzani* (1751), a potboiling account of an Italian male impersonator who "incessantly [followed] the Wenches" and was "barefaced and insatiable" in her lesbian amours. Cleland's last years were spent in jaded penury: Boswell (who enjoyed his company) described him in 1772 as "a fine sly malcontent." He never married, and after meeting him in 1782, Josiah Beckwith wrote that he "[passed] under the Censure of being a Sodomite . . . and in Consequence thereof Persons of Character decline visiting him, or cultivating his Acquaintance."

Memoirs of a Woman of Pleasure contains what is without question one of the most influential scenes of lesbian seduction in eighteenth-century fiction. Early in the novel, which takes the form of a first-person "tell-all" memoir, the virginal heroine, Fanny, living in a household of prostitutes and about to become one herself, is initiated into vice by her bedmate Phoebe, whose business is to "break in" young girls to the trade. While Cleland obviously relishes the opportunity to deliquesce on female-female lovemaking—the scene is salacious in the extreme—it turns out to be but a prelude to greater things: Fanny soon tires of Phoebe's ministrations and begins to long for something more "substantial" than this "foolery from woman to woman." In building in this explicit erototeleology—Fanny will go on to a glorious succession of mightily endowed male lovers—Cleland establishes one of the cherished conventions of pornographic lesbian representation: that female homosexuality is at best a sort of warm-up to heterosexual sex—a necessary but ultimately temporary phase in the apprenticeship of the female libertine.

FURTHER READING: John Cleland, *Memoirs of a Woman of Pleasure* (Oxford and New York: Oxford University Press, 1985); David Foxon, *Libertine Literature in England, 1660–1745* (London: Shenval, 1964); William H. Epstein, *John Cleland: Images of a Life* (New York: Columbia University Press, 1974); Nancy K. Miller, *The Heroine's Text: Readings in the French and English Novel, 1722–1792* (New York: Columbia University Press, 1980); Randolph Trumbach, "Modern Prostitution and Gender in *Fanny Hill*: Libertine and Domesticated Fantasy," in G. S. Rousseau and Roy Porter, eds., *Sexual Underworlds of the Enlightenment* (Chapel Hill: University of North Carolina Press, 1988), pp. 69–85; —, "Erotic Fantasy and Male Libertinism in Enlightenment England," in Lynn Hunt, ed., *The Invention of Pornography: Obscenity and the Origins of Modernity, 1500–1800* (New York: Zone, 1993), pp. 253–82; James Grantham Turner, "'Illustrious Depravity' and the Erotic Sublime," *The Age of Johnson: A Scholarly Annual 2* (1989): 1–38; Donald H. Mengay, "The Sodomitical Muse: *Fanny Hill* and the Rhetoric of Crossdressing," in Claude J. Summers, ed., *Homosexuality in Renaissance and Enlightenment England: Literary Representations in Historical Context* (New York: Harrington Park, 1992), pp. 185–98; Emma Donoghue, *Passions Between Women: British Lesbian Culture 1668–1801* (London: Scarlet, 1993); Felicity Nussbaum, *Torrid Zones: Maternity, Sexuality, and Empire in Eighteenth-Century English Narratives* (Baltimore: Johns Hopkins University Press, 1995); Lisa L. Moore, *Dangerous Intimacies: Toward a Sapphic History of the British Novel* (Durham, N.C. and London: Duke University Press, 1997); Peter Sabor, "From Sexual Liberation to Gender Trouble: Reading *Memoirs of a Woman of Pleasure* from the 1960s to the 1990s," *Eighteenth-Century Studies* 33 (Summer 2000): 561–78.

[*Fanny's "breaking in" by Phoebe*]

To slip over minutes of no importance to the main of my story, I pass the interval to bed-time, in which I was more and more pleased with the views that open'd to me of an easy service under these good people: and after supper, being shew'd up to bed, Miss *Phoebe*, who observed a kind of modest reluctance in me to strip, and go to bed in my shift before her, now the maid was withdrawn, came up to me, and beginning with unpinning my handkerchief, and gown, soon encouraged me to go on with undressing myself, and, still blushing at now seeing myself naked to my shift, I hurried to get under the bed-cloaths, out of sight. *Phoebe* laugh'd, and was not long before she placed herself by my side. She was about five and twenty, by her own most suspicious account, in which, according to all appearances, she must have sunk at least ten good years, allowance too being made for the havoc which a long course of hackney-ship, and hot waters, must have made of her constitution, and which had already brought on, upon the spur, that stale stage, in which those of her profession are reduced to think of *show-ing* company, instead of *seeing* it.

No sooner then was this precious substitute of my mistress's lain down, but she, who was never out of her way when any occasion of lewdness presented itself, turned to me, embraced, and kiss'd me with great eagerness. This was new, this was odd; but imputing it to nothing but pure kindness, which, for ought I knew, it might be the *London* way to express in that manner, I was determin'd not to be behind-hand with her, and returned her the kiss and embrace, with all the fervour that perfect innocence knew.

Encouraged by this, her hands became extremely free, and wander'd over my whole body, with touches, squeezes, pressures, that rather warm'd and surpriz'd me with their novelty, than they either shock'd or alarm'd me.

The flattering praises she intermingled with these invasions, contributed also not a little to bribe my passiveness, and knowing no ill, I fear'd none; especially from one who had prevented all doubt of her womanhood, by conducting my hands to a pair of breasts that hung loosely down, in a size and volume that full sufficiently distinguished her sex, to me at least, who had never made any other comparison.

I lay then all tame and passive as she could wish, whilst her freedom, raised no other emotion but those of a strange, and till then unfelt pleasure: every part of me was open, and exposed to the licentious courses of her hands, which like a lambent fire ran over my whole body, and thaw'd all coldness as they went.

My breasts, if it is not too bold a figure to call so, two hard, firm, rising hillocks, that just began to shew themselves, or signify any thing to the touch, employ'd and amused her hands a while, till slipping down lower, over a smooth track, she could just feel the soft silky down that had but a few months before put forth, and garnish'd the mount-pleasant of those parts, and promised to spread a grateful shelter over the sweet seat of the most exquisite sensation, and which had been, till that instant, the seat of the most insensible innocence. Her fingers play'd, and strove to twine in the young tendrils of that moss which nature has contrived at once for use and ornament.

But not contented with these outer-posts, she now attempts the main-spot, and began to twitch, to insinuate, and at length to force an introduction of a finger into the quick itself, in such a manner, that had she not proceeded by insensible gradations, that enflamed me beyond the power of modesty to oppose its resistance to their progress, I should have jump'd out of bed, and cried out for help against such strange assaults.

Instead of which, her lascivious touches had lighted up a new fire that wanton'd through all my veins, but fix'd with violence in that center appointed them by nature, where the first strange hands were now busied in feeling, squeezing, compressing the lips, then opening them again, with a finger between, till an Oh! express'd her hurting me, where the narrowness of the unbroken passage refused it entrance to any depth.

In the mean time the extension of my limbs, languid stretchings, sighs, short heavings, all conspired to assure that experienced wanton, that I was more pleased than offended at her proceedings, which she seasoned with repeated kisses and exclamations, such as "Oh! what a charming creature thou art!—what a happy man will he be that first makes a woman of you!—Oh! that I were a man for your sake—!" with the like broken expressions, interrupted by kisses as fierce and salacious as ever I received from the other sex.

For my part, I was transported, confused, and out of myself: Feelings so new were too much for me; my heated and alarm'd senses were in a tumult that robb'd me of all liberty of thought; tears of pleasure gush'd from my eyes, and somewhat assuaged the fire that rag'd all over me.

Phoebe herself, the hackney'd, thorough-bred *Phoebe*, to whom all modes and devices of pleasure were known and familiar, found, it seems, in this exercise of her art to break young girls, the gratification of one of those arbitrary tastes, for which there is no accounting: not that she hated men, or did not even prefer them to her own sex; but when she met with such occasions as this was, a satiety of enjoyments in the common road, perhaps too a secret byass, inclined her to make the most of pleasure, wherever she could find it, without distinction of sexes. In this view, now well assured that she had, by her touches, sufficiently inflamed me for her purpose, she roll'd down the bed-cloaths gently, and I saw myself stretch'd naked, my shift being turned up to my neck, whilst I had no power or sense to oppose it; even my glowing blushes expressed more desire than modesty, whilst the candle left, to be sure not undesignedly, burning, threw a full light on my whole body.

"No! (says *Phoebe*) you must not, my sweet girl, think to hide all these treasures from me, my sight must be feasted as well as my touch—I must devour with my eyes this springing *bosom*,—suffer me to kiss it—I have not seen it enough—let me kiss it once more—what firm, smooth, white flesh is here—how delicately shaped!—then this delicious down! Oh! let me view the small, dear, tender cleft!—this is too much, I cannot bear it, I must, I must—." Here she took my hand, and, in a transport, carried it where you will easily guess; but what a difference in the state of the same thing!—a spreading thicket of bushy curls mark'd the full-grown complete woman: then the cavity, to which she guided my hand, easily received it, and as soon as she felt it within her, she moved herself to and fro, with so rapid a friction, that I presently withdrew it, wet and clammy, when instantly *Phoebe* grew more composed, after two or three sighs, and heart-fetch'd Oh's! and giving me a kiss, that seemed to exhale her soul through her lips, she replaced the bed-cloaths over us.

What pleasure she had found I will not say; but this I know, that the first sparks of kindling nature, the first ideas of pollution, were caught by me that night, and that the acquaintance and communication with the bad of our own sex, is often as fatal to innocence, as all the seductions of the other: But to go on:—when *Phoebe* was restor'd to that calm, which I was far from the enjoyment of myself, she artfully sounded me on all the points necessary to govern the designs of my virtuous mistress on me, and by my answers, drawn from pure undissembled nature, she had no reason but to promise herself all imaginable success, so far as it depended on my ignorance, easiness, and warmth of constitution.

After a sufficient length of dialogue, my bed-fellow left me to my rest, and I fell asleep, through pure weariness, from the violent emotions I had been led into, when nature (which had been too warmly stir'd, and fermented to subside without allaying by some means or other) relieved me by one of those luscious dreams, the transports of which are scarce inferior to those of waking, real action.

[*After Fanny and Phoebe spy on the lovemaking of Polly, a prostitute in the house, and a young Italian man, Fanny is disgusted by Phoebe's renewed advances and renounces lesbian passion in the hope of "more solid food."*]

The young foreigner was sitting down, fronting us, on the couch; with *Polly* upon one knee, who had her arms round his neck, whilst the extreme whiteness of her skin was not undelightfully contrasted by the smooth glossy brown of her lover's.

But who could count the fierce, unnumber'd kisses given and taken? in which I could often discover their exchanging the velvet thrust, when both their mouths were double-tongu'd, and seem'd to favour the mutual insertion with the greatest gust and delight.

In the mean time, his red-headed champion that had so lately fled the pit, quell'd, and abash'd, was now recover'd to the top of its condition, perk'd and crested up between *Polly*'s thighs, who was not wanting on her part to coax and keep it in good humour, stroking it with her head down, and receiv'd even its velvet tip between the lips of not its proper mouth, whether she did this out of any particular pleasure, or whether it was to render it more glib, and easy of entrance, I could not tell; but it had such an effect, that the young gentleman seem'd by his eyes, that sparkled with more excited lustre, and his inflamed countenance, to receive encrease of pleasure. He got up, and taking *Polly* in his arms embraced her, and said something too softly for me to hear, leading her withal to the foot of the couch, and taking delight to slap her thighs, and posteriours with that stiff sinnew of his, which hit them, with a spring, that he gave it with his hand, and made them resound again, but hurt her about as much as he meant to hurt her, for she seem'd to have as frolick a taste as himself.

But, guess my surprise, when I saw the lazy young rogue lie down on his back, and gently pull down *Polly* upon him, who giving way to his humour, straddled, and with her hands conducted her blind favourite to the right place, and following her impulse, ran directly upon the flaming point of this weapon of pleasure, which she stak'd herself upon, up-pierc'd, and infix'd to the extremest hair-breadth of it: thus she sat on him, a few instants, enjoying, and relishing her situation, whilst he toyed with her provoking breasts.—Sometimes she would stoop to meet his kiss: but presently the sting of pleasure spurr'd them up to fiercer action: then began the storm of heaves, which, from the undermost combatant, were thrusts at the same time: he crossing his hands over her, and drawing her home to him with a sweet violence: the inverted strokes of anvil over hammer soon brought on the critical period, in which all the signs of a close conspiring extasy, informed us of the *point* they were at.

For me, I could bear to see no more: I was so overcome, so inflamed at this second part of the same play, that, mad with intolerable desire, I hugg'd, I clasp'd *Phoebe*, as if she had had wherewithal to relieve me: pleased however with, and pitying the taking she could feel me in, she drew me towards the door and opening it as softly as she could, we both got off undiscover'd, and she reconducted me to my own room, where unable to keep my legs, in the agitation, I was in, I instantly threw myself down on the bed, where I lay transported, tho' asham'd at what I felt.

Phoebe lay down by me, and asked me archly, if now that I had seen the enemy, and fully considered him, I was still afraid of him? or did I think I could venture to come to a close engagement with him? to all which not a word on my side: I sigh'd, and could scarce breathe. [She takes hold of my hand, and having roll'd up her own petticoats, forced it half-strivingly towards those parts, where now grown more knowing, I mist the main object of my wishes; and finding not even the shadow of what I wanted, where every thing was so flat! or so hollow!] In the vexation I was in at it, I should have withdrawn my hand, but for fear of disobliging her. Abandoning it then entirely to her management, she made use of it as she thought proper, to procure herself rather the shadow than the substance of any pleasure. For my part, I now pin'd for more solid food, and promis'd tacitly to myself that I would not be put off much longer with this foolery from woman to woman, if Mrs. *Brown* did not soon provide me with the essential specific: in short I had all the air of not being able to wait the arrival of my lord *B*----, tho' he was now expected in a very few days: nor did I wait for him, for love itself took charge of the disposal of me, in spite of interest, or gross lust.

ANONYMOUS

"The Game of Flatts" from *Satan's Harvest Home* (1749)

The anonymous pamphlet *Satan's Harvest Home* (1749), an attack on contemporary urban vices, contains passages excoriating both male and female homosexuality. Yet as is often the case in such hortatory subliterature, the author frequently exhibits a prurient interest in that which he seeks to discredit. The rather repellent story of the Turkish male impersonator related in "The Game of Flatts" circulated widely in the eighteenth century and seems to have originated in the sixteenth-century travel account of a Romanian diplomat, A. G. Busbequius. At Turkish bathhouses, asserted an English translator of Busbequius's *Travels into Turkey* in 1744, young girls were "exposed Naked to the view of other Women," causing the women to "fall in Love with them, as young Men do with us, at the sight of Virgins." The "game of flatts" in the title, derived from a seventeenth- and eighteenth-century term for playing cards (*flats*), refers to tribadism, or the rubbing together of two female pudenda. Interestingly, *flat* carries over as a sapphic linguistic marker into nineteenth- and twentieth-century slang: the anonymous author of the Victorian sexual memoir *My Secret Life* (1888–94) refers to lesbian sex as "flat fucking," while in our own day the epithet *flatbacker* remains a popular slang term in the American South for a female homosexual.

FURTHER READING: *Satan's Harvest Home: or the Present State of Whorecraft, Adultery, Fornication, Procuring, Pimping, Sodomy, and the Game at Flatts* (1749; rpt. New York and London: Garland, 1985); Randolph Trumbach, "London's Sapphists: from Three Sexes to Four Genders in the Making of Modern Culture," in Julia Epstein and Kristina Straub, eds., *Body Guards: The Cultural Politics of Gender Ambiguity* (New York: Routledge, 1991), pp. 112–41; Emma Donoghue, *Passions Between Women: British Lesbian Culture 1668–1801* (London: Scarlet, 1993); Lisa L. Moore, *Dangerous Intimacies: Toward a Sapphic History of the British Novel* (Durham, N.C. and London: Duke University Press, 1977); George E. Haggerty, *Unnatural Affections: Women and Fiction in the Later Eighteenth Century* (Bloomington: Indiana University Press, 1998).

I am credibly informed, in order to render the scheme of iniquity still more extensive amongst us, a new and most abominable vice has got footing among the w---- of q----y, by some called the Game at Flatts. However incredible this may appear to some people, I shall mention a story from an author of very great credit, applicable to the matter, who, speaking of the Turks says:

"A Turk hates bodily filthiness and nastiness worse than soul-defilement, and, therefore, they wash very often, and they never ease themselves by going to stool, but they carry water with them for their posteriors. But ordinarily the women bathe by themselves, bond and free together, so that you shall many times see young maids, exceeding beautiful, gathered from all parts of the world, exposed naked to the view of other women, who thereupon fall in love with them, as young men do with us at the sight of virgins.

"By this you may guess what the strict watch over females comes to, and that it is not enough to avoid the company of an adulterous man, for the females burn in love one towards another; and the panderesses to such refined lovers are the bards; and, therefore, some Turks will deny their wives the use of their public baths, but they cannot do it altogether because their law allows them. But these offences happen among the common sort; the richer sort of persons have baths at home, as I told you before.

"It happened one time that at the public baths for women an old woman fell in love with a girl, the daughter of a poor man, a citizen of Constantinople; and, when neither by wooing nor flattering her, she could obtain that of her which her mad affection aimed at, she attempted to perform an exploit almost incredible. She feigned herself to be a man, changed her habit, hired an house near the maid's father, and pretended he was one of the *chiauxes* of the Grand Seignor; and thus, by reason of his neighbourhood, she insinuated herself into the man's acquaintance, and after some time acquaints him with the desire of his daughter. In short, he being a man in such a prosperous condition, the matter was agreed on, a portion was settled, such as they were able to give, and a day appointed for the marriage. When the ceremonies were over and this doughty bridegroom went into the bride-chamber to his spouse, after some discourse, and plucking off her head-gear, she was found to be a woman. Whereupon the maid runs out and calls up her parents, who soon found that they had married her not to a man but a woman. Whereupon they carried the supposed man the next day to the General of Janizaries, who, in the absence of the Grand Seignor, was governor of the city. When she was brought before him he chid her soundly for her beastly love. 'What,' says he, 'are you not ashamed, an old beldam as you are, to attempt so notorious a bestiality, and so filthy a fact?'

"'Away, sir,' says she! 'You do not know the force of love, and God grant you never may.' At this absurd reply the governor could scarce forbear laughter, but commanded her presently to be packed away and drowned in the deep. Such was the unfortunate issue of her wild amours."

DENIS DIDEROT (1713–1784)

From *The Indiscreet Jewels* (1748) and *The Nun* (1760)

Born of bourgeois parents in the Marne, the great French *philosophe* Denis Diderot studied at the University of Paris and worked as a hack writer in Paris in his early years. Commissioned in 1745 to translate Ephraim Chambers's *Cyclopedia* (1728), he devised the idea of an exhaustive reference work that would incorporate within it the whole of practical, philosophical, and scientific knowledge to date. The result was the celebrated *Encyclopédie; ou Dictionnaire raisonnée des sciences, des arts et des métiers* (1751–86), a massive multivolume reference work that he compiled with the help of Voltaire, d'Alembert, Buffon, Montesquieu, Turgot, and various other distinguished collaborators. It remains Diderot's greatest single achievement and the epitome of French Enlightenment culture. Yet Diderot was extraordinarily prolific and published much else besides: novels, essays, plays, art criticism, and a series of philosophical "entertainments" of which *Le Neveu de Rameau* (1762), *Le Rêve d'Alembert* (1769), and *Jacques le fataliste* (1773) are the best known. He married once and died in 1784.

Like Samuel Richardson, whom he greatly admired, Diderot wrote fiction touching on the lesbian theme. Whether it is true, as he was wont to fantasize, that his longtime mistress, Sophie Volland, had a homosexual relationship with her sister, the subject of lesbianism seems always to have held for him a special—if ambiguous—emotional significance. The two excerpts below suggest the complexity of his attitude. The first is from the 1748 novel *The Indiscreet Jewels* (*Les Bijoux indiscrets*)—a lubricious comic fable in which the Turkish sultan Mangogul and his sultana Mirzoza wager over whether there are any virtuous women left in the world. Mangogul, who believes there are not, sets out to prove his case with the help of a magic ring, which when rubbed, forces the genitals (or "jewels") of the woman at whom it is directed to speak the names of all the men with whom she has had sexual relations. He fears the bet is lost when he encounters Fricamona, an apparently chaste woman whose jewels remain mute under interrogation. Yet as he and Mirzoza discover, the comely Fricamona is hardly as innocent as she appears. Embedded in her name, as Diderot's eighteenth-century readers would instantly have recognized, is a bawdy pun on *fricatrice*, a contemporary synonym for tribade or sapphist.

Diderot tackled the lesbian theme rather more disturbingly in *The Nun* (*La Religieuse*), an inflammatory fictional attack on the Catholic church that he began writing in 1760. Here, a young woman named Suzanne Simonin—forced by her family into a convent against her will—falls victim to the seductive wiles of its woman-loving Mother Superior, a character based on the real-life French abbess, Adelaide d'Orléans. While the picture of sexual depravity behind convent walls is ostensibly meant to expose the "unnatural" forms of behavior produced by religious sequestration, Diderot's voyeuristic fascination with the predatory "Madame ----"—as in the scenes below, in which she pursues a bewildered yet aroused Suzanne—subtly undermines any wholesome or enlightening message. Diderot's novel has often attracted the opprobrium of censors: afraid of ecclesiastical reprisals, he was unable to publish it openly during his lifetime; a film by Jacques Rivette based on *The Nun* was banned in France in 1966.

FURTHER READING: Denis Diderot, *Oeuvres complètes*, ed. J. Assezat and Maurice Tourneux (Paris: Garnier, 1875–77); —, *The Indiscreet Jewels*, trans. Sophie Hawkes (New York: Marsilio, 1993); —, *The Nun*, trans. Leonard Tancock, (Harmondsworth, Middlesex: Penguin, 1974); —, *Diderot's Letters to Sophie Volland*, ed. Peter France (London: Oxford University Press, 1972); Vivienne Mylne, "What Suzanne Knew: Lesbianism and *La Religieuse*," *Studies on Voltaire and the Eighteenth Century* 208 (1982): 176–73; Rita Goldberg, *Sex and Enlightenment: Women in Richardson and Diderot* (Cambridge: Cambridge University Press, 1984); Eve Kosofsky Sedgwick, "Privilege of Unknowing," *Genders* 1 (1988): 102–24; Erica Rand, "Diderot and Girl-Group Erotics," *Eighteenth-Century Studies* 25 (1992): 495–516; P. N. Furbank, *Diderot: A Critical Biography* (New York: Knopf, 1993); Terry Castle, *The Apparitional Lesbian: Female Homosexuality and Modern Culture* (New York: Columbia University Press, 1993); Christopher Rivers, "'Inintelligibles pour une femme honnête': Sexuality, Textuality and Knowledge in Diderot's *La Religieuse* and Gautier's *Mademoiselle de Maupin*," *Romanic Review* 86 (1995): 1–29. Irene Fizer, "Women 'Off' the Market: Feminine Economies in Diderot's *La Religieuse* and the Convent Novel," in Thomas DiPiero and Pat Gill, eds., *Illicit Sex: Identity Politics in Early Modern Culture* (Athens: University of Georgia Press, 1997).

From *The Indiscreet Jewels* (1748)

The African author does not tell us what Mangogul did while waiting for Bloculocus. Most likely he went out to consult a jewel or two, and then, satisfied with what he learned, returned to the favorite, emitting the joyous cries that begin this chapter.

"Victory! Victory!" he cried. "You have triumphed, madame, and the château, the porcelains, and the little monkey are yours."

"No doubt it is Eglea?" asked the favorite.

"No, madame, no, it is not Eglea," interrupted the sultan. "It is another."

"Ah, Prince," said the favorite, "do not withhold this paragon's name any longer . . ."

"Very well! It is . . . who would ever have thought it?"

"It is . . . ?" said the favorite.

"Fricamona," answered Mangogul.

"Fricamona!" returned Mirzoza. "I do not find that so difficult to believe. This woman has spent most of her youth in a convent, and since she got out she has led a most exemplary and secluded life. No man has ever set foot in her house; and she, in some measure, has made herself the abbess of a troop of devout young women who constantly fill her house, and whom she educates to perfection. You could hardly find fault with her," added the favorite, smiling and shaking her head.

"Madame, you are right," said Mangogul. "I questioned her jewel, but received no answer. I redoubled the powers of my ring by rubbing and rubbing. Nothing happened. It must be, I told myself, that this jewel is deaf. I prepared to leave Fricamona on the bed where I found her when she began to speak—through the mouth, that is."

"'Dear Acaris,' she cried, 'how happy am I in these moments I snatch from my obligations to devote myself to you! After those I spend in your arms, these are the sweetest moments of my life . . . Nothing distracts me. Silence is all around me. My half-open curtains admit only as much light as I need to move me to tenderness and gaze at you. I command my imagination; it calls you forth and I see you . . . Dear Acaris! You look so beautiful to me! . . . Yes, those are your eyes, your smile, your lips . . . Do not hide those budding breasts from me. Allow me to kiss them . . . I have not seen enough of them . . . Let me kiss them again! . . . Alas, may I die upon them . . . What madness takes hold of me! Acaris! Dear Acaris, where are you? Come to me, dear Acaris . . . Ah! Dear and tender friend, I swear to you, unfamiliar sentiments are taking hold of my soul. It is full of them, overwhelmed, and cannot contain them . . . Flow, sweet tears, flow and ease the passion that devours me . . . No, dear Acaris, no, that Alizali whom you preferred to me will not love you as I do . . . But I hear a noise. Ah! It is no doubt Acaris! . . . Come, sweet soul, come . . .'

"Fricamona was not mistaken," continued Mangogul, "for it was Acaris herself. I left them twined together, strongly persuaded that Fricamona's jewel would continue to be discreet, and I ran to tell you that I have lost my wager."

"But," replied the sultana, "I do not understand a thing about this Fricamona. She must be mad or suffer terrible vapors. No, Prince, no, I have more conscience than you think. I have no objection to this trial. But I feel something that prevents me from taking advantage of it. And I will not take advantage of it. That is settled. I do not want your château, or your porcelains, or I will have them on better grounds than this."

"Madame," answered Mangogul, "I do not understand you. You are unsurpassably difficult. You must not have looked closely at the little monkey."

"Prince, I have looked at him well," replied Mirzoza, "and I know that he is charming. But I suspect that Fricamona is not the person I seek. If you wish him to be mine one day, you must look elsewhere."

From *The Nun* (1760)

I could see the affection the Superior had conceived for me growing from day to day. I was always in her cell or she in mine; for the slightest indisposition she prescribed the sick-room for me, excused me from offices, sent me to bed early or forbade early morning prayers. In choir, refectory or recreation she contrived to show her friendship; in choir, if there was a verse containing some affectionate or tender sentiment, she sang it to me or looked at me if it was sung by another; in the refectory she always sent me part of anything delicious that was served to her; in recreation she would put her arm round my waist and say the sweetest and kindest things; nobody gave her a present that I did not share in: chocolate, sugar, coffee, liqueurs, snuff, linen, handkerchiefs, whatever it was. She stripped her own cell of pictures, china, furniture and a host of pleasant and useful things so as to embellish mine, and I could scarcely leave my room for a moment without finding on my return that it had been enriched with gifts. Then I would go and thank her, and that gave her indescribable pleasure, and she kissed me and hugged me, sat me on her knee, told me all the most confidential secrets of the convent and promised herself a life a thousand times happier than she would have had in the world outside, provided that I loved her. Then she would stop, look at me with eyes of love and say: "Sister Suzanne, do you love me?"

"How could I fail to love you? I would have to be the very soul of ingratitude."

"That is true."

"You are so kind."

"So fond of you . . ."

As she said these words she lowered her eyes and the hand round me tightened still more, and the one on my knee increased its pressure. She pulled me down to her, my face was against hers, she sighed and fell back on her chair trembling. It was as though she had some secret to tell me but dared not, and she shed tears and then said: "Ah Sister Suzanne, you don't love me!"

"I don't love you, dear Mother?"

"No."

"Tell me what I must do to prove it to you."

"That you will have to guess."

"I am trying, but I cannot think of anything."

By now she had raised her collar and put one of my hands on her bosom. She fell silent, and so did I. She seemed to be experiencing the most exquisite pleasure. She invited me to kiss her forehead, cheeks, eyes and mouth, and I obeyed. I don't think there was any harm in that, but her pleasure increased, and as I was only too glad to add to her happiness in any innocent way, I kissed her again on forehead, cheeks, eyes and lips. The hand she had rested on my knee wandered all over my clothing from my feet to my girdle, pressing here and there, and she gasped as she urged me in a strange, low voice to redouble my caresses, which I did. Eventually a moment came, whether of pleasure or of pain I cannot say, when she went as pale as death, closed her eyes, and her whole body tautened violently, her lips were first pressed together and moistened with a sort of foam, then they parted and she seemed to expire with a deep sigh. I jumped up, thinking she had fainted, and was about to go and call for help. She half opened her eyes and said in a failing voice: "You innocent girl! it isn't anything. What are you doing? Stop . . ." I looked at her, wild-eyed and uncertain whether I should stay or go. She opened her eyes again; she had lost her power of speech, and made signs that I should come back and sit on her lap again. I don't know what was going on inside me, I was afraid, my heart was thumping and I breathed with difficulty, I was upset, oppressed, shocked and frightened, my strength seemed to have left me and I was about to swoon. And yet I cannot say it was pain I was feeling. I went over to her and she once again motioned me to sit on her lap, which I did; she was half dead and I felt as though I were dying myself. We remained in that peculiar state for some time. If a nun had come upon us then she would certainly have been scared and would have imagined either that we had fainted or gone to sleep. However, the good Superior, for it is impossible to be so sensitive and not good, seemed to be recovering. She was still lying back in her chair and her eyes were still closed, but her face was lit up with the loveliest colour. She took one of my hands and kissed it, while I said to her: "Dear Mother, you did give me a fright!" She smiled sweetly without opening her eyes. "But haven't you been ill?"

"No."

"I thought you were."

"What innocence! ah, dear innocent child! How she appeals to me!"

As she said these words she sat up straight in her chair, threw her arms round me and kissed me hard on both cheeks, then said: "How old are you?"

"Not quite twenty."

"I can't believe it."

"Dear Mother, nothing is truer."

"I want to know the whole story of your life. Will you tell me?"

"Yes, dear Mother."

"Everything?"

"Everything."

"But somebody might come. Let us sit at the keyboard, and you will be giving me a lesson."

We did so but, I don't know why, my hands shook and the page seemed just a lot of muddled notes and I simply could not play. I told her so and she began to laugh and took my place, but it was still worse, for she could hardly hold out her arms.

"My dear child," she said, "I can see that you are in no fit state to teach me, nor I to learn. I am rather tired, and must have some rest, so good-bye. Tomorrow, and no later, I want to know everything that has gone on in that dear little soul of yours; good-bye . . ."

At other times when I left she came with me to her door and watched me all the way down the corridor as far as mine, blew a kiss at me and only went into her room when

I had gone into mine, but on this occasion she hardly rose, and it was as much as she could do to get to the armchair by her bed, where she sat down, laid her head upon her pillow, blew me a kiss with her hands and closed her eyes as I took myself off.

My cell was almost opposite that of Sainte-Thérèse, her door was open and she was watching for me. She stopped me and said:

"Oh, Sainte-Suzanne, you have come from our Mother's?"

"Yes."

"Did you stay there long?"

"As long as she wanted me to."

"That is not what you promised me."

"I didn't promise you anything."

"Would you dare tell me what you did there?"

Although I had nothing to reproach myself with I will admit, Sir, that her question embarrassed me. She saw it did, and insisted on an answer, so I replied:

"Dear Sister, you may not believe me, but you would believe our dear Mother, and I shall ask her to tell you."

"My dear Sainte-Suzanne," she cut in quickly, "don't do that. You don't want to make my life a misery; she would never forgive me. You don't know what she is, she is capable of passing from the greatest tenderness to ferocity. I don't know what would happen to me. Promise to say nothing to her."

"You mean that?"

"I beg of you on my knees. I am desperate. I see that I must make up my mind, and I will. Promise me you'll say nothing to her."

I helped her to her feet and gave her my word; she relied on it and she was right. We retired to our cells, she to hers and I to mine.

Back in my own room I could not concentrate, I wanted to pray but could not; I tried to find something to do and began one task and gave it up for another, and that for yet another; my hands stopped of their own accord and I was so to speak stupid—I had never experienced anything like it. My eyes closed in spite of me and I fell into a little doze, although I never usually sleep in the daytime. When I woke up I questioned myself about what had passed between the Superior and me and examined my conscience. After a further examination I thought I could glimpse an answer, but they were such vague, crazy, ridiculous notions that I put them out of my mind. The result of my reflections was that it was probably an affliction to which she was subject, then another thought came, that perhaps the malady was catching, and that Sainte-Thérèse had caught it and I should too.

On the following day, after Matins, our Superior said to me: "Sainte-Suzanne, today I hope to know everything that has happened to you. Come along."

I went. She made me sit in her own armchair by her bed, while she sat on a slightly lower chair, so that I dominated her a little, for I am taller and was a bit higher as well. She was so near me that my knees were interlocked with hers, and she leaned on her bed. After a moment's pause I said:

"Although I am so young I have been through a great deal of trouble. I shall soon have been in this world for twenty years, and it has been twenty years of suffering. I don't know whether I shall be able to tell you everything or whether you will have the heart to listen to it: family troubles, troubles in the convent of Sainte-Marie, troubles in the convent of Longchamp, troubles everywhere. Dear Mother, where do you want me to begin?"

"With the first."

"But, dear Mother, it will be very long and very depressing, and I don't want to make you miserable for so long."

"Don't be afraid, I love a good cry, and to be shedding tears is a delicious state for a sensitive soul. You must enjoy weeping too—you will wipe away my tears and I yours, and perhaps we shall be happy in the middle of the tale of your sufferings, and who knows where our emotion may lead us?" As she said these last words she looked at me from top to toe with eyes already wet with tears, took me by both hands and came even nearer until we were touching each other.

"Tell me, my child. I am ready and I feel in the most pressing mood for emotion, indeed I don't think I have ever in my life had a day more full of sympathy and affection . . ."

So I began my story more or less as I have been writing it to you. I cannot describe the effect it produced upon her, the sighs she heaved, the tears she shed, her expressions of indignation against my cruel parents, the horrible women at Sainte-Marie and those at Longchamp. I should be sorry if the smallest part of the ills she wished for them ever befell them, for I would not have wanted to tear a single hair out of the head of my most cruel enemy. Now and again she stopped me, stood up, walked about, then resumed her place, or she would raise her hands and eyes to heaven and then bury her head in my lap. When I told her about the scene in the dungeon and that of my exorcism and my public confession she almost shouted aloud, and when I ended my tale and stopped speaking she remained for some time bent over her bed with her head buried in the coverlet and arms stretched out above her head. I said: "Dear Mother, do forgive me for all the distress I have given you, but I did warn you and you insisted on it." But she only answered with these words:

"What wicked creatures! Horrible creatures! Only in convents can humanity sink so low. When hatred allies itself to habitual ill temper you don't know how far things can go. Fortunately I am a kind woman and I love all my nuns, and they have taken on something of my character, some more and some less, but they all love each other. But how did that poor health of yours manage to stand up to such torments? How comes it that all these fragile limbs were not broken? And that delicate mechanism destroyed? Why was the lustre of those eyes not dimmed for ever by tears? What cruel women! Fancy crushing those arms with ropes!" And she took my arms and kissed them. "Drowning those eyes in tears!" And she kissed them. "Drawing groans and wailing from that mouth!" She kissed that too. "Condemning that charming, serene face to be constantly clouded by sadness!" She kissed it. "Making the roses of those cheeks wither!" She stroked them with her hand and kissed them. "Robbing that head of its beauty! tearing out that hair! loading that brow with sorrow!" She kissed my head, brow, hair. "Fancy daring to put a rope round that neck and tearing those shoulders with sharp points!" She pushed aside my collar and coif, opened the top of my dress and my hair fell loose over my bare shoulders; my breast was half uncovered and her kisses spread over my neck, bare shoulders and half-naked breast.

The trembling that began to come over her, the confusion of her speech, the uncontrolled movements of her eyes and hands, her knee pressing between mine, the ardour of her embraces and the tightness of her arms as she held me, all showed me that her malady was about to come over her again. I don't know what was going on inside me, but I was seized with panic, and my own trembling and faintness justified the suspicion I had had that her trouble was contagious.

I said: "Dear Mother, look what state you have put me in! If anybody were to come . . ."

"Stay here, stay here," she said in a failing voice, "nobody is going to come."

But I struggled to get up and free myself from her, saying: "Dear Mother, do be careful, your illness is coming on. Let me go away . . ."

I wanted to get away, I really did, but could not. I had no strength left and my legs were giving way. She was sitting and I standing up, she pulled me and I was afraid of falling on top of her and hurting her, so I sat on the edge of her bed and said:

"I don't know what's the matter with me. I feel faint."

"So do I, but relax a moment and it will pass. It won't be anything."

And indeed my Superior regained her composure, and so did I, but we were both exhausted. I had my head on her pillow and she rested hers on one of my knees, with her forehead on one of my hands. We remained in that state for some minutes. I wasn't thinking of anything, nor could I, for my weak state took up the whole of my attention. We said nothing, but the Superior was the first to break the silence: "Suzanne, from what you have told me of her I have got the impression that you were very attached to your first Superior."

"Very."

"She did not love you any more than I do, but you loved her more . . . You have no answer?"

"I was unhappy, and she comforted me in my distress."

"But where does your distaste for the religious life come from? Suzanne, you haven't told me everything."

"Excuse me, Madame, I have."

"What! it's not possible, nice as you are—for, my dear child, you are very nice, and you don't realize yourself how nice you are—that nobody has told you so."

"Yes, I have been told so."

"And you didn't dislike the man who told you?"

"No."

"You didn't feel any liking for him?"

"None whatever."

"What, hasn't your heart ever felt anything?"

"No, nothing."

"So it isn't some passion, secret or disapproved of by your parents, which turned you against convents? Let me into the secret, I am indulgent."

"Dear Mother, I have no secret of that kind to confide in you."

"Then once again, where does your distaste for the religious life come from?"

"From the life itself. I hate its duties, occupations, seclusion, constraint, and I feel I am called to do something else."

"But what makes you feel like that?"

"The boredom that overwhelms me; I am bored."

"Even here?"

"Yes, dear Mother, even here, in spite of all your kindness to me."

"But do you feel any urges or desires within yourself?"

"No, none."

"So it seems. It looks to me as though you have a very equable temperament."

"Fairly."

"Even frigid."

"I couldn't say."

"You don't know the world outside?"

"Very little."

"Then what attraction can it have for you?"

"That isn't very clear to me, but there must be some."

"Is it your freedom that you miss?"

"Yes, it is that, and perhaps many other things."

"And what are those other things? My dear, open your heart to me; would you like to be married?"

"I would prefer that to being what I am, for certain."

"Why?"

"I don't know."

"You don't know? Now tell me, what impression does a man's presence make on you?"

"None, but if he is intelligent and speaks well I enjoy listening to him, and if he has a handsome face, I notice it."

"And your heart is untouched?"

"So far it has felt no emotion."

"What! When they have looked into your eyes with ardour, haven't you felt——?"

"Sometimes I have felt embarrassed, and that made me drop my eyes."

"But no stirring of emotion?"

"None."

"Your senses didn't have anything to say to you?"

"I don't know what the language of the senses is."

"And yet they do have a language."

"That may well be."

"But you don't know it?"

"Not at all."

"What! You . . . It is a very tender language. Wouldn't you like to learn it?"

"No, dear Mother, what use would it be to me?"

"It would drive away your boredom."

"It might add to it, though. And then, what does this language of the senses mean, if it has no object?"

"When we talk it is always to somebody, and that is better, surely, than talking to oneself, although that is not altogether without pleasure."

"I don't follow any of this."

"If you wished, my dear child, I would make myself clearer."

"No, dear Mother, no. I know nothing, and I would rather know nothing than acquire knowledge which might make me unhappier than I am now. I have no desires, and I don't want to discover any I couldn't satisfy."

"But why couldn't you?"

"How could I?"

"As I do."

"As you do! But there is nobody in this place."

"I am here, my dear, and so are you."

"Well, what am I to you, and you to me?"

"How innocent she is!"

"Oh yes, I am, it is true, dear Mother, and I would rather die than cease to be so."

I don't know in what way these last words were unpleasant to her, but they made her change her expression at once. She became serious and embarrassed, and her hand, which she had rested on one of my knees, first stopped its pressure and then was moved away. She kept her eyes lowered.

I said: "Dear Mother, what have I done? Has something escaped me which has upset you? Forgive me. I am using the freedom you have given me, and nothing I have to say to you is in any way studied, and besides, if I were to think it out I wouldn't put it any differently and might not do it as well. The things we are discussing are so novel to me! Forgive me . . ."

So saying, I threw my arms round her neck and laid my head on her shoulder. She put her arms round me and held me very tenderly. For a few minutes we remained thus, and then, recovering her calmly affectionate manner, she said:

"Suzanne, do you sleep well?"

"Very well, especially just recently."

"Do you go to sleep at once?"

"Most often."

"But when you don't drop off at once what do you think about?"

"My past life, the life I have still to come, or I pray to God, or I weep—all sorts of things."

"And in the morning when you wake up early?"

"I get up."

"At once?"

"At once."

"You don't like just dreaming?"

"No."

"Enjoying the lovely warmth of the bed?"

"No."

"Never . . . ?"

She paused at that word, and she was right, for what she was about to ask me was not seemly, and perhaps I shall be even more unseemly if I repeat it, but I have resolved to keep nothing back. "You have never been tempted to consider with some self-satisfaction how beautiful you are?"

"No, dear Mother. I don't know whether I am as beautiful as you say, but even if I were, one is beautiful for others, and not for oneself."

"It has never occurred to you to run your hands over that lovely bosom, those legs, that body, that firm, soft, white flesh of yours?"

"Oh no, that is sinful, and if such a thing had happened to me I don't know how I could ever have mentioned it in my confession . . ."

I don't know what else we said to each other, but then she was told she was wanted in the parlour. I thought the arrival of this visitor vexed her and she would have preferred to go on talking to me, although what we were saying was hardly worth regretting. However, we separated.

The community had never been happier than since I had joined it. The Superior seemed to have lost her moody character and they said I had steadied her. She even granted in my honour several recreation days and what are called feasts, that is to say days when the fare is a little better than usual, offices briefer and all the time between given over to recreation. But that happy time was soon to come to an end for the others as well as for me.

The scene I have just described was followed by many others which I pass over. Here is the sequel to it.

The Superior began to give way to restlessness and she lost her gaiety, freshness and sleep. On the following night, when everybody was asleep and the whole house silent, she rose and wandered about the corridors for some time, finally coming to my cell. I am a light sleeper, and I thought I recognized her step. She stopped still. Apparently letting her head fall forward against my door she made enough noise to wake me even if I had been asleep. I made not a sound; I thought I heard a voice lamenting, somebody sighing, and it made me shudder, and then I made up my mind to say *Ave*.

Instead of answering she tiptoed away, but came back a little later, and the moanings and sighings began again. Once again I cried *Ave*, and she went away a second time. I felt reassured and went to sleep. While I was asleep somebody came in and sat by my bed, the curtains were drawn aside and a little candle was held so as to light up my face while the person holding it watched me sleeping. Anyhow, that is what I gathered from her attitude when I opened my eyes, and the person was the Mother Superior.

I sat up at once, and seeing how frightened I was she said: "Suzanne, don't be afraid, it's me." I let my head fall back on the pillow and said: "Dear Mother, what are you doing here at this hour of night? What has made you come? Why aren't you asleep?"

"I can't sleep and I shan't be able to for a long time. I am tormented by bad dreams, hardly do I close my eyes before the agonies you have suffered haunt my imagination. I can see you in the clutches of those inhuman creatures, your hair all over your face and your feet bleeding, torch in hand and a rope round your neck. I am convinced they are about to take your life, and I start and tremble and all my body breaks into a cold sweat. I want to rush to your rescue, I scream and wake up, then wait in vain for sleep to come back to me. This is what has happened to me tonight, and I feared that heaven was warning me of some disaster to my friend, so I got up, came to your door and listened. I had the impression that you were not asleep, you called out and I went away. I came back again and again you spoke. Yet again I went away, but came back for the third time, and thinking you were asleep I came in. I have been here beside you for some time now, afraid of waking you up. At first I hesitated about pulling back your curtains, and wanted to go away for fear of upsetting your rest, but I could not resist a desire to see whether my beloved Suzanne was well, so I looked at you. How beautiful you are to look at, even when asleep!"

"Dear Mother, how kind you are!"

"I am frozen, but now I know I have nothing to fear for you, my dear child, and so perhaps I shall sleep. Give me your hand."

I did so.

"How gentle your pulse is! and regular! Nothing upsets it."

"I sleep pretty soundly."

"How lucky you are!"

"Dear Mother, you will get colder still."

"Yes, you are right. Good-bye, my dear, good-bye. I am going now."

But she did not go; she stayed there looking at me, and a tear fell from each of her eyes. "Dear Mother," I said, "what is the matter? You're crying. How sorry I am to have told you about my troubles!" Thereupon she shut my door, blew out the candle and fell upon me. She lay beside me, outside my coverlet, holding me in her arms, her face was pressed to mine and her tears moistened my cheeks, she sighed and gasped out plaintively: "Dearest friend, take pity on me!"

"Dear Mother, what is the matter? Are you ill? What can I do for you?"

"I am shaking and shivering, and a terrible chill is coming over me."

"Would you like me to get up and give you my bed?"

"No, there is no need for you to get up; just turn back the cover a little so that I can get near you, warm myself and be healed."

"But, dear Mother, that is forbidden. What would they say if it were known? I have seen nuns given penance for far less serious things. It happened in the convent of Sainte-Marie that a nun went into another's cell at night, for they were great friends, and I can't tell you how badly it was thought of. My confessor has sometimes asked me if anybody has ever suggested coming to sleep with me, and solemnly warned me not to allow it. I have even mentioned the caresses you have given me, which I thought quite innocent, but he doesn't think so. I don't know why I have forgotten his advice, for I had made up my mind to speak to you about it."

"My dear," she said, "the whole place is asleep around us, and nobody will know anything. I am the one who rewards and punishes here, and whatever your confessor may say I cannot see what harm there is for one friend to take into her bed another friend who is very distressed and has come in the night in spite of the freezing weather to make sure her dear one isn't in any danger. Suzanne, haven't you ever shared the same bed at home with your sisters?"

"No, never."

"But if there had been occasion wouldn't you have done so without hesitation? If your sister had been very frightened and was freezing cold, and had come and asked for a place beside you, would you have refused?"

"No, I don't think so."

"And am I not your dear Mother?"

"Yes, you are. But it is forbidden."

"My dear, I forbid it in others, but I allow it to you, and am asking you to do so. Just let me warm myself a minute and then I'll go. Give me your hand." I did so. "Feel me, touch me and see for yourself. I am all shivering and stone cold." And it was true. "Oh, poor Reverend Mother," I said, "you will be ill. Just a moment, I will move over to one side and you can put yourself in the warm place." I moved over to the side, lifted the coverlet and she came into my place. Oh, how upset she was! She was shaking in every limb, she wanted to talk to me and come nearer, but could neither say a word nor move. She whispered: "Suzanne, my dear, come a bit nearer." She held out her arms, but I had my back to her; she took me gently and pulled me towards her, passed her right arm under my body and the other above and said: "I am frozen, and so cold that I am afraid to touch you for fear of hurting you."

"Dear Mother, you need not be afraid of that."

Immediately she put one hand on my breast and the other round my waist, her feet were under mine, and I pressed them so as to warm them, and she said: "Oh my dear, see how my feet have warmed up at once because there is nothing between them and yours."

"But," I said, "what is there to prevent you from warming yourself everywhere in the same way?"

"Nothing, if you are willing."

I had turned round, and she had opened her nightdress, and I was on the point of doing the same when suddenly there were two violent blows on the door. I was terrified, and leaped straight out on one side of the bed and the Superior on the other. We listened and heard somebody tiptoeing back to the cell opposite. "Oh," I said, "that is Sister Sainte-Thérèse. She must have seen you go along the corridor and come in here. She must have listened and overheard us. What will she say?" I was more dead than alive. "Yes, it is she," said the Superior angrily, "I am sure it is, and I hope it will be a long time before she forgets her temerity."

"Oh, dear Mother, don't do anything to her."

"Suzanne, good-bye, good night, go back to bed and sleep well. I excuse you from early prayers. Now I am going to see this silly girl. Give me your hand . . ."

I held out a hand from one side of the bed to the other, she pulled my sleeve and kissed my arm all the way up from fingertips to shoulder, then she went out protesting that the impertinent girl who had dared to disturb her would not forget it in a hurry. I at once leaned over on the side of my bed nearer the door and listened: she went into Thérèse's room. I was tempted to get up and go and intervene between her and the Superior if the scene became violent, but I was so worried and upset that I preferred to stay in bed, but I did not sleep. I thought I should become the talk of the convent, and that the episode, which could not have been more simple, would be recounted in the most damning detail, and that it would be even worse here than at Longchamp, where I was accused of something I did not understand; that our offence would come to the knowledge of higher authorities and that our Superior would be dismissed and both of us be severely punished. But I continued to be all ears, and anxiously waited for our Mother Superior to leave Sister Thérèse's room. Apparently the matter needed a great deal of clearing up, for she stayed there almost all night. How I pitied her, in her nightdress, almost naked and numbed with anger and cold.

CHARLOTTE CHARKE (1713–1760)

From *A Narrative of the Life of Mrs. Charlotte Charke* (1755)

The flamboyant Charlotte Charke, actress and memoirist, was the daughter of the English actor and playwright Colley Cibber. Following in her father's footsteps, she began acting on the London stage in 1730 and soon became renowned for her skill in male roles. (It was common for young women to take on so-called breeches parts on the eighteenth-century British stage.) Cibber subsequently disowned Charke, who scandalized contemporaries by appearing in masculine dress offstage as well as on. Charke responded, or so it was rumored, by robbing Cibber at gunpoint, while disguised as a highwayman. After the Licensing Act of 1737 closed down many London theaters, Charke—facing poverty—traveled as a strolling player into the provinces, wrote novels and plays, and worked at various menial occupations, including a stint (in male attire) as a valet to the Earl of Anglesey in 1742. She wrote her autobiography, a lively and often poignant account of her various "mad pranks," as part of a last-ditch attempt to stave off financial ruin, but died indigent in 1760.

Despite the garrulous air adopted in the memoirs, Charke's erotic personality remains a mystery. Her preference for male dress, as she freely acknowledges, was profound and lifelong, but she says little about its meaning or her own emotional history. She married twice and had a daughter, but neither marriage lasted long. During her years as a strolling player, she traveled under the alias "Charles Brown" and lived with a woman she identifies only as "Mrs. Brown." Whether the two had a homosexual relationship has been much debated. Havelock Ellis, in his *Sexual Inversion* (1897), was skeptical; Jeannette Foster, however, author of the pioneering *Sex Variant Women in Literature* (1956), included Charke in her "conjectural record" of female homosexuality before the twentieth century. Charke's memoirs continue to fascinate: the British novelist Maureen Duffy drew on them in her experimental lesbian novel, *The Microcosm* (1966).

In the first excerpt that follows, Charke describes one of her earliest cross-dressing forays; in the second, she relates a comical and somewhat Shakespearean episode from her "Mr. Brown" years. The curious mixture of self-revelation and obfuscation is characteristic.

FURTHER READING: Charlotte Charke, *A Narrative of the Life of Mrs. Charlotte Charke* (1755; rpt. Gainesville, Fla.; Scholars' Facsimiles, 1969); Jeannette Foster, *Sex Variant Women in Literature* (1956; rpt. Tallahassee, Fla.; Naiad, 1985); Fidelis Morgan, *The Well-Known Troublemaker: A Life of Charlotte Charke* (London: Faber and Faber, 1988); Kristina Straub, "The Guilty Pleasures of Female Theatrical Cross-Dressing and the Autobiography of Charlotte Charke," in Julia Epstein and Kristina Straub, eds., *Body Guards: The Cultural Politics of Gender Ambiguity* (New York: Routledge, 1991); Philip E. Baruth, ed., *Introducing Charlotte Charke: Actress, Author, Enigma* (Urbana and Chicago: University of Illinois Press, 1998).

[Charke describes her childhood and first experiment in cross-dressing.]

I confess, I believe I came not only an unexpected, but an unwelcome guest into the family (exclusive of my parents) as my mother had borne no children for some few years before, so that I was rather regarded as an impertinent intruder, than one who had a natural right to make up the circular number of my father's fireside; yet, be it as it may, the jealousy of me from her other children laid no restraint on her fondness for me, which my father and she both testified in their tender care of my education. His paternal love omitted nothing that could improve any natural talents heaven had been pleased to endow me with—the mention of which, I hope, won't be imputed to me as a vain self-conceit, of knowing more, or thinking better than any other of my sister females. No! Far be it from me, for as all advantages from nature are the favourable gifts of the power divine, consequently no praise can be arrogated to ourselves for that which is not in ourselves possible to bestow. [. . .]

As I have instanced that my education was not only a genteel, but in fact a liberal one, and such indeed as might have been sufficient for a son instead of a daughter, I must beg leave to add that I was never made much acquainted with that necessary utensil which forms the housewifery part of a young lady's education called a needle, which I handle with the same clumsy awkwardness a monkey does a kitten, and am equally capable of using the one as Pug is of nursing the other.

This is not much to be wondered at, as my education consisted chiefly in studies of various kinds, and gave me a different turn of mind than what I might have had if my time had been employed in ornamenting a piece of canvas with beasts, birds, and the alphabet; the latter of which I understood in French rather before I was able to speak English.

As I have promised to conceal nothing that might raise a laugh, I shall begin with a small specimen of my former madness, when I was but four years of age. Having, even then, a passionate fondness for a periwig, I crawled out of bed one summer's morning at Twickenham, where my father had part of a house and gardens for the season, and taking it into my small pate that by dint of a wig and a waistcoat I should be the perfect representative of my sire, I crept softly into the servants' hall, where I had the night before espied all things in order, to perpetrate the happy design I had framed for the next morning's expedition. Accordingly I paddled down stairs, taking with me my shoes, stockings, and little dimity coat, which I artfully contrived to pin up as well as I could to supply the want of a pair of breeches. By the help of a long broom I took down a waistcoat of my brother's and an enormous bushy tie-wig of my father's, which entirely enclosed my head and body, with the knots of the ties thumping my little heels as I marched along with slow and solemn pace. The covert of hair in which I was concealed, with the weight of a monstrous belt and large silver-hilted sword that I could scarce drag along, was a vast impediment in my procession, and what still added to the other inconveniences I laboured under was whelming myself under one of my father's large beaver hats, laden with lace as thick and as broad as a brickbat.

Being thus accoutred, I began to consider that it would be impossible for me to pass for Mr Cibber in girl's shoes, therefore took an opportunity to slip out of doors after the gardener, who went to his work, and rolled myself into a dry ditch, which was as deep as I was high, and in this grotesque pigmy state walked up and down the ditch bowing to all who came by me. But, behold, the oddity of my appearance soon assembled a crowd about me, which yielded me no small joy, as I conceived their risibility on this occasion to be marks of approbation and walked myself into a fever in the happy thought of being taken for the squire.

When the family arose, till which time I had employed myself in this regular march in my ditch, I was the first thing enquired after and missed, till Mrs Heron, the mother of the late celebrated actress of that name, happily espied me, and directly called forth the whole family to be witnessed of my state and dignity.

The drollery of my figure rendered it impossible, assisted by the fondness of both father and mother, to be angry with me, but, alas, I was borne off on the footman's shoulders, to my shame and disgrace, and forced into my proper habiliments.

[Charke, disguised as "Mr. Brown," is pursued by a wealthy young lady.]

Notwithstanding my distresses, the want of clothes was not amongst the number. I appeared as Mr Brown (a name most hateful to me now, for reasons the town shall have shortly leave to guess at) in a very genteel manner and not making the least discovery of my sex by my behaviour, ever endeavouring to keep up to the well-bred gentleman, I became, as I may most properly term it, the unhappy object of love in a young lady, whose fortune was beyond all earthly power to deprive her of, had it been possible for me to have been what she designed me, nothing less than her husband.

She was an orphan heiress and under age, but so near it that at the expiration of eight months her guardian resigned his trust and I might have been at once possessed of the lady and forty thousand pounds in the Bank of England, besides effects in the Indies that were worth about twenty thousand more.

This was a most horrible disappointment on both sides; the lady of the husband, and I of the money, which would have been thought an excellent remedy for ills by those less surrounded with misery than I was. I, who was the principal in this tragedy, was the last acquainted with it, but it got wind from the servants to some of the players (who, as Hamlet says, "can't keep a secret"), and they immediately communicated it to me.

Contrary to their expectation, I received the information with infinite concern, not more in regard to myself than from the poor lady's misfortune, in placing her affection on an improper object, and whom, by letters I afterwards received, confirmed me "she was too fond of her mistaken bargain."

The means by which I came by her letters was through the persuasion of her maid, who, like most persons of her function, are too often ready to carry on intrigues. It was no difficult matter to persuade an amorous heart to follow its own inclination and accordingly a letter came to invite me to drink tea, at a place a little distant from the house where she lived.

The reason given for this interview was the desire some young ladies of her acquaintance had to hear me sing, and, as they never went to plays in the country, it would be a great obligation to her if I would oblige her friends, by complying with her request.

The maid who brought this epistle informed of the real occasion of its being wrote and told me, if I pleased, I might be the happiest man in the kingdom before I was eight and forty hours older. This frank declaration from the servant gave me but an odd opinion of the mistress, and I sometimes conceived, being conscious how unfit I was to embrace so favourable an opportunity, that it was all a joke.

However, be it as it might, I resolved to go and know the reality. The maid too insisted that I should, and protested her lady had suffered much on my account from the first hour she saw me, and, but for her, the secret had never been disclosed. She further added I was the first person who had ever made that impression on her mind. I own I felt a tender concern and resolved within myself to wait on her and, by honestly confessing who I was, kill or cure her hopes of me for ever.

In obedience to the lady's command, I waited on her, and found her with two more, much of her own age, who were her confidantes, and entrusted to contrive a method to bring this business to an end by a private marriage. When I went into the room I made a general bow to all, and was for seating myself nearest the door, but was soon lugged out of my chair by a young madcap of fashion, and, to both the lady's confusion and mine, awkwardly seated by her.

We were exactly in the condition of Lord Hardy and Lady Charlotte, in *The Funeral*, and I sat with as much fear in my countenance as if I had stolen her watch from her side. She, on her part, often attempted to speak, but had such a tremor on her voice she ended only in broken sentences. It is true, I have undergone that dreadful apprehensions of a bum-bailiff, but I should have thought one at that time a seasonable relief and, without repining, have gone with him.

The before-mentioned madcap, after putting us more out of countenance by bursting into a violent fit of laughing, took the other by the sleeves and withdrew, as she thought, to give me a favourable opportunity of paying my addresses. But she was deceived for when we were alone I was in ten thousand times worse plight than before, and what added to my confusion was seeing the poor soul dissolve into tears, which she endeavoured to conceal.

This gave me freedom of speech, by a gentle enquiry into the cause and, by tenderly trying to soothe her into a calm, I unhappily increased, rather than assuaged, the dreadful conflict of love and shame which laboured in her bosom.

With much difficulty I mustered up sufficient courage to open a discourse, by which I began to make a discovery of my name and family, which struck the poor creature into astonishment. But how much greater was her surprise when I positively assured her that I was actually the youngest daughter of Mr Cibber, and not the person she conceived me! She was absolutely struck speechless for some little time, but when she regained the power of utterance, entreated me not to urge a falsehood of that nature, which she looked upon only as an evasion, occasioned, she supposed, through a dislike of her person, adding that her maid had plainly told her I was no stranger to her miserable fate, as she was pleased to term it (and, indeed, as I really thought it).

I still insisted on the truth of my assertion, and desired her to consider whether it was likely an indigent young fellow must not have thought it an unbounded happiness to possess at once so agreeable a lady and immense fortune, both which many a nobleman in this kingdom would have thought it worth while to take pains to achieve.

Notwithstanding all my arguments, she was hard to be brought into a belief of what I told her and conceived that I had taken a dislike to her from her too readily consenting to her servant's making that declaration of her passion for me, and for that reason she supposed I had but a light opinion of her. I assured her of the contrary, and that I was sorry for us both, that providence had not ordained me to be the happy person she designed me, that I was much obliged for the honour she conferred on me and sincerely grieved it was not in my power to make a suitable return.

With many sighs and tears on her side, we took a melancholy leave and in a few days the lady retired into the country, where I have never heard from or of her since, but hope she is made happy in some worthy husband that might deserve her.

She was not the most beautiful I have beheld, but quite the most agreeable: sang finely, and played the harpsichord as well, understood languages, and was a woman of real good sense. But she was (poor thing!) an instance, in regard to me, that the wisest may sometimes err.

ANONYMOUS

From *Anecdotes of a Convent* (1771)

The three-volume novel *Anecdotes of a Convent* (1771), which according to its title page is "by the author of the Memoirs of Mrs. Williams," has sometimes been attributed to Helen Maria Williams, the noted English memoirist and partisan of the French Revolution. This attribution seems fanciful, however, given that Williams would only have been about ten years old at the time of the work's putative publication. It is perhaps no matter: the novel itself, a melodramatic love story set in England and France, is a meandering affair, neither compelling nor well-written, with the possible exception of the eponymous "convent" episode excerpted below. In this remarkable sequence, one of the novel's heroines, Louisa Boothby, a beautiful young English orphan placed in a French convent in childhood by her guardian Lady Jane Plumbstead, writes a letter to a friend in which she tells the somewhat startling story of her life there. The titillating descriptions of the "amiable, good-natur'd Ladies" of the convent would seem to owe much at first glance to Diderot's *The Nun* (1760): the nuns are "seductingly *caressante*" and, with one exception, appear to encourage the passionate bonds that grow up between various girls. Louisa herself, we learn, has formed a powerfully eroticized friendship with the dashing Miss Merton, another English girl living in the house. As Louisa's and Miss Merton's strange history unfolds, however, the narrative turns to a kind of Ovidian joke, complete with shifting identities and improbable, last-minute revelations.

The most bizarre element in the episode is undoubtedly Miss Merton's supposedly protracted unawareness of her real sex. Yet it should be noted that in the annals of human sexual foible, such instances of apparent confusion have not been entirely unknown. The situation described in *Anecdotes of a Convent* curiously foreshadows the story of the French nineteenth-century hermaphrodite Herculine Barbin, raised in a convent under the impression she was a girl, yet later forced to adopt male dress and live as a man after she fell in love with a convent companion.

FURTHER READINGS: *Anecdotes of a Convent* (London, 1771); Michel Foucault, ed., *Herculine Barbin*, trans. Richard McDougall (New York: Pantheon, 1980); Emma

Donoghue, *Passions Between Women: British Lesbian Culture, 1668–1801* (London: Scarlet, 1993).

[*Louisa Boothby, the beautiful young ward of Lady Jane Plumbstead, writes to her friend Julia Bolton:*]

When we arrived at that capital, [Lady Jane] kept me with her for a month; at the end of which time, she took me a few miles out of *Paris*, to a Royal Abbey, in order to pay a visit to the Abbess, and Nuns of the Convent, which I was destin'd to reside in for some years. There is nothing I can say, my dear *Julia*, can give you a perfect idea of the insinuating manners of the Nuns; to conceive it, you must have been acquainted with some of them; there is a soft sensibility in their eyes, and in the tone of their voices, which touches the heart. They are, to use a *French* expression, seductingly *caressante*. Such is the exterior of all the Nuns, who are suffered to appear at the grates of their parlours, and such were those I that morning saw. The flattering compliments they paid to my little person, the sense and vivacity they pretended to read in my eyes, the declarations they made of their admiration of my figure, and uncommon understanding, for a child of my age, the numberless presents they made me of beads, housewifes, pincushions, pictures of saints, and sugar plumbs, and you will not be surprized to hear, that all these things put together almost turn'd my head, and entirely gain'd my heart. I wish'd to live with such amiable, good-natur'd Ladies as these Nuns (I took it for granted) were. [. . .]

Upon my being introduced to the schoolroom, I was instantly surrounded by fifty or sixty girls, who all expressed their joy on the acquisition of a new companion. I was gazing about me with wonder at the novelty of the scene, when a well-looking venerable Nun advanced toward me, leading a young Lady by the hand, whom she presented to me, saying, "I beg leave to present a country-woman of yours to you, Miss; she is the only *English* girl we have in the house, consequently is very impatient to be made known to you." I raised my eyes on her, and felt as if my soul at that instant had darted through my breast into hers, there to take up its residence for ever. She flew into my arms, kissing my cheeks and forehead with transport, and expressed her joy on my being an inhabitant of the same house with her, in the most lively and obliging terms. The old Nun checked her vivacity, by saying, "My Dear, the pleasure you feel on seeing an *English* Lady should not make you forget all good manners and decorum." I was sorry she chid this lovely girl, and therefore made some apologies for her. [. . .]

At five o'clock in the afternoon, myself and school-fellows were all summoned, by the ringing of a bell, to supper; an hour so very unusual to me, that you may suppose I did not eat much; it chiefly consisted of fried fish and sallad; Miss *Merton* sat by me; as foreigners we had always the precedency given us, such is the politeness of the *French*. She frequently took my hand under the table, and her every look expressed the lively friendship she had conceived for me. The old Nun before-mentioned stood at her chair back, and seemed to observe us with an attentive, and, I thought, a jealous eye. When we rose from table, we all went into the garden, which was really a fine one and extremely extensive: Some of the young ladies played at ball, others at bowls; in short, everyone amused themselves according to their taste, while the old Nun, whose name was *La Conception* or the Conception (a strange name, you'll say, but a very common one in Convents); Miss *Merton* and I sat in a Chapel (of which there are several in the garden) looking at them. Madam *La Conception* neither spoke, nor understood, one word of *English*, so that my companion and I conversed with perfect ease in that language before her, which seemed to give her pain, for she frequently interrupted us; at last she insisted upon our walking about, fearing, she said, that we might take cold from sitting so long in the air. "The devil take her," said Miss *Merton*, rising; "this old harridan is the plague of my life; she follows me every where like an evil genius, and seems jealous of every body I speak to." [. . .]

My friendship with *Fanny* encreased every hour: I will here, if I am able, introduce her person to your acquaintance. [. . .] Miss *Merton* was taller than me by a head, and near two years older; her carriage was majestic, her eyes were blue, and had a sensibility in them which no painting can express, yet she occasionally could throw a fire into them which dazzled one; her hair was light, and her complexion delicate to an excess; her shape was strait as a pine, but, as she was strongly made, and large, if it had not been for the colour of her hair, and delicacy of her skin, she would rather have been thought too masculine for her sex; then she was active to a degree that never suffered her to sit still two minutes in the same posture. Nothing could fix her attention for any time but myself and her books, both of which were her passions; her temper was as amiable as her figure; she was, however, rather warm, easily moved to anger, and as easily pacify'd by a good-natur'd word. She had an attentive manner of obliging, which captivated my heart; ever ready to succour and relieve distress; polite and insinuating to all, and tender only to me. [. . .]

[Louisa goes on a short trip to Paris with her fashionable guardian.]

During the little time I stayed at *Paris*, we were constantly in a round of company and diversion; in the midst of which, however, I sigh'd in my heart for the hour which was to restore me to Miss *Merton*. At last it came; Lady *Jane* accompanied me to the Convent. On our arrival there, I presented her to my Fanny; she receiv'd her with great politeness, but *me* she embraced with transport, exclaiming, "And are you returned, my *Louisa*! how my heart joys to see you!" Thus we went on, our friendship increasing with our years: We could have wish'd to have spent more of our time together alone, than was in our power to do, though we sought every possible opportunity to this effect, but *Fanny's* old *Argus* effectually defeated all our schemes, by hardly ever suffering her charge to be a moment out of her sight, and though she could not understand what we said, yet she watch'd our every look and gesture. [. . .]

We were one day sitting at work, Miss *Merton*, the old Nun, and myself, when a Sister came to us, saying, somebody at the parlour asks to speak directly with Madam *Conception*, a circumstance I had never observed to have happened before; she looked vastly surprized, crying, "Holy Virgin, who can it be! Is it a man or a woman?" The Sister reply'd, she could not tell; upon which the old woman advanced to a glass, where after having adjusted her guimpe and veil to the best advantage, she ordered us to go that instant into the school room, and then, promising to return in a few minutes, she left us. The moment she had disappeared, *Fanny* came up to me, and, flinging her arms round my neck, almost stifled me with kisses; I gently reproved her for her violence; I felt myself somewhat offended at the manner in which she had expressed the vivacity of her friendship for me, and was hurt and confused at her indelicacy; she, too, look'd confounded at her own behaviour; we gazed on each other—I don't know how, *Julia*, I cannot describe what I don't understand; she knelt, and ask'd my pardon, in a voice so tender and pathetic, that it pierc'd my heart: Her hand, which held mine, trembled; our mutual confusion was incomprehensible to me. I fell into a reverie, from which I perhaps should not so soon have recovered myself, had not I perceived the door thrust open, and the old Nun enter the room with terror (I thought) painted on her face. She cried out, "My God! Holy Virgin! what have you two girls been doing? Why did you not go into the school-room as I ordered you?" Miss Merton, after having pressed my hand to her lips now rose from my feet, where she was kneeling when the affrighted Nun came in. "What's the matter, mother?" said she: "Matter enough," reply'd the old woman, "but I'll have no such doings in the future, I'll take care of that; you shall not see or converse with one another any more." "Softly, Madam," said Miss Merton, (setting one of her arms on her side, and extending the other towards me,) "Neither you, nor all the powers on earth, shall ever deprive me of seeing and speaking to that lovely girl; she is the idol of my heart, and I will defend her with my life, against the united tyranny of you, and all your sisterhood. I will not only see, and converse with her whenever I please, but if any of you should offer to prevent my doing so, I'll murder you, fire the Convent, and escape from this prison, with my treasure in my arms." The Nun was struck dumb with astonishment at the vehemence with which these threats were uttered, and instantly lowered her tone; she even begg'd pardon for her vivacity. Miss Merton told her, she must certainly be either mad, or drunk, to put herself into such a passion, because two girls were left together for a moment alone. I can no way give you a picture of my thoughts during this extraordinary scene; they were a perfect chaos: Miss Merton's figure and attitude, whilst she was speaking to the Nun, were so new to me, that I scarce knew her; I thought she never had look'd so enchantingly handsome, as she did while thus defending our mutual interests; but then, I thought it was done in a manner rather too rough, and not with that delicacy which I had always observed in her; for she really appeared a perfect Virago.

She now came to me, and, taking my hand, said, with a voice replete with more than female softness, "Come, my Louisa, don't be frighted at any thing that old Fury can say; no creature on earth shall ever divide us, nor vex my angel, while I have one drop of blood left in my veins." I begg'd her to be calm; she press'd me to her beating bosom, saying, "Alas! I know not why, *Louisa*, but all your gentle endeavours to sooth me only serve to raise a tempest in my breast, that shakes every fibre in my frame." Alarm'd at what she said, as well as the perturbation of spirits I saw her in, I trembled for her precious health, and, reseating myself, I placed her head upon my bosom; I found her forehead burn, and her heart beat violently, I therefore with tears entreated her to go to bed. She reply'd, "Most willingly, my soul, if you'll go with me." "Alas!" answered I, "that I would with the greatest pleasure, but Mother *Conception* will never suffer it, I fear; I will sit up in the room with you all night, if she will give me leave." "O, they will never let us be together again," said she, with a deep sigh; "I cannot conceive what they mean by all their Care to keep you and I asunder; can you *guess*, *Louisa?*" said the sweet girl, looking full in my face. I blush'd (I know not why,) and answered, "indeed I do not." Here the Abbess came to us; she had been fetch'd (I suppose) by our *Argus*, On looking at Miss *Merton*, she declared her to be in a fever, and therefore had her conveyed to her own apartment, and ordered me into the Class immediately, notwithstanding our earnest solicitations not to be separated, at least for that night. "It is, Ladies," said she, in a resolute tone, "you know, the rule of this Convent, that no two girls shall sleep together, so, Miss *Boothby*, go where I bid you." I obeyed, bath'd in tears at being obliged to quit my sick friend. [. . .]

[*Louisa and Miss Merton continue to communicate secretly, until Miss Merton is abruptly removed from the convent by her mother. not long after Louisa receives the following letter:*]

My dear *Louisa*,

I have been a prisoner ever since the day on which we were so barbarously torn from each other. Sir Francis and Lady Merton have forbid me seeing of you, or rather, the latter has, for my father does not seem so averse to it as she: I shall, however, beg leave to disobey them in this article, as I purpose being at the parlour of the Convent next Thursday afternoon, whilst the Nuns are at Vespers; if any of them tell you, at that time, that a young Gentleman from the Ambassadress asks to speak with you at the grate, make no further enquiries, but run downstairs directly, to, yours eternally,

Francis Merton

In the postscript he wrote, "O, my Louisa, my charming girl, what wonders I have to tell you."

This letter, when I had read it, appeared extremely extraordinary: why did she propose seeing me at the grate, rather than enter into the interior of the Convent? Who was the young Gentleman that was to ask for me? And what were the wonders which he had to relate to me? In this state of perplexity I remain'd till the day came, when, at the appointed hour, I was inform'd, that a young Gentleman, from the Countess of Plumbstead, desir'd to speak to me in the parlour: I rather flew than ran to see him; when, O, *Julia!* Judge, if you can, of my surprize, on perceiving my friend *Fanny*, metamorphos'd into a man. I star'd at her with amazement, and thought she look'd [more] handsome in that dress than any thing human had done before. She caught my hand through the grate, and, pressing it with ardour to her lips, express'd her transports at seeing me again. I wept aloud for joy. When our extasies, occasion'd by the sight of each other, were a little subsided, I ventur'd to ask her why she was thus disguis'd? "I am not disguis'd, my angel," said she, "I was indeed so while in the Convent, but now I wear my proper habit: Ah! my dear girl," continu'd she, (looking tenderly at me,) "why did we not believe our hearts? They would easily have explain'd a mystery, which, I am persuaded, frequently puzzled us both in trying to unravel, and which our extreme innocence hid from our knowledge: Do you understand me, Louisa?" said she. "Indeed I do not," I reply'd, trembling from head to foot, and casting my eyes to the ground; "then I will relate what has happen'd to me, since I was compell'd to leave the idol of my soul, the narration of which will sufficiently explain my meaning." [. . .]

> [*Francis Merton now reveals that his mother, a fanatical "Papist,"*
> *disguised him at birth as a girl in order to contravert the wish of*
> *her Protestant husband, Lord Merton, that his sons be raised as*
> *Protestants. The ruse has been so successful, that neither the*
> *"delicate" Francis himself—installed in the convent at the age of*
> *three—nor any of the nuns in charge of his education have ever*
> *doubted his femininity.*]

"And now, my amiable mistress, as well as friend," (said the sweet youth,) "will you not love me as well as you did when you was ignorant of my sex? Yes, I know you will— you must—my heart is not alter'd by the change, why then should *that* of my beloved *Louisa*'s?" Covered with confusion at all the wonders I had heard, I blushing, answer'd, "It is not in my power, Mr. *Merton*, to cease loving you, you must therefore be ever dear to the heart of your wretched *Louisa*." "Why wretched!" repeated he; "that can never be, since you must, you shall be mine. My father's fondness can refuse me nothing, and my mother has, by the unravelling of her plot, entirely lost his confidence, and (I really fear) his esteem also; so that her opposition to our happiness will be of little or no impediment to it." The rest of our conversation was like that of all lovers, *Julia*, not worth repeating; the evening parted us, he promised to see me frequently, we plighted our mutual vows of love and constancy, and then reluctantly bid each other adieu.

ANONYMOUS

From "Dialogue Between Sappho and Ninon de L'Enclos, in the Shades" (1773)

The "Dialogue Between Sappho and Ninon de L'Enclos, in the Shades" appeared in June 1773 in the *Covent-Garden Magazine; or, Amorous Repository*, a popular London journal of the early 1770s devoted to sexual gossip, rape trial accounts, and gambling advice. Like the pornographic poem *The Sappho-an* (c. 1735), the "Dialogue" confirms the homosexual encoding of the Greek poet Sappho in eighteenth-century popular erotic iconography. Here, in a conversation after death with Ninon de Lenclos, the celebrated seventeenth-century French courtesan and *salonnière*, Sappho describes her youthful love affairs with girls and denies that her unusual tastes were due to hermaphroditism. While the anonymous author is careful to reintroduce the story of Sappho's ill-fated passion for Phaon at the end of the dialogue, he or she presents—for the time—a remarkably tolerant picture of lesbian loves. Unlike many later translators and editors of Sappho, the author also makes clear the female addressee of the "ode so much talked of," the famous Sappho Fragment 31 (familiarly known in English as "Peer of the Gods") reproduced in Longinus's *On the Sublime*.

FURTHER READING: "Dialogue Between Sappho and Ninon de L'Enclos, in the Shades," *Covent-Garden Magazine: or, Amorous Repository* (June 1773): 225–26; David M. Robinson, *Sappho and Her Influence* (Boston: Marshall Jones, 1924); Emma Donoghue, *Passions between Women: British Lesbian Culture, 1668–1801* (London: Scarlet, 1993); Jane McIntosh Snyder, *Sappho* (New York and Philadelphia: Chelsea House, 1995); —, *Lesbian Desire in the Lyrics of Sappho* (New York: Columbia University Press, 1997); Margaret Reynolds, *The Sappho Companion* (New York: Palgrave, 2001).

SAPPHO: How different, my dear Ninon, were our sentiments, with regard to men! — and yet we both liked them to extravagance.

NINON: True, Sappho; but it is said that you had another passion, of a more unaccountable kind. The Lesbian maids can reveal the mystery. For my part I could never form any idea of it.

SAPPHO: I understand you: I was an hermaphrodite.

NINON: I cannot say what you were; but you must have been something very different from other women, or you could never have spoke so feelingly of your own sex.

SAPPHO: That difference consisted only in the warmth of my passions. Hermaphrodites, my dear Ninon, or persons who have the power of *giving* and *receiving* the pleasure of the sexes, be assured, exist only in the regions of romance. I was a mere woman, as the last action of my life strongly shewed.

NINON: I am satisfied as to your womanhood, and not a little pleased to find that you was no more; for, to tell you the truth, I always envied you on account of your supposed superiority. Nothing would have pleased me more than to have been able to communicate the delights I have so often received, to clasp a little creature in my arms, and see her expire, as I have so frequently expired—how flattering to pride!—

I meant to have asked you—but you it seems know as little of that matter as I—whether the men or we receive most pleasure in the moment of extacy. You can inform me, however, what gave rise to the report of your passion for women.

SAPPHO: I can—When a girl I was exceedingly amorous, and used to twine myself round my companions, and load them with caresses, as if I would have devoured them; and this I did intuitively, even before I was sensible of its cause, it had its effect; nature often unburdened herself in those transports.

The younger, and the colder part of my companions, were afraid of me, and supposed I was something more than I should be; but those of similar feelings sympathized with my ardour; they returned my caresses, or were pleased to receive mine; and in the height of desire we often undressed ourselves, we pressed our lips and our breasts to each other, and did all that women can, to imitate real enjoyment. We tried every posture, in short, which imagination can invent, till imagination produced—what we would much rather had been the effect of a less refined, but more vigorous impulse.

NINON: Was that all?—

SAPPHO: All indeed. It was at this period of my life that I wrote the ode so much talked of, and which was preserved by Longinus. Not that I felt all the love and jealousy there described for a girl; but as I was at that time ignorant of any male connection, I addressed it to my favourite female companion, figuring to myself what I would have felt if she had been a man, or I a man, and she in the situation alluded to.

As soon as I met with a man to my mind, I laid aside such trifling.

NINON: I am glad to hear it—for it never would have done for me.—But is it really true that you leaped over the rock of Leucadia, because Phaon deserted?—

SAPPHO: Most assuredly. What is life without those we love?

NINON: *Love*!—could you find nobody to love but him?

SAPPHO: Perhaps I might, if the violence of my passion had not driven me to despair; but it must have been after such a scene of sorrow as I could not think of enduring; I, therefore, leapt off the stage at once.

NINON: A noble exit, truly! [. . .] I wanted likewise [passion's] *demon*: I knew nothing of the torturing jealousy which distracted your bosom. You leapt into the sea in the bloom of life, while I lived among my lovers and my friends, till the age of fourscore and upwards; and, at last, died quietly in my bed, the scene of my former delights. Who was most to be envied?

SAPPHO: You, perhaps, as it happened, but I envy you not; and, were I to appear again on the stage of life, I would not exchange my *sensibility* for your *philosophy*—God give me feeling, tho' it sting me to the heart!

ANONYMOUS

From *The Adulteress* (1773)

The Adulteress, an anonymous imitation of Juvenal's Sixth Satire published in London in 1773, asserts the depravity of the times in conventional Juvenalian terms. Of particular historical interest in the stanza excerpted below is the use of the word *tommy* as a slang term for lesbian or tribade. *Tommy* can be compared with *molly*—used in England from the 1720s on to refer to an effeminate man or male homosexual. In a scurrilous antilesbian pamphlet from 1781, *A Sapphick Epistle, from Jack Cavendish to the Honourable and most beautiful Mrs. D----* (c. 1781)—an attack on the sculptor and womanizer Mrs. Anne Seymour Damer, the cousin of Horace Walpole—the poet Sappho is described as "the first Tommy the world has upon record." A variant of *tommy* survives in early-twentieth-century British slang: in her 1977 biography of the novelist Elizabeth Bowen, Victoria Glendinning reports that "once, staying in Kerry with Norah Preece, [Bowen] heard the young girls of the house announce that they were having such trouble with their boyfriends that they had decided to be 'toms.' Elizabeth and Eddy Sackville-West told them that on no account must they be toms: 'Always,' said Elizabeth, 'having terrible rows about bracelets.'"

FURTHER READING: *The Adulteress* (London, 1773); Randolph Trumbach, "London's Sapphists: From Three Sexes to Four Genders in the Making of Modern Culture," in Julia Epstein and Kristina Straub, eds., *Body Guards: The Cultural Politics of Gender Ambiguity* (New York: Routledge, 1991), pp. 112–41; Rictor Norton, *Mother Clap's Molly House: The Gay Subculture in England, 1700–1830* (London: Gay Men's, 1992); Emma Donoghue, *Passions Between Women: British Lesbian Culture 1668–1801* (London: Scarlet Press, 1993); Andrew Elfenbein, *Romantic Genius: The Prehistory of a Homosexual Role* (New York: Columbia University Press, 1999).

Women and Men, in these unnat'ral Times,
Are guilty equal of unnat'ral crimes:

Women with Women act the Manly Part,
And kiss and press each other to the heart.
Unnat'ral crimes like these my Satire vex;
I know a thousand *Tommies* 'mongst the Sex:
And if they don't relinquish such a Crime,
I'll give their Names to be the scoff of Time.

GIACOMO CASANOVA (1725–1798)

From *A History of My Life* (1789–98)

Giacomo Casanova, the Italian adventurer whose compulsive sexual exploits have made his name a synonym for rakishness, was born in Venice to an actor father and actress mother. Raised to be a priest, he was expelled in his teens from the seminary of St. Cyprian for immoral behavior. He then gambled his way through various European countries, living off his wits, charm, and effrontery. In 1755 he was arrested in Venice for practicing magic and imprisoned for a year. His extraordinary escape from the prison known as the Piombi, or the Leads, is described in his *Histoire de ma fuite* (1788). He later lived in Paris, where he organized the national lottery, and Holland, where he received the title of Chevalier de Seingault. Near the end of his life he retired to Dux in Bohemia, where he became librarian to Count Waldstein and wrote (in French) twelve volumes of memoirs celebrating his various achievements, mercenary and venereal. He died at seventy-three, while carrying on an amorous correspondence with a young woman, Cecilie von Roggendorf.

Casanova's memoirs (1789–98) contain a number of titillating lesbian scenes. (Throughout his erotic career, he particularly enjoyed bedding two women simultaneously.) In the following section from volume 12 Casanova describes a curious evening with the "inseparable companions" Armellina and Scholastica, two nuns who have escaped from a convent. After dressing them in male garments and taking them with him to a masked ball, Casanova—who desires Armellina but fears she is in love with a "Florentine"—seduces her, with Scholastica's somewhat bizarre assistance. Here and elsewhere in the memoirs Casanova seems much influenced by pornographic visual art, and especially the so-called Aretinian or spintrian postures—scenes of multiple copulation—popular in eighteenth-century obscene engravings. Erotic illustrations of one man/two women threesomes can be found in Borel and Elluin's 1785 edition of the anonymous *Thérèse Philosophe* (1747), various late-eighteenth-century editions of Sade's *Juliette* (1792), and certain scurrilous underground pamphlets, such as *La Vie privée de Marie-Antoinette* (c. 1780), in which the French queen Marie Antoinette was accused by Jacobin detractors of having homosexual relations with several female members of her court. Casanova's own memoirs were illustrated—lasciviously—by Chauvet at the end of the century.

FURTHER READING: Giacomo Casanova de Seingalt, *Histoire de ma vie*, 12 vols. in 6 (Wiesbaden and Paris: F. A. Brockhaus and Librairie Plon, 1960–62); —, *History of My Life*, trans. Willard R. Trask, 12 vols. (New York: Harcourt, Brace and World, 1966); François Roustang, *Le Bal masqué de Giacomo Casanova* (Paris: Minuit, 1984); Chantal Thomas, *Casanova: Un voyage libertin* (Paris: P. Denoël, 1985); Peter Wagner, *Eros Revived: Erotica of the Enlightenment in England and America* (London: Secker and Warburg, 1988); Lynn Hunt, "The Many Bodies of Marie Antoinette," in Hunt, ed., *Eroticism and the Body Politic* (Baltimore: Johns Hopkins University Press, 1991), pp. 108–30; —, ed., *The Invention of Pornography: Obscenity and the Origins of Modernity, 1500–1800* (New York: Zone, 1993); Lydia Flem, *Casanova: The Man Who Really Loved Women*, trans. Catherine Temerson (New York: Farrar, Straus and Giroux, 1997); Terry Castle, *Boss Ladies, Watch Out! Essays on Women, Sex, and Writing* (New York: Routledge, 2002).

[*Casanova, in love with the beautiful Armellina, takes Armellina and her fellow nun scholastica to a carnival booth.*]

[. . .] the next day Armellina came to the grating with the Superioress and a new girl, perhaps three or four years older than she, who was very pretty; but she interested me only a little; still in love with Armellina, and hoping to conquer her completely, I could only be indifferent to any other object. The Superioress told me that the girl, whose name was Scholastica, would thenceforth be Armellina's inseparable companion, and that she was sure she would win my esteem, for she was as good as Emilia; but that in return I must do what I could to forward her in her inclination for a young man who had lucrative employment and who would be ready to marry her if he had the three hundred scudi he needed in order to do so. He was the son of a third cousin of Scholastica's; she called him her nephew, though he was older than she; the stipend could easily be bought; but to obtain it for nothing I should have to find someone who would ask the Holy Father for it. I promised her I would speak on his behalf.

The Carnival was nearing its end, and Scholastica had never seen either an opera or a play. Armellina wanted to see a ball, and I had finally found one at which I thought I could be certain that no one would recognize us; but since being recognized could have consequences, it was necessary to take precautions; I asked them if they were willing to dress as men, which I would arrange for them, and they eagerly consented. I had a box at the Teatro Aliberti for the day after the ball, so I told them to ask the Superioress for permission, and to expect me toward dusk, when I would come to fetch them as usual in one of the Santa Croces' carriages. Though disheartened by Armellina's resistance and by the presence of her new companion, who I thought was neither a girl to be hurried into anything nor one to be left to stare at the wall, I nevertheless had everything we needed to dress the two girls as men taken to the inn to which we always went.

Getting into the carriage, Armellina told me the bad news that Scholastica knew nothing about our relation and that we must not permit ourselves the slightest liberty in her presence. I did not have time to answer her. The other girl got in, and we went to the inn, where we had no sooner entered the room in which there was a good fire than I said in a tone which betrayed ill-humor that if they insisted upon being perfectly free I would go into the other room, though it was cold there. So saying, I showed them the men's clothing. Armellina replied that it would be enough if I would turn my back, adding:

"Isn't that so, Scholastica!"

"I'll do as you do; but I'm very sorry, for I'm sure I'm in your way. You love each other, and it's perfectly clear: I prevent you from giving each other tokens of it. I am not a child. I am your friend, but you do not treat me like a friend."

At this discourse, which proceeded from common sense, but which required a good deal of intelligence to be so well expressed, I breathed again.

"You are right, beautiful Scholastica," I said, "I love Armellina and she is looking for an excuse not to give me tokens of it, for she does not love me."

So saying, I left the room and shut the door. I fell to making a fire. A quarter of an hour later Armellina knocked and asked me to open the door. She was wearing breeches. She said that they absolutely needed me because, the shoes being too small, they could not get them on. I sulked, so she threw herself on my neck, and she had no difficulty in soothing me; I was justifying myself to her, at the same time covering everything I could see with kisses, when Scholastica broke in on us, giving a great laugh.

"I was sure," she said, "that I was in your way; but if you do not trust me completely I warn you that I shall not have the pleasure of going to the opera with you tomorrow."

"Very well," said Armellina, "embrace my friend too."

"Here I am."

I was displeased by such generosity on Armellina's part; but that did not keep me from giving Scholastica the kisses which she deserved, and which I would have given her even if she had been ugly, for so much such kind consideration was not to be scorned. I even gave her amorous kisses, intending to punish Armellina; but I was deceived. I saw that she was delighted, she kissed her friend fondly, as if to thank her for her readiness to help, and at that I went to the other room with them to see what was the matter. I made them sit down, and I saw there was nothing for it but to send out for shoes for them; I sent the waiter on the errand, with orders to come back with a shoemaker who would bring all the shoes he had in his shop. While we waited for the shoemaker, love imperiously commanded me not to confine myself to kisses with Armellina. She did not dare to refuse either me or herself; but as if in exculpation, she insisted that I give Scholastica the same caresses I had given her, and Scholastica, to make her easy, eagerly accepted anything I could have demanded of her if I had been in love with her. The girl was charming, she fell short of Armellina only in sweetness and a delicacy of features which was Armellina's alone. The toying, all in all, was not displeasing to me, but my reflections filled me with bitterness. What I saw made me certain that Armellina did not love me, and that if Scholastica made me no resistance it was only to put her friend at ease and to convince her that she could trust her completely. I saw that, before the shoemaker arrived, I must by hook or crook make myself desire Scholastica. I at once became curious to see if Armellina would not change her attitude when I showed that I was really in love with her friend, and if the latter would continue to grant me what could not but seem to her too much, for until then my hands had never gone beyond the boundaries which the belt of her breeches opposed to their reach.

The shoemaker arrived, and in a few minutes they had shoes which fitted them perfectly. After that I helped them on with their coats, and I saw two very pretty girls dressed as elegant young men and such as to make anyone who saw them with me envy my good fortune. After I ordered that supper should be ready at midnight, we went downstairs and on to the house which was to be the scene of the ball and where it was a safe bet that I would not be recognized, for the fiddler whom I had paid for the three tickets had assured me that the company consisted entirely of shopkeepers.

[*Following the ball, Casanova broods over the favor Armellina has shown to a young Florentine whom she wishes to marry. he is cheered, however, by Scholastica's helpful ministrations, and the three of them (who have again retired to an inn) are united in love.*]

The night being very dark, as it was bound to be at the end of the Carnival, I left the house with the two girls, sure that I should not be followed and going to find the carriage where I knew it would be. Escaping from a hell in which I had suffered like one of the damned for four hours, I arrived at the inn without saying a word to either girl, and not answering the reasonable questions which the too natural Armellina put to me. Scholastica avenged me by reproaching her for having obliged me to appear either rude or jealous or ready to break my word.

When we were in our room Armellina all at once changed my jealous rage to pity; I saw her beautiful eyes showing unmistakable signs of the tears which the truths Scholastica had told her had made her shed in the carriage. Supper being already served, they had time only to take off their shoes. I was sad, and I had reason to be so, but Armellina's sadness distressed me; it was a barrier; I had to dissipate it, though the source of it could not but drive me to despair, for I could find it nowhere but in the liking she had taken to the Florentine. Our supper was exquisite, Scholastica did it justice, but for once Armellina ate scarcely anything. Scholastica gave rein to a natural gaiety, she kissed her friend, she begged her to share in her happiness, for, her lover having become my friend, she was sure that I would use my influence for him and for her, just as I had done for Emilia. She blessed the ball and the chance which had brought him there. She proved to Armellina that she had no reason to be sad, since she was sure that I loved her alone.

But Scholastica was mistaken; and Armellina did not dare to enlighten her friend by telling her the real cause of her sadness. On my side, self-esteem prevented me from telling her, for I knew that I was in the wrong. Armellina was thinking of marriage, I was not the sort of man for her, and the handsome Florentine was. Our supper ended without Armellina's having been able to recover her good humor. She drank only one glass of punch, and, since she had eaten very little, I did not urge her to drink more, for fear it would make her ill. Scholastica, on the contrary, who was tasting the delicious beverage for the first time, helped herself to it freely and thought it amusing that instead of going into her stomach it had risen to her head. In this state of gaiety she thought it was her duty to make perfect peace between us and to assure us that she would be no hindrance even if she were present at all the proofs of love which we could give each other.

She rose from the table and, controlling her legs with difficulty, she carried her friend to the sofa, pressing her to her bosom and giving her countless kisses, which made Armellina laugh despite her sadness. She called me, she made me sit down beside her, and put her into my arms. I gave her amorous caresses, which Armellina did not refuse but to which she did not accord the return which Scholastica hoped to see and for which I did not hope, for she would never have granted me in Scholastica's presence what she had not granted me during the three hours I had had her in my arms while Emilia was sound asleep. Scholastica, who did not want to fail in her mediation, put the blame on me: she reproached me with a coldness which I was far from feeling. I told them to take off their disguises and put their dresses on again. So saying, I helped Scholastica to take off her coat and her vest, whereupon Armellina did the same. I offered them their shifts, and at that Armellina told me to go and stand by the fire; but two minutes later the sound of kisses made me curious. Scholastica, more than gay from the punch, was covering Armellina's bosom with kisses, while Armellina, at last become cheerful, did as much to her ardent friend in my presence. The sight so worked upon Scholastica that she did not object to my doing justice to the beauty of her bosom and becoming a babe at the breast. At that Armellina felt ashamed to be less generous to me than her friend, and Scholastica triumphed when she saw for the first time the use to which I put Armellina's hands, whereupon, fearing for her good repute, Armellina demanded that Scholastica serve me in the same way. She did everything, and her astonishment, for though the girl was twenty years of age she knew nothing about such matters, delighted me.

After the explosion I put on their shifts and with the utmost decency took off their breeches. They went to the water closet with their arms around each other, and when they came back they sat on my lap. Scholastica, far from being annoyed at the preference I at once showed for the secret beauties of Armellina, seemed to be fascinated; she watched my maneuvers, and the way in which Armellina lent herself to my undertaking, with the greatest attention, hoping to see the thing which I should have been very glad to show her, but which Armellina would not grant me. Unable to conclude where I wanted to, I called a halt, remembering that I had duties to Scholastica, whose beauties, which were hidden under a long shift, I also wanted to bare for my eyes. Armellina's obliging friend offered me no resistance. She was too sure that she would leave the question unanswered. It was too hard to decide which of the two was the more beautiful; but Armellina had the advantage of being loved, Scholastica's advantage was the beauty of her face. My hand felt that she was as untouched as Armellina, and from the way in which she held herself I clearly saw that she left me the lord of everything; but I hesitated to take advantage of the moment. It was too fine a triumph to owe it to intoxication. However, I ended by doing everything which a skilled practitioner can do to give all the pleasure possible to the charming object whom he deprives of the final pleasure. Scholastica succumbed, voluptuously overcome, and convinced that I had only failed to fulfill her desires from respect and delicacy.

Armellina, all smiles, ingenuously congratulated us both. I felt ashamed. Scholastica begged her pardon. I took them back to their convent, assuring them that I would call for them the next day to take them to the opera, and I went home to bed, unable to decide whether I had won or lost in the game I had played. It was not until I woke the next morning that I was able to decide the question.

MARQUIS DE SADE (1740–1814)

From *Juliette* (1792)

Donatien Alphonse François, Comte de Sade, commonly known as the Marquis de Sade, was born in Paris into an aristocratic family. After serving in the Seven Years War (1756–63) he married a French noblewoman, Renée Pélagie Cordier de Launay de Montreuil, whom he proceeded to torment with his debaucheries. In 1772 he was condemned to death for poisoning and sodomizing a young woman on his estate and fled to Italy. Upon returning in 1777, he was arrested and incarcerated at Vincennes (1778–84) and the Bastille (1784–89), from which he was temporarily liberated during the Revolution. After a brief period of freedom, he was installed in the insane asylum at Charenton and remained there off and on for the rest of his life. All together he spent twenty-seven years in prison for various offences. He used these enforced periods of leisure to write the blasphemous pornographic novels for which he is now fêted and reviled: *Les 120 journées de Sodome* (1785), *Justine, ou les malheurs de la vertu* (1791), *Juliette, ou les prosperités du vice* (1792), *La Philosophie dans la boudoir* (1795), and *La Nouvelle Justine* (1797). He died in 1814, having repented of none of his sins.

Female homosexual acts—along with just about everything else—feature prominently in Sade's alternately fascinating and repellent imaginative world. In the massive, ten-volume *Juliette*, the story of an indefatigable female libertine who takes pleasure in molesting and torturing young girls, lesbianism plays a central and often disgusting part. In the scene below, Juliette has just killed and sodomized her female lover-accomplice Clairwil, and taken up with a new lover, the equally vicious Durand. The image of Durand's grossly distended clitoris harks back to Renaissance descriptions—in Ambroise Paré's *Des Monstres et prodiges* (1573) and elsewhere—of genital malformations associated with hermaphrodites and other sexual "monsters."

FURTHER READING: Marquis de Sade, *La Nouvelle Justine, ou les Malheurs de la vertu, suivie de l'Histoire de Juliette, sa soeur [ou les prosperités du vice]*, 4 vols. (Paris, 1797); —, *Juliette*, trans. Austryn Wainhouse (New York: Grove Weidenfeld, 1968); Angela Carter, *The Sadeian Woman and the Ideology of Pornography* (New York: Pantheon, 1978); Janet Todd, *Women's Friendship in Literature* (New York: Columbia University

Press, 1980); Jane Gallop, *Intersections: A Reading of Sade with Bataille, Blanchot, and Klossowski* (Lincoln: University of Nebraska Press, 1981); Donald Thomas, *The Marquis de Sade* (London: Allison and Busby, 1992); Maurice Lever, *Sade: A Biography*, trans. Arthur Goldhammer (New York: Farrar, Straus and Giroux, 1993); Kathryn Norberg, "The Libertine Whore: Prostitution in French Pornography from Margot to Juliette," in Lynn Hunt, ed., *The Invention of Pornography: Obscenity and the Origins of Modernity, 1500–1800* (New York: Zone, 1993), pp. 225–52.

"No further separation between us ever again," said I to Durand, "leave your inn, come join me in mine; you will take Clairwil's domestics, her carriage, and we shall set off for Paris in two or three days."

The new arrangements were quickly completed; Durand retained but one of her chambermaids, to whom she was especially attached, dismissed all the rest of her household, and came to install herself in what had formerly been Clairwil's quarters.

It was easy to see, from the way that woman devoured me with her eyes, that she was on tenterhooks for the moment when my favors would reward her for her efforts in my behalf. I did not allow her to pine away for long; after the most sumptuous and elegant repast, I stretch forth my arms to her, she leaps into them, we dash to my bedchamber, lock the door, draw the shutters, and I surrender, with inexpressible delight, to the most libertine and the most lustful of women. Durand, in her fiftieth year, was not by any means devoid of merit; her forms were full, shapely, and well preserved; her mouth fresh, her skin soft and showing scarcely a wrinkle; a superb posterior, breasts still firm and very fair, very lively eyes, very fine features; and an energy in her pleasure-taking, tastes so bizarre. [. . .] Capricious Nature had created her with a deformity neither Clairwil nor I had ever noticed: Durand was unable, had never been able, to enjoy pleasure in the conventional manner. Her vagina was obstructed, but (and you will doubtless recall this detail) her clitoris, as long as a finger, gave her the most ardent liking for women. She would flog them, she would embugger them; she held commerce with boys also: I shortly discovered, from the inordinate size of her asshole, that, as regarded intromissions, she was wont to receive there what she was denied elsewhere. The initial advances were made by me, and I thought she was going to swoon from pleasure the moment she felt my hands upon her flesh.

"Let's undress," said she, "one cannot enjoy oneself properly save when naked. I have, moreover, the keenest desire to look again upon your charms, Juliette, I burn to feast upon them."

Everything is removed in a trice. My kisses explore that beautiful body; and I am bound to say that perhaps, had Durand been younger, yes, I might not have found her anything like so interesting. My tastes were beginning to turn to depravation, and entering into my riper years, Nature was providing me with sensations far more intense than anything I had known in my springtime. The unique object of that woman's fiery caresses, great tides of lust boiled up in me; my partner deployed a science and an art that are positively not to be described. Oh, how voluptuous are women seasoned in crime! what dimensions are revealed in their lubricities!

You listless and uninspired prudes, insufferable creatures who dare not even touch the member perforating you, and who would blush to answer fuck with fuck when fucking, cast your eyes this way, come hither for some examples: come take a few lessons from Madame Durand, and learn the extent of your ineptitudes.

After the initial caresses, Durand, less inhibited than when in the past Clairwil had been a party to our affairs, made declaration of her fancies and besought me to submit to them. As she knelt before me, I had, while heaping abuse upon her, to rub her nose now in my cunt, now in my ass; while rubbing my front against her, I had to piss upon her face. That done, I had to strike her all about the body with my fists and kick her everywhere, take up some nettles and flog her till she bled. When by dint of mistreatments I had beaten her down to the floor, I had, with my head between her thighs, to cunt-suck her for fifteen minutes while socratizing her with one hand and exciting her nipples with the other; next, once she was thoroughly heated, I was to let her embugger me with her clitoris the while she tickled mine.

"I apologize for having to ask so much, Juliette," the libertine said, once she had finished outlining the program, "but you know to what satiety can lead us."

"After thirty-five years of sustained libertinage one must offer no excuses for one's tastes," was my reply; "whatever it may be, it is deserving of respect, for it is in Nature; the best of all is the one that pleases us most."

And starting in upon the operation, so amply did I satisfy her that she was nigh to perishing from delight. Durand's voluptuous crises were without parallel. In all my life I had never seen a woman discharge thus: not only would she shoot her fuck forth like a man, but she accompanied that ejaculation by shrieks so loud, by blasphemies so energetic, and by spasms so violent that one could have mistaken her performance for an epileptic attack. I was buggered as solidly as if I had been dealing with a man, and from it experienced the same pleasure.

"Well," said she when she rose to her feet, "how do I strike you?"

"Oh, fuck!" I cried, "you are delightful, you are a very model of lubricity; your passions set me ablaze, do to me everything I have just done to you."

"What! You wish a beating?"

"Beat me, yes."

"And a slapping, a whipping?"

"Make haste."

"Do you want me to piss upon your face?"

"Of course, my darling, be quick, I say, for I'm very hot and I have a discharge pressing."

La Durand, with a longer experience than I in the rendering of these services, proceeds with such consummate skill that the explosion supervenes almost instantaneously, thanks to the heavenly titillations of her voluptuous tongue.

"How you do discharge, my beloved," she said to me; "how vehemently you respond to pleasure! How marvelously we get on!"

"There is no denying it, Durand," I answered her, "you have an astonishing effect upon my imagination: I am overjoyed to be connected with a woman like you. Mistresses of all a universe we shall be; through our alliance I feel we shall become the superiors of Nature herself. Oh, dear Durand, the crimes we are going to commit! the infamies we are going to achieve!"

"THE LADIES OF LLANGOLLEN" [ELEANOR BUTLER (1739–1829) AND SARAH PONSONBY (1755–1831)]

From the journals of Eleanor Butler (1784–1821)

Eleanor Butler (1739–1829) and Sarah Ponsonby (1755–1831), described by a contemporary as "the two most celebrated virgins in Europe," have come to epitomize, however ambiguously, the phenomenon of romantic love between women. Both were members of prominent Anglo-Irish families: Eleanor Butler, daughter of the Earl of Ormonde, was born at the family seat in County Kilkenny; Sarah Ponsonby, an orphan and ward of Sir William and Lady Elizabeth Fownes, grew up in the neighboring village of Woodstock. In May 1778 they astonished their families by eloping together to Wales, where they settled at Plas Newydd in the Vale of Llangollen. For the next fifty years they lived there in a little cottage—genteelly refurbished in the fashionable Gothic style and surrounded by a garden with grottoes and waterfalls—in seemingly blissful rustic retirement. Despite their wish for obscurity, the story of their flight and mutual devotion to one another became legendary, and famous visitors flocked to see them: the poets Wordsworth and Southey, the Duke of Wellington, Josiah Wedgwood, Sir Walter Scott, Anna Seward, Lady Caroline Lamb, and Sir Humphry Davy, among others.

Though Eleanor Butler refers in her journals to sharing a bed with her "Beloved," the exact nature of their relationship is unclear. A number of contemporaries (including the lesbian diarist Anne Lister) thought the "Ladies of Llangollen" might be lovers; the *General Evening Post* published a somewhat prurient account of their "sweet retreat" in 1790. But other commentators have challenged the homosexual designation. Colette, writing about them in *Ces Plaisirs* (*The Pure and the Impure*) in 1932, saw them simply as "two faithful spinsters," untouched by any form of "Sapphic libertinage"— a view most modern biographers have shared. Whatever the facts, their life together continues to inspire lesbian fantasy: the American writer Doris Grumbach published a novel based on Ponsonby and Butler's story in 1984. More risibly, the Japanese lesbian performance art duo, Frank Chickens, recorded a wonderfully absurd song about them—called "Two Little Ladies"—in 1990.

Eleanor Butler's journals—whole or partial daybooks exist for 1784, 1785, 1788–91, 1799, 1802, 1806, 1807, 1819, and 1821—were first collected and published in *The Hamwood Papers of the Ladies of Llangollen and Caroline Hamilton* in 1930. Minute to the point of surrealism, and filled with odd, often Wordsworthian moments of pastoral strangeness and communion, they bear a sublimated yet eloquent witness to two women's lifelong obsession with one another.

FURTHER READING: G. H. Bell, ed., *The Hamwood Papers of the Ladies of Llangollen and Caroline Hamilton* (London: Macmillan, 1930); Colette, *The Pure and the Impure*, trans. Herma Briffault (New York, Farrar, Straus and Giroux, 1966); Elizabeth Mavor, *The Ladies of Llangollen* (Harmondsworth, Middlesex: Penguin, 1973); Lillian Faderman, *Surpassing the Love of Men: Romantic Friendship and Love between Women from the Renaissance to the Present* (New York: William Morrow, 1981); Terry Castle, *The Apparitional Lesbian: Female Homosexuality and Modern Culture* (New York: Columbia University Press, 1993); Ruth Vanita, *Sappho and the Virgin Mary: Same-Sex Love and the English Literary Imagination* (New York: Columbia University Press, 1996).

Saturday, March 29th 1788.—Celestial lovely day. Reading, drawing. Saw a white lamb in the Clerk's hanging Field. The Parlour getting a general scouring, sweeping and cleaning. My Beloved and I went the Home Circuit. Walked round our empty garden many times, liked it infinitely better empty than occupied by that Drunken idle Richard. Sweetest lovely day, close, nay even sultry. Lambs bleating, Birds singing, everything that constitutes the Beauty of solitude and retirement. [. . .] The Irishwoman whom we sent to Wrexham returned. Soft fine rain. Began Les Mémoires de Madame de Maintenon. I doubt whether the Vulgarity of stile, absurd anecdotes, and impertinent reflections will permit me to read it.

Thursday, April 24th.—Soft grave still day. Letter from Miss H. Bowdler, Mr. Wilbraham, Mr. Whitley of Chester. [. . .] Mr. Williams of Ruthin desired to see this cottage and garden. Permitted, though we grumbled not a little. [. . .] My beloved and I went to the shrubbery. While we were thus employed heard loud and repeated lamentations from the Sheep and lambs who were grazing in the little verdant meadow by the Cyflymen. Ran to the pales to see what was the occasion of this plaintive bleating. Saw the entire flock ranged by the brookside, apparently in the greatest distress. At length observed one sheep hanging from the hedge on the other side of the stream just strangling, as the Briar with which it was entangled was got about its neck. Sent instantly and had it released just in time. The moment it was freed all the cries of its companions were appeased. They gazed kindly at it and returned cheerfully to their simple repast. A single lamb attempted to wade over to it, but the tender parent prevented its fond impatience by her own, and rushing thro' the water meekly stood while he plentifully sucked her.

Friday, April 25th.—Reading. Writing. My Beloved and I went the home circuit. A mole caught in the new trap. A Boy in the field with three fine young Thrushes which he took from the nest on Pentrefelin, a piteous sight.

Monday, April 28th.——Rose at six; delicious dewy morning, bright sun, blue sky. From Wrexham new spade. Parcel from Appleyard containing one quire super royal paper for mounting drawings, hundred quill Pens. Parcel for me from B. Denis de la part de St. Stanislas, 'Lettre sur la Mort de Madame Louise Marie de France.' [. . .] Nine Breakfast. Letter from Mrs. Tighe dated Harrow the 25th. Half-past nine till three beauteous day. Wrote to Mrs. Kavanagh, Ballyheil, Thomestown, Ireland. [. . .] My Beloved and I went to the garden, sowed the tender annuals in their hot bed. The Irish-woman whom we sent to Chirk gardens at 7 this morning with a letter to Lever returned with three pots of cucumber plants. Planted them. Sowed three sorts of cucumber seeds. Reading. Drawing. Oiled the Parlour eating table with the Spinham-land receipt. Dined in the kitchen to let the oil soak in it. Shut the shutters of the kitchen window and dined very comfortably on lamb and cold mutton. [. . .] Delicious heav-enly evening. A present from Knight (our late Butcher's Brother) who lives in Corn-wall of the spars and minerals in that county. [. . .] My Beloved and I walked round Edward Evans' meadow, then up the Mill lane, turned into the meadow which slopes from the Blaen Bache hill and hangs over the Mill stream. John Edwards, and his little Son with him, repairing the hawthorn hedge. He moved the Stone from the gate. Walked round the field, returned home by the lane. Found Margaret at the gate waiting for admittance. Opened it for her. Walked round our little demesne. [. . .] In our walk met a little boy, asked him where he was running. To rob a nest which he had observed in the morning. Scolded him and forbad him to molest the birds.

Sunday, May 11th.—— [. . .] As we were returning from the Shrubbery met old Parker, who came with compliments from Mr. and Mrs. Cooper desiring permission to see the cottage and shrubbery. Our compliments. They shall be welcome. We retired to the State Bedchamber till they were come and gone. Observed them from the window. He a tall man (a Clergyman), she a little woman in deep mourning. They left their Compliments and thanks. Said Lady Anne Talbot was very well and with her children would soon be here. [. . .] My Beloved and I walked in Edward Evans' cornfield and meadow. Then before our Cottage. All the pretty neat Peasants in their best apparel returning to their mountains from the Village. The elders soberly conversing returning from the Methodist Chapel.

Monday, May 26th.——My beloved and I went to the sweet hanging meadows over the Mill; what a pretty simple scene did we behold. Between the branching oaks just over the Wheel the Bridge of one arch; the young Miller, his wife and children, sitting on the battlement. An ancient man resting on his crutch, his wallet and faithful dog lying at his feet. Beyond Edward Evans' farm yard; his cows all standing to be milked. The Team led home by his youngest son. Himself bringing out sheaves of straw from the barn. Lovely still night, all the Thunder clouds gone.

Saturday, May 31st.——Compliments from Lord Kenmare on his way to Chel-tenham. Letters for Post written last night and this morning——To Mrs. Tighe, Harrow, Middlesex, Mrs. Goddard, Charles St. Bath, Mrs. Tucker, Nicholas St. Chester. Fair in the Village previous to the Wakes which begin to-morrow. Millions of Country girls and swains hastening down the sides of the mountains to make preparations for the approaching festivity. Letter from Mrs. Keatinge (formerly Miss Bagenal) desiring permission to introduce herself to our acquaintance. She is my relation, but I never saw her. [. . .] We thought it but proper to go down to the Hand to invite her here. We went [. . .] and found Mrs. Keatinge in the Great Parlour of the Hand, writing. A beautiful Tame Fox in one corner of the room. She sent for her daughter who was in her room. She came directly. Very tall fair girl about fifteen years old, very pale and delicate. A beautiful little girl of about five years of age, natural daughter to her Brother Mr. Bagenal. She ordered her servant to bring in her Dogs; three Beautiful harlequins, and a noble newfoundland dog. Then the cat was led in on a Collar. They all came from the Stables where we went also to see her charming Merlins and a magnificent horse which Mrs. Keatinge always rides.

Tuesday, June 3rd.—The Taxgatherer came—paid him. At two retired to Powder and dress our hair, dined at half-past two, at three the Hand Chaise came. My beloved and I went to Hardwick thro' Chirk and Whittington to Halston. Lovely evening. The road new to us after Halston, fine verdure, large enclosures, well planted, cattle grazing, clumps of fine oak. [. . .] Arrived at 5. Mr. Kynaston met us at the hall door. In the Hall we found Mrs. Kynaston, our Barretts, Miss Davies, the three Miss Pigotts of Undervale, Miss Vaughan of Oteley Park, Miss Charlotte Istoyede, Miss Webb, a little Pigott girl, Dr. Boyd, Mr. Blakeway of Shrewsbury. We went to the drawing-room, sat there some time, then went to the Dairy. *Mem.*—I like the Oval Table with the leaden cistern for cream, a plug in the middle by means of which the milk is drawn from the cream. Drank Tea in the Cottage. Miss Webb spoke two Prologues; a scene between Alicia and Jane Shore, the first scene in Lady Randolph, I mean Douglas. Most divinely she looked and spoke, and I pronounce that for beauty and manner I seldom beheld her equal. Tea over we walked round the entire domain, one mile and a half, beautifully wooded. Some good views. In particular one into the Vale of Llangollen, a sweet morning scene. View of Brydon, another of Wrexham Steeple. Saw the cold bath and Mrs. Kynaston's dressing-room. At nine we all dispersed, returned to our several abodes. Miss Vaughan to Oteley Park, the Venerable seat of the Kynastons. Our Barretts to their handsome mansion in Oswestry, and we to our quiet and delicious Cottage. What a night! And what a Country! The Lime Kilns blazing like so many volcanoes, glow worms on the Mountains.

Saturday, June 14th.—Compliments from Mr. and Mrs. Pope and Miss Saville desiring to see the Cottage and Shrubbery. They came. Saw from the State bedchamber window whither we retired till they were gone. Mr. Pope tall gentlemanly handsome man, Mrs. Pope in a green Capotte, Miss Saville scarlet habit. A beautiful large brown and white spaniel which they politely carried in their arms. They expressed the highest admiration of the place.

Beautiful evening. Went to the Shrubbery. Then sat in our delicious seat over the Cyflymen. [. . .] What a scene! On the side of the mountain immediately opposite our hall door a crowd of people, clustered like a swarm of Bees, were seated to behold a

Stage play. The Stage erected under a clump of trees on the edge of the Precipice. A party of recruiting Soldiers, with drums beating and fifes playing, marching up the undulating path of the mountain to join them. Herds of Cattle grazing above their heads and spread over the pasture beneath them. The Shouts of the happy multitude, echo of the drums and fifes, singing of birds. [. . .] I returned to the Shrubbery. My beloved was returning to me when a pretty young woman accosted her and, presenting a neat Basket full of eggs, said: 'They were sent by poor Mary Green who daily prays for you and your companion.' [. . .] Reading. Writing. A lad, quite breathless to let us know our Cow, our Margaret, had just calved in the fields of the Cilmedw. What an event! Sent to desire Mr. Edwards of the Hand would dispatch some careful people to bring her and her calf thence. Sent to the old Man of Bala to know what we should give her. Had her Stable prepared for her, the Turkey Hen and her eleven chickens moved to the loft. About half-past eight Margaret arrived and her Great Son. Put them in the Stable, gave her a drench of warm ale, butter and sugar. Milked her, then at eleven gave her a mash. Delicious night, sun set in flames of crimson and gold. Moon rose calmly and cast her silver light on our Cottage and Shrubbery.

Friday, June 19th.——The evening being Beautiful we walked to the Abbey. We were accompanied by the divinest Rainbow till we had passed the Green, when it began to rain. We took shelter in the farmhouse of Pendile. Found in the Kitchen a Beautiful young woman rocking a Cradle. She appeared so young we could scarcely credit her being the Infant's mother, but the Ring on her finger convinced us of it. In an adjoining house a little woman was winding yarn, two pretty girls standing beside her. We made her Sing. She sang two Welch Songs, rested on her wheel, with such an expressive countenance accompanying the plaintive song she sang.

Saturday, June 27th.——Walked to the white gate, met a country woman going to market. Asked her if she came from Glynn. No——'From the Pengwern hill where the Moon rose last night.'

Tuesday, July 14th.——Sky white. Millions of Rooks on the mountains of Pengwern, consulting I suppose about the weather. I wish they could communicate their observations, or that I could understand their language. Mrs. Kynaston and Miss Mytton came. Never saw Mrs. Kynaston in greater beauty. Her hair surpasses anything I ever saw in that way.

Friday, January 1st 1790.——My beloved and I woke at seven. Found by our bed side Petticoats and Pockets, a new year's gift from our *truest* Friends.

Thursday, January 14th.——A chorus of Throstles, Blackbirds and finches close beside our window. Mr. Lloydde's Hounds in full cry on the opposite mountain. Mists rising from the river. Smoke from the village spinning through the trees.

ANNA SEWARD (1742–1809)

"Elegy Written at the Sea-side, and Addressed to Miss Honora Sneyd"
and excerpt from *Llangollen Vale, Inscribed to the Right Honourable
Lady Eleanor Butler, and Miss Ponsonby* (1796)

The late-eighteenth-century English poet Anna Seward was the daughter of the clergyman and man of letters Thomas Seward. He encouraged her literary endeavors from
an early age. She began writing poetry in the 1780s and published a novel in verse,
Louisa, in 1784. Her poetic productions were highly regarded in their time: her *Original Sonnets* (1799) was instrumental in bringing the sonnet form back into fashion in
English poetry. Popularly known as the "Swan of Lichfield," in honor of the town in
which she resided for most of her life, she remained an influential and respected literary figure until her death, and was particularly admired for her ministrations on behalf
of younger writers.

Despite several marriage proposals and a peculiar platonic attachment to a Lich-
field choirmaster, Seward never married. Her poems testify to close, emotionally intricate, and often exorbitant feelings for women. (She was a self-confessed "idolater" of
the famous tragic actress Sarah Siddons.) "Elegy Written at the Sea-side, and
Addressed to Miss Honora Sneyd" commemorates a youthful romantic friendship with
Honora Sneyd, a young woman raised in Thomas Seward's household, who later—to
Anna's disgust—married Richard Lovell Edgeworth, father of the novelist Maria
Edgeworth. The euphonious *Llangollen Vale*—an epitome of Seward's style at its most
exalted—is a poetic tribute to the celebrated romantic couple, Eleanor Butler and Sarah
Ponsonby, otherwise known as the "Ladies of Llangollen," who lived together for fifty
years at Plas Newydd in North Wales. Seward visited the Ladies at their rural cottage,
and enamored with their way of life, hoped to set up a similar ménage with Elizabeth
Cornwallis, a young woman with whom she became infatuated in 1803 and dubbed
"Clarissa," after the Richardson heroine. Seward died before this scheme could come
to fruition.

FURTHER READING: Anna Seward, *Llangollen Vale with Other Poems* (London, 1796);
Sir Walter Scott, ed., *Poetical Works of Anna Seward*, 3 vols. (Edinburgh, 1810); Margaret Eliza Ashmun, *The Singing Swan: An Account of Anna Seward and Her Acquaintance with Dr. Johnson, Boswell, and Others of Their Time* (New Haven: Yale University

Press, 1931); Elizabeth Mavor, *The Ladies of Llangollen* (Harmondsworth, Middlesex: Penguin Books, 1973); Lillian Faderman, *Surpassing the Love of Men: Romantic Friendship and Love between Women from the Renaissance to the Present* (New York: William Morrow, 1981); Elizabeth Fay, "Anna Seward, the Swan of Lichfield: Reading *Louisa*," in Stephen C. Behrendt and Harriet Kramer Linkin, eds., *Approaches to Teaching British Women Poets of the Romantic Period* (New York: Modern Language Association of America, 1977), pp. 381–91; Anne K. Mellor, "The Female Poet and the Poetess: Two Traditions of British Women's Poetry, 1780–1830," in Isobel Armstrong and Virginia Blain, eds., *Women's Poetry in the Enlightenment: The Making of a Canon, 1730–1820* (New York: St. Martin's, 1999), pp. 81–98.

Elegy Written at the Sea-side, and Addressed to Miss Honora Sneyd

I write, Honora, on the sparkling sand!—
The envious waves forbid the trace to stay:
Honora's name again adorns the strand!
Again the waters bear their prize away!

So Nature wrote her charms upon thy face,
The cheek's light bloom, the lip's envermeil'd dye,
And every gay, and every witching grace,
That Youth's warm hours, and Beauty's stores supply.

But Time's stern tide, with cold Oblivion's wave,
Shall soon dissolve each fair, each fading charm;
E'en Nature's self, so powerful, cannot save
Her own rich gifts from this o'erwhelming harm.

Love and the Muse can boast superior power,
Indelible the letters they shall frame;
They yield to no inevitable hour,
But will on lasting tablets write thy name.

From *Llangollen Vale, Inscribed to The Right Honourable Lady Eleanor Butler, and Miss Ponsonby*

Now with a Vestal lustre glows the Vale,
 Thine, sacred Friendship, permanent as pure;

In vain the stern Authorities assail,
  In vain Persuasion spreads her silken lure,
High-born, and high-endow'd, the peerless Twain,
Pant for coy Nature's charms 'mid silent dale, and plain.

Thro' Eleanora, and her Zara's mind,
  Early tho' genius, taste, and fancy flow'd,
Tho' all the graceful Arts their powers combin'd,
  And her last polish brilliant Life bestow'd,
The lavish Promiser, in Youth's soft morn,
Pride, Pomp, and Love, her friends, the sweet Enthusiasts scorn.

Then rose the Fairy Palace of the Vale,
  Then bloom'd around it the Arcadian bowers;
Screen'd from the storms of Winter, cold and pale,
  Screen'd from the fervors of the sultry hours,
Circling the lawny crescent, soon they rose,
To letter'd ease devote, and Friendship's blest repose.

Smiling they rose beneath the plastic hand
  Of Energy, and Taste;—nor only they,
Obedient Science hears the mild command,
  Brings every gift that speeds the tardy day,
Whate'er the pencil sheds in vivid hues,
Th' historic tome reveals, or sings the raptur'd Muse.

How sweet to enter, at the twilight grey,
  The dear, minute Lyceum of the Dome,
When, thro' the colour'd crystal, glares the ray,
  Sanguine and solemn 'mid the gathering gloom,
While glow-worm lamps diffuse a pale, green light,
Such as in mossy lanes illume the starless night.

Then the coy Scene, by deep'ning veils o'erdrawn,
  In shadowy elegance seems lovelier still;
Tall shrubs, that skirt the semi-lunar lawn,
  Dark woods, that curtain the opposing hill;
While o'er their brows the bare cliff faintly gleams,
And, from its paly edge, the evening-diamond streams.

What strains Æolian thrill the dusk expanse,
  As rising gales with gentle murmurs play,

Wake the loud chords, or every sense intrance,
  While in subsiding winds they sink away!
Like distant choirs, "when pealing organs blow,"
And melting voices blend, majestically slow.

"But, ah! what hand can touch the strings so fine,
  Who up the lofty diapason roll
Such sweet, such sad, such solemn airs divine,
  Then let them down again into the soul!"
The prouder sex as soon, with virtue calm,
Might win from this bright Pair pure Friendship's spotless palm.

What boasts Tradition, what th' historic Theme,
  Stands it in all their chronicles confest
Where the soul's glory shines with clearer beam,
  Than in our sea-zon'd bulwark of the West,
When, in this Cambrian Valley, Virtue shows
Where, in her own soft sex, its steadiest lustre glows?

Say ivied Valle Crucis, time decay'd,
  Dim on the brink of Deva's wandering floods,
Your riv'd arch glimmering thro' the tangled glade,
  Your grey hills towering o'er your night of woods,
Deep in the Vale's recesses as you stand,
And, desolately great, the rising sigh command,

Say, lonely, ruin'd Pile, when former years
  Saw your pale Train at midnight altars bow;
Saw Superstition frown upon the tears
  That mourn'd the rash irrevocable vow,
Wore one young lip gay Eleanora's smile?
Did Zara's look serene one tedious hour beguile?

For your sad Sons, nor Science wak'd her powers;
  Nor e'er did Art her lively spells display;
But the grim Idol vainly lash'd the hours
  That dragg'd the mute, and melancholy day;
Dropt her dark cowl on each devoted head,
That o'er the breathing Corse a pall eternal spread.

This gentle Pair no glooms of thought infest,
  Nor Bigotry, nor Envy's sullen gleam

Shed withering influence on the effort blest,
  Which most shou'd win the other's dear esteem,
By added knowledge, by endowment high,
By Charity's warm boon, and Pity's soothing sigh.

Then how shou'd Summer-day or Winter-night,
  Seem long to them who thus can wing their hours!
O! ne'er may Pain, or Sorrow's cruel blight,
  Breathe the dark mildew thro' these lovely bowers,
But lengthen'd Life subside in soft decay,
Illum'd by rising Hope, and Faith's pervading ray.

May one kind ice-bolt, from the mortal stores,
  Arrest each vital current as it flows,
That no sad course of desolated hours
  Here vainly nurse the unsubsiding woes!
While all who honor Virtue, gently mourn
Llangollen's vanish'd Pair, and wreath their sacred urn.

MARY MATILDA BETHAM (1776–1852)

"In a Letter to A.R.C., on Her Wishing to be Called Anna," "Invitation—To J.B.C.," and "A Valentine" (1797)

Mary Matilda Betham, poet, biographer, and miniature painter, was educated at home by her father, William Betham, rector of Stoke Lacy in Herefordshire. She demonstrated a talent for literature and painting at an early age and published her first book of poetry, *Elegies and Other Small Poems*, in 1797. In 1804 she produced a *Biographical Dictionary of the Celebrated Women of Every Age and Country*. Soon afterwards she traveled to London, where—according to the *Dictionary of National Biography*—she gave public readings from Shakespeare and exhibited some of her miniature portraits at the Royal Academy. These endeavors brought her modest renown: she subsequently became acquainted with Coleridge and Southey, Anna Laetitia Barbauld, Charles and Mary Lamb, and other important literary figures of the day. Her *Poems* appeared in 1808. Over the next decade she supported herself as a portrait painter—she painted Southey and his family in 1809—while also continuing to write poetry. Her *Lay of Marie*, adapted from the work of the thirteenth-century Anglo-Norman poet, was published in 1816, and *Vignettes in Verse* in 1818. She never married and in later years seems to have suffered from poor health and mental instability. She died in London in 1852.

Betham was a feminist of sorts—she included Mary Wollstonecraft in her dictionary of celebrated women—and addressed a number of poems to close female friends. The three poems below—all from her *Elegies*—are remarkable for their freshness, wit, and lack of pretension. As in Anna Seward's love poems to women, the spirit of romantic friendship rules, but it is here transmuted into something less formal and burdensome, at once mischievous and sweet.

FURTHER READING: Mary Matilda Betham, *Elegies and Other Small Poems* (London, 1797); —, *Poems* (London, 1808); Ernest Burton Betham, *A House of Letters* (London: Jarrold, 1905); J. M. S. Tompkins, *The Polite Marriage* (Cambridge: Cambridge University Press, 1938).

"In a Letter to A.R.C., on Her Wishing to be Called Anna"

Forgive me, if I wound your ear,
  By calling of you Nancy,
Which is the name of my sweet friend,
  The other's but her fancy.

Ah, dearest girl! how could your mind
  The strange distinction frame?
The whimsical, unjust caprice,
  Which robs you of your name.

Nancy agrees with what we see,
  A being wild and airy;
Gay as a nymph of Flora's train,
  Fantastic as a fairy.

But *Anna*'s of a different kind,
  A melancholy maid;
Boasting a sentimental soul,
  In solemn pomp array'd.

Oh ne'er will I forsake the sound,
  So artless and so free!
Be what you will with all mankind.
  But *Nancy* still with me.

Invitation—To J.B.C.

Now spring appears, with beauty crown'd,
And all is light and life around,
Why comes not Jane? When friendship calls,
Why leaves she not Augusta's walls?
Where cooling zephyrs faintly blow,
Nor spread the cheering, healthful glow,
That glides through each awaken'd vein,
As skimming o'er the spacious plain,
We look around with joyous eye,
And view no boundaries but the sky.

Already April's reign is o'er,
Her evening tints delight no more;
No more the violet scents the gale,
No more the mist o'erspreads the vale;
The lovely queen of smiles and tears,
Who gave thee birth, no more appears;
But blushing May, with brow serene,
And vestments of a livelier green,
Commands the winged choir to sing,
And with wild notes the meadows ring.

O come! ere all the train is gone,
No more to hail thy twenty-one;
That age which higher honor shares,
And well becomes the wreath it wears.
From lassitude and cities flee,
And breathe the air of heav'n, with me.

A Valentine

What shall I send my sweet today,
  When all the woods attune in love?
  And I would show the lark and dove,
That I can love as well as they.

I'll send a locket full of hair,—
  But no, for it might chance to lie
  Too near her heart, and I should die
Of love's sweet envy to be there.

A violet is sweet to give,—
  Ah, stay! she'd touch it with her lips,
  And, after such complete eclipse,
How could my soul consent to live?

I'll send a kiss, for that would be
  The quickest sent, the lightest borne,
  And well I know tomorrow morn
She'll send it back again to me.

Go, happy winds; ah, do not stay,
  Enamoured of my lady's cheek,
  But hasten home, and I'll bespeak
Your services another day!

The Nineteenth Century

MARIA EDGEWORTH (1767–1849)

From *Belinda* (1801)

The career of the Anglo-Irish novelist and children's writer, Maria Edgeworth, was deeply bound up with that of her father, Richard Lovell Edgeworth—an Irish landowner and educational writer who brought her up along with her twenty-one siblings. (Her mother died when she was six; her father remarried twice.) Her first works—a translation of Madame de Genlis's *Adelaide et Théodore* (1783); *Letters for Literary Ladies* (1795), a defence of female education; and *The Parent's Assistant* (1795), a book of children's stories—were written under his guidance, and some critics have seen traces of his influence in her fiction as well. She never married and lived on her family's Irish estate all of her adult life, with occasional visits to London and Paris. While social and sexual inequities concerned her, her best-known novels—*Castle Rackrent* (1800), *Belinda* (1801), *Ennui* (1809), *Patronage* (1814), and *Ormond* (1817)—are ultimately traditional and conservative in outlook.

Perhaps because of her lifelong psychological subordination to her father, Edgeworth was peculiarly ambivalent about, while also jealous of, independent or assertive women. In a chapter in *Belinda* entitled "Rights of Woman" she offers a violently satirical portrait of one such woman: the aptly named Mrs. Harriet Freke, a contemporary "Amazon" with sapphic leanings. *La* Freke, whom the orphaned heroine, Belinda, encounters at the home of a wealthy relative, is among other things, a duellist, a transvestite, and a fire-breathing proponent of the views of Mary Wollstonecraft, whose support for the French Revolution and controversial feminist treatise, *Vindication of the Rights of Woman*, had prompted public outcry in Britain in 1792. (Edgeworth is one of the first writers to make a satiric connection between lesbianism and feminism.) Having been rejected by her onetime "great friend," Lady Delacour, Mrs. Freke is shown shamelessly pursuing young women. Edgeworth treats her as a sort of sinister buffoon, resulting in a portrait that is is unquestionably one of the most homophobic in polite eighteenth- or nineteenth-century fiction.

FURTHER READING: Maria Edgeworth, *Belinda* (Oxford and New York: Oxford University Press, 1994); Marilyn Butler, *Maria Edgeworth: A Literary Biography* (Oxford:

Clarendon, 1972); O. Elizabeth McWhorter, *Maria Edgeworth* (Boston: Twayne, 1984); Colin B. Atkinson and Jo Atkinson, "Maria Edgeworth, *Belinda*, and Women's Rights," *Eire-Ireland: A Journal of Irish Studies* 19 (winter 1984): 94–118; Elizabeth Kowaleski-Wallace, *Their Fathers' Daughters: Hannah More, Maria Edgeworth, and Patriarchal Complicity* (New York: Oxford University Press, 1991); Lisa L. Moore, *Dangerous Intimacies: Toward a Sapphic History of the British Novel* (Durham, N.C. and London: Duke University Press, 1997).

Rights of Woman

Belinda was alone, and reading, when Mrs Freke dashed into the room.

"How do, dear creature!" cried she, stepping up to her, and shaking hands with her boisterously, "How do? Glad to see you, 'faith! Been long here? Tremendously hot to day!"

She flung herself upon the sofa beside Belinda, threw her hat upon the table, and then continued speaking.

"And how d'ye go on here, poor child! "God! I'm glad you're alone. Expected to find you encompassed by a whole host of the righteous. Give me credit for my courage in coming to deliver you out of their hands. Luttridge and I had such compassion upon you, when we heard you were close prisoner here! I swore to set the distressed damsel free, in spite of all the dragons in Christendom. So let me carry you off in triumph in my unicorn, and leave these good people to stare when they come home from their sober walk, and find you gone. There's nothing I like so much as to make good people stare—I hope you're of my way o'thinking. You don't look as if you were though—but I never mind young ladies' looks—always give the lie to their thoughts. Now we talk o' looks. Never saw you look so well in my life—as handsome as an angel! And so much the better for me. Do you know, I've a bet of twenty guineas on your head—on your face, I mean. There's a young bride at Harrowgate, lady H----, they're all mad about her, the men swear she's the handsomest woman in England, and I swear I know one ten times as handsome. They've dared me to make good my word, and I've pledged myself to produce my beauty at the next ball, and to pit her against their belle for any money. Most votes carry it. I'm willing to double my bet since I've seen you again. Come, had not we best be off? Now don't refuse me and make speeches—you know that's all nonsense—I'll take all the blame upon myself."

Belinda, who had not been suffered to utter a word whilst Mrs Freke ran on in this strange manner, looked in unfeigned astonishment; but when she found herself seized and dragged towards the door, she drew back with a degree of gentle firmness that astonished Mrs Freke. With a smiling countenance, but a steady tone, she said, that she was sorry Mrs Freke's knight-errantry should not be exerted in a better cause, for that she was neither a prisoner, nor a distressed damsel.

"And will you make me lose my bet?" cried Mrs Freke. "O, at all events you must come to the ball! I'm down for it. But I'll not press it now, because you're frightened out of your poor little wits, I see, at the bare thoughts of doing any thing out of rule, by these good people. Well, well it shall be managed for you—leave that to me. I'm used to managing for cowards. Pray tell me, you and lady Delacour are off, I understand? Give ye joy! She and I were once great friends; that is to say, I had over her "that power which strong minds have over weak ones"; but she was too weak for me—one of those people that have neither courage to be good, nor to be bad."

"The courage to be bad," said Belinda, "I believe, indeed, she does not possess."

Mrs Freke stared. "Why, I heard you had quarrelled with her!"

"If I had," said Belinda, "I hope that I should still do justice to her merits. It is said that people are apt to suffer more by their friends than their enemies. I hope that will never be the case with lady Delacour, as I confess that I have been one of her friends."

"Gad, I like your spirit—you don't want courage, I see, to fight even for your enemies. You are just the kind of girl I admire—I see you've been prejudiced against me by lady Delacour. But whatever stories she may have trumped up, the truth of the matter is this; there's no living with her she's so jealous—so ridiculously jealous—of that lord of hers, for whom all the time she hasn't the impudence to pretend to care more than I do for the sole of my boot," said Mrs Freke, striking it with her whip, "but she hasn't the courage to give him tit for tat. Now this is what I call weakness. Pray, how do she and Clarence Hervey go on together? Are they out o'the hornbook of platonics yet?"

"Mr Hervey was not in town when I left it," said Belinda.

"Was not he? Ho! ho! He's off then! Ay, so I prophesied. She's not the thing for him. He has some strength of mind—some soul—above vulgar prejudices. So must a woman be to hold him. He was caught at first by her grace and beauty, and that sort of stuff; but I knew it could not last—knew she'd dilly dally with Clary, till he would turn upon his heel and leave her there."

"I fancy that you are entirely mistaken both with respect to Mr Hervey and lady Delacour," Belinda very seriously began to say; but Mrs Freke interrupted her, and ran on—

"No! no! no! I'm not mistaken; Clarence has found her out. She's a *very* woman—*that* he could forgive her, and so could I. But she's a *mere* woman—and that he can't forgive—no more can I."

There was a kind of drollery about Mrs Freke, which, with some people, made the odd things she said pass for wit. Humour she really possessed; and when she chose it, she could be diverting to those who like buffoonery in women. She had set her heart upon winning Belinda over to her party. She began by flattery of her beauty; but as she saw that this had no effect, she next tried what could be done by insinuating that she had a high opinion of her understanding, by talking to her as an *esprit fort*.

"For my part," said she, "I own I should like a strong devil better than a weak angel."

"You forget," said Belinda, "that it is not Milton, but Satan, who says, 'Fallen spirit, to be weak is to be miserable.'"

"You read I see! I did not know you were a reading girl. So did I once! but I never read now. Books only spoil the originality of genius. Very well for those who can't think for themselves—but when one has made up one's opinions, there is no use in reading."

"But to *make* them up," replied Belinda, "may it not be useful?"

"Of no use upon earth to minds of a certain class. You, who can think for yourself, should never read."

"But I read that I may think for myself."

"Only ruin your understanding, trust me. Books are full of trash—nonsense. Conversation is worth all the books in the world."

"And is there never any nonsense in conversation?"

"What have you here?" continued Mrs Freke, who did not choose to attend to this question; exclaiming as she reviewed each of the books on the table in their turns, in the summary language of presumptuous ignorance. "Smith's *Theory of Moral Sentiments*—milk and water! Moore's *Travels*—hasty pudding! Bruyere—nettle porridge! This is what you were at when I came in, was it not?" said she, taking up a book in which she saw Belinda's mark, "'Essay on the Inconsistency of Human Wishes.' Poor thing! who bored you with this task?"

"Mr Percival recommended it to me, as one of the best essays in the English language."

"The devil! They seem to have put you in a course of the bitters—a course of the woods might do your business better. Do you ever hunt? Let me take you out with me some morning. You'd be quite an angel on horseback; or let me drive you out some day in my unicorn."

Belinda declined this invitation, and Mrs Freke strode away to the window to conceal her mortification, threw up the sash, and called out to her groom,

"Walk those horses about, blockhead!" Mr Percival and Mr Vincent at this instant came into the room.

"Hail, fellow! well met," cried Mrs Freke, stretching out her hand to Mr Vincent.

It has been remarked, that an antipathy subsists between creatures, who, without being the same, have yet a strong external resemblance. Mr Percival saw this instinct rising in Mr Vincent, and smiled.

"Hail, fellow! well met, I say—shake hands and be friends, man! Though I'm not in the habit of making apologies, if it will be any satisfaction to you, I beg your pardon for frightening your poor devil of a black."

Then turning towards Mr Percival, she measured him with her eye, as a person whom she longed to attack. She thought, that if Belinda's opinion of the understanding of *these Percivals* could be lowered, she should rise in her opinion: accordingly, she determined to draw Mr Percival into an argument.

"I've been talking treason, I believe, to miss Portman," cried she, "for I've been opposing some of your opinions, Mr Percival."

"If you opposed them all, madam," said Mr Percival, "I should not think it treason."

"Vastly polite! But I think all our politeness hypocrisy. What d'ye say to that?"

"You know that best, madam!"

"Then I'll go a step farther; for I'm determined you shall contradict me. I think all virtue is hypocrisy."

"I need not contradict you, madam," said Mr Percival, "for the terms which you make use of contradict themselves."

"It is my system," pursued Mrs Freke, "that shame is always the cause of the vices of women."

"It is sometimes the effect," said Mr Percival; "and, as cause and effect are reciprocal, perhaps you may, in some instances, be right."

"O! I hate qualifying arguers. Plump assertion or plump denial for me. You shan't get off so—I say, shame is the cause of all women's vices."

"False shame, I suppose you mean?" said Mr Percival.

"Mere play upon words! All shame is false shame. We should be a great deal better without it. What say you, miss Portman? Silent—hey? Silence that speaks!"

"Miss Portman's blushes," said Mr Vincent, "speak *for* her."

"*Against* her," said Mrs Freke. "Women blush because they understand."

"And you would have them understand without blushing?" said Mr Percival. "So would I; for nothing can be more different than innocence and ignorance. Female delicacy—"

"This is just the way you men spoil women," cried Mrs Freke, "by talking to them of the *delicacy of their sex*, and such stuff. This *delicacy* enslaves the pretty delicate dears."

"No; it enslaves us," said Mr Vincent.

"I hate slavery! *Vive la liberté*!" cried Mrs Freke, "I'm a champion for the Rights of Women."

"I am an advocate for their happiness," said Mr Percival, "and for their delicacy, as I think it conduces to their happiness."

"I'm an enemy to their delicacy, as I am sure it conduces to their misery."

"You speak from experience?" said Mr Percival.

"No, from observation. Your most delicate women are always the greatest hypocrites; and, in my opinion, no hypocrite can or ought to be happy."

"But you have not proved the hypocrisy," said Belinda. "Delicacy is not, I hope, an indisputable proof of it? If you mean *false* delicacy—"

"To cut the matter short at once," cried Mrs Freke, "why, when a woman likes a man, does not she go and tell him so honestly?"

Belinda, surprised by this question from a woman, was too much abashed instantly to answer.

"Because she's a hypocrite. That is and must be the answer."

"No," said Mr Percival, "because if she be a woman of sense, she knows that by such a step she would disgust the object of her affection."

"Cunning!—cunning!—cunning!—the arms of the weakest."

"Prudence!—prudence!—the arms of the strongest. Taking the best means to secure our own happiness without injuring that of others, is the best proof of sense and strength of mind, whether in man or woman. Fortunately for society, the same conduct in ladies which best secures their happiness most increases ours."

Mrs Freke beat the devil's tattoo for some moments, and then exclaimed—

"You may say what you will, but the present system of society is radically wrong: whatever is, is wrong."

"How would you improve the state of society?" asked Mr Percival calmly.

"I'm not tinker general to the world," said she.

"I am glad of it," said Mr Percival; "for I have heard that tinkers often spoil more than they mend."

"But if you want to know," said Mrs Freke, "what I would do to improve the world, I'll tell you: I'd have your sex taught to say, 'Horns! horns!' I defy you."

"This would doubtless be a great improvement," said Mr Percival; "but you would not overturn society to attain it? would you? Should we find things much improved by tearing away what has been called the decent drapery of life?"

"Drapery, if you ask me my opinion," cried Mrs Freke, "drapery, whether wet or dry, is the most confoundedly indecent thing in the world."

"That depends on *public* opinion, I allow," said Mr Percival. "The Lacedæmonian ladies, who were veiled only by public opinion, were better covered from profane eyes, than some English ladies are in wet drapery."

"I know nothing of the Lacedëmonian ladies, I took my leave of them when I was a schoolboy—girl—I should say. But, pray, what o'clock is it by you—I've sat till I'm cramped all over," cried Mrs Freke, getting up and stretching herself so violently that some part of her habiliments gave way. "*Honi soit qui mal y pense!*" said she, bursting into a horse laugh.

Without sharing in any degree that confusion which Belinda felt for her, she strode out of the room, saying, "Miss Portman, you understand these things better than I do; come and set me to rights."

When she was in Belinda's room, she threw herself into an arm chair, and laughed immoderately.

"How I have trimmed Percival this morning," said she.

"I am glad you think so," said Belinda; "for I really was afraid he had been too severe upon you."

"I only wish," continued Mrs Freke, "I only wish his wife had been by. Why the devil did not she make her appearance? I suppose the prude was afraid of my demolishing and unrigging her."

"There seems to have been more danger of that for you than for any body else," said Belinda, as she assisted to set Mrs Freke's *rigging*, as she called it, to rights.

"I do, of all things, delight in hauling good people's opinions out of their musty drawers, and seeing how they look when they're all pulled to pieces before their faces. Pray, are those lady Anne's drawers or yours?" said Mrs Freke, pointing to a chest of drawers.

"Mine."

"I'm sorry for it; for, if they were hers, to punish her for *shirking* me, by the Lord, I'd have every rag she has in the world out in the middle of the floor in ten minutes! You don't know me—I'm a terrible person when provoked—stop at nothing!"

As Mrs Freke saw no other chance left of gaining her point with Belinda, she tried what intimidating her would do.

"I stop at nothing," repeated she, fixing her eyes upon miss Portman, to fascinate her by terrour. "Friend or foe! Peace or war! Take your choice. Come to the ball at Harrowgate, I win my bet, and I'm your sworn friend. Stay away, I lose my bet, and am your sworn enemy."

"It is not in my power, madam," said Belinda calmly, "to comply with your request."

"Then you'll take the consequences," cried Mrs Freke. She rushed past her, hurried down stairs, and called out,

"Bid my blockhead bring my unicorn."

She, her unicorn, and her blockhead, were out of sight in a few minutes.

Good may be drawn from evil. Mrs Freke's conversation, though at the time it confounded Belinda, roused her, upon reflexion, to examine by her reason the habits and principles which guided her conduct. She had a general feeling that they were right and necessary; but now, with the assistance of lady Anne and Mr Percival, she established in her own understanding the exact boundaries between right and wrong. She felt a species of satisfaction and security, from seeing the demonstration of those axioms of morality, in which she had previously acquiesced. Reasoning gradually became as agreeable to her as wit; nor was her taste for wit diminished, it was only refined by this process. She now compared and judged of the value of the different species of this brilliant talent.

Mrs Freke's wit, thought she, is like a noisy squib—the momentary terrour of passengers—lady Delacour's, like an elegant fire work, which we crowd to see, and cannot forbear to applaud—but lady Anne Percival's wit is like the refulgent moon, we "Love the mild rays, and bless the useful light."

"Miss Portman," said Mr Percival, "are not you afraid of making an enemy of Mrs Freke, by declining her invitation to Harrowgate?"

"I think her friendship more to be dreaded than her enmity," replied Belinda.

"Then you are not to be terrified by an obeah-woman?" said Mr Vincent.

"Not in the least, unless she were to come in the shape of a false friend," said Belinda.

"Till lately," said Mr Vincent, "I was deceived in the character of Mrs Freke. I thought her a dashing, free-spoken, free-hearted sort of eccentric person, who would make a staunch friend, and a jolly companion. As a mistress or a wife, no man of any taste could think of her. Compare that woman now with one of our creole ladies."

"But why with a creole?" said Mr Percival.

"For the sake of contrast in the first place. Our creole women are all softness, grace, delicacy—"

"And indolence," said Mr Percival.

"Their indolence is but a slight, and, in my judgment, an amiable defect; it keeps them out of mischief, and it attaches them to domestic life. The activity of a Mrs Freke would never excite their emulation, and so much the better."

"So much the better, no doubt," said Mr Percival. "But is there no other species of activity, that might excite their ambition with propriety? Without diminishing their grace, softness, or delicacy, might not they cultivate their minds? Do you think ignorance, as well as indolence, an amiable defect essential to the female character?"

"Not essential. You do not, I hope, imagine that I am so much prejudiced in favour of my countrywomen, that I can neither see nor feel the superiority in *some instances* of European cultivation? I speak only in general."

"And in general," said lady Anne Percival, "does Mr Vincent wish to confine our sex to the bliss of ignorance?"

"If it be bliss," said Mr Vincent, "what reason would they have for complaint?"

"*If,*" said Belinda; "but that is a question which you have not yet decided."

"And how can we decide it?" said Mr Vincent. "The taste and feelings of individuals must be the arbiters of their happiness."

"You leave reason quite out of the question, then," said Mr Percival, "and refer the whole to taste and feeling? So that, if the most ignorant person in the world assert that he is happier than you are, you are bound to believe him."

"Why should not I?" said Mr Vincent.

"Because," said Mr Percival, "though he can judge of his own pleasures, he cannot judge of yours; his are common to both, but yours are unknown to him. Would you, at this instant, change places with that ploughman yonder, who is whistling as he goes for want of thought? or, would you choose to go a step higher in the bliss of ignorance, and turn savage?"

Mr Vincent laughed, and protested that he should be very unwilling to give up his title to civilized society; and that, instead of wishing to have less knowledge, he regretted that he had not more. "I am sensible," said he, "that I have many prejudices: miss Portman has made me ashamed of some of them."

There was a degree of candour in Mr Vincent's manner and conversation which interested every body in his favour; Belinda amongst the rest. She was perfectly at ease in Mr Vincent's company, because she considered him as a person who wished for her friendship, without having any design to engage her affections. From several hints that dropped from him, from Mr Percival, and from lady Anne, she was persuaded that he was attached to some creole lady; and all that he said in favour of the elegant softness and delicacy of his countrywomen confirmed this opinion.

Miss Portman was not one of those young ladies who fancy that every gentleman who converses freely with them will inevitably fall a victim to the power of their charms, and who see in every man a lover, or nothing.

SAMUEL TAYLOR COLERIDGE (1772–1834)

Christabel (1816)

The Romantic poet and critic Samuel Taylor Coleridge, the son of a vicar, was born in Devon and educated at Christ's Hospital and Jesus College, Cambridge. In his youth he was a political radical and with his friend, the poet Robert Southey, espoused "pantisocracy," an early form of socialism. He began writing poetry in the early 1790s and married Sarah Fricker, the sister of Southey's wife, in 1795. In 1795 Coleridge met the poet William Wordsworth, with whom he developed a close friendship. In 1798 they jointly published *Lyrical Ballads*, one of the imperishable achievements of English romanticism. Three of Coleridge's best-known poems, *The Rime of the Ancient Mariner*, *Kubla Khan*, and the first part of *Christabel*, were written at this time. In 1798 Coleridge visited Germany and became deeply interested in German literature and philosophical thought: he would later translate Schiller and help to popularize German idealistic philosophy in England. Between 1800 and 1804 he lived near Wordsworth, at Keswick, in the Lake District, but subsequently broke with him. He traveled abroad again but returned to England in 1806, suffering from ill health and an incurable opium addiction. In his later years he occasionally gave public lectures on English poetry but devoted himself largely to journalism and criticism, producing his *Biographia Literaria*, a kind of literary and intellectual autobiography, in 1817. Toward the end of his life he left his wife and children and lived mainly with friends, notably his doctor, James Gillman, in whose home he died in 1834.

In his supernatural ballad *Christabel* (1816)—one of the strangest sapphic fantasias in all of European literature—Coleridge reveals something of a lifelong, enigmatic fascination with lesbian sexuality. The poem remains unfinished: when the first two parts, in which the lamialike enchantress, Geraldine, seduces the innocent Christabel, were condemned as obscene in the *Edinburgh Review* in 1816, Coleridge abruptly abandoned it. Even in its truncated form, however, the poem has had a major influence on lesbian literary fantasy. With her elegant, slim shape, mysteriously disfigured breast, and weirdly penetrating "serpent's eye," Geraldine subsequently became the prototype for a host of nineteenth-century lesbian vampires and demonesses. The predatory sapphic wraiths of Baudelaire, Swinburne, Verlaine, Sheridan Le Fanu, Rachilde, and Henry James are unimaginable without the glittering Coleridgean model. In the twentieth century the name Geraldine has continued to function as a synonym for vampiristic female homosexuality: in Rosamond Lehmann's lesbian novel *Dusty Answer* (1927) it is hardly coincidental that the sinister Miss Manners, "tall, dark and splendid," who steals away the heroine's girlfriend, is called Geraldine. In 1998, Karin Kallmaker (writing as Laura Adams) published her own *Christabel*—a lesbian romance novel in which an investment banker, Dina (Geraldine) Rowlands seduces a lovely young supermodel named Christabel.

Scholars have yet to explicate fully the meaning of the lesbian theme in Coleridge's writing. *Christabel*, it turns out, was not his only poem on the subject; a cache of three hundred previously unknown Coleridge verses discovered in the early 1990s included several poems on sapphic love. Even more startling, new evidence uncovered by the scholar Andrew Elfenbein suggests that Coleridge's celebrated friendship with Wordsworth was bolstered in part by a shared interest in lesbian-themed pornography. During the composition of *Lyrical Ballads* the two traded back and forth a volume of lascivious doggerel, *The Frisky Songster*, in which several poems deal with sex between women.

FURTHER READING: Samuel Taylor Coleridge, *The Complete Poetical Works of Samuel Taylor Coleridge*, ed. Ernest Hartley Coleridge, 2 vols. (Oxford: Clarendon, 1912); E. K. Chambers, *Samuel Taylor Coleridge: A Biographical Study* (Oxford: Oxford University Press, 1938); Arthur Hobart Nethercot, *The Road to Tryermaine: A Study of the History, Background, and Purposes of Coleridge's 'Christabel'* (Chicago: University of Chicago Press, 1939); Norman Fruman, *Coleridge: The Damaged Archangel* (New York: Braziller, 1971); Jonas Spatz, "The Mystery of Eros: Sexual Initiation in Coleridge's *Christabel*," *PMLA* 90 (1975): 107–16; Margery Durham, "The Mother Tongue: *Christabel* and the Language of Love," in Shirley Nelson Garner, et al., eds., *The (M)other Tongue: Essays in Feminist Psychoanalytic Interpretation* (Ithaca, N.Y.: Cornell University Press, 1985), pp. 169–93; Camille Paglia, "*Christabel*," in Harold Bloom, ed., *Samuel Taylor Coleridge* (New York: Chelsea House, 1986), pp. 217–29; Bram Djikstra, *Idols of Perversity: Fantasies of Feminine Evil* (New York and London: Oxford University Press, 1986); Paul Magnuson, *Coleridge and Wordsworth: A Lyrical Dialogue* (Princeton: Princeton University Press, 1988); Richard Holmes, *Coleridge: Early Visions* (Harmondsworth, Middlesex: Penguin, 1989); Susan Eilenberg, *Strange Power of Speech: Wordsworth, Coleridge, and Literary Possession* (New York: Oxford University Press, 1992); Daniel P. Watkins, *Sexual Power in British Romantic Poetry* (Gainesville: University of Florida Press, 1996); Andrew Elfenbein, *Romantic Genius: The Prehistory of a Homosexual Role* (New York: Columbia University Press, 1999); Mark M. Hennelly Jr., " 'As Well Fill Up the Space Between': A Liminal Reading of *Christabel*," *Studies in Romanticism* 38 (summer 1999): 203–22; Chris Koenig-Woodyard, "sex–text: *Christabel* and *Christabelliads*," *Romanticism on the Net: An Electronic Journal Devoted to Romantic Studies* 15 (August 1999), n.p.

PART I

'Tis the middle of night by the castle clock,
And the owls have awakened the crowing cock;
Tu—whit!----Tu—whoo!
And hark, again! the crowing cock,
How drowsily it crew.

Sir Leoline, the Baron rich,
Hath a toothless mastiff bitch;
From her kennel beneath the rock
She maketh answer to the clock,
Four for the quarters, and twelve for the hour;
Ever and aye, by shine and shower,
Sixteen short howls, not over loud;
Some say she sees my lady's shroud.

Is the night chilly and dark?
The night is chilly, but not dark.
The thin gray cloud is spread on high,
It covers but not hides the sky.
The moon is behind, and at the full;
And yet she looks both small and dull.
The night is chill, the cloud is gray:
'Tis a month before the month of May,
And the spring comes slowly up this way.

The lovely lady, Christabel,
Whom her father loves so well,
What makes her in the wood so late,
A furlong from the castle gate?
She had dreams all yesternight
Of her own betrothéd knight;
And she in the midnight wood will pray
For the weal of her lover that's far away.

She stole along, she nothing spoke,
The sighs she heaved were soft and low,
And naught was green upon the oak
But moss and rarest mistletoe:
She kneels beneath the huge oak tree,
And in silence prayeth she.

The lady sprang up suddenly,
The lovely lady, Christabel!
It moaned as near, as near can be,
But what it is she cannot tell.—
On the other side it seems to be,
Of the huge, broad-breasted, old oak tree.

The night is chill; the forest bare;
Is it the wind that moaneth bleak?
There is not wind enough in the air
To move away the ringlet curl
From the lovely lady's check—
There is not wind enough to twirl
The one red leaf, the last of its clan,
That dances as often as dance it can,
Hanging so light, and hanging so high,
On the topmost twig that looks up at the sky.

Hush, beating heart of Christabel!
Jesu, Maria, shield her well!
She folded her arms beneath her cloak,
And stole to the other side of the oak.
    What sees she there?

There she sees a damsel bright,
Dressed in a silken robe of white,
That shadowy in the moonlight shone:
The neck that made that white robe wan,
Her stately neck, and arms were bare;
Her blue-veined feet unsandaled were,
And wildly glittered here and there
The gems entangled in her hair.
I guess, 'twas frightful there to see
A lady so richly clad as she—
Beautiful exceedingly!

Mary mother, save me now!
(Said Christabel), And who art thou?

The lady strange made answer meet,
And her voice was faint and sweet—
Have pity on my sore distress,

I scarce can speak for weariness:
Stretch forth thy hand, and have no fear!
Said Christabel, How camest thou here?
And the lady, whose voice was faint and sweet,
Did thus pursue her answer meet—

My sire is of a noble line,
And my name is Geraldine:
Five warriors seized me yestermorn,
Me, even me, a maid forlorn:
They choked my cries with force and fright,
And tied me on a palfrey white.
The palfrey was as fleet as wind,
And they rode furiously behind.
They spurred amain, their steeds were white:
And once we crossed the shade of night.
As sure as Heaven shall rescue me,
I have no thought what men they be;
Nor do I know how long it is
(For I have lain entranced, I wis)
Since one, the tallest of the five,
Took me from the palfrey's back,
A weary woman, scarce alive.

Some muttered words his comrades spoke:
He placed me underneath this oak;
He swore they would return with haste;
Whither they went I cannot tell—
I thought I heard, some minutes past,
Sounds as of a castle bell.
Stretch forth thy hand (thus ended she),
And help a wretched maid to flee.

Then Christabel stretched forth her hand,
And comforted fair Geraldine:
O well, bright dame! may you command
The service of Sir Leoline;
And gladly our stout chivalry
Will he send forth and friends withal
To guide and guard you safe and free
Home to your noble father's hall.

She rose: and forth with steps they passed
That strove to be, and were not, fast.
Her gracious stars the lady blessed,
And thus spake on sweet Christabel:
All our household are at rest,
The hall as silent as the cell;
Sir Leoline is weak in health,
And may not well awakened be,
But we will move as if in stealth,
And I beseech your courtesy,
This night, to share your couch with me.

They crossed the moat, and Christabel
Took the key that fitted well;
A little door she opened straight,
All in the middle of the gate;
The gate that was ironed within and without,
Where an army in battle array had marched out.
The lady sank, belike through pain,
And Christabel with might and main
Lifted her up, a weary weight,
Over the threshold of the gate:
Then the lady rose again,
And moved, as she were not in pain.

So free from danger, free from fear,
They crossed the court: right glad they were.
And Christabel devoutly cried
To the lady by her side,
Praise we the Virgin all divine
Who hath rescued thee from thy distress!
Alas, alas! said Geraldine,
I cannot speak for weariness.
So free from danger, free from fear,
They crossed the court: right glad they were.

Outside her kennel, the mastiff old
Lay fast asleep, in moonshine cold.
The mastiff old did not awake,
Yet she an angry moan did make!
And what can ail the mastiff bitch?

Never till now she uttered yell
Beneath the eye of Christabel.
Perhaps it is the owlet's scritch:
For what can ail the mastiff bitch?

They passed the hall, that echoes still,
Pass as lightly as you will!
The brands were flat, the brands were dying,
Amid their own white ashes lying;
But when the lady passed, there came
A tongue of light, a fit of flame;
And Christabel saw the lady's eye,
And nothing else saw she thereby,
Save the boss of the shield of Sir Leoline tall,
Which hung in a murky old niche in the wall.
O softly tread, said Christabel,
My father seldom sleepeth well.

Sweet Christabel her feet doth bare,
And jealous of the listening air
They steal their way from stair to stair,
Now in glimmer, and now in gloom,
And now they pass the Baron's room,
As still as death, with stifled breath!
And now have reached her chamber door;
And now doth Geraldine press down
The rushes of the chamber floor.

The moon shines dim in the open air,
And not a moonbeam enters here.
But they without its light can see
The chamber carved so curiously,
Carved with figures strange and sweet,
All made out of the carver's brain,
For a lady's chamber meet:
The lamp with twofold silver chain
Is fastened to an angel's feet.

The silver lamp burns dead and dim;
But Christabel the lamp will trim.
She trimmed the lamp, and made it bright,
And left it swinging to and fro,

While Geraldine, in wretched plight,
Sank down upon the floor below.

O weary lady, Geraldine,
I pray you, drink this cordial wine!
It is a wine of virtuous powers;
My mother made it of wild flowers.

And will your mother pity me,
Who am a maiden most forlorn?
Christabel answered—Woe is me!
She died the hour that I was born.
I have heard the gray-haired friar tell
How on her deathbed she did say,
That she should hear the castle bell
Strike twelve upon my wedding day.
O mother dear! that thou wert here!
I would, said Geraldine, she were!
But soon with altered voice, said she—
"Off, wandering mother! Peak and pine!
I have power to bid thee flee."
Alas! what ails poor Geraldine?
Why stares she with unsettled eye?
Can she the bodiless dead espy?
And why with hollow voice cries she,
"Off, woman, off! this hour is mine—
Though thou her guardian spirit be,
Off, woman, off! 'tis given to me."

Then Christabel knelt by the lady's side,
And raised to heaven her eyes so blue—
Alas! said she, this ghastly ride—
Dear lady! it hath 'wildered you!
The lady wiped her moist cold brow,
And faintly said, "'tis over now!"

Again the wild-flower wine she drank:
Her fair large eyes 'gan glitter bright,
And from the floor whereon she sank,
The lofty lady stood upright:
She was most beautiful to see,
Like a lady of a far countree.

And thus the lofty lady spake—
"All they who live in the upper sky,
Do love you, holy Christabel!
And you love them, and for their sake
And for the good which me befell.
Even I in my degree will try,
Fair maiden, to requite you well.
But now unrobe yourself; for I
Must pray, ere yet in bed I lie."
Quoth Christabel, So let it be!
And as the lady bade, did she.
Her gentle limbs did she undress,
And lay down in her loveliness.

But through her brain of weal and woe
So many thoughts moved to and fro,
That vain it were her lids to close;
So halfway from the bed she rose,
And on her elbow did recline
To look at the lady Geraldine.

Beneath the lamp the lady bowed,
And slowly rolled her eyes around;
Then drawing in her breath aloud,
Like one that shuddered, she unbound
The cincture from beneath her breast:
Her silken robe, and inner vest,
Dropped to her feet, and full in view,
Behold! her bosom and half her side—
A sight to dream of, not to tell!
O shield her! shield sweet Christabel!

Yet Geraldine nor speaks nor stirs;
Ah! what a stricken look was hers!
Deep from within she seems halfway
To lift some weight with sick assay,
And eyes the maid and seeks delay;
Then suddenly, as one defied,
Collects herself in scorn and pride,
And lay down by the maiden's side!—
And in her arms the maid she took,
      Ah well-a-day!

And with low voice and doleful look
These words did say:
"In the touch of this bosom there worketh a spell,
Which is lord of thy utterance, Christabel!
Thou knowest tonight, and wilt know tomorrow,
This mark of my shame, this seal of my sorrow;
    But vainly thou warrest,
    For this is alone in
    Thy power to declare,
    That in the dim forest
    Thou heard'st a low moaning,
And found'st a bright lady, surpassingly fair;
And didst bring her home with thee in love and in charity,
To shield her and shelter her from the damp air."

THE CONCLUSION TO PART I

It was a lovely sight to see
The lady Christabel, when she
Was praying at the old oak tree.
    Amid the jagged shadows
    Of mossy leafless boughs,
    Kneeling in the moonlight,
    To make her gentle vows;
Her slender palms together pressed,
Heaving sometimes on her breast;
Her face resigned to bliss or bale—
Her face, oh call it fair not pale,
And both blue eyes more bright than clear,
Each about to have a tear.

With open eyes (ah woe is me!)
Asleep, and dreaming fearfully,
Fearfully dreaming, yet I wis,
Dreaming that alone, which is—
O sorrow and shame! Can this be she,
The lady, who knelt at the old oak tree?
And lo! the worker of these harms,
That holds the maiden in her arms,
Seems to slumber still and mild,
As a mother with her child.

A star hath set, a star hath risen,
O Geraldine! since arms of thine
Have been the lovely lady's prison.
O Geraldine! one hour was thine—
Thou'st had thy will! By tairn and rill,
The night birds all that hour were still.
But now they are jubilant anew,
From cliff and tower, tu—whoo! tu—whoo!
Tu—whoo! tu—whoo! from wood and fell!

And see! the lady Christabel
Gathers herself from out her trance;
Her limbs relax, her countenance
Grows sad and soft; the smooth thin lids
Close o'er her eyes; and tears she sheds—
Large tears that leave the lashes bright!
And oft the while she seems to smile
As infants at a sudden light!

Yea, she doth smile, and she doth weep,
Like a youthful hermitess,
Beauteous in a wilderness,
Who, praying always, prays in sleep.
And, if she move unquietly,
Perchance, 'tis but the blood so free
Comes back and tingles in her feet.
No doubt, she hath a vision sweet.
What if her guardian spirit 'twere,
What if she knew her mother near?
But this she knows, in joys and woes,
That saints will aid if men will call:
For the blue sky bends over all!

PART 2

Each matin bell, the Baron saith,
Knells us back to a world of death.
These words Sir Leoline first said,
When he rose and found his lady dead:
These words Sir Leoline will say
Many a morn to his dying day!

And hence the custom and law began
That still at dawn the sacristan,
Who duly pulls the heavy bell,
Five and forty beads must tell
Between each stroke—a warning knell,
Which not a soul can choose but hear
From Bratha Head to Wyndermere.

Saith Bracy the bard, So let it knell!
And let the drowsy sacristan
Still count as slowly as he can!
There is no lack of such, I ween,
As well fill up the space between.
In Langdale Pike and Witch's Lair,
And Dungeon Ghyll so foully rent,
With ropes of rock and bells of air
Three sinful sextons' ghosts are pent,
Who all give back, one after t'other,
The death note to their living brother;
And oft too, by the knell offended,
Just as their one! two! three! is ended,
The devil mocks the doleful tale
With a merry peal from Borodale.

The air is still! through mist and cloud
That merry peal comes ringing loud;
And Geraldine shakes off her dread,
And rises lightly from the bed;
Puts on her silken vestments white,
And tricks her hair in lovely plight,
And nothing doubting of her spell
Awakens the lady Christabel.
"Sleep you, sweet lady Christabel?
I trust that you have rested well."

And Christabel awoke and spied
The same who lay down by her side—
O rather say, the same whom she
Raised up beneath the old oak tree!
Nay, fairer yet! and yet more fair!
For she belike hath drunken deep
Of all the blessedness of sleep!

And while she spake, her looks, her air
Such gentle thankfulness declare,
That (so it seemed) her girded vests
Grew tight beneath her heaving breasts.
"Sure I have sinned!" said Christabel,
"Now heaven be praised if all be well!"
And in low faltering tones, yet sweet,
Did she the lofty lady greet
With such perplexity of mind
As dreams too lively leave behind.

So quickly she rose, and quickly arrayed
Her maiden limbs, and having prayed
That He, who on the cross did groan,
Might wash away her sins unknown,
She forthwith led fair Geraldine
To meet her sire, Sir Leoline.

The lovely maid and the lady tall
Are pacing both into the hall,
And pacing on through page and groom,
Enter the Baron's presence-room.

The Baron rose, and while he pressed
His gentle daughter to his breast,
With cheerful wonder in his eyes
The lady Geraldine espies,
And gave such welcome to the same,
As might beseem so bright a dame!

But when he heard the lady's tale,
And when she told her father's name,
Why waxed Sir Leoline so pale,
Murmuring o'er the name again,
Lord Roland de Vaux of Tryermaine?

Alas! they had been friends in youth;
But whispering tongues can poison truth;
And constancy lives in realms above;
And life is thorny; and youth is vain;
And to be wroth with one we love
Doth work like madness in the brain,

And thus it chanced, as I divine,
With Roland and Sir Leoline.
Each spake words of high disdain
And insult to his heart's best brother:
They parted—ne'er to meet again!
But never either found another
To free the hollow heart from paining—
They stood aloof, the scars remaining,
Like cliffs which had been rent asunder;
A dreary sea now flows between—
But neither heat, nor frost, nor thunder,
Shall wholly do away, I ween,
The marks of that which once hath been.

Sir Leoline, a moment's space,
Stood gazing on the damsel's face:
And the youthful Lord of Tryermaine
Came back upon his heart again.

O then the Baron forgot his age,
His noble heart swelled high with rage;
He swore by the wounds in Jesu's side
He would proclaim it far and wide,
With trump and solemn heraldry,
That they, who thus had wronged the dame,
Were base as spotted infamy!
"And if they dare deny the same,
My herald shall appoint a week,
And let the recreant traitors seek
My tourney court—that there and then
I may dislodge their reptile souls
From the bodies and forms of men!"
He spake: his eye in lightning rolls!
For the lady was ruthlessly seized; and he kenned
In the beautiful lady the child of his friend!

And now the tears were on his face,
And fondly in his arms he took
Fair Geraldine, who met the embrace,
Prolonging it with joyous look.
Which when she viewed, a vision fell
Upon the soul of Christabel,

The vision of fear, the touch and pain!
She shrunk and shuddered, and saw again—
(Ah, woe is me! Was it for thee,
Thou gentle maid! such sights to see?)

Again she saw that bosom old,
Again she felt that bosom cold,
And drew in her breath with a hissing sound:
Whereat the Knight turned wildly round,
And nothing saw, but his own sweet maid
With eyes upraised, as one that prayed.

The touch, the sight, had passed away,
And in its stead that vision blest,
Which comforted her after-rest
While in the lady's arms she lay,
Had put a rapture in her breast,
And on her lips and o'er her eyes
Spread smiles like light!
            With new surprise,
"What ails then my belovéd child?"
The Baron said—His daughter mild
Made answer, "All will yet be well!"
I ween, she had no power to tell
Aught else: so mighty was the spell.

Yet he, who saw this Geraldine,
Had deemed her sure a thing divine:
Such sorrow with such grace she blended,
As if she feared she had offended
Sweet Christabel, that gentle maid!
And with such lowly tones she prayed
She might be sent without delay
Home to her father's mansion.
            "Nay!
Nay, by my soul!" said Leoline.
"Ho! Bracy the bard, the charge be thine!
Go thou, with music sweet and loud,
And take two steeds with trappings proud,
And take the youth whom thou lov'st best
To bear thy harp, and learn thy song,
And clothe you both in solemn vest,

And over the mountains haste along,
Lest wandering folk, that are abroad,
Detain you on the valley road.

"And when he has crossed the lithing flood,
My merry bard! he hastes, he hastes
Up Knorren Moor, through Halegarth Wood,
And reaches soon that castle good
Which stands and threatens Scotland's wastes.

"Bard Bracy! bard Bracy! your horses are fleet,
Ye must ride up the hall, your music so sweet,
More loud than your horses' echoing feet!
And loud and loud to Lord Roland call,
Thy daughter is safe in Langdale hall!
Thy beautiful daughter is safe and free—
Sir Leoline greets thee thus through me!
He bids thee come without delay
With all thy numerous array
And take thy lovely daughter home:
And he will meet thee on the way
With all his numerous array
White with their panting palfreys' foam:
And, by mine honor! I will say,
That I repent me of the day
When I spake words of fierce disdain
To Roland de Vaux of Tryermaine!—
For since that evil hour hath flown,
Many a summer's sun hath shone;
Yet ne'er found I a friend again
Like Roland de Vaux of Tryermaine."

The lady fell, and clasped his knees,
Her face upraised, her eyes o'erflowing;
And Bracy replied, with faltering voice,
His gracious Hail on all bestowing!—
"Thy words, thou sire of Christabel,
Are sweeter than my harp can tell;
Yet might I gain a boon of thee,
This day my journey should not be,
So strange a dream hath come to me,
That I had vowed with music loud

To clear yon wood from thing unblest,
Warned by a vision in my rest!
For in my sleep I saw that dove,
That gentle bird, whom thou dost love,
And call'st by thy own daughter's name—
Sir Leoline! I saw the same
Fluttering, and uttering fearful moan,
Among the green herbs in the forest alone.
Which when I saw and when I heard,
I wondered what might ail the bird;
For nothing near it could I see,
Save the grass and green herbs underneath the old tree.

"And in my dream methought I went
To search out what might there be found;
And what the sweet bird's trouble meant,
That thus lay fluttering on the ground.
I went and peered, and could descry
No cause for her distressful cry;
But yet for her dear lady's sake
I stooped, methought, the dove to take,
When lo! I saw a bright green snake
Coiled around its wings and neck.
Green as the herbs on which it couched,
Close by the dove's its head it crouched;
And with the dove it heaves and stirs,
Swelling its neck as she swelled hers!
I woke; it was the midnight hour,
The clock was echoing in the tower;
But though my slumber was gone by,
This dream it would not pass away—
It seems to live upon my eye!
And thence I vowed this selfsame day
With music strong and saintly song
To wander through the forest bare,
Lest aught unholy loiter there."

Thus Bracy said: the Baron, the while,
Half listening heard him with a smile;
Then turned to Lady Geraldine,
His eyes made up of wonder and love;
And said in courtly accents fine,

"Sweet maid, Lord Roland's beauteous dove,
With arms more strong than harp or song,
Thy sire and I will crush the snake!"
He kissed her forehead as he spake,
And Geraldine in maiden wise
Casting down her large bright eyes,
With blushing cheek and courtesy fine
She turned her from Sir Leoline;
Softly gathering up her train,
That o'er her right arm fell again;
And folded her arms across her chest,
And couched her head upon her breast,
And looked askance at Christabel—
Jesu, Maria, shield her well!

A snake's small eye blinks dull and shy;
And the lady's eyes they shrunk in her head,
Each shrunk up to a serpent's eye,
And with somewhat of malice, and more of dread,
At Christabel she looked askance!—
One moment—and the sight was fled!
But Christabel in dizzy trance
Stumbling on the unsteady ground
Shuddered aloud, with a hissing sound;
And Geraldine again turned round.
And like a thing, that sought relief,
Full of wonder and full of grief,
She rolled her large bright eyes divine
Wildly on Sir Leoline.

The maid, alas! her thoughts are gone,
She nothing sees—no sight but one!
The maid, devoid of guile and sin,
I know not how, in fearful wise,
So deeply had she drunken in
That look, those shrunken serpent eyes,
That all her features were resigned
To this sole image in her mind:
And passively did imitate
That look of dull and treacherous hate!
And thus she stood, in dizzy trance,
Still picturing that look askance

With forced unconscious sympathy
Full before her father's view—
As far as such a look could be
In eyes so innocent and blue!

And whence the trance was o'er, the maid
Paused awhile, and inly prayed:
Then falling at the Baron's feet,
"By my mother's soul do I entreat
That thou this woman send away!"
She said: and more she could not say:
For what she knew she could not tell,
O'ermastered by the mighty spell.

Why is thy cheek so wan and wild,
Sir Leoline? Thy only child
Lies at thy feet, thy joy, thy pride,
So fair, so innocent, so mild;
The same, for whom thy lady died!
O by the pangs of her dear mother
Think thou no evil of thy child!
For her, and thee, and for no other,
She prayed the moment ere she died:
Prayed that the babe for whom she died,
Might prove her dear lord's joy and pride!
 That prayer her deadly pangs beguiled,
    Sir Leoline!
 And wouldst thou wrong thy only child,
    Her child and thine?

Within the Baron's heart and brain
If thoughts, like these, had any share,
They only swelled his rage and pain,
And did but work confusion there.
His heart was cleft with pain and rage,
His cheeks they quivered, his eyes were wild,
Dishonored thus in his old age;
Dishonored by his only child,
And all his hospitality
To the wronged daughter of his friend
By more than woman's jealousy
Brought thus to a disgraceful end—

He rolled his eye with stern regard
Upon the gentle minstrel bard,
And said in tones abrupt, austere—
"Why, Bracy! dost thou loiter here?
I bade thee hence!" The bard obeyed;
And turning from his own sweet maid,
The aged knight, Sir Leoline,
Led forth the lady Geraldine!

THE CONCLUSION TO PART 2

A little child, a limber elf,
Singing, dancing to itself,
A fairy thing with red round cheeks,
That always finds, and never seeks,
Makes such a vision to the sight
As fills a father's eyes with light;
And pleasures flow in so thick and fast
Upon his heart, that he at last
Must needs express his love's excess
With words of unmeant bitterness.
Perhaps 'tis pretty to force together
Thoughts so all unlike each other;
To mutter and mock a broken charm,
To dally with wrong that does no harm.
Perhaps 'tis tender too and pretty
At each wild word to feel within
A sweet recoil of love and pity.
And what, if in a world of sin
(O sorrow and shame should this be true!)
Such giddiness of heart and brain
Comes seldom save from rage and pain,
So talks as it's most used to do.

"S.T. COLEBRITCHE, ESQ."

Christabess: A Right Woeful Poem, Translated from the Doggerel by Sir Vinegar Sponge (1816)

The comical *Christabess* (1816) is one of several contemporary parodies of Coleridge's sapphic fantasy-poem *Christabel* (1816). The author of this pseudonymous burlesque version, which follows the episodic structure of the original closely, at once exaggerates the lesbian element in Coleridge and exploits it to farcical effect. Adelaide—the Geraldine figure—begins her seduction of the hapless Christabess with the ludicrous verse, "In the tip of this titty there dwelleth a charm," and their mystic coupling is at once ribald and absurd.

FURTHER READING: Samuel Taylor Coleridge, *The Complete Poetical Works*, ed. Ernest Hartley Coleridge, 2 vols. (Oxford: Clarendon, 1912); Bram Djikstra, *Idols of Perversity: Fantasies of Feminine Evil* (New York and London: Oxford University Press, 1986); Richard Holmes, *Coleridge: Early Visions* (Harmondsworth, Middlesex: Penguin, 1989); Andrew Elfenbein, *Romantic Genius: The Prehistory of a Homosexual Role* (New York: Columbia University Press, 1999); Chris Koenig-Woodyard, "sex–text: *Christabel* and *Christabelliads*," *Romanticism on the Net: An Electronic Journal Devoted to Romantic Studies* 15 (August 1999), n.p.

PART I

'Tis a quarter past twelve by the brat that blares,
And the donkey hath waken'd the girl up stairs;
   Ee—eau!----Ee—eau!
Hark!—and the puppy that sleeps down stairs,
   Oh!—what a drowsy snore!

Tom Bottomly, the Tinker fat,
Hath a one-eyed she grey cat,

That, from a hole beneath the stairs,
Answers to the children's blares;
Squall for squall, and howl for howl,
Alternate squall and catterwaul,
In duet grim, so harsh and loud,
'Twould make the dead kick off a shroud.

"Does it rain to-night?—are you asleep?"
"It does not rain, but I'm asleep;"
"This horse-rug is so short and thin,
I scarce can keep my honxes in;
The moon shines in the room; I doubt
That large black cloud will shut it out."
"I'm devilish cold, Nan—hug me, pray;
March comes about a month ere May,
And then comes spring."—"Go to sleep, I say."

That blooming sphinx, Miss Christabess,
Whom her daddy loves to kiss,
Hath she not yet come home to bed?—
What whim is in the numbscull's head?
She dreamt, last night, some stuff, perhap,
About that gawky soldier chap,
Something that made her kick and leap,
And hug the bolster in her sleep;
And that's what keeps her up so late, I think,
For love I wot won't let her sleep a wink.

Along she wends her silent way,
The winds had ceas'd to breathe,
She reach'd, at length, an old oak tree,
All lonely standing on the heath;
Then musing, sat her at the foot
Upon an old grey naked root.

Up suddenly the maiden sprung,
The lovely trembling Christabess!
A squeak is heard to pass along,
But what it is she cannot guess.—
Now all is hush'd—O gemini!
Perhaps some rogue is up the Old Oak tree!

She looks about—no rogue is there—
I'd bet a penny 'twas the wind!—
"There is not wind enough in the air"
To blow away a nasty smell.
From the lovely maid behind,
Which chanced in her fright, poor girl!
There's a last year's leaf on the topmost twig,
That has danced all alone full many a jig,
Now still as the moon, tho' hanging so high,
You would fancy almost that it stuck to the sky.

Now hold your tongue—observe the maid,
Cautious creeping, half afraid;
She pops her head beneath her cloak,
And slowly creeps around the oak,
    Hollo! what now?

A damsel there stood all alone,
With nothing save her *chemise* on,
With heaving breasts, and tearful eyes,
And shift but half way down her thighs;
Oh! had the finder been a he!
Gentle reader, you, or me!—
Vexing; an't it?—"damnably."—

Lud-a-mercy! who are you?
Said Christabess, as back she drew.

Laying her palms upon her neck,
Sweetly thus the damsel spake—
First looking round, as still afraid,
"Oh! have compassion on a maid."—
Christabess stared, and thus began—
"Indeed, sweet maid, I'm not a man,
But tell me whence you are, and who?"—
Her tale then did the sylph pursue.

My Father is a sweep by trade,
And my name is Adelaide,
Five ragamuffins yestermorn,
Seiz'd me a helpless maid forlorn;
And if I spoke they swore they'd stick me,

And so they tied me on a Dickey;
And I was nation vex'd to find
Some walk'd before, and some behind;
One stuck a pin into a stick,
With which he oft would Neddy prick,
We travell'd on all night and day,
Nor can I even guess the way,
Nor who they were, nor how long 'tis,
"(For I have lain in fits I wis)"
Since one, the lankest of the gang,
Took me from the Dickey's rump,
When Neddy giving such a flang,
Kick'd him in his breeches plump,
So sprawling down he threw me thump,
And swore he'd go and get some gin,
And his companions, too, should booze,
And quickly he would come again,
And swing me in a hempen nooze;
So lend your hand, and do not blush,
To help a wretched maiden brush.

Then Christabess stretch'd forth her fist,
And lifted up fair Adelaide,
Saying many a thing I wist,
Of comfort to the wretched maid;
How, safely (as a body-louse)
Should she be in her father's house.

Away they went, and as they flew,
They kick'd the moon-beams from the dew;
Joy warm'd the naked maiden's breast,
And Christabess she softly said,
"All our folks are gone to rest,
Six at least in every bed:
My Father has the belly-ache,
So be as quiet as you can,
For he would hear us, should he wake,
And then he'd shoot you for a man."

They cross'd the ditch—and Christabess,
Who knew the way i'the dark I guess,
From the wicket took the pin,

Which let a brace of maidens in:—
This wicket had lately been broke by the hogs
While clumsily scudding away from the dogs.

The stranger, feeling wearily,
Tumbled down and cut her knee,
The other maiden took her in,
And set her on her legs ag'in,
And wiped the bleeding knee, but which
Was but a little tiny scratch.

They listen'd—all were fast asleep,
Which made their little hearts to leap.
Making the bolts and bars all tight,
"You mus'n't say your prayers to night,"
(Said Christabess unto the maid)
"Lest my Father you should wake."—
"I never do," (says Adelaide)
"God send away his belly ache!"—
They listen'd—all were fast asleep,
Which made their little hearts to leap.

Beneath the stairs grimalkin grey,
Was purring, as asleep she lay,
And all was silent 'neath their feet;
All—save their flutt'ring hearts that beat,
When pussy gave a sudden squeal,
(Whether or no she was asleep,
Egad she made the damsels leap;)
Perhaps she, dreaming, bit her tail,
Else, what the devil can she ail?

They shut the door, that creaking still—
Shut it as softly as you will;
The sticks were out, the embers dying,
All scatter'd 'tween the cob-irons lying.
And when they near the fire-place came,
There flash'd a little flit of flame,
And Christabess saw the maiden's thigh,
But nothing else saw she thereby,
Save a handkerchief red of Tom Bottomly tall,
Which hung like a dirty old clout on the wall.

Said Christabess, "O softly tread,
I heard the creaking of a bed."

Now Christabess took off her shoes,
And crept up stairs upon her toes;
The other maiden held her gown,
Lest she might in the dark fall down—
And at the door they heard a snore.—
Convinced at length her Father was asleep—
More eagerly towards their room
With less of caution now they creep.

"The moon shines dim in the open air,"
But they've a mite of rushlight there;
And by its glimmer they can see
The pictures stuck so curiously:—
Dying speeches, lots of songs,
All placed in order on the wall;
Ditties sweet of maidens wrongs,
Of ravishment, and rape, and all
That to Love's catalogue belongs.

The rushlight in the socket lingers,
And Christabess snuff'd it with her fingers;—
It stuck—she swang it to and fro,
At length she flung it in the po'—
And as the taper burnt more bright,
The stranger sank in weary plight.

"Poor creature!—in your fits again?
Or are you faint from thirst or pain?
Come, sit upon this ban-box—come,
And take a drop of gin or rum."

"O dear, what will your mother say
To me, a maiden all forlorn?"—
Christabess sigh'd— "a-lack a-day!
My mother died when I was born;
And I have heard my grandmother tell,
How she did on her death-bed say,
She should hear the bell that toll'd her knell,
Again upon my wedding-day:

I wish that she were here ag'in,
She us'd to like a drop of gin."

The stranger rose with fixed eye,
Contracted brows and sinews strung,
"Off, grisly ghost! I bid thee fly!
An hour at last from fate I've wrung,"
Alas, what ails poor Adelaide?
Can she espy the shadowy dead?
What means she by the hollow cries—
"Off; take your ashy limbs away,
This hour is mine by stronger ties
Than fate can break—so off I say."—

Then Christabess held by the damsel's smock,
And twitch'd her once, then twitch'd her again,
But listless she, as any stock,
So reckless seemed her brain.
At length she stamp'd and blew her nose,
And cried exulting, "Off she goes."

Again another dram she drank,
Whereby I guess the gin was good,
And by the bed-post where she sank,
Upon her snow white legs she stood,
Oh, she was lovely, sweet, and plump,
Egad—and such a noble rump!

And then she smiled, and thus she spake
To lovely Christa' Bottomly:
"My pretty little virgin bright,
I love you for your kindness sake
And, Oh! how we will hug to night.
With all the skill I have I'll try
To yield your little heart delight,
And I'll unlace your stays, she said,
For I'm in haste to be in bed."

With that she help'd her to undress,
And naked soon was Christabess,
Then nimbly 'twixt the sheets jumpt she,
In spotless, pure virginity.

The other sylphid tore a song,
To curl her hair so black and long;
Nor did she seem, as first she said,
So much in haste to come to bed;
And Christabess almost began
To fancy t'other was a man.

So up she sat upon her bum,
And peep'd behind the curtain sly;
And in the corner of the room,
There she saw the maid untie
A piece of hempen cord, that bound
Her alabaster belly round!
Down dropt her shift, and—-O dear me!
She's naked!—naked!!—naked!!!—see!—
But, reader, turn away your view,
She's not to sleep with me nor you.

Two skips she took and then a straddle,
And tumbled lengthways in the middle;
When in her arms she took the maid,—
    O lork-a-daisy!
And these words she wildly said,
Like one that's crazy:—
"In the tip of this titty there dwelleth a charm,
Which can put out thy senses, or shield thee from harm.
If thou knowest to night, two to one but to morrow
Thou'lt remember this mark of my shame and my sorrow.
    But vainly thou kick'st,
    And vain is thy speaking,
    I'll just tell thee this—
    Thou wert properly fix'd,
    When thou heardest a squeaking,
And found'st a fair maid in nature's best blandishment,
And did'st bring her home with nought else but her smock on,
To shield and protect her from rape and from ravishment."

THE CONCLUSION TO PART THE FIRST

O goodly sight! I fancy yet
I see the lovely Christa' sit

Beneath the tree to rest a bit,
   And see her head recline
   Upon her little fist,
   And see the moon-beams shine
   Upon her heaving breast,
O gentle sighs that swell her breast,
And almost seem her sash to burst!
O lovely face, turned to the skies!
And, O! what modest melting eyes!
Eyes big with tears—it might be said,
They shortly would be brought to bed!
The cloaths were all kick'd off, alack!
And Christabess lay on her back,
With open mouth, and eyes unshut,
Asleep and dreaming—dreaming, yet
Not dreams that mimic fancy drew,
But dreaming what was really true;
And, lo! the worker of the spell
Hugs the maid, and sleepest well;
Sleepest—or else she seems to sleep,
Like a Ram beside a Sheep.

The Moon hath set, the Sun hath risen,
Since Adelaide, O sorceress maid!
Thy arms have been the virgin's prison,
O Adelaide, an hour thou said,
Would suit thy turn, and now 'tis gone,
And all that hour no sound was known!
Charm fraught was every tongue, but now
From Ass and Cur—Ea—eau!—bow—wow!
Bow—wow! and baa! from Calf and Hound.
And see the harmless Christabess
Upon her lovely bottom rise,
She stretches—gapes—and rubs her eyes,
Then trembles—sighs—and cries O dear,
And sheds—or seems to shed a tear;
But now a smile o'erspreads her cheek—
And now again she seems in pain,
As infants with the belly ache.
And now her eye in anguish roves,
Like a little Gipsey witch,
With her lover in a ditch,

Who cries thro' fear of what she loves.
And if she lay there quietly,
Perchance it is because that he,
Having been there with her before,
Cannot fright her any more;
Was this the fate of her I sing?
O gentle reader, no such thing!
Think'st thou she bent to lawless will?
No, reader, she's a virgin still.

ANNE LISTER (1791–1840)

From the *Diaries of Anne Lister* (1824–26)

The recently unearthed diaries of the Yorkshirewoman Anne Lister, a contemporary of Jane Austen and the Brontës, constitute a rich trove of information about upper-middle-class female homosexuality in nineteenth-century England. Lister, the genteel mistress of Shibden Hall, near Halifax, and one of the truly remarkable personalities of the century, led a secret life as a lesbian seductress for over thirty years both in England and on the Continent, where she traveled after 1824. (She died in the Caucasus in 1840.) Throughout her adult life she kept a record of her various attachments in voluminous diaries written partly in code. While scholars have known of the diaries' existence for some time, they were only properly deciphered and published in the 1980s. For historians of sexuality the recovery of the Lister diaries rivals in importance the uncovering of James Boswell's stunningly candid "London Journals" in Ireland in the 1920s.

Lister's attitude toward what she called her "oddity" was both sophisticated and largely guilt-free. An orphan and heiress, she lived with an aunt and uncle who seemed unfazed by her eccentricities, which included a penchant for shooting pistols and dressing in quasi-masculine attire. Lister herself accepted her lifelong homosexual feelings as part of her nature and, while eminently discreet, had little difficulty attracting lovers among her female acquaintances. Indeed, the sheer number and ease of her conquests (in one case she had sexual relations with all four sisters in one family) suggest how common casual homosexuality may have been for putatively *heterosexual* women in earlier centuries, precisely because it involved no danger of pregnancy. The excerpts from Lister's diary below trace a characteristic relationship of the 1820s, with one Mrs. Barlow, a widow whom Lister met while staying for a year at a lodging house in Paris. Particularly noteworthy here is Lister's frank sexual language—she uses the term *queer*, interestingly, as a noun and synonym for the female pudendum—and the confident, even rakish pleasure she takes in recording her erotic exploits.

FURTHER READING: Anne Lister, *I Know My Own Heart: The Diaries of Anne Lister (1791–1840)*, ed. Helena Whitbread (London: Virago, 1988); —, *No Priest But Love: The Diaries of Anne Lister from 1824–1826*, ed. Helena Whitbread (New York: New

York University Press, 1992); Muriel Green, ed., *Miss Lister of Shibden Hall: Selected Letters 1800–1840* (Lewes, Sussex: Book Guild, 1992); Terry Castle, *The Apparitional Lesbian: Female Homosexuality and Modern Culture* (New York: Columbia University Press, 1993); Jill Liddington, *Presenting the Past: Anne Lister of Halifax, 1791–1840* (Hebden Bridge, West Yorkshire: Pennine Pens, 1994); —, ed., *Female Fortune: Land, Gender, and Authority: The Anne Lister Diaries and Other Writings 1833–36* (London and New York: Rivers Oram, 1998); Anna Clark, "Anne Lister's Construction of Lesbian Identity," *Journal of the History of Sexuality* 7 (July 1996): 25–50; Lisa L. Moore, *Dangerous Intimacies: Toward a Sapphic History of the British Novel* (Durham, N.C., and London: Duke University Press, 1999).

THURSDAY 14 OCT. 1824

Went to Mrs Barlow & sat with her an hour. Somehow she began talking of that one of the things of which Marie Antoinette was accused of was being too fond of women. I, with perfect mastery of countenance, said I had never heard of it before and could not understand or believe it. Did not see how such a thing could be—what good it could do—but owned I had heard of the thing. Mrs Barlow asked if Mme Galvani had told me. I said no, & that nobody could be more correct than Mme Galvani. I said I would not believe such a thing existed. Mrs Barlow said it was mentioned in scripture, not in the New Testament not Deuteronomy, nor Leviticus. I said I believed that when reduced to the last extremity—I was going to mention the use of phalli but luckily Mrs Barlow said, "You mean two men being fond of each other?" & I said "Yes," turning off the sentence about being reduced to the last extremity by saying men were often afraid of women for fear of injuring their health. Here Mrs Barlow feigned an ignorance, which gave me the hint that she wanted to pump me but I declared I was the most innocent person in the world considering all I had seen & heard, for everybody told me things. She said she should not have mentioned it but she knew she was not telling me anything I did not know before. I said I read of women being too fond of each other in the Latin parts of the works of Sir William Jones. She told me an old gentleman here, a savant I understand, had made proposals to her to visit her. The French women knew how to manage this without risk of children. All the French ladies, the wives, had two & no more. Mme de Boyve said if she, Mrs Barlow, married again she would tell her how, if she dared. Mme de Boyve had not told her but somebody else has & I understand that old General Vincennes did or was once going to tell her all about it. By the way, it was this—my manner of giving her to understand I knew the secret—that she asked if Mme Galvani had told me. Mrs Barlow said she had learnt all this since she came to France & seemed to insinuate that she knew a great deal. In fact, she suspected me and she was fishing to find it out but I think I was too deep for her. I told her she had more sense than I had & could turn me round her finger & thumb if she liked. "No," she said, "it is Mlle de Sans." "No, no," said I, "you understand this sort of thing better than she does." But I had before said I could go as far in friendship, love as warmly, as most but could not go beyond a certain degree & did not believe anyone could do it. We agreed it was a scandal invented by the men, who were bad enough for anything. She is a deepish hand & I think, would not be sorry to gain me over, but I shall be on my guard. She said, this evening, she never talked of these things except to persons she liked. She was hemming a pocket handkerchief narrow because she thought mine was so, & undoubled the whole to make it broad merely because I asked her. She certainly flirts with me . . . & said sometime afterwards, that she was not so calm and cold as I supposed. [I] made love to Mllc de Sans in the fiacre. Said I began to think I neither knew her nor myself. Knew not what was the matter with me, etc. She owned she had had many offers. Said she was just the sort of girl for it, she could attach anyone, etc. She was poorly & low but still coquetted very well. I cannot help fancying she, too, is a knowing one, considering she is a girl not quite six & twenty.

FRIDAY 15 OCT.

Walked with Mrs Barlow 3/4 hour along the boulevard . . . she did not seem ennuyée with my company & we sat quietly in her room till 1 3/4, when luncheon was announced . . . I asked her for her bible. [I] said I knew what she alluded to as the French way of preventing children. Shewed her Genesis 36, the verse about Onan. I was right, so therefore the French husbands spill their seed just before going to their wives which, being done, they take the pleasure without danger. I wonder the women like it. It must spend the men before they begin. "I must shew you the other passage," said Mrs Barlow, "because I know you wish to know." I asked the chapter. She said Romans, "Yes," said I, "the first chapter" & pointed to that verse about women forgetting the natural use, etc. "But," said I, "I do not believe it." "Oh," said she, "it might be taken in another way, with men." I agreed but without saying anything to betray how well I understood her. "Yes," she said, "as men do with men." Thought I to myself, she is a deep one. She knows, at all rates, that men can use women in two ways. I said I had often wondered what was the crime of Ham. Said she, "Was it sodomy?" "I don't know," said I, then made her believe how innocent I was, all things considered. [I] said we were a cold-blooded family in this particular. Warm as I was in other things, this one passion was wanting. I went to the utmost extent of friendship but this was enough. I should like to be instructed in the other (between two women) & would learn when I could but it would be of no use to me. I had no inclination. Could not imagine what good it could do. Nor could she & thought, therefore, there could be no harm in it. "Oh, no," said I slightly, "they can do no harm." She then shewed me the little book the gentleman had left here for her, "Voyage à Plombières," p. 126, where is the story of one woman intriguing with another. She has lent me the book . . . She gives me to understand she would live with me & is sure I could love very deeply. She believes me tho' that I know nothing about it & is persuaded of what she might have suspected, that I have had no connection with women. But she is decidedly making love to me. I tell her I am more childish than she is—more fond of nonsense after reading, etc. Like to relax in an evening. Should like to have a person always at my elbow, to share my bedroom & even bed, & to go as far as friendship can go, but this is enough. [I] said I was half in love with Mlle de Sans but if I had appointed to go with her & was with Mrs Barlow, I could not keep the appointment. But if sitting with Mlle de Sans I could leave her to go to Mrs Barlow. Mrs Barlow has more tact, more power over me . . . She then told me of her confinement; of Mr Barlow. She did not like honeymoons. How many a man she might have had here. I joked & said if I was my father's son I should be sure I was in love with her—should know what was the matter with me. She said I was crazy, at the same time looking as if she wished to lead me on. [I] laughed & said I was not accustomed to this sort of thing—should take pills or salts, etc., & so we went on till Cordingley, wondering I had not rung, came in to dress me & Mrs Barlow left . . . She sat next me in the evening & every now & then I felt her near me, touching me. My knees, my toes or something . . . Payed [sic] what attention I could to Mlle de Sans but Mrs Barlow evidently wished to engross me. We came up to bed together. Asked her to come into my room & she would but for fear of increasing her cold. She certainly makes absolute love to me. Tells me I don't know her—she can love deeply, etc. All I know about things, I pretend, is a mass of undigested knowledge which I had but know not how to use, for I am a very innocent sort of person. I really must be on my guard. What can she mean? Is she really amoureuse? This from a widow & mother like her is more than I could have thought of. I am safer with Mlle de Sans. I told Mrs Barlow I would not visit her soon again till I felt myself better. I have said & done nothing I cannot & do not lay to simplicity & innocence as yet & I really must take care. I keep telling her she is too deep, too knowing, for me . . . She had said before, this house was a little world & I should think so if I had seen all she had. I begin to think so already.

SUNDAY 17 OCT.

Mrs Barlow & I sat up tête-à-tête till 1—25. My manner towards her kind but proper. Talked rationally of my great want of a companion & how much stronger my friendships were than those of people in general. She could not feel as I did. "Ah," said she, "it is not those that shew the least who feel the least." She put her arm round me. I might have kissed her but contented myself with shaking hands.

TUESDAY 19 OCT.

[Mrs Barlow] sat by while Cordingley curled my hair & afterwards we had a cozy chit-chat. 11—50 when she left me. The thing is decided enough. I am paying regular court to her & she admits it. She said I should soon forget her. I answered, "No, never," & once I was away & recovered from my folly I should always be obliged to her for the kindness with which she treated me. I thought she behaved very well. There was noth-ing for which I could blame [her]. "Perhaps," said she, "you will not always think so." She is evidently aware that I must think she encourages me. Lord bless me, 'tis plain enough she would not allow me to go on in this manner, nor would she put herself so in my way if she did not like it. Just before her going, I put my arm round her waist & tried to pull her on my knee, she resisted & I gave up & apologized. I asked if she was angry as she went out. She said, "No," & was giving me her lips to kiss when she rec-ollected & suddenly turned her cheek, which I kissed, saying "Why did you not do as you were going to do?" I had told her before I wished she could stay all night with me & if she were at Shibden she should, to which she made no objection . . . She is fond of me certainly but I do not pay her attention as if I respect her . . . I ought not to have dared talk to her as I do. What can I think of women in general?

WEDNESDAY 20 OCT.

Began my accounts & had nearly settled them about 2—20 when Mrs Barlow came to me. She asked me if I did not mean to go out & would not sit down but after a long while standing, took her seat close to me & made love in the pathetics. This morning she seems to think she is to blame & expressed her wonder she should allow me to talk so to her. I declared none could behave better. Thanked her again & again. Said how lucky for me that, if I must be foolish, it was with a person so calm, so safe, as herself. Said I should always be obliged to her for this. She would have the thing as not new to me & asked for my word of honour. I pretended I could only give it in part & not altogether & on this account would not give it at all, pretending others had been attached to me but I not to them. Refused to explain because she would even despise me if I did. She observed my wedding ring [given to Anne by Marianna Lawton, a former lover]. [I] said this ought to bind me but this was pure friendship & I began to dread the influence that was greater. She then said, as if a momentary feeling, that the fault was hers. [She] stole over—"But, oh, you are so candid, so open." She knows me not. I am as deep as she . . . I perpetu-ally plead my want of vanity to persuade myself it is possible for her to care for me. She little knows who she has to deal with. Before all this. I had laughed & joked & declared I would go to Italy and try the experiment, that is, get a woman there. She knew what I meant—tho' wrapt up it was plain enough & she only begged me to take care. Should be sorry to see my name in the papers in such a scrape as that would be. I assured her I would manage the thing well & tell her all about it. I would always tell her everything.

THURSDAY 21 OCT.

At 2 1/2, went out with Mrs Barlow. Walked thro' the Tuileries gardens, along the Rue de Seine, direct to the Luxembourgh. Went to see the Observatory. Staid some time on top of it, enjoying the fine air & the fine view of Paris. Then sauntered about the gardens, returned as we went & got home at 5 1/4. Dinner at 5 3/4 . . . Sat with Mlle de Sans (Mrs Barlow had been there ever since dinner) by her bedside till 9—20, when Mrs Barlow & I came up to my room & she sat with me till 10 1/2. A little nonsense as usual. Held her hand & would not let her [go]. "If," said she, "you do in this way, you will prevent my coming again." Of course, I desisted. While with Mlle de Sans, she (Mrs Barlow) let me have my hand up her petticoats almost to her knee. At last, she whispered, "Do not yet." She afterwards let me do it nearly as high. She had before taken away her legs once or twice but always put them back again. Joking about whether my character was respectable, she hoped it was & I joked as if she thought it was a good deal in her power. She has said once or twice if she was not so calm, what would become of me.

TUESDAY 26 OCT.

From 3 to 5, walked [with Mrs Barlow] in the Tuileries gardens . . . Conversation in our usual style. She believes I have had a great deal of experience but acquits all my *friends*. Thinks I respect them too much. Why did I not so respect her? I pretended I respected her as much but liked or loved her better & thus explained all satisfactorily. But whatever experience I had had, she did not blame me more than other men but even thought more allowance was to be made for me than for them . . . She said I astonished Mme Galvani at first, who once or twice said to the Mackenzies she thought I was a man & the Macks too had wondered. Mrs Barlow herself had thought at first I wished to imitate the manners of a gentleman but now she knows me better, it was not put on . . . Asked Mrs Barlow if she thought I was capable of being in love. She thought yes. I said then I was so with her. She said it would soon go off. She thought her being so much with me was the best way of curing me. "Ah," said I, "you know better than that." But she trusted me. Thought me most honourable & that was the greatest obligation by which she could bind me to deserve her confidence. She wondered what Cordingley thought of me. "Oh, merely," said I, "that I have my own particular ways." I happened to say that my aunt often said I was the oddest person she ever knew. Mrs Barlow said, "But she knows all about it, does she not?" "Oh," said I, "she & my friends are all in a mist about it." . . . Mrs Barlow came to me at 7—25. Sat with me here till 8 1/2 & then in her own room till 9, when we went down to join the party . . . On leaving my room, I had before said I liked to see her dressed & put her shawl a little back. She always drew it forward again. Mere coquetry. She begins to blush a little now & then & looks rather pathetic. I asked why she had said last night she could not be happy. She said she was low. She longed to have a home. [I] reminded her she might marry when she likes. She said she might if she had not shut herself up so many years. She likes attention & had not much from the men tonight. After waiting a while she said nobody had given her a word. Of course I gave her one directly. She would not suit me. I would tire of her—but flirting with her amuses me now.

WEDNESDAY 3 NOV.

Mrs Barlow told me this morning she was 21 when she was married in 1808 to Lt. Col. Barlow of the 61st Foot, by special licence in Guernsey. Colonel Barlow was 38, about 18 years older than she. She will be 38 the 28th December next . . . In wishing her good-night she quietly let me put my arms around her waist & gently press her & very gently kiss her. She stood, too, with her right thigh a little within my left, in contact—which she has never permitted before. She likes me certainly.

TUESDAY 9 NOV.

About 7 1/4, Mrs Barlow, Mrs Heath, Mlle de Sans, M. Dacier & myself, set off (in a fiacre) to the Italian [Opera] to see Madame Pasta in "Nina Mad For Love." She was certainly very great. Her voice & singing very fine; she, very graceful. Mme Galvani some time ago said she was decidedly a very much better singer than Catalani. M. Dacier paying attention to Mlle de Sans, to which she shews no dislike, & I to Mrs Barlow. Under our shawls, had my arm round her waist great part of the time. Felt a little excited by the music, etc., & she surely knew it full well. I think she felt something herself. Had my arm round her waist, too, as we returned . . . Got home at 11—20. Went immediately into Mrs Barlow's & sat with her till 12 3/4. We had tea & I had some of my grapes. Dead lovemaking & talked a little foolishly. Said if I could not make a good hit, I should make a bad one, hinting at having a mistress. Seeing her look as if angry, [I] turned it that I should shut myself up from the world . . . I had before told her I had once had a person with me with whom I had gone to bed at ten & lain till one, two, three & later, the next day & my father would not have us disturbed. She looked & said she would not have had such a person in her house. Just before going to the Opera, had come up to put my things on & kissed her left cheek till it was quite sore & three places quite raised. When she shewed me, I laughed heartily, declaring I knew not what I was doing. She said she was ashamed to go downstairs. I believe she was but she was not at all angry.

THURSDAY 11 NOV.

Breakfast at 9—35. Mrs Barlow came at 10—10, ready to go out shopping immediately. Asked her to sit down for one minute & we sat lovemaking till ten minutes before twelve. Went to a shop in the Rue Neuve St Roch (not far from here) & bought 4 ells each of cambric at 18 francs per ell. Mrs Barlow to hem me 6 handkerchiefs. Got back at 12 3/4. Found Mme Galvani waiting for me. Spent all the time in conversation. She left me at 2—10. Then immediately came Mrs Barlow to go out again. She jumped on the window seat to see if it rained. I locked the door as usual, then lifted her down and placed her on my knee. By & by she said, "Is the door fast?" I, forgetting, got up to see, then took her again on my knee & there she sat till four & threequarters, when Mlle de Sans sent to ask if I could receive. [I] told the maid I was sorry, I could not, I had got so bad a headache. The fact was I was heated & in a state not fit to see anyone. I had kissed & pressed Mrs Barlow on my knee till I had had a complete fit of passion. My knees & thighs shook, my breathing & everything told her what was the matter. She said she did me no good. I said it was a little headache & I should go to sleep. I then leaned on her bosom &, pretending to sleep, kept pottering about & rubbing the surface of her queer. Then made several gentle efforts to put my hand up her petticoats which, however, she prevented. But she so crossed her legs & leaned against me that I put my hand over & grubbled her on the outside of her petticoats till she was evidently a little excited, & it was from this that Mlle de Sans' maid roused us. Mrs Barlow had once whispered, holding her head on my shoulder, a word or two which, I think, were, "Do you love me?" But I took no notice, still pretending to be asleep. She afterwards said once or twice, "It is good to pretend to be asleep." & then once, while I was grubbling pretty strongly, "You know you pinch me." From this she never attempted to escape. Before, when rubbing her in front, she had every now & then held my hand but always let me have it back again. After Mlle de Sans' maid roused us, she [drew] her chair close to the bed. I sat on the bed & partly knelt on one knee so as to have her quite close & she began to reproach herself, saying she was a poor, weak creature & what should I think of her. I protested love & respect. Said it was all my fault & I would be miserable if she was too severe to herself. "Can you not love me one little bit for all the great deal I love you? If you do not love me, I cannot forgive you. You are too cruel thus to sport with the feelings of another—but if you do love me, I am happy." "What do you think?" said she. "Oh," I replied, "that you do." She answered that if she did not love me she could not have done as she did. I kissed her mouth several times when it was a little open & rather warmly. Just before she left she said she was a little tired. I asked why. She answered because her feelings had been excited. She told me she had always kept all others at a great distance. I said I did not doubt it for if she could keep me at a distance under present circumstances, she certainly could others when not so tried. I said she frightened me. She had talked to me before we went out this morning about settling near Southampton with the widow of her husband's oldest brother, General Barlow, who was also her aunt, her mother's sister & about fifty. She had a son & daughter grown up. Dinner at 5 1/2. Saying I had a headache, came upstairs immediately after dinner . . . Mrs Barlow came at 10 1/4 & . . . staid with me till 11 3/4. She looked a little grave, as if half-ashamed & wondering how I should treat her. I was very respectful tho' affectionate. Said I had fancied I had much to say to her but all seemed gone & I had not a word to say. I was happy, yet could cry like a child if I chose, little as this was ever my custom. She said this would better suit her. I denied this. Asked her to sit on my knee. She refused, saying she did me harm. I still entreated & she yielded on my promise to behave well. I wished she could remain with me. Instead of expressing any objection, she said, "But as it is impossible, I had better go," & then went. Now that the ice was a little broken, what will it end in? Has she any hope of attaching me really? She is sufficiently yielding. [On my] saying to Mme Galvani that she was pretty, "No, not at all," said she, "beaucoup plus laide que moi," & that she looked eight & thirty. Her skin & complexion were bad. I thought of all this when kissing her & thought it would not do for always . . . Said Mrs Barlow [earlier], "Go to bed early. Do not write tonight." I answered, "I have not much to write. No need of it. I can remember today without writing."

SATURDAY 13 NOV.

At 2—20 went down to Mrs Barlow, meaning to go out. She thought it would be too much for her. I therefore sat with her till 4—35. Lovemaking, vindicating style of conversation respecting myself. A great pickle. "Scaped my maid & got away among the workpeople. My father was one year in the Militia. When my mother thought I was safe I was running out in an evening. Saw curious scenes, bad women, etc. Then went to the Manor school & became attached to Eliza Raine. Said how it [Anne's preference for, or sexual attraction to, women] was all nature. Had it not been genuine the thing would have been different. [I] said I had thought much, studied anatomy, etc. Could not find it out. Could not understand myself. It was all the effect of the mind. No exterior formation accounted for it. Alluded to there being an internal correspondence or likeness of some of the male or female organs of generation. Alluded to the stones not slipping thro' the ring till after birth, etc. She took all this very well. I said ladies could often hear from a man what they could not from a woman & she could from me what she could not from Mrs Mackenzie. She allowed this, saying it depended on how she loved them. Got on the subject of Saffic regard. [I] said there was artifice in it. It was very different from mine & would be no pleasure to me. I liked to have those I loved near me as possible, etc. Asked if she understood. She said no. [I] told her I knew by her eyes she did & she did not deny it, therefore I know she understands all about the use of a --- [The word is not entered in the journal]. Alluded to self-pollution, how much it was practised. Thought my connection with the ladies more excusable than this. She declared she had never heard of this (I was incredulous at heart). From one thing to another. Got to tell her that the business of Thursday was exhausting beyond measure, as it always was to excite & then disappoint nature. Said if a man loved his wife as he ought, he could say anything to her & indelicacy depended on their own minds. Many things might pass between them without indelicacy that might otherwise be shocking. She agreed, tho' hinted at things—sometimes having no night-shift at all for a little while. She said if I wore men's clothes she should feel differently. She could not then sit on my knee. If my father had brought me up as a son she would have married me as I am, had I stated my case to her alone, even tho' she had had rank & fortune & been nineteen & at that age she was well worth having. I thanked her. Happening to say I often told my uncle & aunt how I longed to have someone with me, she wondered what they would think of the person. I said my aunt knew nothing about it, nor would my uncle think anything. Then, expressing my wish to have her, she answered, "But we have had no priest but love. Do you not know the quotation?" I did not yet I said yes. Kissed her repeatedly, rather warmly. We get on gradually. Perhaps I shall have her yet before I go. [I] told her, when speaking of Eliza [Raine], we had once agreed to go off together when of age but my conduct first delayed it & then circumstances luckily put an end to it altogether. Said I had never mentioned this to any human being but herself. At this moment [of writing the journal], I half-fancy I long since told it to Marianna. At 4—35, ran off to the Rue St Honoré for some more flowers. The flower-woman gone, told the porter to get me 2 *very* pretty bouquets, one for Mme de Boyve . . . the other for Mrs Barlow. Did not dress. Sat down to dinner at 5. Immediately on leaving table went with Mrs Barlow to her room & sat with her from 5—50 to 8. Then dressed. Had the hair-dresser after her & paid him 2 francs for making me a terrible grenadier-like looking figure. Mrs Barlow with me here 1/2 hour & we then went down to the party at 9—10. Perhaps about 70 people. They danced quadrilles (in the drawing room, we all sitting round—3 card tables in the room next to us & all the gents who were not dancing) & waltzes. Mme de Boyve & sometimes Mlle de Sans playing on the piano, which was all the music they had. The ladies looked by no means all of them first-rate. The gents appeared most the best of the 2. Mrs Williams, of ridiculous notoriety at Bath in 1813 for dancing cotillons with her monkey-faced husband, etc., formerly Mrs Briscoe, wife to the Governor of St Helena of that name —a dashing person risen, I fancy, from nothing —was here tonight & danced, too, at the close of the evening in the same set with her daughter . . . Tea, bread & butter, & a few sweet cakes. Afterwards, tumbler glasses of common wine & what looked like milk & water. The cakes we had at tea—very indifferent. All the gents held their common round hats in their hands tho' it was professedly a ball—only putting them down while they danced. Mrs Barlow having asked me whether I would have her dance or not, I said no, & she refused, tho' I think with some regrets at doing so &, M. Bellevue, etc., quizzing her, at last I told him it was I would not let her dance. She had a daughter 14. It was time mama gave up dancing. It might do for a Frenchwoman but not for an Englishwoman. She and I left the room at 12—10 & I went into her room & sat with her 1/2 hour, lovemaking. Kissed her neck. She would have me stay no longer. "Go," said she, "remember the servants. Perhaps they do not love each other as we do." I rallied her on having said *we*. "Ah," said she, "I hoped you would not notice it." I perpetually expressed my wish to stay all night with her. She says nothing against it. She said tonight, "Now sit down & compose your-self. You look poorly," meaning empassioned. She told me before dinner I had given her a warm look the first morning she had come to call on me & she had remembered it ever since & always liked me.

WILLIAM WORDSWORTH (1770–1850)

"To the Lady E.B. and the Hon. Miss P., Composed in the Grounds of Plas Newydd, Near Llangollen, 1824" (1824)

William Wordsworth ranks with Shakespeare, Milton, Pope, and Keats as one of the very greatest English poets. He was the son of an attorney and educated at Cambridge. In 1791–92, after a walking tour of France and Italy, he lived for a year in Paris, where he witnessed the early phases of the French Revolution—an experience exultantly commemorated in his magnificent autobiographical poem, *The Prelude*. In 1795 he met Samuel Taylor Coleridge, with whom he formed a deep friendship and produced *Lyrical Ballads*—the first great work of English Romanticism—in 1798. In 1799, after travels with Coleridge and his wife in Germany, Wordsworth settled at Grasmere, in the Yorkshire Lake District, with his sister Dorothy. He married in 1802. Between 1800 and 1814 he produced a series of masterpieces: the famous "Preface" to the second edition (1800) of *Lyrical Ballads*, in which he articulated the guiding principles of Romantic verse; the first version of *The Prelude* (1805); *Poems in Two Volumes* (1807), containing his famous odes "On Duty" and "Intimations of Immortality"; and the meditative nature poem, *The Excursion* (1814). In 1813 he was given the position of commissioner of stamps for Westmorland, a position he held until 1842. Over the next three decades his literary fame grew, even as his verse (and political outlook) became more conservative. He continued to write into the 1840s, when he published *Poems Chiefly of Early and Late Years* (1842) and made extensive revisions to *The Prelude*. He was made Poet Laureate in 1843 and died in 1850.

Wordsworth's sonnet "To the Lady E.B. and the Hon. Miss P." celebrates the famed "Ladies of Llangollen"—Lady Eleanor Butler and Sarah Ponsonby, two Anglo-Irish gentlewomen who ran off to Plas Newydd in Wales together in 1778 and lived in romantic amity there for the next fifty years. Wordsworth was one of many visitors to Plas Newydd to commemorate the Ladies' unusual relationship in verse; his rather saccharine tribute bears comparison with Anna Seward's equally effusive *Llangollen Vale* (1796). While not in any way one of Wordworth's better poems, it captures the air of moral exaltation surrounding the two "fair and noble recluses"—prime exponents of the cult of female romantic friendship in early-nineteenth-century England.

FURTHER READING: William Wordsworth, *The Poetical Works of William Wordsworth*, ed. E. De Selincourt and Helen Darbishire, 5 vols., 2d ed. (Oxford: Clarendon, 1954); George M. Harper, *William Wordsworth: His Life, Works, and Influence* (London: John Murray, 1916); Mary Moorman, *William Wordsworth: A Biography* (Oxford: Clarendon, 1957–65); Geoffrey H. Hartman, *Wordsworth's Poetry, 1787–1814* (New Haven: Yale University Press, 1964); Elizabeth Mavor, *The Ladies of Llangollen* (Harmondsworth, Middlesex: Penguin, 1973); Hunter Davies, *William Wordsworth: A Biography* (London: Weidenfeld and Nicolson, 1980); Juliet Barker, ed., *Wordsworth: A Life in Letters* (New York: Viking, 2002).

A Stream, to mingle with your favourite Dee,
Along the Vale of Meditation flows;
So styled by those fierce Britons, pleased to see
In Nature's face the expression of repose;
Or haply there some pious hermit chose
To live and die, the peace of heaven his aim;
To whom the wild sequestered region owes,
At this late day, its sanctifying name.
Glyn Cafaillgaroch, in the Cambrian tongue,
In ours, the Vale of Friendship, let *this* spot
Be named; where, faithful to a low-roofed Cot,
On Deva's banks, ye have abode so long;
Sisters in love, a love allowed to climb,
Even on this earth, above the reach of Time!

THÉOPHILE GAUTIER (1811–72)

From *Mademoiselle de Maupin* (1835)

The French poet, novelist, and critic Théophile Gautier was born in Hautes-Pyrenées in 1811 and educated in Paris at the Collège Charlemagne. In his youth he was a literary radical and joined with Victor Hugo and other bohemians in championing the new romantic style of French verse over older classical models. His first book of poems, *Poésies*, appeared alongside Hugo's famous drama *Hernani* in a single volume in 1830. Gautier published his best-known work, the comico-historical lesbian romance, *Mademoiselle de Maupin*, in 1835. In a brilliant preface he articulated for the first time in French literature the revolutionary notion of "art for art's sake," soon to become one of the dominant aesthetic concepts of the century. The novel itself was extremely successful, though also widely condemned for its immorality. In subsequent decades Gautier turned to journalism and travel writing, producing a number of books and a corpus of elegant essays on literature and painting. (He ultimately became, like Baudelaire, an esteemed art critic.) His later novels, *Le Roman de la Momie* and *Le Capitaine Fracasse*, appeared in 1856 and 1863; a final book of poetry, *Émaux et Camées* (1852), had a profound influence on the so-called Parnassian poets of the 1860s. Gautier was the dedicatee of Baudelaire's *Les Fleurs du mal* (1859) and the father of the distinguished writer and journalist Judith Gautier (1846–1917).

Although written in part as a manifesto for his aesthetic views, Gautier's *Mademoiselle de Maupin* owes its continuing popularity to its sophisticated handling of the subject of female homoeroticism. Set in a temporally amorphous, romantic-pastoral landscape, the novel tells the story of Madeleine de Maupin, a beautiful young woman who disguises herself as a man in order to travel the world and gain knowledge usually hidden from her sex. Arriving at a château in the country in the guise of "Théodore de Serannes," she immediately attracts the love of an impressionable young man, D'Albert, *and* of his young mistress, the courtesan Rosette. D'Albert fears he has succumbed to an unnatural passion, while Rosette eagerly tries to seduce the mysterious stranger. Both lovers will ultimately be satisfied: the night before Mademoiselle de Maupin rides off in search of new adventures, she reveals her sex and sleeps with both in turn. Rosette is the last to enjoy her caresses; the novel ends with a description of the "imprint of two bodies" found in Rosette's bed the morning after.

Mademoiselle de Maupin has always been a lesbian cult book—and played a talismanic role in nineteenth- and twentieth-century lesbian writing. In James Huneker's *Painted Veils* (1920), a roman à clef about the bisexual turn-of-the-century opera singer Mary Garden, the heroine begins an affair with a masculine-looking woman named Allie after reading it. (She will later taunt a jealous male ex-lover with her passion for Gautier's "sumptuous" descriptions of vice.) In Lillian Hellman's play *The Children's Hour* (1936), a copy of Gautier's novel circulates surreptitiously among the teenaged students at the Wright-Dobie School for Girls, prompting one of them to accuse the two women who run the school of having a homosexual liaison. It crops up in later lesbian fiction too, notably in Rosemary Manning's *The Chinese Garden* (1962) and Brigid Brophy's *The Finishing Touch* (1963).

In the passage below, Madeleine/Théodore, the dashing male impersonator, describes one of Rosette's numerous assaults on her virtue. The scene is typical in its delicious mixture of sensual titillation, poetic fantasia, and the purest bedroom farce.

FURTHER READING: Théophile Gautier, *Mademoiselle de Maupin*, ed. Adolphe Boschot, rev. ed. (Paris: Garnier Frères, 1955); ——, *Mademoiselle de Maupin*, trans. Joanna Richardson (Harmondsworth, Middlesex: Penguin, 1981); Kari Weil, "Romantic Androgyny and Its Discontents: The Case of *Mademoiselle de Maupin*," *Romanic Review* 78 (1987): 348–358; Rosemary H. Lloyd, "Speculum Amantic, Speculum Artis: The Seduction of Mademoiselle de Maupin," *Nineteenth-Century French Studies* 15 (1986/87): 77–86; Janet Sadoff, *Ambivalence, Ambiguity, and Androgyny in Théophile Gautier's "Mademoiselle de Maupin"* (Cambridge: Harvard University Press, 1990); Terry Castle, *The Apparitional Lesbian: Female Homosexuality and Modern Culture* (New York: Columbia University Press, 1993); ——, "Lesbian Aesthetics: A Historical View," in Michael Kelly, ed., *Encyclopedia of Aesthetics* (Oxford: Oxford University Press, 1998), 3:141–44; Christopher Rivers, " 'Inintelligible pour une femme honnête': Sexuality, Textuality, and Knowledge in Diderot's *La Religieuse* and Gautier's *Mademoiselle de Maupin*," *Romanic Review* 86 (January 1995): 1–29; Marlene Barsoum, *Théophile Gautier's "Mademoiselle de Maupin": Toward a Definition of "Androgynous Discourse"* (New York: Peter Lang, 2001).

One day, after having roved about with me for a long time through a pleasance which extended for a great distance behind the mansion, and with which I was unfamiliar, except for those parts bordering on the outbuildings, [Rosette] led me along a tiny path which twined at random and was fringed with elder-trees and hazel bushes, to a small cottage, which might have been a charcoal-burner's hut built of logs arranged crosswise, with a roof of rushes and a door consisting of five or six pieces of wood, scarcely touched by a plane and fastened together in a very rough and ready fashion, the cracks between them being stopped up with moss and wild plants. Close at hand, among the greeny roots of tall ash trees with silvery bark, and flecked here and there with dark patches, gushed a copious spring, which, a few yards farther on, plunged over two marble ledges into a pool filled with water-cress which was greener than any emerald.

At the few spots which were not covered with water-cress could be seen fine, snow-white sand. The water was as clear as crystal and as cold as ice. It issued from the soil in a sudden jet, and amid those dense shadows it was quite beyond the range of even the faintest sunbeam, so that it had no time to become luke-warm or turbid. Although it is apt to be rough to the taste, I am fond of spring-water, and when I saw it there, looking so limpid, I could not resist the temptation to take a drink of it. I stooped down, and as no drinking-vessel was available, I let it flow into the hollow of my hand, and repeated the process several times.

Rosette expressed the wish to quench her thirst with this water, too, and asked me to bring her some, explaining that she could hardly venture to stoop down far enough to reach it herself. I plunged both my hands, which I had linked together as tightly as possible, into the clear fount, then raised them like a goblet to Rosette's lips and held them there until she had drunk every drop of water which was in them. This did not take long, because there was not very much, and some of that trickled away through my fingers, however closely I kept them locked together. It must have been a very engaging sight, and I only wish that a sculptor could have been there to make a sketch of it.

When she had almost finished, her feelings overcame her, and she imprinted a kiss upon my hand which was close to her lips, but she did so in such a way as to try and make me think that she was merely endeavouring to sip the last few drops left in my palm. This did not mislead me, however, and the delightful blush which suddenly over-spread her countenance was sufficient evidence against her.

She took my arm again, and we moved on towards the hut. The fair lady walked as close to me as possible, and while talking to me leaned over in such a way that her bosom rested entirely on my sleeve—a very artfully contrived arrangement, and one which might well have stirred the senses of anyone but myself. I could feel, in every detail, her bosom's form and flawless outline, and also its gentle warmth. Not only that, but I became aware of a sudden throbbing which may have been deliberate or sponta-neous, but by which I was anyhow flattered and gratified.

In this way we reached the door of the hut, which I kicked open. The sight which met my gaze astounded me. I had expected the walls of the shack to be covered with bullrushes, with matting on the floor and a few stools to rest on, but it was not at all like that.

It was a boudoir furnished with the utmost elegance. Above the doors and the mir-rors were portrayed the most lascivious episodes from Ovid's Metamorphoses, Salmacis and Hermaphroditus, Venus and Adonis, Apollo and Daphne, and other love-scenes in bright lilac cameo-painting. The pier-glasses were decorated with small roses, very delicately carved, and daisies, in which love of luxury was carried to its utmost limits, for their heart-shaped centres were gilded and their leaves were silvered. All the furniture was edged with silver braid which set off wall-paper of the softest possible blue, wonderfully suited as a means for making the whiteness and lustre of the flesh stand out. Mantelpiece, shelves, and what-nots were crowded with delightful curios, and there was a lavish supply of settees, couches and sofas, which showed plainly enough that this retreat was not intended for very ascetic pursuits, and that it was no place for those bent on the mortification of the flesh.

A handsome grotto-work clock, standing on a richly-inlaid pedestal, faced a large Venetian mirror, where it was reproduced in a set of glittering vistas which were quite fascinating. I should add that it had stopped, as though to emphasise how pointless it would be to record the hours in a place where they were meant to be forgotten.

I told Rosette that this refinement of luxury was greatly to my liking, that I thought it in very good taste to conceal such studied elegance beneath a primitive exterior, and that I considered it most proper for a woman to wear embroidered petticoats and lace-trimmed body-linen, with outer garments of plain material; that for the lover whom she had or might have, this was a subtle mark of favour which could not be appreciated too highly, and that it was unquestionably better to place a diamond into a walnut, than a walnut into a golden casket.

To prove to me that she shared my opinion, Rosette raised her dress a little and showed me the hem of a petticoat very richly embroidered with large flowers and leaves. It was solely for me to decide whether I wished to be initiated into the secrets of the even greater splendours below, but I showed no eagerness to discover if the glories of the body-linen matched those of the petticoat. I dare say that it was no less sumptuous. Rosette covered her petticoat up again, probably annoyed that she had not shown more.

Nevertheless, this display had enabled her to reveal the beginnings of a flawlessly turned calf which prompted a strong hankering for loftier views. The leg which she stretched forward to show off her petticoat to better advantage was indeed wonderfully delicate and graceful in its pearl-grey silk stocking which fitted to a nicety, while her foot was shod in a tiny slipper, the heel of which was bedecked with a tuft of ribbons, and which resembled the glass slipper worn by Cinderella. I complimented her on it with the utmost sincerity, declaring that I had never come across a prettier leg or a smaller foot, and that I did not see how they could possibly be shapelier. To which she replied with an altogether bright and engaging freedom from pretence and affectation:

"You are right."

Then from a sliding panel in the wall she took one or two bottles of liqueurs and some plates of sweetmeats and cakes, laid it all out on a small stand, and came and sat down beside me on a rather narrow settee, so that in order not to be cramped, I had to slip my arm behind her waist. As she had both hands free, and I could use only my left hand, she filled my glass herself, and put fruit and sweetmeats upon my plate; and presently, when she saw that I was making rather clumsy attempts to deal with them, she said to me: "Come, come now, never mind about that. You're such a baby that you can't feed yourself, so I'm going to feed you." Whereupon she put the morsels into my mouth, and made me gulp them down more quickly than I altogether liked, pushing them in with her dainty fingers, treating me just like a bird that is being crammed, and laughing very heartily about it.

I could scarcely refrain from repaying to her fingers the kiss which, a short while before, she had bestowed upon the palms of my hands, and as though to prevent me from doing so, but in reality to give me a chance of finding a wider scope for my kiss, she slapped my mouth two or three times with the back of her hand.

She had drunk a few nips of curaçao, with a glass of marsala, and I about the same amount. It was certainly not a great deal, but it was enough to exhilarate a couple of women accustomed to drink nothing stronger than water with the merest dash of wine in it. Rosette began to loll backwards and toppled over upon my arm in a most affectionate fashion. She had thrown off her mantle, and in this twisted posture her bosom was thrust forward and squeezed, so that the top of it could be seen. Its flesh-tint was of a captivating sheen and delicacy; its shape was a wonderful blend of the subtle and the ample. I gazed at her for some time with an unaccountable excitement and gratification, and I could not help thinking that, in matters of love, men were more generously treated than ourselves, seeing that we present them with the most delightful of trophies, whereas they have nothing similar to confer upon us.

What bliss it must be for a man to let his lips stray over this smooth fine skin and these rounded curves, which seem to advance towards the kiss and to challenge it; this satiny flesh, these rippling lines which become entwined with each other, these silky tresses, so soft to the touch; what unbounded sources of subtle raptures which we cannot derive from men! Our own caresses can scarcely be other than passive, and yet it is a greater joy to give than to receive.

Last year I would assuredly never have indulged in such reflections as these, and I then might have looked at all the bosoms and shoulders on earth, without stopping to think whether they were shapely or the reverse. But since I have laid aside the garb proper to my sex and have lived among young men, an awareness with which I was previously quite unfamiliar has developed within me—the awareness of beauty. As a rule, it is withheld from women, I know not why, for at first sight they would seem better able to judge of it than men. But as they are the possessors of beauty, and self-knowledge is more difficult than any other kind, it is not surprising that it should be entirely beyond their range.

In general, if one woman thinks another woman good-looking, it may be taken for granted that she is really very ugly, and that not a man will vouchsafe her a glance. On the other hand, all women whose beauty and grace find favour with men are, with one accord, denounced as disgusting hussies by the whole of the petticoated mob, who hoot and hiss at them till further notice. If I were what I appear to be, this is the only standard of taste which I would follow, and I would regard the disapproval of women as a testimonial to a woman's beauty.

I am now familiar with beauty and I cherish it. The garb which I wear sets me apart from my sex, and deadens all feeling of rivalry within me. I am thus better fitted to assess it than anyone else can be. I am no longer a woman, but I am not yet a man, and desire will not blind my judgment so utterly that I shall mistake lay figures for goddesses. I can see with detachment and without bias one way or the other, and my attitude is as impartial as it could possibly be.

The length and delicacy of eyelashes, the pellucid quality of a forehead, the lustre of an iris, the convolutions of an ear, the tint and texture of hair, the elegance of a foot or a hand, the amount of tapering at the joint of the leg or the wrist, a thousand and one items to which I used to pay no attentions, but which are the signs of true beauty and reveal purity of breed, are the details which enable me to form my judgments, and if I keep to them, I can hardly go wrong. I venture to say that if I described a woman as being "really quite nice," that opinion could be implicitly accepted.

It follows as a matter of course that I have a far sounder knowledge of pictures than before, and though I have only a nodding acquaintance with the great masters, it would be difficult to foist off a bad painting upon me as a good one. This is a study which I find downright enthralling, for, like everything else in the world, beauty, moral or physical, needs to be studied, and cannot be mastered without further ado.

But let us return to Rosette; the transition from this subject to her is by no means difficult, for they are two ideas which are closely akin.

As I have said, the fair lady had flung herself back across my arm and her head was resting against my shoulder. Excitement had tinged her lovely cheeks a delicate pink, which was bewitchingly set off by the deep black of a small beauty-patch, placed so as to produce the most coquettish effect. Her teeth gleamed through her smile like raindrops in the depths of a poppy, and the humid splendour of her large eyes was still further heightened by her half-drooping lashes. A ray of light caused countless metallic glints to sparkle upon her hair which shone like watered silk, and a few curls from which had slipped from their proper place, and these stray ringlets, twining along her dimpled neck, enhanced its rich whiteness. A few small fluffy hairs, more rebellious than the rest, had broken loose from the mass, and were twisting themselves in wayward spirals, which were gilded with a strange flickering lustre and which, with a ray of light falling across them, displayed all the hues of the rainbow. They looked just like those golden threads which surround the head of the Virgin Mary in old paintings. Neither of us spoke, and I was intently gazing at the tiny sky-blue veins beneath the pearly sheen of her temples, and the down which softly and gradually faded away on the fringe of her eyebrows.

The fair lady seemed to be engrossed in thought and basking in dreams of boundless bliss. Her arms hung alongside her body, as slack and soft as loosened scarfs; her head was tilted back more and more, as though the muscles which had been supporting it had been severed, or were too weak to do so any longer. She had tucked her dainty feet beneath her petticoat, and had managed to squeeze herself so closely into a corner of the small sofa on which I was seated, although it was extremely narrow, that there was ample room on the other side.

Her body, deft and supple, shaped itself against mine like wax, and adapted itself to its general outlines with the utmost precision. Water could not have flowed more closely round each separate curve. Clinging thus to my side, she resembled that extra stroke which painters add to their pictures on the side where the shadow is, to give them greater fullness and depth. Only a woman eager for love is capable of twining and clinging in such a manner as that. Ivy and willow cannot approach it.

The soft warmth of her body found its way to me. Magnetic currents were radiating from her by the thousand; it was as though the whole of her living essence had passed from her and entered into me. Minute by minute, she drooped and weakened and wilted more and more. Tiny beads of sweat appeared on her lustrous brow; her eyes grew moist, and two or three times she made as though to cover them with her lifted hands, but half-way her wearied arms fell back upon her knees, and each of her efforts proved equally vain—a big tear overflowed from her eyelid and rolled down her burning cheek where it quickly vanished.

My predicament was becoming very awkward, not to say ludicrous. I felt that I must be cutting an extremely poor figure, and that caused me no end of annoyance, although I could not act in any other way. My only appropriate course would have been to show a bold front, and those were the very tactics that were ruled out. I could not afford to risk it, for I felt too sure of meeting with no opposition, and I was, in fact, at my wits' end. At the start, it would have been quite fitting to lavish blandishments and honied words upon the lady, but it would have been the height of silliness at the stage which we had reached. To get up and go out would have been the height of rudeness, and besides, for all I knew, Rosette might have played the part of Potiphar's wife, and caught me by my garment.

I could not claim that my opposition to her wishes was the result of any virtuous promptings; in fact, I must confess it to my shame, this scene, though it placed me in an embarrassing position, was not without a certain lure which appealed to me more than it should have done. The heat of Rosette's craving set me, too, aglow, and I felt a genuine distress at not being able to gratify it. Indeed, I only wished that I were a man, such as I seemed to be, so that I could have consummated this love of hers, for I hated the idea that Rosette should suffer such discomfiture. I began to breathe convulsively, I could feel my face becoming flushed, and I was almost as agitated as the poor love-lorn lady beside me. The knowledge that we were of the same sex gradually ebbed from my mind, and left me with an uneasy sense of something pleasurable. My vision became blurred, my lips trembled, and if Rosette had been a male, I would have assuredly met her more than half way.

At last, unable to bear it any longer, she suddenly stood up in rather a jerky manner, and began to walk about the room with restless steps. Then she stopped in front of the mirror and tidied a few locks of hair which had become uncoiled. During this process I felt very small indeed, and scarcely knew which way to look.

She stopped in front of me and seemed to be pondering.

She must have thought that I was being held back merely by a frantic bashfulness and that I was more of a novice than she had at first supposed. She was now quite beside herself and thoroughly overwrought by her frustrated craving for love, and she decided to make one final effort, like a gambler who stakes everything, either to lose it all or to break the bank.

She came up to me, sat down on my knees and, in a flash, flung her arms round my neck, crossed her hands behind my head, and clung with her lips to mine in a frenzied embrace. I felt her bosom almost bare and wildly aquiver, surging against my breast, and her entwined fingers writhing in my hair. My whole body thrilled and my nipples stiffened.

Rosette remained clinging to my mouth. Her lips were glued to my lips, her teeth were jolting against my teeth, and our very breath was mingled. I shrank back for a brief moment, and turned my head aside two or three times to evade this kiss; but it had an overwhelming fascination which egged me on, and I returned it to her almost as ardently as she had given it to me. Heaven alone knows how all this would have ended, but just in the nick of time we heard a loud barking outside the door, together with the sound of paws scraping against it. The door was thrust open, and a handsome white greyhound came yelping and capering into the hut.

Rosette stood up suddenly, and beat a hasty retreat to the other side of the room. The handsome greyhound frisked gleefully around her, and tried to lick her hands. She was so distraught that it was all she could do to straighten her mantle upon her shoulders.

This greyhound belonged to her brother Alcibiades and was a great pet of his. It was nearly always with him, so that whenever it appeared on the scene, its master was bound to be close at hand. That is why poor Rosette was so scared.

And sure enough, Alcibiades himself turned up a minute later, booted and spurred, and whip in hand. "Ah! there you are," said he, "I've been trying to find you for the last hour, and I certainly shouldn't have found you if my trusty grey hound Snug hadn't run you to earth in your hide-out." And he cast a half-serious, half-playful glance at his sister which made her blush to the roots of her hair. "It looks as if you had some very ticklish subjects to discuss, tucking yourself away like this far from the madding crowd. I suppose you were arguing about theology and the twofold nature of the soul?"

"Good gracious no. Nothing so high-flown as that. We were only taking a little refreshment and having a chat about the latest fashions."

"I don't believe a word of it. It looked to me just now as if you were deep in a confab about love. But it wouldn't be at all a bad idea if you dropped your empty prattle and joined me in a canter. I have a new mare that I want to try. You shall ride her as well, Théodore, and we'll put her through her paces."

The three of us left together, he giving me his arm, and I giving mine to Rosette. The expressions on our faces were remarkably varied. Alcibiades looked thoughtful, I quite happy, and Rosette exasperated.

HONORÉ DE BALZAC (1799–1850)

From *The Girl with the Golden Eyes* (1835)

The phenomenally prolific Honoré de Balzac, one of the great masters of nineteenth-century European fiction, was born into a wealthy middle-class family. While still in his teens, he rebelled against his parents' bourgeois aspirations by deciding to become a writer. He worked as a hack in Paris between 1819 and 1829, publishing a raft of anonymous cheap stories and thrillers. In 1829, however, concerned to produce something of more lasting value, he wrote *Le Dernier Chouan,* the first of the series of great realist novels that would form the celebrated *Comédie humaine* (1842–1850)—a vast fictional panorama of nineteenth-century French moral and social life. Over the next twenty years he wrote a staggering number of interlinked novels and short stories, the best-known of which are *La Peau de chagrin* (1831), *Eugénie Grandet* (1833), *Le Père Goriot* (1834), *Splendeurs et misères des courtisanes* (1838–47), *Illusions perdues* (1843), and *La Cousine Bette* (1847). Though enormously successful and a self-proclaimed "genius"—a point on which history has shown him to be correct—he was constantly in debt and wasted huge sums of money on extravagances and frivolous business ventures. Ugly and plump in appearance, he was as intemperate in love as he was in other aspects of life and had numerous mistresses. He died of apoplexy five months after marrying Evelina Hanska, a wealthy Polish countess whom he had pursued for seventeen years.

Over the course of his prodigious career Balzac—whose frankness on sexual matters was one of his pioneering contributions to the thematics of the novel—touched with some regularity on the subject of desire between women. Lesbianism plays a peripheral role in the fanciful romantic story *Seraphitus-Seraphita* (1834); a rather more telling one in *La Cousine Bette.* (In the latter work the narrator speaks of "the strongest emotion known, that of a woman for a woman.") Yet the celebrated novella *La Fille aux yeux d'or* (*The Girl with the Golden Eyes*), first published in 1835, the same year as Gautier's *Mademoiselle de Maupin,* marks his most provocative treatment of the theme. Though the homosexuality of its two main female characters is insinuated more than described—and will only become fully manifest in the story's shocking final scenes—the story remains one of the classic texts of nineteenth-century lesbian literary decadence. With her "pale sublime" face and murderous appetites, the beautiful Marquise de San-Réal is the prototype for a host of evil girl-lovers in later European literature—

a kind of human pollutant, whose malignant influence can be felt all the way from Baudelaire's *Les Fleurs du mal* and Swinburne's *Lesbia Brandon* to Renée Vivien's *A Woman Appeared to Me* and Djuna Barnes's *Nightwood*.

In the first excerpt below, Henri de Marsay, a jaded Parisian rake and the story's deluded antihero, has a strange love tryst with Paquita, a mysterious young Spanish girl with whom he has become intrigued. Paquita is being kept by a jealous lover, temporarily away in London, who has left her virtually imprisoned in lavish private quarters. De Marsay can only meet Paquita if he agrees to let himself be brought, blindfolded and in secret, to the house where she is hidden away—somewhere on the Rue Saint-Lazare. He complies and is delivered to her exotic boudoir by a mulatto eunuch servant, Cristemio. (In order to keep his own identity secret, De Marsay has told her his name is Adolphe de Gouges.) De Marsay and Paquita then make passionate love, marred only by De Marsay's puzzled awareness that "the girl of the golden eyes might be a virgin, but innocent she was certainly not." When he asks if he might stay with her longer, she is overcome with terror and insists that he leave, telling him her life depends on it. He submits, is blindfolded again, and finds himself, sometime later, on the Boulevard Montmartre.

In the second excerpt—mad with desire and increasingly curious about his unknown rival— De Marsay has another rendezvous with Paquita at her apartment. She begs him to take her away; they wildly embrace. Yet even as his sexual excitement intensifies, so do his suspicions that only something "criminal" can explain Paquita's peculiar sophistication. His worst fear is shockingly realized when Paquita, gazing up into his face, accidentally calls out the name "Margarita" in the act of love. In a rage, he tries to kill her, but is thwarted by Cristemio, the eunuch, and forced to flee. A week later, still determined to kill Paquita, he returns to her hôtel, the address of which Paquita has let him discover. He is accompanied by several members of the Devourers, a secret masculine society to which he belongs. Hearing terrible cries as he runs up the stairway to her room, De Marsay finds that Paquita has already been fatally stabbed— in an orgy of blood and frenzy—by the Marquise de San-Réal, the secret "Margarita," now suddenly returned. In the story's fantastic final twist, De Marsay and the Marquise look into one another's faces and realize that they are half-brother and half-sister, both having been fathered by Lord Dudley, a wayward English aristocrat. The Marquise tells De Marsay she is going to retire to a convent; and De Marsay, feeling no compunction to report Paquita's murder, returns to his old rakish life, his lust for vengeance apparently satisfied.

FURTHER READING: Honoré de Balzac, *Oeuvres complètes*, ed. Marcel Bouteron and Henri Longnon, 40 vols. (Paris: L. Conard, 1912–40); —, *Le Moment de la Comédie humaine: Balzac, oeuvres complètes*, ed. Claude Duchet and Isabelle Tounier (Saint-Denis: Presses Universitaires de Vincennes, 1993); —, *The Girl with the Golden Eyes*, trans. Ernest Dowson (London: n.p., 1929); Jeannette Foster, *Sex Variant Women in*

Literature (1956; rpt. Tallahassee, Fla.: Naiad, 1985); Pierre Michel, "Discours romanesque, discours érotique, discours mythique dans *La Fille aux yeux d'or*," in R. Bellet, ed., *La Femme au XIXème siècle: Littérature et idéologie* (Lyon: P. U. de Lyon, 1979), pp. 179–87; Shoshana Felman, "Rereading Femininity," *Yale French Studies* 62 (1981): 19–44; Pierre Saint-Amand, "Balzac Oriental: *La Fille aux yeux d'or*," *Romanic Review* 79 (1988): 329–40; Owen N. Heathcote, "The Engendering of Violence and the Violation of Gender in Honoré de Balzac's *La Fille aux yeux d'or*," *Romance Studies* 22 (1993), 99–112; Peter Brooks, *The Melodramatic Imagination: Balzac, Henry James, Melodrama, and the Mode of Excess* (New Haven: Yale University Press, 1995).

[*De Marsay arrives at Paquita's strange hideaway for the first time:*]

A woman's hand pushed him on to a divan, and untied the handkerchief for him. Henri saw Paquita before him, but Paquita in all her womanly and voluptuous glory. The section of the boudoir in which Henri found himself described a circular line, softly gracious, which was faced opposite by the other perfectly square half, in the midst of which a chimney-piece shone of gold and white marble. He had entered by a door on one side, hidden by a rich tapestried screen, opposite which was a window. The semi-circular portion was adorned with a real Turkish divan, that is to say, a mattress thrown on the ground, but a mattress as broad as a bed, a divan fifty feet in circumference, made of white cashmere, relieved by bows of black and scarlet silk, arranged in panels. The top of this huge bed was raised several inches by numerous cushions, which further enriched it by their tasteful comfort. The boudoir was lined with some red stuff, over which an Indian muslin was stretched, fluted after the fashion of Corinthian columns, in plaits going in and out, and bound at the top and bottom by bands of poppy-coloured stuff, on which were designs in black arabesque.

Below the muslin the poppy turned to rose, that amorous colour, which was matched by window curtains, which were of Indian muslin lined with rose-coloured taffeta, and set off with a fringe of poppy-colour and black. Six silver-gilt arms, each supporting two candles, were attached to the tapestry at an equal distance, to illuminate the divan. The ceiling, from the middle of which a lustre of unpolished silver hung, was of a brilliant whiteness, and the cornice was gilded. The carpet was like an Oriental shawl, it had the designs and recalled the poetry of Persia, where the hands of slaves had worked on it. The furniture was covered in white cashmere, relieved by black and poppy-coloured ornaments. The clock, the candelabra, all were in white marble and gold. The only table there had a cloth of cashmere. Elegant flower pots held roses of every kind, flowers white or red. In fine, the least detail seemed to have been the object of loving thought. Never had richness hidden itself more coquettishly to become elegance, to express grace, to inspire pleasure. Everything there would have warmed the coldest of beings. The caresses of the tapestry, of which the colour changed according to the direction of one's gaze, becoming either all white or all rose, harmonised with the effects of the light shed upon the diaphanous tissues of the muslin, which produced an appearance of mistiness. The soul has I know not what attraction towards white, love delights in red, and the passions are flattered by gold, which has the power of real-ising their caprices. Thus all that man possesses within him of vague and mysterious, all his inexplicable affinities were caressed in their involuntary sympathies. There was in this perfect harmony a concert of colour to which the soul responded with vague and voluptuous and fluctuating ideas.

It was out of a misty atmosphere, laden with exquisite perfumes, that Paquita, clad in a white wrapper, her feet bare, orange blossom in her black hair, appeared to Henri, knelt before him, adoring him as the god of this temple, whither he had deigned to come. Although De Marsay was accustomed to seeing the utmost efforts of Parisian luxury, he was surprised at the aspect of this shell, like that from which Venus rose out of the sea. Whether from an effect of contrast between the darkness from which he issued and the light which bathed his soul, whether from a comparison which he swiftly made between this scene and that of their first interview, he experienced one of those delicate sensations which true poetry gives. Perceiving in the midst of this retreat, which had been opened to him as by a fairy's magic wand, the masterpiece of creation, this girl, whose warmly coloured tints, whose soft skin—soft, but slightly gilded by the shadows, by I know not what vaporous effusion of love—gleamed as though it reflected the rays of colour and light, his anger, his desire for vengeance, his wounded vanity, all were lost.

Like an eagle darting on its prey, he took her utterly to him, set her on his knees, and felt with an indescribable intoxication the voluptuous pressure of this girl, whose richly developed beauties softly enveloped him.

"Come to me, Paquita!" he said, in a low voice.

"Speak, speak without fear!" she said. "This retreat was built for love. No sound can escape from it, so greatly was it desired to guard avariciously the accents and music of the beloved voice. However loud should be the cries, they would not be heard out-side these walls. A person might be murdered, and his moans would be as vain as if he were in the midst of the great desert."

"Who has understood jealousy and its needs so well?"

"Never question me as to that," she answered, untying with a gesture of wonder-ful sweetness the young man's scarf, doubtless in order the better to behold his neck.

"Yes, there is the neck I love so well!" she said. "Wouldst thou please me?"

This interrogation, rendered by the accent almost lascivious, drew De Marsay from the reverie in which he had been plunged by Paquita's authoritative refusal to allow him any research as to the unknown being who hovered like a shadow about them.

"And if I wished to know who reigns here?"

Paquita looked at him trembling.

"It is not I, then?" he said, rising and freeing himself from the girl, whose head fell backwards. "Where I am, I would be alone."

"Strike, strike! . . ." said the poor slave, a prey to terror.

"For what do you take me then? . . . Will you answer?"

Paquita got up gently, her eyes full of tears, took a poignard from one of the two ebony pieces of furniture, and presented it to Henri with a gesture of submission which would have moved a tiger.

"Give me a feast such as men give when they love," she said, "and whilst I sleep slay me, for I know not how to answer thee. Hearken! I am bound like some poor beast to a stake; I am amazed that I have been able to throw a bridge over the abyss which divides us. Intoxicate me, then kill me! Ah, no, no!" she cried, joining her hands, "do not kill me! I love life! Life is fair to me! If I am a slave, I am a queen too. I could beguile you with words, tell you that I love you alone, prove it to you, profit by my momentary empire to say to you: 'Take me as one tastes the perfume of a flower when one passes it in a king's garden.' Then, after having used the cunning eloquence of woman and soared on the wings of pleasure, after having quenched my thirst, I could have you cast into a pit, where none could find you, which has been made to gratify vengeance without having to fear that of the law, a pit full of lime which would kindle and consume you, until no particle of you were left. You would stay in my heart, mine for ever."

Henri looked at the girl without trembling, and this fearless gaze filled her with joy.

"No, I shall not do it! You have fallen into no trap here, but upon the heart of a woman who adores you, and it is I who will be cast into the pit."

"All this appears to me prodigiously strange," said De Marsay, considering her. "But you seem to me a good girl, a strange nature; you are, upon my word of honour, a living riddle, the answer to which is very difficult to find."

Paquita understood nothing of what the young man said, she looked at him gently, opening wide eyes which could never be stupid, so much was pleasure written in them.

"Come, then, my love," she said, returning to her first idea, "wouldst thou please me?"

"I would do all that thou wouldst, and even that thou wouldst not," answered De Marsay with a laugh. He had recovered his foppish ease, as he took the resolve to let himself go to the climax of his good fortune, looking neither before nor after. Perhaps he counted, moreover, on his power and his capacity of a man used to adventures, to dominate this girl a few hours later and learn all her secrets.

"Well," said she, "let me arrange you as I would like."

Paquita went joyously and took from one of the two chests a robe of red velvet, in which she dressed De Marsay, then adorned his head with a woman's bonnet and wrapped a shawl round him. Abandoning herself to these follies with a child's innocence, she laughed a convulsive laugh, and resembled some bird flapping its wings; but she saw nothing beyond.

If it be impossible to paint the unheard of delights which these two creatures—made by heaven in a joyous moment—found, it is perhaps necessary to translate metaphysically the extraordinary and almost fantastic impressions of the young man. That which persons in the social position of De Marsay, living as he lived, are best able to recognise is a girl's innocence. But, strange phenomenon! The girl of the golden eyes might be virgin, but innocent she was certainly not. The fantastic union of the mysterious and the real, of darkness and light, horror and beauty, pleasure and danger, paradise and hell, which had already been met with in this adventure, was resumed in the capricious and sublime being with whom De Marsay dallied. All the utmost science of the most refined pleasure, all that Henri could know of that poetry of the senses which is called love, was excelled by the treasures poured forth by this girl, whose radiant eyes gave the lie to none of the promises which they made.

She was an oriental poem, in which shone the sun that Saadi, that Hafiz, have set in their pulsing strophes. Only, neither the rhythm of Saadi, nor that of Pindar, could have expressed the ecstasy—full of confusion and stupefaction—which seized the delicious girl when the error in which an iron hand had caused her to live was at an end.

"Dead!" she said, "I am dead, Adolphe! Take me away to the world's end, to an island where no one knows us. Let there be no traces of our flight! We should be followed to the gates of hell. God! here is the day! Escape! Shall I ever see you again? Yes, to-morrow I will see you, if I have to deal death to all my warders to have that joy. Till to-morrow."

She pressed him in her arms with an embrace in which the terror of death mingled. Then she touched a spring, which must have been in connection with a bell, and implored De Marsay to permit his eyes to be bandaged.

"And if I would not—and if I wished to stay here?"

"You would be the death of me more speedily," she said, "for now I know I am certain to die on your account."

Henri submitted. [. . .]

[De Marsay returns to Paquita's apartment the following evening and is increasingly baffled by her mysterious behavior. Then—while they are making love—he makes a horrifying discovery.]

As on the previous night, he found himself on the ottoman before Paquita, who was undoing his bandage; but he saw her pale and altered. She had wept. On her knees like an angel in prayer, but like an angel profoundly sad and melancholy, the poor girl no longer resembled the curious, impatient and impetuous creature who had carried De Marsay on her wings to transport him to the seventh heaven of love. There was something so true in this despair veiled by pleasure, that the terrible De Marsay felt within him an admiration for this new masterpiece of nature, and forgot, for the moment, the chief interest of his assignation.

"What is the matter with thee, my Paquita?"

"My friend," she said, "carry me away this very night. Bear me to some place where no one can say who sees me: 'That is Paquita,' where no one can answer: 'There is a girl with a golden gaze here, who has long hair.' Yonder I will give thee as many pleasures as thou wouldst have of me. Then when you love me no longer, you shall leave me, I shall not complain, I shall say nothing; and your desertion need cause you no remorse, for one day passed with you, only one day, in which I have had you before my eyes, will be worth all my life to me. But if I stay here, I am lost."

"I cannot leave Paris, little one!" replied Henri. "I do not belong to myself, I am bound by a vow to the fortune of several persons who stand to me, as I do to them. But I can place you in a refuge in Paris, where no human power can reach you."

"No," she said, "you forget the power of woman."

Never did phrase uttered by human voice express terror more absolutely.

"What could reach you, then, if I put myself between you and the world?"

"Poison!" she said. "Doña Concha suspects you already . . . and," she resumed, letting the tears fall and glisten on her cheeks, "it is easy enough to see I am no longer the same. Well, if you abandon me to the fury of the monster who will destroy me, your holy will be done! But come, let there be all the pleasures of life in our love. Besides, I will implore, I will weep and cry out and defend myself: perhaps I shall be saved."

"Whom will you implore?" he asked.

"Silence!" said Paquita. "If I obtain mercy it will perhaps be on account of my discretion."

"Give me my robe," said Henri, insidiously.

"No, no!" she answered quickly, "be what you are, one of those angels whom I have been taught to hate, and in whom I only saw ogres, whilst you are what is fairest under the skies," she said, caressing Henri's hair. "You do not know how silly I am. I have learnt nothing. Since I was twelve years old I have been shut up without ever seeing anyone. I can neither read nor write. I can only speak English and Spanish."

"How is it, then, that you receive letters from London?"

"My letters? . . . See, here they are!" she said, proceeding to take some papers out of a tall Japanese vase.

She offered De Marsay some letters, in which the young man saw, with surprise, strange figures, similar to those of a rebus, traced in blood, and illustrating phrases full of passion.

"But," he cried, marvelling at these hieroglyphics created by the alertness of jealousy, "you are in the power of an infernal genius?"

"Infernal," she repeated.

"But how, then, were you able to get out?"

"Ah!" she said, "that was my ruin. I drove Doña Concha to choose between the fear of immediate death and anger to be. I had the curiosity of a demon. I wished to break the bronze circle which they had described between creation and me, I wished to see what young people were like, for I knew nothing of man except the Marquis and Cristemio. Our coachman and the lackey who accompanies us are old men . . ."

"But you were not always shut up? Your health . . . ?"

"Ah," she answered, "we used to walk, but it was at night and in the country, by the side of the Seine, away from people."

"Are you not proud of being loved like that?"

"No," she said, "no longer. However full it be, this hidden life is but darkness in comparison with the light."

"What do you call the light?"

"Thee, my lovely Adolphe! Thee, for whom I would give my life. All the passionate things that have been told me, and that I have inspired, I feel for thee! For a certain time I understood nothing of existence, but now I know what love is, and hitherto I have been the loved one only; for myself, I did not love. I would give up everything for you, take me away. If you like, take me as a toy, but let me be near you until you break me."

"You will have no regrets?"

"Not one!" she said, letting him read her eyes, whose golden tint was pure and clear.

"Am I the favoured one?" said Henri to himself. If he suspected the truth he was ready at that time to pardon the offence in view of a love so single minded. "I shall soon see," he thought.

If Paquita owed him no account of the past, yet the least recollection of it became in his eyes a crime. He had therefore the sombre strength to withold a portion of his thought, to study her, even while abandoning himself to the most enticing pleasures that ever peri descended from the skies had devised for her beloved.

Paquita seemed to have been created for love by a particular effort of nature. In a night her feminine genius had made the most rapid progress. Whatever might be the power of this young man, and his indifference in the matter of pleasures, in spite of his satiety of the previous night, he found in the girl with the golden eyes that seraglio, which a loving woman knows how to create, and which a man never refuses. Paquita responded to that passion which is felt by all really great men for the infinite—that mysterious passion so dramatically expressed in Faust, so poetically translated in Manfred, and which urged Don Juan to search the heart of women, in his hope to find there that limitless thought in pursuit of which so many hunters after spectres have started, which wise men think to discover in science, and which mystics find in God alone. The hope of possessing at last the ideal being with whom the struggle could be constant and tireless ravished De Marsay, who, for the first time for long, opened his heart. His nerves expanded, his coldness was dissipated in the atmosphere of that ardent soul, his hard and fast theories melted away, and happiness coloured his existence to the tint of the rose and white boudoir. Experiencing the sting of a higher pleasure, he was carried beyond the limits within which he had hitherto confined passion. He would not be surpassed by this girl, whom a somewhat artificial love had formed already for the needs of his soul, and then he found in that vanity which urges a man to be in all things a victor, strength enough to tame the girl; but, at the same time, urged beyond that line where the soul is mistress over herself, he lost himself in those delicious limboes, which the vulgar call so foolishly "the imaginary regions." He was tender, kind, and confidential. He affected Paquita almost to madness.

"Why should we not go to Sorrento, to Nice, to Chiavari, and pass all our life so? Will you?" he asked of Paquita, in a penetrating voice.

"Was there need to say to me: 'Will you'?" she cried. "Have I a will? I am nothing apart from you, except in so far as I am a pleasure for you. If you would choose a retreat worthy of us, Asia is the only country where love can unfold his wings . . ."

"You are right," answered Henri. "Let us go to the Indies, there where spring is eternal, where the earth grows only flowers, where man can display the magnificence of kings and none shall say him nay, as in the foolish lands where they would realise the dull chimera of equality. Let us go to the country where one lives in the midst of a nation of slaves, where the sun shines ever on a palace which is always white, where the air sheds perfumes, the birds sing of love, and where, when one can love no more, one dies . . ."

"And where one dies together!" said Paquita. "But do not let us start to-morrow, let us start this moment . . . take Cristemio."

"Faith! pleasure is the fairest climax of life. Let us go to Asia, but to start, my child, one needs much gold, and to have gold one must set one's affairs in order."

She understood no part of these ideas.

"Gold! There is a pile of it her—as high as that," she said, holding up her hand.

"It is not mine."

"What does that matter?" she went on; "if we have need of it let us take it."

"It does not belong to you."

"Belong!" she repeated. "Have you not taken me? When we have taken it, it will belong to us."

He gave a laugh.

"Poor innocent! You know nothing of the world."

"Nay, but this is what I know," she cried, clasping Henri to her.

At the very moment when De Marsay was forgetting all, and conceiving the desire to appropriate this creature for ever, he received in the midst of his joy a dagger thrust, which smote through his heart and mortified it for the first time. Paquita, who had lifted him vigorously in the air, as though to contemplate him, exclaimed: "Oh, Margarita!"

"Margarita!" cried the young man with a roar; "now I know all that I still tried to disbelieve."

He leapt upon the cabinet in which the long poignard was kept. Happily for Paquita and for himself, the cupboard was shut. His fury waxed at this impediment, but he recovered his tranquillity, went and found his cravat, and advanced towards her with an air of such ferocious meaning that, without knowing of what crime she had been guilty, Paquita understood, none the less, that her life was in question. With one bound she rushed to the other end of the room to escape the fatal knot which De Marsay tried to pass round her neck. There was a struggle. On either side there was an equality of strength, agility and suppleness. To end the combat Paquita threw between the legs of her lover a cushion which made him fall, and profited by the respite which this advantage gave her, to push the button of the spring which caused the bell to ring. Promptly the mulatto arrived. In a second Cristemio leapt on De Marsay and held him down with one foot on his chest, his heel turned toward the throat. De Marsay realised that, if he struggled, at a single sign from Paquita he would be instantly crushed.

"Why did you want to kill me, my beloved?" she said.

De Marsay made no reply.

"In what have I angered you?" she asked. "Speak, let us understand each other."

Henri maintained the phlegmatic attitude of a strong man who feels himself vanquished; his countenance, cold, silent, entirely English, revealed the consciousness of his dignity in a momentary resignation. Moreover, he had already thought, in spite of the vehemence of his anger, that it was scarcely prudent to compromise himself with the law by killing this girl on the spur of the moment, before he had arranged the murder in such a manner as should insure his impunity.

"My beloved," went on Paquita, "speak to me; do not leave me without one loving farewell! I would not keep in my heart the terror which you have just inspired in it. . . . Will you speak?" she said, stamping her foot with anger.

De Marsay, for all reply, gave her a glance, which signified so plainly, "You must die!" that Paquita threw herself upon him.

"Ah, well, you want to kill me! . . . . If my death can give you any pleasure—kill me!"

She made a sign to Cristemio, who withdrew his foot from the body of the young man, and retired without letting his face show that he had formed any opinion, good or bad, with regard to Paquita.

"That is a man," said De Marsay, pointing to the mulatto, with a sombre gesture. "There is no devotion like the devotion which obeys in friendship, and does not stop to weigh motives. In that man you possess a true friend."

"I will give you him, if you like," she answered; "he will serve you with the same devotion that he has for me, if I so instruct him."

She waited for a word of recognition, and went on with an accent replete with tenderness:

"Adolphe, give me then one kind word! . . . It is nearly day."

Henri did not answer. The young man had one sorry quality, for one considers as something great everything which resembles strength, and often men invent extravagances. Henri knew not how to pardon. That returning upon itself which is one of the soul's graces, was a non-existent sense for him. The ferocity of the Northern man, with which the English blood is deeply tainted, had been transmitted to him by his father. He was inexorable both in his good and evil impulses. Paquita's exclamation had been all the more horrible to him, in that it had dethroned him from the sweetest triumph which had ever flattered his man's vanity. Hope, love, and every emotion had been exalted with him, all had lit up within his heart and his intelligence, then these torches illuminating his life had been extinguished by a cold wind. Paquita, in her stupefaction of grief, had only strength enough to give the signal for departure.

"What is the use of that!" she said, throwing away the bandage. "If he does not love me, if he hates me, it is all over."

She waited for one look, did not obtain it, and fell, half dead. The mulatto cast a glance at Henri, so horribly significant, that, for the first time in his life, the young man, to whom no one denied the gift of rare courage, trembled. *"If you do not love her well, if you give her the least pain, I will kill you."* Such was the sense of that brief gaze. De Marsay was escorted, with a care almost obsequious, along the dimly-lit corridor, at the end of which he issued by a secret door into the garden of the Hotel San-Réal. The mulatto made him walk cautiously through an avenue of lime trees, which led to a little gate opening upon a street which was at that hour deserted. De Marsay took a keen notice of everything. The carriage awaited him. This time the mulatto did not accompany him, and at the moment when Henri put his head out of the window to look once more at the gardens of the hotel he encountered the white eyes of Cristemio, with whom he exchanged a glance. On either side there was a provocation, a challenge, the declaration of a savage war, of a duel in which ordinary laws were invalid, where treason and treachery were admitted means. Cristemio knew that Henri had sworn Paquita's death. Henri knew that Cristemio would like to kill him before he killed Paquita. Both understood each other to perfection.

"The adventure is growing complicated in a most interesting way," said Henri.

"Where is the gentleman going to?" asked the coachman.

De Marsay was driven to the house of Paul de Manerville. For more than a week Henri was away from home, and no one could discover either what he did during this period, nor where he stayed. This retreat saved him from the fury of the mulatto and caused the ruin of the charming creature who had placed all her hope in him whom she loved as never human heart had loved on this earth before. On the last day of the week, about eleven o'clock at night, Henri drove up in a carriage to the little gate in the garden of the Hotel San-Réal. Four men accompanied him. The driver was evidently one of his friends, for he stood up on his box, like a man who was to listen, an attentive sentinel, for the least sound. One of the other three took his stand outside the gate in the street; the second waited in the garden, leaning against the wall; the last, who carried in his hand a bunch of keys, accompanied De Marsay.

"Henri," said his companion to him, "we are betrayed."

"By whom, my good Ferragus?"

"They are not all asleep," replied the chief of the Devourers; "it is absolutely certain that some one in the house has neither eaten nor drunk . . . Look! see that light!"

"We have a plan of the house, from where does it come?"

"I need no plan to know," replied Ferragus; "it comes from the room of the Marquise."

"Ah," cried De Marsay, "no doubt she arrived from London to-day. The woman has robbed me even of my revenge! But if she has anticipated me, my good Gratien, we will give her up to the law."

"Listen, listen! . . . The thing is settled," said Ferragus to Henri.

The two friends listened intently, and heard some feeble cries which might have aroused pity in the breast of a tiger.

"Your Marquise did not think the sound would escape by the chimney," said the chief of the Devourers, with the laugh of a critic, enchanted to detect a fault in a work of merit.

"We alone, we know how to provide for every contingency," said Henri. "Wait for me. I want to see what is going on upstairs—I want to know how their domestic quarrels are managed. By God! I believe she is roasting her at a slow fire."

De Marsay lightly scaled the stairs, with which he was familiar, and recognised the passage leading to the boudoir. When he opened the door he experienced the involuntary shudder which the sight of bloodshed gives to the most determined of men. The spectacle which was offered to his view was, moreover, in more than one respect astonishing to him. The Marquise was a woman: she had calculated her vengeance with that perfection of perfidy which distinguishes the weaker animals. She had dissimulated her anger in order to assure herself of the crime before she punished it.

"Too late, my beloved!" said Paquita, in her death agony, casting her pale eyes upon De Marsay.

The girl of the golden eyes expired in a bath of blood. The great illumination of candles, a delicate perfume which was perceptible, a certain disorder, in which the eye of a man accustomed to amorous adventures could not but discern the madness which is common to all the passions, revealed how cunningly the Marquise had interrogated the guilty one. The white room, where the blood showed so well, betrayed a long struggle. The prints of Paquita's hands were on the cushions. Here she had clung to her life, here she had defended herself, here she had been struck. Long strips of the tapestry had been torn down by her bleeding hands, which, without a doubt, had struggled long. Paquita must have tried to reach the window; her bare feet had left their imprints on the edge of the divan, along which she must have run. Her body, mutilated by the dagger-thrusts of her executioner, told of the fury with which she had disputed a life which Henri had made precious to her. She lay stretched on the floor, and in her death throes had bitten the ankles of Madame de San-Réal, who still held in her hand her dagger, dripping blood. The hair of the Marquise had been torn out, she was covered with bites, many of which were bleeding, and her torn dress revealed her in a state of semi-nudity, with the scratches on her breasts. She was sublime so. Her head, eager and maddened, exhaled the odour of blood. Her panting mouth was open, and her nostrils were not sufficient for her breath. There are certain animals who fall upon their enemy in their rage, do it to death, and seem in the tranquillity of victory to have forgotten it. There are others who prowl around their victim, who guard it in fear lest it should be taken away from them, and who, like the Achilles of Homer, drag their enemy by the feet nine times round the walls of Troy. The Marquise was like that. She did not see Henri. In the first place, she was too secure of her solitude to be afraid of witnesses; and, secondly, she was too intoxicated with warm blood, too excited with the fray, too exalted to take notice of the whole of Paris, if Paris had formed a circle round her. A thunderbolt would not have disturbed her. She had not even heard Paquita's last sigh, and believed that the dead girl could still hear her.

"Die without confessing!" she said. "Go down to hell, monster of ingratitude; belong to no one but the fiend. For the blood you gave him you owe me all your own! Die, die, suffer a thousand deaths! I have been too kind—I was only a moment killing you. I should have made you experience all the tortures that you have bequeathed to me. I—I shall live! I shall live in misery. I have no one left to love but God!"

She gazed at her.

"She is dead!" she said to herself, after a pause, in a violent reaction. "Dead! Oh, I shall die of grief!"

The Marquise was throwing herself upon the divan, stricken with a despair which deprived her of speech, when this movement brought her in view of Henri de Marsay.

"Who are you?" she asked, rushing at him with her dagger raised.

Henri caught her arm, and thus they could contemplate each other face to face. A horrible surprise froze the blood in their veins, and their limbs quivered like those of frightened horses. In effect, the two Menœchmi had not been more alike. With one accord they uttered the same phrase:

"Lord Dudley must have been your father?"

The head of each was drooped in affirmation.

"She was true to the blood," said Henri, pointing to Paquita.

"She was as little guilty as it is possible to be." replied Margarita Euphémia Porrabéril, and she threw herself upon the body of Paquita, giving vent to a cry of despair. "Poor child! Oh, if I could bring thee to life again! I was wrong—forgive me, Paquita! Dead! and I live! I—I am the most unhappy."

At that moment the horrible face of the mother of Paquita appeared.

"You are come to tell me that you never sold her to me to kill," cried the Marquise. "I know why you have left your lair. I will pay you twice over. Hold your peace."

She took a bag of gold from the ebony cabinet, and threw it contemptuously at the old woman's feet. The chink of the gold was potent enough to excite a smile on the Georgian's impassive face.

"I come at the right moment for you, my sister," said Henri. "The law will ask of you—"

"Nothing," replied the Marquise. "One person alone might ask a reckoning for the death of this girl. Cristemio is dead."

"And the mother," said Henri, pointing to the old woman. "Will you not be always in her power?"

"She comes from a country where women are not beings, but things—chattels, with which one does as one wills, which one buys, sells and slays; in short, which one uses for one's caprices as you, here, use a piece of furniture. Besides, she has one passion which dominates all the others, and which would have stifled her maternal love, even if she had loved her daughter, a passion—"

"What?" Henri asked quickly, interrupting his sister.

"Play! God keep you from it," answered the Marquise.

"But whom have you," said Henri, looking at the girl of the golden eyes, "who will help you to remove the traces of this fantasy which the law would not overlook?"

"I have her mother," replied the Marquise, designating the Georgian, to whom she made a sign to remain.

"We shall meet again," said Henry, who was thinking anxiously of his friends, and felt that it was time to leave.

"No, brother," she said, "we shall not meet again. I am going back to Spain to enter the Convent of *los Dolores*."

"You are too young yet, too lovely," said Henri, taking her in his arms and giving her a kiss.

"Good-bye," she said; "there is no consolation when you have lost that which has seemed to you the infinite."

A week later Paul de Manerville met De Marsay in the Tuileries, on the Terrasse des Feuillants.

"Well, what has become of our beautiful girl of the golden eyes, you rascal?"

"She is dead."

"What of?"

"The lungs."

ELIZA MARY HAMILTON (1807–1851)

"A Young Girl Seen in Church" (1838)

Eliza Mary Hamilton was born into a cultivated Irish Protestant family in Dublin in 1807. Her father, Archibald Hamilton, was an attorney; her brother, the scientist and writer Sir William Rowan Hamilton, later became Royal Astronomer of Ireland. She may have met some of her brother's numerous literary friends—William Wordsworth, Samuel Taylor Coleridge, Felicia Hemans, Robert Southey, and Maria Edgeworth—while living in his household in her early twenties. Between 1833 and 1851 she published a number of poems in the *Dublin Literary Magazine* under the initials "E.M.H." A single volume of her poems was published in 1838. Wordsworth, whom she later visited at Rydal Mount, praised the book.

Apart from the fact that she was devoted to her brother—she dedicated her *Poems* to him—little is known about Hamilton's emotional life. Yet to judge by the poem "A Young Girl Seen in Church"—surely one of the most extraordinarily suggestive English poems of the early nineteenth century—Hamilton was hardly immune to what one might call the "homoerotic romance" of the century.

FURTHER READING: Eliza Mary Hamilton, *Poems* (Dublin, 1838); George M. Harper, *William Wordsworth: His Life, Works, and Influence* (London: John Murray, 1916); Virginia Blain, "Letitia Elizabeth Landon, Eliza Mary Hamilton, and the Genealogy of the Victorian Poetess," *Victorian Poetry* 33 (1995): 31–52.

> Was she an orphan?—can another grief
>   So wholly chasten?—can another woe
> So sanctify?—for she was (as a leaf
>   Of hue funereal mid the Spring's young glow)
> Robed in emphatic black:—the soul of night
>   Filled her rich simply-parted ebon hair,

And raven eye-lashes, and made her bright
    With solemn lustre day can never wear.

Two younger buds, a sister at each side,
    Like little moon-lit clouds beside the moon,
Which up the sky's majestic temple glide,
    Clad darkly too, she led,—but music soon
Moved over her, and like a breeze of heaven,
    Shook from her lips the fragrance of her soul,—
And then, the thoughts with which my heart had striven,
    Spoke in my gaze, and would not brook control.

I bent upon her my astonished eye,
    That glowed, I felt, with an expression full
Of all that love which dares to deify,—
    That adoration of the beautiful
Which haunts the poet,—I forgot the sighs
    Of whispered prayer around me, and the page
Of hope divine, and the eternal eyes
    That look through every heart, in every place and age.
I gazed and gazed as though she were a star,
Unconscious and unfallen, which shone above, afar.—

But eloquently grave, a crimson cloud
    Of deep disquietude her cheek o'erspread
With exquisite rebuke;—and then I bowed
    Like hers my earnest looks and conscious head,
Ashamed to have disturbed the current meek
    Of her translucent thoughts, and made them flow
Painfully earthward. But she veiled that cheek,—
    Veiled even its sweet reproach and sacred glow,
Like those pure flowers too sensitive to brook
    Noon's burning eye, and its oppressive look,
That shut, in beautiful displeasure, up
    Each brilliant petal of their heart's deep cup.

ELIZABETH BARRETT BROWNING (1806–1861)

"To George Sand: A Desire" (1844)

Elizabeth Barrett Browning, born in Herefordshire to well-to-do parents, was the eldest and frailest of eleven children. Precocious as a child, she studied classics with her father and one of her brothers' tutors. After her mother's death in 1828, and a reverse in the Barrett fortunes, her father took the family to London, where they lived on Wimpole Street. Throughout these early years Barrett Browning suffered from lung and other medical problems, necessitating her seclusion. She occupied herself with writing poetry: her *Battle of Marathon* appeared in 1820; a translation of *Prometheus Bound* followed in 1833; and *The Seraphim and Other Poems* in 1838. After the publication of her *Poems* in 1844 she began a correspondence with the poet Robert Browning, with whom she subsequently eloped. They married against her father's wishes in 1846. She settled with Browning in Florence, where her health improved and she lived happily until her death. She published several acclaimed books of verse over the next fifteen years: *Poems* (1850), containing the well-known *Sonnets from the Portuguese*; *Casa Guidi Windows* (1851), in which she celebrated the Italian nationalist movement; and her masterpiece, the long narrative poem *Aurora Leigh* (1857). Though her work has always been overshadowed by that of her husband, her poetry has received renewed attention over the past twenty years especially, as its critical and political aspects have come more clearly into view.

The sonnet entitled "To George Sand: A Desire"—one of several poems Barrett Browning dedicated to the great French writer George Sand (1804–1876)—pays an extravagant, surreal, and curiously homoerotic tribute to its subject. In the image of Sand sprouting angelic wings and being lifted up "above the applauded circus," where "child and maiden," drawn up with her, "kiss upon thy lips a stainless fame," Barrett Browning at once salutes Sand's androgynous style—the French novelist sometimes dressed in male attire and was rumored to have been in love with the actress Marie Dorval—and imagines for her a strange, unsexing, almost cinematic apotheosis as "pure genius." Barrett Browning wrote the poem a year before she began her celebrated love affair with Browning. While the story of her passionate devotion to her husband rightly exerts its romantic force, it has obscured the emotional importance of women in her life. Among her female friends she would later count Sand herself—they met in

France in 1852—and the American writers Harriet Beecher Stowe and Margaret Fuller. Her poetry in turn bears witness to powerful female attachments. In particular, in the marvelous *Aurora Leigh*, a kind of Victorian novel in verse, she depicts an intense cross-class intimacy between Aurora, the poet-heroine, and a young working-class woman, Marian Erle, who accompanies her to Italy and lives with her for much of the poem.

FURTHER READING: Elizabeth Barrett Browning, *The Complete Works*, ed. Charlotte Porter and Helen A. Clarke, 6 vols. (New York: Crowell, 1900); Gardner B. Taplin, *The Life of Elizabeth Barrett Browning* (London: John Murray, 1957); Nina Auerbach, *Communities of Women: An Idea in Fiction* (Cambridge: Harvard University Press, 1978); Barbara Charlesworth Gelpi, "*Aurora Leigh*: The Vocation of the Woman Poet," *Victorian Poetry* 19 (Spring 1981): 35–48; Helen Cooper, *Elizabeth Barrett Browning: Woman and Artist* (Chapel Hill: University of North Carolina Press, 1988); Margaret Forster, *Elizabeth Barrett Browning* (London: Chatto and Windus, 1988); Tess Coslett, *Woman to Woman: Female Friendship in Victorian Fiction* (Brighton: Harvester, 1988); Dorothy Mermin, *Elizabeth Barrett Browning: The Origins of a New Poetry* (Chicago and London: University of Chicago Press, 1989); Marjorie Stone, *Elizabeth Barrett Browning* (New York: St. Martin's, 1995).

Thou large-brained woman and large-hearted man,
Self-called George Sand! whose soul, amid the lions
Of thy tumultuous senses, moans defiance
And answers roar for roar, as spirits can:
I would some mild miraculous thunder ran
Above the applauded circus, in appliance
Of thine own nobler nature's strength and science,
Drawing two pinions, white as wings of swan,
From thy strong shoulders, to amaze the place
With holier light! that thou to woman's claim
And man's, mightst join beside the angel's grace
Of a pure genius sanctified from blame,
Till child and maiden pressed to thine embrace
To kiss upon thy lips a stainless fame.

CHARLOTTE BRONTË (1816–1855)

From *Villette* (1853)

Charlotte Brontë was one of six children born to Patrick Brontë, an impoverished Irishman who served as perpetual curate at the isolated Haworth Parsonage in Yorkshire. Her mother, Maria Branwell, died in 1821; Charlotte and her siblings were raised by her father and an aunt. In 1824 Patrick Brontë sent her and her three sisters to Cowan School, a boarding school for daughters of the clergy: two of the sisters died of consumption the following year, possibly as a result of the fetid and unhealthy conditions at the school. In the aftermath of this trauma, Charlotte and her sister Emily returned home in 1825. For the next ten years she and her surviving siblings—Emily, their sister Anne, and their brother, Branwell—lived at home, collaborating on a voluminous series of romantic stories and poems about an imaginary land named Angria. All four were gifted writers, and all—with the exception of Branwell, who descended into alcoholism and died in his early twenties—would later produce novels of distinction. In 1842, having worked for several years as a teacher and governess, Brontë decided to start her own school and went to Brussels in order to improve her French at a private boarding school. There she fell deeply and unhappily in love with the married headmaster, Constantin Heger, who subsequently became the model for M. Paul in her novel *Villette*. Returning to England in 1843 and unable to find enough money for her own school, she turned again to writing. In 1846 she arranged for the publication—under the pseudonyms "Currer, Ellis, and Acton Bell"—of a book of poems written by herself, Emily, and Anne. While selling poorly, the work was sufficiently intriguing to prompt several London publishers to ask for novels by the mysterious "Bells." Emily's *Wuthering Heights*, Anne's *Agnes Grey*, and Charlotte's *Jane Eyre* were all published the following year.

The years 1847–48 marked a turning point for Brontë. *Jane Eyre* was a huge popular success and her publisher, George Smith of Smith Elder, summoned her to London, where she was enthusiastically embraced by the literary establishment. Tragedy struck again, however, as first Branwell, then Emily, then Anne succumbed to the family curse of tuberculosis between September 1848 and May 1849. Charlotte was forced to settle permanently in the Haworth parsonage and care for her father. She continued to write—her novel *Shirley* appeared in 1849—and made occasional visits to London.

The novelist Elizabeth Gaskell became a good friend and would subsequently write a moving biography of her fellow writer after Brontë's death. In 1852 Brontë refused a marriage proposal from her father's curate, the Reverend Arthur Nicholls. Her final novel, *Villette*, was published in 1853. In 1854 Nicholls proposed again and she married him, only to die the next year from a fever due to pregnancy. Having outlived his wife and all six of his children, Patrick Brontë shared the parsonage with Nicholls until his own death in 1861.

The melancholy *Villette*, considered by many to be Brontë's finest novel, occupies a charismatic place in lesbian literary iconography. Ostensibly an older man–younger woman love story reminiscent of *Jane Eyre*—the narrator, Lucy Snowe, is an independent young English woman teaching at a girls' school in Brussels, who gradually falls in love with her gruff male superior M. Paul—the novel is full of homoerotic elements. Indeed Brontë might be considered the grand progenitrix of a whole corpus of overtly or covertly lesbian "girls' school" texts. Other works in the *Villette* tradition— and they are legion—include Colette's *Claudine à l'école* (1900), Henry Handel Richardson's *The Getting of Wisdom* (1910), Angela Brazil's *The Nicest Girl in the School* (1910) and *A Fourth Form Friendship* (1912), Clemence Dane's *Regiment of Women* (1915), Rosamond Lehmann's *Dusty Answer* (1927), Olive Moore's *The Celestial Seraglio* (1929), Christa Winsloe's *The Child Manuela* (source for the classic German film *Mädchen in Uniform;* 1933), Antonia White's *Frost in May* (1933), Lillian Hellman's *The Children's Hour* (1934), Dorothy Baker's *Trio* (1943), Josephine Tey's *Miss Pym Disposes* (1948), Nancy Spain's *Poison for Teacher* (1949), Dorothy Strachey's *Olivia* (1949), Brigid Brophy's *The King of a Rainy Country* (1956) and *The Finishing Touch* (1963), May Sarton's *The Small Room* (1961), Muriel Spark's *The Prime of Miss Jean Brodie* (1961), Rosemary Manning's *The Chinese Garden* (1962), Violette Leduc's *Thérèse et Isabelle* (1967), Catharine Stimpson's *Class Notes* (1979), Florence King's *Confessions of a Failed Southern Lady* (1985), Fleur Jaeggy's *Sweet Days of Discipline* (1989), and Christine Crow's *Miss X, or the Wolf Woman* (1990).

The following episode from *Villette*—in which Lucy assumes the role of a "fop" in the school vaudeville and plays a passionate love scene opposite her beautiful student, Ginevra Fanshawe—would seem to be the inspiration for a number of similar theatrical cross-dressing episodes in later schoolgirl fiction. (See, for example, Strachey's *Olivia* and Brophy's *The King of a Rainy Country*.) Such scenes usually betoken a moment at which lesbian undercurrents in the narrative come to a crest. Here such undercurrents are kept in check, in part by Brontë's careful orchestration of gazes in the scene—both Lucy and Ginevra are shown playing to chosen men in the audience, M. Paul and Dr. John Bretton—but only just.

FURTHER READING: Charlotte Brontë, *Villette* (1853; rpt. London: The Folio Society, 1967); Elizabeth Gaskell, *The Life of Charlotte Brontë* (1857; rpt. Harmondsworth, Middlesex: Penguin, 1975); Winifred Guérin, *Charlotte Brontë: The Evolution of Genius*

(Oxford: Oxford University Press, 1967); Linda C. Hunt, "Sustenance and Balm: The Question of Female Friendship in *Shirley* and *Villette*," *Tulsa Studies in Women's Literature* 1 (1982): 55–66; Sara M. Putzell-Korab, "Passion Between Women in the Victorian Novel," *Tennessee Studies in Literature* 27 (1984): 180–95; Martha Vicinus, "Distance and Desire: English Boarding School Friendships," *Signs* 9 (1984): 600–22, rpt. in Martin Duberman, Martha Vicinus, and George Chauncey, Jr., eds. *Hidden From History: Reclaiming the Gay and Lesbian Past* (New York: Meridian, 1990), pp. 212–32; Juliet Barker, *The Brontës* (New York: St. Martin's Press, 1994); Corinne E. Blackmer, "*The Finishing Touch* and the Tradition of Homoerotic Girls' School Fictions," *Review of Contemporary Fiction* 15 (1995): 32–39.

In an instant we were out of doors. The cool, calm night revived me somewhat. It was moonless, but the reflex from the many glowing windows lit the court brightly, and even the alleys—dimly. Heaven was cloudless, and grand with the quiver of its living fires. How soft are the nights of the Continent! How bland, balmy, safe! No sea fog; no chilling damp; mistless as noon, and fresh as morning.

Having crossed court and garden, we reached the glass door of the first *classe*. It stood open, like all other doors that night. We passed, and then I was ushered into a small cabinet, dividing the first *classe* from the *grande salle*. This cabinet dazzled me, it was so full of light. It deafened me; it was clamorous with voices. It stifled me, it was so hot, choking, thronged.

"De l'ordre! Du silence!" cried M. Paul. "Is this chaos?" he demanded, and there was a hush. With a dozen words and as many gestures, he turned out half the persons present, and obliged the remnant to fall into rank. Those left were all in costume. They were the performers, and this was the greenroom. M. Paul introduced me. All stared and some tittered. It was a surprise. They had not expected the Englishwoman would play in a *vaudeville*. Ginevra Fanshawe, beautifully dressed for her part, and looking fascinatingly pretty, turned on me a pair of eyes as round as beads. In the highest spirit, unperturbed by fear or bashfulness, delighted indeed at the thought of shining off before hundreds, my entrance seemed to transfix her with amazement in the midst of her joy. She would have exclaimed, but M. Paul held her and all the rest in check.

Having surveyed and criticised the whole troop, he turned to me.

"You, too, must be dressed for your part."

"Dressed—dressed like a man!" exclaimed Zélie St Pierre, darting forwards, adding with officiousness, "I will dress her myself."

To be dressed like a man did not please and would not suit me. I had consented to take a man's name and part; as to his dress—*halte-là!* No. I would keep my own dress, come what might. M. Paul might storm, might rage; I would keep my own dress. I said so, with a voice as resolute in intent as it was low and perhaps unsteady in utterance.

He did not immediately storm or rage, as I fully thought he would. He stood silent. But Zélie again interposed.

"She will make a capital *petit-maître*. Here are the garments, all—all complete; somewhat too large, but I will arrange all that. Come, chère amie, belle Anglaise!"

And she sneered, for I was not "belle." She seized my hand, she was drawing me away. M. Paul stood impassible—neutral.

"You must not resist," pursued St Pierre, for resist I did. "You will spoil all, destroy the mirth of the piece, the enjoyment of the company, sacrifice everything to your *amour-propre*. This would be too bad.—Monsieur will never permit this?"

She sought his eye. I watched, likewise, for a glance. He gave her one, and then he gave me one. "Stop!" he said slowly, arresting St Pierre, who continued her efforts to drag me after her. Everybody awaited the decision. He was not angry, not irritated; I perceived that, and took heart.

"You do not like these clothes?" he asked, pointing to the masculine vestments.

"I don't object to some of them, but I won't have them all."

"How must it be, then—how accept a man's part, and go on the stage dressed as a woman? This is an amateur affair, it is true—a *vaudeville de pensionnat*; certain modifications I might sanction, yet something you must have to announce you as of the nobler sex."

"And I will, monsieur; but it must be arranged in my own way. Nobody must meddle; the things must not be forced upon me. Just let me dress myself."

Monsieur, without another word, took the costume from St Pierre, gave it to me, and permitted me to pass into the dressing-room. Once alone, I grew calm, and collectedly went to work. Retaining my woman's garb without the slightest retrenchment, I merely assumed, in addition, a little vest, a collar, and cravat, and a *paletot* of small dimensions, the whole being the costume of a brother of one of the pupils. Having loosened my hair out of its braids, made up the long back hair close, and brushed the front hair to one side, I took my hat and gloves in my hand and came out. M. Paul was waiting, and so were the others. He looked at me. "That may pass in a *pensionnat*," he pronounced. Then added, not unkindly, "Courage, mon ami! Un peu de sang froid—un peu d'aplomb, M. Lucien, en tout ira bien."

St Pierre sneered again, in her cold, snaky manner.

I was irritable, because excited, and I could not help turning upon her and saying that if she were not a lady and I a gentleman, I should feel disposed to call her out.

"After the play, after the play," said M. Paul. "I will then divide my pair of pistols between you, and we will settle the dispute according to form. It will only be the old quarrel of France and England."

But now the moment approached for the performance to commence. M. Paul, setting us before him, harangued us briefly, like a general addressing soldiers about to charge. I don't know what he said, except that he recommended each to penetrate herself with a sense of her personal insignificance. God knows I thought this advice superfluous for some of us. A bell tinkled. I and two more were ushered on to the stage. The bell tinkled again. I had to speak the very first words.

"Do not look at the crowd, nor think of it," whispered M. Paul in my ear. "Imagine yourself in the garret, acting to the rats."

He vanished. The curtain drew up, shrivelled to the ceiling. The bright lights, the long room, the gay throng, burst upon us. I thought of the black-beetles, the old boxes, the worm-eaten bureaus. I said my say badly, but I said it. That first speech was the difficulty; it revealed to me this fact that it was not the crowd I feared so much as my own voice. Foreigners and strangers, the crowd were nothing to me. Nor did I think of them. When my tongue once got free, and my voice took its true pitch and found its natural tone, I thought of nothing but the personage I represented, and of M. Paul, who was listening, watching, prompting in the side scenes.

By-and-by, feeling the right power come—the spring demanded gush and rise inwardly—I became sufficiently composed to notice my fellow-actors. Some of them played very well, especially Ginevra Fanshawe, who had to coquette between two suitors, and managed admirably—in fact, she was in her element. I observed that she once or twice threw a certain marked fondness and pointed partiality into her manner towards me, the fop. With such emphasis and animation did she favour me, such glances did she dart out into the listening and applauding crowd, that to me, who knew her, it presently became evident she was acting *at* some one; and I followed her eye, her smile, her gesture, and ere long discovered that she had at least singled out a handsome and distinguished aim for her shafts. Full in the path of those arrows—taller than other spectators, and therefore more sure to receive them—stood, in attitude quiet but intent, a well-known form, that of Dr John.

The spectacle seemed somehow suggestive. There was language in Dr John's look, though I cannot tell what he said. It animated me; I drew out of it a history. I put my idea into the part I performed; I threw it into my wooing of Ginevra. In the "Ours," or sincere lover, I saw Dr John. Did I pity him, as erst? No, I hardened my heart, rivalled and outrivalled him. I knew myself but a fop, but where *he* was outcast *I* could please. Now I know I acted as if wishful and resolute to win and conquer. Ginevra seconded me; between us we half changed the nature of the *rôle*, gilding it from top to toe. Between the acts M. Paul told me he knew not what possessed us, and half expostulated. "C'est peut-être plus beau que votre modèle," said he, "mais ce n'est pas juste." I know not what possessed me either, but somehow my longing was to eclipse the "Ours"—that is, Dr John. Ginevra was tender; how could I be otherwise than chivalric? Retaining the letter, I recklessly altered the spirit of the *rôle*. Without heart, without interest, I could not play it at all. It must be played—in went the yearned-for seasoning; thus flavoured, I played it with relish.

What I felt that night, and what I did, I no more expected to feel and do than to be lifted in a trance to the seventh heaven. Cold, reluctant, apprehensive, I had accepted a part to please another; ere long, warming, becoming interested, taking courage, I acted to please myself. Yet the next day, when I thought it over, I quite disapproved of these amateur performances; and though glad that I had obliged M. Paul, and tried my own strength for once, I took a firm resolution never to be drawn into a similar affair. A keen relish for dramatic expression had revealed itself as part of my nature; to cherish and exercise this new-found faculty might gift me with a world of delight, but it would not do for a mere looker-on at life. The strength and longing must be put by; and I put them by, and fastened them in with the lock of a resolution which neither Time nor Temptation has since picked.

CHARLES BAUDELAIRE (1821–1867)

"Lesbos," "Damned Women 1 (Delphine and Hippolyta)," "Damned Women 2" (1857)

Charles Baudelaire, poet, art critic, and genius *maudit*, was born in Paris to genteel bourgeois parents against whom he violently rebelled. Expelled from a military academy in Lyon, he was sent on a voyage to India, but got only as far as the Isle of Mauritius, where he gave himself over to various tropical indulgences. Upon returning to Paris in 1842 he gravitated to the bohemian Latin Quarter, where he smoked hashish and drank, took the first of several mistresses (the mulatto woman Jeanne Duval), and proceeded to run through his family inheritance at mind-boggling speed. His first literary works were published in 1845: the poem "À une dame créole" and a lengthy critical essay on the 1845 Salon. The following year he discovered the short stories of Edgar Allan Poe and immediately began translating them into French, an exhausting labor that occupied him off and on for the next seventeen years. His novel, *La Fanfarlo*, appeared in 1847. Even as his mental and physical health deteriorated, he began to produce poetry and criticism—all of supreme artistic merit—bitterly excoriating middle-class philistinism and hypocrisy. *Les Fleurs du mal* (*The Flowers of Evil*), his still-shocking poetic masterpiece, was published in 1857. Public hostility to his work and the prosecution of *Les Fleurs du mal* for obscenity—Baudelaire was convicted and made to pay a fine—left him emotionally broken. Although he managed to produce *Les Paradis artificiels*, a collection of prose poems, in 1860 and a revised version of *Les Fleurs du mal* in 1861, his final years were ghastly. After an unsuccessful attempt to support himself by lecturing in Belgium, he succumbed to tertiary syphilis and died, a paralytic wreck, in 1867. His *Petits poèmes en prose* (1869) and *Journaux intimes* (1887) were published posthumously.

Thanks to three startlingly frank poems on sapphic love in the first edition of *Les Fleurs du mal*—"Femmes damnées 1 (Delphine et Hyppolyte)," "Femmes damnées 2," and "Lesbos"—Baudelaire had an enormous influence on the evolution of the lesbian topos in nineteenth-century European literature. (The poet seems to have been interested in female homosexuality from early on in his career: in 1846 his publisher, Lévy, announced a forthcoming volume of Baudelaire poems entitled *Les Lesbiennes*, though no such work ever appeared.) Befitting his deeply pessimistic conception of human nature, Baudelaire's vision of lesbian desire is at first view a dark one. Along with Coleridge, whose famous 1816 ballad *Christabel* contained a portrait of a lesbian vam-

pire, Baudelaire is responsible for one of the most enduring of nineteenth-century lesbian literary stereotypes: the woman-lover as seductive yet sterile monster. In the first
"Damned Women" poem she is damned indeed—an exotic and tainted creature whose
unnatural desires result in madness, disfiguration, and death. Yet the darkness should
not be exaggerated: she is also a heroic outlaw, akin, in her magnificent alienation, to
the poet himself. At the end of "Lesbos," when the poet ecstatically identifies himself
with Sappho, or in the final quatrain of "Damned Women 2," when his anguish turns
to eulogy ("Sisters! I love you as I pity you / for your bleak sorrows, for your unslaked
thirsts, / and for the love that gorges your great hearts!") Baudelaire's reveries on lesbian desire remain both morally ambiguous and curiously moving. Walter Benjamin
spoke of "the profound duplicity which animates Baudelaire's poetry." In some sense
Baudelaire was in love with his sapphic monsters—finding in their beauty, unease, and
sensual intransigence a metaphor for his own glittering and rebarbative art.

Baudelaire's spectacular foregrounding of the lesbian theme had numerous liter-
ary-historical ramifications. Swinburne was his most immediate (and inferior) poetic
heir: the English poet's "Faustine" and "Anactoria" are Baudelairean knock-offs bordering on camp. But one can also trace his influence in the writings of Paul Verlaine,
Catulle Mendès, Rachilde, Eugène Sue, Émile Zola, and even Henry James. For a particularly intense and emotionally complex response to the French master, one might
turn to the work of the late-nineteenth-century expatriate Englishwoman Pauline
Tarn, who wrote a series of alternately exquisite and terrifying neo-Baudelairean
verses in French under the name Renée Vivien.

FURTHER READING: Charles Baudelaire, *Oeuvres complètes*, ed. Claude Pichois, 2 vols.
(Paris: Gallimard, 1975–76); —, *Les Fleurs du mal*, trans. Richard Howard (Boston:
Godine, 1982); Arthur Symons, *Charles Baudelaire* (London: E. Mathews, 1920); Jean-
nette Foster, *Sex Variant Women in Literature* (1956: rpt. Tallahassee, Fla.: Naiad, 1985);
Walter Benjamin, *Charles Baudelaire* (Frankfurt: Suhrkamp, 1969); Edwin Morgan,
Flower of Evil: A Life of Charles Baudelaire (Freeport, N.Y.: Books for Libraries Press,
1970); Annette Shaw, "Baudelaire's 'Femmes damnées': The Androgynous Space,"
Centerpoint: A Journal of Interdisciplinary Studies 3 (1980): 57–64; Richard Sieburth,
"Poetry and Obscenity: Baudelaire and Swinburne," *Comparative Literature* 36 (1984):
343–53; Patricia Clements, *Baudelaire and the English Tradition* (Princeton: Princeton
University Press, 1985); A. E. Carter, *Charles Baudelaire* (Boston: G. K. Hall, 1987);
Timothy Raser, "Language and the Erotic in Two Poems by Baudelaire," *Romantic
Review* 79 (1988): 443–51; Richard D. E. Burton, *Baudelaire in 1859* (Cambridge: Cam-
bridge University Press, 1988); —, *Baudelaire and the Second Republic* (Oxford: Claren-
don Press, 1991); Joan DeJean, *Fictions of Sappho, 1546–1937* (Chicago: University of
Chicago Press, 1989); F. W. Leakey, *Les Fleurs du Mal* (Cambridge: Cambridge Uni-
versity Press, 1992); Thais E. Morgan, "Male Lesbian Bodies: The Construction of
Alternate Masculinities in Courbet, Baudelaire, and Swinburne," *Genders* 15 (1992):

37–57; Margery A. Evans, *Baudelaire and Intertextuality* (Cambridge: Cambridge University Press, 1993); Henri Troyat, *Baudelaire* (Paris: Flammarion, 1994); Joanna Richardson, *Baudelaire* (London: John Murray, 1994); Gretchen M. Schultz, "Baudelaire's Lesbian Connections," in Laurence M. Porter, ed., *Approaches to Teaching Baudelaire's "Flowers of Evil"* (New York: Modern Language Association, 2000).

Lesbos

Mother of Latin games and Greek delights,
Lesbos! where the kisses, languid or rapt,
cool as melons, burning as the sun,
adorn the dark and gild the shining days
given to Latin games and Greek delights;

Lesbos, where the kisses, like cascades,
teeming and turbulent yet secret, deep,
plunge undaunted into unplumbed gulfs
and gather there, gurgling and sobbing till
they overflow in ever-new cascades!

Where Phryne's breasts are judged by her own kind
and every sigh is answered by a kiss;
where Aphrodite envies Sappho's rite
at shrines as favored as the Cyprian's own,
and Phryne's judges never are unkind;

Lesbos, where on suffocating nights
before their mirrors, girls with hollow eyes
caress their ripened limbs in sterile joy
and taste the fruit of their nubility
on Lesbos during suffocating nights!

What if old Plato's scowling eyes condemn?
Kisses absolve you by their sweet excess
whose subtleties are inexhaustible!
Queen of the tender Archipelago,
pursue what Plato's scowling eyes condemn

and win your pardon for the martyrdom
forever inflicted on ambitious hearts

that yearn, far from us, for a radiant smile
they dimly glimpse on the rim of other skies—
you win your pardon for that martyrdom!

Which of the Gods will dare to disapprove
and chide the pallor of your studious brow?
Until Olympian scales have weighed the flood
of tears your rivers pour into the sea,
which of the Gods will dare to disapprove?

What use to us are laws of right and wrong?
High-hearted virgins, honor of the Isles,
your altars are august as any: love
will laugh at Heaven as it laughs at Hell!
What use to us are laws of right and wrong?

For Lesbos has chosen me among all men
to sing the secrets of her budding grove;
from childhood I have shared the mystery
of frenzied laughter laced with sullen tears,
and therefore am I chosen among men

to keep my lookout high on Sappho's Cliff,
vigilant as a sleepless sentinel
gazing night and day for the bark or brig
whose distant outline shimmers on the blue;
I keep my lookout high on Sappho's Cliff

to discover if the sea is merciful
and if, out of the sobbing breakers' surge,
there will return to Lesbos, which forgives,
the cherished corpse of Sappho who left us
to discover if the sea is merciful—

of virile Sappho, the lover and the poet,
fairer than Aphrodite whose blue gaze
surrenders to the sombre radiance
of ash-encircled burning eyes—the eyes
of virile Sappho, the lover and the poet!

Fairer than the Anadyómene
scattering her bright serenity

and all the treasures of her golden youth
upon old Ocean dazzled by his child—
fairer than the Anadyómene

was Sappho on the day she broke her vow
and died apostate to her own command,
her lovely body forfeit to a brute
whose arrogance avenged the sacrilege
of Sappho, lost the day she broke her vow . . .

And from that time to this, Lesbos laments.
Heedless of the homage of the world,
she drugs herself each night with cries of pain
that rend the skies above her empty shores,
and from that time to this Lesbos laments!

Damned Women 1

(Delphine and Hippolyta)

Disclosed, though dimly, by the faltering lamps,
Hippolyta rested on a soft and scented couch
reliving those caresses which had raised
the curtains of her inexperience.

Wild-eyed after the storm, she conjured up
already-distant skies of innocence,
just as a traveller might turn back to glimpse
blue horizons lost with the morning's light.

The sluggish tears of her unfocussed gaze,
her eager arms flung down as in defeat—
every trace of voluptuous apathy
served and set off her fragile loveliness.

Reclining at her feet, elated yet calm,
Delphine stared up at her with shining eyes
the way a lioness will watch her prey
once her fangs have marked it for her own.

In all her pride the potent beauty knelt
before the pitiable one, complacently
savoring the wine of her triumph, reaching up
as though to garner fond acknowledgment.

She searched her victim's eyes for evidence
of the silent canticle which pleasure sings
and that sublime and infinite gratitude
which glistens under the eyelids like a sigh.

"Hippolyta, my angel, how do you feel now?
Surely you realize you must not grant
the holy sacrifice of your first bloom
to cruel gales that would disfigure it . . .

My kisses are as light as those May-flies
which graze the great transparent lakes at sunset;
his would trace their furrows on your flesh
like the tongue of some lacerating plough—

as if you had been trampled by a team
of oxen with inexorable hooves . . .
Hippolyta, sister! turn your face to me,
my heart and soul, my other half, my all!

Let me see your eyes, my heaven, my stars!
For one of their healing glances I shall trade
as yet untasted pleasures: you will drift
to sleep in my arms dreaming an endless dream!"

But then Hippolyta looked up: "Delphine,
I am grateful to you, I have no regrets,
yet I am troubled and my nerves are tense,
as if a dreadful feast had fouled the night . . .

Pangs of dread oppress me—I see ghosts
in black battalions beckoning me down
uncertain roads where each horizon ends
abruptly in a sky the color of blood.

What have we done—is it some wicked thing?
Must I endure this turmoil and this fear?

I cringe each time you call me 'angel,' yet
I feel my mouth long for you. No, Delphine—

don't look at me like that! I love you now
and I shall love you always: I choose you,
even if my choice becomes a trap
laid for me, and the onset of my doom."

With adamant eyes and a despotic voice,
Delphine replied, shaking her tragic mane
as if she stirred on the priestess' tripod:
"Who in love's name dares to speak of Hell?

My curse forever on the dreaming fool
who entered first that endless labyrinth
and tried for all his folly to enlist
love in the service of morality!

Whoever hopes to force into accord
day and darkness, shadow and radiance,
will never warm his vacillating flesh
in that red sun our bodies know as love!

Go now—go find yourself some stupid boy
and give his lust your virgin heart to maul;
then, filled with horror, livid with disgust,
bring back to me your mutilated breasts . . .

You cannot please two masters in this world!"
But then the girl, in a paroxysm of grief,
suddenly cried out: "There is emptiness
inside me—and that emptiness is my heart!

Searing as lava, deeper than the Void!
Nothing will satiate this monster's greed,
nothing appease the Fury who puts out
her flaming torch within my very blood . . .

O draw the curtains—leave the world outside!
There must be rest for all this weariness,
Let me annihilate myself upon
your breast and find the solace of a grave!"

Downward, wretched victims! ever down
the path you follow: make your way to hell,
into the pit where crime arouses crime,
seething together in the thunder's maw

and scourged by winds that never knew the sky.
Down, frantic shades, and fall to your desires
where passion never slakes its raging thirst,
and from your pleasure stems your punishment.

Crack by crevice, into your sunless caves
feverish miasmas seep and gather strength
until they catch on fire like spirit-lamps,
imbuing your bodies with their vile perfume.

The harsh sterility of your delight
scalds your throat and desiccates your skin—
and the eyeless cyclone of concupiscence
rattles your flesh like an abandoned flag.

Wandering far from all mankind, condemned
to forage in the wilderness like wolves,
pursue your fate, chaotic souls, and flee
the infinite you bear within yourselves!

Damned Women 2

Pensive as cattle resting on the beach,
they are staring out to sea; their hands and feet
creep toward each other imperceptibly
and touch at last, hesitant then fierce.

How eagerly some, beguiled by secrets shared,
follow a talkative stream among the trees,
spelling out their timid childhood's love
and carving initials in the tender wood;

others pace as slow and grave as nuns
among the rocks where Anthony beheld
the purple breasts of his temptations rise
like lava from the visionary earth;

some by torchlight in the silent caves
consecrated once to pagan rites
invoke—to quench their fever's holocaust—
Bacchus, healer of the old regrets;

others still, beneath their scapulars,
conceal a whip that in the solitude
and darkness of the forest reconciles
tears of pleasure with the tears of pain.

Virgins, demons, monsters, martyrs, all
great spirits scornful of reality,
saints and satyrs in search of the infinite,
racked with sobs or loud in ecstasy,

you whom my soul has followed to your hell,
Sisters! I love you as I pity you
for your bleak sorrows, for your unslaked thirsts,
and for the love that gorges your great hearts!

CHRISTINA ROSSETTI (1830–1894)

Goblin Market (1862)

The English Victorian poet Christina Rossetti came from a gifted and distinguished Anglo-Italian family. Her father, Gabriele Rossetti, an Italian political refugee, was professor of Italian at King's College, London; her mother, Frances Mary Lavinia Polidori, was the sister of the Gothic novelist John William Polidori; her elder brother, Dante Gabriel Rossetti, became a poet, painter, and leading figure in the celebrated Pre-Raphaelite Brotherhood of the 1850s and 1860s. Christina Rossetti was educated at home and began writing poetry in her teens. Her first poem, on her mother's birthday, was privately printed in 1842; her first volume of verse—also published privately— appeared in 1847. In 1850, under the pseudonym Ellen Alleyne, she contributed several poems to her brother's literary journal *The Germ*. Her father's blindness and a resulting decline in the family fortunes prompted Rossetti and her mother to open a day school in London in 1853, but this venture was not a success. Following her father's death in 1854, she was supported mainly by another brother, the critic and translator William Michael Rossetti. A devout High Church Anglican—she refused marriage proposals from two different men on religious grounds—she lived for the rest of her life mostly in seclusion with her mother and her elder sister, to whom she was deeply attached, and devoted herself to literary endeavors. Poetic works published in her lifetime included *Goblin Market and Other Poems* (1862); *The Prince's Progress and Other Poems* (1866), and *A Pageant and Other Poems* (1881), including a sonnet sequence, *Monna Innominata*, inspired by Elizabeth Barrett Browning's 1850 *Sonnets from the Portuguese*. She also wrote a series of devotional works, *Called to Be Saints* (1881), *Time Flies: A Reading Diary* (1885), and *The Face of the Deep* (1892), all published by the Society for the Diffusion of Useful Knowledge, and one novel, *Maude: A Story for Girls*, published posthumously in 1897.

A pious, recessive, and enigmatic personality in life, Rossetti wrote poetry that for all its Christian religiosity is often wildly erotic. She has sometimes been compared on this account to the American poet Emily Dickinson, with whom she shares a sublimated yet potent sensualism. And certainly, like Dickinson, she was also profoundly susceptible to the power of the feminine. (An intense emotional identification with Sappho is visible in two early Rossetti poems of the 1840s, "Sappho" and "What Sappho Would

Have Said Had Her Leap Cured Instead of Killing Her.") The verse parable *Goblin Market*, her most famous poem, manages to be at once both childlike in style and spirit and shockingly homoerotic. With its eerie nursery song rhymes and blatantly cunnilingual imagery, Rossetti's allegory of sisterly devotion has to be one of the strangest of Victorian love poems and a testament to authorial sympathies at once vivid and inscrutable.

FURTHER READING: Christina Rossetti, *The Poetical Works of Christina Rossetti*, ed. William Michael Rossetti (London: Macmillan, 1904); —, *The Complete Poems of Christina Rossetti*, ed. Rebecca Crump (Baton Rouge: Louisiana State University Press, 1979); Margaret Homans, " 'Syllables of Velvet': Dickinson, Rossetti, and the Rhetorics of Sexuality," *Feminist Studies* 11 (Fall 1983): 569–93; Helena Michie, " 'There Is No Friend Like a Sister': Sisterhood as Sexual Difference," *ELH: A Journal of English Literary History* 56 (summer 1989): 401–21; Mary Wilson Carpenter, " 'Eat Me, Drink Me, Love Me': The Consumable Female Body in Christina Rossetti's *Goblin Market*," *Victorian Poetry* 29 (winter 1991): 415–34; Jan Marsh, *Christina Rossetti: A Writer's Life* (New York: Viking, 1995); Germaine Greer, *Slip-shod Sibyls: Recognition, Rejection, and the Woman Poet* (London: Viking, 1995); Yopie Prins, *Victorian Sappho* (Princeton: Princeton University Press, 1999); Mary Arsenau, Antony H. Harrison, and Lorraine Janzen Kooistra, eds., *The Culture of Christina Rosssetti: Female Poetics and Victorian Contexts* (Athens: Ohio University Press, 1999).

Morning and evening
Maids heard the goblins cry:
"Come buy our orchard fruits,
Come buy, come buy:
Apples and quinces,
Lemons and oranges,
Plump unpecked cherries,
Melons and raspberries,
Bloom-down-cheeked peaches,
Swart-headed mulberries,
Wild free-born cranberries,
Crab-apples, dewberries,
Pine-apples, blackberries,
Apricots, strawberries;—
All ripe together
In summer weather,—
Morns that pass by,

Fair eves that fly;
Come buy, come buy:

Our grapes fresh from the vine,
Pomegranates full and fine,
Dates and sharp bullaces,
Rare pears and greengages,
Damsons and bilberries,
Taste them and try:
Currants and gooseberries,
Bright-fire-like barberries,
Figs to fill your mouth,
Citrons from the South,
Sweet to tongue and sound to eye;
Come buy, come buy."
Evening by evening
Among the brookside rushes,
Laura bowed her head to hear,
Lizzie veiled her blushes:
Crouching close together
In the cooling weather,
With clasping arms and cautioning lips,
With tingling cheeks and fingertips.
"Lie close," Laura said,
Pricking up her golden head:
"We must not look at goblin men,
We must not buy their fruits:
Who knows upon what soil they fed
Their hungry thirsty roots?"

"Come buy," call the goblins
Hobbling down the glen.
"Oh," cried Lizzie, "Laura, Laura,
You should not peep at goblin men."
Lizzie covered up her eyes,
Covered close lest they should look;
Laura reared her glossy head,
And whispered like the restless brook:
"Look, Lizzie, look, Lizzie,
Down the glen tramp little men.
One hauls a basket,
One bears a plate,

One lugs a golden dish
Of many pounds' weight.
How fair the vine must grow
Whose grapes are so luscious;
How warm the wind must blow
Through those fruit bushes."
"No," said Lizzie: "No, no, no;
Their offers should not charm us,
Their evil gifts would harm us."
She thrust a dimpled finger
In each ear, shut eyes and ran:
Curious Laura chose to linger
Wondering at each merchant man.
One had a cat's face,
One whisked a tail,
One tramped at a rat's pace,
One crawled like a snail,
One like a wombat prowled obtuse and furry,
One like a ratel tumbled hurry skurry.
She heard a voice like voice of doves
Cooing all together:
They sounded kind and full of loves
In the pleasant weather.

Laura stretched her gleaming neck
Like a rush-imbedded swan,
Like a lily from the beck,
Like a moonlit poplar branch,
Like a vessel at the launch
When its last restraint is gone.

Backwards up the mossy glen
Turned and trooped the goblin men,
With their shrill repeated cry,
"Come buy, come buy."
When they reached where Laura was
They stood stock still upon the moss,
Leering at each other,
Brother with queer brother;
Signalling each other,
Brother with sly brother.
One set his basket down,

One reared his plate;
One began to weave a crown
Of tendrils, leaves, and rough nuts brown
(Men sell not such in any town);
One heaved the golden weight
Of dish and fruit to offer her:
"Come buy, come buy," was still their cry.
Laura stared but did not stir,
Longed but had no money.
The whisk-tailed merchant bade her taste
In tones as smooth as honey,
The cat-faced purr'd,
The rat-paced spoke a word
Of welcome, and the snail-paced even was heard;
One parrot-voiced and jolly
Cried "Pretty Goblin" still for "Pretty Polly";
One whistled like a bird.

But sweet tooth Laura spoke in haste:
"Good Folk, I have no coin;
To take were to purloin:
I have no copper in my purse,
I have no silver either,
And all my gold is on the furze
That shakes in windy weather
Above the rusty heather."
"You have much gold upon your head,"
They answered all together:
"Buy from us with a golden curl."
She clipped a precious golden lock.
She dropped a tear more rare than pearl,
Then sucked their fruit globes fair or red.
Sweeter than honey from the rock,
Stronger than man-rejoicing wine,
Clearer than water flowed that juice;
She never tasted such before,
How should it cloy with length of use?
She sucked and sucked and sucked the more
Fruits which that unknown orchard bore
She sucked until her lips were sore;
Then flung the emptied rinds away
But gathered up one kernel stone,

And knew not was it night or day
As she turned home alone.

Lizzie met her at the gate
Full of wise upbraidings:
"Dear, you should not stay so late,
Twilight is not good for maidens;
Should not loiter in the glen
In the haunts of goblin men.
Do you not remember Jeanie,
How she met them in the moonlight,
Took their gifts both choice and many,
Ate their fruits and wore their flowers
Plucked from bowers
Where summer ripens at all hours?
But ever in the moonlight
She pined and pined away;
Sought them by night and day,
Found them no more, but dwindled and grew grey;
Then fell with the first snow,
While to this day no grass will grow
Where she lies low:
I planted daisies there a year ago
That never blow.
You should not loiter so."
"Nay, hush," said Laura:
"Nay, hush, my sister:
I ate and ate my fill,
Yet my mouth waters still:
To-morrow night I will
Buy more"; and kissed her.
"Have done with sorrow;
I'll bring you plums to-morrow
Fresh on their mother twigs,
Cherries worth getting;
You cannot think what figs
My teeth have met in,
What melons icy-cold
Piled on a dish of gold
Too huge for me to hold,
What peaches with a velvet nap,
Pellucid grapes without one seed:

Odorous indeed must be the mead
Whereon they grow, and pure the wave they drink
With lilies at the brink,
And sugar-sweet their sap."

Golden head by golden head,
Like two pigeons in one nest
Folded in each other's wings,
They lay down in their curtained bed:
Like two blossoms on one stem,
Like two flakes of new-fall'n snow,
Like two wands of ivory
Tipped with gold for awful kings.
Moon and stars gazed in at them,
Wind sang to them lullaby,
Lumbering owls forbore to fly,
Not a bat flapped to and fro
Round their nest:
Cheek to cheek and breast to breast
Locked together in one nest.

Early in the morning
When the first cock crowed his warning,
Neat like bees, as sweet and busy,
Laura rose with Lizzie:
Fetched in honey, milked the cows,
Aired and set to rights the house,
Kneaded cakes of whitest wheat,
Cakes for dainty mouths to eat,
Next churned butter, whipped up cream,
Fed their poultry, sat and sewed;
Talked as modest maidens should:
Lizzie with an open heart,
Laura in an absent dream,
One content, one sick in part;
One warbling for the mere bright day's delight,
One longing for the night.

At length slow evening came:
They went with pitchers to the reedy brook;
Lizzie most placid in her look,
Laura most like a leaping flame.

They drew the gurgling water from its deep.
Lizzie plucked purple and rich golden flags,
Then turning homeward said: "The sunset flushes
Those furthest loftiest crags;
Come, Laura, not another maiden lags.
No wilful squirrel wags,
The beasts and birds are fast asleep."
But Laura loitered still among the rushes,
And said the bank was steep.

And said the hour was early still,
The dew not fall'n, the wind not chill;
Listening ever, but not catching
The customary cry,
"Come buy, come buy,"
With its iterated jingle
Of sugar-baited words:
Not for all her watching
Once discerning even one goblin
Racing, whisking, tumbling, hobbling—
Let alone the herds
That used to tramp along the glen,
In groups or single,
Of brisk fruit-merchant men.

Till Lizzie urged, "O Laura, come;
I hear the fruit-call, but I dare not look:
You should not loiter longer at this brook:
Come with me home.
The stars rise, the moon bends her arc,
Each glow-worm winks her spark,
Let us get home before the night grows dark:
For clouds may gather
Though this is summer weather,
Put out the lights and drench us through;
Then if we lost our way what should we do?"

Laura turned cold as stone
To find her sister heard that cry alone,
That goblin cry,
"Come buy our fruits, come buy."
Must she then buy no more such dainty fruit?

Must she no more such succous pasture find,
Gone deaf and blind?
Her tree of life drooped from the root:
She said not one word in her heart's sore ache:
But peering thro' the dimness, nought discerning,
Trudged home, her pitcher dripping all the way;
So crept to bed, and lay
Silent till Lizzie slept;
Then sat up in a passionate yearning,
And gnashed her teeth for baulked desire, and wept
As if her heart would break.

Day after day, night after night,
Laura kept watch in vain
In sullen silence of exceeding pain.
She never caught again the goblin cry,
"Come buy, come buy;"—
She never spied the goblin men
Hawking their fruits along the glen:
But when the noon waxed bright
Her hair grew thin and grey;
She dwindled, as the fair full moon doth turn
To swift decay and burn
Her fire away.

One day remembering her kernel-stone
She set it by a wall that faced the south;
Dewed it with tears, hoped for a root,
Watched for a waxing shoot,
But there came none.
It never saw the sun,
It never felt the trickling moisture run:
While with sunk eyes and faded mouth
She dreamed of melons, as a traveller sees
False waves in desert drouth
With shade of leaf-crowned trees,
And burns the thirstier in the sandful breeze.

She no more swept the house,
Tended the fowls or cows,
Fetched honey, kneaded cakes of wheat,
Brought water from the brook:

But sat down listless in the chimney-nook
And would not eat.

Tender Lizzie could not bear
To watch her sister's cankerous care,
Yet not to share.
She night and morning
Caught the goblins' cry:
"Come buy our orchard fruits,
Come buy, come buy:"—
Beside the brook, along the glen,
She heard the tramp of goblin men,
The voice and stir
Poor Laura could not hear;
Longed to buy fruit to comfort her,
But feared to pay too dear.
She thought of Jeanie in her grave,
Who should have been a bride;
But who for joys brides hope to have
Fell sick and died
In her gay prime,
In earliest winter time,
With the first glazing rime,
With the first snow-fall of crisp winter time.

Till Laura dwindling
Seemed knocking at Death's door.
Then Lizzie weighed no more
Better and worse;
But put a silver penny in her purse,
Kissed Laura, crossed the heath with clumps of furze
At twilight, halted by the brook:
And for the first time in her life
Began to listen and look.

Laughed every goblin
When they spied her peeping:
Came towards her hobbling,
Flying, running, leaping,
Puffing and blowing,
Chuckling, clapping, crowing,
Clucking and gobbling,

Mopping and mowing,
Full of airs and graces,
Pulling wry faces,
Demure grimaces,
Cat-like and rat-like,
Ratel- and wombat-like,
Snail-paced in a hurry,
Parrot-voiced and whistler,
Helter skelter, hurry skurry,
Chattering like magpies,
Fluttering like pigeons,
Gliding like fishes,—
Hugged her and kissed her:
Squeezed and caressed her:
Stretched up their dishes,
Panniers, and plates:
"Look at our apples
Russet and dun,
Bob at our cherries,
Bite at our peaches,
Citrons and dates,
Grapes for the asking,
Pears red with basking
Out in the sun,
Plums on their twigs;
Pluck them and suck them,—
Pomegranates, figs."

"Good folk," said Lizzie,
Mindful of Jeanie:
"Give me much and many:"
Held out her apron,
Tossed them her penny.
"Nay, take a seat with us,
Honour and eat with us,"
They answered grinning:
"Our feast is but beginning.
Night yet is early,
Warm and dew-pearly,
Wakeful and starry:
Such fruits as these
No man can carry;

Half their dew would dry,
Half their flavour would pass by.
Sit down and feast with us,
Be welcome guest with us,
Cheer you and rest with us."—

"Thank you," said Lizzie: "But one waits
At home alone for me:
So without further parleying,
If you will not sell me any
Of your fruits though much and many,
Give me back my silver penny
I tossed you for a fee."—
They began to scratch their pates,
No longer wagging, purring,
But visibly demurring,
Grunting and snarling.
One called her proud,
Cross-grained, uncivil;
Their tones waxed loud,
Their looks were evil.
Lashing their tails
They trod and hustled her,
Elbowed and jostled her,
Clawed with their nails,
Barking, mewing, hissing, mocking,
Tore her gown and soiled her stocking,
Twitched her hair out by the roots,
Stamped upon her tender feet,
Held her hands and squeezed their fruits
Against her mouth to make her eat.
White and golden Lizzie stood,
Like a lily in a flood,—
Like a rock of blue-veined stone
Lashed by tides obstreperously,—
Like a beacon left alone
In a hoary roaring sea,
Sending up a golden fire,—
Like a fruit-crowned orange-tree
White with blossoms honey-sweet
Sore beset by wasp and bee,—
Like a royal virgin town

Topped with gilded dome and spire
Close beleaguered by a fleet
Mad to tug her standard down.

One may lead a horse to water,
Twenty cannot make him drink.
Though the goblins cuffed and caught her,
Coaxed and fought her,
Bullied and besought her,
Scratched her, pinched her black as ink,
Kicked and knocked her,
Mauled and mocked her,
Lizzie uttered not a word;
Would not open lip from lip
Lest they should cram a mouthful in:
But laughed in heart to feel the drip
Of juice that syruped all her face,
And lodged in dimples of her chin,
And streaked her neck which quaked like curd.
At last the evil people,
Worn out by her resistance,
Flung back her penny, kicked their fruit
Along whichever road they took,
Not leaving root or stone or shoot;
Some writhed into the ground,
Some dived into the brook
With ring and ripple,
Some scudded on the gale without a sound,
Some vanished in the distance.

In a smart, ache, tingle,
Lizzie went her way;
Knew not was it night or day;
Sprang up the bank, tore thro' the furze,
Threaded copse and dingle,
And heard her penny jingle
Bouncing in her purse,—
Its bounce was music to her ear.
She ran and ran
As if she feared some goblin man
Dogged her with gibe or curse
Or something worse:

Nor was she pricked by fear;
The kind heart made her windy-paced
That urged her home quite out of breath with haste
And inward laughter.
She cried, "Laura," up the garden,
"Did you miss me?
Come and kiss me.
Never mind my bruises,
Hug me, kiss me, suck my juices
Squeezed from goblin fruits for you,
Goblin pulp and goblin dew.
Eat me, drink me, love me;
Laura, make much of me;
For your sake I have braved the glen
And had to do with goblin merchant men."

Laura started from her chair,
Flung her arms up in the air,
Clutched her hair:
"Lizzie, Lizzie, have you tasted
For my sake the fruit forbidden?
Must your light like mine be hidden,
Your young life like mine be wasted,
Undone in mine undoing,
And ruined in my ruin,
Thirsty, cankered, goblin-ridden?"—
She clung about her sister,
Kissed and kissed and kissed her:
Tears once again
Refreshed her shrunken eyes,
Dropping like rain
After long sultry drouth;
Shaking with aguish fear, and pain,
She kissed and kissed her with a hungry mouth.

Her lips began to scorch,
That juice was wormwood to her tongue,
She loathed the feast:
Writhing as one possessed she leaped and sung,
Rent all her robe, and wrung
Her hands in lamentable haste,
And beat her breast.

Her locks streamed like the torch
Borne by a racer at full speed,
Or like the mane of horses in their flight,
Or like an eagle when she stems the light
Straight toward the sun,
Or like a caged thing freed,
Or like a flying flag when armies run.

Swift fire spread through her veins, knocked at her heart,
Met the fire smouldering there
And overbore its lesser flame;
She gorged on bitterness without a name:
Ah fool, to choose such part
Of soul-consuming care!
Sense failed in the mortal strife:
Like the watch-tower of a town
Which an earthquake shatters down,
Like a lightning-stricken mast,
Like a wind-uprooted tree
Spun about,
Like a foam-topped waterspout
Cast down headlong in the sea,
She fell at last;
Pleasure past and anguish past,
Is it death or is it life?

Life out of death.
That night long Lizzie watched by her,
Counted her pulse's flagging stir,
Felt for her breath,
Held water to her lips, and cooled her face
With tears and fanning leaves.
But when the first birds chirped about their eaves,
And early reapers plodded to the place
Of golden sheaves,
And dew-wet grass
Bowed in the morning winds so brisk to pass,
And new buds with new day
Opened of cup-like lilies on the stream,
Laura awoke as from a dream,
Laughed in the innocent old way,
Hugged Lizzie but not twice or thrice;

Her gleaming locks showed not one thread of grey,
Her breath was sweet as May,
And light danced in her eyes.

Days, weeks, months, years
Afterwards, when both were wives
With children of their own;
Their mother-hearts beset with fears,
Their lives bound up in tender lives;
Laura would call the little ones
And tell them of her early prime,
Those pleasant days long gone
Of not-returning time:
Would talk about the haunted glen,
The wicked quaint fruit-merchant men,
Their fruits like honey to the throat
But poison in the blood
(Men sell not such in any town):
Would tell them how her sister stood
In deadly peril to do her good,
And win the fiery antidote:
Then joining hands to little hands
Would bid them cling together,—
"For there is no friend like a sister
In calm or stormy weather;
To cheer one on the tedious way,
To fetch one if one goes astray,
To lift one if one totters down,
To strengthen whilst one stands."

ALGERNON CHARLES SWINBURNE (1837–1909)

"Anactoria" (1866) and excerpt from *Lesbia Brandon* (1864–67)

The late Victorian English writer A. C. Swinburne, would-be decadent and occasional flagellant—his poem "Dolores" is a paean to the pleasures of the whip—was born in London and educated at Eton and Balliol College, Oxford. After leaving Oxford without a degree he settled in London, where he became part of the artistic circle around Dante Gabriel Rossetti and William Morris. Despite an unprepossessing appearance (he was tiny and red-headed) and a chaotic personal life (he drank heavily and was addicted to laudanum) Swinburne was quickly recognized as a writer of singular talent. He published his first major work, the verse drama *Atalanta in Calydon*, in 1865. The following year he created a literary sensation with *Poems and Ballads* (1866), a heady, hypnotic, often wilfully shocking celebration of the "pagan" sensuality of the ancient Greeks and Romans. In poems such as "Faustine," a chantlike dirge on the death of the wicked Roman empress, he confirmed his reputation as the enfant terrible of English poetry. Over the next thirty years he added to his fame with a series of accomplished—if sometimes campy—lyric and dramatic poems. His ardent poetic celebrations of the Italian nationalist cause, *A Song of Italy* and *Songs Before Sunrise*, appeared in 1867 and 1871; a second series of *Poems and Ballads* in 1878; and the final play of a romantic verse trilogy about Mary, Queen of Scots, in 1881. Later works included a third volume of *Poems and Ballads* (1889), *Astrophel* (1894), *A Tale of Balen* (1896), *A Channel Passage* (1904), and several works of criticism, including monographs on Elizabethan and Jacobean drama, Shakespeare, Ben Jonson, and Victor Hugo.

Swinburne never married, though he was rumored to have had an affair—or at least a flogging arrangement—with the celebrated variety actress, poet, and stunt rider, Adah Isaacs Menken. In his later years, following an alcoholic breakdown, Swinburne was cared for by a close friend, Theodore Watts-Dunton. Watts-Dunton, in the words of Wolf Mankowitz,

> devoted much time and energy to keeping the little bearded quirky poet safe in his Gothic house in Putney, alive, sober and well away from pretty little boys, for whom he tended nowadays to develop sudden extraordinary passions. Watts kept Swinburne respectable enough to occupy the high place on the

Victorian Parnassus which the academic literary world had now unanimously awarded the middle-aged poet.

Swinburne may be little read today—the self-consciously "decadent" mode has not weathered well—but he is unquestionably a major Victorian writer, whose curious life and oeuvre demand contemporary reevaluation.

Like Baudelaire, who influenced him greatly, Swinburne was deeply attracted by the lesbian theme. And hardly surprisingly, given his own black-sheep tendencies, he reveled in the Baudelairean image of the lesbian as glamorous monster. In "Anactoria," one of several dramatic monologues published in the first *Poems and Ballads*, he assumes the voice of the Greek poet Sappho, who is overheard regaling her lover Anactoria with a series of sadomasochistic sexual fantasies. The sickly, overblown style, intricately worked poetic conceits, and surfeit of images having to do with cruelty and erotic pain ("Ah that my mouth for Muses' milk were fed / On the sweet blood thy sweet small wounds had bled!") are characteristic of Swinburne's poetry at its most morbid and fetishistic. Indeed, were it not so obviously Victorian in its peculiar fusion of high-art ambition and dizzying tastelessness, the poem might well fit into a contemporary collection of glossy upmarket lesbian porn.

In the unfinished novel *Lesbia Brandon* (1864–67), the curious tale of the dark-haired, sexually ambiguous "poet and pagan" Lesbia Brandon, Swinburne took up the same theme in a contemporary (albeit equally decadent) setting. Granted, the overtly lesbian plot elements in this aborted work remain undeveloped; Swinburne abandoned the novel in 1867 when he became absorbed in his Italian poems. But the heroine, as her name and appearance suggest, seems clearly intended to represent a modern-day Sappho. (She may be a fictional portrait of Jane Faulkner, a beautiful yet masculine-looking young woman who at one time rebuffed Swinburne's amorous advances. Faulkner made a study of Sappho's poetry and wrote a number of love poems from the male viewpoint.) In the excerpt below, the hero of the novel, an absurdly effeminate young man named Bertie—whom Swinburne seems to have modeled largely on himself—dresses up as a girl for an evening of private theatricals at Lady Wariston's country house. After being introduced to Lesbia (she is instantly attracted to him because she thinks him a young woman) he falls violently in love with her. His love goes unrequited; in the novel's fragmentary final scene—also reproduced below—she is seen dying of opium addiction and neurasthenia, affirming her horror of men.

FURTHER READING: Algernon Charles Swinburne, *The Complete Works of Algernon Charles Swinburne*, ed. Edmund Gosse and Thomas James Wise, 20 vols. (London: William Heinemann, 1925); ——, *The Novels of A. C. Swinburne: Love's Cross-Currents, Lesbia Brandon*, ed. Edmund Wilson (New York: Farrar, Straus, and Cudahy, 1962); Edmund Gosse, *The Life of Algernon Charles Swinburne* (London: Macmillan, 1917); Georges Lafourcade, *Swinburne, A Literary Biography* (London: G. Bell, 1932); Jean

Overton Fuller, *Swinburne: A Critical Biography* (London: Chatto and Windus, 1968); Wolf Mankowitz, *Mazeppa: The Lives, Loves, and Legends of Adah Isaacs Menken* (New York: Stein and Day, 1982); Frédéric Monneyron, "L'Androgyne dans *Lesbia Brandon* de Swinburne," *CVE* (April 1989): 55–65; Cassandra Laity, "H.D. and A. C. Swinburne: Decadence and Sapphic Modernism," in Karla Jay and Joanne Glasgow, eds., *Lesbian Texts and Contexts: Radical Revisions* (New York: New York University Press, 1990); Joyce Zonana, "Swinburne's Sappho: The Muse as Sister-Goddess," *Victorian Poetry* 28 (spring 1990): 39–50; Robert A. Greenberg, " 'Erotion,' 'Anactoria,' and the Sapphic Passion," *Victorian Poetry* 29 (spring 1991): 79–87; Thais E. Morgan, "Male Lesbian Bodies: The Construction of Alternate Masculinities in Courbet, Baudelaire, and Swinburne," *Genders* 15 (1992): 37–57; —, "Victorian Effeminacies," in Richard Dellamora, ed., *Victorian Sexual Dissidence* (Chicago: University of Chicago Press, 1999); Yopie Prins, *Victorian Sappho* (Princeton: Princeton University Press, 1999).

Anactoria

τίνος αυ τὺ πειθοῖ
μὰψ σαγηνεύσας φιλύτατα;
Sappho.

My life is bitter with thy love; thine eyes
Blind me, thy tresses burn me, thy sharp sighs
Divide my flesh and spirit with soft sound,
And my blood strengthens, and my veins abound.
I pray thee sigh not, speak not, draw not breath;
Let life burn down, and dream it is not death.
I would the sea had hidden us, the fire
(Wilt thou fear that, and fear not my desire?)
Severed the bones that bleach, the flesh that cleaves,
And let our sifted ashes drop like leaves.
I feel thy blood against my blood: my pain
Pains thee, and lips bruise lips, and vein stings vein.
Let fruit be crushed on fruit, let flower on flower,
Breast kindle breast, and either burn one hour.
Why wilt thou follow lesser loves? are thine
Too weak to bear these hands and lips of mine?
I charge thee for my life's sake, O too sweet
To crush love with thy cruel faultless feet,
I charge thee keep thy lips from hers or his,
Sweetest, till theirs be sweeter than my kiss:

Lest I too lure, a swallow for a dove,
Erotion or Erinna to my love.
I would my love could kill thee; I am satiated
With seeing thee live, and fain would have thee dead.
I would earth had thy body as fruit to eat,
And no mouth but some serpent's found thee sweet.
I would find grievous ways to have thee slain,
Intense device, and superflux of pain;
Vex thee with amorous agonies, and shake
Life at thy lips, and leave it there to ache;
Strain out thy soul with pangs too soft to kill,
Intolerable interludes, and infinite ill;
Relapse and reluctation of the breath,
Dumb tunes and shuddering semitones of death.
I am weary of all thy words and soft strange ways,
Of all love's fiery nights and all his days,
And all the broken kisses salt as brine
That shuddering lips make moist with waterish wine,
And eyes the bluer for all those hidden hours
That pleasure fills with tears and feeds from flowers,
Fierce at the heart with fire that half comes through,
But all the flowerlike white stained round with blue;
The fervent underlid, and that above
Lifted with laughter or abashed with love;
Thine amorous girdle, full of thee and fair,
And leavings of the lilies in thine hair.
Yea, all sweet words of thine and all thy ways,
And all the fruit of nights and flower of days,
And stinging lips wherein the hot sweet brine
That Love was born of burns and foams like wine,
And eyes insatiable of amorous hours,
Fervent as fire and delicate as flowers,
Coloured like night at heart, but cloven through
Like night with flame, dyed round like night with blue,
Clothed with deep eyelids under and above—
Yea, all thy beauty sickens me with love;
Thy girdle empty of thee and now not fair,
And ruinous lilies in thy languid hair.
Ah, take no thought for Love's sake; shall this be,
And she who loves thy lover not love thee?
Sweet soul, sweet mouth of all that laughs and lives,
Mine is she, very mine; and she forgives.

For I beheld in sleep the light that is
In her high place in Paphos, heard the kiss
Of body and soul that mix with eager tears
And laughter stinging through the eyes and ears;
Saw Love, as burning flame from crown to feet,
Imperishable, upon her storied seat;
Clear eyelids lifted toward the north and south,
A mind of many colours, and a mouth
Of many tunes and kisses; and she bowed,
With all her subtle face laughing aloud,
Bowed down upon me, saying, "Who doth thee wrong,
Sappho?" but thou—thy body is the song,
Thy mouth the music; thou art more than I,
Though my voice die not till the whole world die;
Though men that hear it madden; though love weep,
Though nature change, though shame be charmed to sleep.
Ah, wilt thou slay me lest I kiss thee dead?
Yet the queen laughed from her sweet heart and said:
"Even she that flies shall follow for thy sake,
And she shall give thee gifts that would not take,
Shall kiss that would not kiss thee" (yea, kiss me)
"When thou wouldst not"—when I would not kiss thee!
Ah, more to me than all men as thou art,
Shall not my songs assuage her at the heart?
Ah, sweet to me as life seems sweet to death,
Why should her wrath fill thee with fearful breath?
Nay, sweet, for is she God alone? hath she
Made earth and all the centuries of the sea,
Taught the sun ways to travel, woven most fine
The moonbeams, shed the starbeams forth as wine,
Bound with her myrtles, beaten with her rods,
The young men and the maidens and the gods?
Have we not lips to love with, eyes for tears,
And summer and flower of women and of years?
Stars for the foot of morning, and for noon
Sunlight, and exaltation of the moon;
Waters that answer waters, fields that wear
Lilies, and languor of the Lesbian air?
Beyond those flying feet of fluttered doves,
Are there not other gods for other loves?
Yea, though she scourge thee, sweetest, for my sake,
Blossom not thorns and flowers not blood should break.

Ah that my lips were tuneless lips, but pressed
To the bruised blossom of thy scourged white breast!
Ah that my mouth for Muses' milk were fed
On the sweet blood thy sweet small wounds had bled!
That with my tongue I felt them, and could taste
The faint flakes from thy bosom to the waist!
That I could drink thy veins as wine, and eat
Thy breasts like honey! that from face to feet
Thy body were abolished and consumed,
And in my flesh thy very flesh entombed!
Ah, ah, thy beauty! like a beast it bites,
Stings like an adder, like an arrow smites.
Ah sweet, and sweet again, and seven times sweet
The paces and the pauses of thy feet!
Ah sweeter than all sleep or summer air
The fallen fillets fragrant from thine hair!
Yea, though their alien kisses do me wrong,
Sweeter thy lips than mine with all their song;
Thy shoulders whiter than a fleece of white,
And flower-sweet fingers, good to bruise or bite
As honeycomb of the inmost honey-cells,
With almond-shaped and roseleaf-coloured shells,
And blood like purple blossom at the tips
Quivering; and pain made perfect in thy lips
For my sake when I hurt thee; O that I
Durst crush thee out of life with love, and die,
Die of thy pain and my delight, and be
Mixed with thy blood and molten into thee!
Would I not plague thee dying overmuch?
Would I not hurt thee perfectly? not touch
Thy pores of sense with torture, and make bright,
Thine eyes with bloodlike tears and grievous light
Strike pang from pang as note is struck from note,
Catch the sob's middle music in thy throat,
Take thy limbs living, and new-mould with these
A lyre of many faultless agonies?
Feed thee with fever and famine and fine drouth,
With perfect pangs convulse thy perfect mouth,
Make thy life shudder in thee and burn afresh,
And wring thy very spirit through the flesh?
Cruel? but love makes all that love him well
As wise as heaven and crueller than hell.

Me hath love made more bitter toward thee
Than death toward man; but were I made as he
Who hath made all things to break them one by one,
If my feet trod upon the stars and sun
And souls of men as his have alway trod,
God knows I might be crueller than God.
For who shall change with prayers or thanksgivings
The mystery of the cruelty of things?
Or say what God above all gods and years
With offering and blood-sacrifice of tears,
With lamentation from strange lands, from graves
Where the snake pastures, from scarred mouth of slaves
From prison, and from plunging prows of ships
Through flamelike foam of the sea's closing lips—
With thwartings of strange signs, and wind-blown hair
Of comets, desolating the dim air,
When darkness is made fast with seals and bars,
And fierce reluctance of disastrous stars,
Eclipse, and sound of shaken hills, and wings
Darkening, and blind inexpiable things—
With sorrow of labouring moons, and altering light
And travail of the planets of the night,
And weeping of the weary Pleiads seven,
Feeds the mute melancholy lust of heaven?
Is not his incense bitterness, his meat
Murder? his hidden face and iron feet
Hath not man known, and felt them on their way
Threaten and trample all things and every day?
Hath he not sent us hunger? who hath cursed
Spirit and flesh with longing? filled with thirst
Their lips who cried unto him? who bade exceed
The fervid will, fall short the feeble deed,
Bade sink the spirit and the flesh aspire,
Pain animate the dust of dead desire,
And life yield up her flower to violent fate?
Him would I reach, him smite, him desecrate,
Pierce the cold lips of God with human breath,
And mix his immortality with death.
Why hath he made us? what had all we done
That we should live and loathe the sterile sun,
And with the moon wax paler as she wanes,
And pulse by pulse feel time grow through our veins?

Thee too the years shall cover; thou shalt be
As the rose born of one same blood with thee,
As a song sung, as a word said, and fall
Flower-wise, and be not any more at all,
Nor any memory of thee anywhere;
For never Muse has bound above thine hair
The high Pierian flower whose graft outgrows
All summer kinship of the mortal rose
And colour of deciduous days, nor shed
Reflex and flush of heaven about thine head,
Nor reddened brows made pale by floral grief
With splendid shadow from that lordlier leaf.
Yea, thou shalt be forgotten like spilt wine,
Except these kisses of my lips on thine
Brand them with immortality; but me—
Men shall not see bright fire nor hear the sea,
Nor mix their hearts with music, nor behold
Cast forth of heaven, with feet of awful gold
And plumeless wings that make the bright air blind,
Lightning, with thunder for a hound behind
Hunting through fields unfurrowed and unsown,
But in the light and laughter, in the moan
And music, and in grasp of lip and hand
And shudder of water that makes felt on land
The immeasurable tremor of all the sea,
Memories shall mix and metaphors of me.
Like me shall be the shuddering calm of night,
When all the winds of the world for pure delight
Close lips that quiver and fold up wings that ache;
When nightingales are louder for love's sake,
And leaves tremble like lute-strings or like fire;
Like me the one star swooning with desire
Even at the cold lips of the sleepless moon,
As I at thine; like me the waste white noon,
Burnt through with barren sunlight; and like me
The land-stream and the tide-stream in the sea.
I am sick with time as these with ebb and flow,
And by the yearning in my veins I know
The yearning sound of waters; and mine eyes
Burn as that beamless fire which fills the skies
With troubled stars and travailing things of flame;
And in my heart the grief consuming them

Labours, and in my veins the thirst of these,
And all the summer travail of the trees
And all the winter sickness; and the earth,
Filled full with deadly works of death and birth,
Sore spent with hungry lusts of birth and death,
Has pain like mine in her divided breath;
Her spring of leaves is barren, and her fruit
Ashes; her boughs are burdened, and her root
Fibrous and gnarled with poison; underneath
Serpents have gnawn it through with tortuous teeth
Made sharp upon the bones of all the dead,
And wild birds rend her branches overhead.
These, woven as raiment for his word and thought,
These hath God made, and me as these, and wrought
Song, and hath lit it at my lips; and me
Earth shall not gather though she feed on thee.
As a shed tear shalt thou be shed; but I
Lo, earth may labour, men live long and die,
Years change and stars, and the high God devise
New things, and old things wane before his eyes
Who wields and wrecks them, being more strong than they—
But, having made me, me he shall not slay.
Nor slay nor satiate, like those herds of his
Who laugh and live a little, and their kiss
Contents them, and their loves are swift and sweet,
And sure death grasps and gains them with slow feet,
Love they or hate they, strive or bow their knees—
And all these ends he hath his will of these.
Yea, but albeit he slay me, hating me—
Albeit he hide me in the deep dear sea
And cover me with cool wan foam, and ease
This soul of mine as any soul of these,
And give me water and great sweet waves, and make
The very sea's name lordlier for my sake,
The whole sea sweeter—albeit I die indeed
And hide myself and sleep and no man heed,
Of me the high God hath not all his will.
Blossom of branches, and on each high hill
Clear air and wind, and under in clamorous vales
Fierce noises of the fiery nightingales,
Buds burning in the sudden spring like fire,
The wan washed sand and the waves' vain desire,

Sails seen like blown white flowers at sea, and words
That bring tears swiftest, and long notes of birds
Violently singing till the whole world sings—
I Sappho shall be one with all these things,
With all high things for ever; and my face
Seen once, my songs once heard in a strange place,
Cleave to men's lives, and waste the days thereof
With gladness and much sadness and long love.
Yea, they shall say, earth's womb has borne in vain
New things, and never this best thing again;
Borne days and men, borne fruits and wars and wine,
Seasons and songs, but no song more like mine.
And they shall know me as ye who have known me here,
Last year when I loved Atthis, and this year
When I love thee; and they shall praise me, and say
"She hath all time as all we have our day,
Shall she not live and have her will"—even I?
Yea, though thou diest, I say I shall not die.
For these shall give me of their souls, shall give
Life, and the days and loves wherewith I live,
Shall quicken me with loving, fill with breath,
Save me and serve me, strive for me with death.
Alas, that neither moon nor snow nor dew
Nor all cold things can purge me wholly through,
Assuage me nor allay me nor appease,
Till supreme sleep shall bring me bloodless ease;
Till time wax faint in all his periods;
Till fate undo the bondage of the gods,
And lay, to slake and satiate me all through,
Lotus and Lethe on my lips like dew,
And shed around and over and under me
Thick darkness and the insuperable sea.

From *Lesbia Brandon*

[*Herbert ("Bertie") meets the poetess Lesbia Brandon at Lady Wariston's fancy-dress party.*]

The house had by this time won a certain repute of an uncertain sort. It amused some; by no means all. It was peopled during the country season by a fair number of passengers. In the September of 1854 it was full of picked guests; very few names of note among them, but a company pleasant and graceful enough within reasonable limits. Charades and proverbs were acted and other small enjoyments found out and gone through. Lady Wariston had grown out of the quiet intolerance of people in general which at first kept her passive and averse to fresh faces. She was seemingly warmer and really brighter. A delicate rapid grace, soft and keen as the play of light flame, moved now with all her emotions. She spoke more and trod quicker than in past years. Her children were now old enough to please her: and her health had been strong and sound ever since the youngest was born.

Herbert was still at home when the house began to fill, and did not enjoy the change. He had fallen into unsocial indolence and the turbid delight of dreams. Quiet usually and excitable always, he grew brilliant all over with pleasure when once in reach of it. He had swum and ridden and lounged through the last month with full content: the new faces and fixed hours that now came into fashion were vexatious. One visitor only he was curious to see. Miss Brandon was of the party this time, as well as her father. The worthy jockey had grown in old age to like a quiet house and old friends. His daughter had published, if not wholly under the rose yet duly under the roseleaf, a volume of verse. Her name had of course taken a veil of disguise, and of course the veil was translucent. This book, among much other worse and better poetry, Bertie had caught up and greedily fed upon. There was a certain fire and music in the verse at its best which had stung and soothed him alternately with gentle and violent delight. Where the writer was weakest, she was weak in a way of her own, rather from the relaxation of nerves overstrung than from the debility of nerves incompetent of passion. She could articulate and attune emotion, and her verse had in it a pulse and play of blood, a sensible if not a durable life. Her first fruits had fervour and fragrance enough to attract the appetite of a boy.

Her arrival was delayed by chance and came by surprise. The afternoon had been wholly absorbed by the elaborate rehearsal of actors in the evening's show-proverb. The whole crew was in full masquerade; Lady Midhurst, a perfect actress at fifty-four as at fifteen, was in rococo costume; which naturally whetted the tongues and lifted the eyes of her coeval friends with depreciation and disgust; Lord Wariston and Mr. Linley in the due powder and red heels, lace and silk; Lady Wariston, who acted in another part of the entertainment, was dressed after a Venetian picture, with Lunsford major as a cavalier and his two brothers as pages; Herbert, who much against his own will had been ousted from a share in this division of the work and voted into a leading female part, was chafing under compliments and chaff from old and young. "*Quem si puellarum insereres choro,*" Mr. Linley had said twice already; and the boy's look was certainly deceptive. His full and curled hair had been eked out with false locks to the due length, and his skin touched up with feminine colours: so that "*solutis crinibus ambiguoque vultu*" he was passable as a girl. Between loyalty to his sister, who abused it by her entreaty and command that he would submit, and a muffled reluctant sense of some comic faculty, he had yielded, and began to catch the infection of amusement.

"How on earth am I to receive these people?" said Lady Wariston. "I can't go down as Lucrezia."

"I don't see why we shouldn't all go as we are," said Lady Midhurst. "It won't help them to guess the word, seeing us all at once. And I will *not* dress more than four times a day: so I for one remain en marquise till the dressing-bell. And you might introduce your sister; he is perfect."

"So is the suggestion," said Mr. Linley; "perfect."

"Not if I know it," said the young lady: "it's nuisance enough to wear this beastliness at all: and they'd see at dinner."

Lady Wariston caught at his hands which were raised to pull out the false hair. "It can't be done again," she said; "you shall wear things of mine at dinner, and put on these again afterwards, but your head must stay as it is, it takes hours to do. You won't ruin the whole thing and miss the best fun?" She was singularly animated all that week, and acted Lucrezia Borgia to young Lunsford's Gennaro with exquisite power and grace. At this minute especially she looked younger than her years, luminous with laughter and excitement. Mme. de Rochelaurier recognized in her a "*grâce fauve*," and would "hardly have given her twenty-four."

"Now do, Bertie, like a good boy: be a good dog, sir," tapping his nose which was not yet on a level with her own. "I'll present you as a rising poetess. You'll be able to sit at her feet and learn her secret: it's a chance for a boy going in for poetry."

"I'm not," said Bertie, who went in but moderately for grammar.

"Introduce him with that blush on," said Mr. Linley, "and the thing's done."

"If Lord Charles were to fall in love with your sister? he always admired you profoundly," said Lady Midhurst.

"A susceptible race," said Linley; "it's in the blood. And meantime they are cooling down I should say for want of a reception."

Not all the boy's rage and scorn after these last remarks could give him nerve or will to resist his sister's. She marched him out before her a slave as of old, amid the due applause. A few of the rest went with them to receive the visitors, who were found expectant. Father and daughter rose to meet them, surprised and smiling.

Miss Brandon was dark and delicately shaped; not tall, but erect and supple; she had thick and heavy hair growing low on the forehead, so brown that it seemed black in the shadow; her eyes were sombre and mobile, full of fervour and of dreams, answering in colour to the hair, as did also the brows and eyelashes. Her cheeks had the profound pallor of complexions at once dark and colourless; but the skin was pure and tender, the outline clear and soft: she was warm and wan as a hot day without a sun. She had a fine and close mouth, with small bright lips, not variable in expression; her throat and shoulders were fresh and round. A certain power and a certain trouble were perceptible in the face, but traceable to no single feature: apart from whatever it might have of beauty, the face was one to attract rather than satisfy.

After the due explanations, Lady Wariston, laughing only with the eyes, did as agreed on present her sister. Lord Charles, who had not seen Bertie for years, and whose memory was known to be loosening, accepted the introduction without a rising eyebrow or questioning lip: it was possible enough that there should be a younger sister now first producible.

"Very like her sister, the young lady is," he discreetly observed. "By the by, where's my old friend—Robert—or Hubert was it?"

"Staying with a schoolfellow," Lady Midhurst thought. "Helen, what have you done with that boy?"

"He's at old Lunsford's," quoth Helen: "hope he likes it."

"The girl talks like a schoolboy while her brother's holidays last," said Lady Midhurst to Miss Brandon. "As her godmother, I ought to look after her language. However, you have a true believer in her for all that; she is verse-mad."

Lesbia looked curiously into the false girl's eyes, and took her hand; it was hard in the palm for a girl's, and specked with sunburns.

"I should have guessed not," she said. "You look fonder of riding, now."

"I like riding, too," said Bertie in a small voice; he began to taste the fun and dread detection.

"Does you brother get on well at school now?" said Lord Charles: "is he in the boat? or only in the bill, eh?"

"Oh, no," Miss Seyton said scornfully; "too much of a muff; they'd have let him steer I daresay if he could, but he shirked it; lazy young brute he is, and doesn't get swished half often enough, *I* think."

"*Par exemple!*" said Lady Midhurst; "he seems to keep you well up to your slang, my dear child, at any rate."

"You are rather hard on him," said Lesbia; "is he older or younger than you?"

"Twin," said Herbert: regaining his lost ground by the happy touch.

"I should like to see him."

"When you've seen her you've seen him," said Lady Wariston.

"He must be a handsome fellow then by this time," said Lord Charles.

"Not enough of him for that," said Linley: "he might be, with more inches."

"I think he must be as it is," said Miss Brandon; "I should like to see him; he must be very fond of you."

"Well, I don't think he hates me," said Herbert, suppressing a puerile grin into a feminine smile.

Lesbia took his cheeks between her hollowed hands and pressed them rather hard, till he looked at her with wide shining eyes from which the light of laughter had vanished and melted into eager and dubious passion.

"You have not really read any verse of mine?" she said.

The query almost throttled Herbert for the minute; then he said: "I thought I had."

"Then you shall tell me later what you like best." Her voice was like a kiss as she said this, the boy thought: remembering the only kisses he knew, his sister's.

[Lesbia, on her deathbed, describes a strange vision of the goddess Proserpine and bids Bertie farewell.]

He had never come near the dead or dying since his tenth year, when his father died at Kirklowes: but he knew there was a savour of death in the room: something beyond the sweet strong smell of perfumes and drugs. The woman's sad and slow suicide had been with time and care duly accomplished. She had killed herself off by inches, with the help of eau-de-Cologne and doses of opium. A funereal fragrance hung about all the air. Close curtains shut out the twilight, and a covered lamp at either end filled the room with less of light than of silver shadow. Along her sofa, propped by cushions and with limbs drawn up like a tired child's, lay or leant a woman like a ghost; the living corpse of Lesbia. She was white, with grey lips; her long shapely hands were pale and faded, and the dark tender warmth of her even colour had changed into a hot and haggard hue like fever. Her beauty of form was unimpaired; she retained the distinction of noble and graceful features and attitudes. She looked like one whom death was as visibly devouring limb-meal as though fire had caught hold of her bound at a stake: like one whose life had been long sapped and undermined from the roots by some quiet fiery poison. Her eyes and hair alone had a look of life: they were brilliant and soft yet, as she reached out her worn hot hands. Herbert came to her with a sense of pressure at his heart, and something like horror and fear mixed with the bitterness of natural pain. The figure and the place were lurid in his eyes, and less fit to make one weep than to make him kindle and tremble. There was an attraction in them which shot heat into his veins instead of the chill and heaviness of terror or grief.

"I'm dying, Bertie," said Lesbia. He sat down by her, silent.

"I'm dying," she said again, playing broken tunes with her fingers in the air.

"It's very like living, do you know? If you stay with me now, mind you don't cry. I've been out of tears myself for a long time—not a sob on hand at any price; and I hate them in others. You look so very sorry."

"Is it quite a sure thing, then?" he said quietly, in a tone which pleased her.

"As sure as death, literally; I suppose the first time that was said it sounded serious. Both doctors told me—Luthrell you know and Sir Thomas Gage. It's a question of hours. I ought to have settled it before now: but I'm as bad a hand at casting up sums as you are. I'd have made an end to-day but I really care little about it and do want to see how long this will hold out—how far the life in me will go. I won't be beaten first—not till it gives in."

[. . .]

Here she began to muse heavily, and her worn eyelids to draw downwards without meeting. He had nothing to say; and after a little she began again.

"If there is such a thing as sound sleep, it must be eternal. The difficulty is to believe in sleep at all."

She stretched out her weary arms, and lifted herself from heel to shoulder, with a great sigh, bending her body like a bow, so that for a minute only the head and feet had any support: then slowly relaxed her lifted limbs, and relapsed into supine and sad prostration.

"I dreamt of the old stories; I was always fond of them. I saw Lethe; it was not dark water, nor slow. It was pale and rapid and steady; there was a smell of meadowsweet on the banks. I must have been thinking of your Ensdon woods. And when one came close there was a new smell, more faint and rank; it came from the water-flowers; many were dead and decaying, and all sickly. And opposite me just across there ran out a wharf into the water: like the end of the pier at Wansdale. I saw nothing anywhere that was not like something I had seen already. I can't get that out my head; as soon as I woke it frightened me: but I didn't wake at once. I remember the green ooze and slime on the piles of the wharf; it was all matted with dead soft stuff that smelt wet. Not like the smell of the sea, but the smell of a lock in a river. And no boat came, and I didn't want one. I felt growing deliciously cold inside my head and behind my eyelids and down to the palms of my hands and feet. I ought to have awaked with a sneeze, and found I had caught cold in fact: but I didn't. And I saw no face anywhere for hours; and that was like a beginning of rest. Then I tried to see Proserpine, and saw her. She stood up to the knees almost in full-blown poppies, single and double. She was not the old Proserpine who comes and goes up and down between Sicily and hell; she had never seen the sun. She was pale and pleased; there was nothing in her like memory or aspiration. The dead element was vital for her; she could not have breathed in higher or lower air. The poppies at her foot were red, and those in her hand white."

"Well?" said Herbert as she paused: her voice had filled him with subtle dim emotions, and he was absorbed at once by the strange sound and sense of the words.

"She had grey eyes, bluish like the mingling of mist and water; and soft hair that lay about her breast and arms in sharp pointed locks like tongues of fire. As she looked at me this hair began to vibrate with the sudden motion of her breast, and her eyes brightened into the brilliance of eyes I knew; your sister's; and I began to wonder if she would melt entirely into that likeness. All the time I knew it was impossible she should, because she was incarnate death; and the other I knew was alive. And behind her the whole place all at once became populous with pale figures, hollow all through like an empty dress set upright; stately shadows with a grey light reflected against them; and the whole world as far as I saw was not in darkness, but under a solid cloud that never moved and made the air darker and cooler than the mistiest day upon earth. And in the fields beyond the water there was a splendid harvest of aconite: no other flower anywhere; but the grass was as pale, all yellow and brown, as if the sun had burnt it. Only where the goddess stood there were poppies growing apart; and their red cups, and the big blue lamps of the aconite, all alike hung heavily without wind. I remember, when I was little, wondering whether those flowers were likest lamps or bells; I thought any light or sound that could come of them must be so like the daylight and the music of a dead world. Well, I don't remember much more: but I was haunted with the fear that there might be nothing new behind death after all; no real rest and no real change. And the flowers vexed me. Only these, and no roses; I thought that white single sort of rose might grow there well enough. And I saw no men there, and no children."

Herbert sat silent; there was nothing to be said in answer. She roamed on through strange byways of sickly thought and channels of straitened speech. Her sleepy delirious eloquence rambled and stumbled to right and left among broken fancies and memories. He saw that her dozing remembrance enlarged and explained the half forgotten dreams of which she spoke. She had not dreamt all this, but something partly like it; and beginning to remember she went on to imagine. There is nothing harder for a child or a sick person than to tell a dream truthfully; for only the clearest and soundest of full-grown minds can safely lay down the accurate landmarks of sleep. Something of this she seemed even to perceive herself as she flowed on fitfully, with sorrowful sudden pauses.

"I tried to sleep again and dream it out; I felt it all going wrong and slipping away from me before I woke; and then I shut my eyes and set my mind steadily upon the dream, but it wouldn't go on: I could only turn over in my head what was past of it. But in a dim way I feel sure about the wharf, and the woman, and the flowers: and for the rest—well, I think it was like that. But I do hope it will not be the same thing afterwards. That would be a terrible sort of hell."

The morbid and obscure fascination of obscure disease began to tell upon her listener: his nerves trembled in harmony with hers: he felt a cruel impersonal displeasure, compound of fear and pain, in the study of her last symptoms. Then by way of reaction came a warm sudden reflux of tenderness; and he clasped one pale restless hand with a sweet acute pang of physical pity.

"My dear brother," she said sadly and softly; then changing her voice to a sudden sharp note of irony—"Bertie, you should have been my lover, sitting here like this. What else would people think if they knew?"

He wrung her hand in his, looking down silent.

"I wonder what it would have been like, to have loved you in that way. I missed of it somehow; I have missed of so many things. But mind I was always fond of you too: and never of any man else. You might give your old sister a kiss now."

A bitter taste came into his mouth and made his cheeks tremble; the bitter water rose against his teeth; he felt his throat compress, and the moist heat of thickening tears swell and beat upon his eyelids. He bowed his face upon her face, his breast across her breast; plunged his lips into hers, hot and shuddering; and devoured her fallen features with sharp sad kisses.

"Lesbia—my dearest and first love in the world—if you could love me at last—you need not die at once surely—and I will go with you.—Oh, only try to love me for five minutes!"

These words came broken between his kisses and her sobs; but as his arms fastened upon her she broke from him sideways, trembling terribly, with widened eyes and repellent hands.

"No, no, Herbert! Let me go! let me die! will you?"

There was a savage terror in her voice and gesture; the hands that thrust him back, the eyes that shone with fear of him, might but have excited him further into a passion of bitter pity and love, but for the mad repugnance, the blind absolute horror, expressed in all her struggling figure and labouring limbs. He let her go, and she cowered away against the wall, moaning and shaking like a thing stricken to death.

When she spoke next her voice was clear and low, pitched in a soft equable key; and never varied again.

"You have done me no harm; don't be vexed. Sit down and listen quickly. Or talk to me if you have anything to say: I like your voice. There is one thing that rather troubles me, the way I shall be buried. I hate all funerals, and all the words read over us: (I feel as if I were one of them, the dead, already;) all the flutter and fuss, all the faith and hope. I have none, and no fear. And if I were to repent of anything I would repent first of my birth. It was no fault of mine. But I think people repent more of their luck than of their faults, as a rule. God knows I repent of living,—if he knows anything about us, or cares. You were very like your sister once about the mouth and eyes. No, not again; when I am dead if you like. I dreamt once that I saw her fall over a cliff. I wish I were dying out of doors, and by day. I should like my body to be burnt and the ashes thrown into the sea. It is I who have taken the leap now, not she. But in my dreams she didn't fall of herself; somebody pushed her, I think I did. My head is full of old dreams, full. I should like to see you as you were that first time. You couldn't go and dress up now, though I have seen women with as much hair about the lips. I should like to die acting; I've heard of people dying on the stage. It would be some relief to have a good part to keep up. Here I am going out by inches, and every minute I feel more alive here, in the head, and less in the body. I think of so many things, and wish I had one to think of: nothing seems worth the trouble it gives."

"I wish to God I could give my life for yours."

"Don't; but I've no doubt you do just now and will for a day or two. I wouldn't have it as a gift."

"I know it's not worth taking," said Herbert, "but it might be worth giving— though it's not worth keeping either."

"Try," she answered smiling. "As for me, I have done with trying, thank heaven, and now I'll go to sleep."

She drank again a shorter draught and turned over lightly but painfully. But she could not sleep or die just yet. For an hour or so Herbert sat by her, watching; her limbs shuddered now and then with a slow general spasm, as though cold or out-tired; but there were no symptoms of a sharper torment. A faint savour of flowers mixed with the smell of drugs as the whitening dusk with the yellow twilight of the lamps. The place seemed ready swept and garnished for death to enter: the light had red and yellow colours as of blood and fog. The watcher felt sad and sick and half afraid; his mind was full of dim and bitter things. He was not in heart to pray; if indeed prayer could have undone things past, he might have believed it could break and remould the inevitable future growing minute by minute into the irrevocable present. The moments as they went seemed to touch him like falling drops of sand or water: as though the hourglass or the waterclock were indeed emptied by grains or gouts upon his head: a clock measuring its minutes by blood or tears instead of water or sand. He seemed in the dim hours to hear her pulses and his own. That night, as hope and trust fell away from under him, he first learnt the reality of fate: inevitable, not to be cajoled by resignation, not to be averted by intercession: unlike a God, incapable of wrath as of pity, not given to preference of evil or good, not liable to repentance or to change.

It was after dawn when Lesbia spoke next. "Keep the curtains drawn," she said; "I won't see the sun again. I mean to die by lamplight." Then after a little: "The room must be dark and warm still, as I like it; though I am getting cold; at last. It will be close and dark enough soon; when I have got to bed again. Keep the light out. There: good-bye." With this she put her hand out, dropped it, turned her face into the cushion, sighing, opened her eyes, and died. He left her in half an hour to the women, having kissed her only twice.

And that was the last of Lesbia Brandon, poetess and pagan.

PAUL VERLAINE (1844–1896)

Scenes of Sapphic Love (1867)

Paul Verlaine, one of the most celebrated of French nineteenth-century poets, was the son of an army engineer and educated in Paris. After rejecting a law career, he published a collection of poems, *Poèmes saturniens*, in 1866, followed by another, *Fêtes galantes*, in 1869. Both books won wide acclaim and Verlaine was taken up by Flaubert, Gautier, and other literary luminaries. In 1870 he married Mathilde Mauté de Fleurville, but quickly became estranged from her after beginning a tumultuous —and ultimately disastrous—homosexual liaison with the sixteen-year-old poet-renegade, Arthur Rimbaud. For several years he and Rimbaud led a rootless and dissipated existence in England, France, and Belgium. During a violent quarrel in 1873 Verlaine wounded Rimbaud with a pistol and was subsequently sentenced to two years in prison. He served out his term, but the experience left him jaded and embittered. In his remaining years he continued to write: over the next two decades he published the verse collections *Sagesse* (1881), *Parallèlement* (1884), *Jadis et naguère* (1884), and *Romances sans paroles* (1887), and a landmark critical study of French nineteenth-century poetry entitled *Poètes maudits* (1888). Even as his literary achievements brought him renewed respect, however, his life was marked by alcoholism, sexual promiscuity, and emotional distress. His health broke down, and he died in poverty in 1896.

Verlaine published *Scènes d'amour sapphique* (*Scenes of Sapphic Love*)—a set of six poems sometimes also referred to as *Les Amies*—in Brussels in 1867. By publishing the work abroad he sought to avoid the kind of trouble with French censors that his contemporary Charles Baudelaire had encountered when he issued his own sapphically themed work, *Les Fleurs du mal*, in 1857. No outcry, as it turned out, resulted, and Verlaine reprinted the poems in *Parallèlement* in 1884. The lack of criticism may have something to do with Verlaine's unambiguously hostile attitude to lesbian sexuality. Unlike Baudelaire, whose representations of Sappho and her ilk are often quasi-eulogistic—Sappho stands in Baudelaire's verse for the rhapsodic power of poetry itself— Verlaine portrays the love of woman for woman as irreparably deranging and defiling. His lesbian couples—such as the incestuous sisters in "Boarding-School Girls"—play at innocence amid the voluptuous signs of their own corruption, while his Sappho is an outright madwoman, whose crazed final love for Phaon is her ironic punishment for indulging in stigmatized lesbian passions.

FURTHER READING: Paul Verlaine, *Oeuvres poétiques complètes*, ed. Jacques Borel (Paris: Gallimard, 1962); —, *La Bonne chanson; Jadis et naguère; Parallèlement*, ed. Louis Forestier (Paris: Gallimard, 1979); Bergen Applegate, *Paul Verlaine: His Absinthe-Tinted Song* (Chicago: Alderbrink, 1916); Harold Nicolson, *Paul Verlaine* (Boston: Houghton Mifflin, 1921); David M. Robinson, *Sappho and Her Influence* (Boston: Marshall Jones, 1924); Jeannette Foster, *Sex Variant Women in Literature* (1956: rpt. Tallahassee, Fla.: Naiad, 1985); Édith Mora, *Sappho: Histoire d'un poète et traduction intégrale de l'oeuvre* (Paris: Flammarion, 1966); Joanna Richardson, *Verlaine* (New York: Viking, 1971); Philip Stephan, *Paul Verlaine and the Decadence, 1882–1890* (Totowa, N.J.: Rowman and Littlefield, 1974); Joan DeJean, *Fictions of Sappho: 1546–1937* (Chicago: University of Chicago Press, 1989); Henri Troyat, *Verlaine* (Paris: Flammarion, 1990); Barbara Milech, " 'This Kind': Pornographic Discourse, Lesbian Bodies, and Paul Verlaine's *Les Amies*," in Thais E. Morgan, ed., *Men Writing the Feminine: Literature, Theory, and the Question of Genders* (Albany: State University of New York Press, 1994), pp. 107–22.

On the Balcony

They both watched butterflies rise in flight:
One pale with hair of jet, the other pink
And blond, their light lace peignoirs waves
Undulating, as clouds might, round them.

And both, with the asphodel's languour,
While the heavens lifted a soft, round moon,
Savoured long draughts of evening's deep
Feeling, and the wan joy of true hearts.

Thus, arms pressing close and moist their supple waists,
Strange couple in sympathy with other couples,
Thus, on the balcony the young women in reverie.

Behind them, in the dark deeps of their sumptuous lair,
Grand as a melodrama's throne and full of scent,
The dishevelled Bed, opening in shadow.

Boarding-School Girls

One at fifteen, the other at sixteen years;
They both slept in the same room.
It was on a ripe and humid September's eve:
Delicate and blue-eyed, a strawberry's blush,

Each, for her comfort, had pulled off
Her thin blouse, with a scent of amber.
The younger's arms held out in gentle camber,
And her sister, touching her breasts, kissed her,

Then fell on her knees, wildly turned
In frenzied tumult where her mouth yet yearned,
Dove into blond filigree to discover shadowed grey;

And all the while, the child counted up
On adorable fingers the promised waltzes,
And, in blushing innocence, smiled.

Per Amica Silentia

The long curtains of white muslin
Undulating in an opaline wave
By the nightlight's pallid gleam
In mysterious, indolent shadows,

The full drapes of Adeline's high bed
Have heard, Claire, your laughing voice,
Your silvery, sweet, seductive voice
Shot through with another, stormy.

"To love, to love!" they said, entwined,
Claire and Adeline, adorable victims
Of the noble promise of your sublime souls.

Love, then, oh love! dear Isolate Girls,
For in these days of misery, yet and still,
The glorious stigmata anoint you.

Spring

Gently the red-head,
Excited by such innocence,
Says to the younger fair-haired girl
These words, in a soft, sweet tone,

"Sap that rises, bloom coming into its own,
Your childhood is an arbour:
Let my fingers roam in the carrageen
Where the rosy button flowers,

"Let me, among the bright leaves of grass,
Drink of the tiny drops of dew
Sprinkled upon this tender blossom—

"Until, my dear, delight illumines
Your spotless brow anew,
As dawn the sky of timid blue.

Summer

And the child answers all aswoon
Beneath the urgent wet caress
Of her breathless mistress:
"I'm dying O my dearest!"

"I die: Your flaming, unrelenting
Breast intoxicates and presses close
Your vivid flesh, a strangely scented
Drunkenness released.

"It has, your flesh, the somber charms
Of summer's ripeness—
The amber of it, its umber hue,

"Your voice sounds clear in the blast,
And your blood-red hair
Flees suddenly in night's slow fall."

Sappho

Frenzied, hollow-eyed and stern of breast,
Sappho, troubled by languorous desire,
Like a she-wolf, she tracks cold furrows,

She dreams of Phaon, forgetting all Ritual,
And, just then seeing her tears disdained,
Tears out her hair in huge handfuls;

In remorse unassuaged, she then recalls
Those times when shone so pure the youthful glory
Of her loves, sung in verse that soul's memory
Will murmur soft to virgins as they sleep:

And see now she lowers her sallow lids
And leaps into the sea where her Fate calls her—
While, in the skies, igniting the black water, bursts
Pale Selene who avenges girlish Loves.

EMILY DICKINSON (1830–1886)

"Her Breast is Fit for Pearls," "Her sweet Weight on my Heart a Night," "Going—to—Her!," "Ourselves were wed one summer—dear—," "Precious to Me—She still shall be—," "The Stars are old, that stood for me—," "Frigid and sweet Her parting Face—," "To see her is a Picture—" (1851–86)

The astonishingly sensual yet elliptical passions recorded in the poems of the great American poet Emily Dickinson have long fascinated biographers and critics, quite as much as her bizarre life story. Born into a well-to-do yet austere New England family, educated at Amherst Academy and the Mount Holyoke Female Seminary, Dickinson chose at the age of thirty to retire from the world and seclude herself in her parents' home with their consent. There she adopted the eccentric habits that subsequently made her a neighborhood legend: dressing all in white, greeting visitors from behind a screen, surreptitiously writing poetry on the backs of envelopes and other discarded scraps of paper that she kept in her room. Though she sent several of her poems to the *Atlantic Monthly* editor Thomas Wentworth Higginson for criticism in the 1860s—he encouraged her to publish her work—she allowed only two poems to appear in her lifetime. She did, however, carry on a voluminous correspondence and enclosed many copies of her poems in letters to friends and relatives after her retreat from the world in 1860. After her death 1,776 poems were found in the drawers of her bureau, neatly stitched into little handsewn books.

Since the 1890s, when selections from Dickinson's poems first became available in a volume edited by Mabel Loomis Todd, readers have sought—with sometimes fanatical partisanship—to identify the real-life individuals to whom Dickinson may be alluding in some of her verses and private papers. On the basis of a group of poems and love letters addressed (but not sent) to a person known only as "Master," a number of male lovers have been proposed for her—notably the Reverend Charles Wadsworth, a married clergyman with whom Dickinson is supposed to have fallen unhappily in love during a sojourn in Philadelphia in 1855, and Samuel Bowles, the editor of an important local newspaper. But an extraordinary series of verses devoted to a beloved "She," dating from 1851 to Dickinson's death, suggest powerful emotional attachments to women as well. So fiercely erotic are some of these female-directed poems, several of Dickinson's early editors felt obliged to alter the pronouns in order to disguise their unusual nature. In the 1950s a critic named Rebecca Patterson hypothesized that Dickinson was for a time passionately in love with Kate Scott Anthon, the widowed former schoolfriend of Dickinson's sister-in-law, Sue Gilbert Dickinson. Recent biographers, however, notably Richard B. Sewall, have argued persuasively that Sue Gilbert herself—whom the poet had known since both were children—was the subject of the "She" poems.

Certainly Dickinson addressed more poems to Gilbert than anyone else: over the course of their lifelong connection Dickinson sent her more than 250 poems in letters. And intriguingly, for reasons that remain unclear, Dickinson was deeply troubled when Gilbert became engaged to Austin Dickinson, Emily's brother, in 1853. After the couple married and moved into the house next door to the Dickinson family home in 1856, Emily refused to correspond with her new sister-in-law for almost two years. When they resumed their correspondence in 1858, Dickinson remained cautious about face-to-face meetings. "Remember," she wrote to Gilbert, "it is idolatry and not indifference." Later she would refer to Sue as that "Siren" for whom she would "forfeit Righteousness." Luckily for posterity, however, and despite the questions that still hover around their relationship, what could not be said in person was channeled into verse: into some of the most amorous, mysterious, and magnificent writing one woman has ever addressed to another.

FURTHER READING: Emily Dickinson, *Poems*, ed. Mabel Loomis Todd and T. W. Higginson (Boston: Roberts, 1890); —, *The Poems of Emily Dickinson*, ed. Thomas H. Johnson, 3 vols. (Cambridge: Harvard University Press, 1955); —, *The Letters of Emily Dickinson*, ed. Thomas H. Johnson and Theodora Ward, 3 vols. (Cambridge: Harvard University Press, 1958); Martha Dickinson Bianchi, *The Life and Letters of Emily Dickinson* (Boston and New York: Houghton Mifflin, 1924); —, *Emily Dickinson Face to Face: Unpublished Letters with Notes and Reminiscences* (Boston and New York: Houghton Mifflin, 1932); Rebecca Patterson, *The Riddle of Emily Dickinson* (Boston: Houghton Mifflin, 1951); Denis Donoghue, *Emily Dickinson* (Minneapolis: University of Minnesota Press, 1969); Richard B. Sewall, *The Life of Emily Dickinson* (Cambridge: Harvard University Press, 1974); Suzanne Juhasz, ed., *Feminist Critics Read Emily Dickinson* (Bloomington: Indiana University Press, 1983); Barton Levi St. Armand, *The Soul's Society: Emily Dickinson and Her Culture* (Cambridge: Cambridge University Press, 1984); Ellen Louise Hart, "The Encoding of Homoerotic Desire: Emily Dickinson's Letters and Poems to Susan Dickinson, 1850–1886," *Tulsa Studies in Women's Literature* 9 (Fall 1990): 251–72; Paula Bennett, *Emily Dickinson: Woman Poet* (Iowa City: University of Iowa Press, 1991); Judith Farr, *The Passion of Emily Dickinson* (Cambridge: Harvard University Press, 1992); Martha Nell Smith, *Rowing in Eden: Rereading Emily Dickinson* (Austin: University of Texas Press, 1992); — and Ellen Louise Hart, eds., *Open Me Carefully: Emily Dickinson's Intimate Letters to Susan Huntington Dickinson* (Ashfield, Me.: Paris, 1998); Sylvia Henneberg, "Neither Lesbian Nor Straight: Multiple Eroticisms in Emily Dickinson's Love Poetry," *Emily Dickinson*

Journal 4 (1995): 1–19; Lena Koski, "Sexual Metaphors in Emily Dickinson's Letters to Susan Gilbert," *Emily Dickinson Journal* 5 (1996): 26–31; Sandra Runzo, "Dickinson, Performance, and the Homoerotic Lyric," *American Literature* 68 (1996): 347–63.

Her breast is fit for pearls,
But I was not a "Diver"—
Her brow is fit for thrones
But I have not a crest.
Her heart is fit for *home*—
I—a Sparrow—build there
Sweet of twigs and twine
My perennial nest.

❧

Her sweet Weight on my Heart a Night
Had scarcely deigned to lie—
When, stirring, for Belief's delight,
My Bride had slipped away—

If 'twas a Dream—made solid—just
The Heaven to confirm—
Or if Myself were dreamed of Her—
The power to presume—

With Him remain—who unto Me—
Gave—even as to All—
A Fiction superseding Faith—
By so much—as 'twas real—

❧

Going—to—Her!
Happy—Letter! Tell Her—
Tell Her—the page I never wrote!
Tell Her, I only said—the Syntax—
And left the Verb and the Pronoun—out!
Tell Her just how the fingers—hurried—
Then—how they—stammered—slow—slow—

And then—you wished you had eyes—in your pages—
So you could see—what moved—them—so—

Tell Her—it wasn't a practised writer—
You guessed—
From the way the sentence—toiled—
You could hear the Boddice—tug—behind you—
As if it held but the might of a child!
You almost pitied—it—you—it worked so—
Tell Her—No—you may quibble—there—
For it would split Her Heart—to know it—
And then—you and I—were silenter!

Tell Her—Day—finished—before we—finished—
And the old Clock kept neighing—"Day"!
And you—got sleepy—and begged to be ended—
What could—it hinder so—to say?
Tell Her—just how she sealed—you—Cautious!
But—if she ask "where you are hid"—until the evening—
Ah! Be bashful!
Gesture Coquette—
And shake your Head!

ॐ

Ourselves were wed one summer—dear—
Your Vision—was in June—
And when Your little Lifetime failed,
I wearied—too—of mine—

And overtaken in the Dark—
Where You had put me down—
By Some one carrying a Light—
I—too—received the Sign.

'Tis true—Our Futures different lay—
Your Cottage—faced the sun—
While Oceans—and the North must be—
On every side of mine

'Tis true, Your Garden led the Bloom,
For mine—in Frosts—was sown—

And yet, one Summer, we were Queens—
But You—were crowned in June—

❧

Precious to Me—She still shall be—
Though She forget the name I bear—
The fashion of the Gown I wear—
The very Color of My Hair—

So like the Meadows—now—
I dared to show a Tress of Their's
If haply—She might not despise
A Buttercup's Array—

I know the Whole—obscures the Part—
The fraction—that appeased the Heart
Till Number's Empery—
Remembered—as the Milliner's flower
When Summer's Everlasting Dower—
Confronts the dazzled Bee.

❧

The Stars are old, that stood for me—
The West a little worn—
Yet newer glows the only Gold
I ever cared to earn—
Presuming on that lone result
Her infinite disdain
But vanquished her with my defeat
'Twas Victory was slain.

❧

Frigid and sweet Her parting Face—
Frigid and fleet my Feet—
Alien and vain whatever Clime
Acrid whatever Fate.

Given to me without the Suit
Riches and Name and Realm—

Who was She to withhold from me
Penury and Home?

≈

To see her is a Picture—
To hear her is a Tune—
To know her an Intemperance
As innocent as June—

To know her not—Affliction—
To own her for a Friend
A warmth as near as if the Sun
Were shining in your Hand.

GEORGE AUGUSTUS SALA (1828–1896)

Translation of Martial's Epigram VII.67 ("Abhorrent of All Natural Joys") from *The Index Expurgatorius of Martial, Literally Translated* (1868)

Since the Renaissance the rediscovered works of ancient Greek and Roman authors have provided educated readers with useful erotic information as well as striking and sometimes liberating images of homosexual love. For sapphically inclined women of the eighteenth and nineteenth centuries, the lesbian writings of the Roman satirists Juvenal and Martial, though flagrantly hostile in tone, were particularly illuminating. References to such writers could sometimes function as a kind of wooing shorthand: in the 1820s the lesbian diarist Anne Lister—who had taught herself Latin—described using discreet conversational references to Juvenal's Sixth Satire to signal her erotic preferences to another woman. The obscene epigrams of Martial (c. A.D. 40–104) were equally significant. It is an odd fact that one can find reassuring confirmation of one's own hidden affective life in the most negative cultural representations. While more explicit than other Victorian translations, the 1868 version below of Martial's notorious Epigram 67 from Book 7 of the *Epigrams*—describing the randy matron Philaenis— suggests just how informative such works could be. The translator, George Augustus Sala, was a well-known Victorian journalist, illustrator, and travel writer, and a friend of the novelist Charles Dickens.

FURTHER READING: Martial, *Epigrams of Martial Englished by Divers Hands*, ed. J. P. Sullivan and Peter Whigham (Berkeley and London: University of California Press, 1987); Sidney Lee, "George Augustus Sala," *Dictionary of National Biography* (London: Smith, Elder, 1897): 50:175–78; Ralph Straus, *Sala: Portrait of an Eminent Victorian* (London: Constable, 1942); Ros Ballaster, "'The Vices of Old Rome Revived': Representations of Female Same-Sex Desire in Seventeenth and Eighteenth Century England," in Suzanne Raitt, ed., *Volcanoes and Pearl Divers: Essays in Lesbian Feminist Studies* (Binghamton, N.Y.: Haworth, 1995), pp. 13–36.

Abhorrent of all natural joys,
  Philaenis sodomises boys,

And like a spouse whose wife's away
  She drains of spend twelve cunts a day.
With dress tucked up above her knees
  She hurls the heavy ball with ease,
And, smeared all o'er with oil and sand,
  She wields a dumb bell in each hand,
And when she quits the dirty floor,
  Still rank with grease, the jaded whore
Submits to the schoolmaster's whip
  For each small fault, each trifling slip:
Nor will she sit her down to dine
  Till she has spewed two quarts of wine:
And when she's eaten pounds of steak
  A gallon more her thirst will slake.
After all this, when fired by lust,
  For pricks alone she feels disgust,
These cannot e'en her lips entice,
  Forsooth it is a woman's vice!
But girls she'll gamahuche for hours,
  Their juicy quims she quite devours.
Oh, you that think your sex to cloak
  By kissing what you cannot poke,
May God grant that you, Philaenis,
  Will yet learn to suck a penis.

THOMAS HARDY (1840–1928)

From *Desperate Remedies* (1871)

The Victorian poet and novelist Thomas Hardy, the son of a stonemason, was born in Dorset and trained in his youth to become an architect. Literature had more appeal, however, and in 1873 he gave up architecture to devote himself wholly to fiction and poetry. He first came to public notice with *Far From the Madding Crowd* (1874), a rural love story set in "Wessex," a thinly disguised version of his native Dorsetshire. Further Wessex novels followed, the best known of which are *The Return of the Native* (1878), *The Trumpet-Major* (1880), *Two on a Tower* (1882), *The Mayor of Casterbridge* (1886), *The Woodlanders* (1887), *Tess of the D'Urbervilles* (1891), *Life's Little Ironies* (1894), and *Jude the Obscure* (1896). Hardy's fiction is typically pessimistic, even fatalistic, in outlook: his characters can do little against the malign forces—inner and outer—ruling human destiny in his bleak fictional world. In *Tess* and *Jude* the bleakness is so pronounced that contemporary readers rebelled: after *Jude* appeared in 1896 critical outcry was so great that a discouraged Hardy gave up novel writing altogether. He turned increasingly to poetry after 1896 and published eight volumes of verse between 1898 and his death. Some of his greatest poetry is contained in *The Dynasts* (1904–08), a huge poetic drama set at the time of the Napoleonic Wars. Hardy married twice—his second wife penned an adoring memoir of him in 1930—and died in Dorset in 1928.

Hardy owes his place in the canon of lesbian literature to his first novel, the 1871 *Desperate Remedies*. The convoluted plot—described by its author as a mixture of "mystery, entanglement, surprise and moral obliquity"—revolves around a genteel young woman, Cytherea Graye, who is forced by the death of her parents to take a position as a lady's maid. Her employer, the beautiful yet peremptory Miss Aldclyffe, both tyrannizes over her and flirts with her. Miss Aldclyffe's wildly seductive behavior on the night of Cytherea's arrival is subsequently explained away as a kind of sublimated pseudomaternal passion—it is revealed that Miss Aldclyffe was once in love with Cytherea's father, who reciprocated her passion but was forced to marry someone else—but not before Hardy manages to bring the two women together in one of the most sexually charged bedroom scenes in all of Victorian fiction. In 1993 a brilliantly comic lesbian-themed film, also called *Desperate Remedies*, parodied this episode along with others from classic nineteenth-century English fiction.

One of the novel's many odd coincidences is that Cytherea and Miss Aldclyffe have the same first name: Cytherea's father, it turns out, secretly named his daughter after his first beloved. Traditionally a name for Aphrodite, the Greek goddess of love—as well as of an island associated with her cult off the southern coast of the Peloponnesus—the name Cytherea has longstanding lesbian connotations. A famous Sappho fragment (Lobel-Page 140) begins, "He is dying, Cytherea, Adonis the delicate." In the nineteenth century the French Parnassian writer and critic Catulle Mendès gave the title "Cytherea" to one of a series of pseudo-Hellenic lesbian reveries he published in *Lila et Colette* in 1885; Renée Vivien entitled a collection of sapphic renderings of poems from the Greek Anthology *Les Kitharèdes* in 1904.

FURTHER READING: Thomas Hardy, *The Works of Thomas Hardy*, 37 vols. (London: Macmillan, 1919); —, *Desperate Remedies* (London: Macmillan, 1951); —, *The Poems of Thomas Hardy*, ed. Kenneth Marsden (New York: Oxford University Press, 1969); Florence Emily Hardy, *The Early Life of Thomas Hardy* (London: Macmillan, 1928); —, *The Later Years of Thomas Hardy* (London: Macmillan, 1930); Richard C. Carpenter, *Thomas Hardy* (New York: Twayne, 1964); Richard Hyde Taylor, *The Neglected Hardy: Hardy's Lesser Novels* (London: Macmillan, 1982); Rosemarie Morgan, *Women and Sexuality in the Novels of Thomas Hardy* (London: Routledge, 1988); Simon Gatrell, *Hardy, The Creator* (Oxford: Clarendon, 1988); Patrick Roberts, "Patterns of Relationship in *Desperate Remedies*," *The Thomas Hardy Journal* 8 (1992): 50–57.

The Events of Twelve Hours

I. AUGUST THE NINTH. ONE TO TWO O'CLOCK A.M.

Cytherea entered her bedroom, and flung herself on the bed, bewildered by a whirl of thought. Only one subject was clear in her mind, and it was that, in spite of family discoveries, that day was to be the first and last of her experience as a lady's-maid. Starvation itself should not compel her to hold such a humiliating post for another instant. "Ah," she thought, with a sigh, at the martyrdom of her last little fragment of self-conceit, "Owen knows everything better than I."

She jumped up and began making ready for her departure in the morning, the tears streaming down when she grieved and wondered what practical matter on earth she could turn her hand to next. All these preparations completed, she began to undress, her mind unconsciously drifting away to the contemplation of her late surprises. To look in the glass for an instant at the reflection of her own magnificent resources in face and bosom, and to mark their attractiveness unadorned, was perhaps but the natural action of a young woman who had so lately been chidden whilst passing through the harassing experience of decorating an older beauty of Miss Aldclyffe's temper.

But she directly checked her weakness by sympathizing reflections on the hidden troubles which must have thronged the past years of the solitary lady, to keep her, though so rich and courted, in a mood so repellent and gloomy as that in which Cytherea found her; and then the young girl marvelled again and again, as she had marvelled before, at the strange confluence of circumstances which had brought herself into contact with the one woman in the world whose history was so romantically intertwined with her own. She almost began to wish she were not obliged to go away and leave the lonely being to loneliness still.

In bed and in the dark, Miss Aldclyffe haunted her mind more persistently than ever. Instead of sleeping, she called up staring visions of the possible past of this queenly lady, her mother's rival. Up the long vista of bygone years she saw, behind all, the young girl's flirtation, little or much, with the cousin, that seemed to have been nipped in the bud, or to have terminated hastily in some way. Then the secret meetings between Miss Aldclyffe and the other woman at the little inn at Hammersmith and other places: the commonplace name she adopted: her swoon at some painful news, and the very slight knowledge the elder female had of her partner in mystery. Then, more than a year afterwards, the acquaintanceship of her own father with this his first love; the awakening of the passion, his acts of devotion, the unreasoning heat of his rapture, her tacit acceptance of it, and yet her uneasiness under the delight. Then his declaration amid the evergreens: the utter change produced in her manner thereby, seemingly the result of a rigid determination: and the total concealment of her reason by herself and her parents, whatever it was. Then the lady's course dropped into darkness, and nothing more was visible till she was discovered here at Knapwater, nearly fifty years old, still unmarried and still beautiful, but lonely, embittered, and haughty. Cytherea imagined that her father's image was still warmly cherished in Miss Aldclyffe's heart, and was thankful that she herself had not been betrayed into announcing that she knew many particulars of this page of her father's history, and the chief one, the lady's unaccountable renunciation of him. It would have made her bearing towards the mistress of the mansion more awkward, and would have been no benefit to either.

Thus conjuring up the past, and theorizing on the present, she lay restless, changing her posture from one side to the other and back again. Finally, when courting sleep with all her art, she heard a clock strike two. A minute later, and she fancied she could distinguish a soft rustle in the passage outside her room.

To bury her head in the sheets was her first impulse; then to uncover it, raise herself on her elbow, and stretch her eyes wide open in the darkness; her lips being parted with the intentness of her listening. Whatever the noise was, it had ceased for the time.

It began again and came close to her door, lightly touching the panels. Then there was another stillness; Cytherea made a movement which caused a faint rustling of the bed-clothes.

Before she had time to think another thought a light tap was given. Cytherea breathed: the person outside was evidently bent upon finding her awake, and the rustle she had made had encouraged the hope. The maiden's physical condition shifted from one pole to its opposite. The cold sweat of terror forsook her, and modesty took the alarm. She became hot and red; her door was not locked.

A distinct woman's whisper came to her through the keyhole: "Cytherea!"

Only one being in the house knew her Christian name, and that was Miss Aldclyffe. Cytherea stepped out of bed, went to the door, and whispered back "Yes?"

"Let me come in, darling."

The young woman paused in a conflict between judgment and emotion. It was now mistress and maid no longer; woman and woman only. Yes; she must let her come in, poor thing.

She got a light in an instant, opened the door, and raising her eyes and the candle, saw Miss Aldclyffe standing outside in her dressing-gown.

"Now you see that it is really myself; put out the light," said the visitor. "I want to stay here with you, Cythie. I came to ask you to come down into my bed, but it is snugger here. But remember that you are mistress in this room, and that I have no business here, and that you may send me away if you choose. Shall I go?"

"O no; you shan't indeed if you don't want to," said Cythie generously.

The instant they were in bed Miss Aldclyffe freed herself from the last remnant of restraint. She flung her arms round the young girl, and pressed her gently to her heart.

"Now kiss me," she said. "You seem as if you were my own, own child!"

Cytherea, upon the whole, was rather discomposed at this change of treatment; and, discomposed or no, her passions were not so impetuous as Miss Aldclyffe's. She could not bring her soul to her lips for a moment, try how she would.

"Come, kiss me," repeated Miss Aldclyffe.

Cytherea gave her a very small one, as soft in touch and in sound as the bursting of a bubble.

"More earnestly than that—come."

She gave another, a little but not much more expressively.

"I don't deserve a more feeling one, I suppose," said Miss Aldclyffe, with an emphasis of sad bitterness in her tone. "I am an ill-tempered woman, you think; half out of my mind. Well, perhaps I am; but I have had grief more than you can think or dream of. But I am a lonely woman, and I want the sympathy of a pure girl like you, and so I can't help loving you—your name is the same as mine—isn't it strange?"

Cytherea was inclined to say no, but remained silent.

"Now, don't you think I must love you?" continued the other.

"Yes," said Cytherea absently. She was still thinking whether duty to Owen and her father, which asked for silence on her knowledge of her father's unfortunate love, or duty to the woman embracing her, which seemed to ask for confidence, ought to predominate. Here was a solution. She would wait till Miss Aldclyffe referred to her acquaintanceship and attachment to Cytherea's father in past times: then she would tell her all she knew: that would be honour.

"Why can't you kiss me as I can kiss you? Why can't you!" She impressed upon Cytherea's lips a warm motherly salute, given as if in the outburst of strong feeling, long checked, and yearning for something to care for and be cared for by in return.

"Do you think badly of me for my behaviour this evening, child? I don't know why I am so foolish as to speak to you in this way. I am a very fool, I believe. Yes. How old are you?"

"Eighteen."

"Eighteen! . . . Well, why don't you ask me how old I am?"

"Because I don't want to know."

"Never mind if you don't. I am forty-six; and it gives me greater pleasure to tell you this than it does to you to listen. I have not told my age truly for the last twenty years till now."

"Why haven't you?"

"I have met deceit by deceit, till I am weary of it—weary, weary—and I long to be what I shall never be again—artless and innocent, like you. But I suppose that you, too, will prove to be not worth a thought, as every new friend does on more intimate knowledge. Come, why don't you talk to me, child? Have you said your prayers?"

"Yes—no! I forgot them to-night."

"I suppose you say them every night as a rule?"

"Yes."

"Why do you do that?"

"Because I have always done so, and it would seem strange if I were not to. Do you?"

"I? A wicked old sinner like me! No, I never do. I have thought all such matters humbug for years—thought so so long that I should be glad to think otherwise from very weariness; and yet, such is the code of the polite world, that I subscribe regularly to Missionary Societies and others of the sort. . . . Well, say your prayers, dear—you won't omit them now you recollect it. I should like to hear you very much. Will you?"

"It seems hardly—"

"It would seem so like old times to me—when I was young, and nearer—far nearer Heaven than I am now. Do, sweet one."

Cytherea was embarrassed, and her embarrassment arose from the following conjuncture of affairs. Since she had loved Edward Springrove, she had linked his name with her brother Owen's in her nightly supplications to the Almighty. She wished to keep her love for him a secret, and, above all, a secret from a woman like Miss Aldclyffe; yet her conscience and the honesty of her love would not for an instant allow her to think of omitting his dear name, and so endanger the efficacy of all her previous prayers for his success by an unworthy shame now: it would be wicked of her, she thought, and a grievous wrong to him. Under any worldly circumstances she might have thought the position justified a little finesse, and have skipped him for once; but prayer was too solemn a thing for such trifling.

"I would rather not say them," she murmured first. It struck her then that this declining altogether was the same cowardice in another dress, and was delivering her poor Edward over to Satan just as unceremoniously as before. "Yes; I will say my prayers, and you shall hear me," she added firmly.

She turned her face to the pillow and repeated in low soft tones the simple words she had used from childhood on such occasions. Owen's name was mentioned without faltering, but in the other case, maidenly shyness was too strong even for religion, and that when supported by excellent intentions. At the name of Edward she stammered, and her voice sank to the faintest whisper in spite of her.

"Thank you, dearest," said Miss Aldclyffe. "I have prayed too, I verily believe. You are a good girl, I think." Then the expected question came.

" 'Bless Owen,' and whom, did you say?"

There was no help for it now, and out it came. "Owen and Edward," said Cytherea.

"Who are Owen and Edward?"

"Owen is my brother, madam," faltered the maid.

"Ah, I remember. Who is Edward?"

A silence.

"Your brother, too?" continued Miss Aldclyffe.

"No."

Miss Aldclyffe reflected a moment. "Don't you want to tell me who Edward is?" she said at last, in a tone of meaning.

"I don't mind telling; only . . ."

"You would rather not, I suppose?"

"Yes."

Miss Aldclyffe shifted her ground. "Were you ever in love?" she inquired suddenly.

Cytherea was surprised to hear how quickly the voice had altered from tenderness to harshness, vexation, and disappointment.

"Yes—I think I was—once," she murmured.

"Aha! And were you ever kissed by a man?"

A pause.

"Well, were you?" said Miss Aldclyffe, rather sharply.

"Don't press me to tell—I can't—indeed, I won't, madam!"

Miss Aldclyffe removed her arms from Cytherea's neck. " 'Tis now with you as it is always with all girls," she said, in jealous and gloomy accents. "You are not, after all, the innocent I took you for. No, no." She then changed her tone with fitful rapidity. "Cytherea, try to love me more than you love him—do. I love you more sincerely than any man can. Do, Cythie: don't let any man stand between us. O, I can't bear that!" She clasped Cytherea's neck again.

"I must love him now I have begun," replied the other.

"Must—yes—must," said the elder lady reproachfully. "Yes, women are all alike. I thought I had at last found an artless woman who had not been sullied by a man's lips, and who had not practised or been practised upon by the arts which ruin all the truth and sweetness and goodness in us. Find a girl, if you can, whose mouth and ears have not been made a regular highway of by some man or another! Leave the admittedly notorious spots—the drawing-rooms of society—and look in the villages—leave the villages and search in the schools—and you can hardly find a girl whose heart has not been *had*—is not an old thing half worn out by some He or another! If men only knew the staleness of the freshest of us! that nine times out of ten the 'first love' they think they are winning from a woman is but the hulk of an old wrecked affection, fitted with new sails and re-used. O Cytherea, can it be that you, too, are like the rest?"

"No, no, no," urged Cytherea, awed by the storm she had raised in the impetuous woman's mind. "He only kissed me once—twice I mean."

"He might have done it a thousand times if he had cared to, there's no doubt about that, whoever his lordship is. You are as bad as I—we are all alike; and I—an old fool— have been sipping at your mouth as if it were honey, because I fancied no wasting lover knew the spot. But a minute ago, and you seemed to me like a fresh spring meadow— now you seem a dusty highway."

"O no, no!" Cytherea was not weak enough to shed tears except on extraordinary occasions, but she was fain to begin sobbing now. She wished Miss Aldclyffe would go to her own room, and leave her and her treasured dreams alone. This vehement imperious affection was in one sense soothing, but yet it was not of the kind that Cytherea's instincts desired. Though it was generous, it seemed somewhat too rank and capricious for endurance.

"Well," said the lady in continuation, "who is he?"

Her companion was desperately determined not to tell his name: she too much feared a taunt when Miss Aldclyffe's fiery mood again ruled her tongue.

"Won't you tell me? not tell me after all the affection I have shown?"

"I will, perhaps, another day."

"Did you wear a hat and white feather in Budmouth for the week or two previous to your coming here?"

"Yes."

"Then I have seen you and your lover at a distance! He rowed you round the bay with your brother."

"Yes."

"And without your brother—fie! There, there, don't let that little heart beat itself to death: throb, throb: it shakes the bed, you silly thing. I didn't mean that there was any harm in going alone with him. I only saw you from the Esplanade, in common with the rest of the people. I often run down to Budmouth. He was a very good figure: now who was he?"

"I—I won't tell, madam—I cannot indeed!"

"Won't tell—very well, don't. You are very foolish to treasure up his name and image as you do. Why, he has had loves before you, trust him for that, whoever he is, and you are but a temporary link in a long chain of others like you: who only have their little day as they have had theirs."

"'Tisn't true! 'tisn't true! 'tisn't true!" cried Cytherea in an agony of torture. "He has never loved anybody else, I know—I am sure he hasn't."

Miss Aldclyffe was as jealous as any man could have been. She continued—

"He sees a beautiful face and thinks he will never forget it, but in a few weeks the feeling passes off, and he wonders how he could have cared for anybody so absurdly much."

"No, no, he doesn't—What does he do when he has thought that—Come, tell me—tell me!"

"You are as hot as fire, and the throbbing of your heart makes me nervous. I can't tell you if you get in that flustered state."

"Do, do tell—O, it makes me so miserable! but tell—come tell me!"

"Ah—the tables are turned now, dear!" she continued, in a tone which mingled pity with derision—

> "Love's passions shall rock thee
> As the storm rocks the ravens on high,
> Bright reason will mock thee
> Like the sun from a wintry sky.

"What does he do next?—Why, this is what he does next: ruminate on what he has heard of women's romantic impulses, and how easily men torture them when they have given way to those feelings, and have resigned everything for their hero. It may be that though he loves you heartily now—that is, as heartily as a man can—and you love him in return, your loves may be impracticable and hopeless, and you may be separated for ever. You, as the weary, weary years pass by will fade and fade—bright eyes *will* fade—and you will perhaps then die early—true to him to your latest breath, and believing him to be true to the latest breath also; whilst he, in some gay and busy spot far away from your last quiet nook, will have married some dashing lady, and not purely oblivious of you, will long have ceased to regret you—will chat about you, as you were in long past years—will say, 'Ah, little Cytherea used to tie her hair like that—poor innocent trusting thing; it was a pleasant useless idle dream—that dream of mine for the maid with the bright eyes and simple, silly heart; but I was a foolish lad at that time.' Then he will tell the tale of all your little Wills and Won'ts, and particular ways, and as he speaks, turn to his wife with a placid smile."

"It is not true! He can't, he c-can't be s-so cruel—and you are cruel to me—you are, you are!" She was at last driven to desperation: her natural common sense and shrewdness had seen all through the piece how imaginary her emotions were—she felt herself to be weak and foolish in permitting them to rise; but even then she could not control them: be agonized she must. She was only eighteen, and the long day's labour, her weariness, her excitement, had completely unnerved her, and worn her out: she was bent hither and thither by this tyrannical working upon her imagination, as a young rush in the wind. She wept bitterly.

"And now think how much *I* like you," resumed Miss Aldclyffe, when Cytherea grew calmer. "I shall never forget you for anybody else, as men do—never. I will be exactly as a mother to you. Now will you promise to live with me always, and always be taken care of, and never deserted?"

"I cannot. I will not be anybody's maid for another day on any consideration."

"No, no, no. You shan't be a lady's-maid, of course. You shall be my companion. I will get another maid."

Companion—that was a new idea. Cytherea could not resist the evidently heart-felt desire of the strange-tempered woman for her presence. But she could not trust to the moment's impulse.

"I will stay, I think. But do not ask for a final answer to-night."

"Never mind now, then. Put your hair round your mamma's neck, and give me one good long kiss, and I won't talk any more in that way about your lover. After all, some young men are not so fickle as others; but even if he's the ficklest, there is consolation. The love of an inconstant man is ten times more ardent than that of a faithful man— that is, while it lasts."

Cytherea did as she was told, to escape the punishment of further talk; flung the twining tresses of her long, rich hair over Miss Aldclyffe's shoulders as directed, and the two ceased conversing, making themselves up for sleep. Miss Aldclyffe seemed to give herself over to a luxurious sense of content and quiet, as if the maiden at her side afforded her a protection against dangers which had menaced her for years; she was soon sleeping calmly.

ELIZABETH STUART PHELPS (1844–1911)

"Since I Died" (1873)

The American novelist, essayist, and short-story writer Elizabeth Stuart Phelps wrote under the same name as her mother, a well-known author of children's books, who died when Phelps was eight. A New England Calvinist by background, Phelps grew up with a strong interest in women's rights and progressive causes; her early literary efforts were encouraged by Harriet Beecher Stowe, the author of *Uncle Tom's Cabin*, and the transcendentalist Harriet Prescott Spoffard. She is primarily remembered today for her bestselling first novel, *The Gates Ajar* (1868), a tale of the supernatural written in the aftermath of the Civil War, but she continued producing fiction until her death in 1911.

"Since I Died," an eerie fantasy in which a woman who has just died silently addresses the beloved female companion who is keeping a vigil over her corpse, was first published in the February 1873 issue of *Scribner's Monthly* and later reprinted in Phelps's 1879 volume of stories, *Sealed Orders*. The strong suggestion that the women have been lovers, or at least partners in a "Boston Marriage"-style relationship, may reflect experiences in Phelps's own life: though later married—unhappily—she lived for a time in her early years with the Andover physician Dr. Mary Briggs Harris.

FURTHER READING: Elizabeth Stuart Phelps, *Men, Women, and Ghosts* (Boston: Fields, Osgood, 1869); —, *Sealed Orders* (Boston: Houghton Osgood, 1879); —, *Chapters from a Life* (Boston and New York: Houghton, Mifflin, 1896); —, *The Gates Ajar* (Cambridge: Belknap, 1964); Carol Farley Kessler, *Elizabeth Stuart Phelps* (Boston: Twayne, 1982); Lori Duin Kelly, *The Life and Works of Elizabeth Stuart Phelps: Victorian Feminist Writer* (Troy, N.Y.: Whitston, 1983); Barbara Patrick, "Lady Terrorists: Nineteenth-Century American Women Writers and the Ghost Story," in Julie Brown, ed., *American Women Short Story Writers: A Collection of Critical Essays* (New York: Garland, 1995), pp. 73–84; Ralph J. Poole, "Body/Rituals: The (Homo)Erotics of Death in Elizabeth Stuart Phelps, Rose Terry Cooke, and Edgar Allan Poe," in Karen L. Kilcup, ed., *Soft Canons: American Women Writers and Masculine Tradition* (Iowa City: University of Iowa Press, 1999), pp. 239–61.

How very still you sit!

If the shadow of an eyelash stirred upon your cheek; if that gray line about your mouth should snap its tension at this quivering end; if the pallor of your profile warmed a little; if that tiny muscle on your forehead, just at the left eyebrow's curve, should start and twitch; if you would but grow a trifle restless, sitting there beneath my steady gaze; if you moved a finger of your folded hands; if you should turn and look behind your chair, or lift your face, half lingering and half longing, half loving and half loth, to ponder on the annoyed and thwarted cry which the wind is making, where I stand between it and yourself, against the half-closed window.—Ah, there! You sigh and stir, I think. You lift your head. The little muscle is a captive still; the line about your mouth is tense and hard; the deepening hollow in your cheek has no warmer tint, I see, than the great Doric column which the moonlight builds against the wall. I lean against it; I hold out my arms.

You lift your head and look me in the eye.

If a shudder crept across your figure; if your arms, laid out upon the table, leaped but once above your head; if you named my name; if you held your breath with terror, or sobbed aloud for love, or sprang, or cried—.

But you only lift your head and look me in the eye.

If I dared step near, or nearer; if it were permitted that I should cross the current of your living breath; if it were willed that I should feel the leap of human blood within your veins; if I should touch your hands, your cheeks, your lips; if I dropped an arm as lightly as a snowflake round your shoulder—

The fear which no heart has fathomed, the fate which no fancy has faced, the riddle which no soul has read, steps between your substance and my soul.

I drop my arms. I sink into the heart of the pillared light upon the wall. I will not wonder what would happen if my outlines defined upon it to your view. I will not think of that which could be, would be, if I struck across your still-set vision, face to face.

Ah me, how still she sits! With what a fixed, incurious stare she looks me in the eye!

The wind, now that I stand no longer between it and yourself, comes enviously in. It lifts the curtain, and whirls about the room. It bruises the surface of the great pearled pillar where I lean. I am caught within it. Speech and language struggle over me. Mute articulations fill the air. Tears and laughter, and the sounding of soft lips, and the falling of low cries, possess me. Will she listen? Will she bend her head? Will her lips part in recognition? Is there an alphabet between us? Or have the winds of night a vocabulary to lift before her holden eyes?

We sat many times together, and talked of this. Do you remember, dear? You held my hand. Tears that I could not see fell on it; we sat by the great hall-window upstairs, where the maple shadow goes to sleep, face down, across the floor upon a lighted night; the old green curtain waved its hands upon us like a mesmerist, I thought; like a priest, you said.

"When we are parted, you shall go," you said; and when I shook my head you smiled—you always smiled when you said that, but you said it always quite the same.

I think I hardly understood you then. Now that I hold your eyes in mine, and you see me not; now when I stretch my hand and you touch me not; now that I cry your name, and you hear it not,—I comprehend you, tender one! A wisdom not of earth was in your words. "To live, is dying; I will die. To die is life, and you shall live."

Now when the fever turned, I thought of this.

That must have been—ah! how long ago? I miss the conception of that for which *how long* stands index.

Yet I perfectly remember that I perfectly understood it to be at three o'clock on a rainy Sunday morning that I died. Your little watch stood in its case of olive-wood upon the table, and drops were on the window. I noticed both, though you did not know it. I see the watch now, in your pocket; I cannot tell if the hands move, or only pulsate like a heart-throb, to and fro; they stand and point, mute golden fingers, paralyzed and pleading, forever at the hour of three. At this I wonder.

When first you said I "was sinking fast," the words sounded as old and familiar as a nursery tale. I heard you in the hall. The doctor had just left, and you went to mother and took her face in your two arms, and laid your hand across her mouth, as if it were she who had spoken. She cried out and threw up her thin old hands; but you stood as still as Eternity. Then I thought again: "It is she who dies; I shall live."

So often and so anxiously we have talked of this thing called death, that now that it is all over between us, I cannot understand why we found in it such a source of distress. It bewilders me. I am often bewildered here. Things and the fancies of things possess a relation which as yet is new and strange to me. Here is a mystery.

Now, in truth, it seems a simple matter for me to tell you how it has been with me since your lips last touched me, and your arms held me to the vanishing air.

Oh, drawn, pale lips! Nerveless, dropping arms! I told you I would come. Did ever promise fail I spoke to you? "Come and show me Death," you said. I have come to show you Death. I could show you the fairest sight and sweetest that ever blessed your eyes. Why, look! Is it not fair? Am I terrible? Do you shrink or shiver? Would you turn from me, or hide your strained, expectant face?

Would she? Does she? Will she? . . .

Ah, how the room widened! I could tell you that. It grew great and luminous day by day. At night the walls throbbed; lights of rose ran round them, and blue fire, and a tracery as of the shadows of little leaves. As the walls expanded, the air fled. But I tried to tell you how little pain I knew or feared. Your haggard face bent over me. I could not speak; when I would I struggled, and you said "She suffers!" Dear, it was so very little!

Listen, till I tell you how that night came on. The sun fell and the dew slid down. It seemed to me that it slid into my heart, but still I felt no pain. Where the walls pulsed and receded, the hills came in. Where the old bureau stood, above the glass, I saw a single mountain with a face of fire, and purple hair. I tried to tell you this, but you said: "She wanders." I laughed in my heart at that, for it was such a blessed wandering! As the night locked the sun below the mountain's solemn watching face, the Gates of Space were lifted up before me; the everlasting doors of Matter swung for me upon their rusty hinges, and the King of Glories entered in and out. All the kingdoms of the earth, and the power of them, beckoned to me, across the mist my failing senses made,—ruins and roses, and the brows of Jura and the singing of the Rhine; a shaft of red light on the Sphinx's smile, and caravans in sandstorms, and an icy wind at sea, and gold adream in mines that no man knew, and mothers sitting at their doors in valleys singing babes to sleep, and women in dank cellars selling souls for bread, and the whir of wheels in giant factories, and a single prayer somewhere in a den of death,—I could not find it, though I searched,—and the smoke of battle, and broken music, and a sense of lilies alone beside a stream at the rising of the sun—and, at last, your face, dear, all alone.

I discovered then, that the walls and roof of the room had vanished quite. The night-wind blew in. The maple in the yard almost brushed my cheek. Stars were about me, and I thought the rain had stopped, yet seemed to hear it, up on the seeming of a window which I could not find.

One thing only hung between me and immensity. It was your single, awful, haggard face. I looked my last into your eyes. Stronger than death, they held and claimed my soul. I feebly raised my hand to find your own. More cruel than the grave, your wild grasp chained me. Then I struggled, and you cried out, and your face slipped, and I stood free.

I stood upon the floor, beside the bed. That which had been I lay there at rest, but terrible, before me. You hid your face, and I saw you slide upon your knees. I laid my hand upon your head; you did not stir; I spoke to you: "Dear, look around a minute!" but you knelt quite still. I walked to and fro about the room, and meeting my mother, touched her on the elbow; she only said, "She's gone!" and sobbed aloud. "I have not *gone!*" I cried; but she sat sobbing on.

The walls of the room had settled now, and the ceiling stood in its solid place. The window was shut, but the door stood open. Suddenly I was restless, and I ran.

I brushed you in hurrying by, and hit the little light-stand where the tumblers stood; I looked to see if it would fall, but it only shivered as if a breath of wind had struck it once.

But I was restless, and I ran. In the hall I met the Doctor. This amused me, and I stopped to think it over. "Ah, Doctor," said I, "you need not trouble yourself to go up. I'm quite well to-night, you see." But he made me no answer; he gave me no glance; he hung up his hat, and laid his hand upon the banister against which I leaned, and went ponderously up.

It was not until he had nearly reached the landing that it occurred to me, still leaning on the banisters, that his heavy arm must have swept against and *through* me, where I stood against the oaken mouldings which he grasped.

I saw his feet fall on the stairs above me; but they made no sound which reached my ear. "You'll not disturb me *now* with your big boots, sir," said I, nodding; "never fear!"

But he disappeared from sight above me, and still I heard no sound.

Now the Doctor had left the front door unlatched.

As I touched it, it blew open wide, and solemnly. I passed out and down the steps. I could see that it was chilly, yet I felt no chill. Frost was on the grass, and in the east a pallid streak, like the cheek of one who had watched all night. The flowers in the little square plots hung their heads and drew their shoulders up; there was a lonely, late lily which I broke and gathered to my heart, where I breathed upon it, and it warmed and looked me kindly in the eye. This, I remember, gave me pleasure. I wandered in and out about the garden in the scattering rain; my feet left no trace upon the dripping grass, and I saw with interest that the garment which I wore gathered no moisture and no cold. I sat musing for a while upon the piazza, in the garden-chair, not caring to go in. It was so many months since I had felt able to sit upon the piazza in the open air. "By and by," I thought, I would go in and upstairs to see you once again. The curtains were drawn from the parlor windows and I passed and repassed, looking in.

All this while, the cheek of the east was waning, and the air gathering faint heats and lights about me. I remembered, presently, the old arbor at the garden-foot, where before I was sick, we sat so much together; and thinking, "She will be surprised to know that I have been down alone," I was restless, and I ran again.

I meant to come back and see you, dear, once more. I saw the lights in the room where I had lain sick, overhead; and your shadow on the curtain; and I blessed it, with all the love of life and death, as I bounded by.

The air was thick with sweetness from the dying flowers. The birds woke, and the zenith lighted, and the leap of health was in my limbs. The old arbor held out its soft arms to me—but I was restless, and I ran.

The field opened before me, and meadows with broad bosoms, and a river flashed before me like a scimitar, and woods interlocked their hands to stay me—but being restless, on I ran.

The house dwindled behind me; and the light in my sick-room, and your shadow on the curtain. But yet I was restless, and I ran.

In the twinkling of an eye I fell into a solitary place. Sand and rocks were in it, and a falling wind. I paused, and knelt upon the sand, and mused a little in this place. I mused of you, and life and death, and love and agony;—but these had departed from me, as dim and distant as the fainting wind. A sense of solemn expectation filled the air. A tremor and a trouble wrapped my soul.

"I must be dead!" I said aloud. I had no sooner spoken than I learned that I was not alone.

The sun had risen, and on a ledge of ancient rock, weather-stained and red, there had fallen over against me the outline of a Presence lifted up against the sky, and turning suddenly, I saw . . .

Lawful to utter, but utterance has fled! Lawful to utter, but a greater than Law restrains me! Am I blotted from your desolate fixed eyes? Lips that my mortal lips have pressed, can you not quiver when I cry? Soul that my eternal soul has loved, can you stand enveloped in my presence, and not spring like a fountain to me? Would you not know how it has been with me since your perishable eyes beheld my perished face? What my eyes have seen or my ears have heard, or my heart conceived without you? If I have missed or mourned for you? If I have watched or longed for you? Marked your solitary days and sleepless nights, and tearless eyes, and monotonous slow echo of my unanswered name? Would you not know?

Alas! would she? Would she not? My soul misgives me with a matchless, solitary fear. I am called, and I slip from her. I am beckoned, and I lose her.

Her face dims, and her folded, lonely hands fade from my sight.

Time to tell her a guarded thing! Time to whisper a treasured word! A moment to tell her that *Death is dumb, for Life is deaf!* A moment to tell her.—

CONSTANCE FENIMORE WOOLSON (1840–1894)

"Felipa" (1876)

The life of the Midwestern-born American writer Constance Fenimore Woolson, great-niece of the novelist James Fenimore Cooper, was marked by tragedy. She was the only one of six daughters to survive into adulthood; her later years, marked by depression and lonely self-exile in Europe after the death of her mother in 1879, culminated with her suicide in Venice in 1894. Yet her misfortunes also enriched her profoundly literary sensibilities, and during the 1870s and 1880s she was one of the most highly regarded of American short-story writers. Henry James was a friend and admirer; his invalid sister, Alice, requested that Woolson's story "Dorothy" be read to her during the last days of her life.

Many of Woolson's stories have regional settings — before moving to Europe, she lived in the Great Lakes area and the American South—and many deal with intimacies between women. In the marvelous "Felipa," the lush Florida setting makes an evocative backdrop for Woolson's intricate tale of triangulated passions. Felipa, the comical little Minorcan girl of the title, is infatuated with Christine, the beautiful friend of Catherine, the narrator. By some curious psychic mechanism, she associates Christine's lover Edward with Christine and begins to "love" him too. Yet the real mystery here is Catherine, a painter drawn to Christine's "pre-Raphaelite" beauty. When Felipa strikes out at Edward—her violence suggesting which of her "two loves" is the stronger—one may discern in her action an allegory of the narrator's own cryptic passional attachments.

FURTHER READING: Constance Fenimore Woolson, *Women Artists, Women Exiles: "Miss Grief" and Other Stories*, ed. Joan Myers Weimer (New Brunswick and London: Rutgers University Press, 1988); Henry James, *Partial Portraits* (London: Macmillan, 1888); Leon Edel, *The Life of Henry James*, 5 vols. (New York: J. W. Lippincott, 1953–72); Rayburn S. Moore, *Constance Fenimore Woolson* (New York: Twayne, 1963); Sharon Dean, "Constance Fenimore Woolson and Henry James: The Literary Friendship," *Massachusetts Studies in English* 7 (1980): 1–9; —, *Constance Fenimore Woolson: Homeward Bound* (Knoxville: University of Tennessee Press, 1995); Mary Kelley, *Private Woman, Public Stage: Literary Domesticity in Nineteenth-Century America* (New York:

Oxford University Press, 1984); Cheryl Torsney, *Constance Fenimore Woolson: The Grief of Artistry* (Athens: University of Georgia Press, 1989); Lyndall Gordon, *A Private Life of Henry James: Two Women and His Art* (London: Chatto and Windus, 1998).

> *Glooms of the live-oaks, beautiful-braided and woven*
> *With intricate shades of the vines that, myriad cloven,*
> *Clamber the forks of the multiform boughs.*
>   *. . . . Green colonnades*
> *Of the dim sweet woods, of the dear dark woods,*
> *Of the heavenly woods and glades,*
> *That run to the radiant marginal sand-beach within*
>   *The wide sea-marches of Glynn.*
>
>   *. . . . Free*
> *By a world of marsh that borders a world of sea.*
> *Sinuous southward and sinuous northward the shimmering band*
> *Of the sand-beach fastens the fringe of the marsh to the folds of the land.*
>
> *Inward and outward to northward and southward the beach-lines linger and curl*
> *As a silver-wrought garment that clings to and follows the firm, sweet limbs of a*
>   *girl.*
> *A league and a league of marsh-grass, waist-high, broad in the blade,*
> *Green, and all of a height, and unflecked with a light or a shade.*
> Sidney Lanier.

Christine and I found her there. She was a small, dark-skinned, yellow-eyed child, the offspring of the ocean and the heats, tawny, lithe and wild, shy yet fearless—not unlike one of the little brown deer that bounded through the open reaches of the pine-barren behind the house. She did not come to us—we came to her; we loomed into her life like genii from another world, and she was partly afraid and partly proud of us. For were we not her guests? proud thought! and, better still, were we not women? "I have only seen three women in all my life," said Felipa, inspecting us gravely, "and I like women. I am a woman too, although these clothes of the son of Pedro make me appear as a boy; I wear them on account of the boat and the hauling in of the fish. The son of Pedro being dead at a convenient age, and his clothes fitting me, what would you have? It was a chance not to be despised. But when I am grown I shall wear robes long and beautiful like the señora's." The little creature was dressed in a boy's suit of dark-blue linen, much the worse for wear, and torn.

"If you are a girl, why do you not mend your clothes?" I said.

"Do you mend, señora?"

"Certainly: all women sew and mend."

"The other lady?"

Christine laughed as she lay at ease upon the brown carpet of pine-needles, warm and aromatic after the tropic day's sunshine. "The child has divined me already, Catherine," she said.

Christine was a tall, lissome maid, with an unusually long stretch of arm, long sloping shoulders, and a long fair throat; her straight hair fell to her knees when unbound, and its clear flaxen hue had not one shade of gold, as her clear gray eyes had not one shade of blue. Her small, straight, rose-leaf lips parted over small, dazzlingly white teeth, and the outline of her face in profile reminded you of an etching in its distinctness, although it was by no means perfect according to the rules of art. Still, what a comfort it was, after the blurred outlines and smudged profiles many of us possess— seen to best advantage, I think, in church on Sundays, crowned with flower-decked bonnets, listening calmly serene to favorite ministers, unconscious of noses! When Christine had finished her laugh—and she never hurried anything—she stretched out her arm carelessly and patted Felipa's curly head. The child caught the descending hand and kissed the long white fingers.

It was a wild place where we were, yet not new or crude—the coast of Florida, that old-new land, with its deserted plantations, its skies of Paradise, and its broad wastes open to the changeless sunshine. The old house stood on the edge of the dry land, where the pine-barren ended and the salt-marsh began; in front curved the tide-water river that seemed ever trying to come up close to the barren and make its acquaintance, but could not quite succeed, since it must always turn and flee at a fixed hour, like Cinderella at the ball, leaving not a silver slipper behind, but purple driftwood and bright seaweeds, brought in from the Gulf Stream outside. A planked platform ran out into the marsh from the edge of the barren, and at its end the boats were moored; for, although at high tide the river was at our feet, at low tide it was far away out in the green waste somewhere, and if we wanted it we must go and seek it. We did not want it, however; we let it glide up to us twice a day with its fresh salt odors and flotsam of the ocean, and the rest of the time we wandered over the barrens or lay under the trees looking up into the wonderful blue above, listening to the winds as they rushed across from sea to sea. I was an artist, poor and painstaking. Christine was my kind friend. She had brought me South because my cough was troublesome, and here because Edward Bowne recommended the place. He and three fellow sportsmen were down at the Madre Lagoon, farther south; I thought it probable we should see him, without his three fellow sportsmen, before very long.

"Who were the three women you have seen, Felipa?" said Christine.

"The grandmother, an Indian woman of the Seminoles who comes sometimes with baskets, and the wife of Miguel of the island. But they are all old, and their skins are curled: I like better the silver skin of the señora."

Poor little Felipa lived on the edge of the great salt-marsh alone with her grand-parents, for her mother was dead. The yellow old couple were slow-witted Minorcans, part pagan, part Catholic, and wholly ignorant; their minds rarely rose above the level of their orange-trees and their fish-nets. Felipa's father was a Spanish sailor, and, as he had died only the year before, the child's Spanish was fairly correct, and we could converse with her readily, although we were slow to comprehend the patois of the old people, which seemed to borrow as much from the Italian tongue and the Greek as from its mother Spanish. "I know a great deal," Felipa remarked confidently, "for my father taught me. He had sailed on the ocean out of sight of land, and he knew many things. These he taught to me. Do the gracious ladies think there is anything else to know?"

One of the gracious ladies thought not, decidedly. In answer to my remonstrance, expressed in English, she said, "Teach a child like that, and you ruin her."

"Ruin her?"

"Ruin her happiness—the same thing."

Felipa had a dog, a second self—a great gaunt yellow creature of unknown breed, with crooked legs, big feet, and the name Drollo. What Drollo meant, or whether it was an abbreviation, we never knew; but there was a certain satisfaction in it, for the dog was droll: the fact that the Minorcan title, whatever it was, meant nothing of that sort, made it all the better. We never saw Felipa without Drollo. "They look a good deal alike," observed Christine—"the same coloring."

"For shame!" I said.

But it was true. The child's bronzed yellow skin and soft eyes were not unlike the dog's, but her head was crowned with a mass of short black curls, while Drollo had only his two great flapping ears and his low smooth head. Give him an inch or two more of skull, and what a creature a dog would be! For love and faithfulness even now what man can match him? But, although ugly, Felipa was a picturesque little object always, whether attired in boy's clothes or in her own forlorn bodice and skirt. Olive-hued and meager-faced, lithe and thin, she flew over the pine-barrens like a creature of air, laughing to feel her short curls toss and her thin childish arms buoyed up on the breeze as she ran, with Drollo barking behind. For she loved the winds, and always knew when they were coming—whether down from the north, in from the ocean, or across from the Gulf of Mexico: she watched for them, sitting in the doorway, where she could feel their first breath, and she taught us the signs of the clouds. She was a queer little thing: we used to find her sometimes dancing alone out on the barren in a circle she had marked out with pine-cones, and once she confided to us that she talked to the trees. "They hear," she said in a whisper; "you should see how knowing they look, and how their leaves listen."

Once we came upon her most secret lair in a dense thicket of thorn-myrtle and wild smilax—a little bower she had made, where was hidden a horrible-looking image formed of the rough pieces of saw-palmetto grubbed up by old Bartolo from his garden. She must have dragged these fragments thither one by one, and with infinite pains bound them together with her rude withes of strong marsh-grass, until at last she had formed a rough trunk with crooked arms and a sort of a head, the red hairy surface of the palmetto looking not unlike the skin of some beast, and making the creature all the more grotesque. This fetich was kept crowned with flowers, and after this we often saw the child stealing away with Drollo to carry to it portions of her meals or a new-found treasure—a sea-shell, a broken saucer, or a fragment of ribbon. The food always mysteriously disappeared, and my suspicion is that Drollo used to go back secretly in the night and devour it, asking no questions and telling no lies: it fitted in nicely, however, Drollo merely performing the ancient part of the priests of Jupiter, men who have been much admired. "What a little pagan she is!" I said.

"Oh, no, it is only her doll," replied Christine.

I tried several times to paint Felipa during these first weeks, but those eyes of hers always evaded me. They were, as I have said before, yellow—that is, they were brown with yellow lights—and they stared at you with the most inflexible openness. The child had the full-curved, half-open mouth of the tropics, and a low Greek forehead. "Why isn't she pretty?" I said.

"She is hideous," replied Christine; "look at her elbows."

Now Felipa's arms *were* unpleasant: They were brown and lean, scratched and stained, and they terminated in a pair of determined little paws that could hold on like grim Death. I shall never forget coming upon a tableau one day out on the barren—a little Florida cow and Felipa, she holding on by the horns, and the beast with its small fore feet stubbornly set in the sand; girl pulling one way, cow the other; both silent and determined. It was a hard contest, but the girl won.

"And if you pass over her elbows, there are her feet," continued Christine languidly. For she was a sybaritic lover of the fine linens of life, that friend of mine—a pre-Raphaelite lady with clinging draperies and a mediaeval clasp on her belt. Her whole being rebelled against ugliness, and the mere sight of a sharp-nosed, light-eyed woman on a cold day made her uncomfortable.

"Have we not feet too?" I replied sharply.

But I knew what she meant. Bare feet are not pleasant to the eye nowadays, whatever they may have been in the days of the ancient Greeks; and Felipa's little brown insteps were half the time torn or bruised by the thorns of the chaparral. Besides, there was always the disagreeable idea that she might step upon something cold and squirming when she prowled through the thickets knee-deep in the matted grasses. Snakes abounded, although we never saw them; but Felipa went up to their very doors, as it were, and rang the bell defiantly.

One day old Grandfather Bartolo took the child with him down to the coast: she was always wild to go to the beach, where she could gather shells and sea-beans, and chase the little ocean-birds that ran along close to the waves with that swift gliding motion of theirs, and where she could listen to the roar of the breakers. We were several miles up the salt-marsh, and to go down to the ocean was quite a voyage to Felipa. She bade us good-bye joyously; then ran back to hug Christine a second time, then to the boat again; then back.

"I thought you wanted to go, child?" I said, a little impatiently; for I was reading aloud, and these small irruptions were disturbing.

"Yes," said Felipa, "I want to go; and still—Perhaps if the gracious señora would kiss me again—"

Christine only patted her cheek and told her to run away: she obeyed, but there was a wistful look in her eyes, and, even after the boat had started, her face, watching us from the stern, haunted me.

"Now that the little monkey has gone, I may be able at last to catch and fix a likeness of her," I said; "in this case a recollection is better than the changing quicksilver reality."

"You take it as a study of ugliness?"

"Do not be hard upon the child, Christine."

"Hard? Why, she adores me," said my friend, going off to her hammock under the tree.

Several days passed, and the boat returned not. I accomplished a fine amount of work, and Christine a fine amount of swinging in the hammock and dreaming. At length one afternoon I gave my final touch, and carried my sketch over to the pre-Raphaelite lady for criticism. "What do you see?" I said.

"I see a wild-looking child with yellow eyes, a mat of curly black hair, a lank little bodice, her two thin brown arms embracing a gaunt old dog with crooked legs, big feet, and turned-in toes."

"Is that all?"

"All."

"You do not see latent beauty, courage, and a possible great gulf of love in that poor wild little face?"

"Nothing of the kind," replied Christine decidedly. "I see an ugly little girl; that is all."

The next day the boat returned, and brought back five persons, the old grandfather, Felipa, Drollo, Miguel of the island, and—Edward Bowne.

"Already?" I said.

"Tired of the Madre, Kitty; thought I would come up here and see you for a while. I knew you must be pining for me."

"Certainly," I replied; "do you not see how I have wasted away?"

He drew my arm through his and raced me down the plank-walk toward the shore, where I arrived laughing and out of breath.

"Where is Christine?" he asked.

I came back into the traces at once. "Over there in the hammock. You wish to go to the house first, I suppose?"

"Of course not."

"But she did not come to meet you, Edward, although she knew you had landed."

"Of course not, also."

"I do not understand you two."

"And of course not, a third time," said Edward, looking down at me with a smile. "What do peaceful little artists know about war?"

"Is it war?"

"Something very like it, Kitty. What is that you are carrying?"

"Oh! my new sketch. What do you think of it?"

"Good, very good. Some little girl about here, I suppose?"

"Why, it is Felipa!"

"And who is Felipa? Seems to me I have seen that old dog, though."

"Of course you have; he was in the boat with you, and so was Felipa; but she was dressed in boy's clothes, and that gives her a different look."

"Oh! that boy? I remember him. His name is Philip. He is a funny little fellow," said Edward calmly.

"Her name is Felipa, and she is not a boy or a funny little fellow at all," I replied.

"Isn't she? I thought she was both," replied Ned carelessly; and then he went off toward the hammock. I turned away, after noting Christine's cool greeting, and went back to the boat.

Felipa came bounding to meet me. "What is his name?" she demanded.

"Bowne."

"Buon—Buona; I can not say it."

"Bowne, child—Edward Bowne."

"Oh! Eduardo; I know that. Eduardo—Eduardo—a name of honey."

She flew off singing the name, followed by Drollo carrying his mistress's palmetto basket in his big patient mouth; but when I passed the house a few moments afterward she was singing, or rather talking volubly of, another name—"Miguel," and "the wife of Miguel," who were apparently important personages on the canvas of her life. As it happened, I never really saw that wife of Miguel, who seemingly had no name of her own; but I imagined her. She lived on a sand-bar in the ocean not far from the mouth of our salt-marsh; she drove pelicans like ducks with a long switch, and she had a tame eagle; she had an old horse also, who dragged the driftwood across the sand on a sledge, and this old horse seemed like a giant horse always, outlined as he was against the flat bar and the sky. She went out at dawn, and she went out at sunset, but during the middle of the burning day she sat at home and polished sea-beans, for which she obtained untold sums; she was very tall, she was very yellow, and she had but one eye. These items, one by one, had been dropped by Felipa at various times, and it was with curiosity that I gazed upon the original Miguel, the possessor of this remarkable spouse. He was a grave-eyed, yellow man, who said little and thought less, applying *cui bono?* to mental much as the city man applies it to bodily exertion, and therefore achieving, I think, a finer degree of inanition. The tame eagle, the pelicans, were nothing to him;

and, when I saw his lethargic, gentle countenance, my own curiosity about them seemed to die away in haze, as though I had breathed in an invisible opiate. He came, he went, and that was all; exit Miguel.

Felipa was constantly with us now. She and Drollo followed the three of us wherever we went—followed the two also whenever I stayed behind to sketch, as I often stayed, for in those days I was trying to catch the secret of the salt-marsh; a hopeless effort—I know it now. "Stay with me, Felipa," I said; for it was natural to suppose that the lovers might like to be alone. (I call them lovers for want of a better name, but they were more like haters; however, in such cases it is nearly the same thing.) And then Christine, hearing this, would immediately call "Felipa!" and the child would dart after them, happy as a bird. She wore her boy's suit now all the time, because the señora had said she "looked well in it." What the señora really said was, that in boy's clothes she looked less like a grasshopper. But this had been translated as above by Edward Bowne when Felipa suddenly descended upon him one day and demanded to be instantly told what the gracious lady was saying about her; for she seemed to know by intuition when we spoke of her, although we talked in English and mentioned no names. When told, her small face beamed, and she kissed Christine's hand joyfully and bounded away. Christine took out her handkerchief and wiped the spot.

"Christine," I said, "do you remember the fate of the proud girl who walked upon bread?"

"You think that I may starve for kisses some time?" said my friend, going on with the wiping.

"Not while I am alive," called out Edward from behind. His style of courtship *was* of the sledge-hammer sort sometimes. But he did not get much for it on that day; only lofty tolerance, which seemed to amuse him greatly.

Edward played with Felipa very much as if she was a rubber toy or a little trapeze performer. He held her out at arm's length in mid-air, he poised her on his shoulder, he tossed her up into the low myrtle-trees, and dangled her by her little belt over the claret-colored pools on the barren; but he could not frighten her; she only laughed and grew wilder and wilder, like a squirrel. "She has muscles and nerves of steel," he said admiringly.

"Do put her down; she is too excitable for such games." I said in French, for Felipa seemed to divine our English now. "See the color she has."

For there was a trail of dark red over the child's thin oval cheeks which made her look unlike herself. As she caught our eyes fixed upon her, she suddenly stopped her climbing and came and sat at Christine's feet. "Some day I shall wear robes like the señora's," she said, passing her hand over the soft fabric; "and I think," she added after some slow consideration, "that my face will be like the señora's too."

Edward burst out laughing. The little creature stopped abruptly and scanned his face.

"Do not tease her," I said.

Quick as a flash she veered around upon me. "He does not tease me," she said angrily in Spanish; "and, besides, what if he does? I like it." She looked at me with gleaming eyes and stamped her foot.

"What a little tempest!" said Christine.

Then Edward, man-like, began to explain. "You could not look much like this lady, Felipa," he said, "because you are so dark, you know."

"Am I dark?"

"Very dark; but many people are dark, of course; and for my part I always liked dark eyes," said this mendacious person.

"Do you like my eyes?" asked Felipa anxiously.

"Indeed I do: they are like the eyes of a dear little calf I once owned when I was a boy."

The child was satisfied, and went back to her place beside Christine. "Yes, I shall wear robes like this," she said dreamily, drawing the flowing drapery over her knees clad in the little linen trousers, and scanning the effect; "they would trail behind me—so." Her bare feet peeped out below the hem, and again we all laughed, the little brown toes looked so comical coming out from the silk and the snowy embroideries. She came down to reality again, looked at us, looked at herself, and for the first time seemed to comprehend the difference. Then suddenly she threw herself down on the ground like a little animal, and buried her head in her arms. She would not speak, she would not look up: she only relaxed one arm a little to take in Drollo, and then lay motionless. Drollo looked at us out of one eye solemnly from his uncomfortable position, as much as to say: "No use; leave her to me." So after a while we went away and left them there.

That evening I heard a low knock at my door. "Come in," I said, and Felipa entered. I hardly knew her. She was dressed in a flowered muslin gown which had probably belonged to her mother, and she wore her grandmother's stockings and large baggy slippers; on her mat of curly hair was perched a high-crowned, stiff white cap adorned with a ribbon streamer; and her lank little neck, coming out of the big gown, was decked with a chain of large sea-beans, like exaggerated lockets. She carried a Cuban fan in her hand which was as large as a parasol, and Drollo, walking behind, fairly clanked with the chain of sea-shells which she had wound around him from head to tail. The droll tableau and the supreme pride on Felipa's countenance overcame me, and I laughed aloud. A sudden cloud of rage and disappointment came over the poor child's face: she threw her cap on the floor and stamped on it; she tore off her necklace and writhed herself out of her big flowered gown, and, running to Drollo, nearly strangled him in her fierce efforts to drag off his shell chains. Then, a half-dressed, wild little phantom, she seized me by the skirts and dragged me toward the looking-glass. "You are not pretty either," she cried. "Look at yourself! look at yourself!"

"I did not mean to laugh at you, Felipa," I said gently; "I would not laugh at any one; and it is true I am not pretty, as you say. I can never be pretty, child; but, if you will try to be more gentle, I could teach you how to dress yourself so that no one would laugh at you again. I could make you a little bright-barred skirt and a scarlet bodice: you could help, and that would teach you to sew. But a little girl who wants all this done for her must be quiet and good."

"I am good," said Felipa; "as good as everything."

The tears still stood in her eyes, but her anger was forgotten: she improvised a sort of dance around my room, followed by Drollo dragging his twisted chain, stepping on it with his big feet, and finally winding himself up into a knot around the chair-legs.

"Couldn't we make Drollo something too? dear old Drollo!" said Felipa, going to him and squeezing him in an enthusiastic embrace. I used to wonder how his poor ribs stood it: Felipa used him as a safety-valve for her impetuous feelings.

She kissed me good night, and then asked for "the other lady."

"Go to bed, child," I said; "I will give her your good night."

"But I want to kiss her too," said Felipa.

She lingered at the door and would not go; she played with the latch, and made me nervous with its clicking; at last I ordered her out. But on opening my door half an hour afterward there she was sitting on the floor outside in the darkness, she and Drollo, patiently waiting. Annoyed, but unable to reprove her, I wrapped the child in my shawl and carried her out into the moonlight, where Christine and Edward were strolling to and fro under the pines. "She will not go to bed, Christine, without kissing you," I explained.

"Funny little monkey!" said my friend, passively allowing the embrace.

"Me too," said Edward, bending down. Then I carried my bundle back satisfied.

The next day Felipa and I in secret began our labors; hers consisted in worrying me out of my life and spoiling material—mine in keeping my temper and trying to sew. The result, however, was satisfactory, never mind how we got there. I led Christine out one afternoon: Edward followed. "Do you like tableaux?" I said. "There is one I have arranged for you."

Felipa sat on the edge of the low, square-curbed Spanish well, and Drollo stood behind her, his great yellow body and solemn head serving as a background. She wore a brown petticoat barred with bright colors, and a little scarlet bodice fitting her slender waist closely; a chemisette of soft cream-color with loose sleeves covered her neck and arms, and set off the dark hues of her cheeks and eyes; and around her curly hair a red scarf was twisted, its fringed edges forming a drapery at the back of the head, which, more than anything else, seemed to bring out the latent character of her face. Brown moccasins, red stockings, and a quantity of bright beads completed her costume.

"By Jove!" cried Edward, "the little thing is almost pretty."

Felipa understood this, and a great light came into her face: forgetting her pose, she bounded forward to Christine's side. "I am pretty, then?" she said with exultation; "I *am* pretty, then, after all? For now you yourself have said it—have said it."

"No, Felipa," I interposed, "the gentleman said it." For the child had a curious habit of confounding the two identities which puzzled me then as now. But this afternoon, this happy afternoon, she was content, for she was allowed to sit at Christine's feet and look up into her fair face unmolested. I was forgotten, as usual.

"It is always so," I said to myself. But cynicism, as Mr. Aldrich says, is a small brass field-piece that eventually bursts and kills the artilleryman. I knew this, having been blown up myself more than once; so I went back to my painting and forgot the world. Our world down there on the edge of the salt-marsh, however, was a small one: when two persons went out of it there was a vacuum.

One morning Felipa came sadly to my side. "They have gone away," she said.

"Yes, child."

"Down to the beach to spend all the day."

"Yes, I know it."

"And without me!"

This was the climax. I looked up. Her eyes were dry, but there was a hollow look of disappointment in her face that made her seem old; it was as though for an instant you caught what her old-woman face would be half a century on.

"Why did they not take me?" she said. "I am pretty now: she herself said it."

"They can not always take you, Felipa," I replied, giving up the point as to who had said it.

"Why not? I am pretty now: she herself said it," persisted the child. "In these clothes, you know: she herself said it. The clothes of the son of Pedro you will never see more: they are burned."

"Burned?"

"Yes, burned," replied Felipa composedly. "I carried them out on the barren and burned them. Drollo singed his paw. They burned quite nicely. But they are gone, and I am pretty now, and yet they did not take me! What shall I do?"

"Take these colors and make me a picture," I suggested. Generally, this was a prized privilege, but to-day it did not attract; she turned away, and a few moments after I saw her going down to the end of the plank-walk, where she stood gazing wistfully toward the ocean. There she stayed all day, going into camp with Drollo, and refusing to come to dinner in spite of old Dominga's calls and beckonings. At last the patient old grandmother went down herself to the end of the long walk where they were, with some bread and venison on a plate. Felipa ate but little, but Drollo, after waiting politely until she had finished, devoured everything that was left in his calmly hungry way, and then sat back on his haunches with one paw on the plate, as though for the sake of memory. Drollo's hunger was of the chronic kind; it seemed impossible either to assuage it or to fill him. There was a gaunt leanness about him which I am satisfied no amount of food could ever fatten. I think he knew it too, and that accounted for his resignation. At length, just before sunset, the boat returned, floating up the marsh with the tide, old Bartolo steering and managing the brown sails. Felipa sprang up joyfully; I thought she would spring into the boat in her eagerness. What did she receive for her long vigil? A short word or two; that was all. Christine and Edward had quarreled.

How do lovers quarrel ordinarily? But I should not ask that, for these were no ordinary lovers: they were extraordinary.

"You should not submit to her caprices so readily," I said the next day while strolling on the barren with Edward. (He was not so much cast down, however, as he might have been.)

"I adore the very ground her foot touches, Kitty."

"I know it. But how will it end?"

"I will tell you: one of these days I shall win her, and then—she will adore me."

Here Felipa came running after us, and Edward immediately challenged her to a race: a game of romps began. If Christine had been looking from her window she might have thought he was not especially disconsolate over her absence; but she was not looking. She was never looking out of anything or for anybody. She was always serenely content where she was. Edward and Felipa strayed off among the pine-trees, and gradually I lost sight of them. But as I sat sketching an hour afterward Edward came into view, carrying the child in his arms. I hurried to meet them.

"I shall never forgive myself," he said; "the little thing has fallen and injured her foot badly, I fear."

"I do not care at all," said Felipa; "I like to have it hurt. It is *my* foot, isn't it?"

These remarks she threw at me defiantly, as though I had laid claim to the member in question. I could not help laughing.

"The other lady will not laugh," said the child proudly. And in truth Christine, most unexpectedly, took up the *rôle* of nurse. She carried Felipa to her own room—for we each had a little cell opening out of the main apartment—and as white-robed Charity she shone with new radiance, "Shone" is the proper word; for through the open door of the dim cell, with the dark little face of Felipa on her shoulder, her white robe and skin seemed fairly to shine, as white lilies shine on a dark night. The old grandmother left the child in our care and watched our proceedings wistfully, very much as a dog watches the human hands that extract the thorn from the swollen foot of her puppy. She was grateful and asked no questions; in fact, thought was not one of her mental processes. She did not think much; she felt. As for Felipa, the child lived in rapture during those days in spite of her suffering. She scarcely slept at all—she was too happy: I heard her voice rippling on through the night, and Christine's low replies. She adored her beautiful nurse.

The fourth day came: Edward Bowne walked into the cell. "Go out and breathe the fresh air for an hour or two," he said in the tone more of a command than a request.

"The child will never consent," replied Christine sweetly.

"Oh, yes, she will; I will stay with her," said the young man, lifting the feverish little head on his arm and passing his hand softly over the bright eyes.

"Felipa, do you not want me?" said Christine, bending down.

"He stays; it is all the same," murmured the child.

"So it is.—Go, Christine," said Edward with a little smile of triumph.

Without a word Christine left the cell. But she did not go to walk; she came to my room, and, throwing herself on my bed, fell in a moment into a deep sleep, the reaction after her three nights of wakefulness. When she awoke it was long after dark, and I had relieved Edward in his watch.

"You will have to give it up," he said as our lily came forth at last with sleep-flushed cheeks and starry eyes shielded from the light. "The spell is broken; we have all been taking care of Felipa, and she likes one as well as the other."

Which was not true, in my case at least, since Felipa had openly derided my small strength when I lifted her, and beat off the sponge with which I attempted to bathe her hot face, "They" used no sponges, she said, only their nice cool hands; and she wished "they" would come and take care of her again. But Christine had resigned *in toto*. If Felipa did not prefer her to all others, then Felipa should not have her; she was not a common nurse. And indeed she was not. Her fair face, ideal grace, cooing voice, and the strength of her long arms and flexible hands, were like magic to the sick, and—distraction to the well; the well in this case being Edward Bowne looking in at the door.

"You love them very much, do you not, Felipa?" I said one day when the child was sitting up for the first time in a cushioned chair.

"Ah, yes; it is so strong when they carry me," she replied. But it was Edward who carried her.

"He is very strong," I said.

"Yes; and their long soft hair, with the smell of roses in it too," said Felipa dreamily. But the hair was Christine's.

"I shall love them for ever, and they will love me for ever," continued the child. "Drollo too." She patted the dog's head as she spoke, and then concluded to kiss him on his little inch of forehead; next she offered him all her medicines and lotions in turn, and he smelled at them grimly. "He likes to know what I am taking," she explained.

I went on: "You love them, Felipa, and they are fond of you. They will always remember you, no doubt."

"Remember!" cried Felipa, starting up from her cushions like a Jack-in-a-box. "They are not going away? Never! never!"

"But of course they must go some time, for—"

But Felipa was gone. Before I could divine her intent she had flung herself out of her chair down on the floor, and was crawling on her hands and knees toward the outer room. I ran after her, but she reached the door before me, and, dragging her bandaged foot behind her, drew herself toward Christine. "You are *not* going away! You are not! you are not!" she sobbed, clinging to her skirts.

Christine was reading tranquilly; Edward stood at the outer door mending his fishing-tackle. The coolness between them remained, unwarmed by so much as a breath. "Run away, child; you disturb me," said Christine, turning over a leaf. She did not even look at the pathetic little bundle at her feet. Pathetic little bundles must be taught some time what ingratitude deserves.

"How can she run, lame as she is?" said Edward from the doorway.

"You are not going away, are you? Tell me you are not," sobbed Felipa in a passion of tears, beating on the floor with one hand, and with the other clinging to Christine.

"I am not going," said Edward. "Do not sob so, you poor little thing!"

She crawled to him, and he took her up in his arms and soothed her into stillness again; then he carried her out on the barren for a breath of fresh air.

"It is a most extraordinary thing how that child confounds you two," I said. "It is a case of color-blindness, as it were—supposing you two were colors."

"Which we are not," replied Christine carelessly. "Do not stray off into mysticism, Catherine."

"It is not mysticism; it is a study of character—"

"Where there is no character," replied my friend.

I gave it up, but I said to myself: "Fate, in the next world make me one of those long, lithe, light-haired women, will you? I want to see how it feels."

Felipa's foot was well again, and spring had come. Soon we must leave our lodge on the edge of the pine-barren, our outlook over the salt-marsh, with the river sweeping up twice a day, bringing in the briny odors of the ocean; soon we should see no more the eagles far above us or hear the night-cry of the great owls, and we must go without the little fairy flowers of the barren, so small that a hundred of them scarcely made a tangible bouquet, yet what beauty! what sweetness! In my portfolio were sketches and studies of the salt-marsh, and in my heart were hopes. Somebody says somewhere: "Hope is more than a blessing; it is a duty and a virtue." But I fail to appreciate preserved hope—hope put up in cans and served out in seasons of depression. I like it fresh from the tree. And so when I hope it *is* hope, and not that well-dried, monotonous cheerfulness which makes one long to throw the persistent smilers out of the window. Felipa danced no more on the barrens; her illness had toned her down; she seemed content to sit at our feet while we talked, looking up dreamily into our faces, but no longer eagerly endeavoring to comprehend. We were there; that was enough.

"She is growing like a reed," I said; "her illness has left her weak."

"-Minded," suggested Christine.

At this moment Felipa stroked the lady's white hand tenderly and laid her brown cheek against it.

"Do you not feel reproached?" I said.

"Why? Must we give our love to whoever loves us? A fine parcel of paupers we should all be, wasting our inheritance in pitiful small change! Shall I give a thousand beggars a half hour's happiness, or shall I make one soul rich his whole life long?"

"The latter," remarked Edward, who had come up unobserved.

They gazed at each other unflinchingly. They had come to open battle during those last days, and I knew that the end was near. Their words had been cold as ice, cutting as steel, and I said to myself, "At any moment." There would be a deadly struggle, and then Christine would yield. Even I comprehended something of what that yielding would be.

"Why do they hate each other so?" Felipa said to me sadly.

"Do they hate each other?"

"Yes, for I feel it here," she answered, touching her breast with a dramatic little gesture.

"Nonsense! Go and play with your doll, child." For I had made her a respectable, orderly doll to take the place of the ungainly fetich out on the barren.

Felipa gave me a look and walked away. A moment afterward she brought the doll out of the house before my very eyes, and, going down to the end of the dock, deliberately threw it into the water; the tide was flowing out, and away went my toy-woman out of sight, out to sea.

"Well!" I said to myself. "What next?"

I had not told Felipa we were going; I thought it best to let it take her by surprise. I had various small articles of finery ready as farewell gifts, which should act as sponges to absorb her tears. But Fate took the whole matter out of my hands. This is how it happened: One evening in the jasmine arbor, in the fragrant darkness of the warm spring night, the end came; Christine was won. She glided in like a wraith, and I, divining at once what had happened, followed her into her little room, where I found her lying on her bed, her hands clasped on her breast, her eyes open and veiled in soft shadows, her white robe drenched with dew. I kissed her fondly—I never could help loving her then or now—and next I went out to find Edward. He had been kind to me all my poor gray life; should I not go to him now? He was still in the arbor, and I sat down by his side quietly; I knew that the words would come in time. They came; what a flood! English was not enough for him. He poured forth his love in the rich-voweled Spanish tongue also; it has sounded doubly sweet to me ever since.

> "Have you felt the wool of the beaver?
> Or swan's down ever?
> Or have smelt the bud o' the brier?
> Or the nard in the fire?
> Or ha' tasted the bag o' the bee?
> Oh so white, oh so soft, oh so sweet is she!"

said the young lover; and I, listening there in the dark fragrant night, with the dew heavy upon me, felt glad that the old simple-hearted love was not entirely gone from our tired metallic world.

It was late when we returned to the house. After reaching my room I found that I had left my cloak in the arbor. It was a strong fabric; the dew could not hurt it, but it could hurt my sketching materials and various trifles in the wide inside pockets—*objets de luxe* to me, souvenirs of happy times, little artistic properties that I hang on the walls of my poor studio when in the city. I went softly out into the darkness again and sought the arbor; groping on the ground I found, not the cloak, but—Felipa! She was crouched under the foliage, face downward; she would not move or answer.

"What is the matter, child?" I said, but she would not speak. I tried to draw her from her lair, but she tangled herself stubbornly still farther among the thorny vines, and I could not move her. I touched her neck; it was cold. Frightened, I ran back to the house for a candle.

"Go away," she said in a low hoarse voice when I flashed the light over her. "I know all, and I am going to die. I have eaten the poison things in your box, and just now a snake came on my neck and I let him. He has bitten me, and I am glad. Go away; I am going to die."

I looked around; there was my color-case rifled and empty, and the other articles were scattered on the ground. "Good Heavens, child!" I cried, "what have you eaten?"

"Enough," replied Felipa gloomily, "I knew they were poisons; you told me so. And I let the snake stay."

By this time the household, aroused by my hurried exit with the candle, came toward the arbor. The moment Edward appeared Felipa rolled herself up like a hedge-hog again and refused to speak. But the old grandmother knelt down and drew the little crouching figure into her arms with gentle tenderness, smoothing its hair and murmuring loving words in her soft dialect.

"What is it?" said Edward; but even then his eyes were devouring Christine, who stood in the dark vine-wreathed doorway like a picture in a frame. I explained.

Christine smiled. "Jealousy," she said in a low voice. "I am not surprised."

But at the first sound of her voice Felipa had started up, and, wrenching herself free from old Dominga's arms, threw herself at Christine's feet. "Look at *me* so," she cried—"me too; do not look at him. He has forgotten poor Felipa; he does not love her any more. But *you* do not forget, señora; *you* love me—*you* love me. Say you do, or I shall die!"

We were all shocked by the pallor and the wild, hungry look of her uplifted face. Edward bent down and tried to lift her in his arms; but when she saw him a sudden fierceness came into her eyes; they shot out yellow light and seemed to narrow to a point of flame. Before we knew it she had turned, seized something, and plunged it into his encircling arm. It was my little Venetian dagger.

We sprang forward; our dresses were spotted with the fast-flowing blood; but Edward did not relax his hold on the writhing, wild little body he held until it lay exhausted in his arms. "I am glad I did it," said the child, looking up into his face with her inflexible eyes. "Put me down—put me down, I say, by the gracious señora, that I may die with the trailing of her white robe over me." And the old grandmother with trembling hands received her and laid her down mutely at Christine's feet.

Ah, well! Felipa did not die. The poisons racked but did not kill her, and the snake must have spared the little thin brown neck so despairingly offered to him. We went away; there was nothing for us to do but to go away as quickly as possible and leave her to her kind. To the silent old grandfather I said: "It will pass; she is but a child."

"She is nearly twelve, señora. Her mother was married at thirteen."

"But she loved them both alike, Bartolo. It is nothing; she does not know."

"You are right, lady; she does not know," replied the old man slowly; "but *I* know. It was two loves, and the stronger thrust the knife."

ÉMILE ZOLA (1840–1902)

From *Nana* (1880)

The French novelist Émile Zola, the son of a Greek-Italian engineer and a French mother, was born in Paris and grew up in Aix, near Marseille. After failing his baccalaureate exam twice, he worked as a journalist in the Latin Quarter in Paris. His first book of short stories, *Contes à Ninon* (*Tales for Ninon*), appeared in 1864. Profoundly influenced by the literary realism of Balzac and Flaubert, Zola held the view that the function of the artist was to describe society with as much "scientific" accuracy as possible. Moralism, fantasy, and sentiment were to be excluded; the novelist's sole responsibility was to explore the human "organism"—and the manifold social and psychological forces shaping its existence—in the way that a biologist might study a specimen under a slide. In the so-called Rougon-Macquart cycle, a series of twenty interlinked novels written between 1871 and 1893, Zola put this ambitious theory into practice. In the greatest works in the series—*La Fortune des Rougon* (1871), *L'Assommoir* (1877), *Nana* (1880), *Germinal* (1885), *La Terre* (1887), and *La Débâcle* (1892), he was largely successful: each of these novels combines powerful storytelling with a penetrating exposé of corruption, hypocrisy, and vice in Second Empire France. Zola was often attacked for his frankness: fastidious critics—Henry James among them—found the emphasis on brutality and squalor in his writing repugnant. Yet Zola was not one to shrink from controversy. In 1898, during the celebrated Dreyfus affair, he published *J'Accuse*, a fiercely polemical open letter to the French President in which he heroically defended Alfred Dreyfus, the Jewish army officer unjustly accused of treason by an anti-Semitic military tribunal. In the resulting fracas, Zola was forced to flee to England, where he lived for a year. He was pardoned by the government in 1900 but had only a couple of years to live; he was accidentally asphyxiated by fumes from a blocked chimney flue in 1902. Only after his death were his remarkable literary gifts unequivocally recognized: he was accorded a state funeral and interred in the Pantheon alongside Victor Hugo and other masters.

The sumptuously obscene *Nana*—perhaps the greatest of the Rougon-Macquart novels—is noteworthy for containing, among other things, the first representation in mainstream European literature of a lesbian bar. In the scene in question, the courtesan Nana, recently initiated into lesbian sex by her fellow prostitute Satin, accompanies

Satin to the infamous Café Laure, a Parisian drinking club for female homosexuals in the Rue des Martyrs. The episode is fascinating from several standpoints. It suggests not only that Paris had a well developed lesbian subculture as early as the 1870s—Zola is seldom inaccurate in his low-life details—but that "butch-femme" role-playing, now usually thought of as a strictly contemporary phenomenon, was already an established convention of underground urban lesbian life by the second half of the nineteenth century. The gritty, unflattering, almost snapshot realism with which Zola captures Café Laure's "bloated clientele" will remind some readers, perhaps, of the famous series of images of male impersonators and their feminine partners taken by the photographer Brassai at Le Monocle, a popular Paris lesbian club in the Boulevard Edgar-Quinet, in the 1930s. Reviewing *Nana* in 1880, Henry James—doubtless with the Café Laure scene in mind—spoke of the "singular foulness" and "monstrous uncleanness" of Zola's imagination.

FURTHER READING: Émile Zola, *Les Rougon-Macquart: Histoire naturelle et sociale d'une famille sous le second Empire*, ed. Colette Becker, et al., 5 vols. (Paris: Robert Laffont, 1991–93); —, *Nana*, trans. George Holden (Harmondsworth, Middlesex: Penguin, 1972); Henry James, *The Literary Criticism of Henry James: European Writers and the Prefaces*, ed. Leon Edel (New York: Library of America, 1984); Bernice Chitnis, *Reflecting on "Nana"* (New York: Routledge, 1991); Henri Troyat, *Zola* (Paris: Flammarion, 1992); Terry Castle, *The Apparitional Lesbian: Female Homosexuality and Modern Culture* (New York: Columbia University Press, 1993); Frederick Brown, *Zola: A Life* (New York: Farrar, Straus and Giroux, 1995).

> [*Abandoned by her lover Fontan, the prostitute Nana goes to Café Laure with her lesbian friend Satin.*]

The next day Fontan informed Nana that he was not coming home to dinner, and she went round early to find Satin, with a view to treating her to a meal in a restaurant. The choice of restaurant posed a difficult problem. Satin proposed various brasseries which Nana considered appalling, and finally persuaded her to dine at Laure's. This was a *table d'hôte* in the Rue des Martyrs where dinner cost three francs.

Tired of waiting for the dinner-hour, and not knowing what to do out in the street, the pair went up to Laure's twenty minutes too early. The three dining-rooms were still empty, and they sat down at a table in the very room where Laure Piédefer was enthroned on a high bench behind a counter. This Laure was a lady of fifty whose swelling contours were tightly laced by belts and corsets. More women came in one after another, and each one craned up to reach over the saucers piled on the counter and kiss Laure on the mouth with tender familiarity, while the monstrous creature tried with tears in her eyes to divide her attentions in such a way as to make nobody jealous. In complete contrast, the waitress who served these ladies was a tall, lean woman, with a ravaged face, dark eyelids and eyes which glowed with sombre fire. The three rooms rapidly filled up. There were about a hundred women there, who had seated themselves wherever they could find a vacant place. Most of them were enormous creatures in their late thirties, with bloated flesh hanging in puffy folds over their flaccid lips, but in the midst of all these bulging bosoms and bellies there were a few slim, pretty girls to be seen. These still wore an innocent expression in spite of their immodest gestures, for they were just beginners in their profession, picked up in some dance-hall and brought along to Laure's by one of her female customers. Here the crowd of portly women, excited by the scent of their youth, jostled one another in order to treat them to all kinds of dainties, paying court to them rather as a group of ardent old bachelors might have done. As for the men, there were very few of them—between ten and fifteen—and apart from four jolly fellows who had come to see the sight, and were cracking jokes, very much at ease, they were behaving very humbly in the midst of an overwhelming flood of petticoats.

"This grub of theirs is all right, eh?" said Satin.

Nana gave a satisfied nod. It was the old substantial dinner you get in a provincial hotel, and consisted of *vol-au-vent à la financière*, chicken and rice, kidney beans in gravy and *crème caramel*. The ladies fell with particular relish on the chicken and rice, almost bursting out of their bodices and wiping their lips with deliberate movements. At first Nana had been afraid of meeting some old friends who might have asked her stupid questions; but she was relieved to discover that there was nobody she knew in that motley throng, where faded dresses and lamentable hats mingled with expensive costumes in the fraternity of shared perversions. For a moment her attention was drawn by a young man with short curly hair and an insolent face, who was keeping a whole tableful of enormous women breathlessly attentive to his slightest caprice. But when the young man began to laugh, his chest swelled out.

"God, it's a woman!" she blurted out.

Satin, who was stuffing herself with chicken, looked up and murmured:

"Oh, yes, I know her. . . . A real good-looker, eh? You ought to see them fighting for her."

Nana pouted in disgust. That was something she still could not understand. However, she remarked in her sensible tone of voice that there was no point in arguing about tastes or colours, because you could never tell what you might like yourself one day. So she ate her *crème caramel* with a philosophical air, well aware that Satin with her big blue innocent eyes was throwing the neighbouring tables into a state of great excitement. There was one woman in particular, a plump blonde sitting near her, who was making herself very agreeable; she was so excited and attentive that Nana was on the point of intervening.

But at that moment a woman coming into the room gave her a shock of surprise, for she recognized her as Madame Robert. The latter, looking like a pretty brown mouse, gave a familiar nod to the tall thin waitress, and then came and leant on Laure's counter. The two women exchanged a lingering kiss. Nana thought that this was a very odd attention on the part of such a distinguished-looking woman, especially as Madame Robert's face no longer wore its modest expression. On the contrary, her eyes roved about the room as she chatted with the proprietress. Laure had just settled down once more with all the majesty of an old idol of vice, its face worn and polished by the kisses of the faithful. Behind the loaded plates she reigned over her bloated clientele of huge women, monstrous in comparison with even the largest among them, and enthroned in the opulence which was the reward for forty years as a hotel keeper.

But Madame Robert had caught sight of Satin. She left Laure and hurried over, full of charm, to tell her how sorry she was that she had not been at home the day before. But when Satin, utterly captivated, insisted on making room for her at the table, she swore that she had already dined: she had simply come along to have a look round. As she stood talking behind her new friend's chair, she leant lightly on her shoulders, smiling and asking her coaxingly:

"Now when shall I see you? If you were free . . ."

Nana unfortunately failed to hear any more. The conversation was annoying her, and she was dying to tell this respectable lady a few home truths. But the sight of a troop of new arrivals paralysed her. It was a group of smart women in evening dress, wearing their diamonds. Under the influence of perverse curiosity they had come as a party to Laure's—whom they all treated with easy familiarity—to eat her three-franc dinner, while flashing a fortune in jewels in the jealous and astonished eyes of poor, shabbily-dressed prostitutes. The moment they came in, talking loudly, laughing merrily and seeming to bring in sunshine with them from the outside world, Nana turned her head away sharply. To her intense annoyance she had recognized Lucy Stewart and Maria Blond among them, and for nearly five minutes—all the time the ladies chatted with Laure before passing into the next room—she kept her head down, and seemed busily engaged in rolling breadcrumbs into balls on the tablecloth. When at last she was able to look round, she was astonished to find the chair beside her empty. Satin had vanished.

"Where the devil has she gone?" she blurted out aloud.

The plump blonde who had been lavishing attentions on Satin laughed at her bad-tempered outburst; and when Nana, irritated by this laugh, scowled threateningly at her, she said in a languid drawl:

"It's not me, you know, that's pinched her from you—it's the other woman."

Nana realized that she would be laughed at if she said any more, and made no reply. She even kept her seat for a little while, not wanting to show how angry she was. She could hear Lucy Stewart laughing at the far end of the next room, where she was treating a whole tableful of girls from the dance-halls of Montmartre and La Chapelle. It was very hot; the waitress was carrying away piles of dirty plates smelling of chicken and rice; while four gentlemen had ended up by treating half a dozen couples to choice wine in the hope of making them tipsy and hearing some juicy titbit. What was annoying Nana now was the thought of paying for Satin's dinner. What a little bitch she was, allowing somebody to buy her a meal, and then scarpering with the first bit of skirt that came along, without so much as a thank-you. Admittedly it was only a matter of three francs, but it annoyed her all the same, the way it had been done. Nevertheless she paid up, throwing the six francs at Laure, whom she despised more at that moment than the mud in the gutters.

[*Returning later to her flat, Nana finds Fontan has locked her out. She goes to spend the night with Satin.*]

When she was out in the street, her first thought was to go and sleep with Satin, provided she had nobody with her. She found her standing outside her house, for she too had been turned out by her landlord, who had just had a padlock fastened to her door. This was illegal, of course, seeing that the furniture was her own; and cursing him roundly, she talked of hauling him in front of the local police commissioner. In the meantime, as midnight was striking, they had to begin thinking of finding a bed. And Satin, considering it inadvisable to involve the police in her affairs, ended up by taking Nana to a little hotel in the Rue Laval kept by a woman she knew. They were given a narrow room on the first floor, the window of which opened on to the yard.

"I'd rather have gone to Madame Robert's," said Satin. "There's always a corner there for me. . . . But with you that's out of the question. She's getting so jealous it's quite ridiculous; she beat me the other night."

When they had locked themselves in, Nana who had not yet relieved her feelings, burst into tears and recounted over and over again the dirty trick Fontan had played on her. Satin listened indulgently, comforting her and railing against the male sex even more indignantly than her friend.

"Oh, the swine, the swine! . . . We'll have nothing more to do with them, that's what we'll do!"

Then she helped Nana undress with all the gentle attentions of an adoring and submissive lover. She kept saying coaxingly:

"Let's go straight to bed, pet. We'll be better off there. . . . Oh, how silly you are to get all worked up! I tell you, they're dirty swine! Forget about them. . . . I'm here, and I love you. Don't cry now—just to please your little darling."

And, once in bed, she took Nana in her arms straight away to comfort her. She refused to hear Fontan's name mentioned again, and every time it returned to her friend's lips, she stopped it with a kiss, pouting in pretty indignation, her hair lying loosely on the pillow, and her face full of tender, childlike beauty. Little by little her gentle embrace persuaded Nana to dry her tears. She was touched, and returned Satin's caresses. When two o'clock struck the candle was still burning, and the sound of muffled laughter was mingling with words of love.

Suddenly a loud noise came up from the lower floors of the hotel, and Satin sat up, half-naked, listening hard.

"The police!" she said, turning pale. "God, that's just our luck! . . . We haven't a chance."

Time and again she had told Nana about the raids the police made on hotels; yet that night, when they had taken refuge in the Rue Laval, neither of them had given a thought to the danger they were running. At the word "police," Nana lost her head. She jumped out of bed, ran across the room, and opened the window with the panic-stricken look of a lunatic on the point of jumping out. Fortunately, however, the little yard had a glass roof which was covered with a wire grating on a level with their bedroom. Without a moment's hesitation she swung her legs over the window-sill, and with her chemise flying and her thighs bared to the night air, she disappeared into the darkness.

GUY DE MAUPASSANT (1850–1893)

"Paul's Mistress" (1881)

The French short-story writer Guy de Maupassant had a short but spectacular career. He was born in Normandy to aristocratic parents; the novelist Gustave Flaubert was a family friend. After serving in the military during the Franco-Prussian War, Maupassant worked as a civil servant (1873–80) and cultivated the relationship with Flaubert, who became his literary mentor. Maupassant's first story, "Boule de suif," was published in 1880 in a collection of short fiction, *Les Soirées de Médan*, edited by Émile Zola. Between 1881 and 1885 he produced nearly three hundred short stories—subsequently collected in *Le Maison Tellier* (1881), *Mademoiselle Fifi* (1882), *Contes de la Bécasse* (1883), and several other volumes—and six novels, including *Une Vie* (1883) and *Bel-Ami* and *Pierre et Jean* (1885). So masterful was the artistic technique displayed in these works—and so vivid the perception of contemporary social life—that Maupassant was quickly acclaimed, along with Flaubert and Zola, as one of the major exponents of the French realist school. He did not live long enough, however, to capitalize on his successes: following a steady physical and mental decline—the result of syphilis contracted in his youth—he was committed to an asylum at Passy in 1892 and died the following year.

Like Zola's *Nana*, the short story "Paul's Mistress" ("La Femme de Paul"), collected in *La Maison Tellier*, firmly, if at times melodramatically, associates lesbianism with moral squalor and degradation. In the picture of the pathetic Paul, driven mad by his jealousy over the faithless prostitute Madeleine, who abandons him for a male impersonator named Pauline at a river resort on the Seine, Maupassant indulges in naturalistic kitsch of a high order. Perhaps the most interesting aspect of the story is its "lesbianization" of those scenes and locales (outdoor cafés, boathouses, public gardens, river banks) typically associated with French impressionist painting. We seem here to look into a Manet or Renoir canvas in which the men, paradoxically, are really women and the women who love them know it.

FURTHER READING: Guy de Maupassant, *Contes et nouvelles*, ed. Louis Forestier (Paris: Gallimard, 1974–79); ——, *Romans*, ed. Louis Forestier (Paris: Gallimard, 1987;

—, *Boule de Suif: The Collected Novels and Stories of Guy de Maupassant*, trans. Ernest Boyd (New York: Knopf, 1924); Henry James, *Partial Portraits* (London: Macmillan, 1888); Francis Steegmuller, *Maupassant: A Lion in the Path* (New York: Grosset and Dunlap, 1949); Jeannette Foster, *Sex Variant Women in Literature* (1956; rpt. Tallahassee, Fla.: Naiad, 1985); C. Scott, "Divergent Paths of Pastoralism: Parallels and Contrasts in Maupassant's 'Une Partie de campagne' and 'La Femme de Paul,' *Forum for Modern Language Studies* 16 (1980): 270–80; Trevor A. Le V. Harris, *Maupassant in the Hall of Mirrors: Ironies of Repetition in the Work of Guy de Maupassant* (New York: St. Martin's, 1990); Rachel M. Hartig, *Struggling Under the Detective Glance: Androgyny in the Novels of Guy de Maupassant* (New York: Peter Lang, 1991); Sharon P. Johnson, *Boundaries of Acceptability: Flaubert, Maupassant, Cézanne, and Cassatt* (New York: Peter Lang, 2000).

The Restaurant Grillon, a small commonwealth of boatmen, was slowly emptying. In front of the door all was tumult—cries and calls—and huge fellows in white jerseys gesticulated with oars on their shoulders.

The ladies in bright spring toilettes stepped aboard the skiffs with care, and seating themselves astern, arranged their dresses, while the landlord of the establishment, a mighty, red-bearded, self-possessed individual of renowned strength, offered his hand to the pretty creatures, and kept the frail crafts steady.

The rowers, bare-armed, with bulging chests, took their places in their turn, playing to the gallery as they did so—a gallery consisting of middle-class people dressed in their Sunday clothes, of workmen and soldiers leaning upon their elbows on the parapet of the bridge, all taking a great interest in the sight.

One by one the boats cast off from the landing stage. The oarsmen bent forward and then threw themselves backward with even swing, and under the impetus of the long curved oars, the swift skiffs glided along the river, grew smaller in the distance, and finally disappeared under the railway bridge, as they descended the stream toward La Grenouillère. One couple only remained behind. The young man, still almost beardless, slender, with a pale countenance, held his mistress, a thin little brunette with the air of a grasshopper, by the waist; and occasionally they gazed into each other's eyes. The landlord shouted:

"Come, Mr. Paul, make haste," and they drew near.

Of all the guests of the house, Mr. Paul was the most liked and most respected. He paid well and punctually, while the others hung back for a long time if indeed they did not vanish without paying. Besides which he was a sort of walking advertisement for the establishment, inasmuch as his father was a senator. When a stranger would inquire: "Who on earth is that little chap who thinks so much of his girl?" some *habitué* would reply, half-aloud with a mysterious and important air: "Don't you know? That is Paul Baron, a senator's son."

And invariably the other would exclaim:

"Poor devil! He has got it badly."

Mother Grillon, a good and worthy business woman, described the young man and his companion as "her two turtledoves," and appeared quite touched by this passion, which was profitable for her business.

The couple advanced at a slow pace. The skiff "Madeleine" was ready, and at the moment of embarking they kissed each other, which caused the public collected on the bridge to laugh. Mr. Paul took the oars, and rowed away for La Grenouillère.

When they arrived it was just upon three o'clock and the large floating café overflowed with people.

The immense raft, sheltered by a tarpaulin roof, is joined to the charming island of Croissy by two narrow footbridges, one of which leads into the centre of the aquatic establishment, while the other unites with a tiny islet, planted with a tree and called "The Flower Pot," and thence leads to land near the bath office.

Mr. Paul made fast his boat alongside the establishment, climbed over the railing of the café, and then, grasping his mistress's hands, assisted her out of the boat. They both seated themselves at the end of a table opposite each other.

On the opposite side of the river along the towing-path, a long string of vehicles was drawn up. Cabs alternated with the fine carriages of the swells; the first, clumsy, with enormous bodies crushing the springs, drawn by broken-down hacks with hanging heads and broken knees; the second, slightly built on light wheels, with horses slender and straight, their heads well up, their bits snowy with foam, and with solemn coachmen in livery, heads erect in high collars, waiting bolt upright, with whips resting on their knees.

The bank was covered with people who came off in families, or in parties, or in couples, or alone. They plucked at the blades of grass, went down to the water, ascended the path, and having reached the spot, stood still awaiting the ferryman. The clumsy punt plied incessantly from bank to bank, discharging its passengers upon the island. The arm of the river (called the Dead Arm) upon which this refreshment wharf lay, seemed asleep, so feeble was the current. Fleets of yawls, of skiffs, of canoes, of podoscaphs, of gigs, of craft of all forms and of all kinds, crept about upon the motionless stream, crossing each other, intermingling, running foul of one another, stopping abruptly under a jerk of the arms only to shoot off afresh under a sudden strain of the muscles and gliding swiftly along like great yellow or red fishes.

Others arrived continually; some from Chatou up the stream; others from Bougival down it; laughter crossed the water from one boat to another, calls, admonitions, or imprecations. The boatmen exposed the bronzed and knotted muscles of their biceps to the heat of the day; and like strange floating flowers, the silk parasols, red, green, blue, or yellow, of the ladies bloomed in the sterns of the boats.

A July sun flamed high in the heavens; the atmosphere seemed full of burning merriment; not a breath of air stirred the leaves of the willows or poplars.

In front, away in the distance, the inevitable Mont-Valérien reared its fortified ramparts, tier above tier, in the intense light; while on the right the divine slopes of Louve-ciennes, following the bend of the river, disposed themselves in a semicircle, display-ing in turn across the rich and shady lawns of large gardens the white walls of country seats.

Upon the outskirts of La Grenouillère a crowd of pedestrians moved about beneath the giant trees which make this corner of the island one of the most delightful parks in the world.

Women and girls with yellow hair and breasts developed beyond all measurement, with exaggerated hips, their complexions plastered with rouge, their eyes daubed with charcoal, their lips blood-red, laced up, rigged out in outrageous dresses, trailed the crying bad taste of their toilettes over the fresh green sward; while beside them young men posed in their fashion-plate garments with light gloves, patent leather boots, canes the size of a thread, and single eyeglasses emphasizing the insipidity of their smiles.

Opposite La Grenouillère the island is narrow, and on its other side, where also a ferryboat plies, bringing people unceasingly across from Croissy, the rapid branch of the river, full of whirlpools and eddies and foam, rushes along with the strength of a torrent. A detachment of pontoon-builders, in the uniform of artillerymen, was encamped upon this bank, and the soldiers seated in a row on a long beam watched the water flowing.

In the floating establishment there was a boisterous and uproarious crowd. The wooden tables upon which the spilt refreshments made little sticky streams were cov-ered with half-empty glasses and surrounded by half-tipsy individuals. The crowd shouted, sang, and brawled. The men, their hats at the backs of their heads, their faces red, with the shining eyes of drunkards, moved about vociferating and evidently look-ing for the quarrels natural to brutes. The women, seeking their prey for the night, sought for free liquor in the meantime; and the unoccupied space between the tables was dominated by the customary local public, a whole regiment of rowdy boatmen, with their female companions in short flannel skirts.

One of them performed on the piano and appeared to play with his feet as well as his hands; four couples glided through a quadrille, and some young men watched them, polished and correct, men who would have looked respectable, did not their innate viciousness show in spite of everything.

For there you see all the scum of society, all its well-bred debauchery, all the seamy side of Parisian society—a mixture of counter-jumpers, of strolling players, of low journalists, of gentlemen in tutelage, of rotten stock-jobbers, of ill-famed debauchees, of old used-up fast men; a doubtful crowd of suspicious characters, half-known, half-sunk, half-recognised, half-criminal, pickpockets, rogues, procurers of women, sharpers with dignified manners, and a bragging air which seems to say: "I shall kill the first man who treats me as a scoundrel."

The place reeks of folly, and stinks of vulgarity and cheap gallantry. Male and female are just as bad one as the other. There dwells an odour of so-called love, and there one fights for a yes, or for a no, in order to sustain a worm-eaten reputation, which a thrust of the sword or a pistol bullet only destroys further.

Some of the neighbouring inhabitants looked in out of curiosity every Sunday; some young men, very young, appeared there every year to learn how to live, some promenaders lounging about showed themselves there; some greenhorns wandered thither. With good reason is it named La Grenouillère. At the side of the covered wharf where drink was served, and quite close to the Flower Pot, people bathed. Those among the women who possessed the requisite roundness of form came there to display their wares and to get clients. The rest, scornful, although well filled out with wadding, supported by springs, corrected here and altered there, watched their dabbling sisters with disdain.

The swimmers crowded on to a little platform to dive. Straight like vine poles, or round like pumpkins, gnarled like olive branches, bowed over in front, or thrown backward by the size of their stomachs, and invariably ugly, they leaped into the water, splashing it over the drinkers in the café.

Notwithstanding the great trees which overhang the floating-house, and notwithstanding the vicinity of the water, a suffocating heat filled the place. The fumes of the spilt liquors mingled with the effluvia of the bodies and with the strong perfumes with which the skin of the trader in love is saturated and which evaporate in this furnace. But beneath all these diverse scents a slight aroma of *poudre de riz* lingered, disappearing and reappearing, and perpetually encountered as though some concealed hand had shaken an invisible powder puff in the air. The show was on the river, where the perpetual coming and going of the boats attracted the eyes. The girls in the boats sprawled upon their seats opposite their strong-wristed males, and scornfully contemplated the dinner-hunting females prowling about the island.

Sometimes when a crew in full swing passed at top speed, the friends who had gone ashore gave vent to shouts, and all the people as if suddenly seized with madness commenced to yell.

At the bend of the river toward Chatou fresh boats continually appeared. They came nearer and grew larger, and as faces became recognisable, the vociferations broke out anew.

A canoe covered with an awning and manned by four women came slowly down the current. She who rowed was petite, thin, faded, in a cabin-boy's costume, her hair drawn up under an oilskin hat. Opposite her, a lusty blonde, dressed as a man, with a white flannel jacket, lay upon her back at the bottom of the boat, her legs in the air, resting on the seat at each side of the rower. She smoked a cigarette, while at each stroke of the oars, her chest and her stomach quivered, shaken by the stroke. At the back, under the awning, two handsome girls, tall and slender, one dark and the other fair, held each other by the waist as they watched their companions.

A cry arose from La Grenouillère, "There's Lesbos," and all at once a furious clamour, a terrifying scramble took place; the glasses were knocked down; people clambered on to the tables; all in a frenzy of noise bawled: "Lesbos! Lesbos! Lesbos!" The shout rolled along, became indistinct, was no longer more than a kind of deafening howl, and then suddenly it seemed to start anew, to rise into space, to cover the plain, to fill the foliage of the great trees, to extend to the distant slopes, and reach even to the sun.

The rower, in the face of this ovation, had quietly stopped. The handsome blonde, stretched out upon the bottom of the boat, turned her head with a careless air, as she raised herself upon her elbows; and the two girls at the back commenced laughing as they saluted the crowd.

Then the hullabaloo redoubled, making the floating establishment tremble. The men took off their hats, the women waved their handkerchiefs, and all voices, shrill or deep, together cried:

"Lesbos."

It was as if these people, this collection of the corrupt, saluted their chiefs like the war-ships which fire guns when an admiral passes along the line.

The numerous fleet of boats also saluted the women's boat, which pushed along more quickly to land farther off.

Mr. Paul, contrary to the others, had drawn a key from his pocket and whistled with all his might. His nervous mistress grew paler, caught him by the arm to make him be quiet, and upon this occasion she looked at him with fury in her eyes. But he appeared exasperated, as though borne away by jealousy of some man or by deep anger, instinctive and ungovernable. He stammered, his lips quivering with indignation:

"It is shameful! They ought to be drowned like puppies with a stone about the neck."

But Madeleine instantly flew into a rage; her small and shrill voice became a hiss, and she spoke volubly, as though pleading her own cause:

"And what has it to do with you—you indeed? Are they not at liberty to do what they wish since they owe nobody anything? You shut up and mind your own business."

But he cut her speech short:

"It is the police whom it concerns, and I will have them marched off to St. Lazare; indeed I will."

She gave a start:

"You?"

"Yes, I! And in the meantime I forbid you to speak to them—you understand, I forbid you to do so."

Then she shrugged her shoulders and grew calm in a moment:

"My dear, I shall do as I please; if you are not satisfied, be off, and instantly. I am not your wife, am I? Very well then, hold your tongue."

He made no reply and they stood face to face, their lips tightly closed, breathing quickly.

At the other end of the great wooden café the four women made their entry. The two in men's costumes marched in front: the one thin like an oldish tomboy, with a yellow tinge on her temples; the other filling out her white flannel garments with her fat, swelling out her wide trousers with her buttocks and swaying about like a fat goose with enormous legs and yielding knees. Their two friends followed them, and the crowd of boatmen thronged about to shake their hands.

The four had hired a small cottage close to the water's edge, and lived there as two households would have lived.

Their vice was public, recognised, patent to all. People talked of it as a natural thing, which almost excited their sympathy, and whispered in very low tones strange stories of dramas begotten of furious feminine jealousies, of the stealthy visit of well-known women and of actresses to the little house close to the water's edge.

A neighbour, horrified by these scandalous rumours, notified the police, and the inspector, accompanied by a man, had come to make inquiry. The mission was a delicate one; it was impossible, in short, to accuse these women, who did not abandon themselves to prostitution, of any tangible crime. The inspector, very much puzzled, and, indeed, ignorant of the nature of the offences suspected, had asked questions at random, and made a lofty report conclusive of their innocence.

The joke spread as far as Saint Germain. They walked about the Grenouillère establishment with mincing steps like queens; and seemed to glory in their fame, rejoicing in the gaze that was fixed on them, so superior to this crowd, to this mob, to these plebeians.

Madeleine and her lover watched them approach, and the girl's eyes lit up.

When the first two had reached the end of the table, Madeleine cried:

"Pauline!"

The large woman turned and stopped, continuing all the time to hold the arm of her feminine cabin-boy:

"Good gracious, Madeleine! Do come and talk to me, my dear."

Paul squeezed his fingers upon his mistress's wrist, but she said to him, with such an air: "You know, my dear, you can clear out, if you like," that he said nothing and remained alone.

Then they chatted in low voices, all three of them standing. Many pleasant jests passed their lips, they spoke quickly; and Pauline now and then looked at Paul, by stealth, with a shrewd and malicious smile.

At last, unable to put up with it any longer, he suddenly rose and in a single bound was at their side, trembling in every limb. He seized Madeleine by the shoulders.

"Come, I wish it," said he; "I have forbidden you to speak to these sluts."

Whereupon Pauline raised her voice and set to work blackguarding him with her Billingsgate vocabulary. All the bystanders laughed; they drew near him; they raised themselves on tiptoe in order the better to see him. He remained dumb under this downpour of filthy abuse. It appeared to him that the words which came from that mouth and fell upon him defiled him like dirt, and, in presence of the row which was beginning, he fell back, retraced his steps, and rested his elbows on the railing toward the river, turning his back upon the victorious women.

There he stayed watching the water, and sometimes with rapid gesture, as though he could pluck it out, he removed with his nervous fingers the tear which stood in his eye.

The fact was that he was hopelessly in love, without knowing why, notwithstanding his refined instincts, in spite of his reason, in spite, indeed, of his will. He had fallen into this love as one falls into a muddy hole. Of a tender and delicate disposition, he had dreamed of liaisons, exquisite, ideal, and impassioned, and there that little bit of a woman, stupid like all prostitutes, with an exasperating stupidity, not even pretty, but thin and a spitfire, had taken him prisoner, possessing him from head to foot, body and soul. He had submitted to this feminine witchery, mysterious and all powerful, this unknown power, this prodigious domination—arising no one knows whence, but from the demon of the flesh—which casts the most sensible man at the feet of some harlot or other without there being anything in her to explain her fatal and sovereign power.

And there at his back he felt that some infamous thing was brewing. Shouts of laughter cut him to the heart. What should he do? He knew well, but he could not do it.

He steadily watched an angler upon the bank opposite him, and his motionless line.

Suddenly, the worthy man jerked a little silver fish, which wriggled at the end of his line, out of the river. Then he endeavoured to extract his hook, pulled and turned it, but in vain. At last, losing patience, he commenced to tear it out, and all the bleeding gullet of the fish, with a portion of its intestines came out. Paul shuddered, rent to his heartstrings. It seemed to him that the hook was his love, and that if he should pluck it out, all that he had in his breast would come out in the same way at the end of a curved iron, fixed in the depths of his being, to which Madeleine held the line.

A hand was placed upon his shoulder; he started and turned; his mistress was at his side. They did not speak to each other; and like him she rested her elbows upon the railing, and fixed her eyes upon the river.

He tried to speak to her and could find nothing. He could not even disentangle his own emotions; all that he was sensible of was joy at feeling her there close to him, come back again, as well as shameful cowardice, a craving to pardon everything, to allow everything, provided she never left him.

At last, after a few minutes, he asked her in a very gentle voice:

"Would you like to go? It will be nicer in the boat."

She answered: "Yes, darling."

And he assisted her into the skiff, pressing her hands, all softened, with some tears still in his eyes. Then she looked at him with a smile and they kissed each other again.

They reascended the river very slowly, skirting the willow-bordered, grass-covered bank, bathed and still in the afternoon warmth. When they had returned to the Restaurant Grillon, it was barely six o'clock. Then leaving their boat they set off on foot towards Bezons, across the fields and along the high poplars which bordered the river. The long grass ready to be mowed was full of flowers. The sinking sun glowed from beneath a sheet of red light, and in the tempered heat of the closing day the floating exhalations from the grass, mingled with the damp scents from the river, filled the air with a soft languor, with a happy light, with an atmosphere of blessing.

A soft weakness overtook his heart, a species of communion with this splendid calm of evening, with this vague and mysterious throb of teeming life, with the keen and melancholy poetry which seems to arise from flowers and things, and reveals itself to the senses at this sweet and pensive time.

Paul felt all that; but for her part she did not understand anything of it. They walked side by side; and, suddenly, tired of being silent, she sang. She sang in her shrill, unmusical voice some street song, some catchy air, which jarred upon the profound and serene harmony of the evening.

Then he looked at her and felt an impassable abyss between them. She beat the grass with her parasol, her head slightly inclined, admiring her feet and singing, dwelling on the notes, attempting trills, and venturing on shakes. Her smooth little brow, of which he was so fond, was at that time absolutely empty! empty! There was nothing therein but this canary music; and the ideas which formed there by chance were like this music. She did not understand anything of him; they were now as separated as if they did not live together. Did his kisses never go any farther than her lips?

Then she raised her eyes to him and laughed again. He was moved to the quick and, extending his arms in a paroxysm of love, he embraced her passionately.

As he was rumpling her dress she finally broke away from him, murmuring by way of compensation as she did so:

"That's enough. You know I love you, my darling."

But he clasped her around the waist and, seized by madness, he started to run with her. He kissed her on the cheek, on the temple, on the neck, all the while dancing with joy. They threw themselves down panting at the edge of a thicket, lit up by the rays of the setting sun, and before they had recovered breath they were in one another's arms without her understanding his transport.

They returned, holding each other by the hand, when, suddenly, through the trees, they perceived on the river the skiff manned by the four women. Fat Pauline also saw them, for she drew herself up and blew kisses to Madeleine. And then she cried:

"Until to-night!"

Madeleine replied: "Until to-night!"

Paul felt as if his heart had suddenly been frozen.

They re-entered the house for dinner and installed themselves in one of the arbours, close to the water. They began to eat in silence. When night arrived, the waiter brought a candle enclosed in a glass globe, which gave a feeble and glimmering light; and they heard every moment the bursts of shouting from the boatmen in the large room on the first floor.

Toward dessert, Paul, taking Madeleine's hand, tenderly said to her:

"I feel very tired, my darling; unless you have any objection, we will go to bed early."

She, however, understood the ruse, and shot an enigmatical glance at him—that glance of treachery which so readily appears in the depths of a woman's eyes. Having reflected she answered:

"You can go to bed if you wish, but I have promised to go to the ball at La Grenouillère."

He smiled in a piteous manner, one of those smiles with which one veils the most horrible suffering, and replied in a coaxing but agonized tone:

"If you were really nice, we should remain here, both of us."

She indicated no with her head, without opening her mouth.

He insisted:

"I beg of you, my darling."

Then she roughly broke out:

"You know what I said to you. If you are not satisfied, the door is open. No one wishes to keep you. As for myself, I have promised; I shall go."

He placed his two elbows upon the table, covered his face with his hands, and remained there pondering sorrowfully.

The boat people came down again, shouting as usual, and set off in their vessels for the ball at La Grenouillère.

Madeleine said to Paul:

"If you are not coming, say so, and I will ask one of these gentlemen to take me."

Paul rose:

"Let us go!" murmured he.

And they left.

The night was black, the sky full of stars, but the air was heat-laden by oppressive breaths of wind, burdened with emanations, and with living germs, which destroyed the freshness of the night. It offered a heated caress, made one breathe more quickly, gasp a little, so thick and heavy did it seem. The boats started on their way, bearing Venetian lanterns at the prow. It was not possible to distinguish the craft, but only the little coloured lights, swift and dancing up and down like frenzied glowworms, while voices sounded from all sides in the shadows. The young people's skiff glided gently along. Now and then, when a fast boat passed near them, they could, for a moment, see the white back of the rower, lit up by his lantern.

When they turned the elbow of the river, La Grenouillère appeared to them in the distance. The establishment *en fête* was decorated with flags and garlands of coloured lights, in grape-like clusters. On the Seine some great barges moved about slowly, representing domes, pyramids, and elaborate monuments in fires of all colours. Illuminated festoons hung right down to the water, and sometimes a red or blue lantern, at the end of an immense invisible fishing-rod, seemed like a great swinging star.

All this illumination spread a light around the café, lit up the great trees on the bank, from top to bottom, the trunks standing out in pale gray and the leaves in milky green upon the deep black of the fields and the heavens. The orchestra, composed of five suburban artists, flung far its public-house dance-music, poor of its kind and jerky, inciting Madeleine to sing anew.

She wanted to go in at once. Paul wanted first to take a stroll on the island, but he was obliged to give way. The attendance was now more select. The boatmen, almost alone, remained, with here and there some better class people, and young men escorted by girls. The director and organiser of this spree, looking majestic in a jaded black suit, walked about in every direction, bald-headed and worn by his old trade of purveyor of cheap public amusements.

Fat Pauline and her companions were not there; and Paul breathed again.

They danced; couples opposite each other capered in the maddest fashion, throwing their legs in the air, until they were upon a level with the noses of their partners.

The women, whose thighs seemed disjointed, pranced around with flying skirts which revealed their underclothing, wriggling their stomachs and hips, causing their breasts to shake, and spreading the powerful odour of perspiring female bodies.

The men squatted like toads, some making obscene gestures; some twisted and distorted themselves, grimacing and hideous; some turned cart-wheels on their hands, or, perhaps, trying to be funny, posed with exaggerated gracefulness.

A fat servant-maid and two waiters served refreshments.

The café boat being only covered with a roof and having no wall whatever to shut it in, this hare-brained dance flaunted in the face of the peaceful night and of the firmament powdered with stars.

Suddenly, Mont-Valérien, opposite, appeared, illumined, as if some conflagration had arisen behind it. The radiance spread and deepened upon the sky, describing a large luminous circle of white, wan light. Then something or other red appeared, grew greater, shining with a burning crimson, like that of hot metal upon the anvil. It gradually developed into a round body rising from the earth; and the moon, freeing herself from the horizon, rose slowly into space. As she ascended, the purple tint faded and became yellow, a shining bright yellow, and the satellite grew smaller in proportion as her distance increased.

Paul watched the moon for some time, lost in contemplation, forgetting his mistress; when he returned to himself the latter had vanished.

He sought her, but could not find her. He threw his anxious eye over table after table, going to and fro unceasingly, inquiring for her from one person and then another. No one had seen her. He was tormented with uneasiness, when one of the waiters said to him:

"You are looking for Madame Madeleine, are you not? She left a few moments ago, with Madame Pauline." And at the same instant, Paul perceived the cabin-boy and the two pretty girls standing at the other end of the café, all three holding each other's waists and lying in wait for him, whispering to one another. He understood, and, like a madman, dashed off into the island.

He first ran toward Chatou, but having reached the plain, retraced his steps. Then he began to search the dense coppices, occasionally roaming about distractedly, or halting to listen.

The toads all about him poured out their short metallic notes.

From the direction of Bougival, some unknown bird warbled a song which reached him faintly from the distance.

Over the broad fields the moon shed a soft light, resembling powdered wool; it penetrated the foliage, silvered the bark of the poplars, and riddled with its brilliant rays the waving tops of the great trees. The entrancing poetry of this summer night had, in spite of himself, entered into Paul, athwart his infatuated anguish, stirring his heart with ferocious irony, and increasing even to madness his craving for an ideal tenderness, for passionate outpourings on the breast of an adored and faithful woman. He was compelled to stop, choked by hurried and rending sobs.

The convulsion over, he went on.

Suddenly, he received what resembled the stab of a dagger. There, behind that bush, some people were kissing. He ran thither; and found an amorous couple whose faces were united in an endless kiss.

He dared not call, knowing well that She would not respond, and he had a frightful dread of coming upon them suddenly.

The flourishes of the quadrilles, with the ear-splitting solos of the cornet, the false shriek of the flute, the shrill squeaking of the violin, irritated his feelings, and increased his suffering. Wild and limping music was floating under the trees, now feeble, now stronger, wafted hither and thither by the breeze.

Suddenly he thought that possibly She had returned. Yes, she had returned! Why not? He had stupidly lost his head, without cause, carried away by his fears, by the inordinate suspicions which had for some time overwhelmed him. Seized by one of those singular calms which will sometimes occur in cases of the greatest despair, he returned toward the ball-room.

With a single glance of the eye, he took in the whole room. He made the round of the tables, and abruptly again found himself face to face with the three women. He must have had a doleful and queer expression of countenance, for all three burst into laughter.

He made off, returned to the island, and threw himself into the coppice panting. He listened again, listened a long time, for his ears were singing. At last, however, he believed he heard farther off a little, sharp laugh, which he recognised at once; and he advanced very quietly, on his knees, removing the branches from his path, his heart beating so rapidly, that he could no longer breathe.

Two voices murmured some words, the meaning of which he did not understand, and then they were silent.

Then, he was possessed by a frightful longing to fly, to save himself, for ever, from this furious passion which threatened his existence. He was about to return to Chatou and take the train, resolved never to come back again, never again to see her. But her likeness suddenly rushed in upon him, and he mentally pictured the moment in the morning when she would awake in their warm bed, and would press coaxingly against him, throwing her arms around his neck, her hair dishevelled, and a little entangled on the forehead, her eyes still shut and her lips apart ready to receive the first kiss. The sudden recollection of this morning caress filled him with frantic recollections and the maddest desire.

The couple began to speak again; and he approached, stooping low. Then a faint cry rose from under the branches quite close to him. He advanced again, in spite of himself, irresistibly attracted, without being conscious of anything—and he saw them.

If her companion had only been a man. But that! that! He felt as though he were spellbound by the very infamy of it. And he stood there astounded and overwhelmed, as if he had discovered the mutilated corpse of one dear to him, a crime against nature, a monstrous, disgusting profanation. Then, in an involuntary flash of thought, he remembered the little fish whose entrails he had felt being torn out! But Madeleine murmured: "Pauline!" in the same tone in which she had often called him by name, and he was seized by such a fit of anguish that he turned and fled.

He struck against two trees, fell over a root, set off again, and suddenly found himself near the rapid branch of the river, which was lit up by the moon. The torrent-like current made great eddies where the light played upon it. The high bank dominated the stream like a cliff, leaving a wide obscure zone at its foot where the eddies could be heard swirling in the darkness.

On the other bank, the country seats of Croissy could be plainly seen.

Paul saw all this as though in a dream; he thought of nothing, understood nothing, and all things, even his very existence, appeared vague, far-off, forgotten, and closed.

The river was there. Did he know what he was doing? Did he wish to die? He was mad. He turned, however, toward the island, toward Her, and in the still air of the night, in which the faint and persistent burden of the music was borne up and down, he uttered, in a voice frantic with despair, bitter beyond measure, and superhumanly low, a frightful cry:

"Madeleine!"

His heartrending call shot across the great silence of the sky, and sped over the horizon. Then with a tremendous leap, with the bound of a wild animal, he jumped into the river. The water rushed on, closed over him, and from the place where he had disappeared a series of great circles started, enlarging their brilliant undulations, until they finally reached the other bank. The two women had heard the noise of the plunge. Madeleine drew herself up and exclaimed:

"It is Paul,"—a suspicion having arisen in her soul,—"he has drowned himself"; and she rushed toward the bank, where Pauline rejoined her.

A clumsy punt, propelled by two men, turned round and round on the spot. One of the men rowed, the other plunged into the water a great pole and appeared to be looking for something. Pauline cried:

"What are you doing? What is the matter?"

An unknown voice answered:

"It is a man who has just drowned himself."

The two haggard women, huddling close to each other, followed the manœuvres of the boat. The music of La Grenouillère continued to sound in the distance, seeming with its cadences to accompany the movements of the sombre fishermen; and the river which now concealed a corpse, whirled round and round, illuminated. The search was prolonged. The horrible suspense made Madeleine shiver all over. At last, after at least half an hour, one of the men announced:

"I have got him."

And he pulled up his long pole very gently, very gently. Then something large appeared upon the surface. The other boatman left his oars, and by uniting their strength and hauling upon the inert weight, they succeeded in getting it into their boat.

Then they made for land, seeking a place well lighted and low. At the moment they landed, the women also arrived. The moment she saw him, Madeleine fell back with horror. In the moonlight he already appeared green, with his mouth, his eyes, his nose, his clothes full of slime. His fingers, closed and stiff, were hideous. A kind of black and liquid plaster covered his whole body. The face appeared swollen, and from his hair, plastered down by the ooze, there ran a stream of dirty water.

The two men examined him.

"Do you know him?" asked one.

The other, the Croissy ferryman, hesitated:

"Yes, it certainly seems to me that I have seen that head; but you know when a body is in that state one cannot recognize it easily." And then, suddenly:

"Why, it's Mr. Paul!"

"Who is Mr. Paul?" inquired his comrade.

The first answered:

"Why, Mr. Paul Baron, the son of the senator, the little chap who was so much in love."

The other added, philosophically:

"Well, his fun is ended now; it is a pity, all the same, when one is rich!"

Madeleine had fallen on the ground sobbing. Pauline approached the body and asked:

"Is he really quite dead?"

The men shrugged their shoulders.

"Oh! after that length of time, certainly."

Then one of them asked:

"Was it not at Grillon's that he lodged?"

"Yes," answered the other; "we had better take him back there, there will be something to be made out of it."

They embarked again in their boat and set out, moving off slowly on account of the rapid current. For a long time after they were out of sight of the place where the women remained, the regular splash of the oars in the water could be heard.

Then Pauline took the poor weeping Madeleine in her arms, petted her, embraced her for a long while, and consoled her.

"How can you help it? it is not your fault, is it? It is impossible to prevent men from doing silly things. He did it of his own free will; so much the worse for him, after all!"

And then lifting her up:

"Come, my dear, come and sleep at the house; it is impossible for you to go back to Grillon's to-night."

And she embraced her again, saying: "Come, we will cure you."

Madeleine arose, and weeping all the while but with fainter sobs, laid her head upon Pauline's shoulder, as though she had found a refuge in a closer and more certain affection, more familiar and more confiding, and she went off slowly.

"WALTER"

From *My Secret Life* (1882–1894)

No one knows who wrote the vastly obscene sexual memoir *My Secret Life*; one modern editor suggests that it may be the work of Henry Spencer Ashbee, the wealthy Victorian book collector who edited several bibliographical volumes on classic pornography under the pseudonym Pisanus Fraxi in the 1870s and 1880s. The work first appeared in eleven volumes between 1882 and 1894 in Amsterdam—Ashbee had numerous contacts there—but any attribution must remain speculative.

Whoever he was—and assuming the events that he relates really happened—the author of *My Secret Life* was unquestionably a man of means and privilege, able to indulge his exorbitant sexual appetites to the fullest. His lubricious adventures are frequently repellent: he is nonchalant about his power over the women he meets (usually prostitutes) and seldom questions his right to exploit those below him on the social scale. Yet he is also a writer of unsettling honesty and intelligence, and for all of its squalors, his book is often surprisingly poignant. At least since the 1960s, when it was published above ground for the first time, *My Secret Life* has proved an invaluable resource for historians of Victorian sexuality and culture, even as it has also been recognized, more generally, as a masterpiece of its kind—surpassed in scope and psychological interest, perhaps, only by Casanova's erotic memoirs.

In the following excerpt from volume 9, "Walter" describes his lifelong interest in what he calls "flat fucking"—women making love to women—and an experimental night spent with his mistress Nellie and her fellow prostitute Rosa B. The Zolaesque portrait of Rosa—drunken, gaunt, and "screeching" with lust—is unforgettable. At the same time, the author confirms several "open secrets" about female same-sex desire: its deeply intoxicating yet psychologically mysterious effect on *men*; its prevalence among women who perform sexual acts for a living; its often melancholy existential undertow.

FURTHER READING: Anonymous, *My Secret Life*, ed. G. Legman, 2 vols. (New York: Grove, 1966); Steven Marcus, *The Other Victorians: A Study of Sexuality and Pornography in Mid-Nineteenth-Century England* (New York: Basic, 1964); Judith R.

Walkowitz, *Prostitution and Victorian Society: Women, Class, and the State* (Cambridge and New York: Cambridge University Press, 1980); —, *City of Dreadful Delight: Narratives of Sexual Danger in Late-Victorian London* (London: Virago, 1990); Colin Wilson, "Literature and Pornography," in Alan Bold, ed., *The Sexual Dimension in Literature* (London: Vision, 1982), pp. 202–19; Walter Kendrick, *The Secret Museum: Pornography in Modern Culture* (Berkeley and Los Angeles: University of California Press, 1987).

A month elapsed, during which I was chaste, then I had an erotic fit which lasted some time. Nelly L---- came to my aid, having long learnt the complete art of love. She took my sperm at times into her cunt, which now tho' so ample in size, was still a delightful grinder, and she was still handsome, and very beautifully formed. My second libation she at times drew labially, for I had now found it a delicious way of finishing the evening when fatigued, and I had several other concupiscent freaks which she satisfied; but being mostly similar to those done with other women, I omit description, two rather novel ones excepted.

I again had been reading about the sexual tricks of women with women, before that having scarcely thought about flat fucking since Sarah F----z----r had disappeared. Now the Lesbian games dwelt in my mind, and I stroked one or two French courtezans, solely to question them closely about the erotic performances of cunt with cunt.

(Just before what is about to be narrated took place, Nelly had been ill and I paid her rent during that time. She shewed her gratitude.)

French women were much more free spoken than the English, who mostly said they disliked to touch another woman's cunt, which I believed was a lie. One or two only, said they'd had a flat fuck with a friend, and what harm was there? One night a woman threw herself upon another before me, and with a sham wriggle said, "That's how we do it."

Nelly one evening in November got me another English woman, and she mounted her and jogged as if fucking, their cunts were close together, but they laughed,—I told her that she shammed, and should go elsewhere where I would see two women really and truly flat fucking. She thought she might lose me and so got serious. The other woman then said, "Nelly does it with Rosa B."—The only time I think I ever saw Nell thoroughly angry was then. She threatened to stick the other for saying so.—The woman who was a little in liquor said, "You do, Rosa flat cocked with me the other night, and told me she did it with *you*, *she* likes it, and *I* like it, I don't care a damn who knows it. Go to the bloody hell and suck her cunt, she says she sucks yours—there."—Nell threw a glass at her head which missed her, and with trouble I pacified them. Another night, Nell confessed that she did flat fuck occasionally with Rosa B. "She came from my village, is fond of me, and likes it, so I let her do it."—I have often found two harlots close friends when they came from the same village or place.

Nelly happened then to be hard up—no unusual thing—I promised her and friend a good fee if they'd flat fuck before me. She didn't think her friend would, but after a time a night was arranged for the entertainment. Nelly then said that the girl did not succeed in harlotting, that she often gave her food, that she sometimes stopped with her from Saturday night until Monday, they had been children together, she wasn't good looking now, and was thin and poorly clothed. She feared I should not like her. She also drank hard and was very fond of brandy, she told me.

One Saturday night I took a bottle of brandy for the tribades, and a bottle of sherry for my own drinking. The girl didn't come, Nell declared she had promised, but she was a funny girl and sometimes would not do it, tho generally she wanted to do it.— Just as tired of waiting, I told her she was humbugging me, she arrived, a middle sized, haggard woman, looking twenty-two or -three years old—with good features, a hectic flush on her cheeks, very thin, sadly shabby, and giving me the impression at once of her being a drunkard, lascivious, and being in a decline. I also recollected her features.

She kissed Nell, said, "Good evening sir," threw off her bonnet and, "Oh my God Nell, I've not had a mouthful to eat, since last night—I didn't get engaged, and hadn't a blessed mag to buy a loaf with—Mrs. ---- wouldn't lend me a penny as I owe a fort-night's rent, give me something to eat." I gave her money to buy with, and back she came with ham, beef, and rolls, and began voraciously to feed before Nell put it on the dish, it was painful to see her.—"Oh you've got brandy, give me a glass."—"Eat first," said Nell.—No, it would do her good to have some at once, or she should have wind on her stomach. In twenty minutes she had drunk three or four glasses, some with, some without water, and eaten a pound of meat. Then she began to laugh, be merry, and her face got very red.

I was impatient to see their flat fucking, and said so. Rising she gave Nell a kiss, and felt her cunt—Nell had only then her chemise on.—It makes me lewed to see a woman feel another's cunt. Then Rosa B. stripped to her chemise which was nice and clean. I pulled it off, and saw a very thin creature but straight and well formed, with a youthful looking cunt, darkish haired, and shewing as she stood with legs closed, a clitoris pro-jecting well from it. I examined her notch which was little enough, but the clitoris and nymphæ full sized. I then stripped Nell and looked at hers. Then we talked about flat fucking, cunt rubbing, clitoris', large and small—cock sucking, and fucking in general whilst we sat by the fire, we two drinking sherry, Rosa brandy and water, till to my astonishment I found her screwed and she'd emptied more than half the brandy bottle. Nell put the bottle out of her way.—"You've had enough, I don't want you tight again," said she.

Nelly was friskier with tipple than usual. I made myself naked, we all felt each other, then I set them to work. They laid on the bed feeling each other's cunts. Rosa was randiest yet for a moment seemed hesitating. "Never mind him,—he knows,—do it properly," said Nell.—Rosa mounted her, her thin thighs fitted in between Nell's fat ones, Nell raised her feet over the other's buttocks and they rubbed cunts together. I put my hand between Rosa's thighs, my thumb up her cunt, two fingers up Nell's, and felt the two cunts joined together. I could even see and feel that they were rubbing against each other. They moved at first quietly with gentle fucking motions, then their arses wriggled, Nell seemed agitated, the other at first noisy, then they breathed short, murmured, and with sighs of pleasure their limbs straightened out and they lay still. Both spent in a few minutes. Encouraged by me, they soon recommenced, Nell again raised her thighs and began moving her legs, but I had been long stiff, excited by the sight of this cunt rubbing, and could wait no longer, so telling my wants and pushing off Rosa, I got on to Nell, fucked her rapidly, and against my will my semen flooded her cunt so quickly, that she had no complete pleasure with me, I had only wound up her lewedness.

Her cunt was running over with my sperm as I slipped off on one side of her.— She was getting up but Rosa rushed at her, pushed her back, and began flat fucking her again.—"Let us do it before you wash," said she. Their cunts squeezed and squashed together with sound, as my mucilaginous libation was pressed between them. Rosa was noisy and ejaculating broken sentences. "His spunk's nice,—oh ain't it nice Nell?—it's on our cunts—what a lot—spend—dear—ohar."—Both now seemed absorbed in lewedness, and rubbed their cunts together furiously till they spent again. I stood with unwashed prick, enjoying the sight, feeling their naked flesh, stimulating their lewedness—"Rub your cunts together, rub my spunk up them—spend Nell—fuck her Rosa,"—I cried, till Rosa rolled off exhausted, their two cunts were in a lather of spendings as I opened their thighs to look, their hair was moist and sticking with sperm. I and Nell washed, but Rosa sitting down naked began eating the remainder of the meat, putting large lumps in her mouth. She had got the brandy and was helping herself, till Nell took it away again. We drank more sherry, Nell put on her chemise—Rosa at Nell's order washed her cunt and sat naked again, eating and drinking, we talked of flat fucking, and prick and cunt exercises of all sorts, for an hour or so.

The sherry was finished by that time, and Nell had had a little brandy and water which finally screwed *her*. Rosa was drunk and as lewed as if she had not been fucked for months. Drink seemed to have roused her to lascivious fury. Why didn't she wait till Nell had washed after I had fucked her? I asked.—Because she'd never done it to a woman who had just had a man.—Never?—Why she had never till tonight done it to a woman at all before a man, she replied. Then she told that she did it to two other girls but liked Nelly best, she loved Nelly, and getting up began spooning, kissing, and feeling her cunt, calling it a lovely cunt—Nell repulsed her but seemed to like it, said she had been asked by men but always denied she ever did it with a woman, and that she hated women. Both their tongues were now loosened, and they told lots about flat fucking until we were all randy again. I put them side by side on the bed, and looking at their cunts prepared to fuck Nell.—Rosa asked me to fuck *her*. "I thought you liked a woman best."—So she did, but she'd like to be fucked by *me*. "I can spend with *you*, I don't spend with men often."

Each then for a minute took my prick in their mouths in turn, such a madly lewed woman I don't recollect as Rosa, at that stage, she was ready for any thing. She dropped on her knees, pulled Nelly to the edge of the bed and gamahuched her. Nelly enjoyed that. Then I began fucking Nell. "Where is the dildo—where is the dildo?" Rosa hollowed.—"Hush don't make that row," said Nell. But Rosa knew where it was, and running to the drawers brought out a largish dildo.—I didn't then know that Nell possessed such a thing—threw herself on the bed half lying, half squatting by the side of us, thrust the dildo up her cunt, and began dildoing violently, looking at us fucking. We spent, and Rosa spent on the dildo, hollowing out baudy words and making such a noise, that Nell more sober, told her not to screech so—for screech it was—Rosa laid back, eyes shut, the dildo still sticking up her cunt, and for a minute or two we all were quiet.—As I pulled my prick out of Nell, Rosa got up to look at Nell's cunt—took the dildo out of her own, and drawing it thro her fingers and thumb to clean it, large drops of spendings dropped off it. She had put it up her cunt quite dry.—"Let's do it in his spunk Nell,—in his spunk"—said she, trying to flat fuck at the bedside—but Nell wouldn't, so she laid herself down on the bed and dildoed herself again—pulled the dildo out, threw it across the room, and dozed off, her face very red, her hair dishevelled. "She's drunk," said Nell.

We roused her by tickling. She got up, pissed and let a volley of farts.—"Go into the other room you dirty beast," said Nell angrily. The girl laughed a drunken laugh and said we all farted at times. Again we talked, I was not even yet satisfied, my voluptuous imagination suggested other baudy acts. Nell and I were still fresh, frisky and quite devil-may-care. Rosa suddenly got wild again on Nelly's cunt, and they flat fucked, Rosa screaming baudily and lovingly when spending.

We finished the brandy, Rosa then threw Nelly lengthwise on the bed, and gamahuched her for a full quarter of an hour. I knelt over her leaning against the head of the bedstead, and she sucked me whilst being gamahuched.—Then I dildoed Rosa's cunt from behind, and she licked Nell's cunt whilst I did it. Then Rosa sucked my cock—"Spend in my mouth, let it come, I like it."—She would have liked any sperm then—but I took it out, fearing that she in her drunkenness might bite it.—I finished by being sucked again by Nell, whilst I felt Rosa's cunt, who knelt on the bed to enable me to feel it easily. She began singing when kneeling and suddenly,—"Oh, you've made me want to piss"—and it began to squirt on to my hand.—"Don't piddle on the bed," said Nell savagely and relinquishing my cock.—"Let *me* suck him," said Rosa, still pissing, whilst turning round and trying to get at my doodle. But I finished in Nell's mouth, whilst Rosa was finishing her piddle in the pot, singing and yelling obscenely as she did so. I was exhausted and disgusted.

When I was leaving, Rosa had got into bed naked, but with her boots on, and was snoring. I thought now that I knew all about flat fucking and should not care about seeing it again, but all my letches seem to resuscitate, there is a periodicity in them. This evening terminated my ultra erotic amusements this year, to be resumed early in the year following.

I was with Nelly one or two days after, she was never shy about flat fucking after that night, and talked about it freely, said she liked a good straight poke with a nice man best, that it was only with Rosa B. she ever did it, that Rosa two years before was a handsome girl, but was killing herself fast with drink and libidinous excesses, would frig herself till nearly dead, would dildo herself by the hour.—She was also fond of flat fucking, there were three or four women who let her do it, and whenever she was dull she flew to her cunt—I never saw her after that night.

Nell some time after that told me that Rosa used to frig her own brother, a boy of fifteen, and he used to feel *her*, till they made better use of their privates, till her brother fucked her. Regular fucking went on for a year or two, for being brother and sister they got opportunity for lots of it, till the mother found them one day copulating. The story got wind in the village and Rosa came to London. One of her uncles came up to town to take her back, instead of which he fucked her into the family way.

This was likely enough, for among the poor, boys and girls amuse themselves with sexual tricks at an early age. They are thrown together, cannot be watched, and nature has its way. How many women I have known, who admitted feeling their brother's pricks, and having had their cunts felt by their brothers, been frigged by them, have frigged their brothers, and frigged themselves.—When such become whores, their craft makes them hide this, they sham ignorance, and men have the felicity of (as they suppose) teaching them.

(Rosa B. died two years after.)

AMY LEVY (1861–1889)

"Sinfonia Eroica (To Sylvia)," "To Lallie," "Borderland," "At a Dinner Party"

The poet and novelist Amy Levy—dubbed a "girl of genius" by Oscar Wilde—was born in London in 1861 and educated in Brighton. Her parents were cultivated English Jews; Levy herself was the first Jewish woman to study at Newnham College, Cambridge. While there she became acquainted with Constance Garnett, Vernon Lee, and the freethinking Olive Schreiner; her first book of poems, *Xantippe and Other Poems* (1881), reflects the ardent feminist views she imbibed from these and other Newnham contemporaries. It is possible (though much about her emotional history remains obscure) that she was for a time in love with Schreiner. Her second book of poetry, *A Minor Poet and Other Verse*—incorporating most of the poems from *Xantippe*— appeared in 1884, and her first novel, *Reuben Sachs*, in 1888. Her critical portrait of the London Jewish community made the latter something of a succès de scandale. It was followed by *The Romance of a Shop* (1888), a novel about three sisters who start a photography business, and *Miss Meredith* (1889), the story of a governess. Like her slightly younger contemporary Charlotte Mew, Levy suffered all her life from bouts of severe depression. In 1889, for reasons that remain unclear, she committed suicide by inhaling charcoal fumes. A final volume of poems, *A London Plane-Tree and Other Verse*, was published posthumously the same year.

Levy's poetry hints frequently at passionate and complex feelings for women. The dedicatee of "Sinfonia Eroica," on Beethoven's symphony, remains unknown; "To Lallie" may be about Vernon Lee. Levy is a master at dramatizing suppressed erotic excitement: a favorite motif—as in the brief yet unforgettable "At a Dinner Party"— is the quickening arousal that results when two people (two women?) exchange secret glances across a crowded room.

FURTHER READING: Amy Levy, *A Minor Poet and Other Verse* (London: T. Unwin, 1884); ——, *Reuben Sachs* (London: Macmillan, 1888); ——, *A London Plane-Tree and Other Verse* (London: T. Unwin, 1889); Melvyn New, ed., *The Complete Novels and Selected Writings of Amy Levy, 1861–1889* (Gainesville: University Press of Florida, 1993); Edward Wagenknecht, *Daughters of the Covenant: Portraits of Six Jewish Women*

(Amherst: University of Massachusetts Press, 1983); Emma Francis, "Amy Levy: Contradictions?—Feminism and Semitic Discourse," in Isobel Armstrong and Virginia Blain, eds., *Women's Poetry, Late Romantic to Late Victorian: Gender and Genre, 1830–1900* (New York: St. Martin's, 1999), pp. 183–204; Linda Hunt Beckman, *Amy Levy: Her Life and Letters* (Athens: Ohio State University Press, 2000).

Sinfonia Eroica

(To Sylvia)

My Love, my Love, it was a day in June,
A mellow, drowsy, golden afternoon;
And all the eager people thronging came
To that great hall, drawn by the magic name
Of one, a high magician, who can raise
The spirits of the past and future days,
And draw the dreams from out the secret breast,
Giving them life and shape.
   I, with the rest,
Sat there athirst, atremble for the sound;
And as my aimless glances wandered round,
Far off, across the hush'd, expectant throng,
I saw your face that fac'd mine.
   Clear and strong
Rush'd forth the sound, a mighty mountain stream;
Across the clust'ring heads mine eyes did seem
By subtle forces drawn, your eyes to meet.
Then you, the melody, the summer heat,
Mingled in all my blood and made it wine.
Straight I forgot the world's great woe and mine;
My spirit's murky lead grew molten fire;
Despair itself was rapture.
   Ever higher,
Stronger and clearer rose the mighty strain;
Then sudden fell; then all was still again,
And I sank back, quivering as one in pain.
Brief was the pause; then, 'mid a hush profound,
Slow on the waiting air swell'd forth a sound
So wondrous sweet that each man held his breath;
A measur'd, mystic melody of death.

Then back you lean'd your head, and I could note
The upward outline of your perfect throat;
And ever, as the music smote the air,
Mine eyes from far held fast your body fair.
And in that wondrous moment seem'd to fade
My life's great woe, and grow an empty shade
Which had not been, nor was not.
    And I knew
Not which was sound, and which, O Love, was you.

To Lallie

(Outside the British Museum)

Up those Museum steps you came,
And straightway all my blood was flame,
   O Lallie, Lallie!

The world (I had been feeling low)
In one short moment's space did grow
   A happy valley.

There was a friend, my friend, with you;
A meagre dame, in peacock blue
   Apparelled quaintly;

This poet-heart went pit-a-pat;
I bowed and smiled and raised my hat;
   You nodded—faintly.

My heart was full as full could be;
You had not got a word for me,
   Not one short greeting;

That nonchalant small nod you gave
(The tyrant's motion to the slave)
   Sole mark'd our meeting.

Is it so long? Do you forget
That first and last time that we met?
   The time was summer;

The trees were green; the sky was blue;
Our host presented me to you—
   A tardy comer.

You look'd demure, but when you spoke
You made a little, funny joke,
   Yet half pathetic.

Your gown was grey, I recollect,
I think you patronized the sect
   They call "esthetic."

I brought you strawberries and cream,
I plied you long about a stream
   With duckweed laden;

We solemnly discussed the—heat.
I found you shy and very sweet,
   A rosebud maiden.

Ah me, to-day! You passed inside
To where the marble gods abide·
   Hermes, Apollo,

Sweet Aphrodite, Pan; and where,
For aye reclined, a headless fair
   Beats all fairs hollow.

And I, I went upon my way,
Well—rather sadder, let us say;
   The world looked flatter.

I had been sad enough before,
A little less, a little more,
   What does it matter?

Borderland

Am I waking, am I sleeping?
As the first faint dawn comes creeping

Thro' the pane, I am aware
Of an unseen presence hovering,
Round, above, in the dusky air:
A downy bird, with an odorous wing,
That fans my forehead, and sheds perfume,
As sweet as love, as soft as death,
Drowsy-slow through the summer-gloom.
My heart in some dream-rapture saith,
It is she. Half in a swoon,
I spread my arms in slow delight.—
O prolong, prolong the night,
For the nights are short in June!

At a Dinner Party

With fruit and flowers the board is deckt,
The wine and laughter flow;
I'll not complain—could one expect
So dull a world to know?

You look across the fruit and flowers,
My glance your glances find.—
It is our secret, only ours,
Since all the world is blind.

CATULLE MENDÈS (1841–1909)

From *Lila and Colette* (1885)

Like many of his literary and artistic contemporaries, the late-nineteenth-century French writer Catulle Mendès—poet, novelist, dramatist, and cofounder in 1866 of the influential literary journal *Le Parnasse contemporain*—was captivated by the theme of love between women. Personal ties may have contributed to his interest: by virtue of his 1868 marriage to Judith Gautier, the daughter of Théophile Gautier, he had a personal connection with one of the founders of the "sapphic" school in France; and after 1870 he was also closely associated with the painter Gustave Courbet, whose 1866 painting *The Sleepers*, depicting two naked women draped in unconscious embrace on a divan together, was one of the most explicitly homoerotic works of art of its day.

Mendès's two most important works dealing with female homosexuality are written in radically contrasting styles. A five-hundred-page novel, *Méphistophéla* (1890), much influenced by Zola and Maupassant, is a flyblown account of a lesbian nymphomaniac whose incessant debaucheries lead to her alcoholism, drug addiction, and death. By contrast, *Lila and Colette* (1885), from which the prose poem "Lesbos" is extracted below, is a piece of flowery yet ingratiating fake Hellenism in a manner subsequently perfected by Pierre Louÿs in *Chansons de Bilitis*.

FURTHER READING: Catulle Mendès, *Histoires d'amour* (Paris: Alphonse Lemerre, 1868); —, *Les Poésies de Catulle Mendès* (Paris: Sandoz et Fischbacher, 1876); —, *Les Boudoirs de verre* (Paris: P. Ollendorf, 1884); —, *Contes choisis* (Paris: G. Charpentier, 1886); *Lila and Colette and The Isles of Love* (1885; rpt. New York: Boar's Head, 1949); —, *Méphistophéla* (Paris: E. Dentu, 1890); —, *Follies of Lovers*, trans. Keene Wallis (New York: Girard, Haldeman-Julius, 1927); Jeannette Foster, *Sex Variant Women in Literature* (1956; rpt. Tallahassee, Fla.: Naiad, 1985).

LESBOS

Muse! Since it is true that the daughters of Lesbos sometimes turn away from the masculine lips which covet them, and wend their way, in pairs, in the evening, conversing in whispers, in lanes of oleander, sing the divine anger from which their crime has arisen, and how they learned the mysteries of feminine hymeneals.

When Lesbos was a savage land, unapproached by man, all-burgeoning among the thorns of virgin lilies and wild roses, the young god Eros, one day, was hunting the boar in the black forests of Pepithymos. While he was sitting, a little tired, not far from a cave shut in by fallen stones, he heard a very soft voice speaking in an answer of sighs:

. . . O beautiful! O blonde! O white! O incomparably more charming than all the beautiful and than all the blonde and than all the white! Why do you turn away from me? Do you believe that I love any the less and that my caresses will be less burning because I am not the same as the detestable men whose embrace binds too painfully and whose kiss bites! It is not in the furious seas that the nymphs love to bathe, but in the calm pools of tepid envelopment; flee those stormy tormentors of the masculine passion, and yield to the cradling of my delicate and languid love.

And then to this voice, tender murmurs of consent replied.

Then Eros was stricken with a great anger! He was not pleased that the laws of eternal love, which he had established, should be transgressed and flouted by the young girls of the earth. He plunged into the cave, resolved to chastise the criminals. But, on seeing them, he stopped, amazed, for one of them—the entreated one who was consenting—he recognized as Kypris herself, against whom his power was naught; as for the temptress, she was a hamadryad called Perystera.

He thought a moment, then he said:

. . . Mother, go away, since punishment cannot touch you. But she there will not escape my vengeance.

He raised his dreaded right hand: Perystera, who never ceased being as white as the swans and snow, was changed into a dove, flapped her wings and flew into the murmuring woods. Through her, her new sisters, soon disdainful of the ring-doves, knew the charm of the guilty kiss, wherein beak glides into beak; and, later the girls of Lesbos, wandering beneath the boughs, felt troubled, on seeing one another beautiful, and on not refusing to one another their mouths, according to the example, alas! of the cooing doves.

HENRY JAMES (1843–1916)

From *The Bostonians* (1886)

Henry James, whom many would call the greatest of American novelists, was born into a wealthy and intellectually distinguished family in New York City in 1843. His father, Henry James Sr., was a Swedenborgian philosopher and friend of Emerson; his older brother was the pioneering psychologist William James. He was educated at home and abroad—he briefly attended Harvard Law School in 1862—and published his first story in 1864. (A back injury kept him out of the Civil War.) Over the next decade he published reviews and stories in the *North American Review* and *Atlantic Monthly* and read voraciously in American and European literature. After making the first of several adult visits to Europe in 1869, he settled permanently in London in 1876. His first important novel, *Roderick Hudson*, appeared in 1875 and was soon followed by *The American* (1877), *The Europeans* (1878), *Daisy Miller* (1879), and his first undisputed masterpiece, *The Portrait of a Lady*, in 1881. While James freely acknowledged his artistic debts to the great European realists—Balzac, Flaubert, George Eliot, and Turgenev especially—these early novels are already quintessentially "Jamesian" in their combination of breathtaking technique, refined psychological insight, and sophisticated international outlook. In the critically acclaimed *Daisy Miller* and *The Portrait of a Lady* in particular—both of which deal with wealthy American ingénues abroad—James first explored in depth the great theme which would preoccupy him for most of his creative life: the confrontation of America and Europe, innocence and experience, the New World and the Old.

In the 1880s, hoping to draw a broader popular audience, James turned to contemporary social and political issues in the three so-called naturalistic novels of his middle years, *The Bostonians* (1886), *The Princess Casamassima* (1886), and *The Tragic Muse* (1889). These works, however, met with only limited success. A six-year foray into theater proved disastrous; his play *Guy Domville* was booed off the London stage in 1895. Traumatized by the debacle, James retired to Rye on the southeast English coast and devoted himself to essays, travel writing, and prose fiction of an increasingly dense, morally complex, and stylistically uncompromising sort. A series of mighty masterpieces ensued: the short novels *What Maisie Knew* (1897), *The Spoils of Poynton* (1897), *The Turn of the Screw* (1898), and *The Awkward Age* (1899), and the three great "late" novels, *The Wings of the Dove* (1902), *The Ambassadors* (1903), and *The Golden Bowl* (1904). James returned to the United States once before his death—he registered his responses in *The American Scene* (1906)—but ultimately came to think of himself as more English than American. He became a British citizen, partly as patriotic gesture, during the First World War. James never married and, despite a series of powerful emotional attachments to handsome younger men—the poet Rupert Brooke, the novelist Hugh Walpole, and the sculptor Hendrick Andersen among them—may have been celibate all his life. He died in London in 1916 and his ashes were buried in Cambridge, Massachusetts.

The Bostonians, James's 1886 fictional study of the late-nineteenth-century women's movement, might be considered the first "lesbian novel" written in English— that is, the first nonpornographic work in Anglo-American literature to engage fully and self-consciously with the love-between-women theme. In that it takes the emotional defeat of a passionate woman as its subject, it is also the first *tragic* lesbian novel. Olive Chancellor, austere scion of a prominent Boston family and ardent proponent of women's rights, finds herself drawn to a beautiful young working-class woman, Verena Tarrant, whose uncanny gift for public speaking makes her—in Olive's view—an ideal worker for the feminist cause. The two become intimate friends and Olive brings Verena to live with her at her house on Charles Street, sublimating her passionate adoration of the younger woman into lavish fantasies about Verena's future as a feminist orator. Before Olive's dreams can be realized, however, fate intervenes in the form of her Southern-born cousin Basil Ransom, who falls in love with Verena and sets about luring her away from Olive. At the end of the novel, just as Verena is about to deliver an important address before a huge audience at the Boston Music Hall, she abandons the mortified Olive and runs off with Basil.

In his notes on the work James wrote that he wished to depict "one of those friendships between women which are so common in New England." So-called Boston Marriages—intense, usually asexual romantic friendships between financially independent educated or upper-class women—were frequent in late-nineteenth-century America: James's own invalid sister, Alice (1848–1892), lived for twelve years with a female friend, Katharine Peabody Loring, who nursed her in her many illnesses. ("There is about as much possibility of Alice's giving Katharine up," wrote James of his sister's relationship, "as of giving her legs to be sawed off.") Other prominent New England women who spent all or much of their lives in Boston Marriage-style arrangements included the journalist and feminist Margaret Fuller, the short-story writer Sarah Orne Jewett, and the actress Charlotte Cushman, who lived for many years both at home and abroad with the celebrated female sculptor Harriet Hosmer.

It is difficult to assess James's attitude toward female homosexuality. (He was later ambivalent about *The Bostonians* itself: it is the only one of his major novels he did not see fit to include in the comprehensive 1907–9 New York edition of his works.) At times he treats the hapless Olive satirically—as when he has a character in the fiction refer to Olive's passion for Verena as "a kind of elderly, ridiculous doll-dressing." Yet at other times—and the novelist's own subtly homoerotic orientation may be a factor here—he displays considerable sympathy for his lonely suffragist. In the two excerpts below—the first describing Verena's initial visit to Olive's house on Charles Street, and the second the older woman's panic and consternation when Verena goes out in a sail-boat with Basil at Cape Cod and doesn't return until dusk—this underlying sympathy manifests itself to particularly moving effect.

FURTHER READING: Henry James, *The Novels and Tales of Henry James*, New York Edition (New York: Scribner's, 1907–9); —, *The Complete Tales of Henry James*, ed. Leon Edel, 12 vols. (Philadelphia and London: Lippincott, 1962–64); —, *Autobiography*, ed. F. W. Dupee (New York: Criterion, 1956); —, *The Bostonians* (New York and Oxford: Oxford University Press, 1984); —, *The Complete Notebooks of Henry James*, ed. Leon Edel (New York and Oxford: Oxford University Press, 1987); Leon Edel, *The Life of Henry James*, 5 vols. (New York: Lippincott, 1953–72); —, *Henry James: A Life* (New York: Harper and Row, 1985); Judith Fetterley, *The Resisting Reader: A Feminist Approach to American Fiction* (Bloomington: Indiana University Press, 1978); Jean Strouse, *Alice James: A Biography* (New York: Houghton Mifflin, 1980); Lillian Faderman, *Surpassing the Love of Men: Romantic Friendship and Love between Women from the Renaissance to the Present* (New York: William Morrow, 1981); Alice James, *The Diary of Alice James*, ed. Leon Edel (Harmondsworth, Middlesex: Penguin, 1982); Esther D. Rothblum and Kathleen A. Brehony, eds., *Boston Marriages: Romantic but Asexual Relationships among Contemporary Lesbians* (Boston: University of Massachusetts Press, 1993); Terry Castle, "Haunted by Olive Chancellor," in *The Apparitional Lesbian: Female Homosexuality and Modern Culture* (New York: Columbia University Press, 1993), pp. 150–85; Lyndall Gordon, *A Private Life of Henry James: Two Women and His Art* (New York: Chatto and Windus, 1998).

[*Verena's arrival at Olive's home on Charles Street*]

"I was certain you would come—I have felt it all day—something told me!" It was with these words that Olive Chancellor greeted her young visitor, coming to her quickly from the window, where she might have been waiting for her arrival. Some weeks later she explained to Verena how definite this prevision had been, how it had filled her all day with a nervous agitation so violent as to be painful. She told her that such forebodings were a peculiarity of her organization, that she didn't know what to make of them, that she had to accept them; and she mentioned, as another example, the sudden dread that had come to her the evening before in the carriage, after proposing to Mr Ransom to go with her to Miss Birdseye's. This had been as strange as it had been instinctive, and the strangeness, of course, was what must have struck Mr Ransom; for the idea that he might come had been hers, and yet she suddenly veered round. She couldn't help it; her heart had begun to throb with the conviction that if he crossed that threshold some harm would come of it for her. She hadn't prevented him, and now she didn't care, for now, as she intimated, she had the interest of Verena, and that made her indifferent to every danger, to every ordinary pleasure. By this time Verena had learned how peculiarly her friend was constituted, how nervous and serious she was, how personal, how exclusive, what a force of will she had, what a concentration of purpose. Olive had taken her up in the literal sense of the phrase, like a bird of the air, had spread an extraordinary pair of wings, and carried her through the dizzying void of space. Verena liked it, for the most part; liked to shoot upward without an effort of her own and look down upon all creation, upon all history, from such a height. From this first interview she felt that she was seized, and she gave herself up, only shutting her eyes a little, as we do whenever a person in whom we have perfect confidence proposes, with our assent, to subject us to some sensation.

"I want to know you," Olive said, on this occasion; "I felt that I must last night, as soon as I heard you speak. You seem to me very wonderful. I don't know what to make of you. I think we ought to be friends; so I just asked you to come to me straight off, without preliminaries, and I believed you would come. It is so *right* that you have come, and it proves how right I was." These remarks fell from Miss Chancellor's lips one by one, as she caught her breath, with the tremor that was always in her voice, even when she was the least excited, while she made Verena sit down near her on the sofa, and looked at her all over in a manner that caused the girl to rejoice at having put on the jacket with the gilt buttons. It was this glance that was the beginning; it was with this quick survey, omitting nothing, that Olive took possession of her. "You are very remarkable; I wonder if you know how remarkable!" she went on, murmuring the words as if she were losing herself, becoming inadvertent in admiration.

Verena sat there smiling, without a blush, but with a pure, bright look which, for her, would always make protests unnecessary. "Oh, it isn't me, you know; it's something outside!" She tossed this off lightly, as if she were in the habit of saying it, and Olive wondered whether it were a sincere disclaimer or only a phrase of the lips. The question was not a criticism, for she might have been satisfied that the girl was a mass of fluent catch-words and yet scarcely have liked her the less. It was just as she was that she liked her; she was so strange, so different from the girls one usually met, seemed to belong to some queer gipsy-land or transcendental Bohemia. With her bright, vulgar clothes, her salient appearance, she might have been a rope-dancer or a fortune-teller; and this had the immense merit, for Olive, that it appeared to make her belong to the "people," threw her into the social dusk of that mysterious democracy which Miss Chancellor held that the fortunate classes know so little about, and with which (in a future possibly very near) they will have to count. Moreover, the girl had moved her as she had never been moved, and the power to do that, from whatever source it came, was a force that one must admire. Her emotion was still acute, however much she might speak to her visitor as if everything that had happened seemed to her natural; and what kept it, above all, from subsiding was her sense that she found here what she had been looking for so long—a friend of her own sex with whom she might have a union of soul. It took a double consent to make a friendship, but it was not possible that this intensely sympathetic girl would refuse. Olive had the penetration to discover in a moment that she was a creature of unlimited generosity. I know not what may have been the reality of Miss Chancellor's other premonitions, but there is no doubt that in this respect she took Verena's measure on the spot. This was what she wanted; after that the rest didn't matter; Miss Tarrant might wear gilt buttons from head to foot, her soul could not be vulgar.

"Mother told me I had better come right in," said Verena, looking now about the room, very glad to find herself in so pleasant a place, and noticing a great many things that she should like to see in detail.

"Your mother saw that I meant what I said; it isn't everybody that does me the honour to perceive that. She saw that I was shaken from head to foot. I could only say three words—I couldn't have spoken more! What a power—what a power, Miss Tarrant!"

"Yes, I suppose it is a power. If it wasn't a power, it couldn't do much with me!"

"You are so simple—so much like a child," Olive Chancellor said. That was the truth, and she wanted to say it because, quickly, without forms or circumlocutions, it made them familiar. She wished to arrive at this; her impatience was such that before the girl had been five minutes in the room she jumped to her point—inquired of her, interrupting herself, interrupting everything: "Will you be my friend, my friend of friends, beyond every one, everything, forever and forever?" Her face was full of eagerness and tenderness.

Verena gave a laugh of clear amusement, without a shade of embarrassment or confusion. "Perhaps you like me too much."

> [*Late in the novel, Verena has gone sailing with Basil Ransom. Olive, aware that her relationship with the younger woman is disintegrating, fantasizes Verena's death.*]

The afternoon waned, bringing with it the slight chill, which, at the summer's end, begins to mark the shortening days. She turned her face homeward, and by this time became conscious that if Verena's companion had not yet brought her back there might be ground for uneasiness as to what had happened to them. It seemed to her that no sailboat could have put into the town without passing more or less before her eyes and showing her whom it carried; she had seen a dozen, freighted only with the figures of men. An accident was perfectly possible (what could Ransom, with his plantation-habits, know about the management of a sail?), and once that danger loomed before her—the signal loveliness of the weather had prevented its striking her before—Olive's imagination hurried, with a bound, to the worst. She saw the boat overturned and drifting out to sea, and (after a week of nameless horror) the body of an unknown young woman, defaced beyond recognition, but with long auburn hair and in a white dress, washed up in some far-away cove. An hour before, her mind had rested with a sort of relief on the idea that Verena should sink for ever beneath the horizon, so that their tremendous trouble might never be; but now, with the lateness of the hour, a sharp, immediate anxiety took the place of that intended resignation; and she quickened her step, with a heart that galloped too as she went. Then it was, above all, that she felt how *she* had understood friendship, and how never again to see the face of the creature she had taken to her soul would be for her as the stroke of blindness. The twilight had become thick by the time she reached Marmion and paused for an instant in front of her house, over which the elms that stood on the grassy wayside appeared to her to hang a blacker curtain than ever before.

There was no candle in any window, and when she pushed in and stood in the hall, listening a moment, her step awakened no answering sound. Her heart failed her; Verena's staying out in a boat from ten o'clock in the morning till nightfall was too unnatural, and she gave a cry, as she rushed into the low, dim parlour (darkened on one side, at that hour, by the wide-armed foliage, and on the other by the verandah and trellis), which expressed only a wild personal passion, a desire to take her friend in her arms again on any terms, even the most cruel to herself. The next moment she started back, for Verena was in the room, motionless, in a corner—the first place in which she had seated herself on re-entering the house—looking at her with a silent face which seemed strange, unnatural, in the dusk. Olive stopped short, and for a minute the two women remained as they were, gazing at each other in the dimness. After that, too, Olive still said nothing; she only went to Verena and sat down beside her. She didn't know what to make of her manner; she had never been like that before. She was unwilling to speak; she seemed crushed and humbled. This was almost the worst—if anything could be worse than what had gone before; and Olive took her hand with an irresistible impulse of compassion and reassurance. From the way it lay in her own she guessed her whole feeling—saw it was a kind of shame, shame for her weakness, her swift surrender, her insane gyration, in the morning. Verena expressed it by no protest and no explanation; she appeared not even to wish to hear the sound of her own voice. Her silence itself was an appeal—an appeal to Olive to ask no questions (she could trust her to inflict no spoken reproach); only to wait till she could lift up her head again. Olive understood, or thought she understood, and the woefulness of it all only seemed the deeper. She would just sit there and hold her hand; that was all she could do; they were beyond each other's help in any other way now. Verena leaned her head back and closed her eyes, and for an hour, as nightfall settled in the room, neither of the young women spoke. Distinctly, it was a kind of shame. After a while the parlour-maid, very casual, in the manner of the servants at Marmion, appeared on the threshold with a lamp; but Olive motioned her frantically away. She wished to keep the darkness. It was a kind of shame.

"MICHAEL FIELD" [KATHERINE HARRIS BRADLEY (1846–1914) AND EDITH COOPER (1862–1913)]

"Erinna, Thou Art Ever Fair," "Atthis, My Darling," "Maids, Not to You," "Power in Silence," "Daybreak," "My Lady Has a Lovely Rite" (1889)

Katherine Harris Bradley, the daughter of a prominent Birmingham tobacco merchant, and her niece, Edith Emma Cooper, eighteen years her junior, formed one of the more unusual literary and emotional partnerships of the nineteenth century. The unmarried Bradley, a young woman with literary leanings and a powerful personality, helped raise Cooper almost from birth; after Cooper's mother, Bradley's married sister, became an invalid in 1865, Bradley moved in with her in order to help raise the infant Edith. Bradley and Cooper subsequently developed a profound romantic attachment to one another during Cooper's adolescence. They would live together for the rest of their lives—first with the Cooper family in Bristol, where both attended classes at University College and were involved in the suffrage and antivivisection movements, and later on their own in Reigate and Richmond. They began writing together in the 1880s, publishing *Bellerophon and Other Poems* under the names Arran and Isla Leigh in 1881. In 1884 they published the historical verse-drama *Callirrhoe* under the name "Michael Field" and kept the pseudonym after the work received good reviews. Under this nom de plume they subsequently produced twenty-six more plays and a series of books of poetry, including *Long Ago*—"an extension of Sappho's fragments into lyrics" (1889)—*Sight and Song* (1892), *Underneath the Bough* (1893), *Poems of Adoration* (1912), and *Mystic Trees* (1913).

The early books were well received—Browning, Meredith, Ruskin, and Wilde were all admirers—but the discovery in 1893 that "Michael Field" was in fact two women aroused hostility and suspicion among many contemporaries. "After the first flush of acclamation," writes the editor of their posthumously published memoirs, *Works and Days*, "their work was treated with ever-increasing coldness by the literary world, and there was no doubt that the discovery that Michael Field was no avatar . . . but two women, was partly responsible." In later years Bradley and Cooper lived in relative seclusion, going by the names "Michael" and "Henry" to each other and among intimate friends. Cooper died of cancer late in 1913, and Bradley, after nursing her, fell victim to the same disease a few months later.

The "Michael Field" poems testify to the intense, almost certainly sexual nature of their lifelong bond. "Of [Michael's] devotion to Henry," wrote their 1922 biographer,

Mary Sturgeon, "its passion, its depth, its tenacity and tenderness, it is quite impossible to speak adequately. From Henry's infancy to her death—literally from her first day to her last—Michael shielded, tended and nurtured her in body and spirit." While never explicit, their poems—lyrical, precise, and emotionally understated—are often strikingly erotic, especially those in *Long Ago* and *Underneath the Bough*. Of the love poems Bradley wrote for the dying Cooper in *Mystic Trees*, the admiring Sturgeon was moved to write, "it is doubtful whether Laura or Beatrice or the Dark Lady had a tenderer wooing."

FURTHER READING: "Michael Field" (Katherine Bradley and Edith Cooper), *A Selection from the Poems of Michael Field* (London: Poetry Bookshop, 1923); Mary Sturgeon, *Michael Field* (London: George Harrup, 1922); T. and D. C. Sturge Moore, *Works and Days* (London: J. Murray, 1933); David M. Robinson, *Sappho and Her Influence* (Boston: Marshall Jones, 1924); Charles S. Ricketts, *Michael Field*, ed. Paul Delaney (Edinburgh: Tragara, 1976); Jeannette Foster, *Sex Variant Women in Literature* (Tallahassee, Fla.: Naiad, 1985), pp. 141–45; Christine White, " 'Poets and Lovers Evermore': The Poetry and Journals of Michael Field," in Joseph Bristow, ed., *Sexual Sameness: Textual Differences in Lesbian and Gay Writing* (London and New York: Routledge, 1992), pp. 26–43; Yopie Prins, "A Metaphorical Field: Katherine Bradley and Edith Cooper," *Victorian Poetry* 33 (1995): 129–48; —, "Sappho Doubled: Michael Field," *Yale Journal of Criticism* 8 (1995): 165–86; —, *Victorian Sappho* (Princeton: Princeton University Press, 1999); Ruth Vanita, *Sappho and the Virgin Mary: Same-Sex Love and the English Literary Imagination* (New York: Columbia University Press, 1996); Emma Donoghue, *We Are Michael Field* (Bath: Absolute, 1998); Bette London, *Writing Double: Women's Literary Partnerships* (Ithaca, N.Y.: Cornell University Press, 1999).

Erinna, Thou Art Ever Fair

Πάρθενον ἀδύφωνον

Erinna, thou art ever fair,
Not as the young spring flowers,
We who have laurel in our hair—
Eternal youth is ours.
The roses that Pieria's dew
Hath washed can ne'er decline;
On Orpheus' tomb at first they grew,
And there the Sacred Nine,
'Mid quivering moonlight, seek the groves
Guarding the minstrel's tomb;

Each for the poet that she loves
Plucks an immortal bloom.
Soon as my girl's sweet voice she caught,
Thither Euterpe sped,
And, singing too, a garland wrought
To crown Erinna's head.

Atthis, My Darling

Τὸ μέλημα τοὐμόν

Atthis, my darling, thou did'st stray
A few feet to the rushy bed,
When a great fear and passion shook
My heart lest haply thou wert dead;
It grew so still about the brook,
As if a soul were drawn away.

Anon thy clear eyes, silver-blue,
Shone through the tamarisk-branches fine;
To pluck me iris thou had'st sprung
Through galingale and celandine;
Away, away, the flowers I flung
And thee down to my breast I drew.
My darling! Nay, our very breath
Nor light nor darkness shall divide;
Queen Dawn shall find us on one bed,
Nor must thou flutter from my side
An instant, lest I feel the dread,
Atthis, the immanence of death.

Maids, Not to You

Ταῖς κάλαις ἴμμιν [τὸ] νόημα τῶμον οὐ διάμειπτον

Maids, not to you my mind doth change;
Men I defy, allure, estrange,
Prostrate, make bond or free:
Soft as the stream beneath the plane
To you I sing my love's refrain;

Between us is no thought of pain,
 Peril, satiety.

Soon doth a lover's patience tire,
But ye to manifold desire
Can yield response, ye know
When for long, museful days I pine,
The presage at my heart divine;
To you I never breathe a sign
Of inward want or woe.

When injuries my spirit bruise,
Allaying virtue ye infuse
With unobtrusive skill:
And if care frets ye come to me
As fresh as nymph from stream or tree,
And with your soft vitality
 My weary bosom fill.

Power in Silence

I

Though I sing high, and chaunt above her,
Praising my girl,
It were not right
To reckon her the poorer lover;
 She does not love me less
For her royal, jewelled speechlessness,
She is the sapphire, she the light,
The music in the pearl.

I I

Not from pert birds we learn the spring-tide
 From open sky.
 What speaks to us
Closer than far distances that hide
In woods, what is more dear

Than a cherry-bough, bees feeding near
In the soft, proffered blooms? Lo, I
Am fed and honoured thus.

III

She has the star's own pulse; its throbbing
   Is a quick light.
She is a dove
My soul draws to its breast; her sobbing
   Is for the warm dark there!
In the heat of her wings I would not care
My close-housed bird should take her flight
   To magnify our love.

Daybreak

Shall there ever be a morn
   I might breathe beside her,
And yet choose to wake forlorn,
And yet choose to wake in death?
Eros, while my Love has breath
   I will breathe beside her.

My Lady Has a Lovely Rite

My lady has a lovely rite:
When I am gone
No prayer she saith
As one in fear:
For orison,
Pressing her pillows white
With kisses, just the sacred number,
She turns to slumber;
Adding sometimes thereto a tear
And a quick breath.

PIERRE LOUŸS (1870–1925)

From *The Songs of Bilitis* (1894)

The fin de siècle writer Pierre Louÿs was born in Belgium and educated in Paris at the École Alsacienne and the Sorbonne. His real name was Pierre Louis. In 1891 he founded a literary magazine, *La Conque*, to which Swinburne, Mallarmé, Valéry, and Gide subsequently contributed. His first book of poems, *Astarté*, appeared in 1891, followed by *Chansons de Bilitis* (*Songs of Bilitis*), a collection of prose poems presented as "translations" from a rediscovered ancient Greek original, in 1894. In 1896 he published the novel *Aphrodite*, a decadent fantasy set in ancient Alexandria; and in 1898, *La Femme et le Pantin*. He married in 1899. Louÿs is often associated with the so-called Parnassian poets of the middle and later nineteenth century (Catulle Mendès, Leconte de Lisle, Théodore de Banville, Théophile Gautier); and indeed his addiction to classical models, mania for form, and heady, often exotic sensualism would seem to place him in that morally inebriating but now little-read school.

Louÿs dedicated *Chansons de Bilitis*, the work by which he is primarily remembered, "to the young ladies of the society of the future." It purports to be a translation of lost Greek poems by one "Bilitis," a courtesan and member of Sappho's lesbian circle on Mytilene. In fact, as contemporary classicists were quick to deduce, Louÿs had written all of it himself. Its inauthenticity in no way diminished its appeal: like many famous literary hoaxes, it had a tremendous vogue in its day. The composer Claude Debussy set three *Bilitis* poems to music ("La Chevelure," "La Flute de Pan," and "Le Tombeau des Naiades"), and the work was quickly translated into English, German, Swedish, and Czech. Despite its campy excesses, the book has always had a powerful cachet in literate lesbian circles: as late as 1955, when the homophile activists Del Martin and Phyllis Lyon founded the first lesbian social and political action group in the United States, they called it (without irony) the Daughters of Bilitis.

Louÿs's sapphic pastiche undoubtedly owed much of its popularity to its lush and overheated eroticism. As Joan DeJean observes in *Fictions of Sappho*, the book was "destined to serve as a source of titillation for more than one generation of readers." But it also added substantially and influentially to the literary mythology of Sappho in the nineteenth century. (The lesbian poet Natalie Clifford Barney would subsequently dedicate her own sapphic fantasy, *Cinq petits dialogues grecs*, to Louÿs in 1902.) More insistently than either Baudelaire or Verlaine, Louÿs homosexualizes the Greek poet—by portraying her as an erotic pedagogue whose special vocation is to initiate young girls into lesbian pleasures. To the extent that *Chansons de Bilitis* tells a story, it has to do with the sexual rivalry of Sappho and Bilitis for Sappho's beautiful young protegée, Mnasidika. Bilitis ultimately wins Mnasidika, and before leaving Lesbos for Cyprus, lives with her for a time, "drunken with her saffron-scented skin."

FURTHER READING: Pierre Louÿs, *Les Chansons de Bilitis; Pervergilium Mortis; avec divers textes inédits*, ed. Jean-Paul Goujon (Paris: Gallimard, 1990); —, *Selections: L'Oeuvre érotique*, ed. Jean-Paul Goujon (Paris: Sortilèges, 1994); —, *The Songs of Bilitis*, trans. Alvah C. Bessie (1926; rpt. New York: Dover, 1988); —, *The Collected Works of Pierre Louÿs*, ed. and trans., M. S. Buck and J. Cleugh (New York: Liveright, 1932); Robert Cardinne-Petit, *Pierre Louÿs intime: Le Solitaire du Hameau* (Paris: J. Renard, 1942); Claude Farrère, *Mon ami Pierre Louÿs* (Paris: Domat, 1953); Édith Mora, *Sappho: Histoire d'un poète et traduction intégrale de l'oeuvre* (Paris: Flammarion, 1966); Harry P. Clive, *Pierre Louÿs (1870–1925): A Biography* (Oxford: Oxford University Press, 1978); Jean-Paul Goujon, *Pierre Louÿs: Une Vie secrète, 1875–1925* (Paris: Seghers, 1988); —, "Pierre Louÿs ou la subversion de la morale," *Europe: Revue Littéraire Mensuelle* 69 (1991): 61–68; Joan DeJean, *Fictions of Sappho 1546–1937* (Chicago: University of Chicago Press, 1989); Lawrence Venuti, "The Scandal of Translation," *French Literature Series* 22 (1995): 25–38; Margaret Reynolds, *The Sappho Companion* (New York: Palgrave, 2001).

Metamorphosis

I formerly was amorous of the beauty of young men, and the memory of their words, one time, would keep me long awake.

I remember having carved a name in the bark of a sycamore. I remember having left a fragment of my gown upon the road where one was wont to pass.

I remember having loved . . . Oh! Pannychis, my child, in what hands have I left you? How could I, unhappy one, have thus abandoned you?

Today Mnasidika alone possesses me, and will forever have me. Let her receive as sacrifice the happiness of those whom I have left for her.

Mnasidika's Breasts

Carefully, with one hand, she opened her tunic and tendered me her breasts, warm and sweet, just as one offers the goddess a pair of living turtle-doves.

"Love them well," she said to me, "I love them so! They are little darlings, little children. I busy myself with them when I am alone. I play with them; I pleasure them.

"I flush them with milk. I powder them with flowers. I dry them with my fine-spun hair, soft to their little nipples. I caress them and I shiver. I couch them in soft wool.

"Since I shall never have a child, be their nursling, oh! my love, and since they are so distant from my mouth, kiss them, sweet, for me."

The Doll

I have given her a doll, a waxen doll with rosy cheeks. Its arms are attached by little pins, and even its little legs can bend.

When we are together she places it between us in the bed; it is our child. At eventide she rocks it and gives it the breast before putting it to sleep.

She has woven it three little tunics, and on the Aphrodisian days we give it little jewels, jewels and also flowers.

She is careful of its virtue, and will not let it out alone; especially in the sun, for the little doll would melt and drip away in drops of wax.

Games

More than her baubles and her doll am I a play-thing for Mnasidika. For hours on end, unspeaking, like a child, she amuses herself with all my body's charms.

She undoes my hair and does it up again according to her fancy, sometimes knotting it beneath my chin like some heavy cloth, or twisting it into a knot behind my neck, or plaiting it until its very end.

She looks with wonder at the color of my lashes, or on the bending of my elbow-joint. Sometimes she places me on hands and knees:

And then (it is one of her games), she slips her little head underneath, and plays the trembling kid at nursing time beneath its mother's belly.

Shadowlight

We slipped beneath the transparent coverlet of wool, she and I. Even our heads were hidden, and the lamp lit up the cloth above us.

And thus I saw her dear body in a mysterious glow. We were much closer to each other, freer, more naked and more intimate. "In the self-same shift," she said to me.

We left our hair done up so that we'd be more bare, and in the close air of the bed two female odors rose, as from two natural censers.

Nothing in the world, not even the lamp, saw us that night. And which of us was loved and which the lover, she and I alone can ever tell. But the men shall never know a thing about it.

Intimacies

You ask why I am now a Lesbian, oh, Bilitis? But what flute-player is not lesbian a little? I am poor; I have no bed; I sleep with her who wishes me, and thank her with whatever charms I have.

We danced quite naked when we still were small; you know what dances, oh, my dear!: the twelve desires of Aphrodite. We look at one another, compare our nakedness, and find ourselves so pretty.

During the long night we become inflamed for the pleasure of the guests; but our ardour is not feigned, and we feel it so much that sometimes one of us entices her willing friend behind the doors.

How can we then love men, who are rude with us? They seize us like whores, and leave before we can attain our pleasure. You who are a woman, you know what I feel. You pleasure others as *you* would be pleased.

AUGUST STRINDBERG (1849–1912)

From *A Madman's Manifesto* (1895)

The Swedish playwright, novelist, and autobiographer August Strindberg, the child of a feckless aristocratic father and a servant woman, suffered all his life from acute shame over his father's mésalliance. His unstable, malignant personality and violent ambivalence toward women—his misogyny is legendary—may have originated in part in these troubling family circumstances. He began writing in the 1870s after leaving the University of Uppsala without a degree. His first important play, *Master Olaf*, was published in 1872, followed by the satirical novel, *The Red Room*, in 1879. He married the actress Siri von Essen, Baroness Wrangel, in 1877; but this union, like two later marriages in 1893 and 1901, ended in bitter divorce. (The fact that Strindberg openly vilified von Essen as a lesbian was undoubtedly a factor in their much publicized breach.) Between 1883 and 1889 he lived abroad and became increasingly notorious across Europe, especially after the appearance of *The Father* (1887), *Miss Julie* (1888), and *The Creditors* (1888), a trio of shockingly cynical naturalistic dramas. After a serious mental breakdown in Paris in 1894–96, Strindberg underwent a religious conversion—described in *Inferno* (1897)—and turned to Swedenborgian mysticism and the occult. His most productive period as a playwright followed. In *Advent* (1898), *There Are Crimes and Crimes* (1899), the three-part *To Damascus* (1898–1904), *A Dream Play* (1902), *The Ghost Sonata* (1907), and *Great Highway* (1909)—devoted primarily to religious and psychological themes—he pioneered modern expressionist and symbolist drama. It has sometimes been said that Strindberg mellowed after his spiritual conversion, but a perusal of *Black Banners*, the vitriolic satiric novel he published in 1907 about his third wife, Harriet Basse, should disabuse anyone of this notion. He died of cancer in 1912.

Strindberg wrote the autobiographical novel *A Madman's Manifesto* in French; it appeared under the title *Le Plaidoyer d'un fou* in 1895. Composed between 1887 and 1888, it is a thinly disguised attack on Siri von Essen, his much loathed first wife. By his own account, Strindberg originally intended to commit suicide after finishing the work and have it issued posthumously as a kind of fictional self-justification. Following his divorce from von Essen in 1892, he abandoned the suicide idea but ended up publishing the book anyway when his former wife's partisans denounced him. The novel

depicts in excruciating detail the collapsing marriage of Axel (Strindberg), a neurasthenic young writer, and the Baroness Maria (von Essen), a cross-dressing actress and
suffragist who repeatedly cuckolds him with various women. In the first of the two
excerpts below, he finds her sporting with their housemaid and begins to suspect her of
"monstrous" desires. In the second, after obsessively interrogating her about her
friendships with fellow actresses, he is forced to confront—glaringly—the further evidences of her homoeroticism. As a whole, *A Madman's Manifesto* powerfully evokes
the turbulent social climate of the 1880s and 1890s, in which so-called New Women—
like Siri von Essen, ardently in search of sexual and moral autonomy—came increasingly into conflict with unsympathetic husbands and fathers. At the same time, the
volatile mixture of sexual grotesquerie, burgeoning paranoia, and emotional violence
is classically Strindbergian.

FURTHER READING: August Strindberg, *Skrifter av August Strindberg*, ed. Gunnar
Brandell, 14 vols. (Stockholm: A. Bonniers Forlag, 1946–53); —, *A Madman's Mani-
festo (Le Plaidoyer d'un fou)*, trans. Anthony Swerling (University: University of
Alabama Press, 1971); —, *The Plays of August Strindberg*, trans. Michael Meyer, 2 vols.
(New York: Random House, 1964); —, *Strindberg's Letters*, ed. and trans. Michael
Robinson, 2 vols. (Chicago: University of Chicago Press, 1992); Michael Meyer,
Strindberg (New York: Random House, 1985); Margery Morgan, *August Strindberg*
(New York: Grove, 1985); John Eric Bellquist, *Strindberg as a Modern Poet* (Berkeley:
University of California Press, 1986); Michael Robinson, *Strindberg and Autobiography*
(Norwich: Norvik, 1986); Frederic Monneyron, "Strindberg et Proust: Deux écritures
de la jalousie au tournant du siècle," *Revue de Littéraire Comparée* 67 (1993): 473–91;
Ross Shideler, *Questioning the Father: From Darwin to Zola, Ibsen, Strindberg, and Hardy*
(Stanford: Stanford University Press, 1999).

[*Axel, a controversial novelist and playwright, struggles to support his
actress-wife and their children through a period of severe financial
hardship. Matters are not helped by his wife's flagrantly scandalous
doings.*]

With the new year, a general crash shook the credit of the old country, and the bank
from which Maria had lent me some shares went bankrupt. The termination of my loan
ensued. I was obliged to cover the guarantee which I had furnished with my effective
responsibility. It was a disaster. Fortunately, after interminable worries, the creditors
granted a settlement, so that I managed to obtain a year's grace.

It was the terrible year, the most terrible of all.

Once calm was re-established, I sought to get back on my feet as soon as possible.

Simultaneously with my duties as librarian, I started a great novel about contemporary behaviour; I filled the newspapers and the reviews with articles, while finishing the composition of my memoir. Maria, whose engagement at her theatre was expiring, obtained, through favour, its renewal for the year with a reduced salary of fourteen hundred francs . . . and there I was above her whom the crash had ruined.

In an execrable mood, she showered me with all her rancour, and, to re-establish equality between us, heeding only her independence, she attempted to obtain loans which only ended, as was to be expected, in recriminations against me. Through lack of intelligence, though motivated by excellent intentions, she was ruining me by seeking to save herself and to facilitate my task. And while being grateful to her for her goodwill, I could not abstain from reproaching her for her conduct.

Her cross-grained character inclined to underhandedness, and new incidents occurred which brutally revealed alarming states of her mind to me.

On the occasion of a masked ball which was given at the theatre, I formally made her promise not to disguise herself as a man. She promised me on oath, for I seemed to insist on it for reasons that I couldn't explain. Didn't I learn the following day that she had presented herself at the ticket office in a black suit and that she had supped with some gentlemen!

Besides the fact that the lie was most displeasing to me, the thought of that supper played on my nerves particularly.

"And so?" she retorted to my observations ". . . Aren't I free?"

"No," I replied, "you are married. And, since you bear my name, there is a solidarity between us. If you lose some of your reputation, my reputation also suffers by it, and even more than yours!"

"Then, I am not free? . . ."

"No, there is no-one who is free in a society where everyone bears the fate of his neighbour rivetted to his own. In short . . . if you had seen me supping with some ladies, what would you say? . . ."

She declared herself free to act all the same, free to destroy my reputation as she liked, free in everything and for everything! Ah! the savage, who understands by liberty the sovereignty of the despot, who tramples the honour, the happiness of everyone underfoot.

After that scene, turning into a quarrel and ending in tears, in a fit of hysteria, another one followed all the more upsetting because I was not initiated into the mysteries of genetic life, the anomalies of which appeared sinister to me as all those which one cannot grasp at first sight.

One evening, then, when the maid was busy making Maria's bed in the room next to mine, I heard small cries of suffocation, smothered, nervous, laughter, as if provoked by ticklings. It produced a strange pain in me, and giving way to an inexplicable anxiety, all ready to dissolve into fury, I brusquely pushed the door, which was pushed to, and I surprised Maria with her hands plunged into the bodice of the open-bloused maid, with her avid lips near to the breasts dazzling with a pearly whiteness.

"What are you doing there, you wretches! You are really mad," I exclaimed with a thundering voice.

"Well! what? . . . I am playing with the maid," Maria answered me brazenly. "Is it your business?"

"Yes, it is my business. Come here."

And, face to face, I explained to her the incorrectness of her conduct.

But she attacked what she grossly called my "dirty fantasy." She accused me of being a depraved person, who only sees shameful actions everywhere. It is dangerous to catch a woman in the act. She poured night-pots of insults on my forehead.

In the course of that discussion, I reminded her of the love that she had formerly confessed, that senseless love for the cousin, pretty Matilda. In the most innocent of tones possible, she replied that she herself had been most astonished at that love, not believing, she said, "that it was possible for a woman to fall in love like that with another woman with such madness."

Calmed by that naïve admission, I recalled, indeed, that right in the middle of a gathering, Maria, at my brother-in-law's, had proclaimed her amorous sentiments for the cousin, without blushing, without even being aware that she was making a mistake.

But I grew angry, however. In restrained terms, I advised her to abstain from those manoeuvres, perhaps innocent in the beginning, but quickly breaking out and capable of having deplorable consequences.

She talked nonsense, called me an imbecile—she always dubbed me as the most ignorant of the ignorant—and finally declared to me that I was lying.

What was the use of explaining to her that the law condemned [those accused of] crimes of this nature to hard labour? What was the use of convincing her that those touchings, exciting the pleasure of the recipient, were, in medical books, classed among the vices?

It was I who was debauched, since I was instructed in all those vices! And nothing was able to drag her from her innocent games.

She was one of those unconscious villains which it would be better to lock up in institutions of special education for women, rather than keeping them in one's home.

[*Having fled to France to escape enemies and creditors, Axel and his wife take up residence in a rackety artists' colony outside Paris. They become acquainted with a pair of Danish women: the bohemian "Miss Z."— painter and "self-styled woman of letters"—and her unnamed female lover. Miss Z., "the lettered friend," "the adventuress," or "friend number one," immediately begins to flatter Axel in order to get close to his wife.*]

Now, in Paris, the friends had become apostates. They made an alliance with my wife against me. Tracked down like a wild animal, I changed my battlefield, and, almost in penury, I managed to reach a neutral port, a village of artists near Paris. I had run into a trap where I remained a recluse for ten months, perhaps the worst in my life.

The society that I met there was composed of young Scandinavian painters, former apprentices to divers trades, of origins as diverse as strange; and, what was worse, of women painters, without scruples, emancipated from everything, frantic admirers of hermaphroditic literatures, so that they believed themselves the equals of men. To distract attention from their sex, they attributed certain male exteriorities to themselves, smoked, got drunk, played billiards, etc., and indulged in the games of love between one another.

That was the last straw!

It was the woman of letters who first paid a visit to me as one does to a great writer, which awoke the jealousy of my wife, at once prepared to attach that ally to herself, who seemed enlightened enough to appreciate the value of my reasons launched against the half-woman.

[*Flouting Axel's authority, Maria and Miss Z. enter into a close correspondence. In a fit of jealous paranoia, Axel unseals one of their letters.*]

The week which followed counts among the bitterest of my bitter life.

It was a question for me of waging a frightful combat against all the principles, inborn, inherited, or else acquired through education, in committing an offence. I resolved to unseal the letters which arrived addressed to Maria, in order to know where I stood! And despite the absolute confidence that I testified to her, for I authorised her to read all my correspondence during my absences, I still recoiled from that infraction of a sacred law, the most delicate obligation of the tacit social contract, never to violate the secret of a letter!

Nevertheless I was sliding down the slope. A day came when I no longer respected the secret. The letter was there, between my trembling fingers, unsealed, trembling as if they had unfolded the paper on which the mortal downfall of my honour could be read.

It was a composition of the adventuress, of the friend number one.

In mocking and scornful terms, she expatiated on my madness, vowing that the good God would soon deliver Maria from her martyrdom by quenching the last flickers of my troubled mind. After having copied down the most shameful phrases, I resealed the envelope and put off the presentation of the letter until the evening post. The moment having come, I gave the missive to my wife and I sat down near her to observe her.

Arriving at the point where a mention was made of the desire which was felt for my death—right on top of the sheet on page two—she laughed, with a ferocious laugh.

So the Adored could not see any other way out of her remorse than my death. Her supreme hope, to extract herself from the consequences of her crimes, consisted in seeing me promptly die. And when that event was accomplished, she would then draw my life insurance, the pension of the famous poet and would marry again or would remain, according to her fancy, a merry widow! The Adored! . . .

So *moriturus sum*, and I was going to hasten the catastrophe by giving myself up to absinthe, which alone made me happy, as well as to billiards which soothed my burning brain.

Meanwhile, a new complication arose, more terrible than all the others. The lettered friend, who affected to have taken a liking to me, made the conquest of Maria, who fell warmly in love with her to the point of giving birth to gossip. At the same time the comrade of the friend became jealous, and that was not conducive to attenuating the ugly rumours.

One evening, in bed, Maria, bewildered by our embraces, asked me if I was not in love with Miss Z . . .

"Ah! no, certainly not! An ignoble drunkard! You can't mean it?"

"I'm mad about her!" she replied. "It's strange, isn't it? . . . I'm afraid of remaining alone with her!"

"Because? . . ."

"I don't know! She's charming . . . An exquisite body . . ."

"Then . . ."

. . . .

[*After a raucous party at which Maria lets herself be fondled by a man, Axel berates her for her many "vices"—including the scandalous friendship with Miss Z. His anger abates when he learns that Miss Z. and her lover— accused of corrupting "a most beautiful local girl"—have been forced to leave the area. Yet when he realizes the apparent depth of Maria's passion for her tribadistic admirer, he gives way to near homicidal frenzy.*]

A week later, we had invited some friends from Paris, artists without scruples, without prejudices, with their wives.

The husbands came, but alone, the wives excusing themselves with pretexts too vague not to wound me cruelly.

It was an orgy. The scandalous conduct of the gentlemen riled me to the marrow.

They treated the two friends of Maria as whores. In the middle of the general drunkenness, I perceived my wife who was letting herself be kissed time and again by a lieutenant.

Brandishing a billiard cue over the heads of the imprudent pair, I demanded an explanation.

"He is a childhood friend, a relative! Don't make yourself ridiculous, my poor friend," retorted Maria. "Besides, it's the custom in Russia to kiss one another like this, point-blank, and we are Russian subjects."

"It's not true! Lie," exclaimed a friend . . . "Relatives, them, not on your life! Lie."
I was *almost* a murderer. I was going . . .

[. . .]

The mere idea of leaving the children without a father or mother held back my raised arm.

Alone together, I avenged myself and I administered to my Maria the chastisement she deserved:

"Whore!"

"Why?"

"Because you let yourself be treated as such!"

"You're jealous?"

"Yes, certainly; I am jealous; jealous of my honour, of the dignity of my family, of the reputation of my wife, of the future of my children! And your bad conduct has just banned us from the society of decent women. To let oneself be kissed like that in public by a stranger! Don't you know that you're nothing but a madwoman, since you can see nothing, can hear nothing, can understand nothing, and renounce all feelings of duty? But I will have you shut away if you don't mend your ways, and to begin with, I forbid your seeing your friends from now on."

"It was you who encouraged me to seduce the latest comer."

"In order to lay a trap for you and surprise you, yes!"

"Besides, have you proof of the nature of the relations which you suspect are established between my friends and myself?"

"Proof, no. But I have your admissions, which you have cynically told me. And then your friend Z . . . , hasn't she declared in front of me that she would be condemned to deportation for her morals if she were living in her own country?"

"I thought that you didn't recognise the 'vice'?"

"Let those wenches enjoy themselves as they like, it doesn't concern me, since it doesn't affect my family! But from the moment that that 'peculiarity,' if you prefer it, causes us trouble it becomes a prejudicial action for us. As a philosopher, there do not exist any vices for me, it's true, except in the sense of bodily or psychic defects. And when the Chamber of Deputies of Paris recently dealt with that question of the unnatural vices, all the noteworthy doctors rallied to this opinion, that the law has no business to interfere with those things, except in the case when citizens are affected in their interests."

But one might as well have preached to the fish! What was the use of thinking one could make that woman who only obeyed the urge of her bestial instinct understand a philosophical distinction!

In order to make a clean breast of those rumours in circulation. I sent off a letter to a devoted friend in Paris, beseeching him to tell me everything.

His reply frankly signified to me that, according to the accepted opinion of the Scandinavians, my wife might have an inclination towards illicit love and that the two

Danish damsels were in any case recognised as established tribads in Paris, where they frequented cafés in the company of other lesbians.

In debt in our pension, without resources, we had no possibility of escaping. Fortunately for us, the Danes, who had seduced a most beautiful local girl, brought the hatred of the peasants upon themselves, and were obliged to decamp. But the acquaintanceship, already formed for eight months, could not be brusquely broken like this, and as those two well-brought-up girls of good family had become companions in misfortune for me, I wanted to prepare an honourable retreat for them. To that end a farewell dinner was served in the studio of a young artist.

At dessert, drunkenness did not fail to appear, and Maria, carried away by her feelings, got up to sing a romance composed by her to the so well-known air of *Mignon*. In it she said her farewells to the Adored.

She had sung with zest, with such a true feeling, with her almond-shaped eyes, moistened with tears, sparkling in the reflection of the candles, she had opened her heart so widely, that, upon my word, I myself was moved and charmed by it! There was such a touching naïvety and sincerity in her song that every licentious idea disappeared on hearing that woman sing amorously of woman! A strange fact, she had not the manner nor the physiognomy of the man-woman, no, she was the loving and tender, mysterious, enigmatic, unfathomable woman.

And one ought to have seen the object of that love! A redheaded type, male face, hooked, hanging nose, fat chin, yellow eyes, cheeks puffed out from an excess of drink, with a flat breast, crooked hands, the most detestable, the most execrable thing it is possible to imagine, a type with which a farm hand would not have contented himself.

Her romance sung, Maria went to sit down beside the monster, who got up in her turn, took her head between her hands and with wide open mouth, sucked her lips by way of a kiss. "It's carnal love at least," I said to myself, and, clinking glasses with the redhead, I got her dead drunk.

She fell on her knees, looked at me with her big frightened eyes, with the hiccuping laughter of a cretin, with her body bundled up against the wall.

Never did I see such a monstrosity in human form and my ideas on the emancipation of women were thenceforth fixed.

After a scandal in the street, where the painter's strumpet was discovered sitting on a milestone and howling terribly between two vomitings, the party was closed, and the following day the two friends had left.

[...]

Maria went through a horrible crisis which only inspired me with pity, so much did she languish for her friend, so much did she suffer, offering the veritable spectacle of an unfortunate lover. She wandered alone in the wood, singing songs of love, sought out the favourite places of her friend, offered all the symptoms of a deeply wounded heart, so much so that I was seized with fear for her reason. She was unhappy and I did not succeed in distracting her. She avoided my caresses, pushed me away when I wanted to kiss her and I held that friend in mortal hatred, for she dispossessed me of the love of my wife.

Maria, more unconscious than ever, did not dissimulate the subject of her grief. Every echo resounded with her plaints and with her amorous pangs. It was unbelievable.

In the course of all these miseries, an assiduous correspondence was kept up between the friends, and one fine day, enraged at the enforced celibacy they made me undergo, I laid hands on a letter from the friend. It was a complete love-letter! My chick, my pet, the intelligent, the delicate Maria, with such noble feelings, etc.; her brutal husband was only a stupid brute! There was a question of attempts at abduction, at escapades . . .

I then rose up against the rival and, that very evening, a struggle, good Lord! a hand to hand struggle, was engaged in the moonlight between Maria and myself. She bit my hands. I dragged her, in order to drown her like a cat, to the edge of the river when all of a sudden the images of the children were evoked and gave me back my reason.

I prepared myself for suicide, but I wanted, before dying, to write the story of my life.

MARCEL PROUST (1871–1922)

"Before Dark" (1896) and two excerpts from *Cities of the Plain* (1921)

Marcel Proust, the greatest of modern European novelists, was raised in Paris by his wealthy bourgeois parents. His mother, who was Jewish, was from a cultured and well-educated family; his father was a professor of public health. At the age of nine Proust developed severe asthma and allergies, the first signs of an acute and lifelong physical frailty. After serving briefly in the military, he studied law and philosophy at the Sorbonne (1893–95) then immersed himself in Paris salon life and fashionable society. Largely in secret—publicly he cultivated the reputation of dandy and dilettante—he began writing a vast autobiographical novel, *Jean Santeuil*. Although this novel was subsequently abandoned, it served as a kind of dress rehearsal for the great creative work of his maturity. He published his first book of stories, *Les Plaisirs et les jours* (*Pleasures and Days*), in 1896.

After his mother's death in 1905, Proust's health worsened and he withdrew from society, ultimately sequestering himself—famously—in a dark, cork-lined bedroom, where he embraced the role of full-time invalid. For almost all of the rest of his life he remained in this womblike retreat, attended by servants and a valet-chauffeur named Alfred Agostinelli, who was also his homosexual lover. Some time around 1909, he began writing his seven-volume masterpiece, *À la recherche du temps perdu* (*Remembrance of Things Past*). Based on his own multifarious experience of the haute monde, the work is at once a scintillating portrait of Parisian high life during the Third Republic and perhaps the greatest autobiographical fiction ever written. Its merits were slow to be appreciated. The complex prose style and boldly experimental narrative technique scared off numerous would-be publishers; Proust had to have the first volume, *Du Côté de chez Swann* (*Swann's Way*), printed at his own expense in 1913. Yet by the time the second part, *À l'ombre des jeunes filles en fleurs* (*Within a Budding Grove*), was published in 1918, the scope of his achievement had begun to come into view. He won the Prix Goncourt the following year. The third and fourth volumes, *Le Côté de Guermantes* (*Guermantes Way*) and *Sodome et Gomorrhe* (*Cities of the Plain*), appeared to international acclaim in 1921. Proust did not live, unfortunately, to see the three final volumes in print: he died in 1922 and *La Prisonnière* (*The Captive*), *Albertine disparue* (*The Sweet Cheat Gone*), and *Le Temps retrouvé* (*The Past Recaptured*)—were published posthumously between 1923 and 1927. The entire work was translated into English by C. K. Scott Moncrieff and Stephen Hudson between 1922 and 1931.

Proust's novels represent one of the richest troves of lesbian-related material in all of nineteenth- and twentieth-century literature. Like Émile Zola, Guy de Maupassant, Paul Bourget, Catulle de Mendès, Rachilde, and countless other late-nineteenth-century "decadent" French writers, Proust was captivated by the lesbian theme, yet exploited it more artfully and intuitively than any of his precursors. It is a central element in *À la recherche du temps perdu*. Proust's psychological epic is at bottom a tale of unrequited (and perverse) passion: Marcel, the sensitive, neurasthenic narrator, is in love with Albertine, a gorgeous young woman of flagrantly sapphic disposition. Even as he pursues her—and she flirts with him—he is agonizingly aware that her love of women makes any real sexual communion between them impossible. Biographers have sometimes read into this scenario a disguised version of Proust's own emotional situation. Homosexual in a society in which such unorthodoxy could seldom be acknowledged, he found little lasting satisfaction in erotic life and was prone to forming masochistic attachments with young men—such as Agostinelli—who humiliated him in one way or another. Rightly or wrongly, it has often been supposed that the attribution of lesbianism to Albertine was a way for Proust of retaining the pathos of the homosexual theme ("that sterile love") without compromising the putative heterosexuality of his autobiographical hero, Marcel.

With this sense of biographical determinants undoubtedly in mind, some readers—Colette and Natalie Barney among them—have found Proust's lesbian character portraits psychologically unconvincing. Yet other readers, such as Jeannette Foster, strongly disagree. "The types he portrays," writes Foster in *Sex Variant Women in Literature*, "their various interconnections, and most of their psychology, ring perfectly true for any group of young female sophisticates." The reader may decide for himself or herself: the two selections below—the ravishing yet enigmatic short story "Before Dark," from *Pleasures and Days*, and Marcel's febrile description of the faithless Albertine from *The Cities of the Plain* (1921)—can be considered characteristic sapphic moments in the Proustian oeuvre.

FURTHER READING: Marcel Proust, *À la recherche du temps perdu*, 15 vols. (Paris: Gallimard, 1954); —, *Remembrance of Things Past*, trans. C. K. Scott Moncrieff and Terence Kilmartin, 3 vols. (New York: Random House, 1982); —, "Before Dark," trans. Richard Howard, in Seymour Kleinberg, ed., *The Other Persuasion: Short Fiction about Gay Men and Women* (New York: Vintage, 1977); —, *Pleasures and Days*, trans. Louise Varese (New York: Ecco, 1984); George Painter, *Marcel Proust: A Biography*, rev. ed. (London: Chatto and Windus, 1989); Jeannette Foster, *Sex Variant Women in Literature* (1956; rpt. Tallahassee, Fla.: Naiad, 1985); J. E. Rivers, *Proust and the Art of Love: The Aesthetics of Sexuality in the Life, Times, and Art of Marcel Proust* (New York: Columbia Press, 1980); Eve Kosofsky Sedgwick, "Proust and the Spectacle of the Closet," in

Epistemology of the Closet (Berkeley: University of California Press, 1990), pp. 213–51; Reginald L. McGinnis, "L'Inconnaissable Gomorrhe: À propos d'*Albertine disparue*," *Romanic Review* 81 (1990): 92–104; Mieke Bal, "Bird Watching: Visuality and Lesbian Desire in Marcel Proust's *À la recherche du temps perdu*," *Thamyris* 2 (1995): 45–66; Gregory Woods, "Marcel Proust," in Claude J. Summers, ed., *The Gay and Lesbian Literary Heritage* (New York: Henry Holt, 1995), pp. 569–74; Colleen Lamos, *Deviant Modernism: Sexual and Textual Errancy in T. S. Eliot, James Joyce, and Marcel Proust* (Cambridge: Cambridge University Press, 1998); Elizabeth Ladenson, *Proust's Lesbianism* (Ithaca, N.Y.: Cornell University Press, 1999); Edmund White, *Marcel Proust* (New York: Viking, 1999); William C. Carter, *Marcel Proust: A Life* (New Haven: Yale University Press, 2000); Tadié, Jean-Yues, *Marcel Proust: A Life*, trans. Euan Cameron (Harmondsworth, Middlesex: Penguin, 2000); Jacqueline Rose, *Albertine* (London: Chatto and Windus, 2001).

Before Dark

"Though I'm still quite strong, you know" (she said to me with something more intimate in her voice, the way we use our inflections to attenuate something we must tell those we love, something too harsh), "I might die from one day to the next—yet I'm still capable of living several months more. So I don't want to wait any longer to tell you something that's weighing on my conscience; you'll understand later how painful it was for me to speak of it." Her pupils, symbolic blue flowers, paled as if they were withering. I thought she was about to cry, but no tears came. "I know I'm deliberately destroying all hope of being admired by my best friend after I die, tarnishing the memory I sometimes imagine he might have kept of my life—a life lovelier, more harmonious than it has really been. But the claims of an esthetic arrangement"—she smiled, uttering the phrase with the tiny ironical exaggeration that always came into her voice at such moments, rare though they were in her conversation—"cannot suppress the need for truth that forces me to speak. Listen to me, Leslie, I must tell you . . . But before I do, give me my coat—it's chilly out here on the terrace, and the doctor doesn't want me getting up and down, if I can help it."

I put her coat around her. The sun had set, and the sea, glimpsed through the apple trees, was mauve. Fragile as withered wreathes and persistent as regrets, tiny pink and blue clouds were floating on the horizon. A melancholy row of poplars led away into the shadows, heads bowed in a churchly pink, resigned. The last rays of the sun, without touching their trunks, tinged their branches, fastening garlands of light to those balustrades of shadow. The breeze mingled three odors: the sea, wet leaves, milk. Never had the Norman countryside sweetened the evening sadness with a more voluptuous touch, but I had no taste for it, so stirred was I by my friend's mysterious words.

"I have loved you a great deal, but I have given you very little, my poor friend—"

"—Forgive me, Françoise, if I break all the rules of this literary form and interrupt a confession I should have heard out in silence," I exclaimed, trying to make a joke to calm her a little, but in reality deadly sad. "How can you say you have given me very little? You have given me all the more in that I asked you for less—much more in fact than if the senses had had a share in our affection. I have adored you, and you have tended me, supernatural as a madonna, gentle as a nurse. I have loved you with an affection whose sagacity was troubled by no hope of carnal pleasure. And in exchange, did you not bring me, over an exquisite tea-table, an incomparable friendship, a conversation embellished by nature herself, as well as by how many bunches of fresh roses? Only you, with your motherly and expressive hands, could have soothed my fevered brow, poured honey between my burning lips, set noble images in my life. Dear friend, I should rather not hear this absurd confession. Give me your hands, let me kiss them. It is chilly out here—let's go inside and talk about something else."

"Leslie, you must hear me out, even so, my poor darling. It must be done. Have you never wondered why I remained a widow, since I was widowed at twenty . . ."

"Suppose I had, it was none of my affair. You are a person so superior to all the rest that what in you was a weakness would have a quality of beauty and nobility lacking in other people's fine actions. You have done as you saw fit, and I am certain you have never done anything but what was delicate and pure."

"Pure! Leslie, your confidence pains me like an anticipated reproach. Listen . . . I don't know how to tell you this. It's much worse than if I had loved you, for instance, or even someone else, yes truly, anyone else."

I turned pale—pale as a sheet, pale as she was, alas, and trembling lest she notice, I tried to laugh and repeated without quite knowing what I was saying, "Oh, 'anyone else'—you really are the strangest creature! . . ."

"I said 'much worse', Leslie, and I'm completely in the dark about it, luminous though the moment is. Evenings, we see things more calmly, but I do not see this thing clearly, and there are exorbitant shadows upon my life. But if in my heart of hearts I believe this was not the worst, why should I be ashamed to tell it to you?—Was it the worst?"

I didn't understand, but at grips with a horrible agitation impossible to conceal, I began to tremble with fear, as if in a nightmare. I dared not look down the row of trees now filled with darkness and dread that stretched before us, and yet I dared not close my eyes. Her voice, which had grown lower, breaking with ever more intense sadness, suddenly rose again, and in quite a natural tone, almost brightly, she said, "You remember when my poor friend Dorothy was caught with a singer—I've forgotten the woman's name . . ." (I was relieved by this digression, which I hoped would distract us from the account of her sufferings) "how you explained to me at the time that we had no right to despise her. I recall your words: How can we be offended by behavior which Socrates—it concerned men in his case, but comes down to the same thing—who drank hemlock rather than commit an injustice, gaily approved in his chosen friends? If love that is fruitful, destined to perpetuate the race, honored as a family duty, a social duty, a human duty, is superior to a purely voluptuous love, on the other hand there is no hierarchy among the sterile loves, and it is not less moral—or rather, no more immoral—that a woman should take pleasure with another woman rather than with a being of another sex. The cause of such love lies in a nervous alteration which is too exclusively nervous to involve a moral content. We cannot say that because most people see things we call red as red that those who see them as violet are mistaken. Moreover—you added, if we refine pleasure to the point of making it aesthetic, since the body of a man and the body of a woman can each be quite as beautiful in its own way as the other, who can say why a really artistic woman would not be in love with another woman. In truly artistic natures, physical attraction or repulsion is modified by contemplation of the beautiful. Most people turn from jellyfish with disgust. Michelet, sensitive to their colors, gathered them with delight. Despite my repulsion for oysters, after I had thought of their life in the sea which their taste would now evoke for me, they have become—especially when I was some distance from the sea—a suggestive treat. Hence with the physical aptitudes, pleasures of contact, cravings for food, delight of the senses—all return to be grafted onto the place where our taste for the beautiful has taken root . . . Don't you suppose such arguments could help a woman physically predisposed to this kind of love to become aware of her vague curiosity, if certain statuettes by Rodin, for instance, had already triumphed—artistically—over her repugnances . . . that such arguments would excuse her in her own eyes, would reassure her conscience: and that this might be a great misfortune!"

I don't know how I kept from crying out, then—simultaneously the meaning of her confession and the sentiment of my dreadful responsibility flashed upon me. But letting myself be directed blindly by one of those higher inspirations which, when we are too far beneath ourselves, too inadequate to play our part in life, suddenly assume our mask and play our role quite eagerly, I said almost calmly: "I assure you I should feel no remorse, for truly I have no feeling of scorn or even of pity for such women."

Mysteriously, with an infinite sweetness of gratitude, she said to me, "You are generous." Then a little lower, and quickly, with a weary expression, as one disdains even while expressing certain earthy details, she added: "You know, I realized perfectly well for all your secret ways with everyone, that the bullet they could not remove and which has determined my illness—that you are still trying to find who shot it at me. And I've always hoped that bullet would never be discovered. Well, since medicine seems so sure of itself nowadays, and because you might suspect certain people who are innocent, I am confessing. But I prefer to tell you the truth . . ." She added, with that sweetness she had in her voice when she began to speak of her imminent death, in order to comfort the pain which what she was saying would cause by the way in which she spoke, "It was I, in one of those moments of despair which are so natural to anyone who really *lives*, it was I who . . . shot myself."

I wanted to go over and embrace her, but though I tried to contain myself, as I stood beside her, an irresistible force choked me, my eyes filled with tears, and I began to sob. At first she wiped my eyes, laughed a little, gently consoled me as she used to do, with a thousand graces. But deep within her a tremendous self-pity—no, a pity for herself and for me as well, welled up, brimming out of her eyes and falling in scalding tears. We wept together: concord of a wide and melancholy harmony! Our mingled pities now had as their object something larger than ourselves and over which we wept gladly, freely. I tried to drink her poor tears out of her hands, but others kept falling, by which she let herself become as if hypnotized. Her hands turned cold as the pale leaves which had fallen into the fountain basin. And never had we had so much pain, so much pleasure.

From *Cities of the Plain*

[The narrator Marcel, in love with Albertine, painfully watches her dance with a girlfriend.]

It was not this evening, however, that my cruel mistrust began to take solid form. No, to make no mystery about it, although the incident did not occur until some weeks later, it arose out of a remark made by Cottard. Albertine and her friends had insisted that day upon dragging me to the casino at Incarville where, as luck would have it, I should not have joined them (having intended to go and see Mme. Verdurin who had invited me again and again), had I not been held up at Incarville itself by a breakdown of the tram which it would take a considerable time to repair. As I strolled up and down waiting for the men to finish working at it, I found myself all of a sudden face to face with Doctor Cottard, who had come to Incarville to see a patient. I almost hesitated to greet him as he had not answered any of my letters. But friendship does not express itself in the same way in different people. Not having been brought up to observe the same fixed rules of behaviour as well-bred people, Cottard was full of good intentions of which one knew nothing, even denying their existence, until the day when he had an opportunity of displaying them. He apologised, had indeed received my letters, had reported my whereabouts to the Verdurins who were most anxious to see me and whom he urged me to go and see. He even proposed to take me to them there and then, for he was waiting for the little local train to take him back there for dinner. As I hesitated and he had still some time before his train (for there was bound to be still a considerable delay), I made him come with me to the little casino, one of those that had struck me as being so gloomy on the evening of my first arrival, now filled with the tumult of the girls, who, in the absence of male partners, were dancing together. Andrée came sliding along the floor towards me; I was meaning to go off with Cottard in a moment to the Verdurins', when I definitely declined his offer, seized by an irresistible desire to stay with Albertine. The fact was, I had just heard her laugh. And her laugh at once suggested the rosy flesh, the fragrant portals between which it had just made its way, seeming also, as strong, sensual and revealing as the scent of geraniums, to carry with it some micro-scopic particles of their substance, irritant and secret.

One of the girls, a stranger to me, sat down at the piano, and Andrée invited Alber-tine to waltz with her. Happy in the thought that I was going to remain in this little casino with these girls, I remarked to Cottard how well they danced together. But he, taking the professional point of view of a doctor and with an ill-breeding which over-looked the fact that they were my friends, although he must have seen me shaking hands with them, replied: "Yes, but parents are very rash to allow their daughters to form such habits. I should certainly never let mine come here. Are they nice-looking, though? I can't see their faces. There now, look," he went on, pointing to Albertine and Andrée who were waltzing slowly, tightly clasped together, "I have left my glasses behind and I don't see very well, but they are certainly keenly roused. It is not sufficiently known that women derive most excitement from their breasts. And theirs, as you see, are com-pletely touching." And indeed the contact had been unbroken between the breasts of Andrée and of Albertine. I do not know whether they heard or guessed Cottard's observation, but they gently broke the contact while continuing to waltz. At that moment Andrée said something to Albertine, who laughed, the same deep and pene-trating laugh that I had heard before. But all that it wafted to me this time was a feeling of pain; Albertine appeared to be revealing by it, to be making Andrée share some exquisite, secret thrill. It rang out like the first or the last strains of a ball to which one has not been invited.

[*Marcel observes, to his unrelenting chagrin, Andrée kissing Albertine.*]

Ever since the day when Cottard had accompanied me into the little casino at Incarville, albeit I did not share the opinion that he had expressed, Albertine had seemed to me dif-ferent; the sight of her made me lose my temper. I myself had changed, quite as much as she had changed in my eyes. I had ceased to bear her any good will; to her face, behind her back when there was a chance of my words being repeated to her, I spoke of her in the most insulting language. There were, however, intervals of calmer feel-ing. One day I learned that Albertine and Andrée had both accepted an invitation to Elstir's. Feeling certain that this was in order that they might, on the return journey, amuse themselves like schoolgirls on holiday by imitating the manners of fast young women, and in so doing find an unmaidenly pleasure the thought of which wrung my heart, without announcing my intention, to embarrass them and to deprive Albertine of the pleasure on which she was reckoning, I paid an unexpected call at his studio. But I found only Andrée there. Albertine had chosen another day when her aunt was to go there with her. Then I said to myself that Cottard must have been mistaken; the favourable impression that I received from Andrée's presence there without her friend remained with me and made me feel more kindly disposed towards Albertine. But this feeling lasted no longer than the healthy moments of delicate people subject to passing maladies, who are prostrated again by the merest trifle. Albertine incited Andrée to actions which, without going very far, were perhaps not altogether innocent; pained by this suspicion, I managed in the end to repel it. No sooner was I healed of it than it revived under another form. I had just seen Andrée, with one of those graceful gestures that came naturally to her, lay her head coaxingly on Albertine's shoulder, kiss her on the throat, half shutting her eyes; or else they had exchanged a glance; a remark had been made by somebody who had seen them going down together to bathe: little trifles such as habitually float in the surrounding atmosphere where the majority of people absorb them all day long without injury to their health or alteration of their mood, but which have a morbid effect and breed fresh sufferings in a nature predisposed to receive them. Sometimes even without my having seen Albertine again, without anyone's having spoken to me about her, there would flash from my memory some vision of her with Gisèle in an attitude which had seemed to me innocent at the time; it was enough now to destroy the peace of mind that I had managed to recover, I had no longer any need to go and breathe dangerous germs outside, I had, as Cottard would have said, supplied my own toxin. I thought then of all that I had been told about Swann's love for Odette, of the way in which Swann had been tricked all his life. Indeed, when I come to think of it, the hypothesis that made me gradually build up the whole of Albertine's character and give a painful interpretation to every moment of a life that I could not control in its entirety, was the memory, the rooted idea of Mme. Swann's character, as it had been described to me. These accounts helped my imagination, in after years, to take the line of supposing that Albertine might, instead of being a good girl, have had the same immorality, the same faculty of deception as a reformed prostitute, and I thought of all the sufferings that would in that case have been in store for me had I ever really been her lover.

WILLA CATHER (1873–1947)

"Tommy, the Unsentimental" (1896)

Born in Virginia, the American novelist and short-story writer Willa Cather was taken as a child by her parents to Red Cloud, Nebraska, where she grew up among the dour yet resilient Central European and Scandinavian immigrant farming families who had settled the prairies in the early nineteenth century. Both the landscape and its tough, soulful occupants had an enduring influence on her fiction. She attended high school in Red Cloud and the University of Nebraska, then worked as a newspaperwoman in Pittsburgh and taught school (1901–1906). Her first book, *April Twilights*, a collection of poetry, was published in 1903. In 1908 Cather joined the staff of *McClure's Magazine* in New York and subsequently became its managing editor. After publishing her first novel, *Alexander's Bridge*, in 1912, she turned to writing full-time. The New England writer Sarah Orne Jewett was both friend and inspiration, and under Jewett's influence Cather began to write about the prairie world of her youth in a series of brilliant novels and short stories—*Oh Pioneers!* (1913), *The Song of the Lark* (1915), *My Ántonia* (1918), *Youth and the Bright Medusa* (1920), *One of Ours* (1922), and *A Lost Lady* (1923). She won the Pulitzer Prize in 1923. In the second half of her career she became increasingly interested in the American Southwest, and two of her greatest novels, *The Professor's House* (1925) and *Death Comes for the Archbishop* (1927), are set, at least partially, in New Mexico, among the dramatic Pueblo Indian ruins that Cather loved. Other important Cather works include the novels *My Mortal Enemy* (1926), *Shadows on the Rock* (1931), *Lucy Gayheart* (1935), and *Sapphira and the Slave Girl* (1940), and the short-story collections *Obscure Destinies* (1932) and *The Old Beauty* (1948). At the time of her death, in 1947, Cather was widely acknowledged as one of the greatest modern American novelists. Her reputation has only been enhanced over time.

Cather's sexuality has been a matter of intense speculation, not least because sexual themes seem so powerfully, if enigmatically, to underlie her imaginative universe. In adolescence she went through a spectacular four-year period of gender rebellion: she cut her hair short, dressed in boys' clothes, and insisted on signing her name "William Cather, Jr." (Several studio photographs from the 1880s showing the juvenile Cather in male attire are reprinted in Sharon O'Brien's biography.) She lived most of her adult life with female companions. In Pittsburgh she lodged for nine years with a wealthy school-friend named Isabelle McClung and her family; she and McClung shared a bedroom. In New York in 1908, she met another woman, Edith Lewis, with whom she lived for the rest of her life. Whether either of these relationships was erotic in nature is unknown; Cather burned her letters to McClung; and Lewis, following instructions in her companion's will, destroyed many other private papers after Cather's death in 1947.

Whatever the link between the work and the life, Cather's fiction is often strikingly homoerotic in atmosphere. The heterosexual lovers in her novels generally fail to convince: the love story in *The Song of the Lark*, for example, between the opera singer Thea Kronberg and a devoted male friend named Fred is so feebly sketched as to be comical. By contrast Cather treats emotional relationships between characters of the same sex with sensuous intensity. In both *Death Comes for the Archbishop* and *The Professor's House*, the primary love relationships are, quite frankly, between male characters. When it came to depicting passion between women Cather was more circumspect, yet the theme is not wholly absent in her writing either, as the 1896 short story "Tommy, the Unsentimental" may illustrate. In the affectionate portrait of the androgynous "Tommy" Shirley, part-time banker and cyclist extraordinaire, Cather at once seems to commemorate her own boyish past and to envision a new-style heroine—in whom virility, stoicism, and discretion combine to produce an authentic (if phlegmatic) lesbian chivalry.

FURTHER READING: Willa Cather, *Willa Cather's Collected Short Fiction 1892–1912*, ed. Virginia Faulkner (Lincoln: University of Nebraska Press, 1965); —, *Early Novels and Stories* (New York: Library of America, 1987); —, *Later Novels* (New York: Library of America, 1990); —, *Stories, Poems, and Other Writings* (New York: Library of America, 1992); Edith Lewis, *Willa Cather Living* (New York: Knopf, 1953); Elizabeth Shepley Sergeant, *Willa Cather: A Memoir* (Philadelphia: J. Lippincott, 1953); E. K. Brown and Leon Edel, *Willa Cather: A Critical Biography* (1953; rpt. New York: Avon, 1980); James Woodress, *Willa Cather: Her Life and Art* (Lincoln: University of Nebraska Press, 1970); Jane Rule, *Lesbian Images* (New York: Doubleday, 1975); Joanna Russ, " 'To Write Like a Woman': Transformations of Identity in the Work of Willa Cather," *Journal of Homosexuality* 12 (1986): 77–87; Sharon O'Brien, *Willa Cather: The Emerging Voice* (New York: Random House, 1987); Hermione Lee, *Willa Cather: A Life Saved Up* (London: Virago, 1989); John March, *A Reader's Companion to the Fiction of Willa Cather* (Westport, Conn.: Greenwood, 1993); Philip L. Gerber, *Willa Cather*, rev. ed. (New York: Twayne, 1995); Guy Reynolds, *Willa Cather in Context* (Basingstoke: Macmillan, 1996); Joan Acocella, *Willa Cather and the Politics of Criticism* (Lincoln: University of Nebraska Press, 2000).

"Your father says he has no business tact at all, and of course that's dreadfully unfortunate."

"Business," replied Tommy, "he's a baby in business; he's good for nothing on earth but to keep his hair parted straight and wear that white carnation in his buttonhole. He has 'em sent down from Hastings twice a week as regularly as the mail comes, but the drafts he cashes lie in his safe until they are lost, or somebody finds them. I go up occasionally and send a package away for him myself. He'll answer your notes promptly enough, but his business letters—I believe he destroys them unopened to shake the responsibility of answering them."

"I am at a loss to see how you can have such patience with him, Tommy, in so many ways he is thoroughly reprehensible."

"Well, a man's likeableness don't depend at all on his virtues or acquirements, nor a woman's either, unfortunately. You like them or you don't like them, and that's all there is to it. For the why of it you must appeal to a higher oracle than I. Jay is a likeable fellow, and that's his only and sole acquirement, but after all it's a rather happy one."

"Yes, he certainly is that," replied Miss Jessica, as she deliberately turned off the gas jet and proceeded to arrange her toilet articles. Tommy watched her closely and then turned away with a baffled expression.

Needless to say, Tommy was not a boy, although her keen gray eyes and wide forehead were scarcely girlish, and she had the lank figure of an active half grown lad. Her real name was Theodosia, but during Thomas Shirley's frequent absences from the bank she had attended to his business and correspondence signing herself "T. Shirley," until everyone in Southdown called her "Tommy." That blunt sort of familiarity is not unfrequent in the West, and is meant well enough. People rather expect some business ability in a girl there, and they respect it immensely. That, Tommy undoubtedly had, and if she had not, things would have gone at sixes and sevens in the Southdown National. For Thomas Shirley had big land interests in Wyoming that called him constantly away from home, and his cashier, little Jay Ellington Harper, was, in the local phrase, a weak brother in the bank. He was the son of a friend of old Shirley's, whose papa had sent him West, because he had made a sad mess of his college career, and had spent too much money and gone at too giddy a pace down East. Conditions changed the young gentleman's life, for it was simply impossible to live either prodigally or rapidly in Southdown, but they could not materially affect his mental habits or inclinations. He was made cashier of Shirley's bank because his father bought in half the stock, but Tommy did his work for him.

The relation between these two young people was peculiar; Harper was, in his way, very grateful to her for keeping him out of disgrace with her father, and showed it by a hundred little attentions which were new to her and much more agreeable than the work she did for him was irksome. Tommy knew that she was immensely fond of him, and she knew at the same time that she was thoroughly foolish for being so. As she expressed it, she was not of his sort, and never would be. She did not often take pains to think, but when she did she saw matters pretty clearly, and she was of a peculiarly unfeminine mind that could not escape meeting and acknowledging a logical conclusion. But she went on liking Jay Ellington Harper, just the same. Now Harper was the only foolish man of Tommy's acquaintance. She knew plenty of active young business men and sturdy ranchers, such as one meets about live western towns, and took no particular interest in them, probably just because they were practical and sensible and thoroughly of her own kind. She knew almost no women, because in those days there were few women in Southdown who were in any sense interesting, or interested in anything but babies and salads. Her best friends were her father's old business friends, elderly men who had seen a good deal of the world, and who were very proud and fond of Tommy. They recognized a sort of squareness and honesty of spirit in the girl that Jay Ellington Harper never discovered, or, if he did, knew too little of its rareness to value highly. Those old speculators and men of business had always felt a sort of responsibility for Tom Shirley's little girl, and had rather taken her mother's place, and been her advisers on many points upon which men seldom feel at liberty to address a girl.

She was just one of them; she played whist and billiards with them, and made their cocktails for them, not scorning to take one herself occasionally. Indeed, Tommy's cocktails were things of fame in Southdown, and the professional compounders of drinks always bowed respectfully to her as though acknowledging a powerful rival.

Now all these things displeased and puzzled Jay Ellington Harper, and Tommy knew it full well, but clung to her old manner of living with a stubborn pertinacity, feeling somehow that to change would be both foolish and disloyal to the Old Boys. And as things went on, the seven Old Boys made greater demands upon her time than ever, for they were shrewd men, most of them, and had not lived fifty years in this world without learning a few things and unlearning many more. And while Tommy lived on in the blissful delusion that her role of indifference was perfectly played and without a flaw, they suspected how things were going and were perplexed as to the outcome. Still, their confidence was by no means shaken, and as Joe Elsworth said to Joe Sawyer one evening at billiards, "I think we can pretty nearly depend on Tommy's good sense."

They were too wise to say anything to Tommy, but they said just a word or two to Thomas Shirley, Sr., and combined to make things very unpleasant for Mr. Jay Ellington Harper.

At length their relations with Harper became so strained that the young man felt it would be better for him to leave town, so his father started him in a little bank of his own up in Red Willow. Red Willow, however, was scarcely a safe distance, being only some twenty-five miles north, upon the Divide, and Tommy occasionally found excuse to run up on her wheel to straighten out the young man's business for him. So when she suddenly decided to go East to school for a year, Thomas, Sr., drew a sigh of great relief. But the seven Old Boys shook their heads; they did not like to see her gravitating toward the East; it was a sign of weakening, they said, and showed an inclination to experiment with another kind of life, Jay Ellington Harper's kind.

But to school Tommy went, and from all reports conducted herself in a most seemly manner; made no more cocktails, played no more billiards. She took rather her own way with the curriculum, but she distinguished herself in athletics, which in Southdown counted for vastly more than erudition.

Her evident joy on getting back to Southdown was appreciated by everyone. She went about shaking hands with everybody, her shrewd face, that was so like a clever wholesome boy's, held high with happiness. As she said to old Joe Elsworth one morning, when they were driving behind his stud through a little thicket of cottonwood scattered along the sun-parched bluffs, "It's all very fine down East there, and the hills are great, but one gets mighty homesick for this sky, the old intense blue of it, you know. Down there the skies are all pale and smoky. And this wind, this hateful, dear, old everlasting wind that comes down like the sweep of cavalry and is never tamed or broken, O Joe, I used to get hungry for this wind! I couldn't sleep in that lifeless stillness down there."

"How about the people, Tom?"

"O, they are fine enough folk, but we're not their sort, Joe, and never can be."

"You realize that, do you, fully?"

"Quite fully enough, thank you, Joe." She laughed rather dismally, and Joe cut his horse with the whip.

The only unsatisfactory thing about Tommy's return was that she brought with her a girl she had grown fond of at school, a dainty, white, languid bit of a thing, who used violet perfumes and carried a sunshade. The Old Boys said it was a bad sign when a rebellious girl like Tommy took to being sweet and gentle to one of her own sex, the worst sign in the world.

The new girl was no sooner in town than a new complication came about. There was no doubt of the impression she made on Jay Ellington Harper. She indisputably had all those little evidences of good breeding that were about the only things which could touch the timid, harassed young man who was so much out of his element. It was a very plain case on his part, and the souls of the seven were troubled within them. Said Joe Elsworth to the other Joe, "The heart of the cad is gone out to the little muff, as is right and proper and in accordance with the eternal fitness of things. But there's the other girl who has the blindness that may not be cured, and she gets all the rub of it. It's no use, I can't help her, and I am going to run down to Kansas City for awhile. I can't stay here and see the abominable suffering of it." He didn't go, however.

There was just one other person who understood the hopelessness of the situation quite as well as Joe, and that was Tommy. That is, she understood Harper's attitude. As to Miss Jessica's she was not quite so certain, for Miss Jessica, though pale and languid and addicted to sunshades, was a maiden most discreet. Conversations on the subject usually ended without any further information as to Miss Jessica's feelings, and Tommy sometimes wondered if she were capable of having any at all.

At last the calamity which Tommy had long foretold descended upon Jay Ellington Harper. One morning she received a telegram from him begging her to intercede with her father; there was a run on his bank and he must have help before noon. It was then ten thirty, and the one sleepy little train that ran up to Red Willow daily had crawled out of the station an hour before. Thomas Shirley, Sr., was not at home.

"And it's a good thing for Jay Ellington he's not, he might be more stony hearted than I," remarked Tommy, as she closed the ledger and turned to the terrified Miss Jessica. "Of course we're his only chance, no one else would turn their hand over to help him. The train went an hour ago and he says it must be there by noon. It's the only bank in the town, so nothing can be done by telegraph. There is nothing left but to wheel for it. I may make it, and I may not. Jess, you scamper up to the house and get my wheel out, the tire may need a little attention. I will be along in a minute."

"O, Theodosia, can't I go with you? I must go!"

"You go! O, yes, of course, if you want to. You know what you are getting into, though. It's twenty-five miles uppish grade and hilly, and only an hour and a quarter to do it in."

"O, Theodosia, I can do anything now!" cried Miss Jessica, as she put up her sunshade and fled precipitately. Tommy smiled as she began cramming bank notes into a canvas bag. "May be you can, my dear, and may be you can't."

The road from Southdown to Red Willow is not by any means a favorite bicycle road; it is rough, hilly and climbs from the river bottoms up to the big Divide by a steady up grade, running white and hot through the scorched corn fields and grazing lands where the long-horned Texan cattle browse about in the old buffalo wallows. Miss Jessica soon found that with the pedaling that had to be done there was little time left for emotion of any sort, or little sensibility for anything but the throbbing, dazzling heat that had to be endured. Down there in the valley the distant bluffs were vibrating and dancing with the heat, the cattle, completely overcome by it, had hidden under the shelving banks of the "draws" and the prairie dogs had fled to the bottom of their holes that are said to reach to water. The whirr of the seventeen-year locust was the only thing that spoke of animation, and that ground on as if only animated and enlivened by the sickening, destroying heat. The sun was like hot brass, and the wind that blew up from the south was hotter still. But Tommy knew that wind was their only chance. Miss Jessica began to feel that unless she could stop and get some water she was not much longer for this vale of tears. She suggested this possibility to Tommy, but Tommy only shook her head, "Take too much time," and bent over her handle bars, never lifting her eyes from the road in front of her. It flashed upon Miss Jessica that Tommy was not only very unkind, but that she sat very badly on her wheel and looked aggressively masculine and professional when she bent her shoulders and pumped like that. But just then Miss Jessica found it harder than ever to breathe, and the bluffs across the river began doing serpentines and skirt dances, and more important and personal considerations occupied the young lady.

When they were fairly over the first half of the road, Tommy took out her watch. "Have to hurry up, Jess, I can't wait for you."

"O, Tommy, I can't," panted Miss Jessica, dismounting and sitting down in a little heap by the roadside. "You go on, Tommy, and tell him—tell him I hope it won't fail, and I'd do anything to save him."

By this time the discreet Miss Jessica was reduced to tears, and Tommy nodded as she disappeared over the hill laughing to herself. "Poor Jess, anything but the one thing he needs. Well, your kind have the best of it generally, but in little affairs of this sort my kind come out rather strongly. We're rather better at them than at dancing. It's only fair, one side shouldn't have all."

Just at twelve o'clock, when Jay Ellington Harper, his collar crushed and wet about his throat, his eyeglass dimmed with perspiration, his hair hanging damp over his forehead, and even the ends of his moustache dripping with moisture, was attempting to reason with a score of angry Bohemians, Tommy came quietly through the door, grip in hand. She went straight behind the grating, and standing screened by the bookkeeper's desk, handed the bag to Harper and turned to the spokesman of the Bohemians.

"What's all this business mean, Anton? Do you all come to bank at once nowadays?"

"We want 'a money, want 'a our money, he no got it, no give it," bawled the big beery Bohemian.

"O, don't chaff 'em any longer, give 'em their money and get rid of 'em, I want to see you," said Tommy carelessly, as she went into the consulting room.

When Harper entered half an hour later, after the rush was over, all that was left of his usual immaculate appearance was his eyeglass and the white flower in his buttonhole.

"This has been terrible!" he gasped. "Miss Theodosia, I can never thank you."

"No," interrupted Tommy. "You never can, and I don't want any thanks. It was rather a tight place, though, wasn't it? You looked like a ghost when I came in. What started them?"

"How should I know? They just came down like the wolf on the fold. It sounded like the approach of a ghost dance."

"And of course you had no reserve? O, I always told you this would come, it was inevitable with your charming methods. By the way, Jess sends her regrets and says she would do anything to save you. She started out with *me*, but she has fallen by the wayside. O, don't be alarmed, she is not hurt, just winded. I left her all bunched up by the road like a little white rabbit. I think the lack of romance in the escapade did her up about as much as anything; she is essentially romantic. If we had been on fiery steeds bespattered with foam I think she would have made it, but a wheel hurt her dignity. I'll tend bank; you'd better get your wheel and go and look her up and comfort her. And as soon as it is convenient, Jay, I wish you'd marry her and be done with it, I want to get this thing off my mind."

Jay Ellington Harper dropped into a chair and turned a shade whiter.

"Theodosia, what do you mean? Don't you remember what I said to you last fall, the night before you went to school? Don't you remember what I wrote you—"

Tommy sat down on the table beside him and looked seriously and frankly into his eyes.

"Now, see here, Jay Ellington, we have been playing a nice little game, and now it's time to quit. One must grow up sometime. You are horribly wrought up over Jess, and why deny it? She's your kind, and clean daft about you, so there is only one thing to do. That's all."

Jay Ellington wiped his brow, and felt unequal to the situation. Perhaps he really came nearer to being moved down to his stolid little depths than he ever had before. His voice shook a good deal and was very low as he answered her.

"You have been very good to me, I didn't believe any woman could be at once so kind and clever. You almost made a man of even me."

"Well, I certainly didn't succeed. As to being good to you, that's rather a break, you know; I am amiable, but I am only flesh and blood after all. Since I have known you I have not been at all good, in any sense of the word, and I suspect I have been anything but clever. Now, take mercy upon Jess—and me—and go. Go on, that ride is beginning to tell on me. Such things strain one's nerve. . . . Thank Heaven he's gone at last and had sense enough not to say anything more. It was growing rather critical. As I told him I am not at all superhuman."

After Jay Ellington Harper had bowed himself out, when Tommy sat alone in the darkened office, watching the flapping blinds, with the bank books before her, she noticed a white flower on the floor. It was the one Jay Ellington Harper had worn in his coat and had dropped in his nervous agitation. She picked it up and stood holding it a moment, biting her lip. Then she dropped it into the grate and turned away, shrugging her thin shoulders.

"They are awful idiots, half of them, and never think of anything beyond their dinner. But O, how we do like 'em!"

ALEISTER CROWLEY (1875–1947)

"The Lesbian Hell" (1898)

The poet, magician, mountaineer, free-love advocate, and drug addict Aleister Crowley—notorious during his own lifetime—remains one of the more curious figures in late-nineteenth and early-twentieth-century English literary history. After studying at Cambridge in the 1890s and publishing several books of verse in the style of Baudelaire and Swinburne, Crowley became interested in the occult and established a mystical neo-pagan order known as the Astrum Argentium in 1908. He settled in Italy after the First World War, but was subsequently deported when it was rumored that he and his disciples were holding black masses and sexual orgies at his Sicilian villa, the "Abbey of Thelema." Crowley later traveled in the Far East, the United States, and Mexico and wrote a series of books on magic, astrology, numerology, and devil worship, as well as an autobiography—*The Spirit of Solitude* (1929)—in which he claimed to be the reincarnation of the sybaritic Pope Alexander VI.

The 1898 poem "The Lesbian Hell" is one of several poems written during Crowley's Cambridge years. Though reminiscent in style and subject of Baudelaire's "Femmes damnées 1 (Delphine et Hippolyte)," the poem exudes a miasma of kitsch, perversity, and sickly religiosity that is distinctively Crowley's own.

FURTHER READING: Aleister Crowley, *White Stains* (London, 1898; rpt. London: Duckworth, 1973); —, *The Spirit of Solitude: An Autobiography: Subsequently ReAntichristened the Confessions of Aleister Crowley* (1929; rpt. London: Routledge and Kegan Paul, 1979); John Symonds, *The Great Beast: The Life of Aleister Crowley* (London: Rider, 1951); —, *The King of the Shadow Realm: Aleister Crowley, His Life and Magic* (London: Duckworth, 1989); —, *Selected Poems of Aleister Crowley*, ed. Martin Booth (Wellingborough, England: Crucible, 1986); Colin Wilson, *Aleister Crowley* (London: Aquarian, 1987); Martin Booth, *A Magick Life: The Biography of Aleister Crowley* (London: Hodder and Stoughton, 2000).

The unutterable void of Hell is stirred
  By gusts of sad wind moaning; the inane
Quivers with melancholy sounds unheard,
  Unpastured woes, and unimagined pain,
  And kisses flung in vain.

Pale women fleet around, whose infinite
  Long sorrow and desire have torn their wombs,
Whose empty fruitlessness assails the night
  With hollow repercussion, like dim tombs
  Wherein some vampire glooms.

Pale women sickening for some sister breast;
  Lone sisterhood of voiceless melancholy
That wanders in this Hell, desiring rest
  From that desire that dwells forever free,
  Monstrous, a storm, a sea.

In that desire their hands are strained and wrung;
  In that most infinite passion beats the blood,
And bursting chants of amorous agony flung
  To the void Hell, are lost, not understood,
  Unheard by evil or good.

Their sighs attract the unsubstantial shapes
  Of other women, and their kisses burn
Cold on the lips whose purple blood escapes,
  A thin chill stream, they feel not nor discern,
  Nor love's low laugh return.

They kiss the spiritual dead, they pass
  Like mists uprisen from the frosty moon,
Like shadows fleeting in a seer's glass,
  Beckoning, yearning, amorous of the noon
  When earth dreams on in swoon.

They are so sick for sorrow, that my eyes
  Are moist because their passion was so fair,
So pure and comely that no sacrifice
  Seems to waft up a sweeter savour there,
  Where God's grave ear takes prayer.

O desecrated lovers! O divine
  Passionate martyrs, virgin unto death!
O kissing daughters of the unfed brine!
  O sisters of the west wind's pitiful breath,
  There is One that pitieth!

One far above the heavens crowned alone
  Immitigable, intangible, a maid,
Incomprehensible, divine, unknown,
  Who loves your love, and to high God hath said:
  "To me these songs are made!"

So in a little from the silent Hell
  Rises a spectre, disanointed now,
Who bears a cup of poison terrible,
  The seal of God upon his blasted brow,
  To whom His angels bow.

Rise, Phantom disanointed, and proclaim
  Thine own destruction, and the sleepy death
Of those material essences that flame
  A little moment for a little breath,
  The love that perisheth!

Rise, sisters, who have ignorantly striven
  On pale pure limbs to pasture your desire,
Who should have fixed your souls on highest Heaven,
  And satiated your longings in that fire,
  And struck that mightier lyre!

Let the ripe kisses of your thirsting throats
  And beating blossoms of your breath, and flowers
Of swart illimitable hair that floats
  Vague and caressing, and the amorous powers
  Of your unceasing hours,

The rich hot fragrance of your dewy skins,
  The eyes that yearn, the breasts that bleed, the thighs
That cling and cluster to these infinite sins,
  Forget the earthlier pleasures of the prize,
  And raise diviner sighs;

Cling to the white and bloody feet that hang,
　And drink the purple of a God's pure side;
With your wild hair assuage His deadliest pang,
　And on his broken bosom still abide
　His virginal white bride.

So in the dawn of skies unseen above,
　Your passion's fiercest flakes shall catch new gold,
The sun of an immeasurable love
　More beautiful shall touch the chaos cold
　Of earth that is grown old.

Then, shameful sisterhood of earth's disdain,
　Your lips shall speak your hearts, and understand;
Your loves shall assuage the amorous pain
　With spiritual lips more keen and bland,
　And ye shall take God's hand.

The Twentieth Century

"MARIE MADELEINE" [MARIE MADELEINE VON PUTTKAMER] (1881–1944)

"Crucifixion," "Beneath the Surface," "The Unfading," "Vagabonds" (1900)

The turn-of-the-century German poet who published under the pseudonym "Marie Madeleine" was born in East Prussia; her maiden name was Günther. In 1900, at the age of eighteen, she married General G. H. von Puttkamer, of the distinguished Prussian military family. Her first and best-known work remains the collection of verse, *Auf Kypros* (1900), written when she was in her teens and subsequently translated into English in 1907 under the title *Hydromel and Rue*. Later works include the play *Das bisschen Liebe* (1906), another book of poems, *Die rote Rose Leidenschaft* (1912), the novels *Frivol: aus dem Leben eines Pferdes* (1906) and *Die heiligen Guter* (1911), and a collection of stories about the First World War *". . . und muss abschiednehmen": Kriegsnovellen* (1915). She spent much of her life in Baden-Baden and Nice and continued publishing poems and stories into the 1930s.

The poems in *Auf Kypros*—full of cries of lust, strange idolatries, and other absinthe-tinted clichés of late-nineteenth-century decadent verse—epitomize the overheated, curiously adolescent quality of fin de siècle European art and sensibility. The sapphic fantasias of Baudelaire and Verlaine are clearly primary influences. (Von Puttkamer translated several books of French poetry into German.) Yet, like those of her contemporary Renée Vivien, the homosexual poems of "Marie Madeleine" are perhaps more than worn-out, second-generation decadent effusions. For all their posturing, they display what their English translator Ferdinand E. Kappey, writing in 1907, called a "strange precocity . . . which, with its amazing intuitions, may be said to forecast an experience and display a knowledge of those psychic influences and sexual emotions either entirely withheld from or but dimly perceived through the channels of normal youth." At their most compelling, the works of "Marie Madeleine" bring to mind the paintings of the Austrian expressionist artist Egon Schiele, whose garish, humorless, yet strangely incisive images of lesbian lovemaking are exactly contemporary with *Auf Kypros*.

FURTHER READING: "Marie Madeleine" (Marie Madeleine von Puttkamer), *Auf Kypros* (Berlin: Vita, 1900); —, *Hydromel and Rue*, trans. Ferdinand E. Kappey (London: Francis Griffiths, 1907); Jeannette Foster, *Sex Variant Women in Literature* (Talla-hassee, Fla.: Naiad, 1985); Gisela Brinker-Gabler, Karola Ludwig, and Angela Wöffen, eds., *Lexicon deutschsprachiger Schriftstellerinnen 1800–1945* (Munich: Deutscher Taschenbuch Verlag, 1986); Lillian Faderman and Brigitte Eriksson, *Lesbians in Germany: 1890's–1920's* (Tallahassee, Fla.: Naiad, 1990).

Crucifixion

Nailed to a cross, your beauty still aglow,
   A fierce incarnate agony you seem;
Like purple wounds upon a field of snow
   My scarring kisses on your body gleam.

How thin your fair young face, your limbs how spare,
   How frail upon your breast the blossom lies!
But oh! the torch of lust is flaming there
   Through darkness and in triumph from your eyes.

When you, a virgin sword unstained, yet fierce
   To brook affront, came thrusting unto me,
Your innocence was like a sword to pierce,
   And I desired to stain your purity.

I gave you of the poison that was mine,
   My sorrow and my passion—all I gave;
And now behold the depth of my design:
   A tortured soul too late for tears to save.

That I might now re-fashion from the dust
   My shattered altars, and redeem the loss!
Madonna, with the kindled eyes of lust,
   'Twas I who nailed you naked to the cross.

Beneath the Surface

All night I saw your vision bright;
Within me snarled the Brute and stirred;
My longing cried to you unheard
Throughout the night—throughout the night.

To you, unwilling amorist!
To you—whose nimble strength I broke!
O how your sleeping passions woke,
And how you knelt to me, and kissed!

I longed for you, remembering
Your body's dear abandonment,
Your sultry boudoir's aching scent,
The wounding rapture and the sting.

"I know it all," you smile and say.
But then you know not how, possest,
I longed to leave upon your breast
The fang-marks of the beast of prey.

The Unfading

The garden of my soul grows duller;
    But one sweet bloom scents all the air;
One scarlet blossom keeps its colour,
    The sinful flower you planted there.

In those cold winter days the willows
    Hung frosted by the river bank,
And virgin snow in drifting billows
    Along the margin rose and sank.

In those cold Winter days and frozen,
    When driving north-winds left their smart,
I—I of all the world was chosen
    To nestle warm against your heart.

And in your room it mattered little
    The cruel ending of the year,
The ice-bound Empire chill and brittle,
    Because I loved, and you were near.

And even to-day as life grows duller,
    The garden of my soul looks fair,
For one deep blossom keeps its colour,
    The scarlet sin you planted there.

Vagabonds

Because mine eyes are fashioned so,
  Shalt thou forsake thy house and hearth,
And like a beggar thou shalt go,
  Despised of men and nothing worth.
Fair fame and fortune—all shall be
  As trodden dust beneath your feet,
      Because of me!

And we shall know the town at eve
  Where, in the gas-illumined street,
Unhappy people make-believe,
  And proven friends are few to meet—
Where lust and hunger, toil and hate,
  In noisy riot pay their due
      To cynic Fate.

Such bitter things and sweet shall fill
  Our souls like hydromel and rue;
The weary hours that others kill
  Shall wing about us strange and new;
No longer shall we need to guess
  Their meaning when poor mortals play
      At "No" and "Yes."

For we shall sound Life's iron strings
  That do not yield to fingers gloved,
And gather from the heart of things
  The most abhorred, the best beloved.
We shall not shrink from bloody strife;
  Not we! Once tasted we will drain
      The Cup of Life.

Contempt will follow at our heel,
  And all will damn us—and in vain!
For us the solemn priests shall kneel
  In prayer again and yet again.
Into the world of night we go
  For ever cursed—because mine eyes
      Are fashioned so!

NATALIE CLIFFORD BARNEY (1876–1972)

"Woman," "Couplets" (1900)

Born in 1876 into a wealthy and distinguished Midwestern family—her mother was the painter Alice Pike Barney and her father the heir to a railroad fortune—the American expatriate writer Natalie Clifford Barney grew up, like a Henry James heroine, in international high society. She left the United States permanently in 1899, settling in Paris, on the Rue Jacob, where she presided for many decades over a celebrated lesbian salon frequented by writers, artists, actresses, opera singers, and bohemians of all stripes. Her sexual conquests were legendary—the painter Romaine Brooks, the courtesan Liane de Pougy, the poets Renée Vivien and Lucie Delarue-Mardrus, Oscar Wilde's lesbian niece, Dolly Wilde, and Elisabeth de Grammont, the duchess of Clermont-Tonnerre, were among her many lovers—and she appears as a character in a host of lesbian literary works of the period, including Liane de Pougy's *Idylle sapphique* (1901), Colette's *Claudine s'en va* (1903), Vivien's *Une Femme m'apparut* (1904), Djuna Barnes's *Ladies Almanack* (1928), Radclyffe Hall's *The Well of Loneliness* (1928), and Delarue-Mardrus's *L'Ange et les pervers* (1930). She was famous, among other frivolities, for the Greek-inspired "Temple de l'Amitié," in the garden at the Rue Jacob, around which she and certain select female friends were wont to disport.

Barney's greatest gift—assisted by wealth, beauty, and much personal flamboyance—was undoubtedly for friendship, but she was also a writer of considerable talent. Over a long life she produced a steady stream of poems, essays, epigrams, and memoirs. Writing in French, her adopted language, she often proselytized on the subject of lesbian love. *Quelques portraits: Sonnets de femmes*, a book of poetic portraits of women, appeared in 1900, followed in 1901 by *Cinq petits dialogues grecs*—a series of pseudo-Greek dialogues, much influenced by Pierre Louÿs's *Chansons de Bilitis*, celebrating Sappho and her love of women. In the teens she formed an important friendship with the French writer and critic Rémy de Gourmont, who dubbed her "the Amazon" and published two collections of his letters to her—*Lettres à l'amazone* (1914) and *Lettres intimes à l'amazone* (1926). In subsequent decades Barney continued to write about her life and loves in a series of sometimes gossipy, sometimes romantic autobiographical books: *Pensées d'une amazone* (1920), *Aventures de l'esprit* (1929), *Nouvelles pensées de l'amazone* (1939), *Souvenirs indiscrets* (1960) and *Traits et portraits* (1963). The poems

606 The Twentieth Century

"Women" and "Couplets" are characteristic both of her nineties-ish poetic sensibility and charming if overweening amorosity.

FURTHER READING: Natalie Barney, *Quelques sonnets et portraits de femmes* (Paris: Société d'Éditions Littéraires, 1900); —, *Cinq petits dialogues grecs (Antithèses et parallèles)* (Paris: Plume, 1902); —, *Actes et entr'actes* (Paris: Sansot, 1910); —, *Pensées d'une amazone* (Paris: Émile-Paul, 1920); —, *Nouvelles pensées de l'amazone* (Paris: Mercure de France, 1939); —, *Souvenirs indiscrets* (Paris: Flammarion, 1960); —, *Traits et portraits* (Paris, 1963; rpt. New York: Arno, 1975); —, *Adventures of the Mind*, trans. John Spalding Gatton (New York: New York University Press, 1992); Rémy de Gourmont, *Lettres à l'amazone* (Paris: Cres, 1914); —, *Lettres intimes à l'amazone* (Paris: La Centaine, 1926); George Wickes, *The Amazon of Letters: The Life and Loves of Natalie Barney* (New York: Putnam's, 1976); Michele Causse and Berthe Cleyrergues, *Berthe ou un demisiècle auprès de l'amazone* (Paris: Tierce, 1980); Shari Benstock, *Women of the Left Bank, Paris, 1900–1940* (Austin: University of Texas, 1986); Karla Jay, *The Amazon and the Page: Natalie Clifford Barney and Renée Vivien* (Bloomington and Indianapolis: Indiana University Press, 1988); Anna Livia, ed., *A Pernicious Advantage: The Best of Natalie Barney* (Norwich, Vt.: New Victoria, 1992).

Woman

Woman, supple frame,
Curving archway, bent for moans
Of love,
My desire will follow your slopes—
The tiny branches of your veins
Where angles join with curves;
Legs enclosing the delta
Of the cherished womanly safe.

—O woman, water and fire—

I pull your head back
In my hand—the human crest,
Cascade of hair!

Couplets

You asked me for a love poem.
Listen, rather, to the love my silence speaks!

I cannot say in steady, docile iambs
The moans of pleasure, the rhythm of our loins.

When beneath my body I feel your beating joy,
Will I say my desire brushing and crushing you?

Come be my love sweet and wild; instead of words
Upon your flesh accept my enraptured sobs.

And when we fall back, spent—if my mouth,
Mute eloquence, still touches you,

Let me explore your body's harmony
From the arch of your foot to your flowing hair.

Senses finely tuned; music, charm,
Harp whose secret chords I hold,

For you, my artful hands, proud instrument,
Make love as a poet, verse as a lover!

RENÉE VIVIEN (1877–1909)

"Sappho Lives Again," "Words to my Friend" (1901)

The turn-of-the-century Anglo-French poet and novelist Renée Vivien was born in 1877 into a crass, exorbitantly wealthy upper-class English family: her real name was Pauline Tarn. She went to school in Paris and as a child developed a profound attachment to French literature and culture. Her father died when she was nine, leaving her a vast fortune. When her mother later attempted to claim some of this legacy for herself—by having her rebellious daughter declared insane—Vivien was made a ward of the court. As soon as she came of age in 1898, she settled permanently in Paris and changed her name to "Renée Vivien" to symbolize both her official escape from familial oppression and her sense of personal rebirth.

Vivien's homosexuality—romantic, fanatical, and libertine in spirit—was from the start an essential and self-conscious part of her being. While still an adolescent she had fallen in love with a school friend, Violet Shilleto, and suffered greatly following Shilleto's premature death in 1901. (The charismatic yet doomed Shilleto appears in a number of lesbian memoirs from the turn of the century: she was the first love also, apparently, of the American writer and bohemian Mabel Dodge Luhan.) Thereafter, in what remained of her own short life, Vivien consoled herself—as best she could—with drink, poetry, and promiscuity.

Vivien's most significant adult love affair was with the flamboyant, American-born *salonnière* Natalie Clifford Barney, whom she met in 1899. Barney introduced her to the poetry of Sappho, and for a time the two dreamed of establishing a modern Sapphic cult on the island of Lesbos. Vivien's first book of poems, *Études et préludes*, containing imitations of Sappho, appeared in 1901. The relationship with Barney was a turbulent one, however, and in the same year Vivien broke with her and began a masochistic emotional liaison with the immensely rich Baroness de Zuylen de Nyevelt (née Rothschild). Vivien's health subsequently declined, her eccentricities proliferated, and she became an alcoholic semirecluse. Yet even as she withdrew from the world—she locked herself up in her apartment on the Avenue Bois de Boulogne and had the windows nailed shut—she continued to write obsessively. She published a *roman à clef* about the relationship with Barney—*Une Femme m'apparut* (*A Woman Appeared to Me*)—in 1904; four volumes of her poetry appeared between 1906 and 1908. After her death in

1909, three more verse collections were published posthumously. Waiflike, absinthe-addicted, sexually compulsive, and probably anorexic—she was believed to have died of pneumonia aggravated by starvation—Vivien was one of the more exotic figures to be found in turn-of-the-century Paris. Colette (who lived for a time next door to her) provides a disturbing—and unforgettable—memoir of her in *Ces Plaisirs* (1932), subsequently published in English as *The Pure and the Impure*.

Renée Vivien's poetry—all of it written in French—has undoubtedly been neglected on account of its forthright celebration of lesbian loves. Sappho was a liberating, ever-present influence; Vivien translated a number of the major Sapphic fragments (creditably) into French in *Sapho* (1903) and *Les Kitharèdes* (1904). Baudelaire and Rimbaud provided her with other, no less crucial, lessons. But Vivien's own lyric voice is a distinctive one. The pseudo-Hellenic poetic style she usually favors has not worn well: at her weakest, she can seem, indeed, a kind of Alma-Tadema in verse—complete with the requisite Greek maidens, urns, and languid ardors. Yet her best poems manage a mood of compelling tenderness and melancholia. It is curious to think what she might have done had she lived: rhetorical excesses aside, surely no other lesbian writer of her time squandered such promising, sophisticated gifts.

FURTHER READING: Renée Vivien, *Études et préludes* (Paris: Alphonse Lemerre, 1901); —, *Brumes de fjords* (Paris: Alphonse Lemerre, 1902); —, *Sapho, traduction nouvelle* (Paris: Alphonse Lemerre, 1903); —, *Une Femme m'apparut* (Paris, 1904; rpt. Paris: Desforges, 1977); —, *Évocations* (Paris: Alphonse Lemerre, 1905; —, *Poèmes en prose* (Paris: Sansot, 1909); —, *Poèmes complètes de Renée Vivien*, 2 vols. (Paris, 1924; rpt. New York: Arno, 1975); —, *A Woman Appeared to Me*, trans. Jeannette H. Foster (Tallahassee, Fla.: Naiad, 1976); André Germain, *Renée Vivien* (Paris: Cres, 1917); David M. Robinson, *Sappho and Her Influence* (Boston: Marshall Jones, 1924); Yves-Gérard LeDantec, *Renée Vivien: Femme damnée, femme sauvée* (Aix-en-Provence: Feu, 1930); Jeannette Foster, *Sex Variant Women in Literature* (1956; rpt. Tallahassee, Fla.: Naiad, 1985); Édith Mora, *Sappho: Histoire d'un poète et traduction intégrale de l'oeuvre* (Paris: Flammarion, 1966); Paul Lorenz, *Sapho, 1900: Renée Vivien* (Paris: Julliard, 1977); Susan Gubar, "Sapphistries," *Signs: Journal of Women and Society* 10 (1984): 43–62; Elyse Blankley, "Return to Mytilene: Renée Vivien and the City of Women," in Susan Merrill, ed., *Women Writers and the City* (Knoxville: University of Tennessee Press, 1984), pp. 45–67; Jean-Paul Goujon, *Tes blessures sont plus douces que leurs caresses: Vie de Renée Vivien* (Paris: Desforges, 1986); Karla Jay, *The Amazon and the Page: Natalie Clifford Barney and Renée Vivien* (Bloomington: Indiana University Press, 1988); Elaine Marks, "Sapho 1900: Imagining Renée Vivien and the Rear of the Belle Époque," *Yale French Studies* 75 (1988): 175–89; Virginie Sanders, *La Poésie de Renée Vivien (1877–1909): "Vertigineusement, j'allais vers les étoiles . . ."* (Amsterdam: Rodopi, 1991); Tama Lea Engelking, "Renée Vivien's Sapphic Legacy: Remembering the 'House of Muses,'" *Atlantis* 18 (1992/93): 125–41.

Sappho Lives Again

In Lesbos long ago the moon would rise
Over the orchard where lovers held their nightly vigil.
Sated passion rose from those sleeping waters
And sobbed deep in the heart of the lyre.

Sappho circled her brow with imperial violets
And celebrated Eros, who swoops down like a wind
Upon the oak trees . . . Attis listened to her pensively
And the torch made her circlets shine brighter still.

The shores were flaming, blond under spots of gold . . .
The virgins taught the lovely foreign maidens
How propitious the shadows are for delicate caresses,
And the sky and sea spread out their decoration.

. . . Some of us have kept the rites
Of that burning Lesbos gilded like an altar.
We know that love is strong and cruel
And our lovers have the white feet of Graces.

Our bodies are for theirs a sisterly mirror,
Our friends, with breasts white as springtime snow,
Know in what strange and suave manner
Sappho used to bend Attis to her will.

We worship with infinite innocence,
Marveling like a wide-eyed child
Given the endless gold of spheres . . .
Sappho lives again, through the grace of harmonies.

We know how to plant a kiss of velvet
And how to embrace with languid ardor;
Our caresses are our lyric poems . . .
Our love is greater than any love.

We repeat those words of Sappho when we lie
Dreaming under a sky shot with silver:
"Oh, lovely ones, toward you my heart remains unchanged . . ."
Those we love have looked with scorn on men.

Our moonlit kisses have a pale gentleness,
Our fingers never crumple the down of a cheek,
And when the sash comes unfastened, we can be
Lovers and sisters all in one.

Desire in us is not as strong as tenderness,
And yet our love for a young girl conquered us
By the will of scathing Aphrodite,
Whose priestess each of us remains.

Sappho lives and reigns in our trembling bodies;
Like her, we have heard the siren,
Like her as well, we have peaceful hearts,
We who never heed insults of passersby.

With fervor we pray: "May night be twice as long
For us whose kisses shun the dawn, for us
Whose knees were parted by mortal Eros,
For us whose flesh is dazzling and unquiet . . ."

And our mistresses cannot disappoint us,
For it is the infinite in them that we adore . . .
And since their kisses make us eternal,
We do not fear the oblivion of Hades' darkness.

Thus we laud them, our hearts overflowing and resounding.
Our days without immodesty, fear, or remorse,
Unfold like vast harmonies,
And we love, as they once loved in Mytilene.

Words to My Friend

Understand me: I am a mediocre being,
Not good, not very bad, peaceful, a bit cunning.
I detest heavy perfume and shrill voices,
And gray is more dear to me than scarlet or ocher.

I love the dying day which grows dim by degrees,
A fire, the cloistered intimacy of a room

Where the lamps, veiling their amber transparencies,
Redden the antique bronze and turn the gray stoneware blue,

My eyes drop to the carpet smoother than sand,
Indolently I evoke rivers flecked with gold
Where the clarity of the beautiful past still floats . . .
And nevertheless, I am quite guilty.

You see: I am at the age when a maiden gives her hand
To the man whom her weakness searches and dreads,
And I have not chosen a companion for the road,
Because you appeared at that turn in the road.

The hyacinth was bleeding on the red hills,
You were dreaming and Eros walked at your side . . .
I am woman, I have no right to beauty.
I had been condemned to masculine ugliness.

And I had the inexcusable audacity of wanting
Sisterly love fashioned with soft whiteness,
The furtive step that didn't trample the fern
And the sweet voice that comes to ally itself with evening.

They have forbidden me your hair, the look in your eyes,
It seems that your hair is long and full of odors
And it seems your eyes reveal strange longings
And grow agitated like rebellious waves.

They have pointed at me with irritated gestures,
Because my eyes searched out your tender look . . .
And seeing us go by, no one wanted to understand
That I had simply chosen you.

Consider the vile law that I transgress
And judge my love that knows nothing of evil,
As candid, as necessary and fatal
As the desire that joins lover to mistress.

They didn't read in my eyes how clearly I saw
The road where my destiny leads me,
And they have said: "Who is this damned woman
Who gnaws blindly at the flames of hell?"

Leave them to the concern of their impure morality,
And let us imagine that dawn has the blondness of honey,
That days without spite and nights without malice
Come, such as lovers whose goodness reassures . . .

We will go to see the clear stars on the mountains . . .
What matters to us, the judgment of men?
And what have we to doubt, since we are
Pure before life and since we love one another? . . .

"LAURENCE HOPE" [ADELA FLORENCE NICOLSON] (1865–1904)

"Kashmiri Song," "From Behind the Lattice" (1901–1905)

Adela Florence Nicolson, the daughter of a British army officer, spent most of her adult life in India, having married a colonel in the Bengal Cavalry in 1889. Under the pseudonym "Laurence Hope" she wrote three books of poetry on Indian themes—*The Garden of Kama* (1901), *Stars of the Desert* (1903), and *Indian Love* (1905). The last work appeared posthumously; Nicolson committed suicide by poison in October 1904, after suffering (according to the writer of her *Dictionary of National Biography* entry) "acute depression" after her husband's death two months earlier.

Nicolson's poems—many written in the masculine voice—suggest a more complex personality than these bare facts might indicate. Most interestingly, it has been rumored that she was romantically involved with the celebrated British composer Amy Woodforde-Finden (1860–1919), who was also the wife of a Bengal Cavalry officer. In 1902 Woodforde-Finden set four of Nicolson's poems to music, including "Kashmiri Song," which under its more familiar title, "Pale Hands I Loved Beside the Shalimar," became the most popular of all Edwardian parlor songs—its putatively lesbian provenance entirely lost on the British musical public.

FURTHER READING: "Laurence Hope" (Adela Florence Nicolson), *The Garden of Kama and Other Love Lyrics from India* (London: William Heinemann, 1901); —, *Stars of the Desert* (London: William Heinemann, 1903); —, *Indian Love* (London: William Heinemann, 1905); —, *Songs from the Garden of Kama* (London: William Heinemann, 1908); F. L. B. [Francis L. Bickley], "Mrs. Adela Florence Nicolson," *Dictionary of National Biography*, 2d Supplement, vol. 3 (London: Smith Elder, 1912), pp. 14–15; Sophie Fuller, *The Pandora Guide to Women Composers: Britain and the United States* (London: Pandora, 1995); Edward Marx, "Reviving Laurence Hope," in Isobel Armstrong and Virginia Blain, eds., *Women's Poetry, Late Romantic to Late Victorian: Gender and Genre, 1830–1900* (New York: Macmillan, 1999), pp. 230–42.

Kashmiri Song

Pale hands I loved beside the Shalimar,
    Where are you now? Who lies beneath your spell?
Whom do you lead on Rapture's roadway, far,
    Before you agonise them in farewell?

Oh, pale dispensers of my Joys and Pains,
    Holding the doors of Heaven and of Hell,
How the hot blood rushed wildly through the veins
    Beneath your touch, until you waved farewell.

Pale hands, pink tipped, like Lotus buds that float
    On those cool waters where we used to dwell,
I would have rather felt you round my throat,
    Crushing out life, than waving me farewell!

From Behind the Lattice

I see your red-gold hair and know
    How white the hidden skin must be,
Though sun-kissed face and fingers show
The fervour of the noon-day glow,
    The keenness of the sea.

My longing fancies ebb and flow,
    Still circling constant unto this;
My great desire (ah, whisper low)
To plant on thy forbidden snow
    The rosebud of a kiss.

The scarlet flower would spread and grow,
    Your whiteness change and flush,
(Be still, my reckless heart, beat slow,
'Tis but a dream that stirs thee so!)
    To one transparent blush.

ANGELINA WELD GRIMKÉ (1880–1958)

"Rosabel," "Brown Girl" (1901)

The African American poet and playwright Angelina Weld Grimké was born into a distinguished mixed-race family. Her great-aunts, Angelina Emily Grimké and Sarah Moore Grimké, were well-known white abolitionists; her father, a lawyer, was the son of a slave. Her mother came from a wealthy white Bostonian background. Grimké attended the Carleton Academy in Minnesota and graduated from Wellesley College in 1902. In 1916 her play *Rachel*, the first drama by an African American to be staged successfully in the United States, brought her considerable recognition; it proved an inspiration to later black women playwrights such as Lorraine Hansberry. In the 1920s, during the heyday of the Harlem Renaissance, Grimké turned increasingly to poetry. Several of her poems were collected in notable "Negro" anthologies of the day, including Alain Locke's *The New Negro* (1925), Countee Cullen's *Caroling Dusk* (1927), and Charles S. Johnson's *Ebony and Topaz* (1927). After 1930, however, she wrote little, possibly as a result of the death of her father, with whom she was extraordinarily close. For the remainder of her life she lived quietly, supporting herself as a schoolteacher while also assuming the role of unofficial spokeswoman and keeper of the flame for her accomplished family.

Grimké never married and left behind a number of unpublished love poems addressed to women. Her editor, Gloria T. Hull, believes that Grimké's relatively small literary output—and silence after 1930—may have been due, at least in part, to a fear of disclosing her homosexuality. Certainly the poems below, thought to have been written around 1901, have an emotional reach not found in Grimké's otherwise careful verse.

FURTHER READING: Angelina Weld Grimké, *Selected Works*, ed. Carolivia Herron (New York: Oxford University Press, 1991); Gloria T. Hull, "Under the Days: The Buried Life and Poetry of Angelina Weld Grimké," *Conditions: Five, The Black Woman's Issue* 2 (1979): 17–25; —, *Color, Sex, and Poetry: Three Women Writers of the Harlem Renaissance* (Bloomington: Indiana University Press, 1987); Yimitri Jayasundera, "Angelina Weld Grimké," in Emmanuel S. Nelson, ed., *African American Authors,*

1745–1945: A Bio-Bibliographical Critical Sourcebook (Westport, Conn.: Greenwood, 2000), pp. 194–98.

Rosabel

1

Leaves, that whisper, whisper ever,
    Listen, listen, pray;
Birds, that twitter, twitter softly,
    Do not say me nay;
Winds, that breathe about, upon her,
    (Since I do not dare)
Whisper, twitter, breathe unto her
    That I find her fair.

2

Rose whose soul unfolds white petaled
    Touch her soul rose-white;
Rose whose thoughts unfold gold petaled
    Blossom in her sight;
Rose whose heart unfolds red petaled
    Quick her slow heart's stir;
Tell her white, gold, red my love is;
    And for her,—for her.

Brown Girl

In the hot gold sunlight,
    Brown girl, brown girl,
        You smile;
    And in your great eyes,
        Very gold, very bright,
            I see little bells,
        Shaking so lazily,
            (Oh! small they are) . . .
            I hear the bells.
But at fawn dusk
    Brown girl, brown girl,

I see no smile,
I hear no bells.
Your great eyes
Are quiet pools;
They have been drinking, drinking,
All the day,
The hot gold of sunlight.
Your eyes spill sunlight
Over the dusk.
Close your eyes,
I hear nothing but the beating of my heart.

FRANK WEDEKIND (1864–1918)

From *Pandora's Box* (1903)

The German playwright, journalist, and cabaret performer Frank Wedekind was born in Hanover and educated in Switzerland. He worked as an actor, publicist, and circus manager as a young man and was one of the founders of the satirical literary journal *Simplicissimus*. His first great success as a playwright came in 1891 with *Frühlings Erwachen* (*Spring Awakening*), a scandalous experimental drama about an adolescent's sexual initiation. Even more popular and controversial, however, were the so called Lulu plays, *Erdgeist* (*Earth Spirit*) and *Die Büsche der Pandora* (*Pandora's Box*)—two interlinked dramas about a ruthless femme fatale and her destructive hold on her various lovers. Stylized, surreal, and shocking in their theatrical effects, the Lulu plays enjoyed an enormous vogue and profoundly influenced the development of German expressionism. Both the great G. W. Pabst silent film *Pandora's Box* (1929) and Alban Berg's magnificent opera *Lulu* (1937) were inspired by the Wedekind cycle. In his later years Wedekind continued to write and perform in cabaret but failed to duplicate his early theatrical coups. He died in Munich in 1918.

The Lulu plays did much to confirm Germany's reputation before and after the First World War as the most sexually progressive and overtly "homosexualized" country in Europe. The modern homosexual emancipation movement began in Germany: at the same time Wedekind was writing the Lulu dramas, the Berlin physician and sexual-freedom activist Magnus Hirschfeld organized a "Scientific-Humanitarian Committee," devoted to the abolition of antisodomy laws. Wedekind's own attitude toward homosexuality was complex but sympathetic. A central character in the Lulu cycle is the Countess Geschwitz, a wealthy lesbian artist and suffragette who falls in love with Lulu and tries to save her from a life of sexual degradation. When Lulu flees to London after murdering one of her male lovers in the second part of the cycle, the countess accompanies her there and helps her to hide in a hospital, allowing herself to be infected with cholera in the process. After Geschwitz recovers, she joins Lulu—who by this time has become a prostitute—and ends up dying alongside her, stabbed to death, when Lulu entertains a client who turns out to be Jack the Ripper.

Defending the Lulu cycle against would-be censors in 1906, Wedekind wrote that the noble yet hapless Geschwitz was his work's "central tragic figure." Her "stoical composure" and "super-human self-sacrifice" gave his drama its moral depth: "It is a matter of fact that the chief protagonists in the old Greek tragedies are almost always beyond the pale of normality. . . . If at the same time the spectator derives aesthetic pleasure from this presentation as well as unqualified spiritual gain, then the presentation is lifted out of the realm of morality into that of art." Although Wedekind seems not to have convinced his critics that "abnormality" might coincide with heroic self-sacrifice, the figure of Geschwitz retains an undeniable tragic pathos—both in the Lulu dramas themselves and in the Pabst and Berg works derived from them. Later in his career, it is worth noting, Wedekind wrote another play in which lesbian relationships featured prominently—the curious *Franʒiska: A Modern Mystery* (1911), featuring a boyish heroine who woos both actresses and heiresses.

In the final act of *Pandora's Box*—the conclusion of which is reproduced here—the countess follows Lulu to the squalid East End hovel in which Lulu sells herself to men. Geschwitz hides and eavesdrops as Lulu tries (unsuccessfully) to seduce a jittery young philosophy lecturer. He flees abruptly when he sees Geschwitz in the corner. In despair over a world in which "Men and women are like animals; not one of them knows what he's doing," Geschwitz then tries to hang herself. While the countess fumbles pitifully in the background with an old rug-cord she has wound around her neck, Lulu admits her next (and final) client, Jack the Ripper. The cycle comes to its bloody close with Geschwitz's death cry ("Lulu!—My angel! Let me see you once more! I am near you—will stay near you—in eternity!"). In Berg's operatic version, the mezzo singing the part of Geschwitz traditionally adds the final blasphemous imprecation: "Verflucht!" [God damn it].

FURTHER READING: Frank Wedekind, *Gesammelte Werke*, ed. Artur Kutscher and Joachim Friedenthal, 9 vols. (Munich: G. Muller, 1924); —, *Werke*, ed. Erhard Weidl, 2 vols. (Munich: Winkler, 1990); —, *The Diary of an Erotic Life*, trans. W. E. Yuill (Cambridge, Mass.: Basil Blackwell, 1990); —, *The Lulu Plays and Other Sex Tragedies*, trans. Stephen Spender (London: Calder and Boyars, 1972); Elizabeth Boa, *The Sexual Circus: Wedekind's Theater of Subversion* (Oxford: Basil Blackwell, 1987); Lillian Faderman and Brigitte Eriksson, *Lesbians in Germany: 1890's–1920's* (Tallahassee, Fla.: Naiad, 1990); Mitchell Morris, "Admiring the Countess Geschwitz," in Corinne E. Blackmer and Patricia Juliana Smith, eds., *En Travesti: Women, Gender Subversion, Opera* (New York: Columbia University Press, 1995), pp. 348–70; Maria Tatar, *Lustmord: Sexual Murder in Weimar Germany* (Princeton, N.J.: Princeton University Press, 1995); Gerald N. Izenberg, *Modernism and Masculinity: Mann, Wedekind, Kandinsky Through World War I* (Chicago: University of Chicago Press, 2000).

GESCHWITZ: [*Alone*]

I'll sit by the door. I'll watch it all without flinching.

[*She sits down on the cane chair by the door*]

—These people don't know themselves, don't know what they are like. Only someone who is not human himself can really know them. Every word they utter is false, a lie. But they don't know it, for today they are like this, tomorrow like that, according to whether they have eaten, drunk and made love, or not. The body alone remains for a time what it is, and only the children are rational. The adults are like animals. Not one of them knows what he is doing. In their happiest moments they groan and moan and in the depths of misery they are delighted by the tiniest trifle. It is strange how hunger deprives men of the strength to be unhappy. But when they have gorged themselves they turn the world into a chamber of horrors, throw their lives away for the satisfaction of a whim. I wonder if there have ever been people who were made happy by love. Their happiness after all consists of nothing more than being able to sleep better and forget everything. Lord God, I thank thee that I am not as other men are. I am not a human being at all—my body has nothing in common with other human bodies. But I have a human soul! The tormented have narrow shrivelled souls within them; but I know it is no merit on my part if I give up everything, sacrifice everything . . .

[Lulu *opens the door and admits* Dr. Hilti. Geschwitz *remains seated motionless by the door, unnoticed by either of them*]

LULU: [*Gaily*]

Come in, come in! You'll stay the night with me?

DR. HILTI: But I have no more than five shillings on me. I never take more with me when I go out.

LULU: That's enough, because it's you. You have such honest eyes!—Come, give me a kiss!

DR. HILTI: Jesus, Mary, Joseph . . .

LULU: Please, please, be quiet!

DR. HILTI: But devil take it, it's the first time I've ever been with a woman. That's really true. By God, I'd imagined it to be quite different!

LULU: Are you married?

DR. HILTI: For God's sake! What makes you think I'm married?—No, I'm a lecturer; I teach philosophy at the University. By God, I come of one of the best families in Basel; as a student I used to get only two francs' pocket money and I had better uses for it than women.

LULU: So that's why you've never been with a woman before?

DR. HILTI: Of course! Of course! But now I need it. I got engaged this evening to a girl from one of Basel's oldest families. She's here as a children's nurse.

LULU: Is your fiancée pretty?

DR. HILTI: Yes, she has two million.—I tell you, I can hardly wait to see what it's like.

LULU: [*Throwing back her hair*]

What luck I have!

[*She rises and takes the lamp*]

Well, if you're ready then, Professor?

[*She conducts* Dr. Hilti *into her chamber*]

GESCHWITZ: [*Pulls a small black revolver out of her pocket and holds it to her forehead*]

Come, come . . . beloved!

DR. HILTI.

[*Snatches the door open from within and rushes out*]

What sort of a dirty business is this!—There's a body in there!

LULU: [*The lamp in her hand, holds him by the sleeve*]

Stay with me!

DR. HILTI: A dead body! A corpse!

LULU: Stay with me, stay with me!

DR. HILTI: [*Freeing himself*]

There's a corpse lying in there in—A dirty business, by God!

LULU: Stay with me!

DR. HILTI: How does one get out of here?

[*Catching sight of* Geschwitz]

And there is the devil!

LULU: Please, please stay!

DR. HILTI: Dirty business, dirty business—My God!

[*Exit by center door*]

LULU: Stop!—Stop!

[*Rushes after him*]

GESCHWITZ: Better to hang! If she sees me lying in my own blood she won't shed a single tear for me. I was never more to her than a willing tool which didn't mind lending itself to the most difficult tasks. From the very first she loathed me from the bottom of her heart. Wouldn't it be better to jump off the bridge? Which is colder, the water, or her heart?—I would dream till I drowned . . . Better to hang! . . . Stab myself?—Hm, nothing to be gained by that . . . How often have I dreamed that she was kissing me! One minute more, then an owl beats against the window and I wake . . . Better to hang! Not into the river; water is too pure for me.

[*Suddenly starting up*]

There!—There!—There it is!—Quickly now, before she comes!

[*She takes the rugstrap from the wall, climbs on a chair, fastens the strap to a hook sticking into the doorpost, puts the strap round her neck, kicks the chair away with her feet, and falls to the ground*]

Accursed life!—Accursed life! . . . could it still be in store for me? . . . Let me appeal once more to your heart, my angel! But you are cold!—I need not go yet! Perhaps I am to have my taste of happiness. Listen to him, Lulu; I need not go yet!—

[*She drags herself over to* Lulu's *picture, sinks onto her knees and clasps her hands*]

My adored angel! My beloved! My star! Have pity on me, have pity on me, have pity on me!

[Lulu *opens the door to admit* Jack. *He is a square-built man, elastic in his movements, with a pale face, inflamed eyes, thick arched eyebrows, drooping moustache, sparse beard, matted sidewhiskers and fiery red hands with gnawed finger nails. His eyes are fixed on the ground. He is wearing a dark overcoat and a small round felt hat*]

JACK: [*Noticing* Geschwitz]: Who is that?

LULU: It's my sister, Sir. She's mad. I don't know how to get rid of her.

JACK: You seem to have a pretty mouth.

LULU: I get it from my mother.

JACK: It looks it.—How much do you want?—I haven't much money left.

LULU: Don't you want to stay all night, then?

JACK: No, I haven't time. I must go home.

LULU: You can tell them at home tomorrow morning that you missed the last omnibus and spent the night with a friend.

JACK: How much do you want?

LULU: I'm not asking for any gold nuggets, but—just a little something.

JACK: [*Turns towards the door*]

Good evening! Good evening!

LULU: [Holds him back]

No, no! Stay, for God's sake!

JACK: [*Walks past* Geschwitz *and opens the closet*]

Why should I stay till morning!—It sounds suspicious!—While I'm asleep my pockets will be turned out.

LULU: No, I shan't do that. No one will do it! Don't go because of that! Please!

JACK: How much do you want?

LULU: Give me half of what I asked before.

JACK: No, that's too much.—You don't seem to have been at this game long.

LULU: Today is the first time.

[*She pulls* Geschwitz *who, still on her knees, has half risen towards* Jack, *back by the strap round her neck*]

Lie down, will you!

JACK: Let her be. She's not your sister. She's in love with you.

[*He strokes* Geschwitz's *hair as if she were a dog*]

Poor creature!

LULU: Why are you staring at me like that?!

JACK: I sized you up by the way you walk. I said to myself you must have a well-made body.

LULU: How can anyone see such things?

JACK: I even saw that you had a pretty mouth.—I've only a silver piece on me.

LULU: Oh, well, what does it matter! Give it to me!

JACK: But you must give half of it back to me in change, so I can take the omnibus tomorrow morning.

LULU: I have nothing in my pocket.

JACK: Have a good look! Go through your pockets! There, what's that? Let me see it!

LULU: [*Holds her hand out to him*]

That's all I have.

JACK: Give me the money!

LULU: I'll change it tomorrow morning; then I'll give you half of it.

JACK: No, give me the whole thing.

LULU: [*Gives it to him*]

For God's sake!—But now, come.

[*She takes up the lamp*]

JACK: We don't need any light. The moon's shining.

LULU: [*puts down the lamp*]

Just as you like.

[*Throws her arms round* Jack's *neck*]

I won't do you any harm! I like you so much. Don't let me beg any longer!

JACK: I'm quite ready.

[*He follows her into* Schigolch's *cubby-hole.*

The lamp goes out. On the boards under both windows appear two harsh squares of light. Everything in the room is clearly visible]

GESCHWITZ: [*Alone, speaks as if in a dream*]

This is the last evening I shall spend with these people.—I shall go back to Germany. My mother will send me money for the fare. I shall take my matriculation. I must fight for women's rights, study jurisprudence.

LULU: [*Barefoot, in chemise and petticoat, tears the door open, screaming, and holds it shut from the outside*]

Help!—Help!

GESCHWITZ: [*Rushes to the door, pulls out her revolver and pushing* Lulu *behind her, aims it at the door. To* Lulu]

Let go!

[Jack, *bent double, pulls the door open from inside and plunges a knife into* Geschwitz's *stomach.* Geschwitz *fires a shot at the ceiling and collapses, whimpering*]

JACK: [*Snatches the revolver from her and hurls himself against the outside door*]

God damn! I've never seen a prettier mouth.

[*Sweat is dripping from his hair, his hands are bloody. He pants as if to burst his lungs and stares at the ground with bulging eyes*]

LULU: [*Trembling in every limb, looks wildly round her. Suddenly she seizes the bottle, dashes it against the table and rushes at* Jack *with the broken-off neck in her hand.* Jack *raises his right foot and sends her hurtling to the floor. Then he picks her up*]

No, no! Have mercy!—Murder!—Police!—Police!

JACK: Shut up! You're not going to get away from me again!

[*He carries her into the closet*]

LULU:[*From within*]

No, no!---Oh! Oh . . .

JACK: [*Returns after a while, and sets the bowl on the table*]

That was a good piece of work!

[*Washing his hands*]

What a damned lucky fellow I am!

[*Looks round for a towel*]

They haven't even got a towel! A miserable hole!

[*He dries his hands on* Geschwitz's *petticoat*]

This monster has nothing to fear from me!—

[*To* Geschwitz]

You're not long for this world, either.

[*Exit through the center*]

GESCHWITZ: [*alone*]

Lulu!—My angel!—Let me see you once more!—I am near you—will stay near you—in eternity!

[*Her arms give way*]

Oh, God!—

[*She dies*]

LUCIE DELARUE-MARDRUS (1874–1945)

"If You Come" (1904)

The author of over seventy books—including forty-seven novels and twelve books of poetry—the prolific French writer Lucie Delarue-Mardrus was born in 1874 in Honfleur on the Normandy coast. In her teens she formed several passionate crushes on older women, including Impéria de Heredia, wife of the poet José-Maria de Heredia. In 1900 she married the scholar Joseph-Charles Mardrus, the French translator of *The Arabian Nights*, and, with her husband, became part of a literary circle that included Gide, Proust, Maeterlinck, Cocteau, and Valéry. Mardrus helped her publish some of her early poems in the influential *Revue Blanche*. Her most profound emotional ties, however, continued to be with women, who responded powerfully to her considerable physical charms. After meeting her in 1902, an early admirer, the famous lesbian *salonnière* Natalie Barney, wrote in her journal, "Mme Mardrus was slim and quite tall in a princess gown which moulded her perfectly symmetrical figure. One felt that in the nude such a body would occasion no disappointment." Other passions included Sarah Bernhardt, the poet Renée Vivien, the novelists Colette and Rachilde, and the actress/journalist Marguerite Durand. The great love of Delarue-Mardrus's life, however, was the Jewish opera singer Germaine de Castro, whom she met in the 1930s. Despite de Castro's great bulk, vulgar manner, and indifferent stage success (her main claim to fame today is that she was Marian Anderson's singing teacher), Delarue-Mardrus was devoted to her and remained with her—courageously—when de Castro was forced into hiding during the Nazi occupation. Delarue-Mardrus's 1935 novel *Une Femme mûre et l'amour* (Love and the Mature Woman) is an autobiographical tribute to the woman whose ripe contralto voice she called "my drug, my morphine!"

Delarue-Mardrus's profuse writings touch often—if discreetly—on lesbian desire. Representative works include the poetry collections *Occident* (1901) and *Horizon* (1904), the play *La Prêtresse de Tanit* (1907), and the novels *Le Roman de six petites filles* (1909), *L'Acharnée* (1910), *Le Pain blanc* (1923), *Graine au vent* (1925), and *L'Ange et les pervers* (1930). The latter (recently translated into English under the title *The Angel and the Perverts*) is at once a lesbian roman à clef—Barney, Vivien, and Vivien's lover, the Baroness de Zuylen de Nyevelt, all make cameo appearances—and an oddly postmodern erotic fable: the central character is a hermaphrodite who passes both as a lesbian and a gay man in the homosexual salons of 1920s Paris.

FURTHER READING: Lucie Delarue-Mardrus, *Mes mémoires* (Paris: Gallimard, 1938); —, *Choix de poèmes* (Paris: Lemerre, 1951); —, *The Angel and the Perverts*, trans. Anna Livia (New York: New York University Press, 1995); Myriam Harry, *Mon amie, Lucie Delarue-Mardrus* (Paris: Ariane, 1946); Pauline Newman-Gordon, "Lucie Delarue-Mardrus, 1874–1945," in Eva Martin Sartori and Dorothy Wynne Zimmerman, eds., *French Women Writers: A Bio-Bibliographical Source Book* (New York: Greenwood, 1991); Hélène Plat, *Lucie Delarue-Mardrus: Une femme de lettres des années folles* (Paris: Grasset, 1994).

If you come, I will meet your lips at the door;
Without a word we will move to shadowy pillows
Where I will lay you out, long as a corpse,
And search, passionately, for your breasts.

Between the flowers at your throat, my mouth
Will take their naked, blushing tips;
Feeling you moan at the touch of every kiss,
I will desire you to the edge of tears!

My lips on your breast, my right hand will arouse
Your quivering body—flawless instrument—
And may all the artistry of sapphic love
Exalt its moist responsive inner flesh.

But when with difficult and painful pleasure
You arch, abandoned, opened wildly,
Can I restrain the mad desiring surge
That clasps my fingers at your lifeless throat!

KATHERINE MANSFIELD (1888–1923)

"Leves Amores" (1907), "Friendship" (1919)

Born in Wellington, New Zealand, where her father was a partner in a shipping company and later chairman of the Bank of New Zealand, the gifted short-story writer Katherine Mansfield—the only writer, Virginia Woolf said, whose style she envied—was educated at Wellington Girls' High School, then at Queen's College, London. She settled permanently in England in 1908, intending to support herself by her writing. Her personal life was difficult. After an unhappy love affair with a New Zealand musician by whom she had become pregnant, she married an Englishman, George Bowden, but left him almost immediately and went to a German spa, where she miscarried. She subsequently became involved—tumultuously—with the English poet and critic John Middleton Murry, whom she married in 1918. A number of her short stories, particularly those in her first short-story collection, *In a German Pension* (1911) and the later collection *Je ne parle français* (1919), bear upon these and other similarly fraught heterosexual relationships.

All her life, however, Mansfield was also powerfully if ambivalently attracted to women. She had several lesbian attachments while at school—including one with a Maori princess, Maata Matapuhu, and another, with a teacher, which may be the model for the Ursula/Winifred episode in D. H. Lawrence's *The Rainbow* (1915). The stories collected in *Prelude* (1918) and *The Garden Party and Other Stories* (1922), based on her childhood and adolescence in New Zealand, testify to the depth and delicacy of these lifelong homoerotic feelings. Later in life Mansfield frequently traveled with a devoted female companion, Ida Baker, and Baker was nearby, along with Middleton Murry, when Mansfield died of tuberculosis, at a spiritual institute run by the mystic Gurdjieff outside Paris, in 1923.

The uncollected story, "Leves Amores," written in 1907, was found among the papers of Vere Bartrick-Baker, one of Mansfield's schoolfriends, and first published as an appendix in Claire Tomalin's *Katherine Mansfield: A Secret Life* in 1987. The poem "Friendship," written in 1919, first appeared in *The Scrapbook of Katherine Mansfield*, a posthumous collection of writings edited by her husband, John Middleton Murry, in 1939.

FURTHER READING: Katherine Mansfield, *The Collected Stories of Katherine Mansfield* (New York: Knopf, 1937); —, *The Stories of Katherine Mansfield*, ed. Antony Alpers (London: Oxford University Press, 1984); —, *The Journal of Katherine Mansfield*, ed. J. M. Murry (London: Constable, 1927); —, *The Scrapbook of Katherine Mansfield* (London: Constable, 1939); —, *The Collected Letters of Katherine Mansfield*, ed. Margaret Scott and Vincent O'Sullivan, 2 vols. (London: Oxford University Press, 1984–87); Jeffrey Meyers, *Katherine Mansfield: A Biography* (London: Hamish Hamilton, 1978); Antony Alpers, *The Life of Katherine Mansfield* (London: Jonathan Cape, 1980); Claire Tomalin, *Katherine Mansfield: A Secret Life* (New York: Viking Penguin, 1987); Angela Smith, *Katherine Mansfield and Virginia Woolf: A Public of Two* (Oxford: Clarendon, 1999); —, *Katherine Mansfield: A Literary Life* (Basingstoke: Palgrave, 2001); David Coad, "Lesbian Overtones in Katherine Mansfield's Short Stories," in Michael J. Meyer, ed., *Literature and Homosexuality* (Amsterdam: Rodopi, 2000), pp. 223–38.

Leves Amores

I can never forget the Thistle Hotel. I can never forget that strange winter night.

I had asked her to dine with me, and then go to the Opera. My room was opposite hers. She said she would come but—could I lace up her evening bodice, it was hooks at the back. Very well.

It was still daylight when I knocked at the door and entered. In her petticoat bodice and a full silk petticoat she was washing, sponging her face and neck. She said she was finished, and I might sit on the bed and wait for her. So I looked round at the dreary room. The one filthy window faced the street. She could see the choked, dust-grimed window of a wash-house opposite. For furniture, the room contained a low bed, draped with revolting, yellow, vine-patterned curtains, a chair, a wardrobe with a piece of cracked mirror attached, a washstand. But the wallpaper hurt me physically. It hung in tattered strips from the wall. In its less discoloured and faded patches I could trace the pattern of roses—buds and flowers—and the frieze was a conventional design of birds, of what genus the good God alone knows.

And this was where she lived. I watched her curiously. She was pulling on long, thin stockings, and saying "damn" when she could not find her suspenders. And I felt within me a certainty that nothing beautiful could ever happen in that room, and for her I felt contempt, a little tolerance, a very little pity.

A dull, grey light hovered over everything; it seemed to accentuate the thin tawdriness of her clothes, the squalor of her life, she, too, looked dull and grey and tired. And I sat on the bed, and thought: "Come, this Old Age. I have forgotten passion, I have been left behind in the beautiful golden procession of Youth. Now I am seeing life in the dressing-room of the theatre."

So we dined somewhere and went to the Opera. It was late, when we came out into the crowded night street, late and cold . She gathered up her long skirts. Silently we walked back to the Thistle Hotel, down the white pathway fringed with beautiful golden lilies, up the amethyst shadowed staircase.

Was Youth dead? . . . *Was* Youth dead?

She told me as we walked along the corridor to her room that she was glad the night had come. I did not ask why. I was glad, too. It seemed a secret between us. So I went with her into her room to undo those troublesome hooks. She lit a little candle on an enamel bracket. The light filled the room with darkness. Like a sleepy child she slipped out of her frock and then, suddenly, turned to me and flung her arms round my neck. Every bird upon the bulging frieze broke into song. Every rose upon the tattered paper budded and formed into blossom. Yes, even the green vine upon the bed curtains wreathed itself into strange chaplets and garlands, twined round us in a leafy embrace, held us with a thousand clinging tendrils.

And Youth was not dead.

Friendship

When we were charming *Backfisch*
With curls and velvet bows
We shared a charming kitten
With tiny velvet toes.

It was so gay and playful;
It flew like a woolly ball
From my lap to your shoulder—
And, oh, it was so small,

So warm—and so obedient
If we cried: "That's enough!"
It lay and slept between us,
A purring ball of fluff.

But now that I am thirty
And she is thirty-one,
I shudder to discover
How wild our cat has run.

It's bigger than a Tiger,
Its eyes are jets of flame,

Its claws are gleaming daggers,
Could it have once been tame?

Take it away; I'm frightened!
But she, with placid brow,
Cries: "This is our Kitty-witty!
Why don't you love her now?"

RADCLYFFE HALL (1880–1943)

"The Spirit of Thy Singing," "Oh! That Thy Lips Were a Goblet of Crystal" (1910), "Miss Ogilvy Finds Herself" (1926)

Radclyffe Hall, author of the classic lesbian novel, *The Well of Loneliness*, is the most important English lesbian writer of the first half of the twentieth century. The daughter of an American socialite mother and a wealthy, ne'er-do-well British father, she was born in Devon and christened Marguerite Radclyffe Hall. Her childhood was unhappy: Hall's father abandoned the family soon after her birth, and after her mother remarried, Hall was raised by a series of governesses. Animals were an early love, and like the heroine of *The Well*, Stephen Gordon, Hall became an accomplished horsewoman in her teens. After inheriting the family fortune at her father's death in 1898 and pursuing some desultory studies at King's College, London, she began writing poetry, publishing several books over the next ten years: *'Twixt Earth and Stars* (1906), *A Sheaf of Verses* (1908), *Poems of the Past and Present* (1910), *Songs of Three Counties* (1913), and *The Forgotten Island* (1915).

While unashamed of her lesbianism—and able to act with relative freedom owing to her wealth and social position—Hall led a turbulent personal life. Her first serious lover, Mabel Veronica ("Ladye") Batten, was a married concert singer, twenty-three years her senior, whom Hall met in 1907 and lived with until Batten's death in 1916. Their last year was difficult: in 1915 Hall (who went by the name of "John" to her friends) began an affair with Una, Lady Troubridge, the wife of a prominent British admiral. Batten's death from a stroke followed soon after. Ridden with guilt, Hall and Troubridge—who would live together for the next twenty-seven years—became dedicated spiritualists and with the help of a medium sought to contact Batten on the "other side." Believing their efforts successful, they wrote up their experiences for the *Journal of the Society for Psychical Research* in 1919. For twenty more years they continued to "communicate" with Batten in this manner. Hall later dedicated *The Well of Loneliness* to "Our Three Selves"—in covert allusion to their odd love triangle.

Hall took up fiction writing in the early twenties, publishing *The Forge* and *The Unlit Lamp* in 1924, *A Saturday Life* in 1925, and *Adam's Breed*—which won both the Prix Femina and the James Tait Black Memorial Prize—in 1926. By 1928 Hall was a well-known and respected author, whose dashingly androgynous looks and fondness for black sombreros made her the darling of London society photographers. Opprobrium awaited, however, with the publication of *The Well of Loneliness* later that same year. In a vicious newspaper attack, James Douglas, the editor of the *Sunday Express,* declared that he would "rather give a healthy boy or a healthy girl a phial of prussic acid than this book" and called for its suppression. Charges were quickly brought against Hall's publishers, and despite letters of protest signed by E. M. Forster, George Bernard Shaw, Virginia Woolf, and nearly forty other prominent writers, the novel was banned in Britain under the Obscene Publications Act of 1857. (The ban remained in place until 1949.) Obscenity charges were also brought against *The Well* in the United States, but attempts to suppress it there were unsuccessful.

Not surprisingly, the prohibition on *The Well of Loneliness* made it an underground bestseller. Hall was deeply shaken by the controversy, however, and came to see herself a martyr to the homosexual cause. She retreated to Rye on the southern coast with Troubridge in 1930. Though she continued to write, publishing *The Master of the House* in 1932, *Miss Ogilvy Finds Herself and Other Stories* in 1934, and a final novel, *The Sixth Beatitude,* in 1936, her last years were marked by depression and inner turmoil. In 1934 she embarked on a tormented love affair with a Russian woman, nearly bringing her long relationship with Troubridge to an end. Troubridge remained loyal, however, and after Hall's death from cancer in 1943 penned an adoring memoir, *The Life and Death of Radclyffe Hall,* subsequently published in 1961.

Hall's minor yet very real gifts as a writer have been obscured by *The Well*'s notoriety. She was, first of all, a poet of distinction, with an old-fashioned, Tennysonian lyrical sensibility and an innate musicality. (A number of her poems were set to music during her lifetime.) And several of the early novels—notably *A Saturday Life* and *The Unlit Lamp*—are surprisingly good. The latter in particular, the stark tale of a daughter who sacrifices her emotional well-being in order to care for her narcissistic mother, attains a degree of psychological pathos seldom found in early twentieth-century popular fiction. As for *The Well* itself, it is not as bad as it is often made out to be. Admittedly the plot is melodramatic; and the 1890s-style sexology—the book is full of grim references to the "third sex" and "the terrible nerves of the invert"—overblown and silly. But decades after its publication *The Well of Loneliness* has not lost its audience or its strange, even startling, power to move.

The terms of Radclyffe Hall's will prohibit the excerpting of material from *The Well of Loneliness*. She is represented here by two love poems from *Poems of the Past and Present* (1910) and the 1926 short story "Miss Ogilvy Finds Herself," completed twelve days before she began the first draft of *The Well*. The poems are characteristic of Hall's late romantic manner: traditional in form yet full of virile (and unselfconscious) erotic fervor. "Miss Ogilvy" anticipates the themes and settings of *The Well*. Like *The Well*'s Stephen Gordon, the story's spinster-heroine serves heroically in an all-woman ambulance brigade on the Western Front—a life-changing experience that leads her to recognize her "inverted" sexual nature. She feels emasculated and confused upon her return to England after the Armistice. The story's ending is spectacularly botched: while visiting a remote island off the Devonshire coast, Miss Ogilvy undergoes a past-life regression in which she imagines herself a caveman making love to a cavewoman. She expires (apparently) in a kind of solitary butch *Liebestod*. Still, despite the final absurdity, the story possesses, like *The Well* itself, an undeniable, if bizarre, emotional pull.

FURTHER READING: Radclyffe Hall, *'Twixt Earth and Stars* (London: Bumpus, 1906); —, *A Sheaf of Verses* (London: Bumpus, 1908); —, *Poems of the Past and Present* (London: Chapman and Hall, 1910); —, *Songs of Three Counties and Other Poems* (London: Chapman and Hall, 1913); —, *The Forgotten Island* (London: Chapman and Hall, 1915); —, *The Unlit Lamp* (1924; rpt. London: Virago, 1981); —, *A Saturday Life* (1925; rpt. New York: Viking Penguin, 1989); —, *The Well of Loneliness* (1928; rpt. New York: Anchor, 1990); Una, Lady Troubridge, *The Life and Death of Radclyffe Hall* (London: Hammond and Hammond, 1961); Vera Brittain, *Radclyffe Hall: A Case of Obscenity?* (London: Femina, 1968); Lovat Dickson, *Radclyffe Hall at the Well of Loneliness: A Sapphic Chronicle* (London and Toronto: William Collins, 1975); Claudia Stillman Franks, *Beyond "The Well of Loneliness": The Fiction of Radclyffe Hall* (Amersham, Bucks.: Avebury, 1982); Esther Newton, "The Mythic Mannish Lesbian: Radclyffe Hall and the New Woman," *Signs* 9 (1984): 557–75; rpt. in Martin Duberman, Martha Vicinus, and George Chauncey Jr., eds., *Hidden from History: Reclaiming the Gay and Lesbian Past* (New York: Meridian, 1989), pp. 281–93; Michael Baker, *Our Three Selves: The Life of Radclyffe Hall* (New York: William Morrow, 1985); Richard Ormrod, *Una Troubridge: The Friend of Radclyffe Hall* (New York: Carroll and Graf, 1985); Rebecca O'Rourke, *Reflecting on "The Well of Loneliness"* (London and New York: Routledge, 1989); Teresa de Lauretis, *The Practice of Love: Lesbian Sexuality and Perverse Desire* (Bloomington and Indianapolis: Indiana University Press, 1994); Terry Castle, *Noël Coward and Radclyffe Hall: Kindred Spirits* (New York: Columbia University Press, 1996); Sally Cline, *Radclyffe Hall: A Woman Called John* (London: John Murray, 1997); Joanne Glasgow, ed., *Your John: The Love Letters of Radclyffe Hall* (New York: New York University Press, 1997); Diana Souhami, *The Trials of Radclyffe Hall* (London: Weidenfeld and Nicolson, 1998); Laura Doan, *Fashioning Sapphism: The Origins of a Modern English Lesbian Culture* (New York: Columbia University Press, 2001); — and Jay Prosser, eds., *Palatable Poison: Critical Perspectives on "The Well of Loneliness"* (New York: Columbia University Press, 2001).

The Spirit of Thy Singing

The spirit of thy singing,
It is as all sweet longing,
A throb through countless ages,
Stirring the sense to aching.

How can I sit and listen
Coldly to that wild music!
How can I stop from kissing
Lips that are half asunder!

Oh! That Thy Lips Were a Goblet of Crystal

Oh! that thy lips were a goblet of crystal,
Holding the priceless wine of thy spirit,
That I might drink there of my belovèd!

Deep would I drink from the marvellous vessel,
Draughts full of rapture and great contentment,
Through the long hours of the throbbing darkness.

Why hast thou hidden thy soul from my vision?
Thou hast revealed to me all thy beauty,
Only thy soul has fled from my kisses!

Miss Ogilvy Finds Herself

Miss Ogilvy stood on the quay at Calais and surveyed the disbanding of her Unit, the Unit that together with the coming of war had completely altered the complexion of her life, at all events for three years.

Miss Ogilvy's thin, pale lips were set sternly and her forehead was puckered in an effort of attention, in an effort to memorise every small detail of every old war-weary battered motor on whose side still appeared the merciful emblem that had set Miss Ogilvy free.

Miss Ogilvy's mind was jerking a little, trying to regain its accustomed balance, trying to readjust itself quickly to this sudden and paralysing change. Her tall, awkward body with its queer look of strength, its broad, flat bosom and thick legs and ankles, as though in response to her jerking mind, moved uneasily, rocking backwards and forwards. She had this trick of rocking on her feet in moments of controlled agitation. As usual, her hands were thrust deep into her pockets, they seldom seemed to come out of her pockets unless it were to light a cigarette, and as though she were still standing firm under fire while the wounded were placed in her ambulances, she suddenly straddled her legs very slightly and lifted her head and listened. She was standing firm under fire at that moment, the fire of a desperate regret.

Some girls came towards her, young, tired-looking creatures whose eyes were too bright from long strain and excitement. They had all been members of that glorious Unit, and they still wore the queer little forage-caps and the short, clumsy tunics of the French Militaire. They still slouched in walking and smoked Caporals in emulation of the Poilus. Like their founder and leader these girls were all English, but like her they had chosen to serve England's ally, fearlessly thrusting right up to the trenches in search of the wounded and dying. They had seen some fine things in the course of three years, not the least fine of which was the cold, hard-faced woman who, commanding, domineering, even hectoring at times, had yet been possessed of so dauntless a courage and of so insistent a vitality that it vitalised the whole Unit.

"It's rotten!" Miss Ogilvy heard someone saying. "It's rotten, this breaking up of our Unit!" And the high, rather childish voice of the speaker sounded perilously near to tears.

Miss Ogilvy looked at the girl almost gently, and it seemed, for a moment, as though some deep feeling were about to find expression in words. But Miss Ogilvy's feelings had been held in abeyance so long that they seldom dared become vocal, so she merely said "Oh?" on a rising inflection—her method of checking emotion.

They were swinging the ambulance cars in midair, those of them that were destined to go back to England, swinging them up like sacks of potatoes, then lowering them with much clanging of chains to the deck of the waiting steamer. The porters were shoving and shouting and quarrelling, pausing now and again to make meaningless gestures; while a pompous official was becoming quite angry as he pointed at Miss Ogilvy's own special car—it annoyed him, it was bulky and difficult to move.

"Bon Dieu! Mais dépêchez-vous donc!" he bawled, as though he were bullying the motor.

Then Miss Ogilvy's heart gave a sudden, thick thud to see this undignified, pitiful ending; and she turned and patted the gallant old car as though she were patting a well-beloved horse, as though she would say: "Yes, I know how it feels—never mind, we'll go down together."

2

Miss Ogilvy sat in the railway carriage on her way from Dover to London. The soft English landscape sped smoothly past: small homesteads, small churches, small pastures, small lanes with small hedges; all small like England itself, all small like Miss Ogilvy's future. And sitting there still arrayed in her tunic, with her forage-cap resting on her knees, she was conscious of a sense of complete frustration; thinking less of those glorious years at the Front and of all that had gone to the making of her, than of all that had gone to the marring of her from the days of her earliest childhood.

She saw herself as a queer little girl, aggressive and awkward because of her shyness; a queer little girl who loathed sisters and dolls, preferring the stable boys as companions, preferring to play with footballs and tops, and occasional catapults. She saw herself climbing the tallest beech trees; arrayed in old breeches illicitly come by. She remembered insisting with tears and some temper that her real name was William and not Wilhelmina. All these childish pretences and illusions she remembered, and the bitterness that came after. For Miss Ogilvy had found as her life went on that in this world it is better to be one with the herd, that the world has no wish to understand those who cannot conform to its stereotyped pattern. True enough, in her youth she had gloried in her strength, lifting weights, swinging clubs and developing muscles, but presently this had grown irksome to her; it had seemed to lead nowhere, she being a woman, and then as her mother had often protested: muscles looked so appalling in evening dress— a young girl ought not to have muscles.

Miss Ogilvy's relation to the opposite sex was unusual and at that time added much to her worries, for no less than three men had wished to propose, to the genuine amazement of the world and her mother. Miss Ogilvy's instinct made her like and trust men, for whom she had a pronounced fellow-feeling; she would always have chosen them as her friends and companions in preference to girls or women; she would dearly have loved to share in their sports, their business, their ideals and their wide-flung interests. But men had not wanted her, except the three who had found in her strangeness a definite attraction, and those would-be suitors she had actually feared, regarding them with aversion. Towards young girls and women she was shy and respectful, apologetic and sometimes admiring. But their fads and their foibles, none of which she could share, while amusing her very often in secret, set her outside the sphere of their intimate lives, so that in the end she must blaze a lone trail through the difficulties of her nature.

"I can't understand you," her mother had said, "you're a very odd creature—now when I was your age . . ."

And her daughter had nodded, feeling sympathetic. There were two younger girls who also gave trouble, though in their case the trouble was fighting for husbands who were scarce enough even in those days. It was finally decided, at Miss Ogilvy's request, to allow her to leave the field clear for her sisters. She would remain in the country with her father when the others went up for the Season.

Followed long, uneventful years spent in sport, while Sarah and Fanny toiled, sweated and gambled in the matrimonial market. Neither ever succeeded in netting a husband, and when the Squire died leaving very little money, Miss Ogilvy found to her great surprise that they looked upon her as a brother. They had so often jibed at her in the past, that at first she could scarcely believe her senses, but before very long it became all too real: she it was who must straighten out endless muddles, who must make the dreary arrangements for the move, who must find a cheap but genteel house in London and, once there, who must cope with the family accounts which she only, it seemed, could balance.

It would be: "You might see to that, Wilhelmina; you write, you've got such a good head for business." Or: "I wish you'd go down and explain to that man that we really can't pay his account till next quarter." Or: "This money for the grocer is five shillings short. Do run over my sum, Wilhelmina."

Her mother, grown feeble, discovered in this daughter a staff upon which she could lean with safety. Miss Ogilvy genuinely loved her mother, and was therefore quite prepared to be leaned on; but when Sarah and Fanny began to lean too with the full weight of endless neurotic symptoms incubated in resentful virginity, Miss Ogilvy found herself staggering a little. For Sarah and Fanny were grown hard to bear, with their mania for telling their symptoms to doctors, with their unstable nerves and their acrid tongues and the secret dislike they now felt for their mother. Indeed, when old Mrs. Ogilvy died, she was unmourned except by her eldest daughter who actually felt a void in her life—the unforeseen void that the ailing and weak will not infrequently leave behind them.

At about this time an aunt also died, bequeathing her fortune to her niece Wilhelmina who, however, was too weary to gird up her loins and set forth in search of exciting adventure—all she did was to move her protesting sisters to a little estate she had purchased in Surrey. This experiment was only a partial success, for Miss Ogilvy failed to make friends of her neighbours; thus at fifty-five she had grown rather dour, as is often the way with shy, lonely people.

When the war came she had just begun settling down—people do settle down in their fifty-sixth year—she was feeling quite glad that her hair was grey, that the garden took up so much of her time, that, in fact, the beat of her blood was slowing. But all this was changed when war was declared; on that day Miss Ogilvy's pulses throbbed wildly.

"My God! If only I were a man!" she burst out, as she glared at Sarah and Fanny, "if only I had been born a man!" Something in her was feeling deeply defrauded.

Sarah and Fanny were soon knitting socks and mittens and mufflers and Jaeger trench-helmets. Other ladies were busily working at depots, making swabs at the Squire's, or splints at the Parson's; but Miss Ogilvy scowled and did none of these things—she was not at all like other ladies.

For nearly twelve months she worried officials with a view to getting a job out in France—not in their way but in hers, and that was the trouble. She wished to go up to the front-line trenches, she wished to be actually under fire, she informed the harassed officials.

To all her enquiries she received the same answer: "We regret that we cannot accept your offer." But once thoroughly roused she was hard to subdue, for her shyness had left her as though by magic.

Sarah and Fanny shrugged angular shoulders: "There's plenty of work here at home," they remarked, "though of course it's not quite so melodramatic!"

"Oh . . . ?" queried their sister on a rising note of impatience—and she promptly cut off her hair: "That'll jar them!" she thought with satisfaction.

Then she went up to London, formed her admirable unit and finally got it accepted by the French, despite renewed opposition.

In London she had found herself quite at her ease, for many another of her kind was in London doing excellent work for the nation. It was really surprising how many cropped heads had suddenly appeared as it were out of space; how many Miss Ogilvies, losing their shyness, had come forward asserting their right to serve, asserting their claim to attention.

There followed those turbulent years at the front, full of courage and hardship and high endeavour; and during those years Miss Ogilvy forgot the bad joke that Nature seemed to have played her. She was given the rank of a French lieutenant and she lived in a kind of blissful illusion; appalling reality lay on all sides and yet she managed to live in illusion. She was competent, fearless, devoted and untiring. What then? Could any man hope to do better? She was nearly fifty-eight, yet she walked with a stride, and at times she even swaggered a little.

Poor Miss Ogilvy sitting so glumly in the train with her manly trench-boots and her forage-cap! Poor all the Miss Ogilvies back from the war with their tunics, their trench-boots, and their childish illusions! Wars come and wars go but the world does not change: it will always forget an indebtedness which it thinks it expedient not to remember.

3

When Miss Ogilvy returned to her home in Surrey it was only to find that her sisters were ailing from the usual imaginary causes, and this to a woman who had seen the real thing was intolerable, so that she looked with distaste at Sarah and then at Fanny. Fanny was certainly not prepossessing, she was suffering from a spurious attack of hay fever.

"Stop sneezing!" commanded Miss Ogilvy, in the voice that had so much impressed the Unit. But as Fanny was not in the least impressed, she naturally went on sneezing.

Miss Ogilvy's desk was piled mountain-high with endless tiresome letters and papers: circulars, bills, months-old correspondence, the gardener's accounts, an agent's report on some fields that required land-draining. She seated herself before this collection; then she sighed, it all seemed so absurdly trivial.

"Will you let your hair grow again?" Fanny enquired . . . she and Sarah had followed her into the study. "I'm certain the Vicar would be glad if you did."

"Oh?" murmured Miss Ogilvy, rather too blandly.

"Wilhelmina!"

"Yes?"

"You will do it, won't you?"

"Do what?"

"Let your hair grow; we all wish you would."

"Why should I?"

"Oh, well, it will look less odd, especially now that the war is over—in a small place like this people notice such things."

"I entirely agree with Fanny;" announced Sarah.

Sarah had become very self-assertive, no doubt through having mismanaged the estate during the years of her sister's absence. They had quite a heated dispute one morning over the south herbaceous border.

"Whose garden is this?" Miss Ogilvy asked sharply. "I insist on auricula-eyed sweet Williams! I even took the trouble to write from France, but it seems that my letter has been ignored."

"Don't shout," rebuked Sarah, "you're not in France now!"

Miss Ogilvy could gladly have boxed her ears: "I only wish to God I were," she muttered.

Another dispute followed close on its heels, and this time it happened to be over the dinner. Sarah and Fanny were living on weeds—at least that was the way Miss Ogilvy put it.

"We've become vegetarians," Sarah said grandly.

"You've become two damn tiresome cranks!" snapped their sister.

Now it never had been Miss Ogilvy's way to indulge in acid recriminations, but somehow, these days, she forgot to say: "Oh?" quite so often as expediency demanded. It may have been Fanny's perpetual sneezing that had got on her nerves; or it may have been Sarah, or the gardener, or the Vicar, or even the canary; though it really did not matter very much what it was just so long as she found a convenient peg upon which to hang her growing irritation.

"This won't do at all," Miss Ogilvy thought sternly, "life's not worth so much fuss, I must pull myself together." But it seemed this was easier said than done; not a day passed without her losing her temper and that over some trifle: "No, this won't do at all—it just mustn't be," she thought sternly.

Everyone pitied Sarah and Fanny: "Such a dreadful, violent old thing," said the neighbours.

But Sarah and Fanny had their revenge: "Poor darling, it's shell shock, you know," they murmured.

Thus Miss Ogilvy's prowess was whittled away until she herself was beginning to doubt it. Had she ever been that courageous person who had faced death in France with such perfect composure? Had she ever stood tranquilly under fire, without turning a hair, while she issued her orders? Had she ever been treated with marked respect? She herself was beginning to doubt it.

Sometimes she would see an old member of the Unit, a girl who, more faithful to her than the others, would take the trouble to run down to Surrey. These visits, however, were seldom enlivening.

"Oh, well . . . here we are . . ." Miss Ogilvy would mutter.

But one day the girl smiled and shook her blond head: "I'm not—I'm going to be married."

Strange thoughts had come to Miss Ogilvy, unbidden, thoughts that had stayed for many an hour after the girl's departure. Alone in her study she had suddenly shivered, feeling a sense of complete desolation. With cold hands she had lighted a cigarette.

"I must be ill or something," she had mused, as she stared at her trembling fingers.

After this she would sometimes cry out in her sleep, living over in dreams God knows what emotions; returning, maybe, to the battlefields of France. Her hair turned snow-white; it was not unbecoming yet she fretted about it.

"I'm growing very old," she would sigh as she brushed her thick mop before the glass; and then she would peer at her wrinkles.

For now that it had happened she hated being old; it no longer appeared such an easy solution of those difficulties that had always beset her. And this she resented most bitterly, so that she became the prey of self-pity, and of other undesirable states in which the body will torment the mind, and the mind, in its turn, the body. Then Miss Ogilvy straightened her ageing back, in spite of the fact that of late it had ached with muscular rheumatism, and she faced herself squarely and came to a resolve.

"I'm off!" she announced abruptly one day; and that evening she packed her kit-bag.

4

Near the south coast of Devon there exists a small island that is still very little known to the world, but which nevertheless can boast an hotel, the only building upon it. Miss Ogilvy had chosen this place quite at random, it was marked on her map by scarcely more than a dot, but somehow she had liked the look of that dot and had set forth alone to explore it.

She found herself standing on the mainland one morning looking at a vague blur of green through the mist, a vague blur of green that rose out of the Channel like a tidal wave suddenly suspended. Miss Ogilvy was filled with a sense of adventure; she had not felt like this since the ending of war.

"I was right to come here, very right indeed. I'm going to shake off all my troubles," she decided.

A fisherman's boat was parting the mist, and before it was properly beached, in she bundled.

"I hope they're expecting me?" she said gaily.

"They du be expecting you," the man answered.

The sea, which is generally rough off that coast, was indulging itself in an oily ground-swell; the broad, glossy swells struck the side of the boat, then broke and sprayed over Miss Ogilvy's ankles.

The fisherman grinned: "Feeling all right?" he queried. "It du be tiresome most times about these parts." But the mist had suddenly drifted away and Miss Ogilvy was staring wide-eyed at the island.

She saw a long shoal of jagged black rocks, and between them the curve of a small sloping beach, and above that the lift of the island itself, and above that again, blue heaven. Near the beach stood the little two-storied hotel which was thatched, and built entirely of timber; for the rest she could make out no signs of life apart from a host of white sea-gulls.

Then Miss Ogilvy said a curious thing. She said: "On the south-west side of that place there was once a cave—a very large cave. I remember that it was some way from the sea."

"There du be a cave still," the fisherman told her, "but it's just above highwater level."

"A-ah," murmured Miss Ogilvy thoughtfully, as though to herself; then she looked embarrassed.

The little hotel proved both comfortable and clean, the hostess both pleasant and comely. Miss Ogilvy started unpacking her bag, changed her mind and went for a stroll round the island. The island was covered with turf and thistles and traversed by narrow green paths thick with daisies. It had four rock-bound coves of which the south-western was by far the most difficult of access. For just here the island descended abruptly as though it were hurtling down to the water; and just here the shale was most treacherous and the tide-swept rocks most aggressively pointed. Here it was that the seagulls, grown fearless of man by reason of his absurd limitations, built their nests on the ledges and reared countless young who multiplied, in their turn, every season. Yes, and here it was that Miss Ogilvy, greatly marvelling, stood and stared across at a cave; much too near the crumbling edge for her safety, but by now completely indifferent to caution.

"I remember . . . I remember . . ." she kept repeating. Then: "That's all very well, but what do I remember?"

She was conscious of somehow remembering all wrong, of her memory being distorted and coloured—perhaps by the endless things she had seen since her eyes had last rested upon that cave. This worried her sorely, far more than the fact that she should be remembering the cave at all, she who had never set foot on the island before that actual morning. Indeed, except for the sense of wrongness when she struggled to piece her memories together, she was steeped in a very profound contentment which surged over her spirit, wave upon wave.

"It's extremely odd," pondered Miss Ogilvy. Then she laughed, so pleased did she feel with its oddness.

5

That night after supper she talked to her hostess who was only too glad, it seemed, to be questioned. She owned the whole island and was proud of the fact, as she very well might be, decided her boarder. Some curious things had been found on the island, according to comely Mrs. Nanceskivel: bronze arrow-heads, pieces of ancient stone celts; and once they had dug up a man's skull and thigh-bone—this had happened while they were sinking a well. Would Miss Ogilvy care to have a look at the bones? They were kept in a cupboard in the scullery.

Miss Ogilvy nodded.

"Then I'll fetch him this moment," said Mrs. Nanceskivel, briskly.

In less than two minutes she was back with the box that contained those poor remnants of a man, and Miss Ogilvy, who had risen from her chair, was gazing down at those remnants. As she did so her mouth was sternly compressed, but her face and her neck flushed darkly.

Mrs. Nanceskivel was pointing to the skull: "Look, miss, he was killed," she remarked rather proudly, "and they tell me that the axe that killed him was bronze. He's thousands and thousands of years old, they tell me. Our local doctor knows a lot about such things and he wants me to send these bones to an expert; they ought to belong to the Nation, he says. But I know what would happen, they'd come digging up my island, and I won't have people digging up my island, I've got enough worry with the rabbits as it is." But Miss Ogilvy could no longer hear the words for the pounding of the blood in her temples.

She was filled with a sudden, inexplicable fury against the innocent Mrs. Nanceskivel: "You . . . *you* . . ." she began, then checked herself, fearful of what she might say to the woman.

For her sense of outrage was overwhelming as she stared at those bones that were kept in the scullery; moreover, she knew how such men had been buried, which made the outrage seem all the more shameful. They had buried such men in deep, well-dug pits surmounted by four stout stones at their corners—four stout stones there had been and a covering stone. And all this Miss Ogilvy knew as by instinct, having no concrete knowledge on which to draw. But she knew it right down in the depths of her soul, and she hated Mrs. Nanceskivel.

And now she was swept by another emotion that was even more strange and more devastating: such a grief as she had not conceived could exist; a terrible unassuageable grief, without hope, without respite, without palliation, so that with something akin to despair she touched the long gash in the skull. Then her eyes, that had never wept since her childhood, filled slowly with large, hot, difficult tears. She must blink very hard, then close her eyelids, turn away from the lamp and say rather loudly:

"Thanks, Mrs. Nanceskivel. It's past eleven—I think I'll be going upstairs."

6

Miss Ogilvy closed the door of her bedroom, after which she stood quite still to consider: "Is it shell shock?" she muttered incredulously. "I wonder, can it be shell shock?"

She began to pace slowly about the room, smoking a Caporal. As usual her hands were deep in her pockets; she could feel small, familiar things in those pockets and she gripped them, glad of their presence. Then all of a sudden she was terribly tired, so tired that she flung herself down on the bed, unable to stand any longer.

She thought that she lay there struggling to reason, that her eyes were closed in the painful effort, and that as she closed them she continued to puff the inevitable cigarette. At least that was what she thought at one moment—the next, she was out in a sunset evening, and a large red sun was sinking slowly to the rim of a distant sea.

Miss Ogilvy knew that she was herself, that is to say she was conscious of her being, and yet she was not Miss Ogilvy at all, nor had she a memory of her. All that she now saw was very familiar, all that she now did was what she should do, and all that she now was seemed perfectly natural. Indeed, she did not think of these things; there seemed no reason for thinking about them.

She was walking with bare feet on turf that felt springy and was greatly enjoying the sensation; she had always enjoyed it, ever since as an infant she had learned to crawl on this turf. On either hand stretched rolling green uplands, while at her back she knew that there were forests; but in front, far away, lay the gleam of the sea towards which the big sun was sinking. The air was cool and intensely still, with never so much as a ripple or bird song. It was wonderfully pure—one might almost say young—but Miss Ogilvy thought of it merely as air. Having always breathed it she took it for granted, as she took the soft turf and the uplands.

She pictured herself as immensely tall; she was feeling immensely tall at that moment. As a matter of fact she was five feet eight which, however, was quite a considerable height when compared to that of her fellow tribesmen. She was wearing a single garment of pelts which came to her knees and left her arms sleeveless. Her arms and her legs, which were closely tattooed with blue zig-zag lines, were extremely hairy. From a leathern thong twisted about her waist there hung a clumsily made stone weapon, a celt, which in spite of its clumsiness was strongly hafted and useful for killing.

Miss Ogilvy wanted to shout aloud from a glorious sense of physical well-being, but instead she picked up a heavy, round stone which she hurled with great force at some distant rocks.

"Good! Strong!" she exclaimed. "See how far it goes!"

"Yes, strong. There is no one so strong as you. You are surely the strongest man in our tribe," replied her little companion.

Miss Ogilvy glanced at this little companion and rejoiced that they two were alone together. The girl at her side had a smooth brownish skin, oblique black eyes and short, sturdy limbs. Miss Ogilvy marvelled because of her beauty. She also was wearing a single garment of pelts, new pelts, she had made it that morning. She had stitched at it diligently for hours with short lengths of gut and her best bone needle. A strand of black hair hung over her bosom, and this she was constantly stroking and fondling; then she lifted the strand and examined her hair.

"Pretty," she remarked with childish complacence.

"Pretty," echoed the young man at her side.

"For you," she told him, "all of me is for you and none other. For you this body has ripened."

He shook back his own coarse hair from his eyes; he had sad brown eyes like those of a monkey. For the rest he was lean and steel-strong of loin, broad of chest, and with features not too uncomely. His prominent cheek-bones were set rather high, his nose was blunt, his jaw somewhat bestial; but his mouth, though full-lipped, contradicted his jaw, being very gentle and sweet in expression. And now he smiled, showing big, square, white teeth.

"You . . . woman," he murmured contentedly, and the sound seemed to come from the depths of his being.

His speech was slow and lacking in words when it came to expressing a vital emotion, so one word must suffice and this he now spoke, and the word that he spoke had a number of meanings. It meant: "Little spring of exceedingly pure water." It meant: "Hut of peace for a man after battle." It meant: "Ripe red berry sweet to the taste." It meant: "Happy small home of future generations." All these things he must try to express by a word, and because of their loving she understood him.

They paused, and lifting her up he kissed her. Then he rubbed his large shaggy head on her shoulder; and when he released her she knelt at his feet.

"My master; blood of my body," she whispered. For with her it was different, love had taught her love's speech, so that she might turn her heart into sounds that her primitive tongue could utter.

After she had pressed her lips to his hands, and her cheek to his hairy and powerful forearm, she stood up and they gazed at the setting sun, but with bowed heads, gazing under their lids, because this was very sacred.

A couple of mating bears padded towards them from a thicket, and the female rose to her haunches. But the man drew his celt and menaced the beast, so that she dropped down noiselessly and fled, and her mate also fled, for here was the power that few dared to withstand by day or by night, on the uplands or in the forests. And now from across to the left where a river would presently lose itself in the marshes, came a rhythmical thudding, as a herd of red deer with wide nostrils and starting eyes thundered past, disturbed in their drinking by the bears.

After this the evening returned to its silence, and the spell of its silence descended on the lovers, so that each felt very much alone, yet withal more closely united to the other. But the man became restless under that spell, and he suddenly laughed; then grasping the woman he tossed her above his head and caught her. This he did many times for his own amusement and because he knew that his strength gave her joy. In this manner they played together for a while, he with his strength and she with her weakness. And they cried out, and made many guttural sounds which were meaningless save only to themselves. And the tunic of pelts slipped down from her breasts, and her two little breasts were pear-shaped.

Presently, he grew tired of their playing, and he pointed towards a cluster of huts and earthworks that lay to the eastward. The smoke from these huts rose in thick straight lines, bending neither to right nor left in its rising, and the thought of sweet burning rushes and brushwood touched his consciousness, making him feel sentimental.

"Smoke," he said.

And she answered: "Blue smoke."

He nodded: "Yes, blue smoke—home."

Then she said: "I have ground much corn since the full moon. My stones are too smooth. You make me new stones."

"All you have need of, I make," he told her.

She stole closer to him, taking his hand: "My father is still a black cloud full of thunder. He thinks that you wish to be head of our tribe in his place, because he is now very old. He must not hear of these meetings of ours, if he did I think he would beat me!"

So he asked her: "Are you unhappy, small berry?"

But at this she smiled: "What is being unhappy? I do not know what that means any more."

"I do not either," he answered.

Then as though some invisible force had drawn him, his body swung round and he stared at the forests where they lay and darkened, fold upon fold; and his eyes dilated with wonder and terror, and he moved his head quickly from side to side as a wild thing will do that is held between bars and whose mind is pitifully bewildered.

"Water!" he cried hoarsely, "great water—look, look! Over there. This land is surrounded by water!"

"What water?" she questioned.

He answered: "The sea." And he covered his face with his hands.

"Not so," she consoled, "big forests, good hunting. Big forests in which you hunt boar and aurochs. No sea over there but only the trees."

He took his trembling hands from his face: "You are right . . . only trees," he said dully.

But now his face had grown heavy and brooding and he started to speak of a thing that oppressed him: "The Roundheaded-ones, they are devils," he growled, while his bushy black brows met over his eyes, and when this happened it changed his expression which became a little sub-human.

"No matter," she protested, for she saw that he forgot her and she wished him to think and talk only of love. "No matter. My father laughs at your fears. Are we not friends with the Roundheaded-ones? We are friends, so why should we fear them?"

"Our forts, very old, very weak," he went on, "and the Roundheaded-ones have terrible weapons. Their weapons are not made of good stone like ours, but of some dark, devilish substance."

"What of that?" she said lightly. "They would fight on our side, so why need we trouble about their weapons?"

But he looked away, not appearing to hear her. "We must barter all, all for their celts and arrows and spears, and then we must learn their secret. They lust after our women, they lust after our lands. We must barter all, all for their sly brown celts."

"Me . . . bartered?" she queried, very sure of his answer, otherwise she had not dared to say this.

"The Roundheaded-ones may destroy my tribe and yet I will not part with you," he told her. Then he spoke very gravely: "But I think they desire to slay us, and me they will try to slay first because they well know how much I mistrust them—they have seen my eyes fixed many times on their camps."

She cried: "I will bite out the throats of these people if they so much as scratch your skin!"

And at this his mood changed and he roared with amusement: "You . . . woman!" he roared. "Little foolish white teeth. Your teeth were made for nibbling wild cherries, not for tearing the throats of the Roundheaded-ones!"

"Thoughts of war always make me afraid," she whimpered, still wishing him to talk about love.

He turned his sorrowful eyes upon her, the eyes that were sad even when he was merry, and although his mind was often obtuse, yet he clearly perceived how it was with her then. And his blood caught fire from the flame in her blood, so that he strained her against his body.

"You . . . mine . . ." he stammered.

"Love," she said, trembling, "this is love."

And he answered: "Love."

Then their faces grew melancholy for a moment, because dimly, very dimly in their dawning souls, they were conscious of a longing for something more vast than this earthly passion could compass.

Presently, he lifted her like a child and carried her quickly southward and westward till they came to a place where a gentle descent led down to a marshy valley. Far away, at the line where the marshes ended, they discerned the misty line of the sea; but the sea and the marshes were become as one substance, merging, blending, folding together; and since they were lovers they also would be one, even as the sea and the marshes.

And now they had reached the mouth of a cave that was set in the quiet hillside. There was bright green verdure beside the cave, and a number of small, pink, thick-stemmed flowers that when they were crushed smelt of spices. And within the cave there was bracken newly gathered and heaped together for a bed; while beyond, from some rocks, came a low liquid sound as a spring dripped out through a crevice. Abruptly, he set the girl on her feet, and she knew that the days of her innocence were over. And she thought of the anxious virgin soil that was rent and sown to bring forth fruit in season, and she gave a quick little gasp of fear:

"No . . . no . . ." she gasped. For, divining his need, she was weak with the longing to be possessed, yet the terror of love lay heavy upon her. "No . . . no . . ." she gasped.

But he caught her wrist and she felt the great strength of his rough, gnarled fingers, the great strength of the urge that leapt in his loins, and again she must give that quick gasp of fear, the while she clung close to him lest he should spare her.

The twilight was engulfed and possessed by darkness, which in turn was transfigured by the moonrise, which in turn was fulfilled and consumed by dawn. A mighty eagle soared up from his eyrie, cleaving the air with his masterful wings, and beneath him from the rushes that harboured their nests, rose other great birds, crying loudly. Then the heavy-horned elks appeared on the uplands, bending their burdened heads to the sod; while beyond in the forests the fierce wild aurochs stamped as they bellowed their love songs.

But within the dim cave the lord of these creatures had put by his weapon and his instinct for slaying. And he lay there defenceless with tenderness, thinking no longer of death but of life as he murmured the word that had so many meanings. That meant: "Little spring of exceedingly pure water." That meant: "Hut of peace for a man after battle." That meant: "Ripe red berry sweet to the taste." That meant: "Happy small home of future generations."

7

They found Miss Ogilvy the next morning; the fisherman saw her and climbed to the ledge. She was sitting at the mouth of the cave. She was dead, with her hands thrust deep into her pockets.

AMY LOWELL (1874–1925)

"Hora Stellatrix," "Stupidity," "Anticipation," "Vintage," "Aubade," "In a Garden," "The Weather-Cock Points South" (1912–1919)

The American poet, critic, and lecturer Amy Lowell, unconventional scion of the wealthy and cultivated Lowell family of Boston, Massachusetts, is primarily remembered as one of the first promoters of the modernist movement in Anglo-American poetry of the teens and twenties. She collaborated with Ezra Pound on several imagist anthologies, was an early supporter of the avant-garde magazine *Poetry*, edited by her friend Harriet Monroe, and championed the radical vers libre of H.D., D. H. Lawrence, John Gould Fletcher, and others in a series of public lectures beginning in 1915. Yet her own poetry, experimental in form and much influenced by H.D. and Pound, deserves rehabilitation. Always prolific—her other works include books of essays and an important biography of Keats—Lowell published nine collections of poetry in her lifetime; two more were issued posthumously. Her best-known books are *A Dome of Many-Coloured Glass* (1912), *Sword Blades and Poppy Seed* (1914), *Men, Women, and Ghosts* (1916), *Pictures of the Floating World* (1919), and *What's O'Clock* (1925) for which she received a posthumous Pulitzer Prize.

Lowell also deserves recognition as a lesbian writer. Her first poem, written in 1902, was a rhapsodic tribute to the actress Eleanora Duse. Later love lyrics, dedicated to her lifelong companion, Ada Dwyer Russell, at times may remind one of Emily Dickinson and Christina Rossetti, so immediate and poignant is the achieved effect. Though Lowell was in life a bold and bluff figure—she smoked cigars, wore mannish clothes, and weighed over 240 pounds—her poems are, by contrast, delicate, filigreed, and often piercingly erotic.

FURTHER READING: Amy Lowell, *Six French Poets: Studies in Contemporary Literature* (New York: Macmillan, 1915); —, *Tendencies in Modern American Poetry* (New York: Macmillian, 1917); —, *John Keats*, 2 vols. (Boston: Houghton Mifflin, 1925); —, *Selected Poems of Amy Lowell*, ed. John Livingston Lowes (Boston: Houghton Mifflin, 1928); —, *Poetry and Poets: Essays by Amy Lowell* (Boston: Houghton Mifflin, 1930); —, *The Complete Poetical Works of Amy Lowell* (Boston: Houghton Mifflin, 1955); S. Foster Damon, *Amy Lowell: A Chronicle* (Boston: Houghton Mifflin, 1935); Jean Gould,

Amy: The World of Amy Lowell and the Imagist Movement (New York: Dodd, Mead, 1975); Lillian Faderman, " 'Warding off the Watch and Ward Society': Amy Lowell's Treatment of the Lesbian Theme," *Gay Books Bulletin* 1 (1979): 23–27; Richard Benvenuto, *Amy Lowell* (Boston: Twayne, 1985); Susan McCabe, " 'A Queer Lot' and the Lesbians of 1914: Amy Lowell, H.D., and Gertrude Stein," in Joyce W. Warren and Margaret Dickie, eds., *Challenging Boundaries: Gender and Periodization* (Athens: University of Georgia Press, 2000), pp. 62–90; William J. Scheick, "Amy Lowell (1874–1925)," in Laurie Champion, ed., *American Women Writers, 1900–1925: A Bio-Bibliographical Sourcebook* (Westport, Conn.: Greenwood, 2000), pp. 198–206; Margaret Homans, "Amy Lowell's Keats: Reading Straight, Writing Lesbian," *Yale Journal of Criticism* 14 (2001): 319–51.

Hora Stellatrix

The stars hang thick in the apple tree,
The south wind smells of the pungent sea,
Gold tulip cups are heavy with dew.
The night's for you, Sweetheart, for you!
Starfire rains from the vaulted blue.

Listen! The dancing of unseen leaves.
A drowsy swallow stirs in the eaves.
Only a maiden is sorrowing.
'T is night and spring, Sweetheart, and spring!
Starfire lights your heart's blossoming.

In the intimate dark there's never an ear,
Though the tulips stand on tiptoe to hear,
So give; ripe fruit must shrivel or fall.
As you are mine, Sweetheart, give all!
Starfire sparkles, your coronal.

Stupidity

Dearest, forgive that with my clumsy touch
   I broke and bruised your rose.
   I hardly could suppose
It were a thing so fragile that my clutch
   Could kill it, thus.

It stood so proudly up upon its stem,
 I knew no thought of fear,
 And coming very near
Fell, overbalanced, to your garment's hem,
 Tearing it down.

Now, stooping, I upgather, one by one,
 The crimson petals, all
 Outspread about my fall.
They hold their fragrance still, a blood-red cone
 Of memory.

And with my words I carve a little jar
 To keep their scented dust,
 Which, opening, you must
Breathe to your soul, and, breathing, know me far
 More grieved than you.

Anticipation

I have been temperate always,
But I am like to be very drunk
With your coming.
There have been times
I feared to walk down the street
Lest I should reel with the wine of you,
And jerk against my neighbours
As they go by.
I am parched now, and my tongue is horrible in my mouth,
But my brain is noisy
With the clash and gurgle of filling wine-cups.

Vintage

I will mix me a drink of stars,—
Large stars with polychrome needles,
Small stars jetting maroon and crimson,
Cool, quiet, green stars.

I will tear them out of the sky,
And squeeze them over an old silver cup,
And I will pour the cold scorn of my Beloved into it,
So that my drink shall be bubbled with ice.

It will lap and scratch
As I swallow it down;
And I shall feel it as a serpent of fire,
Coiling and twisting in my belly.
His snortings will rise to my head,
And I shall be hot, and laugh,
Forgetting that I have ever known a woman.

Aubade

As I would free the white almond from the green
    husk
So would I strip your trappings off,
Beloved.
And fingering the smooth and polished kernel
I should see that in my hands glittered a gem beyond
    counting.

In a Garden

Gushing from the mouths of stone men
To spread at ease under the sky
In granite-lipped basins,
Where iris dabble their feet
And rustle to a passing wind,
The water fills the garden with its rushing,
In the midst of the quiet of close-clipped lawns.

Damp smell the ferns in tunnels of stone,
Where trickle and plash the fountains,
Marble fountains, yellowed with much water.

Splashing down moss-tarnished steps
It falls, the water;

And the air is throbbing with it.
With its gurgling and running.
With its leaping, and deep, cool murmur.

And I wished for night and you.
I wanted to see you in the swimming-pool,
White and shining in the silver-flecked water.
While the moon rode over the garden,
High in the arch of night,
And the scent of the lilacs was heavy with stillness.

Night, and the water, and you in your whiteness,
    bathing!

The Weather-Cock Points South

I put your leaves aside,
One by one:
The stiff, broad outer leaves;
The smaller ones,
Pleasant to touch, veined with purple;
The glazed inner leaves.
One by one
I parted you from your leaves,
Until you stood up like a white flower
Swaying slightly in the evening wind.

White flower,
Flower of wax, of jade, of unstreaked agate;
Flower with surfaces of ice,
With shadows faintly crimson.
Where in all the garden is there such a flower?
The stars crowd through the lilac leaves
To look at you.
The low moon brightens you with silver.

The bud is more than the calyx.
There is nothing to equal a white bud,
Of no colour, and of all,
Burnished by moonlight,
Thrust upon by a softly-swinging wind.

"VERNON LEE" [VIOLET PAGET] (1856–1935)

"The Amazon on the Fountain" (1914)

Of Vernon Lee, the prolific late-Victorian English essayist, novelist, travel writer, aesthetician, controversialist, and all-around difficult personality, Henry James wrote to his brother William: "A word of warning about Vernon Lee . . . because she is as dangerous and uncanny as she is intelligent which is saying a great deal. Her vigour and sweep are most rare and her talk superior, altogether . . . she is by far and away the most able mind in Florence." Lee's real name was Violet Paget; she was the only child of a well-to-do Polish emigré and raised mostly on the Continent. Her first work, *Studies of the Eighteenth Century in Italy* (1880), written when she was twenty-four, established her reputation as a formidable writer on art and culture. Browning, Pater, and the art historian Bernard Berenson were early admirers; later friends included Maurice Baring, Aldous Huxley, and George Bernard Shaw. Lee lived abroad for long periods, particularly in Italy, publishing a series of highly intellectual travel books—*Genius Loci* and *The Spirit of Rome* (1906), *The Sentimental Traveller* (1908), and *The Tower of the Mirrors* (1914)—as well as historical novels, essays on political philosophy, and several volumes of strange, even morbid, supernatural tales. During the First World War she was a staunch pacifist and harshly criticized for her views. Lee's later works had mainly to do with aesthetics: *The Handling of Words, and Other Studies in Literary Psychology* appeared in 1923; *Music and Its Lovers*, on the psychology of musical appreciation, in 1932.

Lee's personal life was tormented in the extreme. Mercurial, sensitive, and passionately drawn to women, she apparently invited, then resisted, physical relationships—to the chagrin of the various women who sought affectionate ties with her. Early in life she loved a woman named Annie Meyer who died young; a photograph of Meyer's corpse, laid out on her bier, hung over Lee's bed for the rest of her life. Lee's most faithful companion was Clementine ("Kit") Anstruther-Thomson, who cared for her devotedly during the nervous breakdown Lee suffered in 1888. Yet after living with Lee for ten years, Anstruther-Thomson finally left her in frustration in 1899. Lee's friend, the robustly sapphic English composer Ethel Smyth, found Lee's love-neurosis "tragic," but it undoubtedly helped to make Lee's writing—represented here by "The Amazon on the Fountain" from *The Tower of the Mirrors*—what it is: weird, formal, acid-tinged, filled with unstated emotion, yet invariably haunting.

FURTHER READING: Vernon Lee, *Studies of the Eighteenth Century in Italy* (London: W. Satchell, 1880); —, *Hauntings: Fantastic Stories* (1892; rpt. Freeport, N.Y.: Books for Libraries, 1971); —, *Genius Loci: Notes on Place* (London: Grant Richards, 1899); —, *Pope Jacynth and Other Fantastic Tales* (London: Grant Richards, 1904); —, *The Tower of the Mirrors, and Other Essays on the Spirit of Places* (London: John Lane, 1914); —, *A Vernon Lee Anthology*, ed. Irene Cooper Willis (London: John Lane, 1929); Peter Gunn, *Vernon Lee: Violet Paget, 1856–1935* (1964; rpt. New York: Arno, 1975); Burdett Gardner, *The Lesbian Imagination (Victorian Style): A Psychological and Critical Study of "Vernon Lee"* (New York and London: Garland, 1987); Diana Maltz, "Engaging 'Delicate Brains': From Working-Class Enculturation to Upper-Class Lesbian Liberation in Vernon Lee and Kit Anstruther-Thomson's Psychological Aesthetics," in Talia Schaffer and Kathy Alexis Psomiades, eds., *Women and British Aestheticism* (Charlottesville: University Press of Virginia, 1999), pp. 211–29; Kathy Alexis Psomiades, " 'Still Burning from this Strange Embrace': Vernon Lee on Desire and Aesthetics," in Richard Dellamora, ed., *Victorian Sexual Dissidence* (Chicago: University of Chicago Press, 1999); Martha Vicinus, "The Adolescent Boy: Fin-de-Siècle Femme Fatale?" in Dellamora, ed., *Victorian Sexual Dissidence*, pp. 83–106; Angela Leighton, "Ghosts, Aestheticism, and 'Vernon Lee,' " *Victorian Literature and Culture* 28 (2000): 1–14.

At Zurich, near that same church of St. Peter's, at the crossing of two steep old-fashioned streets, there stands a fountain; and on it instead of a man-at-arms or some kirtled mediæval virtue, what but a copy of the Polycleitan Amazon! One arm bent over her head, one breast bare, and her chiton belted-up like a man's, there she stands, wounded or captive, on the stumpy Corinthian pillar above the perennial spurt of water and the stone trough shaped like the hollowed-out fir trunk which serves that purpose in an Alpine village. Rains and snows have washed her to a leaden greyness, as if the stone had turned into metal. The eighteenth-century sculptor has placed a fireman's helmet by her side, and also a dragoon's cuirass. And over these alien accoutrements she stands sorrowing between the high-pitched roofs and the turret windows, above the fountain where, no doubt, the Zurich maids, in stomachers and pigtails, were wont to wash the salad and gossip of poor Gretchen's mishap. Perhaps they wondered at so odd and unblushing a female body (*Weibsperson*); and at the taste of some High Herr Master-Cutler or Provost of the Silk Weavers having had her carved out of stone from an engraving brought back from Rome, where the Pope and Cardinals go about dressed like the scarlet woman, and ride in glass coaches with just such brazen hussies, no doubt, as this.

Not a week had passed after my meeting the exiled Amazon when I chanced into the house of that selfsame eighteenth-century dilettante. At least I do not think it could have belonged to anyone else. It was in a place which I shall not name, in order to save inquisitive readers from going there and never finding it; and of which I need only say that it lies about twenty miles west of Zurich. There had been a late fall of snow on the Alps; and in pelting icy rain we stumped to the outskirts of the little town, beyond where a knight armed cap-à-pie sentinels from his fountain column a quincunx of clipped plane trees. Then round the foot of the castle hill, of whose towers and Düreresque rocks and bushes one caught glimpses from under soaked umbrellas; past the gateposts and vases of a Louis XV country house, and in at the narrow passage of what looked like a gabled farm, with great coalscuttle roof and liveried shutters. Then, after groping about in stone passages smelling of kitchen and laundry, we suddenly entered a room: such a room!

It was remote from the rest of the house, and indeed from the world of realities. The faint green light of grassy orchards was filtered through the old bottle windows. And in it shone, unearthly white, the exquisite stucco nudities of goddesses in medallions and cupids dangling free from the ceiling. They smiled upon shelves on shelves of eighteenth-century books, in faded bindings of nosegay-coloured papers. The Herr Doctor lit a faggot of fir branches in the big French fireplace with a helmeted Roman Emperor on its overmantel. The room was filled for a moment with resinous smoke, sweet like some sylvan incense, and the flare struck those long-limbed goddesses and dimpled love-gods overhead, turning their previous pallor (Correggio-greenish from the apple-trees and grass outside) into the divinest rosy blush.

I was just going to ask about the Zurich town councillor who had set up that Amazon above the fountain (since it was evident that this must have been his room) when the Herr Doctor, his successor in that house, looked about him with an air of embarrassment, and said, in that Zurich German which has surely never changed since the eighteenth century: "The ladies will excuse if I now escort them back to their inn. The fact is I have to attend a meeting of Church Elders."

We rose. He snuffed out the flaming wood against the firedogs, turning the goddesses and cupids a ghostly white above the brown book-shelves. And we opened our umbrellas and went forth with him into the chill, rainy twilight of that little mediæval town.

MARINA TSVETAEVA (1892–1941)

"Are You Happy?" "Beneath My Plush Wool Plaid's Caresses," "Tonight, Between Seven and Eight," "How Can I Not Remember" from "The Girlfriend Poems" (1914–15) and *Letter to the Amazon* (1934–36)

Though biographers have often sought to obscure the fact, Marina Tsvetaeva—one of the supreme Russian poets of the century—had several important lesbian relationships over the course of her stark and troubled life. Born in Moscow in 1892, the daughter of a doctor and a classical pianist, she spent much of her childhood abroad in Italy, Switzerland, and Germany. She began publishing poetry as a teenager: her first book, *Evening Album*, appeared in 1910. She was drawn to other girls from an early age, and in "The House at Old Pimen," a prose work from 1933, describes an early crush on an older girl. In 1912 Tsvetaeva married the writer Sergei Efron—possibly to alleviate guilt over her homoerotic feelings—and bore him a daughter, Ariadna. In 1914, however, at the beginning of the First World War, she fell deeply in love with the lesbian poet and translator Sophia Parnok, with whom she carried on a volatile two-year affair. A cycle of poems known as the "Girlfriend" poems—written by Tsvetaeva in 1914 and 1915 but unpublished until the 1970s—commemorates this often anguished relationship.

In 1916 Tsvetaeva and her husband traveled to St. Petersburg, where they became acquainted with the poet Osip Mandelstam and other important writers of the day. (Mandelstam—briefly Tsvetaeva's lover—was a profound poetic influence.) Tsvetaeva's second daughter, Irina, was born in 1917. With the outbreak of revolution and civil war, Efron joined the White Army, leaving Tsvetaeva in famine-ridden Moscow. Struggling to survive the freezing winter of 1919–20, she placed her daughters in an orphanage where she knew they would receive warmth and food. She managed to retrieve Ariadna the following month but abandoned the sickly Irina. Irina died in the orphanage in 1920. Tsvetaeva continued to write—somehow—throughout these appalling events. In 1922, after five years of suffering, she and Ariadna fled Moscow and were reunited with Efron in Prague. They settled in Paris, among other White Russian emigrés, and remained there for the next fourteen years. Tsvetaeva gave birth to a son, Georgy, in 1925.

Tsvetaeva's best-known collection of poems, *Milepost I*, appeared in 1922. It was followed in 1928 by *After Russia*, the second and last volume of her poetry to be published in her lifetime. In the 1930s she turned increasingly to prose and wrote a series of eloquent essays on Russian literature and the role of the artist in society. In the same decade Efron began working for the Soviet secret service. Tsvetaeva gradually found herself ostracized by the Paris emigré community. When her husband and daughter returned to the Soviet Union in 1937, she decided to follow, taking Georgy with her. The move was a disastrous mistake. Her daughter was arrested in 1939 and sent to a concentration camp; Efron was executed a short time later. Unable to find work after being evacuated from Moscow at the beginning of the German offensive, Tsvetaeva hanged herself in Elabuga, in the Tatar Republic, in 1941.

Many of Tsvetaeva's lesbian writings have yet to appear in English. (The elegant translations here are by Diana Lewis Burgin, the first scholar to pursue in depth the subject of Tsvetaeva's relationships with women.) Reproduced first are poems 1, 2, 5, and 10 from the "Girlfriend" sequence. The extraordinary prose piece, *Letter to the Amazon*, originally written in French, dates from the 1930s. This is its first appearance in English. The French version has only been published once before: in an Italian collection of Tsvetaeva's works edited by Serena Vitale, *Le notti fiorentine/Lettera all'Amazone* (Milan: Arnoldo Mondadori, 1983). Tsvetaeva composed her "letter" after meeting Natalie Clifford Barney, the legendary lesbian *salonnière* and author of *Pensées d'une amazone* (1920). Feeling that Barney had rebuffed her friendly advances, Tsvetaeva poured into it all of her fiercely conflicted feelings about love between women. The result is an entirely cryptic, paranoid, overwhelming piece of reverie—all the more powerful for its agonized disquisition on maternity, a subject usually repressed in more conventional writing (such as Barney's) on the nature of lesbian desire.

FURTHER READING: Marina Tsvetaeva, *Stikhotvorenia i poemy v pyati tomakh* [Lyric and narrative poems in five volumes], ed. Alexander Sumerkin (New York: Russica, 1980–83); —, *Izbrannaya proza v dvukh tomakh 1917–1937* [Selected prose in two volumes 1917–1937], ed. Alexander Sumerkin (New York: Russica, 1979); —, *A Captive Spirit: Selected Prose*, trans. J. M. King (Ann Arbor, Mich.: Ardis, 1980); —, *Selected Poems of Marina Tsvetaeva*, rev. ed., trans. Elaine Feinstein (Oxford: Oxford University Press, 1981); —, *Selected Poems*, trans. David McDuff (Newcastle-upon-Tyne: Bloodaxe, 1987); —, *After Russia*, trans. Michael Naydan (Ann Arbor, Mich.: Ardis, 1992); —, *Art in the Light of Conscience: Eight Essays on Poetry by Marina Tsvetaeva*, trans. Angela Livingstone (Cambridge: Harvard University Press, 1992); Simon Karlinsky, *Marina Tsvetaeva: The Woman, Her World, and Her Poetry* (Cambridge: Cambridge University Press, 1985); Elaine Feinstein, *A Captive Lion: The Life of Marina Tsvetaeva* (New York: Dutton, 1987); Viktoria Schweitzer, *Tsvetaeva*, trans. Robert Chandler and H. T. Willetts (New York: Noonday, 1992); Diana Lewis Burgin, *Sophia Parnok: The Life and Work of Russia's Sappho* (New York: New York University Press, 1994); —, "Marina Ivanovna Tsvetaeva," in Claude J. Summers, ed., *The Gay and Lesbian Literary Heritage: A Reader's Companion to the Writers and Their Works from Antiq-*

uity to the Present (New York: Henry Holt, 1995), pp. 706–7; —, "Mother Nature Versus the Amazons: Marina Tsvetaeva and Female Same-Sex Love," *Journal of the History of Sexuality* 6 (1995): 62–88; Jane A. Taubman, "Marina Tsvetaeva," in Christine D. Tomei, ed., *Russian Women Writers, 1–11* (New York: Garland, 1999), pp. 835–44.

From "The Girlfriend Poems"

I

Are you happy?—You won't tell me!—Hardly!
Well, let it be!
You've simply kissed, methinks, too many people.
Hence—your grief.

I see in you the heroines of Shakespeare's
tragic plays.
You, a tragic youthful lady,
whom no one's saved!

You've grown so weary of repeating love's
recitative.
The iron-hued bruise on your pale hand speaks
expressively.

—I love you!—How sin hangs over you like
a thundercloud!—
Because you are sarcastic, searing, and
the best of all,

because we are—because our lives diverge in
a mass of ways,
because of your inspired seductions
and shady fate.

Because to you, my steepbrowed demon, I shall
say goodbye,
because—despite all efforts made to save you!—
you still will die.

Because I feel this thrill because of—can this
be all a dream?—
because of the ironic fascination that
you're not—a he.

October 16, 1914

2

Beneath my plush wool plaid's caresses,
I rouse the dream of yesterday.
What took place? Whose victory was it?
Who was slain?

Again I mull the whole thing over,
I suffer through it all anew.
In what I do not know the word for,
Was there love?

Who was the hunter? Who—the quarry?
It's all demonically reversed!
What knowledge did my cat take in as
She purred and purred?

In that duel of willfulnesses
Who in whose hand was just a ball?
Whose heart went flying off agallop?
Mine, or yours?

And still—what happened really?
What do I so regret and want?
I just don't know: was I victorious?
Or overcome?

October 23, 1914

5

Tonight, between seven and eight,
Headlong down Bolshaya Lubyanka,

Like a bullet, like a snowball,
Sped a sleigh en route somewhere.

I heard a peal of laughter ring . . .
My staring eyes froze solid:
A reddish furry cap of hair,
And someone tall—beside it!

You were already with another,
Off on a sleigh ride with her,
With somebody dear and desired,—
More strongly than I,—desired!

—"I can't take any more,—I'm stifling!"—
At the top of your lungs you shouted,
Sweeping off the heavy fur laprobe,
And wrapping her up in it.

The world was merry, the evening—wild!
Stuff flew out of a muff, unnoticed . . .
You sped through the snowy whirlwind,
Eye to eye and fur to fur.

And there was a most cruel revolt,
And snow blew around you whitely.
For just two seconds—no longer—
My gaze pursued you intently.

I smoothed down the long-haired nap
On my coat—I did not feel angry.
Oh Snow Queen, your little Kai
Has just about frozen to death!

October 26, 1914

I O

How can I not remember
The scent of tea and White Rose,
And the porcelain figures
On the mantel above the blaze.

We wore: me—a splendid dress of
An almost gold faille,
You—a black knit jacket,
With a collar wing-shaped.

I remember your face as you
Came in, no trace of color,
You rose, biting your finger,
Your head slightly inclined.

And your power-loving forehead
Beneath a dense auburn helmet.
—Not a boy and not a woman,
But something stronger than I!

I got up without thinking,
A crowd gathered around us.
"Get acquainted, gentlemen!"
Someone said as a joke.

And with a long, easy motion
You put your hand in my hand,
And my palm felt that ice-sliver's
Tender lingering stroke.

Steeled for a skirmish with
A guest staring sideways,
I sat twisting my wedding
Ring, not knowing why.

You took out a cigarette,
And I lit you a match,
Not knowing what I'd do if
You looked me in the eye.

I remember how our glasses
Clinked—above the blue vase.
"Oh, be my Orestes!" And
I gave you a flower.

Laughing—at what I was saying?—
From your black chamois handbag,

You drew out very slowly
And dropped—a handkerchief.

January 28, 1915

Letter to the Amazon

I have read your book. You are close to me as are all women who write. Do not be offended by that "all"—all women do not write: certain women among all write.

So, you are close to me as is every unique being and especially, every unique female being.

I have been thinking about you since the day I saw you,—was it a month ago? When I was young, I was impatient to have my say, I always feared letting the wave pass that departed from me and carried me toward the other, I always feared not loving any-more, not knowing anything anymore. But I am no longer young, and I have learned to let almost everything pass—irreparably.

To have everything to say—and not loosen one's lips. Everything to give—and not unclench one's hand. That is the sort of renunciation which you call bourgeois virtue and which, bourgeois or not, virtue or not, is the main springboard behind my actions. Springboard?—renunciation? Yes, for the repression of a force requires an infinitely more bitter effort than the free deployment of it—which requires no effort at all. In that sense all natural activity is a passive thing, like any passivity acquired—from activity (effusion—submission, repression—taking action). What is more difficult: to rein a horse in, or let him run, and since the horse we are reining in is ourselves,—which of the two is the more painful: to be reined in, or to give our power full play? To breathe or not to breathe? You may recall that children's game in which the winner is the one who remains longest in a sealed chest *without suffocating*? Cruel game and not at all bourgeois.

To act? To let oneself go. Each time I renounce, I have the sensation of the earth trembling inside me. That is me—an earth that trembles. Renunciation? Petrified struggle.

My renunciation has another name: not stooping to argue with the existing order about the way things are. The existing order in our case? For me to read your book, thank you for it with some words devoid of me, see you from time to time "smiling so that your smile can not be seen,"—act as if you had not written anything, and as if I had not read anything: as if nothing had taken place.

Listen to me, you do not have to respond to me, all you have to do is hear me out. I am dealing a blow straight to your heart, the heart of your cause, of your belief, of your body, of your heart.

Your book contains one omission, one single, immense omission,—is it conscious or not? I do not believe in the unconsciousness of thinking beings, still less—of think-ing beings who write, not at all—in the unconsciousness of a woman writer.

That omission, that white-out, that black gap—is the Child.

You return to it constantly, in frequency of mention you give it what you owe it in importance, you sow it here and there, then in another place, in order not to give it the integrity of the single cry that you owe it.

That cry, have you never, then, at least—heard it? "If I could only have a child from you!"

And that jealousy, savage and unique in the world, implacable because it is incurable, incomparable with the other, "normal" kind, incomparable even with maternal jealousy. That jealousy, that prescience of the inevitable break-up, those large eyes gazing upon the child that she would like to have some day and that you, the older woman, will not be able to give her. Those eyes riveted on the child-to-come.

—"Lovers do not have children." True, but they die. All of them. Romeo and Juliet, Tristan and Isolde, the Amazon and Achilles, Siegfried and Brunhilde (those lovers in their power, those disjointed joined pairs whose amorous disjointedness prevails over the most complete union . . .). And others . . . And others. . . . From all songs, from all eras, from all places . . . They do not have time for the future that is the child, they do not have a child because they do not have a future, they have only the present that is their love and their always present death. They die—or their love dies (degenerates into friendship, into maternal feeling: old Baucis with her old Philemon, old Pulcheria with her old child Afanasy,—couples as monstrous as they are touching).

Love for love's sake is childhood. Lovers are children. Children do not have children.

Or else—like Daphnis and Chloe—we know no more about them: even if they survive—they die, in us, for us.

One cannot *live* on love. The only thing that survives love is the Child.

And that other cry, have you never heard it either? "How I would like to have a child—without a man!" The smiling sigh of a young girl, the ingenuous sigh of an old maid and even, sometimes, the desperate sigh of a woman: "How I would like one who is—uniquely *mine*!"

And so the smiling young girl, who does not want a stranger in her body, who wants no part of him and of what is his, who wants only what is *mine*, meets at a turn in the road an other *me*, a *her*, whom she does not have to fear, against whom she does not have to defend herself, for the other cannot do her harm as one cannot (at least, when one is young) do harm to oneself. A most illusory conviction, and a conviction that will waver at her girlfriend's suspicious gaze and crumble under the major onslaughts of her malice.

But let's not get ahead of ourselves: for the moment she is happy and free, free to love from her heart, without her body, to love without being afraid, to love without doing harm.

And when the harm is done—she discovers it is not harm. Harm—is: shame, regret, remorse, disgust. Harm is the betrayal of one's soul with the enemy. But there is no enemy since what is involved is another *I*, always *I*, a new I, but an I who had been sleeping in the core of my being and was revealed by this other me, out there, in front of me, externalized and finally, *lovable*. She did not have to disavow herself in order to become a woman, she merely had to let herself go (to the depths of her self)—to let herself be. No split, no tear, no stigma.

And those words that sum it all up:

"Oh my own! Oh beloved *me*!"

Oh! It is never shame or disgust that forces her to leave her. It is due to, and for, another reason entirely.

At the outset it is only a kind of joke. "Beautiful baby!" "Would you like a baby like that?" "Yes. No. If it were yours—yes." "But . . ."—But it's all in fun.

The next time it's a sigh. "How I'd like a . . ." "What?" "Nothing." "No, no, I know . . ." "Well, if you know. But only—if it were yours . . ." Silence.

"Are you thinking about that again?" "You brought it up." "But you're the one who keeps bringing it up . . ."

She lacks for nothing, but she still has too much, she still has *everything* to give.— "I would like to love you as you were when you were a little girl"—the same way a woman says: "I would like to love you as you were when you were a little boy." Another you. Another female you. Another female you born from me.

It ends up as a desperate cry, stark and irreparable: "A child from you!"

The one who will never come. The one whose coming cannot even be prayed for. One can ask the Virgin for a child from a lover, one can ask the Virgin for a child from an old man—for evildoing—for a miracle—one cannot ask for something irrational. A union from which the child is simply excluded. A state of things that implies the absence of the child. Unthinkable. Everything except the child. Like the dinner of the Great King and the gentleman: everything except bread. The great daily bread of women.

It is always the desperate desire of one of the women, of the younger, of the more *she*. The older woman, she does not need a child, she has her girlfriend to satisfy her maternal feeling. "You are my girlfriend and my lover, you are my god, you are my everything."

But the other, she does not want to be loved like a child, she wants a child to love.

And the girl who began by not wanting a child from *him* will end up wanting a child from *her*. And because that cannot be, one day she will leave, loving, but crushed by the clear and powerless jealousy of the other—and the day will come when she will run aground, a waif, in the arms of the first man she meets.

(My child, my companioness—lover, my everything, and—as you so splendidly put it, Madame,—my female brother, never: sister. One would think that the word "sister" frightens them, as if it could forcibly reintegrate them into a world which they have left forever.)

At the beginning, the older woman fears it more than the other desires it. It's as if the older woman creates despair in her, transforms her smile into a sigh, her sigh into desire, her desire into obsession. The older woman's obsession creates the obsession of the younger woman. "You'll leave me, you'll leave me, you'll leave me. You want it from me, you'll want it from the first man you meet . . . You're thinking about that again . . . You looked at that man. Aren't you thinking—a fine father for your child! Leave me since I can't give it to you . . ."

Our apprehensions have the power to conjure, our fears to suggest, our obsessions to incarnate. The young girl, forced to be silent, thinks about it constantly, she has eyes only for young women whose arms are full. And she says to herself, "I'll never have a baby since I shall never, never leave her." (That's the very moment when she does leave her.)

The child—a fixed point from which henceforth, her eyes will not stray. The repressed child rises to the surface of her eyes like a drowned person. One has to be blind not to see it there.

And the girl who began by wanting a child from *her* will end up wanting a child from whomever: even from the abhorred him. The persecuting "he" becomes a savior. The Girlfriend—the (Female) Enemy. And the wind retraces its circles . . .

The child begins in us long before its beginning. There are pregnancies that last for years of hope, for eternities of despair.

And all her girlfriends are getting married. And the husbands of those girlfriends, so happy, so open, so close . . . And she says to herself, I would also . . .

She is immured.
Interred alive.

And the other keeps nagging at her. Allusions, suspicions, reproaches. The young girl: "So you don't love me anymore?" "I do love you, but—it's because you'll leave me." You'll leave, you'll leave, you'll leave.

Before leaving, she will want to die. Then, feeling as if she's already dead, without knowing anything, without planning anything in advance, without thinking anything, acting on three pure and vital instincts—youth, life, gut-feeling—at the time of her usual rendezvous which she has never missed, she finds herself laughing and joking at the other end of the city—and of life—with someone or other—perhaps the husband of one of her friends, or the man who works for her father, anyone, just so long as it isn't *she*.

A man, after a woman, what simplicity, what kindness. What openness. What liberty! What purity.

Then, it will be the end. The beginning of a male lover? A series of male lovers? The stability of a husband?

It will be the Child.

I omit the exceptional case: the non-maternal woman.

I also omit the banal case: the girl who is depraved, instinctively, or goes with women to be in fashion: the creature of pleasure who can always be discounted.

I omit, similarly, the rare case of a restless female soul, the woman who in loving is seeking the soul and therefore is predestined for a woman.

And the great female lover, the woman who in loving is seeking love and takes her good where she finds it.

And the woman who cannot have children for medical reasons.

I'm restricting myself to the normal case, the natural and vital case of a young female being who fears men, is attracted to women, and wants a child. The being who, when forced to choose between the stranger, the indifferent one, i.e. the (male) enemy-*revealer*, and the beloved female represser, ends up choosing the enemy male.

Who would rather have a child than love.

Who prefers her child to her love.

For the Child is something innate, it is in us prior to love, prior to having a lover. Its desire to be makes us open our arms. A young girl, I have in mind those from the North, is always too young for love, never for a child. At thirteen—she daydreams about it.

Something innate that must be given to us. Some girls begin by loving the donor, others end up loving him, still others end up submitting to him, and others by not submitting to him any longer.

Something innate that must be given to us. The one who does not give it to us takes it from us.

And we shall meet her again, a baby in her arms, and her heart full of hate for the woman whom henceforth, ungrateful like all women who no longer love, unjust like all women who still love,—she will call an error of her youth.

She will not be taken in again.

Don't be angry with me. I'm responding to the Amazon, not to the pale female vision who asks nothing of me. Not to the woman who gave me the book, to the woman who wrote it.

If you had never mentioned the child, I would have considered that a conscious omission, a last renunciation through silence, a scar that I would respect. But you keep coming back to it, you toss it back and forth like a ball: "By what right do they make and destroy life? Two children—two carefree souls," etc.

That is the only weak point, the only point that can be attacked, the only breach in the perfect entity that is two women who love each other. It is not impossible to resist the temptation of a man, but it is impossible to resist the need for a child.

The only weak point that spoils the whole thing. The only attackable point that allows the enemy corps to enter. For even if someday we shall be able to have a child *without him*, we shall never be able to have a child from her, a little-girl-you to love.

(An adopted daughter? Neither yours, nor mine? With, in addition, two mothers? Better leave it to nature to do what she does.)

The child: the only attackable point that ruins the whole thing. The only point that saves the cause of men. And of humanity.

Wholeness too whole. Oneness too one. ("Two will make only one." No,—two will make *three*.) A road terminating in a deadend. Impasse. Let us retrace our steps.

No matter how beautiful you are, no matter how intensely you embody The Only Woman—the first male nonentity will triumph over you. A nonentity who will be blessed. While you remain cursed.

"But what you are arguing is the same as cases when one cannot have a child with *one particular man*. Is that a reason to leave him?"

An exception to the rule cannot be compared to a rule without exception. The whole race, the whole cause, the whole thing is impugned in each case of love between women.

To leave a sterile man for his fertile brother is different from leaving the eternally infertile woman for the eternally fertile enemy. In the first case, I am merely saying goodbye to one man, in the second, I am saying goodbye to the whole race, the whole cause, all women in a single one.

A change merely of object. A change of coasts and of worlds.

Oh, I know, sometimes it lasts until death. A touching and terrifying vision on the wild Crimean coast, of two women [Polixena Solovyova and Nadezhda Manaseina—trans.], already old, who have spent their life together. One of them was the sister of the great Slav philosopher [Vladimir Solovyov], so read at the moment in France. The same luminous forehead, the same stormy eyes, the same fleshy and bare mouth. But they were surrounded by an emptiness more empty than what surrounds an infertile "straight" old couple, an emptiness more isolating, more desolating.

For no other reason, for none other—a cursed race.

Perhaps, if the young girl happens to be a thoughtful and serious person, it is precisely her horror of that curse that makes her leave.

"What people will say" counts for nothing, should not carry any weight since everything people say is said with malicious intent, everything people see is seen with malice-filled eyes. The spiteful eyes of envy, curiosity, indifference. People have nothing to say, people who wallow in evil.

God? Once and for all, God has nothing to do with carnal love. His name, whether joined or opposed to the name of any loved one, male or female, has the ring of sacrilege. There are things that cannot be compared with one another: Christ and carnal love. God has nothing to do with all those torments except to cure us of them. He said it once and for all: "Love me, the Eternal." Outside of that, everything is vain. Equally, irreparably vain. Simply by loving another human being with that kind of love, I betray The One who died for me and for my other on the cross of the other kind of love.

The Church and the State? They can have nothing to say about it so long as they give their sanction and blessing to millions of young men killing each other.

But what will, what does nature say about it, nature, the sole avengeress of and intercessoress for our physical deviations. Nature says: no. In forbidding it to us, she defends herself. When God forbids us something, He does so out of love for us; when nature forbids us something, she does so out of love for herself, out of hatred for everything that is not she. Nature hates the cloister as much as she hates the island [Lesbos] where the head of Orpheus washed ashore. Her vengeance is our downfall. Except that in a cloister we have God to help us; there, on the Island, there is only the sea for us to drown in.

The Island—an earth that is not earth, an earth one cannot leave, an earth one must love since one is condemned to it. A place where one can see everything, where one can do nothing.

An earth circumscribed by a fixed number of square feet. Impasse.

The great female unfortunate who was the great female poet [Sappho] chose the place of her birth well.

Brotherhood of lepers.

Outside of nature. But how does it happen, then, that the young girl, that creature of nature, loses her way so completely, so confidently?

Because of a trap of the soul. When she falls into the embrace of her older woman, she does not fall into a trap set by nature, or into the snares of the woman she loves, who is too often seen as a bewitching woman, a predatory woman, a rapacious woman, in a word—a vampire, when in reality she is, almost always, simply an acerbic and noble being whose whole crime lies in "seeing ahead" and, let's say it at the start—in foreseeing her young girl's departure. The young girl falls into a trap of the soul.

She wants to love—but . . . , she would indeed love—if . . . and there she is, in her other's arms, her head against her breast where the *soul dwells*.

Can she be repulsed? Ask that question of men young and old.

Then comes the meeting. Unforeseen and inevitable, because—even if one inhabits two separate worlds—the earth is always one: the earth on which one moves.

Her heart feels a shock, her blood ebbs and flows. A woman's first and last weapon—the weapon with which she disarms, believes she will disarm even death— her poor, last bit of courage—a blade that is alive and already red—her smile. Next, there's the small, incoherent torrent of syllables, rushing out one after the other like tiny ripples of water from under pebbles. What did she say? Nothing, because her other, the older woman, heard nothing, as we never hear any of the first words people say to us . . . But, after her other has shifted her eyes away from the mouth that has moved, she notices that the movement has meaning: ". . . for ten months . . . love . . . he likes me more than anybody else . . . he's a man of importance . . . (Take that, take that, take some more, swallow it all—in return for everything you've done to me!) . . . So, as I was saying—he's a man of importance . . ." (More important than the whole earth, more than the whole sea on the heart of the Older Woman.)

What voluptuous revenge! And the hatred—in her eyes! The hatred of a slave who has been liberated at last. The voluptuous pleasure that comes from stomping on another person's heart.

And then the small torrent is finally, at last, dammed up—slow and melodious, crystalline undulations: "Would you like to come visit me, come visit us, my husband and me . . ."

She has forgotten nothing. On the contrary, she remembers too much.

Next comes the bath, the sacred daily bath.

Obvious—and almost indecent—triumph of virility. For it turned out to be a son, always a son, as if nature, impatient to get back her rights, did not slow down enough to take the detour of a daughter. Not the little-girl-you, implored and impossible,—the little-he, the one who ought to have been expected, who arrived without being summoned, on command, a simple result (grandiose goal!).

The female other, clutching at her last hope, or simply not knowing what to say:

"He looks like you." "No" (dry and clipped). A *name* dry and clipped. And the final dart, containing perhaps the last traces of that great poison that is love:

"He looks like his father. He's the spitting image of my husband." There's an intentional vulgarity in this revenge. She says only those words that she knows will be the most wounding, the most common, the most like everyone else's (there you have the typical case that you are so fond of!). Is it choice or instinct? The words all come to her of themselves, she finds herself saying them (just as that day, in the already distant past, she found herself laughing . . .). Then, once the rites are over, Moses is saved and clothed, she gives him her breast and—supreme revenge—as she nurses, she lies in wait behind her lowered eyelashes for the spark of envy to appear in the eyes of the older woman, drowned in a mist of tenderness. For there is in the depths of every woman if she is not a monster, for there is, even in the depths of every monster . . . , for there are no monsters among women.

That spark, that smile—she *knows* them, but—for one reason or another—she will not raise her eyes.

If the man is smart, he will never ask her: "What are you thinking?"

Perhaps, once her other has left, she will want to rack her brains.

Perhaps, once her other has left, she will not want her husband to kiss her.

If the man is smart, he will not kiss her right away, he will wait—to kiss her—until her other is gone—permanently.

(Why did she come? To give herself pain. Sometimes that is all we have left.)

Next will come the other encounter, the counter-encounter, next will come the *payback*.

The same earth (excepting it, nothing is worth mentioning, for everything that happens, happens on the earth).

The same everyone in the role of spectators and listeners. (Nature's final revenge: for having been too alone, too one, too everything for one another, henceforth they will see each other only with everyone and everything between them.)

The same time: youth's eternity for as long as *it lasts*.

"Look, isn't that your ex-girlfriend over there?" "Where?" "There, with that darkhaired woman in blue."

Without having seen her, she knows it's she.

And then the human wave, more inhuman and ineluctable than the waves of the sea, draws her, draws her to her . . .

This time the older woman begins:

"How are you?" (And without waiting, without hearing the response) "Let me introduce my girlfriend, this is Miss So-and-So . . ." (a name).

If the former girlfriend, whose face drains of blood beneath her make-up, "was" a blonde—the new girlfriend, her replacement, will inevitably be a brunette. Desire for a complete death? Or the final blow to memories? Rancor at all blondeness? Killing the blonde with the brown? It's a law. Ask men why.

There are looks that kill. But there are none in this case since the darkhaired woman moves off, extremely animated, on the arm of the older woman—the new beloved. Enwrapping the former girlfriend in the blue waves of her long dress that physically puts entire unnavigable seas between the woman who stays behind and the woman who leaves.

Night, she leans over her adored sleeping child: "Ah! Jean, if you knew, if you knew, if you knew . . ."

It wasn't the day when the child was born, but today, three years later, that she real-izes what he has cost her . . .

So long as the Other remains young, she will always be seen in the company of an animated shade.

The brunette will change: she will become another blonde, or she will become a redhead. The brunette will leave as the blonde left. As all the girls leave who are mov-ing toward their unknown goal—always the same—after they have rested for a time under the tree that never moves.

They will all—pass by. They all would pass through this, if . . . But no one stays young forever.

The other. Let's return to her. The island. The eternally isolated woman. The mother who loses all her daughters, one by one, loses them forever since not only will they not come to put their children in her arms, but when they catch sight of her at a turn in the road, they will make furtive signs of the cross over their children's blonde heads. A Niobe with female descendents, Niobe destroyed by that other hunter, savage in another way. The eternal female loser at the only game worth playing—the only game there is. Shamed. Banished. Cursed. Pale vision without a body, whose race we recog-nize only by that look of the connoisseur, the reconnoiterer, the weigher, that look in which the merchant-pricer is conjoined with the idolatress, the chess player with the person who has tasted bliss,—a look that has various layers of profundity, and in which the last layer always turns out to be the next-to-last, endlessly, bottomlessly, all things that qualify will pass through that look, for it is an abyss,—an ineffable look, effaced by the wintry smile of renunciation.

When these women are young, one recognizes them by their smile, when they are old, it is by their smile that one fails to recognize them.

Young or old, these are the women who have the most soulful look about them. All other women, who have a look of the body about them, *do not have it*, are not of the same stuff, or have it only for the moment.

She lives on an island. She creates an island. She is an island. An island with an infi-nite colony of souls. Who knows if right at this very moment, in India, yonder, at the edge of the world . . . a young girl, knotting up her brown hair . . .

The "who knows's"—provide nourishment.

And are, in addition, the most dependable.

She will die alone, for she is too proud to love a dog, remembers too much to adopt a child. She does not want animals, or orphans, or a lady companion. Nor does she want a young lady companion. King David was a rube when he warmed himself up again from Avizag's inanimate heat. She does not want heat that is paid for, a smile that is put on. She does not want to be either a vampire, or a grandmother. Good for the man who, when he is old, is content with scraps, with elbows elbowing other elbows, hugs hugging other coasts, smiles smiling at other mouths, stopped, stolen by chance.—"Pass by, girls, pass by . . ." She will never be the poor female parent at the banquet of other people's youth. Neither friendship, nor esteem, nor that other abyss that is our own kindness, nothing will she accept in place of love. She will not renounce the splendid blackness, the black and circular burnmark—a circle that is magic in a different way from yours, Faust!—from the fire of her bygone joy. Against all springtimes—she will hold firm.

Even if a young girl throws herself at her the way a child bumps into a passerby or a wall—in passing, she will turn aside, a wall, she will be immovable. That once-frenzied womanlover, when she is old, will be pure out of pride. She who frightened people her whole life will not want to intimidate in that way. The young she-demon will never turn into an aged lamia.

Kindness—condescension—distance.

"Pass by quickly, mad and beautiful girls . . ."

> "Beneath the walls of a powder magazine,
> Walls now nearly wrecked by time,
> With hand held out before your light,
> Pass by, young girls, pass by."

While he, nevertheless,—a he, is able to pass all their passed blondenesses in lawful glory. A she—only in the smoke of horror.

What did not have the power to influence her, or her fatal, natural bent, neither God, nor men, nor her own pity, her pride *will* have the power to influence. And will influence, alone. And will do it so well that the eternal young girl, utterly intimidated, will say to her mother: "That lady frightens me. She has such a hard air about her. How have I displeased her?" . . .

And another girl, whose mother has taken her to "the lady,"—who knows why?—will hear words uttered by a voice in which repression crackles: "Your mother told me that you might have a bent for painting. One must develop one's talents, young lady . . ."

Never painted, never tinted, never made up to look young, never accentuated or falsified, leaving that sort of thing to ageing "normal women," women who, before the eyes of the world, with a priest's benediction, at sixty years of age make lawful marriages with children of twenty. She leaves that sort of thing to the sisters of Caesar.

Fatal and natural bent of the mountain to the valley, of the torrent to the lake . . .

Toward evening, the mountain in its entirety moves back toward its summit. In the evening it is its summit. As if its torrents carry it backwards. In the evening the mountain becomes herself again.

. . . Then, one day still later, the former young girl will learn that somewhere, at the other end of the same earth, her older woman has died. At first, she will want to write in order to know the details. But time rushes on—her letter will be immobilized. The desire will remain desire. The "I want to know" will become "I would like to know"; then—"I don't want to know any longer." "What's the use since she is dead? Since I too shall die some day" . . . And bravely, with the great truth of indifference: "Since she has been dead inside me—for me—hasn't it been twenty years now?"

There is no need to die in order to be dead.

Island. Summit. Alone.

Weeping willow! Willow in tears! Willow tree, the body and soul of women! Weeping nape of a willow. Gray hair spread over the face so as not to see anything anymore. Gray hair wiping the face of the earth.

Waters, air, mountains, trees are given to us so that we may understand the human soul which is so deeply hidden. When I see a willow tree in despair, I understand Sappho.

Clamart, November–December 1932
(recopied and revised in November 1934, with a few more gray hairs. M. Ts.)

SOPHIA PARNOK (1885–1933)

"In Words, in Their Cold Interlacing," "At Times Our Premonitions," "Blindly Staring Eyes," "You Sleep, My Companion-Lover," "You Came In," "I, Like a Blind Woman" (1916–32)

The Russian poet Sophia Parnok was born in the cosmopolitan city of Taganrog, on the inland Sea of Azov, near the Black Sea. Her mother, a physician, died when she was six; she was raised by her father and stepmother, whom she came to loathe. In 1905 she traveled for a year in Europe with a female lover and began writing poetry. Forced to return to Russia for financial reasons, she married a fellow poet but, feeling her own poetic voice stifled, left him in 1909. The same year she moved to Moscow and scrimped out a bohemian living as a poet, journalist, and translator, while also indulging in a number of lesbian affairs. In 1914 she met the charismatic younger poet Marina Tsvetaeva. Tsvetaeva, married and the mother of an infant, fell violently in love with Parnok and was her lover for two years. Both women documented their turbulent affair in verse: Parnok in several works in her first published book of poetry, *Poems* (1916); Tsvetaeva in a series of lyrics (unpublished in her lifetime) written in 1914 and 1915 and now known as the "Girlfriend" poems. Their separation (instigated by Parnok) was painful and left lasting psychic scars on both women.

At the outbreak of the Russian Civil War, Parnok moved to Sudak in the Crimea. For the next five years, often under appalling physical conditions, she continued to write, producing an opera libretto (for Alexander Spendiarov's *Almast*) and two books of poetry, *Roses of Pieria* (1922) and *The Vine* (1923). Increasingly, she looked to Sappho as a model for her own short, refined, yet powerfully homoerotic verses. In 1923, having returned to Moscow, she began a relationship with Olga Tsuberbiller, a mathematician at Moscow University with whom she lived for the rest of her life. In 1926 and 1928 she published two more collections of poetry, *Music* and *Half-Voiced*. Their controversial subject matter prompted the Soviet censors to declare her writing "unlawful," however, and after 1928 she was not allowed to publish. Her last years were spent in poor health and relative isolation, alleviated only by a final love affair, in 1931, with a woman named Nina Vedeneyeva, to whom she dedicated two last cycles of love poetry, "Ursa Major" and "Useless Goods." Parnok died of a heart attack in 1933.

FURTHER READING: Sophia Parnok, *Sobranie stikhotvorenii* [Collected Poems] (Ann Arbor, Mich.: Ardis, 1979); Sophia Poliakova, *[Ne]zakatnve ony dni: Tsvetaeva i Parnok*

(Ann Arbor, Mich.: Ardis, 1983); Rima Shore, "Remembering Sophia Parnok," *Conditions* 6 (1980): 177–93; Diana Lewis Burgin, "After the Ball is Over: Sophia Parnok's Creative Relationship with Marina Tsvetaeva," *Russian Review* 47 (1988), 425–44; —, "Laid Out in Lavender: Perceptions of Lesbian Love in Russian Literature and Criticism of the Silver Age, 1893–1917," in Jane Costlow, Stephanie Sandler, and Judith Vowles, eds., *Sexuality and the Body in Russian Culture* (Stanford: Stanford University Press, 1992), pp. 177–203; —, "Sophia Parnok and the Writing of a Lesbian Poet's Life," *Slavic Review* 51 (Summer 1992): 214–31; —, *Sophia Parnok: The Life and Work of Russia's Sappho* (New York and London: New York University Press, 1994); "Sophia Parnok," in Claude J. Summers, ed., *The Gay and Lesbian Literary Heritage: A Reader's Companion to the Writers and Their Works from Antiquity to the Present* (New York: Henry Holt, 1995), pp. 534–35.

In Words, in Their Cold Interlacing

In words, in their cold interlacing,
your movements' melody and pacing
how can I say?
Your raptures' whims, your passion's slumber,
your power, and the way you tremble
can I convey?
The misty North has not made cooler
your mouth's vermilion, or your golden,
deep suntan's stream;
the sun's warmth, live and animating,
flows on in you without abating,
my very dream.
All of the East's intoxications
I drink in the deep undulations
of your night eyes.
Your spicy smell, can I convey it?
My drunken heart, how shall I say it?
Oh love of mine!

At Times Our Premonitions

At times our premonitions, at times our recollections
uncover to our souls a world beyond our knowledge:

we like the features of the faces we have dreamed of,
the voices and the hues that make our hearts responsive;
and often all our lives, we yearn for them in secret.
We can't resist a thing that resonates their music;
we seek them in all things, the fleeting and eternal,
in pictures, poems, and in our belovèd women. . . .
Is that not why, my darling, you have me in your power?
What voice has made your voice become its repetition?
From whose curved lips have yours retained their obstinacy?
Whose arms encircle me when I'm in your embraces?

Blindly Staring Eyes

Blindly staring eyes of the
Holy Mother and Savior Child.
Smell of incense, wax, and oil.
Sounds of soft weeping filling the church.
Melting tapers held by young, meek women
in fists stiff with cold and roughskinned.
Oh, steal me away from my death,
you, whose arms are tanned and fresh,
you, who passed by, exciting me!
Isn't there in your desperate name a
wind from all storm-tossed coasts,
Marina, named after the sea!

You Sleep, My Companion-Lover

You sleep, my companion-lover, just like
a child on the breast of its mother!
How sweet: for you to fall asleep,
for me to lack strength to awaken,
the sonorous twilight, and you,
and you in my peaceful embrace?
Oh delicately winding tendrils
on your moist temple! Oh violets!
The same as the ones which would bloom
for us in our native meadows.

The two of us wove floral wreaths,
and where there were wreaths there was singing,
and songs came with bliss . . . Oh my last,
my sweet dream, are you finally asleep? . . .
Flow gently, Aeolian sky,
as you drift and drift up above me,
keep blazing, last sunset of mine,
keep foaming, my ancient wine!

You Came In

You came in just as thousands have entered,
but the doors for an instant breathed fire,
and I realized: your hand has been hewn with
that selfsame, prophetic sign.
Yes, I know it, the ring—of Venus
marks your palm in the very same way:
for your walk is entirely too measured,
and the light far too dimmed in your gaze,
and your face powder covers up tear stains,
and your lipstick is smeared over blood—
yes, my sister, I know, that's precisely
how she chokes you with kisses—love!

I, Like a Blind Woman

I, like a blind woman, find my way by touch
to your voice, your warmth, your smell . . .
In Pluto's garden I shall not get lost:
where you went in is East, West where you went out.
All right then, lead me, lead, lead
even through all the circles of hell
to that sandstorm blowing up ahead,
you're the only Virgil that I need!

GERTRUDE STEIN (1874–1946)

From "Lifting Belly" (1915), "Miss Furr and Miss Skeene" (1922),
"As a Wife Has a Cow—A Love Story" from *A Book Concluding with
As a Wife Has a Cow—A Love Story* (1926)

Gertrude Stein—perhaps the most famous lesbian literary eminence of the twentieth
century—was born in Pennsylvania, the child of well-to-do German-Jewish parents.
She briefly attended Radcliffe College in the 1890s, then pursued medical studies (subsequently abandoned) at Johns Hopkins University in Baltimore, where she came under
the influence of the psychologist William James. In 1902, having decided to be a writer
and live in Europe, Stein joined her brother, Leo, who had settled permanently in Paris,
on the rue de Fleurus. The two of them began collecting modern art. They quickly
amassed an extraordinary collection of works—by Picasso, Matisse, Braque, Cézanne,
and others—and their home became an international meeting place for avant-garde
writers, painters, and musicians. Even as Stein assumed the role of patroness, however,
she worked steadily on her own radically innovative writing, trying to find—through
repetition, associative word-play, and severe dislocations of grammar and syntax—an
equivalent in prose for the eloquent abstractions of painters like Picasso and Braque.

Stein's domestic arrangements changed dramatically in 1907, when she met Alice
B. Toklas, who supplanted Leo at the rue de Fleurus and became Stein's lover and companion for the next forty years. With Toklas's devoted assistance—she typed and
proofread all of Stein's manuscripts—Stein began to publish some of her experimental
writings. Early publications included *Three Lives* (1910), *Tender Buttons* (1914), abstract
word "portraits" of her friends Matisse, Picasso, Carl Van Vechten, and Guillaume
Apollinaire, and portions of her dense modernist epic, *The Making of Americans*
(1925). During the First World War Stein and Toklas served as relief workers and
drove a Red Cross ambulance. After the war, they played host to scores of Americans—members of the so-called Lost Generation—who gravitated to Paris in the
aftermath of world conflict. Stein's celebrated friendships with Ernest Hemingway,
Thornton Wilder, Sherwood Anderson, and Virgil Thomson—commemorated in
Hemingway's *A Moveable Feast* (1964) and other memoirs of the time—date from this
period.

The 1930s brought Stein renown, even notoriety, as more of her writings—and the
ardent bohemianism of her personality—became known to the general public. Her
entertaining memoir of her early years in Paris, *The Autobiography of Alice B. Toklas*

(1933), led to a lecture tour of the United States in 1934; her opera *Four Saints in Three Acts*, written with Virgil Thomson, debuted in New York in the same year. In her last decade Stein produced several major experimental works, including *The Geographical History of America or the Relation of Human Nature to the Human Mind* (1936) and *Ida, A Novel* (1940). But she continued publishing more accessible works as well: *Everybody's Autobiography* (1936), *Wars I Have Seen* (1942–44), and numerous writings on her literary aims and methods. She spent the years of the Nazi occupation, unmolested, with Toklas at their country home in Bilignin, but died soon after the end of the war, in 1946.

Stein's homosexuality was an open secret. With her close-cropped hair, massive yet graceful body, mannish clothing, and drolly intransigent manner—documented in a host of portraits and photographs—she was an early and striking epitome of twentieth-century high butch style. But her writings also testified to her love of women. One of her earliest pieces of fiction, the 1903 novel *Q.E.D.* (first published in 1950 under the title *Things As They Are*) is a fairly transparent account of an all-female love triangle in which Stein was involved during her years in Baltimore. Both "Melanctha" and "The Good Anna" in *Three Lives* contain elliptical portraits of women-loving women. Yet even the more experimental writings, as Catharine R. Stimpson has argued, can be read as lesbian "somograms": encrypted messages about new ways of loving. In the short story "Miss Furr and Miss Skeen" (1922) the passionate relationship between the principals is intimated through the giddy repetition of the word "gay." (Stein is one of the first modern writers to use the word as a slang term for homosexual.) And in the rhythmic, rocking devices of *Lifting Belly* (1915) and *As a Wife Has a Cow—A Love Story* (1926)—both love poems to Alice B. Toklas—Stein invents her own private language for lesbian eros: a speech at once abstract and formal, yet instantly and voluptuously comprehensible.

FURTHER READING: Gertrude Stein, *Geography and Plays* (Boston: Four Seas, 1922); —, *Three Lives* (Norfolk, Conn.: New Directions, 1933); —, *Selected Writings of Gertrude Stein*, ed. Carl Van Vechten (New York: Random House, 1946); —, *The Yale Edition of the Unpublished Writings of Gertrude Stein*, 8 vols. (New Haven: Yale University Press, 1951–58); —, *Bee Time Vine and Other Pieces*, ed. Virgil Thomson (New Haven: Yale University Press, 1953); —, *The Making of Americans* (New York: Something Else, 1966); —, *Fernhurst, Q.E.D., and Other Early Writings*, ed. Leon Katz (New York: Liveright, 1971); —, *The Yale Gertrude Stein*, ed. Richard Kostelanetz (New Haven: Yale University Press, 1980); —, *A Stein Reader*, ed. Ulla E. Dydo (Evanston, Ill.: Northwestern University Press, 1993); John Malcolm Brinnin, *The Third Rose: Gertrude Stein and Her World* (Boston: Little, Brown, 1959); Richard Bridgman, *Gertrude Stein in Pieces* (New York: Oxford University Press, 1970); James R. Mellow, *Charmed Circle: Gertrude Stein and Company* (New York: Praeger, 1974); Janet Hobhouse, *Everybody Who Was Anybody: A Biography of Gertrude Stein* (New York: Putnam's, 1975);

Catharine R. Stimpson, "The Mind, the Body, and Gertrude Stein," *Critical Inquiry* 3, no. 3 (spring 1977): 489–506; ——, "Gertrude Stein: Humanism and Its Freaks," *Boundary 2: A Journal of Postmodern Literature and Culture* 12–13, (1984): 301–19; ——, "Gertrude Stein and the Transportation of Gender," in Nancy K. Miller, ed., *The Poetics of Gender* (New York: Columbia University Press, 1986), pp. 1–18; ——, "The Somagrams of Gertrude Stein," *Poetics Today* 1–2 (1985): 67–80; ——, "Gertrude Stein and the Lesbian Lie," in Margo Culley, ed., *American Women's Autobiography: Fea(s)ts of Memory* (Madison: University of Wisconsin Press, 1992), pp. 152–66; Marianne DeKoven, *A Different Language: Gertrude Stein's Experimental Writing* (Madison: University of Wisconsin Press, 1983); Diana Souhami, *Gertrude and Alice* (London: Pandora, 1991); Bob Perelman, *The Trouble with Genius: Reading Pound, Joyce, Stein, and Zukovsky* (Berkeley: University of California Press, 1994); Linda Wagner-Martin, *"Favored Strangers": Gertrude Stein and Her Family* (New Brunswick, N.J.: Rutgers University Press, 1995); Linda S. Watts, *Rapture Untold: Gender, Mysticism, and the "Moment of Recognition" in Works by Gertrude Stein* (New York: Peter Lang, 1996); Corinne E. Blackmer, "Lesbian Modernism in the Shorter Fiction of Virginia Woolf and Gertrude Stein," in Eileen Barrett and Patricia Cramer, eds., *Virginia Woolf: Lesbian Readings* (New York: New York University Press, 1997), pp. 78–94; Stephen Scobie, *Earthquakes and Explorations: Language and Painting from Cubism to Concrete Poetry* (Toronto: University of Toronto Press, 1997); Barbara Will, *Gertrude Stein, Modernism, and the Problem of "Genius"* (Edinburgh: Edinburgh University Press, 2000); Steven Meyer, *Irresistible Dictation: Gertrude Stein and the Correlations of Writing and Science* (Stanford: Stanford University Press, 2001); Juliana Spahr, *Everybody's Autonomy: Connective Reading and Collective Identity* (Tuscaloosa: University of Alabama Press, 2001).

From *Lifting Belly*

Come and sing.
Lifting belly.
I sing lifting belly.

I say lifting belly and then I say lifting belly and Caesars. I say lifting belly gently and Caesars gently. I say lifting belly again and Caesars again. I say lifting belly and I say Caesars and I say lifting belly Caesars and cow come out. I say lifting belly and Caesars and cow come out.

Can you read my print.
Lifting belly say can you see the Caesars. I can see what I kiss.
Of course you can.
Lifting belly high.

That is what I adore always more and more.

Come out cow.

Little connections.

Yes oh yes cow come out.

Lifting belly unerringly.

A wonderful book.

Baby my baby I backhand for thee.

She is a sweet baby and well baby and me.

This is the way I see it.

Lifting belly can you say it.

Lifting belly persuade me.

Leave me to sing about it to-day.

And then there was a cake. Please give it to me. She did.

When can there be glasses. We are so pleased with it.

Go on to-morrow.

He cannot understand women. I can.

Believe me in this way.

I can understand the woman.

Lifting belly carelessly. I do not lift baby carelessly.

Lifting belly because there is no mistake. I planned to flourish.

Of course you do.

Lifting belly is exacting. You mean exact. I mean exacting.

Lifting belly is exacting.

Can you say see me.

Lifting belly is exciting.

Can you explain a mistake.

There is no mistake.

You have mentioned the flour.

Lifting belly is full of charm.

They are very nice candles.

Lifting belly is resourceful.

What can lifting belly say.

Oh yes I was not mistaken. Were not you indeed.

Lifting belly lifting belly lifting belly oh then lifting belly.

Can you make an expression. Thanks for the cigarette. How

pretty.

How fast. What. How fast the cow comes out.

Lifting belly a permanent caress.

Lifting belly bored.

You don't say so.
Lifting belly now.
Cow.
Lifting belly exactly.
I have often been pleased with this thing.
Lifting belly is necessarily venturesome.
You mean by that that you are collected. I hope I am.

Miss Furr and Miss Skeene

Helen Furr had quite a pleasant home. Mrs. Furr was quite a pleasant woman. Mr. Furr was quite a pleasant man. Helen Furr had quite a pleasant voice a voice quite worth cultivating. She did not mind working. She worked to cultivate her voice. She did not find it gay living in the same place where she had always been living. She went to a place where some were cultivating something, voices and other things needing cultivating. She met Georgine Skeene there who was cultivating her voice which some thought was quite a pleasant one. Helen Furr and Georgine Skeene lived together then. Georgine Skeene liked travelling. Helen Furr did not care about travelling, she liked to stay in one place and be gay there. They were together then and travelled to another place and stayed there and were gay there.

They stayed there and were gay there, not very gay there, just gay there. They were both gay there, they were regularly working there both of them cultivating their voices there, they were both gay there. Georgine Skeene was gay there and she was regular, regular in being gay, regular in not being gay, regular in being a gay one who was one not being gay longer than was needed to be one being quite a gay one. They were both gay then there and both working there then.

They were in a way both gay there where there were many cultivating something. They were both regular in being gay there. Helen Furr was gay there, she was gayer and gayer there and really she was just gay there, she was gayer and gayer there, that is to say she found ways of being gay there that she was using in being gay there. She was gay there, not gayer and gayer, just gay there, that is to say she was not gayer by using the things she found there that were gay things, she was gay there, always she was gay there.

They were quite regularly gay there, Helen Furr and Georgine Skeen, they were regularly gay there where they were gay. They were very regularly gay.

To be regularly gay was to do every day the gay thing that they did every day. To be regularly gay was to end every day at the same time after they had been regularly gay. They were regularly gay. They were gay every day. They ended every day in the same way, at the same time, and they had been every day regularly gay.

The voice Helen Furr was cultivating was quite a pleasant one. The voice Georgine Skeene was cultivating was, some said, a better one. The voice Helen Furr was cultivating she cultivated and it was quite completely a pleasant enough one then, a cultivated enough one then. The voice Georgine Skeene was cultivating she did not cultivate too much. She cultivated it quite some. She cultivated and she would sometime go on cultivating it and it was not then an unpleasant one, it would not be then an unpleasant one, it would be a quite richly enough cultivated one, it would be quite richly enough to be a pleasant enough one.

They were gay where there were many cultivating something. The two were gay there, were regularly gay there. Georgine Skeene would have liked to do more travelling. They did some travelling, not very much travelling, Georgine Skeene would have liked to do more travelling, Helen Furr did not care about doing travelling, she liked to stay in a place and be gay there.

They stayed in a place and were gay there, both of them stayed there, they stayed together there, they were gay there, they were regularly gay there.

They went quite often, not very often, but they did go back to where Helen Furr had a pleasant enough home and then Georgine Skeene went to a place where her brother had quite some distinction. They both went, every few years, went visiting to where Helen Furr had quite a pleasant home. Certainly Helen Furr would not find it gay to stay, she did not find it gay, she said she would not stay, she said she did not find it gay, she said she would not stay where she did not find it gay, she said she found it gay where she did stay and she did stay there where very many were cultivating something. She did stay there. She always did find it gay there.

She went to see them where she had always been living and where she did not find it gay. She had a pleasant home there, Mrs. Furr was a pleasant enough woman, Mr. Furr was a pleasant enough man, Helen told them and they were not worrying, that she did not find it gay living where she had always been living.

Georgine Skeene and Helen Furr were living where they were both cultivating their voices and they were gay there. They visited where Helen Furr had come from and then they went to where they were living where they were then regularly living.

There were some dark and heavy men there then. There were some who were not so heavy and some who were not so dark. Helen Furr and Georgine Skeene sat regularly with them. They sat regularly with the ones who were dark and heavy. They sat regularly with the ones who were not so dark. They sat regularly with the ones that were not so heavy. They sat with them regularly, sat with some of them. They went with them regularly went with them. They were regular then, they were gay then, they were where they wanted to be then where it was gay to be then, they were regularly gay then. There were men there then who were dark and heavy and they sat with them with Helen Furr and Georgine Skeene and they went with them with Miss Furr and Miss Skeene, and they went with the heavy and dark men Miss Furr and Miss Skeene went with them, and they sat with them, Miss Furr and Miss Skeene sat with them, and there were other men, some were not heavy men and they sat with Miss Furr and Miss Skeene and Miss Furr and Miss Skeene sat with them, and there were other men who were not dark men and they sat with Miss Furr and Miss Skeene and Miss Furr and Miss Skeene sat with them. Miss Furr and Miss Skeene went with them and they went with Miss Furr and Miss Skeene, some who were not heavy men, some who were not dark men. Miss Furr and Miss Skeene sat regularly, they sat with some men. Miss Furr and Miss Skeene went and there were some men with them. There were men and Miss Furr and Miss Skeene went with them, went somewhere with them, went with some of them.

Helen Furr and Georgine Skeene were regularly living where very many were living and cultivating in themselves something. Helen Furr and Georgine Skeene were living very regularly then, being very regular then in being gay then. They did then learn many ways to be gay and they were then being gay being quite regular in being gay, being gay and they were learning little things, little things in ways of being gay, they were very regular then, they were learning very many little things in ways of being gay, they were being gay and using these little things they were learning to have to be gay with regularly gay with then and they were gay the same amount they had been gay. They were quite gay, they were quite regular, they were learning little things, gay little things, they were gay inside them the same amount they had been gay, they were gay the same length of time they had been gay every day.

They were regular in being gay, they learned little things that are things in being gay, they learned many little things that are things in being gay, they were gay every day, they were regular, they were gay, they were gay the same length of time every day, they were gay, they were quite regularly gay.

Georgine Skeene went away to stay two months with her brother. Helen Furr did not go then to stay with her father and her mother. Helen Furr stayed there where they had been regularly living the two of them and she would then certainly not be lonesome, she would go on being gay. She did go on being gay. She was not any more gay but she was gay longer every day than they had been being gay when they were together being gay. She was gay then quite exactly the same way. She learned a few more little ways of being gay. She was quite gay and in the same way, the same way she had been gay and she was gay a little longer in the day, more of each day she was gay. She was gay longer every day than when the two of them had been being gay. She was gay quite in the way they had been gay, quite in the same way.

She was not lonesome then, she was not at all feeling any need of having Georgine Skeene. She was not astonished at this thing. She would have been a little astonished by this thing but she knew she was not astonished at anything and so she was not astonished at this thing not astonished at not feeling any need of having Georgine Skeene.

Helen Furr had quite a completely pleasant voice and it was quite well enough cultivated and she could use it and she did use it but then there was not any way of working at cultivating a completely pleasant voice when it has become a quite completely well enough cultivated one, and there was not much use in using it when one was not wanting it to be helping to make one a gay one. Helen Furr was not needing using her voice to be a gay one. She was gay then and sometimes she used her voice and she was not using it very often. It was quite completely enough cultivated and it was quite completely a pleasant one and she did not use it very often. She was then, she was quite exactly as gay as she had been, she was gay a little longer in the day than she had been.

She was gay exactly the same way. She was never tired of being gay that way. She had learned very many little ways to use in being gay. Very many were telling about using other ways in being gay. She was gay enough, she was always gay exactly the same way, she was always learning little things to use in being gay, she was telling about using other ways in being gay, she was telling about learning other ways in being gay, she was learning other ways in being gay, she would be using other ways in being gay, she would always be gay in the same way, when Georgine Skeene was there not so long each day as when Georgine Skeene was away.

She came to using many ways in being gay, she came to use every way in being gay. She went on living where many were cultivating something and she was gay, she had used every way to be gay.

They did not live together then Helen Furr and Georgine Skeene. Helen Furr lived there the longer where they had been living regularly together. Then neither of them were living there any longer. Helen Furr was living somewhere else then and telling some about being gay and she was gay then and she was living quite regularly then. She was regularly gay then. She was quite regular in being gay then. She remembered all the little ways of being gay. She used all the little ways of being gay. She was quite regularly gay. She told many then the way of being gay, she taught very many then little ways they could use in being gay. She was living very well, she was gay then, she went on living then, she was regular in being gay, she always was living very well and was gay very well and was telling about little ways one could be learning to use in being gay, and later was telling them quite often, telling them again and again.

From *A Book Concluding with As a Wife Has a Cow— A Love Story*

Nearly all of it to be as a wife has a cow, a love story. All of it to be as a wife has a cow, all of it to be as a wife has a cow, a love story.

As to be all of it as to be a wife as a wife has a cow, a love story, all of it as to be all of it as a wife all of it as to be as a wife has a cow a love story, all of it as a wife has a cow as a wife has a cow a love story.

Has made, as it has made as it has made, has made has to be as a wife has a cow, a love story. Has made as to be as a wife has a cow a love story. As a wife has a cow, as a wife has a cow, a love story. Has to be as a wife has a cow a love story. Has made as to be as a wife has a cow a love story.

When he can, and for that when he can, for that. When he can and for that when he can. For that. When he can. For that when he can. For that. And when he can and for that. Or that, and when he can. For that and when he can.

And to in six and another. And to and in and six and another. And to and in and six and another. And to in six and and to and in and six and another. And to and in and six and another. And to and six and in and another and and to and six and another and and to and in and six and and to and six and in and another.

In came in there, came in there come out of there. In came in come out of there. Come out there in came in there. Come out of there and in and come out of there. Came in there, come out of there.

Feeling or for it, as feeling or for it, came in or come in, or come out of there or feeling as feeling or feeling as for it.

As a wife has a cow.

Came in and come out.

As a wife has a cow a love story.

As a love story, as a wife has a cow, a love story.

Not and now, now and not, not and now, by and by not and now, as not, as soon as not not and now, now as soon now now as soon, now as soon as soon as now. Just as soon just now just now just as soon just as soon as now. Just as soon as now.

And in that, as and in that, in that and and in that, so that, so that and in that, and in that and so that and as for that and as for that and that. In that. In that and and for that as for that and in that. Just as soon and in that. In that as that and just as soon. Just as soon as that.

Even now, now and even now and now and even now. Not as even now, therefor, even now and therefor, therefor and even now and even now and therefor even now. So not to and moreover and even now and therefor and moreover and even now and so and even now and therefor even now.

Do they as they do so. And do they do so.

We feel we feel. We feel or if we feel if we feel or if we feel. We feel or if we feel. As it is made made a day made a day or two made a day, as it is made a day or two, as it is made a day. Made a day. Made a day. Not away a day. By day. As it is made a day.

On the fifteenth of October as they say, said anyway, what is it as they expect, as they expect it or as they expected it, as they expect it and as they expected it, expect it or for it, expected it and it is expected of it. As they say said anyway. What is it as they expect for it, what is it and it is as they expect of it. What is it. What is it the fifteenth of October as they say as they expect or as they expected as they expect for it. What is it as they say the fifteenth of October as they say and as expected of it, the fifteenth of October as they say, what is it as expected of it. What is it and the fifteenth of October as they say and expected of it.

And prepare and prepare so prepare to prepare and prepare to prepare and prepare so as to prepare, so to prepare and prepare to prepare to prepare for and to prepare for it to prepare, to prepare for it, in preparation, as preparation in preparation by preparation. They will be too busy afterwards to prepare. As preparation prepare, to prepare, as to preparation and to prepare. Out there.

Have it as having having it as happening, happening to have it as having, having to have it as happening. Happening and have it as happening and having it happen as happening and having to have it happen as happening, and my wife has a cow as now, my wife having a cow as now, my wife having a cow as now and having a cow as now and having a cow and having a cow now, my wife has a cow and now. My wife has a cow.

D. H. LAWRENCE (1885–1930)

From *The Rainbow* (1915)

The great British novelist, poet, travel writer, and literary critic D(avid) H(erbert) Lawrence was the son of an impoverished Nottinghamshire miner. Thanks in part to his mother's encouragement—she came from a more cultivated background than his father—he won a scholarship to Nottingham University, from whence he graduated in 1908. After a stint as a schoolteacher in Croydon, he published his first book of poems in 1909, followed by a first novel, *The White Peacock*, in 1911. In 1912 he caused a scandal by eloping with Frieda von Richthofen, the German wife of one of his Nottingham professors. Though their subsequent marriage was stormy—both Lawrences were forceful personalities and prone to physical violence—they managed to stay together until Lawrence's death in 1930, she nursing him faithfully through his many bouts of ill-health.

Lawrence's first major literary success was *Sons and Lovers* (1912), an autobiographical novel about a powerful mother/son relationship. During World War I he became a pacifist and retired to Cornwall, where he and Frieda were harassed by British authorities who suspected them of spying for the Germans. This abuse—compounded by Lawrence's moral disgust after his third novel, *The Rainbow* (1915), was suppressed by a court order on grounds of obscenity—prompted him to leave England for good in 1919 and spend the rest of his life wandering. He and Frieda lived for a time in Italy, where he completed *Women in Love* (his masterpiece) in 1920, and *Aaron's Rod* in 1922. Then they moved on to Ceylon and Australia, the inspiration for *Kangaroo* (1923). In 1924, at the invitation of the American writer-bohemian Mabel Dodge Luhan, they traveled to Taos, New Mexico. Lawrence was already suffering from the tuberculosis that would kill him, but was strongly attracted by the harsh and primal desert landscape and remained there for three years. He later visited Mexico—the subject of *The Plumed Serpent* (1926) and *Mornings in Mexico* (1927)—then returned to Italy, where his most controversial novel, *Lady Chatterley's Lover*, was published in 1928. (The latter was banned in England and the United States until the 1960s.) In his last two years he continued to write prolifically: the volumes *Apocalypse* (1931), *Last Poems* (1932), and *The Lovely Lady and Other Stories* (1933) were all published posthumously.

Homoeroticism, male and female, is a recurrent topos in Lawrence's writings.

Lawrence himself was deeply (if ambivalently) attracted to other men; his sexual feelings for John Middleton Murry, for example, the husband of Katherine Mansfield and model for Gerald in *Women in Love*, were lifelong and unresolved. Several of his best-known works of fiction—notably the disturbing short story "The Prussian Officer"—depict painfully homoerotic male-male bonds. But he was also fascinated by lesbianism and wrote about it in considerable psychological depth—most strikingly in *The Rainbow* and the 1921 novella *The Fox*. In the scene below from *The Rainbow*, one of several in the book deemed obscene by contemporary censors, Lawrence describes a brief yet passionate affair between the adolescent Ursula Brangwen and her young teacher, the suffragist Winifred Inger. Although Ursula subsequently rejects Winifred and turns to men—craving, in Lawrence's words, "some fine intensity, instead of this heavy cleaving of moist clay"—their fleeting relationship is treated with remarkable erotic frankness and emotional pertinence. In drawing the scene, as Claire Tomalin and others have suggested, Lawrence may have been inspired by an episode in the early life of his friend Katherine Mansfield.

FURTHER READING: D. H. Lawrence, *The Cambridge Edition of the Works of D. H. Lawrence*, ed. James T. Boulton and Warren Roberts, 21 vols. (Cambridge: Cambridge University Press, 1979–94); —, *The Letters of D. H. Lawrence*, ed. James T. Boulton et al., 4 vols. (Cambridge: Cambridge University Press, 1979–87); John Carter, "The *Rainbow* Prosecution," *Times Literary Supplement*, 27 February 1969, p. 216; Harry Thornton Moore, *The Priest of Love: A Life of D. H. Lawrence*, rev. ed. (New York: Farrar, Straus and Giroux, 1974); Aidan Burns, *Nature and Culture in D. H. Lawrence* (Totowa, N.J.: Barnes and Noble, 1980); Keith M. Sagan, *The Life of D. H. Lawrence* (London: Eyre Methuen, 1989); Claire Tomalin, *Katherine Mansfield: A Secret Life* (New York: Viking Penguin, 1987); Elaine Feinstein, *Lawrence and the Women: The Intimate Life of D. H. Lawrence* (New York: HarperCollins, 1993); Brenda Maddox, *D. H. Lawrence: The Story of a Marriage* (New York: Simon and Schuster, 1994); Mark Kinkead-Weekes, *D. H. Lawrence: Triumph to Exile, 1912–1922* (Cambridge and New York: Cambridge University Press, 1996); David Ellis, *D. H. Lawrence: Dying Game, 1922–1930* (Cambridge and New York: Cambridge University Press, 1998); Allison Pease, *Modernism, Mass Culture, and the Aesthetics of Obscenity* (Cambridge and New York: Cambridge University Press, 2000); Justin D. Edwards, "At the End of the Rainbow: Reading Lesbian Identities in D. H. Lawrence's Fiction," *International Fiction Review* 27 (2000): 60–67; Jan Pilditch, *The Critical Response to D. H. Lawrence* (Westport, Conn.: Greenwood, 2001); Paul Poplawski, ed., *Writing the Body in D. H. Lawrence: Essays on Language, Representation, and Sexuality* (Westport, Conn.: Greenwood, 2001); Fiona Becket, *The Complete Critical Guide to D. H. Lawrence* (London and New York: Routledge, 2002); Michael Squires and Lynn K. Talbot, *Living at the Edge: A Biography of D. H. Lawrence and Frieda von Richthofen* (Madison: University of Wisconsin Press, 2002).

From *The Rainbow*

Shame

Ursula had only two more terms at school. She was studying for her matriculation examination. It was dreary work, for she had very little intelligence when she was disjointed from happiness. Stubbornness and a consciousness of impending fate kept her half-heartedly pinned to it. She knew that soon she would want to become a self-responsible person, and her dread was, that she would be prevented. An all-containing will in her for complete independence, complete social independence, complete independence from any personal authority, kept her dullishly at her studies. For she knew that she had always her price of ransom—her femaleness. She was always a woman, and what she could not get because she was a human being, fellow to the rest of mankind, she would get because she was a female, other than the man. In her femaleness she felt a secret riches, a reserve, she had always the price of freedom.

However, she was sufficiently reserved about this last resource. The other things should be tried first. There was the mysterious man's world to be adventured upon, the world of daily work and duty and existence as a working member of the community. Against this she had a subtle grudge. She wanted to make her conquest also of this man's world.

So she ground away at her work, never giving herself, never giving it up. Some things she liked. Her subjects were English, Latin, French, mathematics and history. Once she knew how to read French and Latin, the syntax bored her. Most tedious was the close study of English literature. Why should one remember the things one read? Something in mathematics, their cold absoluteness, fascinated her, but the actual practice was tedious. Some people in history puzzled her and made her ponder, but the political parts angered her, and she hated ministers. Only in odd streaks did she get a poignant sense of acquisition and enrichment and enlarging, from her studies: one afternoon, reading "As You Like It"; once when, with her blood, she heard a passage of Latin, and she knew how the blood beat in a Roman's body, so that ever after she felt she knew the Romans, by contact; she enjoyed the vagaries of English Grammar, because it gave her pleasure to detect the live movements of words and sentences; and mathematics, the very sight of the letters in Algebra, had a real lure for her.

She felt so much and so confusedly at this time, that her face got a queer, wondering, half-scared look, as if she were not sure what might seize upon her at any moment out of the unknown.

Odd little bits of information stirred unfathomable passion in her. When she knew that in the tiny brown buds of autumn were folded, minute and complete, the finished flowers of the summer nine months hence, tiny, folded up, and left there waiting, a flash of triumph and love went over her.

"I could never die while there was a tree," she said passionately, sententiously, standing before a great ash, in worship.

It was the people who, somehow, walked as an upright menace to her. Her life at this time was unformed, palpitating, essentially shrinking from all touch. She gave something to other people, but she was never herself, since she *had* no self. She was not afraid nor ashamed before trees and birds and the sky. But she shrank violently from people, ashamed she was not as they were, fixed, emphatic, but a wavering, undefined sensibility only, without form or being.

Gudrun was at this time a great comfort and shield to her. The younger girl was a lithe, farouche animal who mistrusted all approach, and would have none of the petty secrecies and jealousies of school-girl intimacy. She would have no truck with the tame cats, nice or not, because she believed that they were all only untamed cats with a nasty, untrustworthy habit of tameness.

This was a great stand-back to Ursula, who suffered agonies when she thought a person disliked her, no matter now much she despised that person. How could anyone *dislike her*, Ursula Brangwen? The question terrified her and was unanswerable. She sought refuge in Gudrun's natural, proud indifference.

It had been discovered that Gudrun had a talent for drawing. This solved the problem of the girl's indifference to all study. It was said of her "She can draw marvellously."

Suddenly Ursula found a queer awareness existed between herself and her classmistress, Miss Inger. The latter was a rather beautiful woman of twenty eight, a fearless-seeming, clean type of modern girl whose very independence betrays her to sorrow. She was clever, and expert in what she did, accurate, quick, commanding.

To Ursula she had always given pleasure, because of her clear, decided, yet graceful appearance. She carried her head high, a little thrown back, and, Ursula thought, there was a look of nobility in the way she twisted her smooth brown hair upon her head. She always wore clean, attractive, well-fitting blouses, and a well-made skirt. Everything about her was so well-ordered, betraying a fine, clear spirit, that it was a pleasure to sit in her class.

Her voice was just as ringing and clear, and with unwavering, finely-touched modulation. Her eyes were blue, clear, proud, she gave one altogether the sense of a fine-mettled, scrupulously groomed person and of an unyielding mind. Yet there was an infinite poignancy about her, a great pathos in her lonely, proudly closed mouth.

It was after Skrebensky had gone that there sprang up between the mistress and the girl that strange awareness, then the unspoken intimacy that sometimes connects two people who may never even make each other's acquaintance. Before, they had always been good friends, in the undistinguished way of the classroom, with the professional relationship of mistress and scholar always present. Now, however, another thing came to pass. When they were in the room together, they were aware of each other, almost to the exclusion of everything else. Winifred Inger felt a hot delight in the lessons when Ursula was present, Ursula felt her whole life begin when Miss Inger came into the room. Then, with the beloved, subtly-intimate teacher present, the girl sat as within the rays of some enrichening sun, whose intoxicating heat poured straight into her veins.

The state of bliss, when Miss Inger was present, was supreme in the girl, but always eager, eager. As she went home, Ursula dreamed of the school-mistress, made infinite dreams of things she could give her, of how she might make the elder woman adore her.

Miss Inger was a Bachelor of Arts who had studied at Newnham. She was a clergyman's daughter, of good family. But what Ursula adored so much was her fine, upright, athletic bearing and her indomitably proud nature. She was proud and free as a man, yet exquisite as a woman.

The girl's heart burned in her breast as she set off for school in the morning. So eager was her breast, so glad her feet, to travel towards the beloved. Ah, Miss Inger, how straight and fine was her back, how strong her loins, how clean and free her limbs!

Ursula craved ceaselessly to know if Miss Inger cared for her. As yet no definite signs had been passed between the two. Yet surely, surely Miss Inger loved her too, was fond of her, liked her at least more than the rest of the scholars in the class. Yet she was never certain. It might be that Miss Inger cared nothing for her. And yet, and yet, with blazing heart, Ursula felt that if only she could speak to her, touch her, she would know.

The summer term came, and with it the swimming class. Miss Inger was to take the swimming class. Then Ursula trembled and was dazed with passion. Her hopes were soon to be realised. She would see Miss Inger in her bathing dress.

The day came. In the great bath the water was glimmering pale emerald-green, a lovely, glimmering mass of colour within the whitish, marble-like confines. Overhead the light fell softly and the great green body of pure water moved under it as someone dived from the side.

Ursula, trembling, hardly able to contain herself, pulled off her clothes, put on her tight bathing suit, and opened the door of her cabin. Two girls were in the water. The mistress had not appeared. She waited. A door opened, Miss Inger came out, dressed in a rust-red tunic like a Greek girl's, tied round the waist, and a red silk handkerchief round her head. How lovely she looked. Her knees were so white and strong and proud, she was firm-bodied as Diana. She walked simply to the side of the bath, and with a negligent movement, flung herself in. For a moment Ursula watched the white, smooth, strong shoulders and the easy arms swimming. Then she too dived into the water.

Now, ah now she was swimming in the same water with her dear mistress. The girl moved her limbs voluptuously, and swam by herself, deliciously, yet with a craving of unsatisfaction. She wanted to touch the other, to touch her, to feel her.

"I will race you, Ursula," came the well-modulated voice.

Ursula started violently. She turned to see the warm, unfolded face of her mistress looking at her, to her. She was acknowledged. Laughing her own beautiful, startled laugh, she began to swim. The mistress was just ahead, swimming with easy strokes. Ursula could see the head put back, the water flickering upon the white shoulders, the strong legs kicking shadowily. And she swam blinded with passion. Ah, the beauty of the firm, white, cool flesh! Ah, the wonderful firm limbs. If she could but hold them, hug them, press them between her own small breasts! Ah, if she did not so despise her own thin, dusky fragment of a body, if only she too were fearless and capable.

She swam on, eagerly, not wanting to win, only wanting to be near her mistress, to swim in a race with her. They neared the end of the bath—the deep end. Miss Inger touched the pipe, swung herself round, and caught Ursula round the waist, in the water, and held her for a moment against herself. The bodies of the two women touched, heaved against each other for a moment, then were separate.

"I won," said Miss Inger, laughing.

There was a moment of suspense. Ursula's heart was beating so fast, she clung to the rail, and could not move. Her dilated, warm, unfolded, glowing face turned to the mistress, as if to her very sun.

"Goodbye," said Miss Inger, and she swam away to the other pupils, taking professional interest in them.

Ursula was dazed. She could still feel the touch of the mistress's body against her own—only this, only this. The rest of the swimming time passed like a trance. When the call was given to leave the water, Miss Inger walked down the bath towards Ursula. Her rust-red, thin tunic was clinging to her, the whole body was defined, firm and magnificent, as it seemed to the girl.

"I enjoyed our race, Ursula," said Miss Inger. "Did you?"

The girl could only laugh with revealed, open, glowing face.

The love was now tacitly confessed. But it was some time before any further progress was made. Ursula continued in suspense, in inflamed bliss.

Then one day, when she was alone, the mistress came near to her, and touching her cheek with her fingers, said, with some difficulty:

"Would you like to come to tea with me on Saturday, Ursula?"

The girl flushed all gratitude.

"We'll go to a lovely little bungalow on the Soar, shall we. I stay the week-ends there sometimes."

Ursula was beside herself. She could not endure till the Saturday came, her thoughts burned up like a fire. If only it were Saturday, if only it were Saturday.

Then Saturday came, and she set out. Miss Inger met her in Sawley, and they walked about three miles to the bungalow. It was a moist, warm, cloudy day.

The bungalow was a tiny, two-roomed shanty set on a steep bank. Everything in it was exquisite. In delicious privacy, the two girls made tea, and then they talked. Ursula need not be home till about ten o'clock.

The talk was led, by a kind of spell, to love. Miss Inger was telling Ursula of a friend, how she had died in childbirth, and what she had suffered: then she told of a prostitute, and of some of her experiences with men.

As they talked thus, on the little verandah of the bungalow, the night fell, there was a little warm rain.

"It is really stifling," said Miss Inger.

They watched a train, whose lights were pale in the lingering twilight, rushing across the distance.

"It will thunder," said Ursula.

The electric suspense continued, the darkness sank, they were eclipsed.

"I think I shall go and bathe," said Miss Inger, out of the cloud-black darkness.

"At night?" said Ursula.

"It is best at night. Will you come?"

"I should like to"

"It is quite safe—the grounds are private. We had better undress in the bungalow, for fear of the rain, then run down."

Shyly, stiffly, Ursula went into the bungalow and began to remove her clothes. The lamp was turned low, she stood in the shadow. By another chair Winifred Inger was undressing.

Soon the naked, shadowy figure of the elder girl came to the younger.

"Are you ready?" she said.

"One moment."

Ursula could hardly speak. The other naked woman stood by, stood near, silent. Ursula was ready.

They ventured out into the darkness, feeling the soft air of night upon their skins.

"I can't see the path," said Ursula.

"It is here," said the voice, and the wavering, pallid figure was beside her, a hand grasping her arm. And the elder held the younger close against her, close, as they went down, and by the side of the water, she put her arms round her, and kissed her. And she lifted her in her arms, close, saying softly:

"I shall carry you into the water."

Ursula lay still in her mistress's arms, her forehead against the beloved, maddening breast.

"I shall put you in," said Winifred.

But Ursula twined her body about her mistress.

After a while the rain came down on their flushed, hot limbs, startling, delicious. A sudden, ice-cold shower burst in a great weight upon them. They stood up to it with pleasure. Ursula received the stream of it upon her breasts and her belly and her limbs. It made her cold, and a deep, bottomless silence welled up in her, as if bottomless darkness were returning upon her.

So the heat vanished away, she was chilled, as if from a waking up. She ran indoors, a chill, non-existent thing, wanting to get away. She wanted the light, the presence of other people, the external connection with the many. Above all she wanted to lose herself among natural surroundings.

She took her leave of her mistress and returned home. She was glad to be on the station with a crowd of Saturday-night people, glad to sit in the lighted, crowded railway carriage. Only she did not want to meet anybody she knew. She did not want to talk. She was alone, immune.

All this stir and seethe of lights and people was but the rim, the shores of a great inner darkness and void. She wanted very much to be on the seething, partially illuminated shore, for within her was the void reality of dark space.

For a time, Miss Inger, her mistress, was gone; she was only a dark void, and Ursula was free as a shade walking in an underworld of extinction, of oblivion. Ursula was glad, with a kind of motionless, lifeless gladness, that her mistress was extinct, gone out of her.

In the morning, however, the love was there again, burning, burning. She remembered yesterday, and she wanted more, always more. She wanted to be with her mistress. All separation from her mistress was a restriction from living. Why could she not go to her today, today? Why must she pace about revoked at Cossethay, whilst her mistress was elsewhere? She sat down and wrote a burning, passionate love-letter: she could not help it.

The two women became intimate. Their lives suddenly seemed to fuse into one, inseparable. Ursula went to Winifred's lodging, she spent there her only living hours. Winifred was very fond of water—of swimming, or rowing. She belonged to various athletic clubs. Many delicious afternoons the two girls spent in a light boat on the river, Winifred always rowing. Indeed, Winifred seemed to delight in having Ursula in her charge, in giving things to the girl, in filling and enrichening her life.

So that Ursula developed rapidly during the few months of her intimacy with her mistress. Winifred had had a scientific education. She had known many clever people. She wanted to bring Ursula to her own position of thought.

They took religion and rid it of its dogmas, its falsehoods. Winifred humanised it all. Gradually it dawned upon Ursula that all the religion she knew was but a particular clothing to a human aspiration. The aspiration was the real thing—the clothing was a matter almost of national taste or need. The Greeks had a naked Apollo, the Christians a white-robed Christ, the Buddhists a royal prince, the Egyptians their Osiris. Religions were local and religion was universal. Christianity was a local branch. There was as yet no assimilation of local religions into universal religion.

In religion, there were the two great motives of fear and love. The motive of fear was as great as the motive of love. Christianity accepted crucifixion to escape from fear: "do your worst to me, that I may have no more fear of the worst." But that which was feared was not necessarily all evil, and that which was loved not necessarily all good. Fear shall become reverence, and reverence is submission in identification; love shall become triumph, and triumph is delight in identification.

So much she talked of religion, getting the gist of many writings. In philosophy she was brought to the conclusion that the human desire is the criterion of all truth and all good. Truth does not lie beyond humanity, but is one of the products of the human mind and feeling. There is really nothing to fear. The motive of fear in religion is base, and must be left to the ancient worshippers of power, worship of Moloch. We do not worship power, in our enlightened souls. Power is degenerated to money and Napoleonic stupidity.

Ursula could not help dreaming of Moloch. Her God was not mild and gentle, neither Lamb nor Dove. He was the lion and the eagle. Not because the lion and the eagle had power, but because they were proud and strong; they were themselves, they were not passive subjects of some shepherd, or pets of some loving woman, or sacrifices of some priest. She was weary to death of mild, passive lambs and monotonous doves. If the lamb might lie down with the lion, it would be a great honor to the lamb, but the lion's powerful heart would suffer no diminishing. She loved the dignity and self-possession of lions.

She did not see how lambs could love. Lambs could only be loved. They could only be afraid, and tremblingly submit to fear, and become sacrificial; or they submit to love, and become beloveds. In both they were passive. Raging, destructive lovers, seeking the moment when fear is greatest and triumph is greatest, the fear not greater than the triumph, the triumph not greater than the fear, these were no lambs nor doves. She stretched her own limbs like a lion or a wild horse, her heart was relentless in its desires. It would suffer a thousand deaths, but it would still be a lion's heart when it rose from death, a fiercer lion she would be, a surer, knowing herself different from and separate from the great, conflicting universe that was not herself.

Winifed Inger was also interested in the Women's Movement.

"The men will do no more—they have lost the capacity for doing," said the elder girl. "They fuss, and talk, but they are really inane. They make everything fit into an old, inert idea. Love is a dead idea to them. They don't come to one and love one, they come to an idea, and they say 'You are my idea,' so they embrace themselves. As if I were any man's idea! As if I exist because a man has an idea of me! As if I will be betrayed by him, lend him my body as an instrument for his idea, to be a mere apparatus of his dead theory. But they are too fussy to be able to act: they are all impotent, they can't *take* a woman. They come to their own idea every time, and take that. They are like serpents trying to swallow themselves because they are hungry."

Ursula was introduced by her friend to various women and men, educated, unsatisfied people, who still moved within the smug provincial society as if they were nearly as tame as their outward behaviour showed, but who were inwardly raging and mad.

It was a strange world the girl was swept into, like a chaos, like the end of the world. She was too young to understand it all. Yet the inoculation passed into her, through her love for her mistress.

CHARLOTTE MEW (1869–1928)

"À Quoi Bon Dire," "On the Road to the Sea," "The Road to Kérity," "My Heart Is Lame" (1916)

The British poet, essayist, and short-story writer Charlotte Mew, born in London to a middle-class family, experienced loss and impoverishment early in life. Of her six siblings, two died in infancy, another at the age of five, and two more succumbed to mental illness. Mew's father died when she was in her twenties, leaving her and her mother in relative poverty. She began publishing fiction and poetry in the 1890s—first in the magazine *Temple Bar*, later in the *Yellow Book*, the *Nation*, and the *New Statesman*. At the urging of Harold Monro, she published her one and only collection of poems, *The Farmer's Bride*, in 1916; an expanded version appeared in 1921. Experimental in technique, dreamlike in setting, and emotionally stark, her poems made an immediate impression. Thomas Hardy declared her "far and away the best living woman poet" of the day; Virginia Woolf, Ezra Pound, H.D., Rebecca West, John Masefield, and Siegfried Sassoon were other admirers. Critical esteem, however, did little to mitigate Mew's chronic melancholia; after the deaths of her mother and sister in 1923 and 1927, she took her own life—by ingesting creosote—at the age of fifty-nine in 1928.

A sense of emotional oddity contributed to Mew's lifelong depression. Short, gruff, ungainly, "neither quite boy nor quite girl," she loved several women passionately yet without satisfying return. As an adolescent she was infatuated with a female teacher; later loves included the editor and *Yellow Book* writer, Ella D'Arcy (1851–1937), and the novelist and feminist May Sinclair (1863–1946). Mew's relationship with the latter was especially painful: after a period of intense friendship in 1914, Mew made physical overtures to Sinclair, which Sinclair violently rebuffed. Sinclair subsequently spread the story of the incident among their mutual friends, one of whom wrote in her diary, "Charlotte is evidently a pervert. Are all geniuses perverts?"

Mew's poems, among the most exquisite and forlorn in the language, allegorize these and other humiliations, and their author's anguished sense of being "the moon's dropped child." Yet the sufferings displayed in them also give them their curious power to haunt. Mew retains her high reputation among poets and poetry lovers: a posthumous collection, *The Rambling Sailor*, appeared in 1929; a *Collected Poems* in 1953; and a *Collected Poems and Prose* in 1981. A number of Mew's poems have been set to music, very beautifully, by the American composer Ned Rorem.

FURTHER READING: Charlotte Mew, *Collected Poems of Charlotte Mew* (London: Manchester, 1953); ——, *Collected Poems and Prose*, ed. Val Warner (London: Carcanet, 1981); Harold Monro, *Some Contemporary Poets* (London: L. Parsons, 1920); Alida Monro, "Charlotte Mew—A Memoir," in *Collected Poems of Charlotte Mew* (London: Manchester, 1953); Theophilus E. M. Boll, "The Mystery of Charlotte Mew and May Sinclair: An Inquiry," *Bulletin of the New York Public Library* 74 (1970): 445–53; Mary C. Davidow, "The Charlotte Mew—May Sinclair Relationship: A Reply," *Bulletin of the New York Public Library*, 75 (1971): 295–300; Penelope Fitzgerald, *Charlotte Mew and Her Friends* (London: William Collins, 1984); Suzanne Raitt, "Charlotte Mew and May Sinclair: A Love-Story," *Critical Quarterly* 37 (1995): 3–17; ——, "Charlotte Mew's Queer Death," *Yearbook of Comparative and General Literature* 47 (1999): 25–40; ——, *May Sinclair: A Modern Victorian* (Oxford: Clarendon, 2000). Jeredith Merrin, "The Ballad of Charlotte Mew," *Modern Philology* 95 (1997): 200–17; Eavan Boland, "Charlotte Mew," *Brick* 67 (2001): 113–14.

À Quoi Bon Dire

Seventeen years ago you said
Something that sounded like Good-bye;
   And everybody thinks that you are dead,
     But I.

So I, as I grow stiff and cold
To this and that say Good-bye too;
   And everybody sees that I am old
     But you.

And one fine morning in a sunny lane
Some boy and girl will meet and kiss and swear
   That nobody can love their way again
     While over there
You will have smiled, I shall have tossed your hair.

On the Road to the Sea

We passed each other, turned and stopped for half an hour, then
went our way,
   I who make other women smile did not make you—

But no man can move mountains in a day.
    So this hard thing is yet to do.

But first I want your life:—before I die I want to see
    The world that lies behind the strangeness of your eyes,
There is nothing gay or green there for my gathering, it may be,
      Yet on brown fields there lies
A haunting purple bloom: is there not something in grey skies
        And in grey sea?
    I want what world there is behind your eyes,
    I want your life and you will not give it me.

Now, if I look, I see you walking down the years,
    Young, and through August fields—a face, a thought, a swinging
        dream perched on a stile—;
    I would have liked (so vile we are!) to have taught you tears
      But most to have made you smile.

To-day is not enough or yesterday: God sees it all—
Your length on sunny lawns, the wakeful rainy nights—; tell me—;
      (how vain to ask), but it is not a question—just a call—;
Show me then, only your notched inches climbing up the garden
      wall,
      I like you best when you are small.

    Is this a stupid thing to say
    Not having spent with you one day?
No matter; I shall never touch your hair
Or hear the little tick behind your breast,
    Still it is there,
    And as a flying bird
Brushes the branches where it may not rest
    I have brushed your hand and heard
The child in you: I like that best

So small, so dark, so sweet; and were you also then too grave and
      wise?
    Always I think. Then put your far off little hand in mine;—Oh!
let it rest;
I will not stare into the early world beyond the opening eyes,
    Or vex or scare what I love best.

But I want your life before mine bleeds away—
   Here—not in heavenly hereafters—soon,—
    I want your smile this very afternoon,
(The last of all my vices, pleasant people used to say,
   I wanted and I sometimes got—the Moon!)

   You know, at dusk, the last bird's cry,
And round the house the flap of the bat's low flight,
   Trees that go black against the sky
And then—how soon the night!

No shadow of you on any bright road again,
And at the darkening end of this—what voice? whose kiss? As if
   you'd say!
It is not I who have walked with you, it will not be I who take away
   Peace, peace, my little handful of the gleaner's grain
   From your reaped fields at the shut of day.

   Peace! Would you not rather die
Reeling,—with all the cannons at your ear?
   So, at least, would I,
And I may not be here
To-night, to-morrow morning or next year.
Still I will let you keep your life a little while,
   See dear?
I have made you smile.

The Road to Kérity

Do you remember the two old people we passed on the road to
   Kérity,
Resting their sack on the stones, by the drenched wayside,
Looking at us with their lightless eyes through the driving rain, and
   then out again
To the rocks, and the long white line of the tide:
Frozen ghosts that were children once, husband and wife, father,
   and mother,
Looking at us with those frozen eyes; have you ever seen anything
   quite so chilled or so old?

But we—with our arms about each other,
We did not feel the cold!

My Heart Is Lame

My heart is lame with running after yours so fast
    Such a long way,
Shall we walk slowly home, looking at all the things we passed
    Perhaps to-day?

Home down the quiet evening roads under the quiet skies,
    Not saying much,
You for a moment giving me your eyes
    When you could bear my touch.

But not to-morrow. This has taken all my breath;
    Then, though you look the same,
There may be something lovelier in Love's face in death
As your heart sees it, running back the way we came;
    My heart is lame.

"CLEMENCE DANE" [WINIFRED ASHTON] (1887–1965)

From *Regiment of Women* (1917)

Clemence Dane, British playwright and novelist, took her pseudonym from St. Clement Danes Church in the Strand near Covent Garden, the area of London in which she lived most of her life. Her real name was Winifred Ashton. After studying art as a young woman in Dresden and at the Slade School in London, she turned to acting, only to have her career ended by ill health during the First World War. While teaching at a girls' school in Ireland, she began to write, publishing her first novel, *Regiment of Women*—based in part on her teaching experiences—in 1917. It was followed by *Legend* in 1919, then a series of plays: *A Bill of Divorcement* and *Will Shakespeare* (1921), *Granite* (1926), *Mariners* (1927), *Wild Decembers* (1932) and *Come of Age* (1933). Of the latter only the first was a decided success, but thanks to her energy and charm and wide circle of acquaintances, Dane remained an important figure in London literary and theatrical circles between the wars. Friends included Vita Sackville-West, Virginia Woolf, Radclyffe Hall (who tried to get her to adapt *The Well of Loneliness* for the stage), Sybil Thorndike, Alfred Lunt, and Noël Coward, who described her as a "unique mixture of artist, writer, games mistress, poet and egomaniac," capable of "[wreaking] more havoc in a small space of time than an army of delinquent refugees." She is said to be the model for Madame Arcati in Coward's *Blithe Spirit* (1941). During and after the Second World War she wrote radio and film scripts and was awarded a CBE in 1953. She never married and lived much of her life with a female secretary-companion, Olwen Bowen.

Paradoxically, given the worldliness of her personal life, Dane's *Regiment of Women* remains one of the more openly homophobic texts of the early twentieth century. The novel features a full-blown lesbian villainess: the "unnatural" Clare Hartill, senior teacher at an exclusive girls' school. After making Alwynne Durand, a former pupil and fellow teacher, fall in love with her, Clare tries to control every aspect of the younger woman's life. Alwynne ultimately spurns her, but not without a fierce emotional struggle. In the scene below, from early in the novel, the head teacher's seductive Machiavellianism is in the ascendant. *Regiment of Women* may have influenced several "girls' school" novels: Christa Winsloe's *The Child Manuela* (1933; made into a film under the title *Mädchen in Uniform*), Dorothy Baker's *Trio* (1945), and Dorothy Strachey's *Olivia* (1949) all take up similar themes.

FURTHER READING: Clemence Dane [Winifred Ashton], *Regiment of Women* (1917; rpt. London: Heinemann, 1966); —, *A Bill of Divorcement* (New York: Macmillan, 1921); Cole Leslie, *The Life of Noël Coward* (London: Jonathan Cape, 1976); Philip Hoare, *Noël Coward: A Biography* (London: Sinclair-Stevenson, 1995); Terry Castle, *Noël Coward and Radclyffe Hall: Kindred Spirits* (New York: Columbia University Press, 1996); Janice Oliver, "Clemence Dane (Winifred Ashton) (1887–1965)," in William Demastes and Katherine E. Kelly, eds., *British Playwrights, 1860–1956: A Research and Production Sourcebook* (Westport, Conn.: Greenwood, 1996), pp. 97–104.

"I had a letter from Louise yesterday," announced Clare.

She was curled up in a saddle-bag before the roaring golden fire, and was busy with paper and pencil. Alwynne, big with her as yet unissued invitation, sat cross-legged on the white bearskin at her feet. The floor was littered with papers and book-catalogues. At Christmas-time Clare ordered books as a housewife orders groceries, and she and Alwynne had spent a luxurious evening over her lists. The vivid flames lit up Clare's thin, lazy length, and turned the hand she held up against their heat into transparent carnelian. Her face was in shadow, but there were dancing specks of light in her sombre eyes that kept time with the leaping blaze. Clare was a sybarite over her fires. She would not endure coal or gas or stove—wood, and wood only, must be used; and she would pay any price for apple-wood, ostensibly for the quality of its flame, secretly for the mere pleasure of burning fuel with so pleasant a name; for she liked beautiful words as a child likes chocolate—a sober, acquisitive liking. She had, too, though she would not own it, a delight in destruction, costly destruction; she enjoyed the sensation of reckless power that it gave her. The trait might be morbid, but there was not a trace of pose in it; she could have enjoyed a Whittington bonfire, without needing a king to gasp applause. Yet she shivered nightly as she undressed in her cold bedroom, rather than commit the extravagance of an extra fire. She never realized the comicality of her contradictoriness, or even its existence in her character, though it qualified every act and impulse of her daily life. Her soul was, indeed, a hybrid, combining the temper of a Calvinist with the tastes of a Renascence bishop.

At the moment she was in gala mood. The autumn term was but four days dead, she had not had time to tire of holidays, though, within a week, she would be bored again, and restless for the heavy work under which she affected to groan. Her chafing mind seldom allowed her indolent body much of the peace it delighted in—was ever the American in lotus-land. It was fidgeted at the moment by Alwynne's absorption in a lavishly illustrated catalogue.

"Did you hear, Alwynne? A letter from Louise."

Alwynne's "Oh?" was absent. It was in the years of the Rackham craze, and she had just discovered a reproduction of the *Midsummer* Helen.

"Any message?" Clare knew how to prod Alwynne.

The girl glanced up amused but a little indignant.

"You've answered it already? Well! And the weeks I've had to wait sometimes."

"This was such a charming letter," said Clare smoothly. "It deserved an answer. She really has the quaintest style. And Alwynne—never a blot or a flourish! It's a pleasure to read."

Alwynne laughed ruefully. She would always squirm good-humouredly under Clare's pin-pricks, with such amusement at her own discomfiture that Clare never knew whether to fling away her needle for good, or, for the mere experiment's sake, to stab hard and savagely. At that stage of their intimacy, Alwynne's guilelessness invariably charmed and disarmed her—she knew that it would take a very crude display of cruelty to make Alwynne believe that she was being hurt intentionally. Clare was amused by the novel pedestal upon which she had been placed; she was accustomed to the panoply of Minerva, or the bow of Dian Huntress, but she had never before been hailed as Bona Dea. It tickled her to be endowed with every domestic virtue, to be loved, as Alwynne loved her, with the secure and fearless affection of a daughter for a newly-discovered and adorable young mother. She appreciated Alwynne's determination of their relationship, her nice sense of the difference in age, her modesty in reserving any claim to an equality in their friendship, her frank and affectionate admiration—yet, while it pleased her, it could pique. Calm comradeship or surrendering adoration she could cope with, but the subtle admixture of such alien states of mind was puzzling. She had acquired a lover with a sense of humour and she felt that she had her hands full. Her imperious will would, in time, she knew, eliminate either the lover or the humour—it annoyed her that she was not as yet quite convinced that it would be the humour. She intended to master Alwynne, but she realized that it would be a question of time, that she would give her more trouble than the children to whom she was accustomed. Alwynne's utter unrealization of the fact that a trial of strength was in progress, was disconcerting: yet Clare, jaded and super-subtle, found her innocence endearing. Without relaxing in her purpose, she yet caught herself wondering if an ally were not better than a slave. But the desire for domination was never entirely shaken off, and Alwynne's free bearing was in itself an ever-present challenge. Clare loved her for it, but her pride was in arms. It was her misfortune not to realize that, for all her Olympian poses, she had come to love Alwynne deeply and enduringly.

Alwynne, meanwhile, laughing and pouting on the hearth, the firelight revealing every change of expression in her piquant face, was declining to be classed with Agatha Middleton; her handwriting might be bad, but it wasn't a beetle-track; anyhow, Queen Elizabeth had a vile fist—Clare admired Queen Elizabeth, didn't she? She had always so much to say to Clare, that if she stopped to bother about handwriting—! Had Clare never got into a row for untidiness in her own young days? Elsbeth had hinted. . . . But of course she reserved judgment till she had heard Clare's version! She settled to attention and Clare, inveigled into reminiscences, found herself recounting quaint and forgotten incidents to her own credit and discredit, till, before the evening was over, Alwynne knew almost as much of Clare's schooldays as Clare did herself. She could never resist telling Alwynne stories, Alwynne was always so genuinely breathless with interest.

They returned to Louise at last, and Alwynne read the letter, chuckling over the odd phrases and dainty marginal drawings. She would have dearly liked to see Clare's answer. She was glad, for all her protests, that Clare had been moved to answer; she knew so well the delight it would give Louise. The child would need cheering up. For, quite resignedly and by the way, Louise had mentioned that the Denny family had developed whooping-cough, and emigrated to Torquay, and she, in quarantine, though it was hoped she had escaped infection, was preparing for a solitary Christmas.

Alwynne looked up at Clare with wrinkled brows.

"Poor child! But what can I do? I haven't had whooping-cough, and Elsbeth is always so afraid of infection; or else she could have come to us. I know Elsbeth wouldn't have minded."

"You are going to leave me to myself then? You've quite made up your mind?"

Alwynne's eyes lighted up.

"Oh, Clare, it's all right. You are coming! At least—I mean—Elsbeth sends her kindest regards, and she would be so pleased if you will come to dinner with us on Christmas Day," she finished politely.

Clare laughed.

"It's very kind of your aunt."

"Yes, isn't it?" said Alwynne, with ingenuous enthusiasm.

"I'm afraid I can't come, Alwynne."

Alwynne's face lengthened.

"Oh, Clare! Why ever not?"

Clare hesitated. She had no valid reason, save that she preferred the comfort of her own fireside and that she had intended Alwynne to come to her. Alwynne's regretful refusal when she first mooted the arrangement, she had not considered final, but this invitation upset her plans. Elsbeth's influence was opposing her. She hated opposition. Also she did not care for Elsbeth. It would not be amiss to make Elsbeth (not her dislike of Elsbeth) the reason for her refusal. It would have its effect on Alwynne sooner or later.

She considered Alwynne narrowly, as she answered—

"My dear, I had arranged to be at home, for one thing."

Alwynne looked hurt.

"Of course, if you don't care about it—" she began.

Clare rallied her.

"Be sensible, my child. It is most kind of Miss Loveday; but—wasn't it chiefly your doing, Alwynne? Imagine her dismay if I accepted. A stranger in the gate! On Christmas Day! One must make allowances for little prejudices, you know."

"She'll be awfully disappointed," cried Alwynne, so eager for Clare that she believed it.

"Will she?" Clare laughed pleasantly. "Every one doesn't wear your spectacles. What would she do with me, for a whole day?"

"We shouldn't see her much," began Alwynne. "She spends most of her time in church. I go in the morning—(yes, I'm very good!) but I've drawn the line at turning out after lunch."

"They why shouldn't you come to me instead? It would be so much better. I shall be all alone, you know." Clare's wistful intonation was not entirely artificial.

Alwynne was distressed.

"Oh, Clare, I'd love to—you know I'd love to—but how could I? Elsbeth would be dreadfully hurt. I couldn't leave her alone on Christmas Day."

"But you can me?"

"Clare, don't put it like that. You know I shall want to be with you all the time. But Elsbeth's like my mother. It would be beastly of me. You must put relations first at Christmas-time, even if they're not first really."

She smiled at Clare, but she felt disloyal as she said it, and hated herself. Yet wasn't it true? Clare came first, though Elsbeth must never guess it. Dear old Elsbeth was pretty dense, thank goodness! Where ignorance is bliss, etcetera! Yet she, Alwynne, felt extraordinarily mean. . . .

Clare watched her jealously. She had set her heart on securing Alwynne for Christmas Day, and had thought, ten minutes since, with a secret, confident smile, that there would not be much difficulty. And here was Alwynne holding out—refusing categorically! It was incredible! Yet she could not be angry: Alwynne so obviously was longing to be with her. . . . Equally obviously prepared to risk her displeasure (a heavy penalty already, Clare guessed, to Alwynne), rather than ignore the older claim. Clare thought that an affection that could be so loyal to a tedious old maid was better worth deflecting than many a more ardent, unscrupulous enthusiasm. Alwynne was showing strength of character.

She persisted nevertheless—

"Well, it's a pity. I must eat my Christmas dinner alone, I suppose."

"Oh, Clare, you might come to us," cried Alwynne. "I can't see why you won't."

Clare shrugged her shoulders.

"If you can't see why, my dear Alwynne, there's no more to be said."

Alwynne most certainly did not see; but Clare's delicately reproachful tone convicted her, and incidentally Elsbeth, of some failure in tact. She supposed she had blundered . . . she often did. . . . But Elsbeth, at least, must be exonerated . . . she did so want Clare to think well of Elsbeth. . . .

She perjured herself in hasty propitiation.

"Yes. Yes—I do see. I ought to have known, of course. Elsbeth was quite right. She said you wouldn't, all along."

"Oh?" Clare sat up. "Oh? Your aunt said that, did she?" She spoke with detachment, but inwardly she was alert, on guard. Elsbeth had suddenly become worth attention.

"Oh, yes." Alwynne's voice was rueful. "She was quite sure of it. She said I might ask you, with pleasure, if I didn't believe her—you see, she'd love you to come—but she didn't think you would."

"I wonder," said Clare, laughing naturally, "what made her say that?"

"She said she knew you better than I did," confided Alwynne, with one of her spurts of indignation. "As if—"

"Yes, it's rather unlikely, isn't it?" said Clare, with an intimate smile. "But you're not going?"

"I must. Look at the time! Elsbeth will be having fits!" Alwynne called from the hall where she was hastily slipping on her coat and hat.

Clare stood a moment—thinking.

So the duel had been with Elsbeth! So that negligible and mouse-like woman had been aware—all along . . . had prepared, with a thoroughness worthy of Clare herself, for the inevitable encounter . . . had worsted Clare completely. . . . It was amazing. . . . Clare was compelled to admiration. It was clear to her now that Elsbeth must have distrusted her from the beginning. It had been Elsbeth's doing, not hers, that their intercourse had been so slight. . . . Yet she had never restrained Alwynne; she had risked giving her her head. . . . She was subtle! This affair of the Christmas dinner for instance—Clare appreciated its cleverness. Elsbeth had not wanted her, Clare now saw clearly; had been anxious to avoid the intimacy that such an invitation would imply; equally anxious, surely, that Alwynne should not guess her uneasy jealousy: so she had risked the invitation, counting on her knowledge of Clare's character (Clare stamped with vexation—that the woman should have such a memory!) secure that Clare, unsuspicious of her motives, would, by refusing, do exactly as Elsbeth wished. It had been the neatest of gossamer traps—and Clare had walked straight into it. . . . She was furious. If Alwynne, maddeningly unsuspicious Alwynne, had but enlightened her earlier in the evening! Now she was caught, committed by her own decision of manner to the course of action she most would have wished to avoid. . . . She could not change her mind now without appearing foolishly vacillating. . . . It would not do. . . . She had been bluffed, successfully, gorgeously bluffed. . . . And Elsbeth was sitting at home enjoying the situation . . . too sure of herself and Clare even to be curious as to the outcome of it all. She knew. Clare stamped again. Oh, but she would pay Elsbeth for this. . . . The *casus belli* was infinitely trivial, but the campaign should be Homeric. . . . And this preliminary engagement could not affect the final issues. . . . She always won in the end. . . . But, after all, Elsbeth could not be blamed, though she must be crushed; Alwynne was worth fighting for! Elsbeth was a fool. . . . If she had treated Clare decently, Clare might—possibly—have shared Alwynne with her. . . . She believed she would have had scruples. . . . Now they were dispelled. . . . Alwynne, by fair means or foul, should be detached . . . should become Clare's property . . . should be given up to no living woman or man.

She followed Alwynne into the hall and lit the staircase candle. She would see Alwynne out. She would have liked to keep Alwynne with her for a month. She was a delightful companion; it was extraordinary how indispensable she made herself. Clare knew that her flat would strike her as a dreary place to return to, when she had shut the door on Alwynne. She would sit and read and feel restless and lonely. Yet she did not allow herself to feel lonely as a rule; she scouted the weakness. But Alwynne wound herself about you, thought Clare, and you never knew, till she had gone, what a difference she made to you.

She wished she could keep Alwynne another couple of hours. . . . But it was eleven already . . . her hold was not yet strong enough to warrant innovations to which Elsbeth could object. . . . Her time would come later. . . . How much later would depend on whether it were affection that swayed Alwynne, or only a sense of duty. . . . She believed, because she hoped, that it was duty—a sense of duty was more easily suborned than an affection. . . . For the present, however, Alwynne must be allowed to do as she thought right. Clare knew when she was beaten, and, with her capacity for wry admiration of virtues that she had not the faintest intention of incorporating in her own character, she was able to applaud Alwynne heartily. Yet she did not intend to make victory easy to her.

They went down the flights of stairs silently, side by side. Alwynne opened the entrance doors and stood a moment, fascinated.

"Look, Clare! What a night!"

The moon was full and flooded earth and sky with bright, cold light. The garden, roadway, roofs, trees and fences glittered like powdered diamonds, white with frost and moonshine. The silence was exquisite.

They stood awhile, enjoying it.

Suddenly Clare shivered. Alwynne became instantly and anxiously practical.

"Clare, what am I thinking of? Go in at once—you'll catch a dreadful cold."

With unusual passivity Clare allowed herself to be hurried in. At the staircase Alwynne said good-bye, handing her her candle, and waiting till she should have passed out of sight. On the fourth step Clare hesitated, and turned—

"Alwynne—come to me for Christmas!"

Alwynne flung out her hands.

"Clare! I mustn't."

"Alwynne—come to me for Christmas?"

"You know I mustn't! You know you'd think me a pig if I did, now wouldn't you?"

"I expect so."

"But I'll come in for a peep at you," cried Alwynne, brightening, "while Elsbeth's at afternoon service. I could do that. And to say Merry Christmas!"

"Come to dinner?"

"I can't."

"Then you needn't come at all." Clare turned away.

Alwynne caught her hand, as it leaned on the balustrade. In the other the candle shook a little.

"Lady Macbeth! Dear Lady Macbeth! Miss Hartill of the Upper Sixth, whom I'm scared to death of, really—you're behaving like a very naughty small child. Now, aren't you? Honestly? Oh, do turn round and crush me with a look for being impudent, and then tell me that I'm only doing what you really approve. I don't want to, Clare, but you know you hate selfishness."

Clare looked down at her.

"All right, Alwynne. You must do as you like."

"Say good-night to me," demanded Alwynne. "Nicely, Clare, very nicely! It's Christmas-time."

Carefully Clare deposited her candlestick on the stair above. Leaning over the banisters, she put her arms round Alwynne and kissed her passionately and repeatedly.

"Good-night, my darling," said Clare.

Then, recoiling, she caught up her candlestick, and without another word or look, hurried up the stairs.

Alwynne walked home on air.

HELEN ROSE HULL (1888–1971)

"The Fire" (1917)

The American novelist and short-story writer Helen Rose Hull was born in Michigan, received a Ph.D. in literature at the University of Chicago, and taught for most of her life—first at Wellesley College in Massachusetts, where she met her life companion, Mabel Louise Robinson, in 1912, and then at Columbia University, where she remained for almost forty years. An active suffragist in her twenties and thirties, she was a member of the feminist club Heterodoxy (founded in New York in 1912) and took a lifelong interest in progressive causes. Hull spent her summer holidays with Robinson in Maine, where she produced essays, short stories, and seventeen novels, including *Quest* (1922), *Labyrinth* (1923), *The Surry Family* (1925), and *Islanders* (1927).

Like Katherine Mansfield, Rose Allatini, and Elizabeth Bowen, Hull wrote movingly about female adolescence, and no more so than in her posthumously published collection of stories, *Last September* (1988). Of the novella of the title, a reviewer for the *New York Times* wrote in 1940 that it placed Hull "in the company of novelists like Edith Wharton and Willa Cather" and compared it favorably with Cather's *Death Comes for the Archbishop*. In "The Fire" (1917), the first of six interlinked tales dealing with Cynthia Bates, a young woman growing up in a midwestern town in America at the turn of the century, Hull delicately explores the subject of adolescent sexuality, as Cynthia struggles to understand her yearning for women—and the harsh social obloquy that such tenderness arouses.

FURTHER READING: Helen Rose Hull, *Islanders* (1922; rpt. New York: Feminist, 1988); ——, *Quest* (1927; rpt. New York: Feminist, 1990); ——, *Writer's Roundtable* (New York: Dodd, Mead, 1960); ——, *Last September*, ed. Patricia McClelland Miller (Tallahassee, Fla.: Naiad, 1988); Jeannette Foster, *Sex Variant Women in Literature* (1956; rpt. Tallahassee, Fla.: Naiad, 1985); Judith Schwarz, *Radical Feminists of Heterodoxy: Greenwich Village 1912–1940*, rev. ed. (Norwich, Vt.: New Victoria, 1986).

Cynthia blotted the entry in the old ledger and scowled across the empty office at the door. Mrs. Moriety had left it ajar when she departed with her receipt for the weekly fifty cents on her "lot." If you supplied the missing gilt letters, you could read the sign on the glass of the upper half: "H. P. Bates. Real Estate. Notary Public." Through the door at Cynthia's elbow came the rumbling voice of old Fleming, the lawyer down the hall; he had come in for his Saturday night game of chess with her father.

Cynthia pushed the ledger away from her, and with her elbows on the spotted, green felt of the desk, her fingers burrowing into her cheeks, waited for two minutes by the nickel clock; then, with a quick, awkward movement, she pushed back her chair and plunged to the doorway, her young face twisted in a sort of fluttering resolution.

"Father—"

Her father jerked his head toward her, his fingers poised over a pawn. Old Fleming did not look up.

"Father, I don't think anybody else will be in."

"Well, go on home, then." Her father bent again over the squares, the light shining strongly on the thin places about his temples.

"Father, please,"—Cynthia spoke hurriedly,—"you aren't going for a while? I want to go down to Miss Egert's for a minute."

"Eh? What's that?" He leaned back in his chair now, and Mr. Fleming lifted his severe, black beard to look at this intruder. "What for? You can't take any more painting lessons. Your mother doesn't want you going there any more."

"I just want to get some things I left there. I can get back to go home with you."

"But your mother said she didn't like your hanging around down there in an empty house with an old maid. What did she tell you about it?"

"Couldn't I just get my sketches, Father, and tell Miss Egert I'm not coming any more? She would think it was awfully funny if I didn't. I won't stay. But she—she's been good to me—"

"What set your mother against her, then? What you been doing down there?"

Cynthia twisted her hands together, her eyes running from Fleming's amused stare to her father's indecision. Only an accumulated determination could have carried her on into speech.

"I've just gone down once a week for a lesson. I want to get my things. If I'm not going, I ought to tell her."

"Why didn't you tell her that last week?"

"I kept hoping I could go on."

"Um." Her father's glance wavered toward his game. "Isn't it too late?"

"Just eight, Father." She stepped near her father, color flooding her cheeks. "If you'll give me ten cents, I can take the car—"

"Well—" He dug into his pocket, nodding at Fleming's grunt, "The women always want cash, eh, Bates?"

Then Cynthia, the dime pressed into her palm, tiptoed across to the nail where her hat and sweater hung, seized them, and still on tiptoe, lest she disturb the game again, ran out to the head of the stairs.

She was trembling as she pulled on her sweater; as she ran down the dark steps to the street the tremble changed to a quiver of excitement. Suppose her father had known just what her mother *had* said! That she could not see Miss Egert again; could never go hurrying down to the cluttered room they called the studio for more of those strange hours of eagerness and pain when she bent over the drawing-board, struggling with the mysteries of color. That last sketch—the little, purpling mint-leaves from the gar-den—Miss Egert had liked that. And they thought she could leave those sketches there! Leave Miss Egert, too, wondering why she never came again! She hurried to the corner, past the bright store-windows. In thought she could see Miss Egert setting out the jar of brushes, the dishes of water, pushing back the litter of magazines and books to make room for the drawing-board, waiting for her to come. Oh, she had to go once more, black as her disobedience was!

The half-past-eight car was just swinging round the curve. She settled herself behind two German housewives, shawls over their heads, market-baskets beside them. They lived out at the end of the street; one of them sometimes came to the office with payments on her son's lot. Cynthia pressed against the dirty window, fearful lest she miss the corner. There it was, the new street light shining on the sedate old house! She ran to the platform, pushing against the arm the conductor extended.

"Wait a minute, there!" He released her as the car stopped, and she fled across the street.

In front of the house she could not see a light, up-stairs or down, except staring reflections in the windows from the white arc light. She walked past the dark line of box which led to the front door. At the side of the old square dwelling jutted a new, low wing; and there in two windows were soft slits of light along the curtain-edges. Cyn-thia walked along a little dirt path to a door at the side of the wing. Standing on the door-step, she felt in the shadow for a knocker. As she let it fall, from the garden behind her came a voice:

"I'm out here. Who is it?" There was a noise of feet hurrying through dead leaves, and as Cynthia turned to answer, out of the shadow moved a blur of face and white blouse.

"Cynthia! How nice!" The woman touched Cynthia's shoulder as she pushed open the door. "There, come in."

The candles on the table bent their flames in the draft; Cynthia followed Miss Egert into the room.

"You're busy?" Miss Egert had stood up by the door an old wooden-toothed rake. "I don't want to bother you." Cynthia's solemn, young eyes implored the woman and turned hastily away. The intensity of defiance which had brought her at such an hour left her confused.

"Bother? I was afraid I had to have my grand bonfire alone. Now we can have it a party. You'd like to?"

Miss Egert darted across to straighten one of the candles. The light caught in the folds of her crumpled blouse, in the soft, drab hair blown out around her face.

"I can't stay very long." Cynthia stared about the room, struggling to hide her turmoil under ordinary casualness. "You had the carpenter fix the bookshelves, didn't you?"

"Isn't it nice now! All white and gray and restful—just a spark of life in that mad rug. A good place to sit in and grow old."

Cynthia looked at the rug, a bit of scarlet Indian weaving. She wouldn't see it again! The thought poked a derisive finger into her heart.

"Shall we sit down just a minute and then go have the fire?"

Cynthia dropped into the wicker chair, wrenching her fingers through one another.

"My brother came in to-night, his last attempt to make me see reason," said Miss Egert.

Cynthia lifted her eyes. Miss Egert wasn't wondering why she had come; she could stay without trying to explain.

Miss Egert wound her arms about her knees as she went on talking. Her slight body was wrenched a little out of symmetry, as though from straining always for something uncaptured; there was the same lack of symmetry in her face, in her eyebrows, in the line of her mobile lips. But her eyes had nothing fugitive, nothing pursuing in their soft, gray depth. Their warm, steady eagerness shone out in her voice, too, in its swift inflections.

"I tried to show him it wasn't a bit disgraceful for me to live here in a wing of my own instead of being a sort of nurse-maid adjunct in his house." She laughed, a soft, throaty sound. "It's my house. It's all I have left to keep me a person, you see. I won't get out and be respectable in his eyes."

"He didn't mind your staying here and taking care of—them!" cried Cynthia.

"It's respectable, dear, for an old maid to care for her father and mother; but when they die she ought to be useful to some one else instead of renting her house and living on an edge of it."

"Oh,"—Cynthia leaned forward,—"I should think you'd hate him! I think families are—terrible!"

"Hate him?" Miss Egert smiled. "He's nice. He just doesn't agree with me. As long as he lets the children come over—I told him I meant to have a beautiful time with them, with my real friends—with you."

Cynthia shrank into her chair, her eyes tragic again.

"Come, let's have our bonfire!" Miss Egert, with a quick movement, stood in front of Cynthia, one hand extended.

Cynthia crouched away from the hand.

"Miss Egert,"—her voice came out in a desperate little gasp,—"I can't come down any more. I can't take any more painting lessons." She stopped. Miss Egert waited, her head tipped to one side. "Mother doesn't think I better. I came down—after my things."

"They're all in the workroom." Miss Egert spoke quietly. "Do you want them now?"

"Yes." Cynthia pressed her knuckles against her lips. Over her hand her eyes cried out. "Yes, I better get them," she said heavily.

Miss Egert, turning slowly, lifted a candle from the table.

"We'll have to take this. The wiring isn't done." She crossed the room, her thin fingers, not quite steady, bending around the flame.

Cynthia followed through a narrow passage. Miss Egert pushed open a door, and the musty odor of the store-room floated out into a queer chord with the fresh plaster of the hall.

"Be careful of that box!" Miss Egert set the candle on a pile of trunks. "I've had to move all the truck from the attic and studio in here. Your sketches are in the portfolio, and that's—somewhere!"

Cynthia stood in the doorway, watching Miss Egert bend over a pile of canvases, throwing up a grotesque, rounded shadow on the wall. Round the girl's throat closed a ring of iron.

"Here they are, piled up—"

Cynthia edged between the boxes. Miss Egert was dragging the black portfolio from beneath a pile of books.

"And here's the book I wanted you to see." The pile slipped crashing to the floor as Miss Egert pulled out a magazine. "Never mind those. See here." She dropped into the chair from which she had knocked the books, the portfolio under one arm, the free hand running through the pages of an old art magazine. The chair swung slightly; Cynthia, peering down between the boxes, gave a startled "Oh!"

"What is it?" Miss Egert followed Cynthia's finger. "The chair?" She was silent a moment. "Do you think I keep my mother prisoner here in a wheel-chair now that she is free?" She ran her hand along the worn arm. "I tried to give it to an old ladies' home, but it was too used up. They wanted more style."

"But doesn't it remind you—" Cynthia hesitated.

"It isn't fair to remember the years she had to sit here waiting to die. You didn't know her. I've been going back to the real years—" Miss Egert smiled at Cynthia's bewildered eyes. "Here, let's look at these." She turned another page. "See, Cynthia. Aren't they swift and glad? That's what I was trying to tell you the other day. See that arm, and the drapery there! Just a line—" The girl bent over the page, frowning at the details the quick finger pointed out. "Don't they catch you along with them?" She held the book out at arm's-length, squinting at the figures. "Take it along. There are several more." She tucked the book into the portfolio and rose. "Come on; we'll have our fire."

"But, Miss Egert,"—Cynthia's voice hardened as she was swept back into her own misery,—"I can't take it. I can't come any more."

"To return a book?" Miss Egert lowered her eyelids as if she were again sizing up a composition. "You needn't come just for lessons."

Cynthia shook her head.

"Mother thinks——" She fell into silence. She couldn't say what her mother thought—dreadful things. If she could only swallow the hot pressure in her throat!

"Oh. I hadn't understood." Miss Egert's fingers paused for a swift touch on Cynthia's arm, and then reached for the candle. "You can go on working by yourself."

"It isn't that——" Cynthia struggled an instant, and dropped into silence again. She couldn't say out loud any of the things she was feeling. There were too many walls between feeling and speech: loyalty to her mother, embarrassment that feelings should come so near words, a fear of hurting Miss Egert.

"Don't mind so much, Cynthia." Miss Egert led the way back to the living-room. "You can stay for the bonfire? That will be better than sitting here. Run into the kitchen and bring the matches and marshmallows—in a dish in the cupboard."

Cynthia, in the doorway, stared at Miss Egert. Didn't she care at all! Then the dumb ache in her throat stopped throbbing as Miss Egert's gray eyes held her steadily a moment. She did care! She did! She was just helping her. Cynthia took the candle and went back through the passageway to the kitchen, down at the very end.

She made a place on the table in the litter of dishes and milk-bottles for the candle. The matches had been spilled on the shelf of the stove and into the sink. Cynthia gathered a handful of the driest. Shiftlessness was one of her mother's counts against Miss Egert. Cynthia flushed as she recalled her stumbling defense: Miss Egert had more important things to do; dishes were kept in their proper place; and her mother's: "Important! Mooning about!"

"Find them, Cynthia?" The clear, low voice came down the hall, and Cynthia hurried back.

Out in the garden it was quite black. As they came to the far end, the old stone wall made a dark bank against the sky, with a sharp star over its edge. Miss Egert knelt; almost with the scratch of the match the garden leaped into yellow, with fantastic moving shadows from the trees and in the corner of the wall. She raked leaves over the blaze, pulled the great mound into firmer shape, and then drew Cynthia back under the wall to watch. The light ran over her face; the delighted gestures of her hands were like quick shadows.

"See the old apple-tree dance! He's too old to move fast."

Cynthia crouched by the wall, brushing away from her face the scratchy leaves of the dead hollyhocks. Excitement tingled through her; she felt the red and yellow flames seizing her, burning out the heavy rebellion, the choking weight. Miss Egert leaned back against the wall, her hands spread so that her thin fingers were fire-edged.

"See the smoke curl up through those branches! Isn't it lovely, Cynthia?" She darted around the pile to push more leaves into the flames.

Cynthia strained forward, hugging her arms to her body. Never had there been such a fire! It burned through her awkwardness, her self-consciousness. It ate into the thick, murky veils which hung always between her and the things she struggled to find out. She took a long breath, and the crisp scent of smoke from the dead leaves tingled down through her body.

Miss Egert was at her side again. Cynthia looked up; the slight, asymmetrical figure was like the apple-tree, still, yet dancing!

"Why don't you paint it?" demanded Cynthia, abruptly, and then was frightened as Miss Egert's body stiffened, lost its suggestion of motion.

"I can't." The woman dropped to the ground beside Cynthia, crumpling a handful of leaves. "It's too late." She looked straight at the fire. "I must be content to see it." She blew the pieces of leaves from the palm of her hand and smiled at Cynthia. "Perhaps some day you'll paint it—or write it."

"I can't paint." Cynthia's voice quivered. "I want to do something. I can't even see things except what you point out. And now—"

Miss Egert laid one hand over Cynthia's clenched fingers. The girl trembled at the cold touch.

"You must go on looking." The glow, as the flames died lower, flushed her face. "Cynthia, you're just beginning. You mustn't stop just because you aren't to come here any more. I don't know whether you can say things with your brush; but you must find them out. You mustn't shut your eyes again."

"It's hard alone."

"That doesn't matter."

Cynthia's fingers unclasped, and one hand closed desperately around Miss Egert's. Her heart fluttered in her temples, her throat, her breast. She clung to the fingers, pulling herself slowly up from an inarticulate abyss.

"Miss Egert,"— she stumbled into words,—"I can't bear it, not coming here! Nobody else cares except about sensible things. You do, beautiful, wonderful things."

"You'd have to find them for yourself, Cynthia." Miss Egert's fingers moved under the girl's grasp. Then she bent toward Cynthia, and kissed her with soft, pale lips that trembled against the girl's mouth. "Cynthia, don't let any one stop you! Keep searching!" She drew back, poised for a moment in the shadow before she rose. Through Cynthia ran the swift feet of white ecstasy. She was pledging herself to some tremendous mystery, which trembled all about her.

"Come, Cynthia, we're wasting our coals."

Miss Egert held out her hands. Cynthia, laying hers in them, was drawn to her feet. As she stood there, inarticulate, full of a strange, excited, shouting hope, behind them the path crunched. Miss Egert turned, and Cynthia shrank back.

Her mother stood in the path, making no response to Miss Egert's "Good evening, Mrs. Bates."

The fire had burned too low to lift the shadow from the mother's face. Cynthia could see the hem of her skirt swaying where it dipped up in front. Above that two rigid hands in gray cotton gloves; above that the suggestion of a white, strained face.

Cynthia took a little step toward her.

"I came to get my sketches," she implored her. Her throat was dry. What if her mother began to say cruel things—the things she had already said at home.

"I hope I haven't kept Cynthia too late," Miss Egert said. "We were going to toast marshmallows. Won't you have one, Mrs. Bates?" She pushed the glowing leaf-ashes together. The little spurt of flame showed Cynthia her mother's eyes, hard, angry, resting an instant on Miss Egert and then assailing her.

"Cynthia knows she should not be here. She is not permitted to run about the streets alone at night."

"Oh, I'm sorry." Miss Egert made a deprecating little gesture. "But no harm has come to her."

"She has disobeyed me."

At the tone of her mother's voice Cynthia felt something within her breast curl up like a leaf caught in flame.

"I'll get the things I came for." She started toward the house, running past her mother. She must hurry, before her mother said anything to hurt Miss Egert.

She stumbled on the door-step, and flung herself against the door. The portfolio was across the room, on the little, old piano. The candle beside it had guttered down over the cover. Cynthia pressed out the wobbly flame, and, hugging the portfolio, ran back across the room. On the threshold she turned for a last glimpse. The row of Botticelli details over the bookcases were blurred into gray in the light of the one remaining candle; the Indian rug had a wavering glow. Then she heard Miss Egert just outside.

"I'm sorry Cynthia isn't to come any more," she was saying.

Cynthia stepped forward. The two women stood in the dim light, her mother's thickened, settled body stiff and hostile, Miss Egert's slight figure swaying toward her gently.

"Cynthia has a good deal to do," her mother answered. "We can't afford to give her painting lessons, especially—" Cynthia moved down between the women—"especially," her mother continued, "as she doesn't seem to get much of anywhere. You'd think she'd have some pictures to show after so many lessons."

"Perhaps I'm not a good teacher. Of course she's just beginning."

"She'd better put her time on her studies."

"I'll miss her. We've had some pleasant times together."

Cynthia held out her hand toward Miss Egert, with a fearful little glance at her mother.

"Good-by, Miss Egert."

Miss Egert's cold fingers pressed it an instant.

"Good night, Cynthia," she said slowly.

Then Cynthia followed her mother's silent figure along the path; she turned her head as they reached the sidewalk. Back in the garden winked the red eye of the fire.

They waited under the arc light for the car, Cynthia stealing fleeting glances at her mother's averted face. On the car she drooped against the window-edge, away from her

mother's heavy silence. She was frightened now, a panicky child caught in disobedience. Once, as the car turned at the corner below her father's office, she spoke:

"Father will expect me—"

"He knows I went after you," was her mother's grim answer.

Cynthia followed her mother into the house. Her small brother was in the sitting-
room, reading. He looked up from his book with wide, knowing eyes. Rebellious
humiliation washed over Cynthia; setting her lips against their quivering, she pulled off
her sweater.

"Go on to bed, Robert," called her mother from the entry, where she was hanging
her coat. "You've sat up too late as it is."

He yawned, and dragged his feet with provoking slowness past Cynthia.

"Was she down there, Mama?" He stopped on the bottom step to grin at his sister.

"Go on, Robert. Start your bath. Mother'll be up in a minute."

"Aw, it's too late for a bath." He leaned over the rail.

"It's Saturday. I couldn't get back sooner."

Cynthia swung away from the round, grinning face. Her mother went past her into
the dining-room. Robert shuffled upstairs; she heard the water splashing into the tub.

Her mother was very angry with her. Presently she would come back, would begin
to speak. Cynthia shivered. The familiar room seemed full of hostile, accusing silence,
like that of her mother. If only she had come straight home from the office, she would
be sitting by the table in the old Morris chair, reading, with her mother across from her
sewing, or glancing through the evening paper. She gazed about the room at the neat
scrolls of the brown wall-paper, at a picture above the couch, cows by a stream. The
dull, ordinary comfort of life there hung about her, a reproaching shadow, within
which she felt the heavy, silent discomfort her transgression dragged after it. It would
be much easier to go on just as she was expected to do. Easier. The girl straightened her
drooping body. That things were hard didn't matter. Miss Egert had insisted upon that.
She was forgetting the pledge she had given. The humiliation slipped away, and a cold
exaltation trembled through her, a remote echo of the hope that had shouted within her
back there in the garden. Here it was difficult to know what she had promised, to what
she had pledged herself—something that the familiar, comfortable room had no part in.

She glanced toward the dining-room, and her breath quickened. Between the faded
green portières stood her mother, watching her with hard, bright eyes. Cynthia's glance
faltered; she looked desperately about the room as if hurrying her thoughts to some
shelter. Beside her on the couch lay the portfolio. She took a little step toward it, stopping at her mother's voice.

"Well, Cynthia, have you anything to say?"

Cynthia lifted her eyes.

"Don't you think I have trouble enough with your brothers? You, a grown girl,
defying me! I can't understand it."

"I went down for this." Cynthia touched the black case.

"Put that down! I don't want to see it!" The mother's voice rose, breaking down the terrifying silences. "You disobeyed me. I told you you weren't to go there again. And then I telephoned your father to ask you to do an errand for me, and find you there—with that woman!"

"I'm not going again." Cynthia twisted her hands together. "I had to go a last time. She was a friend. I could not tell her I wasn't coming—"

"A friend! A sentimental old maid, older than your mother! Is that a friend for a young girl? What were you doing when I found you? Holding hands! Is that the right thing for you? She's turned your head. You aren't the same Cynthia, running off to her, complaining of your mother."

"Oh, no!" Cynthia flung out her hand. "We were just talking." Her misery confused her.

"Talking? About what?"

"About"—the recollection rushed through Cynthia—"about beauty." She winced, a flush sweeping up to the edge of her fair hair, at her mother's laugh.

"Beauty! You disobey your mother, hurt her, to talk about beauty at night with an old maid!"

There was a hot beating in Cynthia's throat; she drew back against the couch.

"Pretending to be an artist," her mother drove on, "to get young girls who are foolish enough to listen to her sentimentalizing."

"She was an artist," pleaded Cynthia. "She gave it up to take care of her father and mother. I told you all about that—"

"Talking about beauty doesn't make artists."

Cynthia stared at her mother. She had stepped near the table, and the light through the green shade of the reading-lamp made queer pools of color about her eyes, in the waves of her dark hair. She didn't look real. Cynthia threw one hand up against her lips. She was sucked down and down in an eddy of despair. Her mother's voice dragged her again to the surface.

"We let you go there because you wanted to paint, and you maunder and say things you'd be ashamed to have your mother hear. I've spent my life working for you, planning for you, and you go running off—" Her voice broke into a new note, a trembling, grieved tone. "I've always trusted you, depended on you; now I can't even trust you."

"I won't go there again. I had to explain."

"I can't believe you. You don't care how you make me feel."

Cynthia was whirled again down the sides of the eddy.

"I can't believe you care anything for me, your own mother."

Cynthia plucked at the braid on her cuff.

"I didn't do it to make you sorry," she whispered. "I—it was—" The eddy closed about her, and with a little gasp she dropped down on the couch, burying her head in the sharp angle of her elbows.

The mother took another step toward the girl; her hand hovered above the bent head and then dropped.

"You know mother wants just what is best for you, don't you? I can't let you drift away from us, your head full of silly notions."

Cynthia's shoulders jerked. From the head of the stairs came Robert's shout:

"Mama, tub's full!"

"Yes; I'm coming."

Cynthia stood up. She was not crying. About her eyes and nostrils strained the white intensity of hunger.

"You don't think—" She stopped, struggling with her habit of inarticulateness. "There might be things—not silly—you might not see what—"

"Cynthia!" The softness snapped out of the mother's voice.

Cynthia stumbled up to her feet; she was as tall as her mother. For an instant they faced each other, and then the mother turned away, her eyes tear-brightened. Cynthia put out an awkward hand.

"Mother," she said piteously, "I'd like to tell you—I'm sorry—"

"You'll have to show me you are by what you do." The woman started wearily up the stairs. "Go to bed. It's late."

Cynthia waited until the bathroom door closed upon Robert's splashings. She climbed the stairs slowly, and shut herself into her room. She laid the portfolio in the bottom drawer of her white bureau; then she stood by her window. Outside, the big elm-tree, in fine, leafless dignity, showed dimly against the sky, a few stars caught in the arch of its branches.

A swift, tearing current of rebellion swept away her unhappiness, her confused misery; they were bits of refuse in this new flood. She saw, with a fierce, young finality that she was pledged to a conflict as well as to a search. As she knelt by the window and pressed her cheek on the cool glass, she felt the house about her, with its pressure of useful, homely things, as a very prison. No more journeyings down to Miss Egert's for glimpses of escape. She must find her own ways. Keep searching! At the phrase, excitement again glowed within her; she saw the last red wink of the fire in the garden.

"A. T. FITZROY" [ROSE ALLATINI] (1890?–1980?)

From *Despised and Rejected* (1918)

"A. T. Fitzroy" is one of several pseudonyms of Rose Laure Allatini. Born in Vienna to a Polish mother and Italian father, Allatini grew up in England. She began writing in the teens and published her first novel, . . . *Happy Ever After*, in 1914. She married the composer Cyril Scott in 1921, and had two children, but left Scott and moved to Rye with another writer, Melanie Mills, in 1941. There, over several decades, both women produced works of romantic fiction under various pseudonyms. Allatini's last novel (written under the name Eunice Buckley) appeared in 1978.

Like D. H. Lawrence's *The Rainbow* (1915) and Radclyffe Hall's *The Well of Loneliness* (1928), *Despised and Rejected* (1918), Allatini's fourth novel, was banned by the British government upon publication. According to government prosecutors, the novel's sympathetic depiction of conscientious objectors—its hero, Dennis Blackwood, is a pacifist and war resister—"was likely to prejudice the recruiting of persons to serve in His Majesty's Forces." Yet Allatini's frank depiction of both male and female homosexuality undoubtedly contributed to the book's seizure as well. Set during the First World War, the story turns upon Dennis's complex relationship with Antoinette de Courcy, a young woman whom he plans to marry. These plans are upset by Dennis's imprisonment as a conscientious objector, as well as the gradual discovery that both he and Antoinette love members of their own sex. A continuing thread in the novel from the start is Antoinette's infatuation with an enigmatic older woman, Hester Cawthorn, whom she meets while staying with her family at a seaside hotel. In the scene below, Allatini depicts the genesis of this attachment in a manner reminiscent of Elizabeth Bowen—at once sensitive and sophisticated and subtly attuned to the exaltations of young female adulthood.

FURTHER READING: "A. T. Fitzroy" [Rose Allatini], *Despised and Rejected*, ed. Jonathan Cutbill (1918; rpt. London: Gay Men's, 1988); Jeannette Foster, *Sex Variant Women in Literature* (1956; rpt. Tallahassee, Fla.: Naiad, 1985); Cyril Scott, *Bone of Contention* (London: Aquarian, 1969).

"Come for a walk with me—do!" The tone was half pleading, half commanding. Hester Cawthorn very slowly closed her book, and from the depths of her chair on the lawn, looked up at Antoinette's eager face. She shook her head, and Antoinette repeated under her breath "Do . . ."

Hester's sullen mouth curved into a smile. "Why should I?"

"Because I—I want you to."

"You seem to consider that an adequate reason!"

"Well—isn't it?"

The hotel visitors, grouped upon the lawn to laze away the hot after-lunch hour, were surprised at seeing Miss Cawthorn and Antoinette de Courcy stroll down the drive together. It was the first time that Miss Cawthorn had been known to set out in company.

"That child has such a way with her, she gets round everybody," murmured Mrs. Blackwood, hoping that Dennis would take notice.

Hester and Antoinette walked in silence down the length of the shady drive. Antoinette was not so sure of herself now; wondered what would be the result of her daring. It had certainly needed daring to ask Hester to come out with her. There was about Hester a nimbus of unapproachability that was recognised by everyone in the hotel, and that had aroused, firstly, curiosity and secondly, interest in Antoinette. Also, she was strangely attracted by this woman with the sombre hooded eyes and down-curved mouth that seemed to speak of much bitterness and disillusion. During her stay at Amberhurst, Antoinette had become amazingly intimate with all the hotel visitors; most of them, at one time or another, had been moved to tell her "the story of my life"; for she was a good listener, and waited with rapt eagerness for the picturesque or the dramatic note that should stamp each story with individuality. Everybody confided in her, petted her, spoilt her. Hester alone had held aloof from her, as she had held aloof from the others. But Antoinette was resolved to make herself the exception to Hester's rule.

"And now—what do you want?" Hester's question, breaking the silence, was abrupt but not discourteous.

Antoinette laughed. "To tell the truth, I don't know. *'Je ne sais pas ce que je veux, mais je le veux absolument.'*"

"Well, then, believe me, you won't get it."

"How can you say that, when you don't know—when I don't even know—what it is I want?"

"I can only warn you that it's useless to expect anything from me—I've nothing to give." Hester's voice was low and beautiful, despite its occasional harshness. Antoinette thrilled at the sound of it, and at the warning that had just been flung at her. Nothing to give—why, she must have worlds to give to one who knew how to claim her gifts. Or perhaps once already she had bestowed them, bestowed them royally upon one unworthy . . . and was cautious now, distrustful of anyone attempting to approach the fortress-gates behind which was locked—herself. Antoinette would lay siege to the fortress with every weapon in her power, with daring and gentleness and subtlety, until the gates were opened to her. She felt confident of success, buoyantly happy as she strode along at Hester's side, hands thrust deep into the pockets of her jersey, the noonday sun beating down upon her bare head.

"You'll catch sun-stroke, child."

"Not I!"

"Haven't you anything to put on your head?"

"I believe so, somewhere in my pocket," Antoinette drew out a crumpled red silk cap and swung it in her hand.

"Put it on," commanded Hester curtly. Antoinette obeyed, enjoying the sensation of being ordered about by Hester.

"Even if you do happen to be possessed of extraordinary vitality," the latter continued, "there's no need to squander it."

"Am I squandering it?" Antoinette asked innocently. She was not introspective, but she was always interested when people told her things about herself.

"Are you squandering it, indeed . . . ? Rushing along a dusty road at the rate of eight miles an hour, at the hottest time of the day—"

"I'm so sorry! Is it too hot for you? Shall we go back?"

"No, I've no objection to it. But then I've not been wearing myself out with emotional acting every night this week."

"Oh, the acting . . . it was such fun! Absolute rot, of course, poor dear Rosabel hasn't the faintest notion how to write a play, but she's written half a dozen different ones about Marie Antoinette. In fact, whenever I meet her, she seems to be in the thick of writing one, and she falls upon my neck with: 'Antoinette darling, I'm writing a tragedy about *her*—it's to be something exquisite . . . six acts and nineteen scenes . . . no, don't ask me anything about it . . . the first scene is in a sort of inn and people come in and talk . . . no, I can't tell you any more, you'd think me so stupid. . . . Another time, perhaps. . . .'"

Hester was laughing outright by now; and thus encouraged, Antoinette went on: "We had an awful business with this particular masterpiece. Rosabel had left all the parts, except the Queen's, quite sketchy; so we had to invent them at rehearsals, and make them fit together as well as we could. Rosabel is never quite successful with anything she attempts. There's a certain blighted perkiness about her, that makes her rather like an early bird that hasn't caught the worm—or perhaps she's the early worm that always gets the bird . . ."

"You're too brilliant, my young friend."

"Am I? Why?"

Hester smiled inscrutably and was silent.

"Why am I too brilliant?" Antoinette was suddenly overwhelmed by the fear of disapproval. "I—I wasn't trying to be."

"No, I daresay you weren't. I was only thinking of that old proverb that was dinned into one's ears in the nursery: 'Sing before breakfast—cry before night!'"

"Oh, do you mean that I shall—'cry before night'?"

Hester looked down at the eager laughing face, the boyish curls surmounted care-lessly by the red cap. "You won't, at all events, cry before—tonight."

"But you think I shall eventually? Can you tell the future, then?"

"Most people's futures are written on their faces, aren't they?"

"For those who are able to read them. . . . So that's how you read mine! Well, I don't care . . ." Antoinette flung her cap into the air and caught it again. "I assure you that if I do have to 'cry before night,' I shall 'sing before breakfast' quite a lot *en attendant*."

"I've no doubt you will," said Hester.

"I'm doing it now—simply having the time of my life."

"And in what," Hester's tone was ironical, "in what, exactly, does the 'time of your life' consist?" Then before Antoinette could answer, she covered up the question with: "Don't tell me if you don't want to—I've no wish to force confidence."

Antoinette smiled involuntarily at the notion that Hester should assume in her a reticence equal to her own. If she had told the truth, she would have answered: "I'm happy because there's so much love in the world, and because so much of it comes to me, and mostly because I'm walking beside you now. . . ."

But she only said, "It's not that I'm really doing anything extraordinary, but this is the first time I've ever stayed away from my people—would you believe it, and I'm nearly twenty-two—but Grand'mère has quite obsolete ideas as to what a *jeune fille* should do and shouldn't do, even though she's lived over here for twenty-five years."

"Were you born in England, then?"

"Yes. And I feel quite English. The others—Grand'mère and Mother and Father are terribly French, though. . . ." Antoinette gave a sigh, and then laughed again. "Being away is such fun, I love sitting down to breakfast in the morning with a differ-ent set of faces, don't you?"

"I never sit down with a 'set of faces' at all."

"Don't you? Not ever? Not even at home?"

Hester was silent. Antoinette tried to imagine the family-circle from which she might have sprung, and gave it up as hopeless: she could not picture Hester in relation to a mother or father, sisters or brothers. She could only see her as an individual, detached from her surroundings, lonely and alone. Her whole heart went out in sym-pathy to this strange woman with the fierce reserve, and the sensitiveness that lay behind her brutally direct manner; in sympathy, and something that was more than sympathy.

After a while, Hester said with quiet bitterness: "I have no home. . . ."

Impulsively Antoinette put out her hand to touch her arm. "I'm sorry—so dread-fully sorry—you must be lonely."

Hester made no movement in response, but replied coldly, "You make a mistake: I am not lonely."

Antoinette, baffled, dropped her hand and was silent. She had been tactless and deserved her rebuff; nevertheless it had hurt—rather. The conquest of Hester, impreg-

nably immured in her fortress, was proving even more difficult than she had anticipated, and therefore ten times more desirable. Antoinette was accustomed to easy victories, victories so easy as scarcely to merit the name, and she was tired of them; but the
prospect of difficulties only stimulated the fighting-instinct in her.

Hester, with an air of detached amusement, was watching her absorbed face. "I
warned you, didn't I . . . ?"

Antoinette flashed out: "If you think I'm frightened of your prickliness—"

"Oh, you hot-headed little fool . . . What's all this for? If you think I'm going to
make a friend or a confidante of you, you're mistaken. Real friendship is, in my experience, a treasure impossible to find, and I've no use for people who want to know my fam-
ily-history, and whence I came and whither I'm going. . . . What concern of theirs can
it be? No, I have no friends and I want none. You're only wasting your time with me."

"I'm not—it isn't waste!" cried Antoinette, "you're so wonderful, and ever since
I've been here I've wanted to talk to you, only I never quite dared till to-day, and then
I simply couldn't stop myself. . . . I noticed you the first evening I came—how could I
help it? All the other people move about in lumps, three or four staying together, three
or four at a table in the dining-room, three or four going out together—and only you
were alone. That was remarkable to begin with."

"I shall always be alone," said Hester.

"Yes—and I know why!" Inspiration seemed suddenly to come to Antoinette.
"Whereas the others want company, want to be together at any price, you only want
what is really good enough for you. It's—it's as if it had to pass through fire before it
could get to you."

"You're fantastic," Hester smiled, but not unkindly, and then, without interrupting
her, she let Antoinette have her say.

"I can understand your keeping the others out and hating them to ask questions—
you know they're only inquisitive, and not asking because it means a great deal to them.
It means a great deal to me, I can't tell you why, but it just does. Please won't you let
me come a little bit closer? You see, I'm not frightened of the prickles or the fire. . . ."
Quite unconsciously she was pleading as a very young boy might plead with his lady-
love.

Hester shook her head. "Even if you do 'come closer,' as you say, you'll only be
disappointed. Go and fall in love with that nice Blackwood boy: it will be much more
profitable than this sort of thing."

"This sort of thing . . . ?" Antoinette repeated with a puzzled frown.

Hester looked at her sharply for a moment, then gave a curt laugh. "Never
mind. . . . Do as I say. Stick to young Blackwood."

"To Clive?" Antoinette exclaimed contemptuously. "Why, he's engaged, Doreen
says, to a girl who studies economics and won't powder her nose."

"I didn't mean Clive, I meant the one who arrived yesterday—Dennis. At any rate,
I'm certain that he's going to fall in love with you."

Antoinette was not interested. Hester continued: "He's quite a character-study. I should like to hear how the affair progresses."

"Would you .. ?" cried Antoinette, overjoyed at the idea that anything connected with herself could be of interest to Hester. "I'd better cultivate him, then."

"I'll leave you my address," said Hester.

"Your address? But you're not going away yet, surely?"

"Going this very evening."

Antoinette stood stock-still in the middle of the road, and gasped. "Not—really?" In the case of anyone but Hester, her plans would have been known by the whole hotel for days in advance. It was but another proof of Hester's aloofness, that the time of her departure came to Antoinette as an absolute shock.

"Don't look so bewildered: it can't possibly matter to you."

"But it does—more than anything else in the world—more than ever now. When I started out with you this afternoon, I was only enormously interested in you, and I admired you—your brains, and the gorgeous way you have of choking off people you don't want. I've watched you do it—Oh, often—but you're not going to choke me off like that, because now, I—I love you. . . ." She had not intended to say those words; a few moments ago they would not have entered her mind; now she had not only said them: she meant them.

Hester looked at her gravely, without curiosity and without astonishment. "If that's the case, I've no right to choke you off. But understand once and for all that you're on a wild-goose chase. You'll find none of the hidden depths in me that you seem to expect to find."

"Whether that's true or not, I'll never expect any confidence or anything that you don't give me of your own free will. But there's nothing on earth that I wouldn't do for you, if I thought it would make you happy."

Hester said with that curious dignity that was hers: "Thank you. . . ."

They walked back then. After some time, Antoinette ventured to ask, "Where is it you're going to-night?"

The answer was: "To Bristol—if the gods are good to me!" and Antoinette saw that Hester's dark eyes were illuminated by a gleam of light, and fixed straight ahead of her, as if in pursuit of some vision whence the light had come. Antoinette longed to know what was portended by that phrase: "If the gods are good to me . . ." wondered what was drawing her to Bristol; if she lived there; if she ever came to London; why she had been staying at Amberhurst. But all these questions remained unasked. She would prove herself worthy of Hester by showing no curiosity, by accepting as a matter of course anything that she might do.

Her offer to help Hester with her packing was declined; but she obtained permission to see her to the station.

"I may be late for dinner," Antoinette flung over her shoulder to Rosabel, as, for the second time that day, she left the hotel in Hester's company. Rosabel stared open-mouthed . . . Hester laughed. "You see, even your friend is struck by the incongruity of seeing us together!"

"It isn't incongruous really. At least I don't think it is. I'm sure I should find much more in common with you, than with Rosabel." Antoinette flushed, fearing that she had said too much; but Hester did not appear to think that she had been guilty of impertinence.

"Perhaps I'm only letting you imagine that you could. . . ." Antoinette pondered on this; then: "No, if you were only acting, just to give me that impression, you'd be so clever that I'd have to adore you all the same. It's no earthly good trying to put me off by pretending you aren't what I know you are."

"I don't know that I am trying to put you off now. . . . I'm only trying to be honest and sincere with you, and to keep you from disappointment."

"Honest and sincere—I should just think you are! I'd follow your lead blindly through anything, and feel that I could trust you."

"Oh, child, child, don't put all that trust in me. No one but a god could be worthy of so much. It's too great a responsibility for a mere human being."

"No trust and no faith could be too great for me to give you—and—and I'll never let you feel the responsibility of me as a drag. I can look out for myself. I want to walk level with you, not hanging on."

"You shall do as you wish," said Hester.

In silence they paced the platform of the little country station. Antoinette's exaltation was shadowed now with the dread of parting from Hester. But she allowed no word of regret to pass her lips. She would be true to her assertion that she would not "hang on" to Hester. Hester's happiness, apparently, lay in going; so, with all her heart, Antoinette tried to want her to go, even though Amberhurst would seem a deserted wilderness without her. She regretted the wasted days that had gone before she had made up her mind to speak to her; the last few hours of joy had passed so swiftly; and now—and now—

Antoinette hastily shook back her curls and smiled, as the train came in. The door of the compartment was slammed between them.

"Well, good-bye," said Antoinette lightly, enjoying the self-imposed necessity of acting up to Hester, "good luck to you."

Hester leant out of the window, and, just as the train started, bent down and kissed her.

LESBIA HARFORD (1891–1927)

"I Can't Feel the Sunshine," "You Want a Lily" (1918)

Little is known about the Australian poet and labor organizer of the 1920s, Lesbia Harford. Although she studied for the bar at Melbourne University during World War I, she gave up the law in order to work as a teacher and a skirt machinist in a textile factory. An ardent socialist, she was active in the Victorian Socialist Party, the anticonscription campaign, and the radical labor group, International Workers of the World. She married in 1920. She wrote one novel—*The Invaluable Mystery*—unpublished in her lifetime. Small, dark, and obsessive in psychological makeup—a kind of Australian precursor of the French philosopher-cum-factory worker Simone Weil—Harford died prematurely in 1927.

Harford's poems, many of which appear to have been written as songs, reflect both her political beliefs and her emotional gravitation toward women. She is known to have had at least one lesbian love affair, with Katie Lush, a philosophy tutor at Melbourne. Harford's editor Drusilla Modjeska notes that Harford's verse radiates questions about "the relationship between popular and literary traditions of writing, the forms of protest poetry and the interconnections between histories of writing, class, and feminism." That she was also a love poet of some power will also be evident, however, to anyone who seeks her out.

FURTHER READING: Lesbia Harford, *The Poems of Lesbia Harford*, ed. Nettie Palmer (Melbourne: Melbourne University Press, 1941); ——, *The Poems of Lesbia Harford*, ed. Drusilla Modjeska and Marjorie Pizer (Sydney: Angus and Robertson, 1985); ——, *The Invaluable Mystery* (Melbourne: McPhee Gribble, 1988); Catherine Cuthbert, "Lesbia Harford and Marie Pitt: Forgotten Poets," *Hecate* 8 (1982): 32–48; Jennifer Strauss, "Stubborn Singers of Their Full Song: Mary Gilmore and Lesbia Harford," in Kay Ferres, ed., *The Time to Write: Australian Women Writers, 1890–1930* (New York: Viking Penguin, 1993), pp. 108–38; Gary Catalano, "Lesbia Harford," *Quadrant* 12 (1998): 53–56.

I Can't Feel the Sunshine

I can't feel the sunshine
Or see the stars aright
For thinking of her beauty
And her kisses bright.

She would let me kiss her
Once and not again.
Deeming soul essential,
Sense doth she disdain.

If I should once kiss her,
I would never rest
Till I had lain hour long
Pillowed on her breast.

Lying so, I'd tell her
Many a secret thing
God has whispered to me
When my soul took wing.

Would that I were Sappho,
Greece my land, not this!
There the noblest women,
When they loved, would kiss.

You Want a Lily

You want a lily
And you plead with me
"Give me my lily back."

I went to see
A friend last night and on her mantle shelf
I saw some lilies,
Image of myself,
And most unlike your dream of purity.

They had been small green lilies, never white
For man's delight

In their most blissful hours.
But now the flowers
Had shrivelled and instead
Shone spikes of seeds,
Burned spikes of seeds,
Burned red
As love and death and fierce futurity.

There's this much of the lily left in me.

VIOLET TREFUSIS (1894–1972)

Letters to Vita Sackville-West (1918–19)

Violet Trefusis is mainly remembered today as the lover of the flamboyant English lesbian writer, Vita Sackville-West (1892–1962). Their turbulent, tragicomic affair—fascinatingly documented by Sackville-West's son, Nigel Nicolson, in his 1973 book *Portrait of a Marriage*—scandalized British high society in the years after the First World War and nearly wrecked both women's marriages. It also lent itself to literary myth-making: Sackville-West's *Challenge* (1924) and Virginia Woolf's *Orlando* (1928) are among several fictional works that allude to the affair.

Yet to view Trefusis merely as a Vita-appendage is to sell her short. The daughter of cultivated (if louche) aristocratic parents—her mother, Alice Keppel, was mistress to King Edward VII—Trefusis was witty, mercurial, musical, highly intelligent, and a connoisseur of beauty in all its forms. Both men and women found her extremely attractive. After meeting her for the first time in the 1930s, Virginia Woolf wrote to Sackville-West:

> I can quite see why you were so enamoured—then: she's a little too full, now, overblown rather; but what seduction! What a voice—lisping, faltering, what warmth, suppleness, and in her way—it's not mine—I'm a good deal more refined—but that's not altogether an advantage—how lovely, like a squirrel among buck hares—a red squirrel among brown nuts.

In France, where she lived for fifty years after separating from Sackville-West in 1921, Trefusis retained a host of distinguished friends and admirers: Proust, Colette, Jean Cocteau, the Sitwells, the Princesse de Polignac, Natalie Barney, Jean Giraudoux, Francis Poulenc, and the future French prime minister François Mitterand.

Trefusis was a fluent writer—at least as talented, some might argue, as the woman with whom her name is most often linked. Trefusis wrote six novels—*Sortie de Secours* (1929), *Echo* (1931), *Tandem* (1933), *Broderie Anglaise* (1935), *Hunt the Slipper* (1937), and *Les Causes perdues* (1941)—three in French and three in English. *Broderie Anglaise* is a thinly disguised roman à clef about the affair with Sackville-West. In 1952 she produced a delightful, yet eminently discreet, autobiography, *Don't Look Round*—a comic highpoint of which is her description of a private meeting with Mussolini during which she accidentally spilled all the contents of her handbag on the marble floor of the Duce's reception room. More revealing are Trefusis's letters—especially to Sackville-West. In the sampling below, written in 1918 at the height of their affair but not published until 1989, Trefusis woos her dark-eyed lover, whom she calls, by turns, "Dmitri" and "Mitya" in honor of her exotic looks, with a mixture of fantasy, flattery, and frank sexual appeal. ("Lushka" was Trefusis's own nickname; the initials "H. N." refer to Sackville-West's then-estranged husband, the diplomat Harold Nicolson.) Farouche, self-dramatizing, yet unfailingly passionate, they are among the greatest of lesbian love letters.

FURTHER READING: Violet Trefusis, *Violet to Vita: The Letters of Violet Trefusis to Vita Sackville-West*, ed. Mitchell A. Leaska and John Phillips (London: Methuen, 1989); —, *Don't Look Round* (1952; rpt. New York: Viking Penguin, 1992); —, *Broderie Anglaise*, trans. Barbara Bray (New York: Harcourt Brace Jovanovich, 1985); Nigel Nicolson, *Portrait of a Marriage: V. Sackville-West and Harold Nicolson* (New York: Atheneum, 1973); Philippe Jullian and John Phillips, *Violet Trefusis: A Biography* (New York: Harcourt Brace Jovanovich, 1976); Henrietta Sharpe, *A Solitary Woman: A Life of Violet Trefusis* (London: Constable, 1981); Victoria Glendinning, *Vita: The Life of V. Sackville-West* (New York: Knopf, 1983); Nigel Nicolson, ed., *Vita and Harold: The Letters of Vita Sackville-West and Harold Nicolson* (New York: Putnam's, 1992); Diana Souhami, *Mrs. Keppel and Her Daughter* (New York: St. Martin's, 1996).

[1918]

. . . I may be writing rubbish, but then I am drunk. Drunk with the beauty of my Mitya! All today I was incoherent. I tell you, there is a barbaric splendour about you that conquered not only me, but everyone who saw you. You are made to *conquer*, Mitya, not be conquered. You were *superb*. You could have the world at your feet. Even my mother, who is not easily impressed, shared my opinion. *You have also changed*, it appears? They said, this evening after you had gone, that you were like a dazzling Gypsy. My sister's words, not mine. A Gypsy potentate, a sovereign—what you will, but still a Gypsy.

They also said they noticed a new exuberance in you, something akin to sheer animal spirits—that never was there before. You may love me, Mitya, but anyone would be *proud* to be loved by you, even if they were to be thrown aside and forgotten—for somebody new. . . .

[30 June 1918]

Men tilich, it was Hell leaving you today. God how I adore you and want you. You can't know how much. . . . Last night was perfection. . . . I am so proud of you, my sweet, I revel in your beauty, your beauty of form and feature. I exult in my surrender, today, not always though. Darling, had your novel been in French, it must inevitably have been christened "Domptée."

Mitya, I miss you so—I don't care what I say—I love belonging to you— I glory in it, that you alone . . . have bent me to your will, shattered my self-possession, robbed me of my mystery, made me yours, *yours*, so that away from you I am nothing but a useless puppet! an empty husk. Alushka need not have been ashamed of being Dmitri's mistress . . . on the contrary! . . .

What do I care what I say to you? I have, if anything, added a few "curtains" to my manners for other people's benefit, but for you there are no curtains, not even gossamer ones! I exult in the knowledge of how little we have in common with the world. . . .

Your Lushka,
BURN THIS! Promise.

1918

This afternoon I steeped myself in music pour revivre, and to forget (a contradiction in terms). The medium was a pianola, but one excused that, it was so well played. . . . O my dear, there is nothing in this world equal to music: "la raison est trop faible, et trop pauvres les mots" alas! for her sister arts— they are nowhere in comparison.

I listened to Grieg, elflike, mischievous, imaginative, romantic—so Latin sometimes despite his Norwegian blood. . . . You would love Grieg. You would love the saccadé rhythm of Anitra's dances, and the grotesque horror of "In the Halle des Bergkonigs." In the fairyland of music, Grieg plays gnome to Debussy's magician. . . .

Then I listened to Debussy, and almost reeled to hear the beauty of *La Mer* (so like Irkutsk) and his *Petite Suite*—which is the epitome of XVIII Century gallantry, joyousness and impudence. O my darling, I could make you love Debussy as much as I do *myself*, only it would take time. Then with an epicureanism worthy of Marius, I selected Brahms, the wild, the "exultant" the free—*your* musician, par excellence. Indeed I played *you* into everything, or almost everything I heard. . . .

22 July 1918

. . . For 16 nights I have listened expectantly for the opening of my door, for the whispered "Lushka" as you entered my room, and tonight I am alone. What shall I do? How can I sleep? . . . I don't want to sleep, for fear of waking up, thinking you near by my side, and stretching out my arms to clasp—emptiness!

Mitya, do you remember this?

All that I know of love I learned of you,
And I know all that lovers can know,
Since passionately loving to be loved
The subtlety of your wise body moved
My senses to a curiosity
And your wise heart adorned itself for me.
Did you not teach me how to love you, how
To win you, how to suffer for you now
Since you have made, as long as life endures,
My very nerves, my very senses, yours?
I suffer for you now with that same skill
Of self-consuming ecstasy, whose thrill
(May Death some day the thought of it remove!)
You gathered from the very hands of Love.

. . . I think you now do realize that this can't go on, that we must once and for all take our courage in both hands, and go away together. What sort of a life can we lead now? Yours, an infamous and degrading lie to the world, officially bound to someone you don't care for, perpetually with that someone, that in itself constitutes an outrage to me, being constantly watched and questioned, watched to see if the expected reaction is not taking place, questioned to make quite sure there is no one else!

I, not caring a damn for anyone but you, utterly lost, miserably incomplete, condemned to leading a futile, purposeless existence, which no longer holds the smallest attraction for me. . . .

A cheery picture, isn't it? And you know how true it is. At all events, I implore you to run the H. N. fiction to death. It is the only thing that can save us, the only thing that will ensure peace for both of us.

En attendant, I think "there is a lot to be said for being (temporarily) dead." Mitya, what stabs me like a knife is to remember you here in this room watching the last things being packed preparatory to going away with you, a fortnight ago. When I think of that and you waiting for me on the stairs, I feel quite faint from the pain of it all. My God, how exultant we were! And now, "la vie est devenue cendre dans son fruit." There is nothing to look forward to, nothing.

I never thought I would (or could) love like this. . . .

14 August 1918

Bacco mio! After I had left you I went to John St. Its châtelaine was out; so I took advantage of her absence to play the pianola. I played Daphnis et Chloe,

very suitable for Bacco, and so lovely! . . . Then suddenly, whilst I was playing it, I found my ideal! You've no idea how exciting it was. My ideal is this,
Mitya: to live far, far away in Greece for preference, Sicily, failing Greece—to
live in the woods, on the mountain slopes, by streams and by rivers—never to
see anyone, save perhaps an occasional shepherd, and to live there with Mitya,
in the spring, only it would have to be always spring! Mitya in his convolvulus
wreath—or, no, Mitya with a faun-skin thrown over his shoulders, with little
gilded hoofs, its head clothing Mitya's head within—Bacchus "sweet upon the
mountains." I quote Euripides. . . .

Oh, Mitya, come away, let's fly, Mitya darling—if ever there were two
entirely primitive people, they are surely us: let's go away and forget the world
and all its squalor—let's forget such things as trains, and trams, and servants,
and streets, and shops, and money, and cares and responsibilities. Oh God!
how I hate it all—you and I, Mitya, were born 2000 years too late, or 2000
years too soon.

14 August 1918, 1 o'clock
My adored beloved, I have come as near to breaking my heart today, as ever I
have. . . . When you said on the telephone that you couldn't come, nay, worse,
that you had hurt yourself badly, everything went quite black, and I felt suddenly sick. I wanted more than I have ever wanted anything before to take the
next train down to Sevenoaks. . . .

. . . I went to Pat's for lunch, still wondering unsociably whether I wouldn't
chuck everything and come by the afternoon train. By the time I had finished
lunch I had made up my mind to do this, and was going to have told you so on
the telephone, when Lily informed me you had gone to Knole, which so
enraged me, that I immediately changed my mind—(Pat did *not* try to deter me
from coming, on the contrary).

I haven't told you the worst, Mitya. I was so utterly miserable when I got
to Pat's before lunch, about 12.30, that I broke down and sobbed my heart out
and told her I couldn't bear going away and why. Darling, you know how generous she is. She was genuinely sorry for me and tried to help me about getting
to you. Then when you said you hadn't really been to Knole, I was again determined to get to you, coûte que coûte. I knew that it was folly and that it would
inevitably be found out, but I didn't care, I resolved to give myself a chance,
not a very good one, but just a chance of catching the train. I felt I would give
the whole of my life to see you for five minutes. I found a taxi and told him to
drive to Charing X; Mitya, I missed the train by two minutes. I don't think if
I could have got to you I would ever have left you again. Mitya, how can I tell
you what I am suffering? . . .

I want to see you. I want to hear your voice. I want to put my hand on your
shoulder and cry my heart out. Mitya, Mitya, I have never told you the whole

truth. You shall have it now: I have loved you all my life, a long time without knowing, 5 years knowing it as irrevocably as I know it now, loved you as my ideal. . . .

And the supreme truth is this: *I can never be happy without you.* I would be quite content to live on terms of purely platonic friendship with you—provided we were *alone* and *together*—for the rest of my days. Now you know everything. You are the *grande passion* of my life. How gladly would I sacrifice *everything* to you—family, friends, fortune, *EVERYTHING.* . . .

Clovelly

25 August 1918

. . . My days are consumed by this impotent longing for you, and my nights are riddled with insufferable dreams. . . . I want you. I want you hungrily, frenziedly, passionately. I am starving for you, if you must know it. Not only the physical you, but your fellowship, your sympathy, the innumerable points of view we share. I can't exist without you, you are my affinity, the intellectual "pendent" to me, my twin spirit. I can't help it! no more can you! . . . Nous nous complétons. . . .

Mitya, we *must*. God knows we have waited long enough! Something will go "snap" in my brain if we wait any longer and I shall tell everyone I know that we are going away and why. Do you think I'm going to waste any more of my precious youth waiting for you to screw up sufficient courage to make a bolt? Not I! . . .

I want you for my own, I want to go away with you. I must and will and damn the world and damn the consequences and anyone had better look out for themselves who dares to become an obstacle in my path.

In the train

15 September 1918

. . . My beautiful, romantic Mitya, our scruples are not worthy of our temperaments. Think of the life we could have together exclusively devoted to the pursuit of Beauty. Oh, Mitya, chepescar! What have we to do with the vulgar, prattling, sordid life of today? What care we for the practical little soigné occupations of our contemporaries? You *know* we're different—Gypsies in a world of "landed gentry."

You, my poor Mitya, they've taken you and they've burnt your caravan. They've thrown away your pots and pans and your half-mended wicker chairs. They've pulled down your sleeves and buttoned up your collar! They've forced you to sleep beneath a self-respecting roof with no chinks to let the stars through—but I, Mitya, they haven't caught *me* yet. I snap my fingers in their faces. Come away, Mitya, come away, when they're all asleep in their snug white beds . . . I'll wait for you at the crossroads. . . . Ah, Beloved!

LIANE DE POUGY (1869–1950)

From *My Blue Notebooks* (1919–41)

After an unsuccessful marriage at the age of sixteen, Anne-Marie Chassaigne, the beautiful daughter of a French army officer, ran away to Paris, renamed herself Liane de Pougy, and became the most celebrated courtesan of the *belle époque*. Life as a busy demimondaine, however, did not keep her from having numerous affairs with women. Her most celebrated female lover was the glamorous American expatriate hostess, Natalie Clifford Barney; de Pougy published a roman à clef about their affair, *Idylle saphique*, in 1901. Later in life, courting respectability, De Pougy married a Rumanian prince and became the Princess Ghika. Even then she remained loyal to her women friends: female admirers were welcome to any of her charms above the waist, she wrote, as long as they realized that her body below the waist belonged to her husband. She became extremely pious in old age and endowed a Trinitarian convent at Bois-Cerf.

Between 1919 and 1941 de Pougy kept a series of gossipy, often hilarious diaries, posthumously collected in a volume entitled *Mes Cahiers bleus* (*My Blue Notebooks*) in 1977. Besides being amusing, the diaries are a trove of information on the international lesbian haute monde between the wars. In the first excerpts below de Pougy reminisces about three former lovers—Valtesse de La Bigne, Émilienne d'Alençon, and "Flossie" (Barney)—and describes a nostalgic visit to the tombs of her friends Maria Bashkirtseff and "Pauline" (Renée Vivien). In subsequent entries she draws an affectionate portrait of "Uncle Max" (Mathilde de Morny), the cross-dressing Marquise de Belboeuf and onetime lover of Colette.

FURTHER READING: Liane de Pougy, *Idylle saphique* (1901; rpt., Paris: J. C. Lattes, 1979); —, *Mes Cahiers bleus* (Paris: Plon, 1977); —, *My Blue Notebooks*, trans. Diana Athill (London: Andre Deutsch, 1979); George Wickes, *The Amazon of Letters: The Life and Loves of Natalie Barney* (New York: Putnam's, 1976); Marianne Rogala, "The Blue Notebooks of Liane de Pougy: The Courtesan Who Became a Princess Who Became a Nun," *Quadrant* 31 (1987): 67–70; Judith Thurman, *Secrets of the Flesh: A Life of Colette* (New York: Knopf, 1999).

13 August 1919

I have had a letter from Marguerite Roquet, née Godard. Her mother was the daughter of my friend Valtesse de La Bigne, the Tesse of the *Idylle saphique*.

That charming woman's death has left a hole in my life which no one else has yet filled. She would have suffered from what is called progress, that's to say from the tendency to accept and excuse shoddiness. She would have suffered but she would not have let it show. She was controlled, self-contained, reserved. Very lovely, sensual and intelligent, making a distinct separation in her life between the pleasures of the body and those of the mind. She never told me she had a daughter, yet we were friends to the limit—both permissible and forbidden. I was unforgiveable. One day I took Flossie to her house, went into a bedroom with Valtesse, locked the door and refused her nothing, highly amused at the thought of Flossie speculating and suffering on the other side of the door. How remote I feel today from the part of me which used to foment such stupid little nastinesses. Valtesse, so haughty and proud, whose motto was a superb "Ego" and who once said to me: "I am a courtesan, and how I do enjoy my work!"

19 August 1919.

The other day someone asked me how old Émilienne d'Alençon is. Fifteen years ago I heard people saying she must be fifty, and she is not that even now. There is just a year between us. How pretty she used to be! Enormous golden eyes, the finest and most brilliant complexion! A proud little mouth, a tip-tilted nose you could eat, an oval face rather in the style of my own.

We were friends, she was my leading light in the ways of the theatre and of our pleasures. She could be beastly, but was really so pretty that one couldn't hold it against her. For instance, she said to me: "I know you are going to be at this big dinner tonight. Don't dress, I shall be wearing just a coat and skirt and a blouse and one row of pearls. You do the same, so that we'll be alike—and send your carriage away, I'll take you home." So at eight o'clock there I am in my simple little suit and one row of pearls—and at nine o'clock in sweeps my Émilienne resplendent in sumptuous white and gold brocade, dripping with diamonds, pearls and rubies, no hat, her curls full of sparkling jewels. "Oh dear—am I late?," with a delicious little pretence at absent-mindedness! One careless, hardly even teasing, glance at me, and she doesn't speak to me for the rest of the evening. But as she leaves she says goodbye and offers me her lips with the choicest nonchalance. And I go home in a cab, confused and cross, brooding bitterly on these lines which I found in a notebook belonging to my grandmother Olympe:

In each young girl with gentle eyes you see
A sister, not a rival . . .

Two days later and it might never have been, on my side as well as hers. With an impudence as great as her beauty she had moved in on me, had installed herself in my bed, at my table, in my carriages, in my theatre boxes—and all, I must confess, to my great pleasure. I couldn't be strict with her. But fore-warned is fore-armed, and I no longer believed what she said.

We went to Nice together, to the casino and to fancy-dress balls. We gambled together at Monte Carlo. Everyone admired us and ran after us; we were fêted, we were spoilt. Darling little Mimi! Last year, at the Majestic, she came to spend an afternoon with me. It was very moving to see each other again after twelve or thirteen years, and we were pleased to find each other still so beautiful. Her face is still ravishing, mine too. We cheered each other up. Our lives have gone completely different ways. She laughs, she dances, she stays up all night, she smokes (opium), she enjoys everything just as she used to do. She is rich, she has lots of friends. Bad friends—but that doesn't worry her. Her expression is still childlike and amused. When you tell her a joke she chuckles like a delightful chicken. She has become a woman of letters and has published a collection of sensitive and well-turned verse. She never stops falling in love, following her whim for better or for worse. She is adored, she's always changing lovers. They weep for her a little—too little—and console themselves rather too soon, but they are proud that she was there. How often have I heard someone drop her name into a conversation with a smug little look! She used to be my favourite model, vicious and ravishing, not like the others. Nothing about her was banal or vulgar, not her face, nor her gestures, nor the things she dared to do. It was she who made me cut my hair. She turned up with a pair of scissors and "snip," it was done. Then she said: "Come along, we'll try some henna." Three months later, we were corn-coloured. Then in a flash we became brunette. We did have such fun with ourselves—and how we laughed at others, both men and women. And then, little Mimi, your lips were so soft, your gestures were so coaxing and . . . but here we are, my dear, a pair of nice little old ladies.

5 October 1919

Salomon came to pick me up most punctually at 9.45. The car was an open one and we glided off to the cemetery at Passy. Dear, brilliant Marie Bashkirtseff; dear, rather brilliant Pauline—you must lend me your beautiful voices for the celebration of this, my first visit to your tombs. I was so much moved when I saw the chapel where my little muse reposes! There are epitaphs in verse round the walls, beautiful poems, sad, desolate, definitive. At the far end, one of her paintings: a desolate woman in a fierce pose, seated, gazing despairingly into the distance. Nearby stands the misty figure of another woman, weeping into her hands. It seems that they put the furniture from her studio into her tomb. There is her bust in white marble, wilful and proud, and a little reading chair covered in bronze plush with a flowered strip down the middle, all buttoned. It was the period for buttoned upholstery. Her chapel is large and was designed by Bastien-Lepage, the ultimate offering of a loving and broken heart. She lies under a little dome, rather Russian: 1860–1884.

Pauline's chapel is long and narrow like a little bed. Yes, like her: long and narrow. A photograph of her, after Levy Dhurmer, is placed in the middle, under the altar; in front of it, an incense burner. The windows are yellow, with figures, bordered with violet; two ivory virgins, one Christ, two old Delft pharmacist's pots containing thistles dyed mauve, church embroideries flung here and there, little bunches of dried violets hung on the grill with lilac ribbons, a selection of her lovely poems carved all around . . . On the exterior wall two verses which went straight to my heart:

> See, I have passed through this door
> Oh my thorn-bedizened roses.
> Gone is what used to be. For ever more
> My dreaming soul with God reposes
>
> Calmly asleep, forgetting strife,
> Having with its last breath,
> For love of death,
> Forgiven that crime, life.

Dear Pauline, have you forgiven me? We were tender rivals for Flossie, then friends. When I was in hospital having been crushed by my car on the public highway, you sent me flowers and copies of your books with beautiful inscriptions. And then one day your intimate friend, that little gnome Janot de Bellune, told me something very tart which you had said about me. I was ruffled and wrote you a letter—also very tart. Later I learnt of your illness and your death. Bitterness vanished from my heart. This morning's little pilgrimage was my symbol of repentance. Pauline died an edifying death. She suffered; she suffered in many ways. The dead are on the road between God and ourselves. . . . .

27 July 1920.
The Duc de Morny died recently. He was the elder brother of our friend Missy, alias Mathilde de Morny. I possess a picture of her as Napoleon. She gave it to me with the inscription "To my daughter, from her father-in-law." It was Missy's way to call nice-looking boys her "sons": Sacha Guitry, Auguste Hériot, Georges, were all her "sons." So when I became the wife of her "son" she called me daughter and signed herself "your father-in-law." She wore men's clothes, cropped her hair, smoked big cigars—and would have let her

mustache grow if she'd had one! She exchanged the name Mathilde for the debonair "Uncle Max." At bottom she was a charming, childlike creature, a bit simple, well brought-up but an exhibitionist and a worry to her family. We gradually let our friendship with her drop, which gave no pain to either party. Max-Mathilde loved dressing up and giving fancy-dress dances; her whole life was a masquerade.

Another of our friends, Sarah Bernhardt's niece Sarita who died some years ago, had the same little kink; although she used to wear skirts and was masculine only in the top half of her clothing, her manner, her style, her rings. She too favoured the cigar, which made her presence very disagreeable to me. Sarita who was intelligent—more intelligent than Missy—was very deeply committed to this line of conduct and used, between ourselves, to make a living by it, whereas Uncle Max was ruined by it. I ought to add that Sarah Bernhardt tried again and again to tear her beloved niece away from those circles and those habits, she reasoned with her, she gave her an allowance, she took her to America, she put her into plays. Nothing worked. Dinner jackets and love nests, short hair and the style of an invert . . . She was still young when she died of intestinal tuberculosis, after appalling suffering. Only when she was in the nursing-home found for her by her aunt, did she become more or less one of my friends.

I shall never understand that kind of deviation: wanting to look like a man, sacrificing feminine grace, charm and sweetness. To help the illusion, Missy used to flatten her breasts under a wide rubber band. How horrible to crush and damage such a charming gift of Nature! And cutting off one's hair when it can be a woman's most beautiful adornment! It's a ridiculous aberration, quite apart from the fact that it invites insult and scandal.

21 January 1921

Charming surprise! My Flossie came to see me, after letting me know by telephone. She was dressed jauntily—Amazon style, what else! in a dark wool dress lightened by a green-embroidered white waistcoat. A caped coat over her shoulders, a plain felt hat on her blonde hair. With her brisk style, her implacable smile, her tenderness towards me, her instinctively caressing little hands, she looked very young and very happy. I plunged into this renewed contact. We spoke about Salomon. She made gentle fun of him, so indignation diminished. She stayed with me for a good hour. She has invited us to attend her Fridays, "I'll have my Chinese music all over again for you, and you must bring Auric."

11 July 1921

Today I want to talk about my conquests. Rediscovered Nathalie comes to coax and caress me, and murmur "My first love, and my last." I see her bending over to enfold me, and it seems that I have never left her arms. Inconstant

Nathalie, so faithful, in spite of her infidelities. She celebrates my body down to the waist. That is all that I allow myself to grant. The rest belongs to Georges and no one else in the world can touch it. The rest would make the sin too big; and anyway that rest is so accustomed to Georges that it throbs for no one but him.

In second place comes Thérèse Diehl of the beaky nose, the wicked eye, the sensual mouth, very chic, candid as a child, unaffected, impudent, artful, simultaneously boring and attractive. She amused me; her skin is resilient. She is a good healthy Basque. She goes to mass every Sunday and doesn't at all allow her disorderly life to disturb her relationship with God. She shares a mad apartment with her brother Carl, a charming and well set-up invert who gets on very well with her and runs the family factory. Thérèse pursues happiness in pleasure, she drinks hard, talks too much, is a bad hostess, pays out generously, but lacks flair. Her head is charming when she tips it back. We went no further than kisses on the mouth. Then I went to dinner with her. There her furniture and her guests enlightened me: I was bored to death. I wrote her very charmingly, truly my letter was a song: "Forgive me for having loved you because I can no longer tell you that I do." That is a splendid sentence and always works. I have used it a good deal in my time.

It was then that poor Dora turned up. I had to pretend that I'd gone away. The telephone rang day and night. Pépé would answer: "The princess is in Saint-Germain for a few days." She loathed Nathalie and would never consent to meet us there. She did, however, bring her orchestra to the Countess de La Béraudière's. Funny little woman; she told me she was forty, because in an attempt to put her off I had advanced my fiftieth birthday. God! when a woman gets something into her head, how hard it is to get it out again!

My other conquest was Madame Bonin, heavy and hot. We met at Nathalie's and sat hand in hand during the whole two hours of that tea party. Another time I invited her to Pépé's house. I was alone. She arrived trembling and panting, fell on my bed and wanted to offer me everything. I drew her attention to the barrier raised by my principles across the bodies of women, just a little below their hearts and their breasts. She tore off her clothes to bare the latter, neither beautiful nor ugly, too big and a bit squeezed together. The top part of her arms was ravishing. She is a woman for men, designed to serve them, amuse them and then, very soon, to bore them. I took it into my head to offer her something to eat and dragged her into the dining-room where she devoured a bowl of cherries, reproaching me the while for getting her "into such a state."

July 12

Nothing amuses me this morning. Still, I would like to talk about my third conquest. At my request I met the daughter of an old friend of mine at Flossie's house. Betsy has her mother's superb fair hair, fashionably cut, a long face, a clear complexion and soft, roving eyes. She gives the impression of tempered steel, an indomitable character. She has her wits about her. At our second meeting, which took place at Pépé's house on a day when I was in bed, she threw herself into my arms, tremulous with passion. Astonished, I held her and began to stroke her hair. She offered me her lips. What could I do but kiss them? I did so with the utmost tenderness and with a touch of alarm, since the vivid impression made by Madame Bonin was still with me. Betsy was gentle and tender, she knew how the situation should be handled. She was a little bit lost for a day or two.

4 October 1921

Here I am with a bad attack of gout in my right big toe. Georges made me smear the sick toe with glycerine and cover it with cotton wool, and the pain disappeared completely in five minutes. Uncle Max [Missy liked to be called Uncle Max] is on to a good thing there; I have just been writing her an unsolicited testimonial. Uncle Max has heaps of good recipes. There's one for polishing fingernails, another for copper, and one for building movable library steps. Tanks, she insists, were her invention. She is much drawn to the cinema.

The other day she caused a great sensation in my room. I was in the dressing-room with Georges when suddenly we heard the dear "old boy's" high-pitched monotonous voice announcing: "Children, I have a confession to make." She's broken something in her bedroom, I thought. "Go ahead," I called. "Well, listen: twice in my life I have slept with men . . ." Hearing that, and imagining it, was so comic that we burst out laughing. She went on: "One of them was my cousin Alexis Orloff. He said he would kill himself if I resisted, so—well, I didn't resist, but I refused any repetition. The second and last was Lord Yume [sic]. He was a very good-looking boy and he adored me, he wanted to marry me. He wore me down, so at last I said 'Let's try,' and I was his mistress for ten days. Then I'd had enough so I refused his proposal."

21 September 1933

Found an article in the *Mercure de France* about the great Sappho, high priestess of lesbian love. It summed up pretty well all that can be said about that legendary and fabulous woman. Miss Barney—the Flossie of my *Idylle saphique*—loved to tell me about her in her own, idealizing way. We began a one-act play in blank verse about Sappho on her island, a happy, flowery island where all the women loved each other like very tender sisters served by almost invisible slaves, nimble, quick and devoted . . . sisters with a natural disposition to every kind of caress. I do not want to expand here on lesbianism, having already said all that I think about it in that same *Idylle saphique*—all, and more. Yes, having been witness to some distressing sights, some sinister results of the practice of that vice, I wanted to drive home my opinion rather fiercely. And anyway it was necessary to do so in those days, in order to find a publisher who would consent to bring out a book on the subject. I made it lyrical and sometimes slightly realistic. That was in the days of the Amazon's youth, and of my own. We were passionate, rebels against a woman's lot, voluptuous and cerebral little apostles, rather poetical, full of illusions and dreams. We loved long hair, pretty breasts, pouts, simpers, charm, grace; not boyishness. "Why try to resemble our enemies?" Nathalie-Flossie used to murmur in her little nasal voice.

VITA SACKVILLE-WEST (1892–1962)

From an unpublished memoir (1920); "She Brought with Careless Hand," "Self-Epitaph, Composed by an Honest Sensualist," "Tess" (1933)

The poet, novelist, biographer, and gardener Victoria ("Vita") Sackville-West, born into one of the most celebrated of Britain's noble families, spent her childhood at the Sackville ancestral home, Knole, in Kent. As a female only child, she grew up with the knowledge she would never inherit Knole, and a sense of disenfranchisement—reinforced early on by a dawning awareness of her homosexuality—haunted her through much of her life. Alienated from her parents, she began writing out of loneliness and completed eight novels and five plays by the age of eighteen. In 1913 she married the diplomat Harold Nicolson (1886–1968) and had two sons by him. Their marriage nearly collapsed several times between 1918 and 1921, when Sackville-West embarked on a tempestuous and protracted affair with a childhood friend, Violet Trefusis—a liaison wryly commemorated in Virginia Woolf's fantasy novel *Orlando*. Yet, bound by shared tastes and a profound affection for one another, Sackville-West and Nicolson—also homosexual—gradually worked out an arrangement by which they would remain married but lead independent sexual lives. Sackville-West took full advantage of the new dispensation, and in the 1920s and 1930s had a number of lesbian liaisons, including one with Woolf (a lifelong friend) and Hilda Matheson, the Talks Director of the BBC. In later years Sackville-West and Nicolson retired to an old Elizabethan house, Sissinghurst in Kent, where together they created one of the great small gardens of Europe.

Although never as brilliant a stylist as Woolf, Sackville-West was nonetheless a writer of fluency and distinction. She was immensely prolific, producing over forty books in various genres. Poetry was especially dear to her, and she wrote a great deal of it, usually in a traditional and pastoral vein. *The Land*, a book-length poetic celebration of the English countryside, won the Hawthornden Prize in 1926; her *Collected Poems* appeared in 1933. She wrote eleven novels, including *Heritage* (1919), *The Edwardians* (1930), *All Passion Spent* (1931), *The Easter Party* (1953), and her last, *No Signposts in the Sea* (1961). Yet some of her best writing is to be found in her numerous biographies, histories, and travel books: *Knole and the Sackvilles* (1922), *Passenger to Teheran* (1926), *Saint Joan of Arc* (1936), *Pepita* (1937), and *The Eagle and the Dove* (1943), a study of St. Theresa of Avila and St. Thérèse of Lisieux. Most compelling of all, perhaps, is an autobiographical account of the affair with Trefusis, written in secret in 1920 and discovered in a locked trunk in her Sissinghurst study after her death in 1962. It was subsequently edited by her son Nigel Nicolson and incorporated into his moving memoir of his parents, *Portrait of a Marriage* (1973).

FURTHER READING: Vita Sackville-West, *Heritage* (London: Collins, 1919); —, *The Land* (London: Heinemann, 1926); —, *Passenger to Teheran* (London: Hogarth, 1926); —, *King's Daughter* (London: Hogarth, 1929); —, *The Edwardians* (London: Hogarth, 1930); —, *All Passion Spent* (London: Hogarth, 1931); —, *Collected Poems* (London: Hogarth, 1933); —, *Saint Joan of Arc* (London: Cobden-Sanderson, 1936); —, *Pepita* (London: Hogarth, 1937); —, *Selected Poems* (London: Hogarth, 1941); —, *The Eagle and the Dove* (London: Michael Joseph, 1943); —, *The Garden* (London: Michael Joseph, 1946); —, *No Signposts in the Sea* (London: Michael Joseph, 1961); Harold Nicolson, *Diaries and Letters*, ed. Nigel Nicolson, 3 vols. (New York: Atheneum, 1966–68); Nigel Nicolson, *Portrait of a Marriage: V. Sackville-West and Harold Nicolson* (New York: Atheneum, 1973); Nigel Nicolson, ed., *Vita and Harold: The Letters of Vita Sackville-West and Harold Nicolson* (New York: Putnam's, 1992); Michael Stevens, *V. Sackville-West: A Critical Biography* (London: Michael Joseph, 1973); Victoria Glendinning, *Vita: A Biography of V. Sackville-West* (New York: Knopf, 1983); Louise DeSalvo and Mitchell A. Leaska, eds., *The Letters of Vita Sackville-West to Virginia Woolf* (London: Hutchinson, 1984); Suzanne Raitt, *Vita and Virginia: The Work and Friendship of V. Sackville-West and Virginia Woolf* (Oxford: Clarendon, 1993).

From an unpublished memoir

27 September 1920

In April [1918], when we were back in the country, Violet wrote to ask whether she could come and stay with me for a fortnight. I was bored by the idea, as I wanted to work, and I did not know how to entertain her; but I could scarcely refuse. So she came. We were both bored. My serenity got on her nerves, and her restlessness got on mine. She went up to London for the day as often as she could, but she came back in the evenings because the air-raids frightened her. She had been here [Long Barn] I think about a week when everything changed suddenly—changed far more than I foresaw at the time; changed my life. It was the 18th of April. An absurd circumstance gave rise to the whole thing; I had just got clothes like the women-on-the-land were wearing, and in the unaccustomed freedom of breeches and gaiters I went into wild spirits; I ran, I shouted, I jumped, I climbed, I vaulted over gates, I felt like a schoolboy let out on a holiday; and Violet followed me across fields and woods with a new meekness, saying very little, but never taking her eyes off me, and in the midst of my exuberance I knew that all the old under-current had come back stronger than ever and that my old domination over her had never been diminished. I remember that wild irresponsible day. It was one of the most vibrant days of my life. As it happened, Harold was not coming down that night. Violet and I dined alone together, and then, after dinner, we went into my sitting-room, and for some time made conversation, but that broke down, and from ten o'clock until two in the morning—for four hours, or perhaps more—we talked.

Violet had struck the secret of my duality; she attacked me about it, and I made no attempt to conceal it from her or from myself. I talked myself out, until I could hear my own voice getting hoarse, and the fire went out, and all the servants had long since gone to bed, and there was not a soul in the house except Violet and me, and I talked out the whole of myself with absolute sincerity and pain, and Violet only listened—which was skilful of her. She made no comments and no suggestions until I had finished—until, that is, I had dug into every corner and brought its contents out to the light. I had been vouchsafed insight, as one sometimes is. Then, when I had finished, when I had told her how all the gentleness and all the femininity of me was called out by Harold alone, but how towards everyone else my attitude was completely otherwise—then, still with her infinite skill, she brought me round to my attitude towards herself, as it had always been ever since we were children, and then she told me how she had loved me always, and reminded me of incidents running through years, which I couldn't pretend to have forgotten. She was far more skilful than I. I might have been a boy of eighteen, and she a woman of thirty-five. She was infinitely clever—she didn't scare me, she didn't rush me, she didn't allow me to see where I was going; it was all conscious on her part, but on mine it was simply the drunkenness of liberation—the liberation of half my personality. She opened up to me a new sphere. And for her, of course, it meant the supreme effort to conquer the love of the person she had always wanted, who had always repulsed her (when things seemed to be going too far), out of a sort of fear, and of whom she was madly jealous—a fact I had not realized so adept was she at concealment, and so obtuse was I at her psychology.

She lay on the sofa, I sat plunged in the armchair; she took my hands, and parted my fingers to count the points as she told me why she loved me. I hadn't dreamt of such an art of love. Such things had been direct for me always; I had known no love possessed of that Latin artistry (whether instinctive or acquired). I was infinitely troubled by the softness of her touch and the murmur of her lovely voice. She appealed to my unawakened senses; she wore, I remember, a dress of red velvet, that was exactly the colour of a red rose, and that made of her, with her white skin and the tawny hair, the most seductive being. She pulled me down until I kissed her—I had not done so for many years. Then she was wise enough to get up and go to bed; but I kissed her again in the dark after I had blown out our solitary lamp. She let herself go entirely limp and passive in my arms. (I shudder to think of the experience that lay behind her abandonment.) I can't think I slept at all that night—not that much of the night was left.

I don't know how to go on; I keep thinking that Harold, if he ever reads this, will suffer so, but I ask him to remember that he is reading about a *different person* from the one he knew. Also I am not writing this for fun, but for several reasons which I will explain. (1) As I started by saying, because I want to tell the *entire* truth. (2) Because I know of no truthful record of such a connection—one that is written, I mean, with no desire to appeal to a vicious taste in any possible readers; and (3) because I hold the conviction that as centuries go on, and the sexes become more nearly merged on account of their increasing resemblances, I hold the conviction that such connections will to a very large extent cease to be regarded as merely unnatural, and will be understood far better, at least in their *intellectual* if not in their physical aspect. (Such is already the case in Russia.) I believe that then the psychology of people like myself will be a matter of interest, and I believe it will be recognized that many more people of my type do exist than under the present-day system of hypocrisy is commonly admitted. I am not saying that such personalities, and the connections which result from them, will not be deplored as they are now; but I do believe that their greater prevalence, and the spirit of candour which one hopes will spread with the progress of the world, will lead to their recognition, if only as an inevitable evil. The first step in the direction of such candour must be taken by the general admission of normal but illicit relations, and the facilitation of divorce, or possibly even the reconstruction of the system of marriage. Such advance must necessarily come from the more educated and liberal classes. Since "unnatural" means "removed from nature," only the most civilized, because the least natural, class of society can be expected to tolerate such a product of civilization.

I advance, therefore, the perfectly accepted theory that cases of dual personality do exist, in which the feminine and the masculine elements alternately preponderate. I advance this in an impersonal and scientific spirit, and claim that I am qualified to speak with the intimacy a professional scientist could acquire only after years of study and indirect information, because I have the object of study always to hand, in my own heart, and can gauge the exact truthfulness of what my own experience tells me. However frank, people would always keep back something. I can't keep back anything from myself.

29 September [1920]

I think Violet stayed on for about five days after that. All the time I was in fantastic spirits; and, not realizing how different she was from me in many ways, I made her follow me on wild courses all over the country, and, because she knew she had me only lightly hooked, she obeyed without remonstrance. There was very little between us during those days, only an immense excitement and a growing wish to go away somewhere alone together. This wish was carried out, by arranging to go down to Cornwall for the inside of a week; it was the first time I had ever been away from Harold, and he obviously minded my going.

We went. We met again in London, lunched at a restaurant, and filled with a spirit of adventure took the train for Exeter. On the way there we decided to go on to Plymouth. We arrived at Plymouth to find our luggage had of course been put out at Exeter. We had only an assortment of French poetry with us. We didn't care. We went to the nearest hotel, exultant to feel that nobody in the world knew where we were; at the booking office we were told there was only one room. It seemed like fate. We engaged it. We went and had supper—cider and ham—over which we talked fast and tremulously; she was frightened of me by then.

The next day we went on to Cornwall, where we spent five blissful days; I felt like a person translated, or re-born; it was like beginning one's life again in a different capacity. We were very miserable to come away, but we were constantly together during the whole of the summer months following. Once we went down to Cornwall again for a fortnight. It was a lovely summer. She was radiant. But I never thought it would last; I thought of it as an adventure, an escapade. I kept telling myself she was fickle, that I was the latest toy; she used to assure me of the contrary. She did this with such gravity that sometimes I was almost convinced; but now the years have convinced me thoroughly.

She no longer flirted, and got rid of the last person she had been engaged to, when we went to Cornwall. But there was a man out in France, who used to write to her; she hardly knew him, and I wasn't jealous. He was called Denzil [Denys Trefusis]. She described him to me as fiery—hair like gold wire, blue eyes starting out of his head, and winged nostrils. I listened, not very much interested. I now hate him more than I have ever hated anyone in this life, or am likely to; and there is no injury I would not do him with the utmost pleasure.

Well, the whole of that summer she was mine—a mad and irresponsible summer of moonlight nights, and infinite escapades, and passionate letters, and music, and poetry. Things were not tragic for us then, because although we cared passionately we didn't care deeply—not like now, though it was deepening all the time; no, things weren't tragic, they were rapturous and new, and one side of my life was opened to me, and, to hide nothing, I found things out about my own temperament that I had never been sure of before. Of course I wish now that I had never made those discoveries. One doesn't miss what one doesn't know, and now life is made wretched for me by privations. I often long for ignorance and innocence. I think that if anything happened to bring my friendship with Violet to an end, I might have the strength of mind to blot all that entirely out of my life.

At the end of that summer Denys came home on leave, and I met him. He was very tall and slender, and had the winged look that she had described—I could compare him to many things, to a race-horse, to a Crusader, to a grey-hound, to an ascetic in search of the Holy Grail. I liked him then (oh irony!), and he liked me. I could afford to like him, because I was accustomed to Violet's amusements. Even now I see his good points, and they are many; but I see them only by translating myself into an impersonal spectator, and I see them, above all, when Violet makes him suffer. I see that he is a rare, sensitive, proud idealist, and I recognize that through me he has undergone months of suffering, and that his profound love for Violet has been thwarted of its fulfilment. And I am sorry enough for him, at moments, just sorry enough to wish vaguely that he could have cared for someone other than Violet. I see his tragedy—for he is a tragic person.

But none of this softens my hatred of him, which is certainly the most violent feeling I have ever experienced. I only hope he returns it in full measure; he has a hundred times more cause to hate me than I to hate him.

He was in London for about ten days. It was already arranged that Violet and I were to go abroad together that winter for a month. There were scenes connected with our going. Violet and I had a row over something; I refused to go abroad; she came round to my house and we made friends again; then I had a dreadful scene with Mother, who was furious at my going; however to make a long story short we left for Paris at the end of November [1918]. I was to be away until Christmas!

5 October [1920]

Paris . . . We were there for about a week, living in a flat that was lent us in the Palais Royal. Even now the intoxication of some of those hours in Paris makes me see confusedly; other hours were, I admit, wretched, because Denys came (the war being just over), and I wanted Violet to myself. But the evenings were ours. I have never told a soul of what I did. I hesitate to write it here, but I must; shirking the truth here would be like cheating oneself playing patience. I dressed as a boy. It was easy, because I could put a khaki bandage round my head, which in those days was so common that it attracted no attention at all. I browned my face and hands. It must have been successful, because no one looked at me at all curiously or suspiciously—never once, out of the many times I did it. My height of course was my great advantage. I looked like a rather untidy young man, a sort of undergraduate, of about nineteen. It was marvellous fun, all the more so because there was always the risk of being found out. Of course it was easy in the Palais Royal because I could let myself in and out by a latchkey; in hotels it was more difficult. I had done it once already in England; that was one of the boldest things I ever did. I will tell about it: I changed in my own house in London late one evening (the darkened streets made me bold), and drove with Violet in a taxi as far as Hyde Park Corner. There I got out. I never felt so free as when I stepped off the kerb, down Piccadilly, alone, and knowing that if I met my own mother face to face she would take no notice of me. I walked along, smoking a cigarette, buying a newspaper off a little boy who called me "sir," and being accosted now and then by women. In this way I strolled from Hyde Park Corner to Bond Street, where I met Violet and took her in a taxi to Charing Cross. (The extraordinary thing was, how natural it all was for me.) Nobody, even in the glare of the station, glanced at me twice. I had wondered about my voice, but found I could sink it sufficiently. Well, I took Violet as far as Orpington by train, and there we found a lodging house where we could get a room. The landlady was very benevolent and I said Violet was my wife. Next day of course I had to put on the same clothes, although I was a little anxious about the daylight, but again nobody took the slightest notice. We went to Knole!, which was, I think, brave. Here I slipped into the stables, and emerged as myself.

Well, this discovery was too good to be wasted, and in Paris I practically lived in that role. Violet used to call me Julian. We dined together every evening in cafés and restaurants, and went to all the theatres. I shall never forget the evenings when we walked back slowly to our flat through the streets of Paris. I, personally, had never felt so free in my life. Perhaps we have never been so happy since. When we got back to the flat, the windows all used to be open onto the courtyard of the Palais Royal, and the fountains splashed below. It was all incredible—like a fairy-tale.

It couldn't go on for ever, and at the end of the week we left for Monte Carlo, stopping on the way at St. Raphael. The weather was perfect, Monte Carlo was perfect, Violet was perfect. Again as Julian, I took her to a dance there, and had a success with a French family, who asked me to come and play bridge with them, and, I think, had an eye on me for their daughter, a plain girl whose head I tried to turn with compliments. They said *"On voit que monsieur est valseur,"* and their son, a French officer, asked me about my *"blessure,"* and we exchanged war reminiscences.

I didn't go back at Christmas. I didn't go back till nearly the end of March, and everybody was very angry with me, and I felt like suicide after those four wild and radiant months. The whole of that time is dreadful, a nightmare. Harold was in Paris, and I was alone with Mother and Dada, who were both very angry, and wanted me to give Violet up. (There had been a lot of scandal, by then.) On the other hand, Denys had been in England a month, and was agitating to announce his engagement to Violet. Violet was like a hunted creature. I could have prevented the engagement by very few words, but I thought that would be too outrageously selfish; there was Violet's mother, a demon of a woman, longing to get her safely married, and having told all London that she was going to marry Denys. She had already so bad a reputation for breaking engagements that this would have been the last straw. Besides, we both thought she would gain more liberty by marrying, and Denys was prepared to marry her on her own terms—that is, of merely brotherly relations.

I was absolutely miserable. I went to Brighton, alone, in a great empty dust-sheeted house, and all night I used to lie awake, and all day I used to wonder whether I wouldn't throw myself over the cliffs. Everyone questioned me as to why I looked so ill. On the fifth day Violet's engagement was announced in the papers; I bought the paper at Brighton station and nearly fainted as I read it, although I had expected to find it there. Not very long after that I went to Paris, to join Harold, who by that time knew the whole truth of the affair. I was terribly unhappy in Paris. When I came back to London, Violet began to declare that nothing would induce her to go through with the thing, and that I must save her from it by taking her away; in fact I believe she used Denys very largely as a lever to get me to do so. Living permanently with me had become an obsession in her mind. I don't absolutely remember the process in detail, but I know that I ended by consenting. After that we were both less unhappy; I could afford to see her ostensibly engaged to Denys when I knew that instead of marrying him she was coming away with me. I really intended to take her; we had every plan made. We were to go the day before her wedding—not sooner, because we thought we should be overtaken and brought back. It was of course only this looking-forward which enabled me to endure the period of her engagement.

Then about five days before her wedding I suddenly got by the same post three miserable letters from Harold, who had scented danger, because, in order to break it to him more or less gently (and also because I was in a dreadful state of mind myself during all that time), I had been writing him letters full of hints. When I read those letters something snapped in my mind. I saw Harold, all sweet and gentle and dependent upon me. Violet was there. She was terrified. I remember saying, "It's no good, I can't take you away." She implored me by everything she could think of, but I was obdurate. We went up to London together, Violet nearly off her head, and me repeating to myself phrases out of Harold's letters to give myself strength. I telegraphed to him to say I was coming to Paris; I had only one idea, to fly as quickly as I could and to put distance between me and temptation. I saw Violet twice more; once in my own house in London; she looked ill and changed; and once in the early morning at her mother's house, where I went to say goodbye to her on my way to the station. There was a dreary slut scrubbing the doorstep, for it was very early, and I stepped in over the soapy pail, and saw Violet in the morning-room. Then I went to Paris, alone. That is one of the worst days I remember. While I was in the train going to Folkestone I still felt I could change my mind and go back if I wanted to, for she had told me she would wait for me up to the very last minute, and would come straightaway if I appeared, or telephoned for her. At Folkestone I felt it becoming more irrevocable, and tried to get off the boat again, but they were moving the gangway and pushed me back. I had Harold's letters with me, and kept reading them until they almost lost all sense. The journey had never seemed so slow; it remains with me simply as a nightmare. I couldn't eat, and tears kept running down my face. Harold met me at the Gare du Nord. I said I wanted to go straight back, but he said, "No, no," and took me out to Versailles in a motor. The next day was Sunday, and he stayed with me all day. By then I had got such a reaction that I was feverishly cheerful, and he might have thought nothing was the matter. I gave him the book I was writing [*Challenge*], because I knew Violet would hate me to do that, as it was all about her. I was awake nearly all that night. Next day was Monday, 16th June [1919]; Harold had to go into Paris, and I sat quite dazed in my room holding my watch in my hand and watching the hands tick past the hour of Violet's wedding. All that time, I knew, she was expecting a prearranged message from me, which I never sent.

I was so stunned by all this at the time that I could not even think; it is only since then that I have realized how every minute has burnt itself into me.

On Tuesday night Violet and Denys came to Paris. On Wednesday I went to see her, at the Ritz. She was wearing clothes I had never seen before, but no wedding ring. I can't describe how terrible it all was—that meeting, and everything. It makes me physically ill to write about it and think about it, and my cheeks are burning. It was dreadful, dreadful. By then I had left Versailles, and was living alone in a small hotel. I took her there, I treated her savagely, I made love to her, I had her, I didn't care, I only wanted to hurt Denys, even though he didn't know of it. I make no excuse, except that I had suffered too much during the past week and was really scarcely responsible. The next day I saw Denys at an awful interview. Violet told him she had meant to run away with me instead of marrying him; she told him she didn't care for him. He got very white, and I thought he was going to faint. I restrained myself from saying much more. I wanted to say, "Don't you know, you stupid fool, that she is mine in every sense of the world?" but I was afraid that he would kill her if I did that. That night I dined at the Ritz, and from the open window of her room Violet watched me, and Denys sobbed in the room behind her. That day seems to have made a great impression upon him, as he constantly referred to it in his letters to her afterwards.

After that they went away to St. Jean de Luz, and I went to Switzerland with Harold, and then back to England alone. After three weeks Violet came back. Things were not quite so bad then. She had a house in Sussex, and Denys only came there for the weekends, and I spent all the rest of the week there. He and I never met, because in Paris he had said to me it must be war or peace. We met once, when he arrived earlier than was expected; I was just leaving, and Violet threw some things into a bag and came with me. I never saw anyone look so angry as he did. He was dead white and his lips were shaking. I tried to make Violet go back, because I thought it was really humiliating the man too much, but she wouldn't. On the whole, however, she was on friendly terms with him, and I am bound to say that he was friendly as an angel to her, and above all he kept the promises he had made, which I think few men would have done. I think on the whole that that was the period when Violet liked him best.

She Brought with Careless Hand

She brought with careless hand
Meadowsweet, cherry,
Orchis and berry,
Agrimony, broom,
And left them in my room
As a token planned.

So that the room was rich
With her memorials,
A store of festivals
For my undoing,
And this bestrewing
Did helpless me bewitch.

She should have brought
Enchanter's Nightshade,
A mandrake's root,
And out of Egypt fruit,

And thus have made
Me turn to naught;
But with such innocent
And wayside blooms
Should not have wrought
Such havoc in my rooms
Or in my heart.
No, I protest
She should have used her utmost art
And cantrip best.
No less did I deserve
Who scornful am, and proud,
If she would have me serve
In love avowed.
She should not tangle me
In simple wreaths,
Nor with such garlands strangle me
To happy deaths.
She cheated in the game,
Sweet rogue, that day she came
And snared me unawares.
Now shall I tell her name and shame,
Or shall I yield me pliant to her snares?

Self-Epitaph, Composed by an Honest Sensualist

If I must lie, who never lied in life,
    Awaiting Judgment-day,
Then lay me here, to lie as others lay
Often with virgin, prostitute, and wife.

Tess

Love thou but me; all other realms I'll give thee,
Realms of the wind, the starlight, and the rain.
Love the whole natural world, and I'll forgive thee,
If thou but love no mortal limbs again.

So generous am I, I would not stint thee;
I spread the whole of nature for thy choice.
Only, with my own cipher would imprint thee,
That thou should'st answer to my single voice.

Oh then beware! for should'st thou stray or falter
From that high mark my arrogance has set,
Stern as a priest I'll stretch thee on an altar
And in revenge all tenderness forget.

Then when the rising sun makes summer shadow,
I'll take a knife and stretch thee on a stone
Scooped for the blood to soak a Wiltshire meadow,
When dawn and death shall find us there, alone.

ROSE O'NEILL (1874–1944)

"A Dream of Sappho," "Death Shall Not Ease Me of You," "Mea Culpa," "But If You Come to Me by Day" (1922)

Born in Pennsylvania, raised in the Midwest by Catholic nuns, the artist, magazine illustrator, novelist, and poet Rose O'Neill was a millionaire by the age of forty, having invented the kewpie—a fey, cupidlike cartoon character subsequently transformed into a doll for children—in the 1890s. Precociously gifted, O'Neill began her career drawing for *Puck*, *Life*, and other New York magazines in 1893, and by 1896 was wealthy enough buy a farm in the Ozark mountains in Missouri, where she moved with her first husband. The kewpie design (which she said came to her in a kind of mystical vision) brought her international fame, as well as a second marriage, in 1902, to Harry Leon Wilson, the editor of *Puck* and author of the popular novel *Ruggles of Red Gap* (1915). She lived with Wilson in Paris for several years, studying painting and exhibiting twice at the Paris Salon. After she ran off with the journalist Booth Tarkington to Capri, Wilson divorced her in 1912—claiming, among other things, that she spoke too often in baby talk. She subsequently divided her time between Missouri, New York, and her villa on Capri, overseeing the worldwide production of kewpie dolls. She was a close friend of the poet and essayist Elinor Wylie (1885–1928).

For all of their author's overt heterosexuality, O'Neill's literary works give evidence of a sexually divided personality. (Jeannette Foster included a long entry on O'Neill in her groundbreaking bibliography, *Sex Variant Women in Literature*, in 1956.) She wrote four novels—*The Loves of Edwy* (1904), *The Lady in the White Veil* (1909), *Garda* (1929), and *The Goblin Woman* (1930). Like the kewpies, her fictional heroes and heroines are often androgynous in looks: in *Garda* the heroine and her twin brother, Narcissus, are described as "the two parts of a single whole." In *The Master-Mistress*— her only book of serious verse—she alternated poems of heterosexual passion and homosexual love lyrics in a manner reminiscent of Shakespeare's sonnets. Clement Wood wrote of the homosexual "note" in her poetry in *Poets of America* in 1925:

> Her poetry will lose a certain Puritan following because of her cryptic frankness on the theme of love. She does not write this across the sky; neither does she, as is the convention, make this creep into a hole and draw the hole in after

it. It is here, in a few poems; those who are not offended by this note in the masters since the Greeks, will not be offended by it here.

Given the unblushing fervor of "A Dream of Sappho" or the poems addressed to "Kallista," however, "cryptic" hardly seems the right word. For wild sapphic ardors, her verses outdo anything in Amy Lowell or Edna St. Vincent Millay, who seem sedate by comparison.

FURTHER READING: Rose O'Neill, *The Kewpies and Dotty Darling* (New York: G. H. Doran, 1912); —, *The Master-Mistress* (New York: Knopf, 1922); —, *The Story of Rose O'Neill: An Autobiography*, ed. Miriam Formaneck-Brunell (Columbia, Mo.: University of Missouri Press, 1997); Clement Wood, *Poets of America* (New York: Dutton, 1925); Jeannette Foster, *Sex Variant Women in Literature* (1956; rpt. Tallahassee, Fla.: Naiad, 1985); Alan McCanse; *Titans and Kewpies: The Life and Art of Rose O'Neill* (New York: Vintage, 1968); Shelley Armitage, *Kewpies and Beyond: The World of Rose O'Neill* (Jackson, Miss.: University Press of Mississippi, 1994).

A Dream of Sappho

She slowly came, I knew her by the sign,
    And fair she was, but far more strange than fair.
        I knew her by the roses in her hair,
        Pierian, and she saluted mine,
Lifting her pale hand in that gesture high
The deathless use to those that cannot die.

        (She bore a purple napkin for her lap;
        Her sandal had a fair-wrought Lydian strap.)

She touched my lyre and listened—while she seemed
    As one dimmed in some doubtful dream re-dreamed;
Then, ah, the voice she from those lips released,
    All birds and bees and singing in a sigh—
"Once, with a thing like this—" she said, and ceased.

    And then,
      That flowery fluting fell again;
"I passed, as some far, careless queen doth pass,
  While, gem by gem, her broken necklace streams:

Perhaps one follows, finding fearful gleams,
  Long after in the pale, pale grass."

  I said, "None with more living lives
  Than those fierce fugitives!"

"But I am dead," she said, "the violet-twined
  Is dead with *that which never man can find*."

  "Rubies enough," I weeping said,
  And red to broider all thy bed!"

Then she, with queenhood most ineffable,
  Put by her golden throat's bereaven swell:
"Stand up, O friend," she said, "stand face to face,
  And of thy hidden eyes unveil the grace!"

Then with what looks we leaned and gazed long while!
  Drunkard meets wreathèd drunkard with *that smile!*
   And what full-lyred beaker brimmèd up,
  With wet lips meeting on the honied cup!
   And as sweet drunkards, reeling, spill
   The crested waves of cups they fill,
  With lovely laughs, inside the purple vest,
So we with laughter, staggered breast to breast.

I wake, the book drops from my dreaming hand,
  As now thy palm august falls out of mine.
Oh, where is that strong singing! Where the wine!
  Prevailing lip! And leafy brow of thine!

Only the long sea and the Lesbian strand!
  Art thou but sand that blows with trodden sand?
   Where is thy burning hand. . . .

Death Shall Not Ease Me of You

To Kallista

Death shall not ease me of you,
No, nor yet

That place where men go to forget:
That curious place
Where beds are made.
It shall not ease me of your face,
Nor I, in darkness laid,
Be ere untied
From the vine of your persisting side,
Nor flowers of your dissuadeless breast,
Nor rest
From wonder. Though I drew
The earthy cover all about
To succour me from you
I shall not keep you out.

Your might
Shall circumvent the night:
While you still press
Upon me obdurate loveliness:
And in your princely fashion
Rend my death
With absolute compassion.

I can not save you Love,
From me, relieve my Dove
Of hovering;
Nor loose your love-arrested wing,
Nor release in any wise
The hold of our tenacious eyes;
But your divine shall tremble me
And break my dead heart endlessly.
Death shall not ease me of you,
No, nor yet,
That place where men go to forget.

Mea Culpa

The night was living, past belief,
The lake was furtive as a thief:
The moon was wading to the knee,
And I was as bad as bad could be.

I was more living than the night,
I made the lilies drown for fright:
I was more furtive than the lake,
I hardly made the water shake.
I lurked, I listened,—touched,—and soon,
I waded deeper than the moon.

But If You Come to Me by Day

But if you come to me by day,
    I shall not know at all,
Nor hark your foot in any hall;
I shall not know your look and way,
    (Unless you kiss and call.)

No daylight-dear are you for loss,
    For man to win or weep,
But one the careful Night shall keep—
A fountain dim that flowed across
    The desert of my sleep.

Oh, draught of dreams! Past sound and sight,
    Where never man could mark—
    Nor listen any drowsy lark—
I held you in the hollow night
    And drank you in the dark!

RONALD FIRBANK (1886–1926)

From *The Flower Beneath the Foot* (1923)

Arthur Annesley Ronald Firbank, the greatest exponent of the camp style in Anglo-American writing, was born in London to wealthy middle-class parents. Between 1906 and 1909, he studied at Cambridge, where he converted to Catholicism and began moving in discreetly homosexual circles. His unmistakable literary manner—a surreal mixture of linguistic preciosity, sexual innuendo, and fey comic incident—developed early: his first published stories, *Odette d'Antrevernes* and *A Study in Temperament*, appeared in 1905. After leaving Cambridge without a degree, he lived in London but traveled frequently on the Continent, where he cultivated the role of post-Wildean dandy-aesthete. Frail health (lifelong) obviated more strenuous pursuits. Grant Richards published his first novel, *Vainglory*, in 1915, but the lukewarm response it received forced Firbank to issue his subsequent stories and novellas—*Inclinations* (1916), *Caprice* (1917), *Valmouth* (1919), *Santal* (1921), *The Flower Beneath the Foot* (1923), *Prancing Nigger* (1924), and *Concerning the Eccentricities of Cardinal Pirelli* (1926)—at his own expense. Only after his death, in Rome at the age of forty, did his extraordinary if idiosyncratic literary gifts begin to be recognized. The works of Evelyn Waugh, Aldous Huxley, Ivy Compton-Burnett, Anthony Powell, and Brigid Brophy, among others, testify to his abiding influence on later twentieth-century British novelists.

Scenes of sapphic intrigue—at once ludicrous and delicious—dot Firbank's fiction. As Brigid Brophy observes in *Prancing Novelist*, her passionate study of the writer, Firbank was deeply interested in the lesbian writers of his time: "I imagine that Miss O'Brookomore and Miss Collins journey to Greece (in *Inclinations*) and that Mrs Thoroughfare sings (in *Valmouth*) of 'White Mit-y-lene' in tribute to the sojourns of Natalie Clifford Barney and Renée Vivien in the villa Renée Vivien owned at Mitylene." Firbank's remarkable "transvestism of the imagination," Brophy suggests, "made him not merely a woman but a queer woman" and his works bear the traces of a lifelong "Sapphic obsession."

In the two excerpts below, both from *The Flower Beneath the Foot*, the obsession is in full fantastic view. In the first, a plush description of "Victoria Gellybore-Frinton" and her husband, the "Hon. Harold Chilleywater," English attaché to the tiny Mediterranean principality of Pisuerga, one of the renowned "faubourgs of Sodom," Firbank offers a satirical portrait of the celebrated lesbian novelist Vita Sackville-West and her diplomat-husband, Harold Nicolson. In the second, he limns a nautical love scene between the dissipated Countess of Tolga ("Vi") and a visitor to the Court of Pisuerga, the innocent yet corruptible German mademoiselle, Olga Blumenghast.

FURTHER READING: Ronald Firbank, *The Complete Ronald Firbank* (New York: New Directions, 1961); —, *Complete Short Stories*, ed. Stephen Moore (Normal, Ill.: Dalkey Archive, 1990); —, *Complete Plays*, ed. Stephen Moore (Normal, Ill.: Dalkey Archive, 1994; Ifan Kyrle Fletcher, *Ronald Firbank, A Memoir* (London: Duckworth, 1930); Jocelyn Brooke, *Ronald Firbank* (London: Arthur Barker, 1951); Miriam J. Benkovitz, *Ronald Firbank: A Biography* (New York: Knopf, 1969); Brigid Brophy, *Prancing Novelist: In Praise of Ronald Firbank* (New York: Harper and Row, 1973); Paul Davies, "'The Power to Convey the Unuttered': Style and Sexuality in the Works of Ronald Firbank," in Mark Lilly, ed., *Lesbian and Gay Writing: An Anthology of Critical Essays* (Philadelphia: Temple University Press, 1990), pp. 199–214; William Lane Clark, "Degenerate Personality: Deviant Sexuality and Race in Ronald Firbank's Novels," in David Bergman, ed., *Camp Grounds: Style and Homosexuality* (Amherst: University of Massachusetts Press, 1993), pp. 134–55; Joseph Bristow, *Effeminate England: Homoerotic Writing after 1885* (New York: Columbia University Press, 1995); Peter Parker, "Aggressive, Witty, and Unrelenting: Brigid Brophy and Ronald Firbank," *Review of Contemporary Fiction*, 15 (1995): 68–7; Steven Moore, *Ronald Firbank: An Annotated Bibliography of Secondary Materials, 1905–1995* (Urbana, Ill.: Dalkey Archive, 1996); Robert L. Caserio, "Artifice and Empire in Ronald Firbank's Novels," *Western Humanities Review* 51 (1997): 227–35; Jonathan Goldman, "The Parrotic Voice of the Frivolous: Fiction by Ronald Firbank, I. Compton-Burnett, and Max Beerbohm," *Narrative* 7 (1999): 289–306.

[. . .] at that instant, the Hon. Mrs. Chilleywater, the 'literary' wife of the first attaché, thrust her head in at the door.

"How are you?" she asked. "I thought perhaps I might find *Harold*. . . ."

"He's with Sir Somebody."

"Such mysteries !" Lady Something said.

"This betrothal of Princess Elsie's is simply wearing him out," Mrs. Chilleywater declared, sweeping the room with half-closed, expressionless eyes.

"It's a pity you can't pull the strings for us," Lady Something ventured: "I was saying so lately to Sir Somebody."

"I wish I could, dear Lady Something: I wouldn't mind wagering I'd soon bring it off!"

"Have you fixed up Grace Gillstow yet, Mrs. Chilleywater?" Lord Tiredstock's third son asked.

"She shall marry Baldwin: but not before she has been seduced first by Barnaby. . . ."

"What are you talking about?" the Hon. 'Eddy' queried.

"Of Mrs. Chilleywater's forthcoming book."

"Why should Barnaby get Grace——? Why not Tex?"

But Mrs. Chilleywater refused to enter into reasons.

"She is looking for cowslips," she said, "and oh I've such a wonderful description of a field of cowslips. . . . They make quite a darling setting for a powerful scene of lust."

"So Grace loses her virtue!" Lord Tiredstock's third son exclaimed.

"Even so she's far too good for Baldwin; after the underhand shabby way he behaved to Charlotte, Kate, and Millicent!"

"Life is like that, dear," the Ambassadress blandly observed.

"It ought not to be, Lady Something!" Mrs. Chilleywater looked vindictive.

Née Victoria Gellybore-Frinton, and the sole heir of Lord Seafairer of Sevenelms, Kent, Mrs. Harold Chilleywater, since her marriage "for Love," had developed a disconcerting taste for fiction—a taste that was regarded at the Foreign Office with disapproving forbearance. . . . So far her efforts (written under her maiden name in full with her husband's as well appended) had been confined to lurid studies of low life (of which she knew nothing at all); but the Hon. Harold Chilleywater had been gently warned that if he was not to remain at Kairoulla until the close of his career the style of his wife must really grow less *virile*.

"I agree with V. G. F.," the Hon. Lionel Limpness murmured, fondling meditatively his "Charlie Chaplin" moustache—"Life ought not to be."

"It's a mistake to bother oneself over matters that can't be remedied."

Mrs. Chilleywater acquiesced. "You're right indeed, Lady Something," she said, "but I'm so sensitive. . . . I seem to *know* when I talk to a man the colour of his braces . . . I say to myself: 'Yours are violet. . . .' 'Yours are blue. . . .' 'His are red.'"

"I'll bet you anything, Mrs. Chilleywater, you like, you won't guess what mine are," the Hon. Lionel Limpness said.

"I should say, Mr. Limpness, that they were *multi-hued* like Jacob's," Mrs. Chilleywater replied, as she withdrew her head.

The Ambassadress prepared to follow.

"Come, Mr. Limpness," she exclaimed, "we've exhausted the poor fellow quite enough—and besides, here comes his dinner."

"Open the champagne, Mario," his master commanded immediately they were alone.

" 'Small' beer is all the butler would allow, sir."

"Damn the b . . . butler!"

"What he calls a *demi-brune*, sir. In Naples we say *spumanti*."

"To — with it."

"Non e tanto amaro, sir, it's more sharp, as you'd say, than bitter. . . ."

". . . . . . !!!!!!"

And language *unmonastic* far into the night reigned supreme.

[. . .]

It had been once the whim and was now the felicitous habit of the Countess of Tolga to present Count Cabinet annually with a bouquet of flowers. It was as if Venus Anadyomene herself, standing* on a shell and wafted by all the piquant whispers of the town and court, would intrude upon the flattered exile (with her well-wired orchids, and malicious, soulless laughter), to awaken delicate, pagan images of a trecento, Tuscan Greece.

But upon this occasion desirous of introducing some new features, the Countess decided on presenting the fallen senator with a pannier of well-grown, early pears, a small "heath" and the Erotic Poems, bound in half calf with tasteful tooling, of a Schoolboy Poet, cherishable chiefly perhaps for the vignette frontispiece of the author. Moreover, acting on an impulse she was never able afterwards to explain, she had invited Mademoiselle Olga Blumenghast to accompany her.

Never had summer shown a day more propitiously clement than the afternoon in mid-autumn they prepared to set out.

Fond of a compliment, when not too frankly racy,** and knowing how susceptible the exile was to clothes, the Countess had arrayed herself in a winter gown of king-fisher-tinted silk turning to turquoise, and stencilled in purple at the arms and neck with a crisp Greek-key design; while a voluminous violet veil, depending behind her to a point, half concealed a tricorne turquoise toque from which arose a shaded lilac aigrette branching several ways.

"I shall probably die with heat, and of course it's most unsuitable; but poor old man, he likes to recall the Capital!" the Countess panted, as, nursing heath, poems and pears, she followed Mademoiselle Olga Blumenghast blindly towards the shore.

Oars, and swaying drying nets, a skyline lost in sun, a few moored craft beneath the little rickety wooden pier awaiting choice :—"The boatmen, to-day, darling, seem all so ugly; let's take a sailing-boat and go alone!"

"I suppose there's no danger, darling?" the Countess replied, and scarcely had she time to make any slight objection when the owner of a steady wide-bottomed boat— the *Calypso*—was helping them to embark.

The Island of St. Helena, situated towards the lake's bourne, lay distant some two miles or more, and within a short way of the open sea.

----

* Vide Botticelli.

**In Pisuerga compliments are apt to rival in this respect those of the ardent South.

With sails distended to a languid breeze the shore eventually was left behind; and the demoiselle cranes, in mid-lake, were able to observe there were two court dames among them.

"Although he's dark, Vi," Mademoiselle Olga Blumenghast presently exclaimed, dropping her cheek to a frail hand upon the tiller, "although he's dark, it's odd how he gives one the impression somehow of perfect fairness." "Who's that, darling?" the Countess murmured, appraising with fine eyes, faintly weary, the orchid-like style of beauty of her friend.

"Ann-Jules, of course."

"I begin to wish, do you know, I'd brought pomegranates, and worn something else!"

"What are those big burley-worleys?"

"Pears. . . ."

"Give me one. . . ."

"Catch, then."

"Not that I could bear to be married; especially like *you*, Vi!"

"A marriage like ours, dear, was so utterly unworthwhile. . . ."

"I'm not sure, dear, that I comprehend altogether?"

"Seagulls' wings as they fan one's face. . . ."

"It's vile and wrong to shoot them: but oh I how I wish your happiness depended, even ever so little, on me."

The Countess averted her eyes.

Waterfowl, like sadness passing, hovered and soared overhead, casting their dark, fleeting shadows to the white, drowned clouds, in the receptive waters of the lake.

"I begin to wish I'd brought grapes," she breathed.

"Heavy stodgy pears. So do I."

"Or a few special peaches," the Countess murmured, taking up the volume of verse beside her, with a little, mirthless, half-hysterical laugh.

To a Faithless Friend.

To V. O. I. and S. C. P.

When the Dormitory Lamp burns Low.

Her gaze travelled over the Index.

"Read something, dear," Mademoiselle Blumenghast begged, toying with the red-shaded flower in her burnished curls.

"Gladly; but oh, Olga!" the Countess crooned.

"What!"

"Where's the wind?"

It had gone.

"We must row."

There was nothing for it.

To gain the long, white breakwater, with the immemorial willow-tree at its end, that was the most salient feature of the island's approach, required, nevertheless, resolution.

"It's so far, dear," the Countess kept on saying. "I had no idea how far it was! Had you any conception at all it was so far?"

"Let us await the wind, then. It's bound to rally."

But no air swelled the sun-bleached sails, or disturbed the pearly patine of the paralysed waters.

"I shall never get this peace, I only realise it *exists* . . ." the Countess murmured with dream-glazed eyes.

"It's astonishing. . . the stillness," Mademoiselle Blumenghast murmured, with a faint tremor, peering round towards the shore.

On the banks young censia-trees raised their boughs like strong white whips towards the mountains, upon whose loftier heights lay, here and there, a little stray patch of snow.

"Come hither, ye winds, come hither!" she softly called.

"Oh, Olga! Do we really want it?" the Countess in agitation asked, discarding her hat and veil with a long, sighing breath.

"I don't know, dear; no; not, not much."

"Nor I,—at all."

"Let us be patient then."

"It's all so beautiful it makes one want to cry."

"Yes; it makes one want to cry," Mademoiselle Blumenghast murmured, with a laugh that in brilliance vied with the October sun.

"Olga!"

"So," as the *Calypso* lurched: "lend me your hanky, dearest."

"Olga—? —? Thou fragile, and exquisite thing!"

H.D. [HILDA DOOLITTLE] (1886–1961)

"Fragment Thirty-Six" from *Heliodora* (1924); from
HERmione (1927)

The American poet-novelist known as H.D., born Hilda Doolittle, grew up in Bethlehem, Pennsylvania, and attended Bryn Mawr College, where she studied literature and Greek mythology. In 1910 she fell in love—painfully—with both a young woman, Frances Gregg, and the poet Ezra Pound. Gregg became her lover, Pound her patron, and bisexuality one of the abiding themes of her art. In 1911 H.D. went to Europe with Gregg and Gregg's mother, and with Pound's help began publishing poems and translations in avant-garde journals. She was quickly recognized as one of the most original and talented of the new "Imagist" poets—a loose grouping of English and American writers devoted to a poetic aesthetic of modernity, concision, and sensuous exactitude in regard to the image. Her first book of poems, *Sea Garden*, appeared in 1916.

H.D. left Gregg in 1912 to marry the writer Richard Aldington, with whom she lived for six years. In turn, after separating from Aldington, she had a brief affair with the musicologist Cecil Gray and bore him a daughter, Perdita. She continued to be drawn to women, however, and in 1919 began a relationship with the poet and shipping heiress, Winifred Ellerman. Ellerman—better known as Bryher—nursed H.D. devotedly when H.D. almost died during the Spanish influenza epidemic that raged across Europe in that year. Following H.D.'s recovery the two women went to Greece—the first of many visits to the eastern Mediterranean. Ancient classical civilization would thenceforth prove to be H.D.'s deepest source of poetic inspiration. Upon returning, she and Bryher set up house together in London and lived there and in Switzerland for the remainder of their lives.

H.D.'s second book of poetry, *Hymen*, subsidized by Bryher, appeared in 1921; *Heliodora*, containing free reworkings of Sappho's fragments, in 1924. H.D. wrote four autobiographical novels in the twenties—*Paint It Today* (1921), *Asphodel* (1921–22), *Palimpsest* (1926), and *HERmione* (1926–27)—though only *Palimpsest* was published during her lifetime. In 1930 she collaborated with the singer Paul Robeson on an experimental film, *Borderline*, and later in the same decade underwent psychoanalysis with Freud, an experience she subsequently commemorated in the lyrical *Tribute to Freud* (1956). After the Second World War—a conflict she found profoundly traumatizing—she continued to write poetry in an increasingly original and visionary mode. Her interest in mythology, especially legends of the Great Goddess and ancient matriarchal cults, deeply informed her later writing, particularly the book-length poetic cycles *Helen in Egypt* (1961) and *Trilogy* (1973). Near the end of her life she turned once again to fiction with the novel *Bid Me to Live* (1960).

H.D.'s writing—both poetry and prose—is difficult and can aggravate even the most forgiving reader. That said, she can also describe things as no one else has described them. The poem "Fragment Thirty-Six," from *Heliodora*, is a case in point. Here, out of the famously cryptic Sapphic utterance—ουκ οιδ οττι θέω δύο μοι τὰ νοήμματα ("I know not what to do: my mind is divided")—she fashions an intimate erotic question-poem of astonishing plangency. In turn, in the gnomic fiction *HERmione*, written around the same time, she explores similar emotions in an explicitly autobiographical mode. The novel is a thinly veiled retelling of the love triangle with Gregg and Pound. In the passage excerpted below, we eavesdrop on a conversation between Her Gart (the H.D. character) and Fayne Rabb (Gregg), with whom Her Gart is in love. Fayne is baiting Her—excruciatingly—over Her's unresolved feelings for George Lowndes (Pound). The style is hermetic indeed, though not enough to obscure the passionate ferocity of the young women's relationship. Caught in a coil of jealousy and resentment, Fayne and Her embody one of the archetypal pairings of lesbian fiction: charismatic bossy schoolgirl and her adoring slave-beginning-to-rebel. That their affair will indeed end badly is intimated by H.D.'s recurrent ironic citation ("curled lips long since half kissed away") of A. C. Swinburne's 1866 poem "Faustine," about the eponymous Roman empress addicted to that "shameless nameless love" that "blew through Mitylene" on "breaths of Sapphic song."

FURTHER READING: H.D., *HERmione* (New York: New Directions, 1981); —, *Collected Poems, 1912–1944*, ed. Louis L. Martz (New York: New Directions, 1983); Bryher, *The Heart to Artemis* (New York: Harcourt, Brace and World, 1962); Barbara Guest, *HERself Defined: The Poet H.D. and Her World* (Glasgow: William Collins, 1984); Thom Gunn, "Three Hard Women: H.D., Marianne Moore, Mina Loy," in Vereen Bell and Laurence Lerner, eds., *On Modern Poetry: Essays Presented to Donald Davie* (Nashville, Tenn.: Vanderbilt University Press, 1988), pp. 37–52; Susan Stanford Friedman, *Penelope's Web: Gender, Modernity, H.D.'s Fiction* (Cambridge: Cambridge University Press, 1990); —, and Rachel Blau DuPlessis, eds., *Signets: Reading H.D.* (Madison: University of Wisconsin Press, 1990); Cassandra Laity, "H.D. and A. C. Swinburne: Decadence and Modernist Women's Writing," in Joanne Glasgow and Karla Jay, eds., *Lesbian Texts and Contexts: Radical Revisions* (New York: New York University Press, 1990), pp. 217–40; Diana Collecott, "What Is Not Said: A Study in Textual Inversion," in Joseph Bristow, ed., *Sexual Sameness: Textual Differences in Lesbian and Gay Writing* (London and New York: Routledge, 1992), pp. 91–110; —, *H.D. and Sapphic Modernism* (Cambridge: Cambridge University Press, 1999).

Fragment Thirty-Six

I know not what to do: my mind is divided.
—Sappho.

I know not what to do,
my mind is reft:
is song's gift best?
is love's gift loveliest?
I know not what to do,
now sleep has pressed
weight on your eyelids.

Shall I break your rest,
devouring, eager?
is love's gift best?
nay, song's the loveliest:
yet were you lost,
what rapture
could I take from song?
what song were left?

I know not what to do:
to turn and slake
the rage that burns,
with my breath burn
and trouble your cool breath?
so shall I turn and take
snow in my arms?
(is love's gift best?)
yet flake on flake
of snow were comfortless,
did you lie wondering,
wakened yet unawake.

Shall I turn and take
comfortless snow within my arms?
press lips to lips
that answer not,
press lips to flesh
that shudders not nor breaks?

Is love's gift best?
shall I turn and slake
all the wild longing?
O I am eager for you!
as the Pleiads shake
white light in whiter water
so shall I take you?

My mind is quite divided,
my minds hesitate,
so perfect matched,
I know not what to do:
each strives with each
as two white wrestlers
standing for a match,
ready to turn and clutch
yet never shake muscle nor nerve nor tendon;
so my mind waits
to grapple with my mind,
yet I lie quiet,
I would seem at rest.

I know not what to do:
strain upon strain,
sound surging upon sound
makes my brain blind;
as a wave-line may wait to fall
yet (waiting for its falling)
still the wind may take
from off its crest,
white flake on flake of foam,
that rises,
seeming to dart and pulse
and rend the light,
so my mind hesitates
above the passion
quivering yet to break,
so my mind hesitates
above my mind,
listening to song's delight.

I know not what to do:
will the sound break,

rending the night
with rift on rift of rose
and scattered light?
will the sound break at last
as the wave hesitant,
or will the whole night pass
and I lie listening awake?

From *HERmione*

"*They* are watching him breathless." "Yes, Fayne." "They see and wonder. Steel flashes and there is some sort of long—long—I mean there is that same green lane and the sea step coming down from the sea wall." "Yes, Fayne." "*You* are not of him being pure, apart. You are the cold ice, the radiant stream head, the very waters of Castilla." "Yes, Fayne." "*He* is beneath you, below you. He has part and parcel of some other fortune. He is not for you." "Yes, yes Fayne." Eyes glared across space, across chasms, across valleys and hills. Eyes stared at Her Gart and eyes caught eyes that lifted mist-blue above frozen waters. Waters were frozen in Her Gart. She was bored with what Fayne was saying. I want to take her hand, press it against my eyes. She will say the moment I let go, get away from this thing. "You are just like *people*. You are like everybody. You can't follow me."

Her Gart lifted eyes and by some dynamic power of readjustment made mist-blue eyes go steel-grey. She felt concentration hold, her head go hard, she would follow Fayne into the space beyond space. "You can't *see* what I see." "No, Fayne. I don't pretend to." "Why do you baffle me, escape me?" "I don't altogether mean to. I don't exactly want to." "You *seem* to see. And then you quite escape me." Light flung upward, fell on the carpet and Her Gart sitting on the carpet was sitting in light reflected from cold paths, from stripped orchard branches, from box trees static and green, more green but cold against autumn branches. Light cast up from beneath was reminiscent of last spring, was prophetic of next winter. Eyes met eyes and the storm held, storm of ice, some storm in an ice crater. "Yes, Fayne."

"But you don't, you don't care. You have so many interests." "I have you, only you Fayne." "And this—this *other*—"

"Other? Do you mean my writing?" "No. Your writing is nothing really. It is the pulsing of a willow, the faint note of some Sicilian shepherd. Your writing is the thin flute holding you to eternity. Take away your flute and you remain, lost in a world of unreality." "It's not—I mean—*all*." "It is all—*all* unreal. You accept false, superimposed standards . . . all these people." "But I'm trying to escape them." "You turn back. Like Lot's wife you are a frozen pillar." "I'm not a frozen pillar. I'm not anything like Lot's wife. I'm not—not anybody's wife." "You jeer at me, make fun of my poor pretences. But there is one grain in me will vanquish, conquer every one of you; one grain, certainly atomic, minute, but very core and center of pure truth. I am pure truth when I *am*." "You so often, Fayne, aren't." "Now little blasphemer—"

This was better. This was real and funny. The hand thrust out made its habitual movement. "But you haven't told me yet if you like George?"

"I don't like George. I don't *care* for him." Words, dynamic twist of a rare mouth. The empress mouth made its down-twist, made its up-twist that scarred the line of the face, that made the face regal. *Curled lips long since half kissed away.* "Wh-aa-at, Her?" "I said *long ere they coined in Roman gold, your face, Faustine.*"

A face drew back, luminous and intense. A head was set on space of blue serge, shoulders rising beneath schoolgirl sort of blue serge one-piece dress, made sort of pedestal for the column that rose above it. The throat rose from squared-in space of shoulders, as if someone had come in, said this thing needs furbishing up, needs sand-papering (what do they do to statues?), needs cleaning, had wondered how to move it, had turned it about, found it was too heavy and finally flung a length of dark cloth on it. Someone had thrown a length of blue dark cloth over marble. The blue cloth was flung across marble nakedness but nakedness remained unclothed, remained pure beneath it. Beneath schoolgirl blue serge a marble from some place (Heliopolis? Perse-polis?) far and far and far. "I don't feel now that at all I want to go to Europe." "Oh— *Europe.*" Fayne spoke, a society debutante, wearied by suggestion of trunk, of box, of maid, of tickets, of orchids. Fayne put into her low voice the sort of scorn that went with *curled lips long since half kissed away.* "I suppose *some* day we'll get there."

"Get where Fayne?" "To Europe, little stupid. Don't you ever listen to what any-one is ever saying?" "George says not." "Oh *George.*" *Curled lips long since half kissed away* came right in the white face. The mouth was straight now, the mouth of a boy hunter. The mouth was a mouth that had hallooed across stones towards some escap-ing quarry. Across the shoulders there was a strap holding arrows. Marble lifted from marble and showed a boy. "You might have been a huntress." "I'm no good—no good at anything." Fayne said "I'm no good at anything" as if one had asked her to play in a tennis tournament or join a bridge club. "I don't mean huntress like that—like that. I don't mean country clubs—not things like that. I mean a boy standing on bare rocks and stooping to take a stone from his strapped sandal. I mean you might wear sandals or else boots laced crossways." "You mean?" "I mean you were so exactly right in that stage tunic. You were so exactly right as that Pygmalion." Her bent forward, face bent toward Her. A face bends towards me and a curtain opens. There is swish and swirl as of heavy parting curtains. Almost along the floor with its strip of carpet, almost across me I feel the fringe of some fantastic wine-coloured parting curtains. Curtains part as I look into the eyes of Fayne Rabb. "And I—I'll make you breathe, my breathless statue." "Statue? You—*you* are the statue." Curtains fell, curtains parted, curtains filled the air with heavy swooping purple. Lips long since half kissed away. Curled lips long since half kissed away. In Roman gold. Long ere they coined in Roman gold your face—your face—your face—your face—your face—Faustine.

Seated in cold steel light, drawn back again, away from that blue-white face, face too-white (eyes too-blue, eyes set in marble, black-glass eyes like eyes set in pre-pyramid Egyptian effigy) Her Gart saw rings and circles, the rings and circles that were the eyes of Fayne Rabb. Rings and circles made concentric curve toward a ceiling that was, as it were, the bottom of a deep pool. Her and Fayne Rabb were flung into a concentric intimacy, rings on rings that made a geometric circle toward a ceiling, that curved over them like ripples on a pond surface. Her and Fayne were flung, as it were, to the bottom of some strange element and looming up . . . there were rings on rings of circles as if they had fallen into a deep well and were looking up . . . "long since half kissed away."

"Isn't Swinburne decadent?" "In what sense exactly decadent, Fayne?" "Oh innocence, holy and untouched and most immoral. Innocence like thine is totally indecent." "Innocence? Indecent? What's the meaning of 'innocence is indecent?'" "I'm being cryptic, pep-igrammatic as George says." "Did George say you were—pep-igrammatic?" "Why yes. Why shouldn't George?" Circles making pool-ripple came close, came close, they were not any more circles, they were a blank pool surface, the rings on rings were not. "I mean what made George exactly say it?"

"George. George. Is there nothing Miss Her Gart for you to talk about but George, but Georgio?" "Do you call him Georgio?" "Why—doesn't everybody?" "No. I did. His mother calls him Ginger." "Oh, his mother. He insisted on her coming to see madre." "To see?" "Mama. His mother is—eccentric." "Eccentric? I thought she was most proper." "That's what I mean exactly." "Why is it eccentric for Lillian to be proper?" "Do you call her Lillian?" "Her name is—" "*Your* name is—" "Is?" "Lily. White out of darkness. You are so simply perfect." "Perfect?" "In your—your idiocy, I mean perfect." "Idiocy?" "Oh do let up Her Gart. You are so simply childish."

Days have done this, said Her Gart sitting upright on the hard floor. She noticed that the floor was hard. The floor didn't used to seem hard. Days are doing things to me. "How long is it since you saw him?" "Saw who?" "George." "Oh, George. It was—it was last week." "He said last week he saw you." "And what aimless irony did he present you, hoping that I would hear it?" "He said you and I ought to be burnt for witchcraft."

VIRGINIA WOOLF (1882–1941)

From *Mrs. Dalloway* (1925) and *Orlando* (1928)

The mercurial Virginia Woolf—novelist, feminist, founding member of the so-called Bloomsbury group, occasional lover of women, and female imaginist extraordinaire— was the daughter of the distinguished Victorian man of letters, Sir Leslie Stephen. Her early years, spent in London and Cornwall, were unhappy: the sudden death of her mother, Julia Stephen, in 1895, when Woolf was thirteen, prompted the first in a life-long series of suicide attempts and mental breakdowns. For the next nine years, despite her own emotional instability, Woolf lived with her depressive widower father, helping her sister Vanessa and half-sister Stella to care for him. Woolf sought refuge in books, taught herself Greek and Latin, and led a relatively secluded life. Her feminism took root early on, despite her obvious intellectual gifts, when her brothers, Thoby and Adrian, went up to Cambridge she was prevented from following them on account of her sex.

Woolf's life changed dramatically upon Sir Leslie Stephen's death in 1904. Eager to cast off the constraints of an oppressive family life, she and her siblings moved to a house in Bloomsbury, near the British Museum, where they began holding weekly intellectual and artistic gatherings. Regular guests—quickly dubbed the "Bloomsbury group" in the London literary press—included the writers and critics Lytton Strachey, Roger Fry, E. M. Forster, and Clive Bell, the economist John Maynard Keynes, and later, the artists Duncan Grant and Dora Carrington. From the start the group devoted itself to social-ism, modern art, sexual freedom, and the self-conscious overthrow of Victorian values. (Woolf's sister, Vanessa, became an important English painter and a leading figure in the famous Omega Workshop design group.) Numerous male members of the Blooms-bury group were homosexual, and Woolf found herself intellectually and emotionally liberated by her friendships with Strachey and Forster in particular.

Woolf began writing seriously in 1905, publishing her first literary essays in the *TLS* the same year. In 1912 she married Leonard Woolf, a left-wing Jewish political writer and onetime colonial administrator who cared for her devotedly when she suf-fered another serious mental breakdown in 1914–15. Her first novel, *The Voyage Out*, appeared in 1915, followed by *Night and Day* in 1919. In 1917 she and Leonard started a small private printing press, the Hogarth Press, which they used to publish both their own and "the best and most original" works of new writers. Running the press proved therapeutic and Woolf enjoyed a period of sustained creativity in the decade that followed. *Jacob's Room*, *Mrs. Dalloway*, and *To the Lighthouse*, her first experimental works, appeared in 1922, 1925, and 1927 and won her international acclaim. In 1928 she published the bestselling *Orlando*, a fantasy novel about a man who lives for three centuries and changes at one point into a woman. Her magnificent (and still influential) feminist treatise, *A Room of One's Own*, appeared in 1929. Her health stabilized, she and Leonard divided their time between London and Monk's House, a cottage they purchased in the Sussex Downs.

The 1930s were less happy: Woolf was deeply grieved by the death of a nephew in the Spanish Civil War and viewed the rise of Hitlerism across Europe with alarm and loathing. She continued, however, to write prolifically. The stream-of-consciousness novel *The Waves* appeared in 1931; the mock biography *Flush* in 1933; the family chronicle novel *The Years* in 1937; and *Three Guineas*, a second feminist treatise, in 1938. Nor were these her only efforts: even as her mental and physical condition slowly worsened over the decade, she produced a steady stream of letters, diaries, book reviews, and literary essays. The outbreak of war in 1939 left her severely depressed, however, and in 1941, fearing another episode of madness, she committed suicide by drowning herself in the River Ouse. She left behind a last (incomplete) novel, *Between the Acts*, published posthumously the same year.

Woolf's sexual orientation remains a topic of extraordinary interest. Her marriage to Leonard Woolf, while eminently companionable, appears to have been largely sexless: repeated sexual abuse in childhood at the hands of two half-brothers seems to have instilled in Woolf a deep-seated repugnance to conventional heterosexual relations. Mental instability compounded her disinclination for passionate attachment. What sensual feelings she did allow herself were plainly evoked by other women. Her relationship with her sister, Vanessa, was powerfully erotic in nature: Woolf's biographer Hermione Lee considers Vanessa to have been the "great love" of Woolf's life. But other women won her affection as well. In youth she loved Violet Dickinson, an old Stephen family friend and onetime Mayoress of Bath; in the early days of her marriage, she was powerfully attracted by the enigmatic Katherine Mansfield. In the mid-1920s she fell in love with the flamboyant writer-seductress Vita Sackville-West, with whom she had a brief affair. (They remained lifelong friends: Woolf subsequently dedicated *Orlando* to her.) And toward the end of her life she formed a chaste yet flirtatious bond—giddily reciprocated—with the lesbian composer and suffragette, Ethel Smyth. Though reluctant to identify herself as a "Sapphist," Woolf found in female love and friendship both a deep personal solace and an inspiration for her art.

Woolf treated the lesbian theme often in her fiction. In the celebrated excerpt below from the stream-of-consciousness novel *Mrs. Dalloway* (1925), Woolf offers perhaps the most sympathetic evocation of female homoeroticism in English fiction before Radclyffe Hall's *The Well of Loneliness*. Returning home at midday after a flower-buying expedition, the eponymous heroine, Clarissa Dalloway, the middle-aged wife of an

M.P., finds herself reflecting, half cynically, half nostalgically, on "this falling in love with women." The sight of her attic bedroom—she and her husband no longer sleep together—prompts memories of the house party years ago at which she became engaged to him. Yet even as she confronts the ghosts of the past, she is forced to acknowledge that it was Sally Seton, the great friend of her youth, with whom she was really in love. The revelation is fleeting—like the chance kiss she remembers Sally giving her. But its psychological aftershocks linger, casting a strange sapphic glow over the rest of Woolf's novel. Men come and go, Woolf intimates, but women's most lasting erotic feelings are inspired by one another.

No less daring, if more playful, is the treatment of lesbianism in the fantasy novel *Orlando*. The book purports to be the biography of a dashing nobleman, born in the Elizabethan age, who undergoes a mysterious sex change at the beginning of the eighteenth century and lives on (as a woman) into the 1920s. It was inspired by Woolf's androgynous lover, Vita Sackville-West. Like Sackville-West, Orlando is handsome, *louche*, and a dedicated seducer of women—even, paradoxically, after he becomes one himself. In the passage below, Orlando—recently reborn as female and disgusted by the constraints of ordinary femininity—longs to relive the erotic pleasures of her (male) youth. Opening "a cupboard in which hung still many of the clothes she had worn as a young man of fashion" a hundred years before, she dons a "black velvet suit richly trimmed with Venetian lace" and ventures out into the streets of eighteenth-century London to look for available women. While Orlando's adventures *en travesti* are both comic and telling—Woolf will use them to make a number of satirical points about the hypocrisy of *heterosexual* relations—they also contain a potent sapphic dimension. In depicting Orlando's drag rambles, Woolf may have had in mind Sackville-West's own adventures in Paris in 1918, when she disguised herself as a demobbed British soldier, "Julian," and exuberantly wandered the streets near the Palais Royal with her then lover, Violet Trefusis.

FURTHER READING: Virginia Woolf, *The Voyage Out* (London: Duckworth, 1915); —, *Night and Day* (London: Duckworth, 1919); —, *Jacob's Room* (London: Hogarth, 1922); *Mrs. Dalloway* (1925; rpt. New York: Harcourt Brace Jovanovich, 1953); —, *To the Lighthouse* (London: Hogarth, 1927); —, *Orlando: A Biography* (1928; rpt. New York: Harcourt Brace Jovanovich, 1956); —, *A Room of One's Own* (1929; rpt. with *Three Guineas*, Harmondsworth, Middlesex: Penguin Books, 1992); —, *The Waves* (London: Hogarth, 1931); —, *The Years* (London: Hogarth, 1937); —, *Between the Acts* (London: Hogarth, 1941); —, *The Diaries of Virginia Woolf*, ed. Anne Olivier Bell and Andrew McNeillie, 5 vols. (New York: Harcourt Brace Jovanovich, 1977–84); —, *The Letters of Virginia Woolf*, ed. Nigel Nicolson and Joanne Trautmann, 6 vols. (New York: Harcourt Brace Jovanovich, 1975–80); —, *The Collected Shorter Fiction of Virginia Woolf*, ed. Susan Dick (London: Hogarth, 1985); —, *The Essays of Virginia Woolf*, 4 vols., ed. Andrew McNeillie (London: Hogarth, 1986); —, *A Passionate*

Apprentice: The Early Journals of Virginia Woolf, ed. Mitchell A. Leaska (London: Hogarth, 1990); Quentin Bell, *Virginia Woolf: A Biography*, 2 vols. (New York: Harcourt Brace Jovanovich, 1972); S. P. Rosenbaum, ed., *The Bloomsbury Group* (London: Croom Helm, 1975); Phyllis Rose, *Woman of Letters: A Life of Virginia Woolf* (London: Routledge and Kegan Paul, 1978); Blanche Wiesen Cook, " 'Women Alone Stir My Imagination': Lesbianism and the Cultural Tradition," *Signs: A Journal of Women in Culture and Society* 4 (1979): 718–39; Jane Marcus, ed., *Virginia Woolf: A Feminist Slant* (Lincoln: University of Nebraska Press, 1983); —, *Virginia Woolf and the Languages of Patriarchy* (Bloomington and Indianapolis: Indiana University Press, 1987); Louise DeSalvo and Mitchell A. Leaska, eds., *The Letters of Vita Sackville-West to Virginia Woolf* (London: Hutchinson, 1984); Alex Zwerdling, *Virginia Woolf and the Real World* (Berkeley: University of California Press, 1986); Sherron E. Knopp, " 'If I Saw You Would You Kiss Me?': Sapphism and the Subversiveness of Virginia Woolf's *Orlando*," in Joseph Bristow, ed., *Sexual Sameness: Textual Differences in Lesbian and Gay Writing* (New York and London: Routledge, 1992), pp. 111–27; Vara Neverow Turk and Mark Hussey, eds., *Virginia Woolf: Themes and Variations* (New York: Pace University Press, 1993); Suzanne Raitt, *Vita and Virginia: The Work and Friendship of V. Sackville-West and Virginia Woolf* (Oxford: Clarendon, 1993); Adam Parkes, "Lesbianism, History, and Censorship: *The Well of Loneliness* and the 'Suppressed Randiness' of Virginia Woolf's *Orlando*," *Twentieth-Century Literature*, 40 (1994): 434–60; Hermione Lee, *Virginia Woolf* (New York: Knopf, 1996); Ruth Vanita, *Sappho and the Virgin Mary: Same-Sex Love and the English Literary Imagination* (New York: Columbia University Press, 1996); Patricia Juliana Smith, *Lesbian Panic: Homoeroticism in Modern British Women's Fiction* (New York: Columbia University Press, 1997); Karen L. Levenback, *Virginia Woolf and the Great War* (Syracuse: Syracuse University Press, 1998); Angela Smith, *Katherine Mansfield and Virginia Woolf: A Public of Two* (Oxford: Clarendon, 1999); Ann Banfield, *The Phantom Table: Woolf, Fry, Russell, and the Epistemology of Modernism* (Cambridge: Cambridge University Press, 2000); Herbert Marder, *The Measure of Life: Virginia Woolf's Last Years* (Ithaca, N.Y.: Cornell University Press, 2000); Natania Rosenfeld, *Outsiders Together: Virginia and Leonard Woolf* (Princeton: Princeton University Press, 2000).

From *Mrs. Dalloway*

Like a nun withdrawing, or a child exploring a tower, she went upstairs, paused at the window, came to the bathroom. There was the green linoleum and a tap dripping. There was an emptiness about the heart of life; an attic room. Women must put off their rich apparel. At midday they must disrobe. She pierced the pincushion and laid her feathered yellow hat on the bed. The sheets were clean, tight stretched in a broad white band from side to side. Narrower and narrower would her bed be. The candle was half burnt down and she had read deep in Baron Marbot's *Memoirs*. She had read late at night of the retreat from Moscow. For the House sat so long that Richard insisted, after her illness, that she must sleep undisturbed. And really she preferred to read of the retreat from Moscow. He knew it. So the room was an attic; the bed narrow; and lying there reading, for she slept badly, she could not dispel a virginity preserved through childbirth which clung to her like a sheet. Lovely in girlhood, suddenly there came a moment—for example on the river beneath the woods at Clieveden—when, through some contraction of this cold spirit, she had failed him. And then at Constantinople, and again and again. She could see what she lacked. It was not beauty; it was not mind. It was something central which permeated; something warm which broke up surfaces and rippled the cold contact of man and woman, or of women together. For *that* she could dimly perceive. She resented it, had a scruple picked up Heaven knows where, or, as she felt, sent by Nature (who is invariably wise); yet she could not resist sometimes yielding to the charm of a woman, not a girl, of a woman confessing, as to her they often did, some scrape, some folly. And whether it was pity, or their beauty, or that she was older, or some accident—like a faint scent, or a violin next door (so strange is the power of sounds at certain moments), she did undoubtedly then feel what men felt. Only for a moment; but it was enough. It was a sudden revelation, a tinge like a blush which one tried to check and then, as it spread, one yielded to its expansion, and rushed to the farthest verge and there quivered and felt the world come closer, swollen with some astonishing significance, some pressure of rapture, which split its thin skin and gushed and poured with an extraordinary alleviation over the cracks and sores! Then, for that moment, she had seen an illumination; a match burning in a crocus; an inner meaning almost expressed. But the close withdrew; the hard softened. It was over—the moment. Against such moments (with women too) there contrasted (as she laid her hat down) the bed and Baron Marbot and the candle half-burnt. Lying awake, the floor creaked; the lit house was suddenly darkened, and if she raised her head she could just hear the click of the handle released as gently as possible by Richard, who slipped upstairs in his socks and then, as often as not, dropped his hot-water bottle and swore! How she laughed!

But this question of love (she thought, putting her coat away), this falling in love with women. Take Sally Seton; her relation in the old days with Sally Seton. Had not that, after all, been love?

She sat on the floor—that was her first impression of Sally—she sat on the floor with her arms round her knees, smoking a cigarette. Where could it have been? The Mannings? The Kinloch-Jones's? At some party (where, she could not be certain), for she had a distinct recollection of saying to the man she was with, "Who is *that*?" And he had told her, and said that Sally's parents did not get on (how that shocked her—that one's parents should quarrel!). But all that evening she could not take her eyes off Sally. It was an extraordinary beauty of the kind she most admired, dark, large-eyed, with that quality which, since she hadn't got it herself, she always envied—a sort of abandonment, as if she could say anything, do anything; a quality much commoner in foreigners than in

Englishwomen. Sally always said she had French blood in her veins, an ancestor had been with Marie Antoinette, had his head cut off, left a ruby ring. Perhaps that summer she came to stay at Bourton, walking in quite unexpectedly without a penny in her pocket, one night after dinner, and upsetting poor Aunt Helena to such an extent that she never forgave her. There had been some quarrel at home. She literally hadn't a penny that night when she came to them—had pawned a brooch to come down. She had rushed off in a passion. They sat up till all hours of the night talking. Sally it was who made her feel, for the first time, how sheltered the life at Bourton was. She knew nothing about sex—nothing about social problems. She had once seen an old man who had dropped dead in a field—she had seen cows just after their calves were born. But Aunt Helena never liked discussion of anything (when Sally gave her William Morris, it had to be wrapped in brown paper). There they sat, hour after hour, talking in her bedroom at the top of the house, talking about life, how they were to reform the world. They meant to found a society to abolish private property, and actually had a letter written, though not sent out. The ideas were Sally's, of course—but very soon she was just as excited—read Plato in bed before breakfast; read Morris; read Shelley by the hour.

Sally's power was amazing, her gift, her personality. There was her way with flowers, for instance. At Bourton they always had stiff little vases all the way down the table. Sally went out, picked hollyhocks, dahlias—all sorts of flowers that had never been seen together—cut their heads off, and made them swim on the top of water in bowls. The effect was extraordinary—coming in to dinner in the sunset. (Of course Aunt Helena thought it wicked to treat flowers like that.) Then she forgot her sponge, and ran along the passage naked. That grim old housemaid, Ellen Atkins, went about grumbling—"Suppose any of the gentlemen had seen?" Indeed she did shock people. She was untidy, Papa said.

The strange thing, on looking back, was the purity, the integrity, of her feeling for Sally. It was not like one's feeling for a man. It was completely disinterested, and besides, it had a quality which could only exist between women, between women just grown up. It was protective, on her side; sprang from a sense of being in league together, a presentiment of something that was bound to part them (they spoke of marriage always as a catastrophe), which led to this chivalry, this protective feeling which was much more on her side than Sally's. For in those days she was completely reckless; did the most idiotic things out of bravado; bicycled round the parapet on the terrace; smoked cigars. Absurd, she was—very absurd. But the charm was overpowering, to her at least, so that she could remember standing in her bedroom at the top of the house holding the hot-water can in her hands and saying aloud, "She is beneath this roof. . . . She is beneath this roof!"

No, the words meant absolutely nothing to her now. She could not even get an echo of her old emotion. But she could remember going cold with excitement, and doing her hair in a kind of ecstasy (now the old feeling began to come back to her, as she took out her hairpins, laid them on the dressing-table, began to do her hair), with the rooks flaunting up and down in the pink evening light, and dressing, and going downstairs, and feeling as she crossed the hall "if it were now to die 'twere now to be most happy." That was her feeling—Othello's feeling, and she felt it, she was convinced, as strongly as Shakespeare meant Othello to feel it, all because she was coming down to dinner in a white frock to meet Sally Seton!

She was wearing pink gauze—was that possible? She *seemed*, anyhow, all light, glowing, like some bird or air ball that has flown in, attached itself for a moment to a bramble. But nothing is so strange when one is in love (and what was this except being in love?) as the complete indifference of other people. Aunt Helena just wandered off after dinner; Papa read the paper. Peter Walsh might have been there, and old Miss Cummings; Joseph Breitkopf certainly was, for he came every summer, poor old man, for weeks and weeks, and pretended to read German with her, but really played the piano and sang Brahms without any voice.

All this was only a background for Sally. She stood by the fireplace talking, in that beautiful voice which made everything she said sound like a caress, to Papa, who had begun to be attracted rather against his will (he never got over lending her one of his books and finding it soaked on the terrace), when suddenly she said, "What a shame to sit indoors!" and they all went out on to the terrace and walked up and down. Peter Walsh and Joseph Breitkopf went on about Wagner. She and Sally fell a little behind. Then came the most exquisite moment of her whole life passing a stone urn with flowers in it. Sally stopped; picked a flower; kissed her on the lips. The whole world might have turned upside down! The others disappeared; there she was alone with Sally. And she felt that she had been given a present, wrapped up, and told just to keep it, not to look at it—a diamond, something infinitely precious, wrapped up, which, as they walked (up and down, up and down), she uncovered, or the radiance burnt through, the revelation, the religious feeling!—when old Joseph and Peter faced them:

"Star-gazing?" said Peter.

It was like running one's face against a granite wall in the darkness! It was shocking; it was horrible!

Not for herself. She felt only how Sally was being mauled already, maltreated; she felt his hostility; his jealousy; his determination to break into their companionship. All this she saw as one sees a landscape in a flash of lightning—and Sally (never had she admired her so much!) gallantly taking her way unvanquished. She laughed. She made old Joseph tell her the names of the stars, which he liked doing very seriously. She stood there: she listened. She heard the names of the stars.

"Oh this horror!" she said to herself, as if she had known all along that something would interrupt, would embitter her moment of happiness.

Yet, after all, how much she owed to him later. Always when she thought of him she thought of their quarrels for some reason—because she wanted his good opinion so much, perhaps. She owed him words: "sentimental," "civilised"; they started up every day of her life as if he guarded her. A book was sentimental; an attitude to life sentimental. "Sentimental," perhaps she was to be thinking of the past. What would he think, she wondered, when he came back?

That she had grown older? Would he say that, or would she see him thinking when he came back, that she had grown older? It was true. Since her illness she had turned almost white.

Laying her brooch on the table, she had a sudden spasm, as if, while she mused, the icy claws had had the chance to fix in her. She was not old yet. She had just broken into her fifty-second year. Months and months of it were still untouched. June, July, August! Each still remained almost whole, and, as if to catch the falling drop, Clarissa (crossing to the dressing-table) plunged into the very heart of the moment, transfixed it, there— the moment of this June morning on which was the pressure of all the other mornings, seeing the glass, the dressing-table, and all the bottles afresh, collecting the whole of her at one point (as she looked into the glass), seeing the delicate pink face of the woman who was that very night to give a party; of Clarissa Dalloway; of herself.

From *Orlando*

It was a fine night early in April. A myriad stars mingling with the light of a sickle moon, which again was enforced by the street lamps, made a light infinitely becoming to the human countenance and to the architecture of Mr. Wren. Everything appeared in its tenderest form, yet, just as it seemed on the point of dissolution, some drop of silver sharpened it to animation. Thus it was that talk should be, thought Orlando (indulging in foolish reverie); that society should be, that friendship should be, that love should be. For, Heaven knows why, just as we have lost faith in human intercourse some random collocation of barns and trees or a haystack and a waggon presents us with so perfect a symbol of what is unattainable that we begin the search again.

She entered Leicester Square as she made these observations. The buildings had an airy yet formal symmetry not theirs by day. The canopy of the sky seemed most dexterously washed in to fill up the outline of roof and chimney. A young woman who sat dejectedly with one arm drooping by her side, the other reposing in her lap, on a seat beneath a plane tree in the middle of the square seemed the very figure of grace, simplicity, and desolation. Orlando swept her hat off to her in the manner of a gallant paying his addresses to a lady of fashion in a public place. The young woman raised her head. It was of the most exquisite shapeliness. The young woman raised her eyes. Orlando saw them to be of a lustre such as is sometimes seen on teapots but rarely in a human face. Through this silver glaze the girl looked up at him (for a man he was to her) appealing, hoping, trembling, fearing. She rose; she accepted his arm. For—need we stress the point?—she was of the tribe which nightly burnishes their wares, and sets them in order on the common counter to wait the highest bidder. She led Orlando to the room in Gerrard Street which was her lodging. To feel her hanging lightly yet like a suppliant on her arm, roused in Orlando all the feelings which become a man. She looked, she felt, she talked like one. Yet, having been so lately a woman herself, she suspected that the girl's timidity and her hesitating answers and the very fumbling with the key in the latch and the fold of her cloak and the droop of her wrist were all put on to gratify her masculinity. Upstairs they went, and the pains which the poor creature had been at to decorate her room and hide the fact that she had no other deceived Orlando not a moment. The deception roused her scorn; the truth roused her pity. One thing showing through the other bred the oddest assortment of feeling, so that she did not know whether to laugh or to cry. Meanwhile Nell, as the girl called herself, unbuttoned her gloves; carefully concealed the left hand thumb which wanted mending; then drew behind a screen, where, perhaps, she rouged her cheeks, arranged her clothes, fixed a new kerchief round her neck—all the time prattling as women do, to amuse her lover, though Orlando could have sworn, from the tone of her voice, that her thoughts were elsewhere. When all was ready, out she came, prepared—but here Orlando could stand it no longer. In the strangest torment of anger, merriment, and pity she flung off all disguise and admitted herself a woman.

At this, Nell burst into such a roar of laughter as might have been heard across the way.

"Well, my dear," she said, when she had somewhat recovered, "I'm by no means sorry to hear it. For the plain Dunstable of the matter is" (and it was remarkable how soon on discovering that they were of the same sex, her manner changed and she dropped her plaintive, appealing ways) "the plain Dunstable of the matter is, that I'm not in the mood for the society of the other sex to-night. Indeed, I'm in the devil of a fix." Whereupon, drawing up the fire and stirring a bowl of Punch, she told Orlando the whole story of her life. Since it is Orlando's life that engages us at present, we need not relate the adventures of the other lady, but it is certain that Orlando had never known the hours speed faster or more merrily, though Mistress Nell had not a particle of wit about her, and when the name of Mr. Pope came up in talk asked innocently if he were connected with the perruque maker of that name in Jermyn Street. Yet, to Orlando, such is the charm of ease and the seduction of beauty, this poor girl's talk, larded though it was with the commonest expressions of the street corners tasted like wine after the fine phrases she had been used to, and she was forced to the conclusion that there was something in the sneer of Mr. Pope, in the condescension of Mr. Addison, and in the secret of Lord Chesterfield which took away her relish for the society of wits, deeply though she must continue to respect their works.

These poor creatures, she ascertained, for Nell brought Prue, and Prue Kitty, and Kitty Rose, had a society of their own of which they now elected her a member. Each would tell the story of the adventures which had landed her in her present way of life. Several were the natural daughters of earls and one was a good deal nearer than she should have been to the King's person. None was too wretched or too poor but to have some ring or handkerchief in her pocket which stood her in lieu of pedigree. So they would draw round the Punch bowl which Orlando made it her business to furnish generously, and many were the fine tales they told and many the amusing observations they made for it cannot be denied that when women get together—but hist—they are always careful to see that the doors are shut and that not a word of it gets into print. All they desire is—but hist again—is that not a man's step on the stair? All they desire, we were about to say when the gentleman took the very words out of our mouths. Women have no desires, says this gentleman, coming into Nell's parlour; only affectations. Without desires (she has served him and he is gone) their conversation cannot be of the slightest interest to anyone. "It is well known," says Mr. S. W., "that when they lack the stimulus of the other sex, women can find nothing to say to each other. When they are alone, they do not talk; they scratch." And since they cannot talk together and scratching cannot continue without interruption and it is well known (Mr. T. R. has proved it) "that women are incapable of any feeling of affection for their own sex and hold each other in the greatest aversion," what can we suppose that women do when they seek out each other's society?

As that is not a question that can engage the attention of a sensible man, let us, who enjoy the immunity of all biographers and historians from any sex whatever, pass it over, and merely state that Orlando professed great enjoyment in the society of her own sex, and leave it to the gentlemen to prove, as they are very fond of doing, that this is impossible.

But to give an exact and particular account of Orlando's life at this time becomes more and more out of the question. As we peer and grope in the ill-lit, ill-paved, ill-ventilated courtyards that lay about Gerrard Street and Drury Lane at that time, we seem now to catch sight of her and then again to lose it. What makes the task of identification still more difficult is that she found it convenient at this time to change frequently from one set of clothes to another. Thus she often occurs in contemporary memoirs as "Lord" So-and-so, who was in fact her cousin; her bounty is ascribed to him, and it is he who is said to have written the poems that were really hers. She had, it seems, no difficulty in sustaining the different parts, for her sex changed far more frequently than those who have worn only one set of clothing can conceive; nor can there be any doubt that she reaped a twofold harvest by this device; the pleasures of life were increased and its experiences multiplied. From the probity of breeches she turned to the seductiveness of petticoats and enjoyed the love of both sexes equally.

So then one may sketch her spending her morning in a China robe of ambiguous gender among her books; then receiving a client or two (for she had many scores of suppliants) in the same garment; then she would take a turn in the garden and clip the nut trees—for which knee breeches were convenient; then she would change into a flowered taffeta which best suited a drive to Richmond and a proposal of marriage from some great nobleman; and so back again to town, where she would don a snuff-coloured gown like a lawyer's and visit the courts to hear how her cases were doing—for her fortune was wasting hourly and the suits seemed no nearer consummation than they had been a hundred years ago; and so, finally, when night came, she would more often than not become a nobleman complete from head to toe and walk the streets in search of adventure.

NAOMI ROYDE-SMITH (1875–1964)

From *The Tortoise-Shell Cat* (1925)

The prolific, now largely forgotten British novelist and playwright Naomi Royde-Smith was educated at Clapham High School and in Geneva. Between 1912 and 1922 she edited the literary magazine the *Westminster Gazette* and was responsible for publishing the first stories of Elizabeth Bowen and Rose Macaulay. She subsequently hosted an important weekly literary salon at her home in Kensington, cultivating friendships with the Sitwells, Walter de la Mare, Hugh Walpole, and Aldous Huxley. Virginia Woolf, who disliked her, offers a satiric portrait in her diary:

> We went to Miss Royde-Smith's party on Thursday to discuss Ireland. Never did I see a less attractive woman than Naomi. Her face might have been cut out of cardboard by blunt scissors. . . . She is slightly furred, too; dressed à la 1860. . . . There she sat in complete command. Here she had her world round her. It was a queer mixture of the intelligent and the respectable. . . . I detest the mixture of ideas and South Kensington.

Royde-Smith's first novel, *The Tortoise-Shell Cat*, appeared in in 1925; she married Ernest Milton in 1926. Over the next four decades she produced a steady stream of novels and plays—some forty-six in all. Historical and literary pastiches were a speciality: witness *The Private Life of Mrs. Siddons* (1933) and *Jane Fairfax* (1940), inspired by Austen's *Emma*.

Both *The Tortoise-Shell Cat* and *The Island* (1930), Royde-Smith's second novel, deal frankly (if negatively) with the lesbian theme. In *The Tortoise-Shell Cat*, excerpted below, an innocent young schoolteacher named Gillian moves into a seedy Chelsea women's residential club in the years before the First World War. She is immediately drawn into a destructive relationship with the older bohemian woman ("V.V.") who lives above her. With her lurid black-and-mauve apartment, decadent tastes, and dark hair "curled like breakers of the sea," the predatory V.V. is pure stereotype: one of that phalanx of lesbian grotesques—including Clare Hartill in Clemence Dane's *Regiment of Women*, Doris Kilman in Virginia Woolf's *Mrs. Dalloway*, Geraldine Manners in Rosamund Lehmann's *Dusty Answer*, and Angela Crossby in Radclyffe Hall's *The Well of Loneliness*—who inhabit so many British women's novels of the teens and twenties. But V.V.'s portrait seems particularly unforgiving: Jeannette Foster thought she might be drawn from life. Interestingly, Royde-Smith was one of the forty or so prominent writers and journalists who volunteered as potential defense witnesses during the obscenity trial of Radclyffe Hall's *The Well of Loneliness* in 1928.

FURTHER READING: Naomi Royde-Smith, *The Tortoise-Shell Cat* (London: Constable, 1925); *The Island* (New York: Harper and Row, 1930); Jeannette Foster, *Sex Variant Women in Literature* (1956; rpt. Tallahassee, Fla.; Naiad, 1985); Michael Baker, *Our Three Selves: The Life of Radclyffe Hall* (New York: William Morrow, 1985); Jane Emery, *Rose Macaulay: A Writer's Life* (London: John Murray, 1991).

She was sitting on her heels, having taken off her hat as soon as she was inside the gateway (Gillian never wore a hat a minute longer than she need, and not always so long as she should), and was watching the cat and admiring the bowl, when the door of the opposite building opened and a tall, dark woman came out and stood at the top of the steps.

Even before she came down to the courtyard and claimed it, Gillian knew that this was the owner of the china bowl, the Providence that dispensed clotted cream to dirty little strays. But as she came with a swift, steady stride, the free rapid movement of a woman who has been much with horses, who has ridden from childhood, Gillian also knew, with a thrill of recognition so strange, so new to her experience that the shock of it took away all sense of any other consideration, that she beheld in the flesh the very image of a perfection wrought by her own imaginings in the secret places of her dreaming mind. This was not a beautiful creature for all the world to see and gape at, it was the figure—unique of its kind—for which the shrine of her spirit had stood empty and waiting till now.

Dark hair "curled like breakers of the sea" away from a low brow under which clear, tawny eyes shone beneath fine, exquisitely arched eyebrows; a wide mouth parted like a ripe pomegranate in a smile that showed white, even teeth, each separated from its fellow; an impression of clear red and white in the complexion, and, above all, that swift, scythe-like movement from hip to knee as the figure approached her where she crouched on the doorstep beside the lapping, oblivious cat, these were the first things Gillian was aware of as she gazed stupidly upwards into the vivid face.

"Is this your little cat?"

The voice was a disappointment: flat, metallic, not coming from any depth, curiously old and lifeless for so vital-seeming a possessor.

"Oh no!" said Gillian, "we aren't allowed to keep cats in the Club; didn't you know?"

"Yes, I knew," said the stranger, "but I thought you might be keeping one."

"You must have thought I was behaving very badly to it," Gillian retorted, "if you've been feeding it too."

"Oh well, I saw it was hungry. It's been about for some days. I can see it from my window." She made no attempt to excuse herself for the implied charge of neglect. Gillian thought she couldn't have noticed it.

"I *heard* it," said Gillian. "I couldn't see it at first. It seems to prefer this side of the yard."

"Yes," said the stranger. "So you live in the Club?"

"I do," said Gillian, "my name is Gillian Armstrong."

"Do you spell it with a J?"

"No," said Gillian, "it's a soft G, like gillyflower. I can see you live in the Club," she went on, "because you've come out without a hat, but I've never seen you before. Are you a new member?"

"Yes, rather new. I came in last year. I know you quite well by sight. I see you from my window."

"That's because I don't have curtains across mine," said Gillian. "Up on the top floor it doesn't really seem necessary. And Mrs. Gordon told me, when I asked if people could see in from below, that she'd never seen nothing wrong in my rooms."

The other laughed, a short dry "honk" that added no more mirth to her steadily smiling eyes.

"Mrs. Gordon is a scream," she said, "so is Mr. Gordon. Do you like his dog?"

"No," said Gillian. "I can't bear Crack, and I don't think you'd better leave this lovely bowl down here. Crack will break it, you know."

The cat had licked the last smear of cream from the sides of the bowl, and was now rubbing itself round the stranger's ankles. Gillian with the bowl in her hands, stood up.

"Shall I wash it for you?" said she; "I'll do it with my tea-things and send it over by the maid who brings my dinner."

"Oh, don't let Mabel bring it," said the stranger, betraying what seemed to Gillian an extraordinary familiarity with the arrangements of the Club under which the four little housemaids revolved from floor to floor with each returning moon, so that you had the same maid for a month at a time and then passed into the hands of one of the other three. Gillian herself was quite incapable of finding out or of remembering which maid was waiting on any other floor but her own, though she had gathered from the verbosities of Mrs. Gordon that some floors were more popular with the servants than others, either because of the kindness of their occupiers or because of the more sensational furniture and adventures which occasionally distinguished one member from another in the gossip of the Club.

"Oh, I'm so sorry," she said. "Mabel is the rough one, she might drop it. How did you know it was Mabel's turn on our landing?"

"Mabel did my floor last month," said the stranger, "and she told me she was going to yours in time for the wedding."

Gillian knew that a wave of resentment flowed through some dim backwater of her mind at this intrusion, but it was drowned in the flood of expectation with which she accepted a suggestion that, if she really insisted on washing out the Chinese bowl, its owner would be delighted to see her with it in her own flat.

"My name is Victoria Vanderleyden," she said, "and I live at Number 36. Do come up to coffee."

Gillian had never been bidden to go anywhere "to coffee" before, but she took the formula to indicate that she would be expected immediately after dinner, and she accepted the invitation saying she would come as soon as she had turned the cat out for the night. For the cat was already inside the door, looking back over its shoulder, a little impatiently at Gillian, and plainly intending to dine with her that night also.

The door of Number 36 stood open and lamp-light poured out from the room over the dark landing where Gordon had not yet lit the gas-jet, when Gillian, carrying the china bowl and a bunch of purple centaureas from a basket of flowers which Sophie had left at the flat on her way from Glynde that afternoon, reached the third floor of the house across the courtyard, soon after eight o'clock.

It was, Gillian saw, one of the large, two-windowed rooms. The windows looked west-ward, across the tops of the trees in the gardens of Cheyne Row, and through them, lower than the lamplight, there still came the glow of a late, red sunset. Accustomed as she was to the roofs and chimneys of the street, or to the windows of the house across the courtyard as the familiar views from the Club windows, Gillian felt, as she entered this lit and quiet room, as though she were going into some far country.

Her own rooms and those of the Countess and of the Middletons, the only flats beside her own and Mrs. Barraclough's into which she had so far entered, were all colour-washed a uniform cream, with white paint on the doors and window-frames and skirting-boards; and this colour scheme was, so Mrs. Barraclough had told the Armstrongs when they took their flat, the rule of the Club.

But Miss Vanderleyden had evidently been allowed to break that rule, for her walls were tinted lavender, and all the woodwork that surrounded them was black. Long curtains, a shade darker than the walls, and touched by the sunset into a rosy mauve, hung at the windows, and two red, wooden candlesticks on the black chimney shelf matched two painted Norwegian chairs which stood on either side of a low black table. A wide divan against the wall at one end of the room was covered with black satin and heaped with red and green cushions, and the bare boards of the floor were black and shining. There were no pictures on the walls, but a mirror in a red frame hung from ceiling to floor between the windows, and over the fire-place there spread a fanshaped case in which hundreds of South Sea Island shells were ranged together in a geometrical pattern. Gillian looked for books, but there were none to be seen. "Perhaps she keeps them behind those strange curtains," she thought, noting that three of the far corners of the long room were curtained off with what was obviously stuff from Burnets in Garrick

Street, a shop into which Lilac, who preferred her cretonnes flowered, had definitely forbidden Gillian to go when they were furnishing Number Seven.

A strong smell of freshly made coffee filled the whole landing; but of Miss Vanderleyden herself there was no trace. Gillian crossed the room and went over to the open window. Between two blocks of houses she saw the river move, still burnished in the fading light, and voices rose faintly from the small gardens under the trees below, where the dwellers in Cheyne Row were sitting out in the cool of the day. In one of the gardens a row of Chinese lanterns had been festooned between the branches, and some one was lighting them as if in preparation for a festivity. One green, one orange and one variegated globe were already swinging in the dusk and Gillian was waiting with absorbed, delightful speculation as to the probable colour of the fourth lantern, when a sound close beside her made her turn. Miss Vanderleyden was standing by the table on which she had placed a Benares tray with coffee cups. She was gazing with lighted eyes, not at Gillian, but at her own reflection in the long, scarlet-rimmed mirror between the windows.

"Come and look," she said, without taking her eyes away from the glass before her.

Gillian obeyed. Miss Vanderleyden had taken the red candlesticks from over the fire-place and had lighted the tall, white candles they held and had placed them on the table so that their wavering flames lit up her face as she leaned between them. The door, still open behind her, showed the dark abyss of the unlit landing beyond, which repeated itself in profound obscurity in the depths of the looking-glass. Out of the heart of the darkness the vivid face floated mid-way on the surface of the mirror—wide, white brow, wide, luminous eyes, wide smiling mouth. Miss Vanderleyden had not changed the soft, dark, brown dress she had been wearing when they first met, and Gillian saw that the large, old-fashioned topaz brooch still fastening the lace at her throat was matched by a pair of heavy gold bracelets which she wore on either arm. The stones in these antique, fetter-like jewels threw out reflections into the mirror and seemed to illuminate the hands which, raised on their finger-tips from the dark surface of the table, as though each had a separate existence in the shadowy picture, completed without belonging to, the whole reflection.

"Look at yourself," laughed the mouth in the mirror, and the mirrored eyes met Gillian's as she gazed.

And Gillian saw herself, a moth-pale phantom behind the radiant head. Her white frock glimmered grey in the background, the candle-light glinted in her hair so faintly that its blondness looked silver above the molten glow of Miss Vanderleyden's topaz and gold. Only her rose-flushed cheeks, and the starry glitter of the eyes she hardly knew for hers, prevailed with the ardent image that challenged her, and proved her able to meet the challenge.

It was the first time in her experience of life that any direct personal appeal had aroused in her this profoundly personal, this intense and definitely physical reply. Miss Vanderleyden's look had, Gillian could see it in her own reflection, changed the colour of her face, the expression of her own eyes and lips. For a moment they stood side by side looking at themselves and at one another in the dark pool of the mirror, and then Miss Vanderleyden spoke.

"Aren't we a nice contrast?" she said in the same flat, shallow voice as had startled Gillian that afternoon with its audible contradiction of all that her eyes could see.

THOMAS BURKE (1886–1945)

"The Pash" (1926)

The novelist and short-story writer Thomas Burke, born in London in 1886 into a shabby-genteel family, found his primary literary inspiration in the city of his birth. In a series of works on urban themes—*Limehouse Nights* (1916), *Twinkletoes: A Tale of Limehouse* (1917), *More Limehouse Nights* (1921), *The Sun in Splendour* (1926), *East of Mansion House* (1926), and *The Real East End* (1932)—he depicted the rough-and-tumble life of London's poorer districts in a gritty and vernacular style owing much to Dickens and the late-nineteenth-century naturalists. In "The Pash," from *East of Mansion House*, the rendering of squalid factory setting and bitter love rivalry between a possessive welfare officer, Miriam Englefield, and the brutal Billy Fishpool over a young limekiln worker, Amy Rainbird, at times suggests a coarser, less metaphysical Lawrence. Yet Burke's story has its moments of delicacy too—as in the sympathetic handling of Miriam's baffled anguish when Amy begins walking out with Billy, or at the final tragic close.

   The use of the slang term "pash" in the title is evocative. In nineteenth-century British slang a "pash" was a small coin, a usage hinted at in the image of Miriam as the infatuated Amy's "silver sixpence." By the turn of the century, however, like "smash" and "crush" (and the German *Schwarm*) it had become a favorite term for feverish homoerotic passions—especially between schoolgirls, or between a girl and an older woman.

FURTHER READING: Thomas Burke, *East of Mansion House* (New York: George H. Doran, 1926); ——, *Son of London* (London: Herbert Jenkins, 1947); Malcolm M. Ferguson, "Thomas Burke of Limehouse," *Romantist* 2 (1978): 41–42; Nancy Sahli, "Smashing: Women's Relationships Before the Fall" *Chrysalis: A Magazine of Women's Culture* 8 (Summer 1979): 17–27.

It was certain that Amy Rainbird had a "pash" for Miss Englefield, the Welfare Officer. Susie Witchett had said so, and Susie saw not only what went on under her nose, but far beyond it. It was a long nose.

It beat her, though, what anybody could see in that Old Thing to rave about; and when little Amy discovered admirable traits in her, and began to rave, Susie looked at her with lowered eyes and chipped her. Susie couldn't understand it and what she couldn't understand she condemned. Why couldn't Amy be ordinary, and come out Sunday nights upon the hills, and have some fun with the boys, instead of always hanging round Miss Englefield? But Amy had no eye for the boys, and no ear for Susie's mutterings.

It was knocking off time, Saturday afternoon, and at the first howl of the hooter the gates of the Clutterfield factories came to life. Flour-faced men and women came from the limestone works. Boys and girls came spectrally from the kilns. Blackfaced men, raddled with sweat, came from the furnaces. Young girls, with yellow skins, came from the filling shed, moving like live things. Smokes from the bottle-necked chimneys wavered and curled among them in changing hues of saffron and olive. They hobbled on clogs or in father's boots, bickering. Their cheeks were harsh, their eyes shrewish, their hands chilblained. The soap advertisements on the walls that exhorted them to Keep That Schoolgirl Complexion were both inept and unkind.

In ones and twos they broke ranks and passed into the side-streets. At the doorways, flanked by the week's washing, children shrilled adenoidally and fought, finding in black mud the only brightness of their kingdom; and from knocker to knocker went the tallyman.

No place for pashes. But Amy Rainbird went through it undismayed. She was not beautiful, but she had youth and ardour, and her statuette figure moved through that crowd with something of the quality of a lantern in a mist. She was noticeable, and she had been noticed. She walked upright. Copper curls dressed her white face; keen eyes lent character to the slack mouth. The more volatile of the men, shaken out of their trolloping by her April ardour, spoke of her as a Nice Bit; she didn't know it, though. She had, as I say, no eye for the men; she had seen too much of them and their ways in home and factory. Assuming that all men were like the men she knew, she turned from their proffered attentions in disgust, and went steadily through them, and crossed to the opposite kerb, and stood looking right and left hungrily. Then, at the sight of a tall gaunt woman, her face lit up; her step took buoyancy; and she sped towards her like a child to a garden. The woman received her with an attitude of ownership, looking down at her with a tolerance that was almost mocking; and Amy was grateful for even this tolerance. To her, Miriam Englefield was not only the most wonderful thing in Clutterfield; she was the most wonderful thing in the world. She was rapture and adventure. Where others saw a tall woman with long face, aimless hands, tight mouth, and drooping eyes that stared always beyond, she saw a goddess. She saw what she sought. The blackest earth will throw up its flower; no corner is too dark to hide the silver sixpence from sharp eyes.

Miriam was her silver sixpence. Her early years had been steeped in smoke and ringed by uncomely spectacles; and she was at that age when girls of her class and temperament want what they call Life. She wanted blithe frocks and company; full contact with the world; Good Times; trips to London. She had no claim by merit or indulgence upon these things; she was set fitly in her station; but she wanted them and fretted for them, and at last, when her employers gave her a Welfare Worker, she found them. Against the dumpling minds of the people about her, the competence and self-sufficiency of Miriam Englefield shone and rang with refreshment for the heart and stimulus for the eye. So she turned to what she saw of beauty, and Susie's irony was toothless.

Miriam? Well, Susie had labelled Miriam, in her first week, a Bit of a Mystery. And Susie was right. She was a mystery to herself and to others. She was hard and cold; as hard as diamonds and with something of their tepid lustre; a good worker on her job but giving nothing beyond the job's requirements; finding nothing in the world that could move her from her state of shuttered calm, nor believing that the world held anything for her of delight or dismay. The other girls couldn't get near her; she wore icicles. But Amy. . . . Somehow the cow-eyed worship of this child *had* moved her. Against her will, she began to notice her, and to find something piquant in the pallor and the orange curls and the hungry face that one look or word of hers could feed. To her, as to Amy, Clutterfield was unkind. They met at a moment when both (one actively, the other unconsciously) were resentful of the smoke and the corroding round of the factory. By ironic chance, their tired eyes fell upon each other, and the thing played itself out as Susie said it would.

Arms linked, they went together down the Stewpony Road, the child of fourteen and the woman of forty, Amy looking up with worship, Miriam looking down with the casual approval of leader to follower. At the car terminus, they halted. Amy's road lay the other way, but always, when permitted, she walked with Miriam to the car, and lingered until she was dismissed. This afternoon the car was waiting; and as she turned regretfully to leave her idol she looked up to her and murmured "Good-bye, Miss Englefield." Then, shyly frivolous: "Happy dreams!"

Miriam gave her one of her white smiles. "You funny little friend! That's what your name means, you know. Amy—little friend. Would you like to be my little friend?"

"Oo—miss!" Paradise opened in her face.

"Call me Miriam if you like, child. That is, when we're not in the factory."

"Oo—Miriam! May I?"

An appraising look from Miriam. "What a funny baby you are! Would you like to come to tea with me to-morrow? You know my rooms? Branksome Street. Number Fifteen."

Amy slid home on the wind. The joy of looking at her beloved, and worshipping from a distance, was now crowned. The gate was opened. This shining creature had stooped and chosen her from other and better people as alone worth notice; had accepted her worship and was rewarding it with the glory of her actual presence. Her store of love had now a direction and a haven. Miriam wanted her. She made images of adventure and sent them floating along the pavement. Against the tormented horizons of Clutterfield she threw up bright dreams centring on Miriam, and saw Miriam as a spreading flower luminous in a midnight garden. She imagined herself rich, and bringing gifts to Miriam; thoughtful gifts; she imagined long talks with Miriam; saw herself saving Miriam from many complex deaths; being praised by Miriam and rebuked by Miriam. At home that night she took from her box a cluster of wax cherries that had fallen one day from Miriam's hat in the cloak-room; and timidly, daringly, she kissed them, and dreamed of to-morrow.

And on that Sunday afternoon she knew six hours of bliss. Six hours in that luminous garden. Six avalanches of confession and devout attention to Miriam's lightest word. Six hours of looking into that wonderful face, and sitting in that room of which every chair, every vase, every picture, every cushion, was Miriam. And under the adoring eyes Miriam sat thinking "Little Fool! Little Fool!"

Yet . . . in those six hours Miriam was conscious of a change. Something in the March beauty of this child, and her morning mind and profuse devotion, seized upon her and swayed her; brought back to her the unbusiness-like perfume of the Spring. She forgot herself and her self-sufficiency and her reserve. The Little Fool was so fresh, so much on tip-toe; so much in need of some star to follow, and so sure that Miriam was that star. There she sat, placing her heart for Miriam to pick up or kick aside.

Miriam picked it up.

All very well if it had stopped at that. But it didn't. After years of solitude, the sense of possession was inspiring. She began to take Amy in hand, and went to improving her speech and her manners and her dress. She lent her magazines and novelettes, and books of poetry by the easier poets, and sent her in for a course in the Pallas School of Memory Training and Efficiency. And when Amy bowed humbly to all reproof and exhortation, though she thought "Little Fool!" the thought was tempered; and she found that, having done so much for the child, she must do more. Soon they were always together, and Miriam felt herself drifting; being led by the child instead of leading; and at last there came an evening when the thing was out of her hands, and she found herself giving secret for secret, confidence for confidence.

She had been fitting Amy with a new frock, and at one moment of the fitting, she held her by the arms. The mutual touch of hand and arm startled them, and they broke away in awkward silence. When the fitting was done, they were still silent, and sat down by the fire, Amy saucer-eyed and meek; Miriam veiled. Then, by chance, each turned secretly to look at the other. Their eyes met, and for some seconds they held each other, telegraphing. Amy broke the spell.

With a queer gurgle she flung herself from the chair towards Miriam, and knelt before her with "Oh, Miriam! Oh, Miriam!" chanting the words. "You won't ever let's part, will you? Ever? It'd be awful without you." And Miriam, speaking from outside herself, cried, "Amy! Oh, Amy . . ." and their lips met and their arms closed upon treasure.

Well, that night the Pash was proclaimed. There was no more patronage of innocence by experience; no more welfare inspector and factory-hand. That night Miriam knew that she was beyond the reach of reason; that Amy was her world; that she would live for Amy; dream of Amy. She had descended from her heights, to snatch at an old dream, and she knew that she would never get back. But she was content; and all that evening she talked and gave her heart away; and in the morning, though she remembered what she had done, and all that it implied, she was not dismayed. She knew that she rejoiced in the idea of Amy as Amy rejoiced in the idea of her.

All through that summer this bond—limp as milk, active as jelly—held them. Evening walks and Sunday teas became fixtures; every parting at night was a heartache. Every Saturday they took the train to Brundle, and had tea there; and paraded the Wide Walk with the young pride of the town; and Susie Witchett became balder and balder in her comments. But they were not as other girl-couples; they had no backward glances for the boys; and even at the Elysée de Danse they danced always together. The factory day became for each of them a necklace of adventure, to be told bead by bead. There were encounters in the corridors—smiles—slippings of notes—flowers for Miriam's table—long walks at night, hand in hand under crimson skies and above valleys that were whirlpools of smoke and glittering windows and flame. Amy's pale face began to wear a bloom; her clear eyes became dusky with wisdom. All life seemed to lie in the drowsy perfume of lavender that came from Miriam's dress; a perfume that set her trembling at every meeting; and she sobbed in her prayers at night for the gift of Miriam's friendship.

But her worship did more than she knew. She brought a battery to a sluggish pulse, and under its touch the pulse stirred and drummed. Her friendship was April; Miriam's was Indian summer. Amy was resilient; Miriam rigid; and Miriam began to hold her in bondage. This was no more a Little Fool, but a treasure to be hoarded. When other girls talked to Amy, or tried to draw her into their parties, she became peremptory. If any boy passed a salutation her eyes went hard; she fumed and fidgeted. Amy's friendship was flame and flash; it had brought something at once vital and restful into her days. At last she found what she had never dared hope for—a friend with a child's beauty and love's mind who could understand the dreams and desires that in a grown woman were ludicrous and shameful; and at the mere thought of losing that wild-flower beauty, she knew fury and dismay. New forces, new passions, from which her level life had protected her, now began to grow. She who had been indifferent to all affection now knew that she had surrendered all hope of peace to the whims of a child.

She began to be bitterly afraid, and to wonder—How long will it last? Will it. . . . ? If it. . . . Oh, my God!

Nature and Billy Fishpool answered her.

One evening, after work, the Little Fool came to Branksome street babbling and singing of a boy.

"Comes from Liverpool, Miriam . . . William Fishpool his name is, but everybody calls him Billy . . . You know him I expect . . . He's in the filling shed t'other—I mean, the other side of the yard. . . . Boy with dark curly hair . . . Always laughing. . . . He's asked me to go to the pictures with him. He says I've got the prettiest eyes in Clutter-field. . . . He looks awfully smart when he's got his best things on, but I like him best when he's working in the yard. . . . He ain't half—I mean, he's awfully strong. . . . I see him—I mean, I saw him lift one of the spudders in the yard and hold it out straight for nearly a minute. . . . He smokes a pipe. . . . He says he likes the way I do my hair. . . . He says . . ."

You know the sort of thing. Miriam, tight-lipped, listened without comment. Once or twice she turned the talk to other matters, but, strangely, all topics impinged at some point or other on Billy Fishpool. At last she dismissed Amy, curtly, and noted that Amy went, not, as at other times, grieved at being shut out of paradise, but brightly, as though to some secret storehouse.

When she was gone, Miriam sat rigid for an hour, staring into the fire and twisting her limp hands. It had come. She had lost her. And not only that. Amy had made her a gift of her love to play with, and she had thought to amuse herself with it, to ease her mind with borrowings from its fresh ripple. But now . . . now it was she who had given her heart into childish hands that would tear it to pieces. She felt suddenly as though she were on a rocking boat.

For two evenings that week Amy was missing. On the Wednesday she came as usual, her eyes bright and set. She said nothing of boys, but sat in her customary place at Miriam's feet, resting her face on Miriam's knees, and glowing with subdued colour, as through a bridal veil. Miriam had to prompt her. Then it came in a cascade, bubbling and falling and . . .

It was only stopped by the sight of Miriam's long white face and twisting fingers.

"Why—Miriam, dear—what's the matter? Whatever's the matter?"

There was a scene; a flood of sobs and phrases; a struggle. Before Amy knew what the trouble was, they were quarrelling. Like most quiet people they started suddenly on the topmost note. They stormed at each other. Their tones cranked. Miriam was like a cat when a bird is taken from it. She turned on Amy a flame of fury. She wept and pleaded. She took the child by the shoulders and shook her. Her face had the hue of red cabbage.

"Amy! Amy! He can't have you.

"He can't! I won't have it. I won't have you going with boys.

"You're mine! You belong to me. Not a silly clod like him. Have you forgotten—!

"Amy—you can't go. You can't leave me. You're the only thing I've got. The only thing I ever loved. *Amy!*"

Her voice went suddenly bleak; then failed. She knelt to Amy with begging hands and whispered, "You're mine, dear. You know you are. Nobody else can have you."

But Amy couldn't see it. Something had happened that had changed her from a Lit-tle Fool, and she stared back at Miriam's antics. As though she were seeing her for the first time, and seeing her suddenly as something small. And when Miriam shook her, and put a tight arm round her neck, and almost wrestled with her, Amy was indignant. She broke free and moved round the table. It seemed that in three days she had achieved competency and self-sufficiency.

"Miriam!" The tones registered surprise and pain. "Whatever's up wi' you, Miriam? What you mean gittin' 'old o' me like that? What you mean—you won't have it? Who are you to say that? I'm not under your orders."

Miriam was gulping. "Mean? What do I mean? You . . . you . . . You—coming here and pretending and—and—and getting what you can—and then—then, when you're tired—you—you leave me for some guttersnipe from the yard. And—and—" She became operatic. "And after all you've said to me. Here. In this room. At nights. All the things you said. About us always being together. The way you came with your sawniness—and—and your innocence and—and—All lies, I suppose it was. Eh? Lies! Just to get what you could out of me. Eh?" She ended on a muffled scream. "You—beast!"

But love had come to Amy, and she hardly followed the outburst. Her worship of Miriam seemed now nothing but a moment's enthusiasm; something behind her that neither of them could be expected to take seriously.

"Why, Miriam . . . Why, I never thought you'd be like this about it . . . Here—don't be silly. Talking like that. Anybody'd think you owned me. That was just my silly-kid ways. Sloppiness. All that poetry and stuff. You don't know what love is. I didn't until now. You didn't ought to 'ave let me talk like that."

"Let? Let? You—you little back-street kid—come to me like you came, and—How was I to know you was pretending? Oh, you little fool. Haven't I got a right? Haven't I made you what you are? Taught you to speak properly. Taught you to dress. Taught you to behave. And now—oh!"

She collapsed, then, and moaned; and at that Amy went to her, and put a hand that was meant to be kind, but was patronising, on her shoulder. "Miriam. I say—Miriam. Here. . . . We shall always be friends."

She calmed a little. She saw a last chance. She took Amy's hand and pressed it. She said she was sorry for what had just happened. She was all worked up, because Amy's friendship meant so much to her. She asked Amy to forget it, and Amy gave her a return squeeze, and sat again at her feet, ready to talk sensibly about Billy. She didn't understand this upheaval, and she really couldn't bother to try. There were more important things.

Miriam, cunning, let her talk. And as the room became dusky and intimate, she dropped words upon Amy. She kept herself out of it, and moralised. Her Little Fool had brought her the tidings of first love; and all that evening, through the twilight, she curdled it with doubt and diffidence. She gathered back the reserve she had lately scattered, and became her old self.

"You see, child, he's a man. Men are different. They don't feel as we do. Love doesn't last with them. They soon get used to it. Make it part of everyday, and then

. . . But as long as you're happy I shan't mind. I expect Billy's different from other men—not such a brute. If he loves you, you'll enjoy washing his clothes and getting his dinner and cleaning the house, and you won't want all the other things. If you can only be sure he's different . . ."

"Oh, he is, Miriam. He is." Within an hour Amy was once again under the influence, and the evening ended in calm and the old domination. Miriam thought she had won.

But that evening was their last. Next morning, in the cold air of October, Billy stepped again into Amy's heart, and she was filled with self-loathing. Looking back at that muggy friendship and the frigid kisses, she felt as though she had fallen into a weedy pond; she wanted to wipe out all memory of it; and when that night she met Billy, and told him of the outburst, and heard his comments on it, his lucid passion cleansed and calmed her. After Miriam, he was as commonplace and sweet as running water.

But Miriam was not plastic. She had no running water to cleanse and calm her; only herself and her thoughts for company; and after meeting Amy and Billy in the street, and receiving turned heads, she knew that she was alone again. It hadn't mattered before, but now something was gone from her and Amy had taken it. Days began to stretch before her like deserts—deserts that had once been green; and Amy loomed in them, and her shadow covered them. She could not turn to novels or poetry or to the streets or to the pictures. Her mind was set wholly upon an adoring and adorable Little Fool; upon the sound of her step on the stairs; upon the warmth of her pale face as she moved chattering about the room, or stood, poised and vibrant in mignon beauty, by the fireplace. The fire was out; but she would still stare at its ghost, and stretch her hands to the cold bars.

She took to wandering about the outskirts of Clutterfield, early and late. On the hills above the valley of flame and smoke, where she had perversely found beauty, she sought now for comfort and inspiration, and in the fantasia of slag-heaps and gasping furnaces she pretended to find symbols of her own state. Even at midnight, when the town's voice was hushed, the valley had not the peace of a village or the suspense of a great city, but lay petulant, waving red tongues, a venomous animal cowed. Like herself.

That guttersnipe. To come between her and her beauty, putting his great hands on her treasure, and claiming it for his own. To take the sensitive plant she had tended so delicately, and set it in coarse ground and fertilise it with worldly knowledge. To soil that grace and purity with his harsh humour. To kiss those orange curls. To poison her against her best friend. Somewhere about the town he would be walking with Amy; and she knew that her own confidences were now doormats for the feet of the boy and girl. And through the nights she gnawed her hands, and called, "Amy! Oh, Amy—you're mine—you're mine!"

But in the factory she took trouble to avoid her. Once or twice, in yard or corridor, they met, and Amy gave her glances that were on the edge of mockery; and other girls noted, and Susie said, that she looked at Amy as though she would like to whip her.

From this thought she drew some solace, and comforted the lonely nights with fancies of Amy returning to her, penitent, and of shaming the child with forgiving kisses.

It couldn't go on like this, though. Somehow she must get her back, or something must happen to end it. She couldn't drag through days and days this clotted longing and despair. And all through that Little Fool. To think that all this misery and self-hatred and horror could be lifted by one movement from a silly factory girl. A life at the mercy of a kid. Somehow it must be snapped short and sharp. Only the faith that something would happen to end it sustained her under its burden. She created the fancy of their dying together. Of compelling Amy to go with her to Skegness, for a last Sunday, and there taking her with her into the sea. Like the poem they'd read together. "She's mine. She must come back. She must."

But she didn't. These things seldom round themselves off like poems.

It was late afternoon in November when the end came. The explosion began in the mixing-shed. There was no warning; no first flash or single detonation, but one boom that shook buildings within a mile and broke windows within many miles; and the shed went up. In a few seconds the air was filled with dust and chipped glass and stones and splinters of steel. The ground was littered with broken men. Three seconds later, many bells rang—alarm-bells, fire-bells, dinner-bells, hooters. From other sheds the workpeople came in clusters. About them moved agitated foremen seeking to hold them in order, calling for positions of fire-drill, and crying—"Safety Shelters! Safety Shelters!"

But rules were forgotten; were, indeed, useless; for, following the great explosion came a wind—a whirr—a flash—a fugue of falling bricks—and darkness covered the laboratory and the power-plant. Random cartridges fired themselves among the crowd. Through the dark, streaked by fire, moved terrible figures, stumbling and falling.

At the first boom, Miriam, they say, went from her office to attend the girls, with the steady step of one who knew her job and was going to do it. In the first shed there were no girls to attend; only a mass of twisted steel and still forms. She went to the second—empty; to the third—that, too, was empty.

In the uncertain light she stood still, peering about her.

She was last seen by Susie Witchett who made picturesque remarks about the sort of figure she cut standing there in that light among those things, and staring as though she was looking for somebody.

And Susie says that while Miriam was standing there a little girl came round a corner, babbling, and fell upon her and kept crying, "Oh, Miriam—save me, save me. Oh, Miriam!" And that while Miriam was holding the girl in her arms and kissing her, a young fellow came up, and got hold of the girl, and pulled her away; and Miriam pulled her back, and the girl held on to her, taking no notice of the boy, and only whimpering "Miriam—oh, Miriam!" And she heard the boy shout, "Let 'er go, damn you. She's my girl. Let 'er go!" But the girl went on saying, "Miriam—I wanta die with Miriam. Oh, Miriam!"

And then, she says, the young chap went for Miriam, as though she were a man. Went straight at her, and they wrestled, and at last he got hold of the girl, and got Miriam down, and picked the girl up, and ran. And Susie ran too. Only just in time. For twenty seconds later there was a red flare and a bang; and where they'd been wrestling there was nothing.

Next morning Susie wanted to know all about it. "How did Miss Englefield come to be killed right outside the safety-shed? Why didn't she go inside? What was she waiting for? What was you all fighting about?"

But Amy Rainbird was suddenly grown-up and reserved. "How should I know? Lorst her nerve, I s'pose. She was a bit loopy, really, when you got to know her. Billy Fishpool says—"

ÉDOUARD BOURDET (1887–1945)

From *The Captive* (1926)

Given the furor surrounding the publication of Radclyffe Hall's *The Well of Loneliness* in 1928, it is sometimes difficult to remember that Hall's novel was not the only lesbian-themed work to create a scandal in the 1920s. Édouard Bourdet's play *La Prisonnière* (*The Captive*), an Ibsenesque shocker about a young woman's sexual obsession with the wife of her fiancé's boyhood friend, preceded *The Well* by three years and was every bit as notorious in its day. A smash hit in Paris, Brussels, and Berlin, despite numerous attempts by political and religious leaders to close it down, it was banned outright in England and raided by police during its sellout run at the Empire Theater in New York in 1927. Along with Mae West's *The Drag*—a comedy-drama about male homosexuality that played in New York the same season—Bourdet's play was responsible for the passage of the so-called Wales Padlock Law, an amendment to the New York state penal code specifically barring plays "depicting or dealing with, the subject of sex degeneracy, or sex perversion." Once on the books, the law helped to keep explicitly gay-themed plays off the stage in the United States for the next forty years.

One can see what the fuss was about: *The Captive* is a well-constructed and effective piece of drama and, for the most part, its author takes an unusually worldly and nonjudgmental view of his characters. Bourdet, a popular playwright of the twenties and thirties and later head of the Comédie Française, claimed that he had been inspired to write the work after meeting a man who had suffered a humiliation similar to that of D'Aiguines, the hapless husband whose wife seduces the play's youthful heroine, Irène de Montcel. Yet if anything the sympathetic focus of the drama falls on Irène, unable to free herself of her infatuation for the invisible Mme. D'Aiguines. (It was Bourdet's brilliant dramatic ploy never to have Mme. D'Aiguines appear onstage.) When the play first ran in France, some critics compared Irène to Racine's Phèdre; after its opening in New York, its star, the actress Helen Mencken, received "on the average fifty letters a day" from lovestruck girls inspired by her portrayal of the heroine. At this late date it is difficult not to hear in the play's final slamming door—as Irène abandons her fiancé forever and rushes off in search of her female lover—both the obvious echo of *A Doll's House* and a portent, perhaps, of less equivocal liberations.

The play's first big revelation scene occurs in act 2. In the excerpt below, Jacques Virieu—fiancé to the affectionate but oddly skittish Irène—fears that a boyhood friend whom he has not seen for many years, the wealthy D'Aiguines, may be Irène's secret lover. He summons D'Aiguines to his house and confronts him with his suspicions. D'Aiguines disabuses him in short order, warning him of the dire fate that befalls any man who tries to interfere in the demonic relations of "two beings" who should be "left to dwell alone among themselves in the kingdom of shadows!" D'Aiguines knows from bitter experience: his own wife is just such a "phantom"—one who can "poison and pillage everything before the man whose home she destroys is even aware of what's happening to him."

FURTHER READING: Édouard Bourdet, *La Prisonnière* (Paris: L. Billaudot, 1926); —, *The Captive*, trans. Arthur Hornblow Jr. (New York: Brentano, 1927); Jonathan Ned Katz, *Gay American History* (New York: Crowell, 1976), pp. 83–91; Kaier Curtin, *"We Can Always Call Them Bulgarians": The Emergence of Lesbians and Gay Men on the American Stage* (Boston: Alyson Publications, 1987); Sherrie A. Inness, "Who's Afraid of Stephen Gordon: The Lesbian in the United States Popular Imagination," *National Women's Studies Association Journal* 4 (1992): 303–20.

JACQUES: [*Talking off*]
   Would you mind coming in here, monsieur?
[Jacques *moves a little away from door.* D'Aiguines *enters past him and turns to* Jacques *with outstretched hand*]
D'AIGUINES: How are you, old boy?
JACQUES: Why, it's—
D'AIGUINES: Of course it is! Didn't you know you were writing to me?
JACQUES: Why, no, otherwise—
D'AIGUINES: Otherwise you wouldn't have been so formal, I hope. But didn't my name mean anything to you?
JACQUES: Of course. But I was led to believe that the D'Aiguines I had to deal with was somewhat older.
D'AIGUINES: Somewhat older? Why?
JACQUES: Well, it doesn't matter. I remember you had some cousins. I thought perhaps it might be one of them.
D'AIGUINES: Ah? . . . But what's the reason for—
JACQUES: I'll tell you.
[*Pause*]
   Do sit down!

D'AIGUINES: [*Puts hat and gloves on desk*]

You're looking at me? ... You find I've changed, eh? ... I'm sure you'd hardly have recognized me?

JACQUES: Yes. . . . I would have.

D'AIGUINES: Good Lord, it's something like twenty years since we've seen each other. Not since the days when we wore our trousers out sitting on the same bench at school. Twenty years leave their mark! On some people at least. . . . But you've hardly changed. I'm very glad to see you again, old chap.

JACQUES: Thanks.

D'AIGUINES: It's strange we shouldn't have met. Of course I haven't been in France much. What have you been doing? Weren't you in Morocco for a time?

JACQUES: Yes.

D'AIGUINES: Who was it told me so?

[*A pause*]

... Ah, yes, I remember; it was Sicard—you remember him—fat Sicard? I met him one day in Madrid. We were staying at the same hotel. He had just returned from Africa, I think, and had seen you there.

JACQUES: Yes.

D'AIGUINES: And now you're living here altogether?

JACQUES: Yes.

D'AIGUINES: Damn funny thing, life. You really didn't know that the D'Aiguines you were writing to for an appointment was I?

JACQUES: No.

D'AIGUINES: Well, the minute I saw your signature I didn't hesitate. That's why I came here right away. If Jacques Virieu wanted to see me I certainly couldn't keep him waiting!

JACQUES: [*Pause*]

Is that the only reason you came here right away?

D'AIGUINES: [*Surprised*]

Good Lord! Since I haven't the least idea what you have to say to me—

JACQUES: You haven't the least idea?

D'AIGUINES: Why, of course not—no.

JACQUES: Ah . . . ?

D'AIGUINES: Well, look here, you arouse my curiosity! Upon my word, you sit there looking like a judge! Come, what's it all about?

JACQUES: Whom is it all about, might be better.

D'AIGUINES: Whom? ... All right, if you prefer it. Well, then, whom is it all about?

JACQUES: [*Pause*]

About Irène de Montcel.

D'AIGUINES: [*Amazed and annoyed*]

Irène de Montcel?

JACQUES: Yes.

[*Pause*]

 You seem to begin to understand!

D'AIGUINES: No. What can you have to say to me about Mademoiselle de Montcel?

JACQUES: You can't guess?

D'AIGUINES: No, I can't!

JACQUES: I'm a distant cousin of hers. But what's more important is that I've been a friend of hers for a long time. One of her best friends—I might even say her best friend, if you wish.

D'AIGUINES: Well?

JACQUES: You knew that, didn't you?

D'AIGUINES: I didn't even know you were acquainted.

JACQUES: Have you never heard her speak of me?

D'AIGUINES: Never.

JACQUES: She hasn't even spoken of the—rôle that some one was playing for her at the present time?

D'AIGUINES: What rôle?

JACQUES: Don't you know that some one is pretending to Irène's father to be engaged to her, or something of the sort?

D'AIGUINES: Engaged to her?

JACQUES: To ward off her father's suspicions; and to permit her to remain in Paris, yes.

D'AIGUINES: [*Pause*]

 She asked you to do that?

JACQUES: Yes.

D'AIGUINES: Did you do it?

JACQUES: Yes.

[*Pause*]

 You knew nothing about all that?

D'AIGUINES: I? Why, of course, I didn't!

JACQUES: Really! I had somehow imagined that you would have known about it.

D'AIGUINES: What are you driving at?

JACQUES: I merely wanted to let you know by what right I say what I shall have to say to you about her.

D'AIGUINES: That's all very well—but I've no right to listen to what you may have to say about the young lady.

[*Rises*]

JACQUES: Sit down, please.

D'AIGUINES: [*Disturbed*]

 What for? I tell you again that it's something which doesn't concern me.

JACQUES: Steady! Otherwise, I'll be forced to think it's something which concerns you deeply.

D'AIGUINES: [*Feelingly*]

What do you mean?

JACQUES: I mean that a suspicion I had before your arrival has become a conviction in the last five minutes.

D'AIGUINES: All right—keep your suspicions to yourself, and allow me to leave?

JACQUES: [*Standing between the door and* D'Aiguines]

I swear that you'll listen to me!

D'AIGUINES: Good God! Are you crazy?

JACQUES: No.

D'AIGUINES: You insist upon my listening to you?

JACQUES: [*Vehemently*]

Yes!

D'AIGUINES: You're wrong, I tell you!

JACQUES: We'll see as to that.

D'AIGUINES: Very well, I've warned you. Do as you like. . . .

JACQUES: I shan't take long, don't worry. If—contrary to what I think—what I have to say doesn't apply to you, at least you'll know to whom it should be repeated. When a man occupies in a girl's life the place which the person I'm referring to occupies in Irène's life—when he makes her do or lets her do what she has done in order not to be separated from him—he has no valid excuse, none, do you hear, for not marrying her. That is to say, if he's free. If he isn't, then he must take steps to become so, at no matter what cost and at the earliest possible moment. Now you have it.

D'AIGUINES: [*Pause*]

Is that all?

JACQUES: Well, just about. For I shouldn't like to think that the person in question were a man without honor. If that were the case then the duty of a friend is clear; to warn Montcel to protect his daughter. But I hope it won't be necessary to go to that extreme.

D'AIGUINES: Have you quite finished this time?

JACQUES: Yes.

D'AIGUINES: Then, unless I'm crazy I must conclude that you believe me to be Mademoiselle de Montcel's lover or something of the sort. That's it, isn't it?

JACQUES: That is the most likely supposition, yes. . . .

D'AIGUINES: [*Earnestly*]

Well, then look at me and despite the high strung condition you seem to be in, try to see things clearly. I give you my word of honor that you're mistaken. I am not and never have been anything but an acquaintance of hers, do you hear . . . not even a friend. You can believe me or not, that's your affair. That's all I've got to say. And please understand that if I've taken the trouble of replying to you at all instead of treating you like a lunatic and leaving here without a word, it's solely because of our old friendship.

JACQUES: [*Impressed by* D'Aiguines' *truthful attitude, but despairing*]

Then . . . who is it?

D'AIGUINES: How should I know? . . . Has she a lover?

JACQUES: Yes.

D'AIGUINES: Did she tell you so?

JACQUES: She let me believe it—which amounts to the same thing.

D'AIGUINES: Not always. You may be too hasty in drawing conclusions.

JACQUES: Well, it's the only possible explanation. If it weren't true, she'd have said so. She couldn't have doubted for a moment that I was convinced of it.

D'AIGUINES: [*Pause*]

Well, in any case, I'm sorry, but I can give you no information. And if you've nothing more to say. . . .

JACQUES: You're not going?

D'AIGUINES: I must. I came as soon as I got your note but I'm leaving Paris in a few days and I've a great deal to do.

JACQUES: Don't go, I beg you! You're the only one who can help me find this man and I *must* find him.

D'AIGUINES: But since I know nothing—

JACQUES: That's not possible! You must have some idea, some suspicion. Seeing her constantly . . . knowing the sort of life she leads . . . whom she sees. . . .

D'AIGUINES: But you're wrong. I don't see her constantly. Once in a while she goes out with us—but I've much less in common with her than you seem to think—

JACQUES: How can that be? You're almost the only people she ever sees—she spends all her time at your house. You can't help knowing *something!*

D'AIGUINES: [*Coldly, not looking at* Jacques]

I know nothing.

JACQUES: I don't believe you!

D'AIGUINES: See here! That's quite enough—

JACQUES: I believed you a moment ago, believed you without proof, when you said you were not her lover. You were telling the truth then. Now, you're not, you're lying. You're lying so as not to betray the secret of some one who is probably your friend. That's it, isn't it?

D'AIGUINES: I know nothing.

JACQUES: Listen: just tell me that he's a decent chap and that he'll marry her—and I'll ask you nothing more.

D'AIGUINES: I have nothing to say. I know nothing.

JACQUES: But don't you understand that this poor girl must be saved, that she can't be allowed to go more deeply every day into an affair that is ruining her! . . . And if it were only that! She has already begun to suffer. What's going on? . . . Has she felt that he wants to be rid of her? I don't know. But what I *do* know is that she spends her time locked in her room, sobbing. That's what she has come to!

D'AIGUINES: Oh! . . .

[*Gesture*]

JACQUES: That doesn't worry you, eh? Well it does me! I'd give my life, do you hear, my life, to make her happy.

D'AIGUINES: [*Looks at him in surprise*]

You mean to say you love her?

JACQUES: I am her friend.

D'AIGUINES: Answer me. One doesn't do what you have done out of mere friend-ship—nor go through with a thing like this pretended engagement. You love her?

JACQUES: Very well, then, I do love her. I've loved her for ten years, and I'll never love any one else. What of it?

D'AIGUINES: You love her? Is that true?

JACQUES: Yes!

D'AIGUINES: Then for Christ's sake, get away from here! Get away! It doesn't matter where—as far as you can and stay away as long as you can! Don't come back until you're cured! That's all I can say!

JACQUES: What do you mean?

D'AIGUINES: I'm giving you some advice, good advice, that's all.

JACQUES: You're going to explain to me exactly what you mean! Aren't you?

D'AIGUINES: [*With hesitation*]

Why—there's nothing to explain—You love this young woman and from what you tell me I gather she loves some one else. That being the case, the best thing to do is clear out. Don't you agree with me?

JACQUES: Clear out and leave her in the hands of some rotter, probably—some rotter who wanted her and so made her believe he'd marry her.

D'AIGUINES: Is she really so simple as that?

JACQUES: A woman is always that the first time she's in love. This is her first experi-ence, I have reasons to know that. If she had loved any one before this, I'd proba-bly have been the man. I adored her and until last year I lived in the hope that some day she'd be my wife. And she would have been, do you hear, if this other man hadn't appeared. I didn't fight against it, there was no use. But since he's been the means of making me unhappy, at least I want him to be the means of making her happy. To do that I must find him.

D'AIGUINES: You can do nothing for her.

JACQUES: How do you know?

D'AIGUINES: No one can do anything for her.

JACQUES: Why?

[D'Aiguines *gestures, but remains silent*]

Ah! You made a slip there! You're not going to keep on pretending that you don't know how things are! You can't keep silent any longer!

D'AIGUINES: Leave her alone! Don't meddle in this, believe me! And don't ask me anything more!

JACQUES: Look here, you don't suppose I'm going to be satisfied with vague warnings that can have only one effect: making me more anxious than ever! I'm not asking for advice, I'm demanding a name!

D'AIGUINES: [*Abruptly*]

The name of her lover? She has no lover! Now, are you satisfied?

JACQUES: What?

D'AIGUINES: It might be better for her if she had one!

JACQUES: I don't understand.

D'AIGUINES: A woman can free herself from a lover—even if he's the worst scoundrel living. She can get over it. Whereas in *her* case—

JACQUES: In her case, what? Finish!

D'AIGUINES: Hers is quite another kind of bondage. . . . And that kind—

[*Gesture*]

JACQUES: Another kind of bondage?

D'AIGUINES: Yes. It is not only a *man* who may be dangerous to a woman. . . . In some cases it can be another woman.

JACQUES: Another *woman?*

D'AIGUINES: Yes.

JACQUES: What are you talking about? You mean to say it's on account of a woman that Irène refused to go with her father to Rome?

D'AIGUINES: Yes.

JACQUES: It's on account of a *woman* that she spends her time crying?

D'AIGUINES: Yes.

JACQUES: What kind of story is this?

D'AIGUINES. The kind of story that often happens—regardless of what men think. The kind of story that people don't believe for the most part, or which makes them smile, half amused and half indulgent.

JACQUES: But it's impossible! Irène is much too well balanced.

D'AIGUINES: What does that prove?

JACQUES: Are you positive of this?

D'AIGUINES: Yes.

JACQUES: Do you—know this woman?

D'AIGUINES: Yes.

[*Looks at* Jacques *quickly, and sees that the latter is not observing him. A great sadness crosses his face*]

I know her.

JACQUES: [*After a moment*]

I am dumbfounded—

D'AIGUINES: And a little relieved . . . aren't you?

JACQUES: Well, good Lord! After what I had feared! . . .

D'AIGUINES: So you'd prefer—?

[*Pause*]

Well, you're wrong to prefer it!

JACQUES: You'd rather she had a lover?

D'AIGUINES: In your place? Yes! A hundred, a thousand times rather!

JACQUES: Are you mad?

D'AIGUINES: It's you who are mad. If she had a lover I'd say to you: Patience, my boy, patience and courage. Your cause isn't lost. No man lasts forever in a woman's life. You love her and she'll come back to you if you know how to wait. . . . But in this case I say: Don't wait! There's no use. She'll never return—and if ever your paths should cross again fly from her, fly from her . . . do you hear? Otherwise you are lost! Otherwise you'll spend your existence pursuing a phantom which you can never overtake. One can never overtake them! They are shadows. They must be left to dwell alone among themselves in the kingdom of shadows! Don't go near them . . . they're a menace! Above all, never try to be anything to them, no matter how little—that's where the danger lies. For, after all, they have some need of us in their lives . . . it isn't always easy for a woman to get along. So if a man offers to help her, to share with her what he has, and to give her his name, naturally she accepts. What difference can it make to her? So long as he doesn't exact love, she's not concerned about the rest. Only, can you imagine the existence of a man if he has the misfortune to love—to adore a *shadow* near whom he lives? Tell me, can you imagine what that's like? Take my word for it, old man, it's a rotten life! One's used up quickly by that game. One gets old in no time—and at thirty-five, look for yourself, one's hair is gray!

JACQUES: Do you mean—?

D'AIGUINES: Yes. And I hope you'll profit by my example. Understand this. they are not for us. They must be shunned, left alone. Don't make my mistake. Don't say, as I said in a situation almost like yours, don't say: "Oh, it's nothing but a sort of ardent friendship—an affectionate intimacy . . . nothing very serious . . . we know all about that sort of thing!" No! We don't know *anything* about it! We can't begin to know what it is. It's mysterious—terrible! Friendship, yes—that's the mask. Under cover of friendship a woman can enter any household, whenever and however she pleases—at any hour of the day—she can poison and pillage everything before the man whose home she destroys is even aware of what's happening to him. When finally he realizes things it's too late—he is alone! Alone in the face of a secret alliance of two beings who understand one another because they're alike, because they're of the same sex, because they're of a different planet than he, the stranger, the enemy! Ah! if a *man* tries to steal your woman you can defend yourself, you can fight him on even terms, you can smash his face in. But in this case—there's nothing to be done—but *get out* while you still have strength to do it! And that's what you've got to do!

JACQUES: . . . Why don't you get out yourself?

D'AIGUINES: Oh, with me it's different. I can't leave her now. We've been married eight years. Where would she go? . . . Besides it's too late. I couldn't live without her any more. What can I do—I love her? . . .

[*Pause*]

You've never seen her?

[Jacques *shakes his head*]

You'd understand better if you knew her. She has all the feminine allurements, every one. As soon as one is near her, one feels—how shall I say it—a sort of deep charm. Not only I feel it. Every one feels it. But I more than the rest because I live near her. I really believe she is the most harmonious being that has ever breathed. . . . Sometimes when I'm away from her, I have the strength to hate her for all the harm she has done me . . . but, with her, I don't struggle. I look at her . . . I listen to her . . . I worship her. You see?

JACQUES: [*Pursuing an idea*]

Tell me . . . why is Irène suffering?

D'AIGUINES: I don't know.

[*Rises*]

You don't suppose I'm confided in, do you? She is suffering probably, as the weak always do, struggling with a stronger nature until they give in.

JACQUES: You think Irène is weak?

D'AIGUINES: Compared to the other? Oh, yes.

[*Pause*]

She is probably still struggling.

JACQUES: Ah!

[*Pause*]

So that's why she is unhappy?

[*Rises*]

D'AIGUINES: For that reason—or some other. She has many to choose from.

JACQUES: You mean—?

D'AIGUINES: Why shouldn't she suffer? I suffer, don't I?

JACQUES: That's not the same thing.

D'AIGUINES: You think so, do you? Well, on the contrary, I believe it's very much the same thing. There's only one way to love, you see, and one way to suffer. It's the same formula for everybody—and in that respect she and I have been in the same boat for some time. Only she hasn't got used to it yet—and I have.

JACQUES: I don't quite follow you.

D'AIGUINES: Haven't you heard any mention of a cruise?

JACQUES: A cruise?

D'AIGUINES: Yes. In the Mediterranean . . . on a yacht, an American yacht?

JACQUES: No.

[*Pause*]

Is she to be one of the party?

D'AIGUINES: I don't know. That's why I'm asking if she spoke of it.

JACQUES: She never speaks to me of anything.

D'AIGUINES: In her place—I'd refuse to go.

JACQUES: You would?

D'AIGUINES: I doubt that she'll be able to refuse. However—that's her affair. What matters most is you. What are you going to do? Will you take my advice and go away for a while?

JACQUES: I don't know yet. I'll think it over.

D'AIGUINES: Don't wait, Jacques. Believe me.

ROSAMOND LEHMANN (1901–1990)

From *Dusty Answer* (1927)

The daughter of an English father, the Liberal M.P. and *Punch* contributor R. C. Lehmann, and an American mother, Alice Marie Davis, the novelist Rosamond Lehmann grew up in a literate and highly cultivated family. She began publishing poetry when she was sixteen and won a scholarship to Girton College, Cambridge, in 1919. Her first novel, *Dusty Answer*, appeared in 1927, followed by *A Note in Music* (1930) and *Invitation to the Waltz* (1932). She was twice married and twice divorced, and had a nine-year love affair in the forties with the poet Cecil Day-Lewis (1909–1972). The death of her daughter, Sally, of polio in 1958 was a severe blow, and later in life Lehmann became increasingly interested in spirituality and mysticism. She published two works on the subject, *The Swan in the Evening: Fragments of an Inner Life* and *Letters from Our Daughters* (with Cynthia Sandys), in 1967 and 1972. Over her long and distinguished career Lehmann produced seven novels, several volumes of short stories, and translated a number of works from the French, including Cocteau's *Les Enfants terribles* in 1955.

Dusty Answer, the sensitive account of a young girl, Judith Earle, moving from adolescence into adulthood, remains Lehmann's most popular work. Published a year before *The Well of Loneliness*, it treats passion between women sympathetically—Judith has a piercing love affair with a female friend, Jennifer, at Cambridge—and invites comparison with Hall's rather more polemical treatment of similar themes. In the excerpts below we see the burgeoning of Judith's infatuation with Jennifer (complete with Lawrentian bathing scene) and subsequent jealousy when Jennifer receives a visit from a glamorous older woman, the seductive yet sinister Geraldine Manners.

FURTHER READING: Rosamond Lehmann, *Dusty Answer* (New York: Henry Holt, 1927); John Lehmann, *The Whispering Gallery* (London: Longmans, Green, 1955); Diana E. LeStourgeon, *Rosamond Lehmann* (New York: Twayne, 1965); Gillian Tindall, *Rosamond Lehmann: An Appreciation* (London: Chatto and Windus, 1985); Ruth Siegel, *Rosamond Lehmann: A Thirties Writer* (New York: Peter Lang, 1989); Judy Simons, *Rosamond Lehmann* (Basingstoke: Macmillan, 1992); Selina Hastings, *Rosamond Lehmann* (London: Chatto and Windus, 2002).

Gradually Judith and Jennifer drew around them an outer circle of about half a dozen; and these gathered for conversation in Jennifer's room every evening. That untidy luxuriant room, flickering with firelight, smelling of oranges and chrysanthemums, was always tacitly chosen as a meeting-place; for something of the magnetism of its owner seemed to be diffused in it, spreading a glow, drawing tired heads and bodies there to be refreshed.

Late into the night they sat about or lay on the floor, smoked, drank cocoa, ate buns, discussed—earnestly, muddle-headedly—sex, philosophy, religion, sociology, people and politics; then people and sex again. Judith sat in a corner and watched the firelight caress and beautify their peaceful serious faces; talked a great deal suddenly now and then, and then was silent again, dreaming and wondering.

Even the most placid and commonplace faces looked tragic, staring into the fire, lit by its light alone. They were all unconscious; and she herself could never be unconscious. Around her were these faces, far away and lost from themselves, brooding on nothing; and there was she, as usual, spectator and commentator, watching them over-curiously, ready to pounce on a passing light, a flitting shade of expression, to ponder and compare and surmise; whispering to herself: "Here am I watching, listening. Here are faces, forms, rooms with their own life, noise of wind and footsteps, light and shadow. What is this mystery? . . ." And even in her futile thoughts never quite stepping over the edge and staring mindlessly and being wholly unaware.

They broke up at last with sighs and yawns, lingered, drifted away little by little. Judith was left alone with Jennifer.

"One more cigarette," she suggested.

"Well, just one."

Jennifer let down her hair and brushed it out, holding it along her arm, watching it shimmer in the fire light with an engrossed stare, as if she never could believe it was part of her.

Always Jennifer. It was impossible to drink up enough of her; and a day without her was a day with the light gone.

Jennifer coming into a room and pausing on the threshold, head up, eyes wide open, darting round, dissatisfied until they found you. That was an ever fresh spring of secret happiness. Jennifer lifting you in her arms and carrying you upstairs, because she said you looked tired and were such a baby and too lovely anyway to walk upstairs like other people.

Jennifer basking in popularity, drawing them all to her with a smile and a turn of the head, doing no work, breaking every rule, threatened with disgrace, plunged in despair; emerging the next moment new-bathed in radiance, oblivious of storm and stress.

Jennifer dispensing her hospitality with prodigal and careless ease, recklessly generous in public and in secret, flashing the glow of her magnetism suddenly into unlit and neglected lives, allowing them to get warm for a little, and then light-heartedly forgetting them. But never forgetting Judith—or not for long; and coming back always to sit with her alone, and drop all masks and love her silently, watchfully with her eyes.

Jennifer singing Neapolitan folk-songs to a be-ribboned guitar. Where she had picked up the airs, the language, the grace and fascination of her manner, no one knew. But when she sat by the window with bright streamers falling over her lap, singing low to her soft accompaniment, then, each time, everyone fell madly in love with her.

Jennifer chattering most when she was tired, or depressed, her words tripping over each other, her absurd wit sparkling, her laugh frequent and excited: so silent, so still when she was happy that she seemed hypnotized, her whole consciousness suspended to allow the happiness to flow in.

Jennifer looking shattered, tortured after a few hours spent by mistake over coachings and time-papers in stuffy rooms; starting up in the end with a muttered: "O God, this place! . . ." wrenching open the door and rushing downstairs, oblivious of all but the urgency of her mood. From the window you could see her in the grounds, running, running. Soon the trees hid her. She was tramping over the ploughed fields, her cheeks glowing, her hair like a light against the dark hedges. She was going, alone, tensely, over the long fields. What was she thinking of? She had her evasions. No good to ask her: her eyes would fly off, hiding from you. She would not let herself be known entirely.

By Judith's shadowy side ran the hurrying flame of Jennifer; and from all that might give her pause, or cloud her for a moment Jennifer fled as if she were afraid.

The lonely midnight clouded her. Jennifer was afraid of the dark.

Was it that people had the day and the night in them, mixed in varying quantities? Jennifer had the strength of day, and you the strength of night. By day, your little glow was merged in her radiance; but the night was stronger, and overcame her. You were stronger than Jennifer in spite of the burning life in her. The light hid the things for which you searched, but the darkness and the silence revealed them. All your significant experiences had been of the night. And there, it was suddenly clear, was the secret of the bond with Roddy. He too had more shadow in him than sun. *"Chevalier de la lune"* that was he— *"Que la lumière importune"*—ah! yes! *"Qui cherche le coin noir"*— yes, yes— *"Qui cherche le coin noir."* Some time—it did not matter when, for it was bound to happen—he would say in the dark, "I love you."

Meanwhile there was Jennifer to be loved with a bitter maternal love, because she was afraid. And because, some day, she might be gone. For Jennifer said "I love you" and fled away. You cried "Come back!" and she heard and returned in anguish, clasping you close but dreading your dependence. One day when you most needed her, she might run away out of earshot, and never come back.

But there was value in impermanence, in insecurity; it meant an ache and quickening, a perpetual birth; it meant you could never drift into complacence and acceptance and grow old.[. . .]

The long days of May stretched out before Judith and Jennifer. Each day was a fresh adventure in the open air, and work an unimportant and neglected nuisance. For weeks the weather remained flawless. Life narrowed to a wandering in a green canoe up small river-channels far from the town, with Jennifer paddling in wild bursts between long periods of inaction. To all Judith's offers of help she answered firmly that a woman should never depart from her type.

They landed finally and made ready to bathe.

"Off, off, you lendings!" cried Jennifer. "Do you know, darling, that comes home to me more than anything else in all Shakespeare? I swear, Judith, it seems much more natural to me to wear no clothes."

She stood up, stretching white arms above her head. Her cloud of hair was vivid in the blue air. Her back was slender and strong and faultlessly moulded.

"Glorious, glorious Pagan that I adore!" whispered the voice in Judith that could never speak out.

Beside Jennifer she felt herself too slim, too flexible, almost attenuated.

"You are so utterly lovely," Jennifer said, watching her.

They swam in cool water in a deep circular pool swept round with willows, and dried themselves in the sun.

They spent the afternoon in the shade of a blossoming may bush. All round them the new green of the fields was matted over with a rich and solid layer of buttercup yellow. Jennifer lay flat on her back with the utter relaxed immobility of an animal, replenishing her vitality through every nerve.

Slowly they opened books, dreamed through a page, forgot it at once, laid books aside; turned to smile at each other, to talk as if there could never be enough of talking; with excitement, with anxiety, as if to-morrow might part them and leave them for ever burdened with the weight of all they had had to tell each other.

Judith crept closer, warming every sense at her, silent and utterly peaceful. She was the part of you which you never had been able to untie and set free, the part that wanted to dance and run and sing, taking strong draughts of wind and sunlight; and was, instead, done up in intricate knots and overcast with shadows; the part that longed to look outward and laugh, accepting life as an easy exciting thing; and yet was checked by a voice that said doubtfully that there were dark ideas behind it all, tangling the web; and turned you inward to grope among the roots of thought and feeling for the threads.

You could not do without Jennifer now.

The sun sank, and the level light flooded the fields and the river. Now the landscape lost its bright pure definitions of outline, its look as of a picture embroidered in brilliant silks, and veiled its colours with a uniform pearl-like glow. A chill fell and the scent of May grew troubling in the stillness. They turned the canoe towards home.

Nearer the town, boats became more frequent. Gramophones clamoured from the bowels of most of them; and they were heavily charged with grey-flannelled youth. Jennifer, observing them with frank interest, pointed out the good-looking ones in a loud whisper; and all of them stared, stared as they passed.

Above the quiet secretly-stirring town, roofs, towers and spires floated in a pale gold wash of light. What was the mystery of Cambridge in the evening? Footfalls struck with a pang on the heart, faces startled with strange beauty, and every far appearing or disappearing form seemed significant.

And when they got back to College, even that solid redbrick barrack was touched with mystery. The corridors were long patterns of unreal light and shadow. Girls' voices sounded remote as in a dream, with a murmuring rise and fall and light laughter behind closed doors. The thrilling smell of cowslips and wall-flowers was everywhere, like a cloud of enchantment.

In Jennifer's room, someone had let down the sun-blind, and all was in throbbing shadow. Her great copper bowl was piled, as usual, with fruit, and they ate of it idly, without hunger.

"Now a little work," said Judith firmly. "Think! only three weeks till Mays. . . ."

But it was impossible to feel moved.

Jennifer, looking childish and despondent, sat down silently by the window with a book.

Judith wrote on a sheet of paper:

Tall oaks branch-charmèd by the earnest stars; and studied it. That *was* a starry night: the sound of the syllables made stars prick out in dark treetops.

Under it she wrote:

> . . . *the foam*
> *Of perilous seas in faëry lands forlorn.*

What a lot there were for the sea and the seashore! . . . The page became fuller.

> *Upon the desolate verge of light*
> *Yearned loud the iron-bosomed sea.*

> *The unplumbed salt estranging sea.*

> *From the lone sheiling of the misty island*
> *Mountains divide us and a world of seas:*
> *But still the blood is strong, the heart is Highland;*
> *And we in dreams behold the Hebrides.*

Ah, that said it all. . . .

The lines came flocking at random.

> *But the majestic river floated on,*
> *Out of the mist and hum of that low land*
> *Into the frosty starlight, and there flowed*
> *Rejoicing through the hushed Chorasmian waste*
> *Under the solitary moon. . . .*

> *Ah sunflower weary of time*
> *That countest the steps of the sun.* . . .

Ah sunflower! . . . Where were they—the old gardens of the sun where my sunflower wished to go? They half unfolded themselves at the words . . .

> *Nous n'irons plus aux bois*
> *Les lauriers sont coupés.*

O mors quam amara est memoria tua homini pacem habenti in substantiis suis. . . .

How with one tongue those both cried alas!
And then in the end, sleep and a timeless peace.

> *Nox est perpetua una dormienda.*

There were so many tumbling and leaping about in your head you could go on for ever. . . .

Now to study them. What did it all mean? Was there any thread running through them with which to make a theory? Anybody could write down strings of quotations,—but a student of English literature was expected to deal in theories. It was something to do with the sound . . . the way sound made images, shell within shell of them softly unclosing . . . the way words became colours and scents . . . and the surprise when it happened, the ache of desire, the surge of excitement, the sense of fulfilment, the momentary perception of something unknowable. . . . Some sort of truth, some answer to the question: What is poetry? . . . No it was no good. But it had been very enjoyable, writing things down like that and repeating them to yourself.

Jennifer was half asleep with her head upon the windowsill. The bowl of fruit burned in the dimness. How like Jennifer was her room! Yellow painted chairs, a red and blue rug on the hearth, cowslips in coloured bowls and jars, one branch of white lilac in a tall blue vase; the guitar with its many ribbons lying on the table; a silken Italian shawl, embroidered with great rose and blue and yellow flowers flung over the screen: wherever you looked colour leapt up at you; she threw colour about in profuse disorder and left it. Her hat of pale green straw with its little wreath of clover lay on the floor. Nobody else had attractive childish hats like hers. A wide green straw would remind you of Jennifer to the end of your life; and beneath it you would see the full delicious curve of her cheek and chin, her deep-shadowed eyes, her lips that seemed to hold all life in their ardent lines.

She turned her head and smiled sleepily.

"Hullo!" said Judith. "Haven't we been quiet? I've done such a lot of work."

"I've done none. I couldn't remember the difference between ethics and aesthetics. What rot it all is! . . . Now listen and we'll hear a nightingale. He's tuning up."

They leaned out of the window.

The icy aching flute in the cedar called and called on two or three notes, uncertain, dissatisfied; then all at once found itself and bubbled over in rich and complicated rapture.

Jennifer was listening, tranced in her strange immobility, as if every other sense were suspended to allow her to hear aright.

She roused herself at last as Judith bent to kiss her good night.

"Good night my—darling—darling—" she said.

They stared at each other with tragic faces. It was too much, this happiness and beauty.

The end of the first year.

It was, of course, Mabel who was the first to hint of ill-tidings. Eating doughnuts out of a bag, late one night, during one of Judith's charity visits, she said:

"Has that Miss Manners been up lately?"

"Who's Miss Manners?"

"Why—that Miss Manners, Jennifer's friend, who stayed with her so much during the Long."

"Oh yes—"

"I was sure you must have heard about her, because they seemed such very great friends. They were always about together and always up to some lark." She gave a snigger. "We used to wonder, we really did, how long it would be before Jennifer got sent down, the way they used to go on, coming in so late and all. But somehow Jennifer never gets found out, does she?" Another snigger. "What a striking-looking girl she is."

"Who?"

"Miss Manners."

"Oh yes. . . . I've never seen her. Only photographs."

"Everybody said what a striking pair they made. . . . I expect she'll be up soon again, don't you?"

"I don't know at all," said Judith. "I expect so." Mabel looked solemn.

"The wrestling matches they used to have out there on the lawn! I used to watch them from my window. I wonder they didn't . . . I really wonder . . . any of the dons . . . It looked so . . . throwing each other about like that. . . . It's not the sort of thing you expect—quite, is it? I mean . . ."

"Oh, wrestling's glorious," said Judith. "I love it. Jennifer's tried to teach me. But I'm not strong enough for her; the—the—Manners girl is much more of a match for her."

Mabel pursed up her mouth and was silent.

It was necessary to leave her quickly for fear of striking her; because her deliberate intent was obvious; because she knew quite well now that you had never before heard of Miss Manners; because you were seeing that girl plainly, tall, dark and splendid, striding on the lawn with Jennifer, grasping her in strong arms, a match for her in all magnificent unfeminine physical ways, as you had never been. Her image was all at

once there, ineffaceably presenting itself as the embodiment of all hitherto unco-ordi-
nated and formless fears, the symbol for change, and dark alarms and confusions. And
the unbearable image of Mabel was there too, watching by herself, gloating down from
the window with glistening eyes that said:

"At last!"

She stopped short in the corridor, and moaned aloud, aghast at the crowding panic
of her thoughts.

Judith, returning from her bath, heard voices and laughter late at night behind Jennifer's door. Should she stop? All the circle must be there as usual, laughing and talking as if nothing were amiss. She alone had excluded herself, sitting with a pile of books
in her room, pretending to have important work. It was her own fault. She had said she
was busy, and they had believed her and not invited her to join their gathering. She
would go in, and sit among them and smoke, and tell them things,—tell them something to make them laugh; and all would be as before. They would drift away in the end
and leave her behind; she would turn and look at Jennifer in the firelight, put out a hand
and say: "Jennifer. . . ."

She opened the door and looked in.

The voices stopped, cut off sharply.

In the strange, charged, ensuing silence, she saw that the curtains were flung back.
Purple-black night pressed up against the windows, and one pane framed the blank
white globe of the full moon. They were all lying on the floor. Dark forms, pallid,
moon-touched faces and hands were dimly distinguishable; a few cigarette points
burned in the faint hanging cloud of smoke across the room. The fire was almost out.
Where was Jennifer?

"Hullo, there's Judith," said one.

"Is there room for me?" said Judith in a small voice. She came in softly among them
all, and went directly over to the window and sat on the floor, with the moon behind her
head. She was conscious of her own unnatural precision and economy of movement; of
her long slender body wrapped in its kimono crossing the room in three light steps, sinking noiselessly down in its place and at once remaining motionless, expectant.

Where was Jennifer?

"All in the dark," she said, in the same soft voice. And then: "What a moon! Don't
you know it's very dangerous to let it shine on you like this? It will make you mad."

One or two of them laughed. She could now recognize the three faces in front of
her. Jennifer must be somewhere by the fireplace. There was constraint in the room.
She thought with awful jealousy: "Ah, they hate my coming. They thought they were
getting rid of me at last. They come here secretly without me, to insinuate themselves.
They all want her. They have all hated me always." She said:

"Give me a cigarette, someone."

Jennifer's voice broke in suddenly with a sort of harsh clangour. From her voice,
Judith knew how wild her eyes must be.

"Here, here's a cigarette, Judith. . . . Have something to eat. Or some cocoa. Oh—there was a bottle of cherry-brandy, but I believe we've finished it."

Horrible confusion in her voice, a stumbling hurry of noise. . . .

"I have just licked up the last dregs," said a deep voice.

"Who's that who spoke then?" said Judith softly and sweetly.

"Oh . . ." cried Jennifer shrilly, "Geraldine, you haven't met Judith yet."

What was she saying? Geraldine Manners was staying the week-end, no, was wrestling on the lawn with her; had just arrived, no, had been in the room for months, since the summer, for they were such very great friends. . . .

"How do you do. I'm guessing what you are like from the way you speak," said Judith softly, laughingly.

"Oh, I'm no good at that."

How bored, how careless a voice!

"Shall I switch on the light?" said someone.

"No!" said Judith loudly.

She lifted up her arm against the window. The kimono sleeve fell back from it, and it gleamed cold and frail in the moonlight, like a snake. She spread out her long fingers and stared at them.

"I would like to be blind," she said. "I really wish I were blind. Then I might learn to see with my fingers. I might learn to hear properly too."

And learn to be indifferent to Jennifer; never to be enslaved again by the lines and colours of her physical appearance, the ever new surprise and delight of them; learn, in calm perpetual darkness, how the eyes' tyrannical compulsions had obscured and distorted all true values. To be struck blind now this moment, so that the dreadful face of the voice by the fireplace remained for ever unknown! . . . Soon the light would go on, and painfully, hungrily, with awful haste and reluctance, the eyes would begin their work again, fly to their target.

"Don't be absurd, Judith," said someone. "You don't know what you're talking about"; and went on to talk of work among the blind, of blinded soldiers, of St. Dunstan's.

The conversation became general and followed the usual lines: it was better to be deaf than blind, blind than deaf. Jennifer and Geraldine were silent.

"Oh, it's time we went to bed," said someone. "Jennifer, I must go to bed. I'm almost asleep. What's the time?"

Now the light would go on.

It went on. The room suddenly revealed its confusion of girls, cushions, chairs, cups, plates and cigarette-ends. Everybody was getting up, standing about and talking.

Jennifer was on her feet, voluble, calling loud goodnights. They made a group round her and round somebody still sitting on the floor beside her. Judith caught a glimpse of a dark head leaning motionless against the mantelpiece. Now they were all going away. Judith followed them slowly to the door and there paused, looking over her shoulder towards the fireplace.

"Stay," said Jennifer shrilly. She was standing and staring at Judith with wild eyes; pale, with a deep patch of colour in each cheek, and lips parted.

"No, I must go. I've got some work," said Judith, smiling over her shoulder. She let her eyes drop from Jennifer's face to the other one.

At last it confronted her, the silent-looking face, watching behind its narrowed eyes. The hair was black, short, brushed straight back from the forehead, leaving small beautiful ears exposed. The heavy eyebrows came low and level on the low broad brow; the eyes were long slits, dark-circled, the cheeks were pale, the jaw heavy and masculine. All the meaning of the face was concentrated in the mouth, the strange wide lips laid rather flat on the face, sulky, passionate, weary, eager. She was not a young girl. It was the face of a woman of thirty or more; but in years she might have been younger. She was tall, deep-breasted, with long, heavy but shapely limbs. She wore a black frock and a pearl necklace, and large pearl earrings.

Judith said politely:

"Is this the first time you have been here?"

"No." She laughed. Her voice was an insolent voice.

"I'm tired," said Jennifer suddenly, like a child.

"You look it," said Judith. "Go to bed."

"I'll get undressed." Jennifer passed a hand across her forehead and sighed.

The woman by the fireplace fitted a cigarette into an amber holder slowly, and lit it.

"I'm not sleepy yet," she said. "I'll wait till you're in bed and come and tuck you up."

"This room feels—" cried Jennifer staring around her in horror. She dashed to the window and flung it wide open; then disappeared into her bedroom; and there was not another sound from her.

The woman started singing to herself very low, as if forgetful of Judith's presence; then broke off to say:

"I like your kimono."

Judith wrapped the long red and blue silk garment more closely round her hips.

"Yes. It was brought me from Japan. I gave Jennifer one. A purple one."

"Oh, that one. She's lent it to me. I forgot to bring a dressing-gown."

She turned her head away, as if to intimate that so far as she was concerned conversation was neither interesting nor necessary.

Judith bit back the "Good-night, Jennifer" which she was about to call; for she was never going to care any more what happened to Jennifer; never again soothe her when she was weary and excited, comfort her when she was unhappy. She would look at Jennifer coldly, observe her vagaries and entanglements with a shrug, comment upon them with detached and cynical amusement: hurt her, if possible, oh, hurt her, hurt her.

Now she would leave her with Geraldine and not trouble to ask herself once what profound and secret intimacies would be restored by her withdrawal.

She smiled over her shoulder and left the room.

COMPTON MACKENZIE (1883–1972)

From *Extraordinary Women* (1928)

The gifted and gregarious Sir Edward Montague Compton Mackenzie, scion of a distinguished theatrical family, chose writing over the stage soon after leaving Magdalen College, Oxford, in 1904. He published his first book of poems in 1907; his first two novels, *The Passionate Elopement* and *Carnival*, in 1911 and 1912. The semiautobiographical *Sinister Street*, whose hero moves from a golden youth at Oxford into the London underworld, appeared in 1913. After serving as an intelligence officer in Greece in the First World War, Mackenzie spent several years with his first wife, Faith Stone, on the Mediterranean island of Capri, where he befriended Norman Douglas, W. Somerset Maugham, Romaine Brooks, Natalie Barney, and other members of the bohemian homosexual colony living there in the postwar years. Two comic novels of that time, *Vestal Fire* (1927) and *Extraordinary Women* (1928), affectionately satirize homosexual highlife on the island. In the 1920s and 1930s Mackenzie worked as a journalist and academic: he founded the musical magazine *Gramophone* in 1922, wrote book reviews for the *Daily Mail*, and was rector of Glasgow University from 1931 to 1934. Later in life he produced novels and popular histories, children's books, song lyrics, and ten volumes of memoirs. He married three times, cofounded the Scottish Nationalist Party, and was also lifetime president of the British Siamese Cat Club.

Extraordinary Women, a comic saga of sapphic shenanigans on the fictional island of "Sirène" (Capri), appeared in September 1928, a month before Radclyffe Hall's famous lesbian novel, *The Well of Loneliness*, was ruled obscene and banned by the British government. Yet unlike *The Well*, Mackenzie's book escaped prosecution—in part, one suspects, because of its author's light-hearted handling of his homosexual characters. (Mackenzie claimed to have been disappointed his novel was not banned; he would have enjoyed, he said, appearing in court in his own defense.) A deliberate mixture of fluff and farce, *Extraordinary Women* has to do with the libidinal havoc wreaked by one Rosalba Donsante, heiress and lady-killer, on Sirène's colony of lesbian expatriates. The novel is a roman à clef. Rosalba is modeled on Natalie Barney's onetime lover, the capricious Mimi Franchetti, and other characters have been variously identified with Radclyffe Hall, her lover Una Troubridge, the painter Romaine Brooks, and the pianist Renata Borgatti. In the passage below, one of Rosalba's many suitors, the hapless yet devoted Aurora "Rory" Freemantle, middle-aged breeder of bulldogs and patroness of lady boxers, attempts—unsuccessfully—to persuade Rosalba to leave her current lover, the obsequious and overpowered Countess Monforte. The effusions of Rory's Swinburnean poetic alter ego, "Demonassa," are clearly meant to bring to mind the scandalous lesbian poems of "Michael Field" (Katherine Bradley and Edith Cooper), "Marie Madeleine" (Marie Madeleine von Puttkamer), Renée Vivien, and other turn-of-the-century female decadents.

FURTHER READING: Compton Mackenzie, *Extraordinary Women: Theme and Variations* (1928; rpt. London: Hogarth, 1986); —, *My Life and Times,* 10 vols. (London: Chatto and Windus, 1963–71); Norman Douglas, *Siren Land* (West Drayton, Middlesex: Penguin, 1948); Christina Foyle, "Compton Mackenzie," *Dictionary of National Biography* (1971–80); D. J. Dooley, *Compton Mackenzie* (New York: Twayne, 1974); Jeannette Foster, *Sex Variant Women in Literature* (1956; rpt. Tallahassee, Fla.: Naiad, 1985); Terry Castle, *The Apparitional Lesbian: Female Homosexuality and Modern Culture* (New York: Columbia University Press, 1993).

Aurora Freemantle was so masculine as almost to convey the uncomfortable impression that she really was a man dressed up in female attire. But she was without doubt an Englishwoman who had lived for over twenty-five years in Paris, where under the pseudonym of Demonassa she had contributed poems to various advanced reviews and under her own name pence to support them. She had begun as a symbolist and was at present an imagist; but through all the mutable fashions of literature she had remained faithful to the breeding of French bulldogs. She was not beautiful, having herself a considerable likeness to the bulldogs she loved. Her prominent chin was as hispid as the leaves of borage. She was indeed, if one may use a botanical family to classify a human being, a boraginacious woman combining in herself the sentimentality of the forget-me-not with the defiance of the bugloss. Like the Demonassa whose name she had borrowed from Lucian she was rich, and like her she could fairly be called a Corinthian inasmuch as she had done more than anybody to promote the sport of boxing among women. She had derived as much pleasure from the protection of likely young feminine featherweights as in the bewhiskered prime of the Victorian era elderly gentlemen derived from the protection of ballet-dancers. In early days she had had some bitter experiences in the way of empirical love-making; but for many years now, until Rosalba Donsante entered her life, she had always been able to feel that she was the protector with perpetual freedom to dismiss the protected. At present, however, Rosalba eluded her. And to the enslavement of Rosalba Rory set that massive and hispid jaw. One of her practical reasons for coming to Sirène (romantically she could not bear the thought of even the briefest separation) was the hope that she might cut Rosalba off from relying too much upon her grandmother's financial help, which was one of the chief bars to the indisputable protection that she had craved ever since she met Rosalba at a friend's house in Paris last October. Under the pseudonym of Demonassa Rory had expressed very frankly her feminine ideal, and there is no doubt that Rosalba came nearer than anybody so far to realizing it. Poems of hers written before Rosalba came into this world foreshadowed her. She might have met her unborn shade and cried "*Tu Marcellus eris.*" There was published privately in the early 'nineties a slim volume of verse bound in sea-green vellum called *Cydro*, which is still met with in second-hand book catalogues under the heading "Curious." Rory Freemantle had not yet assumed the name Demonassa at this period, and the only indication of authorship was a portrait of her at the beginning which in spite of being reproduced from a silver-point, with all the advantages that such an ethereal style of sketching provides, showed a determined young woman quite alien from the Cydro whose beauty and fascination the poems celebrated. This Cydro became in turn Gyrinno, Anactoria, Atthis, Megara, Telesippa, Leaena, Megilla, Gongyla, Ismenodora, or Mnesidice; and she was sometimes a slim anonymous flute-player of Pyrrha or Methymna flitting through the verses of Demonassa as her prototype may have flitted through the olive groves of Mytilene. But whatever her name or occupation she certainly might always have been Rosalba with her upcurving faun's mouth, Rosalba with her long legs and weight of glinting hair. And now when that poetic ideal was incarnate in Rosalba's Greek beauty verse was not sufficient. Rory must take to painting and paint her. She was rich enough to experiment with another art in approaching middle-age, and the fashion of the moment was kind to her lack of technique. She was rich enough to be credited with a freshness of vision, and the portraits she made of Rosalba that first winter had a vogue in her Parisian côterie. They made one feel, her friends assured her, that the war would at last come to an end. Whereupon the Germans nearly broke through again, and the côterie was dispersed. Rory did not allow Rosalba to be dispersed. She had not found the incarnation of her feminine ideal after searching twenty-five years to lose her a few months later. She left her bulldogs and feather-weight female boxers and followed her ideal to Lucerne. Here it was that owing to the restrictions of war-time which made Mytilene a difficult island to reach they planned to spend the late spring and summer in Sirène.

When Rory was presented to the Contessa Monforte and informed that she was to make a third on Sirène, she decided that she could afford to show her jealousy. There were likely to be rivals in the future much more powerful than this soft over-powdered creature, when it might have to be concealed in order not to lose Rosalba. She knew Rosalba would be flattered by a display of jealousy, and she saw quite clearly Rosalba would by no means relish being left alone with the Countess. So she cancelled the tickets and announced she would return to Paris.

"Go," Rosalba invited. "It is quite all the same to me, *mon cher.*"

"And I hope you'll enjoy the company of that idiotic woman who is trailing after you," said Rory, pacing the room with an almost nautical roll.

"She has at least good manners, *mon cher.*"

To Giulia Monforte Rosalba confided that she could no longer put up with Rory's ugliness.

"*Avec sa figure de bouledogue*," she complained. "Let her go. I am sick of her *prepotenza*. You and I will go alone together to Sirène."

"*Oh, cara, sarebbe un sogno*," the Countess sighed.

So Rosalba went to her grandmother to provide herself with the extra amount of ready money Rory's defection made advisable.

"You have had too much money from me this year," said the Baroness unexpectedly. "I think you will be wise to learn a little prudence."

Rosalba frowned. The Countess was not rich. The prospect of a straitened visit to Sirène was by no means to her taste. Perhaps she should be wise not to quarrel with Rory. In spite of her possessive airs she was a more useful companion *en voyage* than poor Giulia.

"I think you are absurd, *mon cher*, to be jealous of Giulia," she told Rory.

"I cannot stand a flabby creature like that daring to follow you about all over Europe."

"But she is so harmless."

"That is precisely what I dislike about her. It's no recommendation of an earthworm to call it harmless."

"Then I suppose I must send her away."

Rory hesitated, turning her bright prominent eyes intently upon Rosalba. She was trying to make up her mind whether this easy victory was worth while. It was clear Rosalba had no interest in the poor Monforte. This was probably a favourable occasion to surrender.

"Oh, let her come, let her come," she said impatiently. "But if she has a headache all the time, my dear, don't expect me to hold her hand."

ANONYMOUS

The Sink of Solitude (1928)

The Sink of Solitude, an anonymous mock-heroic lampoon from 1928, satirizes the principals involved in the public furor over Radclyffe Hall's controversial lesbian novel, *The Well of Loneliness,* in the autumn of that year. Usually attributed to the hack writer P. R. Stephensen, the poem appeared shortly after the muckraking editor of the *Sunday Express,* James Douglas, penned a scathing attack on *The Well* calling for its suppression. Responding to Douglas's screed, the right-wing British Home Secretary, Sir William Joynson-Hicks, popularly known as "Jix," charged Hall's publisher, Jonathan Cape, with violating the Obscene Publications Act of 1857 and the book was subsequently banned in Britain for twenty years. In *The Sink,* as in Pope's *Dunciad,* no one is spared the satirist's lash. If Douglas and Joynson-Hicks are pilloried as forces of cultural reaction, Hall herself ("plodding a road of weariness and gloom / Where boredom unalloyed shall be our doom") is guilty of creating dull art on the subject that once inspired the great Sappho. In Beresford Egan's often-reproduced frontispiece to *The Sink,* Hall is shown groaning Christlike on a cross, while the prune-faced "Jix"— alongside various cupids and *putti*—leers grotesquely from below.

FURTHER READING: *The Sink of Solitude* (London: Hermes, 1928); Paul Allen, *Beresford Egan: An Introduction to His Work* (Lowestoft: Scorpion, 1966); Vera Brittain, *Radclyffe Hall: A Case of Obscenity?* (London: Femina, 1968); Michael Baker, *Our Three Selves: The Life of Radclyffe Hall* (New York: William Morrow, 1985); Laura Doan, *Fashioning Sapphism: The Origins of a Modern English Lesbian Culture* (New York: Columbia University Press, 2001); —, and Jay Prosser, eds., *Palatable Poison: Critical Perspectives on 'The Well of Loneliness'* (New York: Columbia University Press, 2002).

For themes gigantic verse may well be blank;
(SHAKESPEARE and MILTON take the highest rank)
But duller matters duller treatment need

Now English intellects have gone to seed
So in heroic numbers let us sing
Sad songs of those who make no welkins ring,
Plodding a road of weariness and gloom
Where boredom unalloyed shall be our doom,
In wells of loneliness drink draughts, not deep,
But yet Lethean—since we'll go to sleep
And take a long farewell of pleasant mirth
To cool for ages in most earthy earth.
Sing then, O mundane Muse, of RADCLYFFE HALL
And how she wrote a story that should fall
On souls suburban like a ton of bricks,
Crushing JAMES DOUGLAS and SIR JOYNSON HICKS
And how they wound in the Home Office tape
Another soul suburban, Mister CAPE.
But do not let us seek poetic flights
Nor from the gutter hope to scale the heights,
From JIMMY, JIX, and JONATHAN to cull
Bright interludes where everyone is dull.

The Isles of Greece where burning SAPPHO sung
We analyse in terms of FREUD and JUNG;
Though SAPPHO burned with a peculiar flame
God understands her, we must do the same,
And of such eccentricities we say
"'Tis true, 'tis pity: she was made that way."
In a lone hamlet in the Malvern Hills
The LADY ANNA GORDON sits and fills
Her mind for years with thoughts of infant sons,
Pre-natal influence is how it runs.
But even in the best conducted homes
From cruel fact too oft the fancy roams.
The son arrives; the nurse, dull witted finds
It seems a girl to ill-instructed minds.
Well, well; let's call her STEVE and let it go,
The philosophic father wills it so.
She kicks, she thrives, she grows to man's estate,
For trousers love she feels, for knickers hate.
Alas! the weakness of the human will,
Ladies in trousers must be ladies still.
Her father burns the good electric light
In reading HAVELOCK ELLIS all the night,

But though he masters psychopathic lore
He dies the sole possessor of his store
Exclaiming, as we watch his soul depart
"My lips are sealed. 'Twould break my ANNA'S heart!"
And so the maiden grows to man's estate,
(The sequel will be sad to contemplate).

"Anything once," ANGELA CROSSBY said,
A simple rule that suits an empty head,
As now for STEPHEN she displays her charms
And something new attempts in STEPHEN'S arms.
Poor STEPHEN'S heart is lifted to the skies
She decorates herself with shirts and ties,
Buys motorcars, and jewels for her dear,
Thousands of lovers do it every year.
Till ANGELA takes up another scheme
And bursts the bubble of her love's young dream,
Remarking crudely, "Sorry, STEVE, but see
"Business is business—could you marry me?"
Romance is thus flung whop into the dirt
And STEPHEN seeks to soothe her gaping Hurt.
Greyhounds are drawn to the electric hare
The bus-conductor drawn towards the fare,
Strong men at six are drawn towards the bar
And gallery girls at stage doors seek the star,
So all whom life has laid upon the mat
Inevitably seek a Chelsea flat,
To paint the chimneys or to write a book—
The normal course abnormal STEPHEN took.

And so we follow on the common round
Of novels with a much less novel ground
Paris, then war, danger and noble deeds
For STEPHEN follows where the soldier leads,
Comes peace with victory, and well-earned rest
True love at last makes every hero blest,
For every man a damsel, sometimes two,
And STEPHEN to her happiness won through.
She settles with a kind and gentle she
Whose name is MARY, as it ought to be.
Thus adolescence, lost illusions, flight,
Creative struggles and the sterner fight,

Success, the soul-mate, all the course is run;
A happy ending and our story's done.

But happy endings find no place in Art
A far, far better thing is STEPHEN'S part.
When clouds arise upon domestic joys
The world insists that girls shall not be boys—
Though MARY finds convention all absurd
She weakens from the pressure of the herd,
Unhappy if she stay or if she go
Her loyalties conflicting, hence her woe,
Now once upon a time 'twas pointed out
By someone, who if he were still about
Would take an interest in the present case,
That with mankind it is a commonplace
To find that all men kill the thing they love—
No doubt he thinks so still, although above.
But STEPHEN will preserve an equal mind
And not allow the same for womankind
She finds a man, and though it spoil her life
MARY shall be a mother and a wife,
For love's sweet sake she gives her little all,
And goes to tell the tale to RADCLYFFE HALL.

The tragic story of a woman's grief
Misunderstood, or worldly unbelief—
Beneath the author's hands takes rapid shape
Is finished, typed and sent to Mister CAPE
And after hesitation more or less
It gets a preface and is sent to press.
The way to make a modern novel sell is
To have a preface done by HAVELOCK ELLIS.
The book is published and success seems clear
When sympathetic notices appear.
In praise of RADCLYFFE (Gracious, what a nark!)
The TIMES LIT. SUP. is promptly off the mark
In BOOT'S and MUDIE'S the subscribers stand
Supply falls rapidly below demand,
In London streets the groves of Lesbos bloom—
Man-hatted girls, tweed-coated, light the gloom.
Women in love *now* only love themselves
And men are left (like duller books) on shelves.

For loneliness a recipe is found,
And a pale bud opens on barren ground.

But then at last JAMES DOUGLAS sees the work;—
While decadents the moral issue shirk
He girds his loins (if any) for the right
Exclaiming "Onward-Christians-to-the-fight!"
Depress! Repress! Suppress! (Sunday Express)
JAMES DOUGLAS knows what others merely guess—
That woman-interest, sex, and moral ire,
Will set a million readers' veins on fire . . .
Of rhetoric he need not burk a particle
In this week's splurging moral-uplift article.
JIMMY is menaced. He is far from placid.
Ho Ho The Borgias! Who likes prussic acid?
Some women poison with a deadly look,
But RADCLYFFE poisoned JIMMY with a book!
The WELLS OF LONELINESS are far from pure
For poisoned wells JAMES DOUGLAS has a cure,
"Stop up the Well!" is JIMMY'S urgent call
(Inset: A picture of MISS RADCLYFFE HALL)

In JONATHAN's office consternation spreads
And while THE MILLION READERS in their beds
Peruse JAMES' Sunday outburst, weep, and sigh;
JO: CAPE sits down to write a long reply.
But all in vain—poor JO: is in a fix,
Among the Million Readers one is JIX.
From JIX to JIMMY deep calls unto deep
For moral sheep will follow moral sheep;
While rapidly the book sells out of stock,
Two great men quiver with a holy shock,
Two men now burst with holy indignation
To save the morals of the British nation.

Two men in Sodom can avert God's spleen:
Two men can keep the British Empire clean:
Two men by filthy books are never flecked
Two *Good* Men—never mind their intellect!
So JOYNSON HICKS to JONATHAN sent a letter
And CAPE withdrew—he ought to have known better!
No more remains to tell of the brave story

Which covered JAMES and JIX with fleeting glory,
Except that MILTON pleading for the Press
Had never read LORD BEAVERBROOK'S "Express";
Perhaps a certain kind of prejudice
Prevented MILTON reading things so nice
On Sunday as the doings of Society
And chorus-girls and crime. He liked variety.
And so he lustily for Freedom cried
(What *blank* verse he'd have written had he tried
The Areopagitica to revise
To make it fitting for J. Hix' eyes!)

But does an Areopagitic cry
To this dull morbid episode apply?
Did SAPPHO sing, did SHAKESPEARE write for us
Beauty obscenely sweetly amorous,
That DOUGLAS might be born, and JOYNSON HICKS,
And RADCLYFFE HALL put CAPE into a fix?
Can Love thus puddled in a lonely well
In which no more than dead leaves ever fell,
Shake nothing more than DOUGLAS in its mud?
Does beauty course no longer in our blood?
Alas, when JIX who cannot understand
The problem shaking (slightly) all the land,
Wrote notes to CAPE, the pathos of the thing
Is that the poor earth once heard SAPPHO sing. . . . . .

DJUNA BARNES (1892–1982)

"Cassation" (1929)

Born into a wealthy and eccentric family in Cornwall-on-Hudson, New York, in 1892, the American novelist, journalist, short-story writer and dramatist Djuna Barnes was educated at home by her father and grandmother. Evidence suggests that she was raped in childhood either by her father or a step-uncle—a fact that may account for the unease and psychic violence that are so much a part of her fictional world. In her twenties Barnes worked as a journalist in New York, specializing in human interest stories of a grotesque or darkly comic nature. After moving to Paris in 1919 she began a ten-year relationship with the artist Thelma Wood and became part of the expatriate lesbian circle around the wealthy *salonnière* Natalie Barney. Her privately printed 1928 satire, *Ladies Almanack*, written in a fake-seventeenth-century style and decorated with her own woodcuts, is a sapphic mock-tribute to the promiscuous Barney ("the Lady's Lady") and her friends. In the same year Barnes published her first novel, *Ryder*, followed by a book of short stories, *A Night Among the Horses*, in 1929.

Barnes's undisputed masterpiece is her 1936 novel *Nightwood*, singled out by T. S. Eliot as possessing "a quality of horror and doom very nearly related to that of Elizabethan tragedy." Inspired by Barnes's relationship with Wood, the novel depicts—in a dense, baroque, often fantastic prose—the tormented love of Nora Flood, an American painter, for the amoral Robin Vote, "the amputation that Nora could not renounce." Recognized at once as an artistic triumph, the work also spelled Barnes's creative doom. She never wrote anything so powerful again and for the rest of her life mourned the loss of her inspiration. She returned to the United States at the outbreak of the Second World War and lived alone in Greenwich Village for the next forty years, gradually becoming an alcoholic semirecluse—bitter, misanthropic, and increasingly alienated from the world around her.

The 1929 short story "Cassation," from *A Night Among the Horses*, epitomizes Barnes's haunting high modernist mode. Cast as a weird obsessional monologue, a kind of sapphic *Rime of the Ancient Mariner*, it tells of an attachment between two women that is at once binding, maternal, and inexplicably sinister. The dreamlike imagery—of ornate yet dilapidated interiors, Wagnerian swans, strange women, and idiot children—anticipates the death-driven world of *Nightwood*. An ironic, characteristically Barnesian touch: the term "cassation" refers to a type of eighteenth-century musical composition, similar to a divertimento or serenade and often performed outdoors.

FURTHER READING: Djuna Barnes, *A Night Among the Horses* (New York: Boni and Liveright, 1929); —, *Nightwood* (New York: New Directions, 1961); —, *The Selected Works of Djuna Barnes* (New York: Farrar, Straus and Cudahy, 1962); —, *I Could Never Be Lonely Without a Husband: Interviews*, ed. Alyce Barry (London: Virago, 1987); —, *The Book of Repulsive Women: Eight Rhythms and Five Dreamings* (Los Angeles: Sun and Moon, 1989); —, *New York*, ed. Alyce Barry (Los Angeles: Sun and Moon, 1989); —, *Ladies Almanack* (Elmwood Park, Ill.: Dalkey Archive, 1992); —, *Collected Stories* (Los Angeles: Sun and Moon, 1996); Suzanne C. Ferguson, "Djuna Barnes's Short Stories: An Estrangement of the Heart," *Southern Review* 5 (1969): 26–41; Andrew Field, *Djuna: The Life and Times of Djuna Barnes* (New York: G. P. Putnam's Sons, 1983); Hank O'Neal, *Life Is Painful, Nasty, and Short. . . . In my Case It Has Only Been Painful and Nasty* (New York: Paragon House, 1990); Mary Lynn Broe, ed., *Silence and Power: A Reevaluation of Djuna Barnes* (Carbondale: Southern Illinois University Press, 1991); Frau Michel, " 'I Just Loved Thelma': Djuna Barnes and the Construction of Bisexuality," *Review of Contemporary Fiction* 13 (1993): 53–61; Carolyn J. Allen, "Sexual Narrative in the Fiction of Djuna Barnes," in Julia Penelope and Susan J. Wolfe, eds., *Sexual Practice, Textual Theory* (Cambridge, Mass.: Blackwell, 1993), pp. 184–98; —, *Following Djuna: Women Lovers and the Erotics of Loss* (Bloomington: Indiana University Press, 1996); Philip Herring, *Djuna: The Life and Work of Djuna Barnes* (New York: Viking, 1995); Erin G. Carlston, *Thinking Fascism: Sapphic Modernism and Fascist Modernity* (Stanford: Stanford University Press, 1998); Victoria L. Smith, "A Story Beside(s) Itself: The Language of Loss in Djuna Barnes's *Nightwood*," *PMLA* 114 (1999): 194–206.

"Do you know Germany, Madame, Germany in the spring? It is charming then, do you not think so? Wide and clean, the Spree winding thin and dark—and the roses! the yellow roses in the windows; and the bright talkative Americans passing through groups of German men staring over their *steins*, at the light and laughing women.

"It was such a spring, three years ago, that I came into Berlin from Russia. I was just sixteen, and my heart was a dancer's heart. It is that way sometimes; one's heart is all one thing for months, then—altogether another thing, *nicht wahr?* I used to sit in the café at the end of the Zelten, eating eggs and drinking coffee, watching the sudden rain of sparrows. Their feet struck the table all together, and all together they cleared the crumbs, and all together they flew into the sky, so that the café was as suddenly without birds as it had been suddenly full of birds.

"Sometimes a woman came here, at about the same hour as myself, around four in the afternoon; once she came with a little man, quite dreamy and uncertain. But I must explain how she looked: *temperamentvoll* and tall, *kraftvoll* and thin. She must have been forty then, dressed richly and carelessly. It seemed as though she could hardly keep her clothes on; her shoulders were always coming out, her skirt would be hanging on a hook, her pocket book would be mislaid, but all the time she was savage with jewels, and something purposeful and dramatic came in with her, as if she were the centre of a whirlpool, and her clothes a temporary debris.

"Sometimes she clucked the sparrows, and sometimes she talked to the *Weinschenk*, clasping her fingers together until the rings stood out and you could see through them, she was so vital and so wasted. As for her dainty little man, she would talk to him in English, so that I did not know where they came from.

"Then one week I stayed away from the café because I was trying out for the *Schauspielhaus*, I heard they wanted a ballet dancer, and I was very anxious to get the part, so of course I thought of nothing else. I would wander, all by myself, through the *Tiergarten*, or I would stroll down the *Sieges-Allee* where all the great German emperors' statues are, looking like widows. Then suddenly I thought of the *Zelten*, and of the birds, and of that tall odd woman and so I went back there, and there she was, sitting in the garden sipping beer and chuck-chucking the sparrows.

"When I came in, she got up at once and came over to me and said: 'Why, how do you do, I have missed you. Why did you not tell me that you were going away? I should have seen what I could do about it.'"

"She talked like that; a voice that touched the heart because it was so unbroken and clear. 'I have a house', she said, 'just on the Spree. You could have stayed with me. It is a big, large house, and you could have the room just off my room. It is difficult to live in, but it is lovely—Italian you know, like the interiors you see in Venetian paintings, where young girls lie dreaming of the Virgin. You could find that you could sleep there, because you have dedication.'

"Somehow it did not seem at all out of the way that she should come to me and speak to me. I said I would meet her again some day in the garden, and we could go 'home' together, and she seemed pleased, but did not show surprise.

"Then one evening we came into the garden at the same moment. It was late and the fiddles were already playing. We sat together without speaking, just listening to the music, and admiring the playing of the only woman member of the orchestra. She was very intent on the movement of her fingers, and seemed to be leaning over her chin to watch. Then suddenly the lady got up, leaving a small rain of coin, and I followed her until we came to a big house and she let herself in with a brass key. She turned to the left and went into a dark room and switched on the lights and sat down and said: 'This is where we sleep; this is how it is.'

"Everything was disorderly, and expensive and melancholy. Everything was massive and tall, or broad and wide. A chest of drawers rose above my head. The china stove was enormous and white, enamelled in blue flowers. The bed was so high that you could only think of it as something that might be overcome. The walls were all bookshelves, and all the books were bound in red morocco, on the back of each, in gold, was stamped a coat of arms, intricate and oppressive. She rang for tea and began taking off her hat.

"A great painting hung over the bed; the painting and the bed ran together in encounter, the huge rumps of the stallions reined into the pillows. The generals, with foreign helmets and dripping swords, raging through rolling smoke and the bleeding ranks of the dying, seemed to be charging the bed, so large, so rumpled, so devastated. The sheets were trailing, the counterpane hung torn, and the feathers shivered along the floor, trembling in the slight wind from the open window. The lady was smiling in a sad grave way, but she said nothing, and it was not until some moments later that I saw a child, not more than three years old, a small child, lying in the centre of the pillows, making a thin noise, like the buzzing of a fly, and I thought it was a fly.

"She did not talk to the child, indeed she paid no attention to it, as if it were in her bed and she did not know it. When the tea was brought in she poured it, but she took none, instead she drank small glasses of Rhine wine.

" 'You have seen Ludwig,' she said in her faint and grieving voice, 'we were married a long time ago, he was just a boy then. I? Me? I am an Italian, but I studied English and German because I was with a travelling company. You,' she said abruptly, 'you must give up the ballet—the theatre—acting.' Somehow I did not think it odd that she should know of my ambition, though I had not mentioned it. 'And', she went on, 'you are not for the stage; you are for something quieter, more withdrawn. See here, I like Germany very much, I have lived here a good many years. You will stay and you will see. You have seen Ludwig, you have noticed that he is not strong; he is always declining, you must have noticed it yourself; he must not be distressed, he can't bear anything. He has his room to himself.' She seemed suddenly tired, and she got up and threw herself across the bed, at the foot, and fell asleep, almost instantly, her hair all about her. I went away then, but I came back that night and tapped at the window. She came to the window and signed to me, and presently appeared at another window to the right of the bedroom, and beckoned with her hand, and I came up and climbed in, and did not mind that she had not opened the door for me. The room was dark except for the moon, and two thin candles burning before the Virgin.

"It was a beautiful room, Madame, '*traurig*' as she said. Everything was important and old and gloomy. The curtains about the bed were red velvet, Italian you know, and fringed in gold bullion. The bed cover was a deep red velvet with the same gold fringe: on the floor, beside the bed, a stand on which was a tasselled red cushion, on the cushion a Bible in Italian, lying open.

"She gave me a long nightgown, it came below my feet and came back up again almost to my knees. She loosened my hair, it was long then, and yellow. She plaited it in two plaits; she put me down at her side and said a prayer in German, then in Italian, and ended, 'God bless you', and I got into bed. I loved her very much because there was nothing between us but this strange preparation for sleep. She went away then. In the night I heard the child crying, but I was tired.

"I stayed a year. The thought of the stage had gone out of my heart. I had become a *religieuse*; a gentle religion that began with the prayer I had said after her the first night, and the way I had gone to sleep, though we never repeated the ceremony. It grew with the furniture and the air of the whole room, and with the Bible lying open at a page that I could not read; a religion, Madame, that was empty of need, therefore it was not holy perhaps, and not as it should have been in its manner. It was that I was happy, and I lived there for one year. I almost never saw Ludwig, and almost never Valentine, for that was her child's name, a little girl.

"But at the end of that year I knew there was trouble in other parts of the house. I heard her walking in the night, sometimes Ludwig would be with her, I could hear him crying and talking, but I could not hear what was said. It sounded like a sort of lesson, a lesson for a child to repeat, but if so, there would have been no answer, for the child never uttered a sound, except that buzzing cry.

"Sometimes it is wonderful in Germany, Madame, *nicht wahr*? There is nothing like a German winter. She and I used to walk about the Imperial Palace, and she stroked the cannon, and said they were splendid. We talked about philosophy, for she was troubled with too much thinking, but she always came to the same conclusion, that one must be, or try to be, like everyone else. She explained that to be like everyone, all at once, in your own person, was to be holy. She said that people did not understand what was meant by 'Love thy neighbour as thyself.' It meant, she said, that one should be like all people *and* oneself, then, she said, one was both ruined and powerful.

"Sometimes it seemed that she was managing it, that she was all Germany, at least in her Italian heart. She seemed so irreparably collected and yet distressed, that I was afraid of her, and not afraid.

"That is the way it was, Madame, she seemed to wish it to be that way, though at night she was most scattered and distraught, I could hear her pacing in her room.

"Then she came in one night and woke me and said that I must come into her room. It was in a most terrible disorder. There was a small cot bed that had not been there before. She pointed to it and said that it was for me.

"The child was lying in the great bed against a large lace pillow. Now it was four years old and yet it did not walk, and I never heard it say a thing, or make a sound, except that buzzing cry. It was beautiful in the corrupt way of idiot children; a sacred beast without a taker, tainted with innocence and waste time; honey-haired and failing, like those dwarf angels on holy prints and valentines, if you understand me, Madame, something saved for a special day that would not arrive, not for life at all: and my lady was talking quietly, but I did not recognize any of her former state.

" 'You must sleep here now,' she said, 'I brought you here for this if I should need you, and I need you. You must stay, you must stay forever.' Then she said, 'Will you?' And I said no, I could not do that.

"She took up the candle and put it on the floor beside me, and knelt beside it, and put her arms about my knees. 'Are you a traitor?' she said, 'have you come into my house, Ludwig's house, the house of my child, to betray us?' And I said, no, I had not come to betray. 'Then', she said, 'you will do as I tell you. I will teach you slowly, slowly; it will not be too much for you, but you must begin to forget, you must forget *everything*. You must forget all the things people have told you. You must forget arguments and philosophy. I was wrong in talking of such things; I thought it would teach you how to lag with her mind, to undo time for her as it passes, to climb into her bereavement and her dispossession. I brought you up badly; I was vain. You will do better. Forgive me.' She put the palms of her hands on the floor, her face to my face. 'You must never see any other room than this room. It was a great vanity that I took you out walking. Now you will stay here safely, and you will see. You will like it, you will learn to like it the very best of all. I will bring you breakfast, and luncheon, and supper. I will bring it to you both, myself. I will hold you on my lap, I will feed you like the birds. I will rock you to sleep. You must not argue with me—above all we must have no arguments, no talk about man and his destiny—man has no destiny—that is my secret—I have been keeping it from you until today, this very hour. Why not before? Perhaps I was jealous of the knowledge, yes, that must be it, but now I give it to you, I share it with you. I am an old woman,' she said, still holding me by the knees. 'When Valentine was born, Ludwig was only a boy.' She got up and stood behind me. 'He is not strong, he does not understand that the weak are the strongest things in the world, because he is one of them. He cannot help her, they are adamant together. I need you, it must be you.' Suddenly she began talking to me as she talked with the child, and I did not know which of us she was talking to. 'Do not repeat anything after me. Why should children repeat what people say? The whole world is nothing but a noise, as hot as the inside of a tiger's mouth. They call it civilization—that is a lie! But some day you may have to go out, someone will try to take you out, and you will not understand them or what they are saying, unless you understand nothing, absolutely nothing, then you will manage.' She moved around so that she faced us, her back against the wall. 'Look,' she said, 'it is all over, it has gone away, you do not need to be afraid; there is only you. The stars are out, and the snow is falling down and covering the world, the hedges, the houses and the lamps. No, no!' she said to herself, 'wait. I will put you on your feet, and tie you up in ribbons, and we will go out together, out into the garden where the swans are, and the flowers and the bees and small beasts. And the students will come, because it will be summer, and they will read in their books. . . .' She broke off, then took her wild speech up again, this time as though she were really speaking to the child, 'Katya will go with you. She will instruct you, she will tell you there are no swans, no flowers, no beasts, no boys—*nothing*, nothing at all, just as you like it. No mind, no thought, nothing whatsoever else. No bells will ring, no people will talk, no birds will fly, no boys will move, there'll be no birth and no death; no sorrow, no laughing, no kissing, no crying, no terror, no joy; no eating, no drinking, no games, no dancing; no father, no mother, no sisters, no brothers—only you, only you!'

"I stopped her and I said, 'Gaya, why is it that you suffer so, and what am I to do?' I tried to put my arms around her, but she struck them down crying, 'Silence!' Then she said, bringing her face close to my face, 'She has no claws to hang by; she has no hunting foot; she has no mouth for the meat—*vacancy*!'"

"Then, Madame, I got up. It was very cold in the room. I went to the window and pulled the curtain, it was a bright and starry night, and I stood leaning my head against the frame, saying nothing. When I turned around, she was regarding me, her hands held apart, and I knew that I had to go away and leave her. So I came up to her and said, 'Good-bye, my Lady.' And I went and put on my street clothes, and when I came back she was leaning against the battle picture, her hands hanging. I said to her, without approaching her, 'Good-bye, my love,' and went away.

"Sometimes it is beautiful in Berlin, Madame, *nicht wahr?* There was something new in my heart, a passion to see Paris, so it was natural that I said *lebe wohl* to Berlin.

"I went for the last time to the café in the Zelten, ate my eggs, drank my coffee and watched the birds coming and going just as they used to come and go—altogether here then altogether gone. I was happy in my spirit, for that is the way it is with my spirit, Madame, when I am going away.

"But I went back to her house just once. I went in quite easily by the door, for all the doors and windows were open—perhaps they were sweeping that day. I came to the bedroom door and knocked, but there was no answer. I pushed, and there she was, sitting up in the bed with the child, and she and the child were making that buzzing cry, and no human sound between them, and as usual, everything was in disorder. I came up to her, but she did not seem to know me. I said, 'I am going away; I am going to Paris. There is a longing in me to be in Paris. So I have come to say farewell.'

"She got down off the bed and came to the door with me. She said, 'Forgive me—I trusted you—I was mistaken. I did not know that I could do it myself, but you see, I can do it myself.' Then she got back on to the bed and said, 'Go away,' and I went.

"Things are like that, when one travels, *nicht wahr*, Madame?"

ELIZABETH BOWEN (1899–1973)

"The Jungle" (1929)

The novelist and short-story writer Elizabeth Bowen was born into a venerable Anglo-Irish family and spent her early years in Dublin and at the family's ancestral home, Bowen Court. After her father suffered a nervous breakdown, the family moved to England: her mother died when Bowen, an only child, was thirteen. These childhood traumas undoubtedly contributed both to Bowen's lifelong stutter and the undertow of melancholia present in so much of her writing. In 1923 she married an English civil servant, Alan Cameron, who provided the emotional and financial support that enabled her to write. Her first collection of short stories, *Encounters*, appeared in 1923, followed by the novels *The Hotel* (1927), *The Last September* (1929), *Friends and Relations* (1931), *To the North* (1932), *The House in Paris* (1935), and *The Death of the Heart* (1938).

A tall, striking, somewhat masculine-looking woman, Bowen attracted the love of both sexes. Her best-known novel, *The Heat of the Day* (1949), was inspired by an intense wartime romance with a Canadian diplomat, Charles Ritchie. But women too found her compelling: Virginia Woolf, Rosamond Lehmann, and Eudora Welty were devoted friends; the American writers May Sarton and Carson McCullers both fell in love with her. As Bowen's biographer Victoria Glendinning writes: "Enough lesbian sensibility has been discerned in Elizabeth's fiction for at least one critic to include her in a study of lesbian literature; and enough in her manner for some people to have presumed that, however conventional her married life, it was towards women that her true inclinations lay." Erotic attraction between women (often an adolescent girl and an older woman) is a recurrent theme in Bowen's early novels—notably *The Hotel* and *The Last September*—and again in *The Little Girls* (1964) and *Eva Trout* (1969), the last novels she published before her death in 1973.

"The Jungle" appeared first in the short-story collection *Joining Charles*, in 1929. It is the second of a pair of stories—the other is called "Charity"—involving the schoolgirl Rachel, whose skittish friendships with other girls are at once bittersweet, abortive, yet full of emotional portent.

FURTHER READING: Elizabeth Bowen, *The Hotel* (London: Constable, 1927); —, *The Last September* (London: Constable, 1929); —, *The Heat of the Day* (London: Jonathan Cape, 1949); —, *The Little Girls* (London: Jonathan Cape, 1964); —, *The Collected Stories of Elizabeth Bowen*, ed. Angus Wilson (London: Jonathan Cape, 1980); Jane Rule, *Lesbian Images* (Garden City, N.Y.: Doubleday, 1975); May Sarton, *A World of Light: Portraits and Celebrations* (New York: Norton, 1976); Victoria Glendinning, *Elizabeth Bowen* (New York: Knopf, 1978); Hermione Lee, *Elizabeth Bowen: An Estimation* (London: Vision, 1981); Harold Bloom, ed., *Elizabeth Bowen* (New York: Chelsea, 1987); renée c. hoogland, *Elizabeth Bowen: A Reputation in Writing* (New York and London: New York University Press, 1994); Patricia Juliana Smith, *Lesbian Panic: Homoeroticism in Modern British Women's Fiction* (New York: Columbia University Press, 1997); Jane Miller, "Re-Reading Elizabeth Bowen," *Raritan* 20 (2000): 17–31.

Towards the end of a summer term Rachel discovered the Jungle. You got over the wall at the bottom of the kitchen garden, where it began to be out of bounds, and waded through knee-high sorrel, nettles and dock, along the boundary hedge of Mr. Morden's property until you came to a gap in the roots of the hedge, very low down, where it was possible to crawl under. Then you doubled across his paddock (this was the most exciting part), round the pond and climbed a high board gate it was impossible to see through into a deep lane. You got out of the lane farther down by a bank with a hedge at the top (a very "mangy" thin hedge), and along the back of this hedge, able to be entered at several points, was the Jungle. It was full of secret dog-paths threading between enormous tussocks of bramble, underneath the brambles there were hollow places like caves; there were hawthorns one could climb for a survey and, about the middle, a clump of elders gave out a stuffy sweetish smell. It was an absolutely neglected and wild place; nobody seemed to own it, nobody came there but tramps. Tramps, whose clothes seem to tear so much more easily than one's own, had left little fluttering tags on the bushes, some brownish newspaper one kicked away under the brambles, a decayed old boot like a fungus and tins scarlet with rust that tilted in every direction holding rain-water. Two or three of these tins, in some fit of terrible rage, had been bashed right in.

The first time Rachel came here, alone, she squeezed along the dog-paths with her heart in her mouth and a cold and horrible feeling she was going to find a dead cat. She knew cats crept away to die, and there was a sinister probability about these bushes. It was a silent July evening, an hour before supper. Rachel had brought a book, but she did not read; she sat down under the elders and clasped her hands round her knees. She had felt a funny lurch in her imagination as she entered the Jungle, everything in it tumbled together, then shook apart again, a little altered in their relations to each other, a little changed.

At this time Rachel was fourteen; she had no best friend at the moment, there was an interim. She suffered sometimes from a constrained, bursting feeling at having to keep things so much to herself, yet when she compared critically the girls who had been her great friends with the girls who might be her great friends she couldn't help seeing that they were very much alike. None of them any more than the others would be likely to understand . . . The Jungle gave her a strong feeling that here might have been the Perfect Person, and yet the Perfect Person would spoil it. She wanted it to be a thing in itself: she sat quite still and stared at the impenetrable bramble-humps.

On the last day of term Rachel travelled up in the train with a girl in a lower form called Elise Lamartine, who was going to spend the holidays riding in the New Forest. Elise had her hair cut short like a boy's and was supposed to be fearfully good at French but otherwise stupid. She had a definite quick way of doing things and a thoughtful slow way of looking at you when they were done. Rachel found herself wishing it weren't the holidays. She said, off-hand, as she scrambled down from the carriage into a crowd of mothers: "Let's write to each other, shall we?" and Elise, beautifully unembarrassed, said, "Right-o, let's!"

During the holidays Rachel became fifteen. Her mother let down her skirts two inches, said she really wasn't a little girl any more now and asked her to think about her career. She was asked out to tennis parties where strange young men had a hesitation about calling her anything and finally called her Miss Ritchie. Her married sister Adela promised that next summer holidays she'd have her to stay and take her to "boy and girl dances." "Aren't I a girl now?" asked Rachel diffidently. "You oughtn't to be a girl in that way till you're sixteen," said Adela firmly.

Rachel had one terrible dream about the Jungle and woke up shivering. It was something to do with a dead body, a girl's arm coming out from under the bushes. She tried to put the Jungle out of her mind; she never thought of it, but a few nights afterwards she was back there again, this time with some shadowy person always a little behind her who turned out to be Elise. When they came to the bush which in the first dream had covered the arm she was trying to tell Elise about it, to make sure it *had* been a dream, then stopped, because she knew she had committed that murder herself. She wanted to run away, but Elise came up beside her and took her arm with a great deal of affection. Rachel woke up in a gush of feeling, one of those obstinate dream-taps that won't be turned off, that swamp one's whole morning, sometimes one's day. She found a letter from Elise on the breakfast-table.

Elise wrote a terrible letter, full of horses and brothers. So much that might have been felt about the New Forest did not seem to have occurred to her. Rachel was more than discouraged, she felt blank about next term. It was impossible to have a feeling for anyone who did so much and thought nothing. She slipped the letter under her plate and didn't intend to answer it, but later on she went upstairs and wrote Elise a letter about tennis parties. "There has been talk," she wrote, "of my going to boy and girl dances, but I do not feel keen on them yet."

"Who is your great friend now?" asked Mother, who had come in and found her writing. She put on an anxious expression whenever she spoke like this, because Rachel was a Growing Daughter.

"Oh, no one," said Rachel. "I'm just dashing off something to one of the girls."

"There was Charity. What about Charity? Don't you ever write to her now?"

"Oh, I like her all right," said Rachel, who had a strong sense of propriety in these matters. "I just think she's a bit affected." While she spoke she was wondering whether Elise would get her remove or not. Rachel was going up into IVa. It would be impossible to know anybody two forms below.

Next term, when they all came back, she found Elise had arrived in IVb (one supposed on the strength of her French), but she was being tried for the Gym Eight and spent most of her spare time practising for it. Rachel looked in at the Gym door once or twice and saw her doing things on the apparatus. When she wasn't doing things on the apparatus Elise went about with the same rather dull girl, Joyce Fellows, she'd been going about with last term. They sat together and walked together and wrestled in the boot-room on Saturday afternoons. Whenever Rachel saw Elise looking at her or coming towards her she would look in the other direction or walk away. She realized how the holidays had been drained away by imagination, she had scarcely lived them; they had been wasted. She had a useless, hopeless dull feeling and believed herself to be homesick. By the end of the first fortnight of term she and Elise had scarcely spoken. She had not been back again to the Jungle, of whose very existence she somehow felt ashamed.

One Sunday, between breakfast and chapel, they brushed against each other going out through a door.

"Hullo!" said Elise.

"Oh—hullo!"

"Coming out?"

"Oh—right-o," said Rachel, indifferent.

"Anywhere special? I know of a tree with three apples they've forgotten to pick. We might go round that way and just see—"

"Yes, we might," agreed Rachel. They went arm in arm.

It was early October, the day smelt of potting-sheds and scaly wet tree-trunks. They had woken to find a mist like a sea round the house; now that was being drawn up and the sun came wavering through it. The white garden-gate was pale gold and the leaves of the hedges twinkled. The mist was still clinging in sticky shreds, cobwebs, to the box-hedges, the yellow leaves on the espaliers, the lolling staggering clumps of Michaelmas daisies; like shreds of rag, Rachel thought, clinging to brambles.

Elise's apple tree was half way down the kitchen-garden. They looked up: one of the apples was missing. Either it had fallen or some interfering idiot had succeeded in getting it down with a stone. The two others, beautifully bronze, nestled snugly into a clump of leaves about eight feet up. The girls looked round; the kitchen-garden was empty.

"One could chuck things at them," said Rachel, "if one didn't make too much row."

"I bet I could swing myself up," said Elise confidently. She stepped back, took a short run; jumped and gripped a branch overhead. She began to swing with her legs together, kicking the air with her toes. Every times she went higher; soon she would get her legs over that other branch, sit there, scramble up into standing position and be able to reach the apples.

"How gymnastic we are!" said Rachel with the sarcastic admiration which was *de rigueur*. Elise half-laughed, she hadn't a breath to spare. She stuck out her underlip, measured the branch with her eye. Her Sunday frock flew back in a wisp from her waist; she wore tight black stockinette bloomers.

"—*Elise*" shrieked a voice from the gate. "Rachel *Ritchie*! Leave that tree alone— what are you doing?"

"Nothing, Miss Smyke," shouted Rachel, aggrieved.

"Well, don't," said the voice, mollified. "And don't potter! Chapel's in forty minutes—don't get your feet wet."

Elise had stopped swinging, she hung rigid a moment, then dropped with bent knees apart. "Damn!" she said naturally. Rachel said "dash" herself, sometimes "confound." She knew people who said "confound" quite often, but she had never had a friend of her own who said "Damn" before. "Don't be profane," she said, laughing excitedly.

Elise stood ruefully brushing the moss from her hands "Damn's not profane," she said. "I mean, it's nothing to do with God." She took Rachel's arm again, they strolled towards the end of the kitchen-garden. "Are you getting confirmed next term?"

"I think I am. Are you?"

"I suppose I am. Religion's very much *in* our family, you see. We were Huguenots."

"Oh, I always wondered. Is that why you're called—"

"—Elise? Yes, it's in our family. Don't you like it?"

"Oh, I *like* it . . . But I don't think it suits you. It's such a silky delicate kind of a girlish name. You, you're too—" She broke off; there were people you couldn't talk to about themselves without a confused, excited, rather flustered feeling. Some personalities felt so much more personal. "You ought to have some rather quick hard name. Jean or Pamela . . . or perhaps Margaret—*not* Marguerite."

Elise was not listening. "I ought to have been a boy," she said in a matter-of-fact, convinced voice. She rolled a sleeve back. "Feel my muscle! Watch it—look!"

"I say, Elise. I know of a rather queer place. It's near here, I discovered it. I call it the Jungle, just to distinguish it from other places. I don't mean it's a bit exciting or anything," she said rapidly, "it's probably rather dirty; tramps come there. But it is rather what I used to call 'secret.'" She was kicking a potato down the path before her, and she laughed as she spoke. Lately she had avoided the word "secret." Once, at the end of a visit, she had shown a friend called Charity a "secret place" in their garden at home, and Charity had laughed to the others about it when they were all back at school.

"Which way?"

"Over the wall—you don't mind getting your legs stung?"

The nettles and docks were rank-smelling and heavy with dew. One was hampered by Sunday clothes; they tucked their skirts inside their bloomers and waded through. "It's a good thing," said Rachel, "we've got black stockings that don't show the wet. Brown are the limit, people can see a high-water mark." The wet grass in Mr. Morden's paddock squashed and twanged, it clung like wet snakes as they ran, cutting their ankles. She pulled up panting in the lane below. "Sure you're keen?" said Rachel. "There may be blackberries."

When they came to the Jungle she pushed in ahead of Elise, parting the brambles recklessly. She didn't mind now if she *did* find a dead cat: it would be almost a relief. She didn't look round to see what Elise was doing or seemed to be thinking. They were down in a hollow, it was mistier here and an early morning silence remained. A robin darted out of a bush ahead of her. It was an even better place than she had remembered; she wished she had come here alone. It was silly to mix up people and thoughts. Here was the place where the dead girl's arm, blue-white, had come out from under the bushes. Here was the place where Elise, in the later dream, had come up and touched her so queerly. Here were the rags of her first visit still clinging, blacker and limper . . . the same boot—

"Like a nice boot?" she said facetiously.

Elise came up behind her, noisily kicking at one of the tins. "This is an awfully good place," she said. "Wish *I'd* found it."

"It isn't half bad," said Rachel, looking about her casually.

"Do you like this sort of thing—coming here?"

"I bring a book," said Rachel defensively.

"Oh, that would spoil it. I should come here and make camp fires. I should like to come here and go to sleep. Let's come here together one Saturday and do both."

"I think sleeping's dull," said Rachel surprised.

"I love it," exclaimed Elise, hugging herself luxuriously. "I can go to sleep like a dog. If wet wouldn't show too much on the back of my dress I'd lie down and go to sleep here now."

"My dear—how *extraordinary*!"

"Is it?" said Elise, indifferent. "Then I suppose I'm an extraordinary person." She had stopped in front of a bush; there were a few blackberries, not very good ones; just like a compact, thick boy in her black tights she was sprawling over the great pouffe of brambles, standing on one foot, balancing herself with the other, reaching out in all directions. But for that way she had of sometimes looking towards one, blank with an inside thoughtfulness, one couldn't believe she had a life of her own apart from her arms and legs. Rachel angrily doubted it; she crouched beside the bush and began eating ripe and unripe blackberries indiscriminately and quickly. "I am a very ordinary person," she said aggressively, to see what would come of it. She wondered if Elise had a notion what she was really like.

"No, you're not," said Elise, "you're probably clever. How old are you?"

"I was fifteen in August. How old—"

"I shall be fifteen in March. Still, it's awful to think you're a whole form cleverer than I am."

"I'm not clever," said Rachel quickly.

Elise laughed. "One queer thing," she said, "about being clever is that clever people are ashamed of it . . . Look what worms some of these brains here are—I say, if I eat any more of them I shall be sick. They're not a bit nice really, they're all seed, but I never can help eating things, can you?"

"Never," said Rachel. "At home I often used to eat three helpings—I mean of things like *éclairs* or pheasant or treacle tart—our cook makes it awfully well. I don't now that I have started staying up to late dinner. That makes an awful difference to what one eats in a day, helpings apart."

"I'd never eat three helpings because of my muscles. I mean to keep awfully strong, not get flabby like women do. I know all the things men don't eat when they're in training. Do you?"

"No. Do you stay up to late dinner?"

"We don't have late dinner," said Elise scornfully. "We have supper and I've stayed up to that ever since I was eight."

Elise's people must be very eccentric.

They were seen coming breathless across the garden twenty minutes late for chapel and found Miss Smyke at the door with a flaming sword. "What did I say?" asked Miss Smyke, rhetorical. "What did I *tell* you? It's no use going into chapel now," she said spitefully (as though they would want to). "They're at the Te Deum. Go up and change your stockings and stay in your dormitories till you're sent for." She turned and went back into chapel, looking satisfied and religious.

Being punished together was intimate; they felt welded. They were punished more severely than usual because of Elise, who had a certain way with her under-lip . . . She had a way with her head, too, that reminded Rachel of a defiant heroic person about to be shot. It didn't come out, mercifully, that they had broken bounds; the Jungle remained unmenaced. They were ordered apart for the rest of the day (which sealed them as "great friends") and Rachel, usually humiliated by punishment, went about feeling clever and daring. On Monday evening she kept a place beside her for Elise at supper, but after some time saw Elise come in arm in arm with Joyce Fellows and sit down at another table. She looked away. After supper Elise said, "I say, why didn't you come? Joyce and I were keeping a place for you."

Term went on, and it was all rather difficult and interesting. Rachel was a snob; she liked her friends to be rather distinguished, she didn't like being "ordered about" by a girl in a lower form. That was what it amounted to; Elise never took much trouble about one, her down-right manner was peremptory: when she said, "Let's—" it meant (and sounded like), "You can if you like: *I'm* going to." Whenever they did things together it ended in trouble; Rachel began to wish Elise wouldn't stick out her lip at people like Casabianca and look down her nose. Mistresses spoke scornfully about "Going about with the younger ones." They never asked her to "influence" Elise, which showed that they knew. IVb seemed a long way down the school, yet Elise would swagger ahead of one along passages and throw back, without even looking: "Buck up: do come on!" Then there was Joyce Fellows; a silly, blank-faced, rather unhappy "entourage."

One evening in prep Charity did a drawing on a page of her notebook, tore it out and passed it across to Rachel. It was called "Jacob (Rachel's Rajah)," and was a picture of Elise in trousers hanging upside down from a beam in the gym roof and saying, in a balloon from her mouth, "Buck up, come here, I'm waiting." Rachel couldn't climb ropes and hadn't a good head when she did get to the top of things, so this was unkind. The name was stupid but the drawing was rather clever. Rachel showed it to Elise at supper and Elise turned scarlet and said, "What a darned silly fool!" She hadn't much sense of humour about herself.

The next evening there was a drawing of a figure like two tennis balls lying on Charity's desk. (Charity's figure was beginning to develop feminine curves at an alarming rate.) Charity looked, laughed and picked the drawing up with the very tips of her finger and thumb. "Of course I don't *mind* this," she said, "but I suppose you know your beastly little common friend has no business in our form-room?"

Rachel's cheeks burnt. It wouldn't have mattered a bit if the drawing had been clever, but Elise couldn't draw for toffee: it was just silly and vulgar. "I don't know why you should think it was you," she said, "but if the cap fits—"

Later she rounded on Elise. "If you did want to score off Charity you might have invented a cleverer way."

"I don't pretend to be clever," said Elise.

"I'd never have shown you the Jacob one if I'd thought you were going to be such a silly serious ass," stormed Rachel.

Elise stared with her wide-open pale grey eyes that had, this moment, something alert behind them that wasn't her brain. "You knew that wouldn't be my idea of a funny joke," she said, "didn't you?"

Rachel hesitated. Elise, with tight lips, made a scornful little laughing sound in her nose.

"As a matter of fact," said Rachel, "I didn't think it mattered showing you what all my friends in my form think. You know you have got into a fearfully bossy way with everybody."

"I don't know what you're talking about," said Elise. "I don't s'pose you do either. What do you mean by 'everybody'? I never take any notice of anybody unless I happen to like them, and if they think I'm bossy I can't help it. It's not me who's bossy, but other people who are sloppy."

"Do you think I'm sloppy?"

"Yes, you are rather sloppy sometimes."

It was at supper, a dreadful place to begin a conversation of this sort. Rachel and Elise had to remain side by side, staring at the plates of the girls opposite, biting off and slowly masticating large mouthfuls of bread-and-jam. Then Rachel half-choked over a mouthful, turned away quickly and flung herself into the conversation of two girls on the other side. They all three talked "shop" about algebra prep. Elise just sat on there, perfectly natural and disconcertingly close. When Rachel peeped round she did not notice. She sat badly, as always, her head hunched forward between her shoulders, and Rachel knew her lip was out and had a feeling that she was smiling. When grace was over they pushed back their chairs and bolted out in different directions. Out in the hall everybody was crowding up to the noticeboard. Rachel turned away and went into the classroom and sat at her desk. When the others had gone she came out and looked at the notice-board. The lists for the next match were up and Elise was in the Lacrosse Eleven.

The last Sunday but one, in the afternoon, Rachel went back to the Jungle. It was December, goldenly fine; the trees were pink in the afternoon light, rooks circled, grass was crisp in the shadows from last night's frost. She had started out in an overcoat with a muffler up to her nose and rabbit-skin gloves, but soon she untwisted the muffler and stuffed the gloves into her pocket. The lovely thin air seemed to have turned warmer; her breath went lightly and clearly away through it. The wall, the hedge, the gate of the paddock gave her a bruised feeling.

She stumbled across the paddock, tripping up on the long ends of her muffler, with her unbuttoned overcoat flapping against her legs. "It will be a good end to this kind of a term," she thought. "If Mr. Morden catches me."

It really hadn't been much of a term. She hadn't worked, she hadn't been a success at anything, she hadn't made anyone like her. The others in IVa had been nice to her since she "came back," but they forgot her unintentionally; they had got into the way of doing things together in twos and threes since the beginning of term and she got left out—naturally. She felt lonely, aimless, absolutely inferior; she tried a lot of new ways of doing her hair, designed a black velvet dress for herself and looked forward to going home. She brought names, Charity's and the other girls', rather unnaturally into her letters so that Mother shouldn't suspect she was being a failure. She felt so sick for Elise that she prayed to be hit by a ball on the head every time she went out to Lacrosse.

Elise had the most wonderfully natural way of not seeing one. She said "Sorry" when she bumped into one in the passage, shared a hymn-book in chapel when they found themselves side by side, and when she caught up and passed one going out to the playing-field side-glanced indifferently as though one were one of the seniors. She had got her colours after her third match; no one under fifteen had ever got their colours before. All the important people were taking her up and talking about her. IVa agreed that they would not have minded, they'd have been glad, if she'd only been humble and nice to begin with and not such an absolutely complacent pig. They never talked about her in front of Rachel and Rachel never mentioned her.

Down in the lane there were deep ruts; she walked between them on crumbling ridges. A dog was barking somewhere at Mr. Morden's, snapping bits out of the silence, then letting it heal again. The bank to the Jungle was worn slippery; Rachel pulled herself up it from root to root. The Jungle was in shadow; the grass had fallen like uncombed hair into tufts and was lightly frosted. "It's nice to come back," said Rachel. "I never was really *here* that last time, it's awfully nice to come back." She bent down, parting the brambles; the leaves were purple and blackish; some rotting brown leaves drifted off at her touch.

Coming out from the brambles, an arm was stretched over the path. "Not, O God, in this lonely place," said Rachel—"let there not be a body!"

She was shaken by something regularly, put up a hand to her heart with the conscious theatrical movement of extreme fear and found it thumping. The hand lay a yard ahead of her—she could have taken three steps forward and stepped on it—the thumb bent, the red, square-tipped fingers curling on to the palm.

"Elise, is this you?" whispered Rachel. She waited, plucking leaves from the bramble, hearing the dog bark, then went round to where Elise was lying in a valley between the brambles.

Elise lay half on her side, leaning towards the arm that was flung out. Her knees were drawn up, her other arm flung back under her head which rested, cheek down, on a pile of dead leaves as on a pillow and was wrapped up in a muffler. The muffler was slipping away from her face like a cowl. Down in the sheltered air between the bushes she was flushed by sleep and by the warmth of the muffler. She was Elise, but quenched, wiped-away, different; her mouth—generally pressed out straight in a grudging smile—slackened into a pout; thick short lashes Rachel had never noticed spread out on her cheeks. Rachel had never looked full at her without having to pass like a guard her direct look; her face now seemed defenceless. Rachel stood looking down—the only beautiful thing about Elise was the cleft in her chin. She stood till her legs ached, then shifted her balance. A twig cracked; Elise opened her eyes and looked up.

"I told you I'd come here and sleep," she said.

"Yes—isn't it fearfully cold?"

Elise poked up her head, looked round and lay back again, stretching luxuriously. "No," she said, "I feel stuffyish. Have you just come?"

"Yes. I'm going away again."

"Don't go." Elise curled up her legs to make room in the valley. "Sit down."
Rachel sat down.

"Funny thing your just coming here. Have you come much?"

"No," said Rachel, staring into the brambles intently as though she were watching something that had a lair inside them moving about.

"I brought Joyce Fellows once; we came in here to smoke cigars. I hate smoking— Joyce was as sick as a cat."

"How *beastly*!"

"Oh, I don't suppose there's anything left now, we covered it up. Anyhow, I shall never smoke much. It's so bad for the wind."

"Oh, by the way," said Rachel, "congratulations about your colours."

Elise, her hands clasped under her head, had been lying looking at the sky. "Thanks so much," she said, now looking at Rachel.

"Aren't we mad," said Rachel uneasily, "doing this in December?"

"Why shouldn't we if we're warm enough? Rachel, why shouldn't we?— Answer."

"It'll be dark soon."

"Oh, dark in your eye!" said Elise, "there's plenty of time . . . I say, Rachel, I tell you a thing we might do—"

Rachel wound herself up in her muffler by way of a protest. She had a funny feeling, a dancing-about of the thoughts; she would do anything, anything. "'Pends what," she said guardedly.

"You could turn round and round till you're really comfy, then I could turn round and put my head on your knee, then I could go to sleep again . . ."

The round cropped head like a boy's was resting on Rachel's knees. She felt all constrained and queer; comfort was out of the question. Elise laughed once or twice, drew her knees up higher, slipped a hand under her cheek where the frieze of the overcoat tickled it.

"All right?" said Rachel, leaning over her.

"Mm   mmm."

The dog had stopped barking, the Jungle, settling down into silence, contracted a little round them, then stretched to a great deep ring of unrealness and loneliness. It was as if they were alone on a ship, drifting out . . .

"Elise," whispered Rachel, "do you think we—"

But the head on her knees had grown heavy. Elise was asleep.

LESBIAN BLUES LYRICS OF THE 1920S

"Prove It on Me Blues," "B.D. Woman Blues," "Has Anybody Seen My Corinne?"

The African American blues song has often been a vehicle for the expression of sub-versive sexual sentiments, and no more so than in New York City in the 1920s, when an extraordinary number of female blues artists now known to have been lesbian or bisex-ual—Gertrude ("Ma") Rainey, Bessie Smith, Ethel Waters, Alberta Hunter, Gladys Bentley, and Jackie Mabley among them—played to enthusiastic crowds in the speakeasies and jazz clubs of Harlem. In lyrics at once earthy, wry, and full of sexual innuendo, singers like Rainey, Smith, and Bentley boldly challenged the heterosexual norms of the day and got away with it.

A number of lesbian-themed blues songs were recorded in the twenties and thirties on so-called race records—cheap 78 rpm recordings distributed solely to black audi-ences. Ma Rainey's "Prove It on Me Blues," a flamboyant celebration of cross-dressing and "wild womens," came out in 1928; Bessie Jackson's "B.D. Woman Blues"—a driv-ing boogie-woogie on the theme of "bulldaggers" (i.e., mannish lesbians)—in 1935. Both songs can be heard on the 1977 Stash Records compilation, *AC/DC Blues: Gay Jazz Reissues*. Lucille Hegamin recorded "Has Anybody Seen My Corinne?"—a blues transmogrification of a traditional lament—in 1961 for an album entitled *Songs We Taught Your Mother* with Victoria Spivey and Alberta Hunter.

FURTHER READING: Chris Albertson, *Bessie* (New York: Stein and Day, 1972); San-dra Lieb, *Mother of the Blues: A Study of Ma Rainey* (Amherst: University of Massa-chusetts Press, 1981); Linda Dahl, *Stormy Weather: The Music and Lives of a Century of Jazz Women* (New York: Pantheon, 1984); Frank Taylor, *Alberta Hunter: A Celebration in Blues* (New York: McGraw-Hill, 1987); Eric Garber, "Gladys Bentley: The Bulldag-ger who Sang the Blues," *Out/Look* (Spring 1988): 52–61; ——, "A Spectacle in Color: The Lesbian and Gay Subculture of Jazz Age Harlem," in Martin Duberman, Martha Vicinus, and George Chauncey, Jr., eds. *Hidden from History: Reclaiming the Gay and Lesbian Past* (New York: Meridian, 1990), pp. 318–31; Angela Y. Davis, *Blues Legacies and Black Feminism: Gertrude "Ma" Rainey, Bessie Smith, and Billie Holiday* (New York: Pantheon, 1998).

Prove It On Me Blues

Went out last night,
Had a great big fight,
Everything seemed to go a-wrong[?].
I looked up,
To my surprise,
The gal I was with was gone.

Why she went
I don't know,
I mean to follow everywhere she goes.
Folks say I'm crooked[?],
I don't know where she took it,
I want the whole world to know.

[Chorus]
They say I do it,
Ain't nobody caught me,
You all got to prove it on me.

Went out last night,
With a crowd of my friends,
They must bin womens
Cause I don't like no mens.
It's true I wear a collar and a tie,
Make the women-folk[wind blow(?)]
Go all wild.[All the while(?)]
You all say I do it,
Ain't nobody caught me,
You sure got to prove it on me.

[Chorus]
They say I do it,
Ain't nobody caught me,
You all got to prove it on me.

I went out last night,
With a crowd of my friends,
They must bin womens
As I don't like no mens.
Wear my clothes

Just like a man[?],
Talk to the gals,
Just like any old man.
Cause they say I do it,
Ain't nobody caught me,
You sure got to prove it on me.

B.D. Women Blues

Comin' a time,
B.D. women they ain't goin' need no men,
Comin' a time,
B.D. women they ain't goin' need no men,
Oh the way they treat us
Is a lowdown and dirty thing.

B.D. women
You sure can't understand,
B.D. women
You sure can't understand,
They got a head like [a machine gun?]
And they walk just like a natural man.

B.D. women,
They all done laid their claim,
B.D. women,
They all done laid their claim,
They can lay their jive
Just like a natural man.

B.D. women,
B.D. women you know they sure is rough,
B.D. women,
B.D. women you know they sure is rough,
They all drink up many a whiskey
And they sure do strut their stuff.

B.D. women,
You know they work and make their dough,

B.D. women,
You know they work and make their dough,
And when they get ready to spend it,
They know just where to go.

Has Anybody Seen My Corinne?

Has anybody seen my Corinne?
Aw, she's a dream,
Just like a vampire
She set my heart on fire.

I regret the day,
The day that she was born,
Since my lovin' Corinna's been gone.

If anybody sees my Corinne,
No matter where Corinna may be,
Tell my Corinna
To hurry back to me.

My gal went away last night,
I did my best to treat her right,
For no reason I could see,
I was wild about my gal,
Thought she was wild about me.

Has anybody seen my Corinne?
Aw, she's a dream,
Just like a vampire
She set my heart on fire.

I regret the day,
The day that she was born,
Since my lovin' Corinna's been gone.

If anybody sees my Corinne,
No matter where Corinna may be,
Tell my Corinna
To hurry back to me.

Has anybody seen my Corinne?
Aw, she's a dream,
Just like a vampire
She set my heart on fire.

I regret the day,
The day that she's been gone,
Ever since Corinna's been gone.

If anybody sees my Corinne,
No matter where Corinna may be,
Tell my Corinna
To hurry home to me.

NELLA LARSEN (1891–1964)

From *Passing* (1929)

Nella Larsen's story is a sad one. Born in Chicago, the daughter of a Danish mother and West Indian father, she suffered lifelong ambivalence over her mixed-race ancestry. Yet her split heritage was also a source of creative inspiration: both of the novels for which she is remembered today, *Quicksand* (1928) and *Passing* (1929), deal with the conundrums of mulatto identity. Larsen attended both the black-oriented Fisk University and the University of Copenhagen, and later worked as a nurse and a librarian in New York City, where she began writing children's literature. In 1919 she married a wealthy black scientist, published several short stories, and became a well-known figure in Harlem social and artistic life. Her novels of the late twenties met with success and she was the first African American woman to receive a Guggenheim fellowship. Her marriage ended unhappily, however, and in 1930 the public accusation that she had plagiarized a short story—a charge she denied—devastated her. She wrote no more, and returned to nursing for the next thirty years. She died, a mostly forgotten figure, in 1964.

Since the rediscovery of her fiction in the mid-1960s, Larsen's second novel, *Passing*, has attracted wide attention, thanks in part to its powerful yet cryptic representation of desire between women. The story involves a light-skinned black woman, Irene Redfield, who meets an old schoolfriend, the glamorous Clare Kendry, while both are "passing" (for white) in a segregated restaurant. The priggish Irene lives a conventional middle-class life with her husband in Harlem; her passing is of an unusual and impulsive nature. Clare, however, has married a white man—a violent bigot who has no idea his wife is "colored"—and has made such daring pretence a part of daily life. After meeting Irene, Clare tests the limits of her masquerade by openly visiting her friend in Harlem. While Clare claims to be in search of her lost "Negro" identity, she also seems strangely infatuated with Irene, who responds with a mixture of panic and fascination. For much of the book the "passing" metaphor thus works on two levels. Irene and Clare can pass for "white," but one often feels, uneasily, that one or both may be passing for "straight" as well. Irene will later be implicated—in a scene of superb psychological ambiguity—in Clare's accidental death.

In the scene below Clare pays a surprise visit on Irene, who is confused, excited, and repelled by her friend's seductive overtures. The sense here of a fatal repressiveness—both in Irene herself and in the fabric of the narrative—is characteristic of Larsen's disquieting and memorable book.

FURTHER READING: Nella Larsen, *An Intimation of Things Distant: The Collected Fiction of Nella Larsen*, ed. Charles R. Larson (New York: Anchor, 1992); Robert A. Bone, *The Negro Novel in America* (New Haven: Yale University Press, 1965); Barbara Christian, *Black Women Novelists: The Development of a Tradition 1892–1976* (Westport, Conn.: Greenwood, 1980); Cheryl Wall, "Passing for What? Aspects of Identity in Nella Larsen's Novels," *Black American Literature Forum* 20 (1986): 97–111; David L. Blackmore, " 'That Unreasonable Restless Feeling': The Homosexual Subtexts of Nella Larsen's *Passing*," *African-American Review* 26 (1992): 475–84; Jennifer D. Brody, "Clare Kendry's 'True' Colors: Race and Class Conflict in Nella Larsen's *Passing*," *Callaloo: A Journal of African-American and African Arts and Letters* 15 (1992): 1053–1065; Deborah E. McDowell, " 'It's Not Safe. Not Safe at All': Sexuality in Nella Larsen's *Passing*," in Henry Abelove, Michele Aina Barale, and David Halperin, eds., *The Lesbian and Gay Studies Reader* (New York and London: Routledge, 1993), pp. 616–25; Judith P. Butler, "Passing, Queering: Nella Larsen's Psychoanalytic Challenge," in *Bodies That Matter: On the Discursive Limits of "Sex"* (New York: Routledge, 1993), pp. 167–86; Barbara Johnson, "Lesbian Spectacles: Reading *Sula*, *Passing*, *Thelma and Louise*, and *The Accused*," in Marjorie Garber, Jann Matlock, and Rebecca L. Walkowitz, eds., *Media Spectacles* (New York: Routledge, 1993), pp. 160–66; Thadious M. Davies, *Nella Larsen: Novelist of the Harlem Renaissance* (Baton Rouge: Louisiana State University Press, 1994); Corinne E. Blackmer, "The Veils of the Law: Race and Sexuality in Nella Larsen's *Passing*," *College English* 22 (1995): 50–67; Nell Sullivan, "Nella Larsen's *Passing* and the Fading Subject," *African American Review* 32 (1998): 373–86.

The noise and commotion from above grew increasingly louder. Irene was about to go to the stairway and request the boys to be quieter in their play when she heard the doorbell ringing.

Now who was that likely to be? She listened to Zulena's heels, faintly tapping on their way to the door, then to the shifting sound of her feet on the steps, then to her light knock on the bedroom door.

"Yes. Come in," Irene told her.

Zulena stood in the doorway. She said: "Someone to see you, Mrs. Redfield." Her tone was discreetly regretful, as if to convey that she was reluctant to disturb her mistress at that hour, and for a stranger. "A Mrs. Bellew."

Clare!

"Oh dear! Tell her, Zulena," Irene began, "that I can't—No. I'll see her. Please bring her up here."

She heard Zulena pass down the hall, down the stairs, then stood up, smoothing out the tumbled green and ivory draperies of her dress with light stroking pats. At the mirror she dusted a little powder on her nose and brushed out her hair.

She meant to tell Clare Kendry at once, and definitely, that it was of no use, her coming, that she couldn't be responsible, that she'd talked it over with Brian, who had agreed with her that it was wiser, for Clare's own sake, to refrain—

But that was as far as she got in her rehearsal. For Clare had come softly into the room without knocking and, before Irene could greet her, had dropped a kiss on her dark curls.

Looking at the woman before her, Irene Redfield had a sudden inexplicable onrush of affectionate feeling. Reaching out, she grasped Clare's two hands in her own and cried with something like awe in her voice: "Dear God! But aren't you lovely. Clare!"

Clare tossed that aside. Like the furs and small blue hat which she threw on the bed before seating herself slantwise in Irene's favorite chair, with one foot curled under her.

"Didn't you mean to answer my letter, 'Rene?" she asked gravely.

Irene looked away. She had that uncomfortable feeling that one has when one has not been wholly kind or wholly true.

Clare went on: "Every day I went to that nasty little post office place. I'm sure they were all beginning to think that I'd been carrying on an illicit love affair and that the man had thrown me over. Every morning the same answer: 'Nothing for you.' I got into an awful fright, thinking that something might have happened to your letter, or to mine. And half the nights I would lie awake looking out at the watery stars—hopeless things, the stars—worrying and wondering. But at last it soaked in, that you hadn't written and didn't intend to. And then—well, as soon as ever I'd seen Jack off for Florida, I came straight here. And now, 'Rene, please tell me quite frankly why you didn't answer my letter."

"Because, you see—" Irene broke off and kept Clare waiting while she lit a cigarette, blew out the match, and dropped it into a tray. She was trying to collect her arguments, for some sixth sense warned her that it was going to be harder than she thought to convince Clare Kendry of the folly of Harlem for her. Finally she proceeded: "I can't help thinking that you ought not to come up here, ought not to run the risk of knowing Negroes."

"You mean you don't want me, 'Rene?"

Irene hadn't supposed that anyone could look so hurt. She said, quite gently, "No, Clare, it's not that. But even you must see that it's terribly foolish, and not just the right thing."

The tinkle of Clare's laugh rang out, while she passed her hands over the bright sweep of her hair. "Oh, 'Rene," she cried, "you're priceless! And you haven't changed a bit. The right thing!" Leaning forward, she looked curiously into Irene's disapproving brown eyes. "You don't, you really can't mean exactly that! Nobody could. It's simply unbelievable."

Irene was on her feet before she realized that she had risen. "What I really mean," she retorted, "is that it's dangerous and that you ought not to run such silly risks. No one ought to. You least of all."

Her voice was brittle. For into her mind had come a thought, strange and irrelevant, a suspicion, that had surprised and shocked her and driven her to her feet. It was that in spite of her determined selfishness the woman before her was yet capable of heights and depths of feeling that she, Irene Redfield, had never known. Indeed, never cared to know. The thought, the suspicion, was gone as quickly as it had come.

Clare said: "Oh, me!"

Irene touched her arm caressingly, as if in contrition for that flashing thought. "Yes, Clare, you. It's not safe. Not safe at all."

"Safe!"

It seemed to Irene that Clare had snapped her teeth down on the word and then flung it from her. And for another flying second she had that suspicion of Clare's ability for a quality of feeling that was to her strange and even repugnant. She was aware, too, of a dim premonition of some impending disaster. It was as if Clare Kendry had said to her, for whom safety, security, were all-important: "Safe! Damn being safe!" and meant it.

With a gesture of impatience she sat down. In a voice of cool formality, she said: "Brian and I have talked the whole thing over carefully and decided that it isn't wise. He says it's always a dangerous business, this coming back. He's seen more than one come to grief because of it. And, Clare, considering everything—Mr. Bellew's attitude and all that—don't you think you ought to be as careful as you can?"

Clare's deep voice broke the small silence that had followed Irene's speech. She said, speaking almost plaintively: "I ought to have known. It's Jack. I don't blame you for being angry, though I must say you behaved beautifully that day. But I did think you'd understand, 'Rene. It was that, partly, that has made me want to see other people. It just swooped down and changed everything. If it hadn't been for that, I'd have gone on to the end, never seeing any of you. But that did something to me, and I've been so lonely since! You can't know. Not close to a single soul. Never anyone to really talk to."

Irene pressed out her cigarette. While doing so, she saw again the vision of Clare Kendry staring disdainfully down at the face of her father, and thought that it would be like that that she would look at her husband if he lay dead before her.

Her own resentment was swept aside and her voice held an accent of pity as she exclaimed: "Why, Clare! I didn't know. Forgive me. I feel like seven beasts. It was stupid of me not to realize."

"No. Not at all. You couldn't. Nobody, none of you, could," Clare moaned. The black eyes filled with tears that ran down her cheeks and spilled into her lap, ruining the priceless velvet of her dress. Her long hands were a little uplifted and clasped tightly together. Her effort to speak moderately was obvious but not successful. "How could you know? How could you? You're free. You're happy. And," with faint derision, "safe."

Irene passed over that touch of derision, for the poignant rebellion of the other's words had brought the tears to her own eyes, though she didn't allow them to fall. The truth was that she knew weeping did not become her. Few women, she imagined, wept as attractively as Clare. "I'm beginning to believe," she murmured, "that no one is ever completely happy, or free, or safe."

BLAIR NILES (1890–1959)

From *Strange Brother* (1931)

Blair Niles—prolific novelist, explorer, travel writer, and fellow of the Society of Women Geographers—was born in Virginia but spent much of her life traveling, particularly in South America. She married Robert Niles, Jr. in 1913. Her 1931 novel *Strange Brother* is one of a group of early-twentieth-century works—Carl Van Vechten's *Nigger Heaven* (1926) and Claude McKay's *Home to Harlem* (1927) are others—that deal frankly with the gay and lesbian presence in African American urban culture. Set in 1920s New York during the heyday of the Harlem Renaissance, when white sophisticates flocked uptown to the bars and nightclubs of Harlem in order to experience the new and burgeoning "Negro" culture prompted by the huge influx of black migrants into the city after World War I, *Strange Brother* is the sympathetic story of a young white man, Mark Thornton, who comes to recognize his homosexuality after finding himself drawn to the gay clubs and cabarets of black Harlem.

Niles modeled the nightclub in the scene below—the "Lobster Pot"—on the notorious Clam House jazz club on Seventh Avenue. A contemporary journalist described the Clam House as "a narrow room in Jungle Alley catering to a large white patronage and featuring Gladys Bentley, pianist and torrid warbler. A popular house for revelers but not for the innocent young." Bentley (1907–1960), who weighed over 250 pounds, wore men's suits, and "married" another woman in a highly publicized mock-ceremony in the late twenties, appears here as the lesbian nightclub singer Sybil, whose "piercingly sweet call" is "like a love-cry heard far off in some jungle night." Despite Niles's crude handling of her black characters—uniformly presented as glamorous primitives—the portrait of Sybil conveys something of the authentic excitement of Gladys Bentley's lost art.

FURTHER READING: Blair Niles, *Strange Brother* (1931; rpt. New York: Arno, 1975); Harriette Cuttino Buchanan, "Blair Rice Niles," in Lina Mainiero, ed. *American Women Writers*, vol. 3 (New York: Frederick Ungar, 1981), pp. 267–69; Jonathan Ned Katz, *Gay/Lesbian Almanac: A New Documentary* (New York: Harper and Row, 1983); Eric

Garber, "Gladys Bentley: The Bulldagger Who Sang the Blues," *Out/Look* (Spring 1988): 52–61; —, "A Spectacle in Color: The Lesbian and Gay Subculture of Jazz Age Harlem," in Martin Duberman, Martha Vicinus, and George Chauncey, Jr., eds., *Hidden from History: Reclaiming the Gay and Lesbian Past* (New York: Meridian, 1990), pp. 318–31; George Hutchinson, *The Harlem Renaissance in Black and White* (Cambridge, Mass.: Harvard University Press, 1995); Jonathan Goldberg, "Strange Brothers," in Eve Kosovsky Sedgwick, ed., *Novel Gazing: Queer Readings in Fiction* (Durham, N.C.: Duke University Press, 1997); Jon Michael Spencer, *The New Negroes and Their Music: The Success of the Harlem Renaissance* (Knoxville: University of Tennessee Press, 1997); Kevin J. Mumford, "Homosex Changes: Race, Cultural Geography, and the Emergence of the Gay," in Lucy Maddox, ed., *Locating American Studies: The Evolution of a Discipline* (Baltimore, Md.: Johns Hopkins University Press, 1999), pp. 385–407; Paul Allen Anderson, *Music and Memory in Harlem Renaissance Thought* (Durham, N.C.: Duke University Press, 2001).

"Oh, what a scrap of a place!"

The door of the Lobster Pot had swung open to admit them. They had had first to ring a bell, and after a pause June had seen an eye appear at a peep-hole in the door. The eye had peered, had been withdrawn and the peep-hole closed, before finally the door had opened.

Then, while Phil took off his hat and coat, June stood looking about the narrow rectangular smoke-filled room.

She saw three small round tables ranged against one wall, with four tables against the opposite wall. At the end of the room an upright piano stood beside an opening from which a door had been removed. June could see through the opening into the room beyond. It was fitted up as a bar. And through a further opening she looked into a kitchen. She saw it all through smoke so thick that, until her eyes had become adjusted, the details were vague. Even the figures at the tables, and the huge negress at the piano, were like blurred shadows.

But in a moment she began to register the details, noting that the tablecloths were checked red and white, that there was just enough space between the tables to walk the length of the room, and on into the bar, that there was a green glass light in the middle of the ceiling, and small parchment-shaded lights at intervals along the side walls.

And while she took in these items she felt the reverberating beat of the piano throb in her ears.

"Let's take that table, across from the piano," she said.

Then, as she sat down, letting her wrap fall back over her chair, she found herself returning a smile of recognition, for at the next table was the young man she had seen at the Magnolia Club, sitting between the two negroes. And with them now was the girl, Glory, who when she sang had made June know so unbearably what life might give.

June thought that Mark's smile brought a sunlit quality to his face, which in repose was so sad that each time he had smiled she had been surprised. [. . .]

After the first moment of her recognition of Mark Thornton, June had for a time no thought for any one in the room but the strange figure whose hands passed with such incredible speed up and down the piano.

"What rhythm! See, Phil, how she keeps her feet going . . . beating on the floor as if it were a drum. Where on earth could she have come from? She looks like the heart of Africa . . . the heart of darkness! And the way she's dressed!"

June heard a man passing through to the bar greet her as Sybil.

"Sybil . . . her name's Sybil, Phil."

June watched, fascinated at the way rhythm possessed Sybil's great clumsy figure.

"And how she's dressed!"

For Sybil's big feet wore old, down-at-the-heel, black oxford ties. Sybil's legs were in gray cotton stockings. A short tight black cloth skirt was stretched taut about Sybil's heavy thighs. A white blouse and dark coat clothed Sybil's shapeless torso. And set close to her shoulders was Sybil's head; with its protruding lower jaw, its flat receding brow, and its hair, oiled and brushed to an unnatural straightness, as though the hair were Sybil's one vanity.

"Phil, she is extraordinary! Did you ever see a cabaret entertainer before who wasn't dressed up . . . made up? But this Sybil is just an untidy fat woman! Putting herself over by sheer genius . . . nothing but sheer genius!"

"Certainly a contrast to the fuss and feathers of the Magnolia Club," Phil agreed.

Through an opening in the wall above the piano a black hand pushed a glass of whisky and soda. Sybil reached for it and drank, keeping the piano going with her other hand, never pausing in the syncopated beat which pulsed through her body, from her pounding feet to the crown of her sleek oiled head.

Sybil drank. And then Sybil began to sing.

At the sound of her deep man's voice coming suddenly into the room, June started and exclaimed softly, "God!"

"Why was I born?" Sybil sang. "Why am I living?"

Her voice boomed deep and rich.

"What is the good of me by myself?" The tune put all its emphasis on the "me" of that phrase.

"What do I get? . . . What am I giving?"

And then, unexpectedly, the voice rose to a high piercingly sweet falsetto, like a love-cry heard far off in some jungle night.

"Why do I want a thing I daren't hope for?"

And then again that high sweet wordless cry. It was Glory's call, carried back to the source of life, sweet, wild, elemental. Glory's song was human, conscious of itself, as even the most primitive man is conscious of himself. But Sybil's cry was universal, the very birds and beasts cry for each other like that. [. . .]

Sybil danced the length of the room and back, as light on her feet as though she had not weighed nearly two hundred pounds.

"Thank you, Pa, for doing things up just right."

Sybil danced as though to live was so gorgeous an experience that one must dance and sing in thanksgiving. She seemed possessed by an excitement which she communicated to every one in the room.

"God, Phil, how alive she is!" June exclaimed. "So tremendously alive! . . ."

Sybil had dropped her skirt now and was holding her arms as if they encircled an imaginary dancing partner.

And Nelly was again making up her lips, as though to increase vitality by means of a carmine lipstick.

Sybil was clapping her hands in front of her, behind her, in front again, again behind her, and dancing . . . dancing madly.

"Thank you, Grandpa . . . Thank you, Grandma."

[. . .] Sybil clapped her hands, stretching her long arms and clapping, while torso as well as feet danced to the strong monotonous beat of the piano and the insistent rhythm of Carter's banjo.

And then Sybil sunk breathless in the vacant chair beside Ira. Caleb poured out a drink for her.

Later June heard Ira ask, "How's your wife, Sybil? She always used to be here at the Lobster Pot. What's become of her?"

Joe was playing softly, so that June was able to hear the reply. "Amy's well, but the management won't let her come over any more."

"Why not?"

"Oh, Amy's so jealous! She makes trouble. Can't stand it if a woman looks at me. She's as jealous of me, Ira, as you are of Glory. She won't have nobody lookin' at me with a wet eye. The management said she was always makin' trouble. I tell him to pay it no mind . . . but he wouldn't have it. See?"

Sybil drank thirstily. "Gosh, Ira," she went on. "This has been a hard week for me."

"What's been the matter?"

"Mother-in-law, Ira. Amy's mother's been visitin' us. She's goin' home to-morrow. An' that's a good thing. Amy an' I couldn't keep under cover one more day."

"Ho, Sybil, you an' your mother-in-law!" Ira laughed, rocking back and forth. "You an' your mother-in-law! What'll I hear next! Next you'll be tellin' me that you and Amy are expectin' a son an' heir!"

"Amy is talkin' about adoptin' . . . when we can afford it!"

Again the door had opened and a dark youth had come to sit at the table with the negro dandies.

"There's Pansy," Sybil said. "Evenin', Pansy. How're you?"

Pansy waved a greeting with one hand and lovingly smoothed his hair with the other.

June noticed then that he wore pearl earrings.

Sybil had gone back to the piano. She mopped her still dripping forehead and began to play, her fingers running up and down the keys as if she were uncertain what to choose, playing snatches of one thing and another. Joe stood beside her, leaning against the wall. Carter with his banjo was at the other end of the piano, beside the door which led into the bar. Sybil mopped her forehead again, and the three began, at first in slow, carefully enunciated, chanting syllables:

> As I passed St. James infirmary,
> I saw my sweetheart there.
> > Aw-aw-h! Aw-aw-h!
> All stretched out on a table.
> > Aw-aw-h! Aw-aw-h!
> So pale, so cold, so fair!
> > Aw-aw-h! Aw-aw-h!
> So pale, so cold, so fair!
> > Aw-aw-h! . . .

Ira took up the song, repeating, "So cold, so pale, so fair!"

And the youth called Pansy moaned in high soprano, "Aw-aw-h! . . ."

It seemed to June that a corpse actually lay in the room.

"Aw-aw-h! Aw-aw-h!"

Glory, Caleb, Ira . . . there was not a negro, nor a mulatto in the place who was not joining in now.

"Aw-aw-h!"

Surely the corpse seemed to lie in the room, and they were all wailing around it:

"I put my hand on my sweetheart . . . and I saw that she was dead."

"Aw-aw-h! Aw-aw-h! . . ."

June was seeing everything now in detached isolated details. Sybil's gray-stockinged leg, moving up and down to the measure of the tune. Nelly's plucked eyebrows, dark against a white forehead. The girl with her red felt hat askew, too drunk now to kiss her lover. Sybil's sleek black hair with the light glistening on it. The gray stocking always moving up and down to the beat of the piano.

"Aw-aw-h! Aw-aw-h!"

Glory's lips, full and purplish red—pomegranate red. Sybil's black hands, under whose touch the piano keys gave forth that deep monotonous beat. Mark's face, so pale among his companions. Mark's black necktie. Sybil's gray leg moving up and down. . . .

And suddenly an incredibly sweet, prolonged, trembling cry from Sybil.

Pansy took up the cry, higher still and with the illusion of its having come from somewhere far away, as two birds in the jungle answer each other across a distance.

The sandy-haired man was paying for the club sandwich and the ginger ale. He was putting on his hat and coat. The door had opened and he was going out.

How green the light was in the ceiling! And why did the fair young man wear a black necktie? Had some one died?

The bright crescents of Glory's eyes . . . and the smell of fritters and coffee coming from the kitchen . . . and the voices chanting:

"Sixteen coal black horses . . . hitched to a rubber-tired hack . . . took seven girls to the graveyard."

Sybil and Joe and Carter led the singing, answered by repeated phrases, now from Ira, now from Pansy, now from Glory.

"Coal black horses."

"Took seven girls to the graveyard."

"Only six o' them are comin' back."

"Aw-aw-h! Aw-aw-h!"

[. . .]

The answering phrases came from every negro in the room. Only the whites remained expressionless, inarticulate.

To Mark, the piano seemed pounding far away, somewhere deep within him. To June, it seemed as though sand slipped irrevocably through an hourglass, and she longed to live completely while there was yet time.

And all around them, voices alternately swelled and moaned:

"Let her go! Let her go! . . . God bless her!"

It was as if those who sang were draining off all the sorrow of the world. A few moments before they had been singing of fertility, giving thanks for life. Now, though they wailed, they were accepting death. The whole cycle of living had been expressed, there in that smoky little room, led by a fat negress and two lanky mulatto youths. They had recognized, accepted, and given expression to all the elemental human emotions. They had questioned, "Why was I born? . . . Why am I living?" And they had replied with love of life, with love of loving, and now they were accepting death:

"Oh, when I die just bury me!"

"Aw-aw-h! Aw-aw-h!"

MARGARET ANDERSON (1886–1973)

From *My Thirty Years' War* (1930)

The epithet "free spirit" would seem to have been invented for Margaret Anderson. Born into a middle-class Midwestern family, she decided early on that the bohemian life was for her and gravitated to Chicago, where she worked as a freelance journalist and performed briefly as a concert pianist. In 1914, with virtually no financial backing, she founded *The Little Review*, an experimental literary journal destined to become most influential American arts magazine of the first decades of the century. Anderson's venture quickly found supporters: the poet Ezra Pound became a major contributor and the *Review*'s European editor; Jane Heap, a witty young writer and woman about town, became Anderson's lover and coeditor. Soon enough, with Heap's assistance, Anderson was publishing scores of important writers: Sherwood Anderson, Djuna Barnes, T. S. Eliot, Hart Crane, Dorothy Richardson, H.D., Emma Goldman, Wyndham Lewis, William Carlos Williams, and W. B. Yeats among them. Although perennially short of funds, a situation exacerbated when she and Heap serialized part of James Joyce's controversial *Ulysses* and were convicted on obscenity charges at a celebrated trial in Chicago in 1920, the indefatigable Anderson managed to keep the magazine going until 1929.

With the demise of the *Little Review*, Anderson's nine-year relationship with Heap also came to an end and Anderson moved to France with a new companion, the opera singer Georgette Leblanc, widow of Maeterlinck. Together they renovated a lighthouse in Normandy and lived there for the next twenty-one years. (Heap remained a close friend and a frequent visitor.) After Leblanc's death in 1941, Anderson formed a new partnership, equally devoted, with Dorothy Caruso, widow of the singer, which lasted until Caruso's death in 1955. Anderson herself died in 1973.

In three volumes of chatty, entertaining, gloriously self-promoting memoirs—*My Thirty Years' War* (1930), *The Fiery Fountains* (1951), and *The Strange Necessity* (1969)—Anderson detailed these and other loves. While sometimes coy about her homosexuality—her descriptions of Heap, Leblanc, and other "lovely companions" are euphemistic and hagiographical in tendency—she nonetheless casts an indelible light on lesbian artistic and intellectual life between the wars. She knew everybody who was anybody—Gertrude Stein, Colette, Janet Flanner, Isadora Duncan are among the countless friends and acquaintances who appear in the memoirs—and she was passionate in her support of female creativity. In the excerpt below from *My Thirty Years' War*, Anderson describes going with Heap to meet one of their early Chicago heroines, the lesbian opera singer Mary Garden. The rhapsodical mode is characteristic; likewise the cosy gesturing toward Heap, whose own oddball *hommage* to Garden she includes at the end of the piece. At the same time, however, the passage is a neat evocation of Anderson's own quirky charm and devotion to feminine genius.

FURTHER READING: Margaret Anderson, *My Thirty Years' War* (New York: Covici, Friede, 1930); ——, *The Fiery Fountains* (New York: Horizon, 1951); ——, ed., *The Little Review Anthology* (New York: Hermitage House, 1953); ——, *Traits and Portraits* (London: Routledge and Kegan Paul, 1962); ——, *The Strange Necessity* (New York: Horizon Press, 1969); Georgette Leblanc, *Souvenirs: My Life with Maeterlinck*, trans. Janet Flanner (New York: Dutton, 1932); Jane Rule, *Lesbian Images* (New York: Doubleday, 1975); Shari Benstock, *Women of the Left Bank: Paris, 1900–1940* (Austin: University of Texas, 1986); Holly Baggett, "The Trials of Margaret Anderson and Jane Heap," in Susan Albertine, ed., *A Living of Words: American Women in Print Culture* (Knoxville: University of Tennessee Press, 1995), pp. 169–88; Andrea Weiss, *Paris Was a Woman: Portraits from the Left Bank* (London: Pandora, 1995); Nina van Gessel, "Margaret Anderson's Last Laugh: The Victory of *My Thirty Years' War*," *English Studies in Canada* 25 (1999): 67–88.

During our last days in Chicago we met someone who has also loved it above other cities—Mary Garden. Jane had written in the current *Little Review* that Mary made Galli-Curci and other prima donnas look like lost cloak models wandering about the stage.

I sent her a copy of the magazine, telling her we should like to know her, having proselyted for her since the L.R. began. She answered in a swift and beautiful scrawl: Come to-morrow at four.

We went to the Blackstone where she was staying. I was chiefly concerned with the possibility of establishing some real talk with her. Or would she be conventional?

Well, said Jane, she's from the north. I know the people of the north—(Jane is Scandinavian: her mother came from the extremity of Norway that touches Iceland). They know what's what, though they say very little.

She's Scotch, I said. (I am Scotch.) She has the canny Scotch eye. And I think she can be talked to. (It never occurred to me in those days that anyone but Jane would do the talking. It doesn't now.)

We were shown into a salon whose outstanding feature was an enormous photograph of Oscar Wilde on the piano. From an adjoining room a voice of electric vibrations was giving instructions to a waiter, and then Mary pushed open the door and advanced upon us like a battery. The air was charged with an animal magnetism that one rarely has the pleasure of feeling. Paderewski is devitalized by comparison. The challenge of Mary Garden's presence is one of the most thrilling human experiences I remember. She wore a dark blue suit of a cut that is almost never achieved by any tailor, and a small hat made of pale blue feathers. She sat in a chair like Thais in the mirror scene, hips held back, arms dropping straight.

Where did you get such a body? asked Jane.

I don't know, answered Mary simply. They just gave it to me—("they" meaning the gods, we assumed easily). My sisters haven't it. I don't do anything for it—except tennis—

She sat in her chair surveying her body as if it were a separate entity over which she had a perfect control and in which she could take a complete pride. There was nothing of the prima donna about her. If she hadn't been a singer she would have been a great lawyer, she told us, radiating enough energy to have saved Oscar Wilde from the English.

I carry that photograph with me always, she went on, looking toward the piano. A great poet, a great man. If I had only been where I am to-day, I would have gone to the prison when he came out, taken him with me, re-established him before the world.

There was nothing enveloped, nothing enveloping about Mary Garden's charm. It had none of the suavity of Bernhardt's. It was tangible, unadorned, compelling. What I liked most about her was the quality of her attention.

Let's talk about life, I suggested.

What do you mean? asked Mary, looking frightened.

Oh, I mean abstractly. How do you feel about it?

What she means, said Jane, is that you must find the material a little short.

Mary changed to an armchair. She relaxed in it and began to look more direct than people can look.

Go on, she said.

So Jane went on. She sketched an article she meant to write for the L.R., analyzing Mary's art ideas. Mary Garden furnishes a striking example, in the visual arts, of the artist "creating in his own image."

I am going to begin, said Jane, by saying that the art of the actor to-day is concerned only with the reproduction of the few galvanized words and actions of mankind. This attests nothing but a lack of consciousness, lack of movement, lack of ecstasy. As I see it, you alone on the stage are theatric. You summarize, enforce the design, create a new aspect, indicate the infinite from the concrete—by form and movement.

Mary listened intently. She sat deeper in her chair, her head forward and down, her eyes boring up under the eyelids.

Yes, she said when Jane had finished. [. . .]

Excerpts from Jane's article:

... In all the arts, whenever the magic of the artist has been united with this other magic (personality) the possessor has been of the first great ... I wonder why, even in those people to whom has come some appreciation of the magic of the artist, there is still so often such strong resentment and distrust of this other magic. Because of their adventures in the great emotions those who have it loosen new forces of life; they re-create the great passions; they add something to Fate.

Everyone feels that he has a right to a share in that which the millions are working together in uproar to add to existence. Many long for a share in that which the artists are making in silence for the soul. But who is there except the artist who is willing to feel in this thing the imminence of something beyond life and personality? Who else in the world except the lonely insane, because of their adventures in illusions and hallucinations, ever add anything to Fate? How easy to say that genius is akin to madness. All great antitheses are akin: all unknown things are mysteriously akin, as all known things are naturally akin. But how poignantly akin are the known and unknown.

... When I was a little child I lived in a great asylum for the insane. It was a world outside of the world, where realities had to be imagined and where, even through those excursions in illusions and hallucinations, there ran a strange loneliness. The world can never be so lonely in those places where the mind has never come as in a place where the mind has gone. ... There was no one to ask about anything. There was no way to make a connection with "life." ... Very early I had given up everyone except the Insane. The others knew nothing about anything, or knew only uninteresting facts. From the Insane I could get everything. They knew everything about nothing and were my authority; but beyond that there was a silence. Who had made the pictures, the books and the music in the world? And how had they made them? And how could you tell the makers from just people? Did they have a light around their heads? Were there any of them in the world now? And would I ever see one? ... Then a name came across the world, with a new radiance—Mary Garden.

Mary Garden seems to be the only singer who knows that all the arts come from the same source and follow the same laws. ... None of the arts expresses human emotion—they express the *source* of human emotion. To express the emotion of life is to live; to express the life of emotion is to make art. ... I wish I could tell what a great creative artist Mary Garden is. It is one thing for the artist to create a character within the outlines definitely or indefinitely drawn by the composer; to put himself in the place of the character and act as he would act. But the creative artist *takes the character to himself* and then creates from his imagination in his own image. The more universal the artist the greater his power to reveal his soul in different images. . . .

Mary Garden is a great decorative actress. I am using decoration in the sense in which it is used in painting, where elimination and not elaboration is used to emphasize the intention of line and color . . . She can draw in the whole psychology of a scene with one line of her body—the line of her walk. If she is to dominate a situation with her intellect or her beauty she walks from the centre of her intelligence, which is the head; if it is a matter of the soul she walks from the centre of her presence, which is the top plane of the chest . . . This is living painting which moves in rhythm like a frieze.

WYNDHAM LEWIS (1884–1957)

"Lesbian-Ape" from *The Apes of God* (1930)

Born on a yacht off the coast of Nova Scotia—to English parents then living in the U.S.—the artist, novelist, and critic (Percy) Wyndham Lewis was taken back to England at the age of four and raised in London. He displayed artistic talent at an early age, and after a spell at Rugby (1897–98) won a scholarship to the Slade School of Art (1898–1901). He had his first exhibition of paintings in London in 1909. In 1913, in collaboration with the poet Ezra Pound and the sculptor Henri Gaudier-Brzeska, he founded the avant-garde art movement known as Vorticism, an offshoot of futurism and cubism. Together he and Pound published the short-lived but highly influential magazine *Blast: The Review of the Great English Vortex* (1914–15), in which they excoriated the mechanization and commercialism of modern life and called for a revitalization of art and poetry. During the First World War, in which Lewis served as an artillery officer, the Vorticist movement gradually petered out, but Lewis himself never lost his revolutionary fervor. In a series of idiosyncratic postwar novels and political manifestos—*Tarr* (1918), *The Art of Being Ruled* (1926), *Time and Western Man* (1927), *The Childermass* (1928), *Paleface* (1929), *The Apes of God* (1930), and *The Revenge for Love* (1937)—Lewis poured out his scorn for modern civilization in increasingly satiric and rebarbative prose. In his later years he turned to autobiography, publishing *Blasting and Bombardiering* in 1937, *Rude Assignment* in 1950, and *The Writer and the Absolute* in 1952. While never as celebrated as his colleagues Ezra Pound or T. S. Eliot, Lewis must nonetheless be regarded as one of the most important of Anglo-American modernists, and both his paintings and writings continue to arouse interest and controversy.

Lewis's 1930 novel *The Apes of God* is a fierce, surreal, often wildly funny satiric attack on the "Apes of God": self-designated "artists" and "intellectuals" who prostitute their meager talents in order to win bourgeois acceptance and a place in fashionable society. The central character is a moronic young man named Dan Boleyn who is sent by his mysterious mentor, Horace Zagreus, to investigate the habitats of various London "apes." In the chapter below, the feeble Dan, who carries out his researches by posing as an artist's model, goes to visit a female ape named Miss Ansell at her Chelsea studio but ends up, apparently by mistake, in the horrid atelier of a whip-wielding

"Lesbian-Ape." Among other things, the chapter is a comic assault on the lesbian novelist Radclyffe Hall, whose celebrated apologia for female homosexuality, *The Well of Loneliness*, had been published two years before, in 1928. More broadly, it is an attack on postwar English society, in which (according to Lewis) traditional male and female roles had become dangerously confused. The arresting mixture of violence, farce, and grotesque black humor is characteristic: Lewis would not be Lewis without the intention to shock and give offense.

FURTHER READING: Wyndham Lewis, *The Apes of God* (1930; rpt. Santa Barbara, Cal.: Black Sparrow, 1981); —, *Wyndham Lewis on Art*, ed. W. Michel and C. J. Fox (London: Thames and Hudson, 1969); —, *Men Without Art*, ed., Seamus Cooney (Santa Barbara, Cal.: Black Sparrow, 1987); —, *The Art of Being Ruled*, ed. Reed Way Dasenbrock (Santa Barbara, Cal.: Black Sparrow, 1989); —, *Tarr* (Santa Barbara, Cal.: Black Sparrow, 1990); —, *Time and Western Man*, ed. Paul Edwards (Santa Barbara, Cal.: Black Sparrow, 1992); Geoffrey Grigson, *A Master of Our Time: A Study of Wyndham Lewis* (London: Methuen, 1951); Hugh Kenner, *Wyndham Lewis* (London and Norfolk, Conn.: New Directions, 1954); Geoffrey A. Wagner, *Wyndham Lewis: A Portrait of the Artist as the Enemy* (New Haven and London: Yale University Press, 1957); Robert T. Chapman, "Satire and Aesthetics in Wyndham Lewis's *Apes of God*," *Contemporary Literature* 12 (1971): 133–45; Fredric Jameson, *Fables of Aggression* (Berkeley: University of California Press, 1979); Julian Symons, ed., *The Essential Wyndham Lewis: An Introduction to His Work* (London: André Deutsch, 1989); Paul O'Keefe, *Some Sort of Genius: A Life of Wyndham Lewis* (London: Jonathan Cape, 2000); Paul Edwards, *Wyndham Lewis: Painter and Writer* (New Haven: Yale University Press, 2000); Philip Head, *Engaging the Enemy: The Gentle Art of Contradiction in the Work of Wyndham Lewis* (Kent: Green Knight, 2001).

Dan scudded down Launceston Place, a high wind smote its acacia fernery, and he found his way to Ashburn Place, which was up in arms. Two vagabond cripples had seized a basement, into which they had fallen. This Place he descended in quick strides passing to the other side of the road, averting his head from the scene of disorder. Where Ashburn Place ended he hesitated, and then entered Rosary Gardens. Leaving them behind him, and passing over into Chelsea, he consulted his pocket-map.

It was a long way to this spot from Mrs. Farnham's. He could never have done it without the help of a pocket-atlas of London and his natural map-craft. Policemen made him extremely shy. He never spoke to them if he could help it, and avoided their eyes, even, when crossing the tides of traffic. From experience he had found that, on account of his self-consciousness, it was quite impossible to understand their directions at all. Nothing but confusion ensued from asking to be directed by one of these helmeted young men in blue—whose proverbially kind eyes only drew him in, under the cruel peaked eaves of their helmets, and made him forgetful of his duty and feel so terribly hot and ashamed too and only upset him in any case.

Dan went along a tunnel that was an arched way beneath flats. And in the twilight he came to an empty terrace, upon one side of which was a row of liver-umber, brick, geraniumed cottages. Confronting them was a high and gloomy wall, it filled the terrace with premature darkness. Above it Dan could see the tops of the windows of formidable studios.—These were the gardens he was to visit. *A great nest of women Apes!* The studios were secluded.

Turning into a paved court, out of the narrow terrace, there was a row of wicket-gates, cottage-effect. He attempted in spite of the misty dusk to read the numbers upon the small green studio doors. He stopped at the third wicket-gate. He looked over it for a little while, he was satisfied. Although the number was blurred and might be five instead of three, he entered and knocked upon the massive doll's-house entrance.

The door opened very suddenly. Dan at the moment was collapsed, as if deflated, and crumpling at the left side. He had forgotten he was there, about to put his head into the she-ape's den, in a spasm of delicious reminiscence, and of anticipation. Tomorrow Horace would be with him!

With alarm he glanced up. Before him stood a severe masculine figure. In general effect it was a bavarian youth-movement elderly enthusiast. She was beyond question somewhat past mark-of-mouth. But this was a woman, as in fact she had appeared in the typed description. Of that he felt tolerably certain, because of the indefinable something that could only be described as "masculine." An heroic something or other in the bold blue eye, that held an eyeglass, that reminded him of the Old Guard or the Death-or-Glory-Boys, in the house of Mr. Brian Macdonnell, secured for him certainty of the sex at least without further worry. It was She. This was Miss Ansell.

She was wiry and alert with hennaed hair bristling, en brosse. In khaki-shorts, her hands were in their pockets, and her bare sunburnt legs were all muscle and no nonsense at all. There was something that reminded Dan of Dick Whittingdon, for she was bald, he remarked with a deep blush, on the top of her head. Only there the resemblance ended it seemed, for whereas Dick was anxious, that was easy to see, to disguise his naked scalp, *this* strong-minded person had a peculiar air of being proud of it all the time (to be bald, like the ability to grow a moustache, was a masculine monopoly). A march had been stolen, with her masculine calvity. But a strawberry-pink pull-over was oddly surmounted by a stiff Radcliffe-Hall collar, of antique masculine cut—suggestive of the masculine hey-day, when men were men starched-up and stiff as pokers, in their tandems and tilburys. The bare brown feet were strapped into spartan sandals. A cigarette-holder half a foot long protruded from a firm-set jaw. It pointed at Dan, sparkling angrily as the breath was compressed within its bore.

Daniel Boleyn stood simply rooted to the spot. He was frankly dismayed, but could think of nothing to say to excuse himself for having knocked at all. "The wrong door!" he muttered in his mind but he could not utter the apology. He was genuinely sorry he had knocked—but he was quite unable to find his tongue. Could this be Miss Ansell? Surely he would have been warned in his morning duty-sheet. Not even Horace would have been so inhumane as not to whisper a caveat! Why had he been sent to her? He must have mistaken the number. What *was* the number? Was it five? Was it three? He had not looked for some time at his instructions, though he was positive three was the number. What a terrible oversight!—

They stood staring at each other for a momentous half-minute, the woman with the utmost hostility.

"What are you staring at!" at last she asked him, bold and gruff, straight from the shoulder.

A shiver went down Dan's back as he heard this voice, but he was incapable of moving a muscle.

She turned up a wrist-watch towards the sky.

"It's a bit late isn't it?" She pointed out to him gruffly.

Dan blushed. It *was* late.

"Come in, if you're coming in!"

She turned upon her heel and went back into a large lighted studio, which he could perceive beyond. At least it was a studio, even if the wrong one, and should he bolt she would be after him like a flash of greased lightning he was positive and catch him before he had gone far.

But as she left him he did regain the use of his legs. Convulsively he stepped out and it was forward he was moving. He followed the soldierly boy-scoutish fantosh into the artist's-studio, slinking in the wake of its positive strut.

"Shut the door!" she called over her shoulder at him, as she receded.

Dan went back and, with the most anxious attention, he closed the front door without making any noise whatever, as he pushed it into its sleek solid oaken rabbets. Then anew he made his way into the lighted interior, and she faced him in the manner that is indicated by the word *roundly* and by the word *squarely*. There she stood, and avoiding her militant male eye he approached her. Her dander was up.

"Who sent you? Was it Borstie? Was it Miss Lippencott?" she demanded.

"Lip Got!" Dan cooed, with blankest eyes, in Beach-la-Mar.

"Lippencott," she said with a dark puzzled scorn.

He was quite silent. However pressed for an answer, he would have been quite unable to open his lips any more.

She quizzed the drooping six-foot-three of speechless manhood. With vicious eye she wrenched off his four-foot of swaying trouser-leg. She tore to shreds the massive pretences of the male attire.

She snorted a sigh, as she saw the man quail at her glances.

"Well, let's have a look at you!" she then ruggedly exclaimed, as one chap to another. She jerked a thumb backwards, towards a screen, beneath the balcony, which ran the entire length of the long side of the place.

"You can undress there! Look slippy!"

At this Dan's knees in fact did shake. Had he had a tongue in his head he would have told her then and there that she must be mistaken. He was *not* an italian model (such as he had seen leaving the studio of Mélanie). There was some fearful misunderstanding. This was not Miss Ansell, he had been deceived. It was quite a different kind of Ape, that dwelt in this lonely well, to the one it had been Horace's wish he should visit.

But even as these words (which would not materialize) were crying out inside his brain, he was assailed by a new doubt. If this *were* after all Miss Ansell? Horace he said to himself would not have sent him here upon a purposeless errand. There was nothing purposeless about Horace. This was a noted Ape of God no doubt. He had been dispatched to report upon her—he must not leave empty-handed. It was not his place to call in question the arrangements of Horace. Horace, it might very well be, *had* intended him to pose as a nude italian model, to this woman. For the ways of Horace were mysterious in the extreme.

Taken to its ultimatum and crisis, where would this not perhaps lead? The expressive eyes of this dewy colossus, this maidenly great doe, rolled in panic—he saw the path that Horace had, it might be, intended him to tread, but he balked it in one sweeping squirm of lovely revulsion. He writhed, beneath her insulting eyes. *Mustht* I? his eye, in tender obsecration, asked. *Yesth!* her eye signalled in response, in beastly parody—hitting every time below the belt.

In spite of the fact that his glances were downcast mainly, Dan was yet present to every object, and he had immediately observed with terror a large dog-whip upon the model's-throne. Haunted as he was by the memory of the Bokharan oxthong he had been compelled to hold by that grinning old Jenny, the sight of this disciplinary instrument disturbed him extremely. In fancy he could see himself naked, in full flight, before this little hennaed white-collared huntress—her dog-thong cracking about his girl-white surfaces, of Clydesdale proportions, as he rushed round and round her artist's studio—till probably he would fall, panting and exhausted, at her sandalled feet! And vae victis of course—there would be no quarter in this sanguinary munera.

For better or for worse, he must escape at once—he could not go through with it, he had made up his mind—tomorrow he must inform Horace that posing as a nude model was a thing he was quite unable to do. Would Horace excuse him nude-posing please, as a great concession! It would be asking him to suffer the tortures of the Damned! *Please* Horace, do not ask me to strip and nude-pose—not *that*! (It was not as though he were *beautiful*, he added with a secret blush.)

"What are you doing may I ask?" the horrid masculine accents banged out at him ever so loud in the big hollow studio, and caused him a fright-bang too—a discharge of adrenalin. "Look sharp! I can't hang about here all night for you to peel!"

Oh how that dreadful word *peel* left him not only naked, but skinless! What, wrench off his putamen, in obedience to this martinet? Oh what a horrid errand was this, upon which Horace had sent him!—if, that was, he had come to the right address. What an anguishing thought—the real Ape he had been sent in quest of might in fact all the time be expecting him with a glass of sherry, in the studio opposite.

She had been lighting a cigarette, straddling her tiger-skinned hearth, selecting a seasoned cigarette-holder, resembling a Brissago, facing the mantelpiece. Catching sight (out of the corner of her eye) of this maddening male professional lay-figure, who had turned up to offer himself for posing-work, still in the same place (posing as it were already where he stood) she wheeled about in the most savage manner possible. Pointing to the screen, she shouted:

"*There* you idiot—over there!—can't you see the bloody thing! Go over there and peel at once or I'll chuck you out of the bloody studio neck and crop! Yes I mean it! I do believe you're some beastly Fairy! I don't know what possessed Borstie to send a ghastly Fairy round here! It's no use your making sheep's eyes at *me*! Either go in there and peel or else beat it! Do you get me! Jump to it!"

As she said *jump* she jumped herself, and more dead than alive Dan skipped as well. As she took a threatening step in his direction he turned tail, he rushed quickly over straight at the screen. Bolt upright behind it, his heart-rate trebled, he held his breath and bit his lip, rolling frightened eyes. He strained his ears to catch her movements. Oh—what he had gone through for the sake of this man! And did Horace return his devotion? He smiled wanly to himself, in the comparative darkness—no, one would scarcely say Horace *did*, to judge from all he made him suffer!

Dan became slowly aware that his was the opposite case to that of the ostrich. He had achieved the occultation of his body, but the luxuriant summit of his head must be visible above the screen. So he made haste to crouch down, and in that position he placed an eye to a crack, where two of the panels of the screen met. With an intense alarm, he was able now to observe all the movements of the threatening masculine person beyond, in her sports-kit (dressed to kill, by sheer roughness, and to subdue all the skirted kind) scraping a large palette with an ugly looking jack-knife.

He saw her look up, stop scraping, and incline her head to listen. Then she called out sharply.

"I say aren't you ready yet? You take a long time to peel for a man!"

There was a pause in which, knife in hand, she listened.

"I don't believe you *are* peeling!"

He saw her put down the palette upon the model's-throne, next to the dog-whip. She retained, he observed abashed, the long jack-knife in her hand.

In an instant Dan had wrenched off his jacket, torn from his neck his collar and his tie. With hands all thumbs and all a-flutter, he undid, and then in one continuous movement dropped down, and kicked off, his man's long trousers—as if as a symbol of capitulation to the militant feminine-male beyond. Standing white, occult, and quite naked, his teeth chattering, with his vest in one hand and limp shoe in the other, he awaited the next move of the master-spirit—the boy-scout spinster masculine rake. But suddenly he was pulled up sharp with a vengeance, and put to work to think in earnest: he gazed, startled and guilty, blushing unseen, quite lost in thought. Feverishly he turned over in his mind a most knotty problem. It had not presented itself to him before, in the midst of this breathless march of events.

Necessity proved herself once again, upon the spot, the mother of invention, and he put down his shoe and seized the limp empty arms of the thin cotton vest. He held it out, until the square body of it hung like an apron before the midst of his person. With the speed bred of a high sense of decorum, he had passed the shoulder-line of the vest, rolled into a rude rope, about his waist—securing it behind, at the summit of the buttocks, in a large knot. Then he drew the apron that hung down between his legs, and he incorporated its extremity in the large bulging knot behind.

"Look here I've had about enough of this!" came the now familiar bark, from beyond the screen. "Are you coming out or not? Anyone would think you were a bloody woman!"

The imperious tones of crashing command rang out upon the air of this palatial well of stern bachelor loneliness, and they froze his blood.

Blushing a deeper red than any hefty big-handed Susannah could ever compass—surprised by the most designing of Old Elders that ever stepped upon painted canvas, Dan came out into the obscene harsh light of the arc-lamp which hung above the model's-throne.

He gave one dilated terrified glance at the woman standing astride before her easel. Turning swiftly, he rushed back behind the screen. There was a hoarse laugh from the haggard old bachelor-girl in sports-shorts. But her voice pursued him scornfully over the screen, behind which once more he crouched:

"The world's coyest virgin what! Well well well! *Come* out of that! Come out and let's have a look at what all the fuss is about! I'm sure I don't know what the men are coming to!"

Dan stood and shook behind the screen. Wildly he rolled his eyes to himself in a great effort to decide what steps to take, in this fearful emergency—what for a Pelman-brave would have been Kinderspiel. But he simply shook with blank indecision.

"I say, cut this out old bean will you? You've come to the wrong shop!" she raised her voice still more. (The wrong shop indeed! This *could* not be where Horace had sent him!)

"I shall absolutely lose my patience in two shakes of a donkey's tail!" the harpy's voice whipped him like a cat-o'-nine-tails. It had grown ugly too. "Come out unless you want me to step over there and drag you out by the—! Chuck all this jolly rot and roll out, you dirty little sprucer, or I'll stick you up on the jolly old throne myself!"

Upon a terrified sudden impulse Dan came swiftly out from behind the screen. He cast one glance of wild appeal at the woman, and rushed up upon the model's-throne. There, blushing down to his waist line—the "ram and goat" even, of the horrid poetry, suffused with red, his solar plexus flushed, as if it had been punched in boxing—he limply stood, his head turned in the opposite direction from the watching slave-driving person, his body drooped in profile.

"Good!" she rapped at him. "Yes!" she said, with her painter's squint. "Not at all bad!" she informed the nudity before her, with hearty male patronage, as she ran over his points, "you're quite muscular!" she yawned.

The studio was extremely cold, when you were nude, and Dan was beside himself with fear. He shivered without ceasing, occasionally gulping.

"Model! Turn round—do you mind! I've had that view of you long enough."

Slowly Dan moved, until the whole of his back was turned towards her.

"No!" the woman immediately bellowed, as she grasped the manœuvre. "No! Not *that* way! Turn round *this* way. Not your *back*!"

With a fresh spasm of deep-red bashfulness, Dan still more slowly turned about, until he faced her. But he stood with averted face, gazing away to his right flank. He held his chin high, for beneath upon the floor of the throne was the dog-whip, and he wished to forget its presence.

"What on earth have you got there!" he heard her exclaim.

Dan was petrified. The hard white light poured down over him, splitternaked and stark as your fist's-face, he could not move a muscle. Oh, what obedience to Horace (if it were indeed Horace who had planned this) had led him to! In a pose of hieratic stiffness, his head in profile, he awaited her attack. He heard her brisk step and the rigor increased. Marching over with decision to the model's-throne, she did not hesitate a moment. A half-scream, the first sound he had uttered since his entrance, broke from the lips of Dan, as with careless hand she rudely seized the coil of his cotton vest. Then, with a violent tug, she dragged it clean off his shrinking person.

Standing beneath him, his vest in one hand, she fixed him with a chilly masculine eye.

"Listen to me my dear man!" she said: she waved a disdainful hand in his direction, "that is of no interest whatever to *me*. Do you understand me? Put your mind quite at rest! It would take a jolly sight more than the likes of you to vamp me! Get me? So don't let's have any more of this stuff! You come here to *sit*, not to try and seduce me anyway! It's love's labour lost! See? Spare yourself the dérangement!"

She threw down the vest upon a chair.

"Do you want to sit or not?"

Dan violently nodded his head. He desired from the bottom of his heart to sit down.

"Very well. Let's get on with the War then! I shan't pay you for the time you waste while you're trying to vamp me! If you want to sit—sit!"

Dan again nodded his head, without looking at her, with great vehemence. She was appeased.

"Very well!" it became almost a tone of approval. "Here get hold of this!"

To his horror she snatched up the dog-whip and brandished it. He retreated a step, his eyes fixed upon her in terror. She held out to him the handle of the whip. He seized it, and his knees knocking lightly together from mingled cold and dread of what this fearful Ape might not require of him, he held it tightly at his side.

"Take up an attitude like this will you?"

Dan gave her askance one fleeting look of horror—for she had thrown herself into an attitude replete with offence not to some figure but to himself he felt.

"I want you for a figure of a roman soldier threatening Our Saviour. No that whip!"

Dan struck several attitudes. All were designed, as far as possible, to minimize the immodesty of the glaring white crown-to-foot exposure of his animal self. The towering milk-pink declivities of the torso beneath the arc-light, the sectioning of the chest by the upright black feather of body-hair, the long polished blanched stalks of the legs, upon which the trunk oscillated, all moved hither and thither. He threw his head into the scales, first to the left then to the right. Full it is true of earth's old timid grace, as haunted by the feminine irish chastity, he threatened an imaginary Saviour with a whip. But at length the restless evasive bulk fell into an accepted position.

"Stop like that!"

Camped energetically, charcoal in hand, she dropped into a watchful, pouncing attitude. She looked keenly from the white surface of the body to the white surface of the paper, and back. With difficulty Dan came to a halt.

"Can you keep that?" she asked him.

His whip gave a weary upward waggle. His head sank, in melancholy affirmative. For a few seconds he held himself quite still. When he saw her eyes were upon her paper he moved about, seeking a more comfortable arrangement for his twisted nudity—one that might eventually lessen the immodesty.

Now a steady scratching began. A large sheet of paper was fixed upon a board. Her legs wide apart, the busy artist stood before her super-easel—thrusting out at arm's-length a stick of charcoal, from time to time, while she squinted up the eye that was not furnished with the eye-glass She computed relative distances, from one landmark to another, upon the person of her sitter. She joined these major points, upon the paper before her, with sweeping lines.

But for Dan the physical agony, in succession to the mental agony, had now set in. His hips had become still more inconveniently twisted, in order to remove away to the left the greater part of his exposed person, and so present as far as possible an offence-less edge-on object to the eye of the observer. On one foot the heel was gracefully removed from the ground. The other foot received the complete weight of a muscle-laden body rising above two metres into the air.

The staccato rasp, flashed to and fro, of the brittle charcoal, was incessant. A page was whisked off the board with as much force as had been used to remove Dan's vest. It fell to the floor and she stamped upon it as she returned to the attack, dashing dark black lines here and there upon the new page.

But Dan stood bathed in a cold perspiration. His face, from having been a sunset crimson, had become a corpse-like white. Then it became a most alarming pallid green. Holding stiffly at arm's length the whip of the legionary, Dan swayed from side to side, with more and more giddy abandon.

"Keep still can't you!" the enraged employer of labour shouted, from the easel. "I can't draw you if you roll about like that!"

Dan's last thought (before he fell) was of Horace. He had forgotten that this might be the wrong studio altogether. All he could say over and over again to himself was "Horace, why are you *always* so unkind—why—so always—*unkind*!"

Dan reeled, slowly at first. His body with a loud report came in contact with the floor of the model's throne. As his head struck he had a sickly flash of consciousness, and his body turned over, in a slight convulsion. Then he lay relaxed at last in a deep faint.

When Dan came-to there were two voices audible—one soft and one hard. The hard one said,

"Of course I thought you sent him, Borstie. How can you be so stupid!"

The soft voice replied inaudibly, it was a muffled tinkle.

"With *that*? Thank you!"

There was a hoarse whispering, with a snorted laugh or two, also a super-male chuckle, a bald *ha-ha*!

"A more useless piece of goods I've never met with."

"It is certainly a horrid sight."

"You're right. If it could only stand up on its legs!"

"You don't propose to pay it for lying on its back do you!"

"The trouble I had to get the animal to peel! Il s'est fait prié ma chère."

"Isn't he a model?—What does he come for?"

"I think he thought he'd got a *bonne poire*. He tried to vamp me!"

"My *dear*! That!"

"Oh yes. He wanted me to undress him. He was most averse to posing."

"Pah! Turn it over! I don't want to look at that *any* more!"

Opening an eye slightly, Dan perceived a second younger figure, that that possessed the softer voice, beside the first—but dressed with recognized feminine elegance, with a breast visible to the nipple, and with sun-kissed silken legs all-clear to the tenderloin. Then a rough hand seized his shoulders and attempted to roll him along the floor of the throne.

"Don't touch him—he might not like it, if he were conscious," the feminine voice remarked, solicitous for the safety of her mate.

The man-voice snorted defiance, and gave Dan another big shake.

Dan's head and neck were wet with water. He made a slight movement with his arm.

"He is coming round" said the slight voice. "My dear! *Look*!"

"Model! Do you feel better?"

Dan was nearer the edge of the throne now: with an eel-like agility born of shame and terror he rolled off, and as he did so he sprang to his feet. The newcomer started back and uttered a scream. Swiftly Dan regained the cover of the model's undressing screen. His "vanish" was accompanied by two loud shouts of laughter from extraordinary woman No. 1—who, at his bashful exit, indulged in the coarsest mirth, pointing after him with her cigarette-holder to her sweetheart, who tittered sneeringly as the great white mass disappeared, like a rat into its hole.

With a violent head-ache, overwhelmed with shame, Dan got his clothes on very quickly. But the vest remained in the hands of the feminine enemy. When he was quite ready, standing in his hiding-place he waited some minutes. He hoped that the second woman might take herself off. But the terrible voice of the first to bring him to his senses soon rang out.

"How much longer are you going to potter about in there? If I hadn't seen all you've got I should have thought you were a woman. Hallo! Come out! I've had enough of your company. Hop it! Do you hear model?"

Dan came out and went towards the door with averted head.

"Here. Here is a half-crown for you."

She intercepted him and thrust the money up into the occulted palm of his trembling hand.

"Go and have a Scotch."

He held the half-crown in his hand, and he went on towards the door.

"You don't appear satisfied. It's all you'll get! It's a bloody sight more than you deserve!"

She slammed the door upon him, as soon as he had passed out into the garden.

Night had now fallen. In the lighted doorway of the opposite studio stood a dark eminently feminine figure. As he went through the wicket-gate he observed it making signs to him. Without losing time he decamped at the double, but he heard at his back in the darkness a tinkling voice.

"Is that Mr. Bolcyn by any chance?"

That was it! Evidently that could be none other than Miss Ansell, to whom he had been supposed to go after Yarmouth Place. He had got into the wrong studio. *Horace was not to blame!* He did not look back but hastened away from this monstrous colony.

COLETTE (1873–1954)

From *The Pure and the Impure* (1932)

The celebrated French writer Sidonie Gabrielle Colette, prolific author of novels, short stories, essays, and memoirs, was born in the village of Saint-Sauveur-en-Puisaye in Burgundy. The child of an army officer and an adoring mother ("Sido"), whom she later memorialized in some of her most lyrical works, Colette grew up with a profound love of nature, animals, and the French countryside. Memories of her idyllic early years indubitably sustained her over a long and extraordinarily eventful life. In 1893, at the age of twenty, Colette married the older novelist and critic Henry Gauthier-Villars (known as Willy). Dishonest, brutal, and an inveterate womanizer, Willy nonetheless inspired her first literary ventures. At his behest she wrote her first novel, *Claudine à l'école* (*Claudine at School*), an autobiographical account of her schooldays, which Willy then published under his own name in 1900. When the book became a popular success, he forced her to produce a number of sequels—sometimes by shutting her in her room until she wrote—and these too were published under his name.

Willy's exploitation came to an end when Colette ran away from him and divorced him in 1906. While continuing to write, she supported herself, bohemian-style, as a vaudeville dancer and mime. In the same year she took up with Mathilde de Morny, the wealthy, cross-dressing Marquise de Belboeuf, known as Missy, with whom she had a six-year lesbian relationship. (The two became notorious in 1907 when they performed an Arabian Nights-style love scene at the Moulin Rouge in which Missy, dressed as an Egyptian prince, kissed Colette on the mouth.) Colette commemorated this colorful period—and her own itinerant acting career—in the novel *La Vagabonde* (1911). Tiring of theater life, Colette left Missy in 1912 and subsequently married the journalist Henry de Jouvenal, by whom she had a daughter—her only child—at the age of forty. With her new husband's encouragement, she published more novels and *souvenirs*— *L'Entrave* (1913), *L'Envers du music-hall* (1913), *Les Heures longues* (1917), *Chéri* (1920), *La Maison de Claudine* (1922), *Le Voyage égoiste* (1922), and *Le Blé en herbe* (1923). By the mid-1920s she had become internationally famous. Divorcing de Jouvenal in 1924, she lived alone for eleven years, turning increasingly to autobiography in works such as *Sido* (1930), *Prisons et paradis* (1932), *Le Pur et l'impur* (1932), *Mes Apprentissages* (1936), *Belles saisons* (1945), and *Le Fanal bleu* (1949). Late in life she married her third husband, the writer Maurice Goudeket, with whom she lived happily until her death at the age of eighty-one. Elected to the Académie Goncourt in 1945 and made a Grand Officier de la Légion d'Honneur in 1953, she was the first woman in French history to be honored at her death with a state funeral.

Love between women was an important theme in Colette's writing from the beginning. The racy *Claudine à l'école* is one of the first and best of lesbian schoolgirl novels; subsequent works, such as the novel *La Seconde* (1929), contain discreetly sapphic elements. Colette treats the subject most extensively, however, in *Le Pur et l'impur* (*The Pure and the Impure*), a collection of loosely linked, semiautobiographical essays on the pleasures of the flesh. (The book was originally published under the title *Ces Plaisirs* in 1932.) True to her own sophisticated ethos, Colette treats same-sex love as an eminently civilized—and civilizing—passion. The "purity" and "impurity" in the English title, as Ann Cothran has pointed out, have nothing to do with moral judgments: indeed, the desires of the body only become "impure," according to Colette, when pursued to excess. Whatever one's erotic predilection, true purity, she suggests—and true gratification—lie in the rejection of libertinism.

The chapter below—on Colette's onetime friend, Renée Vivien, the short-lived Anglo-French lesbian poet and lover of Natalie Clifford Barney—illustrates the thesis in its negative or critical aspect. Addicted to drink and drugs and the cruel ministrations of an unseen female lover, the exotic Vivien epitomizes for Colette the human "catastrophe" of voluptuousness in excess. So great is Colette's imaginative sympathy, however, that Vivien never comes off as mere caricature. Even as she limns Vivien's suicidal dissipation, Colette treats her subject's complex nature with the piquancy, tact, and moral understanding of the great novelist.

FURTHER READING: Colette, *Oeuvres complètes*, 15 vols. (Paris: Flammarion, 1950); —, *The Pure and the Impure*, trans. Herma Briffault (New York: Farrar, Straus and Giroux, 1966); —, *Earthly Paradise: Colette's Autobiography, Drawn from the Writings of Her Lifetime*, ed. Robert Phelps (New York: Farrar, Straus and Giroux, 1966); Elaine Marks, *Colette* (New Brunswick: Rutgers University Press, 1960); Margaret Crosland, *Colette: The Difficulty of Loving* (New York: Dell, 1973); Yvonne Mitchell, *Colette: A Taste for Life* (New York: Harcourt Brace Jovanovich, 1975); Michèle Sarde, *Colette: Free and Unfettered*, trans. Richard Miller (New York: William Morrow, 1980); Sherry A. Dranch, "Reading through the Veiled Text: Colette's *The Pure and the Impure*," *Contemporary Literature* 24 (1983): 176–89; Shari Benstock, *Women of the Left Bank: Paris, 1900–1940* (Austin: University of Texas Press, 1986); Nicole Ward Jouve, *Colette* (Bloomington: Indiana University Press, 1987); Herbert Lottmann, *Colette: A Life* (Boston: Little Brown, 1991); Ann Cothran, "Colette (1873–1954)," in Claude J. Summers, ed., *The Gay and Lesbian Literary Heritage: A Reader's Companion to the Writers and Their Works, from Antiquity to the Present* (New York: Henry Holt, 1995), pp. 172–73; Judith Thurman, *Secrets of the Flesh: A Life of Colette* (New York: Knopf,

1999); Terry Castle, *Boss Ladies, Watch Out! Essays on Women, Sex, and Writing* (New York: Routledge, 2002).

I still have in my possession some thirty letters Pauline Tarn wrote to me. I had a great many more, but some of them were filched from me, and the shortest, the least attractive, I gave away to "fans" of Renée Vivien. A few of them, too, have been mislaid.

If I were to publish the correspondence of this poet who never ceased claiming kinship with Lesbos, it would astound only because of its childishness. I stress this very particular childish quality, which strikes a false note—dare I say a note of obvious insincerity? The charming face of Renée Vivien reflected only a part of that childlike quality, in the rounded cheek, soft and downy, in the innocent short upper lip, so typically English, curled up and revealing four little front teeth. A bright smile constantly lit up her eyes, a chestnut-brown which became greenish in sunlight. She wore her long, beautiful ash-blond hair, which was fine and straight, massed at the top of her head, from which stray locks came down now and then like wisps of fine straw.

There is not a single feature of her youthful face that I do not vividly recall. Everything in it bespoke childishness, roguishness, and the propensity to laughter. Impossible to find anywhere in that face, from the fair hair to the sweet dimple of the weak little chin, any line that was not a line of laughter, any sign of the hidden tragic melancholy that throbs in the poetry of Renée Vivien. I never saw Renée sad. She would exclaim, in her lisping English accent, "Oh, my dear little Colette, how disgusting this life is!" Then she would burst into laughter. In all too many of her notes, I find that same exclamation repeated, often spelled out frankly in the coarsest words: "Isn't this life sheer muck? Well, I hope it will soon be over!" This impatience of hers amused her friends, but her hope was not dashed, for she died in her thirtieth year.

Our friendship was in no way literary, it goes without saying—or rather, I should say, thanks to my respect for literature. I am sparing of words on that subject, except for occasional exclamations of admiration, and in Renée Vivien I found the same diffidence and well-bred restraint. She, too, refused to "talk shop." Whenever she gave me any of her books, she always hid them under a bouquet of violets or a basket of fruit or a length of Oriental silk. She was secretive with me on the two literary aspects of her brief existence: the cause of her sadness, and her method of work. Where did she work? And at what hours? The vast, dark, sumptuous, and ever changing flat in the avenue du Bois gave no hint of work. That ground-floor flat in the avenue du Bois has never been well described, by the way. Except for some gigantic Buddhas, all the furnishings moved mysteriously: after provoking surprise and admiration for a time, they had a way of disappearing . . .

Among the unstable marvels, Renée wandered, not so much clad as veiled in black or purple, almost invisible in the scented darkness of the immense rooms barricaded with leaded windows, the air heavy with curtains and incense. Three or four times I caught her curled up in a corner of a divan, scribbling with a pencil on a writing pad propped on her knees. On these occasions she always sprang up guiltily, excusing herself, murmuring. "It's nothing, I've finished now . . ." Her lithe body devoid of density languidly drooped, as if beneath the weight of her poppy-flower head with its pale golden hair, surmounted by immense and unsteady hats. She held her long and slender hands in front of her, gropingly. The dresses she wore were always long, covering her feet, and she was afflicted with an angelic clumsiness, was always losing as she went her gloves, handkerchief, sunshade, scarf . . .

She was constantly giving things away: the bracelets on her arms opened up, the necklace slipped from her martyr's throat. She was as if deciduous. It was as if her languorous body rejected anything that would give it a third dimension.

The first time I dined at her place, three brown tapers dripped waxen tears in tall candlesticks and did not dispel the gloom. A low table, from the Orient, offered a pell-mell assortment of *les hors d'oeuvre*—strips of raw fish rolled upon glass wands, *foie gras*, shrimps, salad seasoned with sugar and pepper—and there was a well-chosen Piper-Heidsieck champagne *brut*, and very strong cocktails—Renée Vivien was ahead of her time. Suffocated with the obscurity, mistrustful of the unfamiliar fire of Russian, Greek, and Chinese alcohols, I scarcely touched the food. I remember that Renée's gay laughter, her liveliness, the faint halo of light trembling in her golden hair all combined to sadden me, as does the happiness of blind children who laugh and play without the help of light. I did not believe that this meeting in this luxurious flat submerged in darkness could result in any real friendship with this tall young woman who tossed off her drink with the obliviousness one sees in bridesmaids at a country wedding.

Among the beverages that she raised to her lips was a cloudy elixir in which floated a cherry harpooned on a toothpick. I laid a hand on her arm and cautioned her.

"Don't drink it."

She opened her eyes so wide that the lashes of her upper eyelids touched her eyebrows.

"Why not?"

"I've tasted it," I said, embarrassed. "It's . . . it's deadly. Be careful, it tastes like some kind of vitriol."

I dared not tell her that I suspected a practical joke. She laughed, flashing her white teeth.

"But these are my own cocktails, *ma pethith Coletthe*. They are excellent."

She emptied the glass at one gulp, neither gasping nor blinking, and her rounded cheek kept its floral pallor.

I did not notice that evening her almost total abstention from food, but later on I discovered that she subsisted mainly on a few spoonfuls of rice, some fruit or other, and alcohol—especially alcohol. During this first evening, nothing could dispel the uneasiness engendered by the strangeness of the place, bound to astonish a guest, the semi-darkness, the exotic foods on plates of jade, vermeil, or Chinese porcelain, foods that had come from countries too far away.

However, I was to see Renée Vivien many times afterward.

We discovered that her house and mine communicated, thanks to the two garden courts separated only by a grille, and that the concierge who had the keys was not incorruptible; I could therefore go from the rue de Villejust to the avenue du Bois to visit her without setting foot in the street. Occasionally I used this facility. On my way, I would rap on the windows of the garden flat where Robert d'Humières lived, and he would open his window and hold out an immaculate treasure, an armful of snow, that is to say, his blue-eyed white cat, Lanka, saying, "To you I entrust my most precious possession."

Twenty meters farther on, and I would confront, at Renée's, the air which, like stagnant water, slowed down my steps, the odor of incense, of flowers, of overripe apples. It is an understatement to say that I was stifled in that gloom. I became almost wickedly intolerant there, yet never wore out the patience of the gossamer angel who dedicated offerings of lady apples to the Buddhas. One day, when the spring wind was stripping the leaves from the Judas trees in the avenue, I was nauseated by the funereal perfumes and tried to open the window: it was nailed shut. What a contribution such a detail is, what a flourish it adds to a theme already rich! What a quantity of lurid gleams and glints of gold in the semi-darkness, of whispering voices behind the doors, of Chinese masks, of ancient instruments hanging on the walls, mute, only vaguely whimpering at the banging of a door beneath my heavy hand. At Renée Vivien's I could have wished to be younger, so I could be a little fearful. But impatience got the better of me and one evening I brought an offending, an inadmissible big oil lamp, and plumped it down, lit, in front of my plate. Renée wept big tears over this, like a child—it is only right to add that she consoled herself in like manner.

Try as she would to please me by inviting along with me two or three of my best friends, to make me happy, our intimacy did not seem to make any real progress. At the table in the darkness, or lounging comfortably and provided with exotic food and drink, Turkish cigarettes or Chinese blond tobacco in miniature silver pipes, we remained a bit stiff and uneasy, as if our young hostess and we ourselves apprehended the unexpected return of an absent and unknown "master."

This "master" was never referred to by the name of woman. We seemed to be waiting for some catastrophe to project her into our midst, but she merely kept sending invisible messengers laden with jades, enamels, lacquers, fabrics . . . A collection of ancient Persian gold coins came, glittered, disappeared, leaving in its place glass cabinets of exotic butterflies and other insects, which in their turn gave way to a colossal Buddha, a miniature garden of bushes having leaves of crystal and fruit of precious stones. From one marvel to another Renée moved, uncertainly, already detached, and showing the indifferent self-effacement of a guard in a museum.

When I recall the changes which gradually rendered Renée more understandable, I believe I can link these with certain gestures at first, then with some words that threw a different light on her. Some people become transformed by riches, others acquire a real life only by impoverishment, their very destitution giving them life. When was I able to forget that Renée Vivien was a poet, I mean, when did I begin to feel a real interest in her? No doubt it was one evening when dining at her place, an evening of spicy foods and of disquieting drinks—I risked drinking only two glasses of a perfect and very dry champagne—a gay evening and yet inexplicably strained, when Renée's gaiety expressed itself in laughter, in an eagerness to applaud exaggeratedly any least droll word.

Exceptionally that evening she wore a white dress that bared her delicate and youthful throat and the nape of her neck, where wisps of her soft straight hair were always coming undone. Between two remarks and without warning, she suddenly leaned against the back of her chair, her head bowed, her chin on her thin chest, her eyes closed . . . I can still see her two slender hands resting open and lifeless on the tablecloth.

This fainting spell, or whatever it was, lasted less than ten seconds, and Renée came to without embarrassment.

"Forgive me, my dears, I must have gone to sleep," she murmured, and resumed the argument she had left for the fleeting death from which she had returned fired with a strange frenzy.

"Oh, that B.I.," she exclaimed, "I don't want to hear any more about him or his verses tonight. He has *no* talent. He is—wait, I know what he is, he's a cunt, a cunt with a pen. Yes, a cunt with a pen!"

The word fell into our silence, coarse, blunt. Anyone of us would have been capable of pronouncing that word in an undertone and among ourselves, but as Renée repeated the indecent remark, there reigned on her childlike features a blank expression that set the words outside time, deprived of any significance, and revealed in the speaker a profound disorder.

The wily lunatic is lost if through the narrowest crack he allows a sane eye to peer into his locked universe and thus profane it. Afterward, it is the sane eye that changes, is affected, becomes fascinated with the mystery it has seen and can never cease to question. The more sensitive the lunatic, the less able is he to resist this prying interest of the normal human being. I felt that Renée's change of key—to myself, I compared Renée to a sweet melody, a little flat despite its laborious harmonies—was approaching.

At Pascaud's, where we had gone to hire costumes for the fancy-dress ball Robert d'Humières was giving at the Théâtre des Arts, which he directed, Renée Vivien, as she dressed again after the fitting of her costume—she intended to go as Jane Grey on the executioner's block, exactly, alas, as Paul Delaroche painted her—put on by mistake my black coat instead of her own.

"It almost fits you," I said, laughing. "But for you to look your best in it, something is needed here, and here . . . Otherwise . . ."

"It almost fits me?" Renée repeated.

I can still see how her face clouded, how her mouth fell open in stunned surprise.

"It's a great misfortune," she stammered, "a great misfortune that you've just announced to me . . ."

She turned a gloomy and calculating look upon me—at that period I was a pleasant little cob pony of a person—then rapidly collected herself and we separated. That

evening I was handed a letter she had addressed to me and my friends who were to figure in the *tableau vivant* of Jane Grey. It read:

> *My dears, the worst possible thing has happened to me: I've carelessly put on*
> *weight—ten pounds. But there are still ten days before our ball, in which I can lose*
> *them—that's enough, it's got to be enough, for I must not, at any price, weigh more*
> *than fifty-two kilos. Don't try to find me, I'm going to a place none of you knows.*
> *Count on me, I'll be back in ten days, and all ready for the ball. Yours, Renée.*

She kept her word. We heard later on that she had spent the ten days at the Pavil-
lon Henri IV in Saint-Germain. In the mornings she drank a glass of tea, then walked
in the forest until her strength gave out. Then she drank more tea, this time with alcohol added, and went to bed in an almost fainting condition. Next day it began all over
again. She had the inexhaustible strength of unbalanced people. "We walked perhaps
twenty kilometers every day," her companion confessed to us later on. "I don't know
how mademoiselle kept going. As for myself, I ate normally, yet was exhausted."

The ten days over with, Renée met us at eleven o'clock in the evening at the
Théâtre des Arts. She looked very pretty in her costume, powdered and rouged, hollow-eyed, her hair loose on one shoulder, and she was gay in a distracted kind of way.
She still had the strength to play the part of Jane Grey, her hands tied, her bowed head
revealing a white nape, her fair hair flooding out on the block. But afterward she fainted
backstage, the victim of the saddest and most violent case of alcohol poisoning, aggravated by starvation and some drug or other.

This was her very pathetic secret, the confession of a quite ordinary neurosis. Or
was it? Yes, if one can be satisfied with a single fact, as I was for a time—a rather short
time. Renée was dying when I was told how she had managed in a weirdly simple way
to drink to excess without anyone in Paris or anyone in Nice in the little house in the
Parc Cessole ever being able to catch her at it . . .

Adjoining the bathroom, in a small room that substituted as a linen closet, her
docile chambermaid sat sewing. Quick, maladroit, stumbling against the furniture,
Renée was constantly calling out for help to . . . let us call her Justine, for that was
absolutely not her name.

"Justine, my dear, will you sew on this hook that's come off?" "Justine, dear, have
you ironed my embroidered frock?" "Quick, my slipper ribbon is undone . . ." "Oh!
These new gloves still have a price tag on, do take it off, Justine, will you?" "Please,
Justine, tell the cook that tonight . . ."

Behind the sewing-room door, which remained open, you heard only a murmured
reply: "Yes, mademoiselle. Very well, mademoiselle . . ." And the maid did not leave
the chair where she sat at work. Every time Renée appeared, Justine had only to lean
over to reach, under her chair, one of the filled wineglasses that her skirt concealed. She
held it out in silence to Renée, who emptied it at a gulp and went from the linen closet
to the bathroom, where she found waiting her, punctually renewed, a glass of milky-

looking water clouded with perfumes. She would gargle this and hurriedly spit it out. People who had seen and smelled that glass of perfumed liquid believed and have affirmed that Renée Vivien drank toilet water. What she so foolishly imbibed was no better.

I sometimes met Renée in the mornings, when I led my memorable cat Prrou out on a leash for a walk along the grassy paths in the avenue du Bois, and I recall one such encounter. As usual when she ventured out into the streets, Renée was a bit over-dressed. In getting into the carriage that morning, she stepped on the hem of her long skirt and caught the strap of her bag on the handle of the door.

"Where are you going this early in the day?" I asked.

"To buy my Buddha. I've decided to buy one every day. Don't you think that's a good idea?"

"Excellent. Enjoy yourself!"

She turned to wave goodbye and knocked her hat askew. To hold it on, she raised the hand she had passed through the strap of the bag and it, ill shut, fell open, scatter-ing a quantity of crumpled bank notes. "Oh, *mon Dieu*," she exclaimed, laughing softly. At last the fiacre, the big hat, the dress with the ripped hem went off in the dis-tance, while, close to my cat hygienically scratching the grass, I stood reflecting: "The alcohol . . . the thinness . . . the poetry, the daily Buddha . . . And that's not all. What is the dark origin of all this nonsense?"

May I be excused for having included as an element of "all this nonsense" the word "poetry." Renée Vivien has left a great many poems of unequal strength, force, merit, unequal as the human breath, as the pulsations of human suffering. The cult of which they sing arouses curiosity and then infatuation; today they have disarmed the indig-nation of even the lowest kind of moralists—and this is a fate I would not have dared to promise them if they had lauded only the love of Chloë for Daphnis, since the low-est kind of moralist follows the fashions and makes a display of broadmindedness. In addition, Renée's work inhabits a region of elevated melancholy, in which the *amies*, the female couple, daydream and weep as often as they embrace. Admirably acquainted with our language, broken to the strict rules of French meter, Renée Vivien betrays her foreignness—that is to say, her assimilation of French masterworks relatively late in life—by exuding her Baudelairism in the years 1900–9, which was rather late for us.

When I found out she was so fallible, so faddy, so enslaved to a ruinous habit that she hoped to keep secret, my instinctive attraction to Renée changed into friendship. Friendship is not always circumspect, and one day I went so far as to put a strange ques-tion.

"Tell me, Renée. Are you happy?"

Renée blushed, smiled, then abruptly stiffened.

"Why, of course, my dear Colette. Why would you want me to be unhappy?"

"I didn't say I wanted it," I retorted.

And I went off, dissatisfied with us both. But next day her embarrassed laugh was apologetic and she thrashed the air around me with her long arms, maladroit and affectionate, as if she were looking for a way into my confidence. I noticed her listlessness, the dark rings under her eyes, and I asked her if she was ill.

"Why, not at all," she protested emphatically.

She then yawned behind her hand and explained the reasons for her lassitude in terms so clear that I could not believe my ears. And she did not stop there . . . What new warmth had melted her reserve and encouraged such expansiveness? Unhindered by any ambiguity, she spoke openly, and what she spoke of was not love but sexual satisfaction, and this, of course, referred to the only sexual satisfaction she knew, the pleasure she took with a woman. Then it was a question of the satisfactions of another epoch, another woman, and regrets and comparisons. Her way of talking about physical love was rather like that of little girls brought up for a life of debauchery: both innocent and crude. The most curious thing about her calm and farfetched confessions, during the recital of which Renée never left off the tone of tranquil gossip, strangely in accord with the least ambiguous terms, was that they revealed an immodest consideration for "the senses" and the technique of obtaining physical satisfaction . . . And when, beyond the poet who praised the pallor of her Lesbian loves, their sobbing in the desolate dawns, I caught a glimpse of "Madame How-many-times," counting on her fingers, mentioning by name things and gestures, I put an end to the indiscretion of those young half-conscious lips, and not very tactfully. I believe I told Renée that certain frank remarks she had made were as suitable to her as a silk hat to a monkey . . . As a sequel to this incident, I still have the brief note she sent me, very imposing in its form:

> *You gravely offended me last night, Colette, and I am not one who forgives. Adieu.*
> *Renée*

However, the other Renée, the good and charming Renée, saw to it that I had a second note two hours after the first one. It read:

> *Forgive me, dear little Colette, God only knows what I wrote to you. Eat these lovely peaches as a toast to my health and come to see me. Come dine with me as soon as you can, and bring along our friends.*

I did not fail to do so, although I took exception to the odd, clandestine character of those feasts laid out among three candles, to which sometimes Renée invited a harpist, at other times a soloist. But on the threshold of her apartment, which I always said smelled like "a rich man's funeral," we met Renée in a black evening dress, ready to go out.

"No, my dears," she murmured agitatedly, "you've not made a mistake, I was expecting you tonight. Sit down at the table, I'll be back very soon, I swear it by Aphrodite! There are shrimps, *foie gras*, some Chios wine, and fruit from the Balearic Isles . . ."

In her haste, she stumbled on the steps. She turned her golden head toward me, the luminous heart of a great beehive of dark velvet, then came back to whisper in my ear: "Hush, I'm requisitioned. *She* is terrible at present."

Constrained, mystified, we remained and we waited . . . And Renée did not return.

Another time she was gaily having dinner, I mean to say, she was watching us dine, and at the dessert she stood up, gathered together with a shaky hand her long gloves, a fan, a little silk purse, then excused herself.

"My dears, I have to go . . . *Voilà* . . ."

She did not finish what she had to say but burst into tears and fled. A carriage waiting for her outside bore her away.

In spite of my old friend Hamel (called Hamond, in the *Vagabonde*), who had a paternal affection for Renée and who now interceded for her, I went home with dignity, swearing never to return. But I did return, because the friendship one has given to a human being who is already going to pieces, is already headed toward her downfall, does not obey the dictates of pride. When I went back, urged by Renée in a laconic note, I found her sitting on the rim of the tub in the cold, ugly, and rudimentary bathroom. Seeing her pallor, the trembling of her long hands, her absurd thinness encased in a black dress, I tried to cheer her by addressing her as the Muse of Lévy-Dhurmer. She paid no attention.

"I'm going away," she said.

"Yes? Where are you going?"

"I don't know. But I'm in danger. *She* will kill me. Or else *she* will take me to the other side of the world, to countries where I shall be at her mercy . . . She will kill me."

"Poison? Revolver?"

"No."

In four words she explained how she might perish. Four words of a frankness to make you blink. This would not be worth telling, except for what Renée said then.

"With her I dare not pretend or lie, because at that moment she lays her ear over my heart."

I prefer to believe that this detail and the "danger," which both, alike, seem to have been borrowed from P. J. Toulet's *Monsieur du Paur*, were conceived under the influence of alcohol. Perhaps, even, the exhausting Lesbian lover never existed. Perhaps, invisible, she owed her strength, her quasi-tangibility to the last effort, the last miracle of an imagination which, getting out of hand, brought forth ghouls instead of nymphs.

While I was on tour—the Baret Music Hall Tour—I was unaware that Renée was very close to death. She kept losing weight, always refusing to eat. In her spells of giddiness, in the aurora borealis of starvation, she thought she saw the flames of the Catholic hell. Someone close to her perhaps fanned the flames, or described them to her? Mystery. Enfeebled, she became humble and was converted. Her paganism was so little rooted in her. Fever and coughing shook her hollow chest. I was by chance spared the sight of Renée dying, then dead. She carried off with her more than one secret, and beneath her purple veil, Renée Vivien, the poet, led away—her throat encircled with moonstones, beryls, aquamarines, and other anemic gems—the immodest child, the excited little girl who taught me, with unembarrassed competence: "There are fewer ways of making love than they say, and more than one believes . . ."

Blond, her cheek dimpled, with a tender, laughing mouth and great, soft eyes, she was, even so, drawn down beneath the earth, toward everything that is of no concern to the living. Like all those who never use their strength to the limit, I am hostile to those who let life burn them out. Voluntary consumption is, I always feel, a kind of alibi. I fear there is not much difference between the habit of obtaining sexual satisfaction and, for instance, the cigarette habit. Smokers, male and female, inject and excuse idleness in their lives every time they light a cigarette.

The habit of obtaining sexual satisfaction is less tyrannical than the tobacco habit, but it gains on one. O voluptuous pleasure, O lascivious ram, cracking your skull against all obstacles, time and again! Perhaps the only misplaced curiosity is that which persists in trying to find out here, on this side of death, what lies beyond the grave . . . Voluptuaries, consumed by their senses always begin by flinging themselves with a great display of frenzy into an abyss. But they survive, they come to the surface again. And they develop a routine of the abyss: "It's four o'clock . . . At five I have my abyss . . ." It is possible that this young woman poet, who rejected the laws of ordinary love, led a sensible enough life until her personal abyss of half past eight in the evening. An abyss she imagined? Ghouls are rare.

NOËL COWARD (1899–1973)

From *Spangled Unicorn* (1932)

The English actor, playwright, composer, and cabaret artist Noël Coward was born to working-class parents in London in 1899 and began acting professionally as a child. In 1924 he wrote and starred in *The Vortex* (1924)—a turgid twenties melodrama that nonetheless became a popular hit in London and New York and made him world famous. A series of enormously successful stage comedies and revues followed—*Hay Fever* and *Fallen Angels* (1925), *Easy Virtue* (1926), *This Year of Grace* (1928), *Private Lives* (1930), *Cavalcade* (1931), *Words and Music* (1932), *Design for Living* (1933), *To-Night at* 8:30 (1936), *Present Laughter* (1939), and *Blithe Spirit* (1941)—making Coward one of the wealthiest and most popular artists of his day. Glamorous, soigné, and ineluctably arch, he and his leading lady, Gertrude Lawrence, came to epitomize all that was fashionable in British society between the wars: a world of cocktails, dinner jackets, Bright Young Things, and witty double entendre.

During the Second World War Coward made propaganda tours for the Ministry of Information and began to work in film: he starred in the famous patriotic David Lean film, *In Which We Serve* (1942). After the war his popularity declined—a highly publicized move to Jamaica to avoid British income tax penalties did not help—and he never matched his popular successes of the twenties and thirties. Nonetheless he continued to write prolifically—stories, novels, memoirs, and songs—and remained an important presence in British theater. A lifelong homosexual, he never married and hid his private life from fans and the press. He was knighted in 1970, three years before his death.

Throughout his life Coward had numerous lesbian friends and artistic collaborators. He became friends with the lesbian novelist and poet Radclyffe Hall and her lover Una Troubridge in the early 1920s. While unable to show his support openly during the huge public scandal that erupted over Hall's novel *The Well of Loneliness* in 1928—he feared that his own homosexuality might be revealed were he to defend so notoriously prohomosexual a work—he nonetheless provided support to Hall behind the scenes. (The character of Jonathan Brockett, the glamorous homosexual playwright who appears in the London and Paris scenes of that novel, is largely based on Coward.) At the same time he was not above poking fun at Hall—or indeed at lesbians generally—when it suited him. In *Spangled Unicorn*, a parody anthology of modernist verse by such imaginary luminaries as Crispin Pither and Juanita Mandradagora, he offers a satiric portrait of Hall in the figure "Jane Southerby Danks," an eccentric poetess whose virile exploits mimic events both in Hall's own life and that of Stephen Gordon, the quasi-autobiographical heroine of the *The Well*. The concocted sample of Danks's "poetry" ("Richmond Boating Song") is hardly reminiscent of Hall's poetry, however; despite a possibly sapphic subtext, it resembles the rather more "Elizabethan" abstractions of her contemporary Edith Sitwell.

FURTHER READING: Noël Coward, *Spangled Unicorn* (London: Hutchinson, 1932); Radclyffe Hall, *The Well of Loneliness* (1928; rpt. New York: Anchor, 1990); Cole Lesley, *The Life of Noël Coward* (London: Jonathan Cape, 1976); Philip Hoare, *Noël Coward: A Biography* (London: Sinclair-Stevenson, 1995); Terry Castle, *Noël Coward and Radclyffe Hall: Kindred Spirits* (New York: Columbia University Press, 1996).

Jane Southerby Danks

INTRODUCTORY NOTE

In writing an introductory preface to Jane Southerby Danks it is odd to compare her early environment with that of her artistic contemporaries. Born in Melton Mowbray in 1897 she rode to hounds constantly, wet or fine, from the age of four onwards. Blauie's portrait "Musette on Roan" depicts her at the very beginning of her adolescence. From the first she shunned the company of the male sex, mixing only with her governesses. To one of whom Madeleine Duphotte she dedicated her first volume of Poems, *Goose Grass*. The Dedication is illuminating in its profound simplicity—"To you, Madeleine, from me."

Storm clouds in her relations with her mother began to gather on the horizon as early as 1912, indeed in the May of this year we find her in Florence with Hedda Jennings then at the height of her career. Her emancipation from home ties continued and the breach had obviously broadened in 1916 when we find her writing from a whaler off Helsinforth to Mrs. Hinton Turner (Libelulle) at Saint Cloud. "How I envy you in your green quiet room. Here, no lace no Sheffield plate, only tar and the cry of gulls, but my heart is easier."

1924 finds her cosily ensconced in Boulogne where she first gained from the fisherfolk the appellation "Knickerbocker Lady."

In 1925 she published *Hands Down* to be followed in the Spring of 1926 by *Frustration*.

In 1927 began her most prolific era in Saint Tropez where in company with Zale Bartlett and Thérèse Mauillac she wrote in French her celebrated *Coucher de soleil pour violon* and *Loup de mer*.

The poems included in this volume are selected from her work of 1929–1930 just after her quarrel with La Duchesse de la Saucigny-Garonette (The "Madame Practique" of "Bon Jour") and expressing in their concrete outline her revulsion of feeling against the Sous Realist School.

Richmond Boating Song

Apples and cheese
Come hold my hand
Trip it, Miss Jenkins, to Kew
The Wooden horse is panting—O!
But that's no argument
Look at Frank.
They brew good beer at the "Saucy Sheep"
With a derry dun derry and soon may be
One for all and all for one.
Parrots are blue in old Madrid
And barking tigers screech the song
Rum Tiddy, rum Tiddy
Peculiar.

WILLIAM CARLOS WILLIAMS (1883–1963)

"The Knife of the Times" (1932)

The American poet, novelist, and essayist William Carlos Williams, was born in New Jersey and educated in New York, Switzerland, and France. While studying medicine at the University of Pennsylvania, he met the poet Ezra Pound and began writing verse under his influence. He received his medical degree in 1906 (he would work as a pediatrician for the next forty-five years); his first book, *Poems*, appeared in 1909. He married Florence Herman in 1912. Over a long and distinguished career, Williams published fourteen more books of poetry (two volumes of *Collected Poems* appeared in 1950 and 1951), five novels, numerous volumes of essays, an autobiography, and a book of short stories, *The Farmer's Daughters* (1961). Some of his best writing was inspired by his wife, including the great late love poem, "Asphodel, That Greeny Flower."

Though known primarily as a poet—he published his free-form masterwork, *Paterson*, in five books between 1946 and 1958—Williams deserves to be reckoned a prose writer of some talent. The essays in *In the American Grain* (1925) are deservedly famous; his *Autobiography* (1951) offers a fascinating picture of transatlantic literary culture in the first half of the century. (Describing a visit to Natalie Barney's lesbian salon in Paris in the 1920s, Williams tells of a "red-faced" member of the French Chamber of Deputies, who, upon seeing Barney and her girlfriends dancing gaily on all sides, "took out his tool" and shaking it right and left, "yelled out in a rage, 'Have you never seen one of these?'") Williams's short fiction is typically urban, gritty, and melancholic in mode: a kind of verbal equivalent to the paintings of Edward Hopper. Nor does he shy away from provocative content: "The Knife of the Times"—a crude yet memorable vignette about suppressed sapphic passion—is as sharp and unyielding as its title.

FURTHER READING: William Carlos Williams, *In the American Grain* (Norfolk, Conn.: New Directions, 1948); —, *Selected Poems* (New York: New Directions, 1949); —, *Autobiography* (New York: New Directions, 1951); —, *Paterson* (New York: New Directions, 1951); —, *The Farmer's Daughters* (New York: New Directions, 1961); *The William Carlos Williams Reader*, ed. M. L. Rosenthal (New York: New Directions,

1966); —, *The Collected Poems of William Carlos Williams* (New York: New Directions, 1986–88); Gilbert Sorrentino, "Polish Mothers and 'The Knife of the Times,'" in Carroll F. Terrell, ed., *William Carlos Williams: Man and Poet* (Orono, Me: National Poetry Foundation, 1983), pp. 391–95; Hugh Witemeyer, "William Carlos Williams' Introduction to his Short Stories: A History and Some Interpretative Uses," *Journal of Modern Literature* 18 (1993): 435–46.

As the years passed the girls who had been such intimates as children still remained true to one another.

Ethel by now had married. Maura had married; the one having removed to Harrisburg, the other to New York City. And both began to bring up families. Ethel especially went in for children. Within a very brief period, comparatively speaking, she had three of them, then four, then five and finally six. And through it all, she kept in constant touch with her girlhood friend, dark-eyed Maura, by writing long intimate letters.

At first these had been newsy chit chat, ending always however in continued protestations of that love which the women had enjoyed during their childhood. Maura showed them to her husband and both enjoyed their full newsy quality dealing as they did with people and scenes with which both were familiar.

But after several years, as these letters continued to flow, there came a change in them. First the personal note grew more confidential. Ethel told about her children, how she had had one after the other—to divert her mind, to distract her thoughts from their constant brooding. Each child would raise her hopes of relief, each anticipated delivery brought only renewed disappointment. She confided more and more in Maura. She loved her husband; it was not that. In fact, she didn't know what it was save that she, Ethel, could never get her old friend Maura out of her mind.

Until at last the secret was out. It is you, Maura, that I want. Nothing but you. Nobody but you can appease my grief. Forgive me if I distress you with this confession. It is the last thing in this world that I desire. But I cannot contain myself longer.

Thicker and faster came the letters. Full love missives they were now without the least restraint.

Ethel wrote letters now such as Maura wished she might at some time in her life have received from a man. She was told that all these years she had been dreamed of, passionately without rival, without relief. Now, surely, Maura did not dare show the letters any longer to her husband. He would not understand.

They affected her strangely, they frightened her, but they caused a shrewd look to come into her dark eyes and she packed them carefully away where none should ever come upon them. She herself was occupied otherwise but she felt tenderly toward Ethel, loved her in an old remembered manner—but that was all. She was disturbed by the turn Ethel's mind had taken and thanked providence her friend and she lived far enough apart to keep them from embarrassing encounters.

But, in spite of the lack of adequate response to her advances, Ethel never wavered, never altered in her passionate appeals. She begged her friend to visit her, to come to her, to live with her. She spoke of her longings, to touch the velvet flesh of her darling's breasts, her thighs. She longed to kiss her to sleep, to hold her in her arms. Franker and franker became her outspoken lusts. For which she begged indulgence.

Once she implored Maura to wear a silk chemise which she was sending, to wear it for a week and to return it to her, to Ethel, unwashed, that she might wear it in her turn constantly upon her.

Then, after twenty years, one day Maura received a letter from Ethel asking her to meet her—and her mother, in New York. They were expecting a sister back from Europe on the Mauritania and they wanted Maura to be there—for old times' sake.

Maura consented. With strange feelings of curiosity and not a little fear, she stood at the gate of the Pennsylvania station waiting for her friend to come out at the wicket on the arrival of the Harrisburg express. Would she be alone? Would her mother be with her really? Was it a hoax? Was the woman crazy after all? And, finally, would she recognize her?

There she was and her mother along with her. After the first stare, the greetings on all sides were quiet, courteous and friendly. The mother dominated the moment. Her keen eyes looked Maura up and down once and then she asked the time, when would the steamer dock, how far was the pier and had they time for lunch first?

There was plenty of time. Yes, let's lunch. But first Ethel had a small need to satisfy and asked Maura if she would show her the way. Maura led her friend to the Pay Toilets and there, after inserting the coin, Ethel opened the door and, before Maura could find the voice to protest, drew her in with herself and closed the door after her.

What a meeting! What a release! Ethel took her friend into her arms and between tears and kisses, tried in some way, as best she could, to tell her of her happiness. She fondled her old playmate, hugged her, lifted her off her feet in the eager impressment of her desire, whispering into her ear, stroking her hair, her face, touching her lips, her eyes; holding her, holding her about as if she could never again release her.

No one could remain cold to such an appeal, as pathetic to Maura as it was understandable and sincere, she tried her best to modify its fury, to abate it, to control. But, failing that, she did what she could to appease her old friend. She loved Ethel, truly, but all this show was beyond her. She did not understand it, she did not know how to return it. But she was not angry, she found herself in fact in tears, her heart touched, her lips willing.

Time was slipping by and they had to go.

At lunch Ethel kept her foot upon the toe of Maura's slipper. It was a delirious meal for Maura with thinking of old times, watching the heroic beauty of the old lady and, while keeping up a chatter of small conversation, intermixed with recollections, to respond secretly as best she could to Ethel's insistent pressures.

At the pier there was a long line waiting to be admitted to the enclosure. It was no use—Ethel from behind constantly pressed her body against her embarrassed friend, embarrassed not from lack of understanding or sympathy, but for fear lest one of the officers and Customs inspectors who were constantly watching them should detect something out of the ordinary.

But the steamer was met, the sister saluted; the day came to an end and the hour of parting found Ethel still keeping close, close to the object of her lifelong adoration.

What shall I do? thought Maura afterward on her way home, on the train alone. Ethel had begged her to visit her, to go to her, to spend a week at least with her, to sleep with her. Why not?

SYLVIA TOWNSEND WARNER (1893–1978)

"Since the First Toss of Gale That Blew," "Out of Your Left Eye,"
"I Would Give You Alexander's Bucephalus," "Loved with an
L. . . . ," "Drawing You, Heavy with Sleep" (1933)

Sylvia Townsend Warner, one of the most gifted—and strangely neglected—English
writers of the twentieth century, was born at Harrow School, near London, where her
father, George Townsend Warner, was a history master. A precocious child and adolescent, she originally planned to study music composition in Vienna with Arnold
Schoenberg. When the First World War scotched these plans, Warner went to London,
where she became a coeditor (with Percy Buck) of the ten-volume *Tudor Church Music*
(1923–29) published by Oxford University Press. Her first collection of poetry, *The
Espalier*, appeared in 1925. In 1926 she published *Lolly Willowes*, a whimsical novel
about an English spinster who becomes a witch. The book was an immediate popular
success, especially in the United States, where it became the inaugural selection of the
newly formed Book of the Month Club.

Warner's life changed dramatically in 1930, when she fell in love with Valentine
Ackland, a volatile and boyish young woman prone to drink and depression. The two
bought a cottage in Dorset and lived together—sometimes tumultuously—until Ackland's death in 1969. Ackland was also a writer, and in 1933 she and Warner published
a book of poems, *Whether a Dove or Seagull*, to which the following "Note to the
Reader" was attached:

> No single poem is in any way the result of collaboration nor, beyond the bare
> fact that it contains the work of two writers, is the book collaborative. The
> authors believe that by issuing their separate work under one cover the ele-
> ment of contrast thus obtained will add to the pleasure of the reader. . . . The
> book, therefore, is both an experiment in the presentation of poetry and a
> protest against the frame of mind, too common, which judges the poem by the
> poet, rather than the poet by the poem.

The ploy was unsuccessful—Warner was the more impressive writer and several
reviewers claimed to be able to recognize which poems were hers and which Ackland's.
(In a subsequent edition an appended key identified the author of each contribution.)
A subtle, sometimes painful tension, arising from Warner's greater talent and produc-

tivity—she had by this time also published the novels *Mr. Fortune's Maggot* (1927) and *The True Heart* (1929) and the poetry collections *Time Importuned* (1928) and *Opus 7* (1931)—was to characterize the relationship with Ackland for its duration.

In the 1930s, with the rise of fascism at home and abroad, Warner became a committed leftist, joining the Communist Party in 1935. She and Ackland worked for the Red Cross during the Spanish Civil War, and were part of the British delegation to the International Congress of Writers in Defence of Culture in Barcelona in 1937. Warner's political concerns are reflected in her 1936 historical novel, *Summer Will Show*, about two women who fall in love in Paris during the 1848 Revolution, and *After the Death of Don Juan* (1938), a satiric fable set in eighteenth-century Spain. During the Second World War she continued to write, while also aiding in the war effort. She published the novel many consider to be her masterpiece, *The Corner That Held Them*— about a group of nuns in a fourteenth-century English convent—in 1948. Her translation of Proust's *Contre Sainte-Beuve* appeared in 1958; the short-story collection *A Stranger with a Bag* in 1966. In 1967 she published a biography of the novelist T. H. White. After Ackland's death, she produced two final story collections, *The Innocent and the Guilty* (1971) and *Kingdoms of Elfin* (1977). Her *Collected Poems* was issued posthumously in 1982.

Although Warner's fiction will always be her first claim to importance, her poetry is of considerable interest, not least on account of its frankly sapphic nature. (Not all readers found this aspect of her work pleasing: in a letter to Louis Untermeyer in 1934, Robert Frost, the dedicatee of *Whether a Dove or Seagull*, wrote of Warner and Ackland's lesbian "collusion" and said that he found it "emasculating.") Warner's poetic style, as witnessed by the love lyrics to Ackland below, is very much that of the 1930s— her decade par excellence. As in Auden's "Lay Your Sleeping Head, My Love," we seem to eavesdrop on intimate voicings, at once amorous, philosophic, and subtly disquieting.

FURTHER READING: Sylvia Townsend Warner, *Lolly Willowes* (London: Chatto and Windus, 1926); —, *Mr. Fortune's Maggot* (London: Chatto and Windus, 1927); —, *Whether a Dove or Seagull* (with Valentine Ackland) (New York: Viking, 1933; London: Chatto and Windus, 1934); —, *Summer Will Show* (London: Chatto and Windus, 1936); —, *After the Death of Don Juan* (London: Chatto and Windus, 1938); —, *The Corner That Held Them* (London: Chatto and Windus, 1948); —, *The Flint Anchor* (London: Chatto and Windus, 1954); —, *Letters*, ed. William Maxwell (London: Chatto and Windus, 1982); —, *Collected Poems*, ed. Claire Harman (Manchester: Carcanet, 1982); —, *One Thing Leading to Another*, ed. Susanna Pinney (London: Chatto and Windus, 1984); —, *Selected Poems* (Manchester: Carcanet, 1985); —, *Selected Stories* (London: Chatto and Windus, 1988); —, *Diaries*, ed. Claire Harman (London: Chatto and Windus, 1994); —, *I'll Stand by You: Selected Letters of Sylvia Townsend Warner and Valentine Ackland*, ed. Susanna Pinney (London: Pimlico, 1998); —, *The*

Element of Lavishness: Letters of Sylvia Townsend Warner and William Maxwell, ed. Michael Steinman (Washington, D.C.: Counterpoint, 2001); Wendy Mulford, *This Narrow Place—Sylvia Townsend Warner and Valentine Ackland: Life, Letters, and Politics, 1930–1951* (London: Pandora, 1988); Claire Harman, *Sylvia Townsend Warner: A Biography* (London: Chatto and Windus, 1989); Robert L. Caserio, "Celibate Sisters-in-Revolution: Towards Reading Sylvia Townsend Warner," in Joseph Boone and Michael Cadden, eds., *Engendering Men: The Question of Male Feminist Criticism* (New York and London: Routledge, 1990), pp. 254–74; Terry Castle, "Sylvia Townsend Warner and the Counterplot of Lesbian Fiction," in Joseph Bristow, ed. *Sexual Sameness: Textual Differences in Lesbian and Gay Writing* (London: Routledge, 1992), pp. 128–47; —, *Boss Ladies, Watch Out! Essays on Women, Sex, and Writing* (New York: Routledge, 2002).

Since the First Toss of Gale That Blew

Since the first toss of gale that blew
Me in to you
The wind that our still love awakened
Has never slackened,
But watchful with nightfall keeps pace
With each embrace.
If we love out the winter, my dear,
This will be a year
That babes now lulled on arm will quote
With rusty throat.
For long meeting of our lips
Shall be breaking of ships,
For breath drawn quicker men drowned
And trees downed.
Throe shall fell roof-tree, pulse's knock
Undermine rock,
A cry hurl seas against the land,
A raiding hand,
Scattering lightning along thighs
Lightning from skies
Wrench, and fierce sudden snows clamp deep
On earth our sleep.
Yet who would guess our coming together
Should breed wild weather
Who saw us now?—with looks as sure

As the demure
Flame of our candle, no more plied
By tempest outside
Than those deep ocean weeds unrecking
What winds, what wrecking,
What wrath of wild our dangerous peace
Waits to release.

Out of Your Left Eye

Out of your left eye
Bright behind bar of lovelock tumbled awry
Life looks at me,
Sudden, dauntless and shy
As a bird moving in a tree;
A bird from its depth of sky
On you delighted suddenly alighted,
A wonder beyond why.
And trapped by that freedom I lie unbreathing,
My hand along your thigh
In stillness sheathing,
My desire laid by,
Lest at a movement, at a sigh
Flesh awaken like a tree shaken
And out of its bower affrighted
Shall fly, oh, fly
So rare and renowned a bird—and never again, maybe,
Mine to behold, to hold in my sense's tether.

Hush, for anon, oh, anon, it will be gone!
For sign of its passage bequeathing
—When we have swayed to stillness, and rest together—
You on my breast lying, fallen a bright breast feather.

I Would Give You Alexander's Bucephalus,

I would give you Alexander's Bucephalus,
As, poised on the rise and fall of your varnished grey,

A silence swung on the steam-organ's bray,
A secret brandished round to beholders,
And prize, for term of the two-pennyworth left to us,
Of my following eyes, and prey,
You float within touch of hand and remote as a child at play;
For love of your long legs and your proud shoulders
And the one lappet of hair hanging astray
I would give you Alexander's Bucephalus,
Though you should mount and ride away—
Though you should ride away.

Loved with an L . . .

Loved with an L . . .
Lynx-eye and leopard-thew,
Whom first I knew
Like the crane demoiselle
Long-legged and prim.
Limber in love and light
As lambs that dance in white,
Unmatchable delight
Of lip and limb;
Leda for hue, and fell
As lioness to smite
With lust's renew.
Now, for the world's spite
What more shall I tell?
Loved with an L.

Drawing You, Heavy with Sleep

Drawing you, heavy with sleep to lie closer,
Staying your poppy head upon my shoulder,
It was as though I pulled the glide
Of a full river to my side.

Heavy with sleep and with sleep pliable
You rolled at a touch towards me. Your arm fell

Across me as a river throws
An arm of flood across meadows.

And as the careless water its mirroring sanction
Grants to him at the river's brim long stationed,
Long drowned in thought, that yet he lives
Since in that mirroring tide he moves,

Your body lying by mine to mine responded:
Your hair stirred on my mouth, my image was dandled
Deep in your sleep that flowed unstained
On from the image entertained.

ERNEST HEMINGWAY (1899–1961)

"The Sea Change" (1933)

The American novelist and short-story writer Ernest Hemingway was born in Oak Park, Illinois, and worked in his early years as a newspaperman in Kansas City and Toronto. During World War I he served as an ambulance driver on the Italian front and was seriously wounded in action—an event he later drew upon in the 1929 war novel *A Farewell to Arms*. Following the Armistice, he moved to Paris with his first wife, Hadley Richardson, and became part of a circle of American expatriate writers and artists that included Gertrude Stein, F. Scott Fitzgerald, and Ezra Pound. His first novel, *The Sun Also Rises*, published to great acclaim in 1926, made him famous on both sides of the Atlantic. In the flush of success, he divorced Richardson and married the second of his four wives; his short-story collection, *Men Without Women*, appeared the following year.

Always restless and attracted to danger, Hemingway traveled extensively in Spain and Africa in the 1930s. His lyrical celebration of bullfighting, *Death in the Afternoon*, was published in 1932; *The Green Hills of Africa*, about hunting big game animals, in 1935. During the Spanish Civil War he worked as a war correspondent; the Spanish conflict served as the backdrop for his bittersweet 1940 novel *For Whom the Bell Tolls*. In 1950s, after moving to Key West, Florida, Hemingway published *Across the River and into the Trees* (1950), followed by the Pulitzer-Prize-winning *The Old Man and the Sea* (1952). Considered by many of his contemporaries to be America's greatest living writer—his hard-boiled prose style became the model for a generation of younger male writers—the novelist received the Nobel Prize for Literature in 1954. No accolade could alleviate, however, his growing struggles with depression and alcoholism, and he committed suicide in 1961. A number of Hemingway works appeared posthumously: a memoir of his early days in Paris, *A Moveable Feast*, was published in 1964; and the novel-fragments *Islands in the Stream* and *The Garden of Eden* in 1970 and 1986.

Despite his flamboyant heterosexualism and he-man persona, Hemingway had a lifelong obsession with androgynous, often lesbian women. Curiously, he suspected both his own mother and his second wife, Pauline, of having homosexual tendencies; in the 1920s he fell briefly in love with Gertrude Stein, whom he later savaged (along with her lover Alice B. Toklas) in *A Moveable Feast*. (In the 1930s Robert McAlmon spread the rumor—convincing to many—that Hemingway was himself a repressed homosexual.) The 1933 short story "The Sea Change"—like the posthumous novel *The Garden of Eden*—reflects this sapphic preoccupation. Hemingway later told Edmund Wilson that the immediate inspiration for the story had been an intense, three-hour conversation with Stein about the mechanics of lesbian lovemaking. So stimulating had he found the conversation, he boasted, "I went out that night and fucked a lesbian with magnificent result." Yet the story is a strangely vulnerable one. The lines of poetry misquoted by the humiliated hero—"Vice is a monster of so frightful mien, / As, to be hated, needs but to be seen"—are from Alexander Pope's *Essay on Man* (1733).

FURTHER READING: Ernest Hemingway, *The Sun Also Rises* (New York: Scribner's, 1926); —, *A Farewell to Arms* (New York: Scribner's, 1929); —, *Death in the Afternoon* (New York: Scribner's, 1932); —, *The Green Hills of Africa* (New York: Scribner's, 1935); —, *For Whom the Bell Tolls* (New York: Scribner's, 1940); —, *Across the River and into the Trees* (New York: Scribner's, 1950); —, *The Old Man and the Sea* (New York: Scribner's, 1952); —, *A Moveable Feast* (New York: Scribner's, 1964); —, *Islands in the Stream* (New York: Scribner's, 1970); —, *The Garden of Eden* (New York: Scribner's, 1986); —, *The Complete Short Stories of Ernest Hemingway* (New York: Scribner's, 1987); Gertrude Stein, *The Autobiography of Alice B. Toklas* (New York: Harcourt, Brace and Company, 1933); Michael S. Reynolds, *The Young Hemingway* (New York: Basil Blackwell, 1986); —, *Hemingway's First War: The Making of "A Farewell to Arms"* (Oxford: Basil Blackwell, 1987); —, *Hemingway: The Paris Years* (Oxford: Basil Blackwell, 1989); —, *Hemingway: The American Homecoming* (Oxford: Basil Blackwell, 1992); —, *Hemingway: The 1930s* (New York: Norton, 1997); —, *Hemingway: The Final Years* (New York: 1999); Jeffrey Myers, *Hemingway: A Biography* (New York: Harper and Row, 1987); Mark Spilka, *Hemingway's Quarrel with Androgyny* (Lincoln: University of Nebraska Press, 1989); Marjorie Perloff, " 'Ninety Percent Rotarian': Gertrude Stein's Hemingway," *American Literature* 62 (December 1990): 668–83; James R. Mellow, *Hemingway: A Life Without Consequences* (New York: Addison Wesley, 1992); Nancy R. Comley and Robert Scholes, *Hemingway's Genders: Rereading the Hemingway Text* (New Haven: Yale University Press, 1994); Frederick Voss, *Picturing Hemingway: A Writer in His Time* (New Haven: Yale University Press, 1999); Debra A. Maddelmog, *Reading Desire: In Pursuit of Ernest Hemingway* (Ithaca, N.Y.: Cornell University Press, 1999).

"All right," said the man. "what about it?"

    "No," said the girl, "I can't."

    "You mean you won't."

"I can't," said the girl. "That's all that I mean."

"You mean that you won't."

"All right," said the girl. "You have it your own way."

"I don't have it my own way. I wish to God I did."

"You did for a long time," the girl said.

It was early, and there was no one in the café except the barman and these two who sat together at a table in the corner. It was the end of the summer and they were both tanned, so that they looked out of place in Paris. The girl wore a tweed suit, her skin was a smooth golden brown, her blonde hair was cut short and grew beautifully away from her forehead. The man looked at her.

"I'll kill her," he said.

"Please don't," the girl said. She had very fine hands and the man looked at them. They were slim and brown and very beautiful.

"I will. I swear to God I will."

"It won't make you happy."

"Couldn't you have gotten into something else? Couldn't you have gotten into some other jam?"

"It seems not," the girl said. "What are you going to do about it?"

"I told you."

"No, I mean really."

"I don't know," he said. She looked at him and put out her hand. "Poor old Phil," she said. He looked at her hands, but he did not touch her hand with his.

"No, thanks," he said.

"It doesn't do any good to say I'm sorry?"

"No."

"Nor to tell you how it is?"

"I'd rather not hear."

"I love you very much."

"Yes, this proves it."

"I'm sorry," she said, "if you don't understand."

"I understand. That's the trouble. I understand."

"You do," she said. "That makes it worse, of course."

"Sure," he said, looking at her. "I'll understand all the time. All day and all night. Especially all night. I'll understand. You don't have to worry about that."

"I'm sorry," she said.

"If it was a man—"

"Don't say that. It wouldn't be a man. You know that. Don't you trust me?"

"That's funny," he said. "Trust you. That's really funny."

"I'm sorry," she said. "That's all I seem to say. But when we do understand each other there's no use to pretend we don't."

"No," he said. "I suppose not."

"I'll come back if you want me."

"No. I don't want you."

Then they did not say anything for a while.

"You don't believe I love you, do you?" the girl asked.

"Let's not talk rot," the man said.

"Don't you really believe I love you?"

"Why don't you prove it?"

"You didn't used to be that way. You never asked me to prove anything. That isn't polite."

"You're a funny girl."

"You're not. You're a fine man and it breaks my heart to go off and leave you—"

"You have to, of course."

"Yes," she said. "I have to and you know it."

He did not say anything and she looked at him and put her hand out again. The barman was at the far end of the bar. His face was white and so was his jacket. He knew these two and thought them a handsome young couple. He had seen many handsome young couples break up and new couples form that were never so handsome long. He was not thinking about this, but about a horse. In half an hour he could send across the street to find if the horse had won.

"Couldn't you just be good to me and let me go?" the girl asked.

"What do you think I'm going to do?"

Two people came in the door and went up to the bar.

"Yes, sir," the barman took the orders.

"You can't forgive me? When you know about it?" the girl asked.

"No."

"You don't think things we've had and done should make any difference in understanding?"

" 'Vice is a monster of such fearful mien,' " the young man said bitterly, "that to be something or other needs but to be seen. Then we something, something, then embrace." He could not remember the words. "I can't quote," he said.

"Let's not say vice," she said. "That's not very polite."

"Perversion," he said.

"James," one of the clients addressed the barman, "you're looking very well."

"You're looking very well yourself," the barman said.

"Old James," the other client said. "You're fatter, James."

"It's terrible," the barman said, "the way I put it on."

"Don't neglect to insert the brandy, James," the first client said.

"No, sir," said the barman. "Trust me."

The two at the bar looked over at the two at the table, then looked back at the barman again. Towards the barman was the comfortable direction.

"I'd like it better if you didn't use words like that," the girl said. "There's no necessity to use a word like that."

"What do you want me to call it?"

"You don't have to call it. You don't have to put any name to it."

"That's the name for it."

"No," she said. "We're made up of all sorts of things. You've known that. You've used it well enough."

"You don't have to say that again."

"Because that explains it to you."

"All right," he said. "All right."

"You mean all wrong. I know. It's all wrong. But I'll come back. I told you I'd come back. I'll come back right away."

"No, you won't. Not to me."

"You'll see."

"Yes," he said. "That's the hell of it. You probably will."

"Of course I will."

"Go on, then."

"Really?" She could not believe him, but her voice was happy.

"Go on," his voice sounded strange to him. He was looking at her, at the way her mouth went and the curve of her cheek bones, at her eyes and at the way her hair grew on her forehead and at the edge of her ear and at her neck.

"Not really. Oh, you're too sweet," she said. "You're too good to me."

"And when you come back tell me all about it." His voice sounded very strange. He did not recognize it. She looked at him quickly. He was settled into something.

"You want me to go?" she asked seriously.

"Yes," he said seriously. "Right away." His voice was not the same, and his mouth was very dry. "Now," he said.

She stood up and went out quickly. She did not look back at him. He watched her go. He was not the same-looking man as he had been before he had told her to go. He got up from the table, picked up the two checks and went over to the bar with them.

"I'm a different man, James," he said to the barman. "You see in me quite a different man."

"Yes, sir?" said James.

"Vice," said the brown young man, "is a very strange thing, James." He looked out the door. He saw her going down the street. As he looked in the glass, he saw he was really quite a different looking man. The other two at the bar moved down to make room for him.

"You're right there, sir," James said.

The other two moved down a little more, so that he would be quite comfortable. The young man saw himself in the mirror behind the bar. "I said I was a different man, James," he said. Looking into the mirror he saw that this was quite true.

"You look very well, sir," James said. "You must have had a very good summer."

MABEL DODGE LUHAN (1879–1962)

From *Intimate Memories* (1933)

The extraordinary Mabel (Ganson) Dodge Luhan, writer, bohemian, patron of the arts and would-be revolutionary, was born into a wealthy Buffalo family and educated in New York and Maryland. During frequent trips to France in her teens, she fell in love with Violet Shilleto, a brilliant young American woman—tragically short-lived—who was also one of the lesbian poet Renée Vivien's early loves. In 1900 Luhan married Karl Evans, by whom she had a son, her only child. Following Evans's death, she moved to Florence with a second husband, the architect Edwin Dodge, where she studied art history for several years. In 1912 Luhan divorced Dodge, returned to New York, and started a salon at her home at 23 Fifth Avenue. She became deeply involved in radical social and political causes and had a tempestuous affair with the journalist John Reed—soon to become famous for his eyewitness account of the Russian Revolution, *Ten Days That Shook the World* (1919). Close female friends included the anarchist Emma Goldman and the birth-control advocate Margaret Sanger. Luhan also became a vigorous supporter of the arts and helped to sponsor the celebrated Armory Show of 1913, which introduced postimpressionism into the United States.

In 1917 Luhan married her third husband, the sculptor Maurice Stern, but the marriage was not a success and soon after she moved to Taos, New Mexico, where she lived with a Native American man, Tony Lujan, and established an artists' colony. For the rest of her life Luhan devoted herself to writing and local political projects while also playing hostess to scores of famous painters, writers, and musicians—Willa Cather, Georgia O'Keeffe, Leopold Stokowski, and D. H. Lawrence among them—who visited the colony. She published several books: *Lorenzo in Taos* (1932); *Winter in Taos* (1935); *Taos and Its Artists* (1947); and a delightfully garrulous four-volume autobiography, *Intimate Memories* (1933–37).

In the first volume of her memoirs—one of the rare works that fully lives up to its title—Luhan is startlingly frank about her adolescent passions for girls and women. In the excerpts below she describes her childhood obsession with the "large, ballooning, billowing breast" of a family maid named Elsa; her fascination with the dashing lesbian aunt of two childhood friends; and the affair in France with Violet Shilleto. Writing of the "wild, sweet, enthralling zestfulness" of her early years, Luhan endows her own prose with the same ardor, resource, and scintillating life.

FURTHER READING: Mabel Dodge Luhan, *Intimate Memories*, 4 vols. (New York: Harcourt, Brace, 1933–37); ; Gertrude Stein, *Portrait of Mabel Dodge at the Villa Curonia* (Florence: Tip. Galileiana, 1913); Emily Hahn, *Mabel* (Boston: Houghton Mifflin, 1977); Jane V. Nelson, *Mabel Dodge Luhan* (Boise: Boise State University, 1982); Winifred L. Frazer, *Mabel Dodge Luhan* (Boston: Twayne, 1984); Lois Palken Rudnick, *Mabel Dodge Luhan* (Albuquerque: University of New Mexico Press, 1984); —, *Utopian Vistas: The Mabel Dodge Luhan House and the American Counterculture* (Alberquerque: University of New Mexico Press, 1996); Helen Barolini, "Mabel Dodge Luhan: In Search of a Personal South," *Southwest Review* 83 (1998): 280–94; Lisa Abney, "Mabel Dodge Luhan (1879–1962)," in Laurie Champion, ed., *American Women Writers, 1900–1945: A Bio-Bibliographical Critical Sourcebook* (Westport, Conn.: Greenwood, 2000).

The Breast

If the long quiet hours in the nursery were dull with Mary Ann for my sole companion, anyway they were better than the times when I was left there alone. For often she would say: "Now you be good till I come back. I have to go and iron," or some other excuse like that, and off she would go for a gossip with the other "girls." I found this out very soon by summoning the courage to follow her on tiptoe down the back stairs, and there she would be in the cozy kitchen with a cup of hot tea in one hand and on her pale, thin face a shadow of faint animation hardly ever to be seen in our room.

There was always some play going on among the girls down there. And once they had a visitor, a fat gay female who roistered and teased them and chuckled and nagged until they retaliated with some daring rejoinder, when, to my inexpressible amazement, I saw her rip open the front of her dress and drag her great breast out from the shelving corset that supported it. With a quick pressure she directed a stream of pale milk right across the room on to the three squawking servant girls, who hid their faces from this shower. Such a novelty as this became a matter of conjecture to me that lasted for . . . who knows how long? I couldn't get the picture out of my mind. Continually I saw again the fine stream of grayish milk striking across the room, and I longed to see it again in actuality. That it came like that out of a woman allured my imagination and was fascinating to think about because it stirred something hidden inside me and gave me new feelings.

Some time later I tried to make it happen again. My mother was away visiting Grandma Cook in New York. I do not remember Mary Ann's being about any more at this time, but we had for a "second girl" a big fair Swedish girl named Elsa. I was attracted by her; she seemed to me to have so much life in her. I begged her to sleep with me. I told her I was afraid at night with my mother gone from the room next to mine, so she sat with me until she thought I slept and later she came and got into my big bed: the bed where Mary Ann had slept beside me for years. But I had not gone to sleep. I had been waiting for her; I had no plan, no thought, of what I wanted—I just wanted.

I waited, quiet, until I knew she was asleep and then I drew nearer to her. She lay on her back and in the darkness I felt her soft breath coming from her open mouth. I felt, rather than saw, how stupid she looked, but I liked her so: I liked her stupid, fair, gentle presence that was yet so throbbing and full of life. With a great firmness, I leaned over her and seized her big warm breast in both hands. It was a large, ballooning, billowing breast, firm and resilient and with a stout, springing nipple. I leaned to it and fondled it. I felt my blood enliven me all over and I longed to approach the whole of my body to her bosom, to cover her completely by my entire surface and have the bounding breast touch me at every point. I rolled it ecstatically from side to side and slathered it with my dripping lips. As my sudden new, delicious pleasure increased, I grew rougher. I longed now to hurt it and wring something from it. I wanted to pound it and burst it. Suddenly I remembered that other breast seen long ago in the kitchen, and I wanted to force from this one the same steely stream of milk that I felt within it, resisting me. However Elsa slept through all this is more than I know, but she never became conscious. I and that breast were alone in the night and that was what I wanted. I worked it back and forward; I approached my body to it in every way I could think of doing to see how it would feel. I held it, pushed it up hard and taut between my two small cold feet, and finally I had enough and, relinquishing it, I fell asleep. Of the awakening the next day I remember nothing, only that night, that first battle and thunder of the flesh, I remember as though it were yesterday.

Dorothy and Madeleine

I got out of our house by way of Dorothy and Madeleine Scatcherd and Nina Wilcox. The Scatcherds lived three houses above us on Delaware Avenue in a white wooden frame house that was very small and ordinary on the outside but had a strong particular charm within. They were Canadians and there were two girls and a little boy, Newton, until later, when Emily the baby was born. She was named after Mrs. Scatcherd's sister, who lived with them, Aunty Em Wood—or was it for lovely Emily Cary, Jack's sister?

Mr. Scatcherd was a charming stout, red-faced man with a small turned-up nose and curly hair. A real English country squire of a man. Mrs. Scatcherd was beautiful in all her forms but had no color. Her body was full-breasted, with large sleek hips, and her waist and arms were slender. Her face was very sensitive and thin; she was one of those small-headed women with fine unpadded features and feathery dark hair brushed straight back and wound about her head. Her eyes were clouded nearly always. She was always sitting in her bedroom window dressed in sheer white muslin dresses and sewing on some white lawn or linen thing. She made exquisite white things with tiny invisible stitches, curtains finely hemstitched for all the bedrooms, the children's underclothes, all little tucks and ruffles, and she invented a very pretty kind of apron for the girls of crossbarred dimity with the transparent stuff fulled on to a flat tucked yoke and long bishop sleeves with cuffs buttoning at the wrists. All our mothers copied these aprons for us. We wore them over our woolen dresses in the winter and they always made us feel fresh and clean when we put one on every morning, starched and crisp.

Another thing Mrs. Scatcherd did that our mothers copied was to have the shoemaker cut the two top buttons off the children's shoes, and that took away the ugliness from the high buttoned "kids" we used to wear that finished at the top with scallops lined with light-blue or red leather. It brought the shoes just above the ankle bone and was very becoming and comfortable.

I loved to go over to the Scatcherds' house. Madeleine had wavy hair like dull beaten gold and Dorothy had hair of the palest blond. She had deep-blue eyes and pale cheeks, while Madeleine had green-blue eyes and pink in her face. They both had the small retroussé nose of their father.

Each of these little girls had her own small room in the small house and everything in them was complete and exquisite. White muslin and lace everywhere and green ribbons and little green boxes and bottles surrounded Madeleine, while Dorothy's was all white and blue. These little girls were like beautiful Dresden china figures in their bowery rooms. Everything about them was feminine and dainty.

Newton, the little boy, had the old nursery at the end of the back hall with Sara, the nurse. This was not so nice. It was battered and worn and unstudied and Sara was a fat, short dragon with dark eyes. In half a dozen deep shelves let into the wall were, however, suddenly some marvelous things. The bottom shelves were crowded full of old red fire engines, torn books, and wigless dolls; but the upper shelves, just above the level of our eyes—they began to accumulate the most fantastic little treasures! Tiny golden guitars and banjos three inches long, glistening dragonflies poised on small pink and blue satin boxes, minute painted fans, and then other incomprehensible trifles of silver lace paper, ribbons, beads, and glass—bottles, furniture, toys of all kinds, all diminutive, all fabulously fine and extravagant. The shelves grew all aglitter, a bedazzlement. The array of adorable little things increased. Other children used to come and play at the Scatcherds' for the sake of that long stare upwards, finger in mouth, pigtails or curls flowing down behind the uptilted face. Really we fed upon those shelves, though we were never allowed to *touch* anything.

"Now don't you try to touch things!" We were all used to that remark. And we needed to touch them terribly. We needed to look and add them to ourselves by looking. But just as much we needed to touch things and know how different kinds of surfaces felt. We really itched to handle things. It was the greatest deprivation to us to prevent our explorations when the cushions of the finger tips were fairly burning to feel their way over the world. But no! "Now don't you go touching anything!" That was always in our ears—from the fear that we would break something.

If they had only let us use our hands then, we would have broken far fewer precious things in our lives. But sometimes when we were alone we pulled a chair up and climbed to a level with the precious shelves and we handled them all we wanted to. But, oh! the secrecy, for we knew we would have been punished.

Sometimes Sara, that hard woman, would gingerly pick up some little fragile object from the shelf and hold it over our heads in her coarse finger and thumb so we could see it by itself, separated from the jumble of other delightful fairy things. "Look at that now! Where do you suppose your Aunty Em fetched that from?" she would exclaim, holding up, maybe, a gilt bird-cage as large as an egg, with a glittering blue bird swinging within it!

Aunty Em in Paris! That is where they came from. But where did she get them, these boxes of trifles, so costly and ephemeral, that breathe of the golden vanity of another world than ours? She had been abroad for some years now. The girls had almost forgotten how she looked, but she kept her memory green by sending to them, every once in a while, a box of "souvenirs," as she called them. She never sent anything useful, never any clothes or kid gloves, no, just these adorable little nameless things that heightened the charm of life for us all and made us dream. We hadn't the faintest notion of their origin, where they came from or what they might be when Aunty Em had them. Some one said "Cotillion favors" in our hearing once—but that was nothing to us, words as meaningless and inapplicable as the things we loved there on the shelves.

Aunty Em was in Paris and sent these darling things to Madeleine and Dorothy once in a while. That was all we knew and all we needed to know. Our eager imaginations reached out to a concrete fact like this—and then they ran on and made the rest for themselves. The little dangerous, fascinating boxes and bottles and musical things, all ribbon and flowers and lace and paint. And sweet-smelling too, or maybe we only fancied so as we sniffed the air above us! Of course they grew to exceed in importance everything else in the house. And Aunty Em herself was included in their glamorous influence. Had she not sent them? Doubtless her life was all compounded of such textures and colors.

They stimulated us curiously and made our blood warmer. We grew interested in our own bodies and secretly talked together about them. Our mothers and our nurses seemed to ignore whole areas of us. They worried over our hair, our eyes, our teeth. They hurt us cleaning our nails and our ears. They scrubbed our backs with stiff brushes and our toes with rough washcloths, but the rest they ignored. And yet we had, we little girls, a vital feeling in the small nipples springing from our thin chests, and an interest in them. And in the crevice of our skinny legs we believed there was sheltered a mysterious hidden power.

When Dorothy was eight years old and Madeleine and I were ten, and there was another girl already two years old, that Emily named for her absent aunt, Aunty Em came home from Paris. She was more like a Scatcherd than like a Wood, for she was plump and dusky red in her cheeks and she too had a little upturned nose.

Aunty Em was very fascinating. She had the small room next to Madeleine's and we children used to gather around her there like flies. She filled the space around her with very small interesting things. She had one table covered with wee silver things of all kinds, much like those which covered the toy shelves in the nursery, only these were all of silver, lined with gold. Boxes, frames, vases, animals, furniture—every kind of a silver thing. Then behind the locked glass doors of her desk she had a lot of most enchanting-looking books. Some were in yellow paper and some were in brown leather with gold trimmings, and we felt certain they had lovely pictures in them and begged her often to unlock the doors and let us take out the books and look at them. But she always shook her head and wrinkled up her nose and her eyes would disappear in a bewitching way between the lids till only a shiny twinkle was to be seen of them. And she laughed. "Oh, no, not for little girls! No, indeed !"

Her dressing-table was covered with lovely brushes and many combs. Bottles of scent of all kinds were there and powder boxes with downy puffs in them. And on each side of the glass were photographs of strange-looking women, some in fancy dresses with cocked hats or ruffs, some in high bunched curls, and one in trousers. Yes, one in real men's trousers and taken in the act of lifting a high silk hat from her head, from which all the hair had been clipped! This photograph almost frightened us and yet we were fascinated by it. One day Dorothy asked Aunty Em who it was.

"Who is that lady, Aunty Em?" she inquired.

"That is my dearest friend, sweetheart. That is the Baroness Blanc," she answered.

Katy was brushing out her long crinkly brown hair as she sat before her dressing-table in a white silk nightgown open like a man's shirt at the neck. Her plump breasts were visible to us as we sat in a row on her little bed. A long fine chain was around her rich throat and disappeared down in the warmth of the crease between her breasts. She was smoking a cigarette.

Aunty Em was the first woman who ever smoked a cigarette in Buffalo and she smoked them all the time. She was a being who was full to the brim with a rich liquor of some kind. It must have been hard for her to come back to Buffalo. Almost at once, we knew in the indescribable way by which children know things, that people didn't like Aunty Em. They were afraid of her and disapproved of her. She certainly was too different from them. She was full of laughter, twinkling and dimpling with it, but she and the other Buffalo people didn't laugh at the same things. She knew things to laugh at that they had never heard of.

One day to my inexpressible surprise I came into our house and saw Aunty Em sitting there with my father and mother. I had heard them say vague things against her that I hadn't understood, and now there she sat with them—and they were all rosy and warm with laughter. All loosened up and happy and laughing together! When I appeared at the door Aunty Em dropped her hand and held it behind her chair and presently a long blue plume of smoke arose behind her head. It was an automatic ges-

ture—a habit of concealment that her period had evoked. At home in her little bedroom, she knew, I had seen her smoking over and over again. Her sudden gesture of
concealment seemed to surround her with an added fascination, even a danger, a
wickedness.

"We mustn't corrupt the young," I heard her murmur to my parents with a mischievous giggle.

"Run out now and play. We're busy," said my mother.

Now Aunty Em had a secret. We always felt she had many secrets but we couldn't
imagine what they were. She had reached out around Buffalo for friends when she came
back, but she hadn't found any. She hadn't found a single "pal," as she called it. She had
two young friends on the stage, Della Fox and Johnstone Bennett, the latter a girl too
who with short hair, an eyeglass, and man's clothes always took young men's parts. But
they only came to Buffalo once a year. Aunty Em had really no one to play with, so she
took to us little girls. And one night when we were having dinner over there, Mr. and
Mrs. Scatcherd went to the theatre and Aunty Em and we were left together.

"If you girls won't give me away, I'll show you something," she told us. We were
thrilled. To be in a secret with this fascinating, strange, foreign Aunty Em!

She told us to wait for her and when she came back after a few minutes she had
completely changed! She had on a suit of men's evening clothes. She had a real stiff
shirt, a long-tailed coat, and an eyeglass! In one hand a small, high hat, in the other a
slender cane! Aunty Em! We had never seen a woman dressed anything like a man.
Women wore very full, voluminous clothes in those days. No one even had bloomers.
They came eight or ten years later, though, for use in school gymnasiums.

Well, we all felt immediately we had a man there in the room with us. And she felt
so too. Clothes are so subtle, so mysterious; their influence has never been quite calculated. "Clothes make the man."

Now Aunty Em had to melt our sudden coolness and reserve. She wooed us gently
and tenderly. She had an air of magical attractiveness. She said: "Let us dance. I will
teach you to dance a new dance." This was different from dancing school. This was
queer. She pressed us to her hard shirt front and we felt her breath on our faces. We
gave way to the sweetness of it and felt rather scared. She danced with us each in turn,
and soon we were pushing each other aside to get into her arms again. She wrinkled her
nose at us and laughed a kind of wild laugh and lighted cigarettes one from the other.

And then the telephone rang and my mother told me it was time to come home and
said to run right along and she'd be waiting at the front door for me. For it was only a
step between our houses.

"Wait. I'll go too. But you must remember now. You're not going to tell about these
clothes. Your mother and father would burn them if they knew I had them in the house,
girls," she said, turning to Madeleine and Dorothy.

"No, no, never!" we all promised and she put on a big cape and walked to my gate
with me. And as we walked down the gas-lit street, past the vacant lot and past the Fri-
ars' House, that pompous red brick with turrets with all the windows gleaming behind

the sheltering shades, I thrilled through and through at the thought of her legs in those trousers underneath the cape—that secret, that almost frightening secret that we had to keep.

Now from that very night Aunty Em turned to the children more and more. She liked Dorothy the best, pale Dorothy with deep-sapphire eyes and flaxen hair. Madeleine and I became more intimate friends. We were beginning to love books. We used to take a couple of books and go off together and read whole afternoons away. But Aunty Em took the Scatcherds' old horse Benny and drove away every day out to the country with Dorothy and Emily, the baby, who was going on three years old now. Dorothy and Aunty Em became inseparable and when Dorothy was with us others she was silent and seemed to have nothing to say. She seemed wrapped in a dream.

Aunty Em swaggered a little in her precious diminutive fashion. She twinkled about, she dressed in rough tweed coats and skirts and wore shirts that were plain tailor-made and not like those of other women. She wore an eyeglass on a black ribbon and she carried a gold match box in the front pocket of her skirt. She was curiously interesting to us all. And to Dorothy. Every day we saw them go off in the low buggy—up Delaware Avenue they drove, out past the country club, over the railroad tracks that circled the town, out to the fields and woods.

And then . . . one day . . . I can hardly write it down! It shattered our neighborhood. A train ran along the level crossing just as they were passing—and drove into them and killed them all three: Dorothy and Emily and Aunty Em. The engineer said over and over that he blew his whistle until it was almost in their ears and yet they paid no attention. He could not make them stop, nor could he stop his train. It happened under his eyes. He couldn't avoid the sight. . . .

The three bodies lay together in the front room of the Scatcherd house, covered with flowers. We all went in and out of the room unheeded, for Mrs. Scatcherd was prostrated as though struck down by the same blow as the others and the house was full of relations and neighbors. So we went in and out until my mother made me stay home. Their faces were calm and smooth, though Aunty Em had a white cloth binding her cheeks. They had a look of being lifted somehow into another world. We said this to each other.

Madeleine grew very quiet in the weeks after this. She sat all day long in the chair in the sitting-room window and read Walter Scott. She was silent and motionless. In the spring she began to twitch and shake and they called it St. Vitus's dance and she grew as restless and nervous as before she had been contained. Mrs. Scatcherd's face became like a mask as she sat always sewing in her bedroom window. Mr. Scatcherd stayed away more and more from the dismal house. It was never the same again.

From this time on I noted how things can never remain in the same combinations. Households, groups of friends, no matter what kind of arrangement of human particles; they come together for a little while and then the whole pattern is broken and altered. Like chemical atoms brought into juxtaposition by a scientist that cannot be held together but fly apart and form new conjunctions or disappear altogether. As Deirdre said: "It's a heartbreak to the wise, things are in the same place for a short time only."

PARIS AND VEEOLETTE

[. . .] I went down to Pierrefonds and Mary [Shillito] met me at the station in a pony cart. I had no idea of what Pierrefonds was, though I had heard the girls talk about the château, and when we came in sight of that great gray stone pile with its pointed towers and curve on curve of rounded corners, solid and ponderous and hoary and so static, like a mood of the Middle Ages congealed and left there, I was filled with awe.

I saw Violet against the dark immovable mass of the château as she walked towards us, knee-deep in the grasses already yellowing, for it was July. She had on a soft blue batiste dress open at the neck, and a coarse straw hat trimmed with black velvet bows and a wreath of poppies and wheat. Her arms were bare to the elbow and there was such an expression of something in their soft pink curves, in her substantial wrists and padded, intelligent hands. I could not think what it was they expressed so fluently, but it was something vital and feminine and even matronly. Mary's hands and arms, for instance, had none of this look. They were fluttering and trembling all the time; they had great sensibility and nervousness, and of course were feminine too; but they were more an artist's hands, while, come to think of it, Violet's hands looked like a mother's hands, like the large, capable, tender hands of the Madonnas.

Violet had come across the fields to meet the cart. She stood in the long grass and smiled at me with her deep, intentional, loving smile. Any one to whom Violet has given that look will never forget it. The words "look" or "smile" describe adequately enough the gestures with which people convey themselves outwardly to the world. But what happened between Violet and the one to whom she felt she could give her spirit was so vital and electric and intense that her buried ardor leaping to her eyes seemed to flash past the barrier of her flesh and enter one in a swift possession, and go running into one's secret channels like a permeating, sweet elixir. No, the word "look" cannot tell about it—it made one understand the Immaculate Conception.

Thus Violet, by the bestowal of her love upon me, entered my cosmos, bringing with her all the subtleties and beauties of the ages that were embodied in her. This is the vital transmission of truth and culture forever; by these channels alone the "river of light" flows on in the race. Truth is not to be found sealed in the pages of books; it has to be given by one to another in an embrace of the spirit.

I looked at Violet as she waited in the tall grasses, with the dark masses of the château behind her. And I thought that she looked as though she had come out of the round turrets to meet us, leaving her tapestry frame when she saw us on the road. She was always like that; she belonged to all ages, she was like a synthesis of the past. Sometimes she seemed to be a little Chinese Kwannon with her slanting eyes and the faint, patient smile and her hanging, clasped hands. In memory of that look she had and which I always wanted to see again, I bought one after another whenever I ran across one of them, my white Chinese porcelain Kwannons. They stood in a row on a long carved walnut chest in the Villa Curonia, all sizes and all serene—all looking like Violet. Once in a great while Nature creates a marvelous human being, but very rarely. Most people go through their lives without ever coming across one of these efflorescent souls and never even know what they have missed. After all these years, Violet's great significance lives in me yet and I realize my good fortune. I have never seen a man or a woman who came anywhere near her in development. As Mary said to me at Miss Graham's: *"Elle sait tout."*

I got out and walked with her to the little house where they were living. Mrs. Shillito had leased a small stone cottage that was an actual part of the château in the old days—a dependency where some of the people had lived—and it was like a small ancient farmhouse. I remember only the room in which I spent the night with Violet, Mary sleeping next to us in a small adjoining dressing-room.

The picture comes back to me clearly: Violet and Mary and I standing on the old stone floor that had a few strips of rush matting on it, standing in our little flannel peignoirs, brushing our hair, while two candles on the muslin-covered dresser threw great shadows of us over the whitewashed walls. The smell of it comes as actually as the sight—for Violet was rubbing a thick white cream on her face and hands and as I sniffed its lovely perfume she told me to take some and try it and I took the little white jar. It was Crême Simon. I have used it ever since and it always makes me think of Violet and the Château de Pierrefonds.

When we blew out our candles and lay down together in the bed, the moon slanted in a long beam of white through the oblong of window high up on the wall; such thick blocks of stone composed that wall that the embrasure was twenty inches deep and the moonlight flowing through the opening in the solid, clear-cut form made me realize once for all what a window is. The openings in most people's houses have no expression, no meaning, no reality. They merely let in air and light. But this window let in beauty. It was wonderful. I will never forget it and how that night I took into myself the feeling of the *moyen age*—its solidity and the sense of security built up by the need of it that filled the nights and days of the people who lived within the thick stone walls of the Château de Pierrefonds. The feeling of carefully prepared materials: stones cut out one by one by the careful chisel and fitted in leisure to sustain a length of lives—rooms, corridors, halls, all felt out and laid out by the eye and determined by feeling before the days of exact mechanical measurements. The women's lives within those walls were full of color. Everything counted for them to increase their sense of living. The colors of their wools as well as the colors of their well-baked loaves and cakes and of their bright-colored meadow flowers—they savored all these, letting nothing pass unnoticed, and watched incessantly down the long roads, for their pleasure and their sorrow, indeed their whole destiny, came to them over those narrow paths that led from the château to the world.

Violet and I lay in the quiet stone room, and I let it all drift into myself, all the past of that place.

I turned in my dreams to Violet where she lay beside me, a long, stiff effigy in the white light from the moon shining on the wall. I saw her smile gleaming still and sweet and subtle. She knew me and could read my imaginings as though they unfurled before me in scrolls of thought from behind my brow.

"What?" I asked her tenderly, more to let her know by the tone of my voice that I loved her than that she should tell me what I knew already. I reached out my hand and laid it shyly upon her left breast, cupping it with my palm. Instantly it was attuned to a music of the finest vibration. From between her young breast and the sensitive palm of my hand there arose all about us, it seemed, a high, sweet singing. This response we made to each other at the contact of our flesh ran from hand and breast along the shining passages of our blood until in every cell we felt each other's presence. This was to awaken from sleep and sing like morning stars. We lay in silence that yet was full of shrill, sweet sound, and all that stone room became vital with the overflow of our increased life, for we passed it out of us in rapid, singing waves—an emanation more fine and powerful than that from radium.

We needed no more than to be in touch like that with each other, just hand and breast, to make our way into a new world together. *"Je t'aime,"* murmured Violet, and I answered, *"Et je t'aime."*

I looked at her again across the dim light and I saw her smile once more — a different smile. She looked happy, rueful, merry, and a little resigned.

"Je ne savais pas que je sois sensuelle," she whispered, *"mais il paraît que je le suis."*

"Et pourquoi pas?" I asked, for it seemed to me if that was what was meant by *sensualité* it was exquisite and commendable and should be cultivated. It was a more delicious life I felt in me than I had ever felt before. I thought it was a superior kind of living too. I looked at Violet questioningly. Since she had that music in her, surely she, so cognizant of fine values, would appreciate it as I did. But she didn't answer. She gave a tiny little sigh and continued to smile, but a deeper, a different meaning had come into it now. Something incredibly antique and compassionate, like an unaging goddess fresh and unfaded, yet of the most ancient days, seemed to gaze at me from under her drooping lids. I saw again in her the Kwannon look—Kwannon, the goddess of mercy who knows the meaning of everything and still smiles her small smile, the merciful goddess who has reached the end of her long evolution and who forfeits Nirvana to come back to earth and help men complete their destiny.

Just in flashes like that, we were not together. She was, in her intuitions and her wisdom, infinitely removed from me. The most lonely creatures in the world are at these times—uncompanioned. I felt my own childhood comforted and assuaged when I saw that look on her face. I felt some one there ahead of me in the invisible distance, some one who would be there before me and wait, no matter how slowly I came on behind her, and who would show me the way. As a child I had felt no one in front of me—an unopened space with no paths in it had encircled me; my parents had seemed like dim, dull figures far, far behind. I could not make them a part of my journey. I had to set off alone by myself and I was always alone. But now I knew there was some one on beyond me, that she, not I, knew loneliness.

Craven, I tasted the comfort of this and it was stronger than any sympathy I had for that girl who had taken my place of isolation in the life of the spirit.

Violet did not draw away from me. Our natural harmony sang on through that night and the next, when we came together again. But into her eyes that compassionate look that was like a mother's who knows more than the child can understand and so is mute, that sweet, rueful, loving smile was on her face now all the time we were together, and it was called there by that glad life of our blood, which for want of a better term I must call music—but that she had named to me by the term *sensualité*.

"HENRY HANDEL RICHARDSON" (ETHEL FLORENCE LINDESAY RICHARDSON) (1870–1946)

"The Bathe," "Two Hanged Women" (1934)

Ethel Richardson, the Australian novelist who wrote under the pseudonym Henry Handel Richardson, was born in Melbourne in 1870 and educated at the Presbyterian Ladies' College. She would later commemorate her schooldays in the novel *The Getting of Wisdom* (1910). Intending to become a concert pianist, Richardson studied music at the Leipzig Conservatorium in the early 1890s but gave up her musical ambitions after meeting a Scottish professor of German, J. G. Robertson, whom she married in 1895. After living in Strasbourg for eight years, they moved to London in 1904, where Richardson completed her first novel, *Maurice Guest* (1908). With the exception of a two-month trip to Australia in 1912 to research *The Fortunes of Richard Mahony* (1930)—a trilogy about a man coming of age during the Australian gold rush years— she remained in England for the rest of her life. The success of the latter work led to her nomination for the Nobel Prize in 1932. After her husband's death in 1933 Richardson published a collection of short stories, *The End of a Childhood* (1934), and the novel *The Young Cosima* (1939), based on the life of Cosima Wagner. In her last years she lived with a female companion, Olga Roncoroni, in Sussex. After Richardson's death Roncoroni completed Richardson's unfinished memoir, *Myself When Young*, and it was published in 1948.

Like Katherine Mansfield, Richardson was fascinated by the sensuality of girls and women, and her writing is often vividly homoerotic in feeling. In both "The Bathe" and "Two Hanged Women" (from *The End of a Childhood*) she explores female-female relationships. In the first—a comic vignette about liberation from physical and emotional restraints—the nature of the intimacy between the two bathing women is ambiguous, but may be suggested by their instinctive joining of hands before they plunge, full-breasted, into the sea. In the second, we listen in on the conversation of "two hanged women," whose diffident, emotion-filled relation is limned with its author's characteristic acumen and delicacy.

FURTHER READING: Henry Handel Richardson, *The Getting of Wisdom* (London: W. Heinemann, 1910); —, *The End of a Childhood* (New York: Norton, 1934); —, *Myself*

When Young (New York: Norton, 1948); Vincent Buckley, *Henry Handel Richardson* (Melbourne: Lansdowne, 1961); Dorothy Green, *Ulysses Bound: Henry Handel Richardson and Her Fiction* (Canberra: Australian National University Press, 1973); William D. Elliott, *Henry Handel Richardson* (Boston: Twayne, 1975); Karen McLeod, *Henry Handel Richardson: A Critical Study* (Cambridge: Cambridge University Press, 1985); Carol Franklin, " 'A Depressed Amor': Richardson's 'The Bathe': A Grotesque," *Australian Literature Studies*, 15 (1992): 165–78; —, "Henry Handel Richardson's 'Two Hanged Women': 'Our Own True Selves' and Compulsory Heterosexuality," *Kunapipi* 14 (1992): 41–52; Michael Ackland, *Henry Handel Richardson* (Melbourne: Oxford University Press, 1996).

The Bathe

THE GROTESQUE

Stripped of her clothing, the child showed the lovely shape of a six-year-old. Just past the dimpled roundnesses of babyhood, the little body stood slim and straight, legs and knees closely met, the skin white as the sand into which the small feet dug, pink toe faultlessly matched to toe.

She was going to bathe.

The tide was out. The alarming, ferocious surf, which at flood came hurtling over the reef, swallowing up the beach, had withdrawn, baring the flat brown coral rocks: far off against their steep brown edges it sucked and gurgled lazily. In retreating, it had left many lovely pools in the reef, all clear as glass, some deep as rooms, grown round their sides with weeds that swam like drowned hair, and hid strange sea-things.

Not to these pools might the child go; nor did she need to prick her soles on the coral. Her bathing place was a great sandy-bottomed pool that ran out from the beach, and at its deepest came no higher than her chin.

Naked to sun and air, she skipped and frolicked with the delight of the very young, to whom clothes are still an encumbrance. And one of her runs led her headlong into the sea. No toe-dipping tests were necessary here; this water met the skin like a veil of warm silk. In it she splashed and ducked and floated; her hair, which had been screwed into a tight little knob, loosening and floating with her like a nimbus. Tired of play, she came out, trickling and glistening, and lay down in the sand, which was hot to the touch, first on her stomach, then on her back, till she was coated with sand like a fish bread-crumbed for frying. This, for the sheer pleasure of plunging anew, and letting the silken water wash her clean.

At the sight, the two middle-aged women who sat looking on grew restless. And, the prank being repeated, the sand-caked little body vanishing in the limpid water to

bob up shining like ivory, the tips of their tongues shot out and surreptitiously moistened their lips. These were dry, their throats were dry, their skins itched; their seats
burned from pressing the hot sand.

And suddenly eyes met and brows were lifted in a silent question. Shall we? Dare
we risk it?

"Let's!"

For no living thing but themselves moved on the miles of desolate beach; not a
neighbour was within cooee; their own shack lay hid behind a hill.

Straightway they fell to rolling up their work and stabbing it with their needles.

Then they, too, undressed.

Tight, high bodices of countless buttons went first, baring the massy arms and fat-
creased necks of a plump maturity. Thereafter bunchy skirts were slid over hips and
stepped out of. Several petticoats followed, the undermost of red flannel, with scal-
loped edges. Tight stiff corsets were next squeezed from their moorings and cast aside:
the linen beneath lay hot and damply crushed. Long white drawers unbound and, leg
by leg, disengaged, voluminous calico chemises appeared, draped in which the pair sat
down to take off their boots—buttoned boots—and stockings, their feet emerging red
and tired-looking, the toes misshapen, and horny with callosities. Erect again, they yet
coyly hesitated before the casting of the last veil, once more sweeping the distance for
a possible spy. Nothing stirring, however, up went their arms, dragging the balloon-like
garments with them; and, inch by inch, calves, thighs, trunks and breasts were bared to
view.

At the prospect of getting water playmates, the child had clapped her hands, hop-
ping up and down where she stood. But this was the first time she had watched a real
grown-up undress; she was always in bed and asleep when they did it. Now, in broad
daylight, she looked on unrebuked, wildly curious; and surprise soon damped her joy.
So this was what was underneath! Skirts and petticoats down, she saw that laps were
really legs; while the soft and cosy place you put your head on, when you were
tired . . .

And suddenly she turned tail and ran back to the pool. She didn't want to see.

But your face was the one bit of you you couldn't put under water. So she had to.

Two fat, stark-naked figures were coming down the beach.

They had joined hands, as if to sustain each other in their nudity . . . or as if, in
shedding their clothes, they had also shed a portion of their years. Gingerly, yet in haste
to reach cover, they applied their soles to the tickly sand: a haste that caused unwieldy
breasts to bob and swing, bellies and buttocks to wobble. Splay-legged they were, from
the weight of these protuberances. Above their knees, garters had cut fierce red lines in
the skin; their bodies were criss-crossed with red furrows, from the variety of strings
and bones that had lashed them in. The calves of one showed purple-knotted with
veins; across the other's abdomen ran a deep, longitudinal scar. One was patched with
red hair, one with black.

In a kind of horrid fascination the child stood and stared . . . as at two wild out-landish beasts. But before they reached her she again turned, and, heedless of the prick-les, ran seawards, out on the reef.

This was forbidden. There were shrill cries of: "Naughty girl! Come back!"

Draggingly the child obeyed.

They were waiting for her, and, blind to her hurt, took her between them and waded into the water. When this was up to their knees, they stooped to damp napes and crowns, and sluiced their arms. Then they played. They splashed water at each other's great backsides; they lay down and, propped on their elbows, let their legs float; or, forming a ring, moved heavily round to the tune of: *Ring-a-ring-a-rosy, pop down a posy!* And down the child went, till she all but sat on the sand. Not so they. Even with the support of the water they could bend but a few inches; and wider than ever did their legs splay, to permit of their corpulences being lowered.

But the sun was nearing meridian in a cloudless sky. Its rays burnt and stung. The child was sent running up the beach to the clothes-heaps, and returned, not unlike a depressed Amor, bearing in each hand a wide, flower-trimmed, dolly-varden hat, the ribbons of which trailed the sand.

These they perched on their heads, binding the ribbons under their chins; and thus attired waded out to the deep end of the pool. Here, where the water came a few inches above their waists, they stood to cool off, their breasts seeming to float on the surface like half-inflated toy balloons. And when the sand stirred up by their feet had subsided, their legs could be seen through the translucent water oddly foreshortened, with edges that frayed at each ripple.

But a line of foam had shown its teeth at the edge of the reef. The tide was on the turn; it was time to go.

Waddling up the beach they spread their petticoats, and on these stretched them-selves out to dry. And as they lay there on their sides, with the supreme mass of hip and buttock arching in the air, their contours were those of seals—great mother-seals come lolloping out of the water to lie about on the sand.

The child had found a piece of dry cuttlefish, and sat pretending to play with it. But she wasn't really. Something had happened which made her not like any more to play. Something ugly. Oh, never . . . never . . . no, not ever now did she want to grow up. *She* would always stop a little girl.

Two Hanged Women

Hand in hand the youthful lovers sauntered along the esplanade. It was a night in mid-summer; a wispy moon had set, and the stars glittered. The dark mass of the sea, at flood, lay tranquil, slothfully lapping the shingle.

"Come on, let's make for the usual," said the boy.

But on nearing their favourite seat they found it occupied. In the velvety shade of the overhanging sea-wall, the outlines of two figures were visible.

"Oh, blast!" said the lad. "That's torn it. What now, Baby?"

"Why, let's stop here, Pincher, right close up, till we frighten 'em off."

And very soon loud, smacking kisses, amatory pinches and ticklings, and skittish squeals of pleasure did their work. Silently the intruders rose and moved away.

But the boy stood gaping after them, open-mouthed.

"Well, I'm *damned*! If it wasn't just two hanged women!"

Retreating before a salvo of derisive laughter, the elder of the girls said: "We'll go out on the breakwater." She was tall and thin, and walked with a long stride.

Her companion, shorter than she by a bobbed head of straight flaxen hair, was hard put to it to keep pace. As she pegged along she said doubtfully, as if in self-excuse: "Though I really ought to go home. It's getting late. Mother will be angry."

They walked with finger-tips lightly in contact; and at her words she felt what was like an attempt to get free, on the part of the fingers crooked in hers. But she was prepared for this, and held fast, gradually working her own up till she had a good half of the other hand in her grip.

For a moment neither spoke. Then, in a low, muffled voice, came the question: "Was she angry last night, too?"

The little fair girl's reply had an unlooked-for vehemence. "You know she wasn't!" And, mildly despairing: "But you never *will* understand. Oh, what's the good of . . . of anything!"

And on sitting down she let the prisoned hand go, even putting it from her with a kind of push. There it lay, palm upwards, the fingers still curved from her hold, looking like a thing with a separate life of its own; but a life that was ebbing.

On this remote seat, with their backs turned on lovers, lights, the town, the two girls sat and gazed wordlessly at the dark sea, over which great Jupiter was flinging a thin gold line. There was no sound but the lapping, sucking, sighing, of the ripples at the edge of the breakwater, and the occasional screech of an owl in the tall trees on the hillside.

But after a time, having stolen more than one side glance at her companion, the younger seemed to take heart of grace. With a childish toss of the head that set her loose hair swaying, she said, in a tone of meaning emphasis: "I like Fred."

The only answer was a faint, contemptuous shrug.

"I tell you I *like* him!"

"Fred? Rats!"

"No it isn't . . . that's just where you're wrong, Betty. But you think you're so wise. Always."

"I know what I know."

"Or imagine you do! But it doesn't matter. Nothing you can say makes any difference. I like him and always shall. In heaps of ways. He's so big and strong, for one thing: it gives you such a safe sort of feeling to be with him . . . as if nothing could happen while you were. Yes, it's . . . it's . . . well, I can't help it, Betty, there's something *comfy* in having a boy to go about with—like other girls do. One they'd eat their hats to get, too! I can see it in their eyes when we pass; Fred with his great long legs and broad shoulders—I don't nearly come up to them—and his blue eyes with the black lashes, and his shiny black hair. And I like his tweeds, the Harris smell of them, and his dirty old pipe, and the way he shows his teeth—he's got *topping* teeth—when he laughs and says 'ra-*ther!*' And other people, when they see us, look . . . well I don't quite know how to say it, but they look sort of pleased; and they make room for us and let us into the dark corner-seats at the pictures, just as if we'd a right to them. And they never laugh. (Oh, I can't *stick* being laughed at!—and that's the truth.) Yes, it's so comfy, Betty darling . . . such a warm cosy comfy feeling. Oh, *won't* you understand?"

"Gawd! why not make a song of it?" But a moment later, very fiercely: "And who is it's taught you to think all this? Who's hinted it and suggested it till you've come to believe it? . . . believe it's what you really feel."

"She hasn't! Mother's never said a word . . . about Fred."

"Words?—why waste words? . . . when she can do it with a cock of the eye. For your Fred, that!" and the girl called Betty held her fingers aloft and snapped them viciously. "But your mother's a different proposition."

"I think you're simply horrid."

To this there was no reply.

"*Why* have you such a down on her? What's she ever done to you? . . . except not get ratty when I stay out late with Fred. And I don't see how you can expect . . . being what she is . . . and with nobody but me—after all she *is* my mother . . . you can't alter that. I know very well—and you know, too—I'm not *too* putrid-looking. But"—beseechingly—"I'm *nearly* twenty-five now, Betty. And other girls . . . well, she sees them, every one of them, with a boy of their own, even though they're ugly, or fat, or have legs like sausages—they've only got to ogle them a bit—the girls, I mean . . . and there they are. And Fred's a good sort—he is, really!—and he dances well, and doesn't drink, and so . . . so why *shouldn't* I like him? . . . and off my own bat . . . without it having to be all Mother's fault, and me nothing but a parrot, and without any will of my own?"

"Why? Because I know her too well, my child! I can read her as you'd never dare to . . . even if you could. She's sly, your mother is, so sly there's no coming to grips with her . . . one might as well try to fill one's hand with cobwebs. But she's got a hold on you, a stranglehold, that nothing'll loosen. Oh! mothers aren't fair—I mean it's not fair of nature to weigh us down with them and yet expect us to be our own true selves. The handicap's too great. All those months, when the same blood's running through two sets of veins—there's no getting away from that, ever after. Take yours. As I say, does she need to open her mouth? Not she! She's only got to let it hang at the corners, and you reek, you drip with guilt."

Something in these words seemed to sting the younger girl. She hit back. "I know what it is, you're jealous, that's what you are! . . . and you've no other way of letting it out. But I tell you this. If ever I marry—yes, *marry*!—it'll be to please myself, and nobody else. Can you imagine me doing it to oblige her?"

Again silence.

"If I only think what it would be like to be fixed up and settled, and able to live in peace, without this eternal dragging two ways . . . just as if I was being torn in half. And see Mother smiling and happy again, like she used to be. Between the two of you I'm nothing but a punch-ball. Oh, I'm fed up with it! . . . fed up to the neck. As for you. . . . And yet you can sit there as if you were made of stone! Why don't you *say* something? *Betty*! Why won't you speak?"

But no words came.

"I can *feel* you sneering. And when you sneer I hate you more than any one on earth. If only I'd never seen you!"

"Marry your Fred, and you'll never need to again."

"I will, too! I'll marry him, and have a proper wedding like other girls, with a veil and bridesmaids and bushels of flowers. And I'll live in a house of my own, where I can do as I like, and be left in peace, and there'll be no one to badger and bully me—Fred wouldn't . . . ever! Besides, he'll be away all day. And when he came back at night, he'd . . . I'd . . . I mean I'd—" But here the flying words gave out; there came a stormy breath and a cry of: "Oh, Betty, Betty! . . . I couldn't, no, I couldn't! It's when I think of *that*. . . . Yes, it's quite true! I like him all right, I do indeed, but only as long as he doesn't come too near. If he even sits too close, I have to screw myself up to bear it"— and flinging herself down over her companion's lap, she hid her face. "And if he tries to touch me, Betty, or even takes my arm or puts his round me. . . . And then his face . . . when it looks like it does sometimes . . . all wrong . . . as if it had gone all wrong—oh! then I feel I shall have to scream—out loud. I'm afraid of him . . . when he looks like that. Once . . . when he kissed me . . . I could have died with the horror of it. His breath . . . his breath . . . and his mouth—like fruit pulp—and the black hairs on his wrists . . . and the way he looked—and . . . and everything! No, I can't, I can't . . . nothing will make me . . . I'd rather die twice over. But what am I to do? Mother'll *never* understand. Oh, why has it got to be like this? I want to be happy, like other girls, and to make her happy, too . . . and everything's all wrong. You tell me, Betty darling, you help me, you're older . . . you *know* . . . and you can help me, if you will . . . if you only will!" And locking her arms round her friend she drove her face deeper into the warmth and darkness, as if, from the very fervour of her clasp, she could draw the aid and strength she needed.

Betty had sat silent, unyielding, her sole movement being to loosen her own arms from her sides and point her elbows outwards, to hinder them touching the arms that lay round her. But at this last appeal she melted; and gathering the young girl to her breast, she held her fast.—And so for long she continued to sit, her chin resting lightly on the fair hair, that was silky and downy as an infant's, and gazing with sombre eyes over the stealthily heaving sea.

"M. J. FARRELL" [MOLLY KEANE] (1905–1994)

From *Devoted Ladies* (1934)

The Anglo-Irish novelist and playwright Molly Keane was born into a wealthy landowning family in County Kildare, Ireland, in 1905. She was educated by her mother, Agnes Shakespeare Higginson, a formidable woman who wrote poetry under the name Moira O'Neill. Keane's own writing career began in 1928, when she published her first novel, *The Knight of the Cheerful Countenance*, under the pseudonym M. J. Farrell. Other M. J. Farrell novels quickly followed—*Young Entry* (1928), *Taking Chances* (1929), *Mad Puppetstown* (1931), *Devoted Ladies* (1934), *Full House* (1935) and *Two Days in Aragon* (1941). These early novels at once memorialized and satirized the rich Anglo-Irish hunting set in which Keane had grown up. In 1938 she married Robert Lumley Keane and published her first play, *Spring Meeting*, cowritten with John Perry. She produced three more plays in the 1940s, but following the death of her husband in 1946 wrote no more significant fiction for almost thirty years. In her seventies Keane began writing again—this time under her own name. The brilliantly acidulous comic novels *Good Behaviour* (1981), *Time after Time* (1983), and *Living and Giving* (1988)— inspired once again by the pleasures and follies of the Anglo-Irish gentry—resulted from this second flowering of her art.

Like Compton Mackenzie's *Extraordinary Women*, Keane's 1934 novel *Devoted Ladies* is a satire on women-loving women, though a far more cynical one than Mackenzie's light-hearted confection. Glamorous, boorish, and irretrievably shallow, the lovers Jane and Jessica are the "devoted ladies" in question; the novel turns—darkly— on the collapse of their relationship. The scene below sets the stage: the two are seen, drunk and disorderly, at a fashionable party at the London flat of their homosexual playwright friend, Sylvester. Describing the ensuing mayhem, Keane establishes the novel's tone—cruel yet chic—and hints at its mordant outcome. Though neither woman knows it yet, the young man into whose arms Jane briefly subsides in a "polite almost lady-like coma" is George Playfair, the polo-playing Irish aristocrat who will lure her away from Jessica with fatal results.

FURTHER READING: M. J. Farrell [Molly Keane], *Devoted Ladies* (1934; rpt. London: Virago, 1984); Molly Keane, *Good Behaviour* (New York: Knopf, 1981); —, *Time After Time* (London: André Deutsch, 1983); —, *Loving and Giving* (New York: Dutton, 1988); Bridget O'Toole, "Three Writers of the Big House: Elizabeth Bowen, Molly Keane, and Jennifer Johnson," in *Across a Roaring Hill: The Protestant Imagination in Modern Ireland*, ed. Gerald Dawe and Edna Longley (Belfast and Dover, N.H.: Black-staff, 1985), pp. 124–38; Rachael Jane Lynch, "The Crumbling Fortress: Molly Keane's Comedies of Anglo-Irish Manners," in Theresa O'Connor, ed., *The Comic Tradition in Irish Women Writers* (Gainesville: University Press of Florida, 1996), pp. 73–98.

Sylvester was giving a party.

His guests toiled up flight upon flight of dark stairs.

Jane was so accustomed to the smell of cats and ammonia on the stairs (there was a mews below) that she hardly noticed where they left off and where the expensive smells of Sylvester's rooms began. She had been there very often this summer, for Sylvester preferred to entertain in his own rooms to entertaining in restaurants or night clubs: "It is more me," he would say, "and much cheaper, and much better—don't you agree?"

And here his friends would agree with enthusiasm. His food and his drink were always good. Not that Jane minded about food or drink either (so long as she could have enough drink). If you have always fed on the rarer and more expensive forms of food you will, by the time you are twenty-eight, have developed an intelligence about food or else you simply won't mind. Jane simply didn't mind. And her favourite drink was brandy; brandies and sodas followed by a mass of liqueur brandies rolling pleas-antly in their large hot glasses.

It was not for Sylvester's good food and drink that Jane came to see him whenever she was asked, and often when she was not asked. It was because she hoped on and on in the face of constant disappointment that Sylvester would put her in a book or in a play.

She could never realise that the people Sylvester put in his life he did not put either in his books or in his plays. When he told her this he hoped that the flattery implied in the remark about his life might assuage her dismal greed for seeing herself as she wished him to see her.

But although he spoke to her softly and cunningly: "Jane, you know I never put the people who *matter* to me in my books"; she would answer only: "Oh, you are *horrible* to me," in her rich South American voice, so teeming with feeling and so barren of words.

Yet in spite of his reluctance to enclose the substance of her flesh and her spirit forever in an aspic of words, Sylvester continued to be very sweet to Jane. Although his new revue was playing to good business and his last book doing well, the moment might yet arrive when he would require to borrow money from Jane, or at any rate make use of her cars or her houses or any of the many benefits which providence spends on very rich young women that very poor young men may thereby profit a little.

It was two years now since Sylvester had ceased to be a very poor young man, but he had not yet quite lost the habit. He was genuinely economical, just as he was genuinely a good writer and a competent playwright. But Jane was genuine in nothing. He believed even her complete stupidity was partly a pose of mind.

How much her affection for Jessica was a pose, a queer piece of exhibitionism, that he did not know.

Jessica and Jane were in Sylvester's bedroom now painting up their faces for the party.

Sylvester's bedroom was all shape and no colour. It was decorated in brown and grey and black. Jane always thought it inconceivably dreary, but Jessica, who thought she knew about house decoration, went into sullen rapture over the lighting. She struggled to impart her feeling to Jane in chosen difficult words. She always worked hard and deliberately for words, but Jane only said, "I'll say it's horrible; I'll always say so."

Jessica looked at Jane standing there in the colourless space of Sylvester's room. She looked at her and looked away again and back again. "She's such a good shape," she thought quickly—clothing for herself in words some indefinable excitement—"Wherever she is she makes her own pattern."

In the grey and black and brown room no doubt Jane did look well, for her lines were faintly geometric, as though flesh had been put on her body only to be ruled off again with extreme exactitude. Her bones were no more than small enough to justify the theory that she was ghostlike, not gaunt. As it was she escaped that unattractive state of body by very little. Her coarse fair hair was a lovely blanched colour and she arranged it with much care like a little girl's. Sometimes when in a particularly girlish mood she would even tie a piece of it up with a ribbon. But it was the scar of her harelip that gave to Jane's face its peculiar and distant expression of sadness, entirely redeeming her features from that dreary baby-like prettiness in which but for this they were surely cast—this thread of a scar, pulling her mouth a little to one side and her nose faintly crooked, was fascinating. It compelled curiosity. First it was faintly shocking and then it became enormously amusing. She would paint her mouth as its lines were, a little awry, and this was amusing too. Her eyes were pulled rather open by the scar (if one folds one's upper lip together the reason for this becomes apparent) which lent them a permanent expression as though staring with tears.

Jessica who had lived with Jane for six months now was quite a different sort of girl. She had been well brought up by her rich family and this, since her brain was her obsession, she found not a little tiresome.

Her ideas were well discovered and, if not always original, at least generally easy to coax into importance. For the discovery of ideas, their crystallisation into phrases and the subsequent delivery of such phrases at the right moment (if possible with no one present who had enjoyed them before) she found family life a poor background. In her comfortable and unsympathetic home Jessica's charm was no charm. And charm, of a dark, compelling kind, Jessica possessed without a doubt. But the length of its influence was a very variable matter.

In her friendships with men as well as with women Jessica spent herself so lavishly and so emotionally that soon there was no more she. She had spent what she was in a sort of dreadful effort towards entire mental contact with the person she loved. And having reserved no smallest ledge of herself for herself, no foothold for the last secret feet of her mind, she would retreat in anger and despair from her friendships. Then cruelly, disdainfully and despitefully she would speak against such a one as she had loved.

Her dreary enthusiasms were tolerated by her friends for the sake of those moments when, her lips curled back from her teeth like a dog, saliva in their corners and hysteria in her eyes she would tell and tell and tell of that past moment in her life; with pitiless mimicry and sure malice breaking the one who had shared it with her on the wheel of her words, on the wheel of her own despair.

Venice with the loved one, or a week in somebody's yacht—she would tear their hours apart and show, with screams of insane laughter, how this or that had filled her lover with sentiment and enthusiasm, while for her it had been beyond mockery.

But how would Jane have voiced enthusiasms, they wondered, who had never heard her say more than: "I feel horrible—fix me a brandy and soda." Still, Jessica could be so wildly funny about the least probable people, the tale was worth waiting for, worth the endurance of her prolonged obsession.

Jessica was an intellectual snob. She seldom condescended to be gay, although she would take endless pains to be rude. She loved to express her emotional reactions to people, food, form or colour by word of mouth. Now she said to Jane:

"You're looking very wonderful to-night—don't let's stay at this party too late— Look, Jane, in that silver dress you're terribly exciting—so . . . *Blanched*, so . . . *Tarnished* . . ." Whenever Jessica got into difficulties for words she would create a mental atmosphere of astericks pregnant with meaning.

Jane said: "Tarnished? Aren't you horrible to me?" and they went down to the party.

Sylvester's party had only just begun when they came in, so Jane decided at once that she had come too early, which was a fatal beginning. However, Sylvester was enchanted to see them both. He said to Jessica:

"I hope you have something really rude and unkind to tell me, darling. We must have words together presently when these people have all arrived. I hate being interrupted when I have you to talk to."

Then he said to Jane:

"What lovely beads, Jane. They are divine, aren't they?" He took them in his hands to look at them and suddenly in his long satirical hands Jane's beads, which had up to now only looked expensive, took on a quickened look of beauty that stayed with them even after he gave them back to her.

Although Sylvester had no enthusiasms left—not even dreary ones such as gathering up etchings or rare and ugly china—although he was thirty years of age and a very tiresome young man and a moderately wealthy one, he preserved within himself a respect for things—good beads or horses galloping, properly made toast or the reason why a fly plaits its forelegs together. But he preserved this within himself, for he had a horror of the tiresomely fantastic either in life or in letters.

Perhaps Jane's scar enabled him to look on her as a Thing, faintly worthy of curiosity. Otherwise it is difficult to see how he troubled to retain her friendship—for the faint possibility of future need could scarcely have influenced him so far.

But Sylvester had not much time to spare to the girls now, for he greeted all his guests with old-fashioned politeness, and not until late in the evening did he, at his own parties, indulge in selfish converse with those of his guests who bored him least.

Jessica watched Sylvester talking to the people he'd asked to his party. "She watched him covertly," she said to herself, but, in fact, she was staring at him openly with her jaw rather dropped and her mouth rather slackened, trying for the hundredth time to put a name to that nameless quality which was Sylvester's power over others.

Of all the writers she had known he only could divorce himself from his profession and be Sylvester. Lovely and charming and almost stupid. Kind and sweet and polite . . . Jessica said: "A double gin and tonic water please"—and proceeded to consider the party. She heard Jane's plaintive whine across the room: "Oh, darling—fix me a brandy and soda, I feel *horrible*." She wondered whom she was talking to, but when she saw it was only a handsome young man she felt quite easy in her mind and continued her mental analysis of those present, an analysis which she felt to be a definite importance of the moment.

Jessica was immoderately drunk by now, so drunk that she would have argued reasonably with any one about her entire sobriety. More, she would have sustained with fervour her reputation for carrying her liquor like a gentleman. She was looking splendid. Her dark eyes were full of secrets and her hands teeming with life.

"Go away, for God's sake," she was saying to a young man who had just brought her another double gin and thought he might stay and talk for a little. "I don't want to talk to *you*. I want to talk to this girl. This girl looks more like my cup of tea."

Sylvester, who knew she did not know the girl—a pretty little Hearty (he forgot why he had asked her here to-night—watched and listened with amusement. With enormous enjoyment he heard her begin to abuse his new play. She tore it competently to pieces.

"There's only one phrase in the whole thing," Jessica declared arbitrarily, "and that's the one I lent him—when the girl says: '*Bring me a bottle of beer*'—just a bottle of *beer*, utterly fed up, you see—can't you *see* it—I mean I think—I think the whole thing is in that. I may be wrong. It's just my idea. You know. But—'*Bring me a bottle of beer.*' There are people who affect one just like that aren't there? When one's with them all the time one's thinking—Christ if I had a bottle of beer instead of talking to them. It's rather how I felt about Sylvester's Piece. But of course the *lovely* thing was he couldn't see I meant that. He has quite a thing about his own Pieces—But the lovely part for *me* is I can go as often as I can bear it to that dreary Piece and hear the girl say that every time I go—So *lovely* for me."

Sylvester began to be sorry for the pretty Hearty who had got herself so entangled in Jessica's merciless conversational net. Women like Jessica he considered ought to wear some outward Sign as a warning to those who may then pass by. A wreath of white dahlias perhaps—or a garland, that had been rather a pretty fashion. Anyhow this poor girl was as bored as he was entranced. He would gladly have gone to her relief but Jessica was scarcely drunk enough to continue her abuse of his dreary Piece to his face. Or perhaps she was. No. He would not take the risk of interrupting her enthralling commentary.

But he had hardly arrived to this selfish decision before Jessica ceased to discuss him or any less interesting subject. He saw her morose silence, she could pull silence about her in sullen folds. He observed that she permitted the girl who was so pre-eminently not her cup of tea to manoeuvre and escape her, and then he saw her fixed gaze burning itself out across the room where Jane lay placid and obviously contented in the arms of a young man. It was obvious that he had fixed her a good many brandies and sodas, or at any rate brandies, for she had reached that state of polite almost lady-like coma in which Sylvester found her most tolerable. For then she hardly spoke; indeed she was very peaceful and quiet in liquor and annoyed nobody nor even demanded Love.

Why then should Jessica look upon this quiet interval with eyes of passionate gloom and why should she explain to Sylvester when he came and sat beside her the Evil and the Folly of women drinking.

"You and Jane will have to start putting things in each other's coffee," he said. For if Jessica could be tiresome and boring, then so could he.

But he saw she was in earnest. She sat twisting her great white hands (their painted nails had an obscene quality, half flower half animal) together in her lap—the disarming thing about Jessica was the way in which she could produce suddenly a domestic and pathetic attitude of mind and body, such as a terror of the urge to drink, in the middle of his party—and a lap which would not have disgraced the black silk apron of a long dead housekeeper, in a Molyneux gown.

He wondered if this was the first approach of that inevitable storm which must end this curious friendship. Surely he saw a storm coming, the sky growing black and the leaves turned to a still and icy green against its darkness. Was he to be the first to hear Jessica really break forth upon the subject of Jane? What lovely words might he now gather up and keep for his private entertainment for that lovely Piece of which he would never deliver himself—not to the pen, not to the rarest friend, not for Gold—

well, perhaps for *much* Gold. No. No. Never. These confidences, which he labelled with delight "Sacred and Girlish," were his own, alone and forever.

But Jessica was taking altogether too wide a view of the Drink Evil; he would endure her a little longer, but she must narrow her subject matter down to Jane and the evil effects of drink on Jane, not on a million Janes. "But now look," he said, "at Jane."

Suddenly looking anew as it were on Jane, not just seeing her mildly, he felt almost wounded by his pity for her, poor girl, as she lay on his divan, silver and bark geometrically woven in its fabric. In the mild square lighting of his room her crooked face was as though drowned in water and quite at peace. He looked at Jane as he had directed Jessica and back again on Jessica, on her consuming eyes. He felt supremely concerned for Jane, a concern which filled his mind almost to the exclusion of the hope that Jessica might pour forth to him the first fine torrents of her abuse of Jane.

"I can't bear to see her like that," Jessica went on, "half asleep—half drunk. It disgusts me. Why, I'd rather see her dead, I think." And with this she picked up a bottle of Tonic Water and made menacing gestures with it across the room at Jane.

Jane just had time to scream: "Now, Jessica, don't you throw that bottle at me—" when Sylvester, sitting still in a kind of entrancement from which he could not even rouse himself in time to catch Jessica's upthrown arm (and she had been a noted bowler at Heather Close in her schooldays) saw the crash of broken glass and heard Jane scream: "Oh—you're *horrible* to me," as she bowed her bleeding head upon his divan.

Sylvester's friends were very polite people and paid but little attention to this scene (although there was not one of them who did not cherish his impression of it). They continued to play cards, drink, eat and talk while Jessica and Sylvester supported Jane towards Sylvester's bedroom, and onwards then towards the bathroom, for two of his guests were having a quiet talk in his bedroom and Jane after murmuring, "Oh, you *horrible* boys," staggered on to the bathroom.

Here Jessica bathed her forehead. There was a shallow cut slanting up under her hair and bleeding profusely from the splinter of glass which had struck her. Jessica's aim was not so good as in the days when the full pitches she bowled had been the terror of Heather Close adversaries in the cricket field. She stopped bathing Jane's head to tell Sylvester about this. Sylvester, who could not bear the sight of blood curdling in water, sat swaying backwards and forwards on the edge of his square green bath. He was feeling slightly sick, partly from the sight of Jane's nasty blood and partly from his understanding of that fierce instinct to cherish that Jessica—drunken, pallid and tender— displayed now as she sponged Jane's head with his favourite sponge; dreadfully protective where five minutes ago she had been to all intents and purposes a murderess. He preferred her, he thought, in the swift committal of her *crime passionnel*.

Peroxide, lint, bandages, he had to find them all in turn; and there sat Jane in the coral light of this hot green room, a bath towel fastened about her neck like a man at his barber's, her crooked mouth a little open and her whole attitude as drained of emotion as that of any woman at the conclusion of a blood quarrel with her mate. It was unbearable. But it was none of his business. Jessica would undoubtedly kill Jane before she quarrelled with her. But that was nothing to do with him. Jane might be a lot better dead, anyhow—the dreary little Piece. But that it seemed was for Jessica to decide—Jessica who said: "Sit there, my sweet, while I find our coats and then I'll take you home."

When Jessica had gone he said swiftly, although it was none of his business: "It's nothing to do with me, Jane, I know—but she'll kill you some day."

"Yes," Jane agreed, "she's horrible to me."

"But does she often throw bottles at you?"

"Oh, Sylvester, her temperaments are certainly horrible. I'm very devoted to Jessica, I love having her around, but I'm scared to death she'll kill me."

"But, Jane, you are a fool to go on living with her. Your husband even wasn't such a devastating companion."

"Ah," said Jane, "he was kind of disheartening to live with. I got sort of low-spirited always looking at him. Now Jessica—although she's horrible to me—she's a real live woman. Why, Sylvester, last week she threw such a temperament she just smashed all the china in the bathroom and then she lay and bit the bath till she broke a tooth in it—naturally she did, for my bath is a unique alabaster bath. You've seen it, Sylvester? Well, your bath is nice, you know, but mine's a very lovely bath . . ."

The return of Jessica put a stop to any further confidences and as Sylvester watched her lapping Jane in her coat and taking her away from his party he felt unwarrantably vexed. And why should he feel vexed, for it was none of his business. Not if Jessica drew a revolver from her sac and shot Jane with appropriate words: "Smile, Baby, for the last time, Smile!" and then drove Jane's expensive corpse about in Jane's expensive car till she found a convenient spot to dump it, would it be Sylvester's business. No, he would not become involved.

MARGUERITE YOURCENAR (1903–1987)

"Sappho or Suicide" from *Fires* (1936)

The French novelist Marguerite Yourcenar—first woman writer inducted into the ranks of *les immortels* of the French Academy—was born in 1903 in Brussels. Her real name was Marguerite Cleenewerck de Crayencour; her mother died soon after her birth. A precocious only child, she was educated in Paris and England by her father, a wealthy and somewhat dissolute man of letters with whom she powerfully identified. She quickly revealed a gift for languages: besides her native French, Yourcenar learned English, Italian, Greek, and Latin, and later in life translated Henry James, Virginia Woolf, and Negro spirituals into French. She published her first literary works, a verse drama and a collection of poems, under the pen name Yourcenar—a near-anagram of Crayencour—in 1920 and 1922. Financially independent after her father's death, she devoted herself to writing and travel: her first major work, the novel *Alexis*—about a man who leaves his wife and child on account of his homosexuality—appeared in 1929. Though indebted to Gide and other literary models, the work is characteristic on two counts: it reflects Yourcenar's lifelong fascination with male homosexuality; and it is written in the austere yet perfect French—neoclassical, elegant and severe—which would become her artistic trademark.

Predominantly lesbian and libertine in her sexual tastes, Yourcenar had affairs with both men and women in the twenties and thirties. In 1937, however, she met the American translator and college professor Grace Frick, with whom she lived for the next forty-four years, mostly on Mount Desert Island off the coast of Maine. (Frick would subsequently translate a number of Yourcenar's works into English.) In 1939 Yourcernar published *Coup de Grâce*, a dark fable about revolutionaries in Eastern Europe; she became a naturalized American citizen in 1947. She spent the 1940s composing the book considered to be her masterpiece, the passionate, ruminative *Mémoires d'Hadrien* (*Memoirs of Hadrian*). Cast as a valedictory letter in which the homosexual Roman emperor Hadrian recalls his love for the beautiful Greek youth Antinous, the novel became a bestseller when it appeared in 1951 and made its author famous worldwide.

In the early 1950s Yourcenar taught briefly at Sarah Lawrence College, but soon gave up her position to return to full-time writing. In 1959 she published a much-revised version of her 1934 novel, *Denier du rêve*. The novel *L'Oeuvre au noir* appeared in 1968; two volumes of plays followed in 1971. In the 1970s and 1980s Yourcenar devoted herself to her last work, a multivolume family memoir entitled *Le Labyrinthe du monde*. The first two volumes, *Souvenirs pieux* and *Archives du Nord*, appeared in 1974 and 1977. A third volume, *Quoi? L'Eternité*, was published posthumously in 1988. After receiving the French Academy's Grand Prix de la Littérature in 1980, Yourcenar was inducted into that august body in 1981—just a few months after Frick's death from cancer. In her last years Yourcenar became deeply attached to a young homosexual man, Jerry Wilson, who died of AIDS in 1986. Yourcenar herself died in 1987 at the age of eighty-four.

With one exception, Yourcenar never broached the subject of lesbianism in her work. The exception is "Sappho ou Suicide" (Sappho or Suicide), one of several prose poems she published in 1936 under the title *Feux* (*Fires*). The "Sappho" in question is a modern-day circus artist whose sordid erotic life is a debauched parody of that of her famous namesake. Yourcenar treats her character impassively, even coldly, but in the piece's cryptic postscript ("*I will not kill myself. The dead are so quickly forgotten*") she may nonetheless encode something of her own erotic history.

FURTHER READING: Marguerite Yourcenar, *Memoirs of Hadrian*, trans. Grace Frick (New York: Farrar, Straus and Young, 1954); —, *Coup de Grâce*, trans. Grace Frick (New York: Farrar, Straus and Cudahy, 1957); , *The Abyss*, trans. Grace Frick (New York: Farrar, Straus and Giroux, 1976); —, *Fires*, trans. Grace Frick (New York: Farrar, Straus and Giroux, 1981); —, *Alexis*, trans. Grace Frick (New York: Farrar, Straus and Giroux, 1984); —, *A Blue Tale*, trans. Alberto Manguel (Chicago: University of Chicago Press, 1995); Germaine Brée, *Women Writers in France* (New Brunswick: Rutgers University Press, 1973); Frederick C. Farrell Jr. et al., "Marguerite Yourcenar's *Feux*: Structure and Meaning," *Romance Quarterly* 29 (1982): 25–35; Pierre L. Horn, *Marguerite Yourcenar* (Boston: Twayne, 1985); Georgia Hooks Schurr, *A Reader's Guide to Marguerite Yourcenar* (New York: University Press of America, 1987); Katherine Callen King, "Achilles on the Field of Sexual Politics: Marguerite Yourcenar's *Feux*," *LIT: Literature, Interpretation, Theory* 2 (1991): 201–20; Joan E. Howard, *From Violence to Vision: Sacrifice in the Works of Marguerite Yourcenar* (Carbondale: Southern Illinois University Press, 1992); Josyane Savigneau, *Marguerite Yourcenar: Inventing a Life* (Chicago: University of Chicago Press, 1993); Erin G. Carlson, *Thinking Fascism: Sapphic Modernism and Fascist Modernity* (Stanford, Cal.: Stanford University Press, 1998).

I have just seen, reflected in the mirrors of a theater box, a woman called Sappho. She is pale as snow, as death, or as the clear face of a woman who has leprosy. And since she wears rouge to hide this whiteness, she looks like the corpse of a murdered woman with a little of her own blood on her cheeks. To shun daylight, her eyes recede from the arid lids, which no longer shade them. Her long curls come out in tufts like forest leaves falling under precocious storms; each day she tears out new gray hairs, and soon there will be enough of these white silken threads to weave her shroud. She weeps for her youth as if for a woman who betrayed her, for her childhood as if for a little girl she has lost. She is skinny; when she steps into her bath, she turns away from the mirror, from the sight of her sad breasts. She wanders from city to city with three big trunks full of false pearls and bird wreckage. She is an acrobat, just as in ancient times she was a poetess, because the particular shape of her lungs forces her to choose a trade that is practiced in midair. In the circus at night, under the devouring eyes of a mindless public, and in a space encumbered with pulleys and masts, she fulfills her contract; she is a star. Outside, upstaged by the luminous letters of posters stuck to the wall, her body is part of that ghostly circle currently in vogue that soars above the gray cities. She's a magnetic creature, too winged for the ground, too corporal for the sky, whose wax-rubbed feet have broken the pact that binds us to the earth: Death waves her dizzy scarves but does not fluster her. Naked, spangled with stars, from afar she looks like an athlete who won't admit being an angel lest his perilous leaps be underrated; from close up, draped in long robes that give her back her wings, she looks like a female impersonator. She alone knows that her chest holds a heart too heavy and too big to be lodged elsewhere than in a broad bosom: this weight, hidden at the bottom of a bone cage, gives each of her springs into the void the mortal taste of danger. Half eaten by this implacable tiger, she secretly tries to be the tamer of her heart. She was born on an island and that is already a beginning of solitude; then her profession intervened, forcing on her a sort of lofty isolation every night; fated to be a star, she lies on her stage board, half undressed, exposed to the winds of the abyss, and suffers from the lack of tenderness as from the lack of pillows. Men in her life have only been steps of a ladder she had to climb, often dirtying her feet. The director, the trombone player, the publicity agent, all made her sick of waxed mustaches, cigars, liqueurs, striped ties, leather wallets—the exterior attributes of virility that make women dream. Only young women's bodies would still be soft enough, supple enough, fluid enough to let themselves be handled by this strong angel who would playfully pretend to drop them in midair. She can't hold them very long in this abstract space bordered on all sides by trapeze bars: quickly frightened by this geometry changing into wingbeats, all of them soon give up acting as her sky companion. She has to come down to earth, to their level, to share their ragged, patchy lives, so that affection ends up like a Saturday pass, a twenty-four-hour leave a sailor spends with easy women. Suffocating in these rooms no bigger than alcoves, she opens the door to the void with the hopeless gesture of a man forced, by love, to live among dolls. All women love one woman: they love themselves madly, consenting to find beauty only in the form of their own body. Sappho's eyes, farsighted in sorrow, looked further away. She expects of young women what self-adorning idolatrous coquettes expect of mirrors: a smile answering her trembling smile, until the breath from lips moving closer and closer obscures the reflection and clouds the crystal. Narcissus loves what he is.

Sappho bitterly worships in her companions what she has not been. Poor, held in contempt, which is the other side of celebrity, and having only the perspectives of the abyss in stock, she caresses happiness on the bodies of her less threatened friends. The veils of communicants carrying their souls outside themselves make her dream of a brighter childhood than hers had been; when one has run out of illusions, one can still lend others a sinless childhood. The pallor of these girls awakens in her the almost unbelievable memory of virginity. In Gyrinno, she loved pride, and lowered herself to kiss the girl's feet. Anactoria's love brought her the taste of French fries eaten by handfuls in amusement parks, of rides on the wooden horses of carousels, and brought her the sweet feel of straw, tickling the neck of the beautiful girl lying down in haystacks. In Attys, she loved misfortune. She met Attys in the center of a big city, asphyxiated by the breath of its crowds and by the fog of its river; her mouth still smelled of the ginger candy she had been chewing. Soot stains stuck to her cheeks shiny with tears: she was running on a bridge, wearing a coat of fake otter; her shoes had holes; her face like that of a young goat had a haggard sweetness. To explain why her lips were pinched and pale like the scar of an old wound, why her eyes looked like sick turquoises, Attys had three different stories that were after all only three aspects of the same misfortune: her boyfriend, whom she saw every Sunday, had left her because one evening she wouldn't let him caress her in a taxi; a girlfriend who let her sleep on the couch of her student room had turned her out, accusing her wrongly of trying to steal her fiancé's heart; and finally, her father beat her. Attys was afraid of everything: of ghosts, of men, of the number 13, of the green eyes of cats. The hotel dining room dazzled her like a temple where she felt obliged to speak only in a whisper; the bathroom made her clap her hands in amazement. Sappho spends the money she has saved for years through suppleness and temerity for this whimsical girl. She makes circus directors hire this mediocre artist who can only juggle flower bouquets. With the regularity of change that is the essence of life for nomadic artists and sad profligates, together they tour the arenas and stages of all capitals. Each morning, in the furnished rooms rented so that Attys will avoid the promiscuity of hotels full of too rich clients, they mend their costumes and the runs in their tight silk stockings. Sappho has nursed this sick child so often, has so many times warded off men who would tempt her, that her gloomy love imperceptibly takes on a maternal cast, as though fifteen years of sterile voluptuousness had produced this child. The young men in tuxedos met in the halls of theater boxes, all recall to Attys the friend whose repulsed kisses she perhaps misses: Sappho has heard her talk so often of Philip's beautiful silk shirts, of his blue cuff links, of the shelves of pornographic albums decorating his room in Chelsea, that she now has as clear a picture of this fastidiously dressed businessman as of the few lovers she couldn't avoid slipping into her life. She stows him away absentmindedly among her worst memories. Little by little, Attys' eyelids take on a lavender hue; she gets letters at a post-office box and she tears them up after reading them; she seems strangely well informed about the business trips that might make the young man run into them, by chance, on their nomadic road. It is painful to Sappho not to be able to give Attys anything more than a back room in life, and to know that only fear keeps the little fragile head leaning on her strong shoulder. Sappho, embittered by all the tears she had the courage never to shed, realizes that all she can offer her friends is a tender form of despair; her only excuse is to tell herself that love, in all its forms, has nothing better to offer shy creatures, and were Attys to leave, she would not find more happiness somewhere else. One night Sappho, arms full of flowers picked for Attys, comes home later than usual. The concierge looks at her differently than she ordinarily does as she walks by; suddenly the spirals of the staircase look like serpent rings. Sappho notices that the milk carton is not in its usual place on the doormat; as soon as she is in the entrance hall, she smells the odor of cologne and blond tobacco. She notices in the kitchen the absence of an Attys busy frying tomatoes; in the bathroom the want of a young woman naked and playing with bathwater; in the bedroom the removal of an Attys ready to let herself be rocked. Facing the mirrors of the wide-open wardrobe, she weeps over the disappearance of the beloved girl's underwear. A blue cuff link lying on the floor reveals the cause of this departure, which Sappho stubbornly refuses to accept as final, afraid that it could kill her. Once again, she is trampling alone on city arenas, avidly scanning the theater boxes for a face her folly prefers to all bodies. After a few years, during one of her tours in the East, she learns that Philip is now director of a company that sells Oriental tobaccos; he has just been married to a rich and imposing woman who couldn't be Attys. Rumor has it that the girl has joined a dance company. Once again, Sappho makes the rounds of Middle East hotels; each doorman has his own way of being insolent, impudent, or servile; she checks out the pleasure spots where the smell of sweat poisons perfumes, the bars where an hour of stupor in alcohol and human heat leaves no more trace than a wet circle left by a glass on a black wooden table. She carries her search even as far as going to the Salvation Army, in the vain hope of finding Attys impoverished and ready to let herself be loved. In Istanbul, she happens to sit, every night, next to a casually dressed young man who passes himself off as an employee of a travel agency; his slightly dirty hand lazily holds up the weight of his forehead. They exchange those banal words that are often used between strangers as a bridge to love. He says his name is Phaon, claims he is the son of a Greek woman from Smyrna and of a sailor in the British fleet: once again, Sappho's heart quickens when she hears the delightful accent so often kissed on Attys' lips. Behind him stand memories of escape, of poverty, and of dangers unrelated to wars and more secretly connected to the laws of his own heart. He, too, seems to belong to a threatened race; one that is allowed to exist through a precarious and ever provisional permissiveness. Not having a residence visa, this young man has his own difficulties; he's a smuggler dealing in morphine, perhaps an agent of the secret police; he lives in a world of secret meetings and passwords, a world Sappho cannot penetrate. He doesn't need to tell her his story to establish a fraternity of misfortune between them. She tells him her sorrows; she goes on and on about Attys. He thinks he has met her; he vaguely remembers seeing a naked girl juggling flowers in a cabaret of Pera. He owns a little sailboat that he uses on Sundays for outings on the Bosphorus; together they go looking in all sad cafés along the shore, in restaurants of the island, in the modest boarding-houses on the Asian coast that poor foreigners live in. Seated at the stern, Sappho watches this handsome male face, which is now her only human sun, waver in the light of a lantern. She finds in his features certain traits once loved in the runaway girl: the same pouting mouth that a mysterious bee seems to have stung; the same little hard forehead under different hair that this time seemed to have been dipped in honey, the same eyes looking like greenish turquoises but framed by a tanned, rather than livid, face, so that the pale brown-haired girl seems to have been simply the wax lost in cast-ing this bronze and golden god. Surprised, Sappho finds herself slowly preferring these shoulders rigid as trapeze bars, these hands hardened by the contact of oars, this entire body holding just enough feminine softness for her to love it. Lying down on the bot-tom of the boat, she yields to the new sensations of the floodwaters parted by this fer-ryman. Now she only mentions Attys to tell him that the lost girl looked like him but wasn't as handsome: Phaon accepts these compliments with a mocking but worried sat-isfaction. She tears up, in front of him, a letter in which Attys announces that she is coming back; she doesn't even bother to make out the return address. He watches her doing this with a faint smile on his trembling lips. For the first time, she neglects the dis-cipline of her demanding profession, she interrupts the exercises which put every mus-cle under the control of the spirit; they dine together; and surprisingly, she eats a little too much. She only has a few days left with him in this city; her commitments have her soaring in other skies. Finally he consents to spend the last evening with her in the lit-tle apartment she rents near the port. She watches him come and go in the cluttered room, he is like a voice mingling clear and deep notes. Unsure of his moves, as though afraid of breaking fragile illusions, Phaon leans over the portraits of Attys for a better look. Sappho sits down on the Viennese sofa covered with Turkish embroideries; she presses her face in her hands like someone trying to erase memories. This woman who until now took upon herself the choice, the offer, the seduction, the protection of her more vulnerable girlfriends, relaxes and, falling, yields limply, at last, to the weight of her own sex and of her own heart. She is happy that, from now on, all she has to do with a lover is to make the gesture of acceptance. She listens to the young man prowl in the next room; there, the whiteness of a bed is sprawled like a hope remaining, in spite of everything, miraculously open; she hears him uncork flasks on the dresser, rummage in drawers with the ease of a housebreaker or a boyfriend who feels he is allowed every-thing. He opens the folding doors of the wardrobe, where, among a few ruffles left by Attys, Sappho's dresses hang like women who have killed themselves. Suddenly the ghostly shudder of a silken sound draws near like a dangerous caress. She rises, turns around; the beloved creature has wrapped himself in a robe Attys left behind; the thin silk gauze worn on naked flesh accentuates the quasi-feminine gracefulness of the dancer's long legs; relieved of its confining men's clothing, this flexible body is almost a woman's body. This Phaon, comfortable in his impersonation, is nothing more than a stand-in for the beautiful absent nymph; once again, it's a girl coming toward her with a crystal laugh. Distraught, Sappho runs to the door to escape from this fleshly ghost who will only give her the same sad kisses. Outside, she charges into the swell of bodies and runs down the streets leading to the sea; they are littered with debris and garbage. She realizes that no encounter holds her salvation, since, no matter where she goes, she runs into Attys again. This overwhelming face blocks all openings but those leading to death. Night falls like a weariness confusing her memory; a little blood endures next to the sunset. Suddenly she hears cymbals clashing as though fever hit them in her heart; a long-standing habit has brought her back, unawares, to the circus at the very hour when she struggles with the angel of dizziness each night. For the last time, she is intoxicated by this wildbeast odor that has been the odor of her life, by this music like that of love, loud and discordant. A wardrobe woman lets her into the dressing room, which she enters now as if condemned to death; she strips as if for God; she rubs white makeup all over herself to become a ghost; she snaps the choker of memory around her neck. An usher, dressed in black, arrives to tell her that her hour has come; she climbs the rope ladder of her celestial scaffold; she is fleeing skywards from the mockery of believing that there had been a young man. She removes herself from the yells of orange vendors, from the cutting laughter of pink children, from the skirts of dancers, from the mesh of human nets. With one pull, she brings herself to the last support her will to die will allow; the trapeze bar swinging in midair transforms this creature, tired of being only half woman, into a bird; she glides, sea gull of her own abyss, hanging by one foot, under the gaze of a public which does not believe in tragedy. Her skill goes against her; no matter how she tries, she can't lose her balance; shady equestrian, Death has her vault the next trapeze. She climbs at last higher than the spotlights; spectators can no longer applaud her, since now they can't see her. Hanging on to the ropes that pull the canopy painted with stars, she can only continue to surpass herself by bursting through her sky. Under her, the ropes, the pulleys, the winches of her fate now mastered, squeak in the wind of dizziness; space leans and pitches as on a stormy sea; the star-filled firmament rocks between mast yards. From here, music is only a smooth swell washing over all memory. Her eyes no longer distinguish between red and green lights: blue spotlights, sweeping over the dark crowd, bring out, here and there, naked feminine shoulders that look like tender rocks. Hanging on to her death as to an overhanging ledge, Sappho looks for a place to fall and chooses a spot beyond the netting where the mesh will not hold her. Her own acrobatic performance occupies only half of the immense vague arena; in the other half, where seals and clowns carry on, nothing has been set up to prevent her from dying. Sappho dives, arms spread as if to grasp half of infinity; she leaves behind her only the swinging of a rope as proof of having left the sky. But those failing at life run the risk of missing their suicide. Her oblique fall is broken by a lamp shining like a blue jellyfish. Stunned but safe, she is thrown by the impact toward the netting that pulls and repulses the foamy light; the meshes give but do not yield under the weight of this statue fished out from the bottom of the sky. And soon roustabouts will only have to haul onto the sand this marble pale body streaming with sweat like a drowning woman pulled from the sea.

I will not kill myself. The dead are so quickly forgotten.

One can only raise happiness on a foundation of despair. I think I will be able to start building.

Let no one be accused of my life.

It's not a question of suicide. It's only a question of beating a record.

MARCIA DAVENPORT (1903–1996)

From *Of Lena Geyer* (1936)

Born in New York, the American novelist and journalist Marcia Davenport was the daughter of the celebrated operatic soprano Alma Gluck (1884–1938) and step-daughter of the violinist Efrem Zimbalist. Though uninterested in pursuing a musical career herself, she retained a lifelong love of the art and later counted many important musicians—notably the conductor Arturo Toscanini—among her friends. After dropping out of Wellesley College and an unhappy first marriage, she began writing for the *New Yorker* in the mid-1920s. In 1929 she married the poet and journalist Russell Davenport, and in 1932 published her first major work, a bestselling biography of Mozart. She then turned to fiction, eventually publishing five novels, of which *The Valley of Decision* (1942) is perhaps the best known today. Always active in politics, she worked during the Second World War for the Writer's War Board and other wartime service agencies. At the end of the war, having divorced her husband in 1943, Davenport lived in Prague for several years, where she became close to the anti-Communist Czech leader Jan Masaryk. Masaryk's death under mysterious circumstances in 1948 left her bereft, and after a spell in Italy, she moved back to New York. In the 1960s she published her autobiography, *Too Strong for Fantasy* (1967). She died in 1996.

Reflecting its author's musical background, Davenport's first novel, *Of Lena Geyer* (1936), purports to be the life story of a charismatic turn-of-the-century American opera singer named Lena Geyer. Modeled in part on Davenport's mother, Alma Gluck, and in part on the Swedish-American opera singer Olive Fremstad, Geyer is a formidable figure who casts a powerful erotic spell over men and women alike. Midway through the novel she attracts a wealthy young devotée, Elsie deHaven, who follows her from performance to performance, always sitting in the sixth row. After a London performance of *The Marriage of Figaro* Geyer invites the besotted deHaven to a little "Mozart supper"—described below—and proceeds to captivate her entirely. Following this tête-à-tête Geyer gives up her male lover, the jealous Duc de Chartres, in order to live with deHaven, who thenceforth acts as her secretary-companion.

The quasilesbian relationship depicted between Geyer and deHaven is modeled in part on the lifelong intimacy between Olive Fremstad and Mary Watkins Cushing, an American art student who became infatuated with Fremstad after seeing her debut at the Met and lived with her for many years. Cushing later wrote about her relationship with Fremstad in her 1954 memoir, *The Rainbow Bridge*. Fremstad was also the model for Thea Kronborg, the diva-heroine of Willa Cather's *The Song of the Lark* (1915).

FURTHER READING: Marcia Davenport, *Of Lena Geyer* (New York: Grosset and Dunlap, 1936); —, *Too Strong for Fantasy* (New York: Scribner's, 1967); Mary Watkins Cushing, *The Rainbow Bridge* (New York: Putnam's, 1954); Terry Castle, "In Praise of Brigitte Fassbaender: Reflections on Diva Worship," in Corinne E. Blackmer and Patricia Juliana Smith, eds., *En Travesti: Women, Gender, Subversion, Opera* (New York: Columbia University Press, 1995), pp. 20–58; Susan J. Leonardi and Rebecca A. Pope, *The Diva's Mouth: Body, Voice, Prima Donna Politics* (New Brunswick: Rutgers University Press, 1996).

Elsie deHaven was buying ribbon at Harrods in London one afternoon in early June. She had been making small purchases—bootlaces, veils, hairpins—and now bought some baby ribbon such as ladies used to wear in their under-clothes. She selected several pieces and gave the clerk her name and address, having to spell out the name to the girl. As she did so, she realized that a tall woman who had been standing beside her at the counter was for some reason not moving on. Miss deHaven finished spelling her name and turned, and the tall woman looked straight at her. She was Lena Geyer.

"My knees went weak," Miss deHaven wrote me, "and my eyes filled with tears. I could not speak. She pronounced my name in a deep, liquid voice while I grasped the counter for support. 'Elsie deHaven,' she said. 'Are you the E. deH. who sends me yellow roses?' I was too stupefied to do anything but nod. 'The slender young woman in the black gown that follows me all over Europe? And sits in a sixth-row stall?' She looked hard at me and I was surprised to see that her eyes were green.

"I found a fragment of voice presently and said, 'How did you know?'

"She laughed. I wish I could tell you the quality of that laugh. It was like a glorious red Burgundy flowing into a goblet, rich and lustrous and warm. 'How did I know!' she exclaimed. 'Did you think nobody knew? My dear child, one does not have such an eccentricity without its being noticed. My manager knows it. Monsieur De Reszke knows it. My—my friends know it.'

"I was sick with mortification. I remember hanging my head like a child caught in mischief. I wanted to crawl into a hole and cry. But Lena Geyer put her arm through mine. 'Come along and have tea with me,' she said. 'We can have sandwiches and cake. I'm not singing tonight.' She chuckled and led me through the shop to the door where her carriage was waiting. My own carriage was there but I forgot it. We went to the Savoy where she was staying. All the way there I do not remember saying a word, and if she spoke I cannot remember what she said. Yet I have no recollection of awkward silence.

I felt absolutely at peace, absolutely happy for the first time in my life. This was not like the happiness at the opera. This was something nobody could know but I, alone.

"As we entered her apartment she pulled out her hatpins and lifted off her hat. I found that I was intensely curious to see her hair. I was so accustomed to her wigs that I could hardly realize she had any hair. It was brown, rather darker than mine, and simply dressed in a low pompadour with a chignon at the back. Her figure as she took off her jacket was superb. She stood very straight, with her wide shoulders held back like a soldier, and walked with a free stride that no ordinary woman could have copied. She moved about the room with peculiar litheness, and my first physical impression of her was of tremendous vitality, trained and utilized to a point of driving force. She rang for tea and then came across to me holding out her hands. She asked me for my coat. I was so bewildered with joy that I let her take it as if I had been a child. Then she asked me to come and sit down with her by the window 'and talk,' she said. 'We must get acquainted.'

"I don't know what I meant to say but I blurted out my surprise that she spoke English, and without an accent.

"She threw back her head and laughed. 'Why that's not so odd,' she said. 'You are an American, are you not?'

"I nodded. 'So am I,' she said with a shrug.

"'What?' I sat up as if I had been pinched. 'You an American? I thought you were an Austrian, a German, or something.'

"'I am,' she said, 'but I lived in New York for years. I've never had a home, but New York came nearest to it.'

"I could hardly take this in. 'You mean you have been in New York?' I repeated. She assured me she had, that she had lived there and received most of her training there. I told her I thought she was Lilli Lehmann's pupil. 'I am,' she said, 'but I studied in New York a long time before that.'

"I was too surprised to speak. I watched her hands as she poured the tea, and was suddenly conscious that it was not the sort of thing she enjoyed doing. Her hands were large, unusually so, with square backs and long, rather thick fingers. The tips of them were blunt, heavily cushioned, and her nails were deep and filed quite short. The skin of her hands looked loose, as if they had never completely grown into it, though they were much too large for conventional standards. She wore no rings, and I never knew her to wear one, except her wedding ring after she was married. When some royalty or patron presented her with a ring, which happened rather often, she would have the stones reset into earrings or some ornament for her high collars. She wore high collars long after they went out of fashion.

"That afternoon we talked a good deal, though I can hardly tell you what we said, for we were groping toward an understanding that soon made small talk superfluous. She was very curious about me, and without my realizing it drew most of my story out of me. She seemed to find it completely incredible that anyone should make a whole life out of following her around to hear her sing. She insisted she could not see what I got out of it. I tried to tell her it meant as much to me as parents, a husband, children, or anything most women attach themselves to. She only shook her head and stared. She asked me if I meant to keep it up. I told her so long as she would let me. She smiled and squeezed my hand. 'Better say so long as I please you,' she said.

"Just then her maid came in, a large frowning woman she called Dora, whose story I will tell you later. Dora said in a low voice, 'Monsieur is here.' Madame Geyer grimaced as she bit into a sandwich. 'Tell him I'm resting,' she said shortly. 'I'll dine with him at nine.' She ate with frank relish that I had never seen a woman show. She never nibbled anything, and she was not dainty in her appetite. You could not say she gobbled or did anything ungraceful, but she reminded me of a man when she ate. She grinned at me as she started on her third cake. '*Jour maigre tomorrow*,' she said. 'I'm singing.'

" 'I know,' I said.

"She grinned again. That expression was so free, so *gamine*, it was the last thing one could possibly expect of an opera singer. Everything of that sort about her enchanted and thrilled me. I knew she had a powerful personality, one could not hear her and not know that, but to discover this jolly, almost foolish human simplicity was tremendously exciting and surprising. Since I had never in my wildest dreams thought of meeting her I could not have anticipated her; but if I had, I suppose I would have thought of her as rather distant, rather queenly. She was queenly enough in bearing, and in her manner in public, but alone at home she was a big overgrown girl.

"Presently I realized that I had stayed much too long. As I was drawing on my gloves she smiled at me and said, 'Look here, wouldn't you like to come back after the opera tomorrow night and see me?'

"I nodded, too pleased to speak. She strode over to her writing table and scribbled a note on a pad. She told me to give it to the guard at the stage door, and she would be expecting me. I held out my hand to say good-bye, but she did not take it. She put both her hands on my shoulders and stood a moment looking into my eyes. Then she bent down and kissed me on both cheeks. 'Thank you,' she said suddenly. I never knew what she meant by that. But I was too overwhelmed by my experience to wonder about it.

"The following night she was to sing a part I particularly loved, the Contessa in *Nozze di Figaro*. It was one of the parts that best displayed her wonderful musicianship, superficially simple in comparison with the great, complicated Wagnerian ones, but really much more exacting. She had tremendous respect for it, and I have known her at the height of her fame to practise the phrases of *Dove Sono* with all the earnest humility of a student. In character she was the ideal of the rôle, noble and restrained and deeply emotional. When she made her entrance, my heart leaped with a new sort of recognition. I felt in a way as if something of her belonged to me, and though she was too polished on the stage to do it, I had a feeling she might glance toward the place where she knew I sat. I had sent her that evening not only yellow roses, but a hamper of flowers, losing all sense of proportion in my new excitement about her.

"After the opera I went to her dressing room. When you realize how glamorous a prima donna's dressing room is even to a sophisticated person, you may imagine how I felt. I was goggle-eyed with wonder. I knocked timidly and the door was opened a crack. Dora eyed me through it, then opened the door just wide enough for me to come in. She shut and locked it behind me. Along one wall there was a large dressing table with a huge mirror, entirely surrounded by lights. Madame Geyer sat before it on a stool. I had never seen anyone closely in make-up. (In those days we did not use rouge and lipstick as they do now.) Her face startled me. I could recognize it, and that was about all. Yesterday she had looked natural, and on the stage she had, but at this close range she was so distorted that for a moment I could hardly understand the change. She laughed, and held out one hand. 'Don't come too close till I take off this muck,' she said in a whisper, 'or you'll spoil that beautiful black dress.' She gave me a deliberate wink. I was vainly trying to tell her how beautifully she had sung, but no words seemed to come out.

"Dora was busy unhooking the tight bodice of the eighteenth-century gown. Madame Geyer stood up and shook herself. The whole thing slipped off around her feet, leaving her in a high-busted corset and a pair of lacy cambric drawers. I must have shown the question in my mind—how could she sing in such stays? She answered me by remarking that she was about ready to throw them all into the fire and start a vogue for natural lines on the stage. The sequel to that is that she did. Dora unlaced her, and removed the harness. As she did so, Madame Geyer groaned and stretched delightedly, then slipped a dressing gown over her shoulders and sat down again while Dora took off her white wig. Without the wig, and still with the make-up, she looked too grotesque for words. Her eyes were lined and beaded with black and blue, her eyebrows caricatured in heavy arcs, more awful because of a tight white bandage around her hairline. She dipped her two hands into a big pot of white grease and slapped it all over her face and throat. 'Sit down,' she croaked at me. I was a little puzzled by the voice, but realized that it must be something singers did to rest their throats after singing. As she started to wipe off the thick, dirty mess, her own face emerged, white and fine-textured as I had seen it yesterday. Immediately I felt much better. Then she took the bandage off her forehead, and Dora brushed her hair vigorously.

"Just as she was twisting it up, there was a knock at the door and Dora admitted a tall man in an Inverness cloak, with an opera hat under his arm. He had a short, pointed black beard and a haughty manner. As I recognized him—the Duc de Chartres, whom I had met in Madame de Rancelles' drawing room—he caught sight of me sitting on the divan, and an expression of terrible anger flashed across his face. It was gone at once, and as he bent over to kiss Madame Geyer's hand he fixed me with a cold, narrowed, meaning glance of his eyes. I knew he meant me to gather that we were complete strangers, though I could not understand his motive. I knew of no reason why we should not have met.

"Madame Geyer introduced us and he bowed most coldly. I turned away and he spoke to her in French, telling her that the carriage was ready. At that she almost completely upset my poise by telling him that he must forgive her, she had invited me to go home to supper with her. She had of course done nothing of the sort and I was overcome by surprise. But since she had so thrown the situation into my hands, I could not make my excuses and leave, though that was what he would have had me do. I was learning fast, I realized, when that was my first encounter with anything related to intrigue or the deeper currents of human motives. It was the duke who said good night. As he bent over her hand he asked her something I did not hear. She shook her head and brusquely, I thought, said '*Non, impossible. Bon soir.*' Even an innocent like myself could see that he was receiving a sharp dismissal.

"Madame Geyer washed her face vigorously with soap and water, brushed it over with powder, which she rubbed off with a piece of chamois, and quickly put on the clothes Dora handed her. She wore two or three layers of soft under-clothing, without corsets, and a long, loose dress of dark red wool. She put her feet, still in bedroom slippers, into a pair of velvet carriage boots, and put on a heavy black cloak lined in quilted silk that covered her completely, with a hood over her head. 'Come on,' she said to me. I had not really thought she meant I was to go home with her but when I saw that she did, I went along without hesitation. In the corridor she stopped suddenly with a look of consternation. She had no carriage, she had sent the duke away.

"I told her my carriage would be waiting, which I had completely forgotten, with poor Mademoiselle, my chaperone, inside. We sent the guard to the front door to have it sent round to the stage entrance. When Mademoiselle saw me emerging from the stage door with Lena Geyer (she knew it could be nobody else) she forgot her fright at my disappearance and gaped like an idiot. I presented her to Madame Geyer, who promptly made herself charming to the old spinster. We got out at the Savoy and sent Mademoiselle home. I told her to go to bed and tell the coachman to come back and wait for me at the Savoy. I saw she was shocked at such a departure but I did not care.

"There was a good fire burning in Madame Geyer's sitting room and a supper table set for two drawn up before it. She looked at it and laughed as she threw off her cloak. 'Poor Louis,' she said. 'I am ashamed of myself. You are going to eat his supper.'

"Much to my own surprise I found myself telling her I thought she should indeed be ashamed. I told her she had been cruel, and even rude. Then the enormity of my impudence came over me and I burst into tears. Madame Geyer strode across to me and put her arms around me. She was a head taller than I and I shrank against her. She was strong and warm. She stood there holding me for several minutes while I sobbed like a child. I was so unnerved by the emotions of the past twenty-four hours that I could not regain control of myself. For the first time in my life I was freely and utterly giving way to deep feeling. Lena Geyer pressed my head against her shoulder and murmured to me in German, tender broken phrases that one would use to a child. I felt as if I should die for love of her. I could not get my breath. Presently she drew away and put her hand under my chin and shook her head and whispered, 'You funny little girl.' Of course I know now what was puzzling her, but at that time such was my innocence that I had no idea of the ambiguity of my situation and my emotions. Although the world has since said many cruel things about this strange, almost passionate friendship between Madame Geyer and myself, I need hardly assure you that not one word of the essential accusation is true. Call me a freak if you like—the fact remains that my feeling for Lena Geyer was childlike in its simplicity, and yet more powerful than any other emotion in my life.

"As she held me to her I tried to say something, but could only gasp. She nodded slowly. She said, 'I know. There is no explaining these things. You aren't a child any more. How old are you?'

"'Twenty-two.'

"'Ten years younger than I. Have you any friends?'

"I told her no, no friends anywhere.

"She said she had none either. She had everything else—sponsors, patrons, admirers, her two beloved teachers, a lover—but no friend. She smiled at me with tears in her eyes. 'Perhaps we need each other,' she said. And then, in the next breath, 'But I'm a devil, I warn you! Sometimes you'll hate me!'

"I said I could never hate her. I said—to this day I wonder how I summoned the courage—that I loved her. She put her arms around me again and kissed me. Then she took her handkerchief and dried my eyes with it and flicked the end of my nose. 'Stop crying,' she said. 'It makes your nose red.'

"Our supper came and she sniffed the dishes with delight. She said she really felt very guilty. Louis had ordered her favorite Mozart dishes and she had sent him away. I asked her what she meant by Mozart dishes and she told me that she always preferred certain foods after certain music—special ones for Mozart, Bellini, Verdi, Wagner, and the rest. This sounded too ridiculous to me. Not at all, she said, eating was as much a part of life as singing and she loved to eat. Different music put her in the mood for certain foods just as it made one gay or sad. I had never heard anything so curious. The Mozart supper consisted of a rich consommé with egg balls, fried chicken—*Wiener Backhänderl*, she called it—a delicious mixture of rice and green peas highly seasoned with herbs, asparagus, and a *Himmeltorte*. She said this was a special occasion and she sent for the sommelier and ordered a Johannisberger Vogelsang. I protested that I hardly ever drank wine and that it made me dizzy. Then I would have to learn, she said, if I spent much time with her, because wine was the finest thing in the world and food was meaningless without it.

"I had never had such an evening. Actually I think that was the first meal I had ever eaten; all the others were just food I had consumed in the routine of existence. Her appetite would have made anyone feel good. She picked up her chicken and her asparagus in her fingers and even licked them once or twice, but though this looks terrible written down on paper, she did it with such charm and such childlike relish that it never suggested bad manners to me. My mother would probably have swooned at such a sight. She talked steadily, making an effort to whisper, but often forgetting and bursting into a loud laugh. There was an awkward moment when I asked her something and called her Madame Geyer. She looked at me with a puzzled frown and asked what I meant—I was supposed to call her Lena. She had a way of enveloping me with her enthusiasm and warmth; it was like walking into a warm, beautiful room after being out in a cold rain for a long time.

"When I remembered suddenly that I had a carriage waiting I looked at my watch and it was nearly two o'clock. I had never been up so late in my life. I jumped up, frightened. She looked up at me lazily. 'What difference does it make?' she asked. 'Who is going to punish Cinderella for staying out late?'

"'Why—nobody!' I said with surprise.

"'Exactly,' she nodded. 'You must not be such a timid little mouse. Do as you please. Be careless.' "

H. E. BATES (1905–1974)

"Breeze Anstey" from *Something Short and Sweet* (1937)

Herbert Ernest Bates, one of the most prolific English writers of his generation, was the son of a shoemaker. Born in the Midlands and educated locally, he won a scholarship to Cambridge but was forced to give it up owing to the financial burden that going to university would have imposed on his family. For a while he worked as a warehouseman and began writing poetry and fiction; his first novel, *The Two Sisters*, was accepted by Jonathan Cape in 1925. Thereafter Bates devoted himself exclusively to writing and was subsequently hired as a columnist for the *Spectator*. Over the next fifty years he produced an astonishing number of works: twenty-three novels, nineteen collections of short stories, twenty novellas, a history of the short story, numerous critical essays and books on natural history, as well as a three-volume autobiography.

Though his work is sometimes uneven—several of his novels are little more than potboilers—Bates must be classed among the great short-story writers of the century, equal at his best to D. H. Lawrence and Katherine Mansfield. His characters are often country people; unrealized or botched love affairs a favorite theme. Some of his best writings are to be found in his collections from the 1930s—*The Black Boxer* (1932), *The Woman Who Had Imagination* (1934), *Cut and Come Again* (1935), and *Something Short and Sweet* (1937), from which the story below, "Breeze Anstey," is taken. Although heavily influenced by Lawrence—in particular the 1921 novella, *The Fox*—Bates's dramatization of the title character's emotional self-discovery is unusually sympathetic for its time. As in countless lesbian-themed works of the first half of the century, a bathing scene—here, an evening swim in a secret forest pond—stands as the suggestive emblem of female-female eros.

FURTHER READING: H. E. Bates, *The Black Boxer: Tales* (London: Jonathan Cape, 1932); —, *The Woman Who Had Imagination and Other Stories* (London: Jonathan Cape, 1934); —, *Cut and Come Again: Fourteen Tales* (London: Jonathan Cape, 1935); —, *Something Short and Sweet* (London: Jonathan Cape, 1937); —, *Selected Stories* (London and Baltimore: Penguin Books, 1957); —, *The Watercress Girl and Other Stories* (London: Michael Joseph, 1959); —, *The Vanished World: An Autobiography* (London:

Michael Joseph, 1969); —, *The Blossoming World: An Autobiography* (London: Michael Joseph, 1971); —, *The World in Ripeness: An Autobiography* (London: Michael Joseph, 1972); Henry Miller, Preface to *The Best of H. E. Bates* (Boston: Little, Brown, 1963); Thomas Owen Beachcroft, *The Modest Art: A Survey of the Short Story in English* (London: Oxford University Press, 1968); Dennis Vanatta, *H. E. Bates* (Boston: Twayne, 1983); Dean R. Baldwin, *H. E. Bates: A Literary Life* (Selinsgrove, Pa.: Susquehanna University Press, 1987).

I

The two girls, Miss Anstey and Miss Harvey, had been well educated; but it was another matter getting a job. They first came together one summer, quite casually, and in the August of the same year, having no prospects, began farming together. In this they felt shrewd; their farm was to be so different. Not a common farm, with pigs or corn, sheep or poultry, but a farm for herbs. "Where you will find," they said, "a thousand people farming the ordinary things, you won't find one farming herbs." There was something in this. But in their hearts they liked it because they felt it to be different, a little poetical, charged with some unspecified but respectable romance. They had ideals. And that autumn, when they rented a small cottage in Hampshire, with an acre of land, on the edge of the forest, they felt existence for the first time very keenly; they felt independent; they had only to stretch out and pick up handfuls of sweetness and solitude.

The forest opened into a clearing where their house stood, and oak and rhododendron and holly pressed in and down on them and their land, securing their world. The plot was already cultivated, and they intended to grow the herbs, at first, in small lots, taking variety to be salvation. For the first year they would work hard, cultivating; after that they would advertise; after that sell. They divided responsibility. Miss Harvey, the practical one, took charge of the secretarial work and kept accounts and made plans. Miss Anstey had imagination and knew a little botany; she could talk of carpel and follicle, of glandulosa and hirsutum. In late August, in a world still warm and dark and secure in leaf, the first bundles of herbs began to arrive; and pressing out the small rare sweetnesses and joyfully smelling each other's hands, they felt sure of everything. Above all, they felt very sure of each other.

From the first they were devoted. Miss Anstey was the younger, twenty-three. Miss Harvey was twenty-eight. They called each other Breeze and Lorn. No one seemed clear about the origins and reasons of Miss Anstey's name, which did not express her small, slimmish, very compact and not at all volatile figure. Her hair was almost white; her nostrils were rather arched; she looked Scandinavian. She had a beautiful way of smiling at nothing, absently. She had another way of smiling at Miss Harvey, chiefly when she was not looking. It was a kind of mouse smile, furtive and timid, not fully expressed. It had in it the beginnings of adoration.

Miss Harvey was heavily built, with thick eye-brows and black short hair. She was very strong and wore no stockings and her legs went red, almost ham-coloured, in the sun. She was attractive in a full-blooded, jolly way. She was like some heavy, friendly mare, with her black mane falling over her face, and her thick strong thighs, and her arched way of walking with her shoulders back. Nothing was too much trouble for her, nothing daunted or depressed her.

The two girls at first worked hard, scorning outside help, happy together. They began with three hundred pounds. Breeze said: "We should be very strict and apportion everything out and pay weekly." They did this. Rent would cost them fifty a year, so they opened a new account at the bank, paid in a year's rent and signed a banker's order. That settled, they hoped to live on a hundred a year, the two of them. That left a hundred and fifty for seeds and plants, expenses and saving. "We should save seventy-five." Lorn said. All this was theory. In practice it did not turn out so well.

It was a long time, almost a whole winter and a spring, before they noticed it. In autumn they were pre-occupied. The autumn went on, that year, a long time, drawn up into some too-dreamy twilight of mild airs and leaves that hung on and kept out the low sunlight like blankets of dark leaf-wool. August and September were hot. Planted too soon, their first plants died. In a panic they ordered more, then kept the water bucket going. Their well got low. That was a real problem. They could not bathe. Lorn made little portable tents of lath and newspaper to shade the plants, and by September they had learnt to wash hair, face and feet in one kettle of water. Up to that time they had not worn stockings, and often not shoes. They had to give that up. They wore shoes and washed their feet twice a week. That was real hardship.

But they were not troubled about it. They liked it. It was part of the new life, more still of the new independence. It was fun. It was hardship only by comparison. Instinctively they felt that cleanliness and godliness were one, perhaps, after all. They longed for water, not seeing until then how much life might depend on it.

Then Breeze made a discovery. They felt it to be miraculous. Wandering off the forest path to look for sweet chestnuts, she came upon a pond, not a hundred yards from the house. Shaded by trees, it was quite deep. Round it marsh and sedge were dry, the earth cracked in thick crust blisters, and she could see where wild ponies had broken it up, coming down to drink. She fetched Lorn, who said: "We could fetch twenty buckets in an hour and then bathe." Breeze got some water in her hands. "Why carry it?" she said. The water was brownish, leaf-stained, but clear. "Why take the mountain to Mahomed? We could come down here and bathe."

"Not in daylight."

"Why shouldn't we? We would have costumes on. Who's to say anything?"

"Nobody. But this is the forest. You know people are always wandering about."

"All right. Then we could come when the sun's gone down. It's warm enough."

It was too good to miss. After sunset they took soap and towels and costumes and went into what was already half darkness under the trees. The pond was black, unreflective, and there was some sense, under the pitch dark roof of forest branches, of peculiar secrecy. As she took off her clothes. Breeze said: "I'm going in without anything on." She stood undressing, feet in the water. "It's warm." she said. "It's wonderfully warm. Don't put anything on. It's warm and like silk. It would be wicked to put anything on."

She went in naked, swam round and looked back to Miss Harvey. She was putting her costume on.

"Oh! Don't!"

"What do you think I am?" Lorn said. "Venus?"

"Yes, but it's the feeling. It's wonderful. And it's quite warm."

"Is it swimmable?"

"It's about four feet. Look."

She swam off, turning, breasting back. When she stood up again she saw Lorn knee-deep in water. She had nothing on. Looking at her the girl was struck by an odd spasm of pleasure. It ran up her legs like a hot current of blood and pounded up, finally, in her chest. She felt, for about a second, strange and weak. There was aroused in her an unconscious exquisite capacity for pain and she did not know what to do with it. It was like a shock.

"I thought you said it was warm?"

"Go under."

It was all she could say. She did not know why, but the sight of Lorn filled her with a queer excitement. Lorn was bigger than she had imagined, more mature, more ripe. She felt absurdly young beside her. She looked at her large brown-nippled breasts and saw in them the potential beauty of motherhood. The thick smooth flesh of the whole body had some beautiful power to attract and comfort. Lorn went under, up to her neck. She came up heavily, dripping, to stand in water up to her knees. The girl looked at her again, in a spell of adoration.

"It's muddy!" Lorn said.

"No. Not here. Come over here. It's lovely. Like sand. Why don't you swim?"

"I'll walk. I'm not certain of it."

She took heavy water-bound strides across the pond, arms folded under breasts.

"Shall we wash each other?" Breeze said.

"Puzzle, find the soap."

"I brought it."

"Good. Wash me. Wash my sins away. Wash my back."

The younger girl stood with her habitual absent smile of adoration, rubbing the soap in her hands. "Swim round while I get some lather."

Lorn swam, heavy and white, in a ponderous circle, then came back to Breeze. The water was up to their middles. The young girl's hands were white with the lather. Lorn bent her back. She put her hands on her knees and the girl began to soap her back, absently tender.

"Oh! that's lovely. Lovely. Wash up as far as possible and down as far as possible. Why is it so nice to have your back rubbed?"

"I don't know, why is it? Have the soap and rub your front."

Lorn made lather and rubbed it over her chest, until her breasts were snow bubbles with the brown mouth of nipple alone uncovered. Then she turned, and Breeze stared at her.

"What are you looking at?"

"You're so big. I didn't think you were so big, Lorn."

"Well. I like that! Big. You mean fat."

"No. Lorn, I like it. You look like a woman. Not half of one. Look at me. You could hold what there is of me in one hand."

She looked down at her small, almost stiff breasts, her slight figure.

"I ought to wear more support," Lorn said. "I shall be all over the place. Look at you. You're the ideal of every female in Christendom. All you need wear is half a yard of silk. Turn round and let me scrub you, child."

Breeze turned, bent her back and Lorn rubbed her with large soap-soft hands. The sensation of the soft drawn-down palms was something exquisite, physically thrilling to the girl.

"Harder. I want to get really clean. Harder. Wash me all over. Everywhere."

"Anything else. Madam?"

"Your hands are bigger than mine. Soap me all over."

"Extra charge." They both laughed. "Front portion extra. Owing to my sensibility, Madam."

"Oh! Lorn, you're a dear. It's a grand feeling to be washed again."

She stood with arms over her head, hands clasped on her hair, and turned round, and Lorn soaped her chest and shoulders. Her hands took wide strong sweeps across and down the girl's body. The soap covered the small almost absurd bust in snow froth.

"Oh! it's grand, Lorn. Lovely!"

"We must get out."

"Oh! must we? Need we?"

"I can hardly see you. It must be awfully late."

"It's nice in the twilight. It's warm. That's all that matters. One swim."

She swam round the darkening pond. Above, when she turned and floated, she could see the autumn evening sky colourless beyond the forest branches. The trees seemed very near, the sky correspondingly far off. She felt extraordinarily happy, her mind quiet, the exquisite sensation of shock gone. She floated serenely on the memory of emotions. She could smell the forest, dampish, closed-in, the sweetish odour of living and falling leaves, and she felt almost like crying.

Then she stood in shallow water and, looking up, saw that Lorn was out. She saw the white flap of the towel. Something made her hurry out too, some sudden and not quite conscious impulse to be near her.

She ran out, splashing. She stood quivering on the cracked mud among the sedge, and got her towel. She looked at Lorn and in a moment the sensation of physical shock, like some electric start of nerves, struck her again. She rubbed her body hard, trembling.

"I feel wonderful." Lorn said.

Lorn put her skirt over her head. It was pink, almost colourless in the tree twilight. Breeze did not speak. She felt nearer to Lorn, at that moment, than she had ever done to anyone in her life. It was an attachment not only of emotion, but of body. She felt drawn to Lorn physically, in a beautiful way, by some idealized force of attraction. It elated her and, for a second or two, stupefied her with its strength and gentleness.

It was only when Lorn said at last. "Come on, Breezy, cover your shame, child, do, and get a stitch or two on," that she came back to her normal self. Even then she did not speak. She wanted to speak and she stood trying to speak, to frame some words to express at least a hint of her affection, but nothing came.

In five minutes she was dressed. The forest was then almost dark, and looking up at the fragments of sky above the heavy mass of trees she felt some kind of balm in them. She felt completely herself. At rest again.

2

"Lorn," Breeze said, "you must have been in love, sometime?"

It was early January, and now they had nothing to do, on the long winter nights, except read and talk and evolve unrealized theories about the future, the farm, the world, themselves and men. They argued hard, quarrelled a little; but the central core of affection between them was never soured or shaken. It was dark south-west weather, wild warm days of rain followed by black nights, when they could do very little outside. They settled down after tea and read books, had supper at eight and generally talked till ten. "The less we go out, the less we spend," they said.

"Yes," Lorn said.

"But when was it? You never told me. You never said anything."

"I should have told you if I'd ever told anybody."

"Did it go on long?"

"Two years. If you can call that long."

"Did you—did it ever come to anything?"

"Yes."

Breeze had wanted to know this. She felt somehow that it concerned her, was important. She had felt, sometimes, that it might distress her. Now she felt almost indifferent, only curious. As something in the past, it hardly touched her.

"Only once?"

"No. A lot. Almost every time we saw each other. Almost whenever we could."

"It must be a long time ago, or you couldn't talk about it."

"Three or four years. Four years."

"Who wanted it most? Did he, or you?"

"Both of us. We both did. We couldn't go on without it. It wouldn't have meant anything."

Breeze did not speak. She wanted to ask something else. Lorn said:

"Why this sudden discussion of my affairs, young lady?"

"We swore we'd have no secrets."

"Well, I've told you now."

"Lorn," Breeze said, "what's it like? The loving part. The proper loving."

"Sometimes there's nothing there."

"And others?"

"You must know. I can't explain. It's something you can't tell."

"Like some electric shock?"

"No."

"What then?"

"Partly electric. But more a fulfilment. You take something from each other, and something in you is fulfilled."

"That doesn't make sense."

"I know. It's a thing that doesn't make sense. Why should it?"

Breeze said earnestly: "Does it change you?"

"Yes."

"How? Physically?"

"Partly. It must do. But I don't think you'd notice it anyway, whatever it does."

"Not till afterwards?"

"No." Lorn got up. "I don't think you do till afterwards. Till you must do without it."

She went into the kitchen, gathered plates and knives and forks from the dresser, and came back to lay supper. Breeze looked at her with an absent smile, and said:

"Why is it all over?"

Lorn flacked the cloth, smoothed it, her eyes looking down flat on its dead whiteness.

"I never said it was all over."

Breeze could not speak. She felt it instantly, for some reason, to be something between them. She felt the minute beginnings of a queer jealousy. It was not active; it moved in her consciousness like a remote pain, pricking her.

When it faded, in a moment, and she was able to speak, she said: "I don't see what you mean. How do you mean, it's not all over?"

"Oh! Just that. We had a pact and parted, but very shortly he'll be home again, and then—"

"Home?"

"He's in India."

"India? A soldier?"

"An army doctor."

"Let me make the cocoa," Breeze said.

She bent down before the fire, pushed the kettle against the logs. The kettle sang a little. She straightened up, mixed cocoa and milk in the two cups, on the table, while Lorn cut bread. Breeze felt strangely anxious, as though Lorn had told her she was ill or was going away. Remote, not fully conscious, her anxiety pricked her, as the jealousy had done, like a small pain. The kettle boiled and she made cocoa, half looking at Lorn. How very strong Lorn was: big wind-cut arms, solid neck, such friendly strength, so warm. She stood absently fascinated, the small pain dying away.

"It was a question of finishing his period of service," Lorn said. "He wanted to go back."

"He wanted to go back more than he wanted you."

"No. He wanted to go back. I understood that all right. I wanted him to go back. I was only twenty-three, just out of college."

"What difference did that make? If it was all you say it was?"

"That was just it. We wanted to see if it made a difference. If it made a difference, well, there it was. If it didn't, then he could come back, and we'd get married."

They sat by the fire, with cocoa and bread and cheese, Lorn with her skirts up, warming her knees.

"I think that's awful," Breeze said. "For all it mattered, you were married. Nothing could alter that."

"I don't see it. We'd made love. But that was something we couldn't help. We could help marriage, if we ever got to it. Hence the arrangement."

"It was like making a business of it," Breeze said. She was upset, trembling. "It's a hateful thing. It was like making a business of it, it was like making a business of it! It was awful!"

"Breeze, Breeze."

"You don't deny it, do you?"

"Breeze."

"Who proposed it, he or you?"

"He did. He was older."

"Then he wasn't worthy of you! How could he be? Proposing that. Proposing an awful thing like that. He wasn't worthy of you!"

"Breeze. I can't bear to hear it."

The words were too much for the girl. She began to cry, deeply, with shame and some unhappiness she could not define. She set her cocoa on the hearth, could not see for tears, and spilt it. Lorn put her cup down beside it and put her arms round Breeze's neck. "You're not to cry. Why are you crying? Breeze. It's silly to cry." She held her, strongly, against the warm resilient bulk of her large body. They sat like mother and child, bound by grief and comfort. "You hear me? You're not to cry."

"It does me good," Breeze said. "I shall feel better. Hold me. I shall feel better."

"I'm holding you." Lorn said. "I've got you."

"Hold me tighter."

3

By April things had begun to move. The rows of herbs began to look vigorous and full of promise. Turned over and hoed, the earth was sweet and black. The two girls planted fresh supplies of plants, new varieties, and sowed seeds. They got up early and worked on into the bright spring evenings, and in the evenings, after a warm day, they could smell the forest, the strong, vigorous and yet almost drowsy odour of a great mass of trees breaking into leaf. They were enchanted by the new life, by an existence in which, as never before, they felt they had a purpose. They lived physically. Tired out, earth-stained, they came indoors as darkness came on and sat down in the little kitchen-sitting-room in the cottage and sat on without speaking and watched the fading out of the primrosy twilights, their minds dumbly content. Too tired to talk, they ate supper, went to bed early and were up again at six.

They spent energy needlessly. Lorn did the digging: she had a large four-pronged fork and used it bravely, like a weapon, knocking the soil about, throwing out every stone. She had some strenuous ambition to see the land as smooth as sand, without stones, immaculate. She did a man's work, and her body got to have some kind of male awkwardness about it: a longer stride, cruder grasp, a way of straddling as she stood. Close to her every day, Breeze did not notice it. She did the hoeing, generally, and the labelling and sowing, and the little artistic things: she would have a little rock-garden by the back door, on the south side, with patches of purple horned viola and winey primulas and rock rose, and then lavender hedges down the paths, giving vistas. "You and your vistas," Lorn said. But vistas were important; they had the effect of making things seem, to Breeze, not quite as they were, and the illusion was precious. She felt the beauty of things keenly; she could not bear ugliness, and spring drove her into small inexpressible ecstasies. Beauty was everything. It impinged upon her sharply, with pain, so that she felt something immensely precious and personal about the spring. It was for her and she could not share it. Unlike Lorn, she worked in a kind of semi-consciousness. Not bravely, but with a kind of absent persistence. She spent greater energy of spirit, dreaming as she worked, and it seemed as if the spring days sucked her up, body and spirit and all, leaving her at times almost crying with weariness. She did not understand this supreme tiredness at all. She worked harder to overcome it, splashing her hoe crudely with clenched hands, forcing herself into the full consciousness of the act, breaking down her dreamy passivity. All the time, and all through spring and summer, it seemed to get worse. The great massed ring of forest seemed to shut out life sometimes, so that she felt imprisoned by a wall of wood and leaf, sucked by a beauty that was almost parasitic into an awful listlessness of spirit that she could not understand. All the time, in contrast to Lorn, she seemed to get more and not less feminine: much slighter, very brown and delicate, with a light detached beauty and an almost irritating remoteness of spirit. It was as though she needed waking up: as though the best of her were not alive.

Then Lorn noticed it. By the end of May the oaks were in full flower and the forest stood like an olive cloud. The great polished bushes of rhododendron split pinkly into blossom, and the rare sweet-scented wild azaleas, pale yellow. The forest breathed out its enormous but not quite tangible sweetness and sucked back, in turn, the still more enormous breath of the life about it. There were days when, under the shelter of the too-close trees, life was utterly stupefied.

"I get so tired," Lorn said. "How is it? Do you get tired?"

"Yes. I didn't want to say anything about it. I thought it was just myself."

"But how is it? What's the reason for it?"

"I feel there's no air."

"Possibly we need a change," Lorn said. "We might have been working too hard."

"But it's not the work. I'm tired if I sit still."

"Even so, a change would do us no harm."

So they went, for three days, to London. For economy they stayed at a little scrubby hotel off Guildford Street. They ate cheaply; saw films cheaply. London tired them, but in a new way; it stripped off the old lassitude like a heavy skin. They had a double room with one bed, and they stayed in bed, every morning, as late as they dare. And at night, when Lorn took the younger girl in her arms and mothered her down to sleep, Breeze felt a tender and inexplicable restful transfusion of strength take place. She lay close to Lorn and felt again, still not with full consciousness, that queer stirring of remote affection that was like a small pain. It was beautiful, but it was also reassuring, a very wonderful comfort, a strength against trouble. One night Breeze woke up with a start, frightened, not knowing where she was, feeling alone in a strange place. She started wildly up in bed, and said: "What is it? I don't want it! I don't want it to come, please! I don't want it," but in a moment Lorn stretched out her arms and took her back, saying, "Silly kid, silly kid," in a voice of strong but amused tenderness.

"What made you wake up in the night?" she said next morning.

"I was in trouble," Breeze said. "It was you I wanted. I was all right when I'd got you."

That afternoon they went to see a woman, the secretary of an organization specializing in the distribution of rural products. Lorn had heard of her and had written, asking for an interview. This woman made them see various new aspects of things. She raised hopes. Where they had seen, vaguely, that some day they must organize distribution in order to keep going, they now began to see, rationally, how such organization must be planned, how far ahead it must be planned, how little they had done. They would need, in time, packers, a mail-order system, expert knowledge on this, that and the other. Miss Wills, the secretary, wore light amber rimmed spectacles and spoke in a voice of vinegar and treacle which both Breeze and Lorn disliked. But they felt, beyond the voice and the spectacles, a shrewd, clever, no-nonsense personality. "You're on a good thing, you girls, if you'll work hard, and come to me whenever you're stuck. But don't try to be elegant. You're amateurs and you can't afford to be amateurs. We're in touch with all kinds of markets here and we can take all your stuff, if it's good, on a commission basis. You've got to look at things rationally, Miss Harvey, without a lot of sticky romance. When shall you be ready for production?"

Lorn told her. "We hope to be in a position to do something next year. That's what we thought."

"All right. Up to date, what have you done? I mean regarding organization?"

"Not much."

"Then you must start. I think it might be as well if I came down to see you. Discuss things. I could come"—she looked up a diary, marked it off in blue pencil—"in a fortnight. That is, after Whitsun. I'll say the week-end of June 5. Let me know if that suits you. Drop me a card: yes or no. That'll be enough."

They went away full of hope, excited. They saw the thing in rational outline at last, no longer some cloudy embryo of romance. They saw that they must work hard, plan, think, that it was not enough to waste an energy of body and spirit. They saw that by working in the dark, they had worked for nothing: they had given themselves up, whole-heartedly, to emptiness.

"I think that's what made us so tired," Lorn said. "Working and working and not knowing quite where we were going."

"Oh! let's get home, Lorn. I want to be back, doing something. I don't want to be away any longer."

They went back on the following day, excitement still strong, their whole hopes concentrated on the pole of the ideal pointed out by the secretary. "I didn't like her," Breeze said. "She was too sweet and too sure, but she knew what was what. Oh! Lorn, I'm glad we went. We've *got* something now. We can look forward to something."

When they arrived back at the cottage, in the late afternoon, they found a slip on the front door-mat: a cable awaited Lorn at the post office. She at once got on her bicycle and rode with excitement into Lyndhurst. She was back in half an hour. By that time Breeze had tea laid. Lorn laid the cable on the table, for Breeze to read. The cable had been handed in at Port Said, two days previously, and it said:

> Expect arrive London Friday telegraph me Grosvenor Hotel when and where possible meet you have plans for future: Vernon.

"He's coming home," Lorn said. She stood in silence for a moment, and then began to cry. Her strength seemed to vanish at once, she stood weak and in some way foolish, womanish, miserable with joy. All the time Breeze stood apart from her, repelled by some unaccountable feeling of dislike, not knowing what to do.

4

She was caught up, from that moment, by the force of a peculiar jealousy. She got fixed in her mind, as though by some fierce and abrupt photographic flash, a fully realized picture of the man who was coming. He was about thirty, an easy sociable being, with large, cold medical hands, a man of assurance, with the blond aloof sobriety of the English middle class. She saw also, for some reason, his mother in the background. Why, she did not know, but she saw the mother as some skinny and also aloof halo behind the man. She was holding a cablegram too, and smiling, with indulgent proud stretched lips, like some absurd filmic emblem of maternity and sacrifice: the brave waiting for the brave. She felt that she hated her too.

She saw the change in Lorn with identical clarity. Emotion sharpened her before she knew it. With quiet derision she saw Lorn get on her bicycle, the next morning, to bike off to send her wire. She was not prepared for the sudden switch over from adoration to contempt. She had not time to consider it or defend herself from it when it came. It hit her, striking from within, before she had time to think. "Lorn looks so silly, rushing off. Rushing off like a school-kid." Lorn, getting on her bicycle in a hurry, had got her skirt bundled beneath her, showing the laddered and worn tops of her working stockings. She looked, for a second, ungainly, heavily ridiculous. The darned stockings and the gap of bare red flesh above them looked ugly. "Her legs are ugly. Why doesn't she pull her skirts down?" She rode off with excited haste, her thick legs pounding on the bicycle pedals. "She's got the saddle too low. She hasn't raised it since I used it. Her knees stick out." The impressions were instinctive, having no incentive from the conscious self. She could not control them.

Lorn was gone an hour. Breeze worked, meanwhile, on the plot, hoeing among rows of thyme and parsley. It was warm, heavy weather, weeds were coming fast. Breeze kept looking towards the house. She heard at last Lorn's bicycle bell and, looking up, saw Lorn herself pushing the bicycle up the path: pushing heavily, panting, excited, thick legs lumping down on the path, head forward mouth open. Instinctively the impression leapt to mind: "She thumps her feet down like a horse. Why doesn't she hold herself straight?" Lorn was untidy, hot from the ride. "Her face looks awful. Like raw meat. Has she been to Lyndhurst and back like that?" Lorn almost flung the bicycle against the water-butt at the house corner and thumped into the house, catching her foot against the step, stumbling. "She looks as though she doesn't know what she's doing. She looks stupid. Only half there."

She went on hoeing. Lorn did not come out of the house. For a time Breeze did not take much notice; then half an hour passed, an hour, and it was almost noon. Breeze began to get more and more impatient, hoeing fiercely, chopping the hoe hard against the soft dry earth, raising dust. What was Lorn doing? Why didn't she come out, just to say Hullo? Hungry. Breeze remembered then that it was Lorn's turn to cook. That explained it. Even so, she felt inexplicably and persistently angry, against her will. She hoed until her shoes and legs were soot-powdered with dust and her body muck-sweaty and her insides weak with hunger.

Then at twelve-thirty she dropped the hoe and went into the house. She registered, at once, a number of unpleasant impressions: no smell of dinner, no table laid, no Lorn, nothing. Wherever was Lorn? She wrenched open the stairs door and shouted her name.

"Lorn! Lorn! For goodness sake!"

And at once Lorn replied, easily, almost sweetly: "Yes? Want anything?"

In vacant fury, Breeze stood at the foot of the stairs. "I thought it was your turn to cook? What have you been doing? You've been back from Lyndhurst hours."

"I know. Come up a second. I want to tell you something."

Breeze went upstairs, into Lorn's bedroom. Lorn was sitting at her dressing-table in new peach-coloured skirt and knickers, making up. She had a clean huckaback towel over her shoulders and was rubbing a white skin-cream over her face; then, as Breeze came in, she took the towel off her shoulders and wiped her hands and, very carefully, her lips. Bare again, her shoulders looked heavy and coarse, without grace. Breeze stood still, at the door; she could see Lorn's face in the mirror. She did not know what to do or say or what to make of it. Emotion and face-cream had made Lorn's face some-how shining and puffed. It looked faintly gross: not Lorn's face at all, but the face of some absurd obese stranger.

"What's come over you?" Breeze said.

"He's coming down this afternoon." Lorn said, "by the four o'clock."

"How do you know? I thought you telegraphed."

"I telephoned. I telephoned the hotel instead. I spoke to him."

"Is that why you were gone so long?"

"Not altogether. I had to get something." She was unscrewing a cylinder of lip-stick. "She doesn't know how to hold it," Breeze thought. "She holds it like a stick of kid's rock. What's come over her?"

Lorn's thick strong fingers grasped the lipstick crudely and she began to rub it clumsily, to and fro, on her lips. "She uses it like an indiarubber. She's got no idea. She's never done it before." The lips grew orange, greasy. "She's got the wrong colour. She's daubing it on. She can't know. She's like a kid." All of this continual creation of impressions was unconscious, in some way against her will. It ceased when Lorn said:

"Then I had to order the taxi."

"Taxi?"

"He said order a taxi. It could call for me here, then bring us both back from the station. He said he didn't fancy a tramp with luggage."

"He's staying?"

"Well, I should think so." She was pushing out her lips towards the mirror, in an orange pout; she drew them back, pursed them; she twitched the corners, smiling a lit-tle. The lips seemed enamelled, brittle, like snakeskin. Satisfied, Lorn set them in what she felt was a line of tenderness, naturally. "She looks hopeless, awful," Breeze thought. "She looks pathetic. She's got pimples on her face. She can't know how awful she looks." Suddenly she could not bear it. "Lorn, let me do it," she said. "Let me touch it up. You're too heavy."

She took the lipstick: the tinfoil was warm and sweaty where Lorn had held it in her hot hands, the stick already soft beneath.

"What made you get orange?"

"He likes it."

"It's not your colour."

"I know. I wanted cerise. But he likes flame. He always liked it."

Breeze looked at the stick. Flame-coloured, kiss-proof, it was a symbol of some kind of fatuous hope. She wiped Lorn's lips, until they were clean again except for fissures of orange in the cracks of the skin; then she began all over again, painting them delicately, bringing the mouth into softer, longer line. All the time Lorn was trembling.

5

That afternoon, while Lorn had gone to the station in her taxi, there was a storm. It broke with warm stickiness and a great beat of thick rain that flashed white against the summery dark background of forest. It drove Breeze indoors. She sat miserable, waiting and listening for the taxi beyond the sound of rain and the huge sudden blunderings of thunder. The air was hot and oppressive and the rain, smashing down grass and plants and flowers, made small floods among the flattened rows of herbs. By mid-afternoon the garden looked a desolation, its grace gone, its colours washed out, the forest beyond it a gloomy wall of solid leaf and rain. Waiting, miserable, she felt it to be almost the worst thing that could have happened. The place looked mean and small and dead.

The taxi came at half-past three. Going to the window to watch, Breeze had in her mind her preconceived picture of the man: blond, aloof, coldly medical, about thirty, with the skinny and aloof halo of his mother shining, inexplicably, in the background. She had waited for his arrival with a kind of remote arrogance, in a determination to be aloof also, her preconceived image part of a preconceived hatred.

Looking across the garden, to the gate, she had a great shock. There appeared with Lorn, under her grey umbrella, a man of more than fifty. She could not believe it. She stood and stared at him in a conflict of pain: the pain of unbelief, amazement and the shock of a momentary and stupid terror. Her image of him went black, like a fused light, the halo of the mother fluttering out behind it like a silly candle.

She had not time to think. In a moment he was standing before her, grey-haired, lean, flesh yellow with sun, with the air of some decaying and dictatorial professor, nose slightly askew, eyes having some curious affliction of twitching, so that she could not look at him.

"So this," he said, shaking hands with her, "is Breeze Anstey?"

His voice was nasal, meticulous, a little superior. It was a voice accustomed to speaking obliquely, in innuendoes. She did not trust it. Hearing it, she felt the conception of her hatred of him harden more firmly than ever. At that moment it was the only thing of which she felt quite sure.

Foolishly she said: "I'm sorry it rained like this—I mean in this tropical way."

"Tropical. This?" He was very amused. Greatly. Tropical? Very, very funny. Did she understand, dear young lady, quite what tropical meant? He looked at her with oblique superiority, with a maddening amusement and a thin nasal sneer which she was to discover, later, was habitual.

Explaining to her what tropical rain was really like, he addressed her again as "Dear young lady." She felt furious. She stared at him with crude dislike openly. All the time Lorn was smiling, open-mouthed, teeth gay and white against her absurd lipstick. It was a smile in which there was something like a giddiness of adoration: the smile of utterly silly, uncritical feminine delight. She was in heaven.

It went on all through tea. It was like the functioning of some cheap machine into which Lorn kept pressing unseen coins in order to keep it working. To Breeze it was incomprehensible. It could not be genuine. She could not conceive of it as anything else but forced, the desperate mechanical reaction to the occasion.

The doctor talked. To Breeze he was an old man. He framed his sentences with the slow care of experience, searching for his words, as though engaged on some careful and perpetual diagnosis.

"When I first had—er—intimation of—of this—this project of yours, my dear. I had—er—some notion that you had taken—taken a place of some size."

"It doesn't *look* big, dear," Lorn said, "but you try to work it and see."

"But you said—you said a farm."

"Well?"

"But this is—just a garden."

"We call it a farm. It couldn't very well be bigger because of the forest."

"The—the forest?"

He looked out of the window with a kind of amazed contempt, at their small confined and now rain-flattened plot of earth, with the barricade of trees beyond and the heavy English sky pressing down on it all and giving it some air of civilized meanness. He looked in silence. Then he began laughing. It was, to Breeze, an extraordinary laugh, almost silent, impersonal and yet selfish, as though the joke were for himself alone and yet on them. He laughed for fully two minutes before finally saying anything. Then he repeated "Forest, forest," in the tone of a man who, though knowing everything, has a little pity for the rest of the world.

Breeze understood. She caught the accent, almost the sneer, of pity: pity for them, pity for their so-called farm, for their ideals, for two silly too-earnest Englishwomen with their pretence of ambition. Without saying it, he hinted that there were lives of which they knew nothing, forests beside which their own miserable affair was a shrubbery. He seemed to say: "You may believe in it, but is it worth believing in? It can't be serious. It can't mean anything. And now that I've come it can't go on."

Almost as though she heard it, Breeze said, frankly:

"You came home in a hurry, Dr. Bentley."

He looked at her, then at Lorn, obliquely. "I had business," he said. He kept looking at Lorn, still obliquely, with a soft and almost crafty smile of adoration, until Lorn at last lifted her eyes and smiled back in a confusion of happiness. Their eyes, in silence, telegraphed secrets which were not secrets at all. "Yes," the doctor said, "I had business. It's not—not for me to say how—important—it is, But I had business. That is so—eh, Lorn?"

The system of telegraphy, once begun, went on. After tea, and on into the misty heavy evening, the doctor and Lorn sat about in the little sitting-room and, whenever Breeze was there, sent each other messages of what was almost adolescent adoration. They spoke in riddles: restless, obvious riddles of which they were only too anxious that Breeze should know the meaning. They held out their love to her, as it were, on a plate, like some piece of juicy steak, inviting her to admire and, while indicating that it was not for her, to envy. She responded by muteness. She did not know what to say. Dumbly she sat and waited for the time when she could decently go to bed.

"Tempus fugit," the doctor said, once.

"Yes, but slowly," Lorn said, "when you're waiting."

"Everything comes," the doctor said, "to him who waits."

At eight Breeze pleaded excuses and went up to bed. After lying awake, listening to the slow summer drip of rain from the branches outside, she heard, at nine, the shutting and locking of doors, footsteps on the stairs, whispers, the small shufflings and rustling of retirement. She waited for Lorn to come into her, as always, to say goodnight. They would sit together, talk, confide, discuss the happenings of one day and their plans for another. She cherished the moment jealously.

She waited. Nothing happened. Then, towards ten, she heard a door, footsteps. They approached and went past. She heard the opening and shutting of another door, then silence.

She listened for a long time. There was no other sound. The rain had ceased and she could hear the silence, could feel it as something hard and tangible about her, as a crystallization of emptiness into solidity, into something as light and sharp as a knife, cutting her off from Lorn completely.

6

By innuendoes, half-phrases, gestures of superiority, and above all by the sly oblique smile of pity, the doctor poured contempt on the little farm. For almost a week Lorn, bewildered by the pull of opposing emotions, wavered between the man and the ideal she and Breeze had set themselves. As though aware of it, the doctor said, at last:

"I suppose you two—young things know that this—this place—isn't healthy? It isn't doing either of you any good."

This was a shock; and Breeze at once resented it.

"Who said it wasn't healthy?"

The doctor was patient: which aroused her still more. She detested the assured enamel superiority of the man. Honest, decent anger, resentment, bitterness, had no place in his make-up. He presented only an assured too-smooth egg-like coldness. Her own anger, like some feeble Lilliputian pin, could not even scratch the iron shell of his supreme priggishness. It was all hopelessly beyond her. Lorn and this man, this man for a lover.

Another time he said to her: "Do you feel well?"

"Yes," she said. "As well as I ever did."

"Which means?" He paused, waiting for a reply which did not come. "You feel tired?"

"No."

"Sleepy? No—no energy?"

"No."

"Oppressed?"

"No."

She was lying. He knew it and she, in a moment, knew that he was aware of it. "Lorn tells me—quite—quite otherwise," he said.

"I'm not Lorn," she said.

"Lorn says you are both tired—er—continually—and can't understand it."

"We work hard."

"Perhaps so. But that would not account for this—this extraordinary enervation. The trouble is that there are too many trees in this place. They suck up the air."

"That's your opinion. I like the trees."

"May I take your pulse?" he said.

Before she could resist he had taken her hand, had his thumb on her wrist. It was as though she were held in a clasp of pure dead bone. In the feel of his hands she felt, as it were, the whole essence of his nature: hard, bony, dead, the expression of man seeing life as something to be perpetually diagnosed, the delicacy of human nature as something needing eternal probing and some ultimate interesting operation.

He dropped her hand. She felt, for a few seconds, the small cool point of the thumb's contact. She stood waiting, resentfully, in silence. What had he to do with her? Why did he trouble with her? It was beyond her, this damnable solicitude, and she did not want it.

"You'll be telling me next," she said, "that I've got galloping consumption."

For a moment he did not reply. They were in the little sitting-room. Lorn had gone to cut lettuces for the evening salad. It was a sultry, still evening, breathless.

"No, it's not that you've got," he said. "Will you sit down?"

"Why?"

"Just sit down. I want to ask you the same—er—questions as I asked Lorn."

"What questions?"

"Well—er—just—"

"You're going to ask me to sleep with you perhaps?" she said. She raised her voice, spoke without thinking, the words out of her mouth before she could prevent them. "You're going to ask me to wait seven years for you perhaps? No thank you! Not to-day, thank you! No *thank* you!"

He looked at her, smiling, the small chill oblique smile of professional reticence, as one accustomed to such ill-mannered outbursts. He did not speak. She set her teeth, waiting, meaning the words she had spoken with all her heart, yet wishing, now, that she had not spoken them. She stood poised somewhere between anger and embarrassment.

At that moment Lorn came in, carrying the already dew-wet lettuces.

"Hullo, you two," she said. "Quarrelling?"

"Yes!" Breeze said.

"Breeze!"

"He's got as far as taking my pulse—but that isn't far enough."

Her anger quickened again, fired up in her face.

"He's not satisfied with coming here and taking you away. That isn't enough. He wants to prove the place isn't healthy. He wants to get *me* out of it."

"Breeze, Breeze, I won't have it! I won't have it."

"It's true. He's smashed our life."

"You can't say it. I won't have you saying it."

"Why isn't it true? Before he came rushing home like a lovesick boy we were quite happy here. The farm was our whole life. You know that. We'd planned and schemed and banked on it. We'd arranged for the organizer to come down. Now he comes rush-ing home and it all means nothing."

"You mean you mean nothing!"

"Well, what difference? What difference whether it's me or the farm? He's trying to make you believe it's unhealthy. That means he either wants you to give me up or me to give up the farm. Well, I'll give up the farm."

"Oh! Breeze, please. Please, not now."

"I'll give it up, I tell you! You don't want me! What point in my staying? I'll clear out now—before I can change my mind."

Suddenly she looked from Lorn to the man. He was smiling and the smile had that perpetual as though engraved mockery in it, the slightly oblique sneer of condescen-sion, and she knew that he was not only laughing at her physical self, her behaviour, but her ideals, her anger and the very preciousness of her affection.

Suddenly rage burned up in her to a point when she could not control it. She went across to him and hit him full across the face. For a moment nothing happened. The smile did not change. It remained, like some rotten and yet imperishable engraving of his whole nature. Beside herself, almost crying, she struggled with a terrific desire to hit it again, to smash it out of existence. Then, suddenly, the smile, the rage, the reason for it all had no meaning. She went very weak. She had just strength enough to lift her voice and half shout:

"I'll get out in the morning. I'll go! There's not room for all of us."

Lorn would have spoken, but Breeze ran out of the room. She was already crying. In the second before the door slammed she heard the faint condescending breath of a laugh from the doctor.

She lay in bed and cried with anguish and comfort. She waited for Lorn to come, clinging to the hope of reconciliation. It must have been about eight o'clock, and she lay for two hours, until darkness, before she heard a sound from below. Sounds came, then, and went, but nothing happened. She lay in silence and could not sleep. She thought of Lorn. She saw Lorn, physically, as a constant presence, comforting, large, so soft and maternal. She ached for her. She saw her as she had seen her in the forest, bathing, and she was caught up, unexpectedly, by a return of the same singular moment of acute anguish, almost pain, that had shot through her at the first sight of Lorn's body.

Then, for the first time, she understood herself. She knew, suddenly, what it was she resented, what exactly it was she had wanted, what she was so extraordinarily afraid of losing.

She sat up in bed. She had ceased crying and she felt, now, like a rag that has been wrung out. The cold realization of her feeling for Lorn struck her with fear, almost terror, as though she had suddenly become aware that she was incurably ill.

Simultaneously she saw also the reason for the doctor's smile: that perpetual smile of aloof knowingness. "No, that's not what you've got." He knew. Unconsciously she must have known that he knew. But curiously, for all her knowing, her rage against him did not lessen. He had struck so hard at her ideals, the little and now absurd farm, the business partnership, the hope of success. He had taken, and in a way, destroyed Lorn.

She lay for a long time. She hoped that Lorn would come. She wanted, and for the first time consciously, to be held by Lorn, tenderly, with the same love and strength as she felt in return. Something had taught her that a love of that kind belonged to the limbo of things that were never mentioned. To her, in the full realization of it, it seemed a beautiful thing. She cried tenderly because of it. It comforted her. There was some kind of sad inverted pleasure in the gentle pain of realization and loss.

At one o'clock she got up, lighted her candle and packed her bag. Going to shut the window she caught the great breath of the forest, damp, profound, summer-drenched, the smell of a whole section of her life. She stood for a moment breathing it in, looking over the dark quiet earth of the garden towards the still darker mass of trees. The night was deadly still. As it hung about her, huge and intangible, with an intolerable quality of suspense and comfort, her life seemed very little and not to matter.

She shut the window. She felt, at once, back in the cramped confinement of her own affairs, where things had seemed, a moment before, to be all over, but where they seemed, now, to be just beginning.

And she knew that the rest, whatever it was, lay with herself.

"DIANA FREDERICS"

From *Diana: A Strange Autobiography* (1939)

The individual—male or female—who wrote under the pseudonym "Diana Frederics" remains unknown. *Diana: A Strange Autobiography* purports to be the factual account of a young woman's discovery of her lesbianism; when it first appeared in the United States in 1939 it was accompanied by a preface from a Dr. Victor Robinson, who vouched for its authenticity. ("It is the confession of one who was destined by Nature to gather forbidden fruit from the gardens of deviation, and who saved her life from frustration by knowing herself.") Whether factual or fictional, the work has enjoyed a long life as an underground lesbian classic. Some of its popularity, like that of *The Well of Loneliness*, has to do with its air of painful sincerity: the narrator, a college teacher, is excruciatingly frank about her emotional struggles with her "abnormality." Yet even as it plays into stereotypes—including that of the lesbian as depressive misfit—*Diana* also colorfully illuminates important facets of lesbian life between the wars. In the chapter below the narrator describes her first visit to a women's bar—a café in Paris frequented by American and English students. Though "Diana" will be disillusioned by what she finds there, the place is a revelation—not least for what it suggests about the complex social networks and secret codes of recognition existing between homosexual women in the first half of the century.

FURTHER READING: "Diana Frederics," *Diana: A Strange Autobiography*, ed. Julie Abraham (New York: New York University Press, 1995); Jeannette Foster, *Sex Variant Women in Literature* (1956; rpt., Tallahassee, Fla.: Naiad, 1985), pp. 322–24; Lillian Faderman, *Odd Girls and Twilight Lovers: A History of Lesbian Life in Twentieth-Century America* (New York: Columbia University Press, 1991).

The Café in Paris

Two days after our visit to the lesbian café I wanted to return alone without telling Jane. My first brief glimpse of frankly lesbian women *en groupe* had made me conscious of a tribal similarity I had never before suspected. I wanted to discover those points of common likeness if only to avoid them. Though their resemblance one to the other was entirely spiritual, the thought of an inherent lesbian individuality bothered me.

It was a rainy afternoon at a late tea hour. As I went down the circular stairway, sudden timidity almost turned me back before I could push open the door. I could not explain my fear of the women I saw there, but I sensed their guarded interest in me as I made my way to an inconspicuous table.

Five or six couples were dancing to the music of phonograph records, some few groups were idling in booths, and two women were alone reading. The entire room was not as large as it had at first appeared, and its atmosphere of indolent sensuousness soon calmed me. The hush of night formality had given way to easy sociability. These women, younger than the night clientele, looked my own age and were, obviously, American and English.

I was relieved that none of them were dressed as men, although most of them were mannish in bearing as well as attire. It struck me that the English girls were more earnestly mannish than the Americans who looked, in contrast, only tailored and tomboyish. It was not prejudice which made me observe their certain talent for smartness which the English girls lacked.

An onlooker ignorant of the character of the place would not have caught the significance of the four photographs of young women on the wall, close to my table. Two of them I recognized as American actresses. I was amazed at the boldness of a *propriétaire* who would dare defy the secretive habits of lesbians. Remembering the collegiate penchant for hanging pictures of famous sisters in sorority chapter rooms, I caught myself thinking of them as prominent alumnae.

As I sat sipping tea and occupying myself with a book, a rather strange thing happened: a sensation of almost blood-intimacy came over me and for the first time in my life I had the feeling of being a part of a group of fellow human beings. No normal person could understand the relief I experienced as I looked about me and saw the vividness of faces that knew, as I knew, that here was a haven where social prejudice was only a bad dream of the other world. No pressure here or that constant feeling of separateness; no dread here of shame, not even the mask of bantering smiles. Here I could lose a little loneliness with creatures whose hopes and understanding and passions were my own. Here for an instant I could feel beyond the pain and pale of moral judgment.

These girls were individually vivid and intelligent-looking. The thought had never occurred to me before, but now I wondered why I'd never seen either a drab or a stupid-looking lesbian, and I imagined several reasons. First of all, a stupid girl probably would never ascertain her abnormality if she were potentially homosexual—a fact not at all strange on second thought. Further, the girl who did come to understand her inversion was likely to have character in her face, if no degree of beauty. The very fact of her abnormality assured her of that; her expression would be crossed by a subtle something, according to the measure of her disillusionment. No woman could adjust herself to lesbianism without developing exceptional qualities of courage.

I became interested in an American girl of about twenty-five, whose eyes betrayed a trace of boredom as she danced with a tall blonde. I would not have noticed her apart from the others except for her feminine appearance and the fact that she was, unmistakably, trying to flirt with me. It had never occurred to me that lesbians flirted with one another, I'd never seen it before and I felt a little silly and embarrassed. Yet she excited my curiosity. She had an interesting face—cold and smooth and restless. At last, when she was seated opposite me, several tables away, I managed a smile that I hate to recall for its childish self-consciousness. It must have been effective. Almost at once she came to my table, introduced herself simply as Elizabeth, and asked me to dance.

A stubborn prejudice made me refuse. I had never liked the sight of women dancing together, and lesbian couples, while aping normal privileges, only seemed to emphasize their abnormality. I was glad that Elizabeth took no offense, and accepted my invitation to join me.

Her first formality was charming. Our conversation began quickly over mutual interests; I learned that she was accompanist to an American contralto now in Paris, that she was training for concert work herself. Then, after a pause, a slow smile illuminated her dark eyes and I yielded to sudden excitement as she simply looked at me with questioning candor.

"My friends are suspicious of you," she said. She had to explain no further. I understood. I was new here. I had them at a disadvantage.

I'd not suspected the group animosity of lesbians, but this evidence of their eternal desire for secrecy should not have surprised me. I felt as gauche as if I had walked into a private lodge meeting. Then, suddenly, their suspicion became insupportable. I was moved by a quick desire to prove myself, to make them know, to make sentimental appeals so they would know. Prejudice was no longer important. Impulsively I took Elizabeth's hand and asked her to dance. She smiled, understanding, and led me to the dance floor. As we passed her own table, Elizabeth nodded, still smiling, to her friends there; though I had said nothing I interpreted her nod as an official stamp of approval. Then, in the first overt admission of my own nature, my face went hot with self-consciousness. Elizabeth, seeing my confusion, pressed my arm and whispered, "*Il faut du courage.*"

In a little while I was myself again. Elizabeth's friends began to ask for dances, and I had the extraordinary sensation of feeling like the belle of the lesbian ball.

At first I wondered why Elizabeth asked what kind of cocktail I would like, and hovered near me like a zealous escort. Later, from what her friends told me, I understood, very much amused, that Elizabeth was merely being cautious.

I hated having to dance. But I was learning, a little more from each partner, what I had come to find out—something of the class idiosyncrasies of lesbians, what it was that gave the whole group a subtle mark of similarity. In my eagerness to learn I went on abusing my prejudices.

Without exception my partners gave me the impression of being wild and strong and a little devil-may-care. The more I saw of them the better I could understand. Everything they did seemed vital, every move intense. Their faces were mobile, their eyes sensitive, their conversation spirited, their understanding facile, their sympathy quick. Nor was their spiritual nature any more intense than their physical. Their laugh was a little abandoned, their gestures expansive, their energy nervous and suggestive of strength.

After I'd had time to understand the reasons for these impressions they made perfectly obvious sense. Of course the lesbian's reactions would seem more vigorous than those of a normal woman—her emotional range is wider, is masculine as well as feminine. This fecund sensual nature is exactly what gives her distinction from normal women, and what gives lesbians similarity.

The intensity is understandable. The lesbian is forever conscious of her destiny. Lack of social purpose inspires a self-awareness that naturally intensifies thought and action. No matter what she does in life, society always sees her as a frustrated woman. Her armor may be strong, her philosophy pliant, but the social scheme remains a jump ahead of any compromise she makes. The effect does one of two things, depending on her spirit: it swerves her into silent submission or brings out the intensity of a woman affronted.

I was relieved when at last Elizabeth rescued me from a large-boned English girl who was becoming sentimental with English awkwardness. With scarcely a word Elizabeth led me up a short flight of steps and into an alcove. It had not occurred to me that a lesbian café would have private rooms. Elizabeth lighted candles and all I could make out was a small narrow room, furnished well but simply, with a low couch and a coffee table. Almost at once a *garçon* brought in a bottle of brandy, glasses and incense. I noticed his care in letting Elizabeth select the scent she preferred for the incense burner that hung from the wall. The thought of aphrodisiacs crossed my mind and I wanted to laugh before it occurred to me that perhaps I should be frightened.

When the *garçon* had gone out, Elizabeth held a candle close to the wall and pointed to some writing.

"Wouldn't you like to make a contribution?" she smiled, handing me a pencil from the table.

Curious, I got up to read. There, handwritten on the wall, were a dozen aphorisms and fragments of poems, some faded by time, some in bold script, some in dainty. The type of sentiment almost all of them carried interested me. The first I read was Edna St. Vincent Millay's "Prayer to Persephone." Next to it, scrawled in a different hand, I read: "The wise want love; and those who love want wisdom." Farther on was a sentiment written by a lachrymose admirer of Paul Fort: "*Mon Dieu, qu'il est doux de pleurer sans raisons!*" On the opposite wall, printed in heavy black, and outlined as if it were intended to be the motto of lesbianism, I read: "*Tout comprendre, c'est tout pardonner.*" I recognized the next lines, from Byron's *Manfred*, and I assumed they had been written by an English girl:

> "Thou lovedst me
> Too much, as I loved thee; we were not made

To torture thus each other, though it were the deadliest sin to love as
we have loved."

But most interesting to me was the last I saw, written with a black pencil that must have
been in a stoic mood; even the printing looked determined, and there was a heavy,
round period at the end of the second line, as if for emphasis:

"Then I said: I will eat of this sorrow to its last shred,
I will take it unto me utterly.
I will see if I be not strong enough to contain it."

I should have liked to have known the woman who wrote that; I think I would have
admired her.

Again Elizabeth asked me to write something but I disliked the flavor of exhibitionism and made excuses. My reluctance aroused her curiosity. She sat down beside me
and asked me a surprising question.

"Do you mind telling me," she said, "if you are one of us or a spook?"

I was embarrassed to be ignorant of lesbian jargon. Elizabeth had to explain what
she meant by "spook":

"A woman who for some reason or other strays into lesbianism as second best. And
stays because she likes it better."

I reassured Elizabeth, inwardly exultant that my lesbianism was so well disguised.

"Once a woman is a spook she almost never prefers a man again," she went on like
a teacher. "She may marry if she wants a home and children, but chances are she has a
lesbian lover."

Then the surprising opinion I have heard many times since:

"Women make better lovers."

Elizabeth's tone left no room for argument. Reasonably, I resented this smug attitude. I knew the legend "Once a lesbian always a lesbian"; I had always wondered to
what extent lesbian conceit was responsible for it. It was natural that lesbians should be
proud of converts. The thought that an occasional woman strayed into their ranks was
support to a pride that had little to lean on. And it was true that woman's nature favored
her avoidance of the common mistakes of male lovers—haste and selfishness. As significant for some women, too, was the question of a happy intellectual level. The educated woman often wanted, but seldom got, the intellectual respect accorded her male
consort. This irritant was not a factor in the lesbian relationship.

"But isn't it true," I asked, "that converts would be women who were either too
weak or too scared? Women who are psychologically or physiologically unfitted for
normal love?"

"Yes, of course," Elizabeth said. "Lesbians are mostly spiritual. The Greeks, you
know, called them 'Uranians,' after 'Ouranos,' which meant 'Heaven,' because their
love is a lot more emotional than it is physical. It's nearest the spiritual ideal."

I was struck by the defense mechanism which bound lesbian love all the way through. Unable to conform to the conventions, lesbians took the obvious course of exalting their feelings. That was clear enough. Yet Elizabeth was not idealizing so grotesquely as it might at first appear.

Lesbians idealize because they have to. The homosexual relationship does not have what marriage has to hold it together: property, family, frequently even profession. It doesn't have the blessings of church, law and state; if love goes, the relationship is ended with no more papers than it had to begin. Sentiment has to take the place of all these privileges. It is needed as compensation.

But Elizabeth had not brought me into the alcove for conversation. Soon she began to make love to me, and the ease of her approach was startling. Her eyes were brilliant, her hands beautiful, and their warmth on my arms more exciting than I had expected. Still impersonally, with the mood of the voluptuary, I encouraged her. I was almost fascinated by technique more artful than any I had ever known. Elizabeth was touched by that rare charm that sometimes makes a woman radiant in emotion, and when at last she turned my face and kissed my lips I knew my experimenting had gone too far.

Too excited to think, I do not know how I came to lie in her arms. I hadn't thought I would want to. I had not meant to. Elizabeth was talking to me, whispering and leaning over me.

"Tell me you will go home with me. Tell me I won't lose you as suddenly as I've found you. Diana, we could be so happy for a little while. Until I sail."

Her voice was too seductive, her phrasing too practiced. Chilled now, my mind cleared and desire died. I got up, a little rudely. Without emotion I accepted the fact that I had come into the alcove with Elizabeth wanting something to happen. It had, and I had behaved shamefully. Curiosity had been satisfied with a vengeance. Now I wanted only to go home to Jane, where I belonged.

I had not seen clearly before. My attitude of impersonality quickly changed with Elizabeth's glibness. I looked at her, her eyes shining with invitation, and I knew it would not be easy to tell her I had tried for an instant to see if I could match her own spirit. Now, depressed, I feared as something personal the spirit of the place I first thought of as a haven. Lesbianism became hateful for its lack of discipline, its prodigality of intimacy and sensuality. I even began to hate the ridiculous symbol of the incense pot.

I wonder now what I had expected in the first place. Perhaps I had hoped merely to get away from the ever-present contrast of myself with the normal, to become a part of whatever there was of soul and intelligence of my kind. But it hadn't worked. The illusion of one-ness had gone as quickly as it had come. The salvation of transient love, of desire for the body as a last resort, could not be mine; I could never become a part of that grand looseness with which these girls assuaged their natures.

Elizabeth was still lying where I had left her. I told her I could not see her again. After a long minute she looked up at me, and the quiet regret in her face gave the impression that she had known all along.

"Is your lover here in Paris with you?" she asked.

I nodded, feeling like a child caught sneaking. And then Elizabeth became angry.

"Then why did you come here? Were you just in a playful mood? Or could it be that you are honestly as ignorant of the mart as you seem?"

From Elizabeth's sarcastic remark I learned an astonishing thing. I had not known before that lesbians had both "rendezvous" and a "mart." The former was merely a meeting place for lovers, the latter—the café I had unwittingly chosen—an open house for lesbians who were, as Elizabeth bluntly put it, "single."

I began to despair of ever learning the complexities of lesbian social life. But, disillusioned by my first glimpse of it, I could not persuade myself that my ignorance made much difference.

ELIZABETH BISHOP (1911–1979)

"It Is Marvelous To Wake Up Together" (c. 1942)

Elizabeth Bishop—orphaned, alcoholic, asthmatic, depressive, and a deeply closeted lesbian all her life—is one of America's greatest modern poets. She was born in Worcester, Massachusetts, to Gertrude May Boomer Bishop and William T. Bishop. Her father died when she was eight months old; her mother, distraught at her husband's death, was committed to a mental hospital when Bishop was five. Bishop never saw her again. Bishop was raised by her grandparents in a village in Nova Scotia until 1917, when she was sent to live in Worcester and Boston with an aunt. These various shocks and upheavals brought on the debilitating asthma attacks and depressions from which she later suffered as an adult. In her teens she attended the Walnut Hill School, then went to Vassar, where she began writing poetry. In 1934 the poet Marianne Moore encouraged her literary endeavors and helped her publish her first book of poems, *North and South*, in 1946. Between 1935 and 1948, supported by a family inheritance, Bishop lived a somewhat rootless existence, traveling extensively in Europe before settling with a lover, Marjorie Stevens, in Key West, Florida. When that relationship broke up in 1948–49, she was hospitalized for alcoholism and depression and, despite the success of her poetry, appeared to be on a fatal downward spiral.

Bishop's life changed dramatically in 1951, when she won a traveling fellowship from Bryn Mawr College. She had originally planned to sail around the world, but only got as far as Rio de Janeiro, where she was stricken by a near-fatal allergic reaction to a cashew fruit. A Brazilian friend, the wealthy architect and city planner Lota de Macedo Soares, nursed her back to health. The two women became lovers, and Bishop stayed on in Brazil for the next sixteen years. While living with Soares in Petrópolis—and later in the mountain village of Ouro Prêto—Bishop managed to control her drinking and wrote many of her most celebrated poems, including "At the Fishhouses," about her Nova Scotia childhood, and the exuberant "Invitation to Miss Marianne Moore." Her second poetry collection, *A Cold Spring*, appeared in 1955; *The Diary of "Helena Morley,"* her translation of a nineteenth-century Brazilian girl's journal, in 1957; and *Questions of Travel*, a collection of Brazilian poems dedicated to Lota, in 1965.

The idyll came to an end when Soares—herself suffering from depression and overwork—committed suicide in 1967. A period of emotional chaos ensued, during which Bishop (with a new young American lover) shuttled back and forth between the United States and Brazil. Without Soares, however, her relations with the Ouro Prêto villagers deteriorated, and after the new lover broke with her in 1970, Bishop moved permanently back to the United States. The same year she won the National Book Award for her *Collected Poems* (1969) and accepted a teaching post at Harvard, which she held until her death in 1979. A May-December relationship with Alice Methfessel—her junior by thirty-three years—sustained her through her difficult last years, even as international recognition for her poetic achievements grew. Her final book of poems, *Geography III*, appeared in 1976; she died of a cerebral aneurism three years later.

Toward the end of her life—put off by the radical wing of the burgeoning feminist movement—Bishop refused to allow her poems be included in poetry collections devoted exclusively to women poets. Were she alive today, she would undoubtedly be appalled at being categorized as a *lesbian* poet. Yet such a poet—among many other things—she was. "It Is Marvelous To Wake Up Together"—written during her Key West period but unpublished until the 1980s—is one of her lesbian love poems. Like all of her poems, it is secretive, disturbing, and extraordinarily beautiful.

FURTHER READING: Elizabeth Bishop, *The Complete Poems 1927–1979* (New York: Farrar, Straus and Giroux, 1979); —, *The Collected Prose*, ed. Robert Giroux (New York: Farrar, Straus and Giroux, 1984); Adrienne Rich, "The Eye of the Outsider: Elizabeth Bishop's *Complete Poems*," in *Blood, Bread, and Poetry: Selected Prose 1979–1985* (New York: Norton, 1986); Thomas Travisano, *Elizabeth Bishop: Her Artistic Development* (Charlottesville: University Press of Virginia, 1988); David Kalstone, *Becoming a Poet: Elizabeth Bishop with Marianne Moore and Robert Lowell* (New York: Farrar, Straus and Giroux, 1989); Bonnie Costello, *Elizabeth Bishop: Questions of Mastery* (Cambridge: Harvard University Press, 1991); Lloyd Schwartz "Annals of Poetry (Elizabeth Bishop and Brazil)," *New Yorker*, 30 September 1991, pp. 85–97; Lorrie Goldensohn, *Elizabeth Bishop: The Biography of a Poetry* (New York: Columbia University Press, 1992); Victoria Harrison, *Elizabeth Bishop's Poetics of Intimacy* (Cambridge: Cambridge University Press, 1993); Brett C. Millier, *Elizabeth Bishop: Life and the Memory of It* (Berkeley and Los Angeles: University of California Press, 1993); Carmen L. Oliveira, *Rare and Commonplace Flowers: The Story of Elizabeth Bishop and Lota de Macedo Soares*, trans. Neil K. Besner (New Brunswick, N.J.: Rutgers University Press, 2002).

It is marvellous to wake up together
At the same minute; marvelous to hear
The rain begin suddenly all over the roof,
To feel the air suddenly clear
As if electricity had passed through it

From a black mesh of wires in the sky.
All over the roof rain hisses,
And below, the light falling of kisses.

An electrical storm is coming or moving away;
It is the prickling air that wakes us up.
If lightning struck the house now, it would run
From the four blue china balls on top
Down the roof and down the rods all around us,
And we imagine dreamily
How the whole house caught in a bird-cage of lightning
Would be quite delightful rather than frightening;

And from the same simplified point of view
Of night and lying flat on one's back
All things might change, equally easily,
Since always to warn us there are these black
Electrical wires dangling. Without surprise
The world might change to something quite different,
As the air changes or the lightning comes without our blinking
Change as our kisses are changing without our thinking.

JANE BOWLES (1917–1973)

From *Two Serious Ladies* (1943); "Going to Massachusetts" (1966)

The gifted American writer Jane Auer Bowles was born into a well-to-do middle-class Jewish family in New York City and raised in Long Island. Early traumas undoubtedly contributed to her lifelong battles with alcoholism and emotional instability: her father died when she was thirteen; a horseriding accident two years later left her permanently lame. In 1934, after two years in a Swiss sanatorium, Bowles returned to New York and began frequenting the bars and clubs of Greenwich Village, where she became notorious for her bohemian excesses. Her first literary work—now lost—was an abortive novel in French, *Le Phaéton hypocrite*. In 1937 she met the writer and composer Paul Bowles and married him the following year. Over the next decade they traveled widely in Europe and Central America. She and Bowles were both homosexual, she promiscuously so; each tolerated the other's same-sex partners. Her first important postmarital love affair was with Helvetia Perkins, a divorced woman whom she met in Mexico in 1940. In 1948 Bowles left Helvetia and went to Tangiers with her husband, where she stayed for most of the next decade. While living in Morocco, she took up with an illiterate, sometimes violent Arab woman named Cherifa, who both brutalized and attracted her.

Bowles's longest piece of fiction, the experimental novel *Two Serious Ladies*, appeared, to mixed reviews, in 1943. In the same decade she also published several memorable short stories ("A Guatemalan Idyll," "Camp Cataract," "Day in the Open" and "Plain Pleasures"), a puppet play entitled *A Quarreling Pair* (1945), and the first act of a play, *In the Summer House*, which was subsequently staged in Michigan and New York in 1953. But despite the growing critical acclaim her work received, writing did not come easily to her. She frequently said that without her husband's editorial help she would have written little; later in life, in Morocco, she was afflicted by increasingly severe writing blocks and phobias. After she suffered a stroke in 1957, her mental and physical health began to decline precipitously. Over the next fifteen years she drank to excess and was in and out of hospitals in England and Spain. In 1970 another stroke left her comatose and blind. She lived on for three more years, tended by nuns at a convent hospital in Málaga, where she died in 1973.

Like that of Djuna Barnes, Bowles's fiction is a curious mixture of the comic, the tragic, and the squalid. Part of its strangeness (again as in Barnes) is due the fact that female homosexuality is a central narrative concern but seldom draws any explicit authorial comment. In the excerpt below from *Two Serious Ladies*, the diffident Mrs. Copperfield, traveling with her husband in Panama, falls in love with an Indian woman, Pacifica, when Pacifica teaches her to swim. Yet the motivation behind this improbable coupling is never explained. Similarly, in Bowles's abandoned novel from the 1950s, *Going to Massachusetts*, the hapless Bozoe, Janet, and Sis McEvoy play out what is clearly a homosexual love triangle even as the meaning of their actions remains opaque. The result for the reader is an odd kind of seduction: we are drawn in by the surreal matter-of-factness of it all, even as the eccentricities—narrative and psychological— pile up.

FURTHER READING: Jane Bowles, *Two Serious Ladies* (New York: Knopf, 1943); —, *In the Summer House*, in Louis Kronenberger, ed., *Best Plays of 1953–1954* (New York: Dodd, Mead, 1954); —, *The Collected Works of Jane Bowles* (New York: Farrar, Straus and Giroux, 1966); —, *My Sister's Hand in Mine: An Expanded Edition of the Collected Work of Jane Bowles* (New York: Ecco, 1978); Paul Bowles, *Without Stopping* (New York: Putnam's, 1972); Millicent Dillon, *A Little Original Sin: The Life and Work of Jane Bowles* (New York: Holt, Rinehart and Winston, 1981); —, "Jane Bowles: Experiment as Character," in Ellen G. Friedman and Miriam Fuchs, eds., *Breaking the Sequence: Women's Experimental Fiction* (Princeton: Princeton University Press, 1989), pp. 140–47; Robert Lougy, "The World and Art of Jane Bowles (1917–1973)," *CEA Critic* 49 (1986/87): 157–73; Andrew M. Lakritz, "Jane Bowles's Other World," in Laura L. Doan, ed., *Old Maids to Radical Spinsters: Unmarried Women in the Twentieth-Century Novel* (Urbana: University of Illinois Press, 1991), pp. 213–34; Edouard Roditi, "The Fiction of Jane Bowles as a Form of Self-Exorcism," *Review of Contemporary Fiction* 12 (1992): 182–94; Kathy Justice Gentile, "'The Dreaded Voyage into the World': Jane Bowles and Her Serious Ladies," *Studies in American Fiction* (Carbondale: Southern Illinois University Press, 1997); —, "The Legend of Jane Bowles: Stories of the Female Avant-Garde," *Texas Studies in Literature and Language* 41 (1999): 262–79; George Toles, "The Toy Madness of Jane Bowles," *Arizona Quarterly* 54 (1998): 83–110.

From *Two Serious Ladies*

Early the next morning Mrs. Copperfield and Pacifica were together in Pacifica's bedroom. The sky was beginning to grow light. Mrs. Copperfield had never seen Pacifica this drunk. Her hair was pushed up on her head. It looked now somewhat like a wig which is a little too small for the wearer. Her pupils were very large and slightly filmed.

There was a large dark spot on the front of her checked skirt, and her breath smelled very strongly of whisky. She stumbled over to the window and looked out. It was quite dark in the room. Mrs. Copperfield could barely discern the red and purple squares in Pacifica's skirt. She could not see her legs at all, the shadows were so deep, but she knew the heavy yellow silk stockings and the white sneakers well.

"It's so lovely," said Mrs. Copperfield.

"Beautiful," said Pacifica, turning around, "beautiful." She moved unsteadily around the room. "Listen," she said, "the most wonderful thing to do now is to go to the beach and swim in the water. If you have enough money we can take a taxicab and go. Come on. Will you?"

Mrs. Copperfield was very startled indeed, but Pacifica was already pulling a blanket from the bed. "Please," she said. "You cannot know how much pleasure this would give me. You must take that towel over there."

The beach was not very far away. When they arrived, Pacifica told the cab-driver to come back in two hours.

The shore was strewn with rocks; this was a disappointment to Mrs. Copperfield. Although the wind was not very strong, she noticed that the top branches of the palm trees were shaking.

Pacifica took her clothes off and immediately walked into the water. She stood for a time with her legs wide apart, the water scarcely reaching to her shins, while Mrs. Copperfield sat on a rock trying to decide whether or not to remove her own clothes. There was a sudden splash and Pacifica started to swim. She swam first on her back and then on her stomach, and Mrs. Copperfield was certain that she could hear her singing. When at last Pacifica grew tired of splashing about in the water, she stood up and walked towards the beach. She took tremendous strides and her pubic hair hung between her legs sopping wet. Mrs. Copperfield looked a little embarrassed, but Pacifica plopped down beside her and asked her why she did not come in the water.

"I can't swim," said Mrs. Copperfield.

Pacifica looked up at the sky. She could see now that it was not going to be a completely fair day.

"Why do you sit on that terrible rock?" said Pacifica. "Come, take your clothes off and we go in the water. I will teach you to swim."

"I was never able to learn."

"I will teach you. If you cannot learn I will let you sink. No, this is only a joke. Don't take it serious."

Mrs. Copperfield undressed. She was very white and thin, and her spine was visible all the way along her back. Pacifica looked at her body without saying a word.

"I know I have an awful figure," said Mrs. Copperfield.

Pacifica did not answer. "Come," she said, getting up and putting her arm around Mrs. Copperfield's waist.

They stood with the water up to their thighs, facing the beach and the palm trees. The trees appeared to be moving behind a mist. The beach was colorless. Behind them the sky was growing lighter very rapidly, but the sea was still almost black. Mrs. Copperfield noticed a red fever sore on Pacifica's lip. Water was dripping from her hair onto her shoulders.

She turned away from the beach and pulled Mrs. Copperfield farther out into the water.

Mrs. Copperfield held onto Pacifica's hand very hard. Soon the water was up to her chin.

"Now lie on your back. I will hold you under your head," said Pacifica.

Mrs. Copperfield looked around wildly, but she obeyed, and floated on her back with only the support of Pacifica's open hand under her head to keep her from sinking. She could see her own narrow feet floating on top of the water. Pacifica started to swim, dragging Mrs. Copperfield along with her. As she had only the use of one arm, her task was an arduous one and she was soon breathing like a bull. The touch of her hand underneath the head of Mrs. Copperfield was very light—in fact, so light that Mrs. Copperfield feared that she would be left alone from one minute to the next. She looked up. The sky was packed with gray clouds. She wanted to say something to Pacifica, but she did not dare to turn her head.

Pacifica swam a little farther inland. Suddenly she stood up and placed both her hands firmly in the small of Mrs. Copperfield's back. Mrs. Copperfield felt happy and sick at once. She turned her face and in so doing she brushed Pacifica's heavy stomach with her cheek. She held on hard to Pacifica's thigh with the strength of years of sorrow and frustration in her hand.

"Don't leave me," she called out.

At this moment Mrs. Copperfield was strongly reminded of a dream that had recurred often during her life. She was being chased up a short hill by a dog. At the top of the hill there stood a few pine trees and a mannequin about eight feet high. She approached the mannequin and discovered her to be fashioned out of flesh, but without life. Her dress was of black velvet, and tapered to a very narrow width at the hem. Mrs. Copperfield wrapped one of the mannequin's arms tightly around her own waist. She was startled by the thickness of the arm and very pleased. The mannequin's other arm she bent upward from the elbow with her free hand. Then the mannequin began to sway backwards and forwards. Mrs. Copperfield clung all the more tightly to the mannequin and together they fell off the top of the hill and continued rolling for quite a distance until they landed on a little walk, where they remained locked in each other's arms. Mrs. Copperfield loved this part of the dream best; and the fact that all the way down the hill the mannequin acted as a buffer between herself and the broken bottles and little stones over which they fell gave her particular satisfaction.

Pacifica had resurrected the emotional content of her dream for a moment, which Mrs. Copperfield thought was certainly the reason for her own peculiar elation.

"Now," said Pacifica, "if you don't mind I will take one more swim by myself." But first she helped Mrs. Copperfield to her feet and led her back to the beach, where Mrs. Copperfield collapsed on the sand and hung her head like a wilted flower. She was trembling and exhausted as one is after a love experience. She looked up at Pacifica, who noticed that her eyes were more luminous and softer than she had ever seen them before.

"You should go in the water more," said Pacifica; "you stay in the house too much."

She ran back into the water and swam back and forth many times. The sea was now blue and much rougher than it had been earlier. Once during the course of her swimming Pacifica rested on a large flat rock which the outgoing tide had uncovered. She was directly in the line of the hazy sun's pale rays. Mrs. Copperfield had a difficult time being able to see her at all and soon she fell asleep.

"Going to Massachusetts"

Bozoe rubbed away some tears with a closed fist.

"Come on, Bozoe," said Janet. "You're not going to the North Pole."

Bozoe tugged at the woolly fur, and pulled a little of it out.

"Leave your coat alone," said Janet.

"I don't remember why I'm going to Massachusetts," Bozoe moaned. "I knew it would be like this, once I got to the station."

"If you don't want to go to Massachusetts," said Janet, "then come on back to the apartment. We'll stop at Fanny's on the way. I want to buy those tumblers made out of knobby glass. I want brown ones."

Bozoe started to cry in earnest. This caused Janet considerable embarrassment. She was conscious of herself as a public figure because the fact that she owned and ran a garage had given her a good deal of publicity not only in East Clinton but in the neighboring counties. This scene, she said to herself, makes us look like two Italians saying goodbye. Everybody'll think we're Italians. She did not feel true sympathy for Bozoe. Her sense of responsibility was overdeveloped, but she was totally lacking in real tenderness.

"There's no reason for you to cry over a set of whiskey tumblers," said Janet. "I told you ten days ago that I was going to buy them."

"Passengers boarding Bus Number Twenty-seven, north-bound. . . ."

"I'm not crying about whiskey tumblers." Bozoe managed with difficulty to get the words out. "I'm crying about Massachusetts. I can't remember my reasons."

"Rockport, Rayville, Muriel. . . ."

"Why don't you listen to the loudspeaker, Bozoe? It's giving you information. If you paid attention to what's going on around you you'd be a lot better off. You concentrate too much on your own private affairs. Try more to be a part of the world."

"*. . . The truth is that I am only twenty-five miles away from the apartment, as you have probably guessed. In fact, you could not help but guess it, since you are perfectly familiar with Larry's Bar and Grill. I could not go to Massachusetts. I cried the whole way up to Muriel and it was as if someone else were getting off the bus, not myself. But someone who was in* *a desperate hurry to reach the next stop. I was in mortal terror that the bus would not stop at Muriel but continue on to some further destination where I would not know any familiar face. My terror was so great that I actually stopped crying. I kept from crying all the way. That is a lie. Not an actual lie because I never lie as you know. Small solace to either one of us, isn't it? I am sure that you would prefer me to lie, rather than be so intent on explaining my dilemma to you night and day. I am convinced that you would prefer me to lie. It would give you more time for the garage."*

"So?" queried Sis McEvoy, an unkind note in her voice. To Janet she did not sound noticeably unkind, since Sis McEvoy was habitually sharp-sounding, and like her had very little sympathy for other human beings. She was sure that Sis McEvoy was bad, and she was determined to save her. She was going to save her quietly without letting Sis suspect her determination. Janet did everything secretly; in fact, secrecy was the essence of her nature, and from it she derived her pleasure and her sense of being an important member of society.

"What's it all about?" Sis asked irritably. "Why doesn't she raise kids or else go to a psychologist or a psychoanalyst or whatever? My ovaries are crooked or I'd raise kids myself. That's what God's after, isn't it? Space ships or no space ships. What's the problem, anyway? How are her ovaries and the rest of the mess?"

Janet smiled mysteriously. "Bozoe has never wanted a child," she said. "She told me she was too scared."

"Don't you despise cowards?" said Sis. "Jesus Christ, they turn my stomach."

Janet frowned. "Bozoe says she despises cowards, too. She worries herself sick about it. She's got it all linked up together with Heaven and Hell. She thinks so much about Heaven and Hell that she's useless. I've told her for years to occupy herself. I've told her that God would like her better if she was occupied. But she says God isn't interested. That's a kind of slam at me, I suppose. At me and the garage. She's got it in for the garage. It doesn't bother me, but it makes me a little sore when she tries to convince me that I wouldn't be interested in the garage unless she talked to me day and night about her troubles. As if I was interested in the garage just out of spite. I'm a normal woman and I'm interested in my work, like all women are in modern times. I'm a little stockier than most, I guess, and not fussy or feminine. That's because my father was my ideal and my mother was an alcoholic. I'm stocky and I don't like pretty dresses and I'm interested in my work. My work is like God to me. I don't mean I put it above Him, but the next thing to Him. I have a feeling that he approves of my working. That he approves of my working in a garage. Maybe that's cheeky of me, but I can't help it. I've made a name for myself in the garage and I'm decent. I'm normal." She paused for a moment to fill the two whiskey tumblers.

"Do you like my whiskey tumblers?" She was being unusually spry and talkative. "I don't usually have much time to buy stuff. But I had to, of course. Bozoe never bought anything in her life. She's what you'd call a dead weight. She's getting fatter, too, all the time."

"They're good tumblers," said Sis McEvoy. "They hold a lot of whiskey."

Janet flushed slightly at the compliment. She attributed the unaccustomed excitement she felt to her freedom from the presence of Bozoe Flanner.

"Bozoe was very thin when I first knew her," she told Sis. "And she didn't show any signs that she was going to sit night and day making up problems and worrying about God and asking me questions. There wasn't any of that in the beginning. Mainly she was meek, I guess, and she had soft-looking eyes, like a doe or a calf. Maybe she had the problems the whole time and was just planning to spring them on me later. I don't know. I never thought she was going to get so tied up in knots, or so fat either. Naturally if she were heavy and happy too it would be better."

"I have no flesh on my bones at all," said Sis McEvoy, as if she had not even heard the rest of the conversation. "The whole family's thin, and every last one of us has a rotten lousy temper inherited from both sides. My father and my mother had rotten tempers."

"I don't mind if you have a temper display in my apartment," said Janet. "Go to it. I believe in people expressing themselves. If you've inherited a temper there isn't much you can do about it except express it. I think it's much better for you to break this crockery pumpkin, for instance, than to hold your temper in and become unnatural. For instance, I could buy another pumpkin and you'd feel relieved. I'd gather that, at any rate. I don't know much about people, really. I never dabbled in people. They were never my specialty. But surely if you've inherited a temper from both sides it would seem to me that you would have to express it. It isn't your fault, is it, after all?" Janet seemed determined to show admiration for Sis McEvoy.

"I'm having fun," she continued unexpectedly. "It's a long time since I've had any fun. I've been too busy getting the garage into shape. Then there's Bozoe trouble. I've kept to the routine. Late Sunday breakfast with popovers and home-made jam. She eats maybe six of them, but with the same solemn expression on her face. I'm husky but a small eater. We have record players and television. But nothing takes her mind off herself. There's no point in my getting any more machines. I've got the cash and the good will, but there's absolutely no point."

"You seem to be very well set up," said Sis McEvoy, narrowing her eyes. "Here's to you." She tipped her glass and drained it.

Janet filled Sister's glass at once. "I'm having a whale of a good time," she said. "I hope you are. Of course I don't want to butt into your business. Bozoe always thought I pored over my account books for such a long time on purpose. She thought I was purposely trying to get away from her. What do you think, Sis McEvoy?" She asked this almost in a playful tone that bordered on a yet unexpressed flirtatiousness.

"I'm not interested in women's arguments with each other," said Sis at once. "I'm interested in women's arguments with men. What else is there? The rest doesn't amount to a row of monkeys."

"Oh, I agree," Janet said, as if she were delighted by this statement which might supply her with the stimulus she was after. "I agree one thousand percent. Remember I spend more time in the garage with the men than I do with Bozoe Flanner."

"I'm not actually living with my husband because of my temper," said Sis. "I don't like long-standing relationships. They disagree with me. I get the blues. I don't want anyone staying in my life for a long time. It gives me the creeps. Men are crazy about me. I like the cocktails and the compliments. Then after a while they turn my stomach."

"You're a very interesting woman," Janet Murphy announced, throwing caution to the winds and finding it pleasant.

"I know I'm interesting," said Sis. "But I'm not so sure life is interesting."

"Are you interested in money?" Janet asked her. "I don't mean money for the sake of money, but for buying things."

Sis did not answer, and Janet feared that she had been rude. "I didn't mean to hurt your feelings," she said. "After all, money comes up in everybody's life. Even duchesses have to talk about money. But I won't, any more. Come on. Let's shake." She held out her hand to Sis McEvoy, but Sis allowed it to stay there foolishly, without accepting the warm grip Janet had intended for her.

"I'm really sorry," she went on, "if you think I was trying to be insulting and personal. I honestly was not. The fact is that I have been so busy building up a reputation for the garage that I behave like a savage. I'll never mention money again." In her heart she felt that Sis was somehow pleased that the subject had been brought up, but was not yet ready to admit it. Sis's tedious work at the combination tearoom and soda fountain where they had met could scarcely make her feel secure.

Bozoe doesn't play one single feminine trick, she told herself, and after all, after struggling nearly ten years to build up a successful and unusual business I'm entitled to some returns. I'm in a rut with Bozoe and this Sis is going to get me out of it. (By now she was actually furious with Bozoe.) I'm entitled to some fun. The men working for me have more fun than I have.

"I feel grateful to you, Sis," she said without explaining her remark. "You've done me a service. May I tell you that I admire your frankness, without offending you?"

Sis McEvoy was beginning to wonder if Janet were another nut like Bozoe Flanner. This worried her a little, but she was too drunk by now for clear thinking. She was enjoying the compliments, although it was disturbing that they should be coming from a woman. She was very proud of never having been depraved or abnormal, and pleased to be merely mean and discontented to the extent of not having been able to stay with any man for longer than the three months she had spent with her husband.

"I'll read you more of Bozoe's letter," Janet suggested.

"I can't wait," said Sis. "I can't wait to hear a lunatic's mind at work first-hand. Her letter's so cheerful and elevating. And so constructive. Go to it. But fill my glass first so I can concentrate. I'd hate to miss a word. It would kill me."

Janet realized that it was unkind of her to be reading her friend's letter to someone who so obviously had only contempt for it. But she felt no loyalty—only eagerness to make Sis see how hard her life had been. She felt that in this way the bond between them might be strengthened.

"Well, here it comes," she said. "Stop me when you can't stand it any more. *I know that you expected me to come back. You did not feel I had the courage to carry out my scheme. I still expect to work it out. But not yet. I am more than ever convinced that my salvation lies in solitude, and coming back to the garage before I have even reached Massachusetts would be a major defeat for me, as I'm sure you must realize, even though you pretend not to know what I'm talking about most of the time. I am convinced that you do know what I'm talking about and if you pretend ignorance of my dilemma so you can increase efficiency at the garage you are going to defeat yourself. I can't actually save you, but I can point little things out to you constantly. I refer to your soul, naturally, and not to any success you've had or to your determination. In any case it came to me on the bus that it was not time for me to leave you, and that although going to Massachusetts required more courage and strength than I seemed able to muster, I was at the same time being very selfish in going. Selfish because I was thinking in terms of my salvation and not yours. I'm glad I thought of this. It is why I stopped crying and got off the bus. Naturally you would disapprove, because I had paid for my ticket which is now wasted, if for no other reason. That's the kind of thing you like me to think about, isn't it? It makes you feel that I'm more human. I have never admired being human, I must say. I want to be like God. But I haven't begun yet. First I have to go to Massachusetts and be alone. But I got off the bus. And I've wasted the fare. I can hear you stressing that above all else, as I say. But I want you to understand that it was not cowardice alone that stopped me from going to Massachusetts. I don't feel that I can allow you to sink into the mire of contentment and happy ambitious enterprise. It is my duty to prevent you from it as much as I do for myself. It is not fair of me to go away until you completely understand how I feel about God and my destiny. Surely we have been brought together for some purpose, even if that purpose ends by our being separate again. But not until the time is ripe. Naturally, the psychiatrists would at once declare that I was laboring under a compulsion. I am violently against psychiatry, and, in fact, against happiness. Though of course I love it. I love happiness, I mean. Of course you would not believe this. Naturally darling I love you, and I'm afraid that if you don't start suffering soon God will take some terrible vengeance. It is better for you to offer yourself. Don't accept social or financial security as your final aim. Or fame in the garage. Fame is unworthy of you; that is, the desire for it. Janet, my beloved, I do not expect you to be gloomy or fanatical as I am. I do not believe that God intended you for quite as harrowing a destiny as He did for me. I don't mean this as an insult. I believe you should actually thank your stars. I would really like to be fulfilling humble daily chores myself and listening to a concert at night or television or playing a card game. But I can find no rest, and I don't think you should either. At least not until you have fully understood my dilemma on earth. That means that you must no longer turn a deaf ear to me and pretend that your preoccupation with the garage is in a sense a holier absorption than trying to understand and fully realize the importance and meaning of my dilemma. I think that you hear more than you admit, too. There is a stubborn streak in your nature working against you, most likely unknown to yourself. An insistence on being shallow rather than profound. I repeat: I do not expect you to be as profound as I am. But to insist on exploiting the most shal-*

low side of one's nature, out of stubbornness and merely because it is more pleasant to be
shallow, is certainly a sin. Sis McEvoy will help you to express the shallow side of your
nature, by the way. Like a toboggan slide."

Janet stopped abruptly, appalled at having read this last part aloud. She had not
expected Bozoe to mention Sis at all. "Gee," she said. "Gosh! She's messing everything
up together. I'm awfully sorry."

Sis McEvoy stood up and walked unsteadily to the television set. Some of her drink
slopped onto the rug as she went. She faced Janet with fierce eyes. "There's nobody in
the world who can talk to me like that, and there's not going to be. Never!" She was
leaning on the set and steadying herself against it with both hands. "I'll keep on building double-decker sandwiches all my life first. It's five flights to the top of the building
where I live. It's an insurance building, life insurance, and I'm the only woman who
lives there. I have boy friends come when they want to. I don't have to worry, either.
I'm crooked so I don't have to bother with abortions or any other kind of mess. The
hell with television anyway."

She likes the set, Janet said to herself. She felt more secure. "Bozoe and I don't have
the same opinions at all," she said. "We don't agree on anything."

"Who cares? You live in the same apartment, don't you? You've lived in the same
apartment for ten years. Isn't that all anybody's got to know?" She rapped with her fist
on the wood panelling of the television set. "Whose is it, anyhow?" She was growing
increasingly aggressive.

"It's mine," Janet said. "It's my television set." She spoke loud so that Sis would
be sure to catch her words.

"What the hell do I care?" cried Sis. "I live on top of a life-insurance building and
I work in a combination soda-fountain lunch-room. Now read me the rest of the letter."

"I don't think you really want to hear any more of Bozoe's nonsense," Janet said
smoothly. "She's spoiling our evening together. There's no reason for us to put up with
it all. Why should we? Why don't I make something to eat? Not a sandwich. You must
be sick of sandwiches."

"What I eat is my own business," Sis snapped.

"Naturally," said Janet. "I thought you might like something hot like bacon and
eggs. Nice crisp bacon and eggs." She hoped to persuade her so that she might forget
about the letter.

"I don't like food," said Sis. "I don't even like millionaires' food, so don't waste
your time."

"I'm a small eater myself." She had to put off reading Bozoe's letter until Sis had
forgotten about it. "My work at the garage requires some sustenance, of course. But it's
brainwork now more than manual labor. Being a manager's hard on the brain."

Sis looked at Janet and said: "Your brain doesn't impress me. Or that garage. I like
newspaper men. Men who are champions. Like champion boxers. I've known lots of
champions. They take to me. Champions all fall for me, but I'd never want any of them
to find out that I knew someone like your Bozoe. They'd lose their respect."

"I wouldn't introduce Bozoe to a boxer either, or anybody else who was interested in sports. I know they'd be bored. I know." She waited. "You're very nice. Very intelligent. You *know* people. That's an asset."

"Stay with Bozoe and her television set," Sis growled.

"It's not her television set. It's mine, Sis. Why don't you sit down? Sit on the couch over there."

"The apartment belongs to both of you, and so does the set. I know what kind of a couple you are. The whole world knows it. I could put you in jail if I wanted to. I could put you and Bozoe both in jail."

In spite of these words she stumbled over to the couch and sat down. "Whiskey," she demanded. "The world loves drunks but it despises perverts. Athletes and boxers drink when they're not in training. All the time."

Janet went over to her and served her a glass of whiskey with very little ice. Let's hope she'll pass out, she said to herself. She couldn't see Sis managing the steps up to her room in the insurance building, and in any case she didn't want her to leave. She's such a relief after Bozoe, she thought. Alive and full of fighting spirit. She's much more my type, coming down to facts. She thought it unwise to go near Sis, and was careful to pour the fresh drink quickly and return to her own seat. She would have preferred to sit next to Sis, in spite of her mention of jail, but she did not relish being punched or smacked in the face. It's all Bozoe's fault, she said to herself. That's what she gets for thinking she's God. Her holy words can fill a happy peaceful room with poison from twenty-five miles away.

"I love my country," said Sis, for no apparent reason. "I love it to death!"

"Sure you do, Hon," said Janet. "I could murder Bozoe for upsetting you with her loony talk. You were so peaceful until she came in."

"Read that letter," said Sister. After a moment she repeated, as if from a distance: "Read the letter."

Janet was perplexed. Obviously food was not going to distract Sis, and she had nothing left to suggest, in any case, but some Gorton's Codfish made into cakes, and she did not dare to offer her these.

What a rumpus that would raise, she said to herself. And if I suggest turning on the television she'll raise the roof. Stay off television and codfish cakes until she's normal again. Working at a lunch counter is no joke.

There was nothing she could do but do as Sis told her and hope that she might fall asleep while she was reading her the letter. "Damn Bozoe anyway," she muttered audibly.

"Don't put on any acts," said Sis, clearly awake. "I hate liars and I always smell an act. Even though I didn't go to college. I have no respect for college."

"I didn't go to college," Janet began, hoping Sis might be led on to a new discussion. "I went to commercial school."

"Shut up, God damn you! Nobody ever tried to make a commercial school sound like an interesting topic except you. Nobody! You're out of your mind. Read the letter."

"Just a second," said Janet, knowing there was no hope for her. "Let me put my glasses on and find my place. Doing accounts at the garage year in and year out has ruined my eyes. My eyes used to be perfect." She added this last weakly, without hope of arousing either sympathy or interest.

Sis did not deign to answer.

"Well, here it is again," she began apologetically. "Here it is in all its glory." She poured a neat drink to give herself courage. *"As I believe I just wrote you, I have been down to the bar and brought a drink back with me. (One more defeat for me, a defeat which is of course a daily occurrence, and I daresay I should not bother to mention it in this letter.) In any case I could certainly not face being without one after the strain of actually boarding the bus, even if I did get off without having the courage to stick on it until I got where I was going. However, please keep in mind the second reason I had for stopping short of my destination. Please read it over carefully so that you will not have only contempt for me. The part about the responsibility I feel toward you. The room here over Larry's Bar and Grill is dismal. It is one of several rented out by Larry's sister whom we met a year ago when we stopped here for a meal. You remember. It was the day we took Stretch for a ride and let him out of the car to run in the woods, that scanty patch of woods you found just as the sun was setting, and you kept picking up branches that were stuck together with wet leaves and dirt. . . ."*

MARY RENAULT (1905-1983)

From *The Friendly Young Ladies* (1944)

The bestselling historical novelist Mary Renault—born Eileen Mary Challans—was the daughter of a London physician. After reading English at St. Hugh's College, Oxford, she too opted for a medical career and began training as a nurse. In the thirties she worked in a series of hospitals, ending up at the Winford Emergency Hospital in Bristol, where she worked briefly with Dunkirk evacuees following the outbreak of the Second World War an experience that she would draw upon later in her 1953 novel, *The Charioteer*. She met her lifelong companion, Julie Mullard, another nurse, in 1934.

Renault published her first novel, *Purposes of Love,* in 1939. Like all but one of her other early "English" novels—*Kind Are Her Answers* (1940), *The Friendly Young Ladies* (1944), *Return to Night* (1947), *North Face* (1948), and *The Charioteer*—it is set in a hospital and has to do with emotional complications between doctors, nurses, and patients. Though falling broadly into the category of romantic fiction, *Purposes of Love* already suggests an unconventional authorial personality at work—notably in the way Renault complicates the standard nurse-doctor love plot with curiously insistent homosexual subplots. Similar tensions also appear in the other "English" novels.

Only in the last of them, the aforementioned *Charioteer*, would Renault allow herself to focus on her emerging thematic obsession—same-sex love—openly and explicitly. Quite daringly for the time, she takes for her central character a sensitive young soldier named Laurie, palpably homosexual, who while recovering from wounds suffered in the Dunkirk evacuation falls in love with a conscientious objector serving as an orderly in the hospital.

Renault's new imaginative freedom seems to have come to her as a result of a striking professional coup. In 1948 her novel *Return to Night* won the $150,000 Metro-Goldwyn-Mayer Prize—a windfall that allowed her to leave off nursing. She and Mullard moved to South Africa, where Renault began writing full-time. And in a dramatic creative shift, she turned now to historical fiction—producing seven extraordinarily popular novels set in ancient Greece: *The Last of the Wine* (1956); *The King Must Die* (1958); *The Bull from the Sea* (1952); *The Mask of Apollo* (1966); *The Persian Boy* (1972); *The Praise Singer* (1978); and *Funeral Games* (1981). The Greek novels were immediately hailed for their historical sweep and realistic depiction of ancient society, including its idealization of sexual relationships between men. (Two of them deal with the life and loves of Alexander the Great—about whom Renault published a biography in 1975.) Not surprisingly, given the forthrightness with which she now embraced the homosexual theme, her fiction developed a huge following among gay readers—and gay men especially. As one recent biographer has put it, "the classical settings allowed Renault to mask material too explosive to deal with directly while simultaneously giving her a . . . freedom to write about subjects vital to her—among them war, peace, career, women's roles, female and male homosexuality, and bisexuality." When Renault died in 1983, she was one of the best-selling novelists in the world—precisely, one suspects, because she had found a way of imbuing once-taboo sexual topics with moral sophistication, historical complexity, and a colorful, empathic romance.

The Friendly Young Ladies (1944), published under the title *The Middle Mist* in the United States, is Renault's most "lesbian" work of fiction. Set in England in the 1930s, it depicts a relationship between Leo (Leonora), a tomboyish writer of cowboy romances, and Helen, a nurse-turned-medical illustrator, who live together in pleasant bohemian intimacy on a houseboat near London. Without spelling anything out, Renault makes it overwhelmingly clear the two women are lovers. Their idyll comes to an end, however, when with spectacular implausibility Leo falls in love with another writer living on the river, a young man named Joe. At novel's close, Leo and Joe (who seems himself to have homosexual leanings) make passionate love in a boathouse, then abruptly decamp for Arizona, where they intend to live happily ever after.

Writing about the novel in the 1980s, Renault admitted to the "silliness" of this heterosexual final twist. She had wanted, she said, to write a kind of anti–*Well of Loneliness*—a novel in which two women were shown living in joyful sexual amity, without guilt or self-recrimination—but got cold feet at the end. Nevertheless, despite its obvious plot flaws, *The Friendly Young Ladies* remains a fascinating work—comic, soigné, and marvelously "period" in its details. In the extract below, from the first half of the novel, Leo's sixteen-year-old sister Elsie, a timid and impressionable runaway, has taken refuge with Leo and Helen on the houseboat. Elsie is childishly infatuated with Peter Bracknell, a pompous, promiscuous, conceited young doctor who has counseled her—somewhat irresponsibly—to rebel against her parents. Peter—a Freudian know-it-all with no real interest in Elsie—is himself deeply titillated by the "abnormal" ménage of Leo and Helen and longs to break it up by seducing Leo. When he arrives at the houseboat one day, bringing with him Norah—a nurse from his hospital with whom he is having an affair—Leo and Helen, perturbed by his hypocrisy and heartlessness toward Elsie, conspire between them to humiliate him. While Helen keeps Peter otherwise engaged, Leo—rather in the manner of a cross-dressing heroine in Shakespearean comedy—takes Norah for a romantic canoe ride, much to the smug doctor's mortification. The vulnerable Elsie, naively unaware of the nature of the relationship between Leo and Helen, remains a somewhat befuddled observer to the proceedings.

FURTHER READING: Mary Renault, *Purposes of Love* (London: Longmans, 1939); —, *The Friendly Young Ladies* (1944; rpt. with Afterword by the author, New York: Pantheon, 1984); —, *Return to Night* (London: Longmans, 1947); —, *The Charioteer* (London: Longmans, 1953); —, *The King Must Die* (London: Longmans, 1958); —, "History in Fiction," *Times Literary Supplement*, March 23, 1973, pp. 315–16; —, *The Nature of Alexander* (London: Allen Lane, 1975); Peter Wolfe, *Mary Renault* (New York: Twayne, 1969); Bernard F. Dick, *The Hellenism of Mary Renault* (Carbondale: Southern Illinois University Press, 1972); Peter Green, "The Masks of Mary Renault," *New York Review of Books*, February 8, 1979, pp. 11–14; Claude J. Summers, *Gay Fiction: Wilde to Stonewall: Studies in a Male Homosexual Literary Tradition* (New York: Continuum, 1990); Terry Castle, *The Apparitional Lesbian: Female Homosexuality and Modern Culture* (New York: Columbia University Press, 1993); David Sweetman, *Mary Renault: A Biography* (London: Chatto and Windus, 1993); Erin G. Carlston, "Versatile Interests: Reading Bisexuality in *The Friendly Young Ladies*," in Donald E. Hall and Maria Pramaggiore, eds., *RePresenting Bisexualities: Subjects and Cultures of Fluid Desire* (New York: New York University Press, 1996), pp. 165–79; Ruth Hoberman, "Masquing the Phallus: Genital Ambiguity in Mary Renault's Historical Novels," *Twentieth-Century Literature* 2 (1996): 277–93; Caroline Zilboorg, *The Masks of Mary Renault: A Literary Biography* (Columbia: University of Missouri Press, 2001).

It was Helen who first saw the approach of the ferry-boat. She went up to tell Leo, who, because it was sunny and cool, was working on the roof, lying on her stomach with a cushion under her chest, a position not very favourable to writing but excellent for thought and for intervals of siesta.

"He seems to have someone with him." Helen, standing, was visible from midstream, and returned as she spoke the cheerful salutation which Peter waved to her.

"Really?" Leo levered herself up a little on her elbows. She had an equally good view from between the bars of the balustrade, which, however, screened her effectively from sight. "Well, what do you know?" she said inelegantly, "He's brought a bird along with him. His regular, by the looks of it. How rich." Shading her eyes against the light, she looked again. "A bit on the sturdy side, but quite nice, don't you think?"

"Elsie didn't tell me," said Helen thoughtfully, "that he was bringing anyone. I wonder if she knew."

"Oh, good God. Elsie." The suddenness of Leo's movement dislodged a sheet of manuscript which she saved, just in time, from blowing overboard. "No, but really, you know, this is the limit. Poor little devil. This isn't education, it's butchery."

"I expect," said Helen, "he means it all for the best. She has to wake up sooner or later, you know."

"But, damn it all. No, he ought to know better than this. It—it isn't civilized."

Leo's brows settled into a straight dark line. With sudden decision she said, "I'm not taking it."

"It looks," said Helen mildly, "as if none of us had much choice."

"Does it? I wonder" Leo propped her chin on her hands. Her eyes narrowed; a stranger might have thought her to be daydreaming.

"Think again," advised Helen. "Think several times. And then don't do it."

"Do what?" asked Leo absently.

"Anything you think of doing when you look like that. This is going to be embarrassing enough, without any sideshows from you."

Leo emerged from her meditations.

"Have we got any of that face-pack left?"

"I think so. But surely you—"

"Well, go and spread some on Elsie and make her lie down with it for twenty minutes. Do you want to change?"

"No, why? Is anything the matter with me?"

"You were never lovelier. But if you don't, run along and be there when they arrive, because I do."

"I don't fancy any of this. I don't like you when you behave badly."

"Really I won't. I'll be almost imperceptible. Go and do your stuff. Please. There's a honey."

Helen was unmoved by this, and by the smile which went with it. But the ferry-boat was nearly half-way across. She went, reluctantly.

"I'll show him," said Leo under her breath.

Elsie had just finished her face when Helen arrived in the room. Absorbed in the task, she had not noticed the boat in midstream. She had drawn a cupid's bow which overlapped the line of her mouth in three places, and had attempted to rouge her cheeks with her lipstick, the result being not quite symmetrical either in shape or shade. Seeing that it would all have to come off in any case, Helen reflected that the pack would make a good pretext without hurting her feelings. Elsie accepted it readily. In its cloudy pink jar it looked and smelt exotic, and she found in herself a curious lack of objection to the delay. It was pleasant to lie with the glossy film on her face, feeling it tighten and crackle interestingly here and there, knowing that by now Peter was probably here, within twenty yards of her, but freed from the responsibility of having to do anything but think beautifully about him. Now and again she would anticipate the moment when, all preparations over, she would go downstairs, open the door, be face to face with him; and her heart felt mixed uncomfortably with her diaphragm, both of them throbbing like machinery.

A footstep outside made her open her eyes, the only part of her face at her disposal. Leo was passing the open door, and had paused for a moment to look inside. What a number of clothes she had, thought Elsie, sighing. Here were still more she had never seen. Leo had on a plain cream shirt of dull heavy silk, beautifully cut, with the top button open; trousers of cambridge-blue linen with turn-ups and a knife-edge crease, a broad hogskin belt with two gilt buckles and sandals to match. She smiled encouragingly at Elsie, saying at the same time, "Don't move your face, you'll crack it." She looked quite dashing, thought Elsie (trying unsuccessfully to smile back without moving anything but her eyes) with that brown-gold make-up and russet lipstick. The whole outfit looked quite expensive; how odd to spend money on such things when one could have bought a really lovely frock. Leo waved to her, and went on downstairs.

Meanwhile, the ferry-boat had delivered its load. Peter effected introductions and apologies gracefully, but with that ghost of proprietorship which trickles through good manners, unaware, from the inward soul. Norah was evidently used to it. Helen felt for her, and took to her at once. She led them inside, and produced some beer.

"I've been telling Norah about your work," said Peter, "and she's very interested. We were hoping you'd show us some. Both the technical and the non-technical, of course."

"I don't do any non-technical work now," said Helen untruthfully. She was shy of her efforts, for her standard was high and self-critical, and she had a horror of appearing to pose as a serious artist; she had penetrated a few Bloomsbury backwaters in her day. Especially she did not intend to pose with the object of impressing Norah, who struck her as likeable and genuine. She brought out a file. "These are for a book on eye surgery, by Bryn-Davies. It's coming out next month."

"Bryn-Davies? Do you work for him?" Norah looked up, the last of her shyness gone. "I've taken his cases in the theatre sometimes. He was a houseman when I was training."

"You don't mean to tell me," said Helen, delighted, "that you trained at Hilary's? But this is marvellous. So did I."

"Not really? When did you leave? But I was actually there that year. . . . Not till October? . . . Oh, night duty, that accounts for it, of course. . . . On Kingston? Then do tell me, what was the real truth about that Meredith business? I was too new a pro. to hear the inside story."

Helen knew the inside story, and several others. Norah knew, and was delighted to relate, what had become of dear old Eliot and that bitch of a Sister Tutor. The drawings slipped to the floor, forgotten. Peter picked them up, and studied them with critical aloofness. The godfatherly benevolence he had felt at the start of the reunion was beginning to wear a little thin. He thought poorly of Hilary's, as a Jerome's man should, and Norah rarely mentioned it to him. This sort of thing, he felt, was well enough to set the ball rolling, but was outlasting its function. The number of people, of whom he had never heard, that Norah appeared to have known intimately before she met him, seemed unnecessary, even superfluous. He picked up another drawing, and scrutinized it austerely.

"The other way up," said Helen, interrupting her narrative to turn it over for him. "Well, after some weeks even Matron got to hear about it, so . . ."

"A friend of mine," said Peter with determination, "is thinking of writing a thesis on the psychopathy of matrons." He developed this idea, rather amusingly. They ran it along politely for two or three minutes, and, rounding a corner, were back at Hilary's again.

Behind the screen of the portfolio, Peter glanced unobtrusively at the door. Elsie was most uncharacteristically late. And Leo: could she be out? He had, after all, said that he was coming, so it seemed hardly credible. But he had barely been here ten minutes, though it seemed longer. More probably—much more probably—she was getting herself up a bit. He was seldom wrong in guesses of this kind.

He had scarcely formed the thought when a long light step, definitely not Elsie's, sounded outside. Peter buried himself in the portfolio. After her behaviour last time, he felt that a little initial reserve would not be out of place. He looked up just in time to catch the tail-end of a cursory smile and nod. Leo's eyes were already travelling on. Lounging debonairly in the doorway, in a pose that made the most of very good tailoring, she remained fixed for a moment, returning, under dark half-dropped lashes, Norah's fascinated gaze. Her own stare conveyed a calculated reticence, like that of a poker player trying, without complete success, to suppress his feelings at the sight of a straight flush, or of a bibliophile who has spotted a priceless first edition in a twopenny junk-box. Then, like one awaking from a momentary trance, she turned on Peter a face which was the most formal of interrogation-marks.

Up to this moment, Helen had been making up her mind to disapprove of Leo altogether. It was all somewhat excessive and transpontine, and, besides, she felt she had been managing very adequately on her own. But the brittle bonhomie of Peter's introduction, stretched so tenuously over a sulk, was too much for her sense of humour. He had asked, she decided, for what was coming to him. On Norah's account her qualms had disappeared; Norah was quite well able to look after herself, and would be none the worse for a little encouragement to do so. And, looked at from another point of view, her neck was slightly, but reassuringly, too thick. Necks were a matter on which Leo was fastidious.

Taking one thing with another, Helen decided to stand from under. She got up to dispense more drinks, leaving the seat beside Norah vacant.

Leo sank into it, giving her trouser-knees a neat hitch to ease the crease. As she settled herself, she sent Norah a private little smile, as who should say, "We managed that rather well, didn't we?"

Helen came to rest beside Peter, took up the drawings, and said with confiding charm, "Do these really interest you? The best ones are a little further down. Now here's something that really was rather fascinating to watch, though you've often seen it I dare say . . ."

Peter, his field of vision thus circumscribed by good manners, went through the motions of eager attention and shifted restlessly in his chair. His temper was not improved by a clink of glasses at the other side of the room, accompanied by Leo's voice saying, softly but audibly, "To our better acquaintance."

". . . and these," said Helen, "I did for an American who came over here. . . ." She described, in detail, the surgical procedure, contrasting English with American technique, and trustfully inviting Peter's opinion. Her deference would have been quite gratifying, at almost any different time.

Over in the other corner, things were going like a song. Not for nothing had Leo been meeting Helen's friends, in and out of hospital, for rather more than six years. The time being over-short for finesse, she led with the ace of trumps. "You know," she said, "if I hadn't heard you and Helen talking as I came in, I'd never have guessed, in a thousand years, that you were a nurse."

"Wouldn't you?" Norah's candid face warmed with pleasure. For reasons opaque to the lay mind, but crystal-clear to young women whose names appear on the State Register, she would have taken this for a compliment even if spoken in rebuke. As delivered by Leo, it was devastating. Peter himself had never paid her this tribute; though, as their acquaintanceship had ripened in the anaesthetic lobby of the theatre, the omission was reasonable.

"The great thing," she explained, "is to keep up some sort of life of your own outside the job. When you take to sitting about in uniform in your free time, you may as well be dead. Your friend," she added by way of a graceful return, "isn't at all obvious, either."

"That's why she's a friend of mine," said Leo simply. (To him that hath shall be given was, she had long since discovered, a good rule of thumb.) "I'm like you, I prefer untypical people. You and I are rampant individualists, I suppose. It's not fashionable, but it's a lot more fun. Don't you think so?"

Copying as far as possible Leo's air of negligence, Norah agreed that it was. Helen had judged her correctly; she was well supplied with good sense. Tactics of pursuit would have alarmed her as effectively as they would have bored Leo, who, in any case, rated them abysmally low—not merely vulgar, but amateurish, which was worse. In this case, two exclusive people had naturally drifted together. It worked like bird-lime. Norah had had [from Peter] more than two years of being improved; kindly, tactfully on the whole, amusingly sometimes, but unremittingly. Here was someone, clearly critical to a fault, who seemed not to think that any improvement was called for. It was immense.

"What are you laughing at?" she asked, further intrigued by a deep, *sotto voce* chuckle which Leo made no attempt to explain.

"Sorry. I was just thinking what an amusing time a person like you must have had in hospital. Subtly deflating those pompous sisters and so on. Though I suppose as a rule their hides are so thick you can't get through to them without being depressingly crude. Still, you must have had quite a lot of quiet fun all to yourself."

She had limned, with a few economical strokes, the secret self-portrait of four young nurses out of five. To Norah, such penetration on the part of an outsider seemed quite uncanny. She said, deprecatingly, "Well, you certainly would blow your brains out if you didn't give your sense of humour an airing now and again."

Shreds of this conversation drifted over to Helen, as she shuffled the drawings in search of another suited to exposition. She coughed convulsively into her handkerchief, got up, and made a solicitous fuss over the refilling of Peter's glass, which was only one third down.

"I don't know if orthopaedic surgery is at all in your line. . . ." There were quite a number of orthopaedic drawings, illustrations to a monograph. Helen made the most of them. She had, at last, no reason to complain of an abstracted audience. Peter had become, suddenly, all eyes and ears. His head had come several inches nearer, and his comments were accompanied by intimate little glances. They were received into a blanket of bland, innocent friendliness. Helen had had her share of admiration, unforced to the point of occasional embarrassment; she could well afford to be amused this time, and she was. A small convex glass on the wall enabled her to see, without looking round, that the effect was being sadly wasted in the proper quarter. She felt, for a moment, quite sorry for him; her tender heart was apt to be moved by the most temporary reverses. She even allowed him to collect up her fingers accidentally, along with one of the papers, and returned his pressure with a maternal little squeeze. Then "Hullo," she said over her shoulder. "Where are you people off to?"

Peter, who had not the advantage of the wall-mirror, had been preoccupied with the success of his outflanking move. He looked up. The position at which it had been directed was no longer there.

"Shan't be a minute," said Leo airily. "I'm just taking Norah to have a look at the canoe." They disappeared; Leo motioning Norah, with a slight but gallant gesture, to precede her through the door.

Peter gazed after them. There was a moment in which his jaw actually dropped; an unfortunate moment, for it was an expression which sat so incongruously on his face that it brought Helen's comic sense into play. She observed, with acute enjoyment, his rapid recovery, his thoughtful reorientation, and his too obvious resolve to make the best of a job which might turn out not to be so bad after all. The sound of a shy, hesitant step on the ladder cut short her entertainment; she had quite forgotten, for a while, that the performance had been a benefit one.

Elsie's timing, though unconscious, had been perfect. She hit the exact moment when Peter had re-concentrated all his charm for the new mise en scène. As she appeared in the doorway, Helen stooped to gather in her drawings, moving so briskly that Peter's best smile passed clean over her head. He received it back instead, from Elsie, in a pale tremulous reflection, like sunlight on a pool.

"Well," said Helen, getting up, "I really must be getting something done about the supper. I hope those two on the river won't go too far; but I suppose we shall have to risk having it a bit overdone, shan't we?" She smiled at him with the most innocent sociability. "Hullo, Elsie. You're just in time to look after the company while I'm gone."

She moved smoothly off. Helen never bustled. She could accomplish more than most people without the appearance of effort.

Elsie had Peter quite to herself for more than half an hour. He acquitted himself with what, in the circumstances, amounted to credit, and was never once unkind. The talk was not, perhaps, dynamic; but for this Elsie accepted, very readily, the whole responsibility. Like all shy people, she was used to conversations beginning to sag when she was called upon to support one end of them. Even with Peter it had happened sometimes before, though not for quite so long. She answered the questions he asked about her life and progress, and was saddened a little, but unsurprised, to find him not listening very attentively to the answers. She did not lose sight of the fact that in being thus tête-à-tête with him she was enjoying the highest felicity. But after ten minutes there was a strange intimation at the back of her mind that she had had it now, that she was already happy enough, that no more was necessary for the present. If, even, other people came in, and there were general conversation, it would not plunge her into despair. When, during a lengthy pause, Helen came to lay the table, she was conscious of something absurdly similar to relief, and jumped up to help in spite of Helen's assurance that there was really nothing to do. Here was the moment, she reaffirmed, on which her thoughts had been set for days; but now, in its very shadow, her mind had run ahead again, and she looked forward to she knew not what; to the next meeting or its anticipation; to sitting, this evening, and watching him quietly from a corner; even to looking back on it from the completed security of the past. For only precocity, or maturity, or unreconciled age are choked by biting off more than they can chew; to this, its natural exercise, youth is mercifully adapted, like childhood to green apples. Hunger is not so early awake; the taste and scent of love sustain, and, as with green apples, do it sometimes better than the substance. Cruelty and disillusion are the only untransmutable pains. For cruelty Elsie retained the instinct of a lingering childhood; against it her choice had guarded her safely enough. Disillusion had gone out the door just four minutes before she entered it. Peter's first smile, as she arrived, she had somehow felt at once contained happiness enough to last the evening; and, ever since, an instinct wiser than herself had been advising her not to ask for more. Shakespeare, she remembered (trying to excuse and understand the feeling), had been shy too, like an imperfect actor on the stage. To-morrow, next week, there would be miracles. To-day it was enough to expect them; meanwhile she trotted in and out of the kitchen, busied herself with a dozen small distractions, and brought Helen into the conversation whenever she could.

"Where's Leo?" she asked, as she collected plates from the dresser.

"Out in the canoe," said Helen, "with Norah Haynes. (The cheese is on the top shelf.) Norah trained with me at Hilary's. She and Peter came along together. Have you laid a place for her, by the way?"

"Oh, no," said Elsie cheerfully. "I didn't." She had just made good the deficiency when the canoe returned.

It was audible some minutes before it arrived, for just as it came within earshot, Norah had finished telling an amusing story, and Leo's delighted laugh, crackling like a boy's from deep to high, carried cleanly across the water. Peter, whose perfunctory offer to help had been swept aside, got the full benefit of it through the open door, and felt an uncomfortable prickling at the back of his neck. The whole episode, he decided, was of the sort best ignored by an adult mind. One could only regret that a woman of Norah's native intelligence could, after two years' acquaintance with real values, be capable of such a lapse into the third-rate. He would intimate this to her in due course; she was, at least, capable of taking a hint. Meanwhile . . .

The canoe coasted in towards the bank, kissing it neatly under Leo's practised hand. They were humming, as they landed, a verse of "Home on the Range," which they had been harmonizing further up the river.

> When the graceful white swan goes gliding along
> Like a maid in a heavenly dream. . . .

Elsie thought the soft voices, in the gathering dusk, romantically sweet and sad.

"We must meet again," said Leo, in the voice that means, You cannot step twice into the same river; better not try.

"Yes," said Norah, assenting both to the spoken courtesy and the unspoken truth. She was trying, half-heartedly, to imagine what she would think about all this to-morrow morning. It had been so light, so gracefully unreal, like an indiscretion at a masked ball. She gazed at Leo curiously, over the tie-rope of the canoe. One had thought, as far as one had previously thought at all, of thick women in starched evening shirts, and intense, shy-making confidences. . . . Norah found that, as after a moderate indulgence in champagne, little remained except a general impression that one had been unusually witty and charming, together with a feeling of light-hearted sophistication and no harm done. And indeed, anything that happens in a light canoe, even when moored, must needs be moderate enough.

Leo caught her eye and gave her a broad, outrageous, comprehensive wink.

"Come on in," she said, "and eat your supper like a good girl."

They were both blinking a little in the electric light indoors. Peter ignored Norah's entrance with quiet unobtrusive dignity; so it was Leo who introduced her to Elsie, in a manner which did nothing to alter Elsie's belief that she had been a friend of the household for years. Supper went quite well; for a party of four women and one man, who moreover contributed very little, it had almost a swing. Norah was in excellent form; she was feeling, in fact, rather full of herself, and Peter's disapproval, of which she was quite well aware, she found to her own secret surprise had no effect whatever on her spirits. She was conscious of being one up on him, a most unusual feeling and quite astonishingly satisfactory. For Elsie, it was the best part of the day. When Peter did talk, he talked mostly to her; but these desultory moments, while they uplifted, called for no effort, and the general talk freed her from any responsibility for bridging the intervals between. She could sink into herself, look at him now and again; remind herself that it was she whom he had come to see, a truth evident now beyond mistake and sufficient in itself. Helen's personality at the head of the table was like a bland fluid holding everyone else's in smooth suspension. Only Leo, leading Norah on with concealed ingenuity from strength to strength, but already experiencing the sad ennui of victory, and Peter, who had even passed the stage of thinking what he would say to Norah on the way home, wanted the evening to end.

VALENTINE ACKLAND (1906–1969)

From *For Sylvia* (1949)

The poet Valentine Ackland, life companion of the English novelist Sylvia Townsend Warner, was the daughter of well-to-do parents and grew up in London. A sensitive, lonely, and gifted child, she wrote poetry from an early age and dreamed of becoming a great writer. Her lesbianism first manifested itself in her teens: while at a finishing school in Paris in 1922, she fell in love with another student, throwing her family into consternation. In the chaotic aftermath, she converted to Roman Catholicism and married a young man—also homosexual—although the marriage was annulled in 1927. Throughout the late twenties, Ackland drifted through life, writing occasionally, having affairs with both men and women, and drinking heavily. This feckless existence came to an end in 1930, when she fell deeply in love with Warner, who immediately exerted a stabilizing influence. Ackland and Warner lived together for the next four decades, mostly in Dorset.

Though essential to both, the long relationship between them was not untroubled, especially in its later years. The two women shared similar left-wing political views: both became ardent Communists in the 1930s and were members of a British cultural delegation that went to Spain during the Civil War. One of Ackland's few published prose works is *Country Conditions* (1936), a Marxist tract on economic life in depressed English villages. But Ackland's literary career was always overshadowed by her partner's. In 1933 she and Warner published a joint collection of poems, *Whether a Dove or Seagull*; but Ackland's poetry failed to win admirers, and she published little on her own. Later in life she stopped writing, ran an antique shop—and to the skeptical Warner's horror—became increasingly fanatical about her Catholic faith. She died of cancer in 1969. Some of her poems appeared posthumously in a volume edited by Warner, *The Nature of the Moment*, in 1973.

Ackland's fascinating and bittersweet memoir, *For Sylvia*, unpublished during her lifetime, is unquestionably her most compelling piece of writing. She wrote it in 1949, during a period of intense emotional strain. For some years Ackland had been having an affair with an American woman, Elizabeth Wade White, and after much self-tormenting had decided to leave Warner for White. She intended the book, which she dedicated to Warner, as an apologia. In it she retraces her own lesbian history, from her first affair with "Lana," the friend of her schooldays, through her struggles with alcoholism, to the meeting with Warner in 1930. (The "Lana" episode is excerpted below.) Paradoxically, something in the writing of the book proved cathartic: Ackland changed her mind about leaving Warner and broke with White in 1950. The memoir itself was first published in 1985.

FURTHER READING: Valentine Ackland, *Whether a Dove or Seagull* (with Sylvia Townsend Warner) (London: New York, Viking, 1933); —, *The Nature of the Moment* (London: Chatto and Windus, 1973); —, *For Sylvia: An Honest Account* (London: Chatto and Windus, 1985); Wendy Mulford, *This Narrow Place—Sylvia Townsend Warner and Valentine Ackland: Life, Letters and Politics, 1930–1951* (London: Pandora, 1988); Claire Harman, *Sylvia Townsend Warner: A Biography* (London: Chatto and Windus, 1989); Susanna Pinney, ed., *I'll Stand by You: The Letters of Sylvia Townsend Warner and Valentine Ackland* (London: Pimlico, 1998).

Lana was three years older than me—even a little more. She was in her twentieth year. We considered this to be extraordinarily old. We felt chivalrously sorry for her. To have reached that great age and not to be engaged. My school friend knew that Lana was "common" but I did not. I had scarcely any "class-consciousness" then. I thought Lana frightening at first, because she was so old, because she could speak French accurately and fluently, with a charming accent, and because she curled her short-cut hair. This hair was beguiling; nut-brown, with golden hairs growing in a fine peak from her high forehead. She was very small and delicately made, and she dressed superbly. I did not know that I loved her—perhaps I did not love her—until one afternoon when I was lying down in the room I shared with my school friend, and Lana came to talk to me. It was a warm day in late April or early May. She sat on the bed and we talked for a long time, and I told her about my family and our country house, and slowly became aware that she was staring at me, and something in her regard made me falter and fall silent . . . The last word I said, grotesquely unsuitable, was "lepers," I remember: I had been describing how my mother knew about a leper colony somewhere near London. Lana smiled oddly at me, and said softly, "Go on—Lepers—" and then slowly leaned across and kissed me on the mouth.

I was swept into a wild confusion of ecstasy and shyness; I clasped her in my arms and she kissed me again and again. I had no idea of what had happened; my blood burned me, my heart-beat stifled me; I felt as though something had exploded beside me and I had been blown to atoms—

I remember that I stammered out a desperate question, "What is it?" And Lana said, "I am in love with you, my darling—" and I don't remember anything more until—perhaps hours later—she said we must go down to tea, and laughed because soon we should be in company and pretending to be only casual acquaintances, and would have to ask each other, "Milk, please—" or "Can I have the butter?"

We went down to tea (I was shaking so that I could scarcely walk) and then, across the table, Lana said to me, "Can I have the butter?" and I flushed and pushed it across so rudely that I was reprimanded by whichever of the ladies was superintending us that day.

After this, so far as we could manage to be, we were inseparable. Notes passed, and presents; we walked together; we sat together at the Opéra and at concerts. At last the day came when my sister and mother were arriving to stay a few days and I was to go to the Hotel Roosevelt, Avenue Roosevelt, to stay with them. I could scarcely bear to go; but then, waiting for them to arrive, I changed into my new evening dress and painted my lips as I had been taught, and sat—with my waved hair and made-up face— to wait for them in the lounge of the hotel. They arrived and stood there for some time and then walked past me and never recognized me at all. It was a moment of great triumph and happiness. I was, I thought, really "out" at last. My sister could never catch me again. (That was not true.)

The days of their stay dragged, because I did not see Lana alone. We took her out to tea once, and once they visited Rue Ybry with me. And on that occasion Lana told me that she had arranged to change bedrooms; hitherto she had slept alone and I had shared my room; now she was to replace my school friend, who wanted to go upstairs to share a room with another young woman, a rich, sophisticated, noisy, vulgar young woman too.

"I shall have you to myself every night—" said Lana, and I shook with fear and excitement and could not sleep that night and dared not think about how it would be.

On May 29th I returned to Rue Ybry; the room was full of flowers that Lana had bought; white lilac and white irises; a huge bunch of small rosebuds. She had got a screen too, so that we might dress and undress without being shy. Without this I could not have endured my extreme timidity.

That night I went upstairs first and Lana followed when I was in bed. We were both totally ignorant (innocent is the better word) and all we knew of love-making was to lie close together and kiss; but no two have ever loved more or been more completely, passionately fulfilled.

It was a very brief happiness; in the middle of June we left Paris and returned to England. My parents did not like Lana very much, and her home in one of the Kentish suburbs of London was like nothing I had ever seen before. Her mother was a commanding, stout, over-dressed woman, of infinitely kind heart and ferocious temper; her father drank too much and liked to tell stories about seeing girls' legs in railway carriages; there was a lean, spectacled man whom Lana called "godfather," who was her mother's lover; he was clever and in some kind of wholesale dress business with her mother—he was a typical bourgeois businessman and, with less good fortune, he would have been the chief clerk in some solicitor's office. I liked none of them and they all thought my shyness and strangeness was "side." Beside Lana and her mother I felt very dowdy and poor, for they had luxurious satin underclothes and Lana had astonished me by the marvellous splendours of her printed silk pyjamas and the care she took about making-up, about hair-dressing, nail-varnishing, and the fact that directly she awoke in the morning, before her eyes were properly opened on the world, she sprang out of bed and sat down in front of her mirror, licking her forefinger and rubbing her eyebrows straight because "Peggy" her mother "made me promise always to do that; my eyebrows won't keep a good shape otherwise——"

Lana was typically suburban, typically flippant and silly, but these qualities went with others not so commonplace; she read a great deal and introduced me to many poems I had not heard of—she showed me the way to many things that now are the most precious I have. And she was sensitive, full of delicacy, full of amorousness and subtlety. She made love with an exquisite fervour and abandon and, for that brief time, we loved each other with truth and candour. It was like Daphnis and Chloe. It was classical and had no stain upon it.

That summer I spent in Norfolk and then, in September or October, Lana's mother asked me to go with them on a motoring tour abroad, and after some argument my parents consented—if I would first go to a Hunt Ball in Flintshire—or somewhere like that. I travelled to Symond's Yat with a tall American who was sent with me. I did not like him at all. He was extremely successful and handsome and he must have found me troublesome, for I had no idea of amusing him. I carried letters from Lana and her photograph and thought only of how I would soon see her again.

The Hunt Ball was dreadful. The Great Family was called Scudamore Stanhope and my host and hostess were anxious to prove that they were on familiar terms with the noblemen. I had to dance with a drunk young man, one of the S.S.s, who pulled off my slipper and mumbled my foot, I remember, and I had an embarrassing few moments before I could get him up on his feet again. I returned to my hostess's mother, a nice old lady, and steadily refused to dance with anyone again. Most people got drunk, which was then a strange and unaccustomed sight (I expect it has always happened at Hunt Balls but I had never met the genuine backwoods County before, and the sight appalled me). After a gruesome finale, when they all danced a gallop and many couples fell down flat on the floor, and the place resounded with cat-calls, yells, hunting-horns and a variety of horrible noises, we all returned home. It was about four in the morning, and at nine the American and I caught our train for London. He had been delighted by the company and felt still elated and we had a tiresome journey.

I was then only sixteen; I had weathered my first and last Hunt Ball, and now I was on the way to Europe again, and to Lana.

We crossed the Channel, and at St Omer the Studebaker car broke down. We stayed there for two or three days and then went on, through the battlefields of Flanders (still not tidied up—it was 1922—and so oppressive to the spirit that I even lost any sense of joy in Lana's presence, and could not speak and could not endure to look at any of the people I was with) and went on, over the Simplon, into Italy. We went to the Lakes, to Milan, to Turin, back to Switzerland, to Grindelwald, where Lana's mother and her godfather had to return by train to England for some emergency, and Lana and I were left alone, at the Bear Hotel, in great state, for five wonderful days. Then the others returned and we drove at a leisurely pace through France (we stayed a night at Annecy) and to Paris.

There, at the Hotel Continental, Lana's mother grieved because my clothes were so unsuitable to the splendour around us. She tried to persuade me to let her fit me out, but I would not because I was shy and proud and it seemed to me that to do so would be disloyal to my parents. I had a very childish sense of right and wrong—maybe it is truer to call it a sense of "done" and "not done."

At last we returned home. All the journey we had shared a room, Lana and I, and Peggy had often referred to us as "quite like lovers." She was very kind to me, even when she must have been ashamed of me. I grew to respect and like her.

Meanwhile, at home, my sister (engaged but not yet married) had been reading letters from my desk and had, of course, easily discovered the situation between Lana and me. She told my mother, who tried to hush it up. But at length it got to my father and directly I was home he informed me that I was to be sent to a Domestic Training College at Eastbourne. I did not know why. I was horrified. For a year I had been to dances, opera, concerts; I had evening clothes; I thought of myself as grown up. Now I was to go back to school—worse, to a boarding-school: worst of all, to learn Domestic Economy, which seemed like the lowest degradation to me. I begged to be allowed to take up music again, to have a tutor, to do *anything*; but he would not listen. On the morning of the day we were to leave for Eastbourne, he and my mother and I, my father came into my room as I was packing and began to question me, severely and furiously, about my relationship with Lana. I did not understand at all what he was trying to find out. I told him that we were in love.

I remember very vividly the expression of disgust on his face.

He became very angry indeed—much angrier than I had ever seen him before. He asked if I knew what a filthy thing I had been doing? I answered, No, it had not been at all filthy. It was something very strange, but not at all wrong. I thought one or other of us must have been wrongly made—He asked furiously what I meant? I said that Lana ought to have been a man; I thought she must have been one in a previous incarnation—He muttered something and rushed out of the room. My mother came in and began to question me more gently. I patiently explained that we had fallen in love; no one could help that, could they? It was wonderful. We were very, very happy. We would love each other for ever. What could be wrong in that?

They told me that the train went in half an hour and that Lana had confessed everything and her family were furious. I must not see her nor write to her ever again. I fought back then—and insisted upon telephoning her at once. I did so, and heard her in bitter tears, saying the same thing: we must not meet or write again. I had such complete confidence and trust in her that I never for a moment doubted but that she had been forced to this by her mother's rage. I assured her that I would be constant and not give way for a moment. She wept and reiterated that she had promised—we must never meet or write again. And then I was torn away and bundled into the Pullman coach of the Eastbourne express, where I sat facing my father—his face pale and set into lines of extraordinary anger. And at last we arrived.

We went to the Grand Hotel and my father came straight into my room and began to question me. He asked me if I realized that what Lana and I had done was the worst, filthiest (a word reiterated constantly, shocking me each time afresh) the most unforgivable thing that anyone could do? No decent man would marry me if he knew of it. My father was so horrified he could scarcely endure to see me. And so on. Then he used the word "unnatural"—and I began to argue.

How could it be "unnatural" when neither Lana nor I had any idea of it until we fell in love? We had not done anything wrong, I said; we had only loved each other—

It went on and on until my nerve broke and I wept. Then my mother came in and begged my father to leave me, and took me into her room and talked to me; but I stubbornly refused to admit that anything we had done *could* have been unnatural. How—if it was—had we done it? No one had ever told us anything—

All of these arguments, of course, convinced my parents that we had, in fact, been lovers in their *News of the World* sense of that word. Whereas, all the time, we had been as innocent as Daphnis and Chloe; more innocent, in one sense, because we had never known a moment's uneasiness or wonder or curiosity: we had been wholly satisfied to kiss and fondle and lie in bed close to each other and talk and laugh and be happy. My parents never did believe this, and for a full year I had no idea of their theories—I never moved from my position of absolute conviction that what we had done was right, inevitable and in the circumstances perfectly natural. My father never forgave me. My mother grieved for me and after his death accepted the whole position with a kind of generous shrewdness—adapting herself to the inevitable so as not to lose me, for she loved me very much.

At the College I was completely miserable. All the students were inimical to me and I to them. No one of my own class was there; no one with any interest in literature or painting or music. The place was (by an ironical stroke on the part of God) given over to unnatural vice. The headmistress was a pious, emotional, "manly" bitch and the rest of the staff, with one exception, were delighted to encourage "crushes" and "pashes" and all the rest—At night, after lights out, the house used to echo and re-echo; doors slamming, footsteps, whispers, giggles—I had notes and posies left in my room and vile ogling advances made, and nudges and jokes and taunts. I had an attic room, to which I went whenever I could; I never would go near the Common Room, nor go out with any of the others into the town. At last, I suppose because of reports that I was pining, for I would not eat, my parents did the oddest thing: they sent Lana down to stay for one night and two days with me.

That was a tragic, a heartbroken meeting and parting. Lana told me that her parents had said to her what mine had said to me; but she had believed them. She *must* marry, she said; she *must* find someone who would marry her—Her mother had told her that unless she married she would be an old maid, disgraced, poor and unwanted.

She wept; she lay in my bed and we talked till the day came, and then we wandered through the dismal streets, through a long, cold, autumn Sunday in that dreariest of all seaside towns, and then she went away.

After a few more weeks I was taken away and sent down to Sussex, to stay on a farm with some cousins. There I lived rough and among people who despised all the things I revered; but I had the care of two very handsome polo ponies, of the Argentine polo team, who were boarded there for the winter; these were a delight to me and for a while I and my misery managed to keep alive on the pleasure of having those creatures to ride and handle. But at last it was too much and I ran away. To do this I had to steal some money, for I had none; so I took my aunt's purse and bought a ticket to London and arrived at my parents' flat. They lived, then, in a service flat in a luxurious block in Westminster.

I do not remember the arrival. I remember the letter that came next day, saying that I had stolen this money, and the trouble about that. But by then I was so sick with misery and a kind of deadly, lonely despair, that I cannot remember anything in detail, except that I committed every kind of crime and offence; stealing, lying, romancing, falling into agonies of lust, without any idea of what I lusted for; and I could not seem to speak bare truth, even about the smallest things. I was always caught out; I made little or no attempt to cover my tracks. I read feverishly, all the poems I could get—I went to the forever-blessed Poetry Bookshop and bought cheap Broadsheets to hang on my walls, and learned the poems by heart; I sat for hours at a time, imagining the wildest dramas and being sometimes the heroine and sometimes the hero of them, but most often, I think, the heroine.

Among the dire results of my "unnaturalness" I had been told that I should go blind and go mad. I believed this. In a kind of cold reasonableness, I tried to teach myself to type and play the piano with my eyes shut, against the time I should be blind. But the madness I could not think how to prepare for; and yet it seemed always more sure to come. I knew that everything I did was done without my will. I knew that I could not tell the truth, I could not refrain from buying what I wanted, and I could not control my wants; the oddest things seized upon my imagination.

I remember, for instance, that I saw in a cheapjack shop in Charing Cross Road, an imitation gold half-hunter watch, a man's watch; it cost 10s. (London was full of stores that sold such things just then). I bought it, after agonizing for two days with longing for it. I stole the money to buy it, for I had only 10s. a week, and fares, gloves, stockings, hair-dressing and all etc. had to come out of that. I don't remember how I stole the money. The watch, of course, was immediately noticed and my sister enquired where it had come from. I said that I had known a certain major—for some time now. He was in love with me, I said, and could not marry me because he was married already. Now he had gone abroad for ever, and left me this watch of his as a memento.

That odd, pathetic story caused the utmost consternation. My mother believed it and my sister, as she told me, "made enquiries." I grew alarmed, aware of the utter futility of the romance, and told them the truth. They did not believe the truth, but spent a long time hunting about to discover, if possible, *some* clue to this strange and wicked man . . . And I was so sick, so miserable, so nearly mad that I lost all interest in the whole thing, and to this day I cannot tell what happened to the watch, nor how the story came to an end.

Family confusions added to everything else. My mother and father were unhappy together and my father tried to console himself for his great horror of me (he had loved me very much) by cleaving to my sister and by going off for holidays to France with a disreputable grand friend of his and the friend's mistress. My mother disapproved of those people and there were frequent arguments and miseries.

My sister married, in the April, I think of that year, and my father disliked her husband, and she came to dislike him very soon afterwards. In August of that year my father died, suddenly and most shockingly, of cancer. In September my mother's brother-in-law died suddenly from a heart-attack. In the February her other brother-in-law died. These deaths frightened us all and made all our miseries worse, not better. My sister and my brother-in-law took command of our household for a while and made my life unutterably miserable.

I had been in touch with the young man I had been "engaged" to when he was a schoolboy; at this period he was a planter in Java. One of my letters, after my father's death, was so unhappy that he cabled me to marry him and I cabled back that I would. We had not met since I was eleven or so.

The engagement was announced and presents began to come in. A trousseau was bought, and for a while I was very happy, getting ready and writing and receiving long letters. I would escape from my sister; I would be married; I would be away from everything that had been so nightmarishly miserable; I would have children—I longed passionately for children—And in the spring of the following year, 1924, I went with my mother to Switzerland for the last journey abroad before we sailed for Singapore.

On our return (we were not to sail until June) I had nothing to do and I took up political canvassing, and at that job I met a young woman speaker for the Conservative Party, who was extremely popular and attractive. She showed me great favour. She was twenty-eight at that time, which seemed to me extremely old (I was eighteen). One day she told me that she knew two dear old women, one French and the other English, who lived in Camberwell and kept a lodging house; the Frenchwoman was a marvellous cook. She would love to take me there to stay a night and eat a fine dinner—it would be an adventure, to stay in Camberwell, and fun, wouldn't it?

I was deeply flattered and we went.

That night, as we sat in our dressing-gowns by the fire in her bedroom, she took my hand and later, as I had got up to go to my room, she kissed me.

So it had happened again, and this time not to me innocent but to me sullied by reproaches and arguments and misapprehensions, but as ignorant as ever; for I knew nothing about lesbianism, except that now I knew it existed and was, instead of being something that had miraculously happened to me alone, something almost commonplace, and something that aroused loathing and vituperation.

In the morning, I remember, she woke me in my bed, for after we had talked a little about how we had fallen in love, I had gone back to my room. My first words to her, spoken to give me courage, I fancy, and to show her that I was sophisticated and "hard," were "Well, I suppose it is all over?" And she replied, "No—this is only the beginning of the beginning—"

And so it was.

We were lovers from 1924 until 1930, and in that period I broke one engagement, and married, and left my husband, and fell in love many times, but still she and I remained lovers and again and again I returned to her, until at last I fell in love for life.

DOROTHY STRACHEY (1865–1960)

From *Olivia* (1949)

Dorothy Strachey, one of ten children, grew up in a large and distinguished Victorian family. Her father, Sir Richard Strachey, was a soldier, scientist, and colonial administrator (he spent thirty years in India); her mother, the imperious Jane Maria Grant, was an early supporter of women's education. Her siblings, male and female, were an extraordinarily talented group. Her brother, the playwright and biographer Lytton Strachey, became one of the best-known members of the Bloomsbury circle; her sisters Joan and Philippa were, respectively, principal of Newnham College, Cambridge, and secretary to the London National Society for Women's Service. Another brother, James, was the first English translator and editor of Freud. Amid such company, it is hardly surprising that Dorothy Strachey harbored intellectual and artistic ambitions from an early age.

In 1882 and 1883 Strachey attended Les Ruches, an exclusive girls' boarding school in France founded by Marie Souvestre, a leading progressive educator of the day. Her experiences there—commemorated in her autobiographical novel, *Olivia*—were the most influential of her life. Souvestre was a cultivated and charismatic figure: she counted among her many friends the novelist Marcel Proust, the biographer Sir Leslie Stephen, and the socialist thinker Beatrice Webb. Strachey fell deeply under her personal and intellectual sway. Not surprisingly, when Souvestre (with Lady Strachey's help) founded a new school in England—Allenswood, near Wimbledon—Strachey stayed on with her as teacher and protegée for several years.

For a time Strachey seemed set to devote herself, like her mentor, to academic work and spinsterhood. (Among other things, she tutored her younger brother Lytton in French.) In 1903, however, after having rejected several previous marriage proposals, she scandalized her family and friends by marrying an impoverished French painter, Simon Bussy, with whom she moved to the South of France. There she gave birth to a daughter and devoted herself to motherhood and her writing. In 1918 she met the celebrated French novelist André Gide and quickly became his English translator and intimate friend. Gide was one of the first people to read the manuscript of *Olivia* on its completion in 1933. Despite the French writer's enthusiasm for the book—he read it, he told her, with "keen emotion"—Strachey would not allow it to be published until 1949. When it finally appeared—under the pseudonym "Olivia" and with a dedication to the late Virginia Woolf—it became an immediate bestseller. It was subsequently translated into seven languages and made into a film (directed by Jacqueline Audry, with screenplay by Colette) starring Edwige Feuillère and Simone Simon in 1951.

Though Strachey published other works before her death in 1960, *Olivia* remains her best claim to fame. As she acknowledged in the preface, the book is profoundly personal:

> I have condensed into a few score of pages the history of a whole year when life was, if not at its fullest, at any rate at its most poignant—that year when every vital experience was the first, or, if you Freudians object, the year when I first became conscious of myself, of love and pleasure, of death and pain, and when every reaction to them was as unexpected, as amazing, as *involuntary* as the experience itself.

Strachey's contemporaries were quick to read the work as a roman à clef. Souvestre was easily recognizable in the character of the seductive Mademoiselle Julie, as was Eleanor Roosevelt—another Souvestre student and model for one of the book's numerous secondary characters.

Olivia has its weaknesses: a concocted subplot involving Mademoiselle Julie's doomed lover-companion, the ultrafemme and slightly hysterical Mademoiselle Cara, pulls the work toward the realm of pulp fiction. But the emotional core of the book—the rapturous record of Olivia's passion for Mademoiselle Julie (a section of which is excerpted below)—is exquisitely realized. Few writers have captured as well as Strachey the giddy ardors of adolescence or the shocks of amorous betrayal. Indeed, for all that Strachey documents a vanished world—her fervent, half-comical schoolgirls, falling in love as they read aloud from Racine and de Vigny, seem as far from us today as ancient Greeks—the novel itself remains curiously dateless, as fresh in feeling as it is vivid in detail.

FURTHER READING: "Olivia" (Dorothy Strachey Bussy), *Olivia* (London: Hogarth, 1949); Dorothy Strachey Bussy, *Fifty Nursery Rhymes* (Paris: Gallimard, 1951); Jeannette Foster, *Sex Variant Women in Literature* (1956; rpt. Tallahassee, Fla.: Naiad, 1985); Michael Holroyd, *Lytton Strachey: A Critical Biography*, 2 vols. (London: W. Heinemann, 1967–68); Richard Tedeschi, ed., *Selected Letters of André Gide and Dorothy Bussy* (Oxford and New York: Oxford University Press, 1983); Harald Emeis, "*Olivia*, roman à clef," *Bulletin des amis d'André Gide* 11 (1983): 7–36; Martha Vicinus, "Distance and Desire: English Boarding-School Friendships 1870–1920," *Signs: Journal of Women in Society and Culture* 9 (1984): 600–22, rpt. in Martin Duberman, Martha Vicinus, and George Chauncey, Jr., eds., *Hidden from History: Reclaiming the Gay and Lesbian Past* (New York: Penguin Books, 1990), pp. 212–32; Susannah Clapp, Afterword to *Olivia* (London: Virago, 1987); Blanche Wiesen Cook, *Eleanor Roosevelt: Volume 1, 1884–1933* (New York: Viking Penguin, 1992); Corinne E. Blackmer, "*The Finishing Touch* and the Tradition of Homoerotic Girls' School Fictions," *Review of Contemporary Fiction* 15 (1995): 32–39; Marie-Claire Hamard, "*Olivia* from Bloomsbury to the NRF," *BELLS: Barcelona English Language and Literature Studies* 7 (1996): 117–23; Mary Ann Caws and Sarah Bird Wright, *Bloomsbury and France: Art and Friends* (New York: Oxford University Press, 2000).

It was at this time that a change came over me. That delicious sensation of gladness, of lightness, of springing vitality, that consciousness of youth and strength and ardour, that feeling that some divine power had suddenly granted me an undreamt-of felicity and made me free of boundless kingdoms and untold wealth, faded as mysteriously as it had come and was succeeded by a very different state. Now I was all moroseness and gloom—heavy-hearted, leaden-footed. I could take no interest in my lessons; it was impossible to think of them. When, on Thursdays and Sundays, I sat with the other girls in our study where we were supposed to be writing our *devoirs*, I could not work. I sat for hours, my arms folded on the table in front of me, my head resting on them, plunged in a kind of coma.

"What on earth are you doing, Olivia?" a friend would ask. "Are you asleep?"

"Oh, leave me alone," I would cry impatiently. "I'm thinking."

But I wasn't thinking. I was sometimes dreaming—the foolish dreams of adolescence: of how I should save her life at the cost of my own by some heroic deed, of how she would kiss me on my death bed, of how I should kneel at hers and what her dying word would be, of how I should become famous by writing poems which no one would know were inspired by her, of how one day she would guess it, and so on and so on.

At other times I wasn't even dreaming, but just a mass of physical sensations which bewildered me, which made me feel positively sick. My heart beat violently, my breath came fast and unevenly, with the expectation of some extraordinary event which was going to happen the very next minute. At the opening of every door, at the sound of the most casual footstep, my solar plexus shot the wildest stabs through every portion of my body, and the next minute, when nothing had happened, I collapsed, a pricked bladder, into flat and dreary quiescence. Sometimes I was possessed by longing, but I didn't know for what—for some vague blessing, some unimaginable satisfaction, which seemed to be tantalizingly near but which, all the same, I knew was unattainable—a blessing, which, if I could only grasp it, would quench my thirst, still my pulses, give me an Elysian peace. At other times, it was the power of expression that seemed maddeningly denied me. If only I could express myself—in words, in music, anyhow. I imagined myself a prima donna or a great actress. Oh, heavenly relief. Oh, an outlet for all this ferment which was boiling within me. Perilous stuff. If I could only get rid of it—shout it to the world—declaim it away.

Then there was a more passive, a more languorous state, when I seemed to myself dissolving, when I let myself go, as I phrased it to myself, when I felt as though I were floating luxuriously down a warm, gentle river, every muscle relaxed, every portion of me open to receive each softest caress of air and water, down, down, towards some unknown, delicious sea. My indefinite desire was like some pervading, unlocalized ache of my whole being. If I could only know, thought I, where it lies, what it is. In my heart? In my brain? In my body? But no, all I felt was that I desired something. Sometimes I thought it was to be loved in return. But that seemed to me so entirely impossible that it was really and truly unimaginable. I could not imagine *how* she could love me. *Like* me, be fond of me, as a child, as a pupil, yes, of course. But that had nothing to do with what I felt. And so I made myself another dream. It was a man I loved as I loved her, and then he would take me in his arms . . . and kiss me . . . I should feel his lips on my cheek, on my eyelids, on my—No, no, no, that way lay madness. All this was different—hopeless. Hopeless. A dreadful word, but with a kind of tonic in it. I would hug it to my heart. Yes, hopeless. It was that that gave my passion dignity, that made it worthy of respect. No other love, no love of man and woman could ever be as disinterested as mine. It was I alone who loved—it was I alone whose love was an impossible fantasy.

And yet she sometimes showered me with marvellous kindnesses. Often when she was reading aloud to me in the library, she would drop her hand into mine and let me hold it. Once when I had a cold, she visited me in my room, petted me, brought me delicacies from the table, told me stories that made me laugh, left me cheerful and contented. It was during my convalescence from that little indisposition that she put her head into my room one evening and said:

"I'm going out to dinner in Paris, but I'll look in on you when I get back and see how you are and say good night to you." Her good night was gay and tender and the next day I was well.

A fortnight later she went out to dinner again. The last train from Paris reached the station at about half-past eleven and she used to be up at the house a little before twelve. How could I help keeping awake that night, half expecting her, listening for her? She had to pass my door to go to her room. Perhaps, perhaps she would come in again. Ah, straining ears and beating heart! But why was she so long? What could she be doing? Again and again I lit my candle and looked at my watch. Can she have passed the door without my having heard her? Impossible. At last, at last, the step came sounding down the long passage. Nearer, nearer. Would it stop? Would it go on? It stopped. A breathless pause. Would the handle turn? It turned. She came in in the dim light of the unshuttered room and stood beside my bed:

"I've brought you a sweet, you greedy little thing," she said and pulled it out of her bag.

Oh yes, I was greedy, but not for sweets. Her hands were my possession. I covered them with kisses.

"There, there, Olivia," she said. "You're too passionate, my child."

Her lips brushed my forehead and she was gone.

It was a little later that we had the usual Mardi Gras fancy-dress ball. Oh, yes, it was exactly like all other girls'-school fancy-dress balls. There was a day's disorganization, while the dresses were being made and we were allowed to run about as we would into each other's rooms, chattering, laughing, trying on, madly sewing and pinning. And then came the excitement of the evening. The two ladies sat enthroned with the staff at one end of the music room, which had been cleared for dancing; a march was played on the piano and we filed past them two and two, made our bows and our curtsies, were questioned, complimented, and laughed at. Mlle Julie was in her element on such occasions. Tonight was no exception. There was something happier in the atmosphere, a relaxation of tension. Mlle Cara was smiling and cheerful; Mlle Julie's wit sparkled like her eyes; she was enjoying it all as much as anyone. We could see her curiosity, her interest in the different self that each girl revealed in her disguise, some betraying their secret longings and fantasies, some abandoning themselves recklessly to their own natural propensities.

So, it was Mary Queen of Scots, that poor, plain Gertrude so pathetically aspired to be; Georgie's dark eyes burned mysterious and tragic beneath a top hat; with her false moustache and pointed beard, she made a marvellous romantic poet of 1830. On her arm hung Mimi, a charming little grisette in a poke bonnet, a shawl and a crinoline, and the two flirted outrageously to everyone's delight. Madcap Nina was Puck himself, a torment and an amusement to the whole company. And I? I don't know what my dress revealed. It was a Parsee lady's dress which my mother had brought home from India. Very rich and splendid, I thought. The soft Oriental silk was of deep rose colour and it had a gold band inwoven in the material round the edges of the sari and the long skirt. I wore the sari over my head and managed the clinging folds well enough.

But there was no doubt who was the belle of the ball. Cécile, a lovely and complacent Columbia, swam with swanlike grace, a queen among us all. She was draped in the star-spangled banner. An audacious *décolletage* showed her beautiful shoulders and the rise of her breast. Diamond stars crowned her and sparkled round her long slim throat. She was radiantly beautiful.

I was giving her her due of compliments, when Mlle Julie came up.

"*La belle Cécile!*" she cried. "You do us honour, *chère Amérique*—a beauty worthy of Lafayette's gallantry," she went on, laughing. "Turn round and let me look at you."

She put her hands on Cécile's bare arms and as she twisted her round, bent down and kissed her shoulder. A long deliberate kiss on the naked creamy shoulder. An unknown pang of astonishing violence stabbed me. I hated Cécile. I hated Mlle Julie. As she raised her eyes from the kiss, she saw me watching her. Had she noticed me before? I don't know. Now, I thought, she was mocking me.

"Is Olivia jealous of so much beauty?" she said. "No, Olivia, you'll never be beautiful, but you have your points," appraising me, I thought angrily, as if I had been an animal at a cattle show. "Pretty hands, pretty feet, a pretty figure, grace which is some-times more than—"but then her voice trailed off into a murmur too low for me to hear. "But even if I wanted to kiss you, fair Indian, how could I, wrapped as you are in all those veils? Come though, I'll tell you a secret."

She drew me towards her, pulled back my sari, and whispered close, close in my ear, her lips almost touching me, her breath hot on my cheek:

"I'll come tonight and bring you a sweet."

She was gone.

I remember that I felt as if my whole frame had been turned to water. My knees were giving way. I had to cling to a table and support myself till I recovered strength enough to get to a chair—she was coming—tonight—in a few hours—A paean sang in my heart. Had I been weak before? Now, exhilaration flowed through my veins. Why? Why? I didn't stop to think why. I only knew that there, in the immediate future, soon, soon, something was coming to me, some wild delight, some fierce anguish that my whole being called for. But I mustn't think of it. Now, I must dance. Just then Georgie passed me.

"Why are you so pale?" she asked and looked at me.

"Georgie," I said, "have you ever been in love?"

Georgie's dark eyes gloomed and glowed. I could see her breath quickening.

"Yes," she answered sombrely, "yes."

"And what's it like?"

"Too horrible to speak of." And then, as though some lovely memory were rising from the depths of her heart into the glowing eyes, they softened, melted, shone, behind a veil of tears. "And too delicious. Come, let's dance!"

She put her arm round me and pressed me to her. There was comfort in the con-tact. Comfort, I felt, and pleasure for us both. She was stronger, taller than I. My head could rest on her shoulder; I was conscious of hers bending over me. Our steps, our limbs, harmonized, swayed, quickened, slackened to the music, as if one spirit informed them. I could trust myself to her guiding, I could abandon myself in a trance of ecstasy to the motion, to the rhythm, to the languors and the passions of the waltz.

That evening, we danced every waltz together (Georgie abandoned her grisette—"she can't dance for twopence"—), but we knew well enough that we were not danc-ing with each other, that one of us was clasping, the other being clasped by the phan-tom of her own dreams.

It was the fashion to end every ball with what was called a "galop." I don't think this dance exists nowadays. It was the tempestuous conclusion in those Victorian days to evenings that had been filled with sentimentalities and proprieties—waltzes and Lancers—and people would rush into the frenzy of rapid motion with a fury of excite-ment. When the waltzes were over that night, Nina and I, sped by some magnetic impulse, shot madly into each other's arms for the final galop. Excitement was in the air. Fräulein, at the piano, caught it too and added to it by the *brio* of her playing. But no couple could compete with Nina and me. We rushed and whirled, faster and faster, more and more furiously, our hair, our draperies, streaming like Maenads' behind us, till at last the others gave out exhausted and we were left whirling alone, the only couple on the floor. It was the music that surrendered first, and as, at last, we dropped to the ground, laughing and breathless, all the watching girls applauded.

The evening was over. It was time to go to bed. I should have been glad for it to last longer. There was something coming that I dreaded as much as I longed for it. I was approaching an abyss into which I was going to fall dizzy and shuddering. I averted my eyes, but I knew that it was there.

After all the noisy good nights, I was at last alone in my room. I tore off my veils impatiently. I must make haste. There was no time to be lost. I slipped into my school-girl's nightgown, high to the throat and buttoned to the wrists—and suddenly the vision of Cécile's creamy shoulder flashed upon me. I couldn't bear the hideous night-gown. I took out a clean day-chemise and put it on instead. That was better. My arms and neck at least were bare. I got into bed and blew out the candle.

What had she said? Pretty hands, pretty feet, a pretty figure. Yes, but in French, what strange expression does one use? *Un joli corps*. A pretty body. Mine, a pretty body. I had never thought of my body till that minute. A body! I had a body—and it was pretty. What was it like? I must look at it. There was still time. She wouldn't be coming yet. I lighted the candle, sprang out of bed and slipped off my chemise. The looking glass—a small one—was over the wash-hand stand. I could only see my face and shoulders in it. I climbed on to a chair. Then I could see more. I looked at the figure in the glass, queerly lighted; without head or legs, strangely attractive, strangely repulsive. And then I slowly passed my hands down this queer creature's body from neck to waist. Ah, that was more than I could bear—that excruciating thrill I had never felt before. In a second my chemise was on again, I was back in bed.

And now, I listened, not thinking, not feeling any more, absorbed in listening. The noises gradually died away—slamming doors, footsteps, snatches of talk and laughter. The house was silent now. Not quite. I still heard from time to time a window or a shutter being closed or opened. Now. Yes, now it really was silent. Now was the time to hear a coming footstep, a creaking board. There! My heart beat, stood still, beat. No! A false alarm. How long she was. It must be getting late. How late! How late. And still she didn't come. She had never been as late as this before. I lighted my candle again and looked at my watch. One o'clock. And we had gone to bed at eleven. I crept to the door and opened it gently. I could see her room a little way off, on the opposite side of the passage. There was no light coming from the crack under the door. Nothing was stirring. Everything was wrapped in profound and deadly silence. I went heavily back to my bed. She had promised. She couldn't not come now. I must have faith in her. Or could anything have prevented her? Yet surely not for all this time. She knew I should wait for her. Ah, she was cruel. She had no right to promise and not to come. She had forgotten me. She didn't know whether I existed or not. She had other thoughts, other cares. Of course, of course. I was nothing to her. A silly schoolgirl. She liked Cécile better than she did me. Hark! A sound! Hope rose and died a dozen times that night.

Even when I knew it was impossible—even when the late winter dawn was beginning to glimmer in the room, I still lay, tossing and listening. It must have been five o'clock before I fell asleep.

And yet I was to know other, bitterer vigils, during which I looked back on this one as happy—during which I realized she had never loved me, never would love me as well as on that night.

GERTRUDE LAWRENCE (1898–1952)

"Women Are Like Geography" (1949)

Gertrude Lawrence, one of the best-loved British stage personalities of the first half of the twentieth century, was born in South London and raised by her mother in genteel poverty. At fourteen, while performing in a children's theater troupe, she met the thirteen-year-old Noël Coward, subsequently to become the most important influence on her career. She made her West End début as a soubrette in André Charlot's *Cheep!* in 1917 while understudying for Beatrice Lillie. In 1923 she appeared in Coward's musical revue *London Calling!* and became an overnight sensation. Other successes quickly followed: she starred in the George Gershwin musical *Oh, Kay!* (written expressly for her) in New York in 1926, and played Amanda to Coward's Elyot in Coward's hit comedy *Private Lives* in London and New York in 1930 and 1931. Although her comic and musical gifts did not translate particularly well to the wide screen, Lawrence also appeared in a number of films of the era—including *Mimi* (1935) with Douglas Fairbanks Jr. and *Rembrandt* (1936) with Charles Laughton. Her last major stage role was in Rodgers and Hammerstein's *The King and I* (1950), in which she played Anna to Yul Brynner's King of Siam. She died of cancer two years later at the age of fifty-four.

Though briefly married in her teens and romantically involved later with several of her leading men—Douglas Fairbanks was a favorite beau—Lawrence was bisexual in impulse. In 1949 she began a passionate affair with the British novelist and playwright Daphne du Maurier, author of *Rebecca* (1951). Lawrence wrote the little prose poem "Women Are Like Geography"—which may or may not be her own invention—on the back of a postcard sent to du Maurier in that year. The novelist, infatuated with "dear Gert," was delighted to be found "still high-toned and technical."

FURTHER READING: Gertrude Lawrence, *A Star Danced* (New York: Doubleday, 1945); Sheridan Morley, *Gertrude Lawrence* (New York: McGraw-Hill, 1981); Margaret Forster, *Daphne du Maurier* (London: Chatto and Windus, 1993); Philip Hoare, *Noël Coward: A Biography* (London: Sinclair-Stevenson, 1995).

Women are like geography:

From 16 to 22, like Africa—part virgin, part explored.

From 23 to 35, like Asia—hot and mysterious.

From 35 to 45, like the USA—high-toned and technical.

From 46 to 55, like Europe—quite devastated but interesting in places.

From 60 upwards like Australia—everybody knows about it but no one wants to go there.

"CLAIRE MORGAN" [PATRICIA HIGHSMITH] (1921–1995)

From *The Price of Salt* (1952)

The American novelist Patricia Highsmith—daughter of a British mother and German-descended father—was born in Fort Worth and raised in New York City. She studied classics at Barnard College, graduating in 1942. She had originally intended to become a painter and sculptor but started working for a comic book publisher in her twenties, supplying plots for illustration. She soon moved on to crime fiction, publishing her first novel, the mordantly suspenseful *Strangers on a Train*, in 1950. The work's brilliant central device—two men meet on a train and form a pact in which each agrees to murder a victim of the other's choice—inspired Alfred Hitchcock's classic film of the same name, released in 1951. Highsmith soon followed with *The Blunderer* (1954), *The Talented Mr. Ripley* (1955), and *Deep Water* (1957). The character of Ripley in the second of these—a chillingly amoral young man who kills and then impersonates a wealthy acquaintance living in Europe—became Highsmith's trademark creation: a kind of suave, sociopathic anti–Sherlock Holmes. He reappears—wreaking ever more subtle havoc—in a series of elegant sequels: *Ripley Underground* (1970), *Ripley's Game* (1974), *The Boy Who Followed Ripley* (1980), and *Ripley Under Water* (1991).

Literate, disturbing, and often surreally plotted, Highsmith's novels brought her both financial and critical success. (Graham Greene, Julian Symons, and Gore Vidal were all confessed admirers.) Uncomfortable with fame, however, she moved to Europe in 1963, eventually settling in a remote part of Switzerland. There she continued to write—not only popular thrillers but also a how-to guide, *Plotting and Writing Suspense Fiction* (1966), and several best-selling collections of short stories, including *The Snail-Watcher and Other Stories* (1970), *Little Tales of Misogyny* (1977), and *Tales of Natural and Unnatural Catastrophes* (1987). Her last novel, *Small g: A Summer Idyll*, a quirky tragicomedy about the American expatriate colony in Zurich, was published in 1995; her *Selected Stories* appeared posthumously in 2001.

Highsmith's fiction often features overtly or covertly homosexual characters. (The creepy Ripley, for example, is erotically entangled with several of his male victims.) In 1952, under the name "Claire Morgan," Highsmith published a full-blown sapphic romance: the underground lesbian classic *The Price of Salt*. As she acknowledged when the book was reissued by a feminist press in 1984, she had originally had to publish it under a pseudonym because her regular publisher had rejected it out of hand. The work aroused anxiety, she thought, because it was "the first gay book with a happy ending."

> The homosexual novel then had to have a tragic ending. Usually it was about men. One of the main characters, if not both, had to cut his wrists, or drown himself in the swimming pool of some lovely estate, or one had to say good-bye to his partner, having decided to go straight. One of them had to see the error of his/her ways, the wretchedness ahead, had to conform in order to—what? Get the book published? Make sure the publisher wouldn't give himself a black eye by seeming to condone homosexuality? It was as if youth had to be warned against being attracted to the same sex, as youth now is warned against drugs.

Without being in any way sentimental, Highsmith's own novel rejects such melo-dramatic clichés. The two main characters, Therese and Carol, not only fall in love—happily and passionately—they also manage to outwit Carol's abusive husband, an alcoholic boor intent on humiliating his wife at their upcoming divorce trial. The char-acters are all complex and believable (even the weak husband), and Highsmith handles the lesbian love story with realism and frankness. Though dated in certain respects, *The Price of Salt* continues to please—as much for its emotional intelligence as its sure-footed plotting.

In the excerpt below—from the beginning of the novel—the two women who will become lovers meet for the first time. Therese Belivet, a young would-be theater designer, is working to make ends meet as a salesgirl in the toy department of a large New York department store. In the busy, banal run-up to Christmas, she encounters Carol, an elegant, appraising, somewhat mysterious older woman who comes shopping for a doll-case.

FURTHER READING: Patricia Highsmith, *Strangers on a Train* (New York: Harper, 1950); —, (writing as "Claire Morgan"), *The Price of Salt* (1952; rpt., Tallahassee, Fla.: Naiad, 1984); —, *The Blunderer* (New York: Coward-McCann, 1954); —, *The Talented Mr. Ripley* (New York: Coward-McCann, 1955); —, *Plotting and Writing Suspense Fic-tion* (Boston: Writer, 1966); —, *The Snail-Watcher and Other Stories* (Garden City, N.Y.: Doubleday, 1970); —, *A Dog's Ransom* (New York: Knopf, 1972); —, *Edith's Diary* (London: Heinemann, 1977); —, *Little Tales of Misogyny* (London: Heinemann, 1977); —, *The Black House* (London: Heinemann, 1981); —, *Slowly, Slowly in the Wind* (New York: Penguin, 1982); —, *Tales of Natural and Unnatural Catastrophes* (New York: Atlantic Monthly, 1987); —, *Small g: A Summer Idyll* (London: Bloomsbury, 1995); —, *The Ripley Omnibus: The Talented Mr. Ripley; Ripley Underground; Ripley's Game* (New York: Knopf, 1999); —, *The Selected Stories of Patricia Highsmith* (New York: Norton, 2001); Kathleen Gregory Klein, "Patricia Highsmith," in Jane S. Bakerman, ed., *And Then There Were None . . . More Women of Mystery* (Bowling Green, Ohio: Popular, 1985), pp. 170–97; Odette L'Henry Evans, "A Feminist Approach to Patricia Highsmith's Fiction," in Brian Docherty, ed., *American Horror Fiction: From Brockden Brown to Stephen King* (New York: St. Martin's, 1990), pp. 107–119; Bonnie Zimmerman, *The Safe Sea of Women: Lesbian Fiction, 1969–1989* (Boston, Mass.: Beacon, 1990); Russell Harrison, *Patricia Highsmith* (New York: Twayne, 1997); Sally Munt, "Patricia Highsmith (1921–1995)," in Claude J. Summers, ed., *The Gay and Lesbian Literary Heritage: A Reader's Companion to the Writers and Their Works from Antiquity to the Present* (New York: Henry Holt, 1995), pp. 363–64; David Cochran, " 'Some Torture that Perversely Eased': Patricia Highsmith and the Everyday Schizophrenia of American Life," *Clues: A Journal of Detection* 18 (1997): 157–80; Michael Bronski, "The Subversive Ms. Highsmith," *Gay and Lesbian Review Worldwide* 7 (2000), 13–16.

Roberta Walls, the youngest D.S. in the toy department, paused just long enough in her midmorning flurry to whisper to Therese, "If we don't sell this twenty-four ninety-five suitcase today, it'll be marked down Monday and the department'll take a two-dollar loss!" Roberta nodded at the brown pasteboard suitcase on the counter, thrust her load of gray boxes into Miss Martucci's hands, and hurried on.

Down the long aisle, Therese watched the salesgirls make way for Roberta. Roberta flew up and down counters and from one corner of the floor to the other, from nine in the morning until six at night. Therese had heard that Roberta was trying for another promotion. She wore red harlequin glasses, and unlike the other girls, always pushed the sleeves of her green smock up above her elbows. Therese saw her flit across an aisle and stop Mrs. Hendrickson with an excited message delivered with gestures. Mrs. Hendrickson nodded agreement, Roberta touched her shoulder familiarly, and Therese felt a small start of jealousy. Jealousy, though she didn't care in the least for Mrs. Hendrickson, even disliked her.

"Do you have a doll made of cloth that cries?"

Therese didn't know of such a doll in stock, but the woman was positive Frankenberg's had it, because she had seen it advertised. Therese pulled out another box, from the last spot it might possibly be, and it wasn't.

"Wotcha lookin' fuh?" Miss Santini asked her. Miss Santini had a cold.

"A doll made of cloth that cries," Therese said. Miss Santini had been especially courteous to her lately. Therese remembered the stolen meat. But now Miss Santini only lifted her eyebrows, stuck out her bright red underlip with a shrug, and went on.

"Made of cloth? With pigtails?" Miss Martucci, a lean, straggly haired Italian girl with a long nose like a wolf's, looked at Therese. "Don't let Roberta hear you," Miss Martucci said with a glance around her. "Don't let anybody hear you, but those dolls are in the basement."

"Oh." The upstairs toy department was at war with the basement toy department. The tactics were to force the customer into buying on the seventh floor, where everything was more expensive. Therese told the woman the dolls were in the basement.

"Try and sell this today," Miss Davis said to her as she sidled past, slapping the battered imitation alligator suitcase with her red-nailed hand.

Therese nodded.

"Do you have any stiff-legged dolls? One that stands up?"

Therese looked at the middle-aged woman with the crutches that thrust her shoulders high. Her face was different from all the other faces across the counter, gentle, with a certain cognizance in the eyes as if they actually saw what they looked at.

"That's a little bigger than I wanted," the woman said when Therese showed her a doll. "I'm sorry. Do you have a smaller one?"

"I think so." Therese went farther down the aisle, and was aware that the woman followed her on her crutches, circling the press of people at the counter, so as to save Therese walking back with the doll. Suddenly Therese wanted to take infinite pains, wanted to find exactly the doll the woman was looking for. But the next doll wasn't quite right, either. The doll didn't have real hair. Therese tried in another place and found the same doll with real hair. It even cried when it bent over. It was exactly what the woman wanted. Therese laid the doll down carefully in fresh tissue in a new box.

"That's just perfect," the woman repeated. "I'm sending this to a friend in Australia who's a nurse. She graduated from nursing school with me, so I made a little uniform like ours to dress a doll in. Thank you so much. And I wish you a merry Christmas!"

"Merry Christmas to you!" Therese said, smiling. It was the first merry Christmas she had heard from a customer.

"Have you had your relief yet, Miss Belivet?" Mrs. Hendrickson asked her, as sharply as if she reproached her.

Therese hadn't had it. She got her pocketbook and the novel she was reading from the shelf under the wrapping counter. The novel was Joyce's *Portrait of the Artist as a Young Man*, which Richard was anxious for her to read. How anyone could have read Gertrude Stein without reading any Joyce, Richard said, he didn't know. She felt a bit inferior when Richard talked with her about books. She had browsed all over the bookshelves at school, but the library assembled by the Order of St. Margaret had been far from catholic, she realized now, though it had included such unexpected writers as Gertrude Stein.

The hall to the employees' rest room was blocked by big shipping carts piled high with boxes. Therese waited to get through.

"Pixie!" one of the shipping cart boys shouted to her.

Therese smiled a little because it was silly. Even down in the cloakroom in the basement, they yelled "Pixie!" at her morning and night.

"Pixie, waiting for me?" the raw-edged voice roared again, over the crash and bump of the stock carts.

She got through, and dodged a shipping cart that hurtled toward her with a clerk aboard.

"No smoking here!" shouted a man's voice, the very growly voice of an executive, and the girls ahead of Therese who had lighted cigarettes blew their smoke in the air and said loudly in chorus just before they reached the refuge of the women's room, "Who does he think he is, Mr. Frankenberg?"

"Yoo-hoo! Pixie!"

"Ah'm juss bahdin mah tahm, Pixie!"

A shipping cart skidded in front of her, and she struck her leg against its metal corner. She went on without looking down at her leg, though pain began to blossom there, like a slow explosion. She went on into the different chaos of women's voices, women's figures, and the smell of disinfectant. Blood was running to her shoe, and her stocking was torn in a jagged hole. She pushed some skin back into place, and feeling sickened, leaned against the wall and held on to a water pipe. She stayed there a few seconds, listening to the confusion of voices among the girls at the mirror. Then she wet toilet paper and daubed until the red was gone from her stocking, but the red kept coming.

"It's all right, thanks," she said to a girl who bent over her for a moment, and the girl went away.

Finally, there was nothing to do but buy a sanitary napkin from the slot machine. She used a little of the cotton from inside it, and tied it on her leg with the gauze. And then it was time to go back to the counter.

Their eyes met at the same instant, Therese glancing up from a box she was opening, and the woman just turning her head so she looked directly at Therese. She was tall and fair, her long figure graceful in the loose fur coat that she held open with a hand on her waist. Her eyes were gray, colorless, yet dominant as light or fire, and caught by them, Therese could not look away. She heard the customer in front of her repeat a question, and Therese stood there, mute. The woman was looking at Therese, too, with a preoccupied expression as if half her mind were on whatever it was she meant to buy here, and though there were a number of salegirls between them, Therese felt sure the woman would come to her. Then Therese saw her walk slowly toward the counter, heard her heart stumble to catch up with the moment it had let pass, and felt her face grow hot as the woman came nearer and nearer.

"May I see one of those valises?" the woman asked, and leaned on the counter, looking down through the glass top.

The damaged valise lay only a yard away. Therese turned around and got a box from the bottom of a stack, a box that had never been opened. When she stood up, the woman was looking at her with the calm gray eyes that Therese could neither quite face nor look away from.

"That's the one I like, but I don't suppose I can have it, can I? she said, nodding toward the brown valise in the show window behind Therese.

Her eyebrows were blond, curving around the bend of her forehead. Her mouth was as wise as her eyes, Therese thought, and her voice was like her coat, rich and supple, and somehow full of secrets.

"Yes," Therese said.

Therese went back to the stockroom for the key. The key hung just inside the door on a nail, and no one was allowed to touch it but Mrs. Hendrickson.

Miss Davis saw her and gasped, but Therese said, "I need it," and went out.

She opened the show window and took the suitcase down and laid it on the counter.

"You're giving me the one that's on display?" She smiled as if she understood. She said casually, leaning both forearms on the counter, studying the contents of the valise, "They'll have a fit, won't they?"

"It doesn't matter," Therese said.

"All right. I'd like this. That's C.O.D. And what about clothes? Do these come with it?"

There were cellophane wrapped clothes in the lid of the suitcase, with a price tag on them. Therese said, "No, they're separate. If you want doll clothes—these aren't as good as the clothes in the dolls' clothing department across the aisle."

"Oh! Will this get to New Jersey before Christmas?"

"Yes, it'll arrive Monday." If it didn't, Therese thought, she would deliver it herself.

"Mrs. H. F. Aird," the woman's soft, distinct voice said, and Therese began to print it on the green C.O.D. slip.

The name, the address, the town appeared beneath the pencil point like a secret Therese would never forget, like something stamping itself in her memory forever.

"You won't make any mistakes, will you?" the woman's voice asked.

Therese noticed the woman's perfume for the first time, and instead of replying, could only shake her head. She looked down at the slip to which she was laboriously adding the necessary figures, and wished with all her power to wish anything, that the woman would simply continue her last words and say, "Are you really so glad to have met me? Then why can't we see each other again? Why can't we even have lunch together today?" Her voice was so casual, and she might have said it so easily. But nothing came after the "will you?" nothing to relieve the shame of having been recognized as a new salesgirl, hired for the Christmas rush, inexperienced and liable to make mistakes. Therese slid the book toward her for her signature.

Then the woman picked up her gloves from the counter, and turned, and slowly went away, and Therese watched the distance widen and widen. Her ankles below the fur coat were pale and thin. She wore plain black suede shoes with high heels.

"That's a C.O.D. order?"

Therese looked into Mrs. Hendrickson's ugly meaningless face. "Yes, Mrs. Hendrickson."

"Don't you know you're supposed to give the customer the strip at the top? How do you expect them to claim the purchase when it comes? Where's the customer? Can you catch her?"

"Yes." She was only ten feet away, across the aisle at the dolls' clothing counter. And with the green slip in her hand, she hesitated a moment, then carried it around the counter, forcing herself to advance, because she was suddenly abashed by her appearance, the old blue skirt, the cotton blouse—whoever assigned the green smocks had missed her—and the humiliating flat shoes. And the horrible bandage through which the blood was probably showing again.

"I'm supposed to give you this," she said, laying the miserable little scrap beside the hand on the edge of the counter, and turning away.

Behind the counter again, Therese faced the stock boxes, sliding them thoughtfully out and back, as if she were looking for something. Therese waited until the woman must have finished at the counter and gone away. She was conscious of the moments passing like irrevocable time, irrevocable happiness, for in these last seconds, she might turn and see the face she would never see again. She was conscious, too, dimly now and with a different horror, of the old, unceasing voices of customers at the counter calling for assistance, calling to her, and of the low, humming rrrrrr of the little train, part of the storm that was closing in and separating her from the woman.

But when she turned finally, she looked directly into the gray eyes again. The woman was walking toward her, and as if time had turned back, she leaned on the counter again and gestured to a doll and asked to see it.

Therese got the doll and dropped it with a clatter on the glass counter, and the woman glanced at her.

"Sounds unbreakable," the woman said.

Therese smiled.

"Yes, I'll get this, too," she said in the quiet slow voice that made a pool of silence in the tumult around them. She gave her name and address again, and Therese took it slowly from her lips, as if she did not already know it by heart. "That will really arrive before Christmas?"

"It'll come Monday at the latest. That's two days before Christmas."

"Good. I don't mean to make you nervous."

Therese tightened the knot in the string she had put around the doll box, and the knot mysteriously came open. "No," she said. In an embarrassment so profound there was nothing left to defend, she got the knot tied under the woman's eyes.

"It's a rotten job, isn't it?"

"Yes." Therese folded the C.O.D slips around the white string, and fastened them with a pin.

"So forgive me for complaining."

Therese glanced at her, and the sensation returned that she knew her from somewhere, that the woman was about to reveal herself, and they would both laugh then, and understand. "You're not complaining. But I know it'll get there." Therese looked across the aisle, where the woman had stood before, and saw the tiny slip of green paper still on the counter. "You really are supposed to keep that C.O.D. slip."

Her eyes changed with her smile now, brightened with a gray, colorless fire that Therese almost knew, almost could place. "I've gotten things before without them. I always lose them." She bent to sign the second C.O.D. slip.

Therese watched her go away with a step as slow as when she had come, saw her look at another counter as she passed it, and slap her black gloves across her palm twice, three times. Then she disappeared into an elevator.

And Therese turned to the next customer. She worked with an indefatigable patience, but her figures on the sales slips bore faint tails where the pencil jerked convulsively. She went to Mr. Logan's office, which seemed to take hours, but when she looked at the clock, only fifteen minutes had passed, and now it was time to wash up for lunch. She stood stiffly in front of the rotating towel, drying her hands, feeling unattached to anything or anyone, isolated. Mr. Logan had asked her if she wanted to stay on after Christmas. She could have a job downstairs in the cosmetic department. Therese had said no.

In the middle of the afternoon, she went down to the first floor and bought a card in the greeting-card department. It was not a very interesting card, but at least it was simple, in plain blue and gold. She stood with the pen poised over the card, thinking of what she might have written—"You are magnificent" or even "I love you"—finally writing quickly the excruciatingly dull and impersonal: "Special salutations from Frankenberg's." She added her number 645-A in lieu of a signature. Then she went down to the post office in the basement, hesitated at the letter drop, losing her nerve suddenly at the sight of her hand holding the letter half in the slot. What would happen? She was going to leave the store in a few days, anyway. What would Mrs. H. F. Aird care? The blond eyebrows would perhaps lift a little, she would look at the card a moment, then forget it. Therese dropped it.

On the way home, an idea came to her for a stage set, a house interior with more depth than breadth, with a kind of vortex down the center, from which rooms would go off on either side. She wanted to begin the cardboard model that night, but at last she only elaborated on her pencil sketch of it. She wanted to see someone—not Richard, not Jack or Alice Kelly downstairs, maybe Stella, Stella Overton, the stage designer she had met during her first weeks in New York. Therese had not seen her, she realized, since she had come to the cocktail party Therese had given before she left her other apartment. Stella was one of the people who didn't know where she lived now. Therese was on her way down to the telephone in the hall, when she heard the short quick rings of her doorbell that meant there was a call for her.

"Thank you," Therese called down to Mrs. Osborne.

It was Richard's usual call around nine o'clock. Richard wanted to know if she felt like seeing a movie tomorrow night. It was the movie at the Sutton they still hadn't seen. Therese said she wasn't doing anything, but she wanted to finish a pillow cover. Alice Kelly had said she could come down and use her sewing machine tomorrow night. And besides, she had to wash her hair.

"Wash it tonight and see me tomorrow night," Richard said.

"It's too late. I can't sleep if my head's wet."

"I'll wash it tomorrow night. We won't use the tub, just a couple of buckets."

She smiled. "I think we'd better not." She had fallen into the tub the time Richard had washed her hair. Richard had been imitating the tub drain with writhings and gluggings, and she had laughed so hard, her feet slipped on the floor.

"Well, what about that art show Saturday? It's open Saturday afternoon."

"But Saturday's the day I have to work to nine. I can't get away till nine thirty."

"Oh. Well, I'll stay around school and meet you on the corner about nine thirty. Forty-fourth and Fifth. All right?"

"All right."

"Anything new today?"

"No. With you?"

"No. I'm going to see about boat reservations tomorrow. I'll call you tomorrow night."

Therese did not telephone Stella at all.

The next day was Friday, the last Friday before Christmas, and the busiest day Therese had known since she had been working at Frankenberg's, though everyone said tomorrow would be worse. People were pressed alarmingly hard against the glass counters. Customers she started to wait on got swept away and lost in the gluey current that filled the aisle. It was impossible to imagine any more people crowding onto the floor, but the elevators kept emptying people out.

"I don't see why they don't close the doors downstairs!" Therese remarked to Miss Martucci, when they were both stooping by a stock shelf.

"What?" Miss Martucci answered, unable to hear.

"Miss Belivet!" somebody yelled, and a whistle blew.

It was Mrs. Hendrickson. She had been using a whistle to get attention today. Therese made her way toward her past salesgirls and through empty boxes on the floor.

"You're wanted on the telephone," Mrs. Hendrickson told her, pointing to the telephone by the wrapping table.

Therese made a helpless gesture that Mrs. Hendrickson had no time to see. It was impossible to hear anything on a telephone now. And she knew it was probably Richard being funny. He had called her once before.

"Hello?" she said.

"Hello, is this coworker six forty-five A, Therese Belivet?" the operator's voice said over clickings and buzzings. "Go ahead."

"Hello?" she repeated, and barely heard an answer. She dragged the telephone off the table and into the stockroom a few feet away. The wire did not quite reach, and she had to stoop on the floor. "Hello?"

"Hello," the voice said. "Well—I wanted to thank you for the Christmas card."

"Oh. Oh, you're—"

"This is Mrs. Aird," she said. "Are you the one who sent it? Or not."

"Yes," Therese said, rigid with guilt suddenly, as if she had been caught in a crime. She closed her eyes and wrung the telephone, seeing the intelligent, smiling eyes again as she had seen them yesterday. "I'm very sorry if it annoyed you," Therese said mechanically, in the voice in which she spoke to customers.

The woman laughed. "This is very funny," she said casually, and Therese caught the same easy slur in her voice that she had heard yesterday, loved yesterday, and she smiled herself.

"Is it? Why?"

"You must be the girl in the toy department."

"Yes."

"It was extremely nice of you to send me the card," the woman said politely.

Then Therese understood. She had thought it was from a man, some other clerk who had waited on her. "It was very nice waiting on you," Therese said.

"Was it? Why?" She might have been mocking Therese. "Well—since it's Christmas, why don't we meet for a cup of coffee, at least? Or a drink."

Therese flinched as the door burst open and a girl came into the room, stood right in front of her. "Yes—I'd like that."

"When?" the woman asked. "I'm coming in to New York tomorrow in the morning. Why don't we make it for lunch? Do you have any time tomorrow?"

"Of course. I have an hour, from twelve to one," Therese said, staring at the girl's feet in front of her in splayed flat moccasins, the back of her heavy ankles and calves in lisle stockings, shifting like an elephant's legs.

"Shall I meet you downstairs at the Thirty-fourth Street entrance at about twelve?"

"All right. I—" Therese remembered now she went to work at one sharp tomorrow. She had the morning off. She put her arm up to ward off the avalanche of boxes the girl in front of her had pulled down from the shelf. The girl herself teetered back onto her. "Hello?" she shouted over the noise of tumbling boxes.

"I'm sow-ry," Mrs. Zabriskie said irritatedly, plowing out the door again.

"Hello?" Therese repeated.

The line was dead.

VIOLETTE LEDUC (1907–1972)

From *La Bâtarde* (1964)

The French novelist and autobiographer Violette Leduc, illegitimate daughter of a serving woman named Berthe, was born in Arras in 1907. Her mother resented her, and despite the compensatory affection she received from a grandmother and aunt, Leduc grew up with a painful sense of her own ugliness and insufficiency. In the years immediately following the First World War, she attended the Collège de Douai boarding school, where she had two tumultuous lesbian affairs—one with a schoolmate and one with a teacher—later commemorated in *La Bâtarde* (*The Bastard*). In 1926 she moved to Paris and worked for a meager wage as a copywriter at the Plon publishing house. In 1932 she became painfully infatuated with the homosexual author Maurice Sachs, who encouraged her to write, even as he rejected her sexual advances. With his assistance she managed to support herself as a freelance journalist until the outbreak of war in 1939. After a brief and unsuccessful wartime marriage, Leduc survived the Occupation by working as a black marketeer, though she later lost what money she had earned.

In 1946 Leduc fell in love with the philosopher and novelist Simone de Beauvoir, who, like Sachs, failed to return her affections. De Beauvoir nonetheless became Leduc's literary patron and helped her to publish her first novel, *L'Asphyxie*, with Gallimard that same year. After receiving plaudits from Jean Genet, Albert Camus, and other luminaries, an emboldened Leduc wrote several more works of fiction, including the novels *L'Affamée* (1948), *Ravages* (1955), and *La Vieille fille et la mort* (1958). True popular success, however, only came in 1964, with the publication of the autobiographical *La Bâtarde*. Owing to its sexual frankness and bleak revelation of its author's unhappy love life, the book was an immediate succès de scandale. Ironically, the book had already been expurgated *before* publication: fearing prosecution under French obscenity laws, Leduc's publishers had made her excise the chapter describing her early lesbian affairs. (After the offending chapter was published on its own under the title *Thérèse et Isabelle* in 1965 and failed to draw official complaint, it was reinstated in subsequent editions of *La Bâtarde*.) Sadly, Leduc was unable to enjoy her literary triumph for long. After producing two more volumes of autobiography, *La Folie en tête* (1970) and *La Chasse à l'amour* (1972), she died of cancer in 1972.

The excerpt below from *La Bâtarde*, detailing the beginning of the boarding school affair between the teenaged Violette and her beloved Isabelle, comes from the section of the work omitted in the first edition. Frank it is, though Leduc writes with a rhapsodical afflatus which even in translation sets her storytelling apart from the merely prurient or sensational. True, like other lesbian schoolgirl narratives, Leduc's tale of adolescent sexual obsession will end badly, with Isabelle's ultimate alienation and defection. In this erotic fatalism Leduc seems to reaffirm the dysphoric Law ruling lesbian schoolgirl narrative from Colette's *Claudine à l'école* to Dorothy Strachey's *Olivia*: the body of the Beloved must be foresworn. Yet in her dizzying recollections of lovemaking with Isabelle, Leduc reshapes this imperative into art of extraordinary sensual and emotional power.

FURTHER READING: Violette Leduc, *La Bâtarde*, trans. Derek Coltman (New York: Farrar, Straus and Giroux, 1965); —, *In the Prison of Her Skin*, trans. Derek Coltman (London: Hart-Davis, 1970); —, *Mad in Pursuit*, trans. Derek Coltman (New York: Farrar, Straus and Giroux, 1971); —, *La Chasse à l'amour* (Paris: Gallimard, 1972); Germaine Brée, *Women Writers in France* (New Brunswick: Rutgers University Press, 1973); Jane Rule, *Lesbian Images* (New York: Doubleday, 1975); Elaine Marks, "Lesbian Intertextuality," in Elaine Marks and George Stambolian, eds., *Homosexualities and French Literature* (Ithaca, N.Y.: Cornell University Press, 1979), pp. 353–77; Isabelle de Courtivron, *Violette Leduc* (Boston: Twayne, 1985); —, "From Bastard to Pilgrim: Rites and Writing for Madame," *Yale French Studies* 72 (1986): 133–48; Alex Hughes, *Violette Leduc: Mothers, Lovers, and Language* (London: Maney, 1994); —, "Desire and Its Discontents: Violette Leduc/*La Bâtarde*/The Failure of Love," in Alex Hughes, ed., *French Erotic Fiction: Women's Desiring Writing, 1880–1990* (Oxford: Berg, 1996), pp. 69–92; Carlo Jansiti, *Violette Leduc* (Paris: Grosset, 1999).

We were beginning the week with our usual Sunday evening session in the shoe shop; we had just come back from our half-term holiday. The shoe shop in our school was the room where we cleaned our shoes, not a place of lasts and hammers and nails. We polished away in a vault of monotony, windowless and badly lit; we sat dreaming with our shoes on our knees those first evenings back at school. The virtuous odor of the polish, that odor always associated with tonics in druggists' shops, made us listless. We languished over our brushes and rags. We had filed in, two by two, with the monitor, who was bored. Now the new assistant mistress was there sitting on the bench with us, reading, escaping into her story, away from the school, away from the town itself while we stroked our woolen rags across the leather with desultory gestures. That evening we were ten girls back at school, wan under waiting-room lights; ten girls back at school with nothing to say to each other, ten sulking girls forced into each others' company and avoiding each other.

I can count and recount: it was thirty days since I had been back at boarding school; for twenty-six evenings Isabelle had spat on the school as she spat on her shoe. My polish would be less hard if I were to spit like her. I could spread it more easily. She spits. Can the favorite student be annoyed? I am the bad student, I am the worst student in the whole of the senior dormitory. I don't care one way or the other. I loathe the headmistress, I loathe sewing, I loathe physical training, I loathe chemistry, I loathe everything, and I avoid the other girls. It's miserable, but I don't want to go away from here. My mother is married, my mother has been unfaithful. The shoebrush had fallen from my knees; Isabelle had given my brush a kick while I was brooding.

"My brush! Where is my brush?"

Isabelle spat more vigorously on the box-calf in front of her. My brush was under the assistant's foot. She was going to pay for that kick. I picked up the brush, I tipped back Isabelle's face, I thrust the rag spotted with polish, with dust and red cream, into her eyes, into her mouth. I glimpsed her milky skin through the opening in her uniform, I took my hand away from her face, I returned to my place. In silent fury, Isabelle wiped her lips and eyes. She spat for the sixth time on her shoe and shrugged her shoulders. The assistant closed her book and clapped her hands: the light flickered. Isabelle went on rubbing her shoe.

We were waiting for her. "You must come now," said the new assistant timidly. We had entered the shoe shop with clattering heels but we were ghosts as we left it in our black gym shoes like a line of orphans. The gym shoe, near relation to the espadrille, muffles what it strikes: stone, wood, earth. We borrowed the heels of angels to leave the shoe shop and walked with wads of melancholy in our canvas shoes. Every Sunday we went up to the dormitory with the monitor beside us, we breathed in the faint pink smell of disinfectant. Isabelle had caught up with us on the stairs.

I hate her, I want to hate her. It would be a relief if I could hate her even more. Tomorrow we shall be at the same table in the dining hall again. She smiles vaguely when I come in late. I can't change tables. But I crushed that smile of hers. That natural self-confidence of hers . . . I'll flatten that into her face as well. I'll go to the headmistress if I have to but I will change tables.

We entered the dormitory where the dark shine of the linoleum foretold the loneliness of the center aisle at midnight. We lifted our percale curtains and found ourselves once more in those cubicles without locks and without walls. Isabelle was the last to slide the rings of her curtain along their rod; the monitor made her tour of inspection along the aisle. We opened our suitcases, took out our linen, and put it away on the shelf in our closet, keeping out the two sheets for our narrow beds. We threw the key into the suitcase and closed it again for eight more days. We made our beds. Our things didn't belong to us in that municipal light. We pulled our uniforms back into shape on their coat hangers for the Thursday walk. We folded up our underclothes and put them on the chair, we took our bathrobes from their pegs.

Isabelle left the dormitory with her pitcher.

I am listening to the knot of her bathrobe cord brushing against the linoleum. I can hear her fingers drumming on the enamel. Her cubicle is opposite mine. I have that to face. Her comings and goings. I listen for them, her comings and goings. She laughs because I shut myself in the music room to practice diminished arpeggios. She says I pound, she says she can hear me in the study hall.

I went out into the aisle with my pitcher.

She was still there, always there, still there on the landing. I'd have undressed more slowly if I'd known that she was filling her pitcher at the tap. Shall I turn back? Shall I wait till she's gone before coming out? I won't turn back. I'm not afraid of her: I hate her. She knows there's someone behind her, but that wouldn't make her hurry. What nonchalance . . . She isn't even curious enough to look over her shoulder. I should never have come if I'd known she would dawdle like this. I thought she'd gone: here she is just in front of me. Her pitcher will soon be full. At last. I've seen her long hair let down before; how could I avoid it when she's always parading it up and down the aisle? Excuse me. She said excuse me. She brushed my face with her hair as I was standing thinking about it. It's unimaginable. She tossed back her hair into my face. She didn't know I was behind her and she said excuse me. It's unbelievable. She can't say I made you wait, I'm sorry, the tap isn't working properly. She just throws her hair in your face while she says excuse me. The water is running slower. Of course, because she's fiddling with the tap. I won't speak to you, you won't get a word out of me. You ignore me, I will ignore you. Why are you making me wait? Is that what you want? If you've got the time, so have I.

The assistant on duty in the aisle called to us as though there were some sort of complicity between us. Isabelle walked away.

I could hear her lying: she was explaining to the mistress that the water had stopped running. I went back to my cubicle.

The new assistant came and spoke to her again through her percale curtain. They were confiding in each other that they were both the same age: eighteen. A train whistled in the station and cut them short.

I pulled my curtain aside slightly: the proctor was moving away, he began reading again as he walked down the aisle; one of the girls was rustling the paper in a box of candy.

"I have strict orders," murmured the new assistant. "No visiting. All girls are to stay in their own cubicles."

As soon as we had washed, the assistant inspected us as we lay scrubbed and docile in our beds. Some of the girls gave her candies and delayed her with compliments and flattery, while Isabelle retired into her tomb. As soon as I had made a nest in my cold bed I forgot her, but if I woke up again I would grope for the thought of her in order to hate her. She didn't dream aloud, her bedsprings didn't creak. One night I got up at two in the morning, I went across the aisle, I held my breath and listened as she slept. She was an absence. She was laughing at me even in her sleep. I closed her curtain, I listened again. Yes, she was absent, she was having the last word. I hated her as I lay between sleeping and waking. I hated her in the bell at half-past six every morning, in the deep tones of her voice, in her washing water as it ran away, in her hand as it closed her tin of dentifrice. All you ever hear is her, I said to myself with unreasoning obstinacy. I hated the dust in her cubicle when she slid the mop under my curtain, when she bumped against the partition, when her hand disturbed the folds of my curtain. She didn't talk much, she performed all the required motions in the dormitory, in the dining hall, in classes: she was thoughtful during recreation periods. I wondered where she acquired her arrogance. She was good at her work without being either overzealous or conceited. Isabelle often used to pull the strings of my pinafore undone, then she pretended she hadn't when I turned around. She would begin the day teasing me in this way, like a little girl, and then she would immediately tie my pinafore up again for me, humiliating me twice instead of just once.

I got cautiously out of bed as though I were a smuggler. The new assistant stopped buffing her nails. I waited. Isabelle, who never coughed, coughed: for once she was still awake. I brushed the thought of her from my mind, I plunged my arm as far as the shoulder into an unappealing cloth bag hanging in my closet. I always concealed my flashlight and my books inside my dirty linen bag. I used to read at night. That evening I got back into bed with my flashlight and my book but without any desire to read. I switched on the flashlight, I lay gazing with brooding eyes at my gym shoes under the chair. The artificial moonlight filtering out from the assistant's cubicle gave all the objects in my cell a pale and sickly look.

I put out the flashlight, a girl rustled a piece of paper, I pushed away the book with a disgruntled hand. More like a statue on a tomb than the real thing, I said to myself as I imagined Isabelle lying there stiffly in her nightgown. The book fell shut, the flashlight sank into the eiderdown. I put my hands together, I prayed wordlessly for a world I could not envisage, I listened to the surf in the seashell so close to my belly. The assistant put out her light as well. She has all the luck sleeping there, all the luck, lost in her warm, downy tomb. The limpid tick-tock of my watch on the bedside table spurred me to action. I picked up the book again and began reading under the bedclothes.

Someone was spying on me from behind my curtain. Hidden beneath the bedclothes I could hear the inexorable tick-tock of the watch. A night train rolled out of the station drawn by a whistle that arrowed through shadows unknown to the school. I threw back the covers, I was afraid of the silent dormitory.

Someone was calling behind the percale curtain.

I lay low. I pulled the covers up over my head. I lit my flashlight.

"Violette," someone called inside my cubicle.

I put out the flashlight.

"What are you doing under your bedclothes?" asked the voice I didn't recognize.

"I'm reading."

Someone pulled back the covers. Someone pulled my hair.

"I told you I was reading."

"Not so loud," Isabelle said.

One of the girls coughed.

"You can report me if you want to. . . ."

Isabelle wouldn't report me. I was being unfair to her and I knew it.

"Weren't you asleep?"

"Not so loud," Isabelle said.

I was whispering too loud because I wanted my joy to be over and done with: my ecstasy was becoming an unbearable pride.

My visitor was still by my percale curtain. Her long hair hanging down inside my cubicle filled me with uncertainty.

"I'm afraid you'll say no. Say that you'll say yes to me," Isabelle said breathlessly.

I had switched on my flashlight again, I was being obliging to my visitor despite myself.

"Say yes!" Isabelle begged.

Now she was supporting herself with one finger on my bedside table.

She tightened the cord of her bathrobe. Her hair tumbled down over her ripening breasts, her face grew older.

"What are you reading?" She took her finger off the table.

"I was just beginning when you came in."

I put out the flashlight because she was looking at my book.

"The title . . . Tell me the title."

"*A Happy Man . . .*"

"That's the title? Is it good?"

"I've no idea. I've just begun it."

Isabelle was leaving, one of the curtain rings slid along its rod. I thought she was going back to her tomb. She stopped.

"Come and read in my room."

She was leaving again, she was scattering crystals of frost between her request and my answer.

"Will you come?"

Isabelle left my cubicle.

She had seen me with the bedclothes up to my neck. She didn't know I was wearing a special nightgown, a nightgown from a lingerie boutique. I thought one's personality could be changed by wearing expensive clothes. The silk nightgown brushed against my flanks with the softness of a spider's web. I dressed myself in my regulation nightgown, then I too left my cubicle, wrists gripped tightly by my regulation cuffs. The assistant mistress was asleep. I hesitated in front of Isabelle's curtain. I went in.

"What's the time?" I asked coldly.

I stayed by the curtain, I shone my flashlight toward the bedside table.

"Come over here," Isabelle said.

I didn't dare. Her long hair, all undone, seemed to belong to a stranger and it intimidated me. Isabelle was looking at the time.

"Come closer," she said to her wristwatch.

The luxuriance of the hair sweeping down the bars at the head of the bed. It made a shimmering screen hiding the face of a recumbent girl, it frightened me. I put out the light.

Isabelle got out of bed. She took my flashlight and my book away from me.

"Now come here," she said.

Isabelle was back in bed.

She lay in bed directing the beam of my flashlight.

I sat down on the edge of the mattress. She stretched her arm over my shoulder, took my book from the bedside table and gave it to me. She reassured me. I turned the pages of the book because she was staring at me, I didn't know which page to stop at. She waited for what I was waiting for.

I fastened my eyes on the first letter of the first line.

"Eleven o'clock," Isabelle said.

I gazed at the first page, at the words I could not see. She took the book from my hands and put out the light.

Isabelle pulled me backwards, she laid me down on the eiderdown, she raised me up, she kept me in her arms: she was taking me out of a world where I had never lived so that she could launch me into a world I had not yet reached; the lips opened mine a little, they moistened my teeth. The too fleshy tongue frightened me; but the strange virility didn't force its way in. Absently, calmly, I waited. The lips moved over my lips. My heart was beating too hard and I wanted to prolong the sweetness of the imprint, the new experience brushing at my lips. Isabelle is kissing me, I said to myself. She was tracing a circle around my mouth, she was encircling the disturbance, she laid a cool kiss in each corner, two staccato notes of music on my lips; then her mouth pressed against mine once more, hibernating there. My eyes were wide with astonishment beneath their lids, the sea-shells at my ears were whispering too loud. Isabelle continued: we climbed rung after rung down into the darkness below the darkness of the school, below the darkness of the town, below the darkness of the streetcar depot. She had made her honey on my lips, the sphinxes were drifting into sleep again. I knew that I had needed her before we met. Isabelle thrust back her hair which had been sheltering us.

"Do you think she's asleep?" she asked.

"The new assistant?"

"She's asleep," Isabelle decided.

"She's asleep," I said too.

"You're shivering. Take off your robe."

She opened the bedcovers.

"Come in without the light," Isabelle said.

She lay down against the partition, in her bed, at home. I took off my robe, I felt I was too new on the rug of an old world. I had to get into bed with her quickly because the floor was going away from under me. I stretched myself out along the edge of the mattress: prepared to escape like a thief in the night.

"You're cold. Come close to me," Isabelle said.

A sleeper coughed, trying to separate us.

She was already holding me, I was already held, we were already torturing one another, but the cheerful foot touching mine, the ankle rubbing against my ankle, reassured us. My nightgown occasionally brushed against me as we clutched one another and rolled back and forth. We stopped. Memory and the dormitory about us returned. Isabelle switched on the flashlight: she wanted to see me. I took it back from her. A wave carried her away and she sank down into the bed, then rose up again, plunged her face toward me, and held me to her. There were roses falling from the girdle she put around me. I fastened the same girdle around her.

"The bed mustn't make a noise," she said.

I felt for a cool place on the pillow, as though that would be the place to keep the bed silent. I found a pillow of blond hair. Isabelle pulled me on top of her.

We were still hugging each other, we both wanted to be swallowed up by the other. We had stripped ourselves of our families, the rest of the world, time, and light. As Isabelle lay crushed over my gaping heart I wanted to feel her enter it. Love is a harrowing invention. Isabelle, Violette, I thought to myself, trying to become accustomed to the magic simplicity of the two first names.

She swathed my shoulders in the white softness of her arm as though in a fur, she put my hand in the furrow between her breasts, on top of her muslin nightgown. The enchantment of my hand under hers, of my neck and shoulders clothed with her arm. And yet my face was alone: my eyelids were cold. Isabelle knew they were. Her tongue began to press against my teeth, impatient to make me warm all over. I shut myself up, I barricaded myself inside my mouth. She waited: that was how she taught me to open into flower. She was the hidden muse inside my body. Her tongue, her little flame, softened my muscles, my flesh. I responded, I attacked, I fought, I wanted to emulate her violence. We no longer cared about the noise we made with our lips. We were relentless with each other; then, becoming quieter, methodically, both together, we began drugging each other with our saliva. After the exchange of so much moisture, our lips parted despite themselves. Isabelle let herself fall into the hollow of my shoulder.

"Together," she said to regain her breath.

There was something crawling in my belly. I had a sea monster inside me.

Isabelle with a childish finger on my lips was tracing the outline of my mouth. The finger dropped down onto my neck. I seized it, I drew it across my eyes.

"They're yours," I said.

Isabelle didn't speak. Isabelle didn't move. If she were asleep it would be over. Isabelle was once more as she had always been. I no longer trusted her. I should have to leave. This was her cubicle, not mine. I was unable to move: we hadn't finished. If she were asleep, then she had lured me there on false pretenses.

Make her not be asleep among distant stars. Make the darkness not engender darkness in her.

Isabelle was not asleep!

She lifted my arm, my thigh grew pale. I felt a cold thrill of pleasure. I listened to what she took, to what she was giving, I blinked with gratitude: I was giving suck. Isabelle moved suddenly to another place. She was smoothing my hair, she was stroking the night out of my hair so that it ran all down my cheeks. She stopped, she created an intermission. Brow pressed against brow, we listened to the undertow; we were giving ourselves back to the silence, we were giving ourselves up to it.

A caress is to a shudder what twilight is to a lightning flash. Isabelle was dragging a rake of light from my shoulder to my wrist; she passed with her five-fingered mirror over my throat, over the back of my neck, over my back. I followed the hand, I could see under my eyelids a neck, a shoulder, an arm that didn't belong to me. She was raping my ear with her tongue as earlier she had raped my mouth. The artifice was shameless, the sensation strange. I grew cold again, this refinement of bestiality made me fearful. Isabelle found my head again, she held me by the hair and began again. I was disturbed by this fleshy icicle, but Isabelle's self-confidence reassured me.

She leaned out of the bed and opened the drawer in the bedside table.

"A shoelace! Why a shoelace?"

"I'm tying up my hair. Keep quiet, otherwise we shall be caught."

Isabelle was tying the knot, she was preparing herself. I listened to what is always alone: the heart. I waited: she would come when she was prepared.

A tiny bluish egg fell from her lips onto the spot she had left as her mouth returned to it. She opened the neck of my nightgown, she explored the curve of my shoulder with her cheek, with her brow. I accepted the marvels she was imagining on the curve of my shoulders. She was giving me a lesson in humility. I grew frightened. I was a living being. I wasn't a statue.

She closed the neck of my nightgown.

"Am I heavy?" she asked softly.

"Don't move . . ."

I wanted to squeeze her in my arms but I didn't dare. The quarter-hours were borne into the air, one by one, from the school clock. Isabelle was drawing a snail with her finger on the bare patch we have behind our ear lobes. She tickled me without meaning to. It was silly.

She took my head between her hands as though I'd been beheaded, she thrust her tongue into my mouth. She wanted us to be bony, all cutting angles. We tore each other to pieces with stony needles. The kiss slowed down as it reached my entrails, it disappeared, flowing warmly into the sea.

We stopped kissing one another and lay down; we pressed finger bone against finger bone and charged our knuckles with all we could find no words to say.

Isabelle coughed, our intertwined fingers fell silent.

"Let yourself go," she said.

She kissed the points of the collar, the braid on my nightgown; she molded the charity we have around our shoulders. The careful hand drew lines over my lines, curves over my curves. Behind my eyelids I could see the halo made by my shoulder as it came to life, I listened to the light springing to life under the caress.

I stopped her.

"Let me go on," she said.

The voice was slurred, the hand was sinking into a quicksand. I felt the shape of Isabelle's neck, her shoulder, her arm, along my neck, around my shoulder, along my arm.

A flower opened in every pore of my skin.

I took her arm, I thanked her with a kiss that drew the blood up to her skin.

"How good you are!" I said.

The poverty of my vocabulary made me lose heart. Isabelle's hands were trembling, they pulled a corselet of fine lawn tight over the cloth of my nightgown: her hands trembled with greed like the hands of a maniac.

She pushed herself up, she squeezed my waist. Isabelle, with her cheek pressed to mine, was telling a tale of friendship to my cheek.

Isabelle's fingers opened, closed again like the bud of a daisy and brought my breasts through pink mists out of their limbo. I was awakening to spring with a babble of lilacs under my skin.

"Do it more," I said.

Isabelle stroked my side. My flesh as she caressed it became a caress, my flank as she stroked it sent a soft glow seeping down into my drugged legs, into my melting ankles. My insides were being twisted, gently, gently.

"I can't go on."

We waited. We had to keep watch on the watchful shadows all around us.

I took her in my arms but I couldn't hug her as hard as I should have liked because of the narrow bed; I couldn't embed her in my flesh. A peremptory little girl suddenly pulled herself free:

"I want, I want . . ."

I will want what she wants, if the sea monsters stop their lazy coiling, if the shooting stars stop gliding through my limbs. I yearned for an avalanche of rocks.

"Do some more, do some more. . . ."

"You don't help me," said Isabelle.

Her hand moved forward beneath the cloth. I listened to the coolness of her hand, she listened to the heat of my skin. Her finger ventured onto the spot where the buttocks touch. It went on into the groove, it came out again. Isabelle stroked the two buttocks at the same time with one hand. My knees and feet were deliquescing.

"I can't bear it. I tell you I can't bear it."

Isabelle, unmoved, went on stroking quickly back and forth for a long time.

There were pincers pulling at me, I was being filled with spices. Isabelle fell on top of me.

"Are you all right?"

"Yes," I said, unsatisfied.

She returned to the attack, she offered me a kiss, her lips calmly pressed against mine.

Isabelle was turning her hands into claws in the fabric over my Venus' mound, she was going in and out, though without actually entering me; she was cradling my groin, her fingers, the cloth, and time itself.

"Are you all right?"

"Yes, Isabelle."

I didn't like the polite way it came out.

Isabelle persevered with her task in a new way, with one finger moving rhythmically on one of the lips. My body soaked up the light from the finger as sand soaks up the sea.

"Another time," she said into my neck.

"You want me to go now?"

"It would be more sensible."

I got out of bed.

"You want us to be parted?"

"No."

She wound her arms around me while I pretended to resist. It was the first time she had held me against her standing up.

We listened to the whirlwind turning the nebula in our insides, we followed the circling sails of the dormitory's shadowy windmills.

I brought Isabelle back in my turn from a wintry, windswept beach. I pulled back the covers, I helped her in.

"It's late. I was wrong just now: you must get some sleep."

"No, it's all right."

"You're yawning . . . you're half asleep already. . . ."

I gazed at her as I gaze out at the twilit sea when I can no longer see it.

"Yes, you must go now," Isabelle said.

If I got bored during study periods—and I did so often because I didn't work—I opened the door of my book locker, I passed the time by looking at the labels on the closed books, I thought of my books as standing there asleep. I had written the names of their authors on the labels. I folded my arms, I listened for a long while, and at last I heard the murmur of classical tragedies.

"Lily of the valley!"

The bouquet, just a few slips tied together, was lying on my leather satchel. I saw a green and white crucifix made of leaves and flowers laid out on my satchel. The gift lent me an armor of strength: I was too happy. I closed the door of the locker again, I shut myself up inside myself, I went back to the locker. The bouquet hadn't vanished. She had given me flowers from an old romance. She had set down leaves like lances and a talisman of flowers as one sets down a baby in a basket to abandon it. I fled to the dormitory with my treasure.

What shall we do tonight? Tomorrow in this classroom, in front of this desk, I shall remember what it was we did. I stare at *b* on the blackboard. I shall think quickly of what we did last night. Of everything we did, before the girl on monitor duty picks up the eraser, before she rubs out *b*. We didn't do anything. I'm being unfair. She kissed me, she came to me. Yes, she came to me. What a world . . . She lay on top of me. I throw myself at Isabelle's feet. I don't remember what we did and that's all I can think of. What shall we do tonight? Another girl will rub out the triangle, will rub out *a* and *b* and *c*.

It was all even stricter than in church. Isabelle was studying at the front table near the dais. I sat down in my place, I opened a book so as to be like her, I kept watch, I counted one, two, three, four, five, six, seven, eight. I can't go up to her, I can't make her look up from her book. Another girl went up to Isabelle's table without any hesitation, she showed her some work she'd done. They discussed it. Isabelle was still living as she had lived before she called me into her cubicle. Isabelle was disappointing me, Isabelle was casting a spell over me.

I can't read. Every meandering river in my geography book holds the same question in every loop. What can I do to make the time pass? She turns sideways; she has exposed herself to me but she doesn't know I'm drinking her in. She turns toward where I am sitting, she will never know what she gave me. She is talking, she is far away, she is discussing something, she is working: a foal is gamboling in her head. I'm not at all like her. I shall go to her, I shall force myself on her. She yawns—how human she is—she pulls the pin out of her coiled hair, she pushes it back again. She knows what she will do tonight, but she can think of other things.

Isabelle leaned toward me when the other girl left the study hall. Isabelle had noticed me.

I moved down the aisle, squeezed between the walls of my joy.

"My love. Were you there all the time?" she asked.

My head was suddenly quite empty.

"Bring your books. We'll work together. It's stifling in here."

I opened the window and, for heroism's sake, looked out into the courtyard.

"Aren't you bringing your books?"

"It would be impossible."

"Why?"

"I couldn't work near you."

When she sees me and her face changes like that, it's genuine. When she can't see me and her face is normal, that's genuine too.

"Do you really want me near you?" I asked.

"Sit down."

I sat down next to her, I sobbed a sob of happiness.

"What's the matter?"

"I can't explain."

She took my hand under the desk.

"Isabelle, Isabelle . . . What shall we do during recess?"

"We'll talk."

"I don't want to talk."

I took my hand away.

"Tell me what's the matter," Isabelle insisted.

"Can't you tell?"

"We'll be together again. I promise."

At about seven that evening I was surrounded by other girls suggesting I go for a walk with them or talk to them. I stammered, I moved away from the others. I was no longer free and I was no longer the same age. Shall I ever listen again, as I listened once, outside the kindergarten room, to the young mistress who studies at the Conservatoire and still plays Bach on the piano of her alma mater? Isabelle was putting away her books, Isabelle was near me. I turned to stone.

My peach skin: the light at seven in the evening in the recreation yard. My chervil: the spidery lace floating in the air. My reliquaries: the leaves on the trees making arbors for the breeze to rest in. What shall we do when night comes? What happens in the evening becomes uncertain in the daytime. I feel time caressing me but I can't think what we shall do next time. I can hear the seven o'clock noise and voices smoothing the thoughtful horizon. The gloved hand of infinity is closing over me.

"What are you looking at, Violette?"

"The geraniums . . . Down there . . ."

"What else?"

"The street, the window, they're all you."

"Give me your arm."

The evening came down over us with its velvet coat stopping at the knees.

"I can't give you my arm. People will notice, we would be caught."

"Are you ashamed?" Isabelle asked.

"Ashamed of what? Don't you understand? I'm being sensible."

The courtyard was all ours. We ran with our arms around each other's waist, we tore aside the lace in the air with our foreheads, we heard the pattering of our hearts in the dust. Little white horses galloped in our breasts. The girls, the mistresses all laughed and clapped their hands: they urged us on when we slowed down.

"Faster, faster. Close your eyes. I am leading you," Isabelle said.

There was a wall we had to go along. Then we would be alone.

"You're not running fast enough. Yes, yes . . . Close your eyes, close your eyes."

I obeyed.

Her lips brushed against my lips.

"I'm afraid . . . of the summer vacation, Isabelle. . . . I'm afraid of our last day in the courtyard, in summer. . . . I'm afraid of falling and killing myself," I said.

I opened my eyes: we were alive.

"Afraid? I'm leading you," she said.

"Let's run some more if you like."

"My wife, my baby," she said.

She gave me the words and kept them for herself as well. She held them to her by holding me to her. I loosened my fingers slightly around her waist. I counted: my love, my wife, my baby. I had three engagement rings on three fingers of my hand.

The other girls were standing without speaking, it was the minute of silence. Isabelle changed places. We closed the ranks, we were keeping our distance.

"I love you."

"I love you," I said too.

The juniors were already eating. We pretended to forget what we had both said, we both began talking to other girls.

I reached my percale curtain, following the nightly routine. An iron hand seized me and led me elsewhere. Isabelle threw me down onto her bed and buried her face in my underclothes.

"Come back when they're asleep," she said.

She drove me out again, she chained me to her.

I was in love: there was nowhere I could hide. There would be only the respites between our meetings.

Isabelle was coughing as she sat up in bed, Isabelle was ready beneath her shawl of hair. Her shawl. The picture I was going back to paralyzed me. I collapsed onto my chair, then onto the rug: the picture followed me everywhere.

I undressed in the half darkness, I pressed my chaste hand against my flesh, I breathed, I recognized my existence, I yielded myself. I piled up the silence at the bottom of my basin, I wrung it out as I wrung out my washcloth, I spread it gently over my skin as I wiped myself.

The assistant put out the light in her room. Isabelle coughed again: she was calling to me. I decided that if I didn't close my tin of dentifrice I would remember what everything was like before I went to Isabelle in her room. I was preparing a past for myself.

"Are you ready?" whispered Isabelle on the other side of my curtain.

She was gone again.

I opened the window of my cell. The night and the sky wanted no part of us. To live in the open air meant soiling everything outside. Our absence was necessary for the beauty of the evening trees. I risked my head in the aisle, but the aisle forced me back. Their sleep frightened me: I hadn't the courage to step over the sleeping girls, to walk with my bare feet over their faces. I closed the window again and the curtain shivered, like the leaves outside.

"Are you coming?"

I turned on my flashlight: her hair was falling as I had imagined it, but I had not foreseen her nightgown swollen with that bold simplicity. Isabelle went away again.

I went into her cubicle with my flashlight.

"Take off your nightgown," Isabelle said.

She was leaning on one shoulder, her hair raining over her profile.

"Take off your nightgown and put out the light. . . ."

I put out her hair, her eyes, her hands. I stripped off my nightgown. It was nothing new: I was stripping off the night of every first love.

"What are you doing?" Isabelle asked.

"I'm dawdling."

She stifled her laughter in the bed as I posed naked in my shyness for the shadows.

"What are you doing, for heaven's sake?"

I slid into the bed. I had been cold, now I would be warm.

I stiffened, I was afraid of brushing against her hair beneath the covers. She took hold of me, she pulled me on top of her: Isabelle wanted our skins to merge. I chanted with my body over hers, I bathed my belly in the lilies of her belly. I sank into a cloud. She touched me lightly on the buttocks, she sent strange arrows through my flesh. I pulled away, I fell back.

We listened to what was happening inside us, to the emanations from our bodies: we were ringed around with other couples. The bedsprings gave a groan.

"Careful!" she said against my mouth.

The assistant had switched on her light. I was kissing a little girl with a mouth that tasted of vanilla. We had become good little girls again.

"Let's squeeze each other," Isabelle said.

We tightened the girdles that were all we had in the world.

"Crush me. . . ."

She wanted to but she couldn't. She ground my buttocks with her fingers.

"Don't listen to her," she said.

The assistant was urinating in her toilet pail. Isabelle was rubbing her toe against my ankle as a token of friendship.

"She's asleep again," Isabelle said.

I took Isabelle by the mouth, I was afraid of the assistant, I drank our saliva. It was an orgy of dangers. We had felt the darkness in our mouths and throats, then we had felt peace return.

"Crush me," she said.

"The bed . . . it will make a noise . . . they'll hear us. . . ."

We talked amid the crowding leaves of summer nights.

I was crushing, blotting out, thousands of tiny cells beneath my weight.

"Am I too heavy?"

"You'll never be too heavy. I feel cold," she said.

My fingers considered her icy shoulders. I flew away, I snatched up in my beak the tufts of wool caught on thorns along the hedgerows and laid them one by one on

Isabelle's shoulders. I tapped at her bones with downy hammers, my kisses hurtling down on top of one another as I flung myself onward through quicksands of tenderness. My hands relieved my failing lips; I molded the sky around her shoulders. Isabelle rose, fell back, and I fell with her into the hollow of her shoulder. My cheek came to rest on a curve.

"My darling."

I said it over and over.

"Yes," Isabelle said.

She said: "Just a minute," and paused.

"Just a minute," Isabelle said again.

She was tying back her hair, her elbow fanned my face.

The hand landed on my neck: a frosty sun whitened my hair. The hand followed my veins, downward. The hand stopped. My blood beat against the mount of Venus on Isabelle's palm. The hand moved up again: it was drawing circles, overflowing into the void, spreading its sweet ripples ever wider around my left shoulder, while the other lay abandoned to the darkness streaked by the breathing of the other girls. I was discovering the smoothness of my bones, the glow hidden in my flesh, the infinity of forms I possessed. The hand was trailing a mist of dreams across my skin. The heavens beg when someone strokes your shoulder: the heavens were begging now. The hand moved upward once again, spreading a velvet shawl up to my chin, then down once more, persuasively, heavier now, shaping itself to the curves it pressed upon. Finally there was a squeeze of friendship. I took Isabelle into my arms, gasping with gratitude.

"Can you see me?" Isabelle asked.

"I see you."

She stopped me from saying more, slid down in the bed, and kissed the curling hairs.

"Listen, horses!" a girl cried nearby.

"Don't be afraid. She's dreaming. Give me your hand," Isabelle said.

I was weeping for joy.

"Are you crying?" she asked anxiously.

"I love you: I'm not crying."

I wiped my eyes.

The hand stripped the velvet off my arm, halted near the vein in the crook of the elbow, fornicated there amongst the traceries, moved downward to the wrist, right to the tips of the nails, sheathed my arm once more in a long suède glove, fell from my shoulder like an insect, and hooked itself into the armpit. I was stretching my neck, listening for what answers my arm was giving the wanderer. The hand, still seeking to persuade me, was bringing my arm, my armpit, into their real existence. The hand was wandering through whispering snow-capped bushes, over the last frosts on the meadows, over the first buds as they swelled to fullness. The springtime that had been crying its impatience with the voice of tiny birds under my skin was now curving and swelling into flower. Isabelle, stretched out upon the darkness, was fastening my feet with ribbons, unwinding the swaddling bands of my alarm. With hands laid flat upon the mattress, I was immersed in the selfsame magic task as she. She was kissing what she had caressed and then, light as a feather duster, the hand began to flick, to brush the wrong way all that it had smoothed before. The sea monster in my entrails quivered. Isabelle was drinking at my breast, the right, the left, and I drank with her, sucking the milk of darkness when her lips had gone. The fingers were returning now, encircling and testing the warm weight of my breast. The fingers were pretending to be waifs in a storm; they were taking shelter inside me. A host of slaves, all with the face of Isabelle, fanned my brow, my hands.

She knelt up in the bed.

"Do you love me?"

I led her hand up to the precious tears of joy.

Her cheek took shelter in the hollow of my groin. I shone the flashlight beam on her, and saw her spreading hair, saw my own belly beneath the rain of silk. The flashlight slipped, Isabelle moved suddenly toward me.

As we melted into one another we were dragged up to the surface by the hooks caught in our flesh, by the hairs we were clutching in our fingers; we were rolling together on a bed of nails. We bit each other and bruised the darkness with our hands.

Slowing down, we trailed back beneath our plumes of smoke, black wings sprouting at our heels. Isabelle leaped out of bed.

I wondered why Isabelle was doing her hair again. With one hand she forced me to lie on my back, with the other, to my distress, she shone the pale yellow beam of the flashlight on me.

I tried to shield myself with my arms.

"I'm not beautiful. You make me feel ashamed," I said.

She was looking at our future in my eyes, she was gazing at what was going to happen next, storing it in the currents of her blood.

She got back into bed, she wanted me.

I played with her, preferring failure to the preliminaries she needed. Making love with our mouths was enough for me: I was afraid, but my hands as they signaled for help were helpless stumps. A pair of tweezers was advancing into the folds of my flesh. My heart was beating under its molehill, my head was filled with damp earth. Two tormenting fingers were exploring me. How masterly, how inevitable their caress . . . My closed eyes listened: the finger lightly touched the pearl. I wanted to be wider, to make it easier for her.

The regal, diplomatic finger was moving forward, moving back, making me gasp for breath, beginning to enter, arousing the monster in my entrails, parting the secret cloud, pausing, prompting once more. I tightened, I closed over this flesh of my flesh its softness and its bony core. I sat up, I fell back again. The finger which had not wounded me, the finger, after its grateful exploration, left me. My flesh peeled back from it.

"Do you love me?" I asked.

I wanted to create a diversion.

"You mustn't cry out," Isabelle said.

I crossed my arms over my face, still listening under my lowered eyelids.

Two thieves entered me. They were forcing their way inside, they wanted to go further, but my flesh rebelled.

"My love . . . you're hurting me."

She put her hand over my mouth.

"I won't make any noise," I said.

The gag was a humiliation.

"It hurts. But she's got to do it. It hurts."

I gave myself up to darkness and without wanting to, I helped. I leaned forward to help tear myself, to come closer to her face, to be nearer my wound: she pushed me back onto the pillow.

She was thrusting, thrusting, thrusting. . . . I could hear the smacking noise it made. She was putting out the eye of innocence. It hurt me: I was moving on to my deliverance, but I couldn't see what was happening.

We listened to the sleeping girls around us, we sobbed as we sucked in our breath. A trail of fire still burned inside me.

"Let's rest," she said.

My memories of the two thieves grew kinder, my wounded flesh began to heal, bubbles of love were rising. But Isabelle returned to her task now, and the thieves were turning faster, ever faster. Where did this great wave come from? Smoothly now, into the depths. The drug flowed down toward my feet, my dreaming flesh lay steeped in visions. I lost myself with Isabelle in passion's calisthenics.

A great pleasure seemed to begin. It was only a reflection. Slow fingers left me. I was hungry, avid for her presence.

"Your hand, your face. Come closer."

"I'm tired."

Make her come closer, make her give me her shoulder, make her face be close to mine. I must barter my innocence for hers. She is not breathing: she is resting. Isabelle coughed as though she were coughing in a library.

I raised myself up with infinite precautions, I felt new-made. My sex, my clearing, and my bath of dew.

I switched on the flashlight. I glimpsed the blood, I glimpsed the red hair. I switched it off.

The rustling of the shadows at three in the morning sent a cold shudder through me. The night would pass, the night would soon be nothing but tears.

I shone the flashlight, I was not afraid of my open eyes.

"I can see the world. It all comes out of you."

The dawn trailing its shrouds. Isabelle was combing her hair in a limbo of her own, a no-man's land where her hair was always hanging loose.

"I don't want the day to come," Isabelle said.

It is coming, it will come. The day will shatter the night beneath its wheels.

"I'm afraid of being away from you," Isabelle said.

A tear fell in my garden at three in the morning.

I would not let myself think a single thought, so that she could go to sleep in my empty head. The day was advancing through the dark, the day was erasing our wedding night. Isabelle was going to sleep.

"Sleep," I said beside the flowering hawthorn that had waited for the dawn all night.

Like a traitor, I got out of the bed and went to the window. There had been a battle high up in the sky and its aftermath was chill. The mists were beating a retreat. Aurora was alone, with no one to usher her in. Already there were clusters of birds in a tree, pecking at her first beams. . . . I looked out at the half-mourning of the new day, at the tatters of the night, and smiled at them. I smiled at Isabelle and pressed my forehead against hers, pretending we were fighting rams. That way I would forget what I knew was dying. The lyric downpour from the birds as they sang and crystallized the beauty of the morning brought only fatigue: perfection is not of this world even when we meet it here.

"You must go," Isabelle said.

Leaving her like a pariah, leaving her furtively made me feel sad too. I had iron balls chained to my feet. Isabelle offered me her grief-stricken face. I loved Isabelle without a gesture, without any token of my passion: I offered her my life without a sign.

Isabelle pushed herself up and took me in her arms.

"You'll come every night?"

"Every night."

GRAHAM GREENE (1904–1991)

"Chagrin in Three Parts" (1967)

The English novelist, playwright, essayist, and travel writer Graham Greene was born in Hertfordshire in 1904 and studied at Balliol College, Oxford, where he converted to Catholicism. In 1926 he moved to London and became a subeditor for the *Times*. He married Vivien Dayrell-Browning in 1927 (their marriage would subsequently break up in 1941); his first novel, *The Man Within*, appeared in 1929. In the 1930s he worked as a film critic for the *Spectator* and traveled extensively in Mexico and Africa. After a five-year stint in the Foreign Office and MI6 during the Second World War—he was posted to Sierra Leone—he returned to writing full-time in 1946 and settled in Antibes, on the French Riviera. He lived there for much of the rest of his life, but continued to travel widely, especially in Latin and South America. One of his last works was a memoir of his curious friendship with the Panamanian dictator Omar Torrijos, *Getting To Know the General* (1984).

Though Greene wrote—masterfully—in many genres, he is best known for his novels. These fall into two categories. Early in his career he specialized in what he called "entertainments"—sophisticated thrillers and spy stories such as *Stamboul Train* (1932), *A Gun for Sale* (1936), *The Confidential Agent* (1939), *The Third Man* (1950) and *Our Man in Havana* (1958). Starting with the novel *Brighton Rock* (1938), however, he also began to write more serious fiction, in which moral and religious (and especially Catholic) themes played a prominent part. Works in the latter category include *The Power and the Glory* (1940), *The Heart of the Matter* (1948), *The End of the Affair* (1951), *A Burnt-Out Case* (1961), *The Comedians* (1966), *The Honorary Consul* (1973), and *The Human Factor* (1978). Greene wrote twenty-six novels in all—his last was *The Tenth Man*, published in 1985—as well as five books of short stories, three travel books, numerous plays and film scripts, and three volumes of autobiography.

"Chagrin in Three Parts," from the story collection *May We Borrow Your Husband? and Other Comedies of the Sexual Life* (1967), is a classic Greene miniature—a cocktail-hour vignette in which comedy, satire, and spleen are mixed in equal parts. The solitary, down-at-the-heels narrator, eavesdropping on two women in a restaurant, is a familiar Greene type: misanthropic, self-deprecating, and an expert in sly sidelong glances. ("Like most writers," he confesses, "I have the spirit of a *voyeur*.") In the bibulous

Madame Dejoie, however, he meets his match: a wily seductress whose subtle persuasions ("With a woman you do not have to be content with *une façon classique* three times a day") would seem—after several bottles of *blanc de blancs*—to defy rebuttal.

FURTHER READING: Graham Greene, *The Uniform Edition of the Works of Graham Greene* (London: Heinemann, 1950–54); —, *A Sort of Life* (New York: Simon and Schuster, 1971); Kenneth Allott and Miriam Farris, *The Art of Graham Greene* (London: Hamish Hamilton, 1951); R. W. B. Lewis, "The Fiction of Graham Greene: Between the Horror and the Glory," *Kenyon Review* 19 (Winter 1957): 56–75; David Lodge, *Graham Greene* (New York: Columbia University Press, 1971); Marie-Françoise Allain, *The Other Man: Conversations with Graham Greene* (New York: Simon and Schuster, 1981); Denis Donaghy, *Graham Greene: An Introduction to his Writings* (Amsterdam: Rodopi, 1983); A. A. DeVitis, *Graham Greene* (Boston: Twayne, 1986); Norman Sherry, *The Life of Graham Greene*, 2 vols. (New York: Viking Penguin, 1989–94); Michael Shelden, *Graham Greene* (London: Heinemann, 1994); Robert Hoskins, *Graham Greene: An Approach to the Novels* (New York: Garland, 1999); Cates Baldridge, *Graham Greene's Fictions: The Virtues of Extremity* (Columbia: University of Missouri Press, 2000); Shirley Hazzard, *Greene on Capri: A Memoir* (New York: Farrar, Straus and Giroux, 2000); Julia Llewellyn Smith, *Traveling on the Edge: Journeys in the Footsteps of Graham Greene* (New York: St. Martin's, 2001).

I

It was February in Antibes. Gusts of rain blew along the ramparts, and the emaciated statues on the terrace of the Château Grimaldi dripped with wet, and there was a sound absent during the flat blue days of summer, the continual rustle below the ramparts of the small surf. All along the Côte the summer restaurants were closed, but lights shone in Félix au Port and one Peugeot of the latest model stood in the parking-rank. The bare masts of the abandoned yachts stuck up like toothpicks and the last plane in the winter service dropped, in a flicker of green, red, and yellow lights, like Christmas-tree baubles, towards the airport of Nice. This was the Antibes I always enjoyed; and I was disappointed to find I was not alone in the restaurant as I was most nights of the week.

Crossing the road I saw a very powerful lady dressed in black who stared out at me from one of the window tables, as though she were willing me not to enter, and when I came in and took my place before the other window she regarded me with too evident distaste. My raincoat was shabby and my shoes were muddy, and in any case I was a man. Momentarily, while she took me in, from balding top to shabby toe, she interrupted her conversation with the *patronne*, who addressed her as Madame Dejoie.

Madame Dejoie continued her monologue in a tone of firm disapproval: it was unusual for Madame Volet to be late, but she hoped nothing had happened to her on the ramparts. In winter there were always Algerians about, she added with mysterious apprehension, as though she were talking of wolves, but none the less Madame Volet had refused Madame Dejoie's offer to be fetched from her home. "I did not press her under the circumstances. Poor Madame Volet." Her hand clutched a huge peppermill like a bludgeon, and I pictured Madame Volet as a weak timid old lady, dressed too in black, afraid even of protection by so formidable a friend.

How wrong I was. Madame Volet blew suddenly in with a gust of rain through the side door beside my table, and she was young and extravagantly pretty, in her tight black pants, and with a long neck emerging from a wine-red polo-necked sweater. I was glad when she sat down side by side with Madame Dejoie, so that I need not lose the sight of her while I ate.

"I am late," she said. "I know that I am late. So many little things have to be done when you are alone, and I am not yet accustomed to being alone," she added with a pretty little sob which reminded me of a cut-glass Victorian tear-bottle. She took off thick winter gloves with a wringing gesture which made me think of handkerchiefs wet with grief, and her hands looked suddenly small and useless and vulnerable.

"*Pauvre cocotte*," said Madame Dejoie, "be quiet here with me and forget awhile. I have ordered a bouillabaisse with langouste."

"But I have no appetite, Emmy."

"It will come back. You'll see. Now here is your porto and I have ordered a bottle of *blanc de blancs*."

"You will make me *tout à fait soûle*."

"We are going to eat and drink, and for a little while we are both going to forget everything. I know exactly how you are feeling, for I too lost a beloved husband."

"By death," little Madame Volet said. "That makes a great difference. Death is quite bearable."

"It is more irrevocable."

"Nothing can be more irrevocable than my situation. Emmy, he loves the little bitch."

"All I know of her is that she has deplorable taste—or a deplorable hairdresser."

"But that was exactly what I told him."

"You were wrong. I should have told him, not you, for he might have believed me, and in any case my criticism would not have hurt his pride."

"I love him," Madame Volet said, "I cannot be prudent," and then she suddenly became aware of my presence. She whispered something to her companion, and I heard the reassurance, "*Un anglais*." I watched her as covertly as I could—like most writers I have the spirit of a *voyeur*—and I wondered how stupid married men could be. I was temporarily free, and I very much wanted to console her, but I didn't exist in her eyes, now she knew that I was English, nor in the eyes of Madame Dejoie. I was less than human—I was only a reject from the Common Market.

I ordered two small *rougets* and a half bottle of Pouilly and I tried to be interested in the Trollope I had brought with me. But my attention strayed.

"I adored my husband," Madame Dejoie was saying, and her hand again grasped the pepper-mill, but this time it looked less like a bludgeon.

"I still do, Emmy. That is the worst of it. I know that if he came back . . ."

"Mine can never come back," Madame Dejoie retorted, touching the corner of one eye with her handkerchief and then examining the smear of black left behind.

In a gloomy silence they both drained their portos. Then Madame Dejoie said with determination, "There is no turning back. You should accept that as I do. There remains for us only the problem of adaptation."

"After such a betrayal I could never look at another man," Madame Volet replied. At that moment she looked right through me. I felt invisible. I put my hand between the light and the wall to prove that I had a shadow, and the shadow looked like a beast with horns.

"I would never suggest another man," Madame Dejoie said. "Never."

"What then?"

"When my poor husband died from an infection of the bowels I thought myself quite inconsolable, but I said to myself, Courage, courage. You must learn to laugh again."

"To laugh!" Madame Volet exclaimed. "To laugh at what?" But before Madame Dejoie could reply, Monsieur Félix had arrived to perform his neat surgical operation upon the fish for the bouillabaisse. Madame Dejoie watched with real interest; Madame Volet, I thought, watched for politeness' sake while she finished a glass of *blanc de blancs*.

When the operation was over Madame Dejoie filled the glasses and said, "I was lucky enough to have *une amie* who taught me not to mourn for the past." She raised her glass and, cocking a finger as I had seen men do, she added, "*Pas de mollesse.*"

"*Pas de mollesse,*" Madame Volet repeated with a wan enchanting smile.

I felt decidedly ashamed of myself—a cold literary observer of human anguish. I was afraid of catching poor Madame Volet's eyes (what kind of a man was capable of betraying her for a woman who took the wrong sort of rinse?) and I tried to occupy myself with sad Mr. Crawley's courtship as he stumped up the muddy lane in his big clergyman's boots. In any case, the two of them had dropped their voices; a gentle smell of garlic came to me from the bouillabaisse, the bottle of *blanc de blancs* was nearly finished, and, in spite of Madame Volet's protestation, Madame Dejoie had called for another. "There are no half bottles," she said. "We can always leave something for the gods." Again their voices sank to an intimate murmur as Mr. Crawley's suit was accepted (though how he was to support an inevitably large family would not appear until the succeeding volume). I was startled out of my forced concentration by a laugh: a musical laugh: it was Madame Volet's.

"*Cochon!*" she exclaimed.

Madame Dejoie regarded her over her glass (the new bottle had already been broached) under beetling brows. "I am telling you the truth," she said. "He would crow like a cock."

"But what a joke to play!"

"It began as a joke, but he was really proud of himself. *Aprés seulement deux coups . . .*"

"*Jamais trois?*" Madame Volet asked and she giggled and splashed a little of her wine down her polo-necked collar.

"*Jamais.*"

"*Je suis saoule.*"

"*Moi aussi, cocotte.*"

Madame Volet said, "To crow like a cock—at least it was a *fantaisie*. My husband has no *fantaisies*. He is strictly classical."

"*Pas de vices?*"

"*Hélas, pas de vices.*"

"And yet you miss him?"

"He worked hard," Madame Volet said and giggled. "To think that at the end he must have been working hard for both of us."

"You found it a little boring?"

"It was a habit—how one misses a habit. I wake now at five in the morning."

"At five?"

"It was the hour of his greatest activity."

"My husband was a very small man," Madame Dejoie said. "Not in height, of course. He was two meters high."

"Oh, Paul is big enough—but always the same."

"Why do you continue to love that man?" Madame Dejoie sighed and put her large hand on Madame Volet's knee. She wore a signet ring which perhaps had belonged to her late husband. Madame Volet sighed too, and I thought melancholy was returning to the table, but then she hiccupped and both of them laughed.

"*Tu es vraiment saoule, cocotte.*"

"Do I truly miss Paul, or is it only that I miss his habits?" She suddenly met my eye and blushed right down into the wine-coloured wine-stained polo-necked collar.

Madame Dejoie repeated reassuringly, "*Un anglais—ou un américain.*" She hardly bothered to lower her voice at all. "Do you know how limited my experience was when my husband died? I loved him when he crowed like a cock. I was glad he was so pleased. I only wanted him to be pleased. I adored him, and yet in those days—*j'ai joui peut-être trois fois par semaine*. I did not expect more. It seemed to me a natural limit."

"In my case it was three times a day," Madame Volet said and giggled again. "*Mais toujours d'une façon classique.*" She put her hands over her face and gave a little sob. Madame Dejoie put an arm round her shoulders. There was a long silence while the remains of the bouillabaisse were cleared away.

2

"Men are curious animals," Madame Dejoie said at last. The coffee had come and they divided one *marc* between them, in turn dipping lumps of sugar which they inserted into each other's mouth. "Animals too lack imagination. A dog has no *fantaisie*."

"How bored I have been sometimes," Madame Volet said. "He would talk politics continually and turn on the news at eight in the morning. At eight! What do I care for politics? But if I asked his advice about anything important he showed no interest at all. With you I can talk about anything, about the whole world."

"I adored my husband," Madame Dejoie said, "yet it was only after his death I discovered my capacity for love. With Pauline. You never knew Pauline. She died five years ago. I loved her more than I ever loved Jacques, and yet I felt no despair when she died. I knew that it was not the end, for I knew by then my capacity."

"I have never loved a woman," Madame Volet said.

"*Chérie*, then you do not know what love can mean. With a woman you do not have to be content with *une façon classique* three times a day."

"I love Paul, but he is different from me in every way . . ."

"Unlike Pauline, he is a man."

"Oh Emmy, you describe him so perfectly. How well you understand. A man!"

"When you really think of it, how comic that little object is. Hardly enough to crow about, one would think."

Madame Volet giggled and said, "*Cochon*."

"Perhaps smoked like an eel one might enjoy it."

"Stop it. Stop it." They rocked up and down with little gusts of laughter. They were drunk, of course, but in the most charming way.

3

How distant now seemed Trollope's muddy lane, the heavy boots of Mr. Crawley, his proud shy courtship. In time we travel a space as vast as any astronaut's. When I looked up Madame Volet's head rested on Madame Dejoie's shoulder. "I feel so sleepy," she said.

"Tonight you shall sleep, *chérie*."

"I am so little good to you. I know nothing."

"In love one learns quickly."

"But am I in love?" Madame Volet asked, sitting up very straight and staring into Madame Dejoie's sombre eyes.

"If the answer were no, you wouldn't ask the question."

"But I thought I could never love again."

"Not another man," Madame Dejoie said. "*Chérie*, you are almost asleep. Come."

"The bill?" Madame Volet said as though perhaps she were trying to delay the moment of decision.

"I will pay tomorrow. What a pretty coat this is—but not warm enough, *Chérie*, in February. You need to be cared for."

"You have given me back my courage," Madame Volet said. "When I came in here I was *si démoralisée. . . .*"

"Soon—I promise—you will be able to laugh at the past. . . ."

"I have already laughed," Madame Volet said. "Did he really crow like a cock?"

"Yes."

"I shall never be able to forget what you said about smoked eel. Never. If I saw one now . . ." She began to giggle again and Madame Dejoie steadied her a little on the way to the door.

I watched them cross the road to the car-park. Suddenly Madame Volet gave a little hop and skip and flung her arms around Madame Dejoie's neck, and the wind, blowing through the archway of the port, carried the faint sound of her laughter to me where I sat alone *chez* Félix. I was glad she was happy again. I was glad that she was in the kind reliable hands of Madame Dejoie. What a fool Paul had been, I reflected, feeling *chagrin* myself now for so many wasted opportunities.

ISAAC BASHEVIS SINGER (1904–1991)

"Zeitl and Rickel" (1968)

Isaac Bashevis Singer, the great Yiddish novelist and short-story writer, was born in Leoncin, Poland, in 1904 and spent his childhood in Warsaw and Bilgoray. His father, a Hasidic rabbi, raised his family in what one of Singer's biographers has called "almost medieval Jewish orthodoxy." The ultratraditional world of his Polish-Jewish youth had an incalculable influence on Singer's literary art. After an unhappy year at a rabbinical seminary, he began working as a translator and proofreader for the Yiddish literary magazine, *Literarische Bletter*, in Warsaw in 1923. He published his first stories in the journal in 1925 and 1926. In 1935, a year after the publication of his first novel, *Satan in Goray*, Singer moved to the United States, where he lived for a number of years in poverty and obscurity in the Jewish enclave of Williamsburgh in Brooklyn. He married in 1940; his first novel to be translated into English, *The Family Moskat*, appeared in 1950. In 1953 Saul Bellow's translation of Singer's short story "Gimpel the Fool," published in *Partisan Review*, brought Singer to the attention of the English-speaking literary establishment, which embraced his work enthusiastically. Inspired by his new-found American audience, Singer responded with a plethora of brilliant novels and short-story collections: *Gimpel the Fool and Other Stories* and *Shadows on the Hudson* (1957), *A Ship to America* (1958), *The Magician of Lublin* (1959), *The Spinoza of Market Street* (1961), *The Slave* (1962), *Short Friday and Other Stories* (1964), *The Manor* (1967), *The Seance and Other Stories* (1968), *The Estate* (1969), *A Friend of Kafka and Other Stories* (1970), *Enemies, A Love Story* (1972), *A Crown of Feathers and Other Stories* (1973), *Passions and Other Stories* (1975), and *A Young Man in Search of Love* (1978). Prizes and honors followed: he was elected to the National Institute of Arts and Letters in 1964, received the National Book Award in 1970, and won the Nobel Prize in 1978. Singer remained prolific until his death: among his works of the 1980s are *Lost in America* (1981), *The Golem* (1982), *The Penitent* (1983), *Love and Exile* (1984), and *The Death of Methuselah and Other Stories* (1988).

Singer's 1968 tale "Zeitl and Rickel," a tragicomic miniature about a suicidal folie à deux between two shtetl women, is not the only piece of Yiddish writing in which the lesbian theme figures. In the teens and early 1920s Sholom Asch's *The God of Vengeance* (1907), a shocking melodrama about a girl in a provincial town in Poland who falls in love with a prostitute in her father's brothel, played on numerous stages throughout Europe and in the Yiddish theaters of New York. It became notorious for a scene in act 2 in which the girl and the prostitute embraced on stage, and was indeed shut down and its entire cast arrested when it was first performed in English on Broadway in 1922. There is a similar earthiness of approach in Singer's story. While the unnamed narrator purports not to know what strange bond holds Zeitl and Rickel in its clutches, her fascination is evident, even as the story she tells moves toward its dysphoric and demon-haunted conclusion.

FURTHER READING: Isaac Bashevis Singer, *The Seance and Other Stories*, trans. Mirra Ginsburg, et al. (New York: Farrar, Straus and Giroux, 1968); —, *The Collected Stories of Isaac Bashevis Singer*, trans. Saul Bellow, et al. (New York: Farrar, Straus and Giroux, 1982); —, and Richard Burgin, *Conversations with Isaac Bashevis Singer* (Garden City, N.Y.: Doubleday, 1985); Irving Howe, Introduction to *Selected Short Stories of Isaac Bashevis Singer* (New York: The Modern Library, 1966); Paul Kresh, *Isaac Bashevis Singer: The Magician of West 86th Street* (New York: Dial, 1979); Edward Alexander, *Isaac Bashevis Singer* (Boston: Twayne, 1980); Alida Allison, *Isaac Bashevis Singer* (New York: Twayne, 1996); Evelyn Torton Beck, "Teaching About Jewish Lesbians in Literature: From 'Zeitl and Rickel' to 'The Tree of Begats,'" in Bonnie Zimmerman, et al., eds., *The New Lesbian Studies: Into the Twenty-First Century* (New York: Feminist, 1996), pp. 34–40; Janet Hadda, *Isaac Bashevis Singer: A Life* (New York and London: Oxford University Press, 1997).

I often hear people say, "This cannot happen, that cannot be, nobody has ever heard of such a thing, impossible." Nonsense! If something is destined to happen, it does. My grandmother used to say: "If the devil wants to, he can make two walls come together. If it is written that a rabbi will fall off a roof, he will become a chimney sweep." The Gentiles have a proverb: "He who must hang will not drown."

Take this thing that happened in our own town. If anybody told me about it, I'd say he was a liar. But I knew them both, may they intercede for us in heaven. They've surely served their punishment by now. The older one was called Zeitl; the younger one, Rickel.

Zeitl's father, Reb Yisroel Bendiner, was already an old man of eighty when I knew him. He had buried three wives, and Zeitl was the daughter of the third. I don't know whether he had any children with the others. He was in his late fifties when he came to live in our town. He married a young girl, who died, may God preserve us, in childbirth. Zeitl was taken out of her with pincers. Reb Yisroel's father-in-law had left his daughter a large brick building in the marketplace, with thirteen stores, and Reb Yisroel inherited it.

Strange stories were told in town about Reb Yisroel. There had once lived in Poland a false Messiah, Jacob Frank; he had converted many Jews. After he died, a sect remained. He had a daughter somewhere, and barrels full of gold were sent to her. These people pretended to live like other Jews, but at night they would gather in secret and read forbidden parchments.

Reb Yisroel dressed like a rabbi, in a velvet caftan, a round rabbinical hat, slippers, and white socks. He was forever writing something, standing before a high desk, and people said that Zeitl copied all his manuscripts. He had a wide beard, white as snow, and a high forehead. When he looked at anyone, it seemed as though he saw right through him. Zeitl taught the daughters of rich families to read and write. I was one of her pupils.

It was said of the members of the sect that they liked loose women and secretly practiced all sorts of abominations. But with whom could Reb Yisroel have sinned in our town?

Zeitl got married, but six months later she was divorced. Her husband had come from Galicia, and people whispered that he was one of "the clan"; that was how our townsmen called the sect. Nobody knew why the marriage had come to such a quick end. Everything in Reb Yisroel's house was veiled in secrecy. He had trunks hung with double locks. He had large cases full of books. He came to prayer only on the Sabbath, at the cold synagogue. He seldom exchanged a word with anyone. When the store-keepers came to pay their rent, he would put the money into his pocket without counting it.

In those years it was unheard of that groceries should be delivered to anyone at home. The richest women went to market with baskets to do their own shopping. But Zeitl had everything sent to her from the stores: bread, rolls, butter, eggs, cheese, meat. Once a month she received a bill, as though she were living in Warsaw. She had aristocratic ways.

I remember her as if it were yesterday: tall, dark, with a narrow face and black hair braided like a round Sabbath bread. Imagine, in those years—and she did not shave her hair. When she went out, she wore a kerchief. But when was she seen in the street? Reb Yisroel had a balcony upstairs, looking out upon the church garden, and Zeitl would sit there on summer evenings, getting fresh air.

She would give us girls dictation twice a week, not from a letter book but from her head: "My most esteemed betrothed! To start with, I wish to let you know that I am in good health, pray God that I may hear the same from you. Secondly. . . ." Zeitl also knew Polish and German. Her eyes were wild, huge as a calf's, and filled with melancholy. But suddenly she would burst into such loud laughter that all the rooms would echo with it. In the middle of the year she might take a fancy to bake matzo pancakes. She was fond of asking us riddles and of telling tales that made our hair stand on end.

And now about Rickel. Rickel's father was the town's ritual slaughterer, Reb Todie. All slaughterers are pious men, but Reb Todie had the reputation of a saint. Yet he had bad luck. His son had gone one day to the ritual bath and was found drowned. He must have gotten a cramp. One of his daughters died in an epidemic. A few years later strange noises began to be heard in his house. Something knocked, and no one knew what or where. Something would give a bang so that the walls would shake. The whole town came running, even the Gentiles. They searched the attic, the cellar, every corner.

A regiment of soldiers was stationed in our town. The colonel's name was Semiatitsky. He was supposed to have descended from converted Jews. He had a red beard and cracked jokes till your sides would split with laughter. When Semiatitsky heard that a demon was banging in Todie's house, he brought a platoon of soldiers and commanded them to look into every crack and every hole. He did not believe in devils; he called them nothing but old wives' tales. He ordered everybody out and Cossacks stood guard with whips, allowing nobody to come near. But suddenly there was a crash that nearly brought the roof down.

I was not there, but people said that Semiatitsky called to the unholy one to tell his name and what he wanted and that the spirit gave one knock for yes, and two knocks for no.

Every man has enemies, especially if he has a job with the community, and people began to say that Todie should be dismissed as a slaughterer. It was whispered that he had slaughtered an ox with a blemished knife. Reb Todie's wife took it so hard that she died.

Rickel was small, thin, with red hair and freckles. When her father slaughtered fowl, she would pluck the feathers and do other small chores. When the knocking began, suspicion fell on Rickel. Some people said that she was doing it. But how could she? And why? It was said that when she went away for the night the knocking stopped. There's no limit to what evil tongues can invent. One night there was such a loud bang that three windows were shattered. Before that, the devil had not touched the windows. This was the last time. From then on, it was quiet again.

But Reb Todie was already without his job, and he became a teacher of beginners. The family had gone through Rickel's dowry and she was now affianced to a yeshiva student from Krashnik, a lame young man. He was a Hassid, and soon after the wedding he went on a pilgrimage to his rabbi. At first he would come home for Passover and the High Holy Days. Afterwards he disappeared altogether. Rickel became an abandoned wife. Her father had died in the meantime and all she had left was the old house—little more than a ruin.

What could a husbandless wife do? She went around, teaching girls how to pray. She took in sewing and mending. On Purim she carried presents of holiday delicacies for wealthy families. On Passover she would become a sort of women's beadle and deliver gifts of herbs. When a woman was sick and someone was needed to watch at the bedside, Rickel was called. She learned how to cup and bleed the sick. She did not shave her head but wore a kerchief. She read many storybooks and loved to invent wild and improbable tales.

Old maids, you know, also end up half crazy. But when a woman who has had a man is left alone, it goes to her head. Rickel might have found her husband if she had

had the money to send a messenger to look for him, but Todie left her without a groschen. Why did her husband forsake her? Who can tell? There are such men. They get married and then they tire of it. They wander away and nobody knows where their bones have come to rest.

2

I do not know exactly how Zeitl and Rickel got together. It seems that Reb Yisroel fell ill and Rickel came to rub him down with turpentine. People said he had cast an eye on her, but I don't believe it. He was already more dead than alive. He died soon afterwards, and both girls, Zeitl and Rickel, were left alone in the world. At first people thought that Rickel had stayed on with Zeitl as a servant. But if Zeitl had never had a servant before, why would she need one now?

While Reb Yisroel was alive, few matchmakers came to Zeitl with offers. They knew that Reb Yisroel wanted his daughter for himself. There are such fathers, even among Jews. She waited on him hand and foot. If his pipe went out, she would bring him an ember to relight it. I don't know why, but he never went to the bath, and it was whispered that Zeitl bathed him in a wooden bathtub. I've never seen it, but those false believers are capable of anything. To them, a sin is a virtue.

Anyway, Reb Yisroel gave the matchmakers such a reception that they forswore repeating their visits to the tenth generation. But as soon as Zeitl was alone, they were back at her doorstep. She sent them off with all sorts of excuses: later, tomorrow, it's not yet time. She had a habit, whenever she spoke to anyone, of looking over his head. Rickel had moved in with her, and now whenever anyone knocked, she would answer from behind the door chain: Zeitl is out, she is asleep, she is reading.

How long could the matchmakers keep coming? Nobody is dragged to the wedding canopy by force. But in a small town people have time, and they talk. No matter how you may try to keep away from strangers' eyes, you can't hide everything.

It was said that Zeitl and Rickel ate together, drank together, slept together. Rickel wore Zeitl's dresses, shortened and made smaller to fit her. Rickel became the cashier, and she paid the bills sent by the storekeepers. She also collected the rents. In the daytime the two girls seldom went out together, but on summer evenings they went strolling down Church Street, along the avenues leading to the woods. Zeitl's arm would be around Rickel's shoulders, and Rickel's around Zeitl's waist. They were absorbed in their talk. When people said good evening, they did not hear. Where did two women find so much to talk about? Some people tried to follow them and listen in, but they were whispering, as though they had secrets between them. They would walk all the way to the mill or the woods.

Rumors were brought to Reb Eisele, our rabbi, but he said: "There is no law to keep two women from walking to the mill."

Reb Eisele was a Misnagid, a Lithuanian, and they have a law for everything: either it is permitted or it's a sin.

But the talk would not die down. Naftali, the night watchman, had seen Zeitl and Rickel kissing each other on the mouth. They had stopped by the sawmill, near the log pile, and embraced like a loving couple. Zeitl called Rickel dove, and Rickel called her kitten. At first nobody believed Naftali; he was fond of a drop and could bring you tales of a fair up in heaven. Still, where there's smoke, there must be fire. My dear folks, the two girls seemed so much in love that all the tongues in town started wagging. The Tempter can make anybody crazy in his own way. Something flips in your head, and everything turns upside down. I heard talk of a lady in Krasnostaw who made love with a stallion. At the time of the Flood, even beasts paired themselves with other kinds. I read about it in the Women's Bible.

People went to Reb Eisele, but he insisted: "There is nothing in the Torah to forbid it. The ban applies only to men. Besides, since there are no witnesses, it is forbidden to spread rumors." Nevertheless, he sent the beadle for them. Rickel came alone and denied everything. She had a whittled tongue, that girl. Reb Eisele said to her: "Go home and don't worry about it. It is the slanderers who will be punished, not you. It is better to burn in a lime pit than to put another to shame."

I forgot to mention that Zeitl had stopped teaching the girls how to write.

I was still very young at that time, but something of all that talk had reached me too. You can't keep everything from a child's ears. Zeitl and Rickel, it was said, were studying Reb Yisroel's books together. Their lamp burned until late at night. Those who passed their bedroom window saw shadows moving this way and that behind the drapes, and coming together as in a dance. Who knows what went on there?

Now listen to a story.

One summer it turned terribly hot. I've lived through many a summer, but I don't remember such heat. Right in the morning the sun began to burn like fire. Not only men but even girls and older women would go down to the river to bathe. When the sun blazes, the water gets warm. My mother, may she plead for us, took me along.

This was the first time I bathed in the river. Men went into the water naked, but the girls wore their shifts. The roughnecks came running to peep at them, and it was impossible to drive them off. Each time there'd be a squealing and a panic. One woman started drowning. Another screamed that a frog had bitten her. I bathed and even tried to swim until I was so tired that I lay down among the bushes near the bank to rest. I thought I'd cool off in the shade and go home, but a strange sleep came over me. Not just sleep; may heaven preserve us, it was more like death. I put my head down and remained there like a rock. A darkness seemed to fall over me and I sank into it. I must have slept for many hours.

When I awakened, it was night. There was no moon. The sky was cloudy. I lay there and did not know where I was or who I was. I felt the grass around me, moist with dew, but I did not remember that I was on the outskirts of town. I touched myself; I had nothing on but my shift. I wanted to cry, to call for help, when suddenly I heard voices. I thought of demons and was terror-stricken, yet I tried to hear what they were saying. Two women were speaking, and their voices seemed familiar.

I heard one ask: "Must we go through hell?"

The other answered: "Yes, my soul, but even going through hell together with you will be a delight. God is merciful. The punishment never lasts more than twelve months. We shall be purified and enter paradise. Since we have no husbands, we shall be no one's footstools. We shall bathe in balsam and eat of the leviathan. We shall have wings and fly like birds. . . ."

I cannot recall all their talk. I gasped. I knew who they were now: the questioner was Rickel, and Zeitl gave the answers. I heard Zeitl say: "We shall meet our fathers and mothers there, and our grandparents, and all the generations: Abraham and Isaac, Jacob and Rachel, Leah, Bilhah, Zilpah, Abigail, Bathsheba. . . ." She spoke as though she had just come from there, and every word was like a pearl. I forgot that I was half naked and alone out late at night.

Zeitl went on: "Father is waiting for us. He comes to me in dreams. He is together with your mother." Rickel asked: "Did they get married there?" And Zeitl answered: "Yes. We shall get married up there too. In heaven there is no difference between men and women. . . ."

It must have been past midnight. There was a flash of lightning, and I saw my clothing, shoes, and stockings on the grass nearby. I caught a glimpse of them too. They sat by the river in nothing but their shifts, their hair down, pale as death. If I did not die of fright that night, I'll never die.

"And then?"

Wait a minute. I came home in the middle of the night, but my mother had left earlier in the evening for the fair; she was a storekeeper. My father was spending the night at the study house. I slipped into bed, and when I woke next morning, the whole thing seemed like a dream. I was ashamed to tell anyone about it. However, as the saying goes, heaven and earth conspired that there should be no secrets.

People began to say that Zeitl and Rickel were fasting. They would eat nothing all day and merely take a bite at night. We had pious women in town who would climb up the stairs into the women's section of the synagogue at dawn to pray. Every Monday and Thursday they went to visit graves in the cemetery. Suddenly we heard that Zeitl and Rickel had joined the pious company in lamentations and penitential prayers. They had shaved their heads and put on bonnets, as though they had just gotten married. They omitted no line or word, and wept as on the Day of the Destruction of the Temple. They also visited the cemetery, prostrating themselves on Reb Yisroel's grave and wailing.

People ran to Reb Eisele again, but the rabbi sent them off with a scolding. If Jewish daughters wanted to do penance, he said, was that wrong too? He was fond of poring over his books, but the affairs of the town meant little to him. He was later dismissed, but that's another story.

There are busybodies everywhere, and they took the matter to the colonel. But he said, "Leave me out of your Jewish squabbles. I have trouble enough with my soldiers." Cossacks are good soldiers, but sometimes they got letters from home that their wives were carrying on with other men and they went wild. More than one Cossack would go galloping off on his horse, slashing away with his sword right and left. After they had served their five-year terms, they would come into the stores to buy presents for their mothers and fathers, sisters and brothers, the whole family. The shopkeeper would ask, "And what will you get for your wife, Nikita?" "A horsewhip," he would say. They'd go back to their steppes on the Don and find bastards at home. They'd chop off the wife's head and be sent to Siberia for hard labor. . . .

Where was I? Oh, yes, penance. Zeitl and Rickel clung to each other and spoke only of the next world. They bought up all the books from every peddler passing through town. Whenever a preacher came, they questioned him: How long was the punishment inflicted on transgressors after death? How many hells were there? Who meted out the penalties? Who did the whipping? With what kind of rods? Iron? Copper? The wags had plenty to joke about.

We had many visiting preachers, but one, Reb Yuzel, was famous. Whenever he went up to the lectern, it was like the Day of Atonement all over again. When he painted a picture of hell, everybody shuddered. People said that it was dangerous for pregnant women to hear him; several had had miscarriages after his sermons. But that's how it is: when you must not do a thing, you're sure to do it. When Reb Yuzel preached, the synagogue was full. The railing closing off the women's section was almost bursting with the crush. He had a voice that reached into every corner. Every word cut like a knife.

The last time he came, I also ran to hear him. There was not one hell, he said, but seven, and the flames in each were sixty times hotter than in the last. There was a man in our town, Alterl Kozlover. He had a screw loose, and he figured out that the seventh hell was myriads of times hotter than the first. Men cried like babies. Women screamed and wailed.

Zeitl and Rickel were also there. They had entered among the men and stood on a bench, wrapped in their shawls. Ordinarily, women are admitted in the men's section only on the Festival of Rejoicing in the Law. But when the women's section was too crowded, some women were allowed into the antechamber, and from there they'd move inside.

Reb Yuzel handed out punishment to everybody, but the worst of his wrath was reserved for the women. He described how they were hung by the breasts and by the hair; how the imps laid them out on boards of nails and tore pieces from them. From fiery coals they were thrown into snow, and from the snow back onto heaps of coals. Before they were admitted to hell, they were first tortured in the Sling, by devils, imps and evil spirits. It made your hair stand on end to hear him. I was still a young girl, but I began to sob and choke. I glanced at Zeitl and Rickel: they did not cry, but their eyes were twice as big as usual, and their faces were like chalk. A madness seemed to stare out of them, and I had a feeling that they would come to a terrible end.

On the next day Reb Yuzel preached again, but I had had enough. Someone said later that Zeitl had come up to him after the sermon and invited him to be her guest. Many people asked him to their homes, but he went with Zeitl. Nobody knows what they spoke about. I don't remember whether he had stayed there for the night. Probably not; how could a man remain with two women? Although it's true the Lithuanians have an argument for everything. They interpret the Law as they like. That's why they are nicknamed "heathens." My grandfather, may he intercede for us, used to tell of a Lithuanian Jew from Belaya Tserkov who had married a Gentile woman and had gone on studying the Talmud.

After Reb Yuzel left, the town was quiet again. By then the summer was over.

One winter night, long after all the shutters had been closed, we heard a wild outcry. People ran out in panic. They thought the peasants had attacked. The moon was bright, and we saw a strange sight—Fivel the butcher carrying Rickel in his arms. She screamed and struggled and tried to scratch his eyes out. He was a giant of a man and he brought her straight into the rabbi's judgment chamber. Reb Eisele sat up late, studying and drinking tea from a samovar. Everybody shouted, and Rickel kept fighting to break away and run out. It took two men to hold her. The rabbi began to question her.

I was there myself. Ordinarily I went to bed early, but that night we had been chopping cabbage and all the girls had gathered at our house. This was the custom in our town. We chopped cabbage for pickling in barrels, and everybody ate bread with cracklings and told stories. One day the girls would gather in one house, the next in another. Sometimes they'd break into a dance in pairs. I had a sister-in-law who could play all the dances on a comb: a Scissor Dance, a Quarrel Dance, a Good Day.

When we heard the uproar, we all ran out.

At first Rickel would not say anything. She merely screamed to be allowed to go. But Fivel testified that she had wanted to throw herself into the well. He had caught her when she had already flung her leg over the edge.

"How did it come into your head to do such a thing?" the rabbi asked, and Rickel answered: "I am sick of this world. I want to know what goes on in the next." The rabbi argued: "Those who lay their hands upon themselves do not share the rewards of the next world." But Rickel said: "Hell is also for people, not for goats." She screamed: "I want to go to my mother and my father, my grandmother and grandfather. I don't want to keep wandering in this vale of tears." Those were her words. It was clear at once that she had learned all this from Zeitl, because the other knew the texts printed in small letters too. Somebody asked: "Where is Zeitl?" And Rickel answered: "She is all right, she is already up there. . . ." My dear folks, Zeitl had thrown herself into the well a moment earlier. She had gone first.

Half the town came running. Torches were lit, and we went to the well. Zeitl lay with her head in the water, her feet up. A ladder was lowered, and she was dragged up, dead.

Rickel had to be watched, and the men of the burial society took her to the poor-house. She was turned over to the caretaker, who was told to keep an eye on her. Zeitl was later buried outside the fence. Rickel pretended that she had come to her senses and regretted her deed. But the next day at dawn, when everybody was asleep, she rose from the bundle of straw and went to the river. It was frozen, but she must have bro-ken the ice with a stone. It was only in the afternoon that people realized she was gone. They found her footprints in the snow and ran down to the river. Rickel had followed Zeitl. She was buried near the other one, without a mound, without as much as a board to mark the place.

The burgomaster locked and sealed Zeitl's house, but later on, a letter she had writ-ten was discovered. She explained why she was leaving the world: she wanted to know what went on in the hereafter.

Who can tell what goes on in another's head? A person gets hold of some melan-choly notion and it grows like a mushroom. Zeitl was the leader, and Rickel drank in every word she said. Forty years have gone by since their deaths, and they have prob-ably suffered their allotted share.

As long as I was in the town, Reb Yisroel's house was boarded up and nobody moved into it. People saw lights flickering in the windows. A man said that he was pass-ing by at night and heard Zeitl speak and Rickel answer. They kissed, laughed, cried. Lost souls remain on earth and do not even know they don't belong. . . .

I was told that an officer had later moved into the house. One morning he was found hanged.

A house is not simply a pile of logs and boards. Whoever lives there leaves some-thing behind. A few years later the whole marketplace burned down. Thank God for fires. If it were not for them, the stench that would accumulate would reach high heaven. . . .

JANET FLANNER (1892–1978)

"Memory Is All: Alice B. Toklas" (1975)

The American journalist Janet Flanner, for fifty years the Paris correspondent of the *New Yorker*, was born into a middle-class family in Indianapolis, where her father was a prosperous undertaker. She attended the University of Chicago but never took a degree. After working for a couple of years as a theater critic for the *Indianapolis Star*, she made an impulsive marriage—largely to escape her family—and moved with her new husband to New York in 1918. The marriage ended abruptly when she fell in love with Solita Solano, the flamboyant drama editor for the *New York Tribune*. In 1921 she set off with Solano for Europe, in search, as she put it later, of "Beauty with a capital B." The two women ended up in Paris, where they quickly found their way into the fashionable lesbian expatriate circles around Natalie Clifford Barney and Gertrude Stein. They appear as the eager newspaperwomen "Nip" and "Tuck" in Djuna Barnes's satirical 1928 portrait of Barney and her friends, *Ladies Almanack*.

For a time, intending to be a fiction writer, Flanner worked on a novel, later published as *The Cubical City* (1926). Her real vocation announced itself, however, in 1925, when Harold Ross, the husband of a friend in New York, asked her to contribute an occasional "Letter from Paris" to his new magazine, the *New Yorker*. Flanner obliged, and soon enough was producing regular dispatches on French artistic, political, and cultural life. Glamorous friends supplied her with material: Colette, Picasso, Joyce, Josephine Baker, Maurice Ravel, Sylvia Beach, Gertrude Stein, Margaret Anderson, Ernest Hemingway, and Scott Fitzgerald all make cameo appearances in the early "Letters." Yet however recherché her subject matter, she was able—by dint of wit and sensibility—to translate it into stylish yet accessible prose. A contemporary critic, referring to Flanner's famously fastidious print manner, once dubbed her, along with Edmund Wilson, "the supreme commander of the English sentence in her time."

Flanner's private life was a fulfilling one. Though a loner at heart—she lived much of her Parisian life in a single room at the Hôtel Continental—she enjoyed several long-term lesbian attachments. After separating from Solita Solano in the early 1930s Flanner subsequently became involved with Noel Haskins Murphy, a wealthy American widow living near Paris. At the outbreak of the Second World War, Flanner returned to New York, where she fell in love with Natalia Danesi Murray, an Italian broadcaster and publishing executive. She and Murray—who later published a touching memoir about their relationship in 1985—carried on a transatlantic love affair for the next thirty years. Neither Solano nor Murphy vanished from Flanner's life, however: when Flanner returned to France in 1944 after the Liberation, she remained on affectionate terms with both women until her death.

In her later years—she continued writing her "Letter from Paris" into her eighties—Flanner attracted growing international recognition. In 1948 she was made a knight of the Légion d'Honneur for "services to France"; in 1959 she was elected a member of the National Institute for Arts and Letters; and in 1966, when her Paris letters from 1944 to 1965 were republished as a book (edited by William Shawn), she won the National Book Award. *Paris Was Yesterday*, a collection of her *New Yorker* writings from the twenties and thirties, was published, also to great acclaim, in 1972. She died in 1978, having written her valedictory "Letter from Paris" in 1975.

"Memory Is All: Alice B. Toklas," one of Flanner's last essays, appeared after her death in the volume *Janet Flanner's World: Uncollected Writings, 1932–1975*, edited by Irving Drutman. Flanner and Toklas, the lover and companion of the writer Gertrude Stein, were close friends for over half a century, from the 1920s to the 1970s. Flanner once described the diminutive Toklas—who survived Stein by twenty-one years—as "the most widowed woman I know." "Memory Is All" is at once a poignant souvenir of a famous couple, a nostalgic backward glance at early-twentieth-century lesbian history, and a testament to its author's spirited, generous, and salient view of the world.

FURTHER READING: Janet Flanner, *The Cubical City* (New York: Putnam's, 1926); —, *Paris Journal, 1944–1965* (New York: Atheneum, 1965); —, *Paris Journal: 1965–1971* (New York: Atheneum, 1971); —, *Paris Was Yesterday, 1925–1930* (New York: Viking, 1971); —, *London Was Yesterday, 1934–1939* (New York: Viking, 1975); —, *Janet Flanner's World: Uncollected Writings, 1932–1975* (New York: Harcourt Brace Jovanovich, 1979); —, *Darlinghissima: Letters to a Friend*, ed. Natalia Danesi Murray (New York: Random House, 1985); Shari Benstock, *Women of the Left Bank: Paris, 1900–1940* (Austin: University of Texas Press, 1986); Brenda Wineapple, *Genêt: A Biography of Janet Flanner* (New York: Ticknor and Fields, 1989); Terry Castle, *The Apparitional Lesbian: Female Homosexuality and Modern Culture* (New York: Columbia University Press, 1993); Andrea Weiss, *Paris Was a Woman: Portraits from the Left Bank* (London: Pandora, 1995); William Murray, *Janet, My Mother, and Me: A Memoir of Growing Up with Janet Flanner and Natalia Danesi Murray* (New York: Simon and Schuster, 2000).

December 15, 1975 Gertrude Stein, the mortal center of Alice B. Toklas's existence for the thirty-eight years that the two women lived together in concentrated amity in Paris, died on July 27, 1946, leaving Alice companioned by two dominant preoccupations. One was vast in its scope, encompassing the New Testament belief in life after death, by which, in her interpretation, she and Gertrude were to be united again in Heaven for eternity. The other preoccupation was merely mundane, and thus much more bothersome. It was to prepare literary immortality for Gertrude by seeing that all her unpublished manuscripts were printed; this project would require considerable cash, while the first would require only faith, which cost nothing.

Four days after Gertrude's death, Alice was writing from the apartment they had shared, at 5 Rue Christine, to their friends Carl and Fania Van Vechten, in New York: "I'm here alone. And nothing more—only what was." Two days later, on August 2nd, to Carl Van Vechten: "She gives the Picasso portrait to the Metropolitan—the rest to me—and then to Allan's children—so I definitely stay on." On August 5th, to another pair of old New York friends, W. G. and Mildred Rogers: "I went to the country and got Basket [her and Gertrude's white poodle] Sunday, and he and I will stay on here." And to Bennett Cerf, Gertrude's publisher, thirteen days after that: "And now Basket and I are in the flat alone, where we definitely stay on."

"Staying on alone"—Alice's description of the twenty-one remaining years of her life without Gertrude—is both the heart-catching theme and the title of a book subtitled "Letters of Alice B. Toklas" (Liveright, edited by Edward Burns). It is a rich, emotional volume. The broad sweep of information derived from family and household letters, from letters to prospective publishers of Gertrude's work, and to biographers of Gertrude and to old and new friends on both sides of the Atlantic, gives us a picture not only of the major items in Gertrude's and Alice's lives together, viewed retrospectively, but also of what would likely be the items of prime importance in Alice's future. "I wish to God we had gone together as I always so fatuously thought we would—a bomb—a shipwreck—just anything but this," she wrote somberly to one intimate New York friend a little more than a year after Gertrude's death. But though she had been left bereft, she was not left without occupation. Gertrude had willed her manuscripts and papers to Yale University, and Alice obediently sorted and packed these and shipped them off. "When I've finished sending things to Yale and done some typing and cleaned the flat and caught up with darning and patching," she wrote another old friend, early in her bereavement, "well, then it will be spring, and Basket and I will take walks and be in excellent form." Yale held an exhibit of Gertrude's correspondence, and Alice wrote to Donald Gallup, curator of the university's collection of American literature, "I am so thrilled with your description of the exhibition of the letters. What a variety there is of human nature in them. And your including the rejections—the refusals—how Gertrude would have appreciated that. You must know how those refusals hurt at the time they were received, but one day Blanche Knopf outdid even all Knopf's Knopfishness, and then Gertrude forgot our hopes and bitter disappointment and burst into that loud laughter." Another bequest—the 1905–6 Picasso portrait of Gertrude, which was given to the Metropolitan Museum—elicited from Alice, "They took the Picasso portrait for the Metropolitan ten days ago. It was another parting and completely undid me. Picasso came over to say good bye to it and said sadly—*ni vous ni moi le reverra jamais* [neither you nor I will ever see it again]. It was all there was left of their youth."

Whether dead or alive, Gertrude always had a domesticating influence on her admirers, of whom I was one. At the Stein-Toklas parties, the gentlemen would congregate loyally around Gertrude, while we ladies would be grouped around the tea table presided over by Alice, so we could get the gossip. Alice was a very entertaining purveyor of news. She gave it to you adding item to item, as if she were detailing the recipe for a fruitcake. You always knew where Gertrude was in the room, because she would let out her whoops of laughter; curiously, I don't remember ever hearing Alice laugh, although she had an acute and sharp sense of humor, which, since it was bordered with wit, was quiet in tone. Her conversation had its own pattern—she obtained a variety of effects by setting forth the opposite of what anyone else might have said. Her voice was soft, her California accent agreeable, her vocabulary precise, rhythmic, and possessed of its own sense of speed, with allegro touches. A great deal of this personality, this domestic intimacy, comes through in the printed letters. Alice had adopted the childish clan name of Woojums for Carl Van Vechten, which thereafter figures in their correspondence. The very first letter in the book begins, "Dearest Fania and dearest Papa Woojums," and is signed "Mama Woojums." In subsequent examples, Fania Van Vechten is Madame W., and sometimes the Empress. Gertrude, whenever mentioned to the Van Vechtens, is Baby Woojums, or Baby for short. Other close friends have their own cozy sobriquets: Mr. and Mrs. W. G. Rogers are the Kiddies Rogers was one of the first doughboys she and Gertrude had met during the First World War, and to show their familiarity with American slang they called him the Kiddie, which afterward was extended to "Dearest Kiddies," or "Dear Mrs. Kiddie" when Alice is writing only to Mrs. Rogers, thanking her for a gift and, in return, presenting her with a recipe for an "old old French pastry called Massillon . . . They should be frosted all over with a white rum frosting with chopped pistachio sprinkled on the top but I don't bother to do so."

Gertrude was likely to plunge into intimacies like a bear cub, but with new acquaintances Alice observed the formalities until the friendship had ripened to a first-name basis. Thus, Mina Curtiss, who had been introduced to her in 1948, after Gertrude's death, as a friend of Virgil Thomson and Carl Van Vechten, progressed gradually from "Dear Mrs. Curtiss" to "Dear Mina dear." Referring to Gertrude by her first name was more easily achieved. "Oh but you must say Gertrude—it wouldn't be friendly to do otherwise," Alice wrote Mrs. Curtiss. "You know, it was the very young who explained that, when they started the habit twenty-five years ago. It was quite shocking at first, but they finally convinced me, and in no time it was accepted—historical and no further trouble. It was contagious, so that the G.I.s spoke not of but to her not as Gertrude but Gertie—those at the station when they came—the Seventh Army replacements— through our village. Here in the flat she was very ceremoniously Miss Stein. Afterwards on the stairway? . . ."

Like Gertrude, however, Alice could be ambivalent about friends old and new. To one of the latter—an Italian translator of "The Making of Americans," who had graduated from "Miss Pivano" to "Nanda dear," she wrote in 1950, "Paris has been full of Americans—two million—at least—have come to see me—they bore and exhaust me—though I only see those who were friends of Gertrude whom she would have wanted to see . . . but then in spite of wanting to see them all—some of them used to bore her. Did I ever tell you she once said she was going to put an advertisement in the *New York Herald Tribune* saying Miss Gertrude Stein does not desire to see any friend she has not seen for fifteen years?" Alice also had a gift for keeping the heat on under smoldering vendettas. One was against the Museum of Modern Art, which Gertrude "loathed and despised." When the Metropolitan, in an arbitrary private transaction, agreed to "deposit" the Picasso portrait of Gertrude with the Modern for a period of ten years, Alice coldly informed the Metropolitan that Miss Stein had very deliberately chosen it to receive the portrait, and, had there been any other choice, "the Museum of Modern Art would not have been an alternative . . . indeed [Miss Stein] thoroughly disapproved of its policy and aims." Alice kept up such a vigorous campaign, through lawyers and friends, that the Metropolitan was finally goaded into reclaiming the picture. Having won her victory, Alice yet continued her gibes. To a casual acquaintance, she wrote, some years later, "Please do not ask me to chide your wife about the Metropolitan's giving the portrait to that frightful Museum of Modern Art for ten years—since it got back to where it belongs much more quickly than one had reason to hope for. . . . Is your wife possibly connected with the Museum of Modern Art? If she is she is saving it from damnation." And some years after that, in another letter—Alice could be really hard—she reports that three people from the Museum of Modern Art were brought to see the pictures in her apartment, and said of the Picassos that "they had never seen such fine Braque painting." She goes on, "I held my tongue—that was in the other room. Then they came in here and repeated their error. *Silence de ma part*. They appealed to me—was it not—pointing to the big picture over the fireplace. It would be if it were—I permitted myself to answer. And I plied them with sherry—*pâté brioche* and my best little cakes—allowing myself to tell the story—*sans discrétion*—to anyone who will listen."

Early on, Gertrude, and therefore Alice, had taken an aesthetic stand favoring Picasso's work against that of Matisse, which the latter, not unnaturally, had resented. When Gertrude, in "The Autobiography of Alice B. Toklas," wrote that the beautiful Mme. Matisse was beautiful like a horse—meaning it as a compliment—the comparison was misunderstood. Then the Paris newspapers aggravated the issue, the fat was in the fire, and "there was no further acquaintance" with Matisse. However, with Alice, to be out of sight was not necessarily to be out of mind. In 1950, some seventeen years after the *malentendu*, she was still snipping away, writing to Donald Gallup that Matisse was "amongst the majority—the common-place majority as Gertrude called him—of the sad and mistaken." Even when she is quoting for her own advantage something the painter had said, she cannot resist a sneer: "It's as true and trite as most of Matisse's reflections." About Ernest Hemingway, another of Alice's objects of ill will, she was also implacable: "Did you see *The New Yorker's* profile of Hemingway???!!! Nothing he has said since—not even his novel—will be as complete an exposure of all he has spent his life hiding. It's strange that he should be taking so much pleasure in destroying the legend he worked so patiently to construct. Someone . . . sent an A.P. man to see me, and I got into a frightful row with him about Picasso's painting and Hemingway's new book (as if they could be mentioned in one sentence)—he the A.P. man said he thought Picasso was painting carelessly and Hem was writing carelessly! . . . I liked defending Hemingway—it was the first opportunity I've ever been offered—it will no doubt remain a unique experience." And a few days later, after she had been sent some uncomplimentary reviews of Hemingway's new novel, "Across the River and Into the Trees," she wrote, "People seemed to think they would please me. Far from it—the whole Hemingway legend—which we saw him create and *soigner*—going to pieces as it is under one's eyes is the most pitiable embarrassing thing imaginable. The present Hemingway crack up—one must borrow from the vocabulary of the greatest of his victims—has far too much old-fashioned biblical punishments and rewards for comfort to those living in the present. But of course that is just what he doesn't do—he is hopelessly 1890—and one can damn him no further. He wears like the New Look but he is in the tradition of Kipling."

Interspersed with Alice's malice is Alice the dedicated housewife. "Amateur art isn't satisfactory—is it?" she inquired rhetorically of one correspondent. "When I used to bake a cake for Gertrude I never asked is it good, I always said does it look like one that came from the baker's—it should have tasted better because the material it was made of was of a superior quality to what the baker used but wasn't mixed and baked in a professional way, which was what would make it look like the baker's. Well it was often that Gertrude thought it did. Finally some one said one looked as if it had come from a Women's Exchange and Gertrude said that should satisfy me." She fulminated against the new, postwar indifference in Paris to giving or receiving small change, so atypical of the French: "Having learned the value of *petites économies* in 15, it leaves me flabbergasted—how can one save *sous* (that is present francs) if they aren't returned to one—it's very confusing if not immoral."

Unavoidably, since *la bien-aimée* is never far from her thoughts, Alice reveals certain of Gertrude's personal, eccentric preferences. For instance, Gertrude could not bear having anyone read aloud to her—a habit French authors were addicted to. "I read with my eyes, not my ears," she told Picasso. "Ears are inside me." To which Picasso, who could be as elfin as Gertrude, said, "Of course writers write with their eyes, painters paint with their ears. And further neither painters nor writers have ever been painted with their mouths open." We learn that "Gertrude wouldn't have been amused with the present glorification of Melville—not even of 'Moby Dick'—she thought that he was being grossly overrated. He was not one of the writers whom she chose as examples of expressing our sense of abstraction." Nor did the Joyce novel "Ulysses" please Gertrude: "She once said it was rather more than she could manage of the Irish fairies—that Irish fairies were even less palatable than German fairies." Gertrude did, however, have an "unfailing appreciation" of F. Scott Fitzgerald's work. Ulysses S. Grant she considered our greatest eminence—"not second to Lincoln but first." Picasso she thought of as a younger brother. "They understood each other in spite of saying dreadful things when they were irritated," Alice writes. And, least surprising in this list, it was, Gertrude felt, *un*familiarity that bred contempt.

Gertrude's will stipulated that her executors pay to Carl Van Vechten such sums of money "as [he] shall, in his own absolute discretion, deem necessary for the publication of my unpublished manuscripts." All the rest and residue, "of whatsoever kind and wheresoever situated," was left "to my friend Alice B. Toklas . . . to her use for life" and, "insofar as it may become necessary for her proper maintenance and support," the executors were authorized "to reduce to cash" any of the paintings in the Stein collection, which, at the time the will was drawn, in July, 1946, included twenty-eight Picasso paintings and a portfolio of his drawings, as well as seven Juan Gris canvases. Permission for the sale of any of these art works was to be obtained from a Baltimore-court-appointed estate administrator. Upon Alice's death, the remainder of the estate was to go to Allan Stein, only child of Gertrude's oldest brother, Michael, and, after him, to his three children. Gertrude had told Alice that she wanted everything—every manuscript of hers—published, and Alice quickly set out to implement her desire. Although diminutive in size and rather bent, Alice had the strength of a giant when it came to organization; in her years with Gertrude, she had already made it her function to coördinate the conveniences of daily living to accommodate Gertrude's hours of writing, even when they took place at night. Five weeks after Gertrude's death, Alice informed Carl Van Vechten that the first publication, by the Yale University Press, would be "Four in America," one of the "difficult" Stein manuscripts (the four subjects were George Washington, Ulysses S. Grant, Wilbur Wright, and Henry James), for which Thornton Wilder had offered to write a long introduction. The book appeared in the fall of 1947. "Isn't 'Four in America' perfect?" Alice wrote to Dearest Kiddie. "Isn't Gertrude the essence of U.S.? How I wish she could have seen the book—it was always the happiest day of the year (way back it was of the decade) when a new book of hers came in the post and she spent the morning or the whole day reading it. And then when it was read she would say *oui, c'est cela*." Eventually, through her penury and self-denial, plus her driving determination, Alice saw eight volumes of the unpublished works printed by the Yale University Press. She also helped support herself during some trying times by writing an idiosyncratic, chatty cookbook, which sold well, and "What Is Remembered," a less successful volume of memoirs but, in my estimation, her most entertaining book.

The Baltimore court had appointed an elderly lawyer, Edgar Allan Poe—the poet's great-nephew—as administrator of Gertrude's estate. Gertrude had been precise about how her funds were to be spent, but, unaccountably, Poe proved to be an obstructionist and parsimonious in fulfilling her wishes, of which he seemed to disapprove, although it was none of his business. Alice cajoled and threatened, Poe sent money in driblets, and in 1954 Alice, who was desperate, finally sold about forty Picasso drawings without informing Poe—and, upon what now seems the poor advice of Daniel-Henry Kahnweiler, Picasso's dealer, for considerably less than their market value. The plot machinations that followed would have done credit to a Victorian novel. In Alice's orderly existence with Gertrude, there had never been any melodramatic or violent eruptions. But with Gertrude gone, the difficulties so often attendant upon the inheritance of property and interpretation of testaments were inflicted upon her relict, Alice. Allan Stein's wife, Roubina (referred to scornfully in these letters as the Armenian, although she was in fact Rumanian), kept a beady eye upon the pictures in the interests of her minor children. In 1951, Allan Stein died, and the children were in line to inherit after Alice died. In 1961, while the increasingly infirm Alice was absent in Acqui, Italy, taking a mud-bath cure for her arthritis, Mrs. Stein procured a court order to have the pictures removed from the Rue Christine apartment to a Paris bank vault, on the ground that their security was endangered by Miss Toklas's absence. When Alice returned from Acqui she found the walls bare. "The pictures are gone permanently," she wrote a friend pathetically. "My dim sight could not see them now. Happily a vivid memory does. . . . Don't worry about me—I am 84 years old. All old people fall—an aunt skating on the ice—a granduncle jumping off a streetcar. (Alice's imagination was always lively.)

In going over an inventory of the pictures, Roubina Stein had discovered the Picasso drawings missing. She accused Alice of illegal behavior, which was true enough, since she had not sought Poe's permission before she sold them. Alice, on her side, insisted, with equal truth, that she had been within her rights, according to Gertrude's will. To aggravate the tension, Poe was inexplicably three months behind in Alice's monthly allowance. "My eyes are a great trouble," she informed Russell Porter, the Paris lawyer she had engaged to protect her—and little enough help he was able to be. "I can write only by holding the paper within about ten inches of my eyes under a strong light. . . . It is urgent that he [Poe] sends me the money by wire at once—for I am down to bedrock. . . . Gertrude Stein—in her generosity to me—did not foresee that such an occasion could arise." Her financial situation was so precarious that some of us among her old friends raised a fund for her maintenance. Alice was hospitable; she took to inviting us in turn to *bec-fin* restaurants for lunch, after which, in settling the bill, she was inclined to leave the equivalent of twenty dollars as a tip, in addition to the regular service charge. We also discovered that she would send her servant to Fauchon's fancy shop to buy her weekly groceries. (She thought the best was none too good and, as a matter of fact, sometimes not good enough. One November, I troubled to find her a fresh peach she had requested, vainly hoping she would not notice its flaws.) To protect her—and ourselves—from such civilized improvidence, we were finally forced to dole out her income weekly.

The final calamity was still in store. The building at No. 5 Rue Christine was sold, and each occupant was offered the opportunity to buy his apartment. Alice ignored this opportunity, being of the optimistic opinion that she would not be evicted, because of her advanced age. While she was in Italy for her annual arthritis cure, the new owner of her flat sued for possession and won the case. Although powerful friends intervened—even André Malraux, then Minister of Culture, for Gertrude Stein's name was still potent, and Alice was regarded as her official survivor—the French law was adamant. To rehouse her, the musician Doda Conrad and I, after a fruitless search for the kind of old-fashioned Left Bank quarters she was accustomed to, finally had to settle for a comfortable and modern, if unpicturesque, apartment at 16 Rue de la Convention—a noisy commercial street, several miles from the Rue Christine flat which had been so perfectly peopled with her recollections of Gertrude. Alice was eighty-seven when she was forced to move—bedridden, partially deaf, and almost blind. From her pillow in the new apartment, the only view she had was, ironically, that of the local parish church from which she was to be buried three years later. As a little girl in San Francisco, she had been created a Christian in the most casual way by a Catholic friend of her unorthodox Jewish parents; the friend, Alice once told me, had sprinkled her with holy water, which, with childish faith, she had regarded as a valid baptism. In late 1957, after receiving instruction from a very obliging English priest, who supplied her with a missal and a rosary (which she thereafter wore looped around her left wrist), she was officially admitted into the Church and received Holy Communion. She was now ready to meet Gertrude in "the peopled heaven."

The last letter in "Staying On Alone" was written fourteen months before her death, to a young New York couple, Harold and Virginia Knapik, long devoted to Alice. It reads, "I don't know what is to become of me. . . . The Armenian's lawyer is trying to make some sort of settlement without selling any of the pictures. But how he's going to manage it. I'm sure I don't know. Do come back soon. I shan't last forever." She died on March 7, 1967, just before her ninetieth birthday, and was buried in the tomb that she had purchased for herself and Gertrude in the Père Lachaise Cemetery. "Dead is dead but that is why memory is all and all the immortality there is," Gertrude had written years earlier in "The Making of Americans." It is a quotation not often mentioned and surely it would not have been Alice's choice as the epitaph for their mutual earthly devotion.

With the death of Alice, Gertrude's cherished picture collection, which Alice had fought so bitterly to keep intact as a memorial to her, became the property of Allan Stein's children and was dispersed by them without sentiment. A major selection was purchased for about six and a half million dollars by four trustees and one patron of the Museum of Modern Art, the institution that Gertrude and Alice had so detested, and became the nucleus, in December of 1970, of a spectacular exhibition there—"Four Americans in Paris: The Collections of Gertrude Stein and Her Family." The preview night for privileged members, held in a great storm, with the rain falling in sheets, predictably was a fashionable affair, the ladies and gentlemen arriving in their dampened finery to be greeted by a long, formal receiving line that included the new official owners of Gertrude's art. The smart public atmosphere could never, of course, have substituted for the ambience of the Rue de Fleurus studio, where Gertrude's pictures, discovered by her and bought modestly, and now worth a millionaire's ransom, had originally hung, where they had had the benefit of her pure and sacred passion before price became one of their miraculous merits. In their new, sleek museum showcase, the major value that seemed lacking was private love.

THE EIGHTEENTH CENTURY

Dorothy Strachey (Bussey). Excerpt from *Olivia* published by Hogarth Press. Used by permission of the Random House Group Limited.

Violette Leduc. Excerpt from *La Bâtarde*. English translation by Derek Coltman. Copyright © 1964 by Editions Gallimard. Reprinted by permission of Editions Gallimard and Farrar, Straus & Giroux.

Graham Greene. "Chagrin in Three Parts," copyright © 1966 by Graham Greene, renewed from *Collected Stories of Graham Greene*. Used by permission of Viking Penguin, a division of Penguin Putnam Inc. and David Higham Associates.

Isaac Bashevis Singer. "Zeitl and Rickel" from *The Séance and Other Stories*, published by Jonathan Cape. Used by permission of the Random House Group Limited and Farrar, Strauss & Giroux.

Janet Flanner. "Memory is All: Alice B. Toklas" from *Janet Flanner's World: Uncollected Writings, 1932–1975*, published by Secker & Warburg in the UK and by Harcourt, Inc. in the USA. Copyright © 1979 by Natalia Danesi Murray, reprinted by permission of Harcourt, Inc. and the Random House Group Limited.

INDEX OF SELECTED NAMES, TITLES, AND TOPICS